Mission, Church and State in a Colonial Setting
Uganda 1890–1925

For Inge, Mikkel, Henriette and Marianne

Mission, Church and State in a Colonial Setting

Uganda 1890~1925

Holger Bernt Hansen

Senior Lecturer and Associate Professor in African Studies
Institute of Political Studies, Copenhagen

ST MARTIN'S PRESS

NEW YORK

© Holger Bernt Hansen 1984
All rights reserved. For information, write:
St. Martin's Press, Inc., 175 Fifth Avenue, New York, NY 10010
Printed in Great Britain
First published in the United States of America 1984

ISBN 0–312–53474–4

Library of Congress Cataloguing in Publication Data

Hansen, Holger Bernt.
  Mission, church, and state in colonial setting.

  Originally presented as the author's thesis
(D. Phil.—University of Copenhagen, 1981)
  Bibliography: p.
  Includes index.
  1. Missions—Uganda—History.   2. Church and state—
Uganda—History.   3. Uganda—History—1890–1962.
I. Title.
BV3625.U3H36   1984   322'.1'096761   84–16052

ISBN 0–312–53474–4

Typeset in 10/11 pt Plantin by Inforum Ltd, Portsmouth, UK
Printed in Great Britain by Richard Clay (The Chaucer Press) Ltd,
Bungay, Suffolk, UK

CONTENTS

PART V Indirect inputs: parallelism and reciprocity in the relationship between church and state

PART VI An outline of the church–state relationship in a colonial setting: summary, conclusions and evaluation

TABLES

ILLUSTRATIONS

Cover illustration: the King and Chiefs of Toro with clergy and church workers, c.1920

MAPS

ACKNOWLEDGEMENTS

The author and publishers would like to acknowledge the following sources for illustrations.

J.F. Cunningham, *Uganda and Its Peoples* (London, Hutchinson, 1905) 3; C.W. Hattersley, *The Baganda at Home* (London, Religious Tract Society, 1908) 5, 12, 13, 15; C.W. Hattersley, *Uganda by Pen and Camera* (London, Religious Tract Society, 1906) 10; H. Ingrams, *Uganda A Crisis of Nationhood* (London, HMSO, 1960) 2; A.B. Lloyd, *Dayspring in Uganda* (London, Church Missionary Society, 1921) cover; Mansell Collection 4, 7; G. Portal, *British Mission to Uganda 1893* (London, Edward Arnold, 1894) 6; Royal Commonwealth Society 1, 8, 9, 11; H.T.C. Weatherhead, *Uganda A Chosen Vessel* (London, Church Missionary Society, 1913) 13.

Maps 1, 2 and 4 were drawn by J. Ulrich, Institute of Geography, University of Copenhagen. Map 3 is reproduced with permission from Nelson Kasfir, *The Shrinking Political Arena* (1976).

PREFACE

The research work and collection of material for this book was first started while I was a research fellow at Makerere University 1964–6. It was continued while I held a senior lectureship at the University of Copenhagen, attached first to the Institute of Church History and later to the Institute of Political Studies. In this period I supplemented the source material during two short visits to Uganda and during longer periods of study in England, mainly in London and Oxford. The manuscript was finally completed in August 1981, when it was submitted to the Faculty of Arts and in November 1982 accepted as a thesis for the advanced doctor's degree, Dr. Phil. The language has since been revised and the manuscript has been adapted to appear in book form.

Thus, the research work has stretched over several years. For various reasons I have been on and off the project over the years. In particular engagement in the problems of developing countries in general and in Ugandan affairs in particular carry a heavy responsibility for many delays. The long period of genesis has meant that I have received generous assistance from many quarters and accumulated a large debt of gratitude.

My greatest obligation is to Makerere University, where I was received in 1964 with great hospitality as a post-graduate student, and where I was initiated in my formative years into the world of Africa and the field of African studies. It is difficult to imagine a more stimulating environment than Makerere in those days of its transition from an Oxbridge model to a university with its roots planted in the African soil and represented by scholars like Professor Ali Mazrui, Professor John Mbiti and Professor Bethwell Ogot in the Faculty of Arts and Social Sciences. At the same time Makerere was a cosmopolitan place, attracting staff members and visitors from all over the world who were prepared to share their knowledge and experience with newcomers to the field like myself. I am especially grateful for fruitful discussions with Professor Roland Oliver, Professor Anthony Low, Professor Stephen Neill, Professor Hans-Werner Gensichen, to mention only a few names. Makerere stimulated more than most places the crossing of disciplinary boundaries and facilitated interdisciplinary studies in the best sense of the term. Hence, the present book falls within the broad category of African studies as practised at Makerere University.

My particular thanks are due to my base at Makerere, the then new Department of Religious Studies. I have happy memories of helpfulness and friendship from the multinational community of staff members. The Head of the Department, Professor Noel King, has more than anybody else in his own unorthodox way opened the doors for me to the world of African religions and to the community of Africanists. I would also like to thank Dr Louise Pirouet on whose expert knowledge of church records I could always rely.

Several institutions helped me while I conducted my research in Uganda, apart from the Makerere students who assisted with translations. I would especially like to mention Makerere University Library with its Africana Section and the Entebbe Secretariat Archives (now the Uganda National Archives). A special word of thanks goes to officials of the Church of Uganda. The then Archbishop, Dr Leslie Brown, readily gave me access to valuable documentary material on the CMS mission and the church, and I was greatly assisted by other bishops and provincial officers. When I paid visits to various dioceses within the Church of Uganda I was met with great openness and hospitality, and these visits provided me with invaluable experience in approaching and interpreting my material. The same assistance was rendered me by the local administrations when I paid visits to a number of districts in Southern and Western Uganda.

The many links between Makerere University and British universities have meant that I have also enjoyed much assistance and hospitality in Britain. At the University of London I have made use of the facilities at the Institute of Commonwealth Studies and at the School of Oriental and African Studies, where Professor Richard Gray has been of great help to me. Among the many institutions which have assisted me over the years, I should like to mention the Public Record Office in London and the Rhodes House Library in Oxford. First and foremost I am much indebted to the invaluable CMS Archives and in particular to the archivist Miss Rosemary Keen and the librarian Miss Jean Woods.

Turning to the home base I am grateful to the University of Copenhagen for the facilities for research which I have enjoyed over the years. First at the Institute of Church and Mission History where the late Professor Torben Christensen from the very beginning encouraged my exploration of a field which from a traditional Danish point of view appeared rather exotic. Moving to the Institute of Political Studies and cooperation with new colleagues in the social sciences have influenced my method of analysis and emphasized the interdisciplinary approach which I first learned in my days at Makerere. My major obligation is to Professor Ole Karup Pedersen who acted as my supervisor while I held a senior research fellowship. His manifold experience of research work, including African topics, has been most helpful to me. I should also like to thank my colleague from the Institute of Economic History, Ole Justesen, who has commented on parts of the manuscript. A particular word of thanks is due to James Manley of the Department of English, who has meticulously revised my English and made it more readable, supported by a grant from the Danish Social Science Research Council.

The research work has been supported by funds from many sources. A grant from the Danish Council for Development Research and the Danish International Development Agency (DANIDA) supported a two years' research fellowship at Makerere University, and the same sources made later visits to Uganda possible. Visits to England have been funded by the University of Copenhagen and the Danish Research Council for the Humanities which has also subsidized the acquisition of micro-films of CMS material.

The publication of the hardback edition of this book has been supported by a grant from the Danish Research Council for the Humanities, which I gratefully acknowledge. Following a suggestion from James Currey of Heinemann Educational Books, the book will at the same time be available in a paper-covered edition for countries in East Africa. This special arrangement has made the dissemination of the book possible to those areas where it is of primary interest. The author and the publishers gratefully acknowledge donations for this purpose from the following Danish foundations: Queen Margrethe's and Prince Henrik's Foundation; Bikubenfonden; Carlsen-Langes Legatstiftelse; the Danish Council for Development Research; the Ecumenical Foundation; GEC Gads Fond; Krista og Viggo Petersens Fond; Sparekassen SDS; Svend Viggo-Berendts Hindelegat.

Lastly I should like to mention a few individuals who in different ways have had a profound influence on the whole work. My late teacher at university, Professor

Hal Koch, guided my interest towards Africa and secured funds for my first visit to Makerere. It is also due to his influence that my main field of interest has become the church–state problem and the broader connection between religion and society. When I first arrived in East Africa I came almost immediately into contact with Professor Bengt Sundkler who at that time served as Bishop of the North Western Diocese of Tanzania. Over the years his advice and constant encouragement have been most helpful. Dr Michael Twaddle, now at the Institute of Commonwealth Studies, University of London, has followed and stimulated my work since we first met in the Entebbe Secretariat Archives where we shared our findings and started our many years of cooperation.

My greatest debts are to my wife Inge who has from the beginning taken an active part in the research work. While we were at Makerere it was proved that research into biochemistry and nutrition goes well with studies of the mission and the church. The long term of years has meant sacrifice and inconvenience for the whole family, and it is only a small token of my gratitude that this book is dedicated to Inge and our three children, Mikkel, Henriette and Marianne.

Copenhagen, HBH

ORTHOGRAPHY

Place-names. The spelling adopted is the one used during most of the colonial period, and by the Uganda Lands and Surveys Department until the 1960s.

Personal names and titles. The spelling of personal names follows the most generally used orthography in the contemporary source material. As regards titles I have retained the orthography commonly used during the colonial period.

Prefixes. The general pattern of prefixes in the interlacustrine Bantu languages has been maintained as in the colonial period. Bu- prefixes a country or area (Buganda, Busoga); Mu- prefixes a single person (Muganda, Mukopi); Ba- prefixes persons in the plural (Baganda, Bakopi). O- is often added before the singular forms of official titles, as in Omukama (the King of Toro).

Names for some population groups have the prefixes Munya- and Banya-, for instance Munyankore (plural Banyankore) for the people of Ankole.

Lu- signifies the language of the group in question (Luganda, Lunyoro). Lu- has been retained all through the study, although it has become common in later years to use the prefix Ru- in the Western Bantu areas (for instance Runyoro). In Bantu languages 'r' often takes the place of 'l' after the vowels 'i' and 'e'.

The lingua franca of East Africa is generally called Kiswahili, but I have retained the term Swahili without the prefix, as commonly used during the colonial period.

In accordance with recent literature I use both 'Ganda' and 'Buganda' adjectivally.

GLOSSARY OF AFRICAN TERMS

Bakopi (sing. Mukopi): peasants, persons not of chiefly status.

Bakungu: the most important hierarchy of territorial chiefs in Buganda.

Bamalaki: followers of a sect founded by Malaki Musajjakawa, also called Malakites.

baraza: a meeting, even assuming the character of a council, between African leaders and the colonial representative in the various districts.

Bataka (sing. Mutaka): clan heads, guardians of clan land.

Batongole: a category of chiefs appointed by the Kabaka.

Buddu: a saza in Buganda.

Budo: hill where the Kabaka was enthroned; the site of a leading boarding school (King's College, Budo).

busulu: labour tributes to chiefs levied on occupiers of land, later converted to a ground rent.

gombolola: subdivision of a saza.

Kabaka: King of Buganda.

Kago: saza chief of Kyadondo.

Kaima: saza chief of Mawokota.

Kangawo: saza chief of Bulemezi.

kasanvu: compulsory paid labour introduced by the colonial administration.

Kasuju: saza chief of Busuju.

Katikiro: the Kabaka's Prime Minister(s).

katikiro: within the church, a layman in charge of church estates.

Kiimba: saza chief of Bugangazi.

Kimbugwe: saza chief of Buruli.

Kitunzi: saza chief of Gomba.

lukiko: council.

luwalo: compulsory, unpaid communal labour due to African authorities.

mailo: a square mile of land; freehold land under the Uganda Agreement of 1900.

Mugema: saza chief of Busiro.

Mukwenda: saza chief of Singo.

muluka (plur. miruka): subdivision of a gombolola, equivalent to a parish.

Musalosalo: a principal chief in Buganda.

nvujo: a levy on crops.

Omugabe: King of Ankole.

Omukama: King of Toro and Bunyoro.

Omulamuzi: Chief Justice or Minister of Justice in the Buganda government.

Omuwanika: Treasurer or Minister of Finance in the Buganda government.

Pokino: saza chief of Buddu.

Rukurato: council in Toro and Bunyoro.

saza: county.

Sekibob: saza chief of Kyagwe.

shamba: garden, estate.

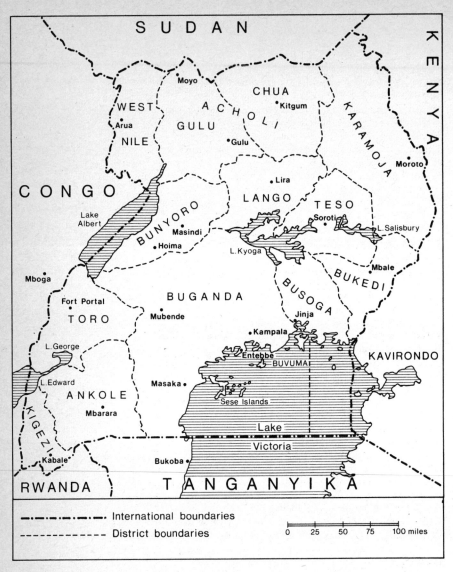

Map 1 *Districts of Uganda Protectorate until 1923*

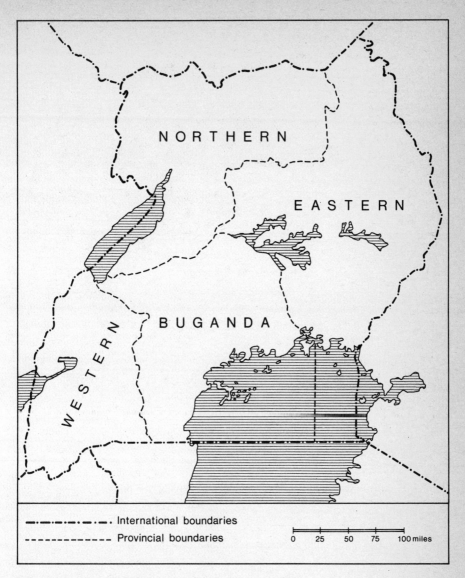

Map 2 *Provinces of Uganda Protectorate until 1932*

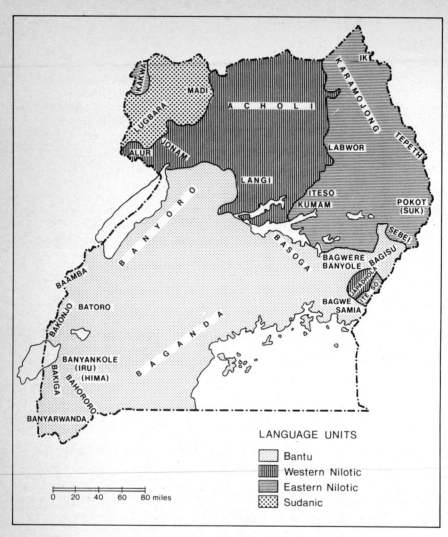

Map 3 *Ethnic and language units in Uganda*

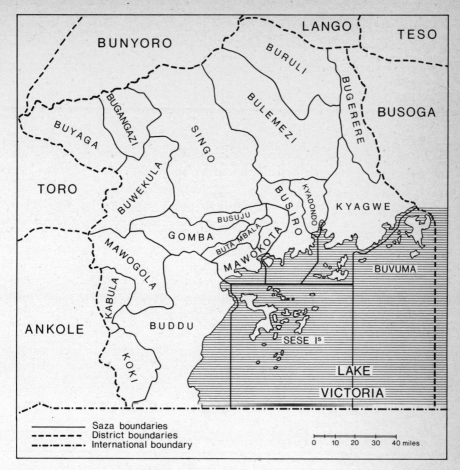

Map 4 *Sazas of the kingdom of Buganda*

PART I

Introduction

Important centres of power in Buganda around 1900

1 (*above*) The Protestant Cathedral and Headquarters on Namirembe Hill

2 (*right*) The Roman Catholic Cathedral and Headquarters on Rubaga Hill

3 (*below*) The Kabaka's Audience-Chamber on Mengo Hill

1

General introduction

The church–state problem in a colonial setting

One of the leading missionaries in Uganda assessed the situation there at the turn of the century as follows: 'Our work here is, on a small scale, so like the work and history of the Church in the 4th and 5th centuries. Many questions are just the same as were then settled. The relation of Church to State is continually cropping up.'[1] He was referring both to the many practical issues which divided the ecclesiastical and political spheres and to the still unsettled relationship between church and state. Later, his successors and their counterparts in the political field compared their own situation to the one obtaining in the Middle Ages. For the Christian leaders the church–state relationship in the Middle Ages almost represented an ideal which they felt ought to inspire the attitudes and policies of the state in their own time. For the representatives of the state medieval history served as a warning against the reintroduction of similar linkages between church and state.[2] Thus both the ecclesiastical and political actors were conscious of the significance and urgency of the church–state problem in the colonial setting and sought guidance in solutions worked out in other areas and ages.

I have taken these contemporary statements as my point of departure. They have served as an impetus to the undertaking of a survey of how the relationship between church and state developed in colonial Uganda, and to the examination of the solutions to the church–state problem. Two analytical themes will provide the general framework. In the first place I will discuss those features of the church–state problem which are peculiar to a colonial society – a theme which may prove to be of general value in the study of colonial Africa as a whole. In the second place, I will assess how far results gained from the study of the colonial situation are comparable with those of well researched areas like Europe and the United States. In practical terms we will ask how far it is possible and justified to explain and interpret the colonial situation by employing generalizations and concepts used in traditional analyses of the church–state problem. The study of the latter theme will add to the comparative value of this survey.[3]

The colonial period, at least in its early phases, was in many respects a formative one, where both the church and the state were in the process of establishing and organizing themselves. This makes it difficult to define the relationship at any given stage, and the changing, dynamic nature of their interrelationship becomes a significant variable. Furthermore, two European agencies, each with different objectives, were appearing on the African stage. The colonial power imposed itself on existing polities and had as its initial goal the maintenance of peace and order, control of political processes and the establishment of a self-supporting colonial unit. The mission had the more specific goal of founding a church, putting it on an independent footing, and in the end making itself superfluous. But the last objective explicitly raises the church–state problem: what rights and status should be granted to such a church, and how should its relationship with the colonial political system and the African polities be defined? Within both the political and the ecclesiastical spheres there were Europeans who maintained lines of communication with Europe. Their links with Europe, their mutual relations and their relationships with their respective African counterparts are all factors which must be taken into consideration. Inevitably we shall find a rather complex relationship. It will in the first place be difficult to define precisely the concepts of church and state. On the ecclesiastical side we must consider the relationship between the missionary society and the newly founded church. We are also faced with a particular type of state formation, the colonial state, comprising both European and African elements, and thus having a dual nature.

Since the specifically colonial situation has to be seen as part of a wider historical process, I employ categories and generalizations which have been developed in other contexts. The comparative framework thus draws on experiences from the American situation. In the United States, the problem of establishment constituted the most important element in the process of solving the church–state problem. One feature of the struggle for independence was the question of disestablishment and the complete separation of church and state. Ever since independence, the United States has stood as an example of innovation as regards the relationship between organized religion and the state. By contrasting the European and the American tradition we can establish a comparative framework where we have 'the ancient European institution of the Establishment' as one extreme, and the total separation of church and state as the other. The latter option naturally precludes an established church. It makes religion a subject of no official concern, relegating it to the sphere of private affairs.[4] Many of the problems raised will be related to these polar standards.

In approaching colonial Uganda, there are first the concrete relational patterns which developed between church and state: formal and informal contacts, economic links, constitutional relationships and the status accorded ecclesiastical organizations (the mission and the church). We may call this the descriptive aspect of the survey. Secondly, there is the question of the political functions which the mission and the church performed in relation to the state. We must identify their political roles and their impact on the state and its policies. We will also discuss the familiar topic of mission and colonialism, and the role of missions and Christian institutions in promoting and sustaining the colonial system. We may call this the functional aspect of the church's relationship with the state. Thirdly, we must attempt to assess the type of relationship which emerges by asking certain more fundamental questions. What factors influenced the relationship and accounted for the process of change? Was there a balance between

the two sides or was it a situation of primacy and subordination? It is also important to examine the impact the ties thus established had on the internal situation of
those involved – the qualitative or evaluational aspects of the relationship. Did
they affect the autonomy of either of the organizations or constitute a relationship
of dependence?

It is important to emphasize two features of this approach to the church–state
problem. First, this survey differs from most other works on the subject of
church–state relations in the colonial setting by including, and ascribing equal
importance to, the third dimension. Previous works have rarely moved beyond
the descriptive level, which establishes points of contact, and the functional level,
which measures the mission's or the church's political impact. One major goal of
the present study will be to include evaluational aspects, to investigate the
anatomy of the interrelationship between church and state, to measure the degree
of interdependence which characterized their relationship, and to define the
constraints which they imposed on each other. Secondly, we will focus on
religious institutions and their interaction with political structures. We will thus
be concerned mainly with the institutional aspects of Christianity, analysing the
relationship between the church, in the main represented by a missionary society,
and a particular type of political system, the colonial state.

The level of inquiry: necessary limitations

The aspects of the church–state problem outlined above have two implications
for the following inquiry. In the first place, we are confining ourselves to the
institutional level of inquiry and this restricts the analysis in certain respects. We
will concentrate on certain topics to the exclusion of others which might appear
just as relevant in another context. In the second place, the way in which we have
defined the church–state problem influences our analytical approach and decides
the method to be employed. We will discuss these two points in turn.

As regards the limitations on this analysis, it is important to be aware from the
outset of the method of selection employed. The church-state problem is only one
aspect of the wider problem of religion and politics, or Christianity and politics.
Beyond the institutional level there are clearly other aspects of religion which
have political significance. But the institutional level will be the focal point of this
study. It follows that we will not be explicitly concerned with the valuational and
societal aspects of missionary activity and the Christian presence. We will not
pursue the possible correlation between religion and political attitudes and
behaviour, nor will we enter into a discussion of religious affiliation as a basis for
group identity and the emergence of interest groups. Consequently, since we
confine ourselves to the institutional level, we will not be able to go into the
question of how Africans responded to missionary penetration, or how the
encounter between African institutions and Christianity began a process of
change. We will concentrate on the fact that religious groups became politicized
to such an extent that they were able to act as interest groups *vis-à-vis* the state and
constituted a political factor which the state could not ignore. It follows that we
will be concerned with those aspects of missionary activity which were related to
the political sphere, or which had some bearing on the mission's position and
attitude towards the state, rather than the wider implications of missionary
activity for African society.[5]

The second limitation inherent in keeping the survey at the institutional level is that it may produce a disproportion between the treatment of European institutions and African ones, between European and African actors. Taking the nature of the early colonial situation into account, there is a risk that African initiatives and achievements may be neglected, as attention is more easily drawn to the two European agencies, which had come with the sole purpose of manifesting themselves within the African surroundings, and therefore displayed a high level of organization. As they also happen to have documented their activities most extensively, the source material suffers from the same bias.[6] This Eurocentric trend is further reinforced by the fact that the organizational patterns of the European agencies, with their hierarchical systems of authority, concentrate focus on the centre of power and decision-making in the colony, and little consideration is given to developments in the various districts, where African initiatives and influence were often quite extensive. This disparity between the central and the local level is again reflected in the available source material. It is difficult to obtain and to make proper use of material on the outlying districts in view of the linguistic diversity and the social, political and cultural heterogeneity in Uganda. To overcome this we need more regional studies which deal in depth with politico-religious developments. Such studies have begun to appear, and I have made some attempt to bridge the gap between the central and local levels by drawing on recent work by Louise Pirouet, Tom Tuma and J. M. Waliggo, who explicitly examine the impact of missionary activity and Christianity in general.[7] A series of recent studies focusing on local politics has also been valuable; reference will be made to works by Martin Doornbos, Tarsis B. Kabwegyere, M. S. M. Kiwanuka, John Tosh, Michael Twaddle, G. N. Uzoigwe *et al.*

Certain general factors must be mentioned which tend to counterbalance the Eurocentric trend and put European activity more into perspective. One basic point is that, unlike some earlier studies, the present study shifts its focus to the African arena and away from the imperial one. The participants all lived, temporarily or permanently, in Uganda. Furthermore, there will be no detailed discussion of the exchanges between those in Uganda and those in London. The latter will only be mentioned when their influence is directly manifested, or when reference must be made to them for explanatory reasons. The 'men on the spot' within both the political and ecclesiastical spheres in Uganda, for a number of reasons, including the long lines of communication between the two arenas, had considerable scope for making their own decisions and formulating policy. This also made them more aware of local conditions.

I have also avoided, as far as possible, giving the impression that European emissaries acted in a vacuum. Their potential, influence and power must not be overestimated, quantitatively or qualitatively. Their scope for action was determined by the continued existence of African institutions and by the reactions, initiatives and opposition of Africans. We must preserve a healthy sense of perspective as regards the European presence in Africa.[8]

Yet, even with these qualifications, this survey may run the risk of being categorized as yet another account of Europeans in Africa, or as colonial history, lacking roots in African soil. In a wider sense, it may be said that it runs counter to current trends in African historiography, as it studies Africa mainly in terms of its invaders.[9] Yet, in spite of these controversial features, it is my contention that a study of the colonial church–state problem along the lines suggested here has relevance for African studies in general.[10] An understanding of the pattern of relationships between church and state laid down in the first half of the colonial period is indispensable for an understanding of later developments before and after independence. The missionaries' attitude to the colonial state and their involvement in state-related secular activities influenced the later position and status of the African church and the scope of Africanization in the ecclesiastical field, as compared to the political one. In that respect the missionary factor helps to complete 'the historical picture of Africa's recent past'.[11] Any study of the special nature of the church-state relationship which has developed in Africa must take into account the fact that the relationship was first worked out in the colonial setting with its highly bureaucratic structure. The mission and the colonial administration were complex bureaucratic organizations, and this fact created a special framework for interaction which left its mark on later developments. While European actors were often influenced by experiences from their own metropolis, events in Uganda were not just reflections of church–state relations in Europe. We must rather take the special situational circumstances of the encounter between European bureaucracies and African realities into account.

In this respect the primary focus on the African arena may admittedly lead to the exclusion of important aspects of the European tradition as explanatory factors. We may assume that the basic attitude of the CMS mission towards the state and its whole conception of the relationship between religion and politics can be explained in terms of the missionaries' roots in the 'Low Church' faction of the Church of England and the position of the CMS within the evangelical tradition.[12] But this dimension is a constant beyond the scope of the present survey.

It follows that since organizations are the major actors, little attention is given to the contributions of individuals, who are seen mainly as spokesmen of the interests of their respective organizational structures. The analysis will only to a limited extent involve an assessment of the significance of individual personalities for any particular line of policy or their overall influence on the course of events. This should be borne in mind, as colonial and missionary history often tends to emphasize the contributions of individuals.

Finally, it is necessary to emphasize here that when we discuss the mission's relations with the colonial administration we are confining ourselves to the Church Missionary Society and the Anglican Church of Uganda, which means that the comparative aspects which might emerge from a study of the Roman Catholic missions and the Catholic Church in Uganda do not figure prominently. This is admittedly a shortcoming, as a comparative study would enable us to penetrate deeper into the nature of the relationship between church and state in a colonial situation, especially in view of the different nationalities of the two missions and their different conceptions of a national church. It proved, however, too great a task to make a detailed study of two missions and two churches, in view of the vast amount of material available, though I will touch on the comparative aspect by inquiring into the colonial government's dealings with the two denominations and by mentioning in passing the results produced by other researchers like J. Cussac, H. P. Gale and J. M. Waliggo.

The period of study

I have taken 1890 as my starting point and have continued to the middle of the 1920s. An embryonic colonial framework was first introduced and both the ecclesiastical and the political fields began to be organized in 1890. The first Anglican Bishop arrived, equipped with sufficient authority to assume the leadership of the missionary work, and to make binding arrangements with the secular power, whether African or colonial. At the same time, the official representative of the Imperial British East Africa Company, empowered with a Royal Charter, concluded a treaty with the Kabaka of Buganda, who acknowledged British protection and placed his Kingdom firmly within the British sphere of interest. It was necessary even at this early stage for the ecclesiastical representatives to consider their relations with the secular authorities and to define the type of relationship they hoped to develop. Consequently, the formative period up to 1900 is included and is subjected to its own specific type of analysis.

The main emphasis, however, is on the first quarter of the twentieth century, a period which has received remarkably little attention so far. It was a phase during which the relationship between church and state assumed a more formalized and permanent character. Furthermore, it is a long enough period to make a longitudinal study possible and register the process of change in the relationship. While the beginning of this period was marked by the conclusion of the Uganda Agreement of 1900, it is more difficult to establish a termination point. World War Two marked a decisive turning-point in the colonial era, but the issues at stake over this span of years proved too many and variegated for the kind of analysis intended here, and the material was much too extensive for a comprehensive study. Another possibility would have been to use 1918 as the year of termination, as has been done in other studies on East Africa.[13] While the war itself was felt mainly indirectly in Uganda, the immediate post-war period appeared for a number of reasons to initiate a new era. At this point a more active approach and a centralizing trend appeared in colonial policy. The colonial system was more firmly established and the administration took a more direct interest, where a *laissez-faire* attitude had prevailed before. Yet all this did not happen from one day to the next. In certain areas it took several years before a new policy was implemented or even formulated. The Protestant mission was in the immediate post-war years faced with the difficulty of adapting means to ends, both because of the expansion of its work and the decline of support in the metropolitan country. Again, events were gradual and were certainly not related to any change in overall missionary policy. On the contrary, continuity was a dominant feature in the mission's approach. As a third criterion we may take the African reaction. It was a commonly held opinion among the colonial officials and the missionaries that a certain amount of anti-European feeling emerged during this period, and that the younger generation had become somewhat restless.

As developments were gradual in the years after 1918 the First World War cannot be regarded as a watershed in the present context.[14] We therefore have to adopt other criteria to establish a demarcation point in the inter-war period. I have here chosen to let the major issues between church and state be decisive. In the middle of the 1920s a number of outstanding issues connected with land, labour and education tended to find solutions, if only provisional ones, or were simply shelved. At the same time new problems and new perspectives began to appear. There was in fact a surprising degree of continuity between the pre-war and post-war periods as regards the substance of the relationship between church and state, and it was only from the middle of the 1920s onwards that new trends appeared or the old ones became intensified. On the other hand, the turning point in about 1925 is of a relative nature. In some instances the narrative stops earlier, while in other cases we pursue processes a little further.

The area of study

The period thus demarcated also has implications for the geographical boundaries – the parts of the Protectorate which are considered. The Kingdom of Buganda receives most attention because of its early contacts with the European agencies and its leading position within the Protectorate. Next, the neighbouring Kingdoms of Ankole, Toro and Bunyoro and the Confederacy of Busoga figure prominently, as they soon became important centres for the activities of both church and state. Mainly because of their later inclusion in the colonial and missionary structures, the eastern and northern parts of the Protectorate earn less comment. The level of analysis and the thematic approach do not require that all areas be given equal consideration in order to accomplish the major objective of the survey.

Related works

The interaction between mission, church and state has attracted interest since African studies became a legitimate field of inquiry for scholars in various disciplines in the period after the Second World War.[15] This survey has been stimulated by a variety of earlier works of which an outline will be given in Appendix 2. In particular two works, appearing as early as 1952, have proved decisive by introducing the church state problem in a colonial setting and outlining relevant topics of research. In his work on missionary activity in Madagascar, Fridtjov Birkeli emphasized the need to consider the political dimension of missionary activity and in particular the inevitable connections between missions and colonialism.[16] He was followed by Roland Oliver, who in his pioneer study, *The Missionary Factor in East Africa*, explicitly formulated the problem of the relationship between mission, church and state.

The present study owes much to Oliver's work, which has remained remarkably relevant, both as regards the formulation of the object of analysis and the pinpointing of the issues which divided church and state, especially as his book was the first which dealt with East Africa, and thus with Uganda. Oliver maintains that the church–state problem was mainly a post-First World War phenomenon, and on this point we differ. Oliver claims that, in the interval between the European occupation and the war, 'missionaries had scarcely needed to consider their relations with the State' (p. 246). I argue that the early, formative period was crucial for the later pattern of church–state relations. One reason for this difference may be that the present study employs a wider definition of the church–state problem. While Oliver's primary concern was to measure missionary impact and the mission's political role, on the basis of the various interactions between mission and state, I adopt a more comprehensive point of view and include all points of contact irrespective of their actual impact in order to assess the nature of the relationship between church and state.

Apart from Roland Oliver's sections on Uganda no really comprehensive study of the church–state problem in Uganda in the colonial period has been made. D. A. Low has pioneered the study of the initial phase in his work on the political impact on the Buganda polity of the arrival of the two missions.[17] But then there is a gap until the decolonization period, which is well covered by more recent studies.[18] This gap has provided one point of departure for me, and has been decisive for the demarcation of the period to be studied.

Source material

A large corpus of source material is available from this period even when I limit myself to material in Uganda and concentrate on 'the men on the spot'. This survey is based primarily on unpublished documents contemporary to the events, while oral material has only been used to a limited extent. Most importance has been attached to the official exchanges between the ecclesiastical and political fields in the Ugandan setting, but documents related to internal policy formulation and decision-making within each sphere have also been considered important (see list of sources).

As the material is distributed over several archives in different countries it represents a scattered corpus of source material of a disparate nature, not least if we compare government and church records. Hence one essential objective of this survey has simply been the collation of material from the various locations. The combinative approach has helped to reveal new aspects of the problem and to throw new light on familiar topics and events. At the same time it has proved necessary in connection with issues like land and labour first to establish the basic facts and the overall course of events, as this information was not available to any substantial extent in other works. This explains the detailed account of some of the subjects at issue between church and state.

Analytical approach

In view of the abundant source material and the lack of guidance from previous works on how to approach the church–state problem in a colonial setting it was necessary to establish an analytical framework within which the survey might be conducted. The analytical approach is again influenced by the way in which I have defined the church–state problem, and by my intention to move beyond the merely descriptive level. As the various kinds of interaction between church and state and an assessment of the flow of influence between them constitute the major subject of inquiry, the solution offered here is to conceive of the church–state problem in terms of systems analysis (see Appendix 1).

The ecclesiastical field can be considered as an essential element in the environment of the political system, and the political dimension of ecclesiastical activity can be seen in terms of inputs to the political system. In the present survey the focus is mainly on the input function and the church's ability to articulate its interests to the state, while the decision-making processes within the state are only discussed in so far as this is necessary for an understanding of the resulting policy. It follows that internal aspects connected with the ability to articulate interests (organizational features, resources and autonomy – in short, capacity) have to be included, as they influence input efficiency.[19]

At the operative level, a distinction is made between three categories of inputs to the political system. As our point of departure we have the mission's fundamental goal: the establishment of an independent church closely integrated with society and state. The realization of this goal requires close links with the economic forces in society, in particular land grants and labour services, the two major economic assets in society. They account for a high degree of interaction between the two spheres and constitute the material basis of the church–state relationship. As a second category of input we have the demands directed to the political system with a view to influencing decisions and allocations. Such demands may be explicitly aimed at special benefits, or be more vague, expressing opinions about distant goals or voicing general grievances. This category may be termed 'direct' input.

Taking into account the fact that the ecclesiastical field in the colonial situation virtually constitutes the only organized structure beside the governmental structures, its existence has political ramifications beyond the level of direct input, and these cannot be neglected. This creates a pattern of interdependence between the two fields: the mere existence of the ecclesiastical structure, and its decisions and actions, has an indirect effect on the political system, and evokes some response from it, whether in the form of special precautionary measures, adjustments of policy, or efforts towards harmonization or coordination of certain areas of policy. This category of interaction may be termed 'indirect' or 'tacit' inputs.

Apart from the formative period where the embryonic church–state relationship requires a different analytical approach, developed in Chapter 3, this tripartite categorization of the interactions between the ecclesiastical and political fields serves as the organizing principle of the survey. In a more general sense the analytical scheme is employed with the aim of sorting and organizing a scattered body of material and to guide the investigation by raising the appropriate questions about the nature of the relationship between church and state in the special colonial situation.

2

The Buganda setting: the emergence of politico-religious parties

In 1877 the first group of Anglican missionaries from the London-based Church Missionary Society (CMS) arrived in the capital of the inter-lacustrine Kingdom of Buganda. They came in response to an invitation from Kabaka Mutesa I, the King of Buganda, which had been forwarded to a British newspaper by the well-known traveller H. M. Stanley during his visit to the court of Mutesa.[1]

The missionaries were not the only 'religious representatives' in Buganda. Since the middle of the century Arab traders from the East African coast and with connections to the Sultanate of Zanzibar had been living at Mutesa's court. Apart from the commercial influence, this Arab presence had also meant a noticeable religious influence, and at one stage Mutesa came close to adopting Islam officially.[2]

In the Buganda setting, however, the function of the foreigners was not only a religious one, nor even primarily so. They were supposed to increase the strength of Buganda in her encounter and rivalry with her neighbours, not least the Kingdom of Bunyoro to the north-west, and to serve as a counterweight against the threat from the north in the shape of Egypt's expansion along the Nile.[3] This assistance could, according to Mutesa's thinking, manifest itself directly through the guns and ammunition the foreigners brought with them, and indirectly because by their presence an alliance was created with an Arab or European power.

It was, therefore, a source of great surprise and suspicion when a group of Catholic missionaries from the Société de Notre-Dame d'Afrique – the so-called White Fathers – arrived in Buganda in 1879. Not only did they come from another European power, France; they also brought with them another version of Christianity which turned out to be hostile to the one the Anglican missionaries had proclaimed.[4]

In the end Buganda benefited very little from the missionaries in the expected fields of politics and weapons. They were, however, allowed to stay on provided that they submitted to surveillance by Mutesa by living in or around his court. Within the field of religion the court from now on became a lively place. Discussions and rivalry were going on continually between the representatives of the three religions. Gradually each of them won a stock of adherents among the young so-called pages, who underwent training at the court in the hope of winning the favour of the Kabaka and later being able to gain an influential position within the Buganda system.[5]

It is important at this stage further to consider the question of the integration of the new religions into the contemporary Buganda system, up to 1884 when Mutesa died. First, these new phenomena and the effects caused by their presence could be contained within the Buganda system as long as the Kabaka managed to manoeuvre between the contrasting factions and as long as his authority was not contested. When the newly converted Muslims showed tendencies towards insubordination, Mutesa did not hesitate to underline his supreme position by instituting purges.

Secondly, these new religious groupings emerging at the court corresponded to tensions already existing within the system between the Kabaka and the leading group of territorial chiefs, the Bakungu. They had the effect of strengthening the position of the Kabaka by constituting an alternative power group to the chiefs, who to a large extent derived their strength from the supporters of the traditional religion.[6] A sort of dual system was coming into being, and the Kabaka was using the new religions and their social manifestations as a means of restructuring the relations of power in the Buganda polity.

When Mutesa's son, Mwanga II, ascended to the throne in 1884 it was as usual difficult for a new Kabaka to establish himself, but especially so in Mwanga's case due to the change and the resultant greater tensions within the system. With the aim of strengthening his own position *vis-à-vis* the chiefs he started to develop a rival hierarchy of personal agents, known as Batongole. For these offices he primarily chose young people from among the adherents of the new religions. As a special precaution he also created armed regiments under his own close control and with leading members of the three religious groups as commanders.[7]

It should be borne in mind that the most important items of trade with the coast, the guns, were now concentrated in the hands of these young converts. The Kabaka's attempt thus to monopolize the new resources underlines more than anything else the shift in the locus of power. The religious divisions begin to emerge as identifiable groupings with political potential. In addition they start to serve as a mechanism for the Kabaka's allocative activity. The newly installed Batongole attracted their respective co-religionists, and this group-formation was further strengthened when Mwanga distributed grants of land and other assets via the Batongole structure. 'Most of those who took possession of these villages were students of European missionary teaching or students of Islam.'[8] Along with these developments came the effects of the traditional patronage and clientship system. This institution had been the backbone of the Bakungu hierarchy, and it was now functioning within – and thereby strengthening – the new religious configurations.

It thus seemed to be within Mwanga's range to obtain the final concentration of power with the assistance of the Batongole while weakening the rival element in the structure, the Bakungu. Mwanga's position was dependent on his ability in the long run to control these new powerful groupings. At this juncture a new factor was beginning to influence the internal power structure – an external factor which made it even more difficult for the Kabaka to keep the system in balance, with himself as the supreme source of authority.

The competition between European powers for possessions in Africa – the so-called 'scramble for Africa' – became more and more perceptible in the interior of East Africa with the British, the Germans and the Belgians actively entering the stage. For Mwanga, as well as for his predecessor, the paramount political goal was to preserve the country's independence, and this goal was identified with the supremacy of the Kabakaship. Accordingly Mwanga was in the present situation seriously alarmed about the possible internal effects of the external threat. First of all, the European missionaries and the Arab traders were no longer simply considered as 'religious representatives'. A political role was ascribed to them, as they were looked upon as representatives of their nations of origin. They came close to being considered as spies in view of the external threat.[9] The second group consisted of the new religious communities. For Mwanga, and even more for the old Bakungu chiefs, it became increasingly doubtful whether the loyalty of the adherents of these religions was primarily directed towards the country and the Kabakaship, since it could be in the interest of any given group to rely on the assistance of an external power. Referring to the earlier purge of the Christians by Mwanga, an Anglican missionary remarked: 'The massacre of the Christians here was very much owing to the suspicions that they were in league with the white man to take the country eventually.'[10] From the Kabaka's point of view it became increasingly doubtful whether the foreign and local representatives of the new religions were any longer controllable.

The situation became more and more critical – it became in fact a question of who would be the first to go into action. The position of the three religious groups *vis-à-vis* Mwanga was very much the same. Contemporary observers labelled them all characteristically under the term 'the Readers', people who had started to learn the new religions.[11] The Readers staged a sort of coup in September 1888. Mwanga went into exile, a new Kabaka was enthroned, and the offices were divided equally between the winners.

This alliance only lasted a month. It came to a new struggle, with the front line running between the Muslims on the one side and the Christians on the other. The Muslims were victorious, resulting in the expulsion of all the missionaries and the leading Christian Baganda going into exile. Buganda was established as a Sultanate, a new Kabaka was installed, and a policy of Islamization was initiated.[12]

It has been a point of discussion among scholars whether the events of 1888 and 1889 can be labelled a revolution, and if so whether it was a Muslim revolution or, taking the final outcome into consideration, a Christian revolution.[13] However, it is a moot question how far the use of these terms will take us in the understanding of the events themselves. It seems sufficient to say that a coup had taken place within the Buganda system. A newly established group had moved in and taken over the centre of power while the office of the Kabaka to some extent had assumed a symbolic character.

It is more important to call attention to two closely related features underlying the tumultuous events. For the first time a particular religious group appears claiming exclusivity at the expense of the two other religious groups. Out of this can be read a clear awareness of the importance of religious affiliation. Moving from the claim of exclusivity it is only a matter of consistency that the winners also institute a monopoly of political power in the sense that the victorious religious group fills all the offices in the state.

It can, therefore, arouse little surprise that the Christians, after their final victory over the Muslims in October 1889, assisted by an internal reaction against the policy of Islamization, tended to use the same prescription. They demanded the same exclusivity by keeping the Muslims away from any influence and even by practising a sort of physical segregation. With regard to the subsequent monopolization of political power the Christians were faced with the difficulty of not being a homogenous group. During the allocation of the various offices the antagonism between the Protestants and the Catholics turned out to be a great impediment. On the intervention of the respective missionaries a treaty was drawn up based on the principle of equal sharing. The arrangement was exceedingly complicated, especially when it came to putting it into practice. Every holder of a position in the hierarchy was to be under a superior of another party – 'alternate ranks in one vertical section of the hierarchy should be held by members of the opposite parties'.[14] But to maintain the balance, which was the main object of this treaty, every chief who changed his religion consequently had to give up his political office. Thus the treaty became the expression of a marked politicization of religion in Buganda and an indication of the fact that religious divisions had by now become the main stratifying principle in society.

It was at this stage of the internal development that envoys from various colonial powers entered Buganda with the purpose of making political treaties. But competition in this respect was rendered superfluous, as an agreement was drawn up between Britain and Germany placing Buganda and her neighbours within the British sphere of interest. The outcome was that Captain Frederick Lugard on behalf of the Imperial British East Africa Company (IBEA Co.), was sent to Buganda. He arrived towards the end of 1890, charged with the task of bringing Buganda within what was later labelled 'the informal British Empire'.[15]

After this short and general outline of the development in Buganda during the years prior to 1890 we may now make an assessment of the situation with which Lugard was faced. First of all, in spite of the upheavals, the structure in the Buganda system remained intact. The various institutions were still functioning, including the Kabakaship, as the Christians had brought Mwanga back and reinstalled him on the throne. His real power was, however, rather limited. The centre of power had by now been taken over by the Christian Batongole leaders who moved into the positions of the Bakungu chiefs. This meant that there was only one hierarchy. The locus of power was now placed in the hands of an oligarchy which was defined by its members' particular religious affiliations. The split between the two Christian groups assumed a special importance in connection with the implementation of the newly won power. The continuous tensions were further increased by the opposing attitudes to the various colonial powers of the two groups.

At the same time these tensions serve to illustrate that the Kabakaship, in spite of the restrictions placed on the incumbent, was not, viewed in a wider context, completely deprived of importance. When Mwanga came back he declared himself to be a Catholic, which meant, in the words of one of the Anglican missionaries, that 'the RCs have a great pull over us in that the King is nominally of their faith, and all the boys and people around him are followers of the Roman religion'.[16] Many people converted to Catholicism, thereby putting great difficulties in the way of the implementation of the 'Lebanon-like' treaty both groups had agreed upon. The Kabaka was still an asset for any of the religious groups as his stand would prove decisive when the bulk of the Baganda had to decide on their allegiance to the new men in power. To this should be added that the split in the victorious Christian group left him a certain amount of room for manoeuvre.

Due to these internal tensions Buganda was particularly vulnerable to the external political forces present in overwhelming numbers in East Africa around 1890. The protagonists themselves consciously tried to involve external forces in the solution of internal problems. At the same time these informal alliances provide for the researcher an indication of where the various groups stand within Buganda society as regards their strategy and final goals.

It is quite clear that Kabaka Mwanga stuck to the same overall goal as his predecessor: to preserve the independence of Buganda without submission to any sort of foreign control. The increasing British activity close to his borders was of increasing concern to him. 'He [Mwanga] sees now that the English mean to govern the country and to curtail his power.'[17] A characteristic feature of the whole situation was that he saw the arrival of Captain Lugard, and the simultaneous arrival of the Anglican Bishop, A. R. Tucker, as parts of the same British push towards Buganda. This was reflected in his refusal to hoist the Union Jack which was forwarded to him by the IBEA Co. Not only would it in his eyes have been a token of submission; it was also a symbol of the Protestant party.[18] It is quite obvious that Mwanga identified British political power with the Protestant religion. In the same way he categorized the missionaries according to their national origin and did not treat them just as religious emissaries. Protestantism was connected with a particular country, and the Protestant envoys were accordingly representatives of this nation. In this respect there was no room for a distinction between the religious and the political aspects.

The same attitude was predominant among the leaders of the two power-holding groups. Among that Catholics it took the form of a strong conviction that the Catholic chiefs would be turned out of office when the IBEA Co. took over. This means that the Catholics expected the same claim to exclusivity from the Protestants as the Muslims earlier insisted upon. Supported by the White Fathers, the Catholics much preferred that the Germans should move in rather than the British.[19] On the other side, the Protestant chiefs were heavily committed to bringing in the IBEA Co., and in the end Britain. In their opinion it was the only possibility of securing peace in the country.[20] The Protestants were also acting on the assumption that the claim to exclusivity would be adhered to; in the case of a negative outcome they were prepared to emigrate.[21]

The Ganda leaders were thus working within a system of assumptions which presupposed a strong connection between political power and religious exclusivity. In this situation the missionaries found themselves placed in a key position. In comparison with the situation before the coup it was now obvious that an expansion of their functions had taken place. Their first role was that of influential advisers for their respective Christian groups. Both sets of missionaries accepted this function, as can be seen from the change in attitude on the part of the Protestant missionaries.

You will be writing and saying I am trying to make myself a sort of Political Agent instead of a Missionary. We try to keep out of all political questions, and matters of internal

Buganda affairs we leave to the people themselves, but outside questions they bring to us, and ask our advice. They know very little about European powers, or the philanthropic motives of the IBEA Co., therefore we are compelled to explain such things to them.[22]

In their second role the missionaries acted as contact men to the representatives of colonialism, who in ever increasing numbers had become interested in Buganda. The Catholic missionaries tried to bar the British from entering Buganda and much preferred to clear the road for French or German interests.[23] The Protestant missionaries on their side were acting even more in accordance with national preferences. They were convinced that peace and reasonable conditions for missionary work would only prevail if the presence of the Company secured a British presence. At the same time their attitude was based on the assumption that the Catholics, on getting the upper hand, would practise a sort of exclusivity and keep the Protestants out.[24]

Finally, the third role is not directly formulated, but it can be deduced from the Protestant material. The missionaries considered themselves as British subjects and in emergencies they claimed the right to call on protection from their home country. They believed at least that their country of origin should accept a special obligation towards her subjects and act accordingly.[25]

The Baganda's conception of the missionaries' political role, and the mission-aries' own views and practices were thus to a large extent identical. In the next stage the decisive thing was to be the extent to which the British authorities accepted this role and especially their willingness to take action in accordance with the presumed national obligation connected with the missionaries' presence in Buganda. In the eyes of the Ganda leaders and of the missionaries the situation was aptly summarized by a leading Anglican missionary: 'The whole country has been divided between the two parties, and whether we like it or not these parties do exist, and we are looked upon as the head of one and the French priests as the head of the other.'[26]

In 1890 it was thus an established fact to everybody that Buganda had been divided into two parties. They were called 'Bakatoliki' and 'Baporostante', the latter also being labelled 'the people of the religion of the Book'.[27] The national association appears from the names 'Fransa' and 'Ingleza'.[28] Both religious and national associations aroused so much antagonism that each party expected the other to claim exclusivity and the monopoly of political power as the logical corollary of this. The pattern initiated by the Muslim party had been accepted by their successors, and the achievement of the aims which had thus arisen was sought through external assistance.

In a situation of this kind Lugard, as the representative of the colonial system, cannot have avoided assuming at the very least a kind of referee function. Whether he could avoid identifying himself with one of the rival groups and thereby swinging the pendulum depended very much on the firmness with which he was able to act. In more general terms Lugard and the succeeding colonial authorities in Buganda in the 1890s were faced with the question of the rela-tionship between church and state, especially with regard to the neutrality of the state's actions under circumstances of great politico-religious polarization. Atten-tion should here be called to a special aspect of the problem, namely the simultaneous and interrelated establishment of church and state in Buganda. In particular, the very special position of the missionaries made it imperative for the secular authorities to decide which sort of role the missionaries, representing the embryonic church, should be allowed to play *vis-à-vis* the state; which position the church should be granted in the future set-up, and last but not least to what extent the missionaries' national origin should influence the attitude and actions of the state, thereby placing the Anglicans and the Catholics on a different footing.

While the problem of the relationship between church and state can mainly be looked upon from an institutional angle the second problem facing the representatives of the colonial power has a more theoretical character. It concerns the overriding question of the relationship between religion and politics. In the Buganda situation there was bound to be some kind of linkage between the two, and it is important at this stage to specifiy which kind of political significance was ascribed to religion in the present context.

It should now have been made clear that the religious divisions had become in 1890 the main stratifying principle in society. No alternative structure proved capable of replacing this religious division in spite of the fact that some other possibilities might be assumed to offer themselves, for instance Bataka versus Bakungu (clan heads versus the chiefly hierarchy), and Bakopi versus Bakungu (the peasants/commoners versus the chiefly hierarchy).[29]

For an explanation of the strength of these religious cleavages one has to point to the contemporary parallel phenomenon of the politicization of religion. Religious divisions became the most important mechanism for allocative activity within the political system. The valued goods were channelled through this structure, and in the eyes of individuals, membership of a religious group served as the obvious means of securing one's fair share. To put it differently, religious factionalism was also political factionalism.[30] The identification of religion and politics was further strengthened in that the formation of groups was strongly influenced by the practice of patronage and clientship. This institution functioned within each religious group when chiefs distributed the goods and when people chose to affiliate themselves to an overlord.[31]

Secondly, one basic attitude which was prevalent within the old relationship to the gods was transferred to the Christian religion. Besides other functions religion is assumed to have practical application, the results of which can be experienced and even measured within society and in daily life. The strength and utility of a religion manifests itself in a concrete way. This attitude has to do with an instrumental emphasis or what can be called a utilitarian principle.[32] This presupposition should be borne in mind when evaluating the Ganda adherence to the Christian denominations. Included is an expectation that goods and results are forthcoming here and now. This basic attitude clearly served as an impetus to join the religious groups and thus to strengthen the link between religion and politics.

Both these aspects of the traditional system and world-view were aptly touched upon by one of the missionaries: 'many are only followers of the Christian chiefs for the sake of the good they thus get in the country . . .'[33] Essential features from the traditional system and the traditional world-view were thus contained within the new structure, and they even had a cementing function. Consequently for a number of Baganda the adherence to one of the religious parties did not necessarily indicate a conscious break with an old pattern. It is of great importance to keep this in mind when we later evaluate the Ganda reaction to demands from the colonial power and from the missionaries that they separate religion and politics.

For the same reason it is important to be quite specific at which level the relationship between religion and politics in this context has been established.[34] To summarize, we are arguing mainly from an empirical–functional point of view. The relationship is explained on the basis of the existence and behaviour of religious groupings within the political system. These groupings quite clearly have a political function and from the members' point of view fulfil essential needs. To some extent religion and politics are pulling together to realize common goals.

An analysis at a functional level imposes certain limitations on the capacity to explain all aspects of the relationship between religion and politics.

(1) Nothing can be said about conversion, its depth and sincerity. The individual's feelings and commitment can neither be proved nor evaluated at this level of analysis. Conversion will have to be placed in a different setting; and it would require an analysis on a more psychological level to be able to say anything about the qualitative aspects of Ganda adherence to Christianity.[35]

(2) Accordingly it would be wrong to conceive of the Baganda within the following pair of alternatives: either the adherence to Christianity is a result of a sincere, personal conversion, or it is due to the attainment of certain goods which the Christian religion can deliver. The Baganda were not placed in a situation of choice such as originates from an individual approach to the change of religion. From the point of view put forward here it is not possible to make such a distinction. It was for contemporary actors and has been in later research work a major subject for discussion. The Protestant missionaries, in particular, inspired by their Low Church background, have laid great emphasis on the individual's conversion. In the Buganda context, this emphasis is also rooted in the legacy of the admirable bravery and endurance which the martyrs displayed during Mwanga's persecution in 1886. Later on the individual's salvation has been measured by the extent to which Christian morality and the rules of the church penetrated into daily life. But such an assessment requires a different set of criteria from the ones employed here.[36]

(3) Nothing can be said about whether religion as such – in this case the content of Christianity – led people towards engagement in politics or to the development of certain political claims or demands. In other words, it is not possible at this level of analysis to establish any correlation between religious ideas and political ideology or consider religion as a source of political values, as is often done within the Weberian tradition.

More than any other, the Buganda situation affords a warning against a conclusion of that sort. It has by now been widely accepted that the Kabakaship was not an expression of the divine kingship which can be found in other places in tropical Africa.[37] The Kabaka was independent of the established religious system and was therefore able, in the beginning, to cope with a difficult pluralistic situation and to move freely between the various religious systems which were offered to the country.[38] It was only when the religious factions took over the centre of power that the religious and the political spheres became closely connected. Elements of the traditional value system give an additional explanation of why the religious grouping obtained such a stranglehold, but these are not sufficient to account for the politicization of religion.

The close connection between the religious and the political spheres cannot be explained in ideological terms. The explanation is, on the contrary, to be drawn from a functional analysis of events over a certain span of years, by primarily using a historical/functional approach. It is within these preconditions that the attempts of the colonial authorities and the missionaries to distinguish between religion and politics must be evaluated and judged. It is further within this level of explanation that the African reaction to these attempts must be judged.

PART II

The formative period: religious liberty and developments in the 1890s

Leading figures of the 1890s

4 Captain F. D. Lugard

5 Bishop A. R. Tucker

6 Kabaka Mwanga

7 Sir Harry Johnston

3

The concept of religious liberty

A characteristic feature of the events in Buganda in the 1890s is that the church, represented by the missionaries, and the state, represented by the IBEA Co. and later by colonial officials, were both in the process of establishing themselves in African society within the same span of years. This parallel development is by no means extraordinary for colonialism in Africa and it is touched upon in many works covering this period.[1] A common perspective has been to investigate the extent to which missionary activity paved the way for colonialism or was even responsible for its introduction and instrumental in its establishment.[2] One particular aspect of this problem has, however, not been dealt with systematically.[3] It concerns the nature of the relationship which was worked out between church and state under these special circumstances prevailing when both were in the process of establishing themselves, and when religion as such did not manifest itself in the shape of one single organization, but took the form of at least three rival factions each of considerable political importance. What were the principles and goals that each part worked towards and what means did they employ to accomplish their goals? These questions gain importance in the longer perspective, when we consider that the 1890s were the founding period for both church and state and that the arrangements worked out during this period proved to be decisive for developments during the following decades of colonialism and right through to independence.

In order to define the actual relationship between church and state in the formative period and to develop some analytical categories we will introduce the concept of religious liberty as the lens through which the events and development in the 1890s may be analysed and evaluated. First of all, the question of religious liberty was brought forward frequently by those involved, primarily the colonial officials and the missionaries, and it was the object of intensive discussion. Therefore, tracing the role of the idea of religious liberty in developments in the 1890s is in itself a relevant task.[4] Secondly, by drawing on experiences from studies of other areas and periods, the concept of religious liberty, which is frequently combined with the ideas of equality and the neutrality of the state, may in the colonial situation prove to be especially applicable in outlining the sort of relationship that exists between church and state and even, on a different level, between religion and politics. This seems to be a useful point of departure for the analysis of the religious policy of the colonial authorities in a pluralistic situation like the one that prevailed in Uganda, and also for the analysis of the aims and expectations of the missionaries as regards the position of the church in society.

Finally, it is well known how significant a factor the concept of religious freedom and tolerance has been for religious and political developments in nineteenth-century Europe. By transferring this concept to Africa and by tracing its effects in African surroundings a small contribution may be made to a comparative study of the interrelationship between religion and politics. There is of course a certain danger in using a concept which is traditionally bound up with a particular historical and geographical development as it may exclude other and more appropriate variables. On the other hand, while acknowledging the uniqueness of the African situation – in this context the special circumstances attendant on the whole colonial setting and the African response – it may be useful to include the comparative perspective by using what is after all a universally applied concept. This has nothing to do with a qualitative devaluation of one area; it is an attempt to show how the experiences from the African setting can contribute to our insight into a universal problem.[5]

In connection with the applicability of the concept of religious liberty in an analysis it is first necessary to specify what is meant by this concept; otherwise it cannot be made operational as an analytical tool. In addition, the legal background for its introduction in the colonial setting will have to be clarified.

The content of religious liberty

Religious liberty is an inclusive concept within which the emphasis can be put on a number of aspects. In the wake of the liberalism of the nineteenth century the normal usage of the term has centred on freedom of conscience and worship, frequently combined with freedom of speech and assembly. This aspect will also be included here, but it does not suffice alone. Taking the colonial situation into account it seems necessary not just to concentrate on the ideal of freedom and the right to live according to this ideal, but also to include the actual possibility of putting it into practice. We should consider how far the ideal can function within a given society and whether any kind of constraints are at work.

Given these premises, it will for analytical reasons be appropriate to subdivide the concept of religious liberty into three interrelated functional levels, and in conjunction with each level to specify the role of the state. In order to do this the ideas of tolerance, equality and neutrality will be included as natural concomitants of religious liberty. They are indicative of the extent to which the commitment to religious liberty is translated into policy. The various components can then be presented as in the schema on p.25.

Functional level	**Role of the state**
Individual level Freedom of conscience and the free exercise of religion. The ideal of *tolerance* has priority at this level.	The state must practise religious tolerance within its area. The state must ensure that religious liberty is respected and safeguard the right of the individual to live according to his convictions.

Societal level
The relationship between civil rights and religious persuasion. Are all citizens placed on an equal footing independent of their religious affiliation? Will there be equal access to office for all, and do there exist privileges or discrimination due to religious persuasion?

Here it is the concept of *equality* which is most relevant, comprising two aspects: equality of opportunity and equality of attainment, or result.[6]

Within the categories of equality of opportunity and equality of result the options of the state can be presented by employing the following continuum:

passive		active
real inequality	formal equality	real equality

real inequality: the state accepts a pattern of inequality in society with respect to the members of the various religious groups.

formal equality: the state declares that all are equal in connection with civil rights and the state does not take religious adherence into account.

real equality: the state is active in redressing an existing pattern of inequality. This category may be labelled affirmative or positive discrimination.[7]

Institutional level
The relationship between the religious bodies (churches)[8] and the state in a pluralistic situation. The extent to which all are placed on equal footing, or any of them have a privileged or established status. At this level the idea of *neutrality* is predominant.

The question of the religious neutrality of the state is involved. Which sort of bonds exist between the state and the individual churches: personal, national, constitutional, financial etc., and how much significance can be ascribed to these bonds? To what extent is the state realizing the ideal of neutrality in relation to each religious body?

Religious liberty as expressed in colonial rules and regulations

The General Act of the Conference of Berlin of February 1885 has often served within the colonial framework as a sort of code to which various participants in colonial affairs have referred. This has especially been the case with article 6, under the characteristic heading 'Provisions relative to Protection of the Natives, of Missionaries and Travellers, as well as relative to Religious Liberty'.[9] The corresponding articles in other treaties have often been based upon the wording in the Berlin Act.

In article 6, freedom of conscience and religious toleration are fully guaranteed to Africans as well as to foreigners within the regions covered by the Berlin Act.[10] This means that the signatory powers accept the basic principle of religious liberty at what has here been called the individual level (see p.25), and acknowledge the accompanying obligations of the state. At the same time it is clearly stated in article 6 that special protection shall be granted to Christian missionaries, together with scientists and explorers. In more general terms there is also included a guarantee of freedom of missionary enterprise irrespective of denominational origin.

In analysing this article, taking into account the fact that all the signatory powers except one (Turkey) at that time counted themselves as Christian nations, it is possible to conclude that one particular religion, Christianity, is placed in a privileged and established position. Using the analytical schema outlined above, this means that at the institutional level the state cannot claim religious neutrality. It acknowledges special bonds to Christianity without, however, making any denominational distinctions. This conclusion is further strengthened by the proceedings of the Berlin Conference. The German Chancellor, Bismarck, who acted as chairman, had originally suggested a wording like 'They [the signatory powers] shall, without distinction of creed or nation, *favour and aid* all religious, scientific, or charitable institutions . . . ' In view of the claim from Turkey that Muslim missionaries should be placed on an equal footing with Christian missionaries, the decisive words were watered down to 'protect and favour'. The Christian powers could not accept that they might be expected to play an active role in promoting Islam and thereby recognize Islam as equal to Christianity.[11]

The reasons for granting Christianity a special position and for looking favourably on Christian missionary activity are manifold and rooted in a mixture of idealistic motives and national and economic interests. One important reason can be read out of article 6 itself. Missionary activity is supposed to contribute to 'instructing the natives and bringing home to them the blessings of civilization'. This idealistic aim is often invoked as the justification for establishing the colonies. From the point of view of the state the Christian missions were important channels for introducing 'the blessings of civilization'. In view of this joint aim it is only natural for the missions and the colonial powers to establish a sort of cooperation and to protect and favour Christian activity.

We are here touching on what may be called the basic philosophy behind the cooperation between the colonial powers and the Christian missions. The two agencies associate to a large extent a common objective with their activities within the colonial framework. We shall see how each side interprets this philosophy and to what extent cooperation between them can function in view of their respective obligations and special interests.

The interpretation of the Berlin Act outlined here is borne out by the fact that at the Brussels Conference in 1889–90, convened to discuss the abolition of the slave trade, the obligation of the signatory powers to protect missions without distinction of creed was even more strongly emphasized, whereas there is no reference to the general principle of religious liberty.[12] This special emphasis on the missions may partly be due to their engagement in the suppression of the slave trade, partly to the supposed threat from Muslim activity in the Congo Basin, which was thought to be detrimental to the establishment of the colonial system and of civilization in general. It appears again that the state and the missions shared vital interests from different points of view, and this can be reckoned as a contributing factor in the special protection afforded by the state to the missions.

Britain followed closely the various international agreements in her own arrangements concerning the East African spheres of interest. In the Royal Charter granted to the IBEA Co. in September 1888, clause 11 requests that the Company adhere to the principle of religious liberty,[13] and that the representatives of the Company in no way interfere with the religion of the inhabitants. In a weak form a request for religious neutrality on the part of the Company is implied in this clause. This interpretation is in accordance with the signal lack of reference in the Charter to missionary activity, unlike the two treaties mentioned above. The omission may, on the other hand, be accounted for in two possible ways. One is that the general reference in the Charter to obligations which Britain has undertaken by signing other treaties was felt to cover this aspect. The second is that the Charter can be considered to be a purely internal arrangement between two British partners. Cooperation with other private agencies such as missions is taken for granted in a British context.

This last suggestion gains some support when we look at the Agreement of 1 July 1890, between Great Britain and Germany, on the partition of East Africa. Besides mentioning adherence to the principle of religious toleration and freedom, article X is quite specific in stating that 'missionaries of both countries shall have full protection'.[14] This means that no country is allowed to grant her own missionaries special privileges different from the ones granted to foreign missionaries. It is the principle of equal treatment that is adopted. Taking this last point one step further it seems that the concept of religious neutrality in this case is understood in a narrow sense and primarily applied within a Christian context. Looking at the whole political atmosphere in which the Anglo-German agreement was worked out,[15] it may further be hypothesized that the interpretation and implementation of the general principles of religious liberty and religious neutrality will often reflect the barometric reading of a given political situation. This assumption gathers some weight when we focus on Uganda and take the instructions to Captain Lugard into consideration.

Before setting off for Buganda in September 1890 Lugard received a letter of instruction from the Administrator-General of the IBEA Co. in East Africa. According to this, approaches to religious problems and methods of dealing with them in practice were closely bound up with an overview of the political situation in Buganda. Anxiety is expressed that Kabaka Mwanga and the Catholic party might oust the Protestants. The Company wanted to preserve both groups and keep a sort of balance between them, as such an arrangement for various reasons was supposed to facilitate the grip of the Company on the country. Based on this judgement the content of the instructions to Lugard can be divided into two parts. First, he should impress on the Catholic missionaries that, contrary to their expectations, the British Company would respect 'all their religious liberties'. Secondly, he should be 'perfectly impartial' and take a reconciliatory attitude to conflicting interests. It is, however, acknowledged that the practice of this impartiality might be hampered by political realities. 'You should therefore *consolidate* the Protestant party and you should attempt by all means in your power to *conciliate* the Roman Catholics.'[16] Political expediency forbids the colonial authorities to stay neutral and the situation prevents them from treating the religious groups equally. The degree of religious neutrality, that is the nature of the relationships between state authorities and various religious bodies, seems to be conditioned by political circumstances. In so far as any tendency is revealed it seems that political ends take precedence over religious neutrality in situations where priorities must be observed. Furthermore, it is evident that the interpretation of religious liberty and religious neutrality is circumscribed in the sense that the concepts only function within the realm of Christianity.

From the various treaties and instructions the impression emerges that the rules and regulations concerning religious liberty and religious neutrality are wide open to different interpretations and divergences in practice when it comes to implementation. Therefore the principle of religious liberty cannot be judged exclusively on its own merits; its interpretation and implementation should be evaluated in the context of the situation in which it actually has to function. This observation is further confirmed by a general trend in some of the treaties. Christian missionary activity is considered to be desirable and to deserve special protection. Christianity is thus placed in a special and often privileged position compared to Islam, not to mention African traditional religion. While adhering to the principle of religious liberty at the individual level the state authorities are facing difficulties in preserving religious neutrality at the institutional level. As a corollary there is the possibility that the concept of religious liberty in certain circumstances is applied only within the confines of Christianity in order to secure the privileges of the various Christian denominations at the expense of non-Christian groups.

4
The era of Company rule: F. D. Lugard in Buganda 1890–2

Lugard's first treaty with Kabaka Mwanga and the first outline of the church–state problem

The fundamental cleavage between Protestants and Catholics and the Christian monopoly of political power seem from the outset to presuppose a narrow interpretation of religious liberty and the limited use of that concept by the colonial representative. That this in fact was the situation with which Lugard had to reckon is confirmed by an interesting letter from the representative of the IBEA Co. at Zanzibar:

My own idea is that it would be very advantageous if you could make terms with the Mahommedan party and secure their friendship and support. No reason why if freedom of religion is allowed the privilege should not be extended to them provided you could quite reckon upon them and be certain they would not play you false. They and the Protestant party on your side would [*illegible*] and keep the Catholics in order and prevent their breaking loose at any time.[1]

There is no doubt in the writer's mind that the restricted use of religious liberty has so far prevailed. It is further characteristic that the suggestion that the Muslims should now be granted this privilege is prompted by political considerations. The idea of religious liberty is implicitly assumed to serve political ends.

The second theme in the letter concerns the principle of freedom of missionary activity as it was first formulated in the Berlin Act and later repeated in other treaties. The writer expresses as his firm opinion that French priests should be banned from extending their activities into the neighbouring area to the east, Busoga, and that the same ban should be enforced upon Protestants and Muslims so as to avoid a Buganda-like situation in Busoga. It is characteristic that this proposed curtailment of missionary activity, which is equivalent to a limitation of one officially accepted aspect of religious liberty, is prompted by political considerations. It shows awareness of the fact that the extension of missionary work will have political consequences which the state cannot ignore.

Shortly afterwards Lugard finds himself involved with these problems. He must decide whether he will base his policy on the narrow interpretation of religious liberty or interpret it in the wider sense. He will also have to determine the scope of missionary activity and the role that should be assigned to European missionaries. The treaty negotiations with Mwanga to which he gives top priority and concludes within a week of his arrival reveal his decision.[2]

The most important aspect of the treaty signed by the Kabaka, as well as the chiefs from the two parties, was that Mwanga acknowledged the suzerainty of the IBEA Co. and that the Kingdom was placed under its protection and within the British sphere of influence as agreed between the European powers.[3] With regard specifically to the question of religious liberty the treaty can be analysed by making use of the three functional levels outlined on p.25.

At *the individual level* it is significant that in the treaty there is no reference to the general principle of religious liberty as stipulated in the Royal Charter and in Lugard's letter of instruction. Clause 4 only refers to the rights of missionaries to stay in the country irrespective of creed and stipulates that their liberties must be respected.[4] The omission of the general principle of religious liberty seems in retrospect all the more remarkable as it was included two years later when the treaty was renewed after the civil war.

The difference between these two treaties, and the narrow interpretation of religious liberty in the first one, can be explained by pointing to Lugard's weak position and the prevailing political realities. This explanation is further borne out by the fact that when we consider the motives behind the legislation as they are set out in Lugard's correspondence with the missionaries it is beyond all doubt that Lugard himself was working with the wide concept of religious liberty and did not want any limitations in this fundamental right.[5]

His reasons for settling for the narrow definition in practice may have been twofold. First, the pressing need of the moment was not so much an insistence upon the fundamental right itself, especially as it could not be implemented before certain conditions at the societal level were fulfilled. Secondly, priority was to be given to placating the Catholic party and to convincing them that the IBEA Co. was not going to encroach on their rights and status by favouring the Protestants. In other words, Lugard's main concern was to write into the treaty the guarantee that the principle of exclusivity would not, contrary to Catholic expectations, be applied by the British Company. The narrow interpretation of religious liberty serves this purpose by emphasizing the equal rights of the two denominations.

This argument is further supported by the codicil which, primarily at the instigation of the Catholic chiefs, was attached to the treaty: 'Now we, the Catholics, want to read and to teach all people in your country as we please.' The right to reside and work in the country was for both the Christian denominations the problem at issue, and this determined the scope of operation for the concept of religious liberty.

At *the societal level* the situation facing Lugard was that offices at all levels were monopolized by the Christians and equally divided between the two Christian parties. It was with this situation in mind that Lugard put clause 9 into the treaty: 'All offices of the State shall be filled by selection, influenced only by merit and qualification, and entirely irrespective of creed.' The same principle was to be applied in the case of the proposed standing army (clause 6).

In stating this principle Lugard had two aims. In a narrow sense he wanted to make it clear that none of the parties would be allowed to monopolize political power however much any of them either wanted or feared this outcome.[6] In a wider sense he aimed at neutralizing or minimizing the political effects of adherence to Christianity. That is, he wanted to separate politics and Christianity at least to the extent that religious liberty would have some chance to function in Buganda society. In order to achieve this, the authorities would prepare the ground for the practice of formal equality and not just accept a situation of real inequality (see the schema).

All this remained, however, a 'declaration of intent'. The Catholic chiefs induced Lugard to sign the codicil in which he confirmed the agreement between the two Christian parties of October 1889 and thereby the provisions for the equitable allocation of all offices in the state. From a position of weakness when confronted with the political realities in Buganda, Lugard was forced to accept the extant politico-religious structure and thereby the association of Christianity with office-holding. He was not strong enough to make the right to office independent of religious persuasion, and he was not able to move from real inequality towards formal equality. Consequently, Christianity had in practice won an entrenched position, and the question of impartiality or neutrality on the part of the authorities was confined to the intra-Christian domain. It is thus in the light of these limitations that *the institutional level* should be considered.

As might be expected, Lugard did not refer to the churches as such, but to the two missions. He negotiated either with the two bishops while they were temporarily in the country, or with individual missionaries.[7] This procedure reflects the low level of organization of the churches. The churches as such were not in a position to negotiate. The Protestants had, since Mwanga's persecutions in 1885, had a Church Council, also called Church Elders, composed primarily of some of the leading Protestant chiefs.[8] These chiefs thus had a double status, holding office both in the state and in the embryonic church. Lugard was, however, dealing with them in their first capacity. Judging by the available evidence, the Church Council does not seem to have been acting politically on behalf of the Protestants. It was first and foremost accountable to the Finance Committee of the CMS in Buganda, which consisted of all the missionaries resident in Buganda.[9]

This organizational set-up confined for the time being the problem of church and state, as far as the institutional level is concerned, primarily to the relationship between the colonial representatives and the missionaries. An overview of the relationship can be obtained by focusing on the following five issues.

(1) In concluding the treaty Lugard made conscious use of the missionaries' good offices. He appealed to them to use their influence with the two parties, especially on the Catholic side, and he used them as go-betweens.[10] Whether this procedure in the end had much influence on the final outcome is difficult to judge. One should, however, not underestimate the ability of the Ganda chiefs to act independently.[11] Lugard was acknowledging the missionaries' advisory role

and their role as links with foreign powers; he was also consciously making use of the religious structure and the religious apparatus in pursuing his political aims.

(2) Concerning the question of impartiality as set out in his instructions and in clause 4 of the treaty, Lugard tried hard to observe this principle and thereby to practise a policy of religious neutrality on behalf of the Company, although he clearly did not do so for idealistic reasons. He was especially aware of the necessity to avoid creating the impression that he was giving the British missionaries preferential treatment and a privileged position. This meant that he refused to acknowledge any special relationship between Anglican missionaries and British officials, nor did he consider it incumbent upon the British authorities to secure favourable conditions for the missionary enterprise of Britain's own nationals. The ideal of religious neutrality militated against such an arrangement, and Lugard tried to avoid appearing to have special bonds with the British missionaries.[12]

It has been much discussed how far Lugard succeeded in preserving a neutral stance.[13] Against the background of the very complicated and often heated Buganda situation this discussion has often given rise to pronouncements of moral judgement and may not in the final analysis be all that fruitful. Instead, contemporary developments are more likely to throw light on the concept of religious neutrality in the situation in which Lugard was placed.

In the first instance, soon after the conclusion of the treaty, the Protestant missionaries, and even more so the Protestant party, started to accuse Lugard of abandoning his neutral stance.[14] They even voiced the suspicion that he was favouring the Catholics. Tensions continued to build up over the first half of 1891 due to Lugard's and his deputy's abortive attempts to resolve various outstanding problems. Things went so far that the Protestant missionaries itemized their complaints in a strongly worded letter to friends in Britain with a view to stimulating further action.[15] Considering the fact that feelings were running high, and the almost daily rows between the two parties,[16] these complaints say less about Lugard's lack of neutrality than about the frustration of the Protestants' expectations that the Company would settle matters in favour of the British missionaries.[17]

This leads directly to the second point. Lugard had very little scope for any sort of neutrality. As we have just seen, any of Lugard's actions or decisions were, against the background of the prevailing tensions, looked upon with great suspicion. In addition, the constant threat of war between the two parties reminded Lugard of his dependence on the Protestants. His weak political and military position made it necessary for him to have allies within Buganda. Every time it came to a real situation of choice Lugard had to admit that he directly or indirectly decided in favour of the Protestants, 'for I do not wish to deal a heavy blow to my own creed, or to the party who saved me, and threw in their lot with me when I came here'. And reflecting his own instructions he added, 'Moreover I think just at present a balance of power in the State is most desirable.'[18]

Lugard's actions at this time are better evaluated in terms of *Realpolitik* than measured with idealistic norms. Impartiality and neutrality require a position of strength which Lugard did not have. His concern was, therefore, more the reduction of the worst inequalities so as to secure a balance and reasonably fair play for the Catholics.

(3) While minimizing the importance of the missionaries' national origin Lugard emphasized their European origin when defining their rights and duties

towards the colonial authorities as represented by himself as the permanent Resident of the IBEA Co. In the treaty with Mwanga there was a provision that the Company would send a fully accredited Resident to the court. His jurisdiction was clearly specified: all Europeans resident in Buganda should refer all disputes to him as arbitrator. According to Lugard's own explanation to the missionaries this power also covered disputes between sects.[19] All decisions made locally were appealable to the Company's officials either at the coast or in England.

The placing of the missionaries under the jurisdiction of the colonial authorities meant that the state took priority over the representatives of the church, even to the extent that matters connected with intra-Christian differences fell within the domain of the state. However implicit this may have been at this early stage, it was certainly an attempt to establish the authority of the colonial representative and reduce the autonomous position which the missionaries enjoyed in a pioneer area.

Secondly, and as a corollary, the missionaries were placed on the same footing as any other Europeans, and all Europeans were considered to be in a different category from Africans. This was probably a sensible arrangement at this stage, but it might have certain repercussions when a church became fully organized and the position of the missionaries within that church had to be specified. Would the missionaries in the eyes of the state still be considered as overseas agents on a par with colonial officials, or would the state be willing to consider them as integrated in the local church? This problem was indirectly touched upon in the treaty, but it was soon to be brought under closer scrutiny: as early as January 1891 the Anglican Bishop Tucker started preparations for the ordination of an African clergy and issued licences to Baganda Christians to go out as evangelists. The position of the missionaries then had to be further clarified taking into account the prevailing theories about the relationship between mission and church.

(4) The missionaries on their part tried to discover what sort of obligations the governing body would undertake and what sort of benefits the missions could expect from the colonial authorities. The first issue brought up for Lugard's consideration was taxation, and in particular the duties on the goods that the missions were bringing into the country. The missions wanted to be exempted and not to be placed in the same category as European traders.[20] It was difficult for Lugard at this very early stage in the setting up of an administration to give a categorical answer, but he expressed the basic principle that 'the originators of this Company have no wish to make money out of Missionaries, but on the contrary would rather go to some expense and inconvenience to assist them'.[21]

In his answer to these inquiries Lugard pointed several times to the fact that the missions as well as the Company were engaged in the work of civilization and that this common aim naturally led to concessions on the part of the Company. In a wider context this is part of a basic problem which already came under consideration during the drawing-up of the Berlin Treaty and has to do with the policy implied in the words 'protect and favour'. Referring to the usefulness of their work from the point of view of the state, the missions claimed special concessions. By granting exemptions from taxes and duties the Company gave in this case a sort of indirect support to the Christian work. This indirect support could, however, manifest itself in a number of different ways, for example in the granting of freehold land. In view of the future arrangement between church and state it is important to take this practice of indirect support into account.

Without actually quoting the Berlin Treaty, the Catholic Bishop did in fact refer to the question of protection as the second item among the obligations that the missions expected the colonial authorities to fulfil. He asked what sort of protection they could expect from the Company when extending their work to remoter parts of Buganda and to areas outside Buganda, but within the British sphere of interest.[22] Again it was difficult for Lugard to give a clear-cut answer. He clearly acknowledged the obligation of the Company to give such protection. When it came to practice the realities were, however, that the Company had no firm power basis and nothing to protect the missions with.

Looking at the problem in a wider perspective, this dilemma suggests two alternative solutions. The colonial authorities could have minimized their obligations, as was the case when the directors of the IBEA Co. in August 1891 turned down Bishop Tucker's call to accept a special responsibility for the Anglican missionaries and let it influence any decision to withdraw from Uganda.[23] Alternatively the colonial authorities could accept full responsibility for the protection of the missionaries, but in return request control over the 'missionary extensions' – the spread of missionary activity into new areas. This would involve a reduction in the freedom of missionary activity otherwise guaranteed in various treaties. There was thus a price to pay for the principle of protection. And if the state took its responsibility seriously, especially with regard to its own nationals, this, in a period of turmoil and scarce resources, could only mean a curtailment of missionary enterprise.[24]

(5) Missionary extension becomes an important factor in itself in clarifying the relationship between the colonial authorities and the missions. When Lugard was briefed before departing for Buganda it was made clear to him that missionary extension might have political repercussions. Immediately after his arrival he was faced with exactly this problem as regards the area of Busoga. The Catholic Bishop inquired about the procedures for the extension of missionary work.[25] This inquiry gave rise to long drawn-out discussions and deliberations, and turned out to be a test-case for the interrelationship between colonial administration and missions. At the same time it focused on the special circumstances arising from the fact that both the missions and the colonial authority were in the process of establishing themselves. Lugard had very few instructions about which rules should be applied in the areas not yet brought under effective administration and where no treaties had been set up with local rulers. On paper the areas were within the British sphere of interest, but no legal code of any sort was in operation.

In this pioneer situation it is apparent that Lugard was not too sure about the best procedure. The lines of communication to the coast and even more to London were so long that he could not await further clarification, especially as the rivalry between the Protestants and the Catholics made quick action necessary. This rivalry was in fact one important motive behind the wish for missionary extension.[26] Lugard felt himself caught in a dilemma between the established right to missionary enterprise and the foreseeable political consequences of it.[27]

Lugard was on safe ground as long as it was the missionaries themselves who claimed the protection of the Company. Then he could dictate conditions and render the departure of missions dependent upon express permission. His scope was more limited when no mutual obligations were involved, as was the case when the missionaries declared that they were going at their own risk. In the period just after his arrival, he was not strong enough to attach firm conditions to their movements within the British sphere of interest. In the attempt to balance the two conflicting interests he confined himself to recommendations and appeals without making any firm decision. He found it desirable that the missions informed the higher authorities at the coast about their planned extensions and waited for their sanction, but he did not explicitly claim the right of prohibition. Instead he asked them to consider, first, that it was beyond doubt that any injury or insult to a European missionary would involve the Company, as in that case European reputation and authority would be jeopardized in the eyes of the Africans. In other words, in Lugard's opinion the distinction between the secular and the ecclesiastical representatives was no longer valid in such circumstances.[28]

Secondly, he enumerated various conditions which in his opinion must be observed if the missions wanted to enjoy the goodwill of the Company. Their centres of activity should clearly manifest themselves as centres of civilization. Then they should make sure that they would be welcomed by the chief of a given community and work in cooperation with him. This political condition was accompanied by another one: they should encourage loyalty towards the Company wherever they went. Finally, they should refrain from interference in politics and, especially, their presence should not lead to 'further discussions between parties'. It was thus with an eye to the Buganda situation that Lugard emphasized that they should come to new places 'with no other object than to preach the Word of God', which was in accordance with his often repeated claim 'that their business was to teach their religion, and ours to settle the country'.[29]

While the Catholic Bishop seemed not unwilling to follow the guidelines laid down by Lugard, the CMS missionaries without any consultation sent two missionaries to Busoga in February 1891.[30] The CMS had, however, some difficulty in maintaining their presence in Busoga. Apart from shortage of manpower it is striking that during most of 1891 and 1892 the Anglican missionary work was carried out without much overall planning, without internal agreement and without any real leadership.[31] It was, therefore, from a weakened position, which seems to have added to Lugard's annoyance,[32] that they were in the beginning of 1892 entering into a head-on collision with Lugard about the right to missionary extension without any interference from the colonial authorities.

In a renewed discussion on the extension to Busoga around New Year in 1891 Lugard's deputy, Captain Williams, tightened the policy of the Company on missionary extension. He requested that the missions accept the right of the Company to prohibit any extension; the Company would not allow the Catholic and the Protestant missions to go to the same place, and a treaty was to be concluded with the chief in question before departure.[33] The explanation of the timing of this change to a more restricted policy can be found in the strengthened position that Lugard and his colleagues now enjoyed in the country. A number of caravans had come up from the coast with new men, arms and equipment, so Lugard, on his itinerary to the western part of the British sphere of interest in the last half of 1891, had concluded treaties with various chiefs and had with the assistance of the Ganda regiments lessened the ever-present Muslim threat in the area bordering on Bunyoro. The Company could now act from a position of greater strength and thereby pursue a firmer policy towards the politico-religious parties and the missions.

The CMS missionaries' local committee (the Finance Committee) could not accept the supremacy of the Company with regard to missionary extension. Their main argument was that these steps violated the principle of religious liberty. They considered themselves, according to their understanding of this principle, free to occupy any opening in the British sphere which they found would benefit their work. Consequently they could not accept any obligation to inform the Company before going, nor could they accept its right of prohibition. Finally, through the association of treaty-making and missionary extension, the Africans could only be left with the impression that religion and politics were inextricably linked, which ran contrary to the intended policy of the Company. The feelings and points of view were aptly set out in the following sentences:

I am obliged to ask for a definite reply or the matter must go home to be decided. The question is this, do you refuse us as British Missionaries the right to extend our Missions anywhere in Imperial British E. Africa without your sanction? If you are unable as the Resident in Buganda to answer this on behalf of the Directors, we have only one course open to us, viz. to refer the matter to our Committee [in London] to be brought before the Houses of Parliament. As a matter of courtesy we should refer any extension to you but not as a matter of right.[34]

The CMS missionaries retreated somewhat from this position by postponing the final decision,[35] and, following the impression made upon them by the tumultuous events of the civil war between the two parties at the end of January 1892, they decided, in deference to Lugard's wishes, to delay the matter until the arrival of the Bishop.[36] In June, however, they returned to their original standpoint in spite of Lugard's attempts at dissuasion,[37] thereby underlining the continued fundamental disagreement on the rights of the missions *vis-à-vis* the colonial authorities.

These issues present various aspects of the relationship between church and state peculiar to the founding period in the colonial situation, though it is striking how similar these problems are in character to the ones normally met elsewhere between church and state, and it is furthermore striking that they emerge at this very early stage of the whole process. We have already seen one typical feature of the colonial and missionary situation. The missionaries as well as the colonial officials had important connections with a much larger political arena, with persons and institutions outside Buganda. In various ways these two lines to Europe had an impact on the local process of policy- and decision-making. Although the long lines of communication made 'the men on the spot' relatively independent they were after all subordinate and responsible to their home authorities. They were at the same time aware of the fact that the question of religious liberty could easily stir up opinion in Britain. This set certain limits to their scope of action and had also the effect of deterring them from going too far to one or the other side. Lugard was conscious of this dilemma, as he showed very clearly in the aftermath of the battle of Mengo (see below). The missionaries were prepared if necessary to use their prerogative of referring matters to headquarters and thereby to public and political opinion in Britain.[38]

Religious liberty and the administration of the law

Caught between the African realities, the missionaries' diverging interests and the latent, and sometimes manifest, impact from the European arena, Lugard had considerable difficulty in establishing any sort of working arrangement as regards the principle of religious liberty. The interrelationship between the two kinds of European envoys, missionaries and Company officials, had not been clarified. More important still, the internal situation in Buganda was characterized by anomalies. On the one hand Lugard had pledged himself to the principle that offices should be filled irrespective of creed; on the other, he had in the codicil to the treaty agreed to the equal distribution of offices between the two politico-religious parties.

The main issue pertinent to the events of 1891 is how Lugard and the IBEA Co., as the secular authority, administered the law as laid down in the treaty, and how they tried to balance the inconsistencies which were implicit in their legal basis. During the first three months of 1891, prior to his expedition to the western part of the British sphere of interest, Lugard was confronted with the question of the equal division of the country between the two parties, and the administration of the law in the case of civil repercussions following upon changes of religion.

The former issue came to a head in connection with the Sese Islands, situated in Lake Victoria close to the mainland. The Protestants claimed that these islands were covered by the agreement of October 1889 between the Christians, and should accordingly be divided equally between the two parties. Mwanga, supported by the Catholics and their priests, contested this interpretation. He asserted that the islands were royal property and consequently at his private disposal, or alternatively that they had the status of a tributary area like Busoga. In both cases they lay outside the jurisdiction of the laws in force in the Kingdom.[39]

Despite the Kabaka's promise of access for both religions to the Sese Islands the Protestant party could not accept such a situation. The islands were of great strategic importance because they controlled the canoes and thereby access to Buganda by water.[40] Characteristically, the Protestant leaders asked the leading Anglican missionary to approach Lugard and request him to exercise his authority in this matter. R. H. Walker's arguments touched upon certain crucial points in the whole legal predicament, and can be divided into three parts.[41]

(1) The question was one of justice and adherence to the October 1889 agreement, according to which the Kabaka renounced his right as owner of all land and agreed to allow the heads of each party to divide the whole country between them, including the Sese Islands.

(2) If the Kabaka kept the islands as his property, they would be given to the Catholics, as the King himself was at least a nominal Catholic and therefore not impartial. In view of the strategic importance of the islands the issue inevitably became a serious political matter.

(3) The question of missionary freedom was hinted at in the following understatement: 'Liberty for propagating their religion at an advantage (by being in the possession of the chieftainships on the Sese Islands) this is a very small matter and one I consider to be of no importance. The Protestant faith requires no civil help to win its way.'

Lugard took the matter up, and succeeded in persuading the Kabaka to give way and agree to a division of the islands.[42] He stood firm on the principle that the laws of the country, however feeble they might be, must be followed and must apply in all parts of Buganda;[43] and he supported the religious division of the islands because religious differences were already firmly entrenched there, and a division was thus necessary.[44]

It is possible to suggest two further reasons for Lugard's religious policy. First, if there was to be a balance between the two parties (and this requirement has earlier been shown to be a cornerstone of Lugard's policy), the Protestants must gain a foothold in these strategically important islands. Secondly, taking up the hint in Walker's third argument, Lugard admitted that without some landed rights, such as the right to chieftainships, it would be impossible for the Protestants to go out and teach.[45] In other words, the expansion of Protestantism was dependent on close cooperation with the traditional office-holders. Lugard was thus fully aware that for all practical purposes missionary expansion was related to the religious division of the country.

While thus supporting the implementation of the equal religious division of the whole country, invoking as his authority the supposed legal basis, Lugard found himself in a much more difficult position when he had to guarantee and defend equal division against a background of frequent changes of religion among office-holders. These changes were causing an ever-increasing numerical imbalance between the two Christian parties. How was Lugard to balance the administration of a law which linked the right to office to particular religious affiliations with the constitutional ideal of religious liberty, according to which the right to office must be independent of religious persuasion? To what extent could he as the secular authority use force to ensure the observance of the law when the same law infringed a basic right, a right which he and the Company claimed to respect? And to what extent could political necessity justify him in upholding such a law? This whole complex of problems underlay the burning issue of the eviction of people from their chieftainships and shambas (gardens or estates) which was a bone of contention right through 1891.[46]

The numerical balance between the adherents of the two parties became increasingly disturbed. The fact that the Kabaka belonged to the Catholic party acted as an inducement for people at the chiefly level as well as commoners to move towards this faction. This resulted in a kind of 'bandwagon effect'.[47] The explanation is straightforward: the Kabaka's membership gave legitimacy to the Catholic party within the traditional structure. Catholics were 'the Kabaka's men', whereas Protestants were labelled 'the Katikiro's men' (the Prime Minister's men).[48] The numerical strength of the former group tilted the balance which was necessary to maintain the system of equal allocation of land and offices, and the system now seemed more and more without foundation in reality.

According to the agreement between the two parties, in order to preserve the equal division of the country, any person changing his religion would have to forfeit his office or shamba. If the individual concerned did not voluntarily take the initiative to this step, the opposite party stepped in, and 'evictions' took place, often by forceful means. To clarify the situation it is necessary to illustrate the impact of party divisions on African society. The chieftainships, estimated to be about 600 in all, were shared out between the two parties in such a way that every holder of a post was to be accountable to a superior of the opposite party.[49] According to the agreement between the two parties of October 1889 (the Bukumbi agreement), this system was to maintain a permanent balance between the parties. Consequently, when an office-holder left his party, as he automatically did if he changed his religion, he must be replaced by another person from the same party. The prerogative of appointment, after the rise of the Christians to power, was invested in the leaders of each party. This was the case in the Sese Islands. In the event, however, it often proved difficult to induce a chief to resign his office and thereby give up the material benefits which accrued from such a position of power. In a number of cases the party claiming the office had to take the matter into its own hands by means of forceful evictions. This problem became especially difficult to handle as the power of the Kabaka was restricted, and in any case he was suspected of Catholic bias. Thus the central authority in Bugandan society was either not functioning or seriously hampered in its functioning. Complaints and requests for assistance in enforcing the law arrived on Lugard's table. He was considered the appropriate authority because, having signed the codicil, he had become a guarantor for the legal system in the country.

Within the newly-established system, and despite the constraints which it imposed, traditional obligations were expected to function as before. This meant that the Bakopi and the sub-chiefs had to work for their superiors and pay tribute to them in accordance with the system of patronage and clientship which permeated the whole of Buganda society. Differences in creed were supposed to be irrelevant within these traditional strings of authority. In practice, however, a number of people gave priority to religious connections and paid tribute to their co-religionists rather than to their superiors by tradition. This could also work from the top downwards, so that a Catholic chief would not want Protestant sub-chiefs within his assigned area.[50] It is clear that a new system of obligations and loyalties was cross-cutting the traditional one and severely disturbing it in its function. The visible result of this was a large number of evictions, more or less arbitrary, from shambas. There was, moreover, no real authority capable of dealing with this problem. It has earlier been shown how Christianity and the two Christian parties could be integrated into the Bugandan power structure at the macro-level. In the present case, however, the two systems of authority worked against one another, and no integration seemed possible. The result was that Lugard was forced into complex situations, as all grievances were referred to him. Because of the treaty and the accompanying codicil Lugard could not simply ignore these evictions. He had of course other reasons for limiting these conflicts, and vital ones. On several occasions they had brought the two parties to the brink of civil war, and violent skirmishes had broken out. Added to this was the fact that rumours, then as ever since in the Buganda context, were in themselves a political factor to be reckoned with.

It was some time before Lugard began to understand the reasons underlying the constant evictions and the grievances of the parties, which often came to his notice through the mediation of the two missions. At first he only grasped the import of the change in obligation and loyalty.[51] Consequently he addressed himself primarily to the problems at the grass-roots level by inducing the chiefs to agree that there were to be no more oustings from shambas, and all persons holding shambas were to fulfil their obligations to their rightful chief irrespective of his creed. In order to back the settlement up with a palpable executive power, he impressed upon the Kabaka that he should be impartial, reinstate the evicted, and pass judgement in future cases; if the necessity arose Lugard himself would step in.[52]

Lugard aimed at restoring the traditional system to such an extent that the original hierarchy of loyalties and obligations could replace once more the newer divisions and attachments based on religious affiliations. Judging from later events, Lugard did not succeed; the arrangement based on alternate layers of office-holders of different creeds had weakened the original system too much. In addition, the centre of power lacked its traditional strength due to the Kabaka's reduced position. The traditional power structure centred on the Kabaka was, as later research has demonstrated, the *sine qua non* for the proper functioning of the Buganda system.[53] Finally, the Kabaka himself was contributing to the vulnerability of the system by belonging officially to one of the parties.

A little later Lugard found himself in an awkward position when he became aware of the full implications of the law behind which he had taken a firm stand. The Protestants, invoking the Bukumbi agreement of October 1889, asked him to effect the forfeiture of office by chiefs who had changed their religions.[54] On the one hand Lugard had to acknowledge the validity of the treaty and the codicil, on the other he was committed to sanctioning absolute freedom of religion.[55] To resolve this dilemma he proposed that only the higher echelons of the hierarchy, that is, the twelve most powerful chiefs, should be subject to the agreement, and even this was to be a temporary measure. Half of the positions were to go to each party, and in the event of a change of religion the official concerned was to resign his office and a new candidate was to be appointed from the same party. People in all other positions were to be free to choose and change their religion without civil consequences. When the Protestant leaders rejected this proposal, Lugard suggested a modified version according to which the number of office-holders liable to be turned out was increased from 12 to 30–40. This was still a great reduction compared with the earlier 600.[56]

Lugard was clearly concerned about the whole problem of eviction from office due to changes in religion. In this newest proposal he attempted to create as much scope as possible for the realization of religious liberty. This would also serve as a means of reducing the political importance of religious factionalism. At the same time, the political consequences of the introduction of religious liberty, even understood in the narrow sense, were clearly grasped by the Catholics. They and the Kabaka were delighted with Lugard's proposals, as this form of religious liberty would mean the removal of hindrances to their expansion by abolishing for all practical purposes the principle of equal division of the country. As they had the Kabaka in their camp, they now expected to sweep the board.[57]

The Protestants were also fully aware that religious liberty would have political effects, so they presented Lugard with a threefold argument.[58] First and foremost, they claimed, the result would be the annihilation of the Protestant party, and the balance which so far had secured peace would disappear. Secondly, freedom of missionary work would be nullified, as access to teaching was closely bound up with the possession of shambas and chieftainships. This is the same argument as was used in the case of the Sese Islands. Thirdly, they said, Lugard was breaking the law by failing to uphold the agreement of 1889. The volte-face in the position of the two parties will readily be seen from these arguments. Whereas the Catholics had earlier stood on the Bukumbi agreement in defence of their position, it was now the Protestants' turn to do so, while the Catholics saw their advantage in the introduction of religious liberty.

The CMS missionaries were strongly in favour of the Protestant cause, to the annoyance of Lugard.[59] Once again the recurrent problem of the claim to exclusivity was rearing its head. R. H. Walker detected a dilemma among the Protestant chiefs; as Christians they were prepared to give up all power and leave the country altogether, handing over power to the Catholics. As Baganda they were inclined to stand on their rights; and the missionaries advised them to choose the last option, for obvious reasons.[60]

Faced with this opposition, Lugard arrived at an accurate evaluation of the whole situation:

I also pointed out that this system of ousting men from their shambas if they changed their nominal creed was entirely opposed to the complete freedom of religion which I had stated in my treaty; and that the only way in which I could reconcile myself to it was as a temporary expedient to preserve the balance of the parties till we were stronger (or rather, as I *really* think, till they are impotent by having no power left) and can dominate both, and I felt that I was compelled to accept the Protestants' decision so far as it was contained in their mutual agreement because at the time that the treaty was signed the Catholics had insisted on my pledging myself to observe this treaty between them.[61]

Four observations may be made on the outcome of this attempt to introduce religious liberty by changing the law and thus, at the societal level, reducing the ties between the holding of office and religious adherence.

(1) Lugard gave priority to *Realpolitik*. His own position was not yet strong enough to allow him to act independently of the internal political situation in Buganda. On the contrary, he was dependent upon the preservation of a certain balance between the various forces, and therefore to some extent had to compromise his impartiality by securing the position of the Protestants when they were on the defensive.

(2) Lugard found himself caught between European norms and African realities. Measured by European standards he knew full well that he was acting contrary to the ideal of religious liberty, even in the narrow sense. The only mitigating factor was that the law's period of validity had been limited to two years. He further tried to put some distance between himself and the administration of the law by constituting a 'Council of State' consisting of the King, the Katikiro and four members from each side to deal with chiefly appointments in the two-year period.[62] Seen with a jaundiced eye, this could appear as an attempt to 'keep his own hands clean' as far as the administration of the law was concerned.[63]

(3) It is once more brought home to us that the realization of religious liberty was conditioned by political circumstances and that the ideal itself cannot have had the required impact on the basis of its own intrinsic qualities alone. This was the case even when the Europeans themselves were supposed to be in control.

(4) The consequence of this was a tendency in Buganda society for freedom of religion to be used as a weapon in the hands of the stronger part with which to threaten the interests of the weaker. This observation must, however, be further substantiated.

The next development occurred when Captain Williams, as Lugard's second-in-command, was left in charge during Lugard's nine-month absence in the western part of the British sphere of influence. During this period the problems connected with religious liberty became more acute, and the positions of the various actors can be more accurately assessed. So far the initiative had mainly been with the Company officials who had acted on more or less clear instructions and had felt themselves under an obligation to administrate in accordance with a basic principle in British colonial policy, at least to the extent that they could avoid public criticism from the European side.

The new development during Williams' period had as its immediate cause the fact that the colonial authority was faced with a direct request for the introduction of absolute 'liberty of conscience' and guarantees that this principle would be observed in practice in Buganda. The request was made by the titular Catholic Bishop, Monsignor Hirth, who shrewdly pointed out that, if the principle was sound, there was no reason to wait for another two years, as Lugard had decided. His line of argument was that the law as expressed in the treaty and codicil, having resulted in evictions, was contrary to the principle of religious liberty. He cleverly added that the existence of two parties was not a necessary condition for the maintenance of Company authority in Buganda, thereby casting doubt upon a point which had so far been a cornerstone in the Company's policy.[64] Whatever value Mgr Hirth attached to the principle of religious liberty, it is beyond all doubt that his timing was prompted by the fact that religious liberty in the circumstances would serve as a vehicle for the growth and expansion of Catholicism; the demand for religious liberty was thus in this context also good strategy.

For the CMS missionaries the only possible interpretation left was that the Catholics' aim was to make 'the R.C. Religion the recognized national religion of Buganda', thereby realizing the old claim to exclusivity, or at least a political monopoly. They substantiated this further by claiming that the Catholic Bishop had accused the Protestants of being in rebellion against Kabaka Mwanga. It is doubtful whether this Protestant interpretation of events was fair towards the Catholics. The argument is interesting, as it illustrates the point mentioned above, that the 'two-party system' in the shape it took at this juncture was in disharmony with the traditional centralized structure with the Kabaka at the apex, and even tended to have a disintegrating effect, while a 'one-party system' could easily be integrated.[65]

Captain Williams was obviously impressed by Mgr Hirth's arguments.[66] He was particularly amenable to them as he was himself faced with numerous claims asking him to act in accordance with the law and enforce evictions from chieftainships and shambas on the grounds of changes of religion. Williams felt uneasy about this and accordingly tried first to change the law by introducing absolute freedom of religion immediately. Faced with strong opposition he next followed in Lugard's footsteps and worked for a limitation of the number of chieftainships allocated to each party.[67]

This attempt failed too, as Williams could not provide the guarantees the Protestant leaders wanted. When Williams placed the strength of the Company behind a guarantee of fair treatment and protection, and even offered to identify himself closely with the Protestants by becoming a member of the Church Council, the Protestant leaders shrewdly asked for a proof of that strength, namely that he induce the Kabaka to hoist the British flag and thereby finally recognize the British as rulers.[68] Mwanga refused, and the Protestants took this to be a token of the Company's weakness. In their eyes it did not have the power to neutralize the political effects of the introduction of religious liberty.[69] Their most secure option was still to rely on the existing law as upheld by the Company. In the end Williams was back at square one, and could only repeat that the arrangement as it stood expired in two years' time.

The deliberations on the Protestant side in response to Williams' religious policy are of special interest. It will therefore be appropriate in this connection to examine more carefully the position of the Protestant Ganda leaders and the Protestant missionaries by investigating to what extent there was or could be a distinction between religion and politics in their minds. As pointed out earlier (p.40) the Protestant missionaries fancied that their converts were being placed in a cleft stick between, on the one hand, the Christian obligation to renounce temporal power, and on the other the desire to maintain their political rights. This dilemma was of course rooted in the double role of the Protestants as Christians and as Ganda nationals. The missionaries were inclined to think that the first consideration ought to take precedence: 'We as Christian missionaries always tell people that political power is undesirable, the truth must triumph finally.'[70] Taken at its face value, this meant that they should stay in Buganda, willingly give up their power and simply live as Christians, thus in practice separating religion and politics.[71]

On closer examination, we find that the Protestant leaders were not really faced with the same options; consequently they were not working with the same distinction between religion and politics. Either they stayed on and claimed their rights or, following the missionaries' recommendations, they renounced their political rights and left the floor to the Catholics, but with the crucial difference from the position of the missionaries that they would then feel obliged to emigrate and found a new state. This was in fact even planned to the extent that they had decided to make their leader, the Katikiro, the new King.[72] However unrealistic this may have seemed in the eyes of the missionaries, the important features to bear in mind are that the Ganda leaders first based their attitude on the concept of exclusivity for both themselves and the Catholics, and secondly were not in a position to separate religion and politics as the missionaries advised.

Moving on from these conclusions, it is possible to formulate some hypotheses about the concept of religious liberty and its applications in African society. First, religious liberty was liable to be conceived of as a tool in the hands of the stronger faction, and not as an end which was intrinsically valuable to work towards. Secondly, the introduction of religious liberty would mean the renunciation of the goods which the Protestants had gained through the exploitation of the religious structure, supposedly with God's blessing. Thirdly, as religion and politics overlapped so much there was hardly any room for a concept like religious liberty. Tolerance could be practised at the individual level, but at the societal level it was difficult to grasp why a change of religion should not be accompanied by corresponding changes in social position, as the influential positions concerned had been acquired on the basis of a particular religious affiliation. And fourthly, seen from the outside, the principle of religious liberty was not compatible with the then structure of Ganda society, with its marked politicization of religion and the corresponding religious factions. For religious liberty to function, an alternative structure would be required, upheld by a powerful centre which could ensure the political neutralization of religion.

The Protestant missionaries saw Captain Williams' policy as a threat to the Protestant party and thereby to their own work in the country. They were once again faced with a dilemma. On the one hand their evangelical background urged them to stay out of politics. 'Spiritual work must be done by spiritual men' was the maxim which they constantly had before their eyes. On the other hand their missionary vocation and the obligations which it entailed did involve the practical necessity of thinking and acting strategically: 'We do not care to see our people strong politically, but we do want to see the pure faith gaining ground and reaching the Dark Corners.'[73] The last consideration proved the more persuasive and became the formula which guided their thinking, and induced them to act politically in at least three respects.

(1) They advised the Protestant leaders to stay on and claim their rights, as the

missionaries themselves, in order to be allowed to carry out their work, were dependent on the secular power of the Protestant chiefs. This meant that they were not likely, given their role as advisers to the Protestant party, to exhibit any exaggerated enthusiasm for the separation of religion and politics.

(2) They were also acting in their second political role as intermediaries between the Protestant leaders and the colonial authorities, and they were in fact being deliberately jockeyed into this position by Captain Williams, so much so that this became one of the reasons for the subsequent animosity between Williams and the missionaries.[74]

(3) More than ever before, they were exploiting their lines of communication with Europe. They informed relatives, friends and the CMS headquarters about the situation, and asked them to do as much as they could to influence developments to their advantage.[75] The reverberations of this correspondence of course reached the ears of the directors of the IBEA Co., who took this opportunity to impress upon their Uganda employees the need for impartiality and respect for freedom of religion in all their activities.[76]

Because of the time-consuming procedure necessary to obtain a response from Europe, the delaying effect of the missionaries' correspondence must be considered an important factor in itself. The missionaries in some cases exploited this factor tactically by notifying Captain Williams of their correspondence and drawing his attention to the possible consequences; 'Again he [Captain Williams] is afraid we Missionaries will report him to the papers as bullying the Protestants and favouring the Catholics.'[77]

The issue of impartiality brings us to two major themes which emerge in connection with the tensions between the missionaries and Williams. The missionaries felt sure that Williams would do his best to prevent an exodus of the Protestants; 'for what would Christian England say if under British rule the Protestants had found Buganda too hot a place for them?'[78] It is first implied, then, that the Company would have to account for its failure to give the Protestants and the British missionaries sufficient protection to carry on their work in a British-administered area: there was thus an implicit reference to the special obligation which the Company, in the eyes of the missionaries, had towards its national and denominational 'kith and kin'.[79] Secondly, it is implied that the Company was not showing impartiality towards the denominations, thereby reneging on the promise of equal treatment irrespective of creed as laid down in various treaties from the Berlin Act onwards. The subsequent reaction from the Head Office in London confirms that this concept of religious liberty was foremost in the minds of the directors.

From an analytical point of view it is interesting that we are here faced with a case where two levels of the religious liberty complex are mutually incompatible in the Bugandan situation. Captain Williams tries at the societal level to cut the ties between the holding of office and religious alignment. This is, however, likely to result in precisely the kind of violation of the principle of missionary freedom with which the European arena is mainly concerned. Without pursuing the matter of the incompatibility of the two levels of religious liberty any further, we now have some indication of the extent to which the Buganda situation ended in a deadlock to which it was difficult for the principals to see any solution.

The CMS missionaries felt somewhat uneasy about the whole question of religious liberty. They wanted the principle to work in Buganda, but on the other hand they recognized that the people did not understand the problem. And they were quite sure that if it was suddenly introduced it would lead to trouble and to the extinction of the Protestant party. However justified the principle might be in theory, there was no justfication for the Protestants having to pay the price alone.[80] Instead the missionaries tried to defuse the issue of religious liberty by suggesting that the two parties should be considered purely political. A change of party would naturally involve the forfeiture of office, just as a politician at home was likely to lose his constituency if he changed his party. The evictions would therefore not be considered a violation of the principle of religious liberty.[81] Lugard was inclined to take a similar view when he commented on Captain Williams' attempt to introduce religious liberty, giving as his reason that the whole matter had nothing to do with freedom of religion, but concerned 'the heathen who belong nominally to either party, and who change with the political horizon, or because the King is a Catholic'.[82]

The model proposed by the missionaries, with purely political parties, was later legitimized further on the basis of another interesting distinction: 'Thus whilst religion is the ground of agreement between the members of the various parties it is not the ground of difference between the opposing parties.'[83] This differentiation between religion as the cohesive principle, but not as the reason for political competition, was certainly an accurate analysis of how the party system functioned, but it presupposed again that there was a distinction between religion and politics which, as we have seen, did not exist in the Ganda context; nor did such a differentiation exonerate the Company from the responsibility of administering a law which stated that change of religion involved the loss of civil rights. A condition for the success of such a solution would be that a stable party system was at work, with insignificant crossings between the two parties.

Hence, it is characteristic that in Lugard's mind the ideal solution seemed to be a one-party system with Mwanga at its head, and full recognition of British supremacy. He was therefore delighted, just before his return to Kampala, to hear rumours to the effect that Mwanga had fallen out with the Catholics and was bent upon joining the Protestants. Such a move would bring the loyal party to power, eliminate the Catholics as a political party and teach the Catholic priests a lesson. He considered the latter responsible for having taught the people to identify religion and politics and thus for the serious factional conflicts in the country. In almost euphoric terms, Lugard came close to supporting the old claims to exclusivity and political monopoly for the Protestant party.[84] The rumours about Mwanga were probably exaggerated; nevertheless Lugard later blamed Captain Williams for not seizing the opportunity at the time and pushing Mwanga in the Protestant direction.[85]

Back at Kampala Lugard was forced to recognize that hardly anything had changed during his first year in Uganda.[86] He may have felt himself in a slightly stronger position due to the recruitment of soldiers from the Sudanese region. Nevertheless, once again he turned impatiently to his old strategy, and in a letter impressed on Mwanga the necessity of finally declaring himself to be under the British, thereby opting for the possibility that everyone could practise whatever religion he wanted without interference.[87] Only such a step could put a stop to the perpetual tensions and the constant threat of open war. It is interesting to notice that the leading Protestant missionary took a somewhat different view, believing that fighting might after all be a better solution than the continued ill-feeling.[88]

To summarize the outcome so far: Lugard recognized that it was necessary to have a stronghold within Bugandan society, and that the Kabakaship provided by far the best solution. When he failed to make any progress in that respect, he sought to secure, as his best alternative, an informal alliance with the Protestant party. He was thus using the power of the Company to maintain a two-party system which was foreign to the Buganda structure, and which was increasingly coming into conflict with forces at work in Buganda society. He was thereby upholding a law which at the societal level was in violation of the principle of religious liberty. He could, however, placate European opinion with the excuse that he was ensuring freedom for the missionaries' work. As regards the specific question of the missions, he had grudgingly had to acquiesce in the political role of the missionaries, directly as regards their activities in the Buganda arena, indirectly as regards their links to the European one. He had not yet solved the problem of defining the relationship between the missions and the colonial authority.

Religious liberty and the change of the law

In view of the course of events during Lugard's first year in Uganda as the representative of the IBEA Co. it comes as little surprise that the deadlocked situation ended, on 24 January 1892, in a warlike clash between the two parties. Nor is it surprising that Lugard, once convinced of the inevitability of war, came down on the side of the Protestant party by handing out weapons to them and by intervening with his own forces at the decisive moment so as to be sure of the outcome. Kabaka Mwanga escaped to one of the islands and later took refuge in German territory, while the Catholic leaders and many of their followers went to the province of Buddu in southern Buganda. The Catholic fathers were caught in a dangerous situation at their headquarters close to the battlefield, but were soon brought to safety at Lugard's fort. From there they later joined their own people.[89]

From Lugard's point of view his weak position made it necessary for him to rely on the only loyal group within Buganda society, the Protestant party. In view of Mwanga's refusal to give the final recognition to British rule, the problem for Lugard now was to ensure continued British supremacy in the face of presumed Catholic hostility. In doing so he at the same time changed the internal power structure and gave the Protestant party the lead in subsequent development. The battle of Mengo, as it came to be called, was fought on the issue of whether there should be European or African leadership in Buganda, but due to the alliance between the Protestants and the Company it tipped the internal political balance in favour of the Protestants.

In considering the aftermath of these dramatic events we will focus on the changes and rearrangements which Lugard attempted to make during the following months. He was now in a stronger position to realize his ideas on religious liberty and the separation of religion and politics. Still, the battle of Mengo had a decisive influence on the conditions under which Lugard had to act.

It was considered quite extraordinary that matters should have come to a head with fighting between two Christian groups with a substantial European involvement. An official inquiry into the events was set up resulting in the Macdonald Report, which blamed Lugard for the war and expressed strong criticism of his handling of the religious parties and the evictions. The report was, however, of little consequence for events in Buganda. The heated discussion sparked off by the report took place a year and a half after the hostilities, and was confined to Europe. Lugard was back in England and could defend himself, but he had already arranged a new settlement in Buganda.[90]

As Lugard expected, the French priests sent gloomy reports home telling of the atrocities they had suffered at the hands of the British, and claiming that they had been forced out of Buganda by the Protestants.[91] The matter was taken up by France in diplomatic representations to Britain claiming an infringement of the Brussels Act, and there were heated debates in Parliament.[92] All this was again a phenomenon within the European arena, and was no more than a matter of curiosity when news of it got back to Uganda nine months after the actual events.[93] But the indirect or deterrent effect of the appeal to Europe seems to have had its effect. Lugard knew that he would have to defend his record, and his treatment of the Catholics after the battle and the reorganization of the country after the upheavals were not unaffected by the inevitable postlude in Britain. He now had a chance to build up a convincing appearance of unbiased treatment of the Catholics.[94]

The Protestant missionaries, too, voiced complaints over Lugard to their home authorities, but on a somewhat different basis. They accused Lugard of not having taken them into his confidence in connection with certain tentative plans which had been drawn up for imminent withdrawal of the Company from Buganda for economic reasons. They reproached him in particular with not giving them sufficient protection during the upheavals, which had involved considerable risk to their lives and property. While the response from Britain could not influence the events in Uganda, the exchange of views and the various accusations levelled none the less strained relations between Lugard and the CMS missionaries. This affected the atmosphere in which the negotiations with the victorious Protestant party were to take place. The missionaries became very suspicious of Lugard's policy in the aftermath of the battle of Mengo, and they had generally lost confidence in him and in the Company as the administrative body of the Uganda region.[95] To this should be added another factor: the missionaries were to some extent reacting on the basis of disappointed expectations, as will be shown below.

The row over the battle of Mengo and Lugard's alleged atrocities coincided in Britain with the controversy over the future of the Uganda region, and these two issues became closely interwoven.[96] When the IBEA Co. was threatened with bankruptcy in the last half of 1891 the CMS, and especially Bishop Tucker, stepped in and raised money, making it possible for the Company to stay another year in Uganda.[97] This period was then devoted to a campaign to persuade the British government to recognize its responsibility for the situation that had developed in Uganda and to put Uganda under direct colonial rule. There was extensive lobbying activity and a large-scale public campaign was launched.[98]

Thus Uganda came very much into focus during 1892 in British politics and in British public opinion. Within Uganda the CMS missionaries came to feel that in this situation they could claim a special status and should be treated accordingly. All actors in Uganda became alert to the fertile soil which this new public interest had created for any information they forwarded to England; though they felt obliged to act in a way which would not bring them into disrepute with British public opinion.[99]

As well as these overall considerations Lugard was faced with a situation where he was the only authority left to create a new equilibrium between the forces at work in Buganda. He would have to withstand the pressure from the various groups, not least the victorious Protestants, and he would have to chair negotiations for a new settlement and the inevitable change of the law.[100] He had from the outset two priorities on which he intended to act. One was that he would have to get the Buganda political and administrative system to function again.[101] The only way to do this was to have the position of the Kabaka filled. Besides the internal dimension there was also an external dimension which was just as important for Lugard. As the representative of the IBEA Co. he needed an authority to negotiate with in order to get the final and formal acceptance of British supremacy. The only suitable candidate was Mwanga, who had fled the country and was now in exile with the French bishop.[102]

Lugard's second priority was closely related to the first one and had to do with the division of the country between the various parties. If there were no Kabaka Lugard could not avoid negotiating with the next on the ladder of authority, the Katikiro, who was also the leader of the Protestant party. Such a procedure would give the appearance that Lugard was willing to grant a political monopoly to the Protestant party after its victory, especially as it was obvious that the Protestants, supported by the missionaries, were pressurizing Lugard to grant such a monopoly.[103]

For both internal and external reasons, Lugard could not afford to accept such a solution, however much he had desired it before the battle. In Buganda it would create continued unrest; in Europe it would confirm the Catholic accusations that Lugard had all the time favoured the Protestants, and it could be seen as an encroachment on religious liberty. His alternative objective was, therefore, to secure with the help of the Kabakaship some kind of division of the country which would enjoy a certain legitimacy in the eyes of the majority of the people and create a stable situation by reflecting the actual numerical strength of each party.[104]

The second treaty with Kabaka Mwanga

After his escape Mwanga was in exile with the French missionaries. There followed protracted negotiations about his return which gradually took the form of a classic bargaining situation. The Catholic bishop attached the condition to Mwanga's return that the Catholics should either be reinstated in their old position or be granted half of the country as their special areas. Lugard on his side refused to negotiate any future arrangement until the Kabaka had returned, and he threatened to choose another candidate, even a Muslim. From the opposite side the threat was that they would set up a Catholic kingdom in Buddu to the south, where most of the Catholics had taken refuge – a possible realization of the old idea of exclusivity.[105]

After more than two months of bargaining the Catholics gave in and Mwanga returned to his throne. Within a few weeks Lugard then finalized the new arrangements for the country. A second treaty was concluded between the Kabaka and the IBEA Co., fully recognizing British protection and the supremacy of the Company.[106] During Mwanga's exile with the Catholics there had developed some tensions in their relationship, and shortly after the conclusion of the new treaty it was announced that Mwanga had changed his religion and had become a Protestant.[107] Setting aside the personal and religious motives in this conversion and judging only from a political point of view two observations may be made. First, it was Lugard's ideal solution that had now come within sight of realization. The strongest and most loyal group was now combined with the centre of power within the Buganda system. Secondly, seen from the internal angle, the victorious and hence strongest party could now take advantage of a Protestant-oriented Kabakaship, whereas other groups must look to another centre of power, the Company, for protection and the guarantee of their rights.[108]

We are confronted once again with the old problem of the relationship between the office of the Kabaka and his supporting, in this case Protestant, party on the one side, and Lugard's power as the Company's Resident on the other. Or in Lugard's own words: 'the radical question at issue was whether they [the Protestant leaders] were to be considered the rulers of Uganda, or I in the name of the Company'.[109] The answer will be sought in an examination of the revised treaty and an analysis of the position of the Kabaka after his restoration.

In the revised treaty, which was generally shorter and less detailed than the first one, there was one noticeable addition. It was specified that the Kabaka should seek advice from the Resident and obtain his consent before 'the appointment of chiefs to higher offices' (clause 4). This refers to the subsequent distribution of offices between the parties, and it was thus a very important prerogative that Lugard preserved for himself. His own motive was that he would then be able to allow the native administrative system to work on its own, provided that it served the interests of all groups and not just one faction.[110] This meant that in practice he could exercise his power by vetoing appointments or decisions.[111] However, the important new development was that it gave the British representative formal access to and influence on the real centre of power in the Ganda political system.

Apart from its legal basis in the treaty, Lugard's position of power was to a large extent a function of the strength of the Kabakaship. It was obvious that, after his flight into exile and his restoration with the assistance of Lugard and the Protestant party, Mwanga's prestige was reduced. The change in his position found expression in the fact that both the Catholic leaders and the Muslim party, which now reappeared on the political stage, bypassed the Kabaka and approached Lugard directly as the most powerful of the two, and from whom they could expect some sort of impartiality.[112] A comment from one of the missionaries confirms that the Kabakaship was devalued, and that he was thus no longer as much of an asset for any party as he had been.[113]

The reduction of the importance of the Kabakaship and the corresponding increase in the Company Resident's prestige provided Lugard with a platform within the Buganda system. The weakening of the old centre of power and the change in the balance of power between the parties thus provide an explanation of the greater strength and authority with which Lugard could act after the battle of Mengo.[114] This internal factor should again be linked with the increased military strength he now had, due to weaponry brought up from the coast, and the image of strength he had projected by deciding the battle.

Lugard made use of his newly won position of power in the negotiations for a political settlement. This time his hands were not bound by any codicil; he was the one who held the initiative and could put forward his own suggestions. As the undisputed leader he could invite any of the three parties for negotiations, and he was even instrumental in the selection of a new Catholic leader.[115] Hence the developments from now on can to a large extent be seen as the expression of his own deliberate policy, and not as something forced upon him by events.

The reorganization of the country

While bringing the Kabaka back had been an important priority, Lugard was fully aware that any reorganization of the country had to be based on the politico-religious parties. He soon became convinced that it was necessary to include the Muslims in any settlement. Since their defeat by the Christians in 1889 they had posed a constant threat to peace and a possible ally for either of the two Christian parties. The Muslims on their part tried to take advantage of the turmoil in Buganda and approached Lugard with an offer to 'replace the Catholics'.[116] Secondly, faced with requests amounting to a demand for political monopoly from the Protestant party supported by the missionaries, Lugard felt obliged to provide for fair treatment of the Catholics, especially as he had become more and more convinced that the strength of the Protestant party had been exaggerated, and that they were fewer in numbers than either the Catholics or the Muslims.[117] The French priests too were not slow to remind Lugard of their appeals to Europe.[118]

As regards the principle to be applied in the sharing of power it was soon agreed by all involved that it was no longer possible to use the chieftainships as a basis. Instead all preferred the territorial principle.[119] The division was consequently put into practice with the help of three different measures.

(1) A treaty was concluded with the Catholic chiefs alone on 5 April 1892[120] assigning to them, with the more or less wholehearted consent of the Kabaka and the Protestant leaders, the southern province of Buddu. Buddu was to be exclusively Catholic in the sense that people of any other religion would have to move to another part of the country.[121]

This treaty, which was limited to a two-year period, had the character of a peace treaty with people who had been in rebellion, and it is significant that Lugard alone and not Mwanga was the signatory. The Catholics were clearly considered by Lugard as the losers and the Protestants as the winners, and any new dispensation would have to reflect this fact.[122]

(2) Parallel with the formal treaty with the Catholics, an informal agreement was worked out between Lugard and the Muslim envoys, assigning to them three small provinces (sazas). It was a deliberate part of Lugard's policy that these provinces should be sandwiched in between the Catholics and the Protestants.[123] After somewhat protracted negotiations, especially with the Protestants, a treaty was officially signed on 3 June 1892.[124]

(3) The real confirmation of the new configurations came with the filling of the important offices in the country. Buganda was at that time divided into ten landed chieftainships, sazas, and the key element in the rearrangement of the country became the appointment to the posts of saza chiefs. Lugard himself called and chaired the decisive meeting on 20 April 1892.[125] The final result was that the Protestants were assigned six saza chieftainships, the Muslims three (the smallest in size), and the Catholics one (Buddu, which was the largest single saza). A further feature of the arrangement was that the Protestant Katikiro continued in office, as did the Catholic Kimbugwe as the next-ranking minister.[126]

The Protestant sazas covered, according to Lugard's own estimate, about 60–70 per cent of Buganda. It is, however, important to investigate further what was implied by this division. It was directly stated that Buddu was to be an exclusively Catholic area whereas there would be no exclusively Protestant area.[127] This meant that Catholics could reside anywhere in the country as long as they maintained no stores of arms and powder.[128] Buddu could in other words be seen as a stronghold for the defeated party.

Also relevant is the question of the religious observance of the petty chiefs, that is, the chiefs in the ranks under each saza chief. From Lugard's own comments it is clear that he expected the practice to be that the petty chiefs would be of the same religion as their respective saza chiefs. At least the leaders of the three parties had the right to interpret the package of treaties and agreements in this way, but they were under no obligation to do so.[129] One of the Protestant missionaries commented upon this point. He estimated that two-thirds of the country had gone to the Protestants.[130] After two years it was possible that the Catholics would try to return and take up positions in other parts of the country: 'Our prayer is that we may be able to flood the country with the Word of God before then.'[131]

The division of the country as set out in the three agreements was carried out under Lugard's own supervision. The result was that the party most loyal to Lugard got the lion's share, in spite of Lugard's annoyance with their exaggerated claims and lack of cooperation, and despite the fact that he was unsure of their numerical strength compared with the other two parties. In order to clarify the wider-ranging aspects of this revision of the administrative system, it will be examined more specifically from the angle of religious liberty.

Religious liberty under the new dispensation

Lugard had completely given up the idea of a one-party system, which he had favoured before the upheavals. One reason was that from an internal point of view he did not find such a solution politically tenable. Also, after the many appeals to Europe and the consequent European interest in the Ugandan situation an exclusion of the Catholics would be considered a violation of religious liberty. Thus developments had made the concept of religious liberty a factor of greater political importance than before. Lugard on more than one occasion drew attention to this fact in his discussions with the Protestant leaders and the CMS missionaries by directly referring to his obligations under the Royal Charter.[132]

On the positive side Lugard, in the renewed treaty with Mwanga, explicitly stated that there was to be freedom of worship and 'no one shall be compelled to follow any religion against his will'. This was a new addition compared with the first treaty, but on the other hand the actual content as well as the implementation of this clause turned out to be somewhat restricted, and the words did not carry much weight beyond the 'individual level'.

The concept of religious liberty was now more clearly specified. It was no longer a question of the narrow interpretation, covering Christians only, as Muslims were now included. It was, however, mainly for reasons of political expediency that they were brought back onto the Buganda stage. Lugard was aware of the paradox that he who had for so many years fought the Muslims as the main traffickers in the slave trade in Africa now appeared to champion their cause. But he added: 'My action is not encouraging Islamism, but rather controlling and limiting it.'[133] We are, therefore, justified in saying that it was a rationalization when Lugard emphasized that the Muslims did not have a European spokesman as the Christians did, and he was consequently obliged to act as their spokesman and defender in the name of religious liberty.[134]

Secondly, it was specifically stated that the Catholics had the right to settle outside their own saza, Buddu, provided they were unarmed. Lugard impressed on Protestant chiefs that it was their duty to protect the Catholics and that no coercion was allowed in matters of religion.[135] But he was here only referring to the treatment of Catholics as individuals.

Finally, as a special category Lugard mentioned the group of people variously labelled 'heathens', 'people who had no religion', or 'people who did not want to read'[136] – in other words those Baganda who still practised the traditional religion. He emphasized that they too were entitled to absolute freedom of religion and must not be subjected to any form of coercion from the Christians.[137]

These measures show that Lugard had now categorically extended the concept of religious liberty well beyond its former area. But the interpretation and implementation of the concept were still circumscribed by the political realities. A closer look at Lugard's measures reveals that freedom of worship was actually only guaranteed, and that protection against coercion could only be afforded within the Protestant sazas. This conclusion is based on the fact that in Catholic Buddu the claim to exclusivity was legalized and with it the right to ask non-Catholics to move out.[138] The same claim to exclusivity was granted to the Muslims in their three sazas. It was not made clear whether they had the same right of eviction, but it was significantly recorded by Lugard himself that after the allocation of the three sazas to the Muslims some 12,000 Protestants moved to other sazas.[139] It was thus only within the Protestant-administered sazas that Lugard could expect the right of individuals to religious liberty to be respected.

Turning to the societal level, and summarizing what has been said above, the Protestants had been given a privileged position compared to the other two parties. The reorganization itself was carried out according to the territorial principle, and by establishing a link between the various offices within the sazas and particular religious alignments, Lugard was thereby sponsoring a system which can best be characterized as *real inequality* (see p.25). Religious criteria decided appointments and, consequently, in the case of a change of religion an appointee would have to forfeit his office. In principle this new arrangement was not much different from the one that was adopted after the first treaty with Mwanga, and it is therefore not surprising that Lugard, in the new treaty, omitted the clause that offices should be filled irrespective of creed. The difference between the old and the new arrangement consisted, first, in the way the new one functioned in Buganda society, and secondly in the arguments with which Lugard justified the partition of the country.

As regards the question of effectiveness, we should first investigate whether Lugard had more success this time in limiting the number of office-holders and others who were affected by the religious criterion. Concerning chieftainships, the agreements show that only the ten saza chiefs and the two leading ministers (the Katikiro and the Kimbugwe) were officially appointed on the basis of their creed. In practice, however, Lugard had to admit that probably all chieftainships – earlier estimated at some 600 – were filled on religious grounds.[140] It has already been pointed out that one consequence of the distribution between the parties was great migrations of people; Lugard himself recorded these movements, and the granting of shambas to co-religionists.[141] A little later, one of the Protestant missionaries confirmed that the practice was that 'No gardens [shambas] are given to men who cannot read,' and he added that 'unless he [the incumbent] is most zealous in teaching he is soon turned out'.[142]

The conclusion to be drawn is that the official pattern of distribution at the top

level spread down through the system to minor chieftainships and to a large extent
to shambas. Consequently, through the use of the territorial principle, the
religious divisions could easily be integrated into the traditional system of
authority. Religious loyalties were not this time in conflict with traditional
obligations, but functioned rather as a reinforcing element. Secondly, the final
pattern of settlement came close to a realization of the principle of *cujus regio ejus
religio*. Within each saza there was a marked tendency for not only office-holders
but also ordinary people to belong to the same religion as the saza chief.

Lugard's own view of the reorganization of the country was based on his
opinion that religion as such was of little significance for the differences between
the three parties. He presented three complementary arguments in support
of this view: first, he repeated the point of view that a distinction had to be
made between religion and political parties, and that he was only concerned
with the latter.[143] Secondly, he tried on several occasions to impress on the Ganda
leaders that religious leaders were different from, and should be appointed
independently of, political leaders.[144] Thirdly, he became more and more
convinced that most of the people who belonged to the Christian parties were only
nominally Christians, and that no more than a handful were sincere Christians.[145]

Lugard thus sought to justify and defend his reorganization of the country by
secularizing the three parties and depoliticizing religious allegiance.[146] Lugard's
biographer, Margery Perham, adds her support to this point of view by pointing
out that a qualitative evaluation of the Christians indicates that they were
primarily political groups who simply followed their leaders (the chiefs); and,
judging by the means the missionaries were prepared to employ, the conflict had a
primarily political character.[147] In considering Perham's argument we may
question the relevance of qualitative evaluations of religious conviction or the
means employed in any given situation. Such evaluations cannot constitute the
sole basis of analysis. We will try to approach the problem from a different angle,
by considering whether the principal premise which seems to underlie Perham's
way of thinking and arguing – the distinction between religion and politics – was
in fact grasped by, or had any practical significance for, the people involved. This
must be a basic requirement for any moral evaluation of Lugard's actions.

The arguments presented above urging the Baganda's failure to distinguish
between religion and politics are still valid. The territorial basis of the redistribution of power and benefits had not brought about any change in this attitude; it
had only removed the main sources of friction. Secondly, the missionaries bear
witness to the fact that the Protestant leaders were still using denominational
criteria in the allocation of shambas. The ability to read, baptism and continuous
Christian activity were conditions of access to the Protestant party and thereby to
the political benefits that the Protestant party was in a position to allocate. The
missionaries, for reasons completely different from Lugard's, raised the question
of the quality and sincerity of belief, and attempted to explain to the Protestant
leaders that their practice was creating large numbers of purely nominal Christians, urging them to allocate offices irrespective of creed. It was to no avail: 'They
are astonished and say they would lose all the country at that rate.'[148] The
Africans were not conscious of the same alternatives as the missionaries, and
consequently did not apply the same distinction between religion and politics.

As far as the European authorities were concerned, it remained incontroverti-
ble that offices, when all was said and done, were still tied to religious alignment,
and that this state of affairs even seemed to meet with the approval of the colonial

administrator. A change of religion might still have political repercussions. As for the missionaries, they may have wanted religious life separated from political activity in the interests of sincerity of belief; but they clearly acknowledged within their own strategy the religious consequences of the political partition of the country, and they were ready to make use of it; for the chieftainships were the key to the opening up of new missionary areas.[149]

These three sets of actors were looking at Buganda from different angles, but had a common awareness of the fact that Lugard had not succeeded in separating religion and politics. It is possible at another level of explanation to make one generalization. As long as religion in a pluralistic situation provided the main structuring principle in society and was not in conflict with the traditional structure of authority, but on the contrary reinforced it, and as long as benefits and rewards were allocated on the basis of this structure, any distinction between religion and politics would remain theoretical. Consequently, it is fair to say that very little had been changed at the societal level during Lugard's reorganization of the country.

Moving on to the institutional level it is interesting to notice the attempts of Lugard himself to link missionary activity to the reorganization of the country and to political realities in general. The concept which became problematical was impartiality, the practice of which was now in jeopardy. It is noticeable that the sentence requiring impartiality which had been included in the first treaty with Mwanga was omitted this time. As the butt of accusations of partiality, Lugard may have felt that it would have been somehwat ironic to repeat such a sentence. The reality behind the omission was, however, that Lugard in his reorganization had not dealt with the missions on equal terms. In the first instance, missionary work was closely connected with the political distribution of offices, and Lugard was well aware that the Protestant missionaries had now been placed in a favourable position.[150] Secondly, Lugard inserted into clause 2 of the treaty with the Catholic chiefs concerning Buddu that if missionary expansion was planned outside Buddu permission was to be obtained beforehand from the Resident. This was a severe restriction on Catholic missionary work, and a clear break with the spirit of the treaty with Mwanga. Later Lugard regretted having enforced these terms on the Catholic priests – this was one of the few occasions on which he admitted himself to have been mistaken. He did however soften the clause considerably by explaining that it should be taken only as an extra underscoring of the understanding already existing between them that expansion to areas outside Buganda required *consultation* with the Resident.[151]

Comparing the position of the Catholics with that of the CMS mission, it is obvious that Lugard took advantage of the Catholics' weakened position to establish the prerogative of the colonial authority to dictate the extent of Catholic missionary enterprise. During this same period, as we have seen, Lugard failed to get the same concession from the local CMS missionaries, with whom he also had a disagreement about missionary expansion (p.34ff.).

Relations between the colonial authority and the missions

By the first half of 1892 it was quite clear that the CMS missionaries now expected an established or at least a privileged position.[152] They no longer limited themselves to the argument that the creed and nationality they shared with the colonial authorities created special bonds between them. They based their claims and expectations on events in both Uganda and Europe. In Uganda the Protestant victory was their point of reference and their main argument for asking Lugard to take them into his confidence rather than that he should rely on the French priests.[153]

It is remarkable how far events in England were now drawn into the negotiations by 'the men on the spot'. By pointing out the fact that the IBEA Co. could only stay in Uganda for another year, thanks to the money collected by the CMS in England, the missionaries argued that these economic bonds justified a special relationship between the local representatives of the two agencies and placed special obligations on the Company towards the mission. One of the missionaries even demanded what was little short of vetoing rights by saying: 'I do not see that it would be too much to ask if the agents of the IBEA Company here should do nothing that the united body of CMS missionaries believe to be disadvantageous to its interests.'[154] To Lugard's considerable annoyance the missionaries even urged the Protestant Katikiro to remind him of the Company's dependence on the CMS, again emphasizing the new strength of the Protestant party, which Lugard would do well not to neglect.[155] The missionaries' arguments show that they were now in fact requesting recognition of their special position as British subjects. They considered that the recent changes and the special circumstances within Europe fully justified the renewal of their claim that the CMS mission should be granted a privileged, or even a semi-established, position within the colonial system. Lugard did in fact, as we have seen, go further in their direction than at any time before, but this made little impression on them because of their increased expectations. Lugard admitted in private that he had yielded to Protestant pressures to grant especially favourable conditions for the Anglican missionary work.[156] This was why he expressed so much disappointment when he was criticized for not going even further in the Protestant direction. He had in fact expected that the Protestants would look on him as 'their deliverer'.[157]

The clash between the missionaries, claiming recognition of their third role, and Lugard, who refused on the grounds of his obligation to practise some sort of impartiality, created serious friction, even to the extent that Lugard began to find his whole work meaningless.[158] The CMS missionaries on their side considered the Company unable to cope with events, and therefore hoped for a direct government takeover.[159]

This conflict over the relationship between the CMS and the IBEA Co. in the local setting cannot be separated from the larger problem of the political role of the missionaries within the Uganda system. It has already been pointed out that the missionaries were here acting in two political roles and that Lugard deliberately made use of their good offices. With the Protestants as the victorious group the missionaries' two roles as advisers and intermediaries were emphasized even more, and took on even greater proportions, as Lugard recorded on several occasions.[160] This development was however counterbalanced by Lugard's stronger position after the devaluation of the Kabakaship. A situation was developing where there appeared to be two European centres of power in Buganda. Lugard began to feel that the real issue was which was to have the primacy. He discovered that the missionaries were at times advising the people to defy him in order to set the two European agencies at odds with one another. If continued, this would inevitably result in a loss of British prestige.[161]

It is important to remember that this problem of the missionaries' political role was becoming acute at the same time as the question of missionary expansion was being discussed.[162] It can thus be seen that the major problem of the position and independence of the ecclesiastical representatives *vis-à-vis* the secular authority was being tackled on two levels at the same time. The root of the problem lay, as we have seen earlier, partly in the lack of a definition of the role of the missions in the colonial setting, partly in the common interests, and thereby in the degree of interdependence that existed between the missions and the colonial authorities. Under these circumstances it was difficult to define the interfaces between church and state in order to work out a clear-cut relationship.

Lugard had thus few guidelines to draw on in solving the problem of the missionaries' political roles. His main aim was, however, clearly defined. He wanted to limit or even to do away with the informal political position that the missionaries enjoyed. After one incident he even went so far as to write directly and inquire whether they would in future continue with their advisory activity, and if so to what extent they would advise their people to ignore the instructions of the Company's Resident.[163] In attempting to do away with the missionaries' political roles he tried to dissuade the leaders of the two Christian parties from always going to the missionaries for advice before coming to him, and warned them not to be led blindly by them in political matters. He tried to explain to them the difference between missionary work and administration.[164] At the more physical level he encouraged the missions to move their headquarters to places at some distance from the political centre. This step was meant to reduce the identification of the two European agencies in the minds of the people, and to make the chiefs' access to the missionaries' political advice more difficult.[165]

Lugard reminded the Protestant missionaries that their Low Church background ought to prevent them from engaging in purely political matters. He quoted some of their earlier statements to that effect, and he even pointed out the possible consequences in Europe if their supporters got to know what was really taking place in Buganda.[166] Lugard apparently met with little response to this line of argument from the missionaries. They simply invoked the intimate connection which existed in Buganda between religion and politics; in spite of admitted opposition from the Parent Committee they had to reserve the right to give advice in all matters when asked.[167] Lugard's attempts only served to worsen the climate between the two sides. Both of them stuck to their positions, and no solution was reached to the problem of the status and independence of the missions.[168]

Summing up the Lugard period

The Lugard period in Buganda covers less than two years, during which time a number of developments occurred.

Taking the strength of Lugard's position as one variable, it is obvious that there was a direct relationship between this factor and the degree of religious liberty in Buganda society. At the individual level, the interpretation of the concept was widened to cover the Muslims as well as the so-called heathens. At the societal level the Muslims were now included in the political process. At the institutional level, however, the degree of impartiality shown by the colonial authority had become somewhat circumscribed because of political developments.

Looking at religious liberty as a concept introduced to Africa from its origins in the European tradition, it emerges that it was a difficult concept to transplant to the African setting, and even more difficult to put into practice. The explanation cannot, however, be found in the foreignness of the concept alone. We must take into account the fact that the various European actors worked with different interpretations of it, and especially that they adapted the concept to the political situation, and incorporated it into the strategies they employed to pursue their own specific goals.

Lugard formalized the three politico-religious parties as the only political structure in the country. He succeeded in integrating the religious allocation of offices into the Buganda hierarchical structure, so that in the end it became less vulnerable to tensions stemming from religious pluralism. His way of achieving this end was to gain a foothold at the centre of power in the Buganda system, thereby reserving for the colonial authority the option of exercising direct influence.

With regard to the problem of religion and politics, we find that Buganda more or less preserved the status quo. Seen from the point of view of the Baganda, the distinction between religion and politics was not making much sense, because of the Baganda's special background and also the impressions they received from the behaviour of the Europeans. The main problem remained: the right to hold office was still linked to religious alignment.

The question of church and state, here represented by the relationship between the missions and the colonial authority, had been presented in its various aspects, but so far only a few solutions had emerged. In the case of the Protestant mission the situation ended in a stalemate, leaving open the question of whether direct government intervention instead of Company rule would make any difference. As regards impartiality towards the missions, the political situation led to an unofficial privileged position for the Protestants at the expense of the Catholics.

There was a growing tendency to appeal to Europe or at least to invoke the possibility of such an appeal. The missionaries' foothold in two countries served as an important channel of communication and was of significance in the decision-making processes. Due to the time-consuming procedure involved in such communication, the importance of this aspect had so far mostly been at the indirect, deterrent level. The concept of religious liberty had been seen to be an effective factor within this framework, in that it could arouse public opinion in Europe.

It is our contention that during the rest of the 1890s, and in some respects even in the period after 1900, the system and structure established in the years 1890–2 are of crucial significance. In many ways developments thereafter take the form of revisions, corrections and improvements rather than radical changes in the foundations already laid. The hypothesis that the historical inertia which dominated the following period has its roots mainly in the short Lugard administration will be substantiated by an analysis of subsequent events.

5

The introduction of direct British rule

The framework and the actors

When Lugard left Uganda for good in June 1892, Captain Williams was left in charge as the representative of the IBEA Co., pending the final decision on the future of the Company in East Africa. This period lasted until the end of March 1893, when the British government decided to pay the Company's expenses for an extra three months.

In the meantime the campaign for British retention of Uganda came to a peak in the autumn of 1892.[1] This campaign, and general government concern about Bugandan events, resulted in the appointment of a Special Commissioner who was to go to Uganda, report on the situation, and recommend on the future status of the country.[2] Lord Rosebery, the Foreign Secretary, appointed Sir Gerald Portal, then Consul-General of Zanzibar, as Commissioner. He arrived in Buganda in the middle of March 1893, and from the first of April took over the government of the country from the Company. This was the real inauguration of direct government administration, even though the future had not yet been formally decided. The British practice of administrating colonies by granting a charter to a private company was now terminated in Uganda and replaced by direct rule.

After a visit of less than three months Portal went home to present his report, leaving in charge Captain Macdonald, who had by then finished his report on Lugard's activities in Buganda. Macdonald was replaced by Colonel H. E. Colvile as Acting Commissioner for the provisional administration from November 1893. It was not until 1894 that the Liberal government had the Protectorate of Uganda ratified by Parliament, the presence of the missionaries and the future of the Christians being decisive factors in the debate. In June the Protectorate, still only covering the Kingdom of Buganda, was gazetted on the basis of Portal's agreement with Kabaka Mwanga, and protectorate status was finalized in Buganda in a treaty between Mwanga and Colvile in August 1894, which basically repeated the

Portal agreement.[3] This sequence of decisions over a period of almost two years led to the establishment of direct British rule in Buganda. The whole process was strongly influenced by the internal British political situation, but there was also heated discussion of where the blame should be laid for internal developments in Buganda. This discussion centred naturally on Lugard's record and the behaviour of the CMS missionaries. On his arrival Portal was carefully briefed by Captain Williams on the subject of the British missionaries, whom the Captain had found difficult and uncooperative.[4]

It would not, however, in this context be particularly fruitful to pursue this moral, and, for the Portal period, largely retrospective question of guilt and responsibility as regards the missionaries' activities and their interference in politics. We will instead concentrate on features which characterized the transition to direct British rule. First, Portal and his successors possessed more power than Lugard and could as government envoys act with greater authority. Portal himself was very conscious of this fact, and it serves to explain his often hasty decisions and actions.[5] At the same time, the CMS missionaries were almost the only group who attached much importance to the fact that there was a distinction between the Company and the British government.[6] Their attitudes towards Portal and Williams could therefore be expected to be different.

This last issue leads us to the question of the leadership within the CMS mission. The CMS mission suffered from a lack of local leadership during the Lugard period, mainly because the Bishop was away for more than two years. This period was characterized by an increasingly deteriorating climate between the missionaries and the representatives of the Company, especially Captain Williams.[7] At Christmas 1892 Bishop Tucker returned to Buganda and stayed on during the Portal visit. He was probably personally more diplomatic than the missionaries: he certainly carried more authority. Even more important, Bishop Tucker had worked less in the Buganda arena than in the European one. After his experiences during the campaign for the retention of Uganda, he was much more inclined to work for good relations and cooperation with the official colonial authorities than the missionaries had been, for the attitude of the missionaries was coloured by their experiences of developments since the battle of Mengo. In short, the difference was one between the men on the spot, who had become engulfed in local events, and the newcomers, who could apply a wider perspective.

The Portal mission to Buganda

During his stay in Buganda, Portal worked very much along the lines already laid down by Captain Williams. He addressed himself to a remarkable extent to the problems that Williams had already identified as the essential ones and tried to solve.[8]

Williams had become more and more convinced that a reorganization of the country was necessary, at least as far as the position of the Catholics was concerned. It was in the first place his firm opinion that the Catholics had not had fair play under the treaty with Lugard, given their numbers and strength.[9] Secondly, Lugard had on his departure impressed on him that he should avail himself of any opportunity to do justice to the Catholics; moreover the Catholics themselves claimed to have been promised a better deal by Lugard.[10] Finally, he felt the present division of the country to be politically unstable. He envisaged a threat from the Catholics to set up a separate Catholic kingdom in Buddu, bordering on German territory, and to legitimize their kingdom by enthroning one of the only two heirs to the Kabakaship, Mwanga's nephews, who were 3–5 years old and were being held by the Catholic priests in German territory.[11] Williams therefore worked hard in the months before Portal's arrival to renegotiate the partition of the country by giving the Catholics more saza chieftainships and other leading offices, thus allowing them 'to have a just weight in the affairs of the country in proportion to their actual power . . . '[12] The Catholics were to be brought into the government of the country, not just treated as the defeated party. In return the priests were to surrender the two nephews to Mwanga's guardianship. To Williams' great annoyance Bishop Tucker and the CMS missionaries refused to renegotiate the partition of the country before the arrival of the Special Commissioner. This is one reason why Williams accused the missionaries of making the administration of the country impossible.[13]

Besides the specifically Catholic question, Williams found it necessary in the interests of peace that spheres of influence outside Buganda proper should be allotted to the two missions. He even suggested specific areas, and envisaged that such an arrangement would remain in force for a ten-year period.[14] Williams was here once again bringing up the question of missionary expansion and suggesting even more official control than Lugard had.

Immediately on his arrival Portal addressed himself to these two mainly local topics, while the third problem of a treaty with Mwanga was given less attention. It is, however, striking that Portal confined himself to the well-known 'Lugardian' issues and that his solutions basically followed the pattern worked out by Lugard. He differed significantly from Lugard only as regards strategy. He was on his arrival struck by the degree of intermixture between religion and politics inherent in the division of the country between the three parties, and the decisive political role that the two groups of missionaries were playing. On the Catholic side they were playing this role quite deliberately, with no feeling of guilt; on the Protestant side they did so with some discomfort, but none the less very efficiently.[15] 'The whole history of Uganda for the last ten years is more worthy of the Middle Ages, or the days of the Edict of Nantes, than the end of the nineteenth century.'[16]

It would not be far from the truth to say that Portal adjusted his strategy to the historical parallel. He differed from Lugard in two ways. First, he accepted the intermixture of religion and politics as the basis for any settlement, and saw little hope of any change in the foreseeable future.[17] Secondly, he accepted the missionaries, and especially the two bishops, as 'the veritable political leaders' of the two parties. Unlike Lugard, he did not seek to neutralize their political roles, but decided to work through the missionary/ecclesiastical structure.[18]

The reorganization of the country

At the earliest opportunity Portal called the two bishops to a meeting, the purpose of which was to come to some agreement on a revision of Lugard's partition of the country, in order to give the Catholics a fairer and more responsible position in Buganda. The bargaining was tough, but the situation was helped by the fact that Bishop Tucker in the end found it necessary to give some concessions to the

Catholics. This amenability can probably be ascribed to his awareness of the European arena and his anticipation of the coming reaction to the Macdonald Report.[19] This meeting, which took place prior to any consultation with the Ganda chiefs, resulted in a signed agreement according to which the Catholics were granted more territory and a larger share of the state offices. This was achieved by doubling the important chieftainships, including the office of Katikiro, so that Catholics and Protestants shared them equally. Bishop Hirth pledged that the Kabaka's nephews would be brought back, and both bishops signed an undertaking that they would use all their influence to get their people to accept these terms.[20]

The agreement thus worked out was accepted by the Protestant chiefs after some further clarifications and guarantees from Portal. It is characteristic that Tucker during this latter phase of negotiations functioned as the intermediary between Portal and the chiefs.[21] A final illustration of the importance of Tucker's role can be drawn from the fact that the agreement was signed by the Protestant chiefs at a meeting in his residence.[22] The agreement on reorganization and the redistribution of offices was formally concluded on 22 April 1893, by the addition of Mwanga's and Portal's signatures.[23] The Catholics acquired one more saza (Kaima), which secured their access to the capital, one district within another saza, and the Sese Islands. The doubling of the principal chieftainships had been the sore point for the Protestants, but Portal was unyielding on this, as he saw this measure as a means of integrating the Catholics into the government of the country. As a corollary it was now specifically stated that the Catholics were henceforth obliged to pay taxes and render other duties to the Kabaka. The Protestants were mollified when Portal stated that the Protestant chiefs were to take precedence over Catholics holding similar offices. One reason he gave for doubling the chieftainships was that it would make it possible for Catholics to be tried and judged by their co-religionists and not by Protestant office-holders.[24]

The burning issue of the Kabaka's nephews, which reflected the struggle for access to the centre of power in Buganda, was solved by a special agreement between the parties most directly involved, Mgr Hirth and Kabaka Mwanga; but Portal was present as a witness and as guarantor for the fulfilment of the pledge. The conditions for the return of the princes were worked out in great detail, even to the extent that it was laid down that no Protestant or Muslim should be allowed to visit them, whereas Catholic chiefs could come for an hour a day.[25] This arrangement later gave rise to much misunderstanding and many opportunities for the deployment of filibustering techniques.

Looking at the more fundamental aspects of this settlement, it is significant that the representative of the British government acknowledged the necessity of a partition of the country based on religious affiliation. He accepted the linkage between office-holding and creed as inevitable. Apart from the more equitable treatment of the Catholics, he was in fact confirming the structure worked out by Lugard, even to the extent that a clause was written into the official treaty with Mwanga which stated that 'the political and *religious* distribution of territory' were among matters on which Mwanga required the consent of the Resident.[26]

It is noteworthy that the colonial authority accepted the political supremacy of the Protestants just as Lugard had done. The additional territory and offices given to the Catholics did not counterbalance the lack of formal equality inherent in the structure. This was confirmed by Bishop Tucker when he privately expressed great satisfaction with the outcome: 'The Protestants are in an immensely better position than they were before the war. Practically the Government of the country is in their hands and two thirds of the country.'[27] It therefore made sense when Tucker warned against publishing anything at present about the proceedings, especially the last sentence above. He referred to the unfortunate effects of the wide publication of the Protestant triumph after Lugard's settlement.[28]

Missionary expansion

As an essential part of any settlement in Uganda, without which there could be no hope of a peaceful future, Portal attached great importance to the resolution of the question of spheres of missionary expansion.[29] He took a step in this direction at his meeting with the two bishops, but the whole matter became rather confused, as Portal gave varying accounts of the outcome.[30] Our presentation will here be based on Portal's official dispatch on missionary expansion, as this was the account which had contemporary impact.

Just after his meeting with the two bishops, Portal sent a dispatch to the Foreign Secretary which was given an official stamp by being published soon afterwards.[31] In this he gave him to understand that the two bishops had entered into a temporary arrangement according to which the Catholic mission would move westward or northward, while the CMS would abstain for some months from entering Toro, and instead concentrate their energies in the eastward direction. Portal made it clear that this was 'a private and verbal understanding' between the two bishops, not committed to paper. He was further at pains to emphasize that he was not a party to any such arrangement, only a witness to the transaction. Thereby he kept himself free from the possibility of any accusation of interference with the established right to freedom of missionary expansion.[32] He did, on the other hand, now think that so much ground had been cleared that he could recommend the Foreign Secretary to make representations to the Vatican and the CMS Committee, to get them to acquiesce in the proposed settlement for a definite period of five to ten years.

The CMS headquarters staff were clearly taken by surprise when they read this dispatch, and found that it was of such a radical nature.[33] Bishop Tucker answered emphatically that there was no agreement whatsoever, only a declaration of intent covering the next few months. Moreover, the anticipated limitation of Protestant missionary activity was more due to lack of manpower than to political considerations.[34] It seems that Portal had either been carried away by his own conception of the urgency of the matter, or that he deliberately tried to push a rather limited declaration of intent in the direction of a more binding agreement. Whatever his motives were, and however strongly Bishop Tucker's denials were phrased, Portal's dispatch did in fact come to function as an official agreement, and the CMS mission observed it for a two-year period.

From the evidence of this phase of negotiations it is apparent that a change in attitude and policy of the CMS mission had taken place. In Lugard's period the missionaries would not acknowledge that the colonial representatives had any authority to influence, much less veto, missionary movements. Instead they claimed absolute freedom of missionary enterprise. In Portal's case, Bishop Tucker could be seen as acknowledging that the colonial power had a legitimate interest in the extent of missionary expansion and its direction, and he was even, if only temporarily, prepared to bend to the wishes of the colonial representative.

This change can be traced back both directly and indirectly to influence from Europe. When the CMS headquarters learned of the rigid stand which their missionaries had taken towards Lugard on the issue of missionary expansion, they instructed the missionaries directly and through Bishop Tucker that as long as the IBEA Co. was responsible for the government of the country, they would require the consent of the Resident before opening up new territory; in general they were to follow the directions of the Company's representatives, pending reference home.[35] This meant that the missionaries, like other Europeans, were still subject to the rules laid down in the treaty with Mwanga. The theory behind this directive was that within any given political unit the question of territorial rights was a matter for the secular authority, and that the missionaries must therefore follow the directives issued by that authority. If they felt that there was any infringement of their rights the matter should be referred to headquarters.

Bishop Tucker, basing his policy on his experiences from England, began in fact, on his own initiative, and before receiving the instructions from London, to carry out this approach to missionary expansion as soon as he arrived in Buganda at Christmas 1892.[36] In two concrete cases, at the request of the Resident, he temporarily postponed setting up new missions inside and outside Buganda, and awaited permission.[37] In neither of these cases was there any problem of security. The Resident waited for purely political reasons because of tension between the Protestants and Catholics. 'In both cases it was in obedience to an expressed desire on the part of the Resident and in both cases done without any prejudice to our claims.'[38] Tucker was thus conceding the point that Lugard had worked for during his time as Resident. To evaluate this step in the proper perspective it is, however, necessary to examine Tucker's motives in a little more detail. He quite obviously chose not to press the claim for missionary freedom as his missionaries had done. Thereby he diverted the mission away from a collision course with the secular authority. From Tucker's point of view, coming as he did from England, it was much more important to be on good terms with the colonial government than to insist on missionary freedom. This was an argument to which he gave, as will emerge below, a high priority.

In his view the problem was not primarily one of missionary freedom, but more a political question of the amount of influence the secular authority should be allowed to exert on missionary expansion. He was therefore willing to comply with the decisions of the colonial authority in concrete situations, as they were best qualified to foresee the purely political implications of any kind of missionary expansion. He was, however, only prepared to comply for a limited period in each case.[39] Looking at Tucker's position from this political angle adds an important dimension to his stand during Portal's attempts to get the two bishops to conclude an agreement on missionary extension. When Portal tried to bring political reasons to bear on the primarily religious area by suggesting an official agreement of a more permanent character, Tucker felt this to be an intrusion and an undue extension of the political realm, which would result in a curtailment of missionary enterprise and the compromise of basic missionary principles. Political reasons could only remain valid for a limited period, and a longer period, as laid down in a fixed agreement, would invalidate missionary freedom.

Tucker's point of view should also be seen in the context of developments inside Buganda. After the war the Protestants were placed in a much more established position, which Portal later confirmed, and of which Tucker was fully aware. It thus became much less of a risk to grant them concessions. The position of the Protestant chiefs provided a firm basis from which to work, and it was no longer imperative to carry the banner of missionary freedom so high. European influence and internal developments in Uganda were now working together towards a solution of one aspect of the problem of the formal relationship between the missions and the colonial power.

The official treaty with Kabaka Mwanga

Just before his departure Portal concluded a provisional treaty with Mwanga, pending ratification by the British Parliament. Its purpose was to define the official relationship between the Kingdom of Buganda as the protected part, and Great Britain as the colonial ruler.[40] In comparison with Lugard's earlier treaties this one provided for much stricter European control, and for more direct rule; hardly anything was left of Lugard's provisions for the continued functioning of the Buganda system. It is remarkable that, apart from the sentence quoted earlier about the religious distribution of territory, nothing was said about religion: neither religious liberty nor the right of missionary enterprise was mentioned.[41] As an explanation of this omission one can point to the special clause (no. 9) which required recognition of all international treaties and agreements to which Britain was a part. Furthermore in the preceding agreement with the two religious parties Portal had inserted the strongest formulation of the principle of religious liberty so far seen in Buganda, probably as a counterweight to the unequal division of offices. In contrast to earlier statements, Portal here enumerated explicitly a number of fields within which the rights of the individual must be safeguarded. This specification made the clause more applicable when it came to concrete administration. As the implementation of religious liberty became problematical mainly after Portal's departure it will be dealt with in the following chapter. It should not, however, be forgotten that the principle was also an issue, if only implicitly, in this settlement.[42]

There was another feature of the treaty with Mwanga which exercised Bishop Tucker, and which occasioned him to express some concern about the future position of the mission *vis-à-vis* the state.[43] Tucker pointed out a new perspective, important from the analytical point of view, in the relationship between church and state in a colonial framework. He attached great importance to the fact that the new treaty had only been signed by Mwanga and not by the chiefs, who had been co-signatories to Lugard's two treaties, and interpreted this as a significant change in the policy of the colonial authority. When Mwanga was restored to power the government consisted of the Kabaka and the chiefs. The Kabaka's previous autocratic power was abolished and replaced by 'something of a popular Government'. But now Portal had ignored 'this constitutional Government'. In view of the colonial officials' prejudice against the CMS missionaries, a legacy from the days of the IBEA Co., Tucker could only draw one conclusion: 'This ignoring the chiefs in my opinion is the first step towards an attempt to break down the power of the Mission.' He could, therefore, only recommend to the CMS Committee to use 'all the legitimate influence available' so that 'a God-fearing man' could be appointed as Resident in Buganda. Unless a man with sympathy towards Christian missions was appointed, more attempts would be made to cripple or at least to hamper the missionary work.[44]

It is not the place here to judge whether Tucker was exaggerating the drawbacks inherent in Portal's treaty with Mwanga. But his remarks are interesting because they give direct expression to several of the premises mentioned above as lying implicitly behind the missionaries' attitudes and actions. There is a clear recognition of the sensitivity of the mission to the prevailing political circumstances. Tucker acknowledged the usual CMS point of view: if it was simply a question of politics he would be glad to keep out of it. But implicitly he recognized that in the Buganda situation the distinction between religion and politics remained theoretical. This is confirmed by the fact that it was strongly emphasized that the chiefs should provide the main lines of access to new communities for the missionaries. Missionary work was therefore dependent on the ascendancy of the chiefly autocracy, and not least on the achievement of Protestant supremacy within the political structure. There was thus a direct relationship between the chiefs' political position and the position and working conditions of the mission. Any change in the chiefs' status and power would therefore affect the mission. This brings us to a further consideration: the fear was expressed that more direct rule by European officials would undermine the position of the chiefs and thereby that of the missionaries. But the effect of direct colonial rule could not be reduced to its *direct* impact on missionary movements. There was also the question of its impact on the African community, and in particular on its pattern of administration – its more indirect impact.

Thus a pattern of church–state relationships emerges which is peculiar to the colonial situation. Bishop Tucker, representing the Protestant mission and the embryonic African church, was working against a background of two political systems: the colonial system and the Buganda system. The leadership had been a major concern in both systems during the Portal period: the Resident's appointment had just been referred by Tucker to Britain; and the religious adherence of Mwanga's two nephews in Catholic hands, one of whom must become his successor, became an important issue.

Relations with both political systems were of cardinal importance for the church. But the church was also affected by a more dynamic factor: the existing and changing relations between the two political systems themselves. The church–state relationship was therefore a complex one. When we add Europe to the two political systems functioning in Buganda we have a three-tiered structure. The dynamic relations between these three have to be taken into account, as the success of the church depended on the pattern which these relations constituted. Bishop Tucker touched on this whole problem, and one aim of the following analysis will be to investigate how the three-tiered system worked in relation to the mission and church.

6

Official colonial rule: the organizational phase, 1893–*c*. 1900

The organizational phase of official colonial rule is here taken to cover the time from the Portal mission until the turn of the century, when a new phase appears. A characteristic feature of this period is the steady expansion of the British Protectorate into the neighbouring Bantu kingdoms and chieftaincies.[1] As the guiding principle we will again employ the schema which examines religious liberty at three levels.

Religious liberty at the individual level

The clearest expression of religious liberty so far seen in Buganda was inserted by Portal into the agreement between the Protestant and Catholic chiefs. We will now examine how the colonial administration interpreted and administrated this clause, which stipulated that 'There shall be absolute freedom of religion throughout Uganda [Buganda]: every person shall be at liberty to follow any religion, creed or superstition, according to his choice: no person shall suffer any injury, loss of property, or restriction of liberty for any such profession or for any change in his belief.'[2]

This clause contains the positive expression of the principle, the safeguarding of the individual, and the statement of rights in the case of change of religion. The new colonial administration was very conscious of the first aspect, in spite of the fact that it appeared in the agreement with the chiefs and not in the treaty with the Kabaka. Captain Macdonald as Acting Commissioner impressed on Bishop Hirth that the administration could not interfere with religious convictions as this would encroach on the right of religious liberty, and he stated explicitly that he was prepared to prosecute anyone who violated this right.[3] His successors even applied the clause outside Buganda proper on two occasions.[4] Colonel Colvile in his turn took this opportunity to emphasize that the administration had a special obligation towards the Muslims and the so-called pagans, as these had no Europeans to take care of them, a fact that had been suggested earlier by Lugard.[5]

The colonial administration was thus upholding the right of religious liberty more extensively than before. This can partly be explained by its stronger position compared to its predecessors. The decisive problem was, however, how to deal with the question of evictions from shambas which arose when the incumbent professed a different religion from his superior in the area. It was in general necessary to clarify the consequences, if any, of a change of religion. The need for clarification became acute as early as December 1893 in connection with two prominent cases. One concerned a Protestant woman of the royal family, with a number of shambas in her possession, who turned Catholic.[6] The other was Mwanga's wish to reconvert to Catholicism. The possibility of the Kabaka moving from one party to the other was looked upon with great concern, as it was thought likely to cause something of an avalanche in the number of religious renegades, and might possibly result in demands for a new reorganization of the country. Colvile was extremely careful in the handling of these cases: he knew that his decisions could create precedents for the future, as they would be the first ones since Portal's 'allotment of Protestant and Roman Catholic spheres'.[7]

Colvile issued a public proclamation dealing with the first case, signed by himself and the Kabaka, and he further worked out a 'Draught of policy to be pursued in the event of any Waganda chiefs changing their religion'. This document was only meant for internal administrative purposes, and was drawn up in order to have a policy laid down in the event of a great number of people changing their religion.[8] Colvile's two documents dealing with his religious policy were forwarded to the Foreign Office. More than six months later he received a sort of approval when the Foreign Office remarked that his policy appeared to be founded 'on just principles'.[9]

The first part of Colvile's policy and guidelines dealt with people who lived on shambas whose possessor was of a different religion, or whose possessor changed his religion, and with people who belonged to the territory of a chief with a different religion from their own. These people were absolutely free to follow the religion of their own choice and could not under any circumstances be evicted. On the other hand, difference or change of religion should not be allowed to affect 'the rights over them now held by chiefs of Districts or Provinces'. Thus the rights of individuals to make a living without being evicted on religious grounds were safeguarded; and the traditional pattern of authority was not to be broken down because of religious differences. Ties and obligations to a chief were to be independent of religious adherence.

From the interpretations given here Colvile's rules and precautions can be seen as a concrete implementation of Portal's clause on religious liberty.[10] He was safeguarding the right to religious liberty, especially as regards the relationship between Protestants and Catholics, at the individual level, while keeping the traditional pattern of authority. He was, in other words, trying to create space for the implementation of religious liberty in Buganda, and there are indications that his endeavours met with some success.[11]

In the case of one issue, however, Colvile was forced to state specifically that the European concept of religious liberty must take precedence over the African structure, thus illustrating how difficult it was, after all, to make this European principle work in the African context. At the instigation of Bishop Hirth another proclamation was issued in the name of Colvile and Mwanga stating that people of a different religion from their chief were not under any obligation to work for him in connection with buildings 'for sectarian purposes'. They could be called upon to work on buildings being erected for the benefit of their own faith, but only after mutual agreement between the two chiefs involved.[12] It can thus be seen that this cardinal point in the European concept of religious liberty, that no one must be forced to contribute to any religion other than his own, ran contrary to the African system of authority and set limitations on the traditional rights of the chiefs. This ruling can further be taken as an indication that the principle of religious liberty had begun to operate at the individual level, resulting in a more mixed pattern of settlement, in the sense that Catholics were now living in areas allocated to Protestants and vice versa.

But a wider consequence of this ruling can also be inferred. In the economic system prevalent so far the contributions of chiefs and their subjects for religious purposes were mainly given in the form of labour, which would be donated by the chief out of the labour tribute to which he was entitled. This meant that ordinary people, by changing their religion at the opportune moment, could invoke this new ruling and thereby avoid doing any religious work. This in turn meant a limitation of the overall amount of work due to their chief. The loophole was soon discovered.[13] As this eroded the wealth of the chief the ruling on religious liberty could result in a weakening of the capacity and inclination of the chiefs to support their churches. This would in turn be detrimental to missionary expansion and could in the end undermine the foundations of an African church structure so closely tied to the chiefly institution.[14]

Another possible consequence of the wider implementation of religious liberty was a change in the respective numerical strengths of the two Christian parties, which would become especially acute if the Kabaka changed his religion. Such a step would lead to political requests for the redistribution of chieftainships and shambas.[15] In the administrative guidelines which Colvile drew up, strictly for internal use, he reaffirmed the territorial distribution as final, and emphasized that changes of religion (in this case from Protestantism to Catholicism or vice versa) would not affect the jurisdiction of the two Katikiros. The Catholic Katikiro was to exercise power over the sazas allocated by Portal to the Catholics, and if any of the inhabitants turned Protestant they would remain under his jurisdiction.[16]

The only possible interpretation of this clause is that the principle of religious liberty and more particularly the subsidiary right to change one's religion was not to be allowed to undermine the territorial organization of the country worked out by Lugard and later revised and confirmed by Portal. This leads us to another observation. The guidelines drawn up by Colvile were implicitly based on a distinction between the rights of the individual on the one hand and civil rights with regard to office-holding on the other, whereas Portal's clause on religious liberty and its implementation was confined to the individual level. This distinction was in fact made explicit some three years later in connection with the allocation of two new sazas annexed from the Kingdom of Bunyoro and handed over to Buganda by the colonial administration. The then Commissioner, E. J. L. Berkeley (1895–1899), stated that the appointment of a Catholic or Protestant saza chief was one thing; but 'apart from this, the inhabitants of, or residents in, each province [saza] must have complete individual freedom to choose or profess each his own religion; no one need . . . be a Catholic or a Protestant because the paramount Chief of the province was a Catholic or a Protestant'.[17] We may, however, question the efficacy of this distinction in practice. Berkeley himself, in another statement, qualified his statement when he admitted that it was a fact of life that ordinary people preferred to settle in the area of a chief of their own denomination. This tendency inevitably caused some movement of people.[18] The end result was thus that the nature of the chiefly institution combined with the denominational distribution of the country, and the practice of tying certain civil rights to specific religious alignments, limited the scope of religious liberty at the individual level. This relationship between the individual and the societal level should be borne in mind as we now turn to the latter.

The societal level: religion and offices

One key point in the colonial administrative policy was the desire to preserve the sharing of the country between the three religious parties, and to avoid any change in the relative positions of the two strongest. Quite obviously this was not a policy which was entirely to the colonial officials' liking, but they regarded it as a heritage of necessity, and were unable to formulate any other policy which would ensure peace and tranquillity.[19] The effect of this policy was, however, that certain civil rights were tied to religious affiliation for reasons of political expediency.

The allocation of new areas

The problem of incorporating new areas became acute in two major cases. First the Muslims, to whom Lugard had granted three sazas, started a rebellion just after Portal's departure, out of dissatisfaction with their allocated area. They were soon defeated.[20] While the loyal group among them was allowed to keep one saza, Macdonald decided that the other two sazas should be shared out between the two Christian parties.[21] Unfortunately the sazas were not of equal size, which led to protracted negotiations with the Catholic Bishop Hirth. Macdonald drew attention to the fact that the Protestants had been most active in the fight against the Muslims and deserved the lion's share. Bishop Hirth contested this indirect accusation that the Catholics had not pulled their weight, and referred in general to the impoverished Catholic position in the country after Portal's settlement. In the event the Catholic Baganda did not take the same firm stand as the Bishop, and were content to settle in the smaller former Muslim saza allocated to them.[22]

Without going further into the details of these negotiations, we may say that their general tenor reveals essential aspects of the colonial policy towards the religious parties and underscores once again the continuity of the problems of Lugard's period. The Protestants had again proved themselves loyal allies, and accordingly deserved more of the spoils. The Catholic party also deserved a share, but the balance of power between the two parties must not be altered, and no revision of Portal's religious settlement could be contemplated. No other principle for a political settlement was suggested.

The same thing happened three years later when the newly annexed part of southern Bunyoro, the so-called 'lost counties', was brought under Buganda's jurisdiction. The two sazas in question were divided between the two Christian parties, and Commissioner Berkeley took this opportunity, as mentioned earlier, to lecture for the Baganda chiefs and representatives of the European missionaries on the implications of this religious partition of the new territory, especially as regards the position of the common people.[23] Officially Berkeley confined the religious partition to the saza chief level, but the real implications of this principle, which had now become an established part of colonial administrative policy, should be examined before returning to the question of its impact on individuals.

The evidence available is somewhat scanty, especially as no official statement was made about the appointment of sub-chiefs. Macdonald did, however, take it for granted, when he reallocated the two former Muslim sazas, that a saza chieftainship carried with it ten sub-chieftainships.[24] Consequently, the former holders of these posts would have to forfeit their offices, as in fact happened when the Catholics, in accordance with Portal's settlement, took over one particular Protestant saza.[25] There are further indications that the normal practice in the case of changes of religion was to resign one's office.[26] As regards the total number of chieftainships, the leading Anglican missionary, R. H. Walker, found in 1896 that 'all the chiefs are baptized and nominally Christians', and he traced this back to the time when the chieftainships were in the hands of the leaders of the two Christian parties.[27]

The silence of the sources about the position of the lower echelons may in part be explained by the fact that the religious partition of the country was so firmly established after 1893 that there were now few changes of religion at the level of the chiefs. Offices were allocated at the level of the parties and people obtained and held them because of their religious affiliation. This was the case with the appointments of new chiefs in the Catholic saza Buddu after Mwanga's rebellion in 1897 (see below). The Acting Commissioner had to admit that he could not appoint Protestants as he had intended. The Protestant party pointed to the possible political complications if Catholic chiefs were not appointed, and they themselves showed reluctance to accept posts in Buddu. The Acting Commissioner conceded the point: 'in order not to weaken the loyal party by internal dissensions, I thought it better to give way, and to adopt another and less sudden method in mixing the creeds'.[28] This example gives the situation in a nutshell. The long-term policy of the government was to put an end to 'the existing isolation of creeds', but it was very difficult to break down the existing pattern of politico-religious partition.

Two conclusions can be drawn from this. In the first place, the number of offices filled on the basis of religious criteria does not seem to have been reduced compared to Lugard's figure; the majority were still tied in practice to a Christian affiliation, however nominal it might be in quality. Secondly, applying the criterion of equality, the colonial administration was still practising real inequality as the Christians had far better power and appointment opportunities than people of other religions. Focusing on the Christians alone, the Protestant hegemony was still upheld.

The privileges which the Christians enjoyed in connection with certain civil rights had some impact at the individual level. The settlement pattern of ordinary people was closely related to the denomination of the chiefs. Religious and traditional bonds tended to work together and reinforce one another. It became a fact of life that the ladder to political power, offices and other benefits was provided by Christianity. The adoption of Christianity conferred social status upon its adherents, and the act of baptism had social consequences. In a situation of choice individuals were likely to take these secondary effects into account, however much the missionaries regretted the consequences for the quality of religious conviction.[29]

The struggle for the centre of power

The balance of power within the Buganda system during the reign of Kabaka Mwanga was not only dependent on the allocation of chieftainships, but equally so on the support given the system by the Kabaka himself. Mwanga's wish to rejoin the Catholics was a politically sensitive question for the colonial administration, as any change at the centre could shatter the precarious balance of power. Looking ahead, a problem of major concern for the administration as well as the missions was the future of Mwanga's two nephews in Catholic custody, the heirs to the throne.

These two factors are not unrelated to one another, as it was assumed that Mwanga's wish to join the Catholics rested on the belief that this step was the only way to get his nephews back.[30] He first mentioned his planned reconversion in December 1893, on the eve of Colonel Colvile's departure on a military campaign against Bunyoro. This timing would in Colvile's opinion have serious consequences, possibly a civil war; so, with a mixture of persuasion, appeals and threats of replacement, he managed to get Mwanga to promise to postpone his change of religion until his return.[31] On this occasion Bishop Hirth accused Colvile of depriving the Kabaka of his right to religious liberty and of mixing religion and politics. The Foreign Office, however, later fully endorsed Colvile's line.[32]

Mwanga returned to the question in July 1894.[33] This time Colvile took an even firmer line and pointed out the risk of a rebellion. He also impressed on Mwanga that it was a bad thing for a kingdom if the King changed his religion as easily as he changed his coat; the British Queen was not allowed to change her religion. But if it was really a matter of conscience and not for the sake of any material gain he should of course do as he wished.[34] From the amount of pressure and persuasion expended on Mwanga it is clear that the colonial administration really felt that this change of religion could lead to unrest, given the number of people who would follow the Kabaka; it could put the politico-religious settlement of the country in jeopardy. In the end Mwanga gave in and announced that he would remain a Protestant.[35]

The problem of the succession bothered the colonial administration just as much as that of the Kabaka's religious affiliation. Bishop Hirth postponed again and again the return of the two nephews. He accused the Protestants of bad faith in the fulfilment of the conditions of the Portal agreement and of misinterpreting Portal's various concessions. The bickering went on for almost a year and a half, and strained relations not only with Colvile, but also with the Foreign Secretary, Lord Rosebery, who was brought into the matter.[36] A solution seemed at last to be in sight when Colvile intervened directly in the Buganda system by issuing a proclamation in his own and Mwanga's name excluding the two princes from the succession to the throne.[37] Events, however, took an unexpected turn when Mwanga in 1896 produced a son and legitimate heir. As he was still nominally a Protestant the birth meant that Protestant succession to the centre of power was ensured. The CMS missionaries, however, had to remain on the alert, as the Catholics were not lying idle.[38]

The problem was to come to a head sooner than anyone had expected. The

Kabaka's wish to change his religion can be seen as a token of his dissatisfaction and an attempt to put himself in a more influential position.[39] He was under pressure from two sides, internally from the chiefs,[40] and externally from the British Resident. Towards the end of 1896 he was even caught smuggling ivory and humiliated by the chiefs of both Christian parties, who on this occasion acted together.[41] The culmination came in July 1897, when Mwanga fled the capital and started a rebellion with Buddu as his base, supported by a number of people who felt the same dissatisfaction with the whole political situation and the ensuing restraints that Christianity had placed on their way of life.[42] It is remarkable that the leaders from all three parties stood by the British 'protectors' and waged war on their own Kabaka for nearly two years, until he was captured and finally deported to the Seychelles, together with the Omukama (King) of Bunyoro and a group of mutinous Nubian soldiers who had joined forces with him. His infant son, Daudi Chwa, was installed as the new Kabaka, 'the first Christian King Uganda [Buganda] has ever had', and ensured a Protestant upbringing.[43] Three regents were appointed pending his coming of age. This development is significant in four respects. In the first place, it marked the culmination of chiefly rule in Buganda at the expense of the Kabakaship. Secondly, taking the composition of the regency (the two Katikiros and one senior Protestant chief) into account, it marked the dominance of the Christians and the hegemony of the Protestants right at the centre of power. Thirdly, all three parties were now loyal to the colonial power, and thanks to their assistance in this difficult period they gained a platform from which to press special claims from Buganda's side in the settlement of the now enlarged Protectorate.[44] Fourthly, the campaign against the rebellious Mwanga created an alliance between the colonial government, the missionaries and the Christian chiefs. The crisis revealed the extent to which they had a shared interest in the preservation of the status quo in Buganda.[45] The new feeling was expressed by a leading Protestant chief when he spoke in a sermon of 'the victory that God has given to the cause of religion, law and order in the country'.[46]

Religious liberty at the institutional level: the relationship between mission, church and state

Moving on from the societal to the institutional level it is appropriate to take as our point of departure the observation just made that Christianity enjoyed a privileged position; further, that within the realm of Christianity the Protestants had emerged as the ruling group and the major political factor. This leads us to a closer analysis of the relationship between the colonial state and the institutional expressions of Protestantism, the mission and the embryonic African church. Important elements are the official nature of direct colonial rule as opposed to that of the Company era, and the more established pattern of colonial administration now coming into effect.

Missionary expansion

During Portal's period the right of the colonial government to control the extent and direction of missionary activity was a prominent issue. As we have seen,

Bishop Tucker conceded that the CMS was under an obligation to obtain permission before any planned extension of missionary work was carried out. The CMS observed this ruling for the rest of the 1890s, seeking permission in each case, and if the government for one reason or another asked them to wait they accepted the postponement.[47] A pattern emerged whereby extensions of both missions followed in the footsteps of the Protectorate's expansion, so that religious expansion paralleled political expansion. The so-called 'Pax Britannica' was certainly a factor that helped the missions in their work.[48]

Portal also had to get the two missions to agree upon spheres of extension. The concrete result was much in doubt, as Portal and Tucker gave somewhat conflicting interpretations in their dispatches home. A tacit agreement seems to have functioned for more than a year in accordance with the 'private and verbal understanding'; and after that period both the CMS mission and the colonial government came to conceive of the agreement as more binding than could have been foreseen.

In July 1894 the local governing body of the CMS, the Finance Committee, asked their headquarters for a missionary to direct the work in Toro. Well aware that Toro, according to the agreement, was reserved for the Catholics, they specifically added that they could not imagine the Bishop and the CMS headquarters extending the agreement for a further period, nor did the government expect such an extension.[49] At the same meeting, the Finance Committee decided to withdraw CMS economic support for the Ganda teachers already working in Toro and leave it to the Church Council to pay for them. The reason given was that it had been brought to their notice that such support, even for African teachers, was not in accordance with Portal's interpretation of his agreement with the bishops.[50] From the correspondence on this issue it is clear that Colvile interpreted the agreement in such a way that neither CMS funds nor personnel must be used for the extension of the Protestant work westwards.[51]

The missionaries were thus in practice complying with the agreement. But they tried to circumvent the problem and keep the work in Toro going on by financing it personally and asking people in England privately 'to help the native church here to extend its influence where the CMS cannot at present go'.[52] The CMS headquarters reluctantly agreed to this proposal, but stipulated that the support should be on a small scale, as the basic principle for all CMS work was that the local church should be made self-supporting.[53]

The distinction between mission and church here emerges very clearly. The interesting new thing is, however, that the colonial government also appears to accept this distinction between the CMS and the Church Council as sponsoring bodies. Colvile emphasized that all Baganda, including teachers, could move freely, and that if they wanted to live outside Buganda 'no one can stop them on the ground of their being Protestants'.[54] For their part the CMS in London found this approach a most encouraging sign that the government viewed the 'Native Church' 'as a body having its own footing and its own rights in the country'.[55]

It remains to be seen how much importance the colonial government attached to what the mission considered a very important distinction. The question arose again and again, in connection with the ownership of land and the general position of the missionaries, whether they belonged exclusively to the mission or were also a part of the church. The problem has been discussed earlier in connection with Lugard's first treaty with Mwanga.

The next development came with the reorganization of Catholic missionary work in the Uganda region, beginning in 1895. For various reasons, not least in order to weaken the prevailing association of Catholicism with French missionaries and Protestantism with British missionaries, it was decided to send Catholic English-speaking missionaries from St Joseph's Foreign Missionary Society of Mill Hill (the Mill Hill Fathers) to Uganda. The whole region was divided between the two Catholic orders by papal decree, and the arrangement was approved finally by the Foreign Office.[56]

Just before leaving for Uganda at the beginning of April 1895 the newly appointed Catholic Bishop Hanlon called on Colvile, who had by then returned to London. It became clear that the new missionary diocese would include not only the regions east of Buganda, but also the eastern sazas of Buganda proper, which under Lugard and Portal had been allocated to the Protestant party. In a report to the Foreign Office Colvile pointed out that the allocation of these sazas to the Mill Hill Fathers was a breach of the verbal agreement between Bishop Tucker and Mgr Hirth of April 1893, and if put into practice would mean the nullification of the agreement on missionary spheres. Colvile did, however, recommend this step as he was against confining religious denominations to special areas, and as he considered 'that the more members of the two principal religions in Uganda [Buganda] are allowed to intermingle the sooner will the ill-feeling with which they regard each other subside'.[57] The Protestants would accordingly be free to set up stations in the Catholic area towards the west. The Foreign Office acted on Colvile's suggestions and informed the CMS that the new Catholic arrangement terminated the agreement of April 1893 and that the Protestants would of course also be free to extend their operations westwards.[58] Thus Colvile attributed, just as he had done a year earlier in Buganda, an official status to the private agreement between the two bishops; and the Foreign Office must have done so too, since it was found necessary to write an official letter about its expiry.

Both Colvile and the Foreign Office took the bishops' agreement on missionary spheres to include Buganda itself.[59] The consequence of this understanding was that the religious division of Buganda not only had a political character, but also demarcated missionary spheres inside the Buganda area. There is no evidence whatsoever that Portal had intended to include Buganda proper in his agreement with the two bishops. He was only thinking of the regions outside Buganda. It is, therefore, understandable that the official handling of the agreement by the Foreign Office and the inclusion of Buganda puzzled the CMS officials, who still remembered Bishop Tucker's strong denials of the existence of any agreement at all.[60] This made it difficult for the CMS, faced with a new request from Tucker, to intervene in the matter. They referred it to the Foreign Office, but the Foreign Office was not helpful in providing further clarification, though it confirmed that the agreement concerning the division of Buganda between the two Christian parties still stood, however much the Foreign Office disliked the idea of chiefs having to give up office when they changed their religions. The answer, couched in diplomatic terms, was as follows: 'I am to state that Lord Salisbury understands from the late Acting Commissioner in Uganda that the custom alluded to has hitherto been a practice rather than a rule, and that it has not always been adhered to.'[61] The Foreign Office took the opportunity to express the hope that the two missions 'will abstain from the admixture of political questions with religious instruction'.[62]

Bishop Tucker's reaction to Catholic expansion in the Uganda region should be seen in the context of this chain of events. In accordance with the stand he had taken earlier he made no reference to the 'Portal agreement' on missionary spheres. In any case, from his point of view, any previous understanding on the extent of missionary activity outside Buganda proper was irrelevant, as the Catholic move should be viewed in a Buganda context. His arguments can further be seen as a continuation of the stand he took during the negotiations with Portal, where two criteria could be singled out: first, that the principle of missionary freedom was not the main problem in Buganda, and secondly that missionary activity was closely related to the political organization of the country. These two criteria underlay the arguments in his strongly-worded letter to the British authorities.[63] First there was the morally-tinged argument that the increase in Catholic missionary activity was 'an act of unprovoked aggression' against the Protestant missionary effort because the Catholics were encroaching on an area where the Protestants were already established, instead of opening up virgin territory. He considered that this went beyond the bounds of decency and was an outright scandal. His second argument was political: to start a Catholic mission in areas which had been assigned to the opposite party under Portal would cause unrest among the inhabitants, and possibly even serious disturbances. In other words, he drew attention to the risk that the Catholic expansion would undermine the laboriously achieved division of the country between the two Christian parties, an arrangement which had so far been cemented by the missions' parallel division of spheres. 'This of course was a political division of the country. But it is one which nevertheless affects missionary work very closely,'[64] he wrote, under-lining the interdependence of missionary work and political organization in Buganda to the detriment of missionary freedom.

What Tucker was asking from the British government was that on the strength of these two arguments they would undertake to control the influx of Catholic missionaries into the country so as to uphold the existing parallel political and missionary structures, and thereby ensure peace and order. Obviously Tucker saw his mission as facing a major Catholic offensive, not just the replacement of one group of missionaries with another. The Protestants could not muster similar resources as a counterbalance, so in this situation he called on the state as secular authority to direct missionary enterprise. As was the case with the principle of religious liberty earlier, absolute freedom of missionary movement involved a risk for the weaker part, which therefore called for government intervention in order to freeze the situation, even if this involved limiting missionary freedom in general. Tucker's moral argument was not acceptable to the government, as constraints on the Catholics would be tantamount to a limitation of missionary freedom. On the contrary, the Foreign Office now took the opportunity to proclaim the principle of missionary freedom in Buganda, thereby separating missionary enterprise from the political distribution of the country. The colonial authority thus seemed to be taking a more active line on the question of freedom for missionary enterprise. It refused to direct the allocation of missionary manpower, and as regards missionary expansion it tried to treat all missions equally, irrespective of creed and nationality.

The real background for the government's line on missionary freedom can be sought in the fact that they were unconvinced by Tucker's second, political argument. Concurring with Colvile's view, the Foreign Office believed that the conflict between the two Christian groups was manageable, and did not call for immediate action. This again reflected the stronger position which the adminis-tration felt itself to be in around 1895.[65]

The new departure in government policy which followed Bishop Tucker's intervention became apparent the following year in connection with the allocation of the two sazas annexed from Bunyoro. It was made quite clear that there would be complete freedom of missionary enterprise in both sazas, just as there was in any other part of Buganda and the neighbouring territories.[66] This policy had noticeable effects in the following years. In 1898 a new Protestant station was opened in the Catholic saza Buddu, where there had been none since Lugard's allocation of Buddu to the Catholic party in 1892. The Protestant Archdeacon alleged that during this period it was not possible to profess the Protestant religion in Buddu. But the government had now built a fort and posted a European Resident to the district. The Protestant move to Buddu was obviously determined by the presence of the government representative, which further illustrates the fact that the degree of implementation of the principle of missionary freedom was related to the strength and presence of the government.[67]

Another effect can be seen from an internal discussion within the Protestant mission on the interpretation of missionary freedom. Apparently Bishop Tucker and some of the missionaries pleaded for a policy of giving no concessions to the Catholics. One method suggested was to induce Protestant chiefs to forbid the building of Catholic churches within their areas of authority. The opposite view was held by Archdeacon R. H. Walker, who wanted people to be free to choose their religion, and did not believe in involving the secular authorities.[68] This discussion seems to have been discontinued without the participants coming to any real conclusion. Bishop Tucker's approach can, however, be viewed as consistent with his earlier attitude: he was inclined to make use of the secular authority in defending and pursuing his own immediate missionary policy. By suggesting the exploitation of the position of the Protestant chiefs he was displaying the same awareness of the importance of the local African political system as he had during the negotiations with Portal. We may here even venture the hypothesis that the neutral stand of the colonial government on the question of missionary expansion would increase the significance which the mission attached to the African political system. This point will be developed further from a different angle. The effect of the stronger and more established position of the official colonial administration was now noticeable and points towards a pattern of relationships between the colonial government and the missions different from the one we have seen so far.

The framework of the relationship between mission, church and state

This framework can, following the analytical pattern established in our discussion of missionary expansion, be examined under three headings: the relationship with the colonial government in the local setting; the role of the European arena; and the relationship with the African political system.

The relationship with the colonial government

We have seen that the missionaries' political role proved to be an important factor in the relationship between mission and government. Here it will be examined in connection with the new factors now operative: the establishment of official colonial rule and correspondingly of a more developed type of colonial administration. The characteristic feature of the period was the foundation of an embryonic legal system with some basic laws and with a procedure for dealing with civil and criminal cases. The difficult thing was clearly how to integrate, or at least adapt to one another, European ideas and principles and the highly developed African tradition of Buganda. A similar problem in connection with the foundation of an administrative practice was the definition of areas of jurisdiction for Europeans and Africans, especially as regards the position of the chiefs and their authority.[69] From what we have seen of the missionaries' position in the Buganda system, this gradual change in the colonial structure was bound to influence their roles. They would especially find themselves cast in the role of interpreters of the two traditions involved, and would be expected to provide some sort of linkage between them.[70] The emphasis now shifted away from the question of expansion to that of the missionaries' political involvement.

The missionaries continued in the main playing their two former political roles, that of advising the leaders of the Protestant party[71] and that of acting as intermediaries to the colonial government. But the issues were now different.[72] In their last capacity they sometimes had special opportunities to exert their influence, when by official request they acted quite literally as interpreters.[73] While they were conscious of the risk of being accused of undue interference,[74] they were quite prepared to criticize, if necessary, the colonial officials' conduct of office.[75] Increasingly, the dominant area for the missionaries' interventions was that of the sentences passed on their own converts by colonial officials. From their point of view they were acting as defenders of the Africans against the new order that had been introduced, especially as they often felt that injustice had been done.[76] An important justification for their attitude was that they knew more about the African tradition and way of thinking from their work than the officials did. They had also, unlike the officials, crossed the language barrier.[77] At the same time they worked to infuse Christian principles deeply into the new societal order which was emerging, not least within the field of family law.[78]

The government officers did not care for this kind of activity on the part of the missionaries. They considered it to be undue interference, often based on insufficient information and misunderstanding, and in any case they thought that it bore an unpleasant similarity to surveillance of their conduct of office. They also accused the missionaries of partisanship towards their own converts, of applying Christian criteria in purely legal matters, and refusing to acknowledge any faults in their protégés. When Colvile finished his term of service in Uganda at the end of 1894 he departed disgusted with the CMS missionaries, just as Lugard and Captain Williams had done before him. Referring to a number of concrete cases, he accused the British missionaries of wilfully creating difficulties for the administration, and of not being capable of accepting 'the extinction of their political power', in which respect they compared unfavourably with the Catholic fathers. He even implied that the CMS missionaries were bent upon 'setting up a Christian party in opposition to the State'.[79]

It would not be particularly profitable to attempt to penetrate further into these matters in order to verify accusations and counter-accusations.[80] The important point to emphasize is that great tensions existed between the two British agencies in Uganda. It was difficult for them to adjust to each other's presence in the changed circumstances and find a *modus vivendi*, though the colonial government attempted to do so by the same means Lugard and Williams had employed earlier. Macdonald and Colvile denounced the line taken by Portal when he gave the two bishops a key position in the negotiations.[81] They impressed on the missionaries that they should stay out of politics,[82] and they tried to cut them off from participation in the political process by encouraging the Ganda leaders not to go to the missionaries first, but to come directly to the government representatives.[83]

Not surprisingly, taking the well-established position of the missionaries into account, the government's measures did not meet with much success. The Commissioner, E. J. L. Berkeley, could on his return home in 1897 give as his impression that each of the Christian parties still referred most questions to its respective mission, 'thus showing the continuance of their belief that religion and politics must necessarily be closely connected'. Things were rather confused, especially as regards jurisdiction and judgements, because of the role of the missions; and he cited the doubts of ordinary people as to where the real authority was to be found.[84] Yet it is not enough, in describing the roles of the colonial government and the Protestant mission, to confine ourselves to the tensions between them and their difficulties in arriving at a *modus vivendi*. It is necessary to extend the analysis and find a formula with whose help their relationship can be presented in more general terms. It is possible to discern two opposite tendencies in the relationship as it has functioned so far: one towards dissociation, the other towards a new awareness of the identity of their interests.

The first trend was a reaction against the over-identification of the British colonial government with the British CMS mission in the minds of the population. Both sides suffered from this near-identity in the post-Portal period, and both for different reasons agreed on the need for dissociation. The government's conscious attempt to bypass the missionaries in political matters should be seen in this context. Colvile tried even more directly to refute the commonly held notion that Protestantism was the English religion and consequently 'Catholicism and anti-English are synonymous'.[85] But it took a long time for this idea to die, not least because of the ingrained Catholic suspicion of the administration when faced with its concrete decisions.[86]

Already at an early stage the mission expressed a general awareness of the need for dissociation from the colonial government.[87] When the administration started, especially from 1894 onwards, to pass sentences in criminal cases the severity of which ran contrary to most Baganda's ideas of justice, the blame for this was laid at the missionaries' door, as they were also British. The people believed that 'the Government officials and we of the CMS are all one lot'.[88] The mission was judged by the actions of the government, with consequences for their work. 'We are openly insulted in the streets, being accused of being the authors of the Musalosalo's sentence. Already this sentence has done much to alienate the sympathies of the people from us.'[89] The strategy of the missionaries was therefore to work for dissociation from the government. To this end they welcomed the arrival of the Mill Hill Fathers, however much they otherwise deplored their intrusion, as it would help to prove that 'nationality has nothing of necessity to do with religion'.[90]

The second thing that made dissociation desirable was the behaviour of the government officers, which was not always as morally exemplary as the missionaries might have wished. The image of the Europeans thus created tended to be extended to the missionaries. The topic was touched upon by Archdeacon Walker in his farewell speech to Commissioner Berkeley, in which he expounded his ideas on the way Europeans ought to behave towards Africans, and suggested that they injured the reputation of their country when they lowered themselves in the eyes of the Africans.[91] What really worried the missionaries was that the government officers were 'people of no religion';[92] they took little or no interest in the work of the mission, and the effect of this was not lost on the Baganda. This presented a bad example for the African leaders of the country, and it served to undermine the Christian ethical imperatives, and in the end the moral authority of the missionaries.[93] The sources suggest that the missionaries felt that they were suffering for the colonial officials' attitude and behaviour, and that the impact it made on the people made it necessary to attempt ameliorating measures.[94] One solution would be to have some real Christians among the officials, and the missionaries tried to achieve this by appealing to their contacts in London.[95]

The second trend at work was sparked off by the course of events in 1897, and made both sides conscious of an interdependence the extent of which they may not have been aware of during the attempts to achieve dissociation. In May–June 1897 both the missions began to detect anti-European feeling among the common people and even among some of the chiefs of both creeds.[96] They were becoming both anti-government/anti-British and anti-religious/anti-Christian. The situation was aptly summarized by Archdeacon Walker: 'in giving up religion they have supposed that of course they will have to fall out with Kampala [i.e. the colonial administration]'.[97] The feeling started as an anti-religious one, expressed in the form of protests against the many restraints that Christian teaching had imposed upon people's lives.[98] The colonial government was equally a target for this sort of dissatisfaction, as the various laws and obligations introduced along with colonial rule were all seen as part of the same European pattern of oppression.[99]

The Protestant missionaries viewed this strong anti-European feeling and the subsequent war exclusively in moral and Christian terms. There was no attempt to seek natural causes for developments, or to see them as to some extent understandable opposition to European tutelage and intrusion. They could see no justification for the reactions of some of the Baganda involved: 'These Europeans have driven away our King and some of the Chiefs and are now "eating" our country.'[100] The missionaries conceived the protests as simple defiance of 'all civil or religious control in the country'. And Archdeacon Walker added: 'From our point of view they have nothing to complain of. I am happy to say that I cannot side with the natives against the English Government as administered here.' He seemed all the same to have some awareness of the inconsistency of this with what he had said a few years before in connection with the administration of justice, and he hastened to add that there was a great difference between the situation now and the one that existed under Colonel Colvile.[101] It should also be noticed that the policy of dissociation was more or less shelved during this development.

This wave of opposition to both mission and government took on proportions that startled the missionaries.[102] First, the colonial government was made aware of the fact that dissatisfaction in the religious field was equally directed towards the government, as the whole system tended towards a close identification of the fields of religion and politics.[103] Secondly, the mission saw how closely Christianity and civilization were associated in the minds of the people, and how dependent the mission was on the secular authority's maintenance of peace and order.[104] These observations are borne out by an examination of the behaviour of the two European agencies during the campaign against Mwanga, the Nubian mutineers and the Omukama of Bunyoro, who formed a loose alliance in their fight against European rule. The government approached the CMS mission with a view to involving some of the missionaries in the campaign in their pastoral capacity. In spite of some heart-searching over the idea of missionaries engaging themselves directly in a war,[105] a number of them accompanied the troops to Busoga. The government found them invaluable in boosting the morale of the Christian Baganda, who constituted a large contingent of the army.[106] The main reason behind the government's seeking direct assistance from the CMS mission was that the existence of both government and mission was considered to be threatened, and that all British subjects must therefore stand together irrespective of profession.[107] It is interesting to notice that the colonial authorities now also saw that it was a question of standing or falling together, and that they based their appeal to the mission on the grounds of common nationality, thus reaffirming the third role of the missionaries mentioned in the discussion of the Lugard period (Chapter 4).

The CMS mission accepted the government's priorities, laying considerable stress on the identical interests of the government, the missions and the Ganda converts.[108] In particular they underlined the key role of the Protestant chiefs, which again reflected the general influence obtained through the groundwork of the CMS, which had not always been given due recognition by the government. 'The Government will never know what they owe to the Missions, and just now to the CMS especially.'[109] This gave the missions cause for reflection on the interdependency and mutual benefit that existed between the two European agencies. The CMS recognized the importance of the Pax Britannica for their continued success.[110] All the same, 'peace and good government' could only provide the framework, which then had to be filled out by the mission: 'the only thing that I can see that will put the country right is the extended work of the Missions'.[111] In particular the personal conduct and contacts of the missionaries would make all the accusations against Europeans appear without foundation, and persuade the people to see 'the great gain Europeans are to a country like this'.

Hence the crisis in 1897 brought both the colonial government and the mission to a clearer perception of their roles *vis-à-vis* each other by putting their relationship in a new perspective. Both seemed now to recognize how much they were 'connected vessels', making some sort of cooperation and mutual understanding imperative. This change of climate was particularly noticeable in the mission's attitude. It has already been pointed out how Archdeacon Walker considered relations with the government to be much improved, and during the following couple of years the mission was at pains to keep on good terms with the government.[112] The crisis in 1897 was not the only reason for this change of attitude, but it takes us much of the way towards an explanation. It also confirms the hypothesis that the two European agencies after all had a lot in common with regard to concrete objectives and even their final goals, the common factor being their work for civilization. They could therefore meet one another in a common strategy to further the cause of civilization. This was not so clearly formulated at the time, but it appears to have been an implicit formula upon which future cooperation could be based. The crisis of 1897 had certainly been instrumental in bringing to the surface some sort of consciousness of joint interests reminiscent of the philosophy behind the Berlin Treaty of some ten years earlier. The validity of such a proposition will, however, have to be examined more carefully.

To return to the two trends earlier described as characteristic of the late 1890s, dissociation and shared interests, it must be emphasized that the latter does not invalidate the former.[113] They can quite easily work at different levels at the same time, ostensibly in conflict with one another, but in fact constituting a dialectical relationship typical of the relations between mission and government in a colonial situation. The African church, organized in the Church Council, was not drawn into the consultations with the colonial government. Contacts with the authorities were handled exclusively by the mission, and nothing can be said in this analysis of the role which the Church Council may have played internally.

The role of the European parent bodies

The importance of the European influence on developments in the Uganda region has been discussed earlier in various connections. We now come to the question whether the European government and mission structure was brought closer to the African arena during the establishment phase of official colonial rule. How much use was made of the parent bodies by those on the spot in Uganda? And how great was the European involvement in policy- and decision-making in Uganda?

With regard to the first question, the missionaries were still using the same technique as before. They were prepared to invoke the home base in cases of dissatisfaction with the administration's handling of specific matters, or if they felt the need to bring pressure to bear on the general policies in the Protectorate. We have seen Bishop Tucker prepared to act in this way in connection with his endeavours to get the Foreign Office to exercise control over Catholic missionary expansion.[114] In another case, Tucker aptly sketched 'the road of recourse'; if all efforts failed at the local level, then 'our course would be clear – to appeal to the Foreign Office and if that failed to Public Opinion'.[115] Or, put more bluntly: 'Mr Berkeley [the Commissioner] will not approve of this, therefore it is not necessary to make a row about it at home.'[116] The missionaries were thus fully aware of the possibility of appealing to Europe. It is difficult to measure the direct effects of this procedure, but indirectly it is beyond all doubt that it had a prohibitive or deterrent effect on the colonial administration. Sir Gerald Portal advised his successor after his departure not to take any immediate action in the case of the Kabaka's two nephews, however justified, so as to avoid any excitement among 'the powerful English Catholics'.[117] The local colonial officials were known to be careful scrutinizers of the statements of Uganda missionaries which appeared in missionary magazines and in the press.[118] This in turn caused leading missionaries to ask their colleagues and correspondents to be careful when publishing information from Uganda, so as to avoid offending the colonial officials unnecessarily.[119]

The colonial officials did not, as government employees, have the same opportunities of appealing to British opinion as the missionaries had. Colvile's bitter remarks about the CMS missionaries, in an official communiqué with the Foreign Office (p.77), can be seen as an isolated attempt in that direction, and more examples may possibly be found.[120] Still, the whole apparatus within which the missionaries worked put them at an advantage over the colonial officials in their recourse to the European arena.

The second question raised was the extent of European involvement in Ugandan affairs in this period. How far had policy- and decision-making been transferred to London as a consequence of direct British rule? The handling of the question of missionary expansion and missionary freedom provides part of the answer. In the first place, the Foreign Office acted on the advice of the

Commissioner, Colvile.[121] He was the one who laid down policy on missionary extensions and spheres of influence. Secondly, as regards the more fundamental question of missionary freedom, the Foreign Office did as much as was in its power to strengthen the principle, but refrained from becoming involved in its implementation at the local level.

It is thus possible to identify a distinction between the main principles in the colonial policy, laid down in London, and the local, individual policy carried out independently in Uganda. The results obtained from the investigation of religious liberty at the individual and societal levels underline the significance of such a distinction. In practice the normal procedure was that the Foreign Office acquiesced in policy and measures already implemented, quite often in the form of a short letter of approval without further comment.[122]

The same pattern was at work within the CMS system. There were a few basic guidelines in accordance with which all missionary work must be conducted. Among these we have already met the principle of self-support. This was part of a larger complex of missionary theories widely accepted around the turn of the century. Adherence to the principle of self-support was especially rigorous within the CMS, as can be seen from developments in Uganda.[123] There was a definite economic ceiling for missionary activity, and when the missionaries reached this ceiling they provoked a reaction from the CMS headquarters. This was again conditioned by the overall direction of finances and manpower by the home board. As the work was financed by voluntary contributions consciousness of spending was very high, and in periods of scarce resources the missionaries were often making a virtue of necessity when they observed the principle of self-support.

Apart from these basic principles it is remarkable how far policy- and decision-making were left to the missionaries in the field, among whom the question of leadership was often an issue of some importance, in view of the fact that the Bishop only paid three visits to Uganda during the years 1890–8. The actual time he spent in Uganda was not more than 15 months altogether.[124] Archdeacon Walker even complained about the response to missionary communications from the CMS headquarters. The answers to his monthly letters were no more than acknowledgements of their receipt, and people at home showed on the whole very little interest in the work, and less knowledge of the details of the situation.[125] With neither the Foreign Office nor CMS headquarters taking over any more of the policy- and decision-making authority than before, it is thus still reasonable to keep this analysis focused on the men on the spot in Uganda.

The importance of the African political system

It has earlier been shown how Bishop Tucker distinguished between the colonial system and the Buganda polity; and when missionary expansion and missionary freedom was at issue it was further suggested that the mission in future would attach greater significance to the African political system. This theme will be further investigated by focusing on the attitude of the CMS mission to the Bugandan political structure. Taking what we have learned from the foregoing developments as the basis of the analysis, it will be convenient to concentrate on two aspects of the African political system: the centre of power, and the position of the chiefs.

The centre of power

We have on several occasions seen the importance attached to the religious affiliation of the Kabaka in spite of the reduction of his political power. This was apparent in connection with Mwanga's wish to change his religion, and again during the period when the two missions were competing for influence over the successors to the throne. In the end the Protestants won, with the baptism of the new-born prince, and later with the enthronement of the infant heir. Examining the missionaries' motives, it is clear that they were very much aware of the political advantages in having the Kabaka in their fold. This emerges from an internal disagreement between the Archdeacon and the Bishop. The former refused at first to have the prince baptized, because the mother was unbaptized, and because of his opposition to 'scheming for one's religion', but Bishop Tucker wrote and impressed upon him the importance of having the child baptized.[126] It should be added that Tucker successfully pursued the same line in the other three interlacustrine kingdoms, Bunyoro, Toro and Ankole.[127]

This policy from the mission's side cannot be regarded as a simple question of strategy due to the importance of the Kabaka in facilitating access to African society. The mission was also working on the assumption that the Kabaka's adherence to Protestantism provided it with an image of being the established religion, even if only unofficially. Some of the endeavours and initiatives of the CMS mission substantiate this proposition. In 1895 there was an ongoing discussion within the mission on whether the Kabaka should be provided with a sort of throne to sit on in the main church. Once again Archdeacon Walker took the opposite view from the others. In principle he was in favour, but in practice he thought that Mwanga's way of life and his unbaptized status made him unworthy of such an arrangement. It would in particular be difficult to explain to people the difference in the treatment of the Kabaka and those baptized Christians who had been excommunicated for leading un-Christian lives. This is a dilemma that has haunted the Church of Uganda even in this century, as well as churches in other parts of the world. The other missionaries took a more institutional view: 'We can do it to the King as King, and not as Mwanga.'[128] Mwanga's participation in the inauguration of the church bell[129] and later the arrangements in connection with the enthronement of the infant Kabaka pointed in the same direction: the CMS mission was clearly conscious of the image of establishment that Protestantism gained by having the Kabaka as a convert.

Such an attitude involved some side effects. The African royal households could have very great influence by standing as examples of the Christian life or otherwise.[130] And life at Mwanga's court gave the missionaries reason for concern. The mission therefore on several occasions attempted to introduce Christian standards at the court,[131] and were careful to take every precaution that Christian principles should have the greatest possible influence on the upbringing of the heir to the Kabakaship.[132] An apt summary of the whole problem of the Kabaka's behaviour, and evidence of the continued affection which Mwanga enjoyed even after his defeat, is provided by a somewhat peculiar discussion between the colonial administration, the leading chiefs, and the mission on the subject of the amenities which were to be provided for Mwanga during his deportation. The chiefs had promised that four girls would accompany him 'to cook for him and to wait on him', and the colonial administration was prepared to concede this request. The Bishop and the Archdeacon protested, 'as the girls could in no sense be looked upon as Mwanga's lawful wives'. They told the chiefs that they should not as Christians allow any girls to go with Mwanga, and they pointed out to the government that it was in fact providing Mwanga with concubines. The government revoked its approval, but the chiefs considered this too hard on Mwanga, especially as the people would now get the impression that they were persecuting a man who was still held in high esteem. In the end, a compromise was reached, allowing Mwanga to be accompanied by two girls who had already been with him during his exile in Bunyoro.[133]

We have here an illustration of the way the mission could make use of both political systems at the same time in a matter which they considered to be of importance for their ends. Their expectations were little short of a demand that both political systems' representatives should act in accordance with Christian principles, or at least that they should not officially violate them. In this case their concern was for the Kabakaship, but it could be extended to other fields, as for example the laws on the family and marriage and general morality in society. The demand for the observation of Christian norms had so far been raised in connection with the centre of power in the African political system, but it also has relevance for the overall relationship between church and state.

The position of the chiefs

The mission's dependence on the Protestant chiefs had so far been expressed most clearly by Bishop Tucker in connection with Sir Gerald Portal's treaty with Kabaka Mwanga in 1893. Tucker at that time presupposed a direct link between the chiefs' political position and the position and working conditions of the missions. He saw certain tendencies, however, which moved him to issue a warning of changes in the chiefs' future position which would come about with the introduction of colonial rule. The first topic to be examined will therefore be the relationship between the mission and the chiefs in the latter part of the 1890s in view of this forecast.

Tucker's prediction that the new colonial government would work through the Kabaka, bypassing the chiefs, appeared to come true when the administration began to manifest itself more directly. From 1895 Archdeacon Walker registered with uneasiness that the new Resident in Buganda, George Wilson, bypassed the chiefs and worked instead through the Kabaka.[134] Walker could only interpret this tendency as a deliberate attempt to weaken the political importance of Christianity and thereby also indirectly the influence of the mission. Wilson kept telling Mwanga that it was not necessary to belong to any religion at all, and Walker added 'anyone who has no definite religion is now worked up into a Government man'.[135] It was therefore a relief to Walker, who was convinced 'that the hope of the country is in the Christian chiefs', that Wilson towards the end of 1896 had come to share his positive view of the chiefs and his negative view of Mwanga.[136] This development culminated in the flight of Mwanga, and the loyal assistance of the chiefs in the fight against the threats to the colonial system.[137]

It is not the place here to go into a review of the administrative principles of the colonial government.[138] The important thing in this context is to notice how closely linked the mission was with the political authorities in Buganda, and how sensitive it was to any change in the position of the chiefs. This is also confirmed in another respect. From time to time the missionaries intervened in the African political system just as they did in the colonial one. This was especially the case when decisions were made in accordance with the traditional law which in their view differed too much from European or Christian norms. They were, however, aware of the possible consequences: such interference could lower the standing of the particular chief concerned in the eyes of his people, and leave the impression that the missionaries could change any judgement.[139] Here we see that their approach to the two political systems was different, and the missionaries gave high priority to the principle that the African system should as far as possible be allowed to continue carrying out its proper functions.[140]

We must supplement our discussion of the chiefs' political status with some account of their economic position. On the evidence of missionary sources, we can for the 1890s identify three phases in the interplay between the growth of the missionary work and the changing role of the chiefs. In the first third of the period, under Lugard and Portal, the basic theme was the relationship between the CMS missionaries and the Protestant chiefs. The chiefs invited the missionaries to start work in their territory, and provided housing and food out of their own resources, which often meant out of the tributes to which they were entitled as office-holders.[141] In that period the missionaries were in great demand, and the competition of the chiefs for the scarce missionary manpower provided to a large extent the only guiding principle in the extension of the work.[142]

After Portal's confirmation of the religious partition of the country another phase began, roughly corresponding with the second third of the 1890s. Archdeacon Walker underlined the basic theme of this period: 'In this country of Buganda there is a general feeling that every Christian chief should build a church.'[143] The churches were built, just as the chiefs' houses were, with the help of the labour tribute which the chiefs had the right to levy on people within their territory. Christian enterprise was thus included among communal obligations. These churches came to be manned by the small number of newly ordained Ganda deacons and priests and the larger number of lay readers, catechists and teachers sent out by the Church Council.[144]

These activities were financed in two ways, and the chiefs were the backbone of both methods. Land was more or less the only wealth to speak of, but the land was only profitable if there were Bakopi on it to provide labour. The chiefs had the right of disposal over the land within their territory, and could therefore give shambas to the church where its servants could live and be sure of a food supply.[145] The mission's attempts to increase the actual value of the land by securing exemptions from public duties is a point which will be dealt with below. Land and labour were clearly reckoned as 'the only certain means of support' but, taken as it was from the chiefs' official tributes, this kind of support did not come 'directly out of their own pockets'.[146]

The second way of financing Protestant activities during this phase was through the funds which the Church Council began to collect in 1894 for the maintenance of teachers and catechists.[147] This fund was supplied by 'collections in church and donations'.[148] The collections were dependent on two things: first, that the Christians knew of, and felt obliged to observe, the custom of contributing to the church. This was only true to a limited extent at this stage.[149] Secondly, it was vital that the economic system made it possible for the ordinary people to contribute. This was hardly the case, as is evident from the comments of Archdeacon Walker. He described what amounted to a typical peasant subsistence economy, where currency (in the form of cowrie shells) played only a peripheral role, as there were very few goods to sell, and little need to buy anything.[150]

Based on such collections, the Church Council's funds could easily run into a deficit, especially as the many demands due to the growth of the work meant a heavy drain on the available resources. Such a deficit brought the principle of self-support into question, as some of the missionaries favoured the idea of trying to obtain outside money.[151] When this was ruled out by the CMS headquarters, the need for donations was increased. These were for all practical purposes gifts from the chiefs, usually in the form of goods (such as ivory). In fact the situation during 1896 seems to have improved because of the long interval of peace in the country. The collection of the Kabaka's taxes was very successful, and 'a good many of the chiefs have sent in part of their tribute [tax] as an offering to the Church'.[152] Hence it can be said that the chiefs still contributed an important part of the economic means for the Protestant work around the middle of the 1890s. Two tendencies, however, were emerging at the end of this period which in their different ways were indicative of future changes. First, Archdeacon Walker registered the increasing spread of the cowrie-based cash economy, stimulated by the presence of a growing number of Europeans and soldiers in colonial service. This in itself meant an increase in the demand for the ability to buy food, and a market for paid labour.[153] Secondly, the missionaries were becoming, after the middle of the 1890s, aware of the increasing numbers of purely nominal Christians. This was especially felt in connection with a number of the chiefs, and can be explained by the fact that the impetus to appear and act like a Christian was no longer so strong after the political stabilization of the country.[154] It is thus possible to trace a lessening in the chiefs' sense of obligation towards the church and Christianity as such, and also a lessening of the emphasis on Christian qualities in the appointment of officers within the Protestant party, all of which could reduce the significance of the economic role of the chiefs for the Protestant effort.

Any foreseeable development was, however, disrupted by the events of 1897, with the flight of Mwanga and the subsequent upheavals, which brought the work to a standstill for more than six months. The third phase of the 1890s was strongly influenced by these events, and the missionaries registered a number of changes amounting to a new departure in society after the restoration of peace. They were inclined to find the causes solely in the political crisis of 1897–8, especially in the case of the changes which had taken place within the economic sphere. But we should also keep in mind the cumulative effect which would manifest itself after a period of standstill. The cash economy, for example, had already begun to spread before 1897.

The new circumstances meant that the mission was once again reminded of the importance of the chiefs for their working conditions. A number of young and inexperienced chiefs were appointed to replace the ones who had either been killed during hostilities or had defected to Mwanga's camp. It took some time before these new chiefs could have any real influence over the people. In other areas the return of the old chiefs soon meant an increase in the presents for the church fund and in the sale of books.[155] Besides the direct political importance of the chiefs and their economic significance, the indirect, catalytic effect of their attitude towards the church was of considerable importance.

The missionaries were however more concerned with the economic changes in the country. 'Suddenly new sources of wealth have opened up to the people.' This was due to the increase in government spending, the presence of more Europeans, a pay rise for the Nubian troops and increased purchasing power. The need for porters, labourers and consumer goods was great, and the ordinary people (the

Bakopi) were now getting money in their hands.[156] The missionaries saw this new development as a transitional stage, and were rather uneasy about the consequences.

The immediate effect was that ordinary people were becoming wealthier by having relatively more at their disposal. They were therefore better able to give more to the church, and church collections indeed increased substantially over the period 1898–9 until they were higher than ever before.[157] This partly counterbalanced the instability caused by the unpredictability of the chiefs' contributions. Having hitherto mostly contributed out of their tributes, there was some doubt whether they would now show genuine willingness to give just as much as before out of their own means.[158] In any case the Bakopi now emerged as a category of independent contributors, instead of figuring as labourers under the chiefs.

The changed economic conditions and the new opportunities for the Bakopi were viewed with anxiety by the mission. They saw the new opportunities as competing with their own work requirements. It was becoming increasingly difficult to recruit teachers, and a number of the teachers already trained took up better-paid jobs with the government, especially as porters.[159] Thus the church framework no longer provided the only ladder to a career and a share of the new possibilities inherent in the emerging new social order in the country. Here the church was at an economic disadvantage as it could not pay its employees more than the principle of self-support allowed. The situation was not helped by the evangelical tradition, which tended to measure spirituality by willingness to forego some of the goods of this world. Thus the missionaries also had moral reasons for their concern over these new developments, as they meant new temptations for their converts, and would cause an increase in the numbers of purely nominal Christians among the Bakopi as well as among the chiefs.[160]

Turning to the more substantial changes that took place in the wake of the altered economic conditions, and which affected both the church and the chiefs, we should first notice that these changes did not tend to reinforce the chiefs' status. On the contrary, they loosened the bonds between the chiefs and the ordinary villagers and peasants. The new income-earning opportunities deprived the chiefs of 'their monopoly of the labour market and their control over the distribution of wealth'.[161] Though this was more a tendency than an established fact, it indicated a step in the direction of independence from the chiefs for the Bakopi, which was manifested in their greater socio-economic and geographical mobility. Their stronger economic position gave them the chance of moving from one chiefdom to another, and the Bakopi became a potential contributing group to the church.

Such mobility was not a new phenomenon in the Buganda tradition. It had long been the practice that people who were dissatisfied with their chief because of his misbehaviour moved to another place. There was no ruling on compulsory residence, and this freedom served as a check on the chiefs' abuse of power, as their authority and wealth were closely dependent on the number of people in their territories. The religious partition of the country created some disturbance in the working of this mechanism, but the implementation of religious liberty worked as a re-establishing factor which worked together with the subsequent economic developments. Christianity itself contributed to the increased mobility in society. People had earlier had few acquaintances outside the circle of the family, but Archdeacon Walker observed changes:

A man on being baptized is written down, receives a name, is soon well known and is admitted into a large family spread all over the country and because he is a Christian finds friends everywhere and a letter from a teacher in the country is an introduction to the chiefs in Mengo the capital.[162]

Membership of the same creed meant that people were less anonymous out in the country, and made it easier for them to move from the territory of one chief to that of another. The Christian community was thus able to cross the boundaries of the family and the clan. Whether this was also the case with ethnic boundaries is a question which will be discussed later.

The substance of the relationship between mission, church and state

Christian principles in the legal and administrative apparatus

This topic has been touched upon earlier in connection with the intervention of the missionaries in cases where their converts were subject to the state's legal or administrative decisions. Their overall aim was clearly that Christian principles and norms should provide the basis for the treatment of Africans and constitute the source of the legal code, especially in the cases of civil law, family law and the work of the judiciary. According to the missionaries' ideas, the colonial government was under an obligation to uphold Christian norms and create conditions which made it possible for people to live a Christian life. Or, defined negatively, the government was expected to refrain from acting in ways that contravened Christian behaviour. This theme will be further developed in Chapter 16.

The status and rights of church personnel

The people involved comprised the missionaries from overseas on the one hand and the African clergy, catechists and teachers on the other. As regards the former, two issues were raised as early as 1890 in connection with Lugard's first treaty with Mwanga. The first was the question of indirect support to the Christian effort, especially of whether the colonial authority would grant the mission exemption from tax and customs duties. The second issue was the role of the missionaries in relation to other Europeans, and whether they should be placed in a special category (p.33).

Both situations reappeared in 1897. In the intervening period the mission had enjoyed the privilege of exemption from customs duties on imported goods and from paying tax. But these concessions were annulled in 1897 on the instructions of the British government, in accordance with its policy of trying to make the Protectorate pay its own way on a larger scale.[163] A five per cent duty was levied on all goods imported by the mission, and each missionary now had to pay a regular annual tax, where before they had paid occasional amounts to the Kabaka, that is, to the African government.[164] The mission accepted these new rulings without much grumbling, in spite of the fact that they hampered the work severely in important areas like the sale of imported books.[165] Their reaction indicates that the mission no longer expected the same concessions and indirect support from the colonial government that Lugard had shown himself willing to grant when he stated that the Company had no intention of making money out of the missionaries, but would rather go to some expense to assist them.

As far as the second issue is concerned, the missionaries were classified as Europeans as opposed to Africans, which meant that their civil obligations were to the colonial government and not to the African authorities. This was clearly confirmed in connection with the possession of land. Whether it was held in the name of the individual missionaries or the local CMS body, the title deeds must be registered with the colonial authority as if the land was alienated from the rest of the country. Africans holding property held it in principle from the Kabaka, which for the time being also meant that most of the church buildings which were the property of 'the Native Protestant Church' had to be registered with the Buganda authorities.[166] The further implications of this distinction between European-owned and African-held land will be discussed below.

Turning to the African church personnel (clergy, catechists and teachers) these were exclusively subject to the African political system, in accordance with a distinction which the colonial authority had drawn since the middle of the 1890s.[167] The principle of self-support further underlined this distinction within the ecclesiastical field. The mission, not surprisingly in view of the rapid growth of the work and the increase in the number of teachers, sought concessions from the Buganda authorities for its African personnel. The main problem was the integration of this new type of work, with its full-time church employees, into the traditional system, and at the same time the securing of reasonable working conditions and direct support on a communal basis.

The whole issue of concessions from the African political system must be seen in the context of the prevailing economic conditions which have been described above, with special reference to the fact that the combination of land and labour constituted the major economic asset in the middle of the 1890s. Chiefs to a great extent provided the teachers with shambas to live on and to provide food, and as church funds were scarce the teachers came very much to depend on these shambas. At that time every possessor of land was expected to pay tribute, not only to the chief in question, but also to the Kabaka. Such tribute consisted mainly of labour services such as the building of houses or roadmaking. One first objective was then to get the clergy, catechists and teachers exempted from public duties to the Kabaka, which were taking teachers away from their stations for long periods and thus interrupting the work. In 1894 the Kabaka promised to exempt them by recognizing shambas granted to teachers as 'church lands' – a concession that amounted to alienation of these shambas from the official system of taxation and tributes.[168] But the Kabaka's promise seems to have remained largely unfulfilled. In many cases teachers were still forced to render labour services to him, and if they could not be found their wives and children were pressed into service instead, in accordance with the custom of the country. This practice was eventually forbidden when Archdeacon Walker got the Sub-Commissioner for Buganda to force the Kabaka to pass a law against the custom of attributing responsibility by association, which had placed undue burdens on people not directly involved.[169] In view of complications like these it was even more necessary to have all teachers exempted from duties and services to the Kabaka, so that they could be free to teach 'without neglecting any civil duty'.[170]

At first the system of exemptions seems to have functioned irregularly. Due to the growth of the work, however, it became essential to lay down more specific guidelines. The mission's only interest was that its teachers should be free to devote all their time to church work. They were apparently unaware of the implications from the African point of view; in particular the concessions they expected meant direct losses and expenses for the African polity.[171] We find confirmation of this in the fact that the chiefs became more hesitant in granting shambas, because granting them involved the alienation of large numbers of workers 'for of course the people on the gardens go with the garden'.[172] It was not sufficient for the missions to have their teachers alone exempted from public duties; the ordinary people who cultivated the shambas must also be exempted, otherwise the church workers would have to take over, and thus have little time for their real work.

Two specific measures were suggested to overcome the hesitation of the chiefs, and to put the matter on a more regular footing. The first one was that the exemptions granted to the shamba cultivators should only apply to the state tributes, whereas they should continue to render local services to the chiefs like anyone else.[173] This was an acknowledgement of the chiefs' continued role as the backbone of the Protestant work. As a second measure the Protestant leaders suggested an upper limit for the scope of the exemptions from service to the Kabaka, whereby the number of people exempted under each teacher should not exceed ten.[174] This had the practical effect that the church could not be accused of taking too many people away from public work, but the mission was also concerned with the moral aspect: by restricting the number of people exempted under each teacher they avoided the danger of people taking refuge in church shambas to escape public duties, which would have had adverse effects on the morality and quality of the workers.[175] The third measure required official approval of the concessions in each case. Only teachers accredited by the Church Council could be granted a shamba, and the arrangement must be registered with the Katikiro.[176] It is difficult to establish whether these suggestions met with the approval of the central authorities in Buganda.[177] The silence of the sources may be due to the fact that the issue of exemptions for church workers was soon to be subsumed under the more general problem of the alienation of land.

Two points of significance for the delineation of the church–state problem should be made. In the first place the mission, with the support of the Church Council,[178] aimed to provide the emergent African church with sufficient status to ensure its support as an official institution from the African polity in the form of land and special privileges for its African personnel, rather than have it depend on gifts from the chiefs on a personal, unofficial basis. Secondly, the fulfilment of this aim proved difficult, in that serious problems were encountered in finding a niche for the church as an institution integrated into the fabric of the Ganda system. Whereas Christianity as such, in the dual form of Protestantism and Catholicism, had been integrated into the political structure, it seemed difficult to integrate its institutional expression in the same way into the prevailing economic system, at least as long as land and labour were the main economic assets and were so closely linked with the chiefly institution. It seemed unavoidable that the granting of privileges to the church would involve some degree of alienation of the land and the people from the traditional system.

These points will be developed in an examination of the role of the two major economic assets, labour and land, and their importance for church work, with particular reference to the economic changes gathering force in the latter part of the 1890s.

The importance of labour services for the mission/church

The definition of labour in the African setting still valid about the middle of the 1890s emerges clearly from the previous section. It was primarily conceived of as the tribute which people rendered to their chief for the use of land under his jurisdiction. This traditional arrangement was so firmly entrenched in the early years that it was impossible for the mission to recruit paid labourers. Labour for wages was at that time foreign to the Ganda mentality. The only way for the mission to find labourers for Christian work was for chiefs to grant the mission some of their tributary rights, or, on a smaller scale, for the mission itself to own land. This would be land registered with the colonial administration, and thus completely alienated from the African system of authority.[179]

From the point of view of European morality, problems arose at this point, as such a labour system was liable to interpretation as forced labour, with all the overtones of slavery that implied. Archdeacon Walker was aware of this risk at an early stage,[180] and not much later the mission was actually officially accused of using forced labour. The accuser was Colonel Colvile, who to the surprise of Walker raised the issue with the Foreign Office after his return to London, saying that the mission's use of forced labour was 'violating the principle of Christianity and civilization', and that it came close to ill-treatment of the Africans.[181] The mission was very sensitive to such an accusation. It detracted from its credibility by threatening to undermine its claim to represent true Christian principles in the colonial situation and its ability to act as the defender of the African population in cases of injustice from the side of the colonial authorities. Furthermore, any risk of the curtailment of the chiefs' supply of labour for church work meant endangering the whole missionary enterprise. Walker was thus very anxious to have the matter clarified at the official level. He took it up with the newly arrived Commissioner Berkeley, and got his seal of approval for the continuation of the practice as before, on the grounds that it was justified by the prevailing circumstances. Berkeley committed himself in somewhat vague terms to the mission's point of view, saying that they had done nothing wrong.[182] The practice therefore continued unchanged over the following years.[183]

This episode illustrates the general problem that concessions granted within the African system could be interpreted as violating Christian, European principles. The missionaries might thus be caught between two incompatible systems of values when they tried to carry out their principal task of founding a Christian church in an African society. This dilemma remained throughout the years, although it was seldom made much of in practice because of the mission's dependence on the chiefs' supply of labour. Only the changes in the economic life of the country after 1897 made it possible to employ paid labour on any substantial scale.[184] This afforded the mission considerable relief: 'The FC [Finance Committee] feel that it is not well to accept unpaid labour, even though the chief himself may be ready to supply it.'[185] The Archdeacon could now report to the CMS headquarters that the new mission hospital in the capital would be built by 'the heathens who are the servants of Christian chiefs', but that it would most likely be the last time that forced labour would be used in church work.[186]

Economic developments and the corresponding reduction of the economic role of the chiefs were thus instrumental in getting the mission 'off the hook'. At the same time another ethical problem was solved: hitherto large numbers of non-Christians had been obliged to work for Christian purposes, and had thus not enjoyed the same liberties as Christians (see p.68ff). [187] In the wider perspective the abandonment of forced labour had far-reaching consequences for the Protestant effort and for the socio-economic position of the church in society. It increased dependence on collections and cash donations, and intensified the importance of exemptions, in this case the right to enjoy the services of the labour force living on church shambas with some degree of exclusivity. This again led to the question whether landholding rights should be extended to cover the right to enjoy all the tributary obligations levied on the people living on the land. This would have the effect of alienating land and labour from the chiefs in the same way as the shambas held exclusively by the CMS were alienated from the Buganda system. The whole concept of landholding thus became an issue in need of clarification in the wake of the economic changes in society. The important question for the present purposes is how far the colonial government would leave this issue to be settled by the mission/church and the African leaders alone, or whether it would feel the need to step in and exercise some control over the concessions to be granted to the church.

The importance of land grants for the mission/church

Before discussing land rights it will be necessary to define the concept of landholding which prevailed in Buganda. It did not include the concept of ownership in the European sense, whereby land is the object of purchase and sale. Land tenure meant usufructuary rights to estates which were mostly attached to particular offices, such as chieftainships. It was, as we have already seen in connection with church land, a question of rights over people in a given area – aptly expressed in the Ganda saying: 'He does not rule land, he rules people.'[188] Ultimately the ownership – or right of disposal – was vested in the centre of power, the Kabaka, who appointed the chiefs at all levels. This explains the fact that emerged during the examination of the politico-economic status of the chiefs – that in Buganda there was 'a close association between political power and the exercise of controlling rights over land'.[189]

For each of the two European agencies, the mission and the colonial government, it became a matter of great importance to have a share in these controlling rights over land. Furthermore, in view of the vital economic interests involved, the land issue became an area within which negotiations between mission and government became frequent.

Introduction of the issue of church land

It had always been the major aim of the CMS to found a self-supporting church integrated with Buganda society. It transpired that this aim could only be realized in practice by making use of the chiefs' position, especially their power to grant sites for churches and shambas for African personnel on a steadily increasing scale corresponding to the rate of growth of the work. During this process the mission seems to have been guided by two strategic principles. The first one has already been seen in function. It was stated explicitly for the colonial authority by Archdeacon Walker when he summed up the requirements of the church in 1899 by underlining 'how absolutely necessary it is for the carrying on of the work of the church that it should own sites for churches and school houses and gardens to supply the food for the teachers'.[190] So far we have seen that these grants were made to the church by African leaders without much involvement of the colonial government. Difficulties arose, however, when land rights had to be defined more specifically against the background of the changing position of the chiefs. The mission's objective was to gain the usufruct of the land for the church wherever possible; but this had the effect of alienating church land from the Buganda system.

The second strategic principle of the mission was therefore to attempt to compensate for the problem of alienation. It was frequently asserted that land granted to the church was not in European hands, but came under the authority of the Africans.[191] Except for a few CMS sites, all land ownership was vested in the Church Council. This presents a clear-cut example of the distinction between the mission as something temporary, and the church as the lasting and independent body to emerge from the missionary enterprise.[192] Acting on this distinction, the mission during the 1890s increasingly used the term 'the Native Church of Uganda' (Buganda), thus indicating their intention of making it the established national church in Buganda, as well as emphasizing its African character in finance and government.[193]

That land rights more and more assumed the key role in the realization of the mission's strategy can be seen from the missionaries' own discussions on the subject. First there was the question of whether the CMS should acquire property at all. One missionary point of view was that the CMS ought to do so in order to safeguard its own buildings in the event of the church's breaking away from the CMS. Others argued that all land should be held in the name of the Church Council. It was claimed that this would provide a strong argument against those who 'say we want to denationalize the church and to eat the country, as long as we can show that all the land belongs to the native church and none of it to that mysterious body called the C.M.S'.[194] This opinion assumed extra significance in the eyes of the missionaries during the period of anti-European feeling aroused at the time of Mwanga's flight from the country. In that atmosphere no land would be granted to the CMS, but African ownership constituted a safeguard for other church property, and answered the accusations of those who accused the Europeans of 'eating the country'.[195] In the long term the Church Council formula served to neutralize the effects of the Africans' change of attitude towards Europeans.

When the question of the drawing up of a church constitution in Buganda was raised as a major issue in 1898 one of the points on which there was strong disagreement was the position of the missionaries themselves: should they be integrated into the church on an equal footing with the Africans, as Bishop Tucker thought? Or should they remain outside the church, preparing to withdraw from the scene? This was the view taken by Archdeacon Walker and the majority of his colleagues.[196] Once again it was the landholding issue and its importance for the continued work of the church that was decisive for most of the missionaries. If the missionaries were included in the church, the distinction between mission and church would be lost. In their capacity as members of the church they figured as owners of church land. Hence it could no longer be claimed that the land was 'a purely native possession'.[197] Since the colonial government was also just at that time expressing concern about the alienation of land acquired for religious purposes, it was of crucial importance that the distinction between mission and church should not be blurred by any constitutional measures.

The acquisition of land rights for the church thus proved indispensable for the

work, and constituted a factor of great significance for the mission's policy-
making. It should be clear from the above that the holding of land almost
inevitably involved its alienation in one way or another, whether it was officially
held from the colonial or from the African authorities. The mission's relationship
was therefore problematical with both these agencies as far as land was concerned.
For the missionaries the distinction between mission and church was a magic
formula which solved the problem of alienation, since they considered that only
land actually owned or held officially by Europeans could properly be considered
alienated, and that land held by the African church could not be so considered.
The relevance in the context of this distinction was determined solely by the
validity of this interpretation of alienation. If, however, the concept of alienation
were to be defined differently, on the basis of the real consequences for the
African polity of the granting of land for religious purposes and the accompanying
exemptions from tributary obligations, then the distinction between mission and
church would not carry the same weight with the colonial and African authorities
as the missionaries were inclined to think. This possibility of a different interpretation of alienation will have to be borne in mind as we examine the problem
from the point of view of the colonial authorities. As we shall see, the colonial
government's and the mission's versions of the concept proved almost diametri-
cally opposite.

Until 1899, in the first period after the establishment of an official colonial
administration, the colonial government appears to have had a relatively *laissez-
faire* attitude to the practice of granting land for the benefit of religious work.
During 1894 Colvile issued an order that the holding of any given piece of land
would only be legal after its registration with the colonial administration. Later,
in connection with his attempt to settle the land problems in more general terms,
Commissioner Berkeley carried out a registration of all lands which had been
transferred to religious work, and gave his approval to shambas and other sites
already used for this purpose.[198] However, the formal procedure for obtaining
approval was changed. When he was asked specifically about 'the property held
by the Native Church of Uganda', Berkeley ruled that such lands should not be
registered at the British Consular Court, but with the Buganda authorities.
Mission land on the other hand should still be registered with the colonial
authorities, as it was supposed to be alienated.[199]

In the eyes of the missionary leaders their fundamental distinction between
mission and church had now acquired an official seal of approval and a legal
status. It is not surprising that they were stimulated by this to lay even greater
weight on the distinction, as it had obviously proved workable at the political
level. But the overall colonial policy on land was still very much in the melting-
pot, as we can see from the many land-policy changes which took place between
1897 and 1899,[200] and the optimism of the missionaries might have been more
restrained, given the instability in this area. In particular the *laissez-faire* attitude
created certain gaps in the clarification of land policy. The commissioners
confined themselves to the question of registration, and did not go into the
problem of whether there should be an upper limit on the amount of land which
could be granted by the African authorities, and whether any strings should be
attached as regards the use of the land. The comparative laxity of the authorities
on these questions explains why the mission was taken by surprise when the
colonial government suddenly in 1899 began to take more interest in the question
of land transfers for religious purposes, demonstrating a singular lack of under-

standing of the basic principle on which the mission had so far based its policy.

The reassessment of religious land grants, 1899

The year 1899 brought a tightening of the overall government policy on land. This primarily took the form of closer surveillance of all land transactions, but involved also the question of whether the colonial administration should participate in the ownership of uncultivated land only, or of all land, irrespective of cultivation or occupation.[201] In the case of the mission, this new departure in government policy directed that, first, any land transaction involving alienation must be submitted to the colonial government before being effected. This meant that the Ganda authorities could no longer handle such matters as the granting of lands to the mission on their own. Secondly, it was found necessary to carry out a survey of the extent of alienation, a measure which indicated the authorities' intention of exercising greater control over methods of acquiring resources for Christian work, and of fixing an upper limit for the total number of land grants.[202]

The first measure came into force in April/May 1899, when the Sub-Commissioner for Uganda, George Wilson, prepared and finally issued a circular introducing new measures of government control in all matters pertaining to the alienation of land. The mission was not opposed to such control in itself, as the church work had progressed sufficiently to justify more independence of the chiefs and their changing attitudes to Christianity. A more important concern for the mission was the attainment of more permanence and a stable legal footing. Archdeacon Walker even suggested measures of his own for inclusion in the new law which, while satisfying the demands for closer government control, still upheld the right of the Buganda government to approve of land grants when the receiver was the African church.[203] A fundamental disagreement between government and mission arose, however, on this last issue. George Wilson's desire for closer surveillance sprang from his conviction that the transfer of land to the church meant alienation, in the sense that it reduced the possibilities of future development for the land concerned. The shambas and other properties possessed by the church could not be sold to traders or settlers, and this might damage the future possibilities of making the Protectorate profitable. Alienation was thus for the colonial administration defined in terms of the economic development of the country, and on the basis of this definition the missionaries' distinction between mission and church could have little relevance.

Archdeacon Walker on the other hand attached little importance to these economic and developmental perspectives, which lay many years ahead. Instead he repeated the usual missionary argument that as church land was not European-owned but solely under African control there could be no question of alienation. The state (that is, the Buganda polity) had in Walker's view kept for itself all the control necessary, and had the right to expropriate church land for national purposes against due compensation if the need arose at any future date.[204] Thus, during this first phase in the revision of land policy, the granting of land for church work was no longer simply a matter between the African authorities and the mission, with the tacit approval of the colonial administration. The latter had begun to take a closer interest in the implications of the establishment of a church in the Buganda society. Questions had now been raised as to how strong the basic principle on which the mission worked, the distinction between mission and church with the latter as the receiver of land, proved to be in reality when brought to the test by the colonial administration, which was working with a different concept of alienation.

The second phase was marked by the colonial government's plans to participate in the ownership of all land. Such a move would have come close to nationalization, even if the formula used was 'shared ownership' between the two authorities involved, African and European.[205] It seems to have been on the basis of these plans that the Acting Commissioner, Colonel Ternan, was acting when he ruled in September 1899 that, while the mission could hold a few properties registered as European, 'no land in Uganda [Buganda] could be called church property', as 'he did not suppose that it would ever be agreed to that there should be an endowment of a native church with state lands'.[206] Consequently the Kabaka and chiefs could not give land away on their own, not even to 'a body of natives', as this meant disposal over rights which the British government possessed.[207] The new departure in colonial land policy apparently meant that all grants of land to the church made in the past were now invalid, and the consequences could well be that the mission's policy over many years as regards the founding of a church would be laid in ruins.[208]

Before going on to the further implications of this ruling, it will be necessary to mention the actual incident which gave rise to it, and which admirably illustrates a number of aspects of the issues of land rights, evictions and religious liberty. In a church shamba which the church had allocated for the support of an ordained African, it happened that one of the inhabitants refused to work for the new clergyman. Originally this worker had moved in as a 'heathen', but had then turned Catholic, and on the grounds of difference in creed claimed the right not to work, referring to the ruling introduced by Colvile that no one was obliged to work for any faith other than his own. As the man also encouraged other 'heathens' to become Catholics and thus be exempted from working for the Protestant church, the clergyman holding the shamba felt that his means of subsistence was being eroded, and evicted the Catholic convert from the shamba. When the man appealed to the colonial administration it ruled that he should be reinstated. When the matter was brought up at the highest level by the mission, the Commissioner confirmed the first decision on the grounds that the church as such could not hold any property, and therefore had no right to evict the man.[209]

This decision clearly reflects the overall policy on land pursued at the time by the Acting Commissioner. It also illustrates the real reason for the negative attitude to the church's holding land. The question at issue was the church's claim to the right of suspension of a law otherwise upheld in society. That this was a question of crucial importance for the colonial administration is borne out by the general remarks which Ternan made while the eviction case was on his table. In connection with the White Fathers' application for a piece of land in Bunyoro, Ternan said:

In granting bases of lands to the Missions it is always necessary to remember that it is their habit to collect their converts about them in their estate as tenants – and that a very undesirable temporal authority is thus required and maintained over a selection of the community who it has been found gradually look upon themselves as more or less outside the jurisdiction of this administration.[210]

Without distinguishing between mission and church Ternan suggested that land leased to the missions should be limited to 'their legitimate requirements' and that they should pay the economic rent.[211] Two motives can be seen as decisive for the colonial administration's policy towards the missions. The first one was the need for a limitation of both the amount of land being granted for religious purposes and the extent to which landholdings were a major economic asset for the church. The second had to do with the rights that accompanied the possession of land. Ternan was obviously concerned with the alienation of people and lands from the jurisdiction of the laws of the state. In this respect – bearing in mind that Ternan was working for state ownership as the ultimate goal – it made no difference whether the land was held by a European or an African body. This concept of alienation was obviously incompatible with that of the missionaries.

The mission was greatly alarmed by this attitude from the colonial administration, and in order to be on the safe side it hastened to have seven of the Protestant properties registered as belonging to the CMS.[212] On behalf of the mission and the church Archdeacon Walker raised the matter with the Acting Commissioner. He laid great weight on the indispensability of the lands so far given by 'the native government' for the support of some 20 clergy and 200 teachers.[213] He argued that the church in fact already had title deeds to the land, which only had to be confirmed; and that all the land was vested in the Church Council and hence in African hands. He suggested that the land endowments should only be valid for as long as they were used for the original purpose.

The Acting Commissioner backed down somewhat from his first position and forwarded Walker's letter to the Foreign Office for decision, as it was a matter of principle whether 'the endowment of the Protestant Church of Uganda with state lands' should be allowed. Ternan recommended in fact that the Foreign Office should endorse the title deeds.[214] In his dispatch he accepted the distinction between the properties occupied by the three missions, which he had investigated and to which he had given statutory approval, and the lands which were wanted by the native churches. In the latter case he pointed out that costs should not only be calculated in terms of acres, but also in terms of the exemptions from tax and feudal labour which could be invoked by the people living on the land.[215]

After being informed of this latest change of attitude on the part of the government, Archdeacon Walker had good reason to be jubilant. He was convinced that his argument that European missionaries stood outside the church and 'that the whole thing is native to the country and not a foreign system introduced here' had carried great weight. He drew comparisons with the Catholic missions, who were not applying the same strict distinction between mission and church, and concluded that the Protestants were in a stronger position.[216] The difference between Walker and Bishop Tucker is again clear here. The latter did not agree with Walker's arguments. He did not attach much importance to whether the missionaries were inside or outside the Church of Buganda. For him the crucial issue was whether there was in fact a properly constituted body in which the ownership of land could be legally vested. As the church as yet had no constitution because of disagreements on the place of the missionaries he believed that the Protestants were in a weak position.[217]

As this takes us right to the nucleus of the relationship between church and state which was emerging parallel with the already more stable colonial system, it will be appropriate first to examine the considerations which influenced the colonial authorities before going on to the outcome of the whole issue of land grants for religious purposes. Ternan's presentation of the issues involved can be summarized thus: first he made it clear to the Foreign Office that the endowment of the Protestant church with a number of shambas would be followed by similar claims from the Catholics and Muslims.[218] It is reasonable to conclude from this statement, even if it is an argument *ex silentio*, that the different patterns followed by Protestant and Catholic missionary work were not assigned any importance by Ternan in reviewing the question of land grants. Bishop Tucker had been nearer to the truth in this respect than Archdeacon Walker. Walker's concept of alienation, derived from the distinction between mission and church, was not referred to, for Ternan was working with a concept whereby any land belonging to agencies other than the state was alienated. Secondly, Ternan's real concern was for the interests of the administration, as is evident from his drive for general state ownership. For the granting of state-owned land to be justifiable it was necessary that the endowment of the Protestant and other churches with properties and the accompanying tributes must be explained and defended in terms of their fulfilling particular official needs. Ternan found a solution in the following remarks of Archdeacon Walker:

I presume that there can be no question as to the value of the work of the native church as an educational and civilizing agency in the country. And on this footing, if on no other, it deserves the support and encouragement that can properly be given to it.[219]

While Walker's reference to educational work was only meant as a secondary, additional argument, it was the only point that figured in Ternan's account to the Foreign Office. He was eagerly clutching at this straw when he stated that both churches 'practically carry on the work of elementary education in addition to their usual functions . . . ' He considered it, therefore, reasonable 'in the interests of progress and civilization' that state aid in some form be provided. As the prevailing economic system in Buganda militated against a money grant, it was natural to turn to the most important economic asset, land, and its accompanying exemptions of the inhabitants from taxes and feudal labour.[220]

It is clear that in Ternan's handling of the issue grants of land were being considered as equivalent to state support, even if the granting authority was the Kabaka and the chiefs. They should therefore take place under the direction and surveillance of the colonial administration, and could no longer be left to the Ganda authorities alone. Secondly, state support to religious bodies was regarded as requiring special justification and explanation. It was difficult to defend it in the case of general missionary work, but activity within the educational field was identifiable and specific, and fell within the range of activities which the administration could reasonably be expected to support, in its own interest and the interests of society. There must necessarily be a ceiling for this kind of support, and educational activity was measurable, thus providing a basis for an estimate of the extent of state support necessary.

Finally, a distinction was being made between mission and church, but was being drawn differently from the one urged by the CMS. A limited number of properties were officially recognized as belonging to the three missions working in the Protectorate. These were clearly demarcated and were in a different category from the land discussed above. They could best be described as the basic, necessary foothold which the missions needed to exist and work in the Protectorate, and which the administration felt under an obligation to provide. Direct aid to church work was quite a different matter, and this was the real issue in 1899. Ternan used in this connection the term 'native churches' about the bodies involved, and noted that they were distinct from the missionary organizations. It is however not entirely clear what significance he attached to this distinction; but it can be taken for granted that it bore no resemblance to Walker's concept of alienation. That the position of the missionaries outside the church meant that the church land was in African hands was not a consideration which figured in Ternan's view of the matter. This is borne out primarily by the fact that he treated Protestants and Catholics alike in spite of their different ways of organizing the work, even in the educational field. It may then be concluded that the CMS mission was labouring under an illusion when it consistently in its dealings with the colonial administration put its faith in its own distinction between mission and church, and argued on that basis that there was no question of alienation of African rights and property. Any further clarification of the matter was however pushed into the background by other events.

The Johnston settlement, 1900

The dispute on land grants to the mission and the church was finally decided by the newly appointed Special Commissioner for Uganda, Sir Harry Johnston, not by the Acting Commissioner's communication with the Foreign Office. Once again the real decisions were being made by the men on the spot, however much they were newcomers. Johnston was appointed by the British government in the middle of 1899 to reorganize the administration of the Protectorate, with special emphasis on the question of possible reductions of the expenses incurred for British taxpayers; the Protectorate was to be set on the road to paying its own way.[221] Johnston set off with few instructions but, basing his approach on his experiences from Central Africa, he had even before arriving in Uganda decided to make use of the introduction of a hut tax and strict surveillance of land transactions in order to ensure the most profitable use of land for the benefit of the colonial administration.

It is therefore not surprising that Johnston, when on the way to Uganda he received Ternan's dispatch to the Foreign Office with Walker's letter enclosed, asked the home authorities to refrain from making any decisions until he had arrived in Uganda. In his comments to Ternan's dispatch he formulated his own ideas on future land policy as regards the mission and the church.[222] It is remarkable how far Johnston adhered to the guidelines already laid down by Ternan. Against the background of the overall aim of self-support he applied from the outset the same two basic principles of state ownership and state control of the disposal of land. The principle of state ownership was to be applied by making all uncultivated areas Crown land. This would at the same time confirm that the cultivated land belonged to the Africans, and would mean the introduction into Uganda of a hitherto unknown concept of ownership.[223] As regards church lands, Johnston pointed out that the granting of Crown land for religious purposes would mean a reduction in the benefits the state would receive from the land and would in fact amount to state support; and that the chiefs would be free to have schools, churches etc. on their private land, and could support whichever denomination they wanted to out of their own personal means.

The second basic principle behind Johnston's thinking, that of state control over the disposal of lands, concerned the more legal aspects of land acquisition. The right to dispose of land was to be vested in the colonial administration. Accordingly, the Kabaka and the chiefs could not grant land to 'any native church' without the approval of the administration. Johnston preferred to exercise the right of disposal by granting sites for schools, churches and houses for teachers, etc., on lease – which was reminiscent of Ternan's plan of charging an economic rent. It follows that Johnston, just like his predecessor, was concerned with the problem of alienation, and it was largely his interpretation of the concept that guided him in finding a solution to the problem of church land. As he saw it, as land was a major economic asset, the possession of land by a native church meant a loss for the state, not least because of the accompanying exemptions. For the purposes of this economic definition of alienation the state was taken to include both the colonial and the African authorities. While this is similar to Ternan's interpretation, Johnston developed a second aspect which we have not met before, and which also ran counter to Archdeacon Walker's employment of the concept:

It would be a fatal step in the future interest of this African dominion that any one section of it or any class of people should occupy a privileged position releasing them from the ordinary obligations of citizens.[224]

Besides the economic aspects, which were ever-present in Johnston's mind, there is a new awareness of the concept of alienation defined in relation to the African community. To emphasize, as Walker did, that the church was still in African hands was not enough. The decisive factor was that the granting of land to the church meant the alienation of a number of people, not just clergymen and teachers, from the obligations of citizens in an African society. As long as the usufruct of land carried with it rights to the labour tributes of the inhabitants the argument that the land was in African hands was of little value. Johnston seems to have grasped the fundamental difference between these two concepts of aliena-tion, at least as far as the economic and administrative aspects were concerned: the second type of alienation meant that church land was drawn out of the organic functioning of Buganda society. From the latter point of view the vesting of land ownership in the African Church Council with its accompanying usufructuary rights presented a serious case of alienation.

It comes therefore as no surprise that Johnston was willing enough to give land to the missionary societies as such: 'This can be done without any appreciable alienation of the bulk of the soil.'[225] He applied, just as Ternan did, a distinction between land granted for missionary work and land granted as an endowment of the native church. In the former case the land represented 'a reasonable endow-ment of missionary societies' and was registered as European-owned, which meant no loss of revenue to the state as people on the land were not exempted from their obligations as citizens. In the case of an endowment of the church Johnston considered the land rather to be privately owned and therefore not at the disposal of the state and without benefit to it, as people on such land would not be obliged to pay taxes and render other services. Hence, support for the native church was not a matter for the state, but rather for the chiefs, as they could allot sites on their own land or grant support by other means.

It was the mission–land formula that prevailed when a new agreement was concluded between Buganda and the Special Commissioner in March 1900. This time there seems to have been virtually no discussion between Johnston and the CMS representatives on the land issue, perhaps because its importance was overshadowed by the more far-reaching issues concerning the whole future political system in Buganda, with particular emphasis on the position of the chiefs. And, what was more important from the CMS point of view, Johnston, unlike Ternan, made it clear from the outset that there was no intention of depriving the Christian effort of the lands already granted. This meant that the missionaries need have no fears of catastrophe ahead.[226] So, in the absence of source material on the discussions which may have taken place on this issue, we can provide little background for the following wording in the Uganda Agreement of March 1900: 'There will be allotted to the three missionary societies in existence in Uganda as private property, and in trust for the native churches, as much as 92 square miles.'[227] Viewing this clause in the light of what we already know about Johnston's point of view, it is clear that he left out all reference to the distinction between mission and church. He dealt with all three missions on the same footing, regardless of their different organizational structures. He was clearly applying the mission formula, as the 92 square miles were set aside for the missionary societies, and even called 'private property'. The last words in the clause are the only reflection of Archdeacon Walker's arguments to be found in the final settlement. They may be seen as a consolation for the CMS. Johnston himself indicated this when he specifically mentioned in his report to the Foreign Office that the CMS held the land 'on its own behalf or on behalf of the Native Church which it represents' – a wording remarkably similar to Walker's when he said that the CMS held the land 'for the advantage of the native Protestant Church . . .'[228] The real purpose behind the mission's holding of land, and their future use of it, were not Johnston's concern at that juncture, but an internal question for the mission. Using the mission–land formula he avoided any alienation from the Buganda political organism, as the inhabitants of mission lands would have to adhere to the normal obligations of citizens.[229] He made it clear that the lawful receiver of the land was the CMS, and applied thereby a concept of ownership which meant that the most important feature was the utilization of the land itself, not the tributes due from its inhabitants. This different concept of ownership, used when Europeans were involved, was not explicitly formulated by Johnston; it is necessary to be aware of it to understand his use of the concept of alienation. In this respect, a crucial difference existed between Johnston and Ternan, in that the former introduced a concept of individual landownership based on the intrinsic value of the land.

Johnston's solution of the problem of land concessions to the Christians can, as just indicated, best be seen in perspective when it is compared with the efforts of his predecessor, Ternan. First, when the granting of land is seen as a form of state support, the question of a ceiling for such support inevitably crops up. Johnston solved this problem once and for all by stipulating the number of square miles available to the missions in the treaty itself. All three missions were presumably better off than they had been before the arrangement.[230] Secondly, by applying the mission–land formula, Johnston avoided giving land to any church as such, thus avoiding also having to recognize the Native Anglican Church as an official, legal body. This leads us to the third point: by granting lands to the missions and not to the native churches he was, unlike Ternan, under no obligation to give specific reasons for state support to church work. This explains the fact that Johnston did not mention the educational work of the church, which had figured prominently in Ternan's exposition. For Johnston it was enough to refer in broad terms to the established pattern of the colonial system in order to secure reasonable working conditions for the Christian missionary work. This followed the pattern laid down in the Berlin Treaty. Fourthly, and probably most fundamentally, Johnston did not include the inhabitants and their labour tributes in his concept of ownership.

As regards the chiefs' landholdings neither Johnston nor the CMS fully understood the far-reaching consequences of the introduction of the concept of freehold land. For both, the important priority was to confirm the chiefs in their present holdings and afford them security from the arbitrary interference of the Kabaka which had characterized the old order. This was what Bishop Tucker had been referring to when he spoke of the abolition of the feudal system; another missionary labelled the introduction of the new system as a bloodless revolution.[231] The parties to the agreement considered the new relationship between the Kabaka and the chiefs the most important feature in it, not the introduction of a new concept of ownership. From the chiefs' point of view, it was their jurisdiction over the people living on the land which was the major issue. If they lost this authority they felt that their position would be put in jeopardy, and that they themselves would be reduced to the status of peasants, mere occupants of a piece of land. Johnston failed to appreciate the close relationship between chiefly authority and land. For him confirmation of the chiefs' land ownership and of their jurisdiction over the people living on the land were two different things. In the end he confirmed both in order to save his agreement, but neither he nor the missionaries seem to have understood that a fundamental contradiction was involved, in the sense that the introduction of private ownership and freehold land severed the old connection between office-holding and land rights.

It seems reasonable to conclude that Johnston was basing his approach to the problem of mission and church land on his short-term experiences from the settlement of the chiefs' landholdings. He conceived, probably vaguely, of the church as an African institution, and calculated with the risk that it as such would claim rights from its landholdings similar to those of the chiefs. This problem, he presumably concluded, would not arise in the case of European ownership. Two points must have been in the forefront of his mind. First, if the church obtained the same rights as the chiefs to receive tributes and impose sanctions on the people living on the land, then there would be a group of people who fell outside the chiefs' jurisdiction (as there already was on the land granted to the Kabaka personally).[232] The church would as an institution be placed in a privileged position, and the effect would be the serious alienation which Johnston was not prepared to accept. Secondly, he wanted to avoid the exemptions which under Ternan had been tolerated in the case of church lands. These ran counter to Johnston's basic aims, as they were a drain on the revenues of the state. In view of these points, it must have seemed safer to invest the ownership of the land in the mission. European ownership would not create problems in relation to the African system, and would make it easier to refuse any claims to exemptions. The reasons for supporting missionary work could be specified and listed without much difficulty, while it was more difficult in the case of a church.

The considerations which thus influenced Johnston's approach to the land issue cannot be found explicitly formulated in the sources, but have been deduced from the tenor of the overall settlement of the land on the chiefs. But these suggestions and conclusions are further confirmed by events which took place some months later. When the titles to the land granted to the CMS were to be issued Bishop Tucker returned to the question and urged once again the claim that the land should be invested in the Mengo Church Council and not in the CMS. He asserted that it had been the firm policy of the CMS in Uganda not to acquire land, with few exceptions. In support of his case he put forward two arguments, neither of which was new. In the first place, he claimed, it would detract from the image of the mission if it appeared to be 'land-grabbing'. For this reason, all the land given for church purposes had been regarded as 'native Church property' controlled by the Mengo Church Council. Secondly, Tucker repeated the argument that the CMS had so far avoided alienation, as the land was the property of an African body. The only European member of the Church Council was the Bishop himself, and 'the idea is that in course of time there may be a native Bishop, in which case the European element – small as it is – would disappear entirely'. On these grounds, Tucker additionally took the opportunity to point out that, as Johnston was dealing with 'a native body', there ought to be a reduction in the survey fee for the church sites, or even a complete exemption from it.[233]

Tucker was working on the assumption that an African church was entitled, if not legally then at least morally, to special, favourable treatment from the administration, in that it was African and not foreign. He was clearly unaware of the intentions behind Johnston's phrasing of the clause on mission land in the Uganda Agreement. Both Johnston and the Bishop seem to have missed one another's main points. This is further confirmed by a second aspect of Tucker's arguments. What he was doing was in fact restating Archdeacon Walker's concept of alienation, even to the extent that he contradicted his earlier opinion by claiming that Europeans stood entirely outside the organization of the church. This change of tune can best be explained by Tucker's unwillingness to leave any argument untried.[234] In addition he rushed through a plan to put the Church Council on a proper constitutional footing. It was openly admitted that this step was taken so that the church could figure as a legal holder of land.[235] But behind all these measures lay Tucker's concept of alienation, so fundamentally different from that of Johnston, and the local CMS was unaware of the fact that this type of alienation was a matter of little concern for the state and African society in general. It was regarded as an internal question for the mission, relevant only for their own peculiar methods of organizing their work.

Faced with these arguments, Johnston gave the following answer, which supports the suggestions above as to the thinking behind his decision to endow the CMS with the Protestant share of the land:

> The CMS I know do not wish to be thought desirous of acquiring land, but in countries like this it must to a certain extent be endowed for the purpose of carrying on its work at less expense, having grounds for plantations etc. . . . The CMS can make any subsequent arrangement it likes, allotting some of this land to the native Anglican Church of Uganda.[236]

Johnston added that landowners would also be free to let the church make use of their own private land. He was here explicitly approving of the mission–land formula and rejecting the church formula, as he refused to accept the Mengo Church Council as a body capable of holding land. He further made it clear that the value of the land was assessed on the basis of its potential agricultural yield. Moreover, he explicitly disapproved of the privileges which the holding of land by the church would entail, in this particular case the exemption from the payment of survey fees which Tucker had requested.

Tucker did not accept Johnston's recommendations; he continued to press his claim that while a few sites should be registered in the name of the CMS, and thus be CMS-owned property, the bulk of the land must be registered in such a way that it would be beyond all doubt that it was held on behalf of the Native Anglican Church (the NAC). The colonial officials were still perplexed by such a distinction, and could not see how it could be applied in land titles.[237] In the end the formula adopted was that the Bishop himself held the land in both cases, on behalf of the CMS and the Native Anglican Church respectively.[238] It may well have contributed to a smoother solution of this problem that all claims were kept within the 40 square miles allotted to the Protestants out of the 92.

Any assessment of this solution should take into account the wording of the clause from the Uganda Agreement quoted above. As the Protestant land was explicitly divided into two categories, even in the title deeds, the last sentence of the clause came to figure more prominently than might originally have been Johnston's intention. So far Bishop Tucker had been successful in his endeavours, if not entirely in the way he had wanted. On the other hand, it was difficult for the colonial authorities to attach any great significance to the division of the Protestant land. The Bishop was in both cases the legal receiver of the land, and also figured as the coordinator between the two bodies involved. Furthermore, the existing Mengo Church Council had not been given any official recognition.[239] The Bishop was considered to be acting on behalf of a Native Anglican Church which had yet to take shape and win a proper constitutional footing. Even more important from the administration's point of view, the distinction between CMS and NAC land had no implications for the actual ownership of the land. That land was held on behalf of the NAC did not mean that special rights or exemptions were attached to it. In this respect the administration lumped all land allotted to missionary work together in the same category, and could not automatically accept any exemptions from civil obligations.

The real difficulty in interpreting the results of the debate on the ownership of mission lands stems from the fact that both parties were arguing from different premises, and had different aims in mind. They did not even understand one another's points of view. For the CMS two aspects were involved, an internal as well as an external one. The former had to do with the relationship between mission and church, and here the distinction between CMS and NAC land was of cardinal importance. As the major economic asset, land was the basis for the realization of the ideal of self-support, and for the future independence of the NAC. The Johnston settlement meant that some ground had been gained in this respect. From the administration's point of view, the whole matter was outside its concern, and it was this attitude that the mission failed to understand. The mission worked on the basis of a linkage between the internal aspect and the external one of the relationship between church and state. The African character of the NAC, preserved inasmuch as the missionaries stood outside it, ought to place it in a special position *vis-à-vis* the state and entitle it to special privileges. The mission failed to realize that the colonial administration's concept of alienation differed so radically from its own, and could not see why it was much less of a problem for the administration to grant land and concessions to a mission than to give state support to a church. This lack of mutual understanding explains why the Bishop and the CMS over the years to come continued to repeat the same arguments in the hope of securing a special position for the church in society.

Conclusions on the land issue

The distinction between mission and church is thus a fundamental issue in dealing with the relationship between church and state in a colonial setting. It has at the same time been established that the secular and the ecclesiastical authorities attached different implications to the distinction. The whole work of the mission was directed both in theory and practice towards the foundation of a future independent church. This involved the principle of self-support and the gradual appearance of an African clergy which could afterwards take over the leadership. But the realization of such a policy meant that the mission was extremely dependent on the politico-economic climate in society. This inevitably raised the question of the emergent church's relationship to the state, insofar as it should be clarified whether it was to have an established status, officially recognized by the state and a privileged position given material expression in the form of concessions from the state. Closely interrelated with this issue was the question of the position the mission should enjoy in relation to the state during the period where it was laying the foundations of the church. This means that two separate institutions were involved, both of whose relationships to the state had to be defined. This duality corresponds to a two-tiered structure in the political field, as there was some doubt whether support and recognition should be sought from the colonial or the African political system. A kind of quadrangular system emerges, within which the lines of connection can be drawn in various ways for different purposes. The picture was particularly complicated because neither the relationship between the mission and the church, nor that between the colonial administration and the African political system was a static, settled one at this period.

From the point of view of the state, the land issue was instrumental in defining its own relationship to both mission and church. The focus was concentrated on the problem of state support for Christian work, the *raison d'être* for such support and its extent. Closely connected to this was the question of whether the mission or the church should be the receiver, and whether the land should be granted by the African political system; and in the latter case, what would be the position of the church within the state? The quadrangle mentioned above was therefore also relevant for the administration, and the lines of connection within it were in need of definition.

The land issue has shown that the years 1899–1900 marked a change in the relationship between mission, church and state. First, the colonial administration began to exercise closer control over the African polity. Its area of authority was, however, somewhat circumscribed, which meant that its authority to give grants to mission and church was substantially diminished. Secondly, the administration took a closer look at the whole question of the granting of support to Christian work, demanded reasonable justification for such support, and also specified an upper limit for it. Thirdly, the mission, for both internal and external reasons, exhibited increasing concern for the future independence of the church. The missionary authorities tried to obtain some measure of official recognition of the church, and made every effort to present the church in such a way that it qualified for support.

7

Colonial rule established: the Uganda Agreement of 1900 and its aftermath

Introduction: the Uganda Agreement

The conclusion of the Uganda Agreement in 1900 is one of the best researched events in Ugandan history.[1] In spite of its name it covered only Buganda.[2] It represented the major outcome of Sir Harry Johnston's mission to the Ugandan Protectorate. The settlement may be divided into three main areas.

There was first an economic settlement. To increase revenue a hut tax and a gun tax were introduced, and all land was divided into two types. This was an arithmetical division, whereby one half was made Crown land and the other half allocated to the royal family and about one thousand chiefs as freehold tenure. The latter was called *mailo land* because it was parcelled out to the individuals concerned in square *miles*. The actual division of the land did not in the event follow the principles originally intended by Johnston. The chiefs were confirmed in their *de facto* holdings, which meant that they still possessed the best parts of the country. As their share amounted to more than the land actually under cultivation they also selected the best areas of uncultivated land and left the least attractive areas to the colonial government. In the long run the effect was that Crown land did not become the economic asset that Johnston had expected it to be.

Secondly, there was a settlement of Buganda's colonial status. The Uganda Agreement superseded all previous treaties and confirmed British authority over Buganda. The Kingdom was made a province within the Uganda Protectorate, like the neighbouring kingdoms and other areas in the sphere of interest, although Buganda enjoyed a very special position in that no other province obtained an agreement with so many concessions and special rights. The British supremacy was, however, marked in various ways, especially by the fact that the colonial administration, not the Kabaka, was the formal recipient of the hut tax. Furthermore, the chiefs functioned as tax collectors and were paid by the colonial administration, which meant that the approval of the colonial authorities was necessary before any appointment to a saza chieftainship was valid.

Thirdly, the Uganda Agreement served as a constitutional settlement of Buganda. The trend noted earlier of shifting the balance of power away from the Kabakaship and towards the chiefly hierarchy was confirmed. The system came to resemble very closely a constitutional monarchy, a fact which was underlined by two particular circumstances. First, a kind of government was formed with executive powers, consisting of the old office of the Katikiro and two new ones: one for judicial matters (the Omulamuzi) and one for finance (the Omuwanika). In the event the three regents appointed for the period of the Kabaka's minority were either confirmed in these posts (as was the Katikiro) or appointed to them. Secondly a *Lukiko* (council) was established to take care of judicial and legislative matters. The members were mainly drawn from the ranks of the chiefs. The three ministers and 20 saza chiefs (a doubling compared to earlier, due to the adminis-trative reorganization of Buganda) were *ex officio* members.

It is apparent that the Uganda Agreement was of special importance for the position of the chiefs. This point deserves further discussion in view of the great importance of the chiefs for the Protestant effort. The chiefs had now become tax collectors and, in view of their various other official responsibilities, they were part of the colonial bureaucracy and were even paid a salary out of colonial revenues. At the same time they were still carrying out political and administra-tive functions within the Buganda system, and as such stood in a special relationship to the Kabaka and enjoyed traditional tributes. This double set of functions marked the beginning of a dual system for the chiefs. Their two roles were not in principle mutually exclusive, but it remained to be seen how the relationship between them would develop – whether the chiefs could function simultaneously at two levels or whether the two roles would have an eroding effect on each other. The picture is further complicated by the fact that the chiefs really derived their power and authority from three different sources.[3] In the first place there was the traditional system with the Kabaka at the top. Here it can be said that in spite of all the changes the chiefs adhered in principle to the continued existence of the traditional institutions. The reduction of the Kabaka's power, however, was an important factor, and this was inevitably tied up with the growth of the second source of authority, the colonial power. Their dependence on a foreign system gave them a fixed salary and the confirmation of certain rights, but at the same time their powers to inflict certain sanctions and penalties were severely limited. While it was difficult to achieve a balance between these two sources of authority, the third source, the holding of freehold land, certainly contributed to the power of the chiefs, at least as far as the first generation of chiefly landowners was concerned. It enabled them to 'rule over people' by making use of rights and sanctions taken from both worlds, the African and the European. Their possession of mailo land provided them with new economic sanctions they could apply in the exercise of their authority. More specifically, they now had a double hold on the people in their areas as they were entitled to collect rent from them as well as chiefly tributes. Their power thus had a basis in the economic system. The new order was aptly summarized by Bishop Tucker: 'Thus it will be seen that the old theory that all land belongs to the King has now been abolished and an order of landed proprietors has been created.'[4]

These changes were bound to exert considerable influence on the role the chiefs would play in relation to the mission and the church, and it will be important to keep them in mind.

Religious liberty at the individual level

The right to religious liberty was not written into the Uganda Agreement, nor can it be found in the corresponding agreements with the neighbouring kingdoms from the same period.[5] The only reference to religious affiliations appeared in the guidelines for the Kabaka's selection of non-*ex-officio* members of the Lukiko (clause 11): 'No question of religious opinion shall be taken into consideration' with regard to appointments. But the Kabaka must abide by the advice of the Commissioner, 'assuring in this respect a fair proportionate representation of all recognized expressions of religious beliefs prevailing in Uganda'.[6] It remained to be seen how this rule would be interpreted and implemented. The colonial administration had here committed itself to a certain extent to securing political representation of the various religions, but it was a moot question what was meant by 'recognized expressions'.

Looking beyond the formal agreements, no public statement seems to have been made on the subject of religious liberty during this period. Attention was, however, called to this matter when Bishop Hanlon of the recently arrived Mill Hill Mission requested in connection with the distribution of saza chieftainships that one of the posts should be given to one of his adherents. This would give his people some representation in the Lukiko.[7] Johnston turned down the request, but tried to reassure the Bishop by adding: 'Naturally any attempt on the part of a Chief of a County to interfere with the free exercise of a man's religion would be regarded by me as a very serious offence.'[8] Thus Johnston continued to adhere to the principles and rules laid down by his predecessors during the 1890s. Just as they did, he also confined his area of concern to that of the safeguard of individuals, in this case the rights of the Bakopi to belong to any religion independently of their chiefs' affiliations.[9] There was thus nothing new in this ruling, and this may be one reason for the absence of any public statements on the issue. Two further reasons for the official silence may be surmised, given the situation about 1900 and the developments in the 1890s leading up to it. In the first instance, the Uganda Protectorate had now become an established part of the British colonial system, and there was no special need to include in any agreement a rule which was supposed to be valid in all parts of the empire. Secondly, judging from the fact that only a few cases were dealt with at the highest level, it seems reasonable to conclude that religious liberty at the individual level was not much of a problem in this period. This may have two explanations: official policy and internal developments in Buganda. As regards the former, the various rules and regulations introduced in the 1890s, especially under Colvile, and the active line which the administration had followed on various occasions in implementing these rules, had started to produce results. As far as the internal developments in

Buganda were concerned, the final allocation of offices accomplished around the middle of the 1890s had meant a more settled situation, where there was less incentive to change one's religion, and consequently less risk of eviction from the shambas. Economic developments had also meant that forced labour was reduced, so all in all there was less chance of people coming into conflict with the various rules.

This should not be taken as an indication that all the problems inherent in the introduction of religious liberty had now been solved. It would be more accurate to say that there were now fewer obstacles in the way of living quietly and privately in accordance with one's own religion. But a final evaluation of the policy of the administration is of course dependent on the definition of religious liberty one uses, whether it is the narrower or the wider one. We have seen that these two options had been available since the Berlin Conference. We may arrive at one kind of answer by examining how the so-called 'pagans' and the Muslims fared under the Johnston settlement. While the former were hardly mentioned, Johnston came up against a problem in the case of the latter in Busoga, the area to the east of Buganda. Bishop Tucker expressed alarm over the apparently dominant position which the colonial authorities had granted to some Muslim Baganda in Busoga. He drew attention to three chieftainships where Muslims had obtained influential positions during the minority of the proper chiefs. This, he claimed, constituted a danger, not just for the missionary work, but for the whole political status quo. Tucker underlined that he was not angling for a favourable position for his mission in Busoga, but was seriously concerned about the Muslims being thus favoured by the administration.[10] Johnston acted promptly, taking immediate measures to remedy the situation in Busoga. It is noticeable that he agreed entirely with the concern expressed by Tucker, and that he did not, in view of his position as the head of the colonial administration, try to defend his own officers in Busoga. Nor did he invoke the necessity of taking a neutral stand in religious matters. The reason was that he took a qualitative view of Islam, and was concerned about the political consequences of its spread:

Finally let me assure you that if there is one thing towards which I am doggedly opposed on political grounds (putting aside religious) it is the Muhammadanising of the Basoga. For this country to become a focus of Muhammadanism would be one of the most dangerous threats to the future prosperity of the Protectorate. In fact it would bring Islam down from the Nile to the Victoria Nyanza [Lake Victoria], and what we want to aim at politically is to thrust Islam as much as possible back into the Sudan.[11]

Johnston's conception of Islam as a political risk caused him to treat the expansion of Christianity and Islam in the Protectorate differently. While he was concerned with Christian missionary freedom,[12] he could not allow the same freedom to the Muslims because of the possible political consequences.

The different treatment of the two religions is underlined by the fact that Johnston and his successor were prepared to tolerate obvious political difficulties created by the spread of Christianity. A case in point was the rivalry between the Catholics and Protestants in the Kingdom of Ankole. Here the distribution of Christian denominations tended to correspond with ethnic divisions. The ruling group, the Bahima, were mostly Protestants; the peasants, the Bairu, were mainly Catholics. As the former group, consisting of the King and the chiefs, favoured the CMS, they protested against the Catholic missionary presence, as it could mean a widening of the existing cleavage in society. Fearing disturbances, the colonial administration barred the Catholic missionaries from going to Ankole. But it is characteristic that this suspension of the Catholic drive in Ankole lasted for less than six months.[13] In contrast with the case of the Muslims in Busoga, the possible political consequences afforded only a short-term argument when Christianity was involved. After a cooling-off period the suspension was lifted in accordance with the primacy given to the principle of Christian missionary freedom.

Judging from these two cases Johnston and his administration were acting on the basis of a qualitative distinction between Christianity and Islam. This meant that their definition of religious liberty was the narrower one, which limited it to the Christian denominations. We see here a marked difference between Johnston and one of his predecessors, Colonel Colvile, who expressed a special concern for the Muslims and 'pagans' as they had no Europeans to speak up for them. This shows how much scope there was for varying interpretations of the concept of religious liberty in colonial policy. In the case of the narrow definition the focus is primarily on the Christian denominations and their respective rights, including freedom of expansion, while people of other religions are guaranteed certain minimum rights like freedom of conscience and worship, and freedom to make a living without undue religious interference. The wider interpretation of religious liberty takes a more active interest in all religious observances, and an administration using this definition will feel concern in the face of existing patterns of inequality between religions in any given area and will take measures to redress the balance as part of its policy. So far it is apparent that the colonial administration in Uganda had for the most part kept to the narrower definition by confining its interest in the issue to the individual level and favouring the Christian denominations.

Religion and office-holding: religious liberty at the societal level

Freehold land was in accordance with the Uganda Agreement distributed mainly among the chiefs of various ranks, which resulted in a close connection between landholding and office-holding. As the chieftainships had all been distributed among the three religious parties throughout the 1890s, it follows that the mailo land would also be allocated according to religious divisions if no other distributive formula was introduced.

Johnston decided to continue the line taken by Lugard and Portal. As already mentioned, he wrote into the Agreement that membership of the Lukiko should reflect 'all recognized expressions of religious beliefs' proportionally. He later confirmed his indebtedness to his predecessors in the 1890s in connection with the question of the allocation of the 20 saza chieftainships:

I have however felt it advisable not to override hastily the policy of Sir Gerald Portal in maintaining to some degree a definite allotment of influence or terrritory to the representatives of the two forms of Christian faith and the Muhammadan religion.[14]

Johnston certainly made no effort to introduce a new distribution formula, although he did add that the arrangement as it stood was not permanently binding on the government, and that it did not militate against freedom of religion. When asked by the Mill Hill Mission to appoint one of their people to a saza chieftainship, he even excused himself from responsibility by replying that the post had been filled in accordance with the wishes of the Catholics and Protestants themselves, and that the matter was really the responsibility of the Lukiko.[15] After the allocation of the old offices and the various new ones instituted by the Agreements, the results of the religious distribution can be presented as in Table 1.

Table 1. Office-holding and religious affiliation in Buganda after the conclusion of the Uganda Agreement[16]

	Protestants	Catholics	Muslims	Traditionalists
Ministers (regents)	2	1		
Saza chiefs	11	8	1	
Members of the Lukiko	49	35	5	

This allocation of the higher offices to the three religious parties, with its exclusion of the adherents of the traditional religion, lasted with few changes for the following half-century. Turning to the lower echelons, one difficulty is that no lists of the minor chiefs were drawn up indicating their religious alignment. It is however possible by consulting the land allotment lists to deduce their religious affiliation. People holding offices below the level of saza chief were each granted a substantial number of acres of freehold land. The higher in rank they were, the more land they were given. The saza chief was responsible for this distribution, and within the bulk allocation of land to his saza he parcelled out the mailo land to his followers. By reading the names of the recipients one can deduce their religious affiliation, and it can be seen that the main beneficiaries were his own co-religionists. It seems therefore reasonable to suggest that the sub-chiefs within each saza were mostly of the same religion as their superiors. It follows that throughout the whole country the majority of the minor chiefs were drawn from the three religious parties, with the Christians predominating.[17] This confirms the continuation of the system initiated with Lugard's and Portal's religious organization of the country.

The chiefs of the lower ranks had thus become landowners, and were ensured a regular income by their entitlement to rents from their peasant tenants.[18] Yet there was no complete congruence between landholding, office-holding and membership of one of the religious parties. People outside these categories, that is, people outside the chiefly hierarchy and in particular non-Christians, had some share in the mailo land. Thus the holding of land could not be fully equated with the holding of office, and this meant that people outside the religious parties also to some extent had a vested interest in the preservation of the new order.[19]

This may also be taken as an indication that more mailo land was available than could actually be shared out among the followers of the three parties. The result was that a number of the so-called pagans, some of these office-holders in the traditional Buganda structure, obtained their shares of the mailo land, although the size of their estates was on average relatively small compared to those of the Christians.

If the strength of the four religions is measured on the basis of the allotment of land it becomes clear that the Christians taken as a whole got the lion's share compared to the Muslims and Traditionalists combined. It is likewise significant that the pagan share of land was much larger than the Muslim one, except within the only Muslim saza. The Muslims were clearly in a minority position if we employ mailo land and offices as criteria.[20] An interesting feature emerges if the pagan share of land is compared with that of the Catholics and Protestants within each saza. There is a clear tendency for Catholic shares in Protestant sazas to be significantly smaller than pagan shares, and vice versa in Catholic sazas.[21] The reason for this pattern may be that Catholics and Protestants preferred to obtain land in sazas where their own religion was predominant, and succeeded in getting it. It was not necessarily the result of a deliberate policy on the part of the party leaders of giving preference to the Traditionalists over their Christian competitors. In any case, the result was that the land settlements served to preserve the distinct religious character of each saza. The pattern of the 1890s was continued, and the previous plans for the intermingling of the two Christian groups went by the board.

The latter point is further underlined when we consider the plight of the Bakopi, who stood outside the distribution of the spoils. After the religious allocation of the new sazas and the land settlement the Bakopi began to migrate in significant numbers, which caused great turmoil in the country, and almost brought the Protestant work to a halt.[22] In many cases chiefs wanted only their own followers on their newly-acquired land, which meant that others were evicted. In other cases the reason for migration was simply that people themselves wanted to live on land belonging to a chief of their own religion.[23] One mechanism which strengthened this settlement pattern was the clientage system, comprising both the traditional ties and the newer religious bonds between chiefs and Bakopi. A movement thus began across the country, especially from east to west and vice versa, because the Catholics had mainly been granted sazas in the western part of the country and the Protestants towards the east. This conformed with the pattern of distribution initiated in Portal's organization of the country.

Summarizing the consequences of Johnston's settlement, it is clear that the effects of the religious division of the country now penetrated far deeper into the fabric of society than hitherto. By giving his approval to the allocation of the highest offices according to the relative strength of the religious parties, and by distributing the mailo land along the same lines, Johnston had employed the religious formula in a way which had ramifications far more complex than he had foreseen or cared to admit. Like his predecessors, he probably did not fully realize the extent to which the religious allocation of offices combined with the traditional clientage system would have far-reaching consequences at most levels of society, especially when the mailo land was added to the benefits to be shared out. More systematically, the outcome may be summarized in the following five points.

(1) The politico-religious division of the country was upheld, and the main

offices within the African political system were tied to particular religious alignments. Although the pattern which had characterized the 1890s was thus confirmed, there were two differences. First, the number of offices concerned had increased substantially both at the top and at the lower levels. Secondly, the combination of the ownership of mailo land and the holding of the various offices had cemented the whole system. The closer interrelationship between the balance of political power and the economic structure made it more difficult to make any changes. For the people involved the consequences of any change of religion for their civil rights would be felt more severely. As for the colonial administration, its political and economic involvement had been increased, which limited its ability to initiate any changes in the status quo. It had accepted the ties between civil rights and religious alignment and had, at least for the time being, given up any ideas of establishing an alternative pattern.

(2) As regards the criterion of equality, the administration's policy can be characterized as coming close to real inequality. During the Johnston period this even manifested itself to some extent in formal procedures. Johnston allowed real inequality to prevail by leaving the distribution of offices to the Baganda themselves, without intervening to redress imbalances. The political victory of Christianity and the Protestant hegemony were confirmed and institutionalized. As the whole pattern was closely identified with the Uganda Agreement, it gained thereby a similar character of permanence and immutability. Apart from the fact that the Muslims were given one of the Protestant sazas some years later, no major incursion was to be made on the Christian monopoly of power for many years to come.

(3) At this stage of our discussion it will be useful to examine the interrelationship between the individual and societal levels. In concrete terms it had become clearer than ever that the road to political influence and economic well-being ran via Christianity. The ruling Christian group possessed most of the benefits available in the form of offices and land. To become a Christian and thereby acquire various skills and behaviour patterns provided the best ladder to a share in the new order. This whole state of affairs had a circumscribing effect on the realization of the ideal of religious liberty. It was attractive to become a Christian, while it was only at some personal cost that one could remain in the traditional sphere. The outlook for someone becoming a Muslim was bleak. Individual choice, faced with such a situation, could not be made in the proper context of religious equity.

In order to develop the relationship between the individual and societal levels, we may attempt to see the problem from a different perspective. Johnston, unlike Lugard when he had to accept the religious division of the country, did not really engage in any discussion of the problem of religion and politics; nor did he feel any need to explain or defend the existing connection between the two areas. This omission may be explained by pointing out that the intermixture of religion and politics had by now become such a regular feature of life in Uganda that it did not call for further comment. It is however possible to suggest another explanation. The relationship between the individual and the societal level had assumed a causative character, in the sense that the more the principle of religious liberty was seen to work at the individual level, safe-guarding the people's basic rights of freedom of conscience and worship, the less acutely would the problem of religion and politics be felt. The former provided in a sense an alibi for measures in the latter field. This tentatively offered proposition may help to explain the fact that the colonial administration chose throughout the following years to accept a situation of real inequality with a minimum of uneasiness, and made only a few attempts to redress the balance.

(4) An evaluation of the role of the religious parties is bound to be somewhat qualified. It follows from the above point that there was no official discussion of the presence and function of these parties. The two Christian parties functioned as the main allocating agencies during the implementation of the Uganda Agreement, and were responsible for the distribution of both offices and land. This again had its effect on the settlement pattern of the Bakopi, which indicates that the system of religious parties had been so far integrated into the traditional structure that the parties now worked in harmony with it instead of being in conflict with it. No other allocating principle was suggested or indeed available, and the importance of the religious parties was increased even more by the inclusion of mailo land among the benefits available.

In the long term the embryonic separation of office-holding and the holding of land, of political and economic power, might weaken the religious parties. But for the first generation of landholders under the Agreement, the combination of office and land tended to strengthen the religious parties. The finality of the land settlement afforded the religious parties an image of stability and permanence. From now on people began to belong to the parties by birth rather than by choice.[24] Hardly anyone could have foreseen that a different concept of ownership, growing up with the development of cash crops, would establish an alternative source of power.

The origin of the Christian parties has been discussed earlier (especially in Chapter 2) and they have throughout this analysis been examined on the basis of their political functions in society. The presence of the two forms of Christianity, despite their differences, served as a cohesive principle, and Christianity itself may have provided a common ideological outlook as a basis for the authority and legitimacy of the leaders.[25] It is however important, in order to explore the relationship of this level to the institutional one, to underline the precise function of the Christian presence. The Christian parties did not pursue Christian goals as such, but directed their activities towards political and social goals. Nor did they work for the establishment of their respective churches, or for special privileges for them. The Christian parties came into being before the churches and did not owe their existence to them. Consequently the intermixture of religion and politics manifest in the Christian parties could not be a function of the existence of the churches as institutions, but was a result of the simultaneous presence of several religious persuasions which constituted the main structuring principle in society. Conversely, the churches were not a direct part of the politico-religious configuration, and there was no question of the direct political involvement of the churches, nor of their clergy taking upon themselves political roles. Instead the churches had a significant auxiliary function in that they provided the educational and other skills which allowed people to take advantage of the new opportunities within the colonial system.[26]

(5) Because of the policy of real inequality the members of the Christian oligarchy were the real winners after the conclusion of the Agreement, and the dominant position of the Protestant leaders was confirmed.[27] Within the ruling group it is possible to distinguish between two layers. The first one consists of the three regents and the 20 saza chiefs, whose absolute leadership had been confirmed. This group got the lion's share of the land, and became in addition salaried

members of the colonial bureaucracy. The second layer consisted of the minor chiefs, who were given less land and no fixed salary. Because of the private ownership of land, however, these two groups constituted a 'permanent aristocracy',[28] quite distinct from the large group of Bakopi who were left in the position of rent-paying tenants. The relationship between these two major strata in society was characterized by the double hold the chiefs from now on had on the Bakopi in their combined roles as landholders and officials.[29]

The chiefs' position had in every respect been strengthened for the moment, which meant that the gradual dwindling of their economic importance observable towards the end of the 1890s had been reversed. This was due to the threefold source from which they now derived their authority, and which served to uphold their 'rule over people'. At the same time hardly anyone noticed the fundamental change in the basis of the relationship between the chiefs and their tenants brought about by the introduction of the individual ownership of land. From the missionaries' point of view, given the importance of the chiefs for their work, their political ascendancy and renewed economic capacity was a positive development. The emergence of the Bakopi as a special category of contributors proved of minor importance. The result was a continued close alliance between the missionaries and the chiefly élite, where the benefits for the missionaries were the possibility of utilizing the chiefs' political influence and economic potential. They could now safely build their strategy around this élite group. The other side of the coin was obviously that the missionaries had linked themselves irreversibly to the existing, now strengthened, power stratum. There was therefore the risk that the high degree of dependence on the Protestant hierarchy would render the Protestant enterprise unduly vulnerable in the case of major changes in the fabric of society. The church might in fact become the victim of tensions between the various layers in society. This problem will be relevant when we turn to an examination of the Protestant mission's policy during the Johnston period.

Relations between mission, church and state: religious liberty at the institutional level

The Uganda Agreement meant a ratification of developments in the 1890s and gave the settlement an air of finality. The privileged position of the Christians had been recognized and the political dominance of the Protestants stabilized. We must now investigate the implications for the missionaries and the church, their mutual relations, and their position *vis-à-vis* the state; a relationship which has been discussed earlier in connection with the land grants for religious purposes, when the CMS representatives failed to gain recognition for the African church from the colonial authorities. It will therefore be appropriate to investigate in a wider context the relationship between mission, church and state in the Johnston period.

The missionaries' political role

Johnston did not feel any need for dissociation from the missions, but used much the same approach as Portal had before him. Immediately after his arrival in Uganda he recognized the missionaries' close knowledge of Buganda society and their influence with the chiefs. The more difficult and protracted his negotiations with the chiefs became, the more he drew upon the CMS representatives, Archdeacon Walker and Bishop Tucker.[30] Making use of their linguistic skills, he used them as intermediaries with the chiefs, especially when he had to have his plans carefully explained, recognizing that it was only through the missionaries that he could carry the chiefs with him.[31] When the Agreement was finally concluded he emphasized the indispensability of the missionaries in arriving at a satisfactory result.[32] From their side the chiefs made just as much use of the CMS missionaries. They took them into their confidence, discussed all important matters with them, and used them as their advocates in the negotiations with Johnston.[33] This time they were not reprimanded for seeking the advice of the missionaries before coming to the authorities.

The missionaries were aware of the semi-official acceptance of their political role: 'Fortunately the Commissioner is large enough minded not to resent missionary interference.'[34] During the negotiations Tucker and Walker made full use of this opportunity to intervene on behalf of the chiefs. They rightly saw that the position and status of the chiefs were at stake, and Walker stated bluntly that his main interest in the negotiations was to secure a fair deal for the chiefs, as they had become his 'most intimate friends'.[35] The close identification with the well-being of the chiefs was almost certainly based on the recognition that the position of the missionaries and the church would also be severely affected by any weakening of the chiefs' standing in the political sphere.[36]

The CMS mission clearly chose sides during these negotiations and stuck firmly to this policy throughout them. They could therefore after the conclusion of the Agreement express great satisfaction with the outcome.[37] Thus a close alliance was here cemented between the CMS mission and the leading chiefs which was bound to have some influence on the future power of the Protestant church. These events probably marked the peak of the CMS missionaries' direct political influence as we have seen it so far. It presented also one of the few occasions where their political role was appreciated by the colonial administration.

The question of neutrality and equal treatment

It would seem that the Protestant missionaries played a more important role than their Catholic counterparts, and were to a greater extent taken into the confidence of the colonial administration. This leads us to the question of whether there was equal treatment of Protestant and Catholic missions during the Johnston period, or whether the authorities demonstrated any lack of neutrality. It has been claimed that Johnston actually showed signs of hostility towards the Catholic missions, in particular to the White Fathers.[38] The evidence for this assertion is not particularly conclusive, and it could just as easily be claimed that Johnston and his colleagues were well aware of the need for equal treatment of the two denominations.[39] It should be pointed out that on at least two occasions he reprimanded both of them for failing to respect one another's rights.[40] An explanation of these conflicting interpretations of Johnston's policy as regards equality can be offered by making a distinction between two levels. At the official, formal level we can enumerate the concrete concessions and benefits which the missions obtained from the administration. Here it is difficult to find any lack of neutrality on the part of the authorities. The granting of land to the three missions affords the best proof of this. As his basic criterion Johnston used the three mission-ary societies' own estimates of the respective requirements, instead of just dis-tinguishing between the two major denominations present in the country. The result was that more land was awarded to the Catholics than to the Protestants. Out of the total 92 square miles to be allotted, 52 went to the Catholics (of which 17 were given to the Mill Hill Fathers) and 40 to the Protestant mission. In view of Bishop Tucker's earlier firm line on the need for equal treatment of the two denominations, it is somewhat surprising that the CMS accepted this. It may have been their preoccupation with the chiefs' problems that prevented them from taking a more active interest in matters affecting their own position. Less than a year later, however, Tucker did become aware of the denominational inequity inherent in the land grants and took swift measures to rectify the situation, as we shall see.

At the unofficial, personal level it is beyond all doubt that there existed closer bonds between the colonial administration and the CMS mission, especially between Johnston and Bishop Tucker, than there were between the administra-tion and the Catholic missions. This was a relatively new state of affairs and began with the events of 1897–8, assuming quite significant proportions during John-ston's stay in Uganda.[41] It is, however, important to remember that this special relationship did not necessarily manifest itself in the form of privileges and concessions. On the other hand, it could have two other effects. First, it gave the colonial administration the image of being biased in favour of the CMS, which gave rise to an attitude of suspicion in the Catholic community and helps to explain the accusations of preferential treatment. Secondly, it could in fact give the CMS leaders more access to the colonial authorities and more opportunity to influence policy-making and concrete decisions at a subtler level. This whole problem should be examined on the basis of specific cases, and it may be of some significance that there was at this time in CMS circles an ongoing discussion on the necessity of strengthening the missionaries' personal relationships with the colonial officials.[42]

This is the old question of the common nationality of mission and colonial power reappearing in a different guise. The common national origin and in most cases the common social and denominational background of the Protestant missionaries and the colonial authorities made for easier communication between the two sets of representatives than there could be with outsiders like the Catholics. The issue was no longer one of special obligations and responsibilities towards the colonial administration's own nationals, as was the case during the introduction of the colonial system. The question at issue now was how far common nationality created a special pattern of personal contacts between the CMS and the colonial authorities.

Exemptions and special concessions

Ths issue of special concessions and exemptions is a further aspect of the problem of the administration's neutrality and the equal treatment of the two main missions, and helps in particular to clarify whether the CMS mission because of its special relationship with the administration gained any advantages or influence at the expense of the Catholics. But first of all, we must examine the extent to which concessions and exemptions were in fact granted, in order to answer the question of whether there had been any significant change in the position of the mission and the church following the introduction of the new order with the Uganda Agreement.

While the land issue was a negotiable one, the introduction of a hut tax fixed at three rupees per hut remained unchanged in accordance with Johnston's primary aim of putting the Protectorate on the road to self-support. The CMS mission agreed with this in principle, but both Bishop Tucker and Archdeacon Walker expressed great concern as to whether the church could bear this financial burden. They felt it would be an especially severe burden for the Protestant effort because of the great number of teachers and evangelists they had to send out – these amounted to about 1,000 people and cost about two hundred pounds a year in hut tax.[43] Apart from the question of whether the mission or the church was to be responsible for the payment of the money, there were other problems. First, many teachers would have to leave their religious work for some months in order to find the tax money which disrupted their work. Secondly, many teachers would have to pay the hut tax twice as they frequently left their families behind while posted to another district.[44] At first Bishop Tucker asked for general exemption for the Protestant teachers, but Johnston turned this request down.[45] As an alternative the CMS asked for a ruling which would exempt teachers from the unreasonable burden of paying the hut tax twice.[46] The colonial administration remained firm, and this concession was also refused. The officials emphasized that tax must be paid for each habitable hut, and they recommended instead that the church should pay it in the second case, as the huts were really church property.[47] This line of argument is interesting, as such an exemption would entail great loss of revenue for the administration. We must remember that the administration considered all exemptions to be a form of indirect support from the state. The authorities also argued that the pagans would find it unfair if a teacher were exempted just because he was preaching the Gospel. This is one of the rare occasions when people belonging to the traditional religion were mentioned at all. Interpreted within the context of the administration's great concern for the proper functioning of the hut-tax system, this reference to the Traditionalists may well have been prompted less by religious considerations than by the intention of the authorities to avoid at all costs any unrest over the question of the hut tax.

This interpretation gains some weight given the failure of a subsequent Catholic attempt to obtain exemptions from the hut tax. The administration took this opportunity to make it clear for all missions that no exemptions would be granted for huts on mission land. The effect of such exemptions would, it was claimed, be that people would settle there to avoid the tax. The approach from the Catholics did, however, raise the question of neutrality on the part of the administration. While the CMS was hit hard because of the great number of teachers they sent out into outlying districts, the dissatisfaction of the White Fathers sprang from the fact that they had a completely different method of working. Instead of sending out teachers they collected their converts at the mission stations for instruction prior to baptism and confirmation. The result of this was that they had great numbers of huts at each station for which they were expected to pay tax. The administration would not grant any exemptions, but for a short period permission was given that four of these huts could count as one if they were situated close to one another.[48]

Thus Johnston certainly gave a sort of concession to the Catholics which it would have been difficult for the Protestants to make use of. If the Protestant method of work had been similar to the Catholic one, they would have saved a lot of money. But their method was based upon the sending of teachers to the villages, and Tucker now reminded Johnston of his earlier refusal to grant exemptions to the teachers. Tucker added significantly that while the Catholics had now been granted a favour on purely religious grounds, he himself had based his application on secular grounds, namely 'the value of these teachers from an educational standpoint'. It would seem, Tucker remarked, that the administration was not prepared to lose one or two thousand rupees a year in return for the advantage of 20–30,000 people learning to read. He would therefore this time ask for a tax reduction of 75 per cent on purely religious grounds, as they seemed to work better with the administration, judging from the Catholic experience.[49]

Though no answer was given to Tucker's renewed request, two things are of special interest here. First, for Tucker there was a marked distinction between basing one's case on secular and religious grounds. He was inclined to assume that the former ought to work best with the authorities, especially the educational argument. Tucker was here following in the footsteps of Archdeacon Walker, in the sense that he was claiming that the mission and the church were carrying out a service function within the educational field for which the administration ought to pay. Unlike Colonel Ternan, Johnston was not prepared to work with such a secular link between church and state, nor to accept this as sufficient reason for granting indirect support to mission work in the form of exemptions. That this is an accurate interpretation of Johnston's attitude is confirmed by his later suggestion with regard to state support for missionary educational work. He recommended that some return should be made in appreciation of their efforts to educate the Africans, but he attached the condition to any such support that 'direct connection . . . with educational purposes can be established'.[50] In other words, funds should be specifically earmarked for educational purposes, and not constitute support for missionary work in general. In this respect the missions would be treated just like any other non-commercial agency undertaking educational work. To make sure that his conditions were adhered to he recommended that support should materialize in the form of reductions in the mission's educational expenditure, such as relief from customs duties on books, stationery and printing presses. Furthermore, in return the administration would require that the missions give instruction in the English language – an item of high priority for Johnston.[51] He thus drew up at this early stage the first outline of an official educational policy based on cooperation with the missions. We shall later deal with this issue in greater detail. It suffices to say here that the question of state support for the missions via exemptions touches on two closely related aspects of the relationship between church and state: the instrumental use of the church by the state, and the church's secular activities as sufficient grounds for direct or indirect support from the state.

The second point arising from Tucker's request concerns the administration's neutrality in its relations with the two denominations. Obviously Tucker was hinting that the colonial authority in granting what amounted to exemptions from hut tax had shown a certain lack of neutrality and favoured the Catholics. Tucker's criticism of the Johnston administration was not however fully justified. First of all, the permission to count four huts as one was a limited, short-term favour to the Catholics. Secondly, Tucker seems to have forgotten that he had obtained a similar concession only a few weeks earlier in connection with registration fees on church land. In accordance with its method of work, the CMS had, unlike the Catholics, divided its allocated land into a number of small plots designed for the teachers, which meant that the required registration of land became quite expensive. While refusing to grant any exemption or reduction Johnston conceded that the small plots within each saza could be regarded as just one plot, which amounted to a substantial saving for the Protestants.[52]

The latter case should also be seen in a wider context. As referred to earlier Tucker used two arguments to back up his request for exemption from registration fees. First, Johnston was this time dealing with a native body, and ought to give it special and favourable treatment. Secondly, the activities of the church were based on the principle of self-support, and the registration fees were an especially heavy burden which put this cardinal principle at risk. Characteristically, Johnston bypassed both arguments by taking the same line as he had done in the land question; the administration did not recognize the African church, but held the mission responsible for all religious activity. The internal division of work was none of his concern.

It is thus apparent that the administration took a firm line on exemptions by hardly granting any. In accordance with its general policy, it upheld the principle of equal treatment. In spite of the more personal informal relationship between members of the colonial administration and of the CMS the latter did not gain any special concessions; the administration maintained a position of neutrality between the two denominations. Johnston was aware that exemptions constituted indirect state support for the Christian effort. He therefore refrained from granting any, probably because he considered that the granting of land was sufficient support for the missionary work. This was consistent with his stand on the land question. Johnston stuck to the mission formula and avoided involving himself in the more complicated issue of the relationship between mission, church and state.

Relationships with the African political system

During the earlier discussion of the role of the chiefs in the furtherance of the Protestant work a distinction was made between their political and economic importance. The same distinction may conveniently be applied again, although it cannot be as clear-cut. Their political importance was accurately described by Bishop Hanlon of the Mill Hill Mission, when he approached Johnston just a couple of weeks after the conclusion of the Agreement and asked for one of the saza chieftainships to be assigned to a man who represented the followers of the Mill Hill Mission. By not having a saza chief, 'our work has been greatly hampered; the interests of our missions have suffered often, and sometimes severely'.[53] Given their close identification with the interests of the chiefs during the negotiation of the Agreement, it is not surprising that the CMS attached great importance to the filling of the leading chieftaincies, and especially the maintenance of the Protestant hold on the ones already assigned to them.[54] Both missions thus considered the chiefs' roles to be of the utmost importance for the Christian effort.

Naturally the chiefs' political importance was closely connected with their economic capacity. The unsettled state of the country after the conclusion of the Agreement, and in particular the great migrations of people, had caused a substantial decrease in gifts to the church funds and had also limited the capacity of ordinary Christians to give.[55] This state of affairs made the Protestant work even more dependent on the Christian chiefs. In some of the sazas things went so far that most of the work was paid for by the saza chief alone.[56] This is again indicative of how much the work of the church was affected by the recent changes in the chiefly hierarchy:

the bulk of the Church's funds are paid in by natives, usually in the form of large gifts by great Chiefs. 3 or 4 of the Great Chiefs pay the whole of the Church's expenses . . . all the money of the country has been put into the hands of 2 or 3 by the English Government. Wages once scattered over 700 chiefs are now concentrated on 20 and on English officials. So only the few can give largely.[57]

These remarks from the missionary A. G. Fraser may be a little exaggerated. All the same they hint at the effect of the Johnston settlement on the chiefs' economic position. They also confirm the fact that two distinct layers in the chiefly hierarchy had emerged. The writer certainly bears witness to the fact that recent developments in the Buganda system had influenced the pattern of the Protestant work and increased its dependence on the chiefly élite.

The close cooperation of the mission with the high-ranking chiefs was demonstratively expressed on the occasion of the building of the new Anglican cathedral in 1901. There were great festivities, the high point of which was the laying of the foundation stone by the five-year-old Kabaka, to the great satisfaction of the Protestant chiefs.[58] The financial means necessary for the erection of the new building were guaranteed by the leading chiefs. They shared the expenses among themselves, the two Protestant Ministers/Regents taking upon themselves the largest share, and the Protestant saza chiefs smaller ones[59]. Besides providing the bulk of the money, the Protestant chiefs also took an active part in providing the clay for the bricks; the Katikiro and all the other leading Protestant chiefs set an example by themselves carrying clay on their heads.[60]

These events provide us with a glimpse of the close association between the Protestant chiefly élite and the work of the mission and the church under the new order. They demonstrate the strength of the relationship between the Anglican mission, the church and the African political system, and illustrate some specific characteristics of that relationship. First, the chiefs provided access to and integration with traditional society. The existing ties between a chief and his subordinates were transferred to the religious field and thus provided the lines of communication to the ordinary people which were essential for the whole missionary effort. The importance of these connections was especially felt by the missionaries when they were broken, as they were when a chief changed his religion.[61] Secondly, there was the practical importance of the chiefs in financial matters, and for working conditions in the sazas, for instance the selection of sites for churches and schools. Their own active participation in church life and in particular their guidance in moral matters should not be underestimated. This was important for the general quality of Christian belief. Thirdly, from the point of view of the mission and church, one important result of their association with the chiefs was that it provided them with an image of establishment. The Protestant mission and church were seen to be closest to the centre of power every time the Kabaka was included on official occasions; and the Katikiro and others of similar rank publicly engaged themselves in the work. The whole framework of the relationship was aptly summarized in Bishop Tucker's comments, which he made before the conclusion of the Uganda Agreement:

The Church of Uganda is co-extensive with the country. The King is a Christian. The majority of the great territorial chiefs are Christians. The Christians are to be found in every province and district in Uganda [Buganda].[62]

The Bishop felt therefore that the time was ripe for 'the founding of a National Church on primitive, natural and truly democratic lines'. In spite of the almost national character of the church thus implied by Bishop Tucker it is necessary for a proper assessment of the nature of its relationship with the African polity to mention two qualifications inherent in the Ganda situation. In the first place, a distinction should be made between Christianity on the one hand and its institutional expressions, the mission and the church, on the other. It has earlier been pointed out that it was Christianity as such which constituted the cohesive principle of the religious parties, and not the church. It was Christianity which legitimized the Christian political apparatus and provided the basis for the power of the chiefs. The church as such was neither a formal nor a real part of the African political system. The chiefs' position was not an effect of the existence of the church, but preceded it. This leads to a second qualification as regards the situation of the church. Given the distinction between mission and church, it was still the former which represented the executive wing of Christianity in its dealings with the African political system. The church was not equipped for such a function, but was mainly concerned with internal and specifically ecclesiastical matters. If we look at the minutes of the Church Council from the 1890s we find that at least 90 per cent of all subjects discussed fall within the category of Christian morality and church discipline: adultery, marriage problems and drunkenness.[63] The mission's aim was accordingly to relate the future church to the already existing Protestant leadership, to utilize the chiefs' economic and political capacities and thus to give the church a proper foundation in African society.

In view of this latter policy it is important to examine the overlap of persons that existed between the African church and the African political system, a factor that is often taken as an indication of the degree of intermingling of church and state.[64] First, there was the practice of switching from an office in one institution to a position in the other, and in some cases back again; sometimes offices were even held in both places simultaneously. Secondly, there was a common source of recruitment to offices in church and state; it is characteristic that most of the saza chiefs and most of the first ordained clergymen were among the group of leading Christians who had gone into exile during the upheavals and civil wars around 1890 (see p.14).[65] The mixture of offices was particularly evident on the occasion of the first ordinations: four out of six of the ordained held chieftainships.[66] There was, however, from the outset a latent possibility for the separation of the work of church and state, and this began to come to the surface around 1900. A number of factors were at work.

(1) A distinction soon appeared between the people who became chiefs and those who became clerics, in spite of the common source of recruitment.[67] The chiefs all had traditional qualifications besides their Christian ones, while the clergymen ordained during the 1890s and in 1901 (27 in all) had no traditional chiefly qualifications.[68]

(2) The church gradually became more institutionalized and its officers had to perform more specialized functions. The same thing happened within the African polity. More and more administrative work fell to the chiefs, a development which culminated in the Agreement of 1900, under which they were included in the colonial bureaucracy. The need for special qualifications and the time-consuming nature of the work forced people to make a choice and decide which of the two careers they would settle for. The result was that the chiefs preferred the secular option. Thus the overlap between the two professions largely remained a first-generation phenomenon.[69]

(3) This trend was further reinforced by the fact that the sources of recruitment for the clergy and for political offices gradually became socially distinguishable. ordinands were classified as having been 'blacksmiths, carpenters, potters or with experience as evangelists and teachers. This meant that the church recruited more and more from her own ranks. Looking at their background, most of the ordinands were classified as having been 'blacksmiths', carpenters, potters or men of some definite occupation'.[70] The growing gulf between the chiefs and the clergy was further widened after the Uganda Agreement, when the chiefs were placed in a privileged and economically safe position, while the clergy in general obtained little or no private land and were, in accordance with the principle of self-support, forced to rely on the scarce resources of church funds. These two identifiable groups, the leaders within their respective spheres, came to stand in a twofold relationship to each other. The chiefs were, as the economic backbone of the church, the main source for the upkeep of the clergy. As they constituted the leading group of laymen in the church they sat together with the clergy in various councils and committees. A more far-reaching consequence of the separation of the chiefs and the clergy was that their different roles and different social and economic statuses increased the chances of a deterioration in the relationships between them.[71]

(4) The CMS missionaries welcomed the separation of the office-holders in church and state. Their evangelical background prompted them to express anxiety about the intermingling of religion and politics that was inevitable when an ordained man became a chief. Yet behind this concern we can detect a conflict of interests between evangelical principles and the desire to gain strategic benefits, the same conflict which had characterized the missionary stance in the Lugard period. The mission expressed great satisfaction on one occasion when a clergymen refused to accept the offer of a chieftainship in spite of a better salary and better conditions of life, thus testifying to the strength of his faith. Despite this some missionaries were not slow in other cases to encourage people to join the secular service so as to promote and safeguard the interests of the Protestants in general, and of the church in particular.[72]

In sum, the practice of holding double offices gradually came to an end. Ordinands who took up offices within the political sphere were appointed on the basis of their traditional qualifications and their connections with the leading group within the Protestant party. They were not recruited in their capacity as Anglican clergymen, and they did not represent the church as such. The church as an institution could not be instrumental in furthering their careers, and insofar as they were able to benefit the Protestant cause and the church it was in an individual, unofficial capacity.

This leads to the observation that, while it was in the interests of the church to have trusted people in leading state posts, it was even more important to have the main actors of the political system associated with the leadership of the church. Around 1900 it was only in rare cases that any of them belonged to the ministry, but they did constitute a prominent part of the lay element of the community, a significant feature of Anglican organization which had little importance in the Catholic system. Bishop Tucker was certainly aware of this and used it as an argument in support of the introduction of his draft constitution.[73] When he attempted to have the African church officially recognized by the colonial government in connection with the registration of land he pointed out that one of the Protestant Regents and two leading chiefs were members of the Church Council.[74] This kind of personal overlapping meant that the church was at the receiving end of this relationship. The participation of secular officers in the church's governing body was not reciprocated by ecclesiastical representation within the African political system. This was in accordance with the CMS's policy; their aim was not for the church to perform a political role, but to give it a position and standing in society which would enable it to carry out its special mission. Their way of securing such a standing for the church was to include influential persons in the Church Council as an important lay element, and in general to maintain close relations between the church and the African political system, for instance by having the Kabaka as a prominent member and letting him take an active part in church life. The mission was not seeking 'the political kingdom' for the church, but rather the image of establishment and the benefits of being closely allied with the centre of power.

This analysis of the amount of personal overlap between the African church and the African polity leads to the conclusion that the African church was placed in a position of dependence in its dealings with the African political system. The separation of office-holding in the two systems and the development of special-ized roles within the church did not change this position. In fact the hierarchy of the church was squeezed between two other hierarchies, the missionaries on the one hand and the chiefly aristocracy which constituted the lay element in the church on the other. From the point of view of the African polity the church was not capable of promoting the interests of the main political actors. To that end the mission had proved useful on several occasions, and was in fact the body most capable of engaging in interaction with the state.

8

Areas outside Buganda: a case-study from Toro

From the middle of the 1890s onwards, after Sir Gerald Portal's mission to Uganda, the colonial government accepted the religious division of Buganda as a necessary frame of reference for its policy. However much it regretted the links between office-holding and religious affiliation, it could not sever them. In the non-Ganda areas, however, the colonial administration was faced with a quite different situation. These societies had not undergone a 'Christian revolution' before the arrival of the colonial power. Furthermore, the colonial authorities arrived ahead of the European missions, who had now accepted the primacy of the secular authority and followed in the footsteps of colonial extension. Hence, as we have shown, the colonial administration acted from a stronger position and with more confidence from the middle of the 1890s, and went out of its way to uphold the principle of missionary freedom, as it felt sure that it would now be able to neutralize the political effects of the dual missionary presence and avoid any repetition of developments in Ganda areas (see Chapter 6). We will now examine the forces at work outside Buganda, and assess how far the colonial government was successful in neutralizing religion as a political factor, in maintaining its own neutrality in religious matters, and in implementing the principle of religious liberty to which it was committed in theory. The western Kingdom of Toro became the first test case for the colonial administration.

Soon after the informal agreement on the distribution of missionary spheres had been annulled in the middle of 1895, both the Catholic and the Protestant missions moved into Toro on a large scale, and each of them stationed a European missionary there.[1] The colonial administration felt sure that it could control the tendency towards polarization which the presence of the two missions would create in Toro, where it was faced with a much more favourable situation than had been the case in Buganda. Lugard had at first restored Toro's independence from Bunyoro and installed Kasagama, one of the exiled heirs to the throne, as ruler. Later, Colonel Colvile had confirmed the restoration by an agreement in March 1894 with Kasagama, and had even extended the Kingdom by creating a confederacy.[2] Toro was thus from the middle of the 1890s onwards a colonial creation under a colonial appointee. But despite the government's tight grip on Toro, there were certain forces at work whose strength the colonial authorities underestimated at first. First of all, a number of more or less manifest linkages were established with Buganda. The colonial administration had the Buganda model in mind when it organized the new Toro confederacy. This element was further reinforced by the fact that the newly installed Omukama (King) and some of his leading chiefs had lived in exile in Buganda. During this period they had established close links with the leading figures within the Buganda Protestant hierarchy, and they had learned some lessons from their stay there. At the same time it is probable that the Baganda leaders saw the Batoro exiles as instrumental in the extension of Ganda influence and thereby in the spread of Protestantism.[3] A second manifestation of Ganda influence was the fact that Kasagama and some of his chiefs, who were being instructed in the Protestant faith, called in Baganda evangelists and were active in promoting Christianity before the arrival of the European missionaries.[4] We have earlier seen that the CMS mission was fully aware of this opening in Toro, and that it gave its active support to these Baganda evangelists (p. 73). Thirdly, the CMS mission was from the beginning in a position both to sustain and to make use of the ruling hierarchy in Toro. This inevitably meant that there was an element of rivalry latent in Toro which would almost certainly break out when the Catholics appeared on the scene. Hence, even before the first colonial officer was sent to Toro in 1894, religious differences were present which could have political effects, just as they had done in Buganda.

The first real move towards the politicization of religion came when the CMS mission intervened on behalf of Kasagama. The officer in Toro, Captain Ashburnham, was very critical of the Omukama's administration, and a severe crisis arose in the latter part of 1895. Kasagama was even imprisoned and had to work in a chain gang for a couple of days, and Ashburnham took similar harsh measures against other Toro leaders.[5] He was convinced that the Ganda evangelists at Kasagama's court had been involved, and he was appalled at the fact that they were stirring up discontent and opposition towards the British Resident, and acting as spies by reporting everything to the CMS mission in the capital.[6] In the end he expelled the Ganda teachers from Toro, while Kasagama himself, fearing worse things to come, sought refuge with the Protestant missionaries in the capital, whom he regarded, according to one of the missionaries, 'as his fathers'.[7] A severe leadership crisis had thus developed in Toro towards the end of 1895, and the otherwise promising work of the Ganda evangelists almost came to a halt. This of course provided the CMS mission with a major reason to take action.[8] It is difficult, given the confusion of the Toro situation, to tell who was really to blame for these unfortunate events, but language difficulties were certainly one major cause.[9] It was also admitted by the Commissioner, E. J. L. Berkeley, and even by Ashburnham himself, that he had been too hasty and had overreacted in handling the situation. All the charges against Kasagama were later withdrawn.[10] At the heart of the matter we may detect different conceptions of a native ruler's sphere of authority. Kasagama, in the Buganda manner, assumed a certain range of power, and acted independently, while Ashburnham conceived of him as a puppet, subject to British officials' control and authority in all matters.[11] This provided another reason for CMS intervention, as the mission had a vested interest in a strong Kingship. This accounts for the element of rivalry between the mission and the colonial administration, and the conception of the mission as an alternative source of authority which was inherent in the Toro crisis in spite of the fact that the mission was not physically present.[12]

Kasagama's flight thus gave the CMS mission, appalled by the government's unfair treatment of Africans, a number of reasons for intervention. But there were also political motives. It was in the interests of the mission to have Kasagama reinstated, and in general to have a strong African leadership on which it could base its work. At the same time the present power vacuum gave the Catholics a great opportunity to exploit the situation, and this too made swift action necessary.[13] In view of the colonial administration's patent mistakes, the CMS mission could act from a strong position and be sure of a positive outcome. It received compensation for the losses its workers had suffered, and Kasagama was virtually acquitted and could return almost in triumph to Toro.[14] Before this happened the CMS made the most of the situation. Kasagama stayed for a while in the capital and was baptized with a magnificent service attended by the Commissioner.[15] Bishop Tucker took the opportunity to visit Toro soon after the Omukama's return, accompanied by A. B. Fisher, who was to be stationed as the first Protestant missionary in Toro (the Catholic Father Achte had already been there for six months). During their visit the alliance between the CMS and the Omukamaship was further cemented.[16]

The crisis in Toro thus accounted for intense exchanges between the CMS mission and the colonial administration, and saw the mission acting in a significant political role. These events emphasized the CMS' strong influence and even privileges as regards 'the native rulers', whose importance for the whole missionary enterprise was clearly demonstrated. Furthermore, everyone was left with the impression that the government had bent to CMS pressure. This would inevitably arouse the suspicions of the Catholic mission, which could easily interpret the outcome as demonstrating a lack of impartiality. All in all, the scene had been set for the transfer of denominational strife to Toro, and it was not long before there was an outbreak of religious conflict.

The immediate cause was the return to Toro of the influential chief of the important county of Mwenge, Yafesi Byakweyamba, who had been a staunch Protestant over the years.[17] In the early stage of the crisis he had been called to the capital for interrogation, and during the temporary vacancy his post had been filled by another chief, who in the meantime had turned Catholic – an indication that the newly arrived Father Achte had not been idle.[18] After the return of Kasagama the CMS mission advocated the return of Byakweyamba too,[19] and the importance the CMS attached to Mwenge was further underlined when contact was established with his Catholic substitute during Bishop Tucker's visit to Toro.[20] Even before this the Catholic Bishop Guillermain had accused the government of a biased handling of the issue of the Mwenge chieftainship, as the removal of the new incumbent was said to coincide with his adoption of Catholicism, and thus to be the result of Protestant agitation.[21] In spite of the Commissioner's firm refutation of the accusation of partiality,[22] Father Achte pursued the issue locally. He accused the CMS mission, and in particular its local missionary, Fisher, of grossly insulting the Catholics and of working with Kasagama to preclude the possibility of Catholics becoming chiefs. He called on the colonial administration to demonstrate its impartiality towards the denominations and to introduce full-scale religious liberty.[23] The incident of the Mwenge chieftaincy set the tone for the rest of 1896, and Toro virtually became a hotbed of religious strife. This caused the local officer, Captain Sitwell, who had replaced

Ashburnham, to lament that: 'All one's time here is taken up by the religious question, one has no time for one's other duties.'[24]

Father Achte accused Kasagama of deliberately excluding Catholics from chieftaincies, claiming that he had said 'there is to be only one religion in Toru and that Protestant'.[25] He also accused Kasagama of withholding support from the Catholic work, regardless of its purpose, while he was generous towards the Protestants.[26] As the CMS mission, and Fisher in particular, were seen as close allies of Kasagama, Father Achte attacked both of them, claiming that they were responsible for the persecution of Catholics which was happening in Toro.[27] The Catholic mission therefore called upon the government to implement the principle of religious liberty actively as a sign of its impartiality, and as the only way of safeguarding the Catholic work in Toro. The CMS mission for its part does not appear to have concerned itself overmuch with religious liberty in the Toro situation. It tacitly supported Kasagama, and worked determinedly to cement its alliance with the ruling hierarchy.[28] It is difficult to assess how far Fisher and his colleagues used the dubious means mentioned by Achte, but it is beyond doubt that the CMS mission worked hard to maintain its monopoly-like position in relation to the chieftainship, and in practice this left little room for religious liberty. It is impossible, on the basis of these allegations and counter-allegations, to pass any fair judgement as to who was really responsible for the deteriorating situation in 1896, or for the increasing politicization of religion. Both Achte and Fisher were zealous adherents of their respective causes, and this provides a partial explanation of the head-on collision which occurred. For his part, Captain Sitwell was inclined to blame Fisher, even to the extent that, when things cooled down and Kasagama apparently 'behaved much better', he ascribed this mainly to Fisher's departure on leave.[29] Still, it is difficult to arrive at the truth, as many of the allegations were based entirely on misinformation, misunderstandings or rumours.[30] For present purposes it will be more profitable to examine how the political authorities (the colonial administration and the Omukama respectively) handled the presence of the two missions and the competition between them, and to examine the options which were open to them as regards the depoliticization of religion.

The colonial administration was concerned about the extent of partisanship in Toro, which was causing unrest and casting doubt upon the impartiality of the authorities. It therefore sought to reduce the mission's political role in Toro affairs. African leaders frequently sought the advice of the missionaries and asked them to voice their grievances, often of a religious nature, with the authorities. The missionaries on their side willingly accepted the role of intermediaries for their converts and even tended to bypass local authorities by taking matters straight to the capital.[31] In the eyes of the Africans the missions became an alternative source of authority, and this tended to reduce the power of the colonial administration. In this area the colonial officials considered that they had made some progress in reducing the significance of religious institutions in politics.[32]

The second, and much more difficult, task was to prepare the way for religious liberty by severing the links between religious affiliation and office-holding. Here the colonial administration addressed itself primarily to the African leaders and the Omukama in particular. Faced with the controversy over the chieftainship in Mwenge and Catholic complaints, Berkeley acted swiftly and issued what he called 'a declaration on religious liberty', in order to dismiss the impression that the colonial administration favoured Protestantism.[33] It was impressed on the Omukama and the chiefs

that religion is a purely personal matter in which each and all are at liberty to follow their private inclinations . . . that this Administration has no sort of bias in favour of any particular religion, that we have no sort of desire to interfere in any way in the question of any individual's religion, and that every one, chiefs and peasants, men and women are perfectly free (without danger or disadvantage to themselves) to choose to follow their own.[34]

And Kasagama in particular was told

that his own religion and that of any individual among his subjects were purely private matters which ought not and must not influence his treatment of his subjects.[35]

In spite of this very clear and detailed declaration there were constant reports that the Omukama was showing intolerance, that he was harassing the Catholics, and that he was forcing people to become Protestants.[36] Apparently the principle of religious liberty did not work in the Toro setting, especially in two respects. First, it was quite obvious that the religious affiliation of individuals had political significance for appointments to chiefly offices, as virtually only Protestants were appointed. There were several reports that Kasagama was threatening the chiefs 'that if they were not Protestants, he would take all their lands from them'.[37] In spite of their protests, officials failed to break the virtual Protestant monopoly of chiefly power.[38]

The second issue was that of public support for the Christian work. As in Buganda, it was proclaimed to be an implication of religious liberty that no one was obliged to support any religion other than his own. This applied primarily to the building of churches.[39] The complexity of implementing such a rule was almost immediately apparent. Father Achte asked the Omukama to procure wood to build sheds for the Catholic mission, as a parallel to the support granted to the Protestants. Kasagama refused, supported by the CMS mission: 'You cannot expect a Protestant King to build sheds for Catholics.'[40] In spite of the fact that Kasagama continued to make Catholics build Protestant churches, the colonial officers did not persuade him to assist the Catholics in the same way.[41] However regrettable the situation was, the Commissioner would not use force, and even admitted that it might be difficult to explain to Kasagama the distinction between public actions in his capacity as a ruler and private actions and feelings as a Protestant.[42] This incident demonstrated the extent of Protestant privileges at the expense of the Catholics in the Toro situation, and the government, in spite of all its good intentions, was powerless to change matters. One remedy would have been to remove Kasagama, abolish the Omukamaship, and impose direct rule or place Toro under Buganda. This was in fact a measure which the colonial administration seriously contemplated, but refrained from in the end, as it was contrary to the principles applied in other areas.[43] It is quite clear that the colonial administration largely ascribed its failure to implement religious liberty properly and to neutralize religion as a political factor to Kasagama's personal behaviour. But we must take a closer look at the circumstances and examine some of the basic structures at work in Toro society, and attempt to assess developments from the point of view of Kasagama himself.

Kasagama was at that juncture faced with the problem of asserting his authority over the newly created Toro confederacy; and there are several indications that some of the county chiefs wanted to pursue their own independent courses.[44] He was therefore very sensitive to any kind of opposition within his area. The controversy over the chieftainship in Mwenge made it quite clear to him what the dual missionary presence and Christian factionalization meant for his own position. The missionaries' competition for influence over the chieftainships, and their efforts to have their own candidates installed, represented an alternative source of authority to his own. Missionary influence and the chiefs' allegiance to the missions clearly reduced his own influence and authority. To make the situation manageable it was essential that there was only one religion, and that the Omukama was identified with it. It is therefore quite likely that Kasagama did say what the colonial authorities claimed, that 'there is to be only one religion in Toru and that Protestant'.[45] A dual power structure was a threat to his own authority. In this respect Kasagama had probably learned a lesson from Buganda. Sitwell quoted many chiefs as asking 'why he [Kasagama] does not do as Mwanga does and let people have what religion they like'.[46] But Ganda developments had shown that a dual system of Christian chiefs was a threat to the Kingship and certainly not in Kasagama's interests. We may also suggest that, in the Toro situation, Protestantism served as a useful ideology to buttress a centralized structure based on the Omukamaship. The CMS laid great weight on a strong Kingship, and the missionaries' support was likely to have a legitimizing and unifying effect which was not to be underestimated, while the religious pluralism which the colonial administration and the Catholics advocated would have had the opposite effect.[47]

There were other hindrances in Toro society to the implementation of religious liberty. The right to refrain from contributing to any religion other than one's own, for instance in connection with the building of churches, was bound to affect the whole pattern of authority in Toro. Contributions for religious purposes mainly took the form of tributes and labour channelled through the chiefs as part of their traditional rights. If individuals were exempted for religious reasons, the result would be that they could evade their obligations to the chiefs and reduce the chiefs' power by showing allegiance to an alternative source of authority. Hence, it was difficult to make allowances for an individualistic concept like religious liberty in a society based upon communal concepts, according to which the ties of loyalty between chiefs and people, and the clientage system, constituted the main structuring principle in society.

The colonial administration was thus faced with difficulties which were immanent in the situation rather than simply due to Kasagama personally. In addition there were some contradictions inherent in its policy. For administrative reasons it was in its interests to have a strong central authority centred on the Omukamaship. At the same time it had to accept the dual missionary presence and secure equal rights for both missions, which was bound to reduce the utility of the central authority. Similarly, the colonial administration made deliberate use of the hierarchical system and the strong ties of loyalty between chiefs and their subjects. At the same time, it was working for the introduction of the individualistic principle of religious liberty, which would tend to dissolve the traditional pattern of authority and the clientage system. The outcome was that the colonial administration in each case gave preference to the first consideration. In spite of all the government's assurances to the contrary, this was what guided its actual policy after 1896. This pragmatic approach was further facilitated by the fact that the pressure from the missionary sector lessened as their mutual relations improved.[48] Hence it became much easier to maintain a low profile on equal rights for Catholics and on the implementation of religious liberty, and Kasagama's rule now appeared in a more favourable light.[49] But nothing had really changed, and the CMS could still look upon Kasagama's authority as their trump card in Toro.[50] It is therefore not surprising that a new round of discussions on these familiar themes was begun in 1899, with a view to improving the Catholic position. Mwenge was again the immediate bone of contention. The Catholic missionary there complained that the Protestant negligence of Catholics had recently taken on greater proportions following the influx of Protestant Baganda into the county.[51] Father Achte, now stationed in the capital, raised the issue with the Commissioner, saying that nothing had changed since 1896. In fact, things had become even worse for the Catholics. His complaint was still directed against the CMS missionaries, and in particular against Kasagama, who was continually harassing the Catholics, whom he considered to be rebels. But it is significant that Achte this time did not demand the right to religious liberty. Instead, he suggested the introduction of the Buganda system with two Katikiros, one for each of the Christian groups. This would reduce Kasagama's abuse of power and provide reasonable protection for the Catholics.[52] We may deduce from this suggestion that Achte no longer believed that a colonial policy based on the principle of religious liberty would work; it was more important to secure a platform for the Catholics close to the centre of power in Toro.

The response of the colonial administration followed the same lines as in 1896, and had the same inconclusive result. The main responsibility for the politicization of religion in Toro was placed with the missionaries and the Omukama. Colonel Ternan, who was Acting Commissioner, therefore took immediate action and impressed on the Catholic mission that it was highly undesirable to revive the old idea 'that the Missionaries are considered the authorized spokesmen on political and judicial matters as well as on those of a purely spiritual character'.[53] When one of the Catholic missionaries apparently could not adapt himself to this ruling, the Commissioner took the unusual step of asking for his removal,[54] which parallelled the frequently expressed concern over the Protestant Fisher's activities in Toro.[55] As regards Kasagama and his treatment of the Catholics, it is significant that the Commissioner did not comment on the proposal to appoint a Catholic Katikiro. To solve the problem of the Omukama's admitted partisanship he suggested, just as he had done in 1896, that the Sub-Commissioner in Toro exercise much more direct rule, even if it meant that Kasagama's influence became little more than nominal. After a time, people of all denominations would then consider the colonial Resident 'as their supreme chief'.[56] The Commissioner was thus prepared to dispense with the local ruler, and this would probably have been the only way to reduce the politicization of religion and secure a reasonable position for the Catholics within the Toro power structure. But the local colonial officer objected to such a drastic move, saying that he was quite satisfied with Kasagama's administration of the country.[57] This meant that in the end things were allowed to go on much as before. It was after all most convenient for the colonial administration to have a strong central authority.[58] The Catholics were considered to be a minority group whose interests the government was obliged to safeguard,[59] but the Protestant monopoly of political power would not be broken to improve the lot of the Catholics.

This state of affairs was given some legitimacy when Sir Harry Johnston, without much consultation, hurried through the Toro Agreement of June 1900.[60] This was a simplified and much shorter version of the Uganda Agreement, and gave the Toro confederacy and the Omukamaship statutory authority. It differed from the Uganda Agreement in that nothing was said about religion, but the Protestant ascendancy was thereby implicitly given legal status. Apart from the Omukama, the Katikiro and other leaders at ministerial level, three out of five county chiefs who were confirmed in their offices and received private as well as official estates, were Protestants; two were Catholics, but one of them had not reached his majority, and his post was in the meantime held by a staunch Protestant.[61] As regards the eight sub-chiefs, who were mentioned as receivers of ten square miles each,[62] four were Protestants, two Traditionalists, and two were Catholics. The dominant position of the Protestant ruling hierarchy was further emphasized by the fact that the leading chiefs were allowed to nominate their successors; office was thus hereditary rather than appointive. This could only serve to cement the Protestant dominance and make it difficult for the Catholics to improve their position. Similarly, the Catholic element in the chiefly hierarchy can be explained to a great extent by hereditary claims to office in the federated counties.

The latter factor kept secessionist tendencies alive within the Toro confederacy even after the signing of the Agreement, and also had the effect that Kasagama tended to pursue a policy of Protestant monopoly. Hence the Catholics still found sufficient reason to complain, in spite of the fact that Sir Harry Johnston had been at pains to impress on them the need to stop their agitation and to accept Kasagama as the ruler of Toro and as a Protestant.[63] But Kasagama's partisanship became so outspoken that the the colonial administration in June 1903 revived an earlier proposal and appointed a special Katikiro to take care of Catholic interests.[64] Kasagama retaliated by working to gain full control of Toro and to change the power relations between himself and the county chiefs. In this campaign he was, as we shall see later, supported by the CMS mission which once again stood for a strong monarchy. Finally, in 1906, the Agreement was amended in accordance with the wishes of Kasagama and the CMS so that the Kingdom became highly centralized under the now strengthened Omukama. The Protestant ascendancy became even more marked with its stranglehold on the chiefly offices and the Rukurato (Lukiko). The number of Catholic county chiefs had been reduced to one by the next year.[65]

Having examined a decade of developments in the Kingdom of Toro, we may conclude that religion was here a factor of great political significance. Christian factionalism was involved in most political activities, and Protestantism had to a great extent become ingrained in the political structure. In spite of its proclamation of religious liberty, and its attempt to use this concept as a means of depoliticizing religion, the colonial administration in the end had to accept a situation which, if less formalized, was similar to the one in Buganda. Although Toro exhibited some special features of its own, it is none the less possible to point out some general factors which account for the extension of missionary rivalry beyond Buganda, and for the government's failure to neutralize this rivalry's wider political consequences.

First, the missions themselves were instrumental in exporting religious factionalism to other areas. The competition between them was enough to create two polar forces within the societies concerned, and this bipolar division was transferred to the political field, as the chiefs were considered to be essential for the progress of the whole enterprise, especially as regards permission to start work, land grants and labour services. As long as the chiefs or other local authorities were the objects of the missions' efforts, there was an inevitable spillover effect into the political arena. This would even have been the case in non-centralized societies, and with offices whose authority was rooted in the colonial system rather than in traditional loyalties.

Secondly, African societies were not geared to the toleration of religious pluralism, which represented a challenge to the traditional system of authority. The missionary presence meant a new source of authority which it was important either to associate with or to exclude from political power. In addition, an individualistic principle like religious liberty tended to erode the traditional network of loyalties and the clientage system, even in small-scale societies. Hence the Africans tended to favour one religion through which they could monopolize the advantages created by the colonial system for the dominant religion's adherents, while people of a different persuasion appeared as opponents. Thus one particular religion became the means of supporting and reinforcing traditional authority.

Thirdly, the colonial administration's policy suffered from certain inherent contradictions which hampered its efforts to neutralize those forces which tended to combine religious and political affiliations. Adherence to the principle of missionary freedom, which inevitably left the way open for religious stratification and a binary division of the societies, presupposed that religious affiliation was a personal or individual matter, and as such was of no political significance. But when the colonial administration at the same time gave priority to the continued functioning of traditional institutions, and utilized customary structures of authority, it was not in the government's own interests to implement the principle of religious liberty effectively, as such an implementation would have undermined these very structures. The contradiction in government policy is further put into perspective if we consider how the government transferred the Buganda concept of chieftainship to non-Ganda areas, and even used Ganda personnel, thus implicitly paving the way for the links between religious affiliation and office-holding. It was therefore a natural consequence that the colonial government was more concerned in its practical policy with the problem of ensuring sufficient minority rights for the Catholics to give it the appearance of neutrality than with any real implementation of religious liberty.

PART III

The material basis of church–state relations: land grants and labour services

The land and labour question involved political leaders at all levels

8 Winston Churchill, Parliamentary Under-Secretary for the Colonies, with the Governor, the Kabaka and Ganda chiefs at a welcoming ceremony, 1907

9 The four kings of the Protectorate and their leading ministers, 1908. Sitting from left to right: the Omukama of Bunyoro, Andereya Duhaga; the Kabaka of Buganda, Daudi Chwa (behind him the Katikiro, Sir Apolo Kagwa); the Omugabe of Ankole, Kahaya II (behind him the Enganzi, Nuwa Mbaguta); the Omukama of Toro, Daudi Kasagama

9
Mission and church land: introduction

The analysis of developments in the 1890s has allowed us to suggest the main features of the relations between church and state. We have seen that the Christian institutions performed a number of roles *vis-à-vis* the political structures, but the exact nature of these roles has not yet been specified. Two aspects of the early colonial system pointed out by F. G. Bailey[1] are relevant here. First, we have a situation where the Christian institutions represented the only organizational structure outside the political sphere proper. This meant that relations between the Christian and the political institutions assumed a special significance, and further that some degree of rivalry could easily develop between the two sides, due to a lack of mutual consent as to their respective areas of influence and activity and disagreement on the proper position of the churches in society. This problem is further put into perspective by Bailey's second point. The transactions between the two sides were conducted in accordance with pragmatic rules. This means that the actors were mainly guided by whatever served their purpose best, in the absence of normative rules of behaviour drawn up on the basis of a procedural consensus. Such normative rules were necessary if the element of rivalry was to be neutralized and a regular pattern of interaction developed.

These two aspects of the early colonial situation provide us with a point of departure for the analysis of the following period. Here the material basis of the church–state relationship presents a field where the transactions between the two spheres were numerous and where the type of relationship which developed between them can most easily be examined. The results of the survey of the formative period suggest that this relationship will in particular be measurable within the interrelated fields of land grants and labour services.

During the first two decades of the twentieth century the interpretation and implementation of the Uganda Agreement of 1900 was one of the major issues in relations between the colonial administration and the Kingdom of Buganda. Given their own contribution to the conclusion of the Agreement, it is not surprising that the local CMS leaders took great interest in this matter. When Sir Harry

Johnston's successor as Commissioner, Colonel Hayes Sadler, who had taken over in 1902, asked for the CMS's opinion of the administrative system as it now stood, Archdeacon Walker warned against any change in the Agreement, and strongly emphasized its finality. Commenting on the Commissioner's concern over discontent among the sub-chiefs, who felt themselves to be unfairly treated in comparison with the higher echelons, Walker made light of their grumbling, thus indirectly confirming the mission's alliance with the new chiefly aristocracy, with its power base in the recently-acquired mailo land.[2]

Besides these political considerations, the CMS had its own share in the mailo land, and therefore had a vested interest in stressing the finality of the Agreement. On the other hand, both the CMS and the Baganda experienced great difficulty in putting Johnston's hastily drawn-up, though in effect revolutionary, land settlement into practice. One issue which had far-reaching implications for the future work of the mission and the church was the geographical location of the mission land. When Johnston allocated 40 square miles to the CMS under the Uganda Agreement he made it clear that it represented a once-and-for-all block grant, and that the area where the land could be chosen covered not only Buganda, but the three western kingdoms (Ankole, Toro and Bunyoro) and the area to the east, Busoga. These were regions in which the CMS mission had begun to work, and which in one way or another had been brought under colonial control.[3] Johnston's ruling thus had the peculiar effect that a clause in a treaty concluded with Buganda alone was considered valid for areas outside Buganda, even to the extent that it was being employed in the disposal of land outside the control of the signatories.

The question of the Agreement land became even more confused in the light of two subsequent developments. First, when Bishop Tucker, a year later than the conclusion of the Agreement, was permitted by the administration, in order to establish a position of equity with the two Catholic missions, to buy at a nominal price a further 12 square miles, Johnston specifically tied this latter grant to the four non-Ganda districts mentioned above.[4] Secondly, a further extension of the area which could be granted as mission land was demanded in 1903, when the CMS asked for one square mile in the newly-occupied Bukedi territory in the eastern part of the Protectorate, giving as their reason that they had taken up all the square miles allotted to them by Johnston in Buganda.[5]

What was meant to be a final settlement of the land question turned out instead to be the beginning of a complicated process of fixing the extent of mission land and its location in the Protectorate. The colonial authorities were inclined to take the stance that, in accordance with Johnston's intentions, the 40 plus the 12 square miles constituted a block grant covering the whole Protectorate as defined by its recognized frontiers.[6] The three missions appear during the first decade more or less consciously to have worked in accordance with this interpretation and to have taken freehold sites outside as well as inside Buganda.[7] Only when the growth of the work, combined with the overall economic growth in the country, increased the competition for land available within the Bantu areas, and when the missions really began to work in the newly opened areas in the north and east, did they feel the need to define what was meant by 'Agreement land',[8] especially as the opening up of new areas coincided with a more restrictive policy on the part of the administration towards new requests for land. From about 1915 the CMS thus took the line that the stipulation of 52 square miles of freehold land was valid for 'Agreement areas', that is, the four kingdoms. Accordingly they considered the

Anglican work to be entitled to 'a fresh concession of land' of not less than ten square miles in the newly opened areas.[9]

The colonial authorities refrained as long as possible from sorting out whether the freehold land granted to the mission under the Uganda Agreement was inside or outside Buganda. For a time the issue was avoided, as the government permitted another 15 square miles to be added to the block grant already held by each of the missions, provided that they were taken up mainly on commercial terms (see below).[10] The practice of allocating Agreement land on a Protectorate-wide basis, yet still relying on a legal arrangement which only covered one part of the Protectorate, backfired in the long run. The concept of individual ownership which Johnston had introduced into Buganda was with a few exceptions not extended into the neighbouring areas, and in particular not into the non-Bantu areas. This meant that it was difficult to find out what was meant by a grant of freehold land outside Buganda, and to specify on what terms any new land could be acquired, especially in the case of gifts of land from the chiefs.[11]

It was only when the Ganda leaders themselves, in 1922–3, brought up the matter in their concern for the preservation of the original Agreement that it was settled. The solution was then arrived at almost by accident. The Kabaka and his chiefs expressed their strong disapproval to the Bishop of the fact that he was letting the Agreement cover more than its own wording implied, and they argued that the 40 square miles which they had granted to the church were originally for the sole use of the church within the Buganda boundaries. The Bishop agreed with the Ganda leaders, and the Land Officer conceded that they had a reasonable case. On the basis of an estimate of the land titles already granted to the church, however, it turned out that church land within Uganda made up practically 40 square miles. This meant that the colonial administration – without any initiation of deliberate policy – could allay any fears which the Ganda leaders had had in this respect.[12] Thus the Uganda Agreement had not in fact been especially final, as the two European agencies involved had chosen to let one of its clauses also be valid in non-Ganda areas. This in turn made the question of mission land part and parcel of the major problem of defining the relationship between Buganda and the rest of the Protectorate. The latter was a problem which also for other reasons exercised the colonial administration and the mission during the first quarter of the century – and for that matter right up to the emergence of an independent Uganda.[13]

The second issue which created difficulties with regard to church land was the Agreement's provision that land granted to the missions was to be considered 'private property'. It was then left to others to establish an interpretation of 'private property' in the Ugandan context, and to determine which rights and privileges went with the land, and in particular whether rights over people on the land were included, in accordance with the traditional system. A partial answer to these questions was provided by the Certificate of Claim which was issued to the missions in granting them 'an Estate in Fee Simple'. Two features emerged from this document and the subsequent Buganda Land Law of 1908. The first, as H. W. West has clearly pointed out, was that a distinction was soon drawn between mailo land, solely owned by Africans, and specific freehold grants mainly given to non-Africans.[14] Now the missions were placed in the same category as other non-African allottees, as their land grants were classified as freehold, not as mailo, land.[15] Thus Johnston's policy of granting land to the European mission and not to the African church had been fully implemented, which meant that the CMS mission was faced with ever-greater difficulties in convincing both African and colonial leaders that land granted for church purposes was African-owned, and not alienated.

Secondly, the Certificate of Claim placed certain restrictions on the use of the freehold land. In the case of abandonment by the mission, the land must be forfeited to the colonial government. It must not be sold, leased or sub-let without the consent of the Governor, and, most important of all, it must not be used without permission for any other purposes other than those 'directly connected with the religious and educational work of the Mission'.[16] The latter part of the restriction was however not much different from the conditions attached to gifts of land before 1900. It soon became a subject of discussion how usufruct of the land should be defined in order to comply with the last sentence in the Certificate of Claim. Did it only cover building sites for churches or schools and the growing of food for the staff, or was the endowment meant to be revenue-producing?[17] In the latter case it was further open to question whether church land could have rent-paying tenants, and whether traditional obligations to the chief, including labour services, were transferred to the church.[18]

Thus the mission was a party to the process of developing an overall concept of ownership which had been left open by the Agreement. This turned out to be of vital importance for the future of the whole missionary effort, of which land constituted an economic cornerstone. At the same time the mission was unavoidably caught up in frictions caused by the incompatibility of the traditional rights accompanying disposal over land and the demands connected with the newly introduced European concept of land ownership. These two major issues, singled out for their relevance to the land question in the post-Agreement period, show clearly that the problem of church land was far from having been solved by Johnston's moves to reach a final settlement. To answer the questions raised by these two introductory issues, the problem may be systematized under three major headings: the mission's demands for more land and the administration's response to these demands; the nature of landholding (the rights and privileges connected with church land); and the question of usufructuary rights to tenant labour.

10

Mission land demands: the government response

Developments up to 1914

The CMS mission spent most of the first decade after the conclusion of the Uganda Agreement securing their sites in the various districts where they had already started working. Meanwhile the colonial administration started on the major operation of surveying all the plots which had been taken over by the large group of people entitled to mailo or freehold land.[1] To cope with the introduction of the new system of landholding, and more generally to put the Protectorate on a proper administrative footing, certain statutory measures were introduced. A major aim of these measures was some degree of uniformity in the land tenure system.[2] An early result was the Crown Land Ordinance of 1903, later amended several times, which was meant to cover the areas now vested in the colonial administration. Another outcome was the Buganda Land Law of 1908 which, as already pointed out, further defined the mailo system.[3] Several similar attempts were made to pass legislation for the remaining parts of the Protectorate, but in spite of the setting up of seven different commissions in the period 1906–19[4] the matter was not settled in the period under survey here. This meant that different landholding practices were allowed to prevail in the various districts, a situation which left loopholes which could be exploited by the missions. Another effect was that the vexed problem of the extension of the mailo system to other parts of the Protectorate continued to rear its head. This lack of results was, however, due not only to factors originating in Uganda, but was closely connected with the overall British colonial policy on the future of the East African colonies. Should they be settlers' areas, or should they be developed in the interests of 'the natives'? Without pursuing this issue further,[5] the significant consequence for Uganda was that the land settlement problem became closely linked with the similar issue in the East African Protectorate (later Kenya).[6] One observation to be made concerning this linkage is that the Colonial Office – which according to our earlier established terminology belonged to the European arena – was much more involved in the policy-making process than hitherto, as for instance when Johnston had concluded the Agreement with the Baganda leaders in 1900. The land question became one of the major issues in the drawing up of overall colonial policy and could not as such be delegated to local representatives of the colonial bureaucracy. The involvement of London was further reinforced by the nature of formal procedures, as most legislative measures were sent to the Colonial Office for approval before coming into force.[7]

During this phase, while the authorities were establishing a proper administrative system and endeavouring to bring the outlying districts under Protectorate rule, the missions were largely engaged in taking possession of the landholdings granted to them under the Agreement, and in securing a firmer foothold in the newly opened districts. At this stage they could count on a relatively lenient attitude from the colonial authorities as regards the number of sites they acquired and their acreage. The officials appeared to be more concerned with the number of yards between the sites of two competing missions, as they wished to forestall too many outbursts of friction or open rivalry.[8]

A gradual change in this pattern became noticeable from about 1910 onwards. First of all, the administration now had to implement its own legislation, and the officials had the necessary legal instruments at hand.[9] Further spurs to action were requests from the Colonial Office for closer scrutiny of the alienation of land; and here the activities of the missions were the most obvious targets, because of their constant demands for land in the recently opened areas.[10] Thus the question gradually arose of how to fix a ceiling to the acreage allotted to the missions in the Protectorate as a whole, and of how to deal with this whole problem while adhering to the guidelines laid down by Johnston in the Agreement.

This more stringent line coincided with moves within the CMS mission to initiate a more active policy with regard to church lands. Over the years the question had been raised of what to do with the valuable land that the church had acquired and how to make it pay.[11] As time went on the need for funds was felt more and more acutely, especially as the disparity between the salary scale in the church's employment and in government service was growing apace and causing a severe manpower drain on the church.[12] As the collections, one of the two previous sources of income, were stagnating, the mission had to concentrate on the second one, its landholdings, if it wanted to make any progress towards the realization of its ideal of self-support.[13]

At this stage, after the first decade of the twentieth century, the outlook for economic development seemed brighter than it had done for a long time. It had been shown, especially by the planters who had taken large holdings of Crown land, that land could be made profitable by growing coffee, cotton and possibly cocoa and rubber on a large scale.[14] Inspired by this successful enterprise, one of the missionaries drew up a scheme for coffee-growing involving the purchase of 800 acres for the church in Bunyoro.[15] This scheme for 'Church Land Development' gained enthusiastic support within the Uganda mission. A detailed timetable for its realization, allowing for a loan from the CMS in London in order to get it started, was drawn up; and there was general agreement that a means had presented itself of putting the church on the road towards self-support. It was even hoped that the church would now be able to pay for some of the European missionaries and thus relieve the CMS of some of its expenses. In addition the opportunities for training and education in such a scheme were emphasized.[16]

The necessary preliminary was that the colonial administration would consent to the purchase of the land, and that it would give its general approval of the perspectives inherent in this new departure in the use made of church land. Accordingly the mission filed an application with the colonial administration to lease an area in Bunyoro with the later option of purchasing it on freehold terms, all in accordance with the usual Crown land conditions.[17] In referring the application to the Colonial Office, the various officials in Uganda expressed warm support both for the educational effect of the actual skilled work involved in such a project and for the work of the mission in general.[18] The local administration was thus in broad sympathy with the developmental-cum-educational aspects of the proposed missionary move, even to the extent that it considered itself justified in relinquishing large tracts of Crown land irrespective of the ceiling on church land fixed by Johnston. There was a similar positive response when the White Fathers applied for land for plantations in 1911 and again in 1914.[19] The missions were clearly seen as vehicles for the furtherance of development in the Protectorate, and useful instruments in the plan to make it pay its own way.[20]

The new colonial policy of 1914

The Colonial Office itself was not so accommodating in the face of the CMS demands for a large estate in Bunyoro, especially as it was faced at the same time with a request for a block grant of ten square miles for the Muslim community, which had received no land under the Agreement;[21] and shortly afterwards there was an application from the White Fathers for a new mission station.[22] The Colonial Office soon came to the conclusion that it was time to work out an overall policy on land grants to missions and religious communities in general; otherwise, it was said, 'if we do not keep an eye on these religious acquisitions, we shall have to have a Mortmain Statute before long'.[23]

In view of the apparent difficulty of coming to grips with the problem of mission landholding as it had developed over the years, the Colonial Office's first move was to ask for more detailed information about the amount of land held by the three missions and other religious communities, the terms and conditions under which it was held, and whether it was used for agricultural purposes or for religious and educational purposes. It was also made clear that the Secretary of State was not inclined to agree to any further grants or leases before he was assured that proper use had been made of the areas already in the possession of the missions; a point which reflected suspicions in the Colonial Office as to whether the CMS had been able to employ usefully the large areas it already held.[24] The Colonial Office also appears to have decided that the CMS had been the object of special and favourable consideration over the years.[25]

In response to the investigative feelers coming from the Colonial Office, the trustees of the Native Anglican Church (the Bishop and two senior missionaries) composed a detailed answer which provided the required information, and stated their case as far as the holding of land was concerned. As this answer turned out to be a document of considerable importance when the Colonial Office framed its general policy on mission land, its contents will be summarized here.[26] The administration's response to it affords us the first real possibility of discerning the British government's fundamental attitude to the missions and their place in the colonial system in Uganda.

In their return the trustees were at pains to show that good use had been made of all the land so far obtained.[27] A small part had recently been set aside for plantation (with coffee), the profits going to the upkeep of the church; another similar part was used for agricultural training; the bulk of the land, however, was divided into small estates of 5–7 acres, containing churches and houses and supplying food for teachers and clergy (that is, it was under native cultivation). It was emphasized that severe restrictions had been placed on the land obtained in freehold, which meant that it could not be used or disposed of for any purposes other than religious or educational ones without the consent of the colonial government.

As regards the amount of land so far obtained, it was made clear that, apart from Agreement land, which amounted to 52 square miles in all, the CMS had only acquired an additional two square miles in freehold tenure since 1900, plus a few small leases. It was at the same time made abundantly clear that this was quite insufficient, taking into account the growth of the work and the opening up of new districts. Permission was therefore asked to acquire more and better land. It was at the same time specified that it could be either on special terms (as a government grant free of charge) or, if that was not possible, on ordinary commercial terms. This drew a distinction between land obtained on special conditions and for special purposes, and land without any restrictions on its use and disposal. In both cases, however, it was to be freehold tenure.

The crucial point then was the strength of the arguments which had been advanced in support of these concessions from the state. First, the educational aspects of the work were pointed out, especially the necessity of supporting the teachers and providing facilities for agricultural training. Secondly, the revenue from the land would enable the church to pay its servants a decent salary and in effect make the church self-supporting; in this connection reference was made to the scheme of growing cash crops.

Both reasons, and especially the second, presupposed that the state owed certain obligations to the church which sprang not only from the direct assistance the church was offering the state, but also from the mission's expectations that the state should provide proper conditions for the existence and work of the church in propagating Christianity. It is striking how similar this line of argument from the CMS mission was to the discussion in connection with the land settlement in 1899–1900 (Chapter 6). Land was still the major economic asset, and the government had the authority to support the Christian effort by granting land. In justifying their land claims the CMS missionaries were again trying to move beyond the mission formula by referring both to their educational work, which was now linked with developmental aspects, and the need to assist the church in realizing the ideal of self-support. It remains to be seen whether the attitude of the colonial authorities had moved beyond Sir Harry Johnston's refusal to act on any other ground than the mission formula.

One way of putting the British government's attitude to the land claims from the various religious bodies into perspective is by examining initially the handling of the Muslim community's request for a grant of land for mosques and schools along the lines of the estates held by the Christian missions. The local officials supported the Muslim request on the basis of two arguments.[28] First, it was necessary to redress some of the imbalance between the Muslims and the Christians, as the former had not been allotted any land under the 1900 Agreement, in spite of their numbers and their support for the government in the preceding critical period; secondly, there was the more political consideration that a grant of 10 square miles (5 less than applied for) would serve to arrest the growing discontent of the Muslims and to secure their loyalty. No importance was attached to these arguments by the Colonial Office. As regards the first one, it was even contested that the Muslims in 1900 had the same rights to free land as the Christians, and it was suggested that it would be preferable to grant them land on leasehold terms only, although at a low rent.[29] In the end the Muslim community was given ten square miles as a free grant, but permission was only given by the government on the basis of a detailed specification of the real needs of the Muslim work and after the government had made sure that the 10 square miles represented a block once-and-for-all grant which covered the whole Protectorate, and not just Buganda. This was in order to avoid the kind of confusion which had arisen in the case of the Christian missions.[30]

What is striking in this procedure, besides a general tightening of control over land granted for religious purposes, is the fact that the formulation of an overall policy on such land was not guided by any principle of equality, despite the reasonableness of the Muslim case. The privileged position of the Christian communities was reaffirmed, and indirectly the assumption of a special relationship between the colonial state and the Christian missions, which underlay the CMS arguments, was confirmed. At this stage there was no attempt to revise the fundamentals worked out in the Uganda Agreement of 1900.

While the Colonial Office adopted without any apparent doubts this positive overall attitude in the formulation of the general policy on land to the Christian missions,[31] it had to consider, first, whether the government had not already been generous enough in its grants of free land, which amounted to direct support for the Christian effort. Secondly, whether the missions had made proper use of the land obtained, and were in a position to utilize further land. Thirdly, what role were the missions to play in the colonial framework in relation to the state?[32] It is evident how closely these three issues were related to the CMS arguments cited above.

Faced with the need to arrive at some definite conclusions and to present them in practical political terms, the Colonial Office reduced the issues to two: the fixing of a ceiling to the amount of land which could be owned by the missions and churches, so as to avoid land-grabbing; and the need for a ruling on the terms and conditions under which land could be held.[33] These issues were clearly reflected in the detailed policy lines laid down by the Colonial Office in May 1914.[34] Most important was the limitation of the total area held by each mission in trust for the churches. Leaving out Agreement land which in the case of the CMS amounted to 40 square miles plus 12 in freehold, each mission was to be allowed to acquire a further area of up to 10,000 acres (15.6 square miles), a figure fixed on the basis of the general ruling on the acquisition of Crown land.[35] This maximum amount covered leasehold and freehold combined, of which not more than 1,000 acres were to be freehold. With regard to the terms on which new land could be acquired within the required limits and the conditions under which it might be held, it was ruled that in new districts into which the missions admittedly had to extend their work, land might be granted on ordinary commercial terms and as leasehold, but could not as before qualify for ultimate freehold by purchase. In the districts where the missions already held land, but wanted to expand their activities, they must be able to prove that more land was really necessary and that they had made the best possible use of the land previously obtained; if so, a lease on commercial terms might be acquired: either a non-assignable lease, or alternatively an ordinary leasehold, if an area of equal value elsewhere was surrendered – some 'sacrifice' would have to be made in either case.[36]

An important point in the new policy was the restriction on freehold land. As the CMS mission already had more than 1,000 acres of Crown land in freehold this issue was closed, with the exception of the difficult question of gifts of land from chiefs. To cover these an extra portion of 591 acres was allowed. The exact amount was fixed on the basis of a rather strange calculation.[37] This new policy, which was fully worked out by the Colonial Office, came very much as a surprise to the local officials. It represented a strict tightening of surveillance over both the total area to be held and the conditions under which it might be held; this was especially true of the virtual ban on acquiring more freehold land. The government considered itself to have been generous both in the past in connection with Agreement land and in its provisions for the future, as it had allowed for 10,000 acres more to be held. In the case of the CMS this was an extension of approximately 30 per cent. This allowed expansion into new districts but fixed limits to the total area. The restrictions meant that there was now a ceiling for direct economic support, as the emphasis was from now on shifted to leasehold on commercial terms and away from free grants.

A second perspective appears when the ruling on mission land is seen against the background of the general land policy which was being worked out at about the same time. As we have already pointed out, the disposability of Crown land was a central issue in the consideration of the missions' requests for additional land; and the issue became even more central in the formulation of the overall land policy. Crown land was increasingly felt to be a major economic asset, which should not be disposed of lightly, for instance as freehold.[38] This policy was put into practice soon afterwards, in 1915, when the Colonial Secretary, to the surprise of local officials, vetoed the extension of the mailo system to districts outside Buganda, as such as extension would have meant a substantial reduction of Crown land.[39] Only a year later this was followed by the announcement that no more grants of freehold land would be made to non-Africans for the time being.[40] These two moves were clearly meant to forestall the alienation of too much land by granting it to non-Africans at the expense of African interests, and to maintain control over the future pattern of economic development in the Protectorate. It had to be decided whether there was to be a plantation economy directed by European planters or a peasant farming system run mainly by the Africans themselves.[41]

The handling of this matter by the Colonial Office provides no evidence that the problem of mission land was causally linked with these two major political moves. The relatively small amount of mission land involved appears to have made the question comparatively insignificant, an impression that is confirmed by the lack of importance attached to missionary enterprise in the field of agricultural development. But the ruling on mission land of 1914 with its abolition of freehold grants stands as an expression of a firmer line on the disposal of Crown land.[42] The later developments in overall land policy could only have the effect of emphasizing the obligation to grant lands to missions in accordance with the new guidelines, as will be seen from the practice of the succeeding years.[43]

One further point to be noticed in reviewing the new policy on mission land against the background of the overall land policy is that land granted for religious purposes was classified and dealt with as non-African land, and derived its legal status mainly from the Crown Land Ordinance, not from the Buganda Land Law of 1908, which covered the mailo land. This observation parallels the conclusion arrived at earlier in our analysis of the first land laws (p. 139). In spite of the renewed arguments which the CMS put to the Colonial Office in 1914,[44] the mission did not succeed in convincing the policy-makers that the land held in trust for the Native Anglican Church was neither European-owned nor alienated. By law both the total amount which could be held and the conditions under which it could be held were covered by the same clauses as the land held by non-Africans.[45]

The CMS mission had placed emphasis on the contribution to agricultural development it was making by starting plantations on a large scale. It is notable that this perspective was not taken into consideration by the Colonial Office when it was fixing the mission land ceiling. Not even the local officials' wholehearted support for the scheme seems to have made an impression. Nor were there any comments on the related argument that the agricultural development of church land would contribute to the self-support of the church. One way of explaining the first omission could well be that the Colonial Office attached little importance to any contribution which the church was in a position to make, and felt that this field was not the concern of the mission or the church. As regards the second issue of self-support, the absence of comment from the Colonial Office may simply have been due to the fact that it was no concern of the government whether the church became self-supporting or not. Self-support for the church would relieve the strain on the funds of the European mission rather than reduce the government's economic burden. These explanations of the government's response must remain hypothetical at this stage. However, as they have an important bearing on the nature of the relationship between state and mission it will be attempted to substantiate them during our discussion of the following period, when the new policies were implemented.

The implementation of the new land policy – a case-study from Busoga

An important element in the new ruling was that the requests of the missions for additional land in the districts outside Buganda might well be met, provided that certain conditions were fulfilled. It was, however, in these same areas that a final settlement of the land question was still pending. The problem was most acutely felt in the three kingdoms of Ankole, Toro and Bunyoro, and in the district of Busoga, where the land issue was a matter of great controversy between the colonial administration and the local rulers. Officially the authorities acted on the assumption that the whole country except Buganda was Crown land, and could accordingly be disposed of by the government. There was at the same time disagreement within the colonial administration on how native rights should be defined, and to what extent, if at all, the mailo system should be extended to these areas.[46] During these efforts to formulate a uniform policy on the land issue, which of course had important implications for the pattern of economic development and for the role of the Africans, the rulers of the three kingdoms and Busoga entertained certain expectations, and certain promises were even given to them.[47] But with the introduction of the new policy on mission land it was far from clear what actual rights the chiefs had to dispose of land and whether their grants to the missions were valid and could be officially recognized.

It was only to be expected that the CMS mission in particular, given its usual pattern of close cooperation with the chiefs everywhere, would be caught up in this muddled situation. The ruling from the Colonial Office had as its basic assumption that all land was Crown land and could be leased out only by the colonial authorities, while the CMS mission took the position that the chiefs had rights over land and could grant it at will, if not as freehold then as leasehold. Acting on these two different premises, and pending a clarification of the whole matter (which was to be drawn out for several years), it is not surprising that the granting of land continuously gave rise to controversy between the CMS mission and the local colonial authorities. The typical pattern was that the CMS claimed that they had taken possession of the permitted 10,000 acres and needed a fresh concession, while the colonial administration contested that the quota had been used up, and accused the mission of having taken possession of plots granted irregularly by chiefs and not registered in the proper way.[48] A retrospective assessment of the whole state of affairs after the 1914 ruling on mission land suggests that much groundwork in the local setting remained to be done before the new policy drawn up in London could begin to function properly.

The district of Busoga became to a great extent the centre of this controversy, and it was especially here that the new policy was put to the test, although the same problems could be found in other districts too. Before the introduction of colonial rule Busoga had never been a political unit, but had consisted of a congeries of small chieftainships, each under a hereditary chief who claimed an authority similar to that of the Kabaka of Buganda. A number of these chieftainships stood in a tributary relationship to Buganda. This tributary obligation was formally brought to an end with the Uganda Agreement of 1900, but no alternative agreement was concluded with the various chieftainships of Busoga, which more or less automatically became part of the Protectorate. The system of ownership of land was therefore unclarified.

The Busoga situation thus left wide scope for close contacts between the various chiefs and the missionaries of the CMS, and resulted in large grants of land to the mission. Acting on the belief that it was within the legal power of the chiefs to grant land as gifts in support of its work, the mission received in the period from 1900 to 1920 about 300 plots, covering an area of 15–20 square miles (or more than 10,000 acres).[49] The Bishop defended these large landholdings by referring to the tremendous growth of the mission's work in Busoga, and added that every plot was a voluntary gift presented without any pressure having been brought to bear on the chiefs.[50] The attention of the colonial officials had been drawn to the situation in Busoga, even before the arrival of the new regulations from London,[51] because the mission seemed to be more demanding here than anywhere else, and because there was great disparity between the actual landholdings and the number of square miles registered with the authorities. In fact, it turned out that less than three square miles were held by certificate of claim as Agreement land.[52] Before any action could be taken by the colonial administration, the detailed rules arrived from the Colonial Office.

Government officials had questioned both the mission's right to most of the plots, claiming that the chiefs had no legal rights to dispose of land, and the need for large plots. It was proposed that apart from the three square miles which had been registered as Agreement land the missions should only be allowed to hold land on lease, and that no plot should exceed five acres.[53] Bishop Willis refrained at this stage from any detailed discussion of the chiefs' rights to dispose of land, and simply suggested that it was in the power of the government to confirm the possession of the plots already used by the church in Busoga. As justification for such a government grant he pointed to the extensive educational work carried out by the church; as the financial situation precluded cash support, land was a reasonable substitute. As regards needs Willis stated bluntly, again invoking the educational argument, that 'without the land the maintenance of native schools becomes a virtual impossibility'. He demanded 'a definite grant in perpetuity' and added a third argument, familiar from the late 1890s and the Johnston period, that such a grant was made to the Native Church and did not in any way involve the alienation of land from African interests.[54]

Each of these arguments was dealt with in turn by the colonial administration over the following period. The Provincial Commissioner within whose region Busoga was situated concentrated in his comments mainly on the needs of the mission. Following the new policy lines, he maintained that the CMS mission had not made proper use of the three square miles so far registered and accordingly did not qualify for any more. Instead, in order to meet their immediate needs, they could acquire unregistered plots of not more than five acres, each of which was sufficient for a church or school building and the maintenance of a teacher.[55] In order to justify this line of argument it was necessary to define what was meant by the proper use of mission land, and this in turn involved a definition of the real purpose of the church's holding land and a specification of the rights accompanying its possession. At this juncture the colonial administration confined itself to stating that proper use was made of a site if it contained a church and a school and provided for a teacher and caretakers for the buildings.[56] Whether this was conceived of as a minimum or a maximum requirement was left open.

Although the government had now brought to light the mission's excessive landholdings in Busoga and pointed out that the legal basis for holding them was doubtful in more than one respect (the Land Officer even claimed that they were rendered invalid by not being registered),[57] no action was taken to rectify the situation. The mission therefore continued to hold the sites given them by the chiefs. Later, as if nothing had happened, the mission again asked on behalf of the church to have the sites in Busoga and other areas legally recognized, apparently in the expectation that in spite of the ruling from the Colonial Office to the contrary they could have them confirmed as freehold.[58] This request was in fact the sequel to a joint action by all three missions. At the first educational conference ever held in Uganda with representatives from both administration and missions in 1917 the missions had asked for a block grant of land in the areas outside Buganda for which no provision had been included in the Agreement.[59] In commenting on these requests a limit of 10,000 acres was quoted by the Land Officer, but no action was taken to make sure that the missions adhered to the rule.[60] Instead it was admitted that the educational argument brought up at the conference (that in view of the lack of cash funds the government should support educational work by way of land grants), might carry some weight. Such a link between education and land was seen as a means of tackling the land problem and possibly of superseding the rules from 1914. But the matter had to be referred to the Colonial Office in order to safeguard those involved from any formal violation of these rules at the outset.[61]

With the value of the educational argument still awaiting assessment, the next round in the controversy came in 1919 when the question of alienation became the dominant issue. In connection with an agreement to exchange land with the administration[62] the CMS mission chose to have some of the estates already granted by chiefs registered. After having investigated the selected sites the District Commissioner for Busoga reported that in all cases a substantial number of tenants would be affected, and that this factor indeed seemed to have been a major criterion for selection. As the chiefs in question were also expressing some discontent, the District Commissioner concluded that there was a gross case of alienation, and recommended that the mission should be asked to choose sites in the large, uninhabited area of Busoga. Anticipating the familiar argument that the land would be held in trust for the Native Church, which was an African institution, he added: 'this I consider is a verbal quibble which leaves the Basoga supremely uninterested'.[63] The Land Officer acted on the recommendation of the DC of Busoga, in that he agreed that alienation occurred when peasants were sequestered from the authority of their chief, and in various other ways were affected unduly by the transfer of the land on which they had settled. He further pointed out that such alienation ran counter to the British government's position on the disposal of Crown land from 1916 onwards[64] as so many people would be affected.[65]

Bishop Willis took exception to this use of the term alienation, and pointed out four characteristics of church land. First of all, the chiefs themselves had been instrumental in selecting the sites, and in many cases the gifts of land had been received years before. This, he considered, disposed of one of the DC's arguments. Secondly, all the land was held in trust for the Native Anglican Church, which meant that it was not European-owned. This was borne out by the fact that church land was under the management of committees in which the majority of the members were Africans. Thirdly, the estates were held for the sole purpose of 'native worship and native education'. Fourthly, 'There is no idea of evicting any tenant, but only a change of landlord from the native Chief to the Native Anglican Church.' The Bishop admitted that the sites had been deliberately selected to include the maximum number of tenants, as land without people would be of little value to the church.[66]

These arguments confirm that the CMS in Busoga had established a close cooperation with the chiefs, which had paid off in grants of land. We may thus surmise that the mission now had vested interests in the outcome of the overall land settlement, and would be especially anxious that the chiefs should not be the losers in the settlement, but should succeed in negotiating a Buganda-type solution. This is, however, a hypothesis which will have to be substantiated further.[67] Secondly, by putting so much emphasis on the tenants and their essential contribution to the value of the land the mission was coming close to the traditional African concept of land ownership: ruling over people. Chiefly rights over tenants were being claimed, and a concept of mission landholding was being employed which differed radically from the one employed by the colonial administration. These two conflicting views account to a great extent for the differing outlooks on the nature of alienation. As they also had some bearing on the larger problem of the status of mission land they will be taken up again in the next chapter.

So far we have seen that the CMS mission contested the accusation of causing alienation largely with arguments of a utilitarian type – the work was exclusively for the benefit of Africans – and by presenting the church as an African institution. The colonial administration was much less consistent in its arguments, since the accusation of causing alienation was related to the still unsolved problems of future landownership and the future position of the chiefs in connection with land. In any case the Land Officer backed down somewhat from his position on the sites selected in Busoga and more accommodatingly recommended that the administration agree to the CMS proposals, giving as his grounds that the mission had agreed to surrender valuable land in exchange in Busoga's most important town and administrative centre.[68] The result was that the mission succeeded in having one square mile registered as freehold land; but because of the special circumstances no precedent was considered to have been established and no principles violated. In particular the question of the chiefs' right of disposal was left in abeyance.

The evidence from Busoga leads to the conclusion that the colonial administration in the latter half of the 1910s was clearly shying away from implementing the 1914 policy on mission land, even to the extent that no attempt was made to reduce the landholdings in accordance with the upper limit fixed by the Colonial Office. It points also to a possible explanation of this *laissez-faire* attitude. The colonial administration lacked sufficient legal grounds for action because the problem of mission land still awaited solution in accordance with the principles laid down for an overall land settlement for the non-Ganda areas. The issue could not be isolated, as is evident from the complications connected with the chiefs' rights. This is confirmed by the contemporary comments of a leading colonial official with regard to Busoga. F. Spire, Provincial Commissioner of the Eastern Province, in commenting on one of the numerous commission reports suggesting the extension of the mailo system to the rest of the Protectorate, said 'that the legal position of land in Busoga has never been defined'. As a first step he therefore suggested a declaration making all land Crown land, which naturally precluded the introduction of the mailo system.[69] The Acting Governor found his view of the situation exaggerated, but admitted that the Crown Land Ordinance was not at all clear, and needed a thorough overhaul.[70] When he suggested the measure, Spire pointed out that it could be done without difficulty as there was no concept of private ownership in Busoga. A chief did not own any land: 'He owns the people rather than the land . . .' But to avoid any sudden upheavals caused by the breaking of the existing feudal ties and the consequent weakening of the chiefs' authority he recommended that there should be a very gradual and cautious process of change with little or no interference in the prevailing functioning of the land system.

These two types of argument, the legal one and the pragmatic one, offer a sufficient explanation of the state of affairs in Busoga as regards mission land. As long as the problem of Crown land versus mailo land had not been solved (and this was a precondition for a workable general land policy), interference with the chiefs' position and rights to dispose of land should be avoided. During such a period of suspension the mission could still claim the so-called 'given land' as the property of the church, on the assumption that a chief still had the authority to transfer his chiefly rights over land to the church for the benefit of his own people, and that such gifts would ultimately qualify as freehold land on the Buganda model.

In addition to the administration's hesitation in fully implementing the 1914 policy, it appears that some of the officials on the spot, with their knowledge of local conditions, had difficulty in understanding and complying with the new regulations. This was especially true of the provision which stated that if a freehold site was surrendered in exchange for another site, the mission only qualified for leasehold on the new site, not for an equal area of freehold Crown land. Some officials even thought that this provision was downright unfair to the missions, and saw it as a hindrance to a final settlement, as it was unlikely that any mission would give up freehold tenure in exchange for leasehold.[71]

Judging from the situation in Busoga, it may be concluded that little of the 1914 policy had been put into practice. Although the Governor later pointed out that the administration had consistently adhered to the regulation prohibiting the granting of more Crown land in freehold,[72] we can also consider what might have been, but was not, done. The most striking feature is, then, that no limitation of the total area was actually enforced, nor were all the sites registered according to their categories. It was only in the most recently opened districts, situated mostly in the Northern Province, that some efforts were made to administrate using the new lines of policy; and this was in fact done primarily as a deliberate measure to guard against the same situation arising here as in the more established districts. It was hoped that laying down firm guidelines from the beginning would help to avoid the misappropriation of land by the missions.[73]

The missionary leaders themselves could hardly be expected to take much interest in the furtherance of the 1914 policy, and it is even doubtful whether they fully understood its implications. During this period they maintained a relatively low profile with regard to the overall land settlement, trusting that, whatever happened, they could hold on to the land gifts from the chiefs on one pretext or another. It was only when the administration finally settled for the Crown land formula instead of the mailo formula that things started to move towards a final settlement of the mission land issue.

The final settlement of the mission–land problem

After protracted discussions and several major changes in policy the pendulum swung in 1922 definitively towards the Crown land formula.[74] It was mainly the four Provincial Commissioners who were responsible for the final outcome,[75] and it is interesting to notice that their proposals followed closely the principles laid down by one of their predecessors, F. Spire, six years earlier.[76] In the proposals submitted to the Colonial Secretary it was definitely stated that it was inadvisable to introduce the mailo system to areas outside Buganda. Instead all land should be made Crown land held in trust for the African population in order to secure its future interests; only a small portion should be available for purposes which would involve alienation, such as leasing to non-Africans.[77] These proposals were approved, and were finally set out in an official statement by the Governor in late 1923.[78] Again the issue of mission land as such formed no part of the deliberations and had no bearing on the final outcome. On the other hand, the principles from the general settlement would inevitably be applied to the question of mission land, and did in fact open up possibilities for the solution of this protracted issue. It was only when the implementation stage was reached that colonial officials began to take in account the position of the missions, especially the CMS; for they realized that their influence with the chiefs, especially in Toro and Ankole, could be of great importance in smoothing the way for the new policies with the local leaders.[79]

Parallel with the adoption of the Crown land policy, the problem of the great number of unregistered plots occupied by the missions in ever-increasing numbers over the years became a matter of great importance, especially for the Provincial Commissioners, who wanted uniform rules for the whole Protectorate.[80] These rules were soon drawn up, and provided for a system whereby sites not exceeding five acres could be held on Temporary Occupation Licences (TOL), on the conditions that a rent was paid and that the sites were only used for the erection of schools and churches and for the growing of food for the teachers.[81] It was in the same memorandum made clear that, as the mailo system was never likely to be applied in Busoga or Bunyoro, all land would be considered as Crown land. Accordingly unregistered sites could only be held on TOL conditions (clauses 4 and 5).

In the confusion of the Busoga situation this was a severe blow to the Anglican work,[82] as the missionaries would have to surrender substantial areas. Bishop Willis intervened and sought clarification of the fundamental question of when and how land in Busoga had become Crown land, as this involved a nullification of chiefs' traditional rights over land.[83] The government stuck to its policy, and was especially adamant that the existence of the unregistered sites made the whole issue of mission land extremely complex and constituted a stumbling-block for a proper settlement in accordance with the 1914 policy.[84] In order to deal summarily with the very worst cases the administration simply cut all discussion short and in 1925 enforced an immediate surrender of all unregistered plots.[85]

The CMS mission protested in the strongest of terms that this step had a crippling effect on their work, both economically and because it suggested in the minds of the people 'that religion, in the thought of the Government, occupied a very unimportant place'.[86] It was impressed on the administration that the mission found its course of action and its claim to all land as Crown land quite unjustified, both because land was taken away 'after an undisputed possession in some cases of over 20 years',[87] and because the chiefs' rights to dispose of land were suddenly being denied them. This had aroused a great deal of ill-feeling. As regards the possible replacement of old, unregistered estates with five-acre sites held under Temporary Occupation Licences, these were considered insufficient, partly because they were considered too small to fulfil their stipulated purposes, and partly because they could not be an economic asset, since no tenants were allowed on them.[88] In spite of several approaches, the CMS's efforts met with no success; the government stood firm on the Crown land formula, which now provided the basis for the settlement of all land problems.[89] By 1926 the colonial authorities could report that the regularization of the holding of land by missions was well under way.[90]

Besides direct approaches to the colonial authorities in Uganda, two other courses of action were open to the CMS in its attempts to have the policy on mission land changed or revised. Both of them serve to illustrate the position of the mission within the state. Soon after the implementation of the 1914 policy was first begun, Bishop Willis made an attempt to have it revised, and this time he went directly to the Colonial Office, bypassing the colonial authorities in Uganda. His first point was related to the upper limit of 10,000 acres. As this limit had already been reached, he asked that additional grants be given in each district in accordance with the needs of the work. It is clear from the context that Willis in this way was trying to circumvent the necessity of accepting many more restricted plots under TOL conditions. He also asked for a revision of the clause which stated that in cases of exchange freehold land could only be exchanged for leasehold land. On the one hand he wanted the flexibility provided by the possibility of exchange; on the other he wanted to keep the original and much more favourable grant of freehold land intact. In support of his claims he placed heavy emphasis on the burden of the educational work which his own and other missions had undertaken; the annual grant from the government was quite inadequate for the purposes intended, but it was on the other hand within the power of the administration to improve this situation by granting sufficient land. In this respect he repeated once more that such land would not be mission property, but would belong to the church.[91]

When the Colonial Office duly consulted the Uganda administration on this matter it was strongly emphasized that the mission could only claim to have reached the limit of 10,000 acres if they included the unregistered sites, 'which have been acquired in a highly irregular manner from native chiefs whose title to give or sell land to the Mission had never been recognized by this Government'. It was pointed out that the most pressing need of the moment was to have missionary landholdings regularized, especially in Busoga, and that this could be done by following the provisions of the 1914 policy and by implementing the later practice of granting plots under TOLs.[92] The Colonial Office then made it clear that it was not prepared to modify the general policy on mission land laid down in 1914.[93] It further found that plots under TOL conditions provided for the desired flexibility in the work, especially as regards educational and religious work in new areas. It is, however, significant that the Colonial Office appears to have shown greater understanding of the mission's land requirements than the local administration did at that time. Concern was expressed that the mission work might be unduly hampered, and this concern was not confined to its educational aspects. Furthermore, the Colonial Office left open the possibility of future acquisition of extra land beyond the 10,000 acres, unrestricted by TOL conditions, provided a real need could be proved.[94] Nevertheless, Bishop Willis did not succeed in having the 1914 policy revised. The mission was still subject to strict surveillance of the total amount of land which it could hold, and any land outside the Agreement area had to be acquired on commercial terms. No extra grant was allowed to the missionary work, not even to the educational part of it, which meant that the unregistered sites would not be legalized.

The second – and supplementary – course of action which was available to the mission in its attempts to retain its landholdings undisturbed was by way of the chiefs. The acknowledgement of the chiefs' right to dispose of land would also mean an approval of their grants to the mission. It is therefore not surprising to learn that close contacts were established between the CMS mission and the chiefs, again most strikingly in Busoga, soon after it became known that the colonial government had settled for the Crown land option and ruled out the extension of the mailo system to areas outside Buganda. One of the chiefs' first actions was to persuade Bishop Willis to intervene with the Governor.[95] As he met with no success, the Busoga chiefs themselves approached the colonial authorities directly, with all due respect for the official ladder: first the Provincial Commissioner, then the Governor, and finally the Secretary of State.[96] During this whole campaign they kept Bishop Willis well informed and asked for his advice and assistance.[97]

The chiefs appear to have been fully aware that they and the mission had common interests in this matter. They saw the annulment of their land grants to the mission as an indication that they could not do as they liked 'with their own land'. But there was also a more subtle aspect to their concern as, according to one of the missionaries, 'the chiefs want to use the Church miles question as a lever in asserting their ownership of the land in opposition to the claims of the Government'.[98] It is significant that the CMS mission accepted both that they and the chiefs had common interests and that the chiefs expected them to play an active role in defending them. Bishop Willis clearly linked the question of church land with that of the chiefs' traditional rights and the broken promises of the administration.[99] Even when the colonial officials pointed out that they were attempting in their land policy to safeguard the interests of the great majority of peasants against the chiefly minority, and expressed the hope that the mission would take this factor into account,[100] Bishop Willis stood firmly by his alliance with the chiefs, and even made an attempt to mobilize public opinion in Britain.[101]

The colonial administration was alert to the reality of the alliance between the CMS mission and the chiefs. Even at the earliest stage, when the government first started to exercise closer control of mission lands, it was aware of 'a number of self-styled chiefs' only recognized by the missions.[102] Later, at the height of the conflict, Bishop Willis' interventions were characterized as representative of 'a body of non-native opinion' which had existed for a long time in support of the chiefs' claims on mailo land.[103] The Governor was even more outspoken when he interpreted a memorandum from Bishop Willis as proof that the Busoga chiefs were primarily urged on by the CMS.[104] In spite of this strongly expressed annoyance, the continued pressure from the CMS and the chiefs, combined with increasing doubts among officials about the fairness of their treatment of the Busoga chiefs,[105] had the effect that official estates were granted to some of the chiefs and private estates to some of the ruling families.[106] As already indicated, this move did not mean that the mission was allowed to maintain unregistered sites in contravention of the regulations laid down in the 1914 policy. The recent confirmation of that policy ensured strict control of gifts of land.[107]

The hypothesis suggested above that the CMS now had a vested interest in the system of mailo land being extended to areas outside Buganda has been confirmed. This was the primary motivation of its interventions with the administration in support of the chiefs, and a successful outcome would have meant the recognition of the gifts of land received over the years. Further, it is evident that the well-established alliance between the Protestant chiefs and the mission in Buganda was now being extended to non-Ganda areas. The parallel is close: we find the CMS intervening in support of the non-Ganda chiefs' rights over land, just as they did in the negotiations with Sir Harry Johnston, leading to the conclusion of the Uganda Agreement. The aim was similarly to preserve the chiefs' status and authority. This leads to a third point. Seen in the wider perspective, it was in the interests of the CMS to have the Buganda type of government extended to other districts as well in order to secure as many chiefs as possible for the Anglican persuasion. This ensured a basis for satisfactory working conditions, primarily in the form of land grants.

Summary and conclusions on the church–state relationship

On the basis of the foregoing we can identify six major themes, all of which touch on various aspects of the church–state relationship.

(1) During the post-Agreement period from 1900 until the mid-1920s a halt was called to the previous *laissez-faire* attitude, and there was a substantial tightening of the administration's policy on mission land involving closer control of missionary activities in this field. A limit was fixed to the total amount of land which any mission was allowed to hold, and the acquisition of more freehold land was virtually blocked. In addition a number of conditions and restrictions were attached to the land already held by the missions, and it was especially made clear that all land other than that which was held under the Agreement must be acquired on commercial terms. The new policy of 1914 thus became in effect an economic limit on indirect government support for missionary work given in the form of land. When the CMS made attempts to have the 1914 policy changed, both directly and indirectly through the chiefs, they met with no success. Only in cases where they were starting work in new areas did the mission obtain some concessions from the administration, but even here the land obtained was limited and controlled by the new practice of granting land under Temporary Occupation Licences. One reason for their lack of success was that the issue of mission land had to be dealt with in accordance with the principles laid down in the overall land policy. The mission land was thus placed in the same category as other non-native-owned land. Granted out of Crown land, it was held on Crown land terms and thus constituted direct state support to the Christian work. This meant that the mission's repeated argument that there was no alienation, as the church and hence the Africans owned the land, did not have much weight. In spite of tighter rules and stricter control the administration considered itself to be acting in a positive and benevolent way: 'the missions, as estate owners, have been very well treated in Uganda'.[108]

(2) In examining the administration's response to the reasons given by the Uganda mission for its requests for more land, it was observed earlier that virtually no attention was paid to the mission's new plan to engage itself in agricultural development; and it was suggested there that the mission was not considered by the Colonial Office to be an agency of any importance in that field. This hypothesis is confirmed by looking at the years after 1914. First of all, the local colonial administration, which had initially lent its enthusiastic support to the agricultural scheme, lost interest and became more concerned with limiting and registering mission land. In that connection there was also much discussion of how to define the proper use of mission land, and the developmental aspect was not mentioned in these considerations.

Secondly, a significant confirmation of this trend can be found in the setting up of the Uganda Development Commission just after the First World War, primarily in order to consider the future economic development of the Protectorate.[109] The Commission had as its members only representatives of the planters and the business community, besides administration officials; and the CMS noted with surprise and regret that there was no representation from the missions.[110] This meant that the missions were not considered indispensable either in their own capacity or on the basis of their knowledge of the Africans.

This exclusion should be contrasted with the contemporary setting up of the Educational Advisory Board, in which the missions naturally constituted the dominant element.[111]

The conclusion to be drawn is that the mission and the church were cut off from direct influence on and direct participation in the developmental sector when the administration began to take the initiative after the war, whereas greater importance was attached to their educational work. Extrapolating from this analysis, it may be said that the colonial administration in this way prescribed the areas of cooperation between church and state in secular matters, and drew a borderline beyond which it was not found necessary to take the advice of the mission. Although the chances of achieving self-support within the church and of introducing a proper salary for church personnel were closely linked with the mission's agricultural scheme, this kind of argument carried no weight with the administration. It did not consider that the relationship between mission and state was such that the authorities were placed under any obligation to grant large estates in the name of self-support for the church. In connection with the work of the Uganda Development Commission, it is clear that the CMS felt that for the first time it was being left out of the policy-making process. This may be taken as the start of a new post-war era in which the state would be more active in seizing the initiative, leaving less scope for missionary activity in societal matters.

The reduced role of the mission in the developmental sector cannot however be exclusively blamed on the official policy. At an early stage some scepticism was being expressed in CMS circles in London over the whole issue of land acquisition: 'Endowments of land would be useless, owing to the difficulty of making them pay.'[112] As regards the plans for agricultural development, increasingly doubts about the feasibility of such schemes were being voiced within the same circles. The CMS Industrial Missions Committee was not convinced that the plan for the development of church lands was sufficiently professional and businesslike, or that the missionaries possessed the requisite managerial skills.[113] Concern was also expressed that spiritual work and evangelical principles might suffer by being combined with such a secular pattern of work.[114] Eventually, the necessary flow of capital was not forthcoming, and the mission itself in the end renounced any direct operative function in the developmental sector. Instead the Uganda mission emphasized the need for the training of skilled workers, thus giving priority to its contribution within the educational sector.[115] This shift in attitude was significantly underlined in 1920 when it was stated that the church estates could only be developed and the church become self-supporting if trained Africans worked on the estates.[116] The church land was thus on the way towards a system of peasant production well before the colonial administration finally decided on the same course in its land policy, and priority was given to Africans instead of European planters and settlers.[117]

(3) While the importance of the mission's developmental contribution was thus dwindling, the educational argument in support of new land concessions assumed increasing significance. At the educational conference in 1917 it was first suggested that support for educational work might be given in the form of land, as no other means were available. This suggestion was most forcefully urged in 1923, when Bishop Willis approached the Colonial Office directly with a view to having the 1914 policy changed. Faced with this line of argument, the colonial authorities accepted educational work as a special sector qualifying for state support. But they did not consider that such support should take the form of land

concessions. In spite of the scarcity of resources, a direct grant, which would be easy to account for, would be earmarked for educational purposes. Thus the educational argument was not accepted as a sufficient reason for a shift in policy on mission land, nor was it taken into consideration in the framing of the policy. The influence of the educational sector on the relationship between church and state will therefore have to be examined in a context not directly connected with the granting of land for church purposes.

(4) To summarize, the colonial administration did not act upon the three arguments so far discussed (development, self-support, education). It was opposed to the possibility of the mission or the church becoming a great landowner. Furthermore, these three different standpoints were based on the assumption that the mission's right to hold land was a revenue-producing endowment. In view of the administration's response, it may be inferred that it hesitated to accept that mission lands in fact were so. Possibly a fundamental difference was appearing here between the mission's and the administration's concepts of landholding; but this new slant is best discussed in connection with the next chapter's analysis of the rights and privileges accompanying the mission's possession of land.

At this stage we can only conclude that the administration was acting on the basis of the most general of all the arguments produced by the mission: that land was granted for ordinary missionary work, or for what in the minutes of the administration was frequently termed 'educational, or educational and religious purposes'. This characteristically reflects the wording in the Certificate of Claim from the beginning of the century.[118] That this represents a basic principle in the policy on mission land is confirmed if we recall how the administration over the years defined the proper use of mission land: it should be divided into small plots of about five acres, large enough to maintain a teacher or catechist and to allow for the erection of a school or church.[119] This definition was not always applicable in the case of freehold land, but it was certainly applied in connection with the granting of land under Temporary Occupation Licences, and later in providing for the extension of the work to newly opened areas.

It is thus possible to arrive at the conclusion that the main principle behind the land policy was that the colonial authorities accepted their obligation to provide proper conditions for the ordinary missionary work in both its religious and educational aspects taken together. On the other hand, it was not part of the obligation to give continuous direct support to this activity in the form of land grants. In pursuing this policy the administration had hardly moved beyond the broad mission formula which had been the basic principle behind Sir Harry Johnston's settlement of the issue of mission land. Thus, during the period under survey (up to the middle of the 1920s), the colonial administration was acting on the premise that missionary work was useful and beneficial within the colonial setting, and aided the administration in fulfilling its aims. Once again the broad line of cooperation established at the Berlin Conference was confirmed. The administration might especially notice the missionary contribution in the field of education, but at the same time it drew no real distinction between the religious and the educational parts of the work as far as land requirements were concerned. A new departure occurred only when the administration demanded more supervision and closer control of the educational system from the lowest levels upwards, and introduced certain qualitative standards for educational work. Inevitably a distinction would have to be drawn between educational and religious activities, and it would be questioned whether land grants, especially those under TOLs, could be justified. Such a new departure would call into question whether the broad conception of missionary work could be maintained. This problem began to make itself felt at the beginning of the 1920s, when colonial officials began to question the standard of the educational work carried out by the missions and its close linkages with religious indoctrination.[120] We will return to this change of attitude below in a different context.

(5) When we focus our attention on the policy- and decision-making processes during the various phases in the history of the land issue, it is striking that the European arena exercised considerable influence. The tightening of the policy on mission land was sparked off by the home authorities, and the new policy of 1914 was entirely the result of deliberations within the Colonial Office, even to the extent that the local authorities were completely overruled. This increased involvement of the home authorities may partly be ascribed to the development of the colonial system with its increasingly bureaucratic structures, and partly to the fact that the land question in general became an issue in which the Colonial Office, because of the economic implications, took great interest.[121] More specifically, the issue of mission land was considered to be most important in the relationship between church and state, which again explains why the Colonial Office for the rest of the period under survey involved itself so closely in the implementation of the 1914 policy, often to the dismay of local officials, who felt themselves to be under too close scrutiny and accordingly asked for greater independence in dealing with mission land claims.[122]

Although a similar degree of control over policy-making cannot be found within the ecclesiastical ranks, it has been noticed that the CMS headquarters made its influence felt in Uganda. It was largely due to its attitude that the agricultural development scheme came to nothing. This specific case has some significance, as it illustrates how, when it came to manpower and resources, the parent institution could wield decisive influence by pulling important strings, in spite of there being a local episcopal authority which might normally be expected to deal with such cases. It is also notable that Bishop Willis deliberately bypassed the local colonial authorities in his direct approach to the Colonial Office, and on another occasion he tried to invoke the assistance of a British-based pressure group; the pattern of communication between the two sides which was characteristic of the formative period was still valid.

(6) The relations between the mission and the African political system will bear further examination. We have seen that the alliance between the CMS mission and the Protestant chiefs established earlier in Buganda also functioned in other areas in connection with the land problem, in particular in Busoga. The chiefs used the good offices of the missionaries to pursue their own goals. On the other hand, the CMS championed the chiefs' cause for reasons both of fairness and expediency, as the chiefs' land gifts were almost indispensable to the missionary enterprise. Thus what we have called the mission's first and second political roles at the turn of the century were still functioning.

But it is noticeable that the mission played these roles with less vigour and less success than it had done at the time of the conclusion of the Uganda Agreement. The leaders of the mission were no longer taken into the government's confidence when the overall land policy was being planned. When the colonial authorities finally settled for the Crown land formula there was hardly any platform left for missionary influence, and the mission had more than enough to do protecting its

own interests. One major explanatory factor here was certainly the more established state of the colonial system, backed up by more effective means of control
and the inclusion of the Colonial Office in policy- and decision-making. Neither
the mission nor the chiefs any longer had the same scope for exerting influence
and pressure.

The developments which we have observed in the handling of the land problem
are further evidenced by the patterns of communication which now emerged.
Negotiations over mission land were dealt with mainly through direct contacts
between the CMS Uganda mission and the colonial administration, while the
chiefs' role was only a minor one, despite the fact that one of the crucial issues was
the validity of the chiefs' gifts of land. This seems indicative of the curtailment of
the chiefs' authority: the African political system no longer had it within its power
to deliver essential benefits. Whether this conclusion is justified in the broader
perspective will emerge from our discussion of the issue of rights and privileges
connected with mission land, where the role of the chiefs will be more in focus.

It was mainly Europeans who took the initiative and represented the ecclesiastical point of view. Hardly anything was heard from African church leaders, and
hardly any approaches to the administration were channelled through church
bodies. The Bishop and the Secretary might think that they were acting in the
capacity of church leaders, but their colonial counterparts clearly conceived of
them as representing the mission.

11

The nature of landholding: rights and privileges connected with mission and church lands

The rights and privileges which accompanied the possession of land are of considerable importance, because the mission's main concern was how to turn the land into a major economic asset alongside voluntary contributions and bring the ideal of self-support close to realization.

So far the mission and church had worked in three ways in order to gain economic benefits from their landholdings: by keeping the expenses as low as possible, for example by acquiring the land on freehold terms; by regarding land as a revenue-producing endowment along European lines; and by using a concept of ownership involving elements of the pre-colonial African tradition, primarily the chiefly right to 'rule over people'. This of course emphasized the role of the tenants. While these ways of turning church land to account were not mutually exclusive, their realization was dependent on the colonial administration in the case of the European concept of landholding, and on the African political system where the status of church land and the possibility of alienation were at issue. Finally, there was a question which touched on a number of aspects of the land-holding problem: the position of tenants on church land. To what extent could the church enjoy usufructuary rights to tenant labour?

The profitability of land in European terms

During the first quarter of the twentieth century two demands in particular were addressed to the colonial authorities with a view to making church land a more profitable asset.

The issue of survey fees

As we have pointed out earlier, the land settlement established by the Uganda Agreement of 1900 sparked off a major surveying operation,[1] which brought home to the CMS missionaries in 1912 that the complete survey of all their sites would cost more than £3,000. When they brought the matter up with the authorities, their initial claim was that, as the church was not a European body but an African one, its estates ought to be classified as African-owned. This would qualify them for free survey, like the official estates of the Kabaka and chiefs.[2] Alternatively, if fees had to be paid, it should be taken into account that the bulk of the land was the property of Africans, not of the CMS, and should therefore not be subject to Crown-land charges. Either the same rates should be charged as for non-official African estates, or a special fee should be introduced. It was recalled that Sir Harry Johnston had in fact promised such a special low rate.[3]

In its handling of this request, the colonial administration ignored the question of whether the church was an African institution, and whether its landholdings should accordingly be categorized as African property instead of Crown land. When a substantial reduction was in fact granted it was solely because the administration felt itself under an obligation to honour Johnston's pledge. The usual charges for the actual survey work were waived and a nominal survey fee, varying according to the size of the estates, was charged.[4]

Yet the burden was still felt to be heavy, and the mission reopened the issue in the post-war period. This time they took a different approach. In the first place, it was maintained that survey fees were a serious burden on 'a struggling native church', whose income was so low that it was hardly able to pay a salary sufficient to cover the minimum needs of clergy and teachers. Secondly, the educational aspects of the work were emphasized. A large number of schools had been built all over the country at no expense to the colonial administration, and the teachers paid far more in poll tax than the official education grant covered. In this field the church contributed so much to the 'uplift and benefit of the whole country' that generous treatment in the question of survey fees was justified. The third argument served in a way to justify the two previous ones, as it dwelt upon the whole purpose of possessing land. The mission maintained that the land granted by Johnston under the Agreement was supposed to be an endowment in support of its work. This purpose, and thereby the spirit of Johnston's policy, was defeated by the imposition of survey fees.[5]

This time the colonial authorities were less inclined to look favourably upon the mission's request; but in the end they recommended a reduction which brought the fees down to the same level as those paid by African landowners under the Agreement.[6] It was not the first of the mission's arguments that influenced this decision. The administration was concerned neither with the African nature of the church, nor with its ideal of self-support: when faced with a request for even lower rates, it decided that the missions could not be charged less than the Africans.[7] The administration was even less interested in the third argument, claiming that land was an endowment which had to be honoured by the authorities. As the mission had been given the land free under the Agreement, it was only reasonable that it should pay for the survey.[8] It was even questionable what kind of endowment the land grant was supposed to be and, as will appear, this issue was also the subject of discussion in a different context.

What really swung the pendulum in favour of the mission in the end was the educational argument, although only after considerable disagreement among colonial officials. Some of them, and in particular the Director of Surveys, maintained that the question of survey fees was quite distinct from that of education, and that the proper course of action would be to increase the educational grant. Others, primarily Governor Coryndon, argued in favour of some reduction to the mission in appreciation of the fact that its educational contribution saved the administration a lot of money.[9] The final decision, however, established a linkage between land and education which seemed to constitute a deviation from the course otherwise followed since the days of Johnston. Before drawing any far-reaching conclusions, however, it will be appropriate to draw attention to three special circumstances. First, the reduction of the survey fees represented an indirect concession on a very limited scale, which had no implications for the overall policy on mission land.[10] Secondly, the concession was granted in the post-war situation, when the mission had admittedly begun to run into financial difficulties. Thirdly, the administration found itself in a kind of vacuum until a real educational policy could be established. While it now acknowledged its responsibility for the educational sector, it did not yet have the means available to fulfil its obligations in this direction (see Chapter 15). A small concession was therefore a token of good will pending a final decision on the extent of the administration's educational engagement. However, the tenability of these suggestions as to the relative significance of the link between land and education will have to be examined in a different and wider context.

The subletting of church sites

We have noticed how closely the mission's agricultural development scheme was tied to the successful cultivation of cash crops. Similarly, the application filed in 1903 for permission to build market stalls in the capital and to let them out was an indication of the beginnings of urbanization and the expansion of trade.[11] The mission saw here an opportunity of obtaining an income for the church, and began to build the stalls even before the answer from the authorities had arrived. When this answer proved to be negative, the mission again countered with the educational argument, claiming that their educational work was such a heavy drain on their resources that it justified any extra income.[12] But the administration argued that the site in question had been granted solely for religious purposes, not in order to provide the church with an income.[13] When the Commissioner visited the site later, however, and saw the stalls virtually finished, he made an exception and granted the necessary permission.

Only three years later, at a time when the church was very short of funds, an application for an expansion of the market area was filed, this time involving a more subtle use of the educational argument: 'I do not like asking the Government to make grants for educational work when the Native Church might get funds out of the land it holds at its disposal.'[14] The newly appointed Commissioner considered it necessary to take legal advice in order to clarify the terms on which mission land was held. The answer was that mission land was meant principally for direct religious and educational work, and that the word 'direct' should be taken at its face value, which ruled out the possibility of making a profit from the land, even if the money was spent on religious or educational projects.[15]

Thus the outcome of the subletting controversy in 1906 was that the Commissioner withheld his permission to diversify the use of church land to include trading purposes; only the few stalls built in 1903 were still allowed to function.[16] As this decision could only be interpreted as a refusal to acknowledge that church land was a revenue-producing endowment, the Uganda mission felt obliged to consult its own legal advisors. This produced the opposite result: that it was legal to use the land 'for the purpose of rendering it profitable'.[17] These conflicting legal opinions may have been the reason why the Commissioner's 1906 decision failed to carry the weight he had expected with the Uganda mission. In any case the administration discovered in 1918 that about 22 shops had been built on church land during the years 1913–16, in areas bordering the municipal market. This was clearly a violation of the 1906 ruling, especially as the church had received 2,343 rupees annually from the leases.[18] The CMS explained that it was ignorant of the earlier correspondence, and that it had acted in good faith, with the one aim of promoting the religious and educational work of the church. It was a temporary expedient that the money was being used to cover the expenses of the church land survey, and permission was asked to continue with the practice of subletting; otherwise the work was bound to suffer seriously.[19]

The colonial officials found it hard to believe that the mission had acted out of ignorance, but in the end the explanation was accepted. After much discussion, the closure of the shops was not requested; but the mission was told that no more shops should be opened, and that the income from those already opened should be used exclusively for missionary work.[20] Soon afterwards it was considered necessary to inform all three missions that subletting was not allowed without specific permission, and that such permission would not be granted in practice.[21] But it proved difficult to stick to this policy, given the various types of missionary landholdings.[22] In 1922 the Land Officer came to the conclusion that the position of the missions with regard to landholding was becoming more and more complicated year by year, and that it was high time to change the conditions under which land could be held.[23] The colonial administration thus made it clear that it did not conceive of mission land as a revenue-producing endowment. In other words it was not prepared to let the mission dispose of its landholdings on the basis of a European concept of ownership. Instead the formula of 'religious and educational work' was stressed, implying that mission landholdings should provide facilities for the mission's general work, and should help to reduce their expenses; but they should not be seen as a means of earning an income. Our earlier suggestion, that there was a fundamental difference between the two agencies' concepts of landholding, is here fully confirmed, even to the extent that the mission felt it necessary on two occasions, and to the great annoyance of the administration, to take the law into its own hands.

Secondly, it is obvious that the administration did not want the mission or the embryonic church to become a major economic force in society. The mission was not to be allowed to become a great landowner, and it was not considered to be a partner in the agricultural development of the Protectorate. The mission was thus barred from using its land in accordance with the new possibilities arising from the general socio-economic development of the Protectorate. The educational argument carried no weight when the mission attempted to obtain permission to make use of the land without restrictions. Educational considerations helped to reduce the direct expenses of acquiring the land, but they had no influence on the overall conditions on which it was held.

The status of church land in relation to the African system: the problem of alienation

The issue of alienation was already to the fore when the mission first received land grants in the 1890s. The problem can be examined by focusing on the chiefs' functions. The chiefs operated within the colonial system, inasmuch as they were part of its bureaucratic apparatus, and the African system, as they performed traditional duties and enjoyed special rights and tributes. How the relationship between these two roles was to be defined had not yet been made clear.[24] However, once the colonial authorities had decided to introduce the Buganda pattern of government in the rest of the Protectorate, and even in a number of cases appointed Ganda agents to the chiefly posts, the chiefs owed their positions mainly to their place within the European-inspired politico-administrative hierarchy, and had very little traditional foundation for their authority. This was especially true in the non-Bantu areas.[25] Following the expansion of the administrative system and the increase in the demands put to its representatives, the bureaucratic role of the chiefs took priority, while the standing and authority which they derived from tradition took on a more auxiliary function.[26] Both aspects of their authority must be taken into account when we examine the rights and privileges connected with church land and how they affected the African political system, in particular the role of the chiefs.[27]

One of the first cases which illustrates this arose as early as 1907, when it was reported that tenants on CMS estates in Buganda were claiming to be exempted from supplying food to passing caravans, and from working in camps established for colonial officials.[28] The mission, in support of the tenants, argued that the church shambas were given solely for religious and educational purposes, and that this included no obligation to supply food,[29] and that the saza chiefs had no authority to order tenants on church estates to do so.[30] The colonial officials could find no basis for such exemptions in the rules. They saw the claims as 'a movement among native occupants of the Church Missionary Society's plantations . . . to act as if they were under a separate Government'.[31] They pointed out that mission estates would attract a great number of people and become sanctuaries for tenants who wanted to be immune from obligations;[32] and the authority of the chiefs, 'through whom we govern the country', would become impossible to uphold.[33]

The administration took a firm stand on this case, and declared: 'It was never intended that mere settlement on Mission lands should interfere in any way with a Uganda native's obligations as a Uganda subject.' It was further pointed out that such an attitude on the part of the CMS was incompatible with its general policy.[34] This was in fact true: the crux of the matter for the CMS at that time was not the general question of exemptions for tenants on church land, but reasonable payment for the food supplied, and the abolition of forced labour without pay.[35] The solution thus seemed straightforward, as the colonial administration was in full agreement on the necessity of paying people for the food supplied to caravans and for their work in camps.

But the settlement arrived at was a partial, *ad hoc* solution. Whether they were paid or not, people on mission land considered themselves to be released from various obligations to their chiefs. This attitude created special difficulties at a time when the chiefs were being asked to produce labourers for public work and work on plantations.[36] A controversial case soon arose in Bunyoro, when two leading chiefs complained that tenants on CMS land were defying their authority, both as regards the traditional obligation to take part in the construction and upkeep of roads and the call from the colonial authorities to work in camps, cotton fields, or transport. The tenants claimed that, as they worked for the mission, they were exempted from obligations to their chiefs, irrespective of whether these were subject to the African or the colonial system. An amicable solution was reached, however, at a meeting of all the parties concerned. The rights of the chiefs to call on people to fulfil obligations within both systems were acknowledged, although certain areas of work under the colonial authorities were made optional. The most significant result of this controversy was that proper channels of communication were established between chiefs and tenants on mission land, making it obligatory for the chiefs to go through the 'headmen' on mission estates. This gave the headmen an official status and placed the tenants on their estates in a relatively privileged position compared with people in the surrounding areas.[37]

It soon became evident that these *ad hoc* arrangements did not define with sufficient stringency the position of the mission estates *vis-à-vis* the chiefs or the obligations owed to the chiefs by mission tenants. As the question constantly recurred, the Chief Secretary of the colonial administration finally sought legal advice, asking whether people were equally subject to the chiefs' jurisdiction whether they lived on mission estates or not, and which labour services and other obligations people living on mission estates and other private estates owed their chiefs.[38] The Crown Agent found it very difficult to give a conclusive answer to these questions. Even from a purely pragmatic point of view there had to be equality; otherwise, if tenants on mission estates were exempted from obligations towards the state, an untoward growth in their number could be expected. From the legal point of view the matter was less clear-cut. First one had to consider the fact that 'a native is subject to all native customs which are lawful and well-established, wherever he lives and whatever his religion'. This meant that obligations to the chief had priority. But it required that the two criteria mentioned by the Crown Agent were fulfilled. While it might not be difficult to decide which customs were well-established,[39] a real difficulty arose in defining what was meant by 'lawful'. Whether a native custom was lawful would have to be decided by examining whether it was in accordance with justice and morality;[40] and here the Crown Agent admitted to being on rather shaky ground. He cited the example of carrying food to the camps on the road. While a government official might think that it was in accordance with old custom that people followed the chiefs' orders, 'a conscientious Church Missionary Society worker' might consider that such a custom smacked of slavery, unless people carried the food of their own free will, not on the orders of the chief. Only the law courts could decide on the basic moral conflicts which these questions raised. The Crown Agent, however, advised strongly against litigation in the circumstances.

Ultimately a reign of pure law, as opposed to custom, will arrive in this country. But in my opinion, the time has not yet arrived in this country when every man's duties and rights can be ascertained by a reference to books or by proceedings before the Courts . . . If I may venture to submit my view of morality, I consider that moral, mental and worldly well-being of the natives as a whole will be best served by supporting as long as possible the system of chiefs, who should have all customary and well-established powers.

The result of these legal deliberations was that in general the obligations of people to their chiefs could not be legally formalized. In particular it was impossible in the case of tenants on mission land who had the missionaries to champion their cause. As regards an arrangement with the missionaries, the only advice that the Crown Agent could offer was that some appeal should be made to their vested interest in the chiefly system.

If the missionaries agree, as I believe they do, that the system of chieftainship is the most beneficial for this country and that its abolition would be deplored, then I think some informal arrangement should be come to with them about these matters.

This meant that in the opinion of the Crown Agent the question of the status of mission land *vis-à-vis* the chiefs could not be settled beyond the level of an informal agreement. He even warned that to press the question further might jeopardize such an arrangement and involve the risk of 'a general break-up of the system of chieftainship', which would be a disaster to be avoided at all costs.[41]

This memorandum bears witness to the virtual indispensability of the civil service chieftaincy within the colonial system, and shows how fragile the system was felt to be at the time, as the chiefs were expected to carry out functions within the colonial framework, but on the basis of an authority originating in the African system and thus assumed to be traditionally founded. The difficulties of formalizing the obligations of the tenants on mission land to their chiefs were further underlined by the administration's inability to provide a firm interpretation of the clause on church land in the Uganda Agreement. In the Luganda translation it was directly stated that *the people* on the land should work for the church, whereas the English version mentioned only that the land was held in trust for the church.[42] The emphasis on people in the Luganda version was taken to have two implications: the first and most far-reaching was that tenants should work exclusively for the church,[43] while the second amounted to an acknowledgement of the fact that land was only of value to the church if people worked on it. Accordingly it was open to various interpretations how this obligation to the church could be combined with obedience to the chiefs.[44] The Provincial Commissioner admitted that the Luganda version of the text was likely to create misunderstandings among Africans, and in the end the administration quietly decided to shelve the problem of interpretation.[45]

It was not long before this policy of inaction was put to the test. Certain people on mission lands in Buganda claimed to be exempted from supplying food to caravans, as they already provided food for the teachers. In one specific area 4,000 people were involved and they were supported in their claim by a CMS missionary.[46] Instead of laying down a definite ruling, the Crown Agent advised the Provincial Commissioner to settle the matter by contacting Archdeacon Walker and impressing on him the necessity for everyone in a given district to follow the instructions of the chief. The Crown Agent's solution was successful. Walker agreed 'that the authority of the Chiefs must be upheld', and he gave an informal promise to instruct his colleagues that tenants on mission land should do their fair share in supplying food in accordance with custom.[47]

This pattern repeated itself with surprising regularity over the following five-year-period. In 1911 it was reported from one saza in Buganda that *gombolola* (sub-county) chiefs,[48] the most recently constituted rank in the chiefly hierarchy, were unable to fulfil their obligations to maintain the roads, as the tenants on the extensive areas taken up by church estates refused to obey their instructions.[49] At the same time it was reported from Busoga that a great number of men were refusing to acknowledge the authority of the chiefs because their shambas and huts were situated on missionary lands; the labour supply and the collection of taxes were especially affected by this refusal.[50] In Bunyoro in 1912 the system worked out some years earlier seems to have collapsed: it was reported that friction had arisen between the chiefs and the headmen on mission estates over the issues of labour, taxes and legal procedure. Events in Bunyoro prompted the District Commissioner there to request a specific answer as to whether tenants on these estates were released from their labour obligations to the administration and from obedience to their administrative chiefs.[51] The friction escalated further when the status of the headmen themselves was called into question: in 1915 the Chief Justice accused them of imposing fines in criminal and civil cases. This was taken to be typical of a tendency for officials on mission land to claim independence of the minor chiefs and to give tenants the impression that they were under the protection of the mission and exempted from a number of obligations.[52]

Even in this last case, where an independent court system could be observed in embryo, the reaction of leading colonial officials was one of moderation and leniency.[53] While they admitted that these were delicate questions, the officials were absolutely unwilling to issue a detailed ordinance at that juncture. In this respect the situation had not changed since the Crown Agent's memorandum in 1909. The overall aim was to preserve the chiefs' authority and status, and this could best be done for the time being by approaching the mission informally.[54] This interest in upholding the chiefs' authority was, not surprisingly, shared by the mission, given the key importance of the chiefs for the Protestant effort. The policy of the mission does not seem to have been formulated explicitly, but one is left with the clear impression that up to 1915 the mission refrained from pursuing too eagerly its claims to an independent status for mission estates and to chiefly rights over tenants.[55] In view of the energy expended in seeking land grants from the colonial system, the mission was caught in a dilemma between its concern for the authority of the chiefs on the one hand, and its wish to secure separate status for church land and chiefly rights on the other. So far the mission's interest in upholding the authority of the chiefs, skilfully exploited by the colonial officials, had restrained it from over-zealousness and allowed the administration to pursue a relatively casual policy.

The departure from this pattern came in 1917 when the CMS mission asked for the recognition of headmen on mission estates. This coincided with the introduction of the lowest rank in the chiefly bureaucracy, the *muluka* chiefs.[56] The old policy of leniency and informality was, therefore, suddenly put to the test. The immediate reason for action at this time was the fact that the Synod of the Anglican Church in 1917 had defined and formalized the position of headmen on church estates (whom they called *katikiros*) and their assistants in the 'Laws and Regulations of the Church of Uganda, 1917'.[57]

The new regulations applied in the first instance to Buganda, where the bulk of the church land held in freehold was situated. For that reason it was the Provincial Commissioner of Buganda who was approached. In presenting his case, Archdeacon Baskerville, who had replaced Walker in 1912, described the system of katikiros on church lands by drawing a parallel with the general administrative system of the country. In each saza there was a katikiro in charge of all church estates, who was accountable to the Diocesan Council. His area was again divided into smaller sections corresponding to gombololas (sub-counties), each under the authority of an assistant who was to function as a link between the church estates and the gombolola chiefs. The katikiros and their assistants attended gombolola courts in cases affecting church estates, and they organized the supply of labour for state purposes (*kasanvu* labour). The request for the official recognition of headmen aimed at establishing appointment procedures, and clarifying the scope of the headmen's functions. With regard to the former, it was suggested that katikiros should be officially recognized in their appointment by the Buganda Lukiko, which should then inform the saza chief concerned. Their assistants should be presented to the saza chief, who would accordingly inform the gombolola chief. If objections were raised by the secular authorities, new nominations would be made. The katikiros and their assistants should be regarded as the official representatives of church interests in the chiefly courts, and as such should be entitled to act as counsel for tenants on church lands. Broadly speaking, they were to be 'in charge of and responsible for the tenants on Church Estates', although the Archdeacon hastened to add that this position would not mean 'a reduction of the Chiefs' authority and prerogative'.[58]

In commenting on this request the Provincial Commissioner, as the Archdeacon had anticipated, saw the last point as the weak link in the argument. 'It must be well known to District Officers that Mission mailos are inclined to be independent of the native administration, a tendency which it is essential to keep under close observation . . .'[59] In this case it was the authority of the muluka chiefs in particular which was being threatened. Approval of the Archdeacon's proposals would be equivalent to granting tenants on church land independence of the muluka chiefs, 'who form an important part of the Administrative framework of the country'. The muluka chiefs would virtually be replaced by the katikiros and their assistants. This would be unacceptable for the additional reason that church lands were classified as private estates whose internal organization was of no concern to the administration.[60]

At first the administration's refusal to recognize the church katikiros was acknowledged by the mission without further comment,[61] but the issue was soon taken up by the Bishop in a wider context. So far we have seen that the mission wanted the church to have jurisdiction over tenants on church land and to act on their behalf in confrontations with the administrative system. It is illustrative to compare this approach with the position the mission took on another contemporary issue: the legality of the gifts of land granted to the church by the chiefs. The mission was adamant that the chiefs had the right to dispose of the land, and did everything in its power to uphold the chiefs' authority, as defined by the traditional system. If the missionaries appear to have contradicted themselves in the case of the church katikiros, the explanation may be that their concern here was with an aspect of the *colonial* administrative structure of which the chiefs at the various levels happened to constitute an essential part. To this should be added that the rights in question were those which the chiefs enjoyed in their capacity as landlords, that is, as mailo owners. The chiefly functions affected by the recognition of church katikiros were mainly those introduced by the colonial system, not traditional ones. Moreover, the chiefly offices involved were those of the lower echelons, and especially the newly created muluka chiefs; there was no conflict with the mission's old familiar allies, the saza chiefs.

Thus the mission could claim that the recognition of katikiros and thereby of church rights over tenants in no way undermined the traditional position of the chiefs, as in this instance they regarded the chiefs as civil servants and landlords. In this way they felt that they could claim special rights connected with church land without affecting the authority of the chiefs. Whether this distinction between the two systems of authority was tenable remains to be seen from a closer examination of the position of tenants on mission land. So far the mission's arguments seem to have had no impact on the attitude of the colonial officials. The authorities' main concern was still the preservation of the status of the chiefs, regardless of its derivation. The elaboration of the administrative system brought about by the inclusion of the chiefs at various levels was thus an indirect factor behind the mission's 1917 request for the official recognition of katikiros on church estates. A more substantial reason appears, however, when we move on to the next phase in the history of the question of church land.

In a joint memorandum to the Governor, the two Catholic bishops and the Anglican bishop expressed great concern over the fact that the conditions for holding church land were deteriorating, and that the administration was becoming more restrictive with regard to the position of tenants. Privileges which mission tenants had enjoyed hitherto had been reduced. The situation in Buganda itself was given special mention: a decision by the Lukiko in August 1917, approved by the Provincial Commissioner, had meant that greater numbers of people were now being called up to do public work. The effect of this on educational work would be disastrous, as the tenants would have less time to work on the church land, which reduced its overall productivity.

The result is that finding themselves called upon to do double duty, to the Church and State, they [the tenants] tend to leave the Church lands, and the purpose for which lands were given, a permanent endowment of the Church, is defeated.[62]

It is here clearly expressed that tenants were indispensable if the church land was to be productive, and it is also implied that the state had an obligation to provide conditions which would attract people to church land, and induce them to stay on. The official recognition of the katikiros and the consequent improvement in the organization and utilization of labour resources was seen as a means of reaching this goal. The link between the request for official recognition and basic economic realities is fully confirmed by the colonial officials' handling of the letter from the three bishops. Two interrelated and fairly familiar problems came to the forefront: the extent to which church land should be regarded as an endowment; and the liability of church tenants to national obligations. The resolution of the latter issue would have consequences for the status of the chiefly element of the administrative system.

While it was generally accepted by leading colonial officials that church land was intended as an endowment, the endowment was considered to embrace land and money (i.e. rents from tenants). Labour services were thus not included.[63] This meant that the missions were not entitled to any exemptions from official labour obligations; otherwise the endowment would be much larger than intended.[64] When the Governor, new to the Protectorate, appeared to be in favour of concessions to the missions in the labour question,[65] he was met with strong opposition, especially from the Provincial Commissioners. They pointed out that it had become common knowledge in the Protectorate that mission land was 'a haven of refuge', where people were free from labour obligations like kasavu and *luwalo* (unpaid labour customarily due to the chief).[66] They emphasized that this was not only a question of resources granted to the missions by the administration; any exemption from national obligations undermined the administrative system of the country, and would 'hasten the decline of tribal control'.[67]

The outcome of this controversy will be taken up separately in the following chapter. It should however be pointed out here that this problem became most acute in 1917–18. In the present context our focus is upon the principles involved in policy-making. The authorities were primarily concerned with the effects any special status for tenants on mission land would have on the whole administrative system, and in particular on the authority of the chiefs. This problem had been raised when the recognition of church katikiros was first requested, and it reappeared again in connection with the bishops' request for special privileges as regards tenant labour. The following remarks by the Provincial Commissioner of Buganda, P. W. Cooper, describe the connection between these two issues admirably, and deserve to be quoted at length:

The fact that a man is a Church tenant in no way frees him from his national obligations as laid down by the Uganda Agreement or sanctioned by the Lukiko in accordance with native custom or from his obedience to his Chiefs. There has been, and still is, a strong tendency for the Missions to try and form a Government within a Government and for their headmen to ignore, and, in some cases, refuse compliance with the orders of the Native Government unless approved of by the European Missionaries; this has been a constant difficulty to the Administration in its endeavours to support tribal control . . . The fact must be recognized that national obligations for the good of the whole country and by which everyone benefits must be carried out by everyone regardless as to his landlord and unless shared equally cause emigration from the native owned land to Church land and destroy the authority of the Chiefs whose duty it is to see that these obligations are performed in the interests of the whole country . . . On no account can it be admitted that such tenants are not liable for their tribal and legal obligations to the Chiefs administering the country under the control and advice of the Government.[68]

It is here made abundantly clear that the Provincial Commissioner of Buganda was against any dual system of authority which would place people on church land in a special category. In this he had the support of his colleagues in other provinces. He was further opposed to the emergence of an independent hierarchy of chiefs with the mission at the apex as the chief executive body. This was not prompted by economic considerations, but by an overriding concern for the maintenance and proper function of the chiefly administrative system at all levels. At the same time he disputed the implicit premise behind the Bishops' arguments: that work for the church was equivalent to work for the national good. National obligations must be carried out through the administrative system and through this system alone.

The administration officials were this time prepared to formalize the status of church land and the position of the katikiros, thus departing from the earlier policy of informality. At a meeting with church katikiros specially called by

Bishop Willis to clarify their situation, Mr Cooper took the opportunity in his capacity as Provincial Commissioner of Buganda to present a memorandum he had drawn up.[69] It summarized the principles already laid down in 1917. Mission land was classified as private land like any other private property, and its internal organization with katikiros and their assistants was a matter for the owner, not for the colonial authorities. This meant that the gombolola and muluka chiefs were responsible for all the people in their areas, regardless of the prevailing type of land ownership. Katikiros on church land had, like any other landholder, the right to appear in court as counsel for their tenants,[70] but this did not entitle them to claim freedom from the muluka chiefs' authority. They were not allowed to collect poll tax from their tenants; this right was vested solely in the gombolola chief, who had the right of access to church estates. Concerning kasanvu (paid labour for the colonial authorities), special rules had been drawn up providing for the possibilities of exemption from the first call to work, but not the second one; whereas no exemptions, not even for katikiros, had ever existed with regard to luwalo.[71]

Bishop Willis was very unhappy with this memorandum and urged on the Provincial Commissioner the inadvisability of issuing it just then. First of all, he pointed out that the question of tenants on church land was still *sub judice*. Apparently he anticipated a more positive attitude from the new Governor. But he was probably closer to the heart of the matter when he stated bluntly that the new ruling would have 'the effect of still further emptying the Church miles'.[72] He was here revealing the real motive behind the drive to have the katikiros officially recognized: such a step would help to create conditions for the tenants which could reverse the present trend towards a steady decrease in their number. On the other hand, the publication of the rules in the form drawn up by the Provincial Commissioner would tilt the balance even further in the wrong direction, as it would draw unwelcome attention to the extra burdens on people living on church land. Bishop Willis succeeded in having the issuing of the memorandum postponed,[73] and it was apparently never published, as it was rendered superfluous by other procedures introduced at about the same time. Foremost among these was the Native Authority Ordinance of 1919, which provided a legal definition of the powers of the chiefs, and at the same time placed them under the strict control of the colonial officials.[74] The ordinance listed the areas in which the chiefs were empowered to make decisions; the fact that quite a number of these were non-traditional functions indicated the extent to which the chiefs had become involved in the colonial administration. It is debatable whether the Native Authority Ordinance was relevant in Buganda.[75] In practice, it seems that the colonial administration in its dealings with Buganda relied to a considerable extent on the Uganda Agreement and other ordinances issued at about the same time as the Native Authority Ordinance.[76] But in whatever way this problem of Buganda versus the rest of the Protectorate was solved, the important point to be made here is that the longer-term goals sketched out by the Crown Agent in 1909 had now come close to realization. The chiefs' duties and rights could now be codified and drawn up in statutory form; it was no longer necessary to invoke custom. The movement towards a more elaborate administrative system, the need for stricter control and the general process of bureaucratization had resulted in an identification and codification of the powers of the chiefs. The issue of the status of tenants on church land had definitely not been an influential element in this whole process, but the outcome was bound to have an important bearing on the whole policy as regards the chiefs' authority over tenants on church land. The codification of the chiefs' powers made it virtually impossible either to grant any special status to these tenants or to give any official recognition to church katikiros.

None the less, efforts were still made during 1919 to secure rights over people living on church land. The Synod asked the bishop to reopen the matter by asking the Governor to permit the church 'to regard people living on Church land as their own people'.[77] Bishop Willis then returned to the argument based on the Luganda version of the Agreement, in which he claimed a clear distinction was made between private estates which were personal property and the land given to the missions, which was not their private property, but was held in trust for the churches.[78] He was thus redeploying the old argument that church land was not alienated from the African system and ought to be officially recognized as the property of an African institution. This argument was soon afterwards taken a step further in a memorandum to the Uganda Development Commission. As church land could not properly be classified as private property, but was meant as a provision for Christian work, an urgent appeal was made that labour on church estates should be left to the disposal of the church.[79] Naturally, the colonial authorities disagreed with this interpretation of the Luganda text. In any case, they said, the English version of the Agreement was the one that counted.[80]

No matter what arguments were presented, the colonial government was prepared to countenance neither an alternative administrative structure in the shape of church katikiros, nor a special position for the tenants on church lands. The legislation of 1919 had provided the administration with the legal basis for turning down any future requests of this kind – a new state of affairs which the mission had not yet fully grasped. Yet, when it came to the implementation of this overall policy, not all problems could be solved so easily. In the outlying districts, not least in the remote areas of the Northern Province, people tended to consider the local missionary as their chief, and 'in many cases the native teacher has a stronger personality than the local chief and natives will crowd on to the Mission land in the hope that they may evade by his instrumentality their obligations to Kasanvu and Luwalo'.[81] The missions' gradual acquisition of chiefly rights for the benefit of their work inevitably had the effect of eroding the power of the newly established chiefs, in contravention of the administration's policy. At the same time it was admitted that the officials, when dealing with cases of alienation, had to take into account 'the civilizing effect of the Missions', and accordingly treat them with general sympathy.[82] Thus the officials found themselves in a dilemma. On the one hand they had to take measures against alienation in order to secure the authority of the chiefs; on the other, they had to demonstrate willingness to ensure favourable conditions for the work of the missions. The kinds of concessions that were actually granted to the mission will be examined in the next chapter.

In spite of vacillation over its implementation, the legislation passed in 1919 demonstrates a correlation between the development of the chiefly administrative system and the prospects for an independent status for church land and its tenants. The more the importance of the chiefs' authority was emphasized, the more acute was the problem of alienation of church land and its tenants felt to be. This pattern of correlation can be further clarified if we summarize two lines of argument from the present chapter.

(1) The tightening of control over African leaders in areas where the mission

was involved, continued, in that the chiefs increasingly became part of the colonial administration, and 'the bureaucratic rather than the traditional character of the native authorities in Uganda' was accented.[83] It therefore became less and less relevant to distinguish between the chiefs' traditionally founded authority and the power they derived from the colonial system. The administration considered traditional chiefly rank mainly as a qualifying criterion and a means of preserving the loyalty of the people. The main objective was less the maintenance of traditional institutions than the building-up of an efficient bureaucracy.

This had three effects on the mission's relations with the African political system. First, there was now less scope for manoeuvre between the two systems, and the mission now played its accustomed roles with less efficacy. Secondly, it was becoming difficult to seek concessions from the African political system, as its leaders had increasingly become civil servants, and had less and less scope for independent action in their chiefly capacity. Thirdly, it became increasingly difficult to argue for concessions and special privileges on the basis of either system alone. The mission was, probably unwittingly, caught in a transitional phase where the choice between one or the other system was no longer of much real importance. When chiefly rights were claimed on church lands, it implied not only the withdrawal of a number of people from the authority of the chief, but also the acquisition of a position equivalent to the chief's new role as a landlord, i.e. a non-traditional function. When church ownership of land was seen in terms of the African concept of ownership with its 'rule over people', there was nevertheless an element of alienation from both the African and the colonial systems, insofar as a number of people were subject to an alternative economic and administrative system. The view that church ownership, unlike mission ownership, should be classified as African ownership, and seen as benefiting African society could not deny this involved the replacement of chiefly authority with a new system. This minimized the value of the argument of non-alienation.

The conclusion must then be that, when three different sources of chiefly authority were involved, and when the chiefs functioned in two different official systems at the same time, it was no longer tenable to claim that rights and privileges connected with landholding could be defined exclusively in terms of either system. Therefore, the policy of establishing the church as an institution in African society by claiming for it a traditionally founded status was difficult to maintain in the face of historical developments; and the mission's familiar arguments carried less and less weight as time went on.

(2) In the earlier section on general land policy it was pointed out how progress towards a more established colonial administration had to be included as an explanatory factor in analysing the changes in the relationship between mission, church and state. We now have an even closer causal connection between the bureaucratic factor and the change in policy on the part of both the mission and the administration from about 1917 onwards, when the informality of the chiefs' authority was replaced by a much more formalized approach. The issue of the church katikiros illustrated a growing correlation between the expansion of the administrative system and the mission's efforts to secure special rights connected with the possession of land. The more elaborate and more efficient administrative system made it difficult to rely on informal arrangements. The general tendency to move from custom to law had its own impact on the practical basis of the Christian work, and especially on the mission's relations with the African system. The initiative on church katikiros and the subsequent break with the policy of

informality are best explained as reactions against the increased pressure from the state. More efficient administration made the land less valuable as an endowment, because it involved closer control of the tenants on church land, the one element that increasingly came to determine its productivity. As a protective measure the mission sought a more official status for church land, and some degree of independence from the colonial bureaucracy. Such a request was, however, the last thing the colonial authorities could grant, as it was committed to its policy, 'whose main direction was towards greater control and increased bureaucratization'.[84] Faced with this initiative from the mission, the officials were bound to be concerned primarily with the protection of their own system. They thus felt driven to replace informal arrangements with a set of rules which specified the exact terms and conditions under which land was held. In a wider sense, we may see this as a codification of the relationship between church and state, and as a transition from pragmatic to normative rules. According to F. G. Bailey, this is a process characteristic of the colonial system (p. 137).

12

Usufructuary rights to tenant labour

Two questions were left open in the last chapter: to what extent could the mission and the church exercise chiefly rights over tenants, and to what extent was the colonial administration willing to grant special concessions? In order to arrive at the answer to these complex questions, we must examine the general obligations to which the Bakopi (the peasants or the ordinary people outside the chief's ranks) were subject.[1]

Obligations on Bakopi in general

So far no systematic work has been done on this topic, and a number of difficulties are involved in sketching a reasonable picture of the situation. First of all, we are faced with a mixture of obligations, some stemming from the colonial system, and others having their origin in the feudal tributes of the traditional system. Secondly, although it is possible to list the most important obligations, it is very difficult to tell to what extent – if at all – they were enforced at any given time in the non-Ganda districts. This somewhat blurred picture is the result of some of the obligations being closely related to the Ganda system of chiefly administration, and their extent and validity being closely linked with the expansion of this system to other districts. Further, a number of the tributes can only be understood by reference to the prevailing system of landholding. As pointed out earlier, even within Buganda it is difficult to decide whether the Bakopi's relationship to their superiors was conditioned by the new system of private landownership or was still derived from the pre-colonial feudal system, where the roles of officeholder and landowner could not be separated. In the non-Ganda areas, the whole question of the extension of the mailo system was controversial, and only found a solution after 1920. These various factors must be regarded as important variables throughout the presentation of the five most important obligations to which the Bakopi were subject.

Hut tax and poll tax

A hut tax of three rupees (15 Rs = the contemporary pound) was introduced as part of the Uganda Agreement in 1900. From 1905 onwards the authorities levied a poll tax of two rupees on bachelors in Buganda, thus introducing a double system of taxation.[2] Soon afterwards, the poll tax was also introduced in the neighbouring areas.[3] However it was increasingly felt that a more uniform system could be established by completely replacing the hut-tax system in Buganda with the poll-tax system. In 1909 a conference was held with the three Regents, the leading chiefs and the heads of the missions. An agreement was reached according to which a poll tax of five rupees was to be introduced for all male adults in Buganda.[4] In the other districts the amount was to be lower in the beginning, with a gradual increase to five rupees.[5] Three motives seem to have prompted the various groups involved to this new departure.

(1) In Buganda the effect of developments in general, and of the growth of trade and the cotton industry in particular, had been that 'the peasantry have become so independent and prosperous that it is becoming, every day, more and more difficult to induce them to engage in any form of regular work'.[6] It was thus the scarcity of labour which prompted the colonial administration to work for a change in the tax system. But the Ganda chiefs had the same problem. They sensed among the Bakopi 'a spirit of independence' growing up in the wake of economic development, which disturbed them.[7] The new and higher poll-tax rates were seen as a means of encouraging the Bakopi to come forward in greater numbers to do paid work.[8] Otherwise, if the people were unable to pay the five rupees, they would have to fulfil their obligation by doing two months' unpaid work.

(2) The chiefly class had a more direct interest in the new arrangement in two different ways. First of all, the Kabaka and the saza chiefs were granted 20 per cent of the amount collected in poll tax in their respective areas. This meant an adjustment of the salary scale laid down in the Uganda Agreement. The latter point may have influenced the Buganda Lukiko to approve of the new poll tax system, as they had to do constitutionally before it could become law.[9] Secondly, the revision of the salary scale and the increase in revenue available from poll tax made it possible to give the minor chiefs a salary, which solved the problem that had arisen soon after the conclusion of the Agreement (cf. p. 138). Because of the increase in administrative work, the saza chiefs themselves now regarded the sub-chiefs as indispensable, and wanted them on the payroll.[10] For other reasons, the colonial administration was even more interested in this matter. It will be remembered that the grade of gombolola chief was formalized in 1909. To avoid irregularities in the collection of taxes it was considered advisable that they should have an officially approved rate of salary; and, significantly, it was added that the sub-chiefs should be made to feel 'that the retention of their position of authority depends more upon the British Government than upon the Saza Chief'.[11] The tax law of 1909 was thus a confirmation of the chiefs' double source of authority and of the government's desire for a 'native civil service'.

(3) One particular feature of the old hut-tax system made the missions favour a change. The hut tax had become a penalty on marriages, in the sense that young men, instead of taking wives, lived together in one hut, paying very little hut tax and doing very little work per head.[12] Both for moral reasons and for the sake of the maintenance of the labour force the mission supported the new tax system in

spite of its severe financial repercussions for themselves.

The new poll tax of five rupees was an important factor in the realization of the principal colonial aim of making the Protectorate self-supporting. This was achieved in 1916.[13] When the colonial administration in the aftermath of the First World War wanted to raise the poll tax to 7.50 Rs, and in fact did so in some districts,[14] the special position of Buganda compared to other parts of the Protectorate proved a major hindrance, and the issue brought the two parties involved close to a constitutional crisis.[15] In accordance with the Uganda Agreement the Ganda leaders could veto any increase in taxation, and actually did so on this occasion because the Governor would not accept a clause in the tax law stating that no increase would be imposed for the next 7–10 years. The Kabaka and his ministers appealed directly to the British government, emphasizing that they considered the Agreement of 1900 to be 'a sacred document'.[16] In the end the Colonial Office accepted the Ganda point of view and overruled the Governor.[17]

This incident shows how jealously the Ganda leaders guarded the special rights they had gained under the Agreement, and how conscious they were of Buganda's special status within the Protectorate.[18] Inevitably this basic attitude would also reflect on their relations with the CMS mission, and their position within the church. Secondly, the controversy on poll tax in 1919 marked the beginning of a new era during which the colonial officials increasingly came to feel that the Agreement was anachronistic, and that Buganda's special status was a nuisance. The Baganda reacted by guarding their rights even more vigorously within both state and church.

Leaving aside the wider consequences of the imposition of poll tax, it becomes clear how difficult it was to standardize administrative measures and Bakopi obligations throughout the Protectorate, although the Buganda model was applied to a great extent to new districts as they were brought under administration during the whole period under survey.[19]

Kasanvu

One reason for the introduction of the poll-tax system in 1909 was the expectation that it would induce the Bakopi to come forward as labourers. But it was also considered necessary to introduce more direct measures in order to secure an adequate supply of labour for government work (porterage, road work, public buildings etc.). In 1909 the Governor, Hesketh Bell, initiated the system which became known as kasanvu, and which rendered all men liable to be called up for one month per year to do public work. In return they would be paid according to current rates fixed by the government.[20] These regulations were duly ratified by the three Regents and the Buganda Lukiko,[21] and, in order to keep a check on the chiefs' adherence to them, registers were drawn up in the various districts, listing the men liable to conscription.[22] At the same time a general exemption was made; no one in permanent employment would be called up.[23] Officially, the new system was justified as furthering the progress of the country; but it had important side effects, as, by exempting men in permanent employment, it made it easier for private employers, especially the European planters, to recruit labour. It enabled them to keep wages fixed at a low level; in addition, conscripted labourers were sometimes handed over to the planters by colonial officials.[24] (See Chapter 13).

Bishop Tucker first protested against the kasanvu principle as such because it was a kind of forced labour, and he took his protest as far as the Colonial Office. (This most important issue in the relationship between the mission and the state will be taken up in a subsequent section, where the issue of forced labour will be discussed in general.) Secondly, the mission approached the colonial administration to ask for exemptions for tenants on mission land (see below). Thirdly, Bishop Tucker asked for a clarification of whether kasanvu was based on native law or on a government ordinance.[25] Tucker was concerned with Buganda alone, as this was the first area where kasanvu was put into practice; but even with this limitation the colonial administration now realized how difficult it was to clarify the legal basis of their measures.[26]

Two alternative solutions were offered to the problem of the legal foundation of kasanvu, the first one suggested by a colonial official, the second by Bishop Tucker himself. The District Commissioner in Kampala made it clear that it was not on the basis of any law or ordinance that people were called up for one month's work; kasanvu was simply founded upon 'the immemorial usage by which the chiefs call upon their people to do work'. It was no new obligation laid upon the Bakopi; what had happened was that the chiefs' customary rights had been limited and defined by the colonial administration. Thus what was happening was simply a redirection of a part of the complex of tributes due to the chiefs. No Muganda had the right to be lazy and refuse to take part in work which he was justifiably obliged to do 'for the progress and civilization of Buganda'.[27] The District Commissioner conceived of the chiefs as officeholders within the traditional system, and not primarily as landowners under the reformed system originating in the Uganda Agreement. Bishop Tucker's reaction to this explanation was that 'the feudal system has been worked to its utmost limits'.[28] When people had paid their poll tax, done their luwalo work in accordance with the Uganda Agreement, and paid their busulu (rent) to the chiefs as landlords, they had no more feudal obligations to fulfil, and should be free to go wherever they wanted. They were none the less sent to Kampala and had to do one month's work to fulfil the government's labour requirements, and if they refused they were punished by the chiefs.[29] Although kasanvu was paid labour, Tucker went so far as to call the whole practice illegal and asked that public attention should be drawn to the situation, so that 'the chiefs shall not be used as Government Agents in what on the Governor's own shewing is an illegality'.[30]

As further proof of his point, Tucker described the chiefs' rights more specifically. Under the feudal system they had had the right to call their tenants to work: 'But this was because the tenants held their land upon a service tenure.' In those early days no distinction had been made between the chiefs as office-holders and as landholders. Now, in accordance with the Johnston Agreement and the land laws, service tenure had been abolished and 'a landed proprietorship' introduced. This meant that in the relationship between tenants and chiefs, the latter now only counted as landlords, and service had accordingly been replaced by rent. Hence, to compel men, when they had paid their rent, to work on the basis of their feudal obligations towards chiefs was simply a violation of the law.[31] This is the most accurate description given by a contemporary observer of Buganda's transition from a feudal system to the restratified social system codified in the Agreement. Tucker here gave a perspicacious analysis of the changed relations between the chiefs and Bakopi which grew up with the new concept of individual land ownership, and he was prepared to face the consequences for the chiefs' position and function.

Faced with Tucker's strongly worded arguments, the colonial administration had to admit that he was right and their colleague wrong. Kasanvu lacked any foundation within the traditional system, and when tenants had fulfilled their luwalo obligation and paid their poll tax and their rent to their landlords, the chief had no right to compel them to do any other public work. 'The influence of the chiefs in this matter is therefore a moral influence.'[32] It is, however, significant that the colonial administration in Uganda was not prepared to take the consequences of their agreement in principle with Tucker. These would have been: first, to admit that the kasanvu system was a misuse of the traditional obligations to chiefs, and then to present kasanvu bluntly as a form of forced labour introduced by the colonial authorities in order to ensure an adequate labour supply for the development of the new order in society. This would have led to a discussion of whether it was at all justifiable to use forced labour within the colonial system.

The authorities certainly refrained from going so far, and instead chose to blur the picture by continuing to relate kasanvu to the traditional system. In practical terms this meant that they accepted the alternative opinion of the District Commissioner of Kampala. An adequate supply of labour was indispensable in order to ensure progress in the country, and the kasanvu system was the one best suited to serve this purpose; therefore, it must be upheld. They expected Bishop Tucker to concur 'that civilization and Christianity alike demand a higher standard of effort than exists among naked savages.'[33] Then, the evolution from the feudal system of labour must be gradual. To sever all the old bonds at once would be harmful to the people. This aspect was developed further in the contention that any relaxation of the bonds would undermine the authority of the chiefs, and would thereby threaten the moral and material welfare of the people.[34]

These arguments provided the substance of a rather inconclusive answer to Bishop Tucker's queries. Not even the Colonial Office found them persuasive, but characterized the answer as being 'of the debating society order'. But when it came to practical policy the Colonial Office was not prepared to face the consequences of the situation as described by Tucker. Instead the following analysis was made of the situation:

As in similar cases in other parts of tropical Africa, the humanitarian has logic on his side, while the man with the practical responsibility of government knows that, logic or no logic, the country would be at a stand-still, if the authority of the chiefs over the labour supply, which Mr Tomkins describes as exercised from time immemorial, were suddenly broken down.[35]

On the basis of this 'Pilate-like attitude' from the Colonial Office[36] the administration in Uganda could uphold the kasanvu system and continue to play down the element of forced labour by presenting it as something based on the traditional bonds between the chiefs and their subordinates. This line of policy was carried further when the Labour Regulations of 1912 introduced a second call to work for the administration, which increased the kasanvu obligation to two months per year if necessary. Once again the regulations were ratified by the Regents of Buganda on behalf of the Lukiko.[37]

During the First World War particularly extensive use was made of the kasanvu obligation by the Protectorate government. It therefore became unpopular among the Bakopi,[38] and abuses and negligent administration spread among the chiefs. Special difficulties were caused by the many exemptions for people in full employment and tenants on mission land.[39] There arose once more a need for clarification of the nature of kasanvu and the rights of the chiefs.[40] During the renewed discussion it is significant that Bishop Tucker's views were ignored. The officials settled for the definition which stated that the kasanvu system was legitimized by the chiefs' customary right to call up labour for official purposes. That this was the administration's basis of legitimacy was now made clearer than ever before, as kasanvu was described as 'merely an extension on organized lines of the hereditary rights of the ruling class due to advancing needs and changed economic conditions of the country'. Kasanvu was thus considered a national obligation redirected towards the fulfilment of responsibilities towards the new unit, the Protectorate.[41]

To support this view the same utilitarian arguments as before were used. First, it was simply necessary to preserve the kasanvu system in order to maintain an adequate labour supply, especially in the non-Ganda districts to which kasanvu had been extended over the years, and where it had proved necessary to apply some form of coercion to bring people forward.[42] Secondly, the chiefs' position was threatened by the modernization process (including education and economic development) and this trend would be accelerated if the customary bonds between chiefs and Bakopi were suddenly severed.[43] It was already noticeable

that a large number of the young men of the country are drifting away from the control of their Chiefs who are no longer considered by them in loco parentis; this tendency is inevitable in a country advancing so rapidly as this Province [Buganda] is, but, in view of this fact, it is of the utmost importance that the ruling Chiefs should not increase this tendency by voluntarily throwing away a power which is theirs by right and theirs by duty in their position as rulers, a right which is recognized as the one bond which, if properly used, can keep the country together and check undue independence which in many cases leads to idleness, selfishness and failure to undertake a fair share in the national responsibilities.[44]

While the incipient erosion of the chiefs' customary authority is admitted here, it is also emphasized that the balance should not be tilted further in that direction by depriving them of one of their rights. This concern is expressed at the same time and by the same official whom we have earlier seen opposing government recognition of katikiros on church land for exactly the same reasons (cf. pp. 171ff). In view of this attitude from the colonial officials, it is not surprising that the authority to continue recruiting labour through the kasanvu system, and even to apply a mild form of force, was written into the Native Authority Ordinance of 1919, and thus became institutionalized in the codification of the chiefs' customary rights.[45]

In spite of this defence of kasanvu, doubts increased in the minds of colonial officials as to how long the system could continue.[46] Internal changes in the country made it more and more difficult for the chiefs to use the system. This was due not least to the chiefs' own shrinking authority over the younger generation and the increasing number of exemptions. A different policy was then suggested: that kasanvu should gradually be phased out, and a permanent labour force introduced.[47] This change of attitude among government officials followed queries from leading Baganda chiefs. They deplored in strong terms the continuation of the kasanvu system, and pointed out its serious economic, social and moral consequences. Kasanvu was even seen as a kind of slavery; it caused the peasants to question whether 'the English freedom' was only accorded to the chiefs and not extended to the peasants. Significantly, the chiefs also called upon Bishop Willis to support them in their campaign against kasanvu.[48] While the abolition of kasanvu was thus requested by the Baganda themselves, its timing was almost certainly influenced by the ban on the official recruitment of forced labour to the settlers in the neighbouring East African Protectorate (later Kenya).[49] Hence, it was only from the beginning of 1922 that kasanvu was finally abolished. It was on that occasion specifically stated that the increasing numbers of voluntary labourers had made the system superfluous.[50]

A number of factors were thus at work in bringing the kasanvu system to an end. But it was probably the inner process of change which had started long before which was of real significance. It was no longer possible to legitimize kasanvu by reference to customary obligations to the chiefs and by playing down the element of forced labour. The fact of the erosion of the chiefs' customary authority, which seems to have reached a critical stage at the beginning of the 1920s, brought the element of forced labour into starker focus, and showed the need for a reappraisal of Bishop Tucker's judgement of the situation. The issue is thus a useful index of the gradual change in the chiefs' position under changing economic circumstances, and points the way towards new departures in administrative policy. It is evident that the administration during the 1910s turned a blind eye to the element of forced labour in the kasanvu system first pointed out by Bishop Tucker, until it was forced to acknowledge it at the beginning of the 1920s. The kasanvu issue thus became an important touchstone for the mission's handling of the forced labour issue after Bishop Tucker's first initiative. At the same time it brought home the difficulties of defining what was meant by the exercise of chiefly rights over people on mission land.

Luwalo

While kasanvu was introduced by the colonial administration and mainly served state purposes, there existed within the African system a different type of labour obligation, known as *luwalo*. This was geared towards public works within the local community. Luwalo had developed from the communal labour principle, and was thus sanctioned by long tradition before it was written into the Uganda Agreement. By definition luwalo was forced, but unpaid, labour, and according to clause 14 of the Agreement saza chiefs were entitled to call up labourers in the proportion of one man for every three huts, to maintain the roads within the saza and to do other kinds of public work, the period of service being one month in each year. This system was later copied in other districts in the Protectorate.[51]

In spite of the fact that it was unpaid, luwalo was much less resented than kasanvu, and accordingly much less controversial.[52] It was generally accepted as a traditional Buganda custom, not as something originating solely in the Agreement.[53] When the Colonial Office in 1919 hesitated to accept the clause on unpaid compulsory labour in the Native Authority Ordinance, it was the argument that luwalo did not go beyond the traditional obligations placed on the Bakopi that won the day.[54] Also, luwalo was visibly for the benefit of the local community, and at least not directly for the private economic benefit of the chiefs. It was not felt to be too burdensome, as it was carried out near the homestead, and allowed people to go home at night.[55]

Even after the war, when kasanvu was much resented, luwalo was not considered much of a burden. There was, however, a tendency for exemptions from kasanvu to be taken to be valid for luwalo too: fewer workers presented themselves, and the same few were called up again and again, over and above the limit of one month a year.[56] In practice the luwalo system thus suffered from the same difficulties as kasanvu, except that it was not disputed that it derived its legitimacy from a customary obligation. This may explain why it was not seriously suggested that luwalo should be discontinued, but only that some of the difficulties connected with it should be alleviated by introducing the possibility of the payment of money in commutation of the labour obligation.[57] This again reflected the increasing prosperity of the Bakopi after the rise in cotton prices which followed the war. It would also mean that the responsibility for public works within a given district could be distributed more evenly.[58]

Acting on the initiative of the colonial administration, the Buganda Lukiko passed a law in February 1920 which made luwalo an obligation on all males over 18 years old for one month each year. The law also had the general aim of increasing the voluntary supply of labour by allowing people in permanent employment (i.e. people who were employed for more than three months a year) to commute the labour obligation for a cash payment of five rupees.[59] These rules were later extended to other parts of the Protectorate.[60] It should be observed that the option of commutation was possible only under certain conditions, and was not open to everyone. Both the colonial officials and the major chiefs agreed that a liberal policy on commutation would mean that too few people would actually come forward for luwalo; this would hamper the building of roads and other public works in the various districts. And although the acceptance of the principle of commutation depended upon the economic changes in society, allowing it to take on too great proportions would involve the risk that the traditional bonds cementing society would be further weakened, and the authority of the chiefs reduced.[61] But the restrictive policy adopted proved to be little more than a holding operation. The pressure of economic growth increased, and from 1922 onwards the Governor accepted the principle of an optional cash commutation of luwalo, which was gradually put into practice in the various districts during the next few years. The last area to be included was the Eastern Province, where permission was given in 1926.[62]

The issue of luwalo commutation shows the dilemma of the colonial administration at the beginning of the 1920s. Should priority be given to the preservation of the chiefs' authority, in spite of the changes in society which had been so decisive for the fate of kasanvu, or should the administration accept economic realities and show more concern for the situation of the Bakopi than for that of the chiefs? Thus while luwalo was affected by the same factors as kasanvu, there were nevertheless two differences which influenced the mission's approach. First of all, luwalo was much less bound up with the chiefs' personal authority, in that it was always geared to identifiable public purposes in local communities. Secondly, luwalo was not, despite the fact that it was unpaid, primarily considered as forced labour, but as a legitimate duty in the context of the traditional system.

Busulu

In pre-colonial and pre-Agreement days, people owed a labour tribute to the chief under whose jurisdiction they lived. This tribute, later known as *busulu*,[63] was an obligation to the chief in his capacity as officeholder, which meant that it was a tribute to the state and a contribution towards the running of the political and administrative system in return for its protective powers. This custom was most prevalent in Buganda, but was presumably also observed in the three interlacustrine kingdoms and Busoga, which had a similar political structure.[64]

With the introduction of the concept of private ownership by the Uganda Agreement of 1900, the busulu obligation was no longer simply a question of the relationship between the Mukopi and his political overlord, but also of the relationship between a tenant and his landlord – though it is difficult to tell to what extent this transition was recognized by the persons involved. The Buganda Lukiko seems to have been aware towards the end of 1901 of some of the consequences of the new order, when it decided that tenants on mailo land should pay two rupees a year as rent, or the equivalent in the form of one month's labour. This decision was prompted by grumblings among the minor chiefs, and the move was clearly aimed at securing for them some sort of fixed income or tribute from their newly obtained mailo estates.[65] It is difficult to avoid the impression that the chiefly aristocracy, at least in Buganda, was fully aware at that early stage of the economic potential of the mailo system, rather than conceiving of landholding in the old political terms, as 'rule over people'.[66]

Once a cash payment instead of a labour tribute could fulfil the busulu obligation, the next logical step was to draw a distinction between the chiefs as officeholders and as landholders. But neither the colonial officials nor the missionaries seem to have been aware of this distinction. Both of them saw the new arrangement as rent to chiefs,[67] and the explanation can only be that, for almost the first two decades of the century, in Buganda there was simply no need to operate with such a distinction. The two roles were played by the same persons, because the mailo land was distributed among the ruling class of officeholders, which was thus transformed into a landed aristocracy. This combination of roles made it unnecessary to define whether busulu, which had earlier been the expression of an exclusively political relationship between clients and chiefs, now signified an economically based relationship between tenants and landlords.[68] In the early period, only Bishop Tucker, as with the issue of kasanvu, appears to have drawn the right conclusions concerning the new system of landholding. He made it clear, as early as 1910, that busulu could no longer be regarded as a feudal tribute based on the 'service tenure' of land, but must be considered as a rent paid to a private landowner for tenancy. In other words, the chiefs' transition to a 'landed proprietorship' ruled out the concept of a customary, feudal tribute.[69] Yet the colonial administration persisted throughout the following years in considering busulu primarily as a feudal tribute, without relating it to the system of landownership. Thus, no distinction was made between people as followers of a chief and as tenants on his land.[70] On this basis the difference between Buganda and the neighbouring districts was felt to be marginal, although it was admitted that the tribute was less well defined outside Buganda.[71] This inconclusive state of affairs was afterwards felt to be untenable: first, there was no consensus on the extent to which the Buganda model, with its system of landownership, could be expanded; secondly, the chiefs' rights and duties in connection with the supply of labour had yet to be defined, as we have seen in connection with kasanvu;[72] and thirdly, the economic growth of the Protectorate had rendered the labour supply unstable by providing for the possibility of commuting a labour obligation to a financial one.

All three anomalies were acutely felt in the Eastern Province. In 1918 the

Provincial Commissioner requested the administration's permission to introduce the Buganda system of commuting the one month's busulu obligation to a cash payment of five rupees, to be levied on all, even those who were in permanent employment, and thus normally exempted from customary tributes. The reasons for this request were manifold. With the introduction of cotton-growing and the corresponding growth in the number of permanent employees, the chiefs' disposal over busulu labour was reduced at a time when their estates were becoming a substantial source of income. Busulu in the form of a cash tribute would constitute compensation for this, or alternatively provide the means of obtaining a labour supply, and would in general strengthen the bonds between the chiefs and the people. Secondly, the introduction of the Buganda busulu practice would help to pave the way for a 'Native Land Tenure' along Buganda lines.[73] In answer to this request, the Chief Secretary pointed out that a Ganda-type arrangement in Busoga would be taken to indicate tacit approval of the chiefs' ownership of land. This should be avoided at all costs, as it would place obstacles in the way of a later land settlement. He stated specifically that there was a fundamental difference between the Eastern Province and Buganda: in the former, land was considered to be Crown land; while in the latter, land of any value was owned in freehold by the Baganda themselves.[74] It was thus here admitted that busulu was linked to land tenure, and that it could only be defined according to the prevailing system of landholding. It was also clearly stated that an extension of the Buganda model would prejudice the final land settlement in other areas. In both respects the issue of busulu was therefore closely linked with the ongoing discussions of land policy in the Protectorate.

This linkage added to the complexity of the busulu issue during the next few years, when colonial officials were attempting to clarify the factors involved.[75] The matter was only settled when it was accepted that the two prevailing systems of landholding in the Protectorate, the mailo system and the Crown land system, necessitated two different definitions of busulu. In principle busulu was a feudal right over people, not over land, and people were expected to pay the tribute in cash or labour. Accordingly, busulu had nothing to do with rent.[76] But this definition was only valid for people living on 'tribal lands', i.e. land held on Crown land terms. In areas like Buganda, where individual ownership prevailed (either over mailo land or freehold), busulu had become synonymous with rent payable to the owner or the lessee of the land, and was no longer a tribute to the chief as officeholder.[77] Thus Bishop Tucker's interpretation of 1910 came into its own. The matter could only be solved by accepting a differentiation between the two main types of landholding, and subsequently defining busulu in two different ways.

Closely linked with these deliberations was the problem of the commutation of busulu in the non-Ganda areas.[78] The increased pressure to meet the widespread demand for commutation in the immediate post-war period was sparked off by three interrelated factors: first, economic growth, especially in the Eastern Province, where there was now extensive cotton-growing, which meant that the peasants had more money, and were better able to pay for commutation; secondly, the growing demand for a labour supply meant that the labour duties to chiefs were now seen as an impediment to labour mobility, and were likely to affect the quality of the work performed by the peasants; thirdly, it was simply becoming more and more difficult to organize any kind of obligatory labour like busulu.[79] The administration clearly considered commutation to be one important means of solving the last two problems.[80] On the other hand, a certain hesitation was expressed: in the first place, the option of commutation could affect the position and authority of the chiefs by its depersonalization of the bonds between them and their subjects; this was especially a risk in the Eastern Province because of the recent introduction of the chiefly offices into the colonial administrative bureaucracy.[81] In the second place, in the event of commutation it had to be established whether the chiefs themselves should receive the vastly increased tribute. While the former problem could be reduced in scale by allowing a gradual and selective access to commutation, the latter one was more fundamental and had more far-reaching implications. When busulu was a feudal tribute to the chief in his capacity as officeholder, it was a contribution to the upkeep and functioning of the traditional administrative system. Therefore, the administration was unwilling to let the cash payment go directly to the chiefs, but thought that it should be paid into a central fund for the maintenance of the chiefly administrative system. In this latter respect it would be correct to speak of the 'nationalization' of busulu.[82] Secondly, the introduction of commutation would entail that the chiefs would be paid a fixed salary, instead of being paid directly by busulu and by poll-tax rebates.[83] Measures were accordingly taken to put this into practice. Salary scales were drawn up, and the so-called Lukiko funds were established in the various districts.[84]

We may conclude that busulu was preserved for its original purpose outside Buganda, but that it was transformed and reinterpreted over the years, mainly because of economic growth in these districts. To define busulu as a tribute one had to take into account the prevailing system of landholding. Hence, the interpretation of busulu in Buganda, with its mailo system, had to be quite different from its interpretation in the other districts. This is why it was so difficult to put the Buganda model into operation in the rest of the Protectorate. Taking the gradual introduction of commutation into account, the issue of busulu illustrates how difficult it is for any given time to conceive of the Protectorate as a uniform entity. The history of the busulu obligation can finally be seen as an important strand in the process registered earlier, whereby the chiefs were subjected to stricter surveillance by being integrated into the colonial civil service, so that their authority derived from the colonial administration, not from their customary position. Commutation of feudal tributes and the fixed salary scheme were clear expressions of the chiefs' increasing dependence on the Protectorate bureaucracy.

Nvujo

The *nvujo* tribute played no significant economic role during most of the period under survey. It is included here partly for the sake of completeness, partly because of the significance it took on in the 1920s. Originally nvujo was a tribute in kind levied on the production of food and beer, and it was mainly a Buganda phenomenon, although it did exist to some extent in the neighbouring areas. In the Buganda Land Law of 1908 it was stipulated that a mailo owner could not be compelled to give his chiefly superior 'any portion of the produce in money or kind' (clause 2j).[85] This meant that nvujo was henceforth mainly seen as a tribute due to mailo allottees, and not as before to the chiefs as officeholders. As in the case of busulu, this decision was not thought to have any great significance at the time.

The real change came with the expansion of cotton cultivation and the extension of the nvujo concept to cash crops. It became the practice of the mailo owners to exact a tithe of the cotton produced by the tenants on their land.[86] Thanks to their majority in the Buganda Lukiko, the mailo owners were able to have this 10 per cent levy on cash crops made statutory.[87] This unpopular levy was one of the reasons for the strength of the Bataka movement, an organization which campaigned against the mailo system and opposed the chiefly landlords' abuses of their tenants.[88] The colonial administration regarded this exploitation of the Bakopi with increasing concern, and when the Lukiko some years later passed a new law, forcing the peasants to give about a third of their cotton crops to the landlords, the law was vetoed by the administration. Attention was thus drawn to the fact that the colonial authorities in Buganda hardly had any measures at their disposal to limit the burden of nvujo and busulu imposed on the Bakopi. In this respect Buganda differed from the other parts of the Protectorate, where the Crown land type of landholding prevailed, and the administration was in full control. To remedy this unfortunate situation the Buganda Lukiko was constrained in 1927 to pass the Busulu and Nvujo Law, which fixed the amount of busulu and nvujo which could be charged.[89] This law has later been called 'a Peasants' Charter'[90] as it signified two important trends in the colonial policy of the 1920s: the priority given to the Bakopi in the cultivation of cash crops, and the shift of emphasis away from the chiefs' rights and claims to the protection and furtherance of the interests of the Bakopi.[91] The handling of the issue of nvujo thus increased the attrition of the chiefs' customary authority, and widened the gap between their roles as chiefs and as mailo owners.

Summary and conclusions

An outline of the nature of the various obligations on the Bakopi is presented in Table 2. The picture which emerges is fluid and inconclusive. There was, for example, the problem of Buganda as opposed to the rest of the Protectorate. Nvujo

Table 2. Obligations and tributes on the Bakopi, 1900–20

	Origin		Basis		Area	
Name of obligation or tribute	Introduced by colonial authority	Originating in traditional system	Rendered to chiefs as office-holders	Determined by type of landholding	Most of Protectorate	Confined mainly to Buganda
Hut tax and/ or poll tax	+				+	
Kasanvu	+		(+)		+	
Luwalo		+	+		+	
Busulu		+	+	+	+	
Nvujo		+	+	+		+

was levied mainly in Buganda, while the other tributes spread to the rest of the country, although often very gradually and with different rates or different labour obligations. This was of course part of the more general problem of how far the Ganda model was applicable in other districts. The decisive factor here was the concept of landholding. Failure to recognize the important consequences of the mailo system for the definition of the traditional tributes (busulu and nvujo), and in particular to clarify whether they were due to the chiefly officeholders or the newly created group of individual landowners, was largely responsible for the unstable state of affairs which characterized most of the period. It was only towards the end of this period that more clear-cut solutions were proposed, and these involved the recognition of two definitions of busulu.

There was a further, related dichotomy between the traditionally rooted system and the colonial one. It became essential to clarify which of the two systems rights and obligations were derived from. Kasanvu, for instance, was introduced by the administration, but justified by reference to the chiefs' customary powers; but this proved untenable in the long run. All these difficulties in establishing what was meant by chiefly rights over land inevitably affected the mission's position when it laid claim to such rights.

Two other factors at work involved changes over the years: the economic growth which came with the spread of cash crops, and which provided a basis for labour commutation on an increased scale; and the increased bureaucracy in the state, which allowed the authorities more control over the burdens placed on the Bakopi, and cast the chiefs in the role of civil servants. Both factors affected the chiefs' rights to tributes and made the administration aware of the need to redefine these tributes; for the maintenance of the chiefs' authority was a matter of prime concern for most colonial officials. All in all, we may say that the post-war period was characterized by an accumulation of effects.

Turning to the actual extent of the burdens placed on the Bakopi, Table 3 shows the amount of money they had to pay or the amount of work they were expected to do per year, in the years 1910 and 1919. Labour requirements of at

Table. 3   Obligations on Bakopi measured in rupees and/or labour duties

Name of obligation or tribute	1909–1910[92]		1919[93]	
	Cash	Labour	Cash	Labour
Poll tax	5 Rs	2 months	7.50 Rs	2 months
Kasanvu		1 month		1 (+ 1) month
Luwalo		1 month		1 month
Busulu	2 Rs	1 month	5 Rs	1 month
Total	7 Rs	5 months	12.50 Rs	5 (6) months

Note: Nvujo was not measurable in rupees or labour until a later period. The figures are based on Buganda rates, and these may have been lower in other districts. Labour obligations were the same in most districts, but may, even as late as 1919, not have been introduced in the remoter areas.[94]

least five months annually, plus some additional duties (such as food supply and porterage) constituted a substantial burden on the Bakopi, and help to explain the unrest among them which found expression in the Bataka movement.[95] For the missions, such a heavy burden made it virtually impossible for them to impose extra obligations on their tenants. As church land had very little intrinsic value, it became essential to establish which tributes could be levied on people on church land. One guiding principle was that obligations on church, mailo and Crown land must be harmonized; otherwise the church land would be emptied of tenants. The most obvious line for the missions to take was to try to secure for themselves a share of the various dues and tributes and to obtain exemptions for their tenants.

Obligations on church tenants

The mission's efforts to obtain a share in the obligations levied on people on their land and the problem of exemptions will have to be examined against the background of overall government policy on alienation (Chapter 11). It will be recalled that the administration was concerned that the authority of the chiefs should not be eroded, a situation which could easily develop if the church tenants were made independent of their chiefs. The local administrative system should not be weakened by the alienation of a group of people who considered themselves accountable to a special system of authority, that is, a 'Government within a Government'. While the administration might be willing to relieve the burden on the missions as much as possible, it could do so only insofar as these principles were not violated. The CMS was hardly aware of the constraints which dictated the administration's policy, and made continuous efforts to obtain exemptions and special concessions for people on church land in spite of all signs that such concessions would not be granted.

Poll tax and educational work

Over the first two decades of the century every change in poll-tax policy and rates was typically followed by demands from the mission for special concessions. When hut tax was first introduced as part of the Uganda Agreement of 1900 the mission foresaw disastrous consequences for its educational work, and accordingly requested full exemption, or at least a substantial reduction, for its teachers. Both requests were refused by Sir Harry Johnston, and his lack of response to the educational argument was particularly striking. It was therefore something of a volte-face when the Commissioner, introducing a poll tax of two rupees on bachelors in 1905, granted exemptions for all unmarried teachers. This saved the mission and church about 800 rupees (£53).[96] It is difficult to say whether this was intended primarily as indirect support for education; it seems rather to have been part of a deal between Bishop Tucker and the Commissioner. According to the Bishop the promise of exemption was an acknowledgement of his efforts to persuade the Ganda chiefs to accept the new poll tax.[97] The events of 1904–5 are thus an indication of the CMS mission's continued political influence in Uganda after the late 1890s and the conclusion of the Agreement. Only a few years later, however, colonial officials were clearly unhappy about these exemptions, although they were hesitant to renege on the promise given by the Commissioner in 1904.[98] Only when poll tax fully replaced hut tax in 1909 was there a chance to rectify the situation.

While the mission much preferred poll tax to hut tax, Bishop Tucker was quick to point out the disastrous consequences for education if teachers were not exempted. Primary education was run without any government support whatsoever, and the teachers were paid a salary which was barely sufficient for subsistence. The Bishop wondered if the government really expected these people to work on the roads. This would be the consequence if no exemptions were granted, and many schools would have to be closed down. He much preferred a direct grant for primary-school work, which now involved 35,000 children; but if that was not possible the second best thing was an exemption from poll tax of the order of £350 per annum.[99]

The local administration persisted in its opposition to any kind of exemption and refused to insert any such clause into the new poll-tax ordinance.[100] On the other hand, they expressed their appreciation of the mission's educational work, and said that they were willing to grant it support in view of its benefit for the whole country.[101] Some surprise was even expressed that the mission had not asked much earlier for direct support for its extensive educational work; direct support had consisted hitherto of a few scholarships and grants for school buildings.[102] Now, in view of the new poll-tax system, the mission gave priority to direct support; its hesitation during the earlier years, as will be seen later, was due to its fear that the administration, if it had to spend money on primary education, might prefer to set up its own secular system instead of using the missions as educational agencies. Such a solution had in fact been suggested at one stage, and had been opposed by the mission.[103] In the meantime the mission-run educational system had expanded so much that it would be very costly to replace or duplicate. At the same time the government, which was trying to pursue a policy of retrenchment, was very happy to be relieved of educational expenses.[104]

Once exemption from poll tax had been ruled out, the problem was to find a formula for granting direct support. An upper limit had to be fixed, and Bishop Tucker here offered his assistance by suggesting that the church should be granted a sum large enough to pay the teachers' poll tax, and that the actual amount should be determined on the basis of the average number of teachers active over the previous five years. If the number of teachers increased in future it would be up to the church to find the extra poll tax.[105] This formula was immediately adopted by the colonial administration, and approval was obtained from London.[106] Instead of exemptions, the CMS mission was granted £300, a sum equivalent to the amount of poll tax paid by the teachers; but the money had to be earmarked for strictly educational purposes.[107] This new departure marked the government's official acceptance of its responsibility for the educational advancement of Uganda, and the grant was soon increased to £850 in support of other specific educational activities.[108] It then remained stable at this level until the end of the First World War in spite of several attempts to have it increased.[109] The poll tax arrangement of 1909 confirmed at the same time that it was from now on the government's intention to fulfil its educational responsibilities through the agency of the missions; and it was regarded as no more than a formality when the Colonial Office reserved for itself the right to discontinue the grant in the event of the administration itself undertaking educational work.[110]

The settlement on teachers' poll tax, which initiated a new era in the relationship between church and state, involved three aspects which deserve emphasis:

(1) The administration made it a point of policy to rule out exemptions and instead 'to give the Mission grants by way of compensation for this taxation on the teachers'.[111] There was also the minor problem of exemption from poll tax of pupils over eighteen years old. This was approved, but the exemption was subject to strict conditions.[112] Apart from this the issue of the teachers' exemption from poll tax was no longer considered relevant, and was not taken up again. This policy thus continued the approach adopted earlier by Sir Harry Johnston when the problem first arose, and was observed consistently in the government's dealings with the missions, except in the case of the unmarried teachers in 1904 which was, as already explained, part of a political deal. Instead of exemptions, the solution adopted was a form of reimbursement of the paid poll tax – a kind of tax rebate (similar to the modern practice in many states).

(2) This reimbursement was regarded as part of the administration's direct support for the mission's educational work, and was specifically directed at primary schools. Thus, although the administration was accepting direct responsibility for the educational sector, it would not simply hand out a block grant. That the support must be earmarked for specific purposes (to facilitate accountability) was made quite clear when some local officials suggested that grants should be given for 'general educational purposes' and that the mission should be left to allocate the money at its own discretion. The Colonial Office preferred that the old practice of allocating grants for specific purposes should continue.[113] This also meant, of course, that the policy of direct support instead of the granting of exemptions represented an increase in the control of parts of the missionary work by the colonial administration.

(3) The poll-tax issue showed the real force of the educational argument. The mission had constantly used this argument to back up its land demands, but it had counted for little with the administration. Nor did it in the case of poll tax produce any exemptions for teachers. The administration clearly preferred direct support, and separated thus educational support from the issues of land grants and tenant exemptions. The mission may not fully have understood this attitude, as it persisted during the 1910s and even later in employing the educational argument in support of other claims. An additional explanation may be that the mission believed that indirect support for education was easier to extract from the administration in a period of scarce resources.

The next phase in the history of the poll-tax issue came with its increase in 1919 from five rupees to 7.50 Rs. Bishop Willis reacted immediately, pointing out the crippling effect such an increase would have on the work of the missions. This time he did not raise the question of exemptions, but concentrated on the grant in lieu of poll tax which had been received since 1910. He asked for this to be adjusted so that the rebate should correspond to the new poll-tax rates; and so that the increase in the number of teachers should be taken into account.[114] The approval of both claims would give an increase of £400.[115] While the Governor recognized that an increase in the poll-tax rebate was justified, he accepted only the first of the two arguments, and approved an increase of £200 only.[116] The increase in the teachers' poll-tax rebate was thus an adjustment of, not a break with, the previous policy. The intention behind the reimbursement of poll tax had never been full coverage of the poll-tax expenses. The system was mainly designed as a method of calculating government support for primary education; the number of teachers was a convenient basis for measuring roughly the extent of educational activity. It was further specified that the case in question must not be taken as a general approval of the principle that the size of the educational grant was tied to the poll-tax rate.[117]

The only significant new departure in government policy was that the European missionaries themselves were somewhat surprisingly exempted from poll tax. This revived a privilege which had been cancelled in the late 1890s.[118] The matter was raised first by the Catholic bishops, who argued that their missionaries received no remuneration, only subsistence expenses, and that all the missions were supported by charitable contributions from overseas. The fact that the Governor agreed to this concession can best be explained as a token of good will at a time when educational grants were insufficient and there was little prospect of any increases.[119] That this was in fact the case is confirmed by the fact that the concession was annulled again in 1925, when the education grants were increased.[120]

The latter decision ushered in a new practice, whereby the teachers' poll tax was no longer used as the basis for calculating the administration's subsidies to education.[121] As we have pointed out in a different context (p. 158), the transition to a new phase of cooperation between mission, church and state started soon after the war, when the administration began to take a more active interest in educational matters. This topic will be discussed in a special chapter on education. For the present it is enough to suggest that a distinction between the mission's educational and religious work would be a natural consequence of the state's involvement in education. The severing of the link between the teachers' poll tax and the government education grant can best be seen as an expression of this new era, when teachers were officially recognized and were paid a fixed salary, and were no longer considered primarily as church workers.

Kasanvu

Bishop Tucker denounced kasanvu because it was falsely derived from the chiefs' customary rights. But the CMS mission was also very concerned about the drain on its labour supply which would occur if tenants were called up to do one month's paid labour for the administration. The mission therefore sought exemptions for its full-time staff (clergy and catechist/teachers) and especially for its tenants. The missionaries asked for the concession that, if the tenants had done one month's labour for the church, they would not be called up.[122] The two issues thus raised were dealt with separately. The first one was covered by the general ruling that people in permanent employment would not be called up, which meant that all teachers, clergy and church keepers (there were generally two for each church) were exempted.[123] The number of people covered by this ruling soon turned out to run into several thousands in the whole Protectorate, with its more than 1,200 Anglican churches.[124] Also included later in this group of permanent employees were the church katikiros and headmen discussed earlier.[125] The exemption from public work of these people was not disputed by the government, and the inclusion of the latter category in particular serves to emphasize that the exemption was not a special concession to the mission, but part of a general ruling valid for all who had permanent employees, including the planters.

The problem proved less straightforward for the ordinary tenants on church land. In the first instance the government responded positively to the mission's claim that it needed the labour badly and had no other means of recruitment than the disposal over the kasanvu obligation. The ruling was made that every tenant who had done one month's manual labour for the church (to be confirmed by a European missionary) would not be called up for kasanvu; but it was emphasized that this rule should be applied with caution so as not to undermine the chiefs' authority.[126] The result of this exemption, although this was not recognized at the time, was that the administration had in effect granted the mission the disposal of the tenants' kasanvu obligation without stipulating any conditions of payment.

When the kasanvu obligation was increased in 1912 to include the possibility of a second month if necessary, the mission was once more on the alert, and requested that tenants who had done two months' work for the church over and above their other obligations be exempted. Otherwise, the badly needed labour supply would be diverted away, and the educational work would suffer.[127] This time the colonial authorities took a less positive line. While the mission's right to dispose of one month's labour was upheld, the tenants were still liable to be called up for the second month. In addition it was required that the one month's labour granted for church purposes should be paid for at normal kasanvu rates, three rupees.[128] This was something new, as the mission had never paid for its tenant labour hitherto. The new ruling seems however to have been applied with some leniency in the following years, and there were few checks, especially as regards the payment of the three rupees.

It was only in 1917–18, with the general tightening of administrative procedures, that the authorities, out of concern for the chiefs' position, began to enforce the 1912 regulations. It was in particular the interpretation of the criterion of permanent employment that caused disagreement between the mission and the administration. It was discovered that tenants, especially in Buganda, were not doing the minimum three months' work (including one month's luwalo) and were not being paid in accordance with the current rates. The officials invoked the restatement of the kasanvu regulations issued in 1917,[129] and the result was that church tenants were now called up to do kasanvu, from which they had hitherto been exempted.[130]

The three bishops, representing all the Christian missions, pointed out the disastrous effects of this on religious work in general, and on educational work in particular. It was felt that conditions on church and non-church land were no longer equal. When the missions continued to call on their tenants to do their usual work and the government also called them up for kasanvu, it was seen as double duty, and people started to leave church lands.[131] In order to restore equality of conditions and ensure that church land could be used for its intended purpose, the bishops suggested that a quota list should be drawn up each year showing how many tenants in permanent employment were necessary for the work to be done properly. In addition they wished to reserve the right to pay the three rupees at their own discretion. The missions were in effect requesting the final authority to decide their own needs for kasanvu labour, although they were willing to submit to an annual check. Similarly, they were asking for the right not to have to pay their tenants for kasanvu labour, evidently assuming that doing kasanvu on church land, close to home would be much more attractive than having to travel in order to do it for the administration. In general the bishops left no doubt that they considered the colonial administration to be under a moral obligation to help stop migration from church estates. This would mean that the transfer of a certain amount of kasanvu labour from the state to the missions was fully justified by the missions' beneficial work for society.

The Governor's attitude to these labour demands was positive, in view of the missions' educational work,[132] whereas other officials were much opposed to granting other concessions than those already in existence, as they saw the matter as part of a much wider issue, and were worried that exempting church tenants from national obligations might have serious repercussions for the whole administrative system.[133]

The discussion in 1918 had no discernible outcome. This was primarily because the much wider issue of abolishing kasanvu altogether now dominated the scene. Meanwhile, the colonial administration seems to have returned to a more lenient practice, which meant that tenants on church land were generally exempted from the first call, but were liable to be called up the second time, unless they could certify that they had been fully employed for three months (including one month's luwalo).[134] By using the concept of permanent employment, the government aimed at dealing with tenants on church land in the same way as, for example, tenants on planters' estates, so as to avoid as far as possible having to make special regulations for church tenants.[135] And when the government, despite its intentions, had to introduce a special ruling for church land in order to procure a reasonable labour supply for the mission's work, it was less a question of exemptions from the work as such, as the church tenants really were expected to do one month's labour, than a transfer of the disposal over kasanvu from the state to the mission.[136] In spite of the limitations, the mission benefited substantially from the disposal over their tenants' kasanvu labour.[137] It is difficult to measure the exact value of this usufruct either in rupees or in man-hours,[138] but it is possible to get some idea by looking at the consequences of the abolition of kasanvu in 1922. Shortly after this, Bishop Willis complained that it had become virtually impossible to keep the schools functioning and to keep up the general work. He suggested that tenants on church land could fulfil their luwalo obligation by being allocated to the building of schools.[139] This suggestion raised a number of important issues concerned with the distinction between religious and educational work which belong mainly to the following period. It does, however, indicate the loss which the mission had suffered by no longer having access to regular, cheap labour from the kasanvu quota. It is signficiant that a substitute was sought in the other labour obligation, luwalo, even though it was strictly for educational purposes. Otherwise, the mission now had to compete for labour in the open market, and had to pay the current wages.

In characterizing the relationship between the mission and the administration on the basis of the kasanvu issue, it is first of all noticeable that the government was willing to do what it could to ensure a reasonable labour supply for the mission and facilitate its conditions of work. The formula used is less clear, though it may be said that it was not primarily a question of granting exemptions, but much more a transfer of government labour to the mission. At the same time, the amount of labour available was limited, and the whole arrangement was subject to strict supervision to ensure that a reasonable balance was maintained between conditions on church and non-church land. The chiefs, too, were affected. Connected with the transfer of the labour supply was the transfer of the right to call people up for work, which entailed some attrition of the chiefs' rights. This again explains why most government officials were very anxious to limit the extent of the transfer; for otherwise the chiefs' authority would be undermined too much.

Looking at the issue from the point of view of the mission, it is characteristic that the missionaries considered kasanvu transfer as a type of exemption from an obligation to the colonial administration, and failed to see the disposal over kasanvu as a chiefly right. This was why the mission did not tackle the problem raised by Bishop Tucker of whether the administration was justified in legitimizing the kasanvu system on the basis of customary obligations to the chiefs. The main aim of Bishop Tucker's successors was clearly to secure the kasanvu labour levied on church tenants for their own purposes, not to dispute its legitimacy. This leads to the tentative conclusion, which will be examined further later, that the mission, by placing itself in such a position, was accepting the forced-labour element in the kasanvu system, even to the extent that it did not necessarily pay the full current rate, and thereby lost its right to deplore compulsory labour as practised by the government. It is further significant that when kasanvu was abolished the Bishop immediately turned to luwalo as a substitute.

Luwalo

As shown earlier, luwalo was, in comparison with kasanvu, easily defined as an official obligation to the local administration, and its legitimacy was not disputed. The mission's acceptance of luwalo was also strongly influenced by the fact that it was written into the Uganda Agreement (clause 14).[140] These factors explain why there were virtually no exemptions or special regulations in connection with luwalo,[141] and why the mission sought none. In practice, however, the situation was slightly different, because the various rulings on kasanvu tended to have a secondary effect on the luwalo obligation:[142] clergy, catechist/teachers, church katikiros and their headmen were not called up for any form of public work; and it was conceded that tenants on church land could confine luwalo work to the neighbourhood of their own homes. This enabled them to meet the considerable demands of the church.[143]

With the general tightening of policy on labour obligations in 1917–18 these two privileges came under close scrutiny, and the three bishops accordingly asked to have them reaffirmed by the government.[144] As this would amount to the formalization of what had hitherto been a practice unofficially condoned by a lenient administration, strong opposition was expressed, especially by the Provincial Commissioners, who were concerned about the effects on the native administrative system and the chiefs' authority. Apart from those connected with kasanvu, there were no other privileges for tenants on church lands.[145] Hence, no exemptions from luwalo should be granted,[146] and the missions' request for preferential treatment ought to be rejected.[147]

The latter point of view prevailed: no special legislation on luwalo was introduced for church tenants, and the mission seems to have accepted the duty of its tenants to fulfil the luwalo obligation.[148] This acceptance may, however, have been due to a tacit return to the earlier lenient practice on the part of the administration.[149] It was a more serious matter for the mission when the new luwalo law of 1920 defined the obligation more accurately, and made it optional for people in permanent employment (those who worked more than three months a year) to commute the labour obligation with a cash payment of five rupees. Tenants on church land could thus no longer avoid the luwalo obligation. Moreover, if clergy, teachers and other employees were not to be taken away from their work, they would have to make use of the commutation option. The CMS mission, again jointly with the two other missions, immediately reacted against this new prospect.[150] It was pointed out that elementary educational work would suffer substantially, as teachers either worked for nothing or were paid 2–4 rupees a month, and therefore could not raise the money necessary for commutation. To make matters worse, they also had to pay the increased poll tax. Either they would have to give up their work, or the missions would have to raise the money, which in the case of the CMS would mean an extra burden of 10,000 rupees (£666) a year. Accordingly, they asked for exemptions for teachers, as they were already doing 'work of national importance'.[151] The ordinary tenants were this time not included in the request.

The colonial administration was thus forced to assess the importance of the combined evangelizing and educational work for society, and to consider whether it could qualify as fulfilment of the luwalo obligation. In the first instance the Provincial Commissioners were consulted. While expressing sympathy for the request, they found themselves in the same dilemma as before. On the one hand they were adamantly against any kind of exemption, on the other they wanted to help the missions. The result was that the basic question was not really answered; in the end clergy, teachers at a certain level and church katikiros were granted exemptions from luwalo.[152]

The lack of clarification of the formula according to which these exemptions were granted became crucial when the concession was to be extended to provinces outside Buganda. In the Western Province, the Provincial Commissioner was a strong supporter of the principle that exemptions could not be granted, as luwalo was a national obligation.[153] The Governor was in favour of a uniform policy for the whole Protectorate, and added that exemption from luwalo would be a recognition of 'certain special unpaid services rendered by individuals to the community'.[154] It was further made clear that when teachers at some future date were paid an adequate salary the concession would expire, as they would no longer be doing 'beneficial services to the community' without payment.[155] In view of the Bakopi's increasing access to the commutation of luwalo it was, however, difficult to have special rules for the church employees, because the basic principle was that every African in the Protectorate was expected to do luwalo work.[156] In the end it was made quite clear that there was really no question of exemptions as such:

The principle in Buganda is that nobody can be 'exempted' from Luwalo, but that in the case of certain persons (i.e. Miruka Chiefs, School Masters, Katikiros of Mission Mailos, etc.) who render substantial *unpaid* services to the community in which they live, these unpaid services are accepted as Luwalo services. They are thus not exempted from Luwalo, but they are regarded as having performed their Luwalo by these unpaid services. This principle should be applied to all other districts of the Protectorate, and the term 'exempted' should be avoided.[157]

While the church employees' services to the community were thus officially recognized in broad terms by the administration, the tenants were not taken into consideration during the discussion of the luwalo obligation. The mission refrained from asking for any special concessions on their behalf, as there was no chance of success. What mattered more for the mission was that tenants could stay on church land and be available as ordinary labourers instead of going away to do a month's luwalo labour. Accordingly the mission's interest was to have the commutation option extended as soon as possible to everybody, instead of being confined to people in permanent employment.[158] Here the colonial authorities had other interests, because of their overriding concern for the customary system of administration and the chiefs' authority.[159] The course of commutation was in fact inevitable; but the change only came gradually.

It is noticeable that the luwalo system was kept as a government prerogative, unlike kasanvu. No rights, either to call up their own tenants, or to have the first option on their luwalo labour, were transferred to the mission. In this respect, neither the mission nor the church was granted any recognized position. In fact, the administration was unusually strict in its opposition to any exemption. When the mission requested some formalization of the leniency which had existed in the administration of luwalo, its request was refused. When the luwalo obligation, following the introduction of commutation, was felt to be a heavy burden, the government was willing to relieve the strain on missionary resources to some extent, but it was very reluctant to grant any exemptions this time, and settled in the end for another formula. Aware of this policy, the mission from its side avoided pressing its claims. It neither requested exemptions for the tenants, nor the right to call on luwalo labour for church purposes at any point in the discussions. It sought certain concessions for the permanently employed so that they could carry out their work. It is difficult to measure the exact value of these concessions. Assuming that 1,200–1,300 people were involved (clergy, teachers and katikiros), the amount saved can be estimated at about 6–7,000 rupees.[160]

The fact that both mission and government acted with restraint can best be explained by luwalo's undisputed link with the traditional political system, and its continued importance for the functioning of the local administration. This was indicated directly by its legalization in the Uganda Agreement, and later in the Native Authority Ordinance. From different angles, both the government and the mission had vested interests in the proper functioning of luwalo in the local community.

The most significant new departure was the recognition that the church employees' work was beneficial to the community, and thus qualified as luwalo services. In this instance the colonial administration did not distinguish between the educational and the religious aspects of the mission's work. But this was only a temporary state of affairs. As in the case of poll tax and kasanvu, a comprehensive view of the mission's work could not survive the advent of a more active colonial educational policy, and the handling of the luwalo issue was one aspect of this process of transition. As soon as the educational grant was increased, and sufficiently qualified teachers were paid a fixed salary, they could no longer be considered as fulfilling their luwalo obligation. Consequently, they would have to pay the commutation rate. Unavoidably, a distinction would then be drawn between teachers and other church workers, and it would then have to be considered whether the clergy and other church employees not directly involved in educational work could be said to be doing unpaid services for the benefit of the community.

How far the work of the church could be considered beneficial to the whole community, and thus of national importance, was a question which also arose in a different context. When kasanvu was abolished the mission asked, in order to secure a sufficient supply of labour for the building of schools, to have luwalo labour allocated to replace the lost kasanvu labour. The workers would in the first instance be recruited from among the mission's own tenants; but as their number was too small, a quota was required from the general call-up; in particular it was desirable that the chiefs should be allowed to use luwalo labour for building schools.[161] This raised the question of whether an official institution for the benefit of the local community should be used for denominational educational purposes instead of general state purposes, as for example a secular school system. In spite of the reduction of the chief–tenant bond which followed the introduction of the commutation option, luwalo's special status and links with the African administrative system made it difficult to use it (or the commutation money) for the benefit of a limited section of the total community.

Busulu

During the first two decades of this century it was never made clear whether busulu was a feudal tribute or a rent paid for the tenancy of land; whether it was related to the traditional administrative system or to the new system of private ownership. The mission and the church had no need of such a clarification, and in spite of Bishop Tucker's doubts it was taken for granted that they had the right to receive busulu from tenants on church land in the same way as the chiefs did, and on the same terms. Hence, a parallelism was maintained between the two kinds of tenants, even to the extent that the mission, like the chiefs, in 1915 raised the rent to five rupees.[162]

The equality of the two categories of tenants was confirmed in 1914, when the Colonial Office inquired about the situation of people living on European-held land. In his reply, the Governor pointed out that it was customary all over the country to charge people a rent or one month's labour in lieu of rent, and that it should not surprise anyone that this custom was also upheld on church land.[163] He was thus implying that church land was classified as European-owned land; whether the church itself was an African institution or not was irrelevant.[164] When asked for a more detailed statement,[165] the Governor made it clear that he was equating the obligations of church tenants with feudal tributes payable to chiefs, and thus admitted that the mission in this respect had the right to exercise chiefly authority over their tenants. From a more pragmatic point of view he argued that it was necessary to harmonize the demands made upon tenants by the mission with those made by the chiefs; otherwise the former's land would become overcrowded and the latter's would be emptied of tenants.[166]

As the Colonial Office was at this point mainly concerned with the problem of the eviction of tenants from European-owned land, in which respect the mission was already subject to restrictions specified in the Certificate of Claim,[167] the matter was not pursued any further. But it is interesting that the Colonial Office in its handling of this issue touched on two points of importance for the following period. First, it was seen as a complicating factor that the chiefs were also large landowners, and thus received tribute from tenants who settled on their privately owned estates. It was therefore difficult to say whether busulu was simply a rent paid by the occupiers of the land, or a feudal tribute to the chief as officeholder. Secondly, it was asked what tenants on church land were getting in return for their tribute. A chief's tenants had 'the benefit of a highly organized system of native administration and justice, probably also a certain fixity of tenure'. But the benefits tenants on mission land enjoyed were doubtful.[168] Thus the Colonial Office was becoming vaguely aware that a distinction was needed between tribute and rent compatible with the prevailing system of land tenure; and that it was inappropriate for the mission to receive a feudal tribute and exercise chiefly rights when it was not in a position to deliver the corresponding benefits.

The outcome of the 1914 discussion was that the mission continued to exact busulu from its tenants without specifying whether it was rent or tribute, and irrespective of freehold or leasehold tenure. Hence it covered all the areas of work in the Protectorate. Thus busulu was being exacted from people living on estates which were not officially authorized, and which were in fact in excess of what the mission was allowed to hold.[169] The levying of busulu by the mission functioned as a chiefly right, and the tenants were thereby exempted from paying busulu to their chiefly overlords. It was only when general guidelines for a land settlement were agreed upon, and officials became aware of the distinction between tribute and rent, that it was felt necessary to clarify and formalize the payment of busulu to the mission. As a first step, it was made clear that on the five-acre plots on Temporary Occupation Licences the tenants were not exempted from 'any tribal obligations', including busulu, and that the mission had no right to labour or rent from these tenants.[170] The next development arose, not surprisingly, out of the confused situation in Busoga (see Chapter 10), and the Busoga controversy ultimately led to the drawing up of uniform rules for the whole Protectorate. It was discovered that the mission was taking busulu from people living both on registered and unregistered plots, and thus receiving a much larger income than it was entitled to.[171] It was therefore laid down as a general rule that a missionary body had the right to demand busulu/rent from tenants on officially recognized church lands held in freehold or leasehold. If any tenants paid their tributes to chiefs, the amount should be given back to the mission. This was tantamount to saying that church tenants were exempted from busulu obligations to their chiefs.[172]

Two things about the busulu ruling should be emphasized. First, tribute and rent were still unseparated, although busulu was now considered primarily as connected with land and not with office. Secondly, tenants on church land were now alienated from the chiefly administrative system to which they were otherwise supposed to belong. The payment of busulu to the mission created the impression that the mission had chiefly rights over people and land. That this last point made the 1924 decision on busulu appear somewhat paradoxical was soon pointed out by the District Commisioner in Bunyoro, who asked for a reclarification of the busulu issue, mentioning that busulu was either a tribute levied for the benefit of the native administration, or a rent payable for the tenancy of land. In his own opinion rent paid to a missionary society could only be a supplement to, and not a substitute for, the payment of dues to the native administration. Busulu ought therefore to be paid by everyone, including church tenants. The proper way to help the mission was either to grant official exemptions from tribal obligations such as busulu, or to grant money for educational and other purposes.[173] Soon after this, the confusion over busulu was aptly illustrated by a case from Bunyoro. A group of people who had earlier lived on church land continued to pay their busulu to the mission instead of the appropriate chief, thus indicating who they considered had chiefly status. One consolation in this case was that it showed that busulu in the minds of the people was really a tribute and not a rent.[174]

In the event, it was finally confirmed that busulu outside Buganda was a tribute to the chiefs, and that it was intended to convert it to a permanent duty payable to the local government, since the latter now provided the services formerly provided by the chief. Until this objective could be realized, church tenants should continue to pay rent to the mission, not a tribute to 'native dignitaries'.[175] This suspension of government policy lasted for only a short period. During 1927 and 1928, in the three provinces outside Buganda, busulu was also payable by tenants on church land to the local Lukiko funds.[176] While recognizing that this meant hardship for the missions, especially as teachers now had to pay busulu, the government agreed to give the missions compensation in the form of additional grants over a limited period. This provoked a highly critical reaction from the CMS mission. Bishop Willis contested the principle of distinguishing between tribute and rent, and claimed that busulu was in origin a tribute payable to the actual owner of the land on which the tenant lived. Since the compensation promised would be paid as part of the educational grant, there would be a reallocation of funds away from general missionary work to the strictly education-al area. What he was in fact saying was that everything which had made the land of any value was now being taken away, because it would be very difficult to ask tenants to pay a rent for land they occupied over and above their busulu, or to do extra work for the mission.[177]

Taking the history of the busulu issue forward as far as 1928 allows us to make two observations. First, the long and strenuous process of defining busulu shows how difficult it was for those involved to come to terms with the mixture of African and European concepts of landownership and the related issue of the chiefs' status. It was particularly difficult to establish whether the mission by collecting busulu was exercising a chiefly right or a landowner's usufruct. When the government finally decided that busulu was in essence a customary tribute, the mission was placed outside the realm of customary rights, and was therefore not qualified to receive such a tribute, however much it had been modernized and nationalized. For the missionaries this came as a shock, as they had never recognized that they were trying to combine chiefly rights with a system of private ownership and claiming that church land was not alienated. Yet the tenants on the land were quite clearly alienated, since they were not fulfilling their traditional obligations to their chiefs.

Secondly, the mission's embattled opposition to its abolition confirms that, of all the various concessions and privileges connected with landholding and tenants, busulu was by far the most valuable, and was in fact the mission's only direct source of income and labour. While indirect support had existed in the form of kasanvu and luwalo concessions and poll-tax rebates, the right to busulu was what really made church land a direct asset in the period under survey.[178]

It is difficult to arrive at an estimate of the total value of busulu in cash and labour in the years when it was neither disputed as a right nor differentiated by being linked with particular types of landownership. This is mainly because the number of tenants then living on church land is not known with any accuracy. We must also take account of the fact that the procedures of rent collection left much to be desired.[179] The figures in Table 4 cover the original 40 square miles of freehold land granted under the Agreement (mainly situated in Buganda) and give some impression of the value of the land as a source of income, especially when we compare these figures with the resources stemming from collections and con-tributions. The direct busulu revenue from the remaining 27 square miles held in freehold and leasehold in other parts of the Protectorate should be added to these figures from Buganda in order to arrive at the total value of busulu. No estimate is however available, because the number of people on these estates and their status within the framework of the church are not known with sufficient accuracy. But there is no reason to believe that busulu was less important in the non-Ganda areas than in Buganda. If we project the Buganda figures to the whole Protectorate we can estimate that busulu supplied about 35 per cent of the church's income, and that its total value was equal to that of the revenue from collections. It should be added that in certain deaneries busulu and the usufruct of church land in general were even more important, for example when the presence of a lukewarm Protestant chief or of a chief of another denomination meant that direct contributions were even smaller.[180]

Table 4. Income from collections and church land

	Collections and voluntary contributions		Rent from church land in Buganda	Total value of busulu in Buganda (from 40 sq.m in freehold)
	Whole diocese	Buganda alone		
1913–14	33,284 Rs[1]		10,000 Rs[1]	
1914–15	29,784 Rs[1]		7,300 Rs[1]	
1916–17	39,270 Rs[2]	18,410 Rs[2]		
1917–18	46,108 Rs[2]	19,432 Rs[2]		
1918–19	44,207 Rs[2]	20,467 Rs[2]		
1920	43,148 Rs[2]	20,708 Rs[2]	12,666 Rs[3]	21,421 Rs[3]

Note: The figures have been compiled from a number of different sources:
(1) Secretary to the Finance Board, Revd F. Rowling: 'Finance in the Ugandan Church', in *Uganda Notes*, Jan. 1916, p. 11 (cf. also statistics in Bishop's Files).
(2) Bishop's Files – S: Statistics 1907–17, Statistics 1882–1935, Namirembe Archives. See also *Diocesan Gazette* from the respective years. The Financial Secretary of the NAC commented on the figures in his Financial Report of 1922 (copy in SMP 7998) and explained the decline in 1920 by referring to cattle plague and the failure of the cotton crop.
(3) Estates Board's Report to the Synod in 1921 (enclosed in Minute Book, MUL). The rent of 12,666 Rs is based upon 2,593 rentpayers. But the Estates Broad tried to calculate the total value of the 40 sq.m of freehold land for the church by estimating the amount which the church would have paid in busulu if it had had no land of its own. The amount of 21,421 Rs was arrived at in the following way:

Rentpayers	12,666 Rs
Teachers/catechists, church katikiros and their assistants (1,239 people)	6,195 Rs
Old people exempted (512 people)	2,560 Rs
Total	21,421 Rs

Summary and conclusions

It is difficult to arrive at an overall estimate of the benefits ensuing from the possession of church land. Neither the actual number of tenants, nor the ratio of

Table 5.   Conditions for people living on church land around 1920

Obligations	Permanently employed: teachers/catechists, katikiros	Tenants	Estimated value for the church
Poll tax	No exemptions, reimbursement for the teachers	No exemptions, 7.50 Rs or 2 months' labour	£300–500 (4,500–7,500 Rs) in reimbursement for the teachers
Kasanvu	None called up	1 month (first call) transferred to work on church land; liable to second call	A saving, as either nothing or a lower rate than the standard 3 Rs per head was paid
Luwalo	In principle, liable to be called up for 1 month in the year, but rarely so in practice; later classified as engaged in public work	Called up for 1 month to work in the vicinity of their church estates	6,000–7,000 Rs, equivalent to 1 month's labour from the permanently employed
Busulu	Exempt	At the disposal of the church	1 month's labour, or the equivalent of 5 Rs from cash-paying (commutating) tenants
Special labour obligations to the church		Liable to 1 month's labour	Paid at current rates

ordinary tenants to the permanently employed, is known. In some cases the rights and obligations of the ordinary tenants were never made clear, or were conceived of differently by mission and government. In addition there was a certain laxity in the implementation of regulations. In spite of all these difficulties, Table 5, summarizing the administrative practices relating to the two categories of people on church land presents a rough picture of the situation throughout the 1910s, and gives some impression of the church's direct and indirect resources in labour and/or cash.

The church tenants were in principle liable for one month's labour more than the ordinary Bakopi because of their labour obligation to the church (see Tables 3 and 5). In practice, however, the church's disposal over one month's kasanvu labour tended to render the special obligation to the church superfluous. At all events the church had at its disposal two months' labour, or one month's labour and five rupees in rent (busulu) from its tenants. To this should be added some fringe benefits and the indirect support represented by concessions to the permanently employed, especially the teachers. Measured on the basis of the tenants' situation, there was thus some degree of equivalence between living on church and non-church land, although this was based on a precarious balance which was sensitive to any change in the government's administrative rules or practice, as for example had happened with kasanvu. None the less, for most of the time up to 1920, the balance was upheld, primarily by the transfer of or exemption from certain public duties. Thus the administration in the main accepted its obligation to secure reasonable working conditions for the mission by making it possible for the land to be a source of income and labour supply. In this respect it may be said that the government had moved beyond the concept of the intrinsic value of church land (as sites for buildings and food production) and had come closer to acceptance of the mission's claim that the land was an endowment involving 'rule over people'.

This point is further put into perspective when we take the mission's concept of landholding into account. The missionaries clearly conceived of the land grant as an endowment, and they wanted the government to provide conditions that enabled them to reap the benefits of this endowment. What they wanted in fact amounted to the recognition of a double concept of landholding: church land, they seem to have thought, should be covered both by a European concept of landownership (free transfer of freehold land, subletting) and also have elements from the African system (chiefly rights to such tributes from tenants as kasanvu and busulu); they wanted the best of both worlds. But it is doubtful how far the mission was actually aware of this manoeuvring between two systems in its attempts to maximize the usufruct of its land. Only Bishop Tucker seems to have understood the precariousness of the situation and to have understood the new 'rules of the game' entailed by the introduction of individual ownership in Buganda. Not even the colonial administration seems to have been fully aware of the fundamental difference between the African and the European concept, as revealed by its handling of the busulu issue and its belated discovery of the need to distinguish between tribute and rent. This may again be related to the fact that colonial policy during the 1910s was based on an undefined synthesis between the preservation of traditional authority and the establishment of a workable administrative system.

While this lack of conceptual clarity resulted in some degree of leniency in government policy on church tenants, the colonial administration was prevented from becoming too lenient by certain basic constraints. One was its concern for the authority of the chiefs. This explains why it was unwilling to grant any exemptions to the tenants and searched instead for another formula, often settling for an *ad hoc* arrangement or informal concessions. In practical terms this resulted in a policy whose aim was to achieve a reasonable degree of harmony between the burdens imposed on people inside and outside church land. It worked reasonably well during the 1910s, but the post-war period revealed how precarious the balance was, and how vulnerable it was to variations in external circumstances. Three factors which contributed to this have been isolated. In the first place, the more elaborate administrative system, with its greater capacity for scrutiny, and its more careful application of the rules and regulations, left less room for informality and leniency. Secondly, the economically determined possibility of commuting labour obligations with cash payments shifted the emphasis from the labour supply to the more easily accountable situation where each individual paid a definite sum. This evened out the inequities between the permanently employed and the ordinary tenants and involved a substantial reduction of the indirect benefits accruing from church lands. Thirdly, the clarification of which obligations were traditional and which the responsibility of the colonial system (busulu interpreted as a tribute to the local authorities, kasanvu abolished as forced labour) meant a reduction in the sum of privileges and concessions obtainable for church tenants. All these developments, working with cumulative effect in the post-war period, aggravated the situation for church tenants. Their burdens were increased, and when they were asked to do church work it was often considered to be a gratuitous extra imposition. Conditions were no longer as attractive as those in the surrounding areas, neither materially nor indeed in terms of lifestyle, given the special standards of conduct the tenants were expected to observe.[181] The consequence was often considerable migration from church lands.[182]

The tilting of the internal/external balance which had formerly existed and the subsequent decline in the value of church land came at an awkward time for the mission, as it was very dependent on the value of the land in the immediate post-war period. Support from overseas was cut down because of the CMS's financial difficulties,[183] and the collections, the second major interior source of income, were hit both by the general economic decline in the Protectorate which began in about 1921,[184] and by the decrease in the chiefs' contributions due to the accession to power of a new generation of chiefs who proved to be 'poor givers'.[185] The prospects for self-support were now anything but encouraging.

The mission tried, of course, to re-establish the balance on a new basis. They also asked for more privileges and concessions, invoking the need for expansion within the educational sector. The government response, however, did indicate that the relationship between the state and the mission had moved into a new phase with a clear-cut distinction between educational and religious work. The latter development, which belongs mainly to the succeeding period, will serve to illuminate the basic premises which had so far lain behind the administration's policy on church land as an endowment for missionary work. Mission landholdings were recognized as a contribution to 'the religious, educational and moral development of the country'.[186] This was the formula which Sir Harry Johnston had applied in 1900, and its origin has been traced to the Berlin Conference of 1884–5. It had ever since provided the guiding principles for policy on mission land from the chiefs was virtually cancelled, and when the two real assets of administration was prepared to grant to mission tenants. But the formula in its general form became less applicable in the post-war situation, and this marked the beginning of a new period when it would become necessary to specify in more detail the aspects of missionary work which the state would be willing to support.

The mission took a gloomy view when in the 1920s the right to receive gifts of land from the chiefs was virtually cancelled, and when the two real assets of church land, labour supply and rent from tenants (chiefly rights over land) were almost cut off. 'If the available labour is diverted, and the payment of rents prohibited, the whole intention of the original gift, confirmed as it has been under the Uganda Agreement and hitherto recognized by Government, namely, provision for the support of the Church in Uganda, is defeated, and the lands cease to be of any practical value.'[187]

PART IV

Direct inputs: demands to the colonial state

10 Collections were essential for educational and other activities of the church: counting the collection (mainly cowrie shells) outside Namirembe Cathedral, 1902

11 Combining secular and religious education: Bible lesson in Mengo High School, 1906

13

The issue of forced labour

While the issue of land grants and landholdings mainly concerns the economic bonds between church and state and allows us to analyse the the position and status of the mission and the church within the colonial state, it reveals only a little about their political role within the colonial system. The survey of church land has indicated that dependence on land meant a high degree of economic dependence on the state, but it does not answer the question whether this dependence had a constraining effect on the mission's ability to act vis-à-vis the state. In order to examine the demands the mission and church presented to the political system, and to what extent they were able to influence, challenge, modify or even hinder any given policy, a number of cases will be presented which illustrate efforts to make an impact on specific political decisions or longer-term policy. These cases have been selected after the examination of a large corpus of source material which is assumed to include most of the direct contacts between the mission and the administration during the first quarter of the 20th century.[1]

It has earlier been shown (Chapter 6) how the issue of forced labour arose as early as the last half of the 1890s, when no wage labourers were available. This meant that the only source of labour was the customary labour tribute due to the chiefs. The mission got its labour force either through concessions from the chiefs or as tribute from people living on church estates. In either case it became open to question whether tributary labour was identical to forced labour, and no real answer was arrived at in the 1890s. This may be ascribed to the fact that two definitions of forced labour, based on two different criteria, were possible, and the missionary actors did not distinguish between them. The mission's use of labour conscripted on the basis of traditional tributes, and thus not voluntary, was apparently the criterion which Colonel Colvile applied when he accused the mission of using forced labour (see p. 91). The second and narrower criterion was that of payment; the argument that only unpaid labour was forced labour. For a time these two definitions were used indiscriminately, but it seems that the mission, and in particular Archdeacon Walker, settled for the second one, as they considered that they had solved the problem of forced labour when they introduced payments.

Bishop Tucker, on the other hand, was more concerned with the problems inherent in the first definition. It is important to examine his attitude more carefully, since he was the key figure when forced labour became a central issue in connection with kasanvu. During his whole episcopate he was seriously concerned with the problem of labour because this seemed to him to be the area where the protection of Africans from injustice was most needed. At first he engaged himself, in accordance with the CMS tradition, in a campaign against the institution of slavery, and he became known within the colonial administration in East Africa as well as in Britain as a keen and serious campaigner. He hailed it as his first victory that in 1893 he got the Ganda Protestant chiefs to emancipate their slaves voluntarily.[2] His main work against slavery was related to the East African coast, and he acted as the chief spokesman for a number of pressure groups in their campaign for the complete abolition of slavery in British dependencies.[3]

Soon after the turn of the century Tucker's attention turned to the labour problem. He was especially concerned with the possible exploitation of Africans, and sent a strongly worded protest to *The Times* in March 1903 denouncing the recruitment of labour from East Africa to the mines in South Africa.[4] The protests of Tucker and others led to a decision that no such recruitment should take place without prior notice to Parliament.[5] Some years later, due to the increasing demand for labour and the lack of volunteers, the practice of forced labour became more widespread. Tucker became increasingly concerned with the burdens currently placed on Africans. He recognized that luwalo was in accordance with custom and law, but held any additional labour obligation to be indefensible. When some people in Bunyoro were called up for road work after they had done their one month's luwalo he immediately raised the matter with the Governor, who then gave 'the most satisfactory assurances' that there would be no further call for this kind of labour.[6]

Tucker stated his motives for taking such a strong stand against forced labour in another context at about the same time. The Governor had suggested that Indians should be allowed to settle in Busoga, which had become severely depopulated because of sleeping sickness and famine. In letters to the Colonial Office and British-based associations Tucker argued strongly against this plan, saying that it was tantamount to depriving the Basoga of their land by taking advantage of their temporary distress, and that the Basoga themselves would consider this an act of robbery. He pointed out that the use of forced labour was in fact a major reason for the famine. It had withdrawn thousands of men from agricultural work and severely hampered the usual pattern of production in Busoga. He also cited the forced cultivation of cotton practised by the government as a reason for the famine.[7]

Nothing came of the plan for Indian immigration to Busoga, but Tucker's stand on these issues in 1909 established him in the eyes of the colonial administration as a spokesman for African interests to be reckoned with, and generally as someone who was well-informed about 'native affairs'.[8] The colonial authorities now realized that he could influence opinion in Europe on issues which he felt strongly about. On the other hand, he was careful to adapt his means to the ends he wanted to achieve. He became very angry when the CMS president independently raised the issue of forced labour in Bunyoro in Parliament. Tucker feared that such a move could harm his own relations with the Protectorate government as it unnecessarily transferred to the European arena a case which could better be settled in the local setting.[9]

The whole of Bishop Tucker's register came into play when the issue of forced labour came to a head with the introduction of kasanvu. It has earlier been shown in detail (Chapter 12) how Tucker disputed the legitimacy of kasanvu as a customary tribute, and how the colonial officials in Uganda as well as in London halfheartedly concurred with him. The importance of this in the present context is that Tucker, using the same kind of arguments, could draw a clear distinction between labour obligations rooted in customs such as luwalo, and newer obligations like kasanvu which had been introduced by the government and could only be characterized as forced labour. Tucker thus isolated and defined the forced-labour element, as the mission had previously failed to do. And so he created for himself a firm basis from which to campaign against forced labour, because kasanvu represented for him such a significant escalation in the use of forced labour that he now felt that the time had come to take action.[10]

After the kasanvu system had been in force for less than a year Tucker raised the issue with the colonial administration, pointing out the unfortunate consequences of forced labour, in particular the depopulation of Buganda due to the migration of large numbers of young men.[11] He foresaw that the current policy would lead to catastrophe and perhaps rebellion. He considered the principle of forced labour to be a violation of the principle of freedom and justice for 'subject races' which was supposed to guide the whole colonial enterprise. Among the types of forced labour he condemned, he laid special emphasis on the forced cultivation of cotton and the supply of conscripted labour to private individuals (Europeans and Indians). As an alternative to this system, Tucker suggested that market mechanisms and normal economic laws should be allowed to prevail: if fair wages were offered, an ample supply of voluntary labour would be forthcoming.[12] After receiving a first, provisional answer, Tucker restated his opinion in even stronger terms.[13] He criticized the former Governor for his 'hustling' of the country by the extended use of forced labour, and pointed out the inconsistency of the government's policy of using coercion, which resulted in depopulation and a lower marriage rate, and thereby threatened the life of the very people in whose interests the country ought to be governed. He showed how strongly he felt about the issue of forced labour when he compared the situation in Uganda with that in the Congo:

To my mind it is little less than hypocrisy for Great Britain to allow this sort of thing to go on in Uganda whilst taking up so different an attitude with regard to the Congo. Had it not been that I am anxious not to weaken the hands of the Government in its action in the Congo I should have drawn public attention to Uganda some time ago.[14]

Faced with Tucker's arguments and demands, the local administration conceded two of his points. As we have already seen, the Acting Governor had to admit that demanding additional work from men who had paid their poll tax and busulu and done their luwalo was unjustifiable, and that it was wrong to request the chiefs to call these people up for public work. Accordingly, instructions were issued that these practices should cease. Secondly, it was agreed that it was not the government's place to supply labour for merchants, traders and other private individuals. The government could make the needs of these people known, but recruitment was their own affair. As regards the forced cultivation of cotton, the Acting Governor argued that in this case the government was *in loco parentis*, and was under an obligation to teach the people what was in their own best interests.

Finally, he was opposed to an increase in the present scale of wages. This would have unfortunate repercussions for economic development in the Protectorate and for the whole feudal system of labour, and could undermine the chiefs' authority.[15]

Tucker apparently received assurances that the labour policy would be substantially changed, although the system of kasanvu was not officially revoked, nor was the forced cultivation of cotton given up.[16] It seems, however, that when it came to actual implementation very little was changed. While in London at the end of 1910 and the beginning of 1911, Tucker found it necessary to approach the Colonial Office directly.[17] He concentrated on the two points on which he had previously met some positive response in Uganda, even if no real action had been taken. First of all, he maintained that it was not the government's business to supply forced labour to private employers[18] – hereby touching on an issue which was much discussed in the East African Protectorate at about the same period because of the influx of settlers.[19] As his second point he cited repeatedly the admission of the Acting Governor, quoted above. In fact, the system as practised now was illegal. This second point was the cardinal one, as the government's acknowledgement of it would have made it indefensible to maintain the kasanvu system.[20]

Bishop Tucker's initiative met with no success in Britain, and the Uganda administration blatantly reneged on the two promises given only a year earlier. The Acting Governor disputed Tucker's claims of large-scale emigration from the Protectorate,[21] and made much of the unfortunate effects any sudden change in the labour policy would have on the chiefs' authority and the whole system of feudal tributes. The sudden cancellation of age-old obligations would hinder progress towards a higher standard of living.[22] It is evident from the Acting Governor's response, in which he did not touch directly on Tucker's two requests, that for the moment a system of forced labour was indispensable for the functioning of the government and for the economic development of the Protectorate. The Colonial Office on its side more or less washed its hands of the whole affair when it confined itself to confronting Bishop Tucker with the admittedly inconclusive answer from Uganda (see p. 180).[23] Tucker's arguments were given a polite hearing, but no action was taken. It was possible for the Colonial Office to keep such a low profile, because at that time the issue of forced labour was not attracting the attention in British circles which it would later in the post-war period. By the same token there is no indication that Tucker made any attempt to involve politicians or other influential groups in his efforts to bring the practice of forced labour to an end. A second factor which may have been important in both Britain and Uganda was that it was officially known that Tucker was resigning his post as Bishop of Uganda for health reasons,[24] and had taken little part in recent developments.

While these two factors may explain why Tucker personally did not pursue the matter any further, it is extraordinary that the local CMS mission did not protest against the administration's abandonment of the two promises earlier given to Tucker. The Acting Governor left no doubt, however, as to why his administration no longer felt obliged to comply with the earlier declarations on kasanvu and the supply of labour to private employers. He pointed out that missionaries themselves applied for labour, like any other employers, through the chiefs. 'I am sure that they would be the first to discontinue this practice if it could be considered reprehensible.'[25] Tucker's own missionaries had in fact undermined his initiative in the forced-labour issue. The mission was divided internally, and the government did not hesitate to make use of this. It was thus limited how far the mission could hope to exert any political influence with regard to labour.

Turning to a closer examination of the mission's later approach, which differed considerably from that of Bishop Tucker, it is important to recall that, apart from the wider definition of forced labour, the mission employed a narrower one based upon the criterion of payment. This was the one Archdeacon Walker used when he discussed forced labour with the colonial administration in 1907. It was the duty of the mission to protect Africans against unfair burdens, and among these were forced labour and other insufficiently paid services.[26] That Walker did not oppose forced labour as such was fully confirmed when kasanvu was introduced in 1909. He accepted that it was necessary for the time being, and for the general good of the country, that large numbers of men were forced to work, provided they received a fixed rate of pay.[27] What really concerned the mission was the question of their own labour supply. They had obtained exemptions for their permanent employees and the right to one month's kasanvu labour from the tenants on church land – and these concessions amounted in fact to their implicit recognition of the system of kasanvu. They apparently consoled themselves with the fact that it was not unpaid labour. Thus, at the same time as Bishop Tucker was working with some success to have forced labour completely abolished, the mission was making use of compulsory labour for its own purposes, and was not even paying the official rate. The colonial administration was thus fully justified when it found no reason to do away with forced labour because of arguments from missionary circles. That the missionary leaders mainly conceived of kasanvu within the perspective of their own labour requirements was fully confirmed when a second call to kasanvu was introduced in 1912. Again the issue for the mission was exemptions for tenants on church lands, and no general protest was expressed against this new burden on the Bakopi. Such an omission would have been unthinkable if Bishop Tucker had still been in charge.

On the contrary, the mission identified itself even more closely with the practice, as it realized that kasanvu meant more labourers for the church, and the missionaries were grateful for any workers the officials could procure.[28] There was even an official request from Bishop Willis to the Governor for the government to grant 10 per cent of its kasanvu labour to the building of the new Namirembe Cathedral.[29] While it was admitted that it was virtually impossible for Bishop Willis to recruit labour in any other way, his request nevertheless caused great surprise among government officials, in view of Bishop Tucker's protest against forced labour in 1909–10. Now the mission seemed to be giving the kasanvu institution its seal of approval. All the same, in view of the large number of exemptions granted to mission tenants, it was not considered advisable to grant it 10 per cent of the government's short supply of kasanvu labour.[30] Apart from this specific request which could not be met, there is no doubt that the mission made considerable use of kasanvu over the years, and the government drew attention to this when the kasanvu obligation was written into the Native Authority Ordinance in 1919.[31] Hence, it comes as no surprise that the mission did not take up Tucker's second major point and protest against the practice of supplying kasanvu labour to private employers, especially the planters. The extent of this practice will be evident if we turn to the situation in Busoga. When the administration tightened up the kasanvu regulations in 1917, the Busoga Planters Association protested and asked that they should have the same share of the kasanvu labour as before.[32] The government would not admit that the planters had any such right; previous practice had consisted of the handing over of surplus labour to assist them in getting their estates properly started.[33] Nevertheless, the Provincial Commissioner of the Eastern Province later thought it necessary to inquire whether, in view of the limited supply of kasanvu labour, the government or the planters in Busoga should have the first option on the labour quota. The Governor answered that the government requirement should be met first.[34] It appears, however, to have been common practice at the time that men called out to do kasanvu for the government were handed over to planters and traders.[35]

Besides the practice of supplying labour to private employers, about which the mission must have known, a second issue became closely linked with the system of kasanvu: in Busoga it was discussed to what extent coercion could be employed in the process of recruitment. It was conceded that it was impossible to get a reasonable supply of labour without the use of some kind of force, but it appeared that government officials in the Eastern Province had gone so far as to use the seizure of cattle as a means of persuasion.[36] While this was deplored, the principle of using mild forms of force was upheld and written into the Native Authority Ordinance of 1919.[37] As the issue of coercion became controversial in the immediate post-war period it provides us with an opportunity to test the opinion of the mission on this important question, where the protection of African interests was really at stake.

The mission became involved in the labour issue on two occasions during 1919: first in connection with the work of the Uganda Development Commission, secondly by being drawn into the much more serious labour problem in the East African Protectorate (known from 1920 onwards as Kenya). The former issue provided an important platform for the European planters to air their grievances about the labour supply.[38] In its report, the Commission mentioned two methods of increasing the labour supply: by indirect and direct pressure. While the former was much to be preferred it was emphasized that there was no injustice in compulsion as such, and that it could easily be justified by the circumstances.[39] The Commission referred specifically to a memorandum which Bishop Willis had written six months earlier, in which he had analysed the whole issue of labour and made his opinion on coercion clear.[40] Willis considered the kasanvu system unsatisfactory and wanted it dropped as soon as possible. Therefore, unlike the Development Commission, he fully supported the campaign of the leading Ganda chiefs to have kasanvu abolished.[41] He did not, however, dispute its immediate necessity, and in general he accepted the need for some compulsion, provided that it was carried out with certain safeguards and according to special regulations. His argument was that, first, there was nothing wrong with compulsion as such: it was sanctioned by ancient custom. Secondly, it was a practical necessity, if the potential wealth of the country was to be developed. And thirdly, there was nothing in the nature of compulsory work which was 'essentially at variance with the Christian law'.[42] This approval of coercion in order to ensure an adequate labour supply for the good of the country was later echoed by other members of the CMS mission when they gave evidence to the Uganda Development Commission in 1919. They denounced unpaid labour, and were unhappy about forced labour when practised in the form of kasanvu, but they clearly recognized the need for coercion in order to get everyone to do some work for the country.[43]

It follows that it is necessary to draw a distinction between the issue of kasanvu and the issue of compulsion. The recommendation to abolish kasanvu was not equivalent to a denunciation of the use of coercion in ensuring an adequate labour supply. Rather, the system of kasanvu, with its element of forced labour, was no longer considered to be a suitable method of recruiting labourers for government purposes, mainly because of its unfortunate social and moral consequences. On the basis of earlier results (p. 193), we may here infer that it would have been in the mission's own interests at that time to have the kasanvu system discontinued. When the kasanvu regulations were strictly enforced and unmitigated by corresponding concessions and exemptions, the mission was left at a disadvantage, as the obligation meant a double burden on church tenants and tended to empty the estates. It may in this respect be significant that the CMS mission did not take the lead in the campaign against kasanvu despite the determined course earlier pursued by Bishop Tucker. His successors settled for less than the ultimate objective. They were satisfied that the obligation was no longer levied on all males, and that the regular conscription of monthly kasanvu labourers ceased. But the mission still accepted the need to ensure an adequate labour supply for the good of society, and in that respect the use of coercion was justified if the actual circumstances required it. It took the Colonial Office by surprise when Bishop Willis suggested direct pressure to obtain labour. This was contrary to their experiences from Kenya, where humanitarians such as the Anti-Slavery and Aborigines' Protection Society had taken the opposite view.[44] Prior to Bishop Willis' own involvement in the controversial labour problems in the East African Protectorate, he had thus endorsed the use of compulsion in recruitment and failed to dissociate himself from the prevailing practice of supplying labour to planters and settlers.

The involvement of the Uganda mission in matters in the neighbouring Protectorate was primarily due to two factors: first, the series of conferences during the 1910s attended by the various missions in East Africa with a view to establishing closer cooperation and possibly setting up an ecclesiastical province; Bishop Willis had been a driving force in these efforts, and had established a number of personal contacts with the missionary leaders in the East African Protectorate.[45] Secondly, the Western Province of the East African Protectorate, Kavirondo, belonged ecclesiastically until 1921 to the Diocese of Uganda, although it had been transferred politically to the East African Protectorate in 1902. This meant that the Church of Uganda in 1919 was still directly affected by the labour question in the neighbouring Protectorate.[46]

Like the planters in Uganda, the settlers in the East African Protectorate raised the labour question. Their attitude towards the government was tougher, and their influence greater, because of their large numbers and their important position in the economy of the country.[47] When the labour shortage became acute in the immediate post-war years the government took action by issuing the well-known 'Northey Circulars', named after the Governor, General Northey. The most important of these, issued in October 1919, introduced two special measures meant to increase the labour supply for both the government and the settlers.[48] First, all males between 17 and 37 were required to do public work for two months in the year, provided they were not in permanent employment. The similarity to the kasanvu system in Uganda is striking, as the circular legalized compulsory paid labour for state purposes. Secondly, district officers, chiefs and elders were instructed to exercise 'every lawful influence' and 'encouragement' in order to augment the supply of labour for private employers, who were mainly

European farmers. With the machinery of government thus involved in the recruitment, what was being endorsed was tantamount to the use of coercion in supplying labour to private employers. The principle underlying this legislation was that it served to combat idleness and to teach Africans the dignity of work.[49]

The October circular elicited a joint response from the Anglican Bishops of Uganda and Mombasa and the senior missionary of the Church of Scotland Mission, Dr J. W. Arthur. These three constituted the core of the newly founded Alliance of Protestant Missions, which enabled them to act with much greater authority. They pointed out that, while coercion was not mentioned, the authorization of colonial officials and chiefs as recruiting agents for European farmers would amount to the same thing. As regards the principle involved, they expressed themselves unequivocally: 'Compulsory labour is not in itself an evil, and we would favour some form of compulsion, at any rate for work of national importance . . .' They nevertheless expressed great concern over the risk of abuses, especially if it was left to the chiefs and headmen to exercise pressure. Their recommendation was therefore that some kind of legal compulsion was preferable, as this would include legal safeguards, which were especially necessary in view of the references to women and children in the labour circulars.[50]

It is useful to compare the content of this memorandum with the attitude of the Uganda mission to forced labour, and in particular to ask whether Bishop Willis had changed his opinion. Comparing the two main issues at stake in both countries, there was in both cases an acceptance of the necessity of compulsion, and there was no denunciation of the supplying of labour to private employers. In neither area was there any fundamental opposition to the principle of forced labour. It was not the policy as such that was being disputed, but the question of how forced labour should be applied, and what safeguards and controls were necessary. Bishop Willis' involvement in the labour problems in the neighbouring Protectorate therefore indicated no new departure in the conception of forced labour; on the contrary the memorandum reflected to a great extent the phrases which he had used in the Uganda context.

The Bishops' Memorandum is rather wordy and somewhat ambiguous, and students of the period disagree on how it should be interpreted and how much influence it really had on the outcome of the forced-labour controversy in Kenya.[51] But in order to put the Uganda mission's attitude to the crucial issue of forced labour in a wider perspective we may record some of the contemporary reactions to the Memorandum and try to ascertain whether these caused the Uganda mission to change its attitude to the government's labour policy. The Memorandum itself caused little stir in government circles. Officials tried to make light of the bishops' alarmist view of the opportunities for abuse,[52] and limited reforms to a few adjustments in the labour policy.[53] Severe criticism of the bishops' position came, however, from colleagues and humanitarians in Britain. The Bishop of Zanzibar, Frank Weston, accused them bluntly of having 'played traitors'.[54] Dr Norman Leys, a leading opponent of compulsory labour and the pro-settler policy in Kenya, had some very harsh comments on the bishops' letter.[55] He compared compulsory labour to slavery and denounced the missions' alliance with the Kenya government, attacking in particular Bishop Willis.[56] It was, however, J. H. Oldham, the influential secretary of the Conference of Missionary Societies in Great Britain and Ireland, who was the driving force in the campaign against the forced-labour policy in Kenya which began in 1920, when the Bishops' Memorandum became the subject of heated discussion among humanitarians.[57] Oldham was surprised by and critical of the bishops' attitude, and thought that they had failed to see the implications of their statement.[58] He thus considered Bishop Willis and his colleagues to be out of tune with the prevailing opinion in Christian circles in Britain; but he tried to neutralize the political impact of their Memorandum by emphasizing some positive features. For instance, he tried to soften Leys' statement that the bishops 'advocated compulsion' by substituting the phrase 'reluctantly accepted'.[59] He also tried to involve Willis and his co-signatories in the campaign to have the Northey Circulars withdrawn.[60] Still, the Memorandum remained a bone of contention during the whole campaign mounted by Oldham.[61]

We may conclude from the contemporary reactions to the Bishops' Memorandum that Bishop Willis and with him the Uganda mission had so far been consistent in their attitude to forced labour, but that this attitude differed considerably from that of the Christian–humanitarian groups in Britain with whom they normally associated, and whose assistance they had often invoked. The major difference was that Bishop Willis had a narrow and somewhat moralistic conception of forced labour. He accepted that it was economically necessary without taking the wider implications for the African population into account. He acquiesced in the conditions set by the government without questioning the basic trend of government policy, and he considered that his own and the mission's essential contribution was to prevent abuses and repair any damage that might be done. His involvement in the Kenya controversy meant that he became exposed to the wider, more serious perspectives of the forced-labour issue, and Oldham clearly tried to get him to revise his attitude and take a more active stand in influencing government policy.[62] Oldham would in fact have liked Willis to adopt a position like the one Bishop Tucker had adopted earlier. It now remains to be seen whether events in Kenya caused the Uganda mission to change its approach to forced labour.

The campaign in Britain, mounted by Oldham, had the effect that the new Colonial Secretary, Winston Churchill, ordered a substantial modification of the labour policy in Kenya in September 1921.[63] In future, government officers were to play no part in the recruitment of labour for private employers; they were to restrict themselves to providing mutual intelligence about the requirements of prospective labourers and employers. Compulsory labour should not be used for government purposes unless this was absolutely necessary. In such cases the public benefit of the work should be carefully specified, and the approval of the Colonial Secretary obtained.[64] It was made clear that the same principles would be applicable in Uganda.[65]

In order to assess the impact on Uganda of these rulings we must first look at the local government's response. The role of government officials in recruiting labour for private employment had now been given up in the more developed districts. But the Acting Governor asked for permission to let the District Commissioners take an active part in assisting employers to obtain labour in the less advanced districts, where the cotton industry would be severely jeopardized by the absence of a voluntary labour force. In justification of this proposal special emphasis was laid on the fact that in these districts only peasant producers benefited from the ginneries.[66] It was with the greatest reluctance that the Colonial Office acquiesced in this proposal, as it conflicted with the general policy laid down in the dispatch to Kenya. However, 'the welfare of the community' overruled all objections provided that district officers confined their assistance to 'general exhortation'.[67] As for compulsory paid labour for the government (kasanvu), it was pointed out that in Uganda, unlike Kenya, the Africans were producers of cash crops. This meant that it was difficult for the government to obtain labourers without compulsion. The abolition of compulsory labour in accordance with the ruling from the Colonial Office could therefore mean a slowing-down, and in certain districts even the complete cessation, of all public works. The Africans would suffer most from this. Instead permission was asked to phase out kasanvu gradually, in accordance with the scheme which had already been initiated in response to demands from Ganda chiefs (p. 181).[68] The Colonial Office then agreed to a longer period of transition from a compulsory to a voluntary labour system.[69] It was later indicated that no difficulty had been experienced in obtaining voluntary labour in the districts where kasanvu had been abolished; the supply had even exceeded the demand. It was admitted, however, that the transition had been considerably facilitated by the prevailing economic conditions; the low price of cotton and the partial failure of the crop meant that people had to undertake wage labour in order to pay the poll tax; also the closing-down of plantations owing to the recession had resulted in a decreased demand for labour.[70] So the abolition of compulsory paid labour for public works presented the government with no difficulty and, as wages were kept at the same level, the expenditure was not increased. But the same economic conditions had the paradoxical effect that compulsory, unpaid labour for the chiefs and the local community (luwalo) had to be retained, as people were unable to pay commutation rates. But luwalo was not much of a problem for the colonial authorities, as it was firmly rooted in tradition.[71] We may thus conclude that labour policy in Uganda, in that it was adapted to local circumstances, differed considerably from the principles laid down for Kenya in 1921. This inconsistency in policy and the slow progress in its implementation clearly caused anxiety at the Colonial Office, especially as officials were very sensitive to possible missionary reactions.[72]

Apart from the question of Kenya there was not much reason for alarm, as labour policy in Uganda was not exposed to missionary criticism. The CMS mission in Uganda appears to have been influenced neither by the critical attitude held by missionary circles in Britain, nor by the resultant new departure in labour policy in Kenya. This may of course be explained by the different circumstances in Uganda, where the revision of policy was much less significant, and where the issue of the settlers was less acute. Still, there are some factors which suggest that the Uganda mission took a different attitude and was influenced by other, much more pragmatic considerations. The government's endorsement of compulsion and the involvement of district officers in recruitment did not provoke any missionary reaction. Although direct evidence of this is lacking we may argue *ex silentio*: when the Colonial Office in 1922 expressed its anxiety over the inconsistencies in policy in Uganda, and the local authorities felt called upon to defend themselves, there was not a single reference to missionary opinion, let alone criticism. This absence is quite significant, in view of the missionary pressure which had been experienced in Kenya, and taking into account how sensitive colonial officials were otherwise to missionary opinion on the labour issue.

To assess the situation from the mission's angle, we must first of all recall that the CMS mission did not take the lead when the Ganda chiefs resumed their efforts to have kasanvu abolished in 1921 (pp. 181–2).[73] Nor did they, unlike Tucker earlier, advocate better working conditions and higher wages as a means of attracting the labourers needed. Their attitude to the use of compulsion was discussed more directly on two occasions in 1921, after Bishop Willis' return from his discussions with Oldham. At the missionaries' conference it was decided unanimously that 'all forms of forced unpaid labour ought to cease, but that forced paid labour might be used . . . within reasonable limitation as to the number of days per annum'.[74] At the following Synod satisfaction was expressed that the British government had ruled that women and children must not be forced to work on plantations, and that the local councils were asked not to employ women and children on the roads.[75] The Synod was thus mainly concerned with abuses and not with the principle of compulsion as such. This whole trend was later confirmed when Bishop Willis, after kasanvu had been abolished in most of the Protectorate, asked to have luwalo labour allotted to the educational work of the church. This move met with the disapproval of one of the missionaries who found it inconceivable that the mission, given its earlier criticism of forced, paid labour, was now willing to use forced, unpaid labour. Not even the planters did this.[76] Willis differed also in this respect from Oldham, who advocated the discontinuation of the luwalo system on the grounds that it was open to abuses by the chiefs and that it was resented by the younger generation.[77]

In general we may conclude that external factors, stemming from the controversy on forced labour in Kenya, had virtually no influence on the Uganda mission, in spite of the fact that Bishop Willis was familiar with, and could have served as a channel for, newer trends in the thinking on forced labour. The mission's attitude to the labour issues was conditioned by local needs, and this accounts for its accommodating attitude *vis-à-vis* the government. The Kenya controversy did not prompt the Uganda mission to change its course and take a more active line in relation to the government's labour policy. The real change in the mission's policy, and subsequently in its approach to the government, took place when Bishop Tucker was succeeded by Bishop Willis in 1911–12. This change cannot be ascribed to the difference in personalities alone, as we have seen that even Tucker's contemporaries, who were more concerned about the prevention of abuses than about the wider matter of principle, worked with a narrower definition of forced labour than the Bishop did. But it remains a significant feature of the period under survey that Bishop Willis and his contemporaries not only dropped the issues which Tucker had raised with some success, the use of coercion and the supply of forced labour to private employers but even went so far as to approve of them, and saw no reason to give priority to the protection of African interests, despite missionary circles in Britain denouncing the same two practices as detrimental to the interests of the African population. We may here offer two other explanations of this attitude to forced labour and to the government's policy in general. These will help us to bring out those factors which determined the mission's policy-making on a crucial issue like labour and decided its ability to influence government policy.

(1) The first explanation presupposes that the scope for the mission to exert political influence or play a role in the policy-making process depended on how it conceived of the state and defined its own relationship with the government. In this respect there was a difference between Tucker and Willis. Tucker, complaining about forced labour in Bunyoro, pointed out the mission's constant dilemma: on the one hand it must 'keep on the best of terms with the Government and at the same time . . . guard carefully the interests of the natives'.[78] While stressing that care and caution were needed in this situation, he had no doubt that it was the duty of the mission to champion the cause of the Africans, and he need not be

ashamed of his own record in this respect. When necessary the mission should take complaints to the government, and his experience was that they were always listened to. Tucker thus expected the mission to play an active role in safeguarding the Africans' interests.

Willis placed the emphasis differently when he, as the new Bishop, delivered his first Episcopal Charge to the missionaries.[79] He pointed out the mission's duty to mediate between the Africans and the colonial government and its responsibility for fostering a spirit of loyalty and contentment. The situation was the happy one that 'whatever may be the occasional failure on the part of individual officers, we have over us a Government just, sympathetic, and emphatically friendly to the best interests of the native'. It was a much more accommodating and conciliatory role which Willis was here ascribing to the mission, although he would not rule out intervention on behalf of the Africans in rare cases. The salient feature of his attitude was confidence in the colonial state. The administration's measures were basically benevolent and in the best interests of the Africans, and the mission and the colonial state were to a great extent working towards a common goal. This was aptly expressed in a review of the Synod in 1921, which mentioned 'the growing realization that the Administration and the Missions . . . (together with every rightminded Britisher of the country) . . . are working shoulder to shoulder for the uplift of Uganda . . .'[80] This was markedly different from the Tucker line, and represented a reappraisal of the mission's role *vis-à-vis* the colonial state. Government measures, including the use of coercion to ensure an adequate labour supply, were accepted as being for the good of the country, in that they taught Africans the value of work. This basic attitude may also account for the fact that Bishop Willis and the Uganda mission did not show any real understanding of the wider implications of the Kenya controversy on forced labour for the development of African society and for the chances of Africans to achieve equality with other groups. It may be said that Willis' line reached an apogee in the idealizing and ideologizing of the relationship between the mission and the colonial state. As the mission moved closer to the government its scope for political influence and intervention on behalf of the Africans was diminished. Instead the mission saw it as one of its functions to legitimize colonial rule in the eyes of the Africans. This trend was reinforced by the mission's material dependence on the government.

(2) We have seen how members of the mission, while Bishop Tucker was campaigning against forced labour, sought exemptions for their personnel and their tenants, and how Bishop Willis soon after applied for a share in the government's kasanvu labour and later gave his unequivocal approval to the use of coercion. Kasanvu was beyond all doubt an essential element, both directly and indirectly, in the work of the church and was looked upon as an important means of furthering the principle of self-support. Certain special circumstances increased the importance of kasanvu when Willis took over. In the first place, he and his colleagues recognized that, unlike Bishop Tucker, he had little access to private funds for the support of particular aspects of the missionary work. Tucker had used his Diocesan Fund for special purposes, and this had not been considered incompatible with the principle of self-support. The drain on local resources would thus now become heavier, and the expansion of the work, especially in the educational sector, would reinforce this tendency.[81] The building of a new cathedral was another expensive project which swallowed funds throughout the second decade. These pressures meant that it was very difficult for Willis to relinquish the resources available from forced labour. On the

contrary, the mission was dependent on and therefore had a vested interest in it. This was not only a question of the labour supply; there was also the more indirect factor that wages were kept at a low level by not being a function of normal market mechanisms.[82]

The mission's dependence did not pass unnoticed by government officials, and it coloured their image of the mission. This weakened the mission's moral stand on the labour issue, compromised its independence and left it little scope for protest. In fact, its members ended, as we have seen, by supporting the principle of coercion. Judging from the labour issue, we may conclude that economic dependence on forced labour had considerable influence on the mission's political standing within the colonial system, and reduced its ability to protect African interests in a field to which Bishop Tucker and his contemporaries in Britain accorded the highest importance. Whether this situation was fully recognized by the missionaries involved is doubtful, as they glossed over the difference between the Tucker and the Willis epochs by rationalizing and redefining the political role of the mission within the colonial system.

The mission had gradually, both ideologically and economically, acquired a vested interest in the status quo. It was inclined to be hesitant in campaigning for the abolition of forced labour and more cautious about taking a direct stand against the colonial government. Bishop Tucker had made considerable progress towards greater influence, whereas his successor neither had nor seemed to wish such influence, despite the fact that, unlike Tucker, he could have counted on support from Britain.

14

Excess land and alienation

Closely linked with the problem of forced labour was the question of the government's confiscation of excess land, following the survey of the chiefs' estates. Just as the European planters needed labour, they also required land. As the government was bent on a dual system of African peasant production and a European plantation economy (pp. 146, 157), it was necessary for it to have at its disposal Crown-land areas which could be sold or leased to the European planters who began to arrive in the last three years of the first decade.[1] It was a major obstacle to these aims that in Buganda, which was the first area to attract the attention of prospective planters, the government did not have much Crown land. Although half of the Buganda area was theoretically made Crown land by the Uganda Agreement of 1900, the government had, apart from forests, mainly hilltops, swamps and wastelands. In addition, as the survey of the chiefs' estates was as yet incomplete, the government did not know how much productive land was actually at its disposal as Crown land. In order to remedy this situation, the administration induced the Buganda Lukiko to pass a law – the Land Law (Survey) of 1909 – under which any excess land (that is, land in excess of the amount granted by the Agreement) shown by the survey to be held by the chiefs was to be converted to Crown land and put at the disposal of the government. On the other hand, any shortages would only be remedied after the completion of the survey, and at the discretion of the government.[2] In order to further facilitate access to the disposal of Crown land, an amendment to the Crown Land Ordinance was passed the following year which allowed the government to sell or lease land to Europeans without regard to the people living on the land, provided that the latter were fully compensated.[3] Both the chiefs and the Bakopi thus fell victim to the drive for a European plantation economy.

When the full implications of the first law dawned upon the Ganda chiefs, they protested and began to work for a change in the law, and it was at this stage that Bishop Tucker took the matter up, combining it appropriately with the issue of forced labour. When the Acting Governor, in his private correspondence with Tucker on the latter issue, complained that the government did not have the confidence of the Ganda chiefs, Tucker was quick to point out that the main cause of this was their uncertainty over land. Speaking as a confidant of the chiefs, he voiced their grievances, mentioning especially the confiscation and sale of excess land which they thought belonged properly to the Baganda under the terms of the Agreement.[4]

The issue of excess land simmered all through 1910, and the leading Protestant chiefs tried in vain to have the legislation changed. They even went so far as to hire one of the newly-arrived European lawyers to put their case, and also attempted to involve Sir Harry Johnston in the affair.[5] The crux of the matter was that the chiefs were convinced that the government was violating the Uganda Agreement by declaring some of the 8,000 square miles allotted to them as mailo land to be Crown land, and by disposing of it to Europeans.[6] When Bishop Tucker returned to London towards the end of 1910 he brought the matter to the notice of the Colonial Office, together with the issue of forced labour.[7] Tucker supported the chiefs' complaint that the Protectorate government had violated pledges given earlier, and drew attention to the fact that the Baganda clearly felt that they were being robbed of land so that it could be sold to Europeans.[8] He suggested a new rule: that land which the Baganda lawfully regarded as theirs and which was held in accordance with the Agreement could only be disposed of with the explicit approval of the Kabaka and the chiefs.[9]

For Tucker this was more than a question of excess land and broken pledges to the chiefs. He was generally concerned about the colonial administration's eagerness to sell or lease land to Europeans. This was equivalent to the transfer of disposal over land which rightly belonged to the people of the country. Not only the chiefs, but also the Bakopi, were bound to be affected by the influx of European planters and the development of a plantation economy. Accordingly he saw the amendment to the Crown Land Ordinance as a radical change in the wrong direction, and referred exclusively to this ordinance in his intervention with the Colonial Office, but failed to mention the Land Law (Survey) of 1909, which affected the chiefs' interests.[10] This was a mistake with regard to the legal basis of the government's policy which would have consequences later. His emphasis on the Bakopi created confusion among colonial officials and made it difficult for them to grasp what he was aiming at. They came to believe that he was solely concerned with the hardships of 'the squatters' on Crown land, and they considered him to be mistaken on this score, as they had taken a number of precautions and ensured fair compensation for these people in the event of the sale of Crown land.[11] They failed to understand Tucker's general anxiety over the whole principle of allotting land to Europeans, and his concern for the interests of the chiefs.

A solution was first arrived at when the newly appointed Governor, F. J. Jackson, a Uganda veteran who had acted as Sub-Commissioner to Sir Harry Johnston at the time of the conclusion of the Uganda Agreement, officially appealed the case to the Colonial Secretary at the request of the Protestant chiefs. Jackson upheld the claims of the chiefs and denounced his predecessor's point of view. He mentioned Bishop Tucker's intervention, and said that he was especially disturbed by the feeling of discontent and suspicion now spreading among the Baganda, who were afraid that the government would sell or lease the surplus land after the survey of the estates. Even in Busoga and Bunyoro people had begun to fear that the government would take away their land, making it impossible for them to plant cotton and other crops.[12] Privately, Jackson was even more outspoken, and characterized the previous policy as an expression of the drive to amass revenue at any cost, in this case by an act of injustice, as the land was acquired for the Crown at the expense of the Baganda. The law of 1909 had been forced on the Baganda, and was a catastrophe, as it was an unjustifiable exploitation of African interests. Jackson went so far as to imply that this, taken together with the issue of forced labour, made Uganda seem little better than the Congo Free State.[13]

Governor Jackson thus supported to a great extent Tucker's criticism of the policy on surplus land. But he did not comment directly on Tucker's more general concern about the sale of land to Europeans and the position of the Bakopi. It is evident that Jackson's reference to Tucker's view had some impact at the Colonial Office, where officials were now belatedly made aware of Tucker's intent in criticizing the handling of the excess land question.[14] But it is equally clear that it was not due to Tucker's intervention that the law of 1909 was revised,[15] but to the Protestant chiefs' own efforts and the support they received from Jackson, with his profound knowledge of Ugandan affairs and his concern to arrest the growing feeling of discontent among the chiefs. The outcome was that the Colonial Office accepted Jackson's interpretation of the Uganda Agreement. It was now written into the law that the Ganda authorities themselves had the right to dispose of the excess land.[16]

Excess land became a problem for the mission itself some years later. The survey of church lands revealed that some of their estates comprised more acreage than had been registered. The government regarded this surplus as Crown land, in accordance with the Certificate of Claim. The mission then requested that these small strips of land should be restored to the original donors, the chiefs, who had granted the land on the understanding that in the event of abandonment it would be returned to them, and were now much aggrieved that excess land was to become Crown land.[17] The administration acquiesced in this, apparently because the landholdings in question were of little significance.[18] The issue demonstrates once more the alliance between the mission and the Ganda chiefs as regards land, and the mission's efforts to secure for the chiefs what was considered to be their rightful property. In a wider sense the whole issue of excess land confirms the impression gained from the study of the overall land question: that the mission and the Protestant Ganda chiefs closed their ranks around the Uganda Agreement in order to exert political influence for the benefit of the chiefs.

It is noticeable that while Tucker expressed general concern about the sale of land to Europeans, because of the vulnerability of the Bakopi, similar concern for the Bakopi on the part of the mission was not evident in the succeeding period. The mission was mainly concerned with obtaining more land on the best possible terms, and therefore went out of its way to prove that in the case of church land no problem of alienation was involved. It should further be remembered that when the British government reversed its policy on the sale of land to Europeans, and later adopted the Crown-land formula in order to safeguard the interests of the peasantry, these decisions were not due to any missionary pressure or intervention, nor did the mission express any special interest in the matter. The mission's engagement in the problem of alienation seems primarily to have been geared towards its own immediate interests, which happened in this case to coincide with those of the chiefs. In the years after Bishop Tucker's involvement the mission appears to have been more concerned with the chiefs' rights to the disposal of land than with the fate of the Bakopi when the land was sold to Europeans. In the absence of concrete evidence, this line of argument must remain speculative, but it accords well with the result of the previous analysis of the forced labour issue.

A further suggestion arising from the investigation of the issue of excess land is related to the change in the mission's ability to play a significant political role. First, Tucker's mistaken view of the legal basis of the government's policy confused the whole matter and made his intervention pointless. One possible explanation is that the more developed state of the colonial system made it more difficult to step in on behalf of the Africans. Greater expertise (for example, legal knowledge) was necessary if intervention was to have any impact on the more technically complex system which had now arisen, and the mission became less useful in a mediatory capacity. This was also evident to the Africans themselves. While Tucker acted as spokesman in Britain for the leading Protestant chiefs, they themselves sought the advice of a lawyer. The mission was no longer the only channel through which to approach the authorities either in Uganda or in Britain. There were now other and often more effective ways of approaching the government, especially as technical knowledge and experience became more and more of an asset.

Generally, we may notice a tendency for the mission to have less scope to assume its usual role as the chiefs' confidant in political matters. This accords well with the developments observed in the discussion of the land question: the more established state of the colonial administration left less scope for the mission to influence politics. This trend cannot solely be ascribed to the difference in attitudes and personality between Tucker and Willis, nor can it be attributed to the higher degree of dependence we have seen in connection with forced labour. A more general factor was at work; changed circumstances within the whole colonial system were responsible.

15

Education as an issue between church and state

The CMS mission's educational work, and the importance of the educational argument in the mission's approaches to the colonial administration have been touched upon on various occasions.[1] We are here concerned with the extent to which education provided a platform for presenting demands to the political system, and the state's response. And, in a wider sense, the question of whether the resultant linkage between mission and government led to a relationship of dependence for the mission.[1]

The establishment of an educational monopoly

Around the turn of the century the CMS mission began consciously to make education an essential part of its work, and substantial resources were allocated to the future expansion of the educational system in Uganda.[2] The use of the educational argument in support of claims began at an early stage, and continued during the negotiation of the Uganda Agreement and the disputes over its implementation. Soon afterwards it was possible to define four main areas of educational work.

(1) The expansion of the primary sector. This had initially been initiated in response to the baptismal requirement of being able to read at least two Gospels in the vernacular.[3]

(2) The training of catechists and teachers, which also reflected the integration of the educational and the evangelical work.[4]

(3) The technical training of craftsmen.[5]

(4) At the highest level, the education of the sons of chiefs with a view to their

becoming future chiefs themselves, and the general training of young people who aimed at employment at the lower levels of the colonial administrative system (as, for instance, interpreters or clerks). In other words, it was the Christian training of the African leaders of the future that was at stake here.[6]

The last two were of direct interest to the colonial administration for the recruitment of qualified African manpower.

The colonial authorities, both in Uganda and London, looked with great favour upon the educational enterprise of the three missions, especially that of the CMS. The Commissioner of Uganda pointed out that there was now no need for the government to start schools of its own, as the missions had undertaken secular as well as religious education.[7] The Foreign Office was even prepared to make an effort to get the Treasury to grant facilities to the missions.[8] In spite of the risk of denominational rivalry the Foreign Office was in no doubt as to the usefulness of the missions' educational efforts. 'The sound policy is to seek neutrality by helping *all* useful educational work by missionary bodies, instead of helping *none*.' What really counted was the usefulness of missionary zeal and missionary funds, especially in a time of scarce resources.[9]

In spite of this enthusiasm for missionary efforts, officials in Uganda were in some doubt as to the responsibility of the government for the education of those people who did not want to attend missionary schools. Some officials were at an early stage in favour of a government school in Kampala, independent of the missions, to cater for the Muslims and in general to avoid denominational rivalry in education.[10] While they had no wish to belittle the value of the missionary effort, it was pointed out that the Muslims and the Swahili and Indian traders had no educational facilities. In order to remedy this situation, as these people could not afford to establish their own schools, it was suggested that the government should start two non-sectarian schools at the two economic and political centres, Kampala and Entebbe.[11]

When Bishop Tucker heard of this suggestion, he took strong exception to it, and demanded that his letter of protest should be forwarded to the Colonial Office. As a matter of principle he argued that, however small a matter the establishment of two non-sectarian schools might appear to be, it would be taken as a sign that the government was committing itself to a policy of non-sectarian education. More pragmatically, he added that the government did not for the moment have the machinery necessary to set up its own educational system, and could not even supplement the existing missionary system. Instead he recommended the improvement of the existing missionary apparatus by means of grants-in-aid, and even a system of inspection.[12] It should be emphasized that Tucker was not primarily against the education of Muslims as such, although he did think that they were able to pay for their own educational facilities. His main concern was to preserve the missionary monopoly of general education at the various levels; and to that end he had to fight against the establishment of a non-sectarian school system, as the result could be a government board of education which would not countenance the teaching of religion in schools. Consequently it became a major political goal for the mission to prevent the establishment of a state system of education, and to persuade the government instead to use the missions as educational agencies. This can de deduced from the discussions on the two non-sectarian schools in 1905–6, and provides the most likely explanation of the mission's hesitation over the following years in asking for any substantial state support, a fact mentioned later with some surprise by the colonial authorities.[13] A request for support might give the impression that the mission was not as capable as it claimed of undertaking the educational work.

The same unwillingness to allow any government influence emerged in connection with the issue of compulsory education. This was discussed within the mission as early as 1904, but the question was left in abeyance, as it would be very difficult to introduce compulsory education by law for all denominations. The basis of teaching in all schools at that point was Christianity, and the consequence of compulsory education for all denominations would be the setting up of secular government schools.[14] The matter was raised again at the Synod in 1909, when a resolution was passed, mainly at the initiative of the African members, requesting that the Buganda Lukiko pass a law compelling all children to attend schools.[15] When it transpired at the 1910 Synod that nothing had been done to implement the recommendation, it was decided to send a delegation to discuss the matter with the Lukiko; but it was specifically stated that it was inadvisable to approach the colonial government. Nor was it found advisable to have a government Board of Education which might not approve of the teaching of religion in schools as it had been practised so far.[16] The same opinion was expressed later by Bishop Willis: to make education compulsory would be to invite the government to set up a purely secular system.[17]

Tucker's fear that a dual educational system could easily become a single, secular system was partly vindicated by the reaction of local officials. The Acting Governor, George Wilson, like his predecessor, expressed concern not only for the Muslim population, but also for the vast number of people 'without any religion' – the term employed for those belonging to traditional African religions. If they too were to be catered for, the outcome was bound to be a government system of schools which would take over from the sectarian ones. The growing feeling of wider responsibility for non-Christians has been discussed earlier (p. 118), but the Acting Governor added two more arguments for a greater government share in education. In the first place he questioned the wisdom of leaving the training of the coming generations entirely in missionary hands, as it was doubtful whether the religious bodies would further national interests and pursue their work in harmony with the development of the whole nation. This echoed a classic issue with which most governments of the twentieth century have been concerned. In the second place, he mentioned denominational rivalries and expressed the fear that the well-known Ganda dissensions of the 1890s would be exported to the neighbouring areas with the expansion of education, to the detriment of the preservation of peace and good order. He cited an example from Bunyoro, where the chiefs had asked on two occasions for the establishment of government schools, so as to avoid dissension on the Ganda pattern. Although he was in principle in favour of a state-controlled system, the Acting Commissioner had to admit that it was difficult at that early stage to imagine any other system which could compete with that of the missionaries, especially as any such system would mean a heavy drain on funds in Britain. As a second-best solution, he was willing to leave education in the hands of the missions, provided they would secularize their teaching so much that the spread of partisan feelings was avoided. He foresaw a future need for the government to take on more responsibility for education by giving grants-in-aid to the missions, and by setting up a government inspectorate.[18]

Although the information coming from Uganda suggested clear-cut alternatives, the Colonial Office was aware that its freedom of action on educational
policy was limited, both by financial considerations and by practical realities. The
Colonial Office first had to make a decision on the advisability of starting a school
for the Muslims, which would mean government acceptance of a certain responsibility for their education. Such a school was in fact approved of as an experiment
in accordance with the proposals of the Uganda administration. On the other
hand, the interests of the Muslims in Uganda did not weigh so heavily that the
Colonial Office took any real action, and the scheme was quietly dropped.[19] The
second issue was whether a government school system should be started. This was
hardly discussed, despite the opposition of Tucker and George Wilson's counter-
proposal. It was only remarked that because of lack of funds there was no
intention of starting such a system.[20]

Lack of funds became the most important influence on policy in the following
period, and rendered it out of the question for the state to engage in any
educational activity of its own.[21] Education was a low priority, even when it
was confined to the bare minimum of catering for the Muslim community.[22]
Secondly, it was made abundantly clear that no considerable grant-in-aid would
be made to the missions for educational purposes as long as the Protectorate was
not self-supporting, but administered mainly at the expense of the British
taxpayer, which again meant close control by the Treasury.[23] Instead, the colonial
government expressed its appreciation of the remarkable progress made under
the missionary education system and congratulated itself on the fact that it had
been relieved of educational expenses.[24] The desire of the CMS to reserve for
itself and the other missions a virtual educational monopoly was realized, but this
was not primarily due to Bishop Tucker's intervention, nor can it be ascribed to
deliberate policy on the part of the government, as the Acting Governor's
recommendation for a secular educational system was hardly discussed. The
outcome, so satisfactory from the missionary point of view, was mainly due to
pragmatic considerations, and was forced upon the government by economic
imperatives. Within the colonial framework, any savings and any services
rendered free of charge were most welcome; but this meant that any overall
political decision on the use of the missions as educational agencies was postponed. As time went on, the range of the government's options was narrowed
considerably. As early as 1905 the Acting Governor, commenting on Tucker's
protest against non-sectarian schools, saw the connection between the extent of
the missions' educational engagement and the government's prospects of setting
up a purely secular system. The more highly developed the former was, the more
difficult and costly it would be for the government to get its own system started.

The strength of this inverse proportion between the two options was even more
evident during the phase from 1909 to 1912, a period marked by the government's
provision of a more substantial but still limited support for the missions'
educational work. After the introduction of the poll-tax system in 1909 the CMS
mission's demand for direct support for primary education had met with approval; and on the recommendation of local officials the grant was soon afterwards
increased in order to cover other sectors as well as the primary one.[25] No other
method of undertaking responsibility for education was discussed, and colonial
officials were full of praise for the good work done by the missions.[26] They were
still assuming that the government was thus being relieved of considerable
expense, and that this made it easier to achieve the principal goal, financial

self-sufficiency.[27] The government's awareness of the inverse proportion was fully confirmed when it was stated that as long as the missions received educational grants from the government the Treasury was not prepared to spend money on government training schools.[28] Still, it was a strictly pragmatic approach, and not the officially endorsed policy, to use the missions as educational agencies, and the Colonial Office reserved for itself the option of discontinuing the educational grants in the event of its setting up a secular system.[29]

Government support for the educational monopoly

In spite of the government's reservations, the CMS mission carried out its educational work from 1912 onwards with great confidence. It was fully aware of the fact that the missions, Protestant and Catholic, constituted the sole educational agency, and that it could therefore more justifiably address demands to the state for an increase in the highly insufficient grant-in-aid.[30] This phase lasted until after the First World War, when new conditions made themselves felt.

The mission was aware in the pre-war period of the risk of a state system of education, but it was at the same time confident that the government had as yet insufficient resources to establish one.[31] The mission therefore felt free to impress on the government its obligation to engage itself more in African education, especially in view of the usefulness to the government of the well-trained people now leaving high schools. The mission pointed to the disparity between the government grant of £850 annually, of which £450 was returned in poll tax,[32] and the £2,350 which the CMS paid in salaries alone to missionaries in charge of schools.[33] Requests for an increase in the educational grant were put forward on a number of occasions both in Uganda and London.[34] Bishop Willis even suggested a formula which would allow for greater government influence, in order to ease the way for an increase in the grant. He proposed that subsequent grants should depend on educational standards reached, and should take the form of a capitation grant, that is, a grant per head for each pupil. At the same time he proposed that a government inspectorate of schools should be set up.[35] Willis thus indicated that he was aware that increased state support involved increased government control, and that the government would have a legitimate interest in the quality and content of the education provided. On the other hand, the mission hoped to be given a freer hand in spending the money by receiving grants which were not earmarked for specific purposes.[36]

The local colonial administration gave their general support to the missionary demands. It was emphasized that the appointment of a government inspectorate was the only satisfactory method of tackling the educational issue, but it was also admitted that this would involve expenditure which the Protectorate could not bear. The only comment from the Colonial Office was, however, that it was too early to put Willis' proposal into practice.[37] The pattern repeated itself as far as the increase in the grant was concerned. The local administration recommended a modest increase from £850 to £1,000 in educational support both to the CMS and the Catholic missions. The Colonial Office agreed, but the Treasury refused the increase. The Colonial Office acquiesced in the Treasury's decision, and pursued the matter no further.[38] The situation did not even change when the Protectorate finally became self-supporting in 1915–16. This time the war was used as an argument against any immediate increase.[39] In spite of substantial pressure, the mission could thus not breach the barrier constituted by the principle of self-sufficiency and defended by the Treasury. The state acted on the assumption that the mission had such a vital interest in the educational enterprise that it would, in spite of all its grumbling, carry on and find the necessary means. Bishop Willis remarked scornfully that the government's frequently expressed gratitude for the mission's efforts ought to take a more practical form and materialize in increased grants.[40]

This state of affairs proved untenable in the long run, and things came to a head in 1917. Differences arose between the mission and the colonial administration over educational cooperation in the newly opened districts, especially whether the building of denominational schools was for the public good and could thus qualify for luwalo labour and other concessions related to the chiefly authority. This particular case will be discussed below when we come to analyse the government's religious policy (Chapter 25). It certainly demonstrated the need for better communication between the missions and the government, and to that end the first conference was called with representatives from all three missions.[41] Bishop Willis repeated on their behalf that the government did not do its fair share in the education of the people, and said that the drain on mission resources was so heavy that they could no longer cope with the increasing demands for education or the requests for trained people from the government and others. They were in fact coming close to a situation where, if grants were not increased, they would actually have to cut down on their activities. In concrete terms, the increase requested by the mission was the rather modest sum of £150 (making a total grant of £1,000) plus a higher poll-tax rebate in view of the greater number of teachers. The last request was presented more forcefully than on previous occasions, and was accompanied by a specification of exactly what would happen if the government did not respond positively.[42]

Although he hinted that the government might in future take over the control of education, the officer representing the colonial administration made it clear that he was happy, in view of past experiences, to leave educational matters in missionary hands.[43] He regretted that for financial reasons the grant had not been more liberal, and a recommendation was forwarded to London in support of the requested increase.[44] It cannot have been all that difficult for the colonial authorities to approve this surprisingly modest request, since it did not exceed what had already been requested in 1912.[45] The important feature of the events of 1917 was that the colonial administration openly accepted that it was under an obligation to take on a greater share of the educational responsibility. It did not, however, consider any possibility other than the channelling of its additional funds for the support of education through the missions. The following statement seems characteristic of the government's attitude: 'The machinery already exists; what is required is strong financial support combined with Government inspection and control.'[46] While the suggestion of a government inspectorate, which reflected Willis' proposal some five years earlier, was not taken up, the Colonial Secretary wholeheartedly gave his approval to this policy; in view of the mission's good work, there was no need for the government to take direct responsibility for education.[47]

This pragmatic approach remained the official policy in the immediate postwar period, and was further reinforced in 1920. The government then impressed on the Colonial Office the benefit of the missions' educational activities for the Protectorate, and stated frankly that the government grant was far too small. The missions had over the years relieved the government of an obligation 'which it could not itself have carried out at anything like the cost of our total contributions, direct and indirect, to the Missions'.[48] The Governor even went so far as to enter into a kind of tactical alliance with the CMS in order to help them obtain a larger grant,[49] and the mission both locally and in London continued throughout these years to address requests to the colonial authorities for a steady increase in the educational grant.[50] In retrospect, these appeals may have reflected the beginning of the financial crisis for the CMS system, but they were put forward from a position of strength at the time. Up until about 1920 the mission had strong cards in its hand because of its possession of the only educational machinery. It could be confident that the government had no other option but to support the missionary system of schools. It relieved the government of substantial expenses, and this was a feature which carried great weight with policy-makers.[51] It should be added that the local missionaries also used the educational argument in their approaches to the CMS headquarters when they requested more resources, and in particular more missionaries. It was pointed out that if the mission did not provide really good education the government would take over, and in that case the result would be secular schools. 'So far the entire education in Uganda is in the hands of the Mission. It will be disastrous if we lose it, through failure to use our present God-given opportunity.'[52]

The erosion of the educational monopoly in the post-war period

The position of strength began to be eroded even before 1920. The process, which culminated in the first half of the 1920s, was due to changing attitudes and the resultant reversals of government and mission policy.

The loss of the educational monopoly

The immediate post-war period saw an increase in the demand for trained people within almost every field, and the government realized that these people were simply not available. It was assumed that the necessary supply of trained personnel was beyond the present capacity of the missions' educational system. The provision of more advanced, specialized technical training was furthermore considered to be outside the proper sphere of the missions.[53] A detailed scheme for the establishment of government institutions for advanced education in practical fields was worked out in connection with the plans for a Native Civil Service. It was recommended that institutions should be set up to cater for medical, clerical, technical, mechanical and agricultural trainees.[54] Special care was taken to ask the missions whether they could provide such services, but it was found that from a financial point of view the government could do it, if not more cheaply, at least more efficiently at the same cost. In the end these plans materialized in the establishment of the government institution for higher education and technical training now known as Makerere University.[55]

The government took great care to consult the missions and ensure their cooperation,[56] and later a Technical School Board was set up, which included one representative from each of the three missions.[57] It was also made clear that the new training institutions were not in any way duplicates of missionary schools, but should be seen as supplementary to these, in the sense that the best pupils would be recruited from the missionary schools. In a further attempt to placate the missions, some broad guidelines were suggested which defined the two spheres of work and the relationship between them.[58] Some sort of division of work was attempted within certain fields; most importantly, the training of elementary schoolmasters was left to the missions, und they were guaranteed government support for this.[59] Finally, the key issue of religious instruction at government schools was discussed, and it was suggested that the missionary societies should be invited to give lessons, in view of the importance of religion in character formation.[60] After some disagreement among officials it was finally decided to make provisions for religious instruction by the missions.[61] In spite of all these placatory measures, the mission had to reckon with a new situation from the beginning of the 1920s onwards. First, the colonial authorities had undertaken direct responsibility for education and had become operative in its own right. Secondly, a non-sectarian educational system had been started, although it was so far confined to the top of the educational pyramid. The CMS mission's reaction was not one of hostility and opposition, despite the fact that the mission had its own well-developed plans to engage in technical training,[62] and had previously made several attempts to introduce skilled training schemes, although none of their plans had ever really come to fruition. It is probably indicative of the mission's attitude that, in view of the great need for technical education, it did not consider that the government's plans would render their own efforts superfluous.[63] Such an approach to skilled training was in harmony with a trend within the mission's educational thinking which can be traced right back to Bishop Tucker.

The mission accordingly had to adapt its own plans for technical education to those of the government and to establish the best possible pattern of cooperation.[64] In the event the mission was willing to leave technical training to the government,[65] a solution which was influenced to a great extent by a contemporary financial crisis in the CMS, which began to make itself felt in 1921–2. Technical training and more advanced education in general were thus not a field where the mission felt it necessary to protect its monopoly-like position, unlike the elementary and secondary sectors.

While the mission thus reacted in a spirit of cooperation, and conceived of the arrangement as a division of labour, the government had now begun to apply new criteria in its evaluation of the mission's general educational work. First, in view of the missions' constant demands for increases in educational grants and for defrayment of expenses for pioneering work in new fields, the government began to make economic calculations on the basis of a kind of cost-benefit analysis. Where the missions' programmes were deemed too expensive, an alternative government programme was set up.[66] In general, as the missions could no longer afford to expand their services, the government was forced to consider whether it would be cheaper and more effective to begin on its own instead of relying on the missions.[67] The old view that the missions' contribution relieved the state of substantial expense was no longer necessarily valid.

Secondly, these economic calculations led to a qualitative assessment of the missions' educational contribution. Taking the missions' limited resources into account, the government's assessment was somewhat negative. Boys coming out of the schools lacked training for any real professional work,[68] and the need for closer government control was strongly felt. What the Deputy Commissioner had hinted at as early as 1905, when he questioned the wisdom of leaving the entire educational work in missionary hands, was now clearly expressed by a later generation of colonial officials as they began to ask whether the present educational system furthered the interests of the state, and whether it was really geared to the needs of government and society. Young people were leaving school with considerable disrespect for manual labour, and they therefore formed 'an element of discontent and unrest in the tribe'.[69] State control might make for better discipline and a higher degree of fitness to meet the government's requirements.[70] The mission had thus lost ground *vis-à-vis* the state in the field of education, and its political strength and its bargaining position were weakened. The educational monopoly had been broken and replaced by a division of labour where the government ran the higher levels of the educational system. This marked the beginning of a separation of religious and educational work which was new in Uganda.

Change of attitude among government officials

From the immediate post-war period onwards government officials felt that a change in the prevailing educational system was necessary. Prompted by the need for trained manpower, and despite admiration for the mission's great services, the Provincial Commissioner of Buganda came to the conclusion that it was time for the government to take upon itself its proper educational responsibilities, to exercise some control of educational work and to formulate a consistent educational policy. It was not clear how this should be done, but one method suggested was that the 'Native Governments' should set up non-sectarian schools especially for artisan training, which would be subject to government inspection.[71] The idea of non-sectarian schools was repeated only a little later by the Principal Medical Officer, who preferred the establishment of government medical schools to providing scholarships to the CMS for the training of medical assistants.[72] At that juncture the Colonial Office was still continuing with its usual line, and was not prepared to pay the extra money which was necessary to go beyond the missionary facilities; it was quite content to rely on these facilities as they were.[73] While this proposal concerned more advanced technical training, the significant point in the support for non-sectarian schools was that they were considered to be more flexible than missionary schools, and would provide a better source of recruitment for government institutions.[74]

Much more far-reaching was the suggestion from the District Commissioners in the Northern Province that the time had come for the government to take over all education and achieve a definitive separation of religious and secular training. They conceded, however, that ministers of all religions should be allowed to give instruction in government schools.[75] This proposal was far too radical for the colonial government,[76] but it was probably the most logical solution to the problem of government involvement in education, and it was especially favoured by officials in newly opened districts with pluralistic religious situations. The same point of view, more moderately expressed, was put to Bishop Willis a little later, on the basis of experience from the Northern Province. The Provincial Commissioner disputed the link between land and education and pointed out that the mission's educational work did not justify the possession of a large number of unregistered estates in Bunyoro or vast areas of excess land. The government and the chiefs could not afford to lose busulu from so many tenants, and in any case educational support ought to be direct, not indirect in the form of concessions. Finally, he said that education, in accordance with the trend in the rest of the world, was really the duty of the state, and not of 'a self-supporting religious community'.[77] This line of reasoning was underscored by the argument that the missions lacked the funds to cope with educational demands, and a higher degree of government involvement was necessary in any case.[78]

According to a number of government officials, especially in the Northern Province, the principles of direct educational support and the strict control of missionary landholdings meant that it was necessary to separate educational and religious work. In particular the system of holding plots under Temporary Occupation Licences and the mission's constant requests to be allowed to occupy these plots without paying any rent made them question whether the state had much to gain by channelling support to the comprehensive missionary work through land concessions.[79] In other words, the land issue made officials question the feasibility of the combination of evangelical and educational work. Finally, in 1923, the Provincial Commissioners' Conference suggested that secondary education could be improved either by establishing government schools or subjecting the existing missionary ones to much stricter government supervision.[80]

The officials who put forward these views were below the real decision-making level; they had gained their experience from local administration in the districts, in particular in the Northern and Eastern Provinces, where the problem was felt to be most acute, because educational work was still in the initial phase. Their local perspective may also account for the fact that no uniform solution to the educational problem had as yet crystallized. While there was a general consensus on the need for greater government involvement and some degree of separation of religious and educational work, it was not yet clear whether there should be a state system proper, or one based on cooperation between the missions and the government.

Recommendations from the Uganda Development Commission

The Uganda Development Commission in its report in 1920 also maintained that education was primarily the duty of the government, but that elementary education should for the time being be left to the missionary societies, who should receive government support. The mission schools should, however, be subject to government inspection. The Commission was most concerned with the technical training necessary to procure skilled manpower, especially artisans. Within the technical field the government ought to start its own institutions without delay, but in order to meet current demands cooperation with the missions was still advisable, and assistance could be granted, provided that the missionary institutions throughout the Protectorate functioned on a non-denominational basis. This would lessen the risk of duplication and ensure a pooling of the available resources.[81] In this respect the Commission, which had no missionary representation, publicly voiced what government officials had suggested earlier, indicating that the present competitive system meant a waste of resources.

Although they were quite satisfied with the Commission's report in general, the missionaries stood firm on their view that missionary-run schools could not under any circumstances be non-denominational.[82] One high-ranking official agreed that to talk about non-denominational mission schools was self-contradictory. The denominational constraints on access to the various institutions was the price which had to be paid when cooperating with the missions.[83] Another government official stated emphatically that the only realistic solution was for schools to be open to all, without distinction of creed.[84] The dilemma inherent in a competitive missionary system was thus brought into focus. The Uganda Development Commission's recommendation of non-denominational institutions provided the mission with an opportunity to make its views abundantly clear: that they found this formula for educational cooperation unworkable and unacceptable.

African attitudes and initiatives

The Africans too began at about the same time to express doubts as to the missions' capacity to deal with the growing demand for more advanced education in the post-war period. Some even questioned the expediency of the existing dual-denominational system. At an early stage the Ganda leaders said that it was the government's duty to undertake skilled training so that their people could engage profitably in trade.[85] This indicated indirectly that Ganda leaders considered technical training to be beyond the scope of the missions. At the same time they expressed dissatisfaction both with the educational standards prevailing in the schools and with the lack of facilities for higher education.[86] The Kings and the leading chiefs in the Bantu areas tried to remedy this weakness by sending their sons overseas, and the government was faced with an increasing number of applications for passages to universities and higher educational institutions in the USA, UK, Ceylon and the Sudan.[87]

This stated need for higher education was taken seriously by the colonial administration,[88] which was especially concerned about the risk of disorientation and 'detribalization' facing the rising generation during their stay abroad.[89] The government also realized that to meet 'the ambitions of the ruling classes'[90] it was necessary to found a university for East Africa,[91] but in the meantime all possible influence was to be exerted to limit or at least control these movements abroad.[92] The CMS mission was just as concerned as the government was about the unfortunate consequences of these stays abroad,[93] and offered advice on the most suitable places of study. In many cases former Uganda missionaries acted as guardians for young Africans.[94] At the same time the mission supported the establishment of a university-like institution in Uganda or East Africa,[95] thus acquiescing in the division of labour seen earlier in connection with plans for technical education.

Africans were not only concerned about advanced education. They also regretted the dual system of schools caused by Catholic and Protestant competition. A more radical solution, characteristically suggested by the chiefs in the scattered district of the Sese Islands, was that the government should start a non-denominational school providing periods for religious instruction.[96] Even more significantly, the younger generation of Baganda pointed out the same deficiency in the educational system, but they were more radical in their approach. A group of young Baganda, products of the missionary schools, had in 1918–19 founded the Young Baganda Association with the aim of working for the progress of their people, especially in education.[97] Their activities and attitudes also showed some opposition to the dominance and conservatism of the chiefly hierarchy.[98] In a memorandum to the Uganda Development Commission the Young Baganda Association requested that the government establish technical schools, which should be open to people of all faiths and all parts of society (not only to the sons of chiefs). Although the missionary schools were doing well, they were not producing people qualified to take up good jobs and receive good salaries.[99] Unofficially it was intimated that the standard in the mission schools was very low, and that the only remedy would be to establish government schools.[100]

In 1921 the Young Baganda Association made its criticism of the denominational system much more specific, calling it a hindrance to the general progress of the country. One main concern was its lack of uniformity. Accordingly the Association requested that all schools should be standardized and graded; that each province should have enough educational facilities, especially boarding schools for boys and girls; that all teachers should be examined and given certificates by the government, and paid in accordance with their qualifications from public funds; and that they should as far as possible be allocated to schools by the government. In addition, special provisions should be made by the government for schools for women and for the Muslim community. The only way to implement such a programme would be a policy of centralization. The government ought to set up an education department to take charge of the necessary inspection and supervision.[101] In fact, the Association stopped just short of proposing the complete nationalization of all schools, conceding that it was best for the time being to use the existing machinery and leave the schools under missionary leadership.[102]

The Governor was impressed by, and sympathetic towards, the suggestions of the Young Baganda Association. He went out of his way to meet some of its demands, although lack of funds limited his range of action, and made it impossible for the government either to take over the existing machinery or to establish a system of its own.[103] The Educational Advisory Board, which was largely composed of the missions' representatives, was called to its second meeting since its establishment in 1917 to discuss the matter. While they expressed the same sympathetic attitude as the Governor, the missions could not help but express disappointment that the Young Baganda Association had omitted any reference to the fact 'that the country is entirely indebted to Missionary enterprise for whatever education the Natives have so far received in the Protectorate'. In addition the missions made it quite clear that a complete separation of educational and missionary work, as suggested by the Young Baganda Association, was not possible, nor was it desirable, and further that the allocation of teachers must remain in the hands of the agencies which were responsible for the particular schools.[104] The missions thus drew certain boundaries which they felt must not be overstepped, even in the case of increased government participation in education.

The impatience of the younger Africans and their critical attitude to the missionary educational system were also voiced publicly in one of the African-run newspapers which appeared in the post-war period in increasing numbers.[105] A former student of the Anglican King's College, Budo, wrote an open letter to the headmaster, Canon H. T. C. Weatherhead, who had warned the Ganda chiefs in a lecture against sending their sons to the USA for higher education.[106] The writer, Z. K. Sentongo, disputed this point of view, referring to the young people's great eagerness to learn everything as soon as possible, and maintained that the Canon's attitude was wrong, in view of the present inadequate facilities in Uganda. He doubted whether it was true that the education of Africans should be left to the missionaries. In the long run, he argued, this was something which should be undertaken by the Africans themselves. The missions might not be able to secure the necessary means, and more importantly, 'perhaps we shall become crippled by your kindness and we ourselves shall not take any trouble to upraise our nation . . .'[107]

One common feature which influenced the different African attitudes to missionary education was that there was a great demand and great pressure for more and better educational facilities.[108] The way the various African spokesmen placed the mission within this new context was indicative of the mission's changed position in society. The first group, the Ganda chiefs, called on the government to support missionary educational efforts, but at the same time asked the government to undertake on its own the more advanced and specialized sectors. The chiefs no longer relied automatically on the mission. The mission's lack of funds and capacity forced them to assign a more important role to the government in a field where the missions had previously held a monopoly-like position. This did not in itself indicate a rupture in the old alliance between the mission and the chiefly aristocracy, but it meant a reduction of the mission's role in secular matters in the eyes of the chiefs.

More significant was the reaction from the younger generation, with its possible consequences for the alliance between the mission and the future chiefs. Underneath the smoothly-functioning alliance between mission and chiefs, other African forces had begun to operate which only began to make themselves felt in the post-war period. In the first instance they directed their activities either against the chiefly aristocracy (the Bataka Movement)[109] or against aspects of the missionary system. But even within the framework of the church the mission had already experienced African protest against the long-established alliance between the mission and the Protestant chiefs. The otherwise obscure controversy about whether there should be a cross on the altar in the new Cathedral, which ran from 1919–21, may best be interpreted as the clergy's protest against the dominance in the Native Anglican Church of the chiefs and missionaries.[110]

The Young Baganda Association was a group with quite a different position in society, which raised its voice in criticism of the denominational basis of the educational system. The members were mainly products of the CMS mission's schools, and belonged accordingly to the Christian middle class which the mission had deliberately fostered in its educational work.[111] But this younger generation proved far from docile, and was disinclined to follow slavishly in the footsteps of the older generation, for whom praise of the mission's work was the order of the day. They had not themselves experienced the value of the alliance with the mission, and did not develop the same affection towards the missionaries.[112] They had more independent minds, and their educational background enabled them to express themselves well enough to make an impact outside their own circles. Though hardly revolutionary, they desired reform. They represented an influence which was beyond missionary control, as evidenced by their direct approach to the government without going through missionary channels.[113] Their emergence placed the mission in a dilemma: should they stick to the well-established alliance with the chiefly aristocracy, or should they side with the rising generation in order to influence it? This dilemma became a major theme of the 1920s, and presented the mission with considerable problems. The issue requires more thorough investigation than space allows here, but it is important to take into account the fact that the attitudes and behaviour of the younger generation in Buganda already exerted some influence on decision-making.

These African educational demands, which received a positive hearing in the first instance from the Governor, added a new dimension to the cooperation between mission and government. In such situations there is no doubt that the government gave priority to considerations of national security, which meant that it examined on each occasion whether an African initiative involved, immediately or in the longer term, a risk to the peace and tranquillity of the colonial state.[114] In the case of the younger generation, the government had an interest in cooperating with the mission in order to make use of its moral influence. This could be observed in their joint efforts to control the flow of students going abroad to study.[115] Such considerations would inevitably also influence the government's willingness to back up the missions in the educational field, as it could be expected that their educational work would have a socializing effect, in the sense that it would induce the younger generation to conform to the requirements of the colonial state.[116] We may thus conclude that the government's concern for the control of the young, which really made itself felt in the post-war period, became a factor that pulled in the direction of a continued educational cooperation with the missions,[117] who shared its concern. The mission was alarmed by independent behaviour which was beyond its control, by the young Africans' lack of appreciation of the mission's efforts over the years, and by the example which these young people could set for ordinary members of the church.[118] The effects which this new spirit could have were viewed with anxiety,[119] and education was considered to be the best means of control. Cooperation in the educational field came to be seen as a key instrument in furthering the mission's overall aims.

This new educational perspective signified a change in the position of the mission. Whereas in the previous decades its advisory and protective role had indicated to the Africans that the mission stood at a certain distance from the government, the mission now seemed to be moving into a controlling role which brought it closer to the state. For the Africans, this tended to confirm the idea that the mission was part of the colonial system and exerted a stabilizing influence. This whole process gained momentum throughout the 1920s, and the provisional observations made here can be seen as a parallel to our conclusion on the forced-labour issue. In the early 1920s the mission was becoming increasingly aware of the interests it shared with the government, and this was bound to affect its capacity to act as defender of, or spokesman for, African interests. This again is part of the whole problem of dependence, to which we will return below.

The change in CMS policy

Within CMS circles in Britain doubts began to arise as to whether the Uganda mission could cope with the increasing demands from the Africans and the colonial authorities, and whether it was proper to engage the mission and church so heavily in educational activity. Faced with constant requests for more teaching missionaries from Bishop Willis and others in the Uganda mission,[120] the Educational Sub-Committee at the CMS headquarters questioned the wisdom of expanding in just that sector which required most Europeans.[121] The Committee suggested that the mission, instead of channelling resources and manpower into high schools (which were boarding schools with a European in charge) should give priority to the central schools, which were day schools run by the best-trained African teachers. Apart from difficulties in recruitment and shortage of funds, the Committee was especially concerned with the longer-term effects on the church. It would become difficult for the African church to take over schools which had been under European direction for a long time. The more heavily engaged the mission was in educational work, the more difficult it would be to realize the principle aims of self-support and self-government. The Educational Sub-Committee made one more point of great importance. It suggested that the government should be pressed for larger grants earmarked for the partial maintenance of European staff in those high schools which the government still wished should carry on functioning. At the same time they warned that the government should not be pressed so far that it would opt for strict government control of education. While it was thus aware of the precarious balance involved in receiving government support, the Sub-Committee suggested none the less a break with the basic principles of the past, by recommending the use of public funds for the maintenance of the teaching missionaries. The implications of this suggestion will appear below.

The Uganda mission's reaction to these proposals was characteristic of its whole conception of the educational work. The missionaries disagreed on the question of central schools, which the Committee had seen as 'a native organization': 'We feel that these Boarding Schools should for these peoples do what our Public Schools have done for the British nation.'[122] The notion that the schools were a hindrance to the future independence of the church was not discussed; nor was any attention paid to the risk of over-strict government control. As for the future, the main emphasis was placed on the missionaries' efforts to win the coming leaders and the emerging class of businessmen for the church by means of the high schools. This would enable the church to pay its clergy and teachers.[123] With this aim the missionaries went ahead with the boarding schools and used them as an argument for increased support. Here the local mission went further than the London Sub-Committee, as it impressed on the government the need to find salaries for teaching missionaries independently of the CMS funds. This meant in reality that they wanted these missionaries to be paid fully by government grants.[124]

On the basis of this strong commitment to the high schools and the principle that they should be staffed by Europeans, the Uganda mission discussed during the next few years whether parts of the government grant should be used to cover the expense of maintaining teaching missionaries.[125] This issue came to a head in 1922, when the CMS headquarters, because of severe financial difficulties, had no option but to reduce the number of teaching missionaries, especially in high schools. The only alternative was to pay them with the government grant. Of the £2,200 granted for unspecified purposes for 1922, a considerable portion would have to be redirected for this purpose, as the teachers' salaries now totalled to £5,000 a year.[126] It was essential for the Society to save £800 (equivalent to the cost of maintaining two married missionaries) in 1923, and if external resources were not forthcoming, a number of high schools would have to be closed down following the withdrawal of European teachers.[127]

The problem posed by the redirection of government grants to the educational missionaries' salaries was taken up both locally and with the Colonial Office.[128] The Diocesan Board of Education, composed equally of Europeans and Africans, allocated £300 out of the government grant for 1922 to the salary of one missionary working in a Teachers' Training College.[129] But the CMS leadership pointed out that allocating part of the government grant to missionary salaries could be understood as the provision of government support for general missionary purposes, which was considered unacceptable. They suggested that this could be avoided by continuing with the present system and increasing the educational grant; the actual allocation would then as before be the responsibility of the mission and the church.[130] A second objection was on the surface a purely internal one, but proved to be linked with the first. In connection with the demand from the CMS that part of the government grant should be allocated to missionary salaries, it was pointed out that the control of finances was not the responsibility of the mission, but of the Diocesan Board of Education, in which the membership was equally divided between Europeans and Africans. If the matter was taken to the superior body, the Diocesan Council, where the missionaries were in a minority, the outcome could not be taken for granted. But if support for the European teachers was approved by the two Boards, this would constitute African control over Europeans. The risk of such a situation had been a major obstacle to the full integration of the missionaries into the church when Bishop Tucker had attempted to introduce a church constitution.[131] In fact the missionaries had with the establishment of the Missionary Committee been given explicit guarantees against such a thing happening, as their primary accountability was to the CMS Parent Committee in its capacity as the sending, sponsoring and paying agency.[132]

The Parent Committee dismissed the last point. It failed to see how the missionaries' position would in any sense be changed by the new practice of paying some of them out of the government grant. It felt confident that its people in Uganda could easily convince the Board of Education of the necessity of devoting public funds to the upkeep of the European missionaries to avoid the teaching capacity being seriously reduced.[133] A different formula, however, was discussed provisionally with the Colonial Office. The CMS Secretary suggested that the government grant could be divided in two, up to half of it to be paid directly to the CMS in defrayment of its educational expenses, and the remainder to be paid to the Native Anglican Church for a similar purpose. Even though this suggestion met with sympathy in the Colonial Office the CMS Secretary made it clear at the same time that he did not at present wish any change which would disturb the existing relations between the CMS and the NAC.[134] The most significant feature of this exchange of views was that the CMS was fully aware of the possible consequences for the relationship between mission and church of transferring the payment of missionaries to government funds. This throws a special light on the solutions found to both the problems raised.

The government in Uganda made its position on the issue very clear. The mission was free to use from that part of the government educational grant which was not earmarked for specific purposes as much as was necessary to cover the salaries of European teachers. This new departure made no difference to the government, and did not constitute official support for ordinary missionary work, as the money had been granted beforehand for educational purposes alone. From the government's point of view the basic principle involved was that the grant was given to the CMS and not to the NAC. It came apparently as a surprise for the mission that this was stressed.[135] But viewed in the context of the previous analysis this attitude from the government's side accorded well with the results at which we have already arrived. First of all, the government dealt with the mission as such, and did not recognize the church officially, in spite of all the mission's attempts to obtain such recognition. The actual working relationship between the two institutions was an internal matter beyond the scope of the government's concern. Secondly, support for educational work was always specified as such, and given directly, not indirectly in response to the mission's broad use of the educational argument. The possibility of confusing missionary and educational work was therefore in this connection irrelevant. The government was thus simply reaffirming its usual stand.

The Missionary Committee decided on its own, without referring the matter to the Board of Education, which was empowered by the church constitution to handle such questions, to allocate £800 from the 1923 government grant to European salaries in accordance with the demand from the CMS Parent Committee.[136] When some missionaries contested this new principle and suggested that the government should be asked to make all grants payable to the Native Anglican Church, the motion was lost on the basis of the clear line taken by the government and the more pragmatic consideration that the money was in any case for the direct benefit of 'Native Education'.[137]

It is apparent that a very high priority was given to the high schools, which were considered 'the greatest asset in formation of Christian character'.[138] In order to keep up the present level of activity, however, the mission demonstrated willingness to comply with government demands and to accept openly its dependence on government support, even to the extent that cardinal principles in the work of the mission were sacrificed. As far as the decision-making process was concerned, an essential area had been removed from the authority of church bodies and reserved for the mission. This meant a change in the relations between the mission and the church. Such a move could only be a step backwards from the realization of the principal goal of self-government, and confirmed the relevance of the warning given earlier by the Educational Sub-Committee, that a heavy engagement in education might delay the arrival of independence for the church.

Developments in Uganda were fully endorsed from Britain. The Parent Committee of the CMS attached great importance to the fact that the Colonial Office had stated that the educational grant was made to the CMS, not to the Native Anglican Church.[139] The allocation of the grant was thus a matter for the Missionary Committee, and its recommendations should be submitted to the Parent Committee, although the suggestions of the Board of Education would not be ignored. The final authority was however with the Parent Committee, especially as regards the amount earmarked for missionary salaries.[140] The clear statement of policy from the Colonial Office thus influenced the CMS authorities to accept the changes in intra-organizational relations between the mission and the church which the CMS had at first envisaged with great reluctance.[141]

The full consequences of this do not seem to have dawned on the Uganda missionaries until they saw it written down in the form of short, clear-cut resolutions.[142] They felt it to be wrong, both in principle and for practical reasons, that the Board of Education and thereby the NAC were excluded from the decision-making process. It appears also that the missionaries' annoyance was rooted in the fact that London now had the final authority instead of themselves, although they did agree that the £800 or more needed for the Europeans' salaries should remain at the disposal of the Parent Committee.[143] The CMS home authorities were very reluctant to make any changes in the procedure now laid down,[145] and in the end the Uganda mission seems to have acquiesced.[146] Thus, the urgent need for an increase in the government's educational grant and its reallocation to missionary salaries, and the government's emphasis on the CMS as the only receiver meant that the missionaries had to sacrifice important principles in their own work. They had to accept the reduction in the authority of the church organization and recognize the fact that it was not only at the personal level, but also at the institutional level that contact with the colonial government was channelled through the missionary structure.

Finally, three aspects of this issue should be emphasized.

(1) There was now a greater dependence on the state than before, and a willingness to comply with state demands in exchange for continued resources to run the high schools. At first the CMS headquarters showed some reluctance in accepting this, but in the end they followed the men in the field, as the outcome was that the CMS was relieved of a heavy drain on its scarce resources.

(2) The introduction of the principle of paying some of the Uganda missionaries from non-CMS funds marked an increase in the specialization of the missionary work, and laid the foundations of a distinction between two categories of missionaries. In a wider sense, this emphasized the lack of integration between the evangelizing and the educational sectors, a feature which was otherwise considered a hallmark of the work in Uganda. The educational work was directed towards society at large and aimed at introducing Christian principles and creating a Christian ruling and middle class. On the other hand the missionary work had as its major goal the conversion of people to Protestantism and the establishment of the church on a self-supporting basis. The allocation of missionaries to one or the other category increased the gap between these two otherwise related goals. Secondly, it was only education that benefited from state support. General missionary work was self-supporting. In practice the church was thus dependent on people's willingness and capacity to contribute to it, while the educational branch was not subject to the same restrictions, and could expand in accordance with the state's willingness to offer its support.

(3) The consequences of placing these two sectors on a different footing were reflected in a change in the relations between the mission and the church. By taking the administration of the government grant away from the Board of Education it was indicated that educational work, at least at the higher levels, was a mission-directed activity. The distinction between the CMS mission and the Native Anglican Church was thus made sharper, and this was a step backwards from the realization of the stated goals of the CMS. It is, however, significant that most of the CMS missionaries accepted the reduction of African influence, though on several occasions the CMS authorities inquired whether it was not possible to place more responsibility in African hands, on the assumption that this would help to relieve the Society of some of its expenses.[147] The answer from the field was invariably that this line had been followed to the greatest possible extent, given the Africans' 'present state of inefficiency'.[148] This confirms the conclusion reached elsewhere that the European attitude to the Africans and the European conception of the Africans' capabilities were significant factors in the relationship between mission and church.[149]

The impact of the financial crisis in the CMS

Demands for increased educational grants were no longer routine after 1920, and the CMS no longer attempted to justify them by referring to the expansion of the educational sector. The emphasis was now on avoiding severe reductions, and even ensuring the continued functioning of parts of the missionary work.[150] Some of the high schools had already been closed, and more closures would follow if demands were not met.[151] The urgency of the matter was further underlined by the pressure that was exerted on the government both in Uganda and London.[152] This campaign culminated in 1922 and had as its result that the grant for 1923 was increased by 25 per cent, to £4,688.[153]

The mission could no longer argue from a position of strength as the only dispenser of education. On the contrary, it exposed its own weakness by its almost desperate need for increased support, revealing how much it depended on the state, if it was to continue its educational work on the same scale as hitherto. This dependence clearly provided an opening for government influence on the mission's work, and the missionary leaders were fully aware of this. On several occasions they demonstrated their awareness that increased state support might also involve increased government control and supervision. They saw it as a legitimate and inevitable requirement from the state, and they willingly accepted it as the price of support,[154] thus disregarding the CMS headquarters' earlier warning about the correlation between government support and government control. At the same time the mission does not seem to have fully recognized that increased grants and the corresponding increase in control tended to separate the religious and educational work by placing the latter in a special category. The same tendency towards increased control applied to the holding of plots under Temporary Occupation Licences. The allocation of government grants for missionary salaries had the same effect. Financial difficulties and increased state support thus caused some fragmentation of activities which had earlier been considered as an integrated whole. The educational work came to be evaluated by secular criteria which were not necessarily in full harmony with the mission's interest in the establishment of an independent church.

For the government the minimum demand, when faced with urgent requests for educational support, was stricter supervision, so as to ensure that the state got something for its money.[155] The colonial officials were, however, fully aware of the mission's difficulties in running the educational system at all, and they noticed with concern that in several districts it had even been necessary to close down the high schools, as no European staff were available.[156] The situation had deteriorated so much that there was a widespread feeling in the administration that the time had now come to formulate 'a definite educational policy'.[157] The missions' weakened position meant that the government felt that it was forced to make a choice: it must either start its own educational system or let the existing agencies carry on under closer supervision than before.[158] In either case a higher degree of state involvement was presupposed, and the government's serious consideration of the first option indicates the shift in bargaining power that had taken place in the relationship between mission and government.

The emergence of an official educational policy: continued cooperation between mission and government

The mission was clearly on the defensive. It was faced on the one side with the Africans' demands for more and better education and on the other with the government's need for trained and skilled manpower, at a time when it was least able to provide these due to its own severe financial crisis.[159] It was thus widely accepted that some change in the system was necessary, and this meant that the government had to establish an overall educational policy for the first time. The main problem was the position of the missions in the educational system. The government was left with a number of different, mutually incompatible suggestions.

(1) State-run non-sectarian schools and other educational institutions at all levels. This could be achieved by starting a new system to replace the missionary one, or by nationalizing the mission schools. In either case religious instruction was not precluded.

(2) The separation of religious and educational work by making the schools non-denominational, i.e. open to all without distinction of creed. The missions would still be in charge, but would be subject to strict government control.

(3) A division of work between the missions and the government along both horizontal and vertical lines. The missionary schools would be supplemented at most levels and non-Christians would be catered for. The result would then be a dual system of educational institutions, but this would not rule out government support for the missionary ones.

(4) A continued cooperation between mission and government, i.e. use of the existing machinery with state support, but under stricter control, so as to ensure a higher and more uniform standard. The establishment of an Inspectorate of Education was considered a suitable means of serving this purpose.

Of these four formulae, two could be dismissed immediately as being either unacceptable or unworkable under the circumstances. Non-denominational schools (2) were seen as a way of counteracting the denominational rivalries between Catholics and Protestants inherent in the dual system of institutions at most levels and in most areas. All this meant a waste, instead of a much-needed pooling, of resources. For the missions, however, non-denominational schools would have meant the complete separation of the educational and evangelizing work, which from their point of view would make the educational work almost meaningless. The government, too, accepted that it was impossible for the missions to separate the two aspects of their work.[160]

As regards (3), a division of areas of responsibility along horizontal lines had already been put into practice with technical and other advanced education. So far there had been full agreement between the missions and the government on this score. But it was doubtful whether this practice could be extended to other types of education without protests from the missionaries. It was the government's impression in 1923 that the missions were concerned with elementary education only in order 'to secure their religious influence over the rising generation', which left the field clear for government action in other sectors.[161] Had this proposal been made public, it would almost certainly have been met with strong opposition from the CMS mission, in view of the importance it attached to the high schools. At a different level, the government's interest in sharing educational responsibility was prompted by its concern for the Muslims. As no one was meeting their educational requirements, it was the government's responsibility to step in and take appropriate measures.[162] This last proposal involved the division of work areas along vertical lines, which would lead to the establishment of parallel and perhaps rival institutions at the same levels as the existing ones. This was not acceptable to the mission, who feared that it would tend to secularize the whole educational system. The Governor had to admit that it would be difficult to run two parallel systems without any real, formalized cooperation between them,[163] and the possibility of continued government support for the missionary schools helped to confuse the issue even more.

The crucial political decision must therefore be made between the two remaining formulae. These represented the only real alternatives, especially in view of the mission's financial crisis: either there must be an entirely state-run educational system, or one based on close cooperation between the missions and the state, involving a sharing of responsibility along horizontal lines. This choice was the basic subject of discussion for the Uganda administration; but no decision could be reached without the involvement of the Colonial Office, both because of the financial considerations and because of the need for a coordinated policy for all the colonies, which was a primary issue at that time. This involved a very long and complicated procedure which we will not dwell upon here.[164] We will restrict ourselves to a brief outline of the decision-making process in Uganda, and a discussion of the most important factors influencing the government's final decision on educational policy.

In 1923 the newly-arrived governor was faced with the choice between the possible courses just outlined. He was inclined to recommend the setting-up of a secular state system of education which would replace, or reduce the extent of, the missionary system. He was especially concerned about the lack of congruence between society's needs and expectations and the low educational standards of the children then leaving the missionary schools. He feared the emergence of 'a large and discontented class'.[165] Before arriving at any final recommendation he asked for a report on the existing system. To that end an educational expert from the Sudan, E. R. J. Hussey, was appointed as his adviser;[166] in the meantime any consideration of increased support in response to the mission's demands was postponed.[167] Hussey recommended, and the governor agreed, that in principle the cooperation between the missions and the government should continue, but on a different footing. The first step would be the introduction of extensive government supervision of grants. Quality was to take priority over quantity. Secondly, there would be, as before, a division of work along horizontal lines; but this would be supplemented to a limited extent by a division along vertical lines so as to cater for non-Christians and ensure a proper standard of efficiency.[168] A secular state educational system was thus rejected as a workable solution, even though it was recognized that it was beyond the mission's capacity to fulfil the demands of the government and the Africans.[169] This solution was based on the principle of cooperation, but the governor knew it to be a compromise.[170] Two internal factors, and possibly one external, seem to have been important.

(1) When the suggestion of a state system of schools was put forward on various occasions in the early 1920s its implementation was prevented every time by the existence of an economic barrier. The Young Baganda Association was told in 1921 that there was no money available for the establishment of the new system;[171] and the following year the governor had to admit that it was not possible for the time being for the government to replace the missions in higher education.[172] In spite of the new governor's initial critical attitude towards the missions' engagement in education, and his preference for a state system,[173] and in spite of his educational adviser's recommendation of a complete system of government education to supplement, if not to replace, the missionary one,[174] both of them had to admit that it was not a realistic educational policy 'to go it alone'.[175] The replacement of the missions would mean a reallocation of Protectorate resources which was not feasible in the foreseeable future. Such a radical step would also cut off the flow of missionary resources into the educational sector, and the government would lose the missions' manpower and their services as recruiting agencies.[176]

The government was thus not prepared to pay the price of establishing a secular system. The CMS mission was aware of this and used it in their arguments, pointing out how much it would cost in public money if the missionaries withdrew, and how much more the government would have to pay in salaries to secular teachers than to missionaries.[177] The mission's extensive use of this somewhat negative argument adds significance to the government's decision. The missionaries felt that the moment was now critical,[178] though they had no stronger basis to exert pressure from than the hope that economic considerations would prevent the government from setting up a state system. The initiative remained with the government, and there can be little doubt that if it had started from scratch just then, it would have settled for a system independent of missionary influence. That this was not realistic policy in 1923–4 shows the weight of the economic argument, and indicates the extent to which the government was the captive of the previous two decades of policy-making. It is worth remembering that the Acting Commissioner had predicted as early as 1905 the future inverse relationship between the extent of the missionary educational work and the scope for government action within this field. Now, almost 20 years later, this inverse relationship had become a reality, and circumscribed the government's freedom of policy-making. The mission's strategy, especially during the 1910s, had been vindicated to a remarkable extent, and was now paying off, even in the present defensive position.

(2) While the choice which the government faced in 1923–4 was mainly determined by economic factors, the solution was also facilitated by a more positive evaluation of the mission's contribution to the educational development of the Protectorate, engendered by the government's concern about the influences at work on the rising generation. This attitude was broadened and generalized over the following years and became part of the commonly held European belief that, in the upheaval of African society caused by the influx of Europeans and the impact of European civilization, religious teaching had a stabilizing effect and played an important role in character formation.[179] The governor and Hussey shared this belief, and they were guided by it in working out

the new educational policy.[180] While religious teaching did not necessarily mean denominational teaching, the realities of the Uganda situation required that the missions become the key instruments in implementing this philosophy. The government was disinclined to exclude the missions from the educational system, as it was the general opinion that the missions and government shared the same ideals and were working together towards progress for the Africans.[181] This line of reasoning meant that the missionaries played a special role to which they were not averse, and which would ensure continued cooperation with the government:[182] 'It was the combination of common goals pursued at the minimum cost to government that became the decisive factor.'[183]

(3) The first two factors influencing the government's decision not to start a separate education system were internal ones. But we must also ask whether missionary pressure was exerted via Britain, and accordingly whether external factors were important. Were the actors in Uganda anticipating outside opinion and influence which would have made it difficult to cut off the missions from direct participation in education? It is difficult on the basis of the evidence to answer this question, as documents from the governor and his educational adviser have little to say on the subject. It is none the less significant that the policy of cooperation with the missions corresponded with the principles for an overall colonial policy already laid down in London. The guidelines for educational policy were finalized in June 1923, more than six months before the recommendations came from Uganda. The deliberations which determined policy in London were remarkable for the amount of influence they granted to missionary circles. Missionary influence was fairly strong in the first report of the Phelps–Stokes Commission on Education in Tropical Africa. More important still was the fact that the most influential leader in the missionary movement, the Secretary for the International Missionary Council, J. H. Oldham, virtually laid down at the invitation of the government the future guidelines for colonial education.[184] The first guiding principle was that, wherever possible, government and mission should cooperate, and that it was better to develop existing institutions than to found new ones. Secondly, an Advisory Committee on Native Education in Tropical Africa was established, composed of government officials, leading educationalists, and representatives of the missions, including Oldham. The significance of this Committee was that it provided the machinery for a regular, institutionalized missionary influence on educational policy in British Dependencies.[185]

It is difficult to tell to what extent the policy of cooperation already endorsed in London influenced policy-making in Uganda.[186] Officials in Uganda were probably aware of how the pendulum was swinging in Europe; though this knowledge alone is unlikely to have turned the tide in Uganda, it would have given the government even stronger motives for cooperation with the mission. It would in any case have been difficult for the Uganda administration to recommend an educational policy which was not based on the recognition of the missions as the agencies through which government expenditure on education could best be channelled.

When the major principles in the new educational policy had been worked out in Uganda, and confirmed by the policy-makers in London, the problem remained of how to implement the cooperation between mission and government in practice. Ways and means were debated throughout most of the 1920s, and cannot be discussed here, except insofar as the discussion sheds light on the changes in the relationship between mission and government caused by new departures in educational policy on both sides.[187] One characteristic feature of the new situation was the mission's suspicion of the government's intentions. Misunderstandings arose again and again in connection with the changes suggested by Hussey.[188] The new educational policy had given the government the initiative, while the mission was on the defensive, trying in spite of scarce resources to cope with the government's increasing demands for an effective system of education.[189] Nor had the mission lost its old fear of secular education. There was a strong suspicion that Hussey, who was appointed shortly after his survey as the first Director of Education, aimed after all at setting up a parallel system of government schools which would gradually replace the missionary ones.[190] This fear was given some support by the statements of outside analysts, who said that the Uganda mission 'should put its educational house in order' before the government worked out its own schemes. If the necessary reorganization was not undertaken there was a great risk that the government would either take over the various missionary institutions or start its own competing system.[191] All this meant that the Uganda mission was inclined to interpret every initiative coming from the government in the light of their fear of a secular system of education.[192] That there was a considerable strain on the mission is borne out by its reaction to Hussey's specific plans for the government's participation in education and for the pattern of future cooperation. While adhering to the cooperation formula in principle, he made extensive use of the division-of-work formula when it came to actual practice. What really put the mission on its guard was that he did not confine himself to the horizontal line of division, but made extensive use of the vertical principle. The former principle in itself provided sufficient grounds for disagreement. Technical training and higher education had already been set up in the only government educational institution in the Protectorate, Makerere College. Apart from the question of religious instruction, and whether the missions should cater for their own students by means of hostels, there were two issues which brought out the difficulties of putting the horizontal principle into practice. The first one was that the missions feared that Makerere would function as a secondary school, and thus be regarded as a rival institution to the existing high schools. The second was the risk that Makerere would absorb all available public funds and deprive the existing missionary institutions of government assistance. There was accordingly a need for a clearer definition of areas of responsibility at the advanced levels, in order to allay the mission's fear of government intrusion into schools hitherto run by the mission.[193]

This last point was even more important when it came to the demarcation of areas of responsibility along vertical lines. Hussey wanted to establish non-denominational elementary and intermediate schools run by the state, arguing that, in the first place, the present ones were unequally distributed, with a high concentration in Buganda. To secure better geographical coverage he felt the government ought to start schools in various districts, especially in the north, where the missions had barely provided any educational facilities. Secondly, there was a need for non-denominational schools, even in areas where the missions were active, because of the presence of large numbers of Muslims and Traditionalists who were anxious that their children should not receive Christian training. According to Hussey, the government was obliged to cater for this group, who were left without any educational opportunities.[194] It was therefore important for Hussey to establish what in fact amounted to a dual system of education. In addition he hoped that government schools would set better standards and help to reduce denominational competition within elementary education. He thus seems to have expected that the non-denominational schools would prove superior in the long run to the denominational ones.[195] It is remarkable that Hussey spoke out so explicitly for the education of the Muslims, in whose interests government officials had occasionally spoken during the preceding two decades, but no action had ever been taken. The government did not consider the matter urgent enough to justify a clash with the missions or the reallocation of the necessary funds. Hussey, probably prompted by his experiences in the Sudan, was the first official with the necessary conviction to be willing to face a showdown with the missions. He was the first official in Uganda who was prepared, in order to secure the rights of a religious minority, to apply a kind of positive discrimination, and in fact Bishop Willis accused him of this.[196]

Faced with these proposals, the mission resorted to its old defences, and firmly opposed the idea of non-denominational schools. The missionaries denounced any attempt to set up a two-tiered elementary system, as this would lead to the introduction of a purely secular system of elementary education. Instead they requested that the previous educational practice, with its division of educational work along horizontal lines, should continue. This would in fact amount to the preservation of their monopoly-like position within the elementary and secondary sectors, but this time with government support.[197] The mission's protests were successful, but although Hussey had to modify his plans, he maintained his influence over the actual educational work because of the conditions he could attach, as Director of Education, to the granting of the essential government support – an issue which became crucial over the following years.[198]

The mission's success may be ascribed partly to its own efforts, but it was certainly helped by the economic factor, which was again decisive in the sense that only one of the six elementary schools planned by Hussey mainly for the benefit of the Muslim community was started, and even this proved short-lived.[199] The government's freedom of action was again curtailed by its shortage of funds and its dependence on the missionary contribution. Secondly, African opinion was mobilized, mainly that of the leading chiefs in Buganda. They protested against the principle of spending government money on non-denominational schools, and said that they were against secular education in general. They expressed their grievances through the Buganda Lukiko and, significantly, through the Synod of the Native Anglican Church.[200] One reason for the chiefs' protest was probably that they had some influence on the schools under the old system, because of their association with church committees. Such influence was less likely under a government system. The African protests were given great prominence by the mission when the European arena was mobilized.[201]

The third and most remarkable feature of the controversy on the pattern of educational cooperation was the influence of the European arena, and the use made of it by the Uganda mission. The mission made its anxiety known through the usual missionary channels of communication, to the London-based Advisory Committee on Native Education. This appeal to London seems to have worked so well that it almost compensated for the mission's weakened position in Uganda. There can be little doubt that the Committee's missionary representatives, by supporting the Uganda mission's point of view and stressing the need for continued cooperation between the government and the missions, exerted great influence on educational policy in Uganda, and brought pressure to bear on Hussey which he could not ignore.[202]

One additional factor has to be taken into account. The Catholic and Protestant representatives were in full agreement on these aspects of educational policy, and could act in concert both in Africa and in Europe.[203] This gave their arguments greater weight, and was of great significance in Uganda. They had previously acted together at the first Educational Conference in 1917, and also when the three bishops sent a joint letter the following year to the government, touching on a number of issues, among these the need for an increased government grant for education. They also presented a united front when non-denominational schools were suggested, and were equally opposed to the establishment of a dual system of education, or the establishment of any secular institutions apart from those at the advanced level. It is not possible to measure here the real impact of this united front. But it prevented the government, if it had so wished, from applying divide-and-rule tactics, and made it more difficult to lay down an educational policy without taking the missions into account.[204]

The new educational policy formulated in 1924 marked in many ways a change from the previous period, but did not seriously affect the missions' monopoly-like position within elementary and secondary education. The mission thus managed to 'stay in business'. But the real change was that the work now had to be carried on under government pressure to meet specific qualitative requirements. The way in which the new educational requirements increased the mission's dependence on the government will be discussed separately below. The mission's commitment to education was still undiminished, in spite of the strain it put on resources and on missionary work in general. The idea of secularizing education after the pioneer stage was now ruled out, as was the idea of a gradual phasing-out of the mission's educational work. The mission for its part considered education so important for the future of the church and the inculcation of Christian norms that it was prepared to go a long way to maintain its position, even to the extent of entering into an unequal alliance with the state. It is this feature of the relationship between mission and state with which we shall now be concerned.

The price of educational cooperation: the question of dependence

Education was a field where numerous and important inputs were directed to the political system. The response to these demands in the form of financial support and extensive cooperation suggests a special kind of relationship between the mission and the colonial state, and provides us with an opportunity to examine the influence which this exerted on the mission's status and work. At the outset we must clarify the motives and aims behind the mission's educational work, which we have so far only touched upon in passing.

The position of education within the whole complex of CMS activities was defined at first on the basis of a comprehensive view of missionary work. While the overall aim was always defined in spiritual terms, aptly summarized in the words: instruction, conversion and the formation of character,[205] this aim could not be implemented by directing all activity towards the founding of a church in accordance with the 'three-selves-formula' (self-support, self-government, self-extension). It was also within the scope of missionary work to attempt to transform the whole of society in the direction of Christian civilization, and this was seen in the long run as a precondition for the existence of a church and the realization of a mode of life compatible with Christian norms.[206] The role of education within this comprehensive conception of missionary work was clearly set out in the first major statement on educational activities in 1909, initially influenced by Bishop Tucker, and later given an authoritative endorsement by Bishop Willis:

We should certainly go as far as possible in our education, and appoint to such work our best available men, with a view to improving the whole nation by turning out, not only a number of well-trained clergy and teachers, but perhaps a far larger number of well-principled, moral, upright Christian traders, clerks, interpreters, and also chiefs, for we should aim specially at gaining the attendance at our schools of chiefs who are still minors, and sons of chiefs.[207]

Some dissenting voices were raised against this comprehensive view. It was suggested from one side that there ought to be a separation of the religious and educational aspects of the work, and that the resources available should be spent on direct religious instruction. According to this view, educational work belonged properly to the secular sphere, not to missionary work.[208] In a different context disappointment and criticism were expressed because students from the newly founded King's School, Budo, an institution modelled on the English public school, were not entering the service of the church. This criticism implied that education should be more closely linked with the objectives of the church, so that results could be measured in terms of direct utility for the church, rather than evaluated in a wider societal setting; only the needs of the church could justify the allocation of resources to the educational sector. Education carried out by the mission ought to be an instrument for the achievement of religious objectives rather than secular ones.[209] These two poles of opinion dominated discussions over the years, and it is interesting to note that the same issues exercised the Catholic leaders. Because they doubted the value of the combined training of people for secular and religious purposes, the Catholics initially chose a different pattern for their educational work, and this had far-reaching consequences for the standing of their converts in society.[210] Within the CMS mission it was the comprehensive attitude that prevailed in the 1910s.[211]

The importance of education and the legitimacy of aiming at supplying both church and society with manpower were reiterated and made more specific in Bishop Willis' first Episcopal Charge to the Uganda mission, in which he bluntly stated that 'Education is and must remain the backbone of our work.' By being the sole educating agency besides the Catholic missions, the CMS mission had 'a marvellous opportunity of moulding a nation at its most formative age . . . We need in all the training of our boys to remember the nation as well as the Church.' Though the schools must be Christian institutions, they must not exclusively provide religious teaching or aim at purely religious objectives. It was important to secure well-trained manpower for both church and state, and thereby to contribute to the emergence of a Christian nation.[212] The two dimensions in the missionary work were here clearly distinguished. If doubt was expressed sometimes with regard to the societal dimension, especially in view of its heavy drain on resources, it was stated that education was 'the backbone of all missionary work', no other branch being more directly productive.[213]

In the schools of Uganda we have, from the missionary point of view, a unique opportunity, for practically all the future leaders of the country in Church and State pass through the Mission Schools. The future of the country lies in the hands of those responsible for these Schools.[214]

This quotation explains the obstinacy with which the mission, as we have seen, clung to the high schools. The more advanced institutions were an investment in the future, as they trained individuals to enter two groups in society. The first group was the future leaders:

The High Schools cater for the sons of chiefs, clergy and other influential natives with the object of making Christians and developing Christian character in those who will eventually rule in Church and State in this country.[215]

This shows how important the mission felt it was that the future élite became Christians.[216] It followed that the future leaders in church and state were trained together in the same schools, and would reach the same educational standard.

The second group was defined by its role in the economic development of society. As early as 1909, Christian traders were mentioned as possible products of the school system, and the target was later expanded to 'the raising of a native class of artisans, shopkeepers . . .'[217] Consequently, technical training was emphasized as an important element in the curriculum. It was not enough to look at things from a spiritual point of view, to teach the Africans reading and writing and how to be earnest Christians. In view of the surrounding conditions and temptations they could easily become lapsed Christians if they were not offered something more substantial. The way to impress the benefits of Christianity on an African was to 'let him see that he has something others have not, that it comes with the Gospel message'. The role of this group in economic life was well-defined. They were to replace the Indians and Goans as middlemen in trade and crafts, and in government service as clerks and interpreters.[218] From an economic point of view their contribution would be to keep profits in the country instead of letting them go abroad.[219] Finally, the emergence of this stratum was seen as a longer-term benefit for the church, as it represented a potential fund-raising source which would help to pay the clergy and teachers.[220] The mission thus saw itself as instrumental, because of its educational involvement, in creating a kind of middle class which would act as the leavening in both church and society.[221]

The direct effects of this societal dimension in the missionary work were soon to become apparent. It has earlier been mentioned that candidates from the high schools were in great demand in the colonial administration. Government officials soon became aware of the difference between the Protestant and the Catholic modes of working, as well-trained Protestant Africans were available in substantial numbers, whereas it was difficult to recruit their Catholic counterparts.[222] The difference of emphasis within education was also observable in the districts,[223] and the fact that leading posts like chieftaincies were increasingly filled by Protestants was further testimony to the success of the CMS.[224] In this respect the high schools, to which the mission had always given high priority, had paid off, as they had virtually secured the leadership of society for the Protestant community. 'Experience has shown that, where there is no Boarding School in a given language area, leadership tends to pass out of the Mission's hands, there being no boys from C.M.S Schools qualified to take up chieftainships . . .'[225] On the basis of the comprehensive conception of educational work, and of its effects on society, it is fair to say that the CMS educational system had an élitist bias. It was deliberately geared to the creation of a political élite, and a middle class in the socio-economic sense, although the ground level of elementary education was not neglected. It became, however, a crucial question whether this élitist bias was detrimental to a proper balance between the two dimensions in the educational work, the one directed towards the church, the other towards society at large.

The question was taken up by the CMS mission's Educational Conference in 1915, which identified the two potential extremes inherent in the educational pattern. Either the instruction could become purely religious in schools which would thereby become theological seminaries 'training for the ministry of the Church, forgetting the ministry of the larger world outside the Church'.[226] (There is here a clear allusion to the Catholic practice.) Alternatively, schools could become secular institutions which mainly trained people for secular employment. A true balance had to be struck between these two extremes, and this meant a reaffirmation of the comprehensive concept of education, with its two dimensions. While this may have been the theoretical policy pursued throughout the period here surveyed, we must ask whether the reality corresponded with the ideal, and in this respect the Conference in 1915 painted a rather gloomy picture. During the review of the relations between the theological/ pastoral and the educational aspects of the work – the relationship between African clergy/catechists and African schoolmasters – it became clear that no one from the high schools, including King's College, Budo, had so far joined the ministry of the church.[227] The candidates had been attracted to government service, service within the chiefly system, or to the teaching profession at the more advanced level. The conclusion to be drawn was that the educational sector had so far failed to fulfil its obligation to the pastoral work of the church, and had rather benefited the state and society at large. In spite of this clear recognition of the problem in 1915, and in spite of all efforts to remedy it, it remained throughout the following years. A similar educational conference in 1921 could only state laconically that, in spite of the opportunity for an educated ministry afforded by the fact that every educated man in the country had passed through the mission schools, 'we have so far failed to make use of this opportunity'.[228]

The great vision of the fruitful combination of education for church and state had fallen short of reality – a risk which the Catholic bishop had envisaged as early as 1906, and which had instigated him to separate the two types of training.[229] This failure was now recognized fully by the leaders within the mission and the church, and adds a special significance to the contemporary struggle to keep the high schools in missionary hands: these had so far failed to achieve one of their main objectives.[230] This leads us to a discussion of the real causes of this unsatisfactory outcome and of its more far-reaching consequences for the missionary work. In this respect we must consider whether the close relationship with the state in the field of education had exerted any influence.

The lack of any personal link between the higher levels of education and recruitment to the ministry can be related to two closely linked factors, both of which were touched upon at the Educational Conferences of 1915 and 1921. First of all, jobs in the service of the church had never achieved any recognized status; they had not really been fitted into the African social system, nor were they imbued with any great prestige.[231] In order to develop this theme further, we must return to an observation made earlier, and explain the low status of clergy and catechists compared to that of secular functionaries in terms of the separation between the chiefly and ecclesiastical career which the missionaries had at first desired for theological reasons about the turn of the century (Chapter 7). This separation was later reinforced by economic developments, especially the land reforms of the Uganda Agreement. One or the other career had to be chosen, and the qualifications required were different. While spiritual qualities were given priority in the service of the church, training, education and traditional status were the major criteria in the secular sector, more so in the colonial system as it became more established. The difference in qualifications reflected a difference in the source of recruitment. The church recruited from the less influential layers of society, not from the ruling group of chiefs, who looked to the secular sphere.[232] This meant that candidates could not carry with them to the ministry any *ascribed status* from the traditional society which, in the case of Buganda, would have counted for much. Because of the primary emphasis on spiritual qualities, there soon developed an internal career ladder, starting from the catechists' ranks.[233] This created a relatively closed system into which it was difficult to introduce purely educational criteria of selection and appointment. The consequence of this was that the clergy not only brought no ascribed status with them to the church, but also no *achieved status* based on their having attended the mission's highest educational institutions. The result was thus a spiritual ministry rather than an educated one.[234]

Apart from going into the service of the state, educated people were attracted to the profession of qualified schoolmaster which was also considered more prestigious than the church. So two classes of church workers grew up side by side, widely separated by their different educational backgrounds, and often by their age. The schoolmaster was 'conscious of an intellectual superiority to, and jealous of any interference from, the older catechists'.[235] These two groups tended to drift apart, and this had repercussions for society in general. The spread of education and the fact that it was geared towards the new élite meant the emergence of an educated laity and a less educated body of clergymen who would often be 'below the present educational standard of many of the boys and girls in their congregations', to quote Bishop Willis' summing-up in 1922.[236] Thus the mission's educational activity itself contributed to the widening of the gap between the two sectors of the mission's work, even at the interpersonal level. The status and prestige of the church employees were rooted neither in the values of the traditional system nor in the newly introduced and highly valued educational skills. A second factor which reinforced this pattern of development, and one to which the missionaries themselves attached considerable importance, was the low pay of church employees. Over the first two decades it was claimed repeatedly in internal discussions that the low salaries of church workers were the real cause of the failure to recruit from the ranks of the educated, and that this, in spite of the fact that the mission itself was responsible for education, caused a 'brain drain' to the teaching profession and the public service, leaving the church to recruit from the poorer classes.[237] As early as 1904 it was discussed whether the number of teachers should be reduced in order to increase the salaries of the clergy; but such a change in priorities was found unacceptable.[238] In periods of financial strain, for instance in connection with the rise in the poll-tax rate, people even deserted the service of the church in order to be able to meet their financial obligations, and church workers sometimes had to engage in part-time trade to make a living. Faced with these conditions, the missionaries were fully aware that they could not expect to attract people 'from the higher social grades',[239] nor from among the well-educated.

If the missionaries were fully aware over the years of the negative effect of the economic factor, the inevitable question is: why did they not make every effort to counteract this? An improvement in the pay of the clergy, to place them in the same salary bracket as the teaching profession, would almost certainly have neutralized the status barrier. It was often suggested that one way of obtaining an educated ministry was to offer a decent salary or even introduce a graded scale based on qualifications and responsibility,[240] but the various measures suggested were of the traditional type. A campaign would be mounted to promote recruitment and an increase in voluntary contributions, and a meeting would be held with the leading chiefs, the old pillars of church work, in order to consider how the needs of the clergy could best be met. The key word was still 'vocation' and the best remedy was thought to be a deepening of the spiritual quality.[241] 'The most essential thing is the revival of spiritual life in the Uganda Church; the giving will follow,' concluded Bishop Willis.[242] But some members of the mission were less sanguine about this prospect. They pointed out a vicious circle: the better-educated could not be expected to offer themselves for the ministry while church salaries remained at their present low level; on the other hand it was doubtful whether any marked increase in giving would materialize before there was a better-educated ministry, in that the rising generation coming out of the mission schools, which constituted the ruling élite and middle class, could not be expected to fulfil their obligations towards the church in its present state.[243]

At that time no further action was taken, in spite of the mission's correct analysis of the situation and its full recognition of the root of the evil. Hopes for improvement were still pinned on a spiritual awakening, and the expectation that the educational investment in the secular side of society would some day begin to pay off. It is significant that this analysis of the past two decades of educational activity was made at the same time as the mission was making every effort to keep the high schools in their own hands. It was not suggested for a moment that the time might have come to reconsider priorities and place resources, scarce as they were, at the disposal of the church. This would have been an investment in the future realization of independence for the church. Such a major structural change in the pattern of work was clearly beyond the imagination of the missionaries. The commitment to the societal sector of the work remained unchanged, and the means of relieving the economic strain were sought in closer cooperation with the state. This cooperation increased the mission's dependence by opening the way for closer government control and influence, and widened the already existing gap between the two sectors of the missionary work.

It was suggested above, in connection with the transfer of the teaching missionaries' salaries from mission funds to the government grant, that the activities directed towards influencing society at large were run on principles quite different from those prevailing within the church. In the latter case, increased spirituality, and a consequent increase in contributions, were assumed to be the proper way of tackling the problem. This precluded any suggestion of seeking external support to break the vicious circle. The upholding of the principle of self-support limited the church's range of action considerably. Freedom of action was further curtailed by economic difficulties, which only made it seem even more essential to uphold the primacy of self-support. At the same time the educational sector was run on different lines and was becoming increasingly dependent on the support and good will of the government for its very existence. The result was a fragmentation of the work which ran counter to the whole idea of integrated educational activities. That this worked against the final goal of the missionary work can be seen from the emergence of another vicious circle. Adherence to the principle of self-support made it almost impossible to obtain an educated ministry which could keep up intellectually with the generation being educated by the other sector. This was a hindrance to the Africanization of the church leadership, and thus caused a significant postponement of the realization of the ideal of self-government.[244]

When the situation came to a head at the beginning of the 1920s the mission deliberately chose to continue its work along the previous lines. This was a choice whose significance they certainly did not fully grasp. It had far-reaching internal consequences, as it furthered a development which, although it had been acknowledged as unfortunate, had not been faced with sufficient determination. The priority given to the societal aspect of the work turned out to be detrimental to the realization of the mission's principal goal. It was initially justified as an investment in the future of the church and Christianity, but in this respect it turned out to be a rather bad investment, as it proved an extreme case of diminishing returns.

Apart from these internal factors, the educational work was a mechanism which automatically involved cooperation with the state. With the rapid increase in the disproportion between the scope of the objectives and the means at hand, this relationship inevitably became one of dependence. The mission's freedom of action became more limited, and it became committed to a specific, inflexible pattern of work. The claim that the mission's emphasis on the societal dimension in education involved *a priori* a close relationship with the state with far-reaching consequences can be substantiated by summarizing some of the results reached earlier in the analysis.

(1) It was recognized at an early stage by the mission that education was an activity for which the state ought to accept some responsibility by granting direct support. As the work expanded quantitatively and institutions for more advanced education were founded, the nature of the government's responsibility was made more specific. The mission acted as the educational agency of the state, and fulfilled an obligation to society which the state would otherwise have had to undertake. The mission could therefore, on the basis of this clarification of its role and the government's moral duty, approach the government with demands for larger grants with more authority. But it was aware at the same time that this was likely to result in closer official control of its educational activities. Up until the post-war period the interrelationship between mission and government was a relatively balanced one, as long as the mission could cope with educational demands, and as long as the government lacked funds and a proper educational policy. In the post-war period this balance could no longer be maintained. African demands for more and better education and the government's need for skilled manpower were beyond what the mission, which was badly hit by a shortage of resources, could provide. The reversal of the relationship was marked by the fact that the government, now in a position to dictate terms, produced an educational policy. Looking at the relationship from a chronological perspective, there was a progression from cooperation between equals in a field for which they were jointly responsible to a situation where the superior authority and responsibility rested with the one partner, while the other was left in a position of dependence. Within

government circles it was fully recognized how dependent the mission was on state support, and it was even suggested that the grant-in-aid could be stopped if the mission did not comply with government instructions.[245] The conception of the state's responsibility had thus clearly changed with the years, and this influenced the nature of the relationship between mission and government.

(2) Over the years the mission used its educational activities as a supposedly strong argument for the granting of support and concessions by the colonial administration. It was also assumed that its undertaking of a task of such public importance would help to ensure the church an officially acknowledged position within the colonial state. This was especially evident in connection with the issues of land and labour: it was clearly believed that such a secular argument would make the greatest impact on the government. The mission was thus prepared to adapt its arguments in order to present its activities in the light which it assumed would count most with the state. The paradox inherent in this, unnoticed by the mission, was that the government responded on the basis of the comprehensive conception of the missionary work earlier called the 'mission formula'. Various limited concessions were granted, not exclusively, or even primarily in support of the educational work, but in support of the missionary work in general, because it constituted an important element within the whole colonial framework and was also considered to promote state interests. While this failure to understand the true nature of state support was at first harmless because of its limited scale, the ramifications were much more serious when the government finally responded to the educational argument and provided substantial support for education *per se*. The mission was caught unprepared and was rather surprised at the effects of state support. In two ways the mission had to accept conditions which had profound internal consequences. First, its own comprehensive conception of the work was distorted, and it now had to accept a sharper distinction between pastoral and educational work. Secondly, educational support was granted solely to the CMS mission, and not to the Ugandan church. Hence, education was categorized as the task of the mission, not of the church. This increased the gap between the CMS mission and the Native Anglican Church, in complete contrast to the mission's original intentions.

(3) Whatever the pretext on which educational support was granted, it allowed the mission to keep up a higher level of activity than otherwise would have been the case. The poll-tax rebate provided an example of this (Chapter 12). It was granted to teachers in elementary schools, but there is plenty of evidence all through the period that the educational and evangelizing work could not be separated at the local level, and were in fact deliberately combined by the mission.[246] This combination of the available resources made it possible to keep up a higher level of activity in a sector where activity would otherwise have been limited by the economic considerations imposed by the principle of self-support. It was, in other words, possible to bypass this otherwise strictly applied principle. This explains why the mission at one stage wanted a free hand to spend the government grant for education as it wished, and provides a partial explanation of the mission's opposition to the proposals to separate the religious and educational work. But the mission was only able to maintain this line as long as the necessary funds were forthcoming. The CMS headquarters' austerity programme meant that the mission could no longer provide its own contributions to the upkeep of its present activities, and the only alternative to a severe cutback was to rely even more on state support. The government's new response to the educational

argument automatically meant a shift in emphasis towards the educational sector. The paying of missionaries out of the government grant rather than mission funds marked this enforced change clearly. In order to keep up the previous level of activity, the mission's activities were redirected to the state-supported sector.

Thus the mission geared its activities to the support on which it depended. The implications of accepting state funds were less obvious as long as the mission was able to fund a major part of the work from its own sources, and as long as the educational enterprise was still in the pioneer period. When this was no longer true, the mission was caught in a trap: it wanted to maintain the same level of activity and to continue its engagement in the societal dimension of the work, and it wanted the sole responsibility for developing the educational sector beyond the pioneering stage. To do this it had to assume the role of a servant being paid for services rendered, and this could only mean a reduction of its independent range of action.

These three features show how the mission's educational enterprise, as a state-related activity, necessarily brought increased involvement with the state. The stronger ties to the state affected the mission's ability to decide its own course of action and achieve its own goals. There were wider implications for the mission's internal situation and its relationship with the colonial state. First, within the ecclesiastical sphere the effect was a changed relationship between mission and church and a fragmentation of their work. This was manifested in the transfer of parts of the power earlier invested in church organs to the mission, and a consequent fading of the prospect of independence for the African church. The stronger ties with the state thus had intra-organizational effects and represented a step backwards from the realization of one of the major goals of the missionary work.

Secondly, the mission's autonomous position in the colonial setting was affected politically by its educational engagement. To justify its running of the more advanced educational institutions the mission had to supply the state with skilled manpower, and in general had to adapt the educational system to the government's overall development policy. As was the case with forced labour, this reduced the mission's capability to act independently, and in particular to act as spokesman for those African interests which came into conflict with government policy. This was demonstrated by the mission's attitude to the increased independence of the rising generation. Here the mission moved closer to the colonial authorities, and undertook a controlling function.

Thirdly, it follows that the mission became associated ideologically with the colonial system. One implicit argument for the continued missionary responsibility for education was that the mission's moral guidance was able to exert a stabilizing influence on the rising generation which would make it conform to the requirements of the colonial state. The mission itself was aware of the potential it had for fostering loyalty towards the colonial state and contributing to the legitimacy of colonial rule.[247] In that the mission's educational engagement was undertaken by deliberate choice, not by historical accident, the mission itself came to be linked with the colonial philosophy and the colonial presence.

To conclude on the issue of education and the mission's increased dependence on the state, we may explain the Uganda situation by employing two generalizations about church–state relationships taken from a different context. First, the kinds of linkage which a church has with society affect its ability to determine its own course of action. A high degree of interdependence between church and state provides a channel for outside influence on the church, which reduces its power to act independently. This is especially evident when the linkages undergo changes over a period of time.[248] In the Uganda situation, education created a number of linkages between mission and government and a high degree of interdependence. We have observed the inverse relationship between the mission's secular engagement with the state and capability to act independently of the state. The more the state's responsibility was extended into the educational field, the higher was the degree of dependence for the mission.

Secondly, when a religious institution undertakes secular objectives like education for which it is not fully equipped beyond what Ivan Vallier has called 'the demonstration point', it falls prey to a form of dependence.[249] In Uganda the pursuit of educational activities beyond the pioneering stage clearly overstrained the mission's capacity in various respects. When the mission, in spite of warnings and in spite of observable repercussions for its work, deliberately chose to carry on, it placed itself in a position of organizational and financial dependence on the state, and compromised its own priorities. The alternative of disengagement, or even of allowing for some degree of secularization, was rejected, and the extent of the secular engagement forced the mission into a dependent position.

16

Demands for a Christian nation: the Christianization of law and administration

One major reason why the CMS missionaries took the educational burden upon themselves was, as we have seen, that they felt that Christian education served the purpose of instilling Christian principles into society and furthering the creation of a Christian nation. The mission sought to realize the same goal more directly, again with the educational system as the vehicle, by creating a Christian ruling class and a Christian economic middle class. By relying on the missions from the outset, the government showed its sympathy towards these efforts. It was only a short step from this for the mission to demand that the positive influence of Christianity should be supported more actively and officially by the state, in the sense that the secular authority should be guided by Christian norms in its policy, its decisions and its legislation.

The object of the present chapter is to examine how and to what extent the mission requested the state to favour the emergence of a Christian society, and to what extent the colonial state was willing to comply. To answer these questions we will turn to the process of legislation and examine in particular the laws relating to the family. We have already seen that the legal issues of the 1890s provide an important criterion for evaluating the government's response to demands of a specifically Christian nature (Chapter 6). However, the missionaries could no longer be content with intervention in individual cases. The colonial system had developed so far that it had become necessary to introduce a more uniform code of law and to consider how far the European legal tradition should be applied.

Marriage

The passing of the marriage laws

The introduction of a marriage law presented, not surprisingly, the first occasion when the CMS mission's drive to Christianize society by legal means was put to the test. Although the church had of course from a very early stage performed a marriage ceremony, this seems to have had no legal consequences,[1] as people who violated Christian marriage were only subjected to church discipline in the form of suspension from Holy Communion or excommunication. This could of course affect their social standing, especially in the case of the chiefs.[2] The only official recognition of Christian marriage seems to have been a law passed by the Buganda Baraza in 1893. This was only valid for Buganda, and stated that women in polygamous households were free to leave their husbands if they wished 'to get married in a Christian way', and be free to lead a Christian life.[3] This established the primacy of Christian marriage over the customary institution. Apart from wishing to have this rule extended to the neighbouring areas, the mission expressed no desire for a marriage law.

It took the mission by surprise, therefore, when a Marriage Ordinance was gazetted in November 1902.[4] Even in this case the local administration had taken no initative. The Ordinance was solely the work of the Foreign Office, which felt that it was time to introduce marriage legislation in Uganda as in other Protectorates.[5] The Foreign Office suggested a Colonial Office model (as used in the West African Dependencies) and this was with a few adaptations promulgated in Uganda by the newly-arrived Commissioner without any previous consultation with the missions. The new Ordinance introduced statutory, monogamous marriage, and it was assumed that Christians would avail themselves of it.[6] The country was divided into five Marriage Districts, with government officials as registrars to take care of all the preliminaries, while public places of worship could be licensed for the celebration of marriages. Marriage was thus considered to be primarily a civil institution and the responsibility of the state. Recognition of customary marriage precluded a statutory marriage. As a corollary to this, it constituted bigamy if persons living in a statutory marriage contracted a marriage under 'native law or custom'. In effect the Uganda Marriage Ordinance of 1902 provided Africans with the option of monogamy irrespective of whether they were Christians or not.

This legislative procedure, as well as the content of the Ordinance and the role granted to the church, prompted Bishop Tucker to mount a formidable campaign against the implementation of the Ordinance on the planned date. His activities on that occasion demonstrate all the strings which the mission could pull when it wanted to influence or change government policy, and provide an almost perfect illustration of the various lines of communication between the ecclesiastical and the political fields already seen at the turn of the century. First of all, Tucker approached the Commissioner by way of telegrams, letters and personal interviews, all within a few weeks and in the middle of the Christmas celebrations. This was because he found the matter of 'vital importance' for the church.[7] He informed the CMS headquarters and asked the Africa Secretary to exert pressure on the Foreign Office.[8] He wrote directly to the President of the CMS asking him as a Member of Parliament to use his influence with the Secretary of State.[9] Spurred by the existence of a clause on 'kindred and affinity' in the Ordinance,

Tucker mobilized a British pressure group,[10] and this led to a direct approach to the Archbishop of Canterbury, who took the matter to the House of Lords.[11] Tucker also hinted at the possibility of a clash with the African political system, as the Ordinance violated its interests and authority.

Tucker pointed out that the *effect* of the Ordinance, because of 'the impracticable character of its main provisions', would be to impose 'an embargo on Christian marriage', making it 'an incentive to immorality'.[12] First, the preliminaries to marriage, especially the registration with the civil authorities in the various Marriage Districts, were simply unworkable, and had been formulated with complete disregard for factors such as distance and means of communication. Secondly, the marriage fee of 4 rupees, payable to the government, would work as a deterrent, and would encourage people to marry by customary law instead of contracting statutory, monogamous marriages. The impracticability of the proposed marriage fee was akin to that of the recently introduced three-rupee hut tax.[13]

As regards the *content* of the Ordinance, Tucker protested strongly against the legalization of marriage with a deceased wife's sister or niece.[14] He considered this to be an insult to the mission, as it was against the laws of both the Anglican and the Catholic churches in Uganda. To understand the real significance of this question of prohibited degrees, two points of clarification should be added. In the first instance, it appears that this kind of affinity was not considered to be an impediment to marriage under customary law, at least in Buganda.[15] The church law against this kind of marriage was the result of missionary influence and represented one of the hard-won gains for which they had managed to get the support of the chiefs.[16] To change it now could only detract from the credibility of the mission. Secondly, at the same time as the question arose in Uganda, a proposal for a 'Deceased Wife's Sister Bill' was being discussed by Parliament in London,[17] and was the subject of public controversy. This gave the mission a special reason for referring the matter to the European arena. The CMS home authorities preferred to remain aloof because of the controversial nature of the matter, and referred it to the ecclesiastical authority – the Archbishop of Canterbury.[18]

Tucker tried to strengthen his position by saying that there would be opposition from the leading chiefs of both denominations: 'Practically the whole political power of the country is in the hands of the members or adherents of these two churches.' They would certainly turn down such a proposal in the Lukiko, and the outcome would inevitably be that the British government would unite the two churches 'in a position of antagonism' with one stroke of its pen.[19] The alliance between the mission and the leading chiefs which had existed at the time of the Uganda Agreement was being invoked again.

As for the *political consequences* of the introduction of the Marriage Ordinance, Tucker questioned the legality of the proposed legislation, as it violated the Uganda Agreement in two respects. First, a marriage fee of four rupees could only be regarded as internal taxation, and could not be imposed without the agreement of the Kabaka (clause 12).[20] Secondly, various clauses in the ordinance violated the provisions for the Kabaka's direct administration of justice over his people (clause 6). Even if the Bishop's interpretation of these two clauses was mistaken, it was a matter of fact that the government had not submitted the proposed legislation for consideration by the Kabaka and the Lukiko, as it was obliged to under the terms of the Agreement.[21] Tucker pointed out that this could cause discontent and shake the Ganda leaders' confidence in the British government. He further reminded the Commissioner of his own key role in the conclusion of the Agreement: he had persuaded the chiefs to sign it by pointing to the large measure of self-government which was thereby granted to Buganda.[22] That the alliance with the chiefs was a reality and not just an empty threat transpired later, when the chiefs in the Lukiko objected to the introduction of even a reduced marriage fee of one rupee. 'In bringing forward this objection, they told me it was only a reflection of the views taken by the Missionaries.'[23]

As regards the *procedural aspects*, the government had failed either to consult the African leaders or the ecclesiastical authorities.[24] Tucker was undoubtedly hinting here at the difference between the present administration and that of Sir Harry Johnston only three years earlier. Two major concerns seem to have prompted Tucker's criticism. First of all, the exclusion of the mission from the deliberations on the Ordinance could only be taken as a step backwards from the cooperation between mission and government. Tucker was very conscious of the political position of the mission in Uganda, and the potential benefits to be derived from it. He was ready to go to great lengths to defend this position, and the marriage issue presented a good opportunity, as it clearly fell within the field of the mission's legitimate interests.

Closely linked with this was a second aspect of Tucker's disapproval of the government. Not only the position of the mission, but that of the church too, was at risk, if the Ordinance came into force. The church was not centrally placed in the planned procedure for contracting marriages. It was completely excluded from the preliminaries, which were seen as a civil task, to be performed by Marriage Registrars. No use was to be made of the church's much more widespread and elaborate network.[25] Though churches might be licensed as places for the celebration of marriages, the Ordinance did not primarily identify monogamous marriage with Christian marriage.[26] In this respect there was a clear secular bias in the Ordinance. Tucker wanted the church to be more centrally placed if monogamous marriage was to be given statutory force.

Tucker's objections are summarized in his statements that the proposed Ordinance represented 'a heavy blow to the cause of Christianity and morality',[27] and the greatest possible blow to the work of the mission.[28] Accordingly, Tucker asked for the withdrawal of the Ordinance, or at least for radical modifications. The government was in reality faced with three major political problems. First, whether it could deliberately retard the work of promoting morality by discouraging monogamous marriage among the population; secondly, whether the Ordinance would hinder the work of the mission for the good of the Protectorate; and thirdly, whether the government was risking a crisis in its relations with the mission and the African polity. The more general questions raised by the relatively trivial question of the proposed marriage ordinance were: how much importance should be attached to the Christian factor in framing policy? And to what extent did the mission have the same goals as the government?

These more fundamental aspects of the controversy were clearly recognized by one of the most senior and experienced colonial officials, Sub-Commissioner George Wilson, when he expressed complete agreement with Tucker's criticism of the Marriage Ordinance and the procedure for its introduction.[29] The Commissioner was at first highly alarmed by Tucker's protests, and immediately asked for permission to postpone the Ordinance to allow for consultations with Tucker and the leading chiefs.[30] He agreed to a great extent with Tucker on the substance of the matter, and recognized its wider political implications.[31] His main problem was in fact to find a formula which could save face for the Foreign Office, which had patently acted in haste.[32] He kept in close contact with the mission, and even went so far as to ask Tucker to set out his views in writing,[33] at the same time asking the Ganda leaders to furnish him with information about customary law.[34] Tucker did as the Commissioner suggested,[35] and a new Ordinance was drafted for African Christian marriages, replacing that of 1902. This included all of Tucker's proposals except one.[36] The church was to have full responsibility for performing marriages between Christians at all phases, including the preliminaries and the official registration, just as in Britain. All ministers of the church were to be recognized as Registrars of Marriages, which meant that full use was made of the church network. The marriage fee was lowered to 1 rupee, although Tucker and the chiefs wanted it to be half a rupee. Tucker even pointed out that more marriages meant more huts and therefore an increase in hut-tax revenue. The government knew, however, that the church had its own separate marriage fee, and therefore had some material interest in the size of the official one.[37]

The one point which the government did not accept in Tucker's criticism was the legalization of marriage with a deceased wife's sister, and this remained unchanged in the draft Ordinance. This was quite clearly a reflection of the ongoing discussion in London, for even the Commissioner himself was against such a legalization at present. It was first of all repugnant to the missions, who had the whole educational system in their hands. Secondly, the measure was not wanted by the Africans, so it was unwise to draw too much attention to the existence of the clause. Here the Commisioner certainly demonstrated how much importance he attached to the combined opinion of the missionaries and chiefs. On the other hand, as the law had passed its second reading in the House of Commons, it would be inappropriate to forbid marriages of this kind in Uganda, especially as foreigners could claim that such marriages were perfectly legal under British law. Under these circumstances one solution could be that, if an African wanted such a marriage and the church refused, a Government Registrar would perform a civil marriage.[38] Tucker had made it quite clear that the church would refuse to celebrate such marriages,[39] and he had the backing of the Archbishop of Canterbury in this.[40]

Apart from pursuing his own more general aims, then, Tucker made special efforts to have the legalization of marriage with a deceased wife's sister repealed. His concern should be seen in an even wider context, as this particular kind of marriage had already been legalized in the East African Protectorate,[41] and as plans were being made to merge the two Protectorates.[42] The question of uniformity was therefore highly relevant, and could influence events in Uganda.[43]

Tucker proved highly successful in invoking London. The issue of marriage with a deceased wife's sister in the two East African Dependencies was discussed in the Lords,[44] and the Foreign Secretary, answering a question in the Commons, had to admit that the whole Marriage Ordinance had been suspended in Uganda because of Bishop Tucker's objections.[45] The Foreign Office was taken aback by this turn of events and had great difficulty in coming to terms with the whole issue.[46] The matter aroused great public interest, and even the Prime Minister, A. J. Balfour, commented on it. He stated bluntly that the government's handling of the matter had got it into a mess. In his view the best solution would be to respect representative local opinion; legislation with regard to such marriages should be framed in accordance with local wishes.[47] In accordance with this principle the Foreign Office could only ask the Commissioner to repeal the clause on marriage with a deceased wife's sister before the Marriage Ordinance came into force in Uganda.[48] The result of this controversy can thus only be taken as a victory for Tucker's strategy of referring to London.[49]

The Foreign Office approved the Commisioner's proposal to issue a special Ordinance covering marriage between African Christians, incorporating the suggestions of Bishop Tucker.[50] Tucker was naturally full of praise for the trouble the Commissioner had taken to adapt the marriage regulations to local conditions.[51] There was, however, one change in the final version of the new Ordinance which received surprisingly little attention at the time. The government decided to include Muslim marriages in the same Ordinance which covered Christians. Initially this was because in both cases ministers of religion had to act as Marriage Registrars.[52] Later, the measure was seen as a way of putting the two types of religious marriages on the same footing as regards fees. The three missions had expressed anxiety that Christian marriages would be placed at a disadvantage compared with Muslim and traditional ones. While the missions were thus placated as regards fees, the Commissioner rejected the suggestion that Christian marriage was at a disadvantage compared to customary marriages. In the case of Christian marriage 'a higher degree of civilization has attached to it higher obligations in addition to greater rights'.[53] The CMS mission did not find this argument convincing, and still feared that the fee for Christian marriage would cause people to revert to the customary form.[54]

The outcome of the marriage issue was paradoxical in two respects. Marriages performed under the auspices of the two immigrant religions were singled out and placed in one Ordinance, called 'The Native Marriage Ordinance (1903)'. Here a Christian monogamous form and a Muslim polygamous form were combined, the common denominator being that they could be categorized as 'religious marriages'. Secondly, Ugandan society was left with three different systems of marriage at the same time. Besides the religious type applying only to Africans, there was a statutory type of marriage based upon the original 'Uganda Marriage Ordinance (1902)', which was now held to cover monogamous civil marriages.[55] Finally there was the indirectly recognized customary marriage law, which was potentially polygamous. These three systems of marriage legislation were inconsistent inasmuch as they comprised several legal traditions with no clear separation of their areas of function, and no provisions for converting marriages from one system to the other. This was especially unfortunate in the case of transitions from polygamy to monogamy, which it was almost certainly the intention to encourage.

The first bone of contention which arose was the question of divorce; the second and major one was related to the definition of the relationship between statutory and customary marriage. It was found necessary at an early stage to include a divorce law in the marriage legislation.[56] A draft Ordinance was again forwarded to the Foreign Office,[57] but this time the local administration was careful not to make the same mistakes as before. First of all, they were now aware of the need to adapt the Ordinance to local conditions.[58] Secondly, they were anxious not to violate agreements with Buganda, Ankole and Toro by taking areas of jurisdiction away from the African authorities. As it was impossible to leave the jurisdiction in Christian divorce cases with the saza chiefs or Lukikos, because of the antagonistic feelings which would arise if the cases were tried by a chief of a different denomination from the parties involved, it was suggested that the power to grant divorces should rest with the High Court.[59] Thirdly, it was emphasized that a Divorce Ordinance should be linked with the two Ordinances which covered monogamous marriages, and not, as the Foreign Office had suggested, only with the one covering Christian marriages.[60] Fourthly, in order to prevent future disagreements, comments were invited from the missions,[61] inasmuch as divorce was a particularly sore point with the Christian churches.[62] In the CMS response, Bishop Tucker felt bound in principle to accept the proposed Ordinance, as it simply corresponded with English practice. It was therefore 'no use struggling against the inevitable'.[63] As regards the details of the provisions, Tucker suggested first that the divorce fee ought to be fixed as high as possible, as divorce should not be 'cheap and easy'. Secondly, when conversion from Christianity to another religion was listed among the reasons for obtaining a divorce, the laws should require something more than just a statement of conversion; if a husband converted to Islam, the wife should only be able to obtain a divorce if it could be proved that the man had not only gone through the required rites such as circumcision, but had also contracted a legal marriage with another woman.

To summarize Tucker's attitude, it is characteristic that, while he attempted to make marriage easier, his main concern in the case of divorce was naturally to set up prohibitive measures in order to secure the continuance of marriages once they had been contracted. In this respect he was not successful. The Commissioner did not report any of Tucker's suggestions to the Foreign Office,[64] and they were not taken into account when the Divorce Ordinance was enacted in 1904.[65] The colonial authorities were not prepared to introduce special protective measures for Christian marriage in Uganda. This was significantly different from the outcome of the controversy on the Marriage Ordinance, but it should be noticed that Tucker kept a relatively low profile on the divorce question, and did not himself take the matter to London.

Tucker's second point, the change of religion as sufficient reason for a divorce, turned out soon afterwards to be highly relevant, as it touched on the unsolved problem of the relationship between the Native Marriage Ordinance (1903), which applied to both Christian and Muslim marriages, and Muslim law. The issue was really the inconsistency of including the two types of religious marriage in one Ordinance. The Ordinance allowed the Muslims to contract polygamous marriages in accordance with Muslim law, although Muslim marriages were not granted full official validity. In practice a number of people converted from Christianity to Islam in order to avail themselves of provisions within Muslim law;[66] they could now convert their marriages to polygamous ones without violating the Ordinance. Most important of all, husbands who had originally contracted a Christian marriage could now easily obtain a divorce from their Christian wives under the relatively lenient stipulation of Muslim law.[67] The easy transition to another system served to devalue the Christian marriage law, and pointed in fact to the advantages in following the Muslim one. In addition, as the Catholic Bishop Streicher pointed out, it discriminated against wives, and in most cases there was no question of faith involved.[68]

The Uganda administration found this situation embarrassing, and realized that it was necessary to establish a firm legal basis for Muslim marriages.[69] Bishop Tucker, asked for his opinion, found it a scandal that most people simply converted to Islam in order to get rid of their wives. It was all too simple, and he suggested that the man should really prove his conversion to Islam (for instance by undergoing circumcision) and that a Christian turning Muslim should be under an obligation to pay his Christian wife a monthly sum.[70] The local administration now drafted a new Ordinance applying solely to Muslim marriages, but did not go as far as Tucker had requested. The 'Mohammedan Marriage and Divorce Ordinance (1906)' granted full validity to Muslim marriages, but included clauses aimed at preventing abuses such as the 'conversion of convenience'. Muslim marriages and divorces had to be registered from now on just like the Christian ones, and the Registrar had to satisfy himself in each case that the marriages or divorces had in fact taken place.[71] In this way the loophole in the Christian Marriage Ordinance was closed and the two kinds of marriage were placed on an equal footing. Tucker's prohibitive measures were not included, but the same purpose may well have been served by the fact that the marriage fee weighed heavier on the Muslims if they contracted polygamous marriages.[72]

With the passing of this Ordinance, the whole complex of marriage laws was completed. The significance of these events and the influence of the missionaries on them emerge when we remember that, apart from an ordinance on Hindu marriage and divorce, the various laws discussed here remained in force almost unchanged during the whole colonial period, and even after independence in 1962.[73] It is therefore especially important to reach some final conclusions on the Christian factor and the impact of the mission's demands on the legislative process. That great importance was attached to this issue was confirmed by Bishop Tucker himself, when he commented on the introduction of the Muslim Marriage Law. He remarked that Uganda is not a Mahomedan country, and that in my opinion Mahomedan law should not be applied as, say, in Zanzibar or the Mahomedan countries, but as say in England and other Christian countries'.[74] The demand that Uganda be treated as a Christian country is here quite clearly formulated and impressed on the colonial authorities. It is suggested that the Muslims as a matter of tolerance be granted minority rights rather than equal rights. The government did not follow the Bishop's advice, but aimed at placing Christian and Muslim marriages on an equal legal footing. Nor did it follow the mission in all its demands for specific provisions in the Muslim marriage legislation. On the other hand, the colonial administration was very concerned that no undesirable advantage should be given to the Muslims by making the registration of their marriages optional, when the registration of Christian marriages was compulsory.[75] Similarly, it was specifically stated that Muslim law applied in Uganda only in cases where both parties involved professed Islam. Otherwise 'the general (Christian) law of the Protectorate' took priority.[76]

We may here notice a general trend in the policy of the colonial administration. By giving priority to monogamous marriages in its legislation, the government was clearly expressing its belief that Christian values should be the norm in African society. It was also prepared to undertake some responsibility for the furtherance of a general Christian morality, both positively by easing the conditions for its realization, and negatively by removing the obstacles to it. Hence, the colonial state was prepared to further the Christian cause and let Christian ideas influence its policy and actions, in short to attach great importance to the Christian factor. This basic attitude made the state highly responsive to missionary demands, and in many ways the outcome of the marriage issue was a great victory for Bishop Tucker. He had a decisive influence on the marriage laws; he secured a central position for the church in society by ensuring that it was responsible for the contraction of monogamous marriages; he underlined the political influence of the mission and its natural consultative status; and he demonstrated the strength of the ever-present alliance between the mission and the African political leaders. His position was further strengthened by the fact that he could now also act as spokesman for the two Catholic missions and draw on their support, a fact that did not escape the notice of the government.[77]

Thus the Christian and missionary factor appears here to have been remarkably significant. It would, however, be dangerous to over-generalize on the basis of the Christian influence in the case of marriage legislation. The marriage question was accepted from the start as falling within the mission's and the church's legitimate domain, and the government was therefore more likely to respond positively to their suggestions. Secondly, the time when these events happened must be taken into account, in two senses. The introduction of marriage laws came immediately after the conclusion of the Uganda Agreement, so the memory of the decisive role played by Bishop Tucker and the CMS was still vivid. The marriage laws were also one of the first areas where legislation was passed, which meant that the colonial administration still lacked experience in handling such matters. Thirdly, Bishop Tucker's personality was an important factor, and it may also have been of some significance that Colonel Hayes Sadler was a new and inexperienced Commissioner, and personally very sympathetic towards the CMS mission.[78] These three factors lead to the conclusion that, before the basic questions raised at the beginning of this chapter can be convincingly answered, the examination of the marriage laws will have to be supplemented by a discussion of cases of a different category, covering a longer span of years.

The conflict between Christian and customary marriage laws

While the marriage laws were being discussed, the problem of the potentially polygamous customary marriages was more or less left in abeyance. No stand was taken on the official recognition of these marriages, their legal status and their relationship to the statutory form of marriage. This was unsatisfactory, as a number of issues inevitably arose which called for a clearer definition of the status of these marriages. But it proved difficult to provide such a definition, as many conflicting interests were involved. Government officials, the missionary representatives and the African leaders all had different views on the matter. Two factors stand out particularly when we look for an explanation of why people combined elements from Christian and customary marriages: the dowry system and the transition from polygamous to monogamous marriage in the event of baptism. The examination of these two issues will help to show the extent to which the mission sought, and succeeded in getting, government backing for marriage as a Christian institution.

Dowry, often somewhat misleadingly called bride-price or bride-wealth, was regarded under customary law as essential for the validity of a marriage. Dowry thus quite clearly had a *legal* function, and this was especially true in the case of divorce. In addition it had a *social* function, in that it signified that a special relationship had been established between two families, when the man presented gifts to the family of the woman and pledged himself to take good care of her.[79] But at first the mission was mainly concerned with the assumed *commercial* aspects of the dowry institution, as they interpreted it as a kind of payment for the girl. For this reason they tried to persuade the Mengo Church Council to abolish the custom altogether in 1897.[80] This move was not successful, and leading Christians then convinced the mission of the social value of the dowry, of its contribution to a strengthening of the marriage bonds, and its providing security for the girl.[81] The mission's main concern then became the fixing of a limit to the number of gifts to be handed over when marriages were contracted, as a high dowry worked as an impediment to marriage, especially when the hut tax increased the overall burden on Africans. In November 1899 a Council of the Baganda chiefs finally approved a maximum rate of ten rupees for ordinary people and a somewhat higher rate for the various grades of chiefs.[82] These limits were upheld during the discussion of the Marriage Ordinances in 1903, and were considered by government officials to be part of African marriage law.[83]

While the mission had been persuaded of the social value of the dowry institution, and made every effort to have the fixed limit upheld, they clearly underestimated the significance of its legal function, to their own disadvantage. A government official observed in 1903 that in every case of marriage in church the dowry custom was observed.[84] In the African setting this meant that a marriage was validated within two legal traditions, and that it was not removed from the domain of the 'native and customary law' just because there was a fixed limit for the dowry. People thus worked with two laws and could if necessary choose at their own convenience which of the two they would observe. They might choose customary law if they wanted to marry additional wives or if they wanted a divorce, in which case the return of the dowry was a token of the legality of the divorce. By paying the dowry the Christians coupled their statutory marriages with customary marriage contracts and established an undefined link between two legal traditions, the result being a kind of 'dual marriage'.[85]

The second important point was that, while the mission accepted the dowry because of its social implications, it insisted that the limit on the dowry fixed by the African leaders should be endorsed by the colonial authorities.[86] In this respect the government responded positively, although its legal basis for doing so was rather dubious;[87] the government had an interest in furthering monogamous marriages, Christian morality and the development of a European family pattern. In 1906 the Catholic Bishop Streicher asked the government, in view of the many violations, to raise the limit of the dowry from 10 to 15 rupees, and the Acting Commissioner asked for Bishop Tucker's reaction. Tucker replied that he opposed any change, as a higher rate would be prohibitive. Instead he asked for the present rule to be enforced more vigorously.[88] Tucker took the same line at the Synod in 1909, which clearly indicates that, in his opinion, the fixing of the dowry rate and its enforcement were part of the secular authorities' obligation towards the church.[89] The government was willing, in cooperation with the African leaders, to undertake the responsibility. It may have been influenced to some extent by its own vested interest (by way of hut tax) in furthering statutory marriages. But the political authorities could do little more than make recommendations. Their powers of enforcement were practically non-existent, and this may be one reason why little was heard of the dowry rate after 1910. A later attempt to fix the dowry rates also misfired, and it remained the official attitude not to become involved in this matter.[90] It was almost impossible to keep a check on actual practice, and this may be why Tucker's motion at the Synod in 1909, asking the government to enforce the fixed rate of 10 rupees, was lost. The

African majority in the Synod found it beyond the bounds of practicality to enforce the observation of the rule, and it was remarked that it would only 'put the Church to shame to ask the Native Government to enforce a law that people did not wish to keep'.[91]

While the issue of dowry rates was thus played down, the continued existence of the dowry practice, even in the case of Christian marriage, indicated the ease with which it was possible to move from one legal system to another, especially from the statutory to the customary form of marriage. The dowry institution further served to obscure the clauses in the Marriage Ordinances of 1902 and 1903 which stated that people were subject to prosecution if they contracted a marriage under customary law while their statutory marriage was still undissolved, and vice versa. The continuation of the dowry practice impressed constantly on the mission that it was necessary to stop easy access to switching between statutory and customary marriage, and to define the validity of the customary marriage. It was necessary to have both these issues clarified before preconditions connected with marital status could be attached to baptism. In more concrete terms: what was the church to do with people from polygamous marriages when they came forward for baptism? To settle these matters, it was necessary to call upon the government to clarify the legal situation and pass the necessary laws.

The confusion on these issues was felt at an early stage both by African church workers and by missionaries.[92] It often happened that two people came forward as husband and wife in accordance with customary law, and were baptized as such. Only a few months later they would then be divorced by a native court under customary law. The following quotation sums up the problem: 'What exactly constitutes a legal heathen marriage is at present a moot point; yet very much hangs on the answer to that question.'[93] As already pointed out, no real answer was provided by the Marriage Ordinances of 1902 and 1903, and this was duly admitted by a government official.[94] This lack of clarification made missionary attempts to reach clear-cut solutions somewhat confused. The most radical solution would have been to ask the government to forbid polygamy. This was in fact what the government at first suspected the mission of wanting, but the mission denied that it had any such aim. All they were asking was that women outside Buganda (in Busoga in the actual case in question) be granted the same freedom as the Ganda women to leave their husbands and live a Christian life.[95] The mission did not recognize that such a move indirectly amounted to a denial of the validity of customary marriages, in that it rendered them dissoluble according to criteria from a completely different legal tradition.

The problem was faced more directly at the Missionary Conference of 1904, when it was specifically asked how heathen marriages could best be registered in cases when people came forward for baptism. The answer was that only Christian marriage and civil marriage, in accordance with the Ordinances of 1902 and 1903, were considered legally binding; consequently a marriage contracted under native law was not so, and its registration with the saza chief could not change its status. Therefore, the solution suggested was that no one claiming to be married under customary law could be baptized before the saza chief had confirmed in writing that the marriage had been properly performed according to customary law; and that the couple should marry in church as soon as possible after baptism. It was even suggested that all Christians who had married earlier according to 'heathen custom' should be encouraged to come forward and be married in church.[96]

It was considered important to check whether baptismal requirements were met; in particular whether the couple were living in a polygamous relationship. In general, it was important that people could not later invoke any customary rule as an excuse for dissolving their marriages. This meant that proper customary marriage functioned in the first instance as a preliminary to baptism. In short, the principal aim was to preclude the possibility of switching back to the domain of customary law. A new marriage in church in fact constituted a remarriage, which entailed that the old customary marriage was thenceforth considered invalid. Furthermore, a Christian marriage was a statutory marriage, which came under the terms of the Ordinance. This meant that anyone who committed a violation, for example by contracting a new marriage under customary law, would be liable to prosecution.

In order to safeguard Christian marriage and put a stop to transitions between the two legal systems, the secular authority would have to be prepared to prosecute in the case of infringement of the Ordinance. It is quite obvious that the government, if only for practical reasons, was unable to do so,[97] and the resolution of the Missionary Conference of 1904 could have very little impact. Under a strict interpretation of the Ordinances of 1902 and 1903, remarriage was against the law, but because of the general lack of clarification of the validity of customary marriage, this point was hardly taken into account by anyone at the time.

Over the following years it was therefore very difficult for the mission to handle cases connected with the undefined status of customary marriages.[98] Naturally, the question was put on the agenda for the newly established Diocesan Synod. It was again discussed whether a native marriage, if registered, could be considered as binding. Bishop Tucker agreed once more to take the matter up with the government.[99] Apparently, no further clarification was achieved, for the practice laid down by the Missionary Conference of 1904 was reaffirmed at the Synod in 1909, although some of the delegates felt uneasy about the invalidation of customary marriages which this practice implied.[100] A major revision of the marriage policy was only carried out when Bishop Willis succeeded Bishop Tucker in 1912.[101] Willis took the initiative in his first address to the Missionary Conference immediately after taking office, and later brought the matter before the Synod. His new departure in the marriage question may well have been substantially influenced by the views of one of the missionaries, who had criticized the previous policy in the strongest of terms, and called it a scandal. Basing his arguments on his experiences in Toro, the Rev. W. E. Owen pointed out the need for a system of registration for customary marriages when they were converted into monogamous marriages. Such a transition, he claimed, must be placed on a proper legal footing, so that it would be possible to take legal action in cases where baptized people broke their pledges, sent away their wives and married again according to customary law. The present practice had 'resulted in an open door being left open to immorality of the most serious kind among the baptized members of the Church'.[102] Willis himself aptly summarized the policy of the previous period by stating: 'It does not seem to me that we have hitherto been guided by any very clear principle in facing the infinitely complex questions connected with native marriages.'[103] The guiding principle was that 'marriage is not essentially a Christian institution'; it was an institution common to all peoples, only the method of effecting it and the value attached to it differed. The special significance of Christian marriage was that it was monogamous, and that it initiated a lifelong union. But it was none the less subject to the general dictum that 'religion sanctifies, it does not destroy every legitimate relationship of life'.[104]

Given this conviction, Willis could only conclude that a customary marriage was fully valid, just like a Christian one, and supported his conclusion by adding that to denounce a customary marriage would be to destroy 'the fundamental idea of native morality'. Secondly, the Marriage Ordinances did in fact recognize the validity of 'the native marriage' by making it punishable to contract a statutory marriage whilst still married to a woman under customary law, and vice versa.[105] The practical results of this reversal of attitude were that Willis suggested a new policy as regards the baptismal conditions laid upon people who had married earlier under customary law, and his suggestions were endorsed by the Synod. The main stipulation was that such a marriage should be formally registered with the government after its correctness had been certified by the saza chief. When both parties had been baptized their marriage could be given the blessing of the church. This meant that, unlike before, any remarriage was ruled out. As this new policy could not be put into effect without government approval, the matter was referred to the Governor, who was asked to authorize the saza and gombolola chiefs as Registrars of Marriages contracted under customary law.[106]

One problem which would have to be solved in connection with the new legislation was: which wife should be retained from a polygamous household? This problem of selection had arisen constantly over the years, and it was now necessary to make a definite ruling in connection with the transfer to a registered, monogamous marriage. While the earlier practice had been that the husband could choose freely among his wives,[107] Willis was now strongly in favour of the principle that the first wife should be retained. He considered this to be a reflection of the African concept of the special status of the first wife. This was also the practice followed by the Catholic mission, and constituted a clearly defined principle.[108] But Willis was outvoted on this issue by the African majority in the Synod, and also by some of the missionaries, much to his regret.[109]

The Bishop and the Synod asked the government to decide in detail on the rules for converting a polygamous marriage into a monogamous one in view of the requirement of a statutory, monogamous marriage as a precondition of baptism.[110] The government was clearly somewhat perplexed by the Bishop's request for a registration of customary marriages, and found it a complicated issue to tackle.[111] The matter was sent to the Provincial Commissioners for comment,[112] and one major difficulty turned out to be the lack of inner consistency in Willis' approach. On the one hand he recognized the validity of customary marriage, on the other he only did so insofar as it involved only one wife. This was borne out by the fact that he wanted marriages to be registered under the Marriage Ordinance of 1902, which only covered civil, monogamous marriages. It was not the first time the government had been asked to recognize customary marriages within such limitations. In Toro, Owen had requested this form of registration as a precondition for baptism in cases where only one of the parties wanted to become a Christian and the marriage could therefore not be ratified in church.[113] It was thus a qualified recognition of marriages contracted under customary law which was included in Willis' new policy. Hence, it was only natural that some government officials expressed doubt as to whether the parties involved in such a registration realized the gravity of moving from one legal tradition to another, for instance in cases of divorce, where a marriage could only be dissolved by the High Court.[114]

This lack of clarity and consistency in Willis' proposal had the effect that two closely interlinked questions arose in the handling of the issue. First, should the registration of customary marriages be carried out irrespective of the number of wives? Secondly, what procedure should be followed as regards wives when a transition from a polygamous marriage to a monogamous, statutory one was required in order to meet the conditions for baptism? The Provincial Commissioners came to the conclusion that the only logical solution would be to register native marriages under customary law rather than statutory law. In practice this meant that a special ordinance covering customary marriages would have to be issued, parallel to the one for Christian marriages. Registration would be compulsory and the saza chiefs would be the Registrars. It was thought that such a system of registration would make the marriages more binding, and thus serve to reduce the number of broken marriages with their unfortunate social repercussions.[115] It was, however, recognized that such legislation would entail the official recognition of polygamy, or at least the sanctioning of polygamy for non-Christian Africans. In short, the state would grant full validity to polygamous marriage, but would at the same time give it a proper legal basis and thus hinder abuses.[116] One of the Provincial Commissioners could even claim that the measure had the support of one of the missionaries, W. E. Owen in Toro, although he doubted very much whether Owen's point of view could be harmonized with that of Bishop Willis.[117] The Bishop did not express his own opinion publicly at this stage, perhaps because Owen's views represented a faction of opinion within the mission. At any rate Willis confined himself to welcoming further discussions in committee.[118] His concept of registration was clearly almost exclusively conditioned by his concern for the fulfilment of the baptismal requirements. Christian husbands should be monogamous, and other wives should be divorced in accordance with native custom. For him there was no doubt that a number of evils were 'inseparable from polygamous life'.[119]

As for transition from customary to statutory marriage, it is characteristic that the Provincial Commissioners in the end assessed the requests for registered, monogamous marriages qualitatively. As such a rule would require the sending away of all a man's wives except one, and as the future welfare of these discarded wives was thereby endangered, one of the Provincial Commissioners wrote: 'To my mind the dissolution of marriages under native custom for no other reason than that a man wants to be baptized, tends to both immorality and injustice and should not be allowed.'[120] The Buganda Regents, with the support of the mission, denied that any hardships were involved for the women, but the officials were adamant that the married women's rights should be considered in any future legislation, and that proper protection should be given to them. As one possible solution to this complex problem it was suggested that the church should recognize polygamy for Christians for the time being, and accordingly baptize a polygamist while allowing him to keep all his wives.[121] This suggestion was rejected by Willis as being absolutely contrary to Christian teaching.[122]

No solution was reached during the first round of talks. Instead the government set up a committee with missionary representation to examine the problem in more detail.[123] The questions to be discussed could now be reduced to two: should the state grant official and direct recognition to customary and potentially polygamous marriages, and how far should the state favour monogamous marriage at the expense of polygamous marriage by only dealing with the former in its laws, and by allowing for the conversion of one to the other in accordance with the church's conditions for baptism? In both cases the importance attached to

Christian opinion would have to be weighed against concern for the Africans' interests and for the continued functioning of their institutions, as the Provincial Commissioners had already indicated. It is therefore of special interest to examine whether the lack of unity within the mission, of which the government was well aware, exerted any influence on the final outcome by weakening the mission's bargaining position.

In the course of the committee work in 1913, when Owen put his views on marriage legislation more firmly, and tried to influence the attitude of the mission,[124] he stressed two issues similar to the ones raised by the Provincial Commissioners. First of all, he found it absolutely necessary that the state should introduce compulsory registration of all native marriages, his main motive being that this was the only way to safeguard the rights of wives in divorce cases.[125] Eighty per cent of all marriages in the Protectorate were not yet covered by any law and were thus open to all kinds of abuses. The legal state of affairs amounted to a 'situation of content' which was almost immoral, and the only logical solution would be either to recognize customary marriage fully or get the government to forbid polygamy.[126] Owen was fully aware that the proposed registration amounted to an official recognition of polygamy, and would interfere with the baptismal requirement of monogamy. But he was also convinced that it would 'manifest in a very much stronger way the Christian abhorrence of polygamy and ultimately lead to a truer morality'.[127] Whether he was right in his analysis was not discussed. The missionary representative on the Government Committee, the Rev. E. Millar, was exclusively concerned with the political consequences of the official recognition of polygamy, and was adamantly against it: 'I shall most certainly object to a man being written down with more than one wife as such a thing would give the natives the idea that the Government wanted polygamy in the country. I had rather wreck the Committee than that should pass.'[128] Millar also referred to support from the Buganda Katikiro, who agreed that people would interpret such a step as a government approval of polygamy. Any registration should for that reason be confined to the situations where one man and one wife were involved.[129]

Owen's second point was related to the rules on divorce in cases where a polygamist wanted to be baptized and thus had to send his separated wives away. Again his main concern was the welfare of the women. He protested against the Synod's decision not to recognize the first wife as the true wife,[130] and insisted on 'just principles controlling the divorce of surplus wives'. Otherwise the church should refuse to baptize the polygamist.[131] Owen thus reflected the Provincial Commissioners' concern about the mission's insistence on monogamous status before baptism. Although he did not attack the baptismal requirement as such, he tried to establish a proper procedure for cases of transition from polygamy to monogamy which would make it more difficult to divorce additional wives simply out of a desire to be baptized.[132] Owen was on dangerous ground, and his views were firmly repudiated by the missionary representative on the Government Committee: 'The matter of surplus wives was *deliberately left out* of the ordinance as it would have been impossible to get the ordinance made had such clauses been put in, the Missionaries and the Government being absolutely opposed to each other.'[133] In other words, pursuing this matter would have brought negotiations to a halt, and it was therefore dropped completely. In Owen's eyes this meant that none of the obvious abuses in the present practice was redressed, so he wanted to go directly to the government to secure, at least for Toro, a proper procedure for the dissolution of polygamous marriages.[134] But this would have drawn unwelcome attention to the disagreements within the mission, and it was firmly vetoed by the Bishop, in spite of the fact that he shared Owen's opinions on the status of the first wife. Willis' main concern was, however, to obtain an ordinance which legalized the conversion of a customary to a statutory marriage without invalidating the former entirely. He therefore wished for 'no obstacles whatever to be put in the way of this ordinance becoming law'.[135]

This whole chain of events shows how deeply split the mission was over the whole marriage problem, although it is difficult to say how much support Owen had from other missionaries.[136] It also indicates that the mission succeeded in keeping the controversy internal, so as not to weaken its position unduly in relation to the government. In any case the disagreements do not seem to have influenced the final outcome, although they do help to put it into perspective.[137] Having failed to make his point in the Uganda arena, Owen recognized that the only possibility left for him was to appeal to the leaders at home.[138] When on leave in Britain in 1914 he engaged in busy activity, writing manuscripts for publication in order to start a debate on the polygamy question and induce the Uganda mission to change its attitude,[139] but he was restrained, partly by the CMS authorities,[140] and partly by his loyalty to the Uganda mission. Bishop Willis in particular persuaded him to refrain from mounting a public campaign.[141] After some hesitation he returned to Uganda in 1915 and took up work in a new area where, as we shall see later, he began, true to his nature, to implement the marriage policy with great consistency.[142] His activities in Europe did not exert any visible influence on mission or government marriage policy. His case serves to show that when an ordinary, individual missionary tried to influence events through the European arena, he could not, despite the strength of his engagement, have the same impact as a missionary leader like the Bishop, working with the support of the whole missionary apparatus.[143]

The final outcome of the Bishop's and the Synod's demand in 1912 for the official registration of monogamous customary marriages was that the Uganda Marriage (Amendment) Ordinance of 1914 was passed, and came into effect on 1 July.[144] The main provision was that a marriage under customary law could be registered as 'a permanent and monogamous marriage' and would from then on be legally valid within the terms of the Marriage Ordinance of 1902. This was a confirmation of monogamous customary marriage, and the legalization of the conversion of a customary marriage to a statutory, monogamous one. Nothing was said about the procedures involved in the latter conversion, but it was tacitly presupposed that a polygamist should be separated from all his wives except one in accordance with customary law before coming forward for registration.[145] This meant that the wish to be baptized and to live in a monogamous marriage was recognized as sufficient reason for obtaining a divorce under customary law.[146]

We may now examine the outcome of these events from two different angles. First, how far did the mission succeed in persuading the government to pass a law in accordance with its demands, and to what extent did the government at the instigation of the mission favour Christian, monogamous marriage? Secondly, what were the longer-term effects of the new legislation?

In answer to the first question, the mission had succeeded in preventing the authorities from granting general recognition to all native marriages; the government seems to have come close to such a recognition at one stage,[147] and the Provincial Commissioners were certainly in favour of it. Customary marriages as such gained no legal status, and remained subject to customary law. Polygamy thus failed to obtain the prestige which could have followed on official recognition. Secondly, by legalizing the conversion of a customary marriage to a statutory one, the state demonstrated its willingness to support Christian monogamy. It should be remembered that this new legal departure was introduced on the basis of the mission's baptismal requirement, and was seen as a means of stopping random transitions from one legal system to another. The law as it now stood was likely to work in favour of monogamy with the general public, and this was what the missionaries intended. The state can thus be said to have responded positively to the mission's demands by refraining from the general recognition of polygamous marriage despite the fact that some officials thought this was the only logical solution.

Thirdly, it is significant that the state refused to involve itself in the 'surplus wives' issue. The mission was fully aware that this was the one point of disagreement with the government which could have wrecked negotiations. The government's attitude had both a negative and a positive aspect. Negatively speaking, what had happened was simply that the government had turned a blind eye, and left the mission to continue with a practice which was known to be causing hardships for those women who were sent away. Some government officials even called the system immoral; but no colonial legislation was proposed, in compliance with the mission's efforts to introduce monogamous marriage. Positively, it may be said that the government deliberately refused to give direct support to this aspect of the missionary policy. People had the option of converting their customary marriages to monogamous civil marriages, but beyond that the government allowed the customary system to operate as before, and refused to legislate on any detailed process of conversion from one marriage law to the other. The fact that the saza and gombolola chiefs were deliberately excluded from the process of registering customary marriages under the Ordinance of 1902 is indicative of the government's attitude to the missionary drive to encourage monogamy. These negative and positive trends in government policy were not necessarily incompatible. Taken together they serve to illustrate the fact that the government was only prepared to support missionary efforts to Christianize society up to a point. The government was also anxious to make sure that African institutions were not demolished all at once on the sole ground that they were not compatible with Christian morality. Some government officials had already expressed reservations about missionary policy, and this trend became even more marked over the following years.

The missionaries on their side attached great importance to the legal procedures for converting marriages, and to the fact that the church's baptismal requirements now had some degree of support in law.[148] This positive result was however only obtained by the mission at a price. Bishop Willis had at first suggested the introduction of certain rules about which wife should be chosen from a polygamous household when the husband became monogamous, but he was overruled by his own Synod when he suggested that the first wife should take priority. Owen pointed out the unfortunate position of the separated wives, and argued that the church had a responsibility for their welfare, even if it meant slowing down the movement towards monogamy. But Willis and the mission in general sacrificed these interests in favour of the passing of the amended Ordinance of 1914. Owen was right in characterizing the result as one which did not alter the old conditions; on the contrary, the mission allowed admitted abuses to continue, and the present policy could in Owen's view be summarized with the words 'the more expediency, the less justice'.[149] It did not change much that church regulations now stipulated that no polygamist could be baptized 'until he had formally separated from, and adequately provided for, the wife or wives other than the one with whom the marriage has been registered'.[150] The enforcement of this rule still fell under customary law. It seems odd that the mission was in this case willing to rely on customary law, while it opposed it on principle in other cases. The mission thus sacrificed certain principles in accepting the new legislation, and the price paid appears in a somewhat ironic light when the benefits of the new law are taken into account.

As for the second main question posed above, one way of measuring the benefits for the Christian marriage institution which arose from the new and much-desired law is to examine how much use was actually made of it, and how it came to work in practice. No statistics are available for this, but we can reach some conclusions by looking into the procedure laid down for the conversion of customary marriages. Neither the clergy nor the saza or gombolola chiefs were involved, as the conversions were ratified by the District Officers of the colonial administration, before whom it was necessary to appear in person. The procedure for converting marriages was similar to the one stipulated in the Marriage Ordinance of 1902 for civil marriages, and accordingly involved an administrative apparatus which the missions had denounced as unworkable ten years earlier, because of its disregard for the conditions prevailing in the Protectorate. At the practical level, therefore, the new Ordinance was likely to have a limited effect even for purely procedural reasons, despite every effort from the church to assist in administrating it. It was pointed out at an early stage that very few people had availed themselves of the new Ordinance.[151] The mission ascribed this mainly to the cumbersome procedure required by the law, and pointed out that if no changes were made by way of introducing better facilities for the conversion of customary marriages the law would remain 'a Dead Letter'.[152] At the Synod in 1921 African members also called for an easier conversion system for marriages, and suggested that saza and gombolola chiefs should be authorized as Registrars.[153] Some years later Bishop Willis confirmed that the 1914 Ordinance had not worked satisfactorily, and that few people had made use of it. He considered that the sole reason for this was the impracticability of registration written into the law.[154]

The paradoxical situation had thus arisen that, while the missionaries in their drive for monogamy required the conversion of customary marriages as a condition of baptism, it was impossible for ordinary people to fulfil this condition without great effort and some expense. This situation was bound to have a devaluating effect on the new law. To this should be added a second factor: even if people came forward at the instigation of the mission and the church to ratify their customary marriages, it proved almost impossible to administrate the law in practice, at least in certain districts. A case from the Eastern Province seems to have been typical. Soon after the passing of the 1914 law the missionary in charge had issued 26 notices to people requiring ratification of their marriages; but after having performed one legal ceremony the District Commissioner refused to perform any more, and asked the mission not to enforce the rule that people could only be baptized when they had ratified their customary marriages. The missionary in charge was inclined to agree with the District Commissioner, in spite of the fact that it was the latter's duty to convert the marriages, and that he could even be compelled to do so.[155] Two interrelated issues were at stake. First of all, it proved impossible to check whether the transition from one legal system to the other had been carried out in the prescribed way. It was particularly difficult to find out whether a husband had really separated from all his wives but one in the correct manner; and afterwards it was impossible to check whether a man had taken back his former wives, or taken new women into his household. Any check would involve a detailed investigation of concrete cases, which was impossible given the number of people involved. It would also have presupposed that there was a definite answer to the question of what, in a given area, constituted a true customary marriage. For instance, must the dowry have been paid before the law could be said to have been broken? In such situations the District Commissioner simply characterized any official registration as 'a wicked action' which would have meant imprisonment for the man involved if the law was enforced.[156] This leads to the second issue. A necessary condition for the functioning of the law was that people were punished when they violated it. The missionary in the case mentioned above raised a crucial question: why did the church not prosecute, as a failure to take action definitely weakened morality? He was not himself in favour of taking such a hard line, preferring to rely on better instruction.[157]

Following this line of reasoning it may be said in general that a necessary precondition for the proper functioning of all the marriage laws would have been the enforcement of the penalty clauses, especially in cases of bigamy, which occurred when people married under the statutory and the customary law at the same time. We must therefore now ask how far the mission and the government were willing to take such a course of action. The 1914 law was aimed exclusively at defining the relationship between the two legal traditions, and was thus supposed to provide a better basis for prosecutions.

Faithful to his earlier convictions, and unlike his colleague in the Eastern Province, Owen felt it necessary to take action in accordance with the law, at least as a preventive measure, in spite of the fact that he considered the law as it stood to be quite inadequate. He still believed that the official registration of all customary marriages was necessary, and envisaged that this would have to be done within the next ten years, as conditions could not go on as they were for very much longer.[158] In the meantime he prosecuted and obtained convictions in six cases of bigamy in less than one year,[159] and, although the sources do not say as much, it is likely that Owen in this respect acted on his own initiative, and not in accordance with a general policy of the mission.[160] This line of action was not welcomed by all his colleagues, and there is some indication that members of the mission found it inappropriate to invoke the secular authorities in order to further the cause of morality.[161] The missionary leaders were also aware of the difficulties of obtaining the evidence necessary for such prosecutions, and defining whether a violation of customary law provided sufficient grounds for legal action.[162]

Leading government officials were much more outspoken in their attitude to prosecution under the marriage laws in general, and to Owen's initiatives in particular. Following one conviction, the Puisne Judge objected to Owen's actions, and stated that he would ask the Privy Council to repeal the two clauses on bigamy.[163] The Chief Justice showed the same disinclination to prosecute for bigamy when he stated: 'I agree with my colleague in thinking it hard that a man should be punished for doing a little more decently and in a manner to satisfy the pagan parents what he can do without punishment by taking a concubine.'[164] It is quite obvious that the leading members of the judiciary in Uganda considered prosecution under the Marriage Ordinances to be incompatible with the realities of daily life. In a wider sense, it went against the prevailing conception of law and justice among the people. In both respects the gap was so wide that prosecution made little sense. It is further remarkable that Owen's point of view found no support from the two most prominent Protestant chiefs and leading laymen in the church. One of the missionaries, giving evidence to the Uganda Development Commission, argued that it should be a penal offence for a Christian to contract a customary marriage;[165] but both the Katikiro, Sir Apolo Kagwa, and the Sekibobo, Ham Mukasa, were against punishment for this type of bigamy: 'Don't see why action should be taken against Xtian man who takes wife by native custom after being married according to Xtian religion. If his wife wishes to take action she can do so but it is no one else's business.'[166] African leaders do not seem to have been interested in furthering the cause of monogamy and Christian marriage by way of the courts. This unwillingness from the government to use the penal clauses, and the lack of pressure from the mission and African leaders, substantially weakened the impact of the marriage laws in general and hampered the proper functioning of the new Law of 1914 in particular.

As regards the latter point, one further aspect should be mentioned. When the issue of converting and registering customary marriages first arose in 1912 some government officials considered it to be immoral of the mission to request the dissolution of such marriages in order to further monogamy. In the following years a more outright scepticism and concern appeared among officials, especially those working in the districts, over the mission's marriage policy and its consequences at the local level. At the time of the passing of the 1914 Law it was pointed out that too many changes had occurred within too short a time as a consequence of hurried baptisms and the subsequent introduction of monogamy.[167] The missionary policy of 'enforcing monogamy among polyga-mous people' was deplored even more strongly in a report from the Northern Province. It was said that such a policy detracted from the value of the missionary presence, as it led to hypocrisy and other misdeeds, especially at a time when the government was trying to eliminate such evils, in particular among the new chiefly generation. Religious norms were required which corresponded better with the traditional way of life.[168] A few years later the same official stated that one of the chief causes of the existing deplorable social situation was 'the too hasty insistence on monogamy for polygamy'.[169] This opinion seems to have been shared by a number of colonial officials with experience from the districts.[170]

That such an attitude existed in the administration and the judiciary leads to the conclusion that the mission could now rely less and less in the second decade of the century on the active support and cooperation of the government in the furthering of monogamy. This was a change in the government's attitude, as compared with the Law of 1914, and it meant that there was no real willingness to give the conversion option the necessary backing and thus make the Law work as the mission intended. In this respect the whole process remained a somewhat futile exercise. The Law did not solve the problem which it was meant to solve, the transition from a polygamous to a monogamous type of marriage. In spite of the mission's qualified recognition of the validity of customary marriages, the two systems of marriage persisted almost unaffected side by side with their mutual relationship undefined, as features such as the continuation of the dowry system demonstrate. The new Law did not provide for a smooth transition from customary to statutory marriage, and, worse still, it did nothing to stop the reverse process, which was the mission's main problem with the marriage institution.

Christian values in law and administration

The subject of marriage is indicative of the extent to which the state was willing to take on responsibility for morality in society and to support the mission in its efforts to introduce Christian norms into African society. But before we can arrive at any conclusions on this, it will be necessary to broaden our perspective and discuss other areas where the mission applied Christian moral principles in its demands to the government. At an early stage the mission expressed serious concern over the decline in moral standards.[171] It was suggested that, aside from the mission's own drive for increased spirituality, the government could do much to remove hindrances to the Christian way of life. As we have seen, hut tax was considered a deterrent to marriage, and this prompted the mission to support the levying of poll tax instead, first on bachelors and later on all adults. The request for a maximum limit on the dowry rate was an expression of the same concern. It was also argued that forced labour like kasanvu and luwalo tended to have adverse effects on family life and morality. In sum, the mission reminded the government on several occasions of its duty to incorporate Christian morality into its legislation and administration, even if this involved the introduction of special preventive measures. For the sake of clarification, these various demands to the colonial state can be divided into two categories: demands for the passing of specific laws, and demands for special administrative measures.

The passing of specific laws

The various issues were first discussed in the Synod and then forwarded to the state. The Synod thus acted as a major policy-making body, just as the Mengo Church Council had done with moral issues in the 1890s. There was no doubt in the Synod as to the responsibility of the government to take action on moral issues.[172] The actors themselves divided their legislatory requirements into three main groups: measures to uphold marriage and hinder adultery; measures to combat drunkenness; and measures which were meant to stop the tendency 'to revert to heathen customs'.[173]

Cases involving adultery arose constantly and led to demands for enforcement or improvement of the existing legislation. Thus in 1919 two resolutions were passed: one asking the various Lukikos to pass a law prohibiting women from leaving their gombolola without a permit; the other asking chiefs and parents not to allow boys to build their own huts before reaching marriageable age.[174] The same pattern was apparent in connection with the problem of drunkenness. It was felt to be increasing over the years,[175] not least due to foreign influence, and the authorities were asked to enforce the laws more rigorously, to restrict beer clubs, and to ban the import of whisky. In general the Synod called for regulations against drunkenness in areas where the existing legislation was insufficient.[176]

The last major area where legislative measures were demanded by the church was that of the continuation of 'heathen customs', when new converts fell back to their old religion. This was a rather complicated problem to tackle, first of all because it was difficult to tell in a transitional period to what extent customs and practices were so closely associated with 'heathen' customs, or were of such an indecent nature, that they represented a danger to Christians. The feelings and prejudices associated with totemistic beliefs, with their importance for the coherence of the clan, were one aspect of this dilemma. The social significance of customs and rites, for instance the succession ceremonies, were such that a ban might disrupt valuable institutions and destroy the social balance which the Christian leaders otherwise wanted to preserve. The discussion of the extent to which legal measures should be taken against old customs and traditions came to a head in 1912–13, when a special committee set up by the Synod investigated customary behaviour.[177] During the discussion of the succession celebrations in particular, the church leaders began to realize the dilemma which faced them. These celebrations were considered to be deplorable, but it would not be realistic to try to abolish them. Instead it was decided to approach the Buganda Lukiko and ask it to pass a law making it the chiefs' responsibility to control the celebrations and prevent the usual immorality connected with them.[178]

The main criterion used in evaluating the various traditional customs was the degree of immorality and adultery involved. This explains why the Buganda Lukiko was asked to pass a law against the singing of indecent songs,[179] and why a ban on the use of harps at marriage feasts was requested later, because of their association with immoral 'heathen' customs.[180] But the crux of the matter was the belief in evil spirits which was supposed to be inherent in a number of customs and ceremonies. It was admitted that it might be difficult to combat this by means of legislation. The most malign expression of this belief was the practice of witchcraft, and it was considered necessary to make this a criminal offence. Later the local Lukikos were asked to pass laws forbidding both witchcraft as such and the general belief in pagan deities (*lubale*), and at the same time to authorize the gombolola chiefs to hear the cases.[181]

In assessing the impact of these demands for legislation we should make it clear from the outset that the source materials available seldom allow us to establish a direct cause-and-effect relationship. This may be ascribed to the following two factors, which show how the framework for direct inputs differed from those we have met in other fields. First, most of the demands for laws and regulations were directed to the Buganda Lukiko, not to the government, because this particular field of legislation was placed, in accordance with the Uganda Agreement, under African authority, although it was still subject to the approval of the colonial administration.[182] The same practice was later extended to the neighbouring areas. This clearly makes it more difficult to examine the importance of the church's interventions. The situation is further complicated because in some cases it is difficult to tell whether a law was passed by a local council with the necessary approval – this would sometimes be the case even if it did not appear in the book of laws – or whether it took the form of a recommendation which was then considered equivalent to a law by some people, and was acted upon accordingly.[183]

The second factor is the amount of overlap among Christian chiefs between the African polity and the church. As we will show below (Chapter 17) they constituted the leading lay element in the various bodies of the church, and played as such an essential role in decision-making processes. This means that they were fully informed about the needs for legislation from the Christian point of view, and could give advice and even exert influence when various demands were put forward. They could also promise to take action without any specific request from the church. One clear example of this was the Buganda Katikiro, Sir Apolo Kagwa.[184] It should further be added that these Christian leaders were fully able and prepared to act in accordance with Christian norms and values without any direct backing or request from the church. This means that it is not always necessary to look for direct demands from the mission and church when faced with laws reflecting Christian principles of morality.[185] This does much to explain many of the laws passed in the first few years after the conclusion of the Agreement, when the Christian chiefs made use of their newly won power and tried to apply their Christian ideals to society.[186]

In order to assess direct and indirect influence on laws passed during the first two decades of the twentieth century, the division into three groups employed above may be used again. As regards the first group of laws, those on marriage, family matters and morality, one early case exemplified, among other things, the problem of gaining the approval of the colonial administration. In November 1901 the Buganda Lukiko passed a law on 'Marriage and the Religion of Children'. The aim of the law was to fix the age when children should be allowed to leave their parents and change their religion.[187] It was discovered, however, in 1903 that the law had never received official sanction.[188] It was only put on the statute books after consultation with Bishop Tucker, which had the effect that the age when a child could choose a religion different from that of its parents was now fixed at 14, while 18 was fixed as the age when children were free to leave home.[189] After this decision the mission was anxious to safeguard parental rights with regard to religion, in view of the competition from the Roman Catholics. When the law was contravened by a saza court in 1917 the mission protested successfully.[190] The Provincial Commissioner upheld parental rights under the terms of the law, but it is significant that the Buganda Lukiko was divided when it discussed the case.[191] Though the evidence is scanty, this seems to suggest that some disagreement existed among the Ganda leaders themselves about the suitability of this early law and its enforcement. A few years later a more general law, the Coming of Age Law of 1920, was passed, which fixed the age of 'legal maturity' at 20. The age of 'religious maturity' and the relationship of this law to the earlier one were not mentioned.[192] This may indicate a change in the Ganda leaders' powers to legislate on specifically religious matters, but a final conclusion must await further evidence.

Two early measures in support of Christian marriage should be mentioned. Even before the Protectorate laws on statutory marriage and divorce were introduced, the Lukiko passed a law which virtually ruled out divorce in the case of Christian marriages; a couple could only be separated by death.[193] As the law was framed, it effectively abolished the traditional right of women to return to their parents.[194] This change from marriage by the old custom to 'marriage by religion' was further confirmed by a second law which placed severe restrictions on the movements of married women, and left the exercise of control entirely in the hands of their husbands.[195] Most of these laws aimed principally to secure a Christian morality in society, and especially a Christian sexual morality. This aim was more explicit in two special laws. The first one, passed by the Buganda Lukiko in 1901, introduced severe penalties for any man assisting in an abortion.[196] A few years later, the law was endorsed by the Lukiko and promulgated by the colonial administration.[197] A second law dealt with the more general problem of adultery and fornication. It was passed with the explicitly stated aim of hindering immorality in the country and dealt with the various forms of illegal relations both within and outside marriage.[198] This kind of law should be seen as an attempt to alter the existing customary law in accordance with the new Christian norms. When the law was expanded and amended in 1917–18 a special clause was inserted stating that this was 'the whole law about sexual offences and all native customs relating to such offences are hereby abolished'. This latter law imposed heavier penalties than before for adultery committed with married women and was thus aimed at safeguarding the institution of marriage, whether statutory or customary.[199]

The 1906 Law against the use of indecent language also comes under the provisions guarding morality.[200] The general impression is that the Buganda Lukiko was very responsive to Christian ideals and took the initiative to incorporate them in its legislation, although it is difficult to say exactly which laws were actually sanctioned by the colonial government.[201] There was a noticeable tendency towards more detailed measures in the earlier years, whereas more general codes of law on the European model were passed towards the end of the period.

Some confirmation of the pattern outlined above is provided by the second type of legislation, the measures against drunkenness. In 1901 the Buganda Lukiko passed laws against the sale of beer in the capital and along the main roads. The latter provision was aimed to encourage husbands working on the roads away from home to remain faithful to their wives.[202] It is difficult to say whether these laws ever received official sanction or were ever enforced. At the Synod in 1909 reference was made to a clause forbidding the sale of European spirits, and the Bishop asked for witnesses to come forward so that he could take the matter to the government.[203] The next legal move came in 1917, when a general law, the Native Liquor Law, was passed by the Buganda Lukiko. It contained a number of regulations on the making and selling of liquor manufactured in accordance with African tradition, but it did not include any direct measures to combat drunkenness.[204] This law was only a partial response to the Synod's serious concern about the problem of excessive drinking, as it did not go as far as the Synod wanted. Nor does it appear to have had any tangible result, as the Synod called for the enforcement of the existing laws, and in particular for a ban on the import of whisky, in 1924.[205]

Moving to the field of traditional customs, the results seem just as meagre from the point of view of the church. A witchcraft ordinance was issued by the government in 1912, making it an offence to practise witchcraft, or more precisely to give advice or provide materials with intent to injure anyone. It was also considered an offence to impute the use of witchcraft to another person.[206] This ordinance was an initiative of the administration itself, and was prompted by experiences in Buganda. It has not been possible to trace any special influence from the mission or church, although their tacit approval could be reckoned on.[207] In 1920, the official administrating the newly opened district of Kigezi asked for an amendment providing for heavier penalties: witchcraft was considered to be the reason for unrest and hostility towards the government.[208] On the other hand it is characteristic that when the Synod in 1924 asked for changes which amounted to increased local involvement in combatting divination and witchcraft, the government did not take any action, as the existing ordinance was considered sufficient.[209] A change along the lines suggested would have meant more direct official involvement in the suppression of 'heathen customs'. This was not considered advisable.

The second major issue raised by the Synod in relation to heathen customs was connected with immorality during celebrations and rites. The demand that the chiefs be made responsible for moral standards at succession celebrations had proved fruitless. A more limited result of the efforts to outlaw heathen practices was the Law for Preventing the Native Tabulu Dance and Certain Other Native Dances, passed by the Buganda Lukiko in 1916.[210] No explicit religious criterion was applied. The crux of the matter was the 'indecent or immoral nature' of the dances, although the Buganda Lukiko in its comments did refer to wider consequences for the nation and for religion.[211] The rather limited success of the church here was further underlined by the final clause of the law which implicitly refused the request for a ban on harps, stating that 'this law does not apply to the playing of native harps . . . provided it is not accompanied by dancing in an indecent or immoral way'.[212]

We have now examined a number of the laws passed during the first few decades of the twentieth century within the three areas of legislation of most relevance for the church: family matters, moral issues like drunkenness, and traditional religious practices. If we compare results with the demands addressed to the political system, we may say that only a few were met in full. In a number of cases, limited action or no action at all was taken. This might suggest that legislative methods for furthering Christian norms and morality were of limited value. It certainly seemed this way to leading missionaries.[213] However, the lack of results and the disappointment of the mission should be contrasted with the African leaders' willingness to use civil authority in support of Christian values and morality. In this context we have seen a pattern of exchanges between the ecclesiastical and political fields which differed considerably from what we have seen otherwise. The church's demands for specific legislation in support of Christian norms were channelled through the Synod to African institutions, primarily the Buganda Lukiko. It was not the European agencies which took the lead in these matters, and this is a point of some importance in evaluating the legislative approach to the problems.

From the beginning the Buganda Lukiko showed great willingness to comply with the church's demands and passed a number of very specific laws. This was made easier because there was a high degree of overlap between the leading members in the Synod and the Lukiko. This certainly produced results on paper, but it is difficult to evaluate the longer-term effects at a more concrete level. One important factor was that the colonial administration both had to approve and enforce laws once they were passed. In both respects there is little direct evidence of the extent to which the colonial administration supported the use of legislative methods to further Christian norms. In the latter part of the period under survey there were three trends which indicate that the government was critical of the legislative method as such and of the church's influence on local legislative processes.

First, we have already noticed the difference between the early laws, which contained a number of detailed provisions and were geared to specific cases, and later laws of a more general nature, less specifically geared to religious and moral issues. This shift may in itself be a reflection of the development of the administrative system. In the earlier period, much of the initiative was left to the Buganda Lukiko, whereas the later period saw an increase in centralization.[214] This was especially so after the extension of legislative measures to the neighbouring areas, which necessitated greater uniformity.

Alongside this administrative development there was a more qualitative trend among colonial officials, parallel to their change in attitude to the drive for monogamy. At an early stage some scepticism was expressed over the detailed provisions in many of the laws. In many cases it was impossible to enforce the laws, and some of them had become obsolete.[215] This attitude was later made explicit when the Provincial Commissioner of Buganda stated that, as laws on family matters were difficult to enforce, it was better not to legislate in the first place, and to leave such matters to public opinion.[216] There was, then, a general feeling among officials that legislation was not the way to further Christian morality.[217]

This scepticism may be combined with a third factor, the growing concern of officials over the procedures employed by the church in presenting its demands to the African authorities. The detailed discussion of this issue belongs, however, with an examination of the importance of the personal bonds between the Protestant church and the African political system (Chapter 17). In the present context it is enough to say that colonial officials in the post-war period expressed a growing concern over the dual role of the leading chiefs in church and state, fearing that it would mean an excessive Christian influence on legislation connected with moral issues. They also questioned the fact that the Synod forwarded resolutions demanding legislation directly to the various African political organs. It was felt that the direct access of church bodies to the various Lukikos, facilitated by the overlap of members, placed too much political activity beyond the control of the government. Accordingly, new rules of procedure were laid down, stipulating that the church had to consult colonial officials before approaching African political bodies. The government's involvement in these procedures lessened the scope of the church to have legislation passed on moral issues.

While these changes limited the efficacy of the legislative method they did not imply any denial of the mission's and the church's legitimate right to express views on moral and social problems. The colonial administration wanted the process to be under government control; it was also considered doubtful whether legislation based primarily on Christian values was advisable. The latter issue may be examined further by investigating the church's more general drive to incorporate Christian principles into the administration of the country.

Demands for special administrative measures

Turning to the mission's and the church's approaches to the political system and their demands for Christian principles in administration, we may concentrate on two issues: Sunday labour and the morality of the chiefs. The issue of Sunday labour arose again and again. The matter was first discussed in 1905, when Bishop Tucker sent a circular letter on the observation of the Sabbath, stating that it was disgraceful for Christians to work on the Lord's Day.[218] In one area, where Christians were asked to do road work on Sundays, the saza chief answered that this was done by order of the Commissioner, and that the Bishop's letter had no authority, as it was not countersigned by the Commissioner.[219] The episode prompted Tucker to take the case to the government. Tucker was as careful as he had been on other occasions, such as the forced labour issue, to avoid giving the impression that he was interfering. He made it quite clear that his recommendation rested on moral authority alone, and that the saza chief had misunderstood his letter. At the same time he asked the government to confirm that it did not order road work on Sundays, as no urgency could possibly justify such a step.[220] The Commissioner admitted that the government had ordered the Sunday work in the saza in question, but only as an exception. While agreeing in principle with Tucker on the observance of holidays, he said that no strict rule of law could prevail here; even in England certain public works had to be carried out on Sundays.[221]

It is significant that the Bishop did not ask for any specific law to be passed. He saw the question as a general administrative one, in the sense that the government was being asked to respect a time-honoured Christian principle. The Commissioner was sympathetic, but did not commit himself further. The following year, at one of the first of the regular Synod meetings, it was again asked why saza chiefs required men to work on Sundays. The Buganda Katikiro, Sir Apolo Kagwa, immediately placed the responsibility with the colonial administration, claiming that it was forcing the chiefs to do so by giving them too short notice and requiring the work to be done at once.[222] In the following year the Synod again named government officials as the chief offenders. A resolution was sent to the Commissioner expressing deep regret that Sunday labour was carried out throughout the Protectorate, and asking the government to respect what was a well-founded right for the Christian population.[223] The Commissioner again responded positively. He sent the Synod's resolution on to his officers, and impressed on them his wish that they should not oblige porters and others to work on the Sabbath by travelling on Sundays.[224] Apparently these attempts at moral persuasion did not have much effect. The matter was discussed again in an atmosphere of even greater distress at the Synod in 1909, when Bishop Tucker recommended legislative methods. To solve the usual dilemma of whether to place the responsibility with the saza chiefs or the colonial officials, it was decided to ask the Buganda Lukiko to pass a law that no man should be compelled to work on Sundays. If it was beyond the authority of the Lukiko to pass such a law, the request would be forwarded to the Governor. In addition all Christians, and especially chiefs, were asked to be more active in their refusal to undertake any work on Sundays.[225]

No law appears to have resulted from this initiative, but the Governor once again expressed his opposition to Sunday labour and sent a circular to all officials telling them not to enforce it. As a more concrete measure he ordered the closing of the markets in all major towns on Sundays.[226] The real problem was, however, that European officials did not comply with these moral appeals. Accordingly, at the initiative of one of the leading Protestant chiefs, the Sekibobo, Ham Mukasa, the Synod approved an even stronger and highly unusual measure in 1910. The Governor was asked to send a letter in English and Luganda to all chiefs, telling them that they need not work on Sundays, even if ordered to do so by 'irresponsible men' (i.e. European officials).[227] Although the sources tell us nothing about the Governor's response, it is most unlikely that he would have issued such a letter, as it would have tended to undermine European authority. The move does however demonstrate the importance attached to the personal attitudes of European officials towards Christian values in an area where no legislation had been endorsed.

The Synod addressed itself once more to the problem of Sunday labour in 1917. The Governor was approached and asked to order the closing of shops and markets on Sundays.[228] Again the results appear to have been meagre, and in

1921 the Synod did not even approach the government, but confined itself to expressing its deep regret that Christians were working on Sundays, and to demanding that members of the church itself at least did not request others to do such work.[229]

In the drive to uphold the principle of the Christian Sabbath the church thus invoked the assistance of the secular authorities. The church was clearly hampered in its efforts by the existence of two systems of authority, and we may even infer that chiefs used this ambivalence to pass responsibility on to the government. In this case, at any rate, it was of little use that the chiefs themselves were members of the Synod, and the church learned from experience that the colonial administration was the important institution. The government did not respond by passing any law or making detailed regulations, nor did it follow up its own circulars by imposing penalties. Repeated complaints that the shops and markets remained open on Sundays provide an illustration of official laxity in this respect. What the church was left with was a moral appeal from the Governor to officials to keep the Christian Sabbath; but the value of this assistance proved to be somewhat limited. The government was hesitant to commit itself beyond the level of moral persuasion.

The second issue which prompted approaches to the government was that of the chiefs and morality in society. It has been shown earlier how the chiefs' economic potential was of great importance in furthering the goals of the mission, and how the decline in their commitment meant a reduction in the funds available for the work. The position and influence of the chiefs were also considered to be a guarantee of moral standards and discipline in society, even to the extent that the increase in immorality was seen as an effect of the 'waning power of chiefs'.[230] It was only a short step from this emphasis on the chiefs' official position to the positing of a correlation between their personal behaviour and the furtherance of Christian morality. Their personal conduct was seen as setting standards for the rest of the community and became therefore the concern of the church authorities. At the Synod in 1909 it was stated that an immoral chief meant an immoral people, and that the state should be asked to take action to remove such chiefs.[231] Bishop Tucker emphasized, however, the necessity of caution in these matters, as the church could not compel the government to do anything. The government must be convinced that 'immorality of life renders a man unfit to rule others under him'. Tucker shrewdly added a tactical argument which would appeal to the government's economic self-interest. Immorality meant the spread of disease, and this in turn meant a heavy drain on government resources. 'Of course we cannot compel the government to do anything, but when their pockets are touched we may be sure they will act at once.'[232] It is difficult to say whether this argument worked. While Bishop Tucker was convinced that the state had an obligation to secure proper standards among its African officials, he was also fully aware of the delicacy of the matter, and of the need for the church to proceed with caution, as any approach to the government might be interpreted as interference in matters of appointment and therefore resented. The effect of this was that increased emphasis was placed on internal church measures for improving discipline, such as suspension from Holy Communion, the publication of the names of offenders, and finally excommunication. But this created yet another dilemma for the church. At the Synod in 1910 it was agreed that the chiefs were the greatest offenders with regard to polygamy. Deprived of legal expedients, the ecclesiastical authorities could only subject them to church discipline and publish their names. But this involved the risk of losing them for the church and thereby reducing the church's social standing. Some thought that this price was too high; others argued that 'the Church does not stand or fall with the chiefs, and a small Church and a holy one is better than a large and sinful one'.[233]

This difference of opinion sums up the dilemma of the church on the issue of the chiefs' morality. Should priority be given to the quality of the church by dispensing with these chiefs, or should the benefits of having people of official standing as leading members take priority, and a blind eye be turned to their moral lapses? Only the state could effectively solve this dilemma by sacking unworthy incumbents and installing new people with high moral standards. But appeals to the state were made only with great caution, as this was not considered by the government to be a field where the church could claim to have legitimate interests. Bishop Willis alluded to the complexity of the whole issue in his first statement of policy in 1912. He was vague about the extent to which the civil authorities should be invoked, and pointed out 'the danger of alienating the chiefs, on whom humanly speaking so much of the future of the country depends'.[234] This left little room for direct action; but it was with great satisfaction that the church observed some years later that the government itself removed a number of sub-chiefs because of fraud and incompetence; for the same officials were 'usually those who have been living bad lives otherwise'.[235] It was thus seen that the best way to approach the government was to appeal to its self-interest, as Bishop Tucker had already suggested. The church employed this pragmatic approach in 1924 when it called on the government to assist in combating excessive drinking by not appointing known drunkards as chiefs and by dismissing those who were so from office.[236]

Despite these appeals to the government, it is remarkable how little correspondence there was in general between the importance attached by the church to the chiefs' moral standards and the number of demands for changes addressed to the government. Although they were aware of the seriousness of the matter, the leaders of the church exercised great caution.[237] This pattern of behaviour stands in marked contrast to the many initiatives within the fields of marriage law and the rules guiding personal conduct. In the first place, the Christian leaders were aware of the government's resentment of any interference as regards the incumbents to chieftainships. As will be seen later (Chapter 17), the church had learned from its experiences in the first few years after the conclusion of the Agreement, when the government had discouraged the missionary societies from involving themselves in the appointment or dismissal of chiefs. Such involvement was considered to be interference in politics.[238] The demands for action on moral grounds were equally open to accusations of interference.

Secondly, as we have seen, the risk of alienating the chiefs and the unfortunate consequences of this for the church were never far from the minds of the Protestant leaders, and had a restraining effect. This problem became even more acute when the private life of the Kabaka himself became the object of more or less hidden criticism from the beginning of the 1920s onwards; this, more than anything else, drew attention to the dilemma of the church. Some kind of action was necessary when it became widely known that the Kabaka's private life was incompatible with reasonable Christian standards. On Christmas Day, 1921, the Bishop felt obliged to suspend the Kabaka from Holy Communion. A little later the prevailing morality at court caused three young Baganda Protestants to write a highly critical letter to various authorities. While the Baganda leaders disagreed amongst themselves on how to handle the issue, the mission took a sympathetic attitude towards the three letter-writers, and even intervened on their behalf when they were prosecuted and accused of contempt for the Kabaka. But the mission was in a precarious position, as it could be accused of undermining native authority by supporting people who gave undue priority to Christian morality.[239] This dichotomy between the ideal of furthering Christian morality at any cost and the more pragmatic need to maintain the status of the church by relating it to the traditional system of authority continued to haunt the church all through the 1920s and 1930s – and in fact continued to do so in the 1950s and 1960s. When the church tacitly, if uncomfortably, settled for the latter option, and tolerated the situation at the Kabaka's court, it was easy for the colonial administration to accuse it of showing preferential treatment when it demanded an immoral chief removed from his post.[240] The privilege of having the Protestant leaders within the Protestant ranks thus hampered the church in its drive to uphold reasonable moral standards among the same leaders.

Thirdly, the church was hampered in these efforts by the fact that European officials did not always set the best possible example. At an early stage the Governor himself pointed out the difficulties of promoting morality among the people when Europeans persisted in doing what Africans were told not to do.[241] This was later underlined by Bishop Willis when he stated that it was very difficult even to attempt to deal with European officers in the same way as Africans, indicating that it was necessary to apply different moral codes to the two groups.[242] In 1924 the Synod blamed government officials for the lack of success in combating drunkenness, because of their failure to set the good example expected of them. Apart from this general appeal for a better moral example from European officials, the mission did not criticize individuals on moral grounds during these years, at least not publicly. This was clearly considered to be beyond the duty of the mission, but an obvious consequence was that it was difficult to ask for disciplinary action to be taken against African chiefs when their superiors were behaving hardly less reprehensibly by mission standards. This would have necessitated a double standard of a type later characterized by the government as unfortunate.[243]

It has in most cases been possible to deduce the government's response only indirectly by focusing on the church's restraint in presenting its demands. We must also ask how far the colonial administration felt itself responsible for the moral condition of the people, and to what extent it was prepared to show its preference for a Christian morality and to operate the machinery of government in such a way that it really promoted Christian moral principles. An answer to these questions emerged in 1918, when the three missions impressed on the government that it could not remain indifferent to the moral character of the people.

Attempts at a definition of the state's Christian responsibility

In 1918 the opportunity arose to test the government's basic willingness to further Christian morality when the three bishops in Uganda presented the matter in general terms rather than by reference to specific cases in a joint letter to the Governor. They called on the colonial administration to come out from behind its wall of benevolent neutrality. The discussion of this issue may be supplemented by reference to developments in the field of marriage law which will enable us to define the limits within which the government acted when it came to actual practice.

We have seen how the informal alliance between the Catholic and Protestant missions was strongest in the latter part of the 1910s when they united over the issues of land and education. The moral welfare of the country was another issue on which they had good reason to cooperate. While presenting a request for a more generous land grant, the three bishops took the opportunity to call attention to the moral climate in the Protectorate.[244] The letter's negative assessment of the situation as well as the remedies suggested were not surprisingly almost identical with the demands for special legislation formulated over the years by the Anglican Synod. Drink and immorality were singled out as the most obvious dangers. Elements cited as typical of the moral malaise of the country were the decline in the number of marriages registered by the churches, the alarmingly high infant mortality rate due to the spread of venereal disease, and the general decrease in the population, especially in Buganda, caused mainly by emigration.

It was suggested that people's movements, and especially those of women, should be restricted, and that the government should do whatever was in its power to uphold 'the sanctity of home life' by introducing steps to encourage marriage and by making the charging of exorbitant dowry rates a penal offence. The bishops also asked for the legislative measures already introduced to be enforced in actual practice.[245] It was admitted that some of the unfortunate features of the situation were either inherent in the people themselves, or caused by 'the overpowering influence of a civilization' which had shaken the social and moral foundations of African society, and was therefore almost impossible to change. But some of them were definitely remediable by the measures suggested.

This analysis of causes and remedies was however not considered sufficient. The bishops implicitly placed a heavy responsibility with the state itself, and their criticism amounted to a call for the government to choose sides and put the force of its authority behind the furtherance of morality in society.

It is an unfortunate necessity that the attitude of strict religious neutrality, rightly maintained by the Government, leaves the people singularly unprotected just at a time when they need most protection. The natives who have come under Christian instruction have always been taught to connect morality with religion, the one in fact being practically impossible without the other. The attitude of religious neutrality has been misunderstood as identical with religious indifference and misinterpreted as implying indifference also as to moral character . . . We cannot forget how far otherwise was the course of Christian Civilization in Europe during the Middle Ages, when the authority of the State went hand in hand with the influence of the Church in doing at least what was possible to produce moral conditions in the people.[246]

One area where neutrality had been misconceived as indifference was, according to the bishops, the government's attitude to the moral character of the chiefs. While admitting that the government had to be neutral in its appointments of chiefs, the bishops nevertheless claimed that this had left the impression that the government was indifferent as to their moral character as long as they did their official work satisfactorily. Such an impression was disastrous in a country where the influence of the chiefs counted for so much. While the bishops did not actually demand dismissals, they called on the government to back the cause of morality actively and publicly by securing 'chiefs of moral character' at any cost. They even suggested that the names of chiefs should be published in the Gazette before the final confirmation of their appointments, allowing people to raise objections 'that might exist on moral or other grounds'. In the opinion of the bishops such an active line from the government would help to counteract the impression of indifference and could not in any sense be said to violate the principle of religious neutrality in appointing chiefs. Included in this explicit request to the government was a call for closer cooperation between missions and government. The bishops concluded their remarks about the happy conditions in the Middle Ages by saying: 'Without some such cooperation neither the authority of the State, nor the moral influence of the Church, working single-handed, will be able to stem the present current.'[247]

This approach to the government was a strong plea for cooperation and for the state's active engagement in improving moral standards in society. It also impressed on the government the need to consider whether the missions were right in claiming that religious neutrality under the circumstances was equivalent to indifference. The reaction of the government is therefore of considerable interest, but at the official level the moral issues were overshadowed by the land issue (the other major topic of the bishops' letter) and it was on this that the colonial administration clearly chose to concentrate. Official reaction came rather from the Provincial Commissioners, to whom the letter was also sent, and whom we have earlier met as outspoken critics of the mission's efforts to introduce a Christian morality.

It emerges clearly that the missions and the colonial officials employed different definitions of morality. The Provincial Commissioner of Buganda made this abundantly clear when he took exception to the way morality was defined by the missions.[248] They applied, he thought, an all too narrow definition by confining themselves to sexual morality, and pursuing this as their major goal. The government made use of a broader definition and aimed at a general morality, which included such features as 'upright public and private life' and a sense of integrity and honour. The government could not primarily, and certainly not exclusively, concern itself with marriage problems. If the missions would take the same strong stand on general morality as they did on sexual morality they would be doing the country an incalculable benefit. A policy along broader lines could facilitate closer cooperation with the government, which was also concerned with improving general social conditions.

The same Provincial Commissioner's comments on the morality of chiefs serve to illustrate the practical consequences of the distinction between these two different concepts of morality. It was made clear that chiefs' morality could not be judged solely on the basis of their sexual habits. A chief's private life was beyond the concern of the government, provided that it did not 'adversely affect his work and his influence as a public man.'[249] It is thus apparent that the colonial administration primarily applied pragmatic, utilitarian criteria to the question of the chiefs' morality. This confirmed Bishop Tucker's supposition of ten years earlier: the colonial government and the missions had subtantially different views of the chiefs' moral role. The government did not conceive of the chiefs as moral examples for the rest of society or as special guardians of morality, and accordingly refused to apply such criteria when appointing chiefs; it may be true to say that the government exhibited a neutrality which came close to indifference.

This leads to a discussion of a second concept, that of *neutrality*. The Provincial

Commissioner of Buganda admitted that the government took a neutral stand on the narrow concept of morality, because recent experience had shown that 'the too hasty insistence on monogamy for polygamy' had shaken the foundations of African society.[250] The accusation of indifference in moral questions in general was, however, disputed. If one employed the broader definition of morality, the government was working towards the same goals as the missions, but with different methods. If the missions would only widen their scope, there would be sufficient grounds for active cooperation, and the government would exhibit neither indifference nor neutrality.

While it could thus reject the accusation of neutrality and aloofness in matters of general morality, the colonial administration still had to answer the accusation that its neutral attitude to religion amounted to religious indifference. The Provincial Commissioners saw this as an unfortunate misunderstanding founded upon a confusion of religious neutrality with religious indifference.[251] The government clearly connected morality with religion, but in a broader sense than the missions did, and had therefore granted concessions in support of various aspects of the missionary work. The confusion in the bishops' arguments stemmed from the fact that they confused the government's neutral attitude to religion in its sectarian aspect with religious indifference, for example in cases involving the appointment of chiefs on denominational grounds. In such cases it was absolutely impossible for the government to declare a religious interest 'by taking an active part in sectarian strife'.[252] Neutrality was absolutely necessary, but it had nothing to do with religious indifference.

We may thus arrive at the tentative conclusion that the presence of more than one religion, in particular the split between Protestants and Catholics, forced the government to exercise more caution and stricter neutrality in religious matters than would otherwise have been the case. This is however a theme which will be taken up in the following chapter when we discuss demands for a Christian state. So far the most important result of our analysis of comments on the letter from the three bishops has been the distinction made between a narrow and a broad definition of morality – a distinction between a primarily sexual and marital morality emphasizing Christian norms and a morality emphasizing more general, even secular ideals, with a bearing on life in society at large. The employment of such a distinction was bound to exert a substantial influence on the government's response to the mission's demands for support for Christian morality. How far this wider concept of morality actually affected government policy, and was not just a convenient way of circumventing the missions' demands, was not made clear in the response to the bishops' letter, as this was mainly concerned with land and labour problems. But the government's position would soon have to be clarified in connection with a new round of discussions on the important issues of polygamous and monogamous marriage.

In 1919 there was a lengthy discussion in the Buganda Lukiko on whether Christians, irrespective of their marital status, were obliged to observe the legislation which applied to Christian marriages. If this was so, it would mean that Christians were not entitled to contract valid marriages under customary law and could not have their cases heard by the native courts.[253] This problem became particularly relevant when Christians who wanted to contract a marriage under customary law first had to have an earlier marriage dissolved. In such cases they would turn to the native courts to secure a proper divorce involving the return of the dowry. At first the Lukiko came to the conclusion that the legal position of

Christians, even if they had not married in church, was such that it was illegal for the native courts to hear their cases, and the Omulamuzi (the Catholic Minister of Justice) instructed the gombolola and saza chiefs accordingly.[254] There was, however, no legal basis for such a decision, and it clearly involved a misinterpretation of the marriage laws, as legal consequences were imputed to the mere conversion to Christianity, not just to the contraction of a Christian marriage. The Provincial Commissioner intervened, and this prompted the Lukiko to pursue the case further and raise new questions, as it felt that the relationship between the two marriage systems was rather confusing. The Provincial Commissioner tried to clarify the situation by sending the Lukiko a note giving answers to the various questions raised.[255]

Meanwhile various rumours had been circulating,[256] which caused the CMS mission to issue a warning against the reintroduction of polygamy in the country.[257] This indicated how the mission was likely to interpret any government move in the controversy with the Lukiko. When the Provincial Commissioner's memorandum finally fell into missionary hands, there was a new concerted action from the Catholic and Protestant missions.[258] They were convinced that this initiative represented an attempt from the government's side to introduce new legislation re-establishing or at least condoning polygamy. The CMS was once more prepared to invoke the European arena by having questions asked in parliament,[259] and at the local level strong protests were lodged with the government. The colonial officials accused the mission of being misinformed, as any new legislation was out of the question; the memorandum to the Lukiko was simply a clarification of the existing legal position. Whatever the status of the memorandum, it was seen by the mission as an official statement indicating the limited responsibility the government was prepared to undertake for the furtherance of Christian morality.[260]

The mission based its assumption on the first of the three major points in the document. It was here stated that if a man who had earlier married in church took an additional wife in accordance with customary law he could not obtain any redress in the courts if she proved unfaithful. In the eyes of the statutory law she was only his concubine. It was, however, added that if the first wife (from the Christian marriage) died, then the man was entitled 'to take any number of wives by native law and custom', and that he could obtain redress in the native court if any of them were unfaithful. The remarkable thing about this document was that there was no mention of the fact that the Christian husband who took an additional wife under customary law was guilty of bigamy under the Marriage Ordinance of 1902 (par. 52), and had thus committed a criminal offence carrying a penalty of up to five years' imprisonment. Bishop Willis expressed surprise at this omission, and said that it could only encourage people to marry a second or more wives openly.[261] No explanation was offered by the government officials, but it is most reasonable to view this omission as an expression of the same unwillingness to prosecute at all which had already been evident among government officials and the judiciary. What was of special concern for Bishop Willis in this case was the fact that the silence of the government neutralized the value of the penalty clauses as deterrents, as they were here obviously being treated as dead letters. The implications were spelled out in the second main paragraph of the Provincial Commissioner's memorandum, which stated: 'The fact that a man has been baptized or confirmed as a Christian does not disentitle him to marry by native law and custom.' Even from a detached, analytical point of view, it is difficult not to agree with Bishop Willis: the phrasing of this 'clarification of the legal position' could only encourage Christians to believe that 'the way of return to polygamy' was now open.[262] It was being made abundantly clear that being a Christian did not in the eyes of the state have any legal consequences in itself. The government was officially taking a neutral stand in the conflict between monogamy and polygamy, and was thus no longer giving first priority to Christian morality.

These wider implications were confirmed by the third and last point in the memorandum: 'A pagan is entitled to take any number of wives by native law and custom.' This prompted the laconic comment from Bishop Willis that Africans had no need of guidance from the government as to how far they might go in 'free marriage'. But it was apparently considered necessary for the sake of consistency to clarify the legal status of polygamous marriage. In the circumstances this was bound to leave the impression that the government considered the two types of marriage not only equally legal, but also equally good. This was at least how Bishop Willis saw it.[263] Whereas the government had previously supported the drive for monogamy, at least tacitly, it now explicitly placed the two types of marriage on an equal footing. Bishop Willis now asked on behalf of the mission whether it was proper for a Christian government to sanction and even encourage an African to do what a European Christian would be punished for.[264]

The question of the obligations of a Christian government became the main issue in the CMS mission's approaches to the government. This was significantly different from the reaction of the Catholics – a fact which was probably minimized or even went unnoticed at the time. The Catholic mission concerned itself almost exclusively with the institution of marriage, and denied the validity of any other kind of marriage than that celebrated in the church. Therefore to say that baptism did not prevent a Christian from marrying under customary law was the expression of an anti-Christian principle and was contrary to Divine Law, as polygamy was forbidden for all Christians.[265] The CMS mission on the other hand concerned itself mainly with the actions of the government, and tried to define the responsibility of a Christian government for furthering Christian morality. This difference in approach to the government may be explained by different attitudes to the validity of customary marriage. While Bishop Willis soon after his investiture reversed the Protestant policy on marriage and based his new policy on some degree of recognition of the customary marriage law, it was very difficult for the Catholics to grant it the same kind of recognition.[266] Catholic requests to the government were therefore of a much more absolute nature than Protestant ones, as they demanded that human laws should not conflict with the Law of God.

The Protestant intervention with the government was concerned with the government's special responsibility for the furthering of Christian morality, and the concept of Christian morality as defined by the mission.[267] As regards the first issue, the memorandum to the Lukiko was seen as a severe setback for the Christian cause, as it could only have a detrimental effect on Christian marriage in a Protectorate which had become at least nominally monogamous.[268] It was impressed on the government that it had assumed 'the position of a Protector of a semi-Christian and semi-Pagan country'.[269] As Christians constituted almost half of the population, Uganda should be considered a Christian nation. Given its role as Protector, the government ought to act as a Christian government, and the laws guiding morality should be rooted in Christian principles.

There is but one Divine Law, and all the legal systems of Christian nations are built upon it and though one cannot claim that every enactment of a Christian nation is in accordance with the Divine Law and notably our Divorce Laws yet on the whole the laws of the British Empire tend to uphold and further righteousness and moral living.[270]

The government proposals amounted to the re-establishment of polygamy, and were therefore a gross abuse of the powers of a Christian government in a Christian nation. If they were approved it would alter the mission's whole relationship with the government.[271] One consequence already pointed out by Bishop Willis was that the government would allow Africans to do what Europeans received heavy penalties for. This amounted to an abandonment of Christian principles and an intolerable double standard.

The mission's arguments were thus quite clear. It called on the government to fulfil its obligations and treat Uganda as a Christian nation. The concept of 'Christian nation' involved two criteria: the religious composition of the population and the Christian character of the British Empire. It was part of the overall colonial mission to develop the Protectorate as a Christian nation, and the government, coming as it did from a Christian country, was in its role as Protector bound to adhere to Christian values and act as a Christian government. This is certainly reminiscent of the philosophy behind the declaration from the Berlin Conference (pp. 26f) and of earlier approaches to the government in the 1890s. We are thus faced here with a basic theme in missionary thinking on relations with the state; on the occasion in question it was simply spelt out in more concrete terms than before.

As for the second area for Protestant intervention, the actual implementation of the ideal of a Christian nation, the subject of morality was here considered to be the main issue. The morality which was prevalent in the country was seen as the major criterion in assessing whether the nation could be called Christian, and whether the government fulfilled its proper function as a Christian government by providing legal support for Christian morality. Therefore a neutral or even positive attitude to customary marriage, such as had been expressed in the Provincial Commissioner's memorandum, could only be seen as a breach of the government's obligation with potentially grave consequences for Christianity in Uganda. Archdeacon Baskerville called the proposals 'immoral suggestions' and said that they would strike 'such a blow at public morality as has not been struck at any rate during the last thirty years whilst I have been in the country'.[272] In fact, he claimed that their mere publication was enough to have a very bad moral effect.[273]

The most significant feature here was that the mission defined morality exclusively in terms of Christian marriage, which it saw as the true foundation of family life. The government had therefore been right in claiming that the mission employed a narrow definition of morality centring on sexual questions, and on home and family life. The emphasis on the narrow concept of morality may be explained by the special circumstances of the case in question, but that this was a general and permanent trend in the mission's conception of morality is borne out by the fact that the same attitude emerged during the discussion of morality started by the letter from the three bishops to the government in 1918. Furthermore, later events point in the same direction. At the Synod in 1921 much time was devoted to the standards of sexual morality in the country. It was decided to mount a campaign explaining the dangers that could arise from immorality and pointing out 'how detrimental those dangers can be to the country's well-being'.[274] The same theme was stressed even more at the Synod in 1924. Again the causal relationship between marriage and morality in general was emphasized and the wider consequences for the nation pointed out: 'The Bishop reminded the Synod that the true foundation of any nation is true and permanent marriage, and without that foundation a nation cannot survive.'[275] When the government seemed to be on the way to ascribing equal value to customary and Christian marriage, the mission, given its basic premises, could only deplore the government's policy. As far as the mission was concerned it was acting in a way which was unworthy of a Christian government by not supporting the moral principles which constituted the very essence of a Christian nation.

The government's response was not as conclusive as might have been expected, given the mission's detailed arguments. It refused to discuss the concept of a Christian nation and its own role in this respect; and it touched only indirectly on the concept of morality.[276] One obvious reason for this was that the government thought that the mission's criticism was based on a misunderstanding, as the Provincial Commissioner's memorandum did not in any sense reflect a desire for new legislation. It was simply meant to clarify the existing legal situation; and in the circumstances the official in question could hardly have acted in any other way. It was however conceded indirectly that the wording might have been unfortunate, and the statement somewhat perfunctorily drawn up. The government not only admitted and regretted that adverse effects might result from such a clarification of the existing law and the ensuing public discussion; it even took active steps to reduce the negative effects by instructing the Provincial Commissioner at the next Lukiko meeting to explain the origin and status of his memorandum and to clarify at the same time the government's position on Christian marriages.

He will remind them that the Civil Law is not in all respects similar to the Church Law and that, although the marriages indicated in (b) and (c) [Christians who had married under customary law] may not be punishable under Civil Law, they are most reprehensible in the eyes of the Christian Churches and that it must not be assumed for a moment that the Government in any way approves of such marriages.[277]

Two conclusions may be drawn from this reply. In the first place, compared with the memorandum, it was a retreat from the public assertion that Christian and customary marriages were equally good. Now the government was prepared to distance itself from Christians marrying in any other way than in the church. We may thus say that the government gave some moral support to Christian marriage. Bishop Willis considered this a satisfactory outcome of the mission's intervention, and this may explain why the matter was not after all taken to Europe.[278] But this positive result must be qualified. The two types of marriage remained equally legal, and accordingly Christians could still contract legal marriages under customary law.[279] The Provincial Commissioner found reason soon afterwards, at a Lukiko meeting, to reaffirm that Christians were not compelled to marry in church and that they were free to marry in accordance with native custom.[280] This meant that the government still upheld the previous legal position, but this time without the use of qualitative terms. This state of affairs was in fact endorsed by Bishop Willis, as it was based upon the principle of the validity of customary marriage; but he hastened to add that it remained a penal offence to be married at the same time under Christian and customary law (according to the bigamy clause).[281]

Throughout this whole clarification of the legal position of Christians as regards marriage, it was directly stated, as quoted above, that civil law and Christian law were not identical. In the wider sense this meant that civil law did not always reflect Christian morality, as it did not provide full legal support for the most essential element in such a morality, Christian marriage. This was fully confirmed when the Omulamuzi made an attempt to interpret the law as only applying to monogamous marriages. It was made quite clear on that occasion that such a practice required the passing of a new law.[282] This was in fact what Bishop Willis now started to work for. Although he was in the first instance satisfied with the government's retraction from its earlier position, the whole controversy had drawn attention to the inadequacy of the existing law as regards the contraction of marriages by Christians. He raised the issue at the next session of the Synod, by saying how much he regretted the fact that, although it was highly necessary, no law had yet been passed 'binding a man to one woman'.[283] This was followed by the adoption of a resolution calling on all local African Councils to pass a law to the effect that people should marry according to the tenets of their own religion only.[284] It may be taken for granted that the main intention behind this resolution was to stop Christians marrying under customary law and thus contracting potentially polygamous marriages. This demonstrated more than anything else the lack of congruence between the law and Christian morality.

Again the government's response was confused by the fact that the approach from the Synod was subsumed in the procedural controversy mentioned above between the church and the government. The same Provincial Commissioner who had taken so much interest in the discussion of morality and neutrality a few years earlier, P. W. Cooper, said that no local Council with a mixed religious composition should be asked to use compulsion in questions of religion. A Council's only duty was to see that the existing law of the Protectorate was upheld.[285] Nonetheless the Buganda Lukiko, strongly encouraged by Bishop Willis, went ahead with its planned legislation against polygamy.[286] The result was a draft law which was submitted for the Governor's approval in late 1921. It contained three main provisions:

(1) It reaffirmed in more absolute terms than the existing Protectorate law that a Christian, once married in church, could not take another woman as his legal wife. This clause can only be interpreted as an attempt to support Christian marriage, as it emphasized the illegality of contracting an additional, customary marriage.

(2) As for those Christians who did not marry in accordance with the Christian rite, they were to have the option of having their marriages registered with the District Commissioner or the chiefly courts. But such registration could only apply to one wife. If anyone took another wife he was not entitled to any hearing in the courts, i.e. he had no legal rights as far as extra wives were concerned. On the contrary, the first wife was entitled to institute legal proceedings. The Lukiko clearly intended with this provision to encourage all Christians to contract monogamous marriages, by making registration easier for Christians than it had been under the law of 1914.

(3) When 'pagans' married one or more women under customary law the wife was to be free to leave her husband and marry another, and he would not be entitled to start legal proceedings to recover her. Only if such a marriage had been

registered in the same way as Christian marriages was he entitled to take legal action. The intention of this clause was clearly to reduce legal protection for polygamists and make polygamy seem less attractive than civil or Christian monogamous marriage.

While it encouraged Christian, or at least monogamous, marriage, the draft law did not explicitly forbid polygamy. This was made quite clear by the Kabaka and his two Protestant ministers in order to secure the Governor's approval of the measures.[287] The third minister, however, the Omulamuzi (a post traditionally held by a Catholic), returned the draft law unsigned as it did not go far enough in its support of Christian marriage. It allowed Christians to marry as they wished to, rather than in accordance with their religion, as they could register their marriages with the civil authorities.[288] That this was the real issue was confirmed by the Provincial Commissioner's actions. He stated outright that the ultimate aim was to have a law passed which would compel Christians to marry according to Christian rites, thus barring them from their present option of marrying under customary law.[289] He believed that such a law was eagerly awaited by all three missions, but he was just as sure that it was resented by a very large number of Baganda of both denominations. As it was also likely to increase prostitution, he and his District Commissioners could not recommend it for approval.

This opposition, and the government's general line, meant that the initiative of the Buganda Lukiko and the Bishop came to nothing and no law was approved.[290] As far as the District Officers were concerned, the whole issue simply served to reaffirm Christians' right to marry legally outside the church in accordance with customary rules. The same issue continued to cause difficulties with the chiefs at the local level. Soon afterwards it was again found necessary for the Omulamuzi to issue a circular in order to clarify the legal position. Christians who had earlier married in church persisted in contracting new marriages with other women under customary law while the first wife was still alive. The Omulamuzi stated that it should be remembered that such marriages were null and void. The chiefly courts were not authorized to hear cases connected with them, as when such a wife left her husband; and the husband was not entitled to any assistance in the recovery of the dowry.[291]

This statement was again no more than a reaffirmation of the existing laws, and was approved as such by the Provincial Commissioner. It said nothing about the rights of those Christians who had *not* contracted a legal Christian marriage, and there were soon complaints that some chiefs were refusing to hear the cases of these Christians on the basis of the Omulamuzi's circular.[292] This was clearly a misinterpretation of the circular, but it bears witness to the complexity of an issue which almost drove even experienced officials to despair.[293] In the end the government upheld the right of Christians to marry outside the church in accordance with customary law.[294]

Thus the mission and the Synod, despite the support of the Buganda Lukiko, did not succeed in their efforts to obtain legal support for the Christian marriage institution. First of all, the legal equality between Christian and customary marriage was upheld. No law was passed giving legal priority to monogamy by removing legal protection from polygamy. Attempts to do so by Baganda ministers were blocked by the government. In the second place, not even the more limited goal of obliging all Christians to marry in accordance with their religion was achieved. This would have given baptism explicit legal consequences. The government rigorously upheld the right of Christians to marry both inside and outside the church and made it clear that it considered the two types of marriage to be equally legal.

The latter point remained a key issue for the mission, and one which caused the greatest confusion among African leaders. It meant, as Bishop Willis had pointed out, that the government was treating European and African Christians different-ly, by allowing Africans to do what was illegal for Europeans. In a wider sense, this attitude indicated the extent to which the government was prepared to enforce Christian morality on people by legal means, and thus to act as a Christian government in a Christian country, an issue which will be dealt with in a concluding section. It remains to be pointed out here that the queries and suggestions which were initially raised by the three bishops' joint letter of 1918 met with no real government response. In fact, they were rejected in practice, if not explicitly, judging from the government's decisions in specific cases. The status quo prevailed in 1923 and 1924, so there was plenty of scope left for complaints and new initiatives. One of the district missionaries complained that Christians were taking such liberties without being prosecuted that it could not be long before 'the marriage vows and the marriage laws become an utter farce'.[295] The decrease in the number of marriages in church and the increase in immoral-ity were discussed again at the Synod in 1924, and it was decided to ask the Governor to convene a committee consisting of the Bishops, the Kings and the Provincial Commissioners to examine the issue.[296] The whole discussion thus began all over again with renewed pressure on the government.

Matters were not helped by a High Court judgement of 1923. According to H. F. Morris, the judgement said that Christians could only contract a legal marriage in accordance with the Marriage Ordinance. Marriages contracted by Christians under customary law were null and void and were no more than extramarital liaisons. By implication this meant that the penal clauses in the Marriage Ordinance were all but suspended. This judgement thus enforced on Christians the monogamy which the church had demanded over the years, but which the government had opposed. But the victory would have been of little value for the church in practice if the ruling was not supported by penal enforcement. If a Christian lapsed and took more wives in accordance with customary law, he was committing no offence. Such a 'marriage' was mere concubinage, since he was a Christian.[297] Further research will show what effects this extraordinary judgement had in practice over the years. It certainly under-lines the difficulty of harmonizing two legal traditions in one country, especially when one of them was considered to take priority over the other.

Conclusions: Uganda as a Christian nation?

The concept of the Christian nation has been used as a frame of reference as this term was used by the missionaries themselves. Bishop Tucker introduced the concept in 1906, when he called on the government to treat Uganda as a Christian country in which the Christians rather than the Muslims should constitute the group towards which government measures should be directed. Later the definition was made more specific by the mission when two features were added: the fact that the Christians actually constituted a large part of the population, at least in the Bantu areas; and the reference to the Christian element in the empire's colonial philosophy. The concept of a Christian nation thus provided a basis both for the formulation of the mission's demands to the state and for its conception of the state's responsibility towards Christianity.

In the second place, the concept of the Christian nation may help us to arrive at a final interpretation of the government response to missionary demands. As these were mainly within the field of morality, it is possible to test the extent to which the government was prepared to work for the Christianization of the nation by supporting Christian morality and Christian values; for the mission claimed that these values were the touchstone of a Christian nation. We will however employ a wider and more commonly accepted definition of the Christian nation, in order to make some generalizations and facilitate comparisons with other surveys not so firmly rooted in the colonial situation. The main question will then be whether the government considered the Christians, although they did not constitute a majority of the population, to have such a clear preponderance over the Muslims and other groups that it was justified in making the interests of this group its primary concern and allowing Christian values to guide its policy. In other words, if the Christian factor counted for so much that it became a guiding principle in formulating policy, Uganda could be considered a Christian nation, or at least a Christian nation in the making. This concept of a Christian nation must be kept distinct from that of a Christian state, which implies the Christianization of institutions in the state and the establishment of institutionalized linkages between church and state.[298]

In the investigation of efforts aimed at the emergence of a Christian nation we have examined three areas to which the mission and the church gave high priority: they worked for legislation in accordance with Christian morality, administrative measures that reflected Christian values, and a Christian marriage institution. We have met these three themes, which were considered to be essential factors in the creation of a Christian society in the African context, continually during the whole period under survey. Although there was no clearly marked turning-point, rather a gradual development, in these three areas, it is possible to observe a noticeable change in the government's response to missionary demands in the discussions which took place between 1912 and 1914 on the subject of the recognition and registration of customary marriages. A closer analysis of the phases before and after this change will help to illustrate the government's attitude to the idea of Uganda as a Christian nation.

The first phase was mainly, though not exclusively, characterized by the government's positive response to missionary demands. The government endorsed, or at least tacitly approved of, a number of laws passed by the Buganda Lukiko. As regards Sunday labour, it was sympathetic, but not to the extent of actually passing any laws. Although the first proposals for marriage legislation went in the direction of civil marriage, the government soon began to legislate for religious marriages; and though the marriage laws also covered Muslim marriages, they were mainly geared towards monogamous Christian ones, in that special concern was shown both for facilitating them and protecting them from abuses. The fact that Christian marriage was brought within the terms of statutory law, which customary marriage was not, meant that the former was placed in a position of greater prestige by the state. Also, church ministers were recognized as Marriage Registrars, and the church was authorized to perform the marriage ceremonies which had civil as well as religious consequences. The church was thus given a special legal position, as its widespread and elaborate machinery was connected with the contraction of valid marriages. This could only work in favour of monogamous Christian marriages. All in all, one is left with the impression that the government preferred the latter type of marriage to the other two possibilities.

To summarize the results of the first phase, the government seemed prepared to accept that society should develop according to Christian principles, and that this development should be openly and actively sponsored. Thus the mission had reason to believe that the government would fulfil its expectations of a Christian government in a future Christian nation. This attitude was combined with the acceptance of the fact that the mission had legitimate interests in certain areas of public importance which had to be taken into account in the policy-making process. At the same time, the mission on its side recognized a certain division of responsibility, in the sense that it avoided interference in matters outside its legitimate sphere of interest. Its reluctance in asking for the dismissal of immoral chiefs, in spite of the crucial importance attached to the chiefs' moral example and guidance, was indicative of the mission's caution in this respect. Although the government thus appeared to be following the path towards a Christian nation, this first phase provides no grounds for a final conclusion. Many of the steps taken were no more than preliminary ones, and needed to be followed up by more concrete measures. A number of problems were left unsolved. The relationship between Christian and customary marriage illustrates this better than any other issue, and the discussion of this problem between 1912 and 1914 marked the beginning of the second phase in the government's attitude to Christian morality.

The regulation of transitions from one kind of marriage to the other became a matter of the utmost importance for the Christian leaders over the years. People who had been married in the Christian way frequently returned to the customary marriage system. Even more acute was the problem of people who were living in polygamous marriages but wanted to be baptized. In both cases the main issue was the status of customary marriage and the legal consequences attached to it. The mission tried to solve the problem by recognizing the validity of the customary union, but only in its monogamous form, and the government was subsequently asked to register such marriages officially so that they could fulfil the Christian requirements for baptism. The mission was in fact demanding that the government recognize customary marriages only in so far as they corres-ponded with baptismal requirements. This was the basic criterion with which the mission thought the government should work, and it was expected that a government which had identified itself with the goal of a Christian nation would officially state its preference for monogamy and thereby distance itself, if only implicitly, from polygamy.

The government failed to fulfil these expectations. In its view the mission's recognition of customary marriage was illusory, because it involved the deplor-able practice of sending away surplus wives. Faced with this contradiction, the government took the stand that any recognition of customary marriage should be based on the traditional view of such marriages, even if this meant the official recognition of polygamy. The government's attitude was a severe setback for the cause of monogamy, and it was feared that the government was not prepared to outlaw polygamy, even indirectly, and let marriage legislation be guided by Christian principles alone. Instead, a compromise was reached: customary marriages (about 80 per cent of all marriages in Uganda) remained outside the law. Thus the mission avoided the state's recognition of polygamous marriages, but did not succeed in persuading the government to adopt monogamy as the only basis for marriage legislation.

One more tangible outcome of the lengthy discussions of 1912–14 was that a provision for converting a customary marriage into a statutory one was included in the law, which made it possible for people to comply with the church's conditions of baptism. Here the government certainly showed some willingness to support the Christian cause. But it is important to emphasize that this provision only provided an *option*, and had no compulsory force. The government did not engage itself actively in this matter, for instance by making such conversions easier, or by establishing a procedure for selecting one wife and dealing with the surplus ones. The final outcome of these discussions allows us to identify a basic trend in government policy which again throws light upon the previous marriage legislation. There were two different possible courses of action: on the one hand the government could confine itself to making something legally possible; on the other it could forcibly influence developments by writing them directly into the laws, thus letting the law lead rather than follow. In other words, there was a distinction between what was *optional* and what was *compulsory*. In accordance with its conception of a Christian nation the mission wanted the latter kind of legislation, while the government preferred the former. During the first, introductory phase, such a distinction was not relevant, and the two agencies' activities and aims appeared to be complementary.[299] As soon as more specific requests were directed to the government, the distinction took on new significance. The government could give sympathy and moral support to the furtherance of a Christian morality, but would not itself, in the pluralistic Uganda society, enforce such a morality by legal means. This distinction serves to explain the limits within which the government supported Christian morality. The government's preference for the first course also helps to explain its unwillingness to prosecute under the marriage laws. The 1914 regulations provided for prosecution in cases of violation, as did the previous marriage ordinances; otherwise the penalty clauses were pointless. By not prosecuting, except in a few rare cases where it was forced to do so, the government clearly indicated that Christian morality was not to be furthered by the legal means available to the secular authorities. The same reluctance to undertake moral obligations was evident at a more practical level in connection with the issue of the moral role ascribed to the chiefs by Christian leaders. The government was not much concerned with moral criteria in defining the chiefs' role in society.

This was the beginning of a new phase in government policy, and a marked retraction from the government's earlier position. It was their awareness of this change, and of the deterioration in moral standards in general, which caused the three bishops to complain in their joint letter that they received too little support from the government in their work to improve moral and social conditions. They accused the government of an indifference in moral matters which was interpreted by the people as religious indifference. While religious neutrality was essential, it was nevertheless the duty of the government to act as a Christian government in a Christian country. There was no direct response to this joint approach. That it did not bring about any change in the government's basic attitude was evident from later developments in the marriage issue. The legality of customary, and thus potentially polygamous, marriages was finally recognized in the sense that they were given legal protection by the local courts. Christian and customary marriages were thus declared equally legal. The mission could not prevent this move, nor did it succeed in having monogamy adopted as the only legally valid kind of marriage. Secular law and Christian marriage doctrine were not in harmony. But although it failed to obtain legal support for monogamy as such, the mission succeeded in persuading the government to endorse officially a qualitative difference between the two types of marriage. This gave at least some moral support to Christian marriage.

The mission thus failed to alter the balance between monogamy and polygamy in favour of the Christian view. It was also unsuccessful in persuading the government to accept as a kind of minimum requirement that baptism should have legal consequences, in the sense that all Christians should be obliged to marry in accordance with their religion, and should enjoy no legal protection if they contracted customary marriages. This would have been a basic step towards the Christianization of the marriage law, and the government would have proved that it was prepared after all to treat Uganda as a Christian nation. But the government did not identify itself closely enough with the cause of the church to attach legal consequences to the rite of baptism. Thus it was not really fulfilling the role of a Christian government. This again leads to the more far-reaching conclusion that it was not willing to use the legal system to set standards and constitute society solely along Christian lines.

While we have examined the government's position mainly on the basis of its marriage policy, the problem has wider aspects. In order to illustrate the government's attitude further it will be useful to reiterate some of the factors involved in the policy-making process. Two main ones were at work: first, officials became increasingly doubtful of the value of the legal method in furthering morality, as it obviously produced very limited results; secondly, experience had proved it difficult, if not impossible, to implement detailed regulations on moral conduct in the African context. Accordingly a number of laws became obsolete, as no one paid any attention to them, and this could only diminish the government's willingness to pursue this method further. Apart from these pragmatic considerations, the government had grave doubts about the expediency of the aim for which the mission was most anxious to obtain government support: the introduction of a monogamous marriage system, at least for Christians. Colonial officials pointed out the disturbing effects which this could have on African society, and the immorality of pursuing a goal which would leave redundant wives so helpless. In order to measure the importance of this negative attitude to the mission's major goal, two additional questions should be raised: first, was the government's opposition to the introduction of monogamy based on its concern for African institutions? And secondly, did government officials dispute the value of Christian morality?

In dealing with the first question, we must ask whether the government was guided by a genuine concern for African institutions, and whether it tried to ensure their continued functioning by assuming a protective role in view of the danger of disruption due to the changes caused primarily by missionary activity. Judging from the various statements of colonial officials mentioned above, the government's supposed role as defender of African institutions was not due to any special appreciation of African culture and traditions, but was first and foremost rooted in administrative self-interest. The transition to monogamy struck at the heart of African society, and was likely to cause upheavals and the break-up of the traditional pattern of authority. The chiefs' position in particular would be eroded, and this was considered to be fatal, as it constituted the cornerstone of the administrative apparatus. If the missionary work was likely to make it more difficult to carry out administrative functions, government officials, especially those stationed in the outlying districts, would react against it.[300]

Administrative self-interest thus provides part of the explanation for the negative reaction to the mission's drive for a Christian morality, but we must also ask whether the government in fact doubted the societal value of Christian morality as such, and hence acted from a position of moral indifference, as the mission claimed. In order to answer this question properly, the distinction between two concepts of morality, first suggested by one of the Provincial Commissioners, may be helpful. As long as the mission worked on the basis of a narrow definition of morality centring on sexual issues the government took a neutral stand, insofar as it refused to give legal support to the realization of missionary goals defined in these narrow terms. It was not the function of the law, it was argued, to take the initiative in setting moral standards. This was not the same as indifference, and the government was willing to express its preference for Christian marriage and give it some degree of moral support. The government's position is best explained by the distinction between the optional and the compulsory conception of the legislative process. The government would go so far as to facilitate Christian marriage and establish procedures for the conversion of customary marriages, but it would not use the state apparatus to secure adherence to specific Christian doctrines. These matters were left to the moral authority of the missions. On the basis of the mission's narrow definition of morality there was little scope for active cooperation between mission and government. According to the mission's criteria, then, the government did not act as a Christian government: its position was seen as one of benevolent neutrality.

If one employs a wider, less specific definition of morality, the government's position was different. It was in full sympathy with the idea of constituting an African society on basic moral principles, and it offered the mission a platform for cooperation if it would settle for less than its ideal goals. What this general concept of morality implied was never explicitly spelled out, but it seems fair to define the government's idea of morality by saying that the emphasis was on civilizing rather than Christianizing society. Its concept of morality was more secular than Christian. It was not rooted in Christianity and the Gospels as such, but in the Christian civilization of Western European society.[301] This may be further illustrated by considering the methods the government was prepared to employ to further its general moral principles. Again there was no question of enforcing morality by legal means and sanctions. The government was more interested in a gradual process based on the prevailing opinion among the people. It therefore seemed appropriate in this context to concentrate on education. It has earlier been shown that one reason for the government's support for the mission's educational work was its socializing effect and its moral influence on the younger generation. A certain discipline was instilled in mission schools which was useful to the state in a number of ways, and which ensured decent moral standards based on Christian precepts. It is appropriate to recall here the motives behind the support for the mission's educational efforts, as the underlying civilizing objective was in full harmony with its broader definition of morality. Hence, educational support was the government's best means of obtaining its limited moral aims.

We may thus conclude that the colonial administration was not, like most political authorities, indifferent to the morality of the people. But its concept of morality was not identical with that of the mission. This was a fundamental difference between Uganda and the European situation in the Middle Ages invoked as a parallel by the three bishops. The close cooperation between church and state in the Middle Ages presupposed near-congruence between their aims and methods, and this did not exist in the African colonial setting. The government was not working for a Christian nation according to the mission's definition, and it was not prepared to enforce Christian morality by legal means.

The next question will then be whether the government accepted the concept of a Christian nation according to a broader definition. This may be answered in'the affirmative, if two factors are taken into consideration: first, that a Christian nation could be defined as a nation constituted on the broad principles of Christian civilization; secondly, that such a nation did not yet exist in Uganda, but constituted a possibility for the future. Accordingly, the government could not be guided exclusively by Christian morality in all its actions; the introduction of Christian civilization was a gradual process which could not be hurried along by legal means. Hence, it was not the function of the law to set the standards of public morality; the law must follow, not lead. The educational method was seen as better suited to guiding development in the direction of a Christian nation. The government thus envisaged a Christian nation, but in the longer term and on a different scale than the mission. On the other hand, if the government moved slowly, it was hardly out of concern for people of other religions like the Muslims and the Traditionalists. Administrative considerations and the conviction that legal methods would not work in the African context counted for more in the framing of government policy.

The government's attitude to the concept of a Christian nation can be put further into perspective if we compare it with the policy of the Buganda government. The latter's actions were more in keeping with the three bishops' Middle Ages analogy. At an early stage the Buganda Lukiko passed a number of detailed laws within areas of special concern for the mission and the church. Because of the Christian majority among its members, the Lukiko was also prepared to support the Christian marriage institution in a number of ways. This was demonstrated by its efforts to fix maximum limits to dowry rates, and by the proposed marriage law of 1920 which came close to making monogamy the only legal kind of marriage in Uganda. In addition, one of the Kabaka's ministers tried to have administrative measures introduced obliging Christians to marry according to their religion. We may therefore conclude that the Ganda leaders tried to further the cause of Christian morality according to the mission's narrow definition, with its main emphasis on marriage. In this respect the Buganda officials took the responsibility for acting as a Christian government in a Christian nation.

There are two ways of explaining the difference between the African and colonial administrations. First, there was to a large extent agreement between the mission and the Buganda government as regards ends and means. Secondly, there was the linkage between church and state within the Buganda framework constituted by the personal overlap between the Protestant Synod and the Lukiko, with the Katikiro as the outstanding example (Chapter 17). There was no such agreement or linkage with the colonial administration, and this goes far to explain the different responses of the two agencies. It is further significant that it was precisely these two factors which caused the government concern, as we shall see in the following chapter, when we examine whether the mission demanded not only a Christian nation, but also a Christian state.

17

Demands for a Christian state: the Christianization of political institutions and institutionalized linkages between church and state

While the attempts to establish a Christian nation primarily had a societal dimension, in the sense that Christians were assumed to constitute the most important group in society, and policies were measured against Christian principles, the notion of the Christian state will be used to examine aspects of the institutional dimension. In this context the concept of the Christian state will be taken to involve two closely related questions. First, what attempts were made to Christianize institutions within the political system so as to emphasize the special status of Christianity, and in particular of the Protestant church? Secondly, what institutionalized linkages were there between church and state which could provide the church with a platform from which to exert influence on the political system?

It should be remembered from the outset that, by concentrating on these two aspects, we are employing a wider definition of the Christian state than is usually the case.[1] Usually, a Christian state is a nation which is proclaimed in its constitution to be Christian. This may find concrete expression in an established church, as in England. The use of a modified definition introduced here is due to the fact that results produced in the earlier part of the analysis, focusing on developments in the 1890s and the conclusion of the Uganda Agreement in 1900, showed that the mission was unsuccessful in its attempts to obtain any official recognition, either for itself or for the church. This state of affairs prevents us from employing the stricter definition of the Christian state, and was in fact fully understood by some of the principal actors within the mission and the church. At the second meeting of the newly established Synod in 1906, some delegates called for closer cooperation between the church and the Buganda political system. It was suggested that the church ought to be an integral part of the Buganda system and that its legal status should be such that the decisions of the Synod, especially on matters of finance, could be enforced by law.[2] In the Bishop's absence Archdeacon Walker pointed out that there was no established church in Uganda, and therefore no state church, as both Catholics and Protestants were present in the country.[3] It was thus fully recognized that there neither was nor could be an established church in Uganda; the denominational factor was absolutely prohibitive. That the mission was right to ascribe so much importance to the denominational factor was shown by the government's concern to preserve a position of neutrality and to grant any concessions equally to all concerned. This is why we must employ the concept of Christian state in a modified version, comprising the two aspects indicated above. We have seen that the mission did not regard an established church as a major goal around 1900. The aim was rather to Christianize certain institutions within the political system and thus to establish formal links between church and state, thus securing a platform from which to exert political influence, and projecting an image of establishment which would give the Protestants an advantage over the Catholics in the public consciousness. We will examine examples of how this programme worked out in the following two decades.

Approaches to the colonial state

The Christianization of institutions and institutionalized links

The following remarks made by a leading missionary on the occasion of the laying of the foundation stone of a church near Government Headquarters illustrate the thinking behind the strategy of the mission in its approaches to the government:

It was impossible to foretell what an immense effect the presence of so many Europeans and the fact of the Commissioner laying this stone, would have throughout the country. The Baganda were a warmhearted race, and such marks of sympathy were greatly valued by them, as they were by the members of the CMS.[4]

The fact that government officials undertook special functions within the church in an official capacity was seen as an asset by the mission. Over the following years a number of efforts were made to encourage this kind of activity, and the mission's special interest centred on the Governor as the local Head of State.[5] Accordingly, when the Synod met, the Governor was either invited to attend the opening sessions and greet the assembly or, in his absence, a special message was sent to him.[6] This system worked very well under the governorship of the Uganda veteran, F. J. Jackson, although he did resent on one occasion being involved too closely with the Anglican cause (see below p. 319). The importance attached by the ecclesiastical authorities to this post is demonstrated by the fact that, when his successor had to be appointed, the Synod was very anxious that the new incumbent would be as good a Christian as Jackson.[7]

The event which best demonstrated attitudes on both sides was the consecration of the new cathedral in 1919. The Governor was invited to take part in the processions and the ceremony with the Kings and leading chiefs. According to the mission this would stress the exceptional nature of the occasion and, even more essentially, 'It will be a unique opportunity for those who govern and those who are governed to meet together as members of the Christian Church professing a Common Creed.'[8] Active participation by the Governor and other officials would inevitably have given the impression of close identity between the Anglican church and the secular authorities, so close that it would seem like the official church of the Protectorate. The Governor himself was well aware of this, and made the following comment: 'It is very official so far as the Church is concerned, but not as to the State.'[9] He therefore agreed to be present, but would not participate or even wear his uniform. To make the situation even more clear he issued a statement afterwards expressing his appreciation of the growing spirit of cooperation between the government and *all* the missionary societies and its importance for the progress of the country.[10]

This illustrates a dichotomy in the government's position which appeared when it was faced with missionary demands for closer links. On the one hand, it was careful not to accept any institutionalized linkages with the mission or the church which might give the impression of a special relationship with, or official support for, any particular church. On the other hand, the Governor appreciated the need for cooperation with the mission. The colonial administration made strenuous efforts over the years to steer a middle course between these two extremes. In some cases, especially at the local level, personal relations between the mission and the government gave the impression that the balance had tipped in favour of close association with the Anglican church. But in general government officials were conscious of the extent to which they could engage themselves formally in the work of the church.[11] In this respect they were also guided by official British colonial policy, which warned against direct religious engagement on the part of the government. This line of policy was influential in Uganda on several occasions, especially as regards financial involvement. When Bishop Tucker asked for a subscription for the building of a church at Government Centre in 1904, the request was firmly refused in London.[12] An answer to a Colonial Office inquiry in 1910 made it clear that no government money was being paid for the maintenance of religious services or buildings; nor were there any official chaplains in the Protectorate.[13] The latter issue re-emerged several times over the years,[14] and in the end the local administration asked for a special grant to support a Church of England chaplain's work at headquarters in Entebbe.[15] In refusing this request, the Colonial Office restated its policy. It aimed at 'the gradual withdrawal of State aid for purely religious purposes in the Colonies', in view of Parliamentary opposition to the endowment of particular denominations.[16]

Little room for manoeuvre was thus left to the local administration, even when it was prepared on rare occasions to support a purely religious activity. In general the Uganda administration shied away from any kind of official involvement or any institutionalized link with the Anglican church. There was thus little opportunity for the mission to play what we have called its third political role, based on its common nationality and creed with the government, (see Chapter 4). The mission was fully aware of the limitations inherent in colonial policy, and the measures examined above were not aimed at obtaining an established position within the colonial state. The mission had settled for a less ambitious way of establishing linkages, although its ultimate aims were still the same: to exert some influence on government policy in various matters, and to present the image of having a special relationship with the colonial state.[17] We must therefore employ a new approach to the mission's role in order to assess the kind of linkages which existed between church and state in the colonial setting.

The quest for consultative status

In our attempt to identify the mission's role *vis-à-vis* the colonial state we must move beyond the level of institutionalization. We may here turn to Bishop Tucker, who outlined the special tasks of the mission on two occasions. The first time was when the government unexpectedly introduced the Marriage Ordinance of 1902, when he protested because the mission had not been consulted beforehand; he considered this to be a breach of well-established practice. A second issue which helped to make the mission more aware of its own role in the colonial state was that of forced labour and excess land. Tucker indicated more or less directly that the government did not have the confidence of the chiefs. As he himself had their confidence, he felt obliged to present their point of view.[18] In Tucker's obituary, Archdeacon Walker testified to the importance of the Bishop's role as a confidant of the chiefs and as spokesman for them with the government.[19]

These two issues suggest that the mission, and in particular Bishop Tucker, claimed a special position within the colonial political system. We may call this the quest for consultative status. The mission believed that it was authorized to act in a capacity different from that of an ordinary interest group. While an interest group is free to present its views and concerns to the political authorities on particular issues the mission expected to be consulted on more general questions. It further claimed the right to raise issues and make suggestions in areas which lay outside its generally recognized spheres of interest, such as marriage laws, morality in general and education. As members of a Christian organization the missionaries took it for granted that they had a special role to play in a Christian state. They assumed the right to direct and unlimited access to the political decision-makers. They conceived of themselves as intermediaries between those who governed and those who were governed, in other words as advocates of African interests.[20] Although this claim to quasi-official status was not explicitly formulated by any of the actors, it has proved fruitful to posit such a role for the mission. We can thus account for those parts of the mission's activities *vis-à-vis* the state which could not be directly ascribed to its search for institutionalized linkages between the church and the political system.

Using the concept of consultative status we can identify certain patterns in the mission's relations with the state and arrive at a more precise description of the position of a Christian institution like the mission in a colonial setting. A number of initiatives, especially in Bishop Tucker's time, helped to establish the mission and the church in this role. Whilst striving for the introduction of a church constitution Tucker even argued that, without a properly constituted church, it would be difficult to protect Christian interests and influence the government.[21] Both procedural and personal factors were repeatedly emphasized as important in gearing the missionary apparatus to this political role. As regards procedure, a centralized structure was considered to be most appropriate. All communications to the government were passed through the Secretary of the mission or handled by the Bishop himself;[22] it was deplored if an individual missionary approached government officials concerning matters of general importance for the mission.[23] Leaders of both church and state were in full agreement on this, and the Commissioner therefore had the full sympathy of the mission in one particular case, when he returned the letters forwarded by an individual missionary.[24] The same case, the Purvis controversy (see below), revealed the need for a more efficient organization of the missionary work, and the Governor himself called for such an improvement. Bishop Tucker found this sufficient reason to create an Archdeaconry of Busoga.[25]

There were also other, more practical procedural considerations. It was considered damaging for the mission's standing if a 'sufficiently respectful style' was not maintained.[26] More important still, the mission must follow certain basic 'rules of the game' and exercise diplomacy if it was not to lose its credibility.[27] The forced-labour issue showed how conscious Bishop Tucker was of this, and he was also very careful about which cases he chose to pursue with the government. One of the important points to be considered was the chance of success: lost battles tended to erode the mission's authority. The case of the Rev. J. B. Purvis in the eastern part of the Protectorate (Bugishu and Bukedi) in 1906–7 illustrates the importance of correct procedure for the mission. In connection with the killing of a Ganda agent in the area of the mission station at Nabumali, the local government officer retaliated by sending a punitive expedition, and a number of people were killed. Purvis, as missionary in charge, protested in strong terms to the government, and a Commission of Inquiry was set up which exonerated the official involved.[28] During his campaign Purvis broke most of the procedural rules,[29] and this proved decisive for Bishop Tucker's stand: 'Mr. Purvis has a good case, but it has been mismanaged.'[30] Tucker knew that the state could use strong measures in such situations: 'The Commissioner has protected himself by his Court of Inquiry.'[31] To pursue the matter under these circumstances, as the CMS headquarters was prepared to do,[32] would be 'like running your head against a brick wall'. Faced with the state's stonewalling tactics, Tucker was fully aware that there were several severe limitations on the mission's ability to perform its role as a consultative body voicing genuine African grievances. He therefore thought an accommodating strategy to be more profitable in the long run.[33]

This aspect of the mission's strategy is even more evident when we turn to the significance of the personal element in the mission's relations with the state. It was soon recognized by the mission that good relations between government officers and missionaries were essential for the furtherance of Christianity, especially in the outlying districts, and this concern had some influence on the locating of missionary manpower on several occasions. A rather trivial altercation between the two sides, for which both the missionary and the official were to blame, took place in the newly occupied Acholi district in 1904.[34] Tucker admitted that the missionary in question could not take up a new post in the same area, as all the officials there had 'got their knife in him'; instead he looked for another missionary who was on better terms with the government officers.[35] The same criterion was used when Tucker established the new post of Archdeacon of Busoga in the wake of the Purvis affair. He laid special stress on the fact that his appointee was *persona grata* with the government.[36]

The mission was so interested in good relations with the government that it accepted direct intervention from it in the question of the allocation of missionaries. When it became known in 1908 that the CMS mission planned to post the Rev. H. Clayton to Ankole, there was some alarm among local officials, as Clayton had taken part in an inquiry some three years before into the murder of a European officer; the events of that time would make it difficult for them to cooperate amicably with him.[37] The Commissioner put the facts before the mission, and outlined the important principle behind his intervention: 'I am sure that you will agree with me in thinking it very desirable, for the good of the natives, that the Missionary and the officials in a district should, if possible, be in complete sympathy and accord with each other.'[38] This corresponded in any case with certain unwritten rules for the allocation of missionaries, so the mission did not take offence at this somewhat surprising intervention; Clayton was not sent to Ankole.[39] In the following year the matter was reopened for a number of reasons, and the mission went out of its way to secure the government's approval for its decision. The way they approached the problem secured not only the government's acceptance, but also the highest commendation of the mission's cooperative spirit.[40] That direct intervention of this kind from the government was exceptional is indicated by a similar case some four years later when officials in the Northern Province protested against the appointment of the Rev. A. B. Fisher to Acholi because of his reputation for interference in administrative matters. In spite of vehement protests, leading members of the administration did not find the evidence strong enough to justify intervention, not even in the form of an informal approach to the Bishop.[41] Although the government was careful in general not to interfere in internal missionary matters, the mission was at the same time well aware of the importance the government attached to personal relations. The cases discussed above show that the mission was willing to a great extent to be accommodating, in that it would allow the government's probable reaction to count as a decisive factor in its own planning of its work.

It is evident that the emphasis on proper procedure and amicable personal relations narrowed the mission's scope as a consultative body. Its acceptance of these conditions and its compliance with a 'safety margin' fixed by the government limited the issues in which the mission would involve itself, and the strength with which it could pursue those issues which it did take up. To this should be added the overall consideration that a consultative role presupposes a certain distance from the government and independence of it. Whether this latter condition was fulfilled all through the period in question will be discussed later. First we must examine some concrete issues which show how the mission handled its more or less self-assumed role as a consultative body.

The analysis of concrete issues in a context such as this must by its nature be selective; the material available is all too scanty to provide wide coverage. In spite of this qualification it is possible to observe two trends in the mission's handling of its consultative status which accord well with previously noted tendencies. First we must consider the mission's relationship with the chiefs. In a number of cases the mission acted as the confidant and adviser of the chiefs to such effect that it influenced government policy. The administration was at any rate highly conscious of this kind of missionary influence. The key question of poll tax is illustrative here.

When hut tax was first introduced as part of the Uganda Agreement of 1900 the missionary leaders played an important role in persuading the Baganda chiefs to accept it (Chapter 7). The same reliance on the good offices of the mission was evident when the poll tax on bachelors was introduced in 1904–5. On that occasion the government was even prepared to make a political deal with Bishop Tucker in return for his contribution in persuading the Baganda leaders to accept the revision of the tax system. A somewhat different pattern emerged with the introduction of the general poll tax in 1909. The government suggested that all males over fourteen should be liable to the new tax. This proposal came at a time when Bishop Tucker was fighting against forced labour. He took up the tax issue with equal vigour, and compared the government's policy with that of the Congo Free State. Children of fourteen, who would be unlikely to be able to pay in cash, should not be expected to work on the roads or as porters, as this would be disastrous for them both physically and morally. He insisted on a minimum age of eighteen, and persuaded the Baganda leaders to stand firm on this in spite of the fact that they themselves would lose money, as they were entitled to 20 per cent of all tax paid. At Tucker's instigation they even refused to compromise when the government suggested a lower age limit of sixteen or seventeen.[42] In the end, the Governor, with the approval of the Colonial Office, gave in, 'as we don't want to quarrel with the chiefs and the Bishop'.[43] Evidently the colonial authorities recognized the strength of the alliance between the chiefs and the mission and the strong political influence which Bishop Tucker was able to exert on the chiefs.

It was therefore to be expected that when the poll-tax system was extended to the neighbouring areas the mission maintained a close interest in its implementation.[44] One important issue was the securing of the usual poll-tax rebate for the chiefs. The mission's own interest in the scheme was that it wanted to have the katikiros on church land accepted as tax-collectors to the exclusion of other possible collectors. In both cases the mission had considerable success in reaching a compromise.[45] Remarkably, when the dispute over poll-tax increases between the government and Buganda developed in 1919 the mission did not act in its advisory capacity to the Baganda leaders, nor was it used as an intermediary between the two parties. This stands in marked contrast to earlier occasions. While one should not conclude too much from a negative observation like this, the impression of the mission's reduced role is increased by its exclusion from the Uganda Development Commission. More evidence in support of this observation was provided by the issue of excess land dealt with in Chapter 14. This was particularly illustrative of the mission's growing difficulties in keeping the confidence of the chiefs. We will return later to this change in the mission's position when more cases have been examined.

The mission undertook a great variety of functions in championing the cause of the chiefs with the government, and two cases will be singled out here. The first one was an intervention in 1904 aimed at reorganizing and improving the whole administrative system in the Kingdom of Toro. The mission voiced the grievances of the Omukama and the chiefs on two scores.[46] First there was considerable variation in administrative practice among officials and a tendency to ignore the Omukama and the chiefs.[47] Secondly, the Toro Agreement was ambiguous on the question of the position of the Omukama and on the land settlement provisions, which promised official and private estates.[48] Under these circumstances it was extremely difficult for the mission to fulfil its task of interpreting the law and the actions of the government and encouraging the Batoro to follow contradictory instructions loyally and patiently.[49] Over the next two years the mission kept up its pressure for the desired reforms in Toro and convinced officials of the necessity for action.[50] In the end the Toro Agreement was revised to the advantage of the Omukama and the chiefs, except as regards the land issue, which was postponed until a settlement could be reached for the whole Protectorate.[51] The mission's support was of considerable importance for the settlement.[52] Evidently the government accepted the mission's mediating role in this case, possibly because of its importance in preventing further agitation among the Toro leaders.[53]

The second case shows the mission in the role of an agency of appeal. It concerns the chiefs deported from Bunyoro to the East African Protectorate after their agitation against the Baganda agents in 1907 (see Chapter 22). Bishop Tucker supported their appeal and recommended that they should be allowed to return home, as they had learned their lesson, and were in any case harmless as they had been stripped of their chieftainships.[54] A similar case was the protest against the injustice done to the Omukama of Toro when his palace was searched for ivory.[55]

There was always the danger that chiefs might use the mission for their own ends rather than to appeal against real injustice. Such cases occurred often in the districts, but it is difficult to get any clear picture of them.[56] It is evident, however, that one important aspect of the mission's role as a consultative agency was that the initiative was not on the European side alone. The African leaders were fully aware of the possibility of using the mission's good offices. There was yet another aspect of the situation which makes any assessment of the mission's motives more complicated. Sometimes the mission had its own interests in helping the chiefs, one obvious example being the issue of church land.[57] The mission's interest in the preservation of chiefly rights over land stemmed from its dependence on the chiefs' economic potential and the need to have the chiefs' gifts of land legitimized. Hence, sometimes the mission could not avoid playing its consultative role less neutrally. This also made it more vulnerable in the sense that its independence and even its capacity to play this role at all could be called into question.[58]

The second major object of the mission's consultative activity was the protection and defence of African rights against any violation by the colonial administration. The mission believed firmly that it ought to help Africans in general to fight against unreasonable demands and behaviour from the state.[59] One early case in the newly-occupied Acholi district has already been mentioned; the missionary in charge protested strongly against what appeared to be the unjustified arrest of Africans. The case was in fact rather trivial as it was based on rumours and misunderstandings, and involved an element of rivalry between the representatives of the mission and the government, as was often the case in pioneer districts. None the less it shows that the mission was ready to intervene when it felt that injustice was being done. The presence of European commercial interests could also have unwelcome consequences for the Africans. For instance, in 1907 Bishop Tucker accused the agents of an Italian trading company of exploitation.[60] But otherwise the main target was the colonial administration itself, as in the case of the Purvis affair, when the mission raised the question of whether it was justifiable to blame a whole clan or village for the misdeeds of individual members, as the government officer had done on that occasion.[61] Although peace was desirable in the districts, and punitive expeditions were sometimes necessary, there was no justification for using methods which completely ignored the rights of the Africans. In other cases the mission took great interest in the way the legal apparatus was operated at the local level, and did its best to procure justice for the ordinary people.[62]

The most outstanding example of the mission's engagement in the protection of African interests against exploitation was the issue of forced labour. The same issue showed however how much the mission's political role was affected by a number of factors. Among these was the mission's conception of the state's intentions. If the mission and the government had different views of the interests of the Africans, the mission would be more critically inclined than if it felt that the government and itself had the same basic aims. A second factor brought out by the forced-labour issue was the extent to which the mission had vested interests in the existing system. Both factors must have limited the mission's capacity to perform a political role based on the safeguarding of African interests. It is doubtful whether the mission itself recognized these limitations, even though they affected its whole function within the colonial state. This will be discussed separately in a concluding section, when the results obtained from the analysis of the mission's approaches to the colonial state will be reviewed.

The doubts expressed by local officials in the controversy in the Acholi district as to whether the mission was overstepping the boundaries set by the colonial system were assuaged by the Deputy Commissioner. Although the missionary in question had overestimated his right to intervene, the Deputy Commissioner did not consider that he had acted subversively.[63] Bishop Tucker was fully aware of the risk of being accused of subversive activity when protecting African interests. On more than one occasion he was therefore at pains to emphasize that 'From the first establishment of the Mission it has been our constant endeavour to [imbue?] the peoples with whom we are in contact with entire loyalty and submission to the powers-that-be.'[64] The mission clearly tried to keep its work within the framework of the colonial order, and felt that it was its duty to foster loyalty among the people towards the colonial state. The claim to consultative status involved no questioning of the colonial system as such. This is hardly surprising, in view of the developments of the 1890s and the missionary approval of the Uganda Agreement of 1900. We have already pointed out, on the basis of events in 1897, that the mission had good reasons to appreciate the peace and order which the colonial system provided. But it is important to emphasize this point again in a context where the mission's criticism of the government is under discussion. The mission was outspoken in its criticism of the government's methods at the time of the Purvis affair in 1906. The following year, after the punitive expedition to Bunyoro and the deportation of the rebellious Nyoro chiefs, Bishop Tucker congratulated the officer in charge of the affair and specifically expressed his approval of the methods used on that occasion.[65] Only six months later, Tucker forwarded and supported the deported chiefs' appeal for clemency. These two cases illustrate the fact that when the mission defended African interests it was done on the basis of an acceptance of the colonial system. The aim was to secure reasonable and decent conditions for Africans *within* the colonial order, but it was not the mission's place to question that order's existence as such.

While the government thus had no reason to doubt the mission's support in principle, it did claim that the mission's advisory activities sometimes had unfortunate political consequences. Officials observed that some people, especially teachers, displayed an independence of the representatives of the government which could only be ascribed to the presence of the local missionary, and that they even used this presence to evade their proper duties.[66] Also, when Africans noticed rivalry or even outright enmity between the two European agencies, they could easily feel insecure about who was the superior authority.[67] The government was afraid that Africans were being given the impression that there was a dual system of authority. The situation was of course aggravated in newly opened districts where there was no proper demarcation between the functions of the two agencies; government officers also indicated that the mission deliberately overstepped the bounds of its proper sphere by interfering in government business and thus creating a situation of rivalry.[68] Bishop Tucker was fully aware of the risk of being accused of undue intrusion into government affairs, and tried to forestall such accusations by carefully defining the boundaries between the two spheres of authority. In one situation he advised the local Church Council to refuse to have anything to do with political or administrative issues, and to refer such matters to the chiefs.[69] Later, when asked by a government official to undertake a special inquiry, Tucker refused angrily, as it would give the impression that he 'had a power of supervision and control which it is my constant endeavour to disclaim and repudiate'.[70]

While the problem of rivalry was alleviated over the years with the establishment of a more efficient administrative system, there remained the fear in government circles that people might misconceive the position of the mission and the church and make them the focus of opposition towards the government. During the controversy between missionaries and government officials in Acholi, concern was expressed that chiefs from one district might unite and exploit the protection of the mission in their fight against another faction of chiefs, and the latter might react by forming a party based on Islam.[71] Anger was also expressed elsewhere over the fact that the leading missionary in Toro acted more like a 'leader of the opposition' than as a 'passive supporter of the District Officer' in providing a rallying-point for African discontent.[72] One obvious field of concern was education: 'Purely Mission-controlled systems of education in Uganda are fraught with possibilities seriously affecting the future peace and good order of the country'.[73] The political authorities must have become aware relatively early of the phenomenon which has been an important feature in Uganda's later history: the indirect and unintentional effect of missionary work and religious factionalism. The grouping potential of religious persuasion was politically significant, and the church and the mission, as institutionalized expressions of religion, were used as means to political ends, or at least as a focus for future opposition to the political office-holders. The government's awareness of this risk coloured its attitude to the mission's advisory activities.

The key word in the government's reaction to the mission's self-imposed consultative status was interference. In spite of all affirmations to the contrary, and in spite of the mission's caution and its strict adherence to the procedural rules, this was how the government frequently interpreted the mission's advisory activities.[74] Whenever the mission was critical the accusation of interference was almost unavoidable, given the difference in the two attitudes towards the Africans. This was one side of the official attitude to the mission, but there was also another side which made the relationship something of a dilemma. On several occasions the government on its own initiative invited the cooperation of the mission in solving problems.[75] It often had to rely on individual missionaries, too, for information, because of their profound knowledge of local affairs and African languages.[76] The risks involved in this cooperation with the mission were fully recognized by one official: 'there have emerged from that long-sustained friendly association rather suspicious signs that ecclesiastical bodies have held our consultations with them to imply joint administrative powers, and this assumption has reflected itself upon the actions of the natives.'[77]

It was therefore difficult for the government to strike the necessary balance between cooperation and the need to keep the mission in its proper place. It accepted that the mission had legitimate interests in certain spheres, and a supportive function where issues like poll tax, and to a certain extent education, were concerned.[78] On some occasions it was even willing to take the missionary factor into account when explaining and justifying its actions, insofar as it hoped that the evidence produced would stand up to missionary scrutiny.[79] But beyond this the mission's political activity was likely to be seen as interference, and resented accordingly. The boundary between cooperation on the government's terms and interference was an extremely fluid one. This was not a new problem for the government. It was strikingly similar to the dialectical relationship of the late 1890s, and seems to have been a basic characteristic of the relations between mission and state in the colonial situation.[80] But the dilemma was not a static one. It seems to have lessened somewhat over the years because of changes both in the colonial system and the attitude of the mission.

Changing prospects for the mission's political influence

In examining the demands for a Christian state we have concentrated on two aspects: the linkages established between the CMS mission and the colonial state, and the consultative status of the mission within the colonial state. As regards the former we have seen that the mission gained very little ground, just as it gained little ground on the issues of church land and the position of the katikiros on church estates. The CMS mission may have succeeded in giving the impression of a special relationship with the colonial state through its frequent contacts and personal linkages, but results were otherwise scanty. We have instead focused on the mission's consultative status and its claim to play a special role within the framework of a Christian state. This has allowed us to demonstrate that the mission had attained a position from which it could influence policy-making and decisions. As the confidant of African chiefs and protagonist of African interests the mission definitely played a political role, but it did not do so on the basis of an institutionalized position. Its influence with Africans and its knowledge of local matters meant that the government could not ignore it, and that it was even sometimes dependent on it. From the available evidence we cannot measure this influence exactly; nor can we compare it quantitatively with the influence of other interest groups. We have, however, identified a number of areas within which the mission was active and influenced government decisions. All we can do at present is to investigate how far the mission impressed on the colonial administration its obligation to act as a Christian government. Here we must first consider the limitations on the mission's ability to play this role, and secondly the changes which took place in this ability throughout the first quarter of the twentieth century.

It has already been argued that the emphasis on proper procedure in approaching the colonial administration, and the importance attached to personal relations, had a directly limiting effect on the mission's political influence. To this should be added a certain amount of indirect pressure from the government's side, which caused the mission to exercise a modicum of self-censorship. It was natural for the state to limit the mission's political influence by confining its activities to areas within which it was supposed to have legitimate interests, or could be expected to carry out a supportive function. Whenever it crossed this ill-defined boundary, the mission encountered the government's resentment, and was accused of inciting rivalry and interfering unduly. One obvious consequence was that the mission made sure that it was on firm ground before it involved itself in issues, and was careful to avoid providing justification for the accusation of interference.[81] At the same time there was always the latent possibility that matters could be referred to London. The mission was fully aware that the public and politicians in Britain remembered past events and were ready to criticize the CMS whenever it gave the impression of interfering for its own ends. Such criticism could of course also be prompted by denominational bias.[82] The fact that these groups were sensitive to religious interference in the political sphere inevitably tempered the mission's willingness to undertake a political role. The strength of these restraints, and the extent to which the mission heeded them, were conditioned by the seriousness of the issues involved, and the prevailing attitude to the government at any given time.

From the quantitative point of view it is significant that the majority of the cases discussed above fell within the first half of the period. The number of issues decreased as time progressed. Furthermore, most of them fell within Bishop Tucker's period, whereas his successor, Bishop Willis, appeared less frequently in the same role. This difference is underlined even more by the fact that some issues to which Bishop Tucker gave high priority were more or less shelved by Willis. The problem of forced labour was a typical example. This suggests that there was a significant difference between the two bishops' conception of the mission's consultative status and political role.

First of all the difference between the two bishops raises the question of the importance of the personal element. We have already seen that there was a difference in personalities which should not be overlooked. Examining the various issues, one is left with the impression that Tucker showed great subtlety and skilful diplomacy in performing his critical role, whereas Willis was less inclined to be critical of the colonial state.[83] Although the difference in personalities was by no means a negligible factor in a small colonial community, its importance should not be exaggerated. We must also show that there was a substantial difference in the two bishops' attitudes to the government. Our analysis of the forced labour issue showed how Willis redefined the mission's role *vis-à-vis* the colonial state, took a much more positive view of its dealings with Africans, and placed more emphasis than Tucker on the joint interests of mission and government. The difference may be accurately described as a move from a position where the critical role was given priority to one where a legitimizing function was predominant. Willis himself came close to confirming this change of priority in his first Episcopal Charge; and on later occasions, when missionary representatives set out to define the mission's role, there was greater emphasis on the task of interpreting the government's laws and actions to the Africans.[84] One might say that the direction of missionary mediation was now from government to Africans, rather than vice versa as it had been in the days of Bishop Tucker. The supportive function constituted by the educational system pointed in the same direction. Such a conception of the state and of its own position was bound to affect the mission's advisory function. These developments go far to explain the reduction in the number of cases in which the mission intervened on behalf of Africans. They also explain why the government had less reason than in the time of Bishop Tucker to impose restraints on the mission's pro-African activities. The problem of interference became less relevant.

Apart from this more or less self-imposed change in the mission's role, a second factor was also at work. With the bureaucratic elaboration of the colonial system there was less need and less scope for the mission's advisory contribution and political engagement. General legislation was laid down, and administrative measures were strengthened and made more uniform. The mission certainly played a part in this process, as we have seen in the preceding chapter, but at the same time its acceptance of the framework of the colonial system reduced its ability to criticize the government and to intervene on behalf of the Africans. The increased bureaucracy brought the chiefs into the administrative system, and in this position they had less need of the mission as an intermediary and defender. As administration became more complex, more technical expertise became necessary to carry out the political role the mission had performed previously. The issue of excess land underlined the difficulties of the situation (see Chapter 14). Changing conditions inevitably narrowed the scope of the mission's advisory activity within the colonial system, and the cumulative effects of these developments became particularly evident during Bishop Willis' period.

A third, more abstract factor should be considered. It has been remarked that the critical role of the mission presupposed a certain amount of distance between the mission and the political authorities. We have also shown how the mission's dependence on the state increased during the 1910s, and how this affected its actions directly and indirectly. The issue of forced labour was a very clear case of this, and those of excess land and education pointed in the same direction. There was also the problem of the mission's own vested interests. Whenever these were involved, as with the issues of land and education, the mission's attitude, capacity and actions were affected. We may generalize, and say that over the years the mission's independence, especially as regards financial matters, was increasingly curtailed, and that its capacity to maintain its consultative status was reduced in so far as it involved criticism of the government. Such a causal relationship is of course difficult to substantiate in detail, as it was neither fully recognized nor directly admitted by the participants themselves. But the various cases examined, especially in the field of education, seem to justify such a suggestion.

By focusing on the changes in the mission's consultative status we have been able to identify the major variables which determined the scope of the mission's political role. The main variables were the state's superior strength, including its access to repressive measures; the stage which the development of the colonial state had reached; the prevailing attitude to the state within the mission; and the extent of the mission's dependence on the state. These factors, both internal and external, supplemented one another. At the same time each variable represented a potential for change, so the resultant picture, rather than being static, was the outcome of a continuous dynamic process. The mission's political role within the colonial system was therefore bound to undergo changes through time, and in this context the trend had clearly been towards the erosion of its political role.

Approaches to the African polities

In dealing with the mission's relations with the African polities it will be appropriate to examine the Christianization of institutions within the African political system, and thereafter the institutionalized linkages between that system and the mission and church.

The Christianization of institutions within the African political system

The Kabakaship

It will be recalled that the Kabakaship was the subject of controversy during the turmoil of the 1890s between the Roman Catholic and the Protestant missions, and that the latter in the end won the battle over the religious affiliation and upbringing of the infant Kabaka (Chapter 6). The CMS mission's interest in the Kabakaship was not only prompted by the strategic consideration that building on the Kabaka's inherited authority would facilitate access to Buganda society, but also by the assumption that a Protestant Kabaka would give the impression that Protestantism was the established religion of Buganda. It was obviously important for the CMS mission to preserve and utilize this advantage by making sure that the incumbent to the Kabakaship was a Christian in fact, not only in name. A number of CMS initiatives from the period just after the turn of the century reveal this aim clearly.

As early as 1901, in fact, when Kabaka Daudi Chwa was approaching the age of five, CMS circles were discussing what education the young King should receive in view of the importance of his future position.[85] There was no doubt that his education should be based upon Christian principles. But it was felt that a CMS missionary would be the wrong choice for a tutor, as this could lead to misunderstandings with regard to the Society's links with a purely political institution. 'The Society scrupulously abstains from any interference with political or other matters relating to the civil administration of the country.' Although it refrained from direct personal involvement in the Kabaka's education, the CMS was quite clear about the interests it wanted to pursue more indirectly.

On the other hand it is of great importance that whoever is appointed should be a man of religious feeling and in sympathy with that predominant type of Christianity which is represented by Bishop Tucker and the Missionaries. The present order and civilization of the country are mainly the result of this Christianity.[86]

The CMS mission was, then, clearly taking a narrowly denominational line. It was not enough that there was a Christian King on the throne of Buganda: he must also be a Protestant King. It is difficult to say whether these issues were communicated to the government;[87] but the CMS mission was certainly well pleased when a young member of the colonial administration, J. C. R. Sturrock, was appointed as tutor for the Kabaka. He was both an Anglican and an English gentleman, and had the full confidence of the mission.[88]

Apart from its interest in the personal qualities of the incumbent, the mission was also intent on identifying the Kabakaship as closely as possible with the

Protestant Church. An early initiative was taken by both the religious and the secular leaders, the Bishop and the Katikiro. In 1900 they introduced for the first time the feature that the Kabaka's Accession Day was celebrated in church.[89] Over the following years the celebration of the Kabaka's birthday and Coronation Day began with a service in the Cathedral, somewhat presumptuously called 'the usual State service'.[90] On this, as on other similar occasions, a public event became a Christian/Protestant event which helped to underpin the central position of the Protestant church.

The Christianization of the Kabakaship came to a peak in 1910 in connection with the burial of the remains of the late Kabaka Mwanga, who had died in exile in the Seychelles in 1903 after having been baptized according to the Anglican rite. At that time the government would not permit the return of his remains to Buganda. The result was that the local Bakopi did not believe that Mwanga had really died, and therefore refused to recognize his successor, Daudi Chwa, and accused the chiefs of failing to adhere to tradition.[91] As it was in the interests of both the mission and the government to enhance the Kabaka's authority, permission was finally given for the proper burial of Mwanga in 1910, once the mission had been assured that no heathen rites would be permitted.[92] Mwanga was given a full Anglican funeral with the Bishop officiating in the Cathedral and at the royal tombs.[93] Only then was it possible to hold a proper succession ceremony for the new Kabaka. This took place the next day in accordance with tradition, accompanied by some discussion among Baganda Christians of whether the ceremony involved heathen rites.[94] The full Christian 'imprimatur' on the young Kabaka came only a week later when he was confirmed by Bishop Tucker.[95]

The whole process of establishing a virtual Protestant monopoly of the Kabakaship was apparently carried out without objections from the government and the Catholic mission. These came, however, shortly afterwards and manifested an accumulated annoyance from both of them. At the time of the succession ceremony the three Regents suggested that the young Kabaka should pay a visit to Britain on the occasion of the Coronation of King George V. The government approved of the idea, although it wanted to play down the official nature of the visit.[96] It was therefore thought that none of the leading Baganda chiefs ought to accompany the Kabaka, but the Regents disagreed, as they attached great official importance to the visit. Accordingly, they wished to be represented at the highest possible level, but could not agree among themselves who to nominate. The Katikiro, supported by his Protestant Co-Regent, suggested the leading Protestant chief, the Sekibobo, Ham Mukasa; while the Catholic Regent, Mugwanya, supported his own candidate. When this state of affairs was brought to the notice of the Provincial Commissioner, he immediately detected the influence of the CMS mission on the Katikiro's faction in the Lukiko, and recommended a cancellation of all further plans.[97] The administration was extremely annoyed at this alliance between the Protestant chiefs and the CMS mission, and there was even talk of 'teaching them a lesson':

I do not see why this should be dropped merely because the Katikiro and the CMS want a course which is not desirable. I think the time has come to make the principle that the Katikiro and the CMS are not the governors, pastors and masters of the Kabaka – and that there is an exterior power to which they must bow.[98]

The administration was thus aware of the need to weaken the strong ties between the Protestants and the Kabakaship. At first the problem was easily solved, as the British government decided not to invite African rulers to the Coronation.[99] But the issue was not forgotten over the next two years. The Regents remained divided among themselves for denominational reasons, and suggested two different candidates for the task of accompanying the Kabaka.[100] This long drawn-out issue involved more than the Protestant monopoly of the Kabakaship; it touched on many of the fundamental problems inherent in the Buganda situation. Religious factionalism continued to be the basis of the political sharing of power, and the government was constantly reminded how easy it was for religious factors to influence politics.[101] Protestant dominance raised two problems for the government: it had to strengthen the position of the Catholic leader, Mugwanya, in the Lukiko; and it had to curtail correspondingly the power of the Katikiro and instil in him more respect for the colonial authorities.[102]

The issue of the Kabaka's visit came to a head when both Bishop Willis and the Catholic Bishop Biermans intervened. Willis supported the Protestant faction,[103] and Biermans demanded that at least one representative of the Catholic party be included in the Kabaka's entourage, claiming that failure to do so would be a gross insult to the large Catholic majority in Buganda.[104] This rather trivial problem had thus entered a phase where the government was forced to consider how much importance should be granted to religious factors in arriving at political decisions. First, the government officials ascribed the actions of the Baganda chiefs to exclusively religious motives, and had to decide whether they should ignore their recommendations and arrive at a decision based on purely secular considerations. Secondly, they now realized that the Protestant establishment, with its alliance between the mission and the chiefs, was a force to be reckoned with: 'The Katikiro backed by the Namirembe Missionaries is practically challenging the Government to a contest; the result of which is to decide whose authority in native affairs is paramount.'[105]

The government felt that its authority was now at stake. In spite of this serious assessment of the situation, and in spite of its recognition of the two dimensions of the religious problem outlined above, the government did not really tackle the problem, but sought a compromise by making a Catholic saza chief from one of the minor sazas a member of the Kabaka's entourage. Catholic participation was thus ensured to the full satisfaction of the Catholic party. Yet the Protestants still constituted the bulk of the entourage and held the most important positions in it.[106] The Governor was extremely angry with what he called the disrespectful behaviour of the two Protestant Regents,[107] but apart from his outbursts and the sending of a conciliatory, explanatory letter from the two Protestant Regents, nothing more happened.[108] In terms of these problems, it meant that the government had not succeeded in neutralizing the religious element in political decision-making, but accepted its existence as a necessary basis for action. Nor did it succeed in reducing the importance of the Protestant establishment in Buganda. It secured certain minority rights for the Catholic faction, but the Protestant hegemony at the centre of power represented by the Kabakaship was untouched. In this case the government worked within a framework formed by a high degree of religious involvement in politics and Protestant political dominance. Whether this was typical will emerge from the investigation of other cases.

The next manifestation of the Protestant involvement with the Kabakaship occurred soon afterwards, when Daudi Chwa came of age in August 1914 and was thus able to take over full power from the three Regents. Bishop Tucker and his successor, Bishop Willis, expressed Protestant concern about this event when they brought the matter to the notice of the Secretary of State. While the latter was in favour of a Christian accession ceremony, he also grasped the crux of the matter when he expressed the hope that there would be Catholic participation in the ceremony.[109] The problem was all the more acute, as the official swearing-in, which signified obedience to the colonial state, and the Christian ceremony, had to be separated by three months in the absence of the Bishop.[110] Both the mission and the Protestant Baganda leaders felt his presence to be of the utmost importance if the ceremony was to have the required impact. All planning was therefore left in the hands of the CMS mission and the Protestant chiefs.[111] This reaffirmed the Protestant monopoly of matters relating to the Kabakaship.[112]

This was a quite deliberate Protestant initiative. Again and again they emphasized that this was 'the first coronation of a Christian Kabaka',[113] thereby indicating that Buganda had virtually become a Christian kingdom. The event was clearly seen as a symbolic affirmation of a Christian Kabakaship; the Bishop drew implicit parallels to European monarchies by speaking of the Kabaka's 'responsibilities as a Christian prince'.[114] But it was also considered necessary to reaffirm the Kabakaship's traditional basis. The Coronation was not only carried out in accordance with Anglican prescriptions; a number of traditional elements were included to underline its legitimacy, first and foremost the fact that the ceremony was held at the traditional site, Budo Hill. The Kabaka ruled not only by the grace of God, but also with the blessing of his ancestors.[115] The circumstances of Mwanga's funeral may have brought home to the mission the need for a traditional rooting of the Kabakaship. But some of the Baganda leaders found themselves in a serious dilemma, which was not solved simply by stripping the ceremony of so-called heathen practices. The use of the traditional site, the sacred Budo Hill, appeared to acknowledge the continued strength of the old gods.[116] But for the organizers of the ceremony, the necessity of respecting some of the old traditions counted for more.[117]

The cooperation between the mission and the Protestant leaders worked perfectly, but there was strong opposition from the Catholic Regent, the Catholic mission and the government. The Governor refused to attend, and ordered the Provincial Commissioner and his staff, who did attend, to come in their second-best uniforms.[118] This marked an unequivocal official disapproval of the Protestants' *tour de force*.[119] But the mission rested content in the belief that all its difficulties had been overcome, and that a precedent had been set for future occasions. The following year, the Synod of the Anglican Church jubilantly welcomed the first Christian Kabaka into their midst.[120]

The investiture of the Kabaka in 1914 represented the crowning achievement of the mission's attempts to create a Christian state, at least as far as the African political system was concerned. Buganda could now be considered a Christian Kingdom, and this was symbolized by its Head of State, who was, moreover, in accordance with unwritten law, a Protestant.[121] The mission had also reaffirmed the indispensability of the church on such official occasions. There was now a clear parallel with those nations where there was a state church, with the monarch as the *ex officio* head. The parallel was further reinforced by the close cooperation between the mission and the Protestant élite, who had responded positively to the drive to give Protestantism an officially established position by means of the Kabakaship. For them, this was a means of strengthening the Protestant cause and the Protestant party in Buganda. Thus the Kabaka became a pillar of the religious as well as of the political system.

But problems were bound to arise if the Kabaka failed to adhere to the rules which guided the whole Ganda system. We will in this context pass over the relationship between the chiefs and the Kabaka,[122] but it is clear that one precondition for the proper functioning of the Kabakaship in relation to the church was that the incumbent to the throne was seen to possess Christian qualities and set a proper Christian example for his subjects. If this precondition was no longer fulfilled, as happened at the beginning of the 1920s, the value of having the Head of State as an official figurehead within the church could be called into question. This diminished the institutional value of the Kabaka's presence, and the church was left in a serious dilemma. Should it continue to ally itself publicly with the Kabakaship, while privately and unofficially criticizing and correcting him? Or should it dissociate itself from him and thereby damage its image of establishment? The mission chose the first option, and this created a number of difficulties with sincere rank-and-file Christians (see one example, p. 287 above) in relation to the mission's own demands for high moral standards among officials. The priority given to the image of establishment weakened the moral voice with which the mission and church could speak and linked them to an institution which could prove more of a liability than an advantage in furthering the Anglican cause in the longer term.

The drive to Christianize the traditional centre of power was not confined to Buganda, but also took place in the neighbouring Kingdoms. It has on earlier occasions been noticed that the Omukama of Toro, Daudi Kasagama, was a close ally of the CMS mission, and that it assisted in preserving and strengthening his position (see Chapter 8). A clear-cut example was provided by the mission's efforts to have the Toro Agreement of 1901 revised. One motive for this was certainly the need to clarify the Omukama's position, and the successful outcome of these efforts in 1906 served to enhance Kasagama's authority. It may not have been unrelated to this event that Kasagama soon afterwards decided that the time had come for a revival of an ancient coronation ceremony (the Empango ceremony). It is further characteristic that this celebration should have taken place on the anniversary of his baptism, on which occasion a special service had been held throughout the previous 12 years.[123] The same pattern was thus emerging as in Buganda: the institution of the Kingship was supported by two pillars, one traditional and the other Christian. Similarly, the close relationship between church and state was emphasized by the fact that the missionary delegated to Toro was called in to officiate, as 'the Christian King wanted a Christian priest to place the crown upon his head'.[124] What is most remarkable is that all this was done on the initiative of the Omukama himself. It confirms what has already been said about Buganda: that African political leaders were fully aware of the possibility of using the mission and the church for their own purposes. There were mutual benefits to be gained, not just a one-way traffic directed by the missionary leaders.[125]

Developments in Bunyoro were almost parallel to those in Toro. When the turmoil of the late 1890s came to an end with the defeat and capture of the Omukama Kabarega, one of his young sons was appointed King by the government. He had been educated by the CMS mission while staying in Buganda, and was soon after his enthronement baptized by Bishop Tucker.[126] Here the mission had to face, even earlier than elsewhere, the fact that the young Omukama did not set a Christian example.[127] They therefore had no objections when the government deposed him in 1902 and appointed his brother, Andereya Duhaga, in his place.[128] Duhaga was a sincere Christian, carefully educated by the CMS mission, and had even at one stage worked as a teacher.[129] He certainly did all that was expected of a Christian monarch,[130] and his relationship with the mission was so close that, during his leading chiefs' rebellion against the dominance of the Baganda agents in Bunyoro in 1907, he joined forces with the mission and accordingly with the government.[131]

When things had returned to normal in 1908 the time was considered ripe to perform the ancient coronation ceremony as in Toro. At the insistence of the Omukama the dedication of the new Anglican church was combined with the Coronation. The missionary in charge of Bunyoro, the Rev. A. B. Fisher, crowned the Omukama with the full approval and active participation of the government. Once more a church event and a state event had been combined. According to the Sub-Commissioner, this symbolized the progress of Bunyoro and marked the common aim towards which the mission and the government were working: the welfare of the country and the happiness of the people.[132]

The Christianization of the Kingship probably succeeded in Bunyoro more than anywhere else, and it is therefore hardly surprising that the mission used the same approach elsewhere over the following years, regardless of changing conditions. The mission's commitment to the value of the Kingship on the one hand, and the secular authorities' changed attitude to the missionary involvement on the other, were clearly revealed in Bunyoro, when a new investiture was due in 1924, on the occasion of the Omukama's death. Yet another son of Kabarega, Tito Winye, was installed on the throne. But this time the Governor himself officiated, and advised the new Omukama in his speech that it was in the interests of his country that he showed the same loyalty to British officials as his predecessor had done.[133] Later the ancient coronation ceremony was performed, this time apparently with no mission or church involvement.[134] Afterwards the CMS mission suggested that the Bishop should crown the new Omukama in the church in accordance with Anglican tradition.[135] Colonial officials were adamantly opposed to this:

I consider any further form of coronation unnecessary and any further form of coronation by the C.M.S. as quite undesirable, as tending to cause confusion in the minds of the natives as to who are the Governors of the Protectorate.[136]

On the basis of this attitude the government took two precautionary measures. First, the Governor wrote to the Bishop that any further ceremony would be a mistake, as two had already taken place.[137] Secondly, in order to stop the Omukama from taking any initiative of his own, it was decided to let it be known indirectly that the Governor was opposed to another ceremony.[138] The aim here was clearly to cut the mission off from direct involvement in the accession celebrations. This should be seen against the background of the government's irritation over the mission-organized Coronation of the Kabaka of Buganda ten years earlier. The government was unwilling to recognize the element of Anglican establishment which such a coronation ceremony, with the Bishop officiating, would imply; nor was it willing to countenance the implication of a rival 'king-making institution'.

The mission seems to have been blind to the writing on the wall provided by the changes that had occurred over the years. Even the combination of the traditional and Christian ceremony seen in earlier years in Buganda, Toro and Bunyoro was discontinued. Instead the mission clung to the old pattern of putting its trust in its close association with the centre of power. This was to be a permanent feature of missionary policy during the period under survey. It was never questioned whether the close alignment with the various courts which had some benefits but also involved severe disadvantages was worth the price the mission had to pay. Nor was it questioned whether it was feasible to be so closely identified with a political structure whose basis was unstable, in view of the shifting balance of power within the colonial system. Although, as we shall see in the next section, on the chiefly institution, rivalry with the Catholics was an important factor for developments in Uganda, events were inevitably influenced by the mission's automatic application of an Anglican/monarchic model in its dealings with the institution of the Kingship in Uganda.

The last point is illustrated by events in the Kingdom of Ankole.[139] In keeping with the mission's usual approach, great importance was attached to the fact that the Omugabe (King) was a member of the Protestant church. Accordingly, the most important church in the Kingdom had been built in the compound of the Royal Palace. In 1916 it was suggested that the church should be moved to a better location, but the Bishop was against the idea because the transfer would give the impression that the Omugabe had lost interest in the church. The Bishop thought this would be detrimental to the progress of Christianity in Ankole. It is interesting to notice that the Ankole chiefs did not support the almost automatic reaction of the Bishop; nor did the Omugabe himself have any objection to moving the church to a new site. He was even willing, if necessary, to build a new church in the Palace.[140] This difference of opinion between the church's central authority and the leaders in one of the districts suggests that the importance attached to the Kingship model in the mission's work may have been exaggerated.

The Lukiko

In view of the importance attached to the Kabakaship it is not surprising that a similar interest was directed towards the Lukiko institution, where the Christians were in the majority. Naturally the question was raised, initially by representatives to the Synod from Bunyoro, of whether Lukiko meetings should begin with prayers.[141] In 1916 a number of Protestant clergymen also suggested this; it was only reasonable, they claimed, that God's blessing, in view of its importance for the country, should be sought. The Katikiro and other Ganda leaders welcomed the suggestion, and it was fully endorsed by Bishop Willis, who argued that the Kabaka and 18 out of 20 saza chiefs were Christians, and that the majority of the population now professed Christianity.[142] He wrote to the Archbishop of Canterbury enquiring whether Roman Catholics had ever expressed disapproval of the prayers used in Parliament, acknowledging that this could be a sore point in the Buganda context.[143] Receiving an assuring answer, Willis then gave his support to the Ganda leaders.

The Provincial Commissioner, however, was against the idea for two reasons. First of all, it would give the impression that religion was closely connected with state matters, and thereby breach a basic principle in government policy; in particular it would leave the government open to the accusation of favouring the Anglican church. Secondly, strong religious feelings in the country meant that there was a risk of creating discontent among the Catholic and Muslim representatives in the Lukiko.[144] Willis repeatedly attempted to win over his counterpart in the government by referring to the parallelism between Parliament in London and the Lukiko at Mengo, and to the Ganda leaders' positive response; but he did not succeed in Christianizing the procedure, despite the fact that the absolute majority in the Lukiko were Christians.

The existence of religious factionalism and the risk of denominational rivalry thus had a deterrent effect on government policy. We must also give some consideration to similar problems at the chiefly level, and ask whether the government took any positive measures to neutralize the religious factor in politics, or if it was content to remain passively on guard against initiatives such as the Protestant demand for prayers in the Lukiko.

Religion and chieftainship

Close links had been established between the chieftainships in Buganda and Toro and Christianity during the 1890s. The great majority of chiefs in the two areas were Christians and this in turn influenced the composition of the local Lukikos. In addition the state had accepted that religious criteria must play a role in appointments, as religious divisions were the main structuring principle in society and were accordingly of great political significance. The state had even accepted that certain posts naturally went to particular religious parties, so that the Protestants, irrespective of their strength among the people, were placed in a dominant position, while the Catholics were reduced to a minority position, and the Muslims even more so.[145]

For the CMS mission there was thus no need to Christianize this important institution within the state. Its major aim was rather to *maintain* the dominant position already gained. In the following we will investigate how far the mission succeeded, by asking whether changes occurred which affected the balance of power within the denominational field. We have already seen how important a role denominational rivalry played in the educational field, where the missions, and in particular the CMS, were prepared to channel much of their resources into the training of future chiefs (p. 250ff.). We must therefore ask how far the government accepted the Christian recruitment of chiefs, with its built-in Protestant dominance. Did it attempt to rectify imbalances by neutralizing the denominational factor in the appointment of chiefs? Some of these questions have already been posed in connection with developments in Buganda up to 1900, and the first task will be to examine the state of affairs there during the following two decades. Thereafter, other parts of the Protectorate will be examined in turn.

Buganda

The Uganda Agreement of 1900 had confirmed the division of saza chieftainships between the three religious parties (Chapter 7). This meant that the minor chiefs within each saza in most cases professed the same religion as their superiors. Political and administrative power was thus structured by a framework which made changes in personnel extremely difficult. A case in point occurred as early as 1907–8, when the Catholic saza chief of Mawokota was persuaded to resign his post. Although the Catholic Bishop, Henry Streicher,[146] cooperated in persuading him to leave, the event involved some typical problems both for the mission and the government. Bishop Streicher expressed concern that a non-Catholic might be appointed to the vacant post, whereupon the Catholics would lose the saza.[147] The Sub-Commissioner resented the involvement of the Bishop, as it was incompatible with the principle of missionary non-interference in politics, and in particular in the selection and dismissal of chiefs.[148] A crucial problem for the government rising out of this case was the appointment of a new saza chief for Mawogola. The post had fallen vacant following a reshuffle of saza chieftainships after the above-mentioned resignation. Mawogola had over the years been considered a Catholic saza, and any change was expected to cause ill-feeling in the country.[149] It came therefore as a surprise when the three Regents, in accordance with their rights under the Uganda Agreement, recommended not only two Catholics, but also two Protestants for the post.[150] This brought the religious question out into the open; it placed the government in a situation where it had to decide whether to give priority to religious adherence or qualifications. Government officials were highly suspicious of the fact that the Regents suggested Protestant names for a saza which had hitherto been Catholic. Their suspicions were not least directed towards the Katikiro, Apolo Kagwa, and his party in the Lukiko.[151]

The Governor found it difficult under the circumstances to arrive at a decision. His conclusion was of great importance for policy-making over the following years and deserves to be quoted in full:

I consider it very advisable that the balance of influence between the two religious parties should be maintained, as far as possible, at its existing degree. I am anxious therefore that the vacancy, in this instance, should be filled by a Roman Catholic. The Lukiko is meant to be a representative body, and we must try to see that the balance between the parties is a fair one, and that neither of them should gain a preponderance which might hamper us hereafter.[152]

Given these premises the colonial administration had only one solution open to it: the appointment of a Catholic candidate. The government was thus forced to acknowledge that it could not bypass the religious allocation of offices. On the contrary, it had to make it the main criterion in the appointment procedure, however much the Governor later claimed 'that all private feelings were merged into a desire to select the best man available, irrespective of creed or of other interests',[153] and however much his Deputy tried to exonerate the colonial administration by placing the full responsibility for local government procedures on the Lukiko.[154]

The Lukiko's composition was of crucial importance in view of its influence on appointments. The problem of maintaining a balance between the two parties arose again soon afterwards in an even more acute form when the issue of the religious allegiance of minor chiefs was discussed. In the unruly saza of Bugangazi, one of 'the lost counties' (see p. 69), a Protestant candidate had virtually been approved as gombolola chief by the Protestant majority in the Lukiko; but the Catholic Regent, Mugwanya, protested, saying that Bugangazi had always been ruled by Catholic chiefs. The Protestant nominee then complained to the government, asking whether it approved of this rejection on religious grounds. He pointed out that 'the Government pays for work, but not for any religion'.[155] Mugwanya answered quite explicitly that he saw the issue in purely religious terms.[156] The Provincial Commissioner could only express his deep regret that the question of religion always entered these matters; but it was a fact, dating back to Lugard's organization of the country, that certain sazas were held at all levels by certain of the three religious parties. He could only add:

I fear that it is impossible at the present juncture to induce the natives to absolutely dissociate the question of religion in these matters, and the preponderance of professed Protestants among the members of the Lukiko is therefore apt to favour adherents of that sect.[157]

Instead of trying to neutralize the religious factor in general, the government now directed its efforts towards limiting the power of the Protestant party in the Lukiko. It was considered whether the appointments of minor chiefs could be made directly by the government, without consulting the Lukiko.[158] But in the end the old procedure prevailed. In accordance with the Governor's almost ritual preference for 'the better and more worthy man',[159] Mugwanya's candidate was appointed, the justification being that the Protestant nominee's criticism of the Catholic Regent, Mugwanya, had shown him to be unworthy of a chieftainship.[160]

This illustrates how deeply ingrained the religion-based allocation of offices was in the Buganda system; even at the gombolola level the religious factor could not be avoided. Any appointment contrary to established practice became the subject of dispute at the highest level of the political apparatus. It also demonstrates how little room the government had for manoeuvre in spite of its discomfort over the fact that religion was so directly involved in the administration of the country. The government could not act independently; it had to take the Ganda leaders into account, and they opted firmly for candidates from their own parties. The government might be able to act more independently and break down the rigid adherence to the religious allocation of offices if it could exploit the disunity and rivalry between the Ganda leaders. Such a chance came in 1913 in connection with the saza chieftainship of Kabula, which had hitherto been held by the Protestants. The three Regents were as usual at odds over the list of candidates, but suggested a Protestant and a Catholic for the post.[161] Mugwanya, however, went a step further, and, in view of the lack of consensus, suggested a Muslim candidate. In his opinion this would make all ill-feeling disappear.[162] This idea was welcomed by the government with great enthusiasm. It opened up the possibility of bypassing the usual rivalry between the two main contestants.[163] In particular it afforded an opportunity of teaching the two Protestant Regents, who had begun to act as if they alone ruled the country, a lesson, especially after their disrespectful treatment of Mugwanya.[164] Moreover, the administration now suddenly became aware of its responsibility towards the Muslims. According to the latest census there was a clear lack of correspondence between the number of offices held by Muslims and their percentage of the population. Now there was a chance to correct this situation to some extent, and to demonstrate to the Christians how intolerant their whole attitude was.

It is simply bigotry and religious intolerance. To penalize a man because he chooses to embrace the Muhammedan Religion is un-Christianlike and contrary to the principles of the British constitution throughout the Empire . . . I think this is a grand opportunity to show the chiefs of this Protectorate that the British Government regards with strong disfavour anything in the shape of religious intolerance or persecution and that a deserving chief should not be debarred from promotion because he chooses to follow the Crescent and not the Cross.[165]

This was virtually the first time after the turn of the century that the ideals of religious freedom and tolerance were expressed as clearly as they had been in the 1890s. The government even seemed prepared to exercise some form of positive discrimination. In any case the Governor agreed that any list of candidates for the Kabula saza chieftainship should contain representatives of all three denominations, so as to include the possibility of a Muslim appointment.[166]

This was certainly an attempt to reduce the importance of the religious factor, but it was also a revision of the previous policy of maintaining the balance between the two main parties, and the Muslims were being used as a lever. The new policy was not, therefore, generally welcomed within the colonial administration. There were those who felt that the time had not yet come to abolish religious distinctions. If the Protestants were deprived of the relatively insignificant saza chieftainship of Kabula they would put up a Protestant candidate again the next time a large Catholic or Muslim chieftainship fell vacant. This could revive dormant religious friction.[167] In any case a policy directed at the improvement of the Muslim position was not considered realistic at present. If the Muslims were under-represented in the various sazas, it was not due to discrimination, but simply to the fact that their candidates were not as well educated as the Christians. Even in the case in question the Muslim candidate lacked the required qualifications.[168] Moreover, it was questioned whether the emphasis on religious differences and the interpretation of the conflict in purely religious terms were justified: 'there is no doubt that it is now a matter of party feeling more than that of religious differences which has caused these unfortunate disputes'.[169] The latter interpretation was significant in that it attempted to defuse the whole issue of religious involvement in Uganda politics; the emphasis on competition between *parties* rather than religious factions was reminiscent of a similar attempt in the late 1890s (pp. 45, 53). But in spite of these objections the Governor was bent upon securing fair, proportional representation of all recognized religions in the country, and went ahead with his plans to appoint a Muslim.[170]

This implied a change in the religious composition of the saza chieftainships; but we must ask whether this move represented a genuine change in policy, or was no more than a token gesture, a demonstration of the Governor's accumulated annoyance with the whole Buganda situation.[171] The revised policy aimed to improve the situation of the Muslims, and to cut the Protestant leaders down to size. These aims might well prove counter-productive in the end, as they failed to transcend the existing framework of religious factionalism. Moreover, the objections voiced within the colonial administration itself and outlined above indicated some opposition within official circles to the new policy, which might work against its implementation in the future.

To this last point should be added yet another factor which was important in the policy-making process. So far virtually nothing had been heard from the CMS mission itself in connection with the appointment of chiefs; so we may assume that the Ganda Protestant leaders had so far been able to handle their own affairs. But when the Protestants were actually deprived of a saza the missionary leaders decided that the time had come to take the matter to the Colonial Secretary. The issue was not discussed in detail, but, in the interview between Bishop Tucker, Bishop Willis and the Colonial Secretary, the bishops made the general claim that the Ugandan government had compelled the Lukiko to elect Muslim and Catholic chiefs where the Lukiko wished to elect Protestants, even though there was a Protestant majority in the Lukiko.[172] But the intervention was in vain: the

Colonial Office left the matter to the discretion of the Governor.[173] The initiative probably served, however, as a reminder of the mission's presence and of its continued interest in the Ganda political scene, and of its readiness to intervene directly whenever its tacit support of the Protestant chiefs no longer seemed sufficient.

It is therefore of special interest to consider the first case where the new policy was put to the test. Towards the end of 1916 the saza chieftainship of Bugangazi again fell vacant. The post had always been held by a Catholic, but the Lukiko now suggested that both a Catholic and a Protestant should be candidates. The Provincial Commissioner recommended that the best man should be appointed irrespective of religion. It so happened that the Protestant candidate was the only Ganda agent left in Toro, and this placed him in a difficult position.[174] He was, therefore, appointed Kiimba of Bugangazi, and the event was hailed in the annual report as a significant deviation from former practice. Religion had been kept out of the matter, the appointment showed 'a forward step in the development of native administration'.[175] The new policy seemed to have been a success, but we must qualify this conclusion somewhat, inasmuch as his appointment solved an acute administrative problem, the extent of which is clear from a letter from the Omukama of Toro thanking the government for the removal of a great burden.[176]

Only a year later the repercussions of this appointment and of the new policy in general became apparent. When the important post of Kago (saza chief) of the large saza of Kyadondo fell vacant,[177] the Catholic Omulamuzi, Mugwanya, refused to sign the list of nominees, in the first place because he now felt that it was time for a Catholic to be promoted to a saza which had hitherto belonged to the Protestants; and secondly because the Kiimba of Bugangazi, who had been appointed to that post only the year before, was among the nominees.[178] Both reasons weighed so much more heavily on Mugwanya as he had been accused by his own party of having 'sold out' over Bugangazi.[179] It did not help much that the Provincial Commissioner tried to explain the government's policy of eliminating the religious element from appointments. In the eyes of the Baganda, appointments to chieftainships were still religious party issues. While this reaction surprised the colonial administration, in view of the expectations raised by the case of Bugangazi, it should not have proved an insurmountable obstacle to the implementation of the new policy. But after considering objections already raised in connection with the saza of Kabula, the Provincial Commissioner himself backed down:

[With regard to] the larger and more important Sazas as Kyadondo, I do not consider it advisable to push this policy with undue haste, and, in the present instance, I consider that it would be unwise to appoint a Roman Catholic Chief to Kyadondo when there is a Protestant candidate available who is equally suitable.[180]

Accordingly the Kiimba was transferred to Kyadondo and was replaced in Bugangazi by a Catholic. The return of Bugangazi to the Catholic party left the new policy in disarray. Mugwanya, probably unwittingly, made matters worse by writing a letter of thanks which cast the whole situation in an ironic light. On behalf of the Catholic community and the Catholic saza chiefs he expressed great satisfaction at the decision to give Bugangazi back to the Catholics and to allow things to remain as they had been before. Recalling past history, the letter emphasized how excellent the system of religious allocation had been for the welfare of Buganda.[181] Mugwanya finally made it perfectly clear that he saw appointments to political offices in purely denominational terms by enumerating the grievances which the Catholics had accumulated against the Protestants over the years.

Some colonial officials thought that Mugwanya's letter was 'distinctly disloyal in character' and represented an outburst of the old spirit of religious animosity.[182] They also assumed that the missions were the driving force behind this spirit, and that this made it all the more urgent to impress once more upon the people the guiding principle in the government's policy: that appointments could not be made on the basis of religion,[183] and 'that education, ability and integrity are the sole determining factors'.[184] This was a restatement of a policy whose credibility had been dealt a fatal blow by recent events. The Acting Governor apparently felt that such an attitude from the government would seem hypocritical. He therefore took the opportunity to formulate what he considered to be a realistic policy.

The policy which, I consider, should be followed is that of maintaining in so far as possible the existing balance between the two religions – Protestant and Roman – as there is little doubt that promises were made in the past by the various Governors and Administrators that this would be done . . . Religious animosity in Buganda is dormant, but it is always there and requires to be very tactfully handled. It cannot be ignored, hence, whilst I am in sympathy with the Provincial Commissioner's desire that only the best men should be selected, I am of opinion that, in making such selections, the balance of power should be maintained in so far as circumstances allow.[185]

This was in fact a full recognition of the old religious basis for the allocation of offices and signalled a return to the policy of maintaining the balance between the main parties. Whether the revision of policy was related to the departure of Governor Jackson, in whose period the change was made, is difficult to say. In any case his governorship came to be regarded as a parenthesis, as far as attempts to eliminate the religious factor from Buganda politics were concerned. Developments over the following years confirmed this assessment.

The Acting Governor's statement, outlining the return to previous policy, was not communicated to Mugwanya. He was only told in vague terms that the government would take all circumstances into consideration when making appointments, and that the Governor reserved the right to select from among the nominees the one most suitable for the post.[186] This could hardly have been very reassuring, and Mugwanya remained on guard, in view of his earlier experiences in the case of Bugangazi. When the saza chieftainship of Busuju fell vacant soon afterwards, he again refused to sign the list of nominees because it included Protestants, and Busuju was an established Catholic saza.[187] In this case his own candidate was appointed, although there were the usual reassurances that the criterion employed had been the selection of the best man, irrespective of his religion.[188] The next time he voiced the Catholic grievances and expressed his fear that the Protestant majority in the Lukiko were trying to reduce the number of Catholic sazas,[189] the Kabaka repeated the government policy to him: that religion, in accordance with clause 11 of the Uganda Agreement, was irrelevant.[190] It now dawned on the Acting Governor that neither the Provincial Commissioner nor the Kabaka and his ministers had understood the recent change in government policy. He therefore made it quite clear that the guiding principle was the preservation of the existing balance between Protestants and

Catholics, as it had been outlined in 1918. If developments in recent years had skewed the balance, steps should be taken to readjust it. Finally, he admitted openly what was an inevitable consequence of such a policy of balance: 'The above policy [reaffirms?] that in some cases the very best man for the post may not be chosen.'[191] The main emphasis thus had to be on religious affiliation if the existing balance was to be maintained, and any deficit in the proportion of Catholics would be due solely to the fact that they lacked suitable candidates. Hence, it would be up to them to train such candidates for chiefly posts. The Provincial Commissioner could only add that at the saza level the Catholics had the same eight chieftainships as they had had in 1900, and that no Protestant was likely to be appointed to a recognized Catholic saza, except in exceptional circumstances, as in Bugangazi in 1916.[192]

Before Mugwanya received these assurances from the government he described the Catholic position in even more pessimistic terms. As victims of Protestant domination they were in danger of losing all their chiefly posts. They were treated in general as outcasts, and there was even a rumour circulating that a person who professed Catholicism could never be 'a great chief'.[193] While it was easy enough for the government to repudiate the anxiety and suspicion of the Catholic community, it was in a serious dilemma when it came to making a public statement of policy. It was all very well to say within government circles that the main aim of the policy was to maintain the balance between the two parties. But as this was a plain admission that the government selected chiefs according to religious criteria the administration was extremely reluctant to make an official statement.[194] Instead, the government repeated once more in an answer to Mugwanya that vacancies were filled by candidates with the best qualifications irrespective of their religion. Immediately afterwards this overall aim was substantially qualified when it was added that the Governor wished as far as possible to maintain the balance between Catholics and Protestants required by Clause 11 in the Uganda Agreement.[195]

Not surprisingly, Mugwanya was still unable to grasp the meaning of the government's statement of policy, as the official version clearly contained two incompatible elements (although both of them appeared in the same clause in the Agreement). Mugwanya was on the defensive once again in connection with a new appointment in the Sese Islands, and asked for a confirmation of the policy of balance.[196] Finally he obtained a clear assurance from the government; but now the two Protestant ministers, with the support of the Kabaka, asked scornfully, with reference to Clause 11, if it was proper to require information about the religious beliefs of candidates, as this could only introduce religious elements into the selection procedure.[197] The government was once more placed in an impossible situation, but it confined itself to repeating the two incompatible aims described above.[198] In spite of all the government's attempts over the following years to play down the religious factor,[199] the religion of every candidate for both saza and gombolola chieftainships was recorded from 1921 to 1924, and the religious affiliation of each post was fully respected: Catholics succeeded Catholics, and Protestants Protestants.[200]

Thus the government shelved all its attempts to eliminate the religious factor in appointments to offices. The consistency with which they did so will be evident when we consider the fate of another ambition, the achievement of proportional representation for the Muslims. The Muslim community had had little to say over the years, but in 1923 its leaders made certain quite specific demands.[201] They were fully aware that chieftainships were allotted on religious grounds, and that the various sazas had been divided between the three religions so as to preclude Protestants from obtaining offices in Catholic sazas and vice versa. They also knew that Muslims could not hold office in sazas dominated by the other two religions. But the Muslims were at a further disadvantage in this respect, as Christians held office in the two Muslim sazas. Accordingly they asked 'whether arrangements will be made to take away all Non-Moslem Gombolola Chiefs from our two counties so that we may fairly follow the suit of our friends.'[202]

The Muslim leaders were in other words asking for equal treatment from the government. They further pointed out that a number of Muslims had now learned to read and write in English, which dispensed with the handicap alluded to earlier by colonial officers. At first the government asked for time to give the matter further consideration.[203] When requested not to delay the matter any longer,[204] the Governor refused the Muslim request, saying that too many years had elapsed to justify any attempt to reallocate offices to the various denominations; besides, these issues were left so much in the hands of the Kabaka and the Lukiko that the government had no authority to interfere with the present distribution of saza chieftainships.[205] This statement may be taken as an authoritative confirmation of the government's policy on the allocation of chieftaincies. The aim was to preserve the status quo; the basis of the policy had been laid down during the 1890s and confirmed by the Uganda Agreement in 1900. Except for the transfer of the saza of Kabula to the Muslims in 1913, the distribution of the sazas remained exactly the same as that approved by Sir Harry Johnston. This meant that the composition of the Lukiko was also virtually the same. At one stage the government considered securing a higher degree of proportional representation for the Muslims through positive discrimination, but these deliberations were completely forgotten when the Muslims themselves took the initiative.

This leads to the inevitable conclusion that government policy was conducted almost exclusively within denominational guidelines aimed at preserving the balance between the two Christian parties. In this respect the policy certainly had a Christian bias: for all practical purposes the chieftainship was considered essentially a Christian institution. Within this framework there was again a Protestant bias, as the settlement of 1900 had ensured Protestant dominance despite the fact that the Protestants, according to the government's own census list, were fewer in number than the Catholics.[206]

The government's acceptance of the 1900 settlement and its continued efforts to preserve the balance between the two Christian parties help to explain the almost passive role played by the two missions. Except for one particular occasion (pp. 328–9), there was no need for the mission to intervene directly in public. Their apparent inactivity can be further explained by the fact that the African leaders were firmly committed to the status quo, and fully capable of serving their own interests, which were identical with those of the missions. The Catholic Regent and Omuwanika, Mugwanya, was particularly active in defending the Catholic position against encroachment from the Protestants, in spite of the latter's near-monopoly of the Ganda political apparatus.

It remains to be established whether the policy pursued in Buganda was more or less forced upon the government by developments and special circumstances such as the terms of the Uganda Agreement. This question can best be answered by comparing Buganda with other parts of the Protectorate, where circumstances were different in many ways, and the government had a freer hand to develop its policies. We must also examine whether the missions, in areas where they arrived later than, or at least simultaneously with, the government, played a different and more active role.

Toro

Although the Toro Agreement of 1900 was neither as extensive nor as detailed as the Uganda one we have seen that there developed a Buganda-like situation in Toro none the less. All the chieftainships were filled by Christians, and the Protestants were even more predominant than in Buganda.[207] Christian rivalry had been particularly fierce in Toro, and the Catholics were full of grievances about their inferior position. The Protestant stranglehold on the political structure and the CMS mission's great influence were particularly in evidence on the occasion of the revision of the Toro Agreement in 1906 and the Coronation of the Omukama Kasagama in 1908. The key issue in Toro over the following two decades was therefore the possibility of improving the Catholic position.

The first initiative came from the Governor, and developed into a discussion among colonial officials of the fitness of the Catholics to hold office. When one of the leading Protestant chiefs had to be replaced the Governor stated that he did not find the Catholics sufficiently represented in Toro.[208] While admitting that the Protestants were over-represented in the Rukurato (Lukiko), the District Officer maintained that there simply were no sufficiently qualified Catholics available. The admission of more into the Rukurato at that juncture would inevitably make for more inefficiency among the chiefs. The backwardness of the Catholics was explained by the fact that they had earlier been grossly neglected by the Omukama so that the most able of them had joined the ranks of the Protestants.[209]

The Catholics' inferior position was thus claimed to be due to a kind of 'bandwagon effect' caused by Kasagama's partisan policies. The Deputy Commissioner also pointed out the inherent deficiency in the Catholic system as it functioned in the Uganda Protectorate. If so few able Catholic chiefs were forthcoming – and Mugwanya was in fact almost the only exception – the explanation was to be found in the strict obedience required of Catholics by their missionary leaders. Such a system either produced puppets unable to act on their own or simply kept people away. 'It would seem, in short, that capable men do not accept the servile position expected of them by the Catholic leaders.'[210]

In view of these strong ties of obedience to 'white sectarian leadership', there was some risk involved in appointing Catholics rather than people who came out of the Protestant system. The former would continue to be guided by the missionaries, which meant that 'that party gains an advantage by white leadership which directs policy on sectarian lines'.[211] The argument was that proportional representation for the Catholics would increase sectarian strife rather than reduce it. Whether this was justified or not, it is evidence of the rather negative view of the Catholics held by some colonial officials, compared to their positive view of the Protestants. It was in effect casting doubt upon the Catholics' fitness to hold office at all. Besides the opposition from the Protestant party, the Catholics thus had a barrier to overcome within the colonial administration itself. Although the Governor in this case repeated that the Catholics in Toro had not been given a fair chance, and that it was undesirable that all power should be in the hands of the Protestant faction, nothing happened at the local level.[212]

Yet another move from the Protestant leadership put the Catholic community at a disadvantage, although it was meant in the first instance to strengthen the Christian position in general. With the full approval of the Omukama, the Toro Rukurato approved the rule that persons who could not read or write could not become chiefs.[213] Although the Governor acknowledged that it would be a good thing if all chiefs could read and write, he found the rule too harsh, as it might exclude a number of able people, especially Muslims, in favour of Christians who had been taught by the missions. But the emphasis on literacy and education would also give the Protestants an advantage over the Catholics as the educational system founded by the CMS mission had from the outset aimed at training chiefs and sons of chiefs.[214] The application of such a criterion would once again make the Protestants appear as the most efficient and best qualified party. Although this conclusion was not explicitly drawn at the time, the colonial administration was well aware that the Omukama and his leading chiefs were much inclined to favour people of their own creed at the expense of those of others on this pretext.[215]

However much the colonial administration regretted the inferior position of the Catholics in Toro, nothing was done to ameliorate it. The situation was so distressing to the Catholics that their Bishop, John Forbes, requested the government to ensure that Kasagama followed the 'British Fair Play policy'. When there were vacancies, he claimed, the Protestant saza chiefs in the Rukurato always nominated people of their own creed and barred Catholic candidates. Although there were considerably more Catholics than Protestants in Toro, the Protestants had more than four times as many chieftainships.[216] When the local administration looked into the matter in order to check the figures, the Bishop's claim was seen to be fully justified. Table 6 shows the distribution of chieftainships among the various religions in Toro in 1920.

Table 6.   Religious distribution of chieftainships in Toro, 1920

	Protestant	Catholic	Muslim	Traditionalist
Chieftainships	47	10	0	2

Note: The table comprises saza and gombolola chiefs in 10 sazas. Only one or two saza chiefs were Catholics. The list of chiefs in Toro District is enclosed in PC Western Province to Chief Secretary, 20 July 1920, SMP 330; see also Report of Toro Deanery to the Synod 1919, in Bishop's Files: Synods. Except for some slight variation in the number of chieftainships the religious distribution of offices given here remained stable during the following decades; see the sample from the late 1950s in E. A. Richards (1960), p. 143; and see also K. Lockard (1974), p. 77.

No immediate initiative was taken to improve the Catholic position, and the Protestants were left in full control of the political and administrative system in Toro. No real agreement had been drawn up here, as it had in Buganda, on the religious allocation of offices, so the colonial administration had less opportunity for control. It was therefore only natural that the Catholics not only fought to maintain their existing position, but that the Catholic Bishop tried to obtain a more reasonable share of offices for the Catholics; but he was not very successful.[217] One reason for this failure was possibly the fact that the administration in Toro put greater emphasis than the Buganda one on the candidates' educational background, and this favoured the Protestants.

Bunyoro

The situation in Bunyoro differed substantially from that in Toro, because of the many years of warfare in the latter part of the 1890s between the Omukama Kabarega and the combined British/Buganda forces.[218] When peace was finally restored at the turn of the century with the latter group victorious, there remained the task of making Bunyoro function again. This meant that the government exercised much stricter control in Bunyoro than in any of the other Kingdoms. One example has already been mentioned: the forced retirement of the young Omukama and the installation of a successor. The government employed, as it invariably did, the Buganda model, when it restored the Bunyoro institutions; a number of sazas were created and chiefs appointed by British officials, some of them Baganda. Naturally, the people appointed were mainly Christians who had remained loyal to the British during the upheavals, and who had, thanks to the pioneer missionary work, acquired some education. Because of the CMS mission's early interest in the Omukama and the leading chiefs, the majority of chieftainships were held by Protestants.[219] Furthermore, the local representative of the CMS mission was firmly bent on maintaining the Protestant hegemony, so the missionary education system was primarily geared to the training of future leaders in both state and church.[220]

Both these factors were evident when the Deputy Commissioner, George Wilson, reorganized the whole saza system in 1905 and replaced a number of chiefs.[221] During the reshuffle the leading CMS missionary was taken into full confidence and his advice on the selection of chiefs was taken. The CMS mission was left with the clear impression that 'Mr Wilson has done his very best to help us'.[222] Of the six sazas created the Protestants took four, the Catholics one, and one was given to a Traditionalist chief. In addition the majority of the minor chiefs (the Myukas) were Protestants, and sometimes constituted a kind of safeguard in sazas not held by Protestant saza chiefs.[223] Nevertheless the Bishop supported one missionary in Bunyoro who complained that his district now fell under the Catholic saza.[224] The complaint was sent to the government, but it evoked no response. However, the fact that it was sent illustrates the great interest the CMS took in the religious affiliation of the chiefs. It also gives us a hint of the strength of the mission in a pioneer district and its readiness to intervene when necessary.

After the agitation against the Ganda agents in 1907 and the deportation of a number of chiefs, another round of appointments to the chieftainships became necessary.[225] This strengthened the Protestant position, as they obtained all six saza chieftainships, which meant that almost all the members of the Rukurato (Lukiko) were Protestants.[226] If we include the recognized minor chiefs (the Myukas) the results of the reorganization can be presented in Table 7, which was drawn up by the local administration on the basis of information provided by the Omukama. The figures were provided at the request of the Governor, who wanted to know the number of Catholic chiefs, significantly enough at the same time as he was expressing dissatisfaction with the low number of Catholic chiefs in Toro.[227] The Deputy Commissioner recommended that the information be obtained discreetly

Table 7:   Religious distribution of chieftainships in Bunyoro, 1908

	Protestant	Catholic	Muslim	Traditionalist
Chieftainships	83	25	6	41

Note: The figures are from Collector, Hoima, to Deputy Commissioner, 11 February 1908, SMP Conf. 7/1908. At that time there were apparently only two categories of chiefs: saza chiefs and myukas; see Fisher to Baylis, 12 July 1907 (n. 226). The last column is headed 'professing no religion' in the letter.

so as not to stir up religious feelings. He also hoped that the figures were for the personal use of the Governor, and that they were 'not likely for the present to be made the basis of any marked administrative action'.[228] In this respect his hopes were confirmed, as no initiative was taken to achieve better proportional representation for the Catholics. We may thus conclude that, although the government had a closer grip on political institutions in Bunyoro than in Toro, denominational strife was as prevalent in Bunyoro as elsewhere. Offices were filled on the basis of religious adherence and were conceived of in denominational terms; and Protestant control of the political apparatus was firmly established.

The process of inertia which was operative in Bunyoro was confirmed in 1915, when it was noticed in the provincial administration's annual report that, while most of the chiefs were Protestants, the Catholic White Fathers did good work 'especially among the peasants'.[229] There was thus a prejudicial factor in the colonial officials' conception of the White Fathers' work which made it difficult for the Catholics to qualify for chieftainships. It is therefore not surprising that Bishop John Forbes asked the Governor in 1919, just as he had done before in Toro, to put pressure on the Omukama to give the Catholics fairer treatment. All the saza chiefs were Protestants and only 7 of the 42 gombolola chiefs were Catholics, although there were just as many Catholics as Protestants among the population.[230] The government answered that its principal aim, here as in Buganda, was to reduce 'undue sectional influences', and to select the best man in each case, regardless of his religion;[231] however, steps would be taken to improve the Catholic position at the gombolola level.[232] In practice these two aims were incompatible. The best man would in most cases be a Protestant, as the Catholic candidates were seldom sufficiently qualified.[233] In other words, in the eyes of most officials, the educational system established by the CMS mission was better suited to training people for public office than the Catholic one. In spite of the government's recognition of the Catholics' under-representation, their position was therefore not likely to be much improved.

The educational handicap was not the only hindrance to the fulfilment of the promise made to Bishop Forbes. The inertia of the Bunyoro political system and the appointment procedure established over the years also played their part. In the event the improvement of the Catholic position at the gombolola level was very limited, as Table 8 shows.

The biggest change came in 1920, when the Catholics finally obtained one of the six saza chieftainships, although they lost one gombolola chieftainship at the same time.[234] In spite of all its claims to the contrary, the government could not

Table 8. Changes in the religious distribution of gombolola chiefs in Bunyoro, 1919

	Previous Holders	New Holders	Difference
Protestant	30	26	−4
Catholic	7	8	+1
Muslim	2	3	+1
Traditionalist	1	1	
Total	40	38	

Note: The figures are from Ag. Chief Secretary to Bishop Forbes, 1 November 1919, min. 269, SMP 1251. The term 'pagan' was used for Traditionalist.

improve the Catholic situation without relating appointments to denominational background. The lack of consistency in government policy was apparent when one of the White Fathers later asked the Governor publicly in the Rukurato to instruct the Omukama and his leading chiefs to appoint Catholics as well as Protestants. Faced with this public request, the Governor had to disclaim the use of religious criteria in appointments and claim religious neutrality: the best man was selected regardless of religious persuasion.[235] But the Governor failed to understand that this statement of principle was of little practical value to the Catholics. It would not alter the Protestants' established position or diminish their political and educational advantages.[236] The denominational grouping therefore remained the decisive political structure in Bunyoro,[237] and the Protestant party retained its powerful position, mainly because of its control of the political apparatus.[238]

Ankole

The pattern seen in the two other Western Kingdoms repeated itself in the last interlacustrine Kingdom to be discussed, Ankole. The CMS mission concentrated on the Omugabe (King) and his leading chiefs, and won them for the Protestant cause.[239] The benefits of this access to the centre of power became evident when the Ankole chiefs protested against the establishment of a Catholic mission in 1901 and succeeded in delaying its arrival for almost a year (pp. 109–10).[240] They were clearly afraid that Catholicism might become a rallying-point for opposition. The lessons of Buganda and Toro had not been lost upon them. If denominational differences became acute in Ankole, this must be ascribed to the peculiar socio-political structure of the Kingdom. The Banyankore consisted of two easily identifiable groups which have been variously labelled as 'classes' or 'ethnic groups'. There were the mainly pastoralist Bahima, who constituted the ruling élite, and the Bairu, who were mostly agriculturalists and were excluded from direct political involvement.[241] There was a similar stratification in Toro and Bunyoro, but it never achieved the vast political significance which it had in Ankole.[242]

Inevitably, the activities of the two missions tended to stabilize and even

Table 9.   Religious distribution of chieftainships in Ankole, 1920

Chieftainships	Protestant	Catholic	Muslim	Traditionalist
Saza	10	0	1	0
Gombolola	71	6	13	6

Note: The figures appear in a minute from the Ag. Governor, dated 21 May 1920; see Bishop John Forbes to Governor Coryndon, 18 September 1920, both in SMP 2071. One saza chieftainship was vacant at the time.

reinforce the existing differences between the two groups. The Protestants concentrated on the ruling élite and strengthened its political hegemony. The Catholics gained ground primarily among the Bairu; later the CMS mission also made considerable progress with the Bairu. This might have been expected to promote some 'unity of interests' between the Bahima élite and the Protestant Bairu;[243] yet during the first decades of the twentieth century religion was not the most important stratifying factor at work in Ankole. Religious factionalism had to contend with an already existing stratification in society based on occupation, status and ethnicity. This may explain why little was heard of religious reallocation of offices after colonial rule had first been imposed. In spite of the Catholic Bairu's many grievances against the Bahima élite, the problem was not interpreted in religious terms. The Bahima dominance could best be explained in historical terms within the socio-political structure of Ankole.[244]

Hence it was only after the controversies over the religious affiliation of chiefs in the neighbouring Kingdoms in 1919–20 that the issue was raised in Ankole. A list (Table 9) was then produced and shows clearly the Protestant supremacy in Ankole. The Catholics, despite their majority among the population, were thus placed in a minority position, even compared with the Muslims, and on an equal footing with the group which still professed the traditional religion. It was against this background that Bishop John Forbes again intervened and stated the Catholic grievances. Having learned from his experiences in Toro and Bunyoro, Forbes made it clear that this time it was not sufficient for the government to answer that it was interested in efficiency and character irrespective of creed. The problem was the attitude of the Omugabe and the Lukiko, who deliberately excluded Catholics.[245] In his answer the Provincial Commissioner said once more that the issue should not be seen primarily in terms of religious categories:

The question of the bias of the Omugabe and the Lukiko is well known and is carefully watched and controlled, but I think this is not so much because he and his leading chiefs are keen pillars of the Church but that they favour men who are Bahima and of their own class.[246]

Again the government was presented with a dilemma. On the one hand it had to demonstrate that chieftainships were open to all groups of Banyankore and to all religions. It did so on two occasions. First a Catholic Muiru was appointed to a saza chieftainship, and later a Muslim Muganda was reappointed to a similar post.[247] On the other hand these criteria could not be allowed to retard the progress of the country by allowing the selection of chiefs who were unsuitable and had no influence in the Kingdom. The government was aware that for administrative reasons priority in appointments had to be given to people who could act with sufficient authority by drawing upon traditional allegiances. This meant favouring the ruling Bahima class, who also happened to be Protestants.[248] The Ankole chiefs themselves were also quick to use the government's dilemma for their own ends: they reminded the Provincial Commissioner that in Ankole, unlike Buganda, there was no agreement allocating sazas to particular religions.[249] The Ankole situation thus differed from that in Buganda and the other two Western Kingdoms in the sense that it was very difficult to pin down the significance of the religious factor. It was confused too much with the ethnic stratification and the traditional system of authority and legitimacy. There was no question of maintaining a balance as in Buganda, nor was it possible to improve the Catholic position by simply neutralizing the Protestant educational prerogative. The Protestant stranglehold on power reflected the traditional pattern of authority, which the government had its own reasons for wishing to preserve. Therefore there were only minor changes during the following years.[250] Later, when educational qualifications counted for more, and colonial officials considered the Bairu eligible for the chiefly ranks, they were still only admitted at the lower levels. But even then it was the Protestants among the Bairu who were the main beneficiaries, as they were considered to be best educated and consequently best suited to the posts.[251] Hence in Ankole educational, ethnic and political criteria all underpinned the Protestant hegemony and constituted an almost insurmountable barrier to Catholic advancement.

The Eastern Province

Although the Eastern Province was anything but homogenous as regards traditional social and political structures, one common feature was the absence of centralized political systems in the various districts which comprised this Province during most of the period under survey: Busoga, Bukedi, Teso and Lango.[252] In this respect the Eastern Province differed greatly from the four interlacustrine Kingdoms. Initially one might think that the colonial government would stand a better chance of neutralizing the religious factor in these areas with no central authority, because of its greater freedom to build up a suitable administrative apparatus. A brief survey will help us to examine whether the distinction between centralized political systems and the so-called 'stateless' or 'acephalous' societies helped the government to avoid the political consequences of denominational rivalry which had created so many problems in the interlacustrine Kingdoms.[253]

Busoga was divided into a number of small independent Kingdoms, some of them in a tributary relationship to Buganda.[254] When the CMS began working in this area, they naturally concentrated on the ruling families. As the older chiefs were reluctant to join the church, the mission concentrated instead on their sons and made earlier and more thorough use of the educational method than in most other districts.[255] The sons of chiefs and future rulers were taken, with the full approval of the government, to Buganda to be educated.[256] During their minority the offices were in many cases filled with Protestant Ganda agents.[257] As the CMS started earlier than the Mill Hill Mission, they gained the lead and succeeded in associating Protestantism with power and chieftainship. The Protestant lead was reinforced by the activities of the Ganda agents and both together accounted for

Table 10.   Religious distribution of chieftainships in Busoga, 1920

	Protestant	Catholic	Muslim	Traditionalist
Chieftainships	45	4	4	1

Note: The list is from PC Eastern Province to Chief Secretary, 1 May 1920, min. 313, SMP 2070. It comprises people at the saza and gombolola levels. Dan Mudoola has worked out a table showing the religion of gombolola chiefs 1910–40, and his result is in full correspondence with the figures reproduced here (Mudoola (1978), p. 26).

the widespread conviction that only Protestants were eligible for chieftaincies.[258] When the sons then returned and took up office their hereditary claim to the posts cemented the Protestant hegemony.[259] For these reasons the Catholics stood a very slim chance of obtaining any of the leading chieftaships. When the Mill Hill Mission attempted to do so in 1913, on the occasion of the early death of one of the young rulers, they were unsuccessful, although they had a well qualified candidate, and despite their appeal to the government's religious impartiality.[260] The government preferred a candidate with a hereditary claim, the three-year-old Protestant son of the deceased chief.[261] Hence the Catholics obtained no more than a few minor posts. In 1920 the government, asked for a survey by a Catholic missionary, obtained figures (Table 10) showing the religious affiliation of office-holders.[262] In spite of these figures no attempt was made to improve the Catholic position, nor were any changes introduced over the following decades.[263] The pattern so firmly established at the beginning of the century and reinforced by the traditional legitimization of office-holders within the small Busoga units proved too strong for government attempts to introduce a more reasonable allocation of offices.[264]

The situation may seem quite different when we consider the other districts of the Eastern Province. These areas had no traditional chiefs who could be used as a basis for administrative structure on the Buganda model,[265] although it was possible in these so-called segmentary societies to identify figures with traditional claims to leadership. But the CMS' usual method of concentrating on the chiefly families was not particularly suitable here. Nevertheless the pattern from Busoga repeated itself in the neighbouring districts thanks to the Ganda agents and the employment of the educational method.

The local administration was built up on the Ganda model by dividing the districts into sazas and putting Ganda agents in charge. These were in most cases Protestants, and they transplanted the Buganda political structure with its built-in Protestant supremacy to these districts.[266] The presence of the Ganda agents gave the CMS mission a strong advantage over the Catholics. This position was then utilized to found an educational system especially geared to the training of a group of youngsters, whether they were sons of traditional leaders or had been selected according to other criteria, to take over from the Ganda agents in due time.[267] The transfer of power was therefore very gradual in these areas,[268] but the Protestantism of the Ganda agents and the CMS lead in education meant that the Protestant ascendancy was unaffected by the change in personnel.[269] When the government surveyed the religious allegiance of the chiefs in Bukedi, Teso and Lango in 1920 the results were as shown in Table 11.

Table 11.   Religious allegiance of gazetted chiefs in Bukedi, Teso and Lango, 1920

	Protestant	Catholic	Muslim	Malakite	Traditionalist
Bukedi	11 (+ 2 unbaptized)	6	19	2	38
Teso	35	2	1	4	9
Lango	8	0	0	0	45

Note: The table comprises all gazetted chiefs and no distinction is made between saza chiefs and other categories. On the Malakite (Bamalaki) Movement, which had seceded from the Anglican Church in Buganda in 1914 and had since spread to other parts of the Protectorate, see below, Chapter 25. The material for the table may be found in PC Eastern Province, Eden, to Chief Secretary, 1 May and 12 June 1920, min. 313 and 321, SMP 2070.

The process was most marked in Teso, while the high number of Traditionalist chiefs in Bukedi and Lango shows that the availability of Protestant candidates was somewhat limited. The picture was soon to change in Bukedi, however, as samples from 1921 and 1923 show that the number of Muslim and Traditionalist chiefs declined rapidly.[270] But the number of Catholic chiefs seems to have remained almost static over the years,[271] while the Protestant ascendancy continued to increase.[272]

In spite of the segmentary societal structures and the lack of the stabilizing hereditary claims to office, the influence of the Ganda agents and of education proved just as effective in Bukedi, Teso and Lango as in Busoga, although the process was slower in Bukedi. In these areas there was apparently little direct missionary intervention, so the colonial administration could claim that the people they had selected were simply the best qualified, and that the fact that they were Protestants was irrelevant. But there can be no doubt that the CMS mission deliberately aimed from the outset at placing itself in a position where its candidates for public office were the natural and only possible choice.[273] So the religious factor was still introduced, and appointments came to be seen by the people involved as denominationally conditioned.[274]

Conclusions on the Christianization of chieftainships

This survey of the chiefly institution does not pretend to cover all of Uganda or all aspects of the problem. But on the basis of what we have we may draw two conclusions. First of all, the chiefly institution had become a predominantly Christian one, in the sense that the absolute majority of offices at all levels were held by Christians. In Buganda, and to some extent in Toro, this meant the continuation of the situation that had developed in the 1890s; in the other two Kingdoms, and to a great extent in Busoga, Christian candidates were given preference, as they were considered the people best qualified to fill both the hereditary and the newly-created offices. Finally, in the Eastern Province, where the colonial system was established mainly with the help of Christian Ganda agents, there was a tendency to favour Christian candidates as the local administration was gradually 'indigenized'. The first conclusion is qualified by the second. The Christianization of the chiefly institution would be more accurately described as its Protestantization, in the sense that Protestant chiefs were in the overwhelming majority. This was moreover clearly recognized at the time by most of those involved. The chiefly institution was conceived of in all areas in denominational terms, and people acted on this assumption (witness the attempts of Catholic leaders to rectify their minority position). Thus religious and denominational differences became the primary allocational principle in society.

All through the period it was deliberate CMS policy to concentrate on the chiefs, to win them for the Protestant cause and to secure Protestant candidates for the chiefly offices.[275] A characteristic feature from the first two decades of the twentieth century was, however, that neither the mission nor the African church leaders had to make direct efforts to pursue this policy, whereas the Catholic mission made its presence felt by direct intervention on a number of occasions. This absence of Protestant demands, which stands in direct contrast with the Protestant initiatives in connection with the Kabakaship, can be explained partly by the fact that Protestant influence had become so firmly established by 1900 that things could only progress along the lines already laid down. Moreover, the Ganda pattern was almost automatically transplanted to other areas of the Protectorate because of the employment of the Ganda administrative model and the use of Ganda agents.

But several other factors were also at work. The Africans themselves conceived of the denominational differences in partisan terms, and saw it as their aim to preserve and maximize the power of their respective parties. They were fully capable of working towards this end, and the Protestants in particular were very successful; so there was no need for the mission to step in publicly, although government officials harboured some suspicion that missionaries were often 'pulling the strings'. Secondly, the control of the centre of power, manifested by a comfortable majority in the various Lukikos, gave the Protestants a firm base from which to exercise decisive influence on appointments: the initial Protestant lead in local politics created an inertia in various African polities in favour of the Protestant community. The tendency was moreover sometimes strengthened by hereditary claims. Thirdly, the Protestant educational system, introduced soon after the turn of the century, gave the Protestant candidates a definite advantage over the Catholics. It was employed so successfully that government officials took it for granted that Protestants were better qualified than Catholics for chiefly office. In this way the CMS mission indirectly created the conditions for Protestant ascendancy. Fourthly, the administrative preference for the Ganda model and the employment of Ganda agents, not least in the Eastern Province, helped to export the image of a 'natural' Protestant political establishment.

These four factors allowed the CMS mission to stay more or less in the background as regards the chiefly institution, so that it ran no risk of being accused of interference in politics. Finally, the four factors, which functioned in various combinations and with varied importance in each area, tended to even out the substantial differences which had existed beforehand between different parts of the Protectorate. The difference between centralized systems like the Kingdoms and the segmentary societies of the Eastern Province, and the difference in time between the arrival of the government and the missions, had little influence on the picture which gradually emerged of political conflict along denominational lines and Protestant supremacy.

The government's policy should therefore be viewed in the light of the frequent

Catholic requests for more proportional representation. These demands forced the government to decide whether it would accept the denominational partition of society as the major framework for political action or banish the religious factor from politics altogether. The dilemma was first felt strongly in Buganda, but it appeared in all the other districts in turn. When it stated its policy in Buganda, the government felt compelled to emphasize that, in cases of appointment, it selected the best qualified candidate irrespective of religion; but this proved an unattainable ideal, except for a short period when it was put into practice with very limited success. When it came to *Realpolitik* the government drew back from any real confrontation with the two Christian parties. Instead it attempted to maintain the balance between the two parties required by the 1900 Agreement, even though this in some cases meant violating the ideal of selecting the very best man for the job. In its practical policy the colonial administration stuck firmly to this 'balance-of-power' policy. It was even reaffirmed as late as 1932, when the government stated that it still felt that it was necessary to uphold the politico-religious balance in Buganda.[276]

While the government in Buganda excused itself from ignoring the religious factor in appointments by reference to the earlier agreement on religious balance, the same approach was not possible in non-Ganda areas.[277] Here there were no guarantees for the Catholics. If left to work alone, the above-mentioned factors inevitably led to absolute Protestant supremacy, and this is in fact what invariably happened. When Catholic leaders complained, the government had to consider whether it should take positive action to secure reasonable Catholic representation. But this would amount to admitting that the official policy of 'selecting the best man' did not work in practice. The government did take certain steps to improve the Catholic position, but by doing so it tacitly reaffirmed the denominationally based political structure and worked against its own aim of neutralizing the religious factor in appointments.[278] But by confining itself to very limited measures which did not go much beyond token gestures, the government gave the impression of inconsistency and left itself open to the accusation of favouring the Protestants at the expense of the Catholics. Vague references to the lack of qualified Catholics and to the Protestants' educational merits and traditional legitimacy could not satisfy the Catholic community, which was numerically equivalent, if not superior, to the Protestants, and which conceived of politics in denominational terms.

The Protestant hegemony within the chiefly hierarchy was thus left unchallenged by the government. The absence of any direct Protestant pressure on the government was therefore not surprising. This raises the question of whether there was any alliance between the Protestant mission and the colonial administration. While a formal alliance can safely be ruled out, it will be appropriate to ask whether an informal alliance existed, in the sense that CMS missionaries were taken into the government's confidence and their advice frequently accepted in connection with specific appointments. We have seen one such example in Bunyoro in 1905, and other similar examples may emerge from detailed studies of other districts. As in Bunyoro, however, this sort of informal relationship would be more likely in the initial phase of the establishment of the administrative system. Later the government's resentment of missionary interference, as demonstrated on other occasions, would rule out even an informal alliance. So this line of argument does not take us far in explaining the growth of the Protestant ascendancy. In any case the factors discussed above do not need to be supplemented by any 'conspiracy theory'. Taken together with the government's reluctance to sever the connection between religion and politics in the African polities, and its outright lack of initiative, they are sufficient to explain the Protestant success. On the other hand, this does not rule out the possibility that people in general, and Catholics particularly, were left with the impression that the government, while favouring Christian applicants in general for public offices, nourished a special bias towards Protestants and all too willingly accepted their stranglehold on offices in the African polities.

Linkages between the church and the African polities: the Protestant use of African political institutions

Important institutions within the African political system, then, were not only Christianized, but to a large extent Protestantized. In many ways we are therefore justified in saying that Uganda bore many resemblances to a Christian state, although the Christianity of the state had no constitutional expression, nor was it accompanied by the existence of an established church. As the two latter criteria cannot be applied in this context the crucial questions are then: how was the Protestant power within the state used by the mission and the church? What linkages were established between the African political system and the church? This approach should be kept distinct from the more qualitative one which sets out to assess whether it really served the interests of the Christians to have the chiefs and other political dignitaries within their fold, and whether the underlying premise, that clients of a chief would take their lead from him also in matters of religion, was after all correct. In the second case one would have to ask whether the advantages were real or only imaginary, and whether they outweighed the risks and setbacks involved in the close alignment with a particular political system. To answer these questions a different level of analysis would be necessary and we would have to cover a longer span of years beyond the scope of this study.[279]

The Protestant structure had a built-in mechanism for using its domination within the African political system. It was part of the Anglican tradition to have a lay element in the government of the church. From an early stage the CMS mission was fully aware of the special advantages in the Uganda setting of creating a platform for political leaders within the framework of the church. This approach allowed the Protestant church to exploit its advantages over the Catholics in the political sphere, and it served to institutionalize the linkages between the two systems. It has earlier been noticed that the leading members of the Mengo Church Council were identical with the influential Protestant chiefs (Chapters 7, 16). Bishop Tucker expressed the mission's thinking on this issue when he argued for the introduction of a church constitution. He said then that it was necessary to have a platform within the church for prominent laymen,[280] and when the constitution was passed in 1909 Tucker mentioned as one of its main features 'its thoroughly representative character on democratic lines'.[281] By this he meant that in the various Councils there would, besides ex officio members like the clergy, be a substantial group of laymen elected by the communicants. Within the church's elaborate pyramidal structure, with the Synod at the apex, down through the Diocesan Council, the Ruridecanal Councils (from 1915 onwards), the District Councils and, at the bottom, the Parochial Councils, there were a large number of seats to which political leaders could naturally be elected.[282] In addition, various special committees were set up: the Estates Board, the Board of Education, etc. In some cases the lay representatives equalled or even exceeded in number the clergy and other ex officio members. There were thus excellent opportunities for African political leaders to play a prominent role as laymen within the church. We will now examine how far this option was put into practice by the kingship and the chieftainship.

The Kabaka of Buganda was welcomed into the Synod in 1915, soon after his accession, as the first Christian Kabaka. Over the following ten years he was present at every Synod, and on some occasions even played an active role in the proceedings by tabling motions.[283] There was a similar involvement of the rulers in the neighbouring Kingdoms, reaching a peak at the Synod of 1919, which was combined with the inauguration of the new Cathedral. Besides the Kabaka of Buganda, the Omukamas of Toro and Bunyoro, the newly installed President of Busoga and a number of katikiros were present. At the same Synod the participation of the rulers and the Katikiro of Buganda was formalized in the sense that they were thenceforth considered as members of the Synod, although their inclusion meant that the maximum number of members, which had been fixed at 300, was exceeded.[284] On a later occasion they were referred to as 'honorary members'.[285]

The presence of the rulers in the church organization was even more marked at the local level. The Omukama and the leading chiefs were present at some of the meetings of the Toro Church Council,[286] and the importance attached to the Omukama's close connection with the work of the church was emphasized more than once.[287] In Bunyoro the Omukama had been a member of the Church Council since its foundation shortly after 1900.[288] Over the following years the Church Council made use of this linkage by asking the Omukama to use his influence and grant support to certain aspects of the church's work.[289] His positive response emerges clearly from a 1919 report: 'the Mukama is a progressive man and the support and maintenance of the Church is largely due to his inspiring example and advice'.[290] In Ankole the Omugabe had also been an active member of the Church Council since the beginning in 1914, and took part in most of the meetings up until 1920.[291] A contemporary account stated: 'Nothing could exceed the generosity and help received from the King and Katikiro.'[292] From this brief survey it is evident that the efforts to Christianize the centres of power in the African polities created institutionalized links with the church. At the same time it is obvious from the statements quoted that the results justified the effort invested.

Turning to the chiefs, we may apply the same criteria. Although nothing was written into the constitution about chiefly representation in the Church Councils, the leading chiefs were obvious candidates, both in the initial phase when the missionaries hand-picked the Councillors, and later when they were elected. In the case of Bunyoro it was reported that the Church Council consisted in 1905 of three saza chiefs and four minor chiefs.[293] In Toro the leading chiefs took part in the meetings,[294] and the tendency was even stronger in Ankole from 1914 to 1920.[295] In Buganda we have seen that the Mengo Church Council also had the leading chiefs among its members. The situation in Buganda changed, however, with the introduction of the church constitution. The Mengo Church Council was replaced by the new Diocesan Synod, which no longer covered the Kingdom of Buganda as such,[296] and this change had two important implications. First,

Buganda, unlike the other Kingdoms, no longer had its own national body within the church organization. While Church Councils were approved in Toro, Bunyoro and Busoga in 1910, and in Ankole in 1913, Buganda was divided into six Rural Deaneries when these units were introduced in 1915.[297] This helps to explain why Ganda Protestants tended to conceive of the Diocesan Synod as still being a Ganda institution. Likewise there was a tendency in the three other Kingdoms to see the Diocesan Synod as a Ganda-dominated institution, because of its origin and the Ganda majority among the members, itself originally due to the strong Protestant presence in Buganda. Consequently, the Protestant leaders in the three Western Kingdoms tended to attach great importance to their own Church Councils, and tried to work independently of the central church authorities as far as possible. This lack of integration within the organization of the church gives us an angle from which to analyse chiefly representation in bodies at the Diocesan level. The inclusion of all the rulers as members of the Synod has already provided one example of an attempt at integration; and representation at the chiefly level from other areas than Buganda could have an even stronger integrative effect.[298] We will return to the issue of the church's contribution to national integration later (Chapter 19).

According to the church constitution there were two ways in which chiefs could be members of church bodies. They could be elected directly to the Synod by the Anglican community in their area of jurisdiction, and from there to the Diocesan Council (which functioned as a standing committee for the Synod). They could also be selected in their capacity as communicants to the various Advisory Boards, independently of their membership of the Synod. The chiefly presence in the church organization will be measured by examining the membership of each of these bodies in turn.

For the period from 1909, when the constitution for the whole Diocese was passed, until 1924, there exists little source material on the composition of the entire Synod which could provide us with a breakdown of its lay members. We must therefore establish the chiefly presence by more indirect means. One characteristic of the minutes of the Synod is that it was almost always the leading chiefs among the lay representatives who took part in discussions and tabled or seconded motions.[299] In reports from the sessions of the Synod the role of these chiefs was frequently emphasized.[300] At the important 1919 Synod a special welcome was extended to all chiefs coming from outside Buganda, as their presence was taken to indicate the unity of the Diocese.[301] How much importance was attached to the presence of chiefs from all over the country is evident from the fact that applications were sent to the government well in advance of each Synod, requesting permission for the chiefs to be away from their districts while attending the meetings.[302] This also served to underline the church view that the sessions of the Anglican Synod were to be considered as official events. Finally, the official list of members for the 1924 Synod shows that ministers and leading chiefs from all the Kingdoms and Busoga were present.[303] The presence of chiefs in the Synod is thus clearly registrable, but no detailed figures can be given; nor is it possible to establish whether there was any variation in the degree of chiefly representation over the period 1909–24. But the presence of the leading chiefs was taken as proof that the Synod 'could speak with very considerable weight to the country at large'.[304]

Source material on the composition of the Diocesan Council, the executive body of the Synod between sessions, allows a more thorough description of chiefly representation of the highest rank; but it is less informative as regards the lower levels, and it is difficult to say whether lay members below the highest chiefly rank were minor chiefs or lay readers/teachers. Members of the Diocesan Council were elected from and by the Synod. In view of changes in the constitution as regards the number of ex officio members and changes in the electoral rules, the examination of the chiefly presence in the Diocesan Council in the period from 1909 to 1924 must be divided into three parts. In the first period, covering the three sessions from 1909 to 1912, all 24 Councillors were elected from among the Synod's members without regard to lay or clerical status. A breakdown of the Councillors is presented in Table 12.

Table 12.   Members of the Diocesan Council, 1909–12

European Missionaries	African Clergy	Laymen
8	7	9 (8 chiefs, 3 of the highest rank)

Note: Lists of members are given in the Minutes of the Synod in 1909 and 1912, Minute Book, MUL. The membership was remarkably stable over the three years. Only the names of the missionaries changed, in cases of leave or retirement.

Of the three high-ranking chiefs, one was the Katikiro and Regent, Sir Apolo Kagwa; the other two were leading saza chiefs, the Sekibobo and the Kago. The importance of having leading political figures among the members was the subject of discussion when the Diocesan Council was first constituted in 1909. Apolo Kagwa was asked whether he could combine the membership of the Council with his official position in Buganda. The Katikiro himself admitted that it could affect his relationship with the Roman Catholics and the Muslims. In the end, strongly urged by Bishop Tucker, who pointed out the advantage of his presence when important matters relating to the state were discussed, he accepted the seat in the Diocesan Council.[305]

As all the African members of the first Diocesan Council were Baganda, it was not really representative of the whole Diocese.[306] To improve this situation it was decided at the Synod in 1913 that the chairmen of the Church Councils in Bunyoro, Toro, Ankole and Busoga would be made ex officio members. The number of such members was then further increased by the addition of the two Archdeacons and the Secretaries of the five Advisory Boards under the Synod, and the Secretary of the Missionary Committee.[307] As all the secretaries were missionaries, and as the chairmen of the four Church Councils also happened to be missionaries, the European element in the Diocesan Council became quite substantial. Twenty-four members were still elected from the Synod, and in practice twelve laymen and twelve clergymen were appointed. Of the latter, four were missionaries and the other eight were Baganda, although they had some experience of the neighbouring areas (see Table 13). Of the four leading chiefs two, the Katikiro and the Omuwanika, belonged to the Kabaka's ministers and were also Regents until 1914; the other two, the Sekibobo and the Kago, were saza chiefs. At the highest level the membership thus remained fairly stable, and high-level representation was even reinforced; but this level still consisted entirely of Baganda.[308]

Table 13.   Members of the Diocesan Council, 1913–16

European Missionaries	African Clergy	Laymen
12 ex officio 4 elected	8	12 (9 chiefs, 4 of the highest rank)

Source: Minutes of the Synod, July 1913, Minute Book, MUL.

The reorganization of the Diocesan Council in 1913 thus hardly satisfied the demands for better representation of the non-Ganda districts. Growing resentment of the Buganda dominance in the church was expressed by Bunyoro, Toro and Ankole before the 1917 Synod.[309] This resulted in a number of measures granting more independence to the various districts.[310] As an extra concession non-Ganda districts were to be represented by their own people in the Diocesan Council.[311] Subsequently, a rule was made that each Rural Deanery should nominate from among its Synod members two representatives to the Diocesan Council, one of whom must be a layman.[312] Including the twelve ex officio members, the composition of the Diocesan Council in 1917 and 1919 is shown in Table 14.

Table 14.   Members of the Diocesan Council, 1917 and 1919

	European Missionaries	African Clergy	Laymen
1917	12 ex officio 3 elected	7	14 (7 chiefs, one of whom was a saza chief)
1919	12 ex officio 1 elected	10	13 (6 chiefs, one of whom was a saza chief)

Note: The figures for 1917 are based upon lists in the minutes of the Synod, June 1917, and the *Diocesan Gazette*, August 1917. The figures for 1919 are from the *Diocesan Gazette*, October 1919. It is difficult to say anything about the representation of chiefs from the non-Ganda areas, but there were at any rate no leading figures among them.

The change in the electoral procedure made the Diocesan Council more representative of all the districts by removing Ganda clergy and Ganda lay representatives. The Ganda clergy could be replaced by colleagues from the various Deaneries, but it was only in rare cases that lay representatives were elected from the chiefly ranks. This meant that the great majority of the remaining chiefly representatives were Baganda. Two observations should be made concerning this last group. First, the overall number of chiefly members had decreased. This was reflected in the new ratio between ordinary lay representatives and chiefs. While the chiefs constituted 75 per cent or more of the total number of lay representatives before 1917, they constituted 50 per cent or less after 1917 (see Tables).[313] Secondly, a most significant change was that the number of leading chiefs was substantially reduced. For the first time none of the

Kabaka's ministers were members of the Diocesan Council. The one saza chief left in 1919 was the Mukwenda, and although the Kago remained a member, he was only elected as an interim measure by the outlying district of Kavirondo.

The loss of the most influential chiefs was the one effect of the application of the representative principle which was much regretted by the mission.[314] It loosened the ties between the chiefs and the executive body of the church, and could have repercussions on chiefly representation in the Synod itself. It was certainly not the result of deliberate policy on the part of the mission that this happened; nor was it due to any pressure from the government. The change was rather forced upon the mission by the prevailing anti-Ganda feeling which had been so strongly expressed by the three Western Kingdoms before the 1917 Synod. It may be seen as a sacrifice which had to be made for the sake of unity and integration within the church. That the mission's motive cannot have been a desire to dissociate itself and the church from its close identification with Buganda is demonstrated by an analysis of the composition of the Advisory Boards over the corresponding period.

Table 15.   Chiefly membership of the Church Advisory Boards 1909–19

	1909–1912		1917		1919	
	highest rank	lower ranks	highest rank	lower ranks	highest rank	lower ranks
Board of Education	Katikiro Sekibobo Kago	0	Katikiro Sekibobo Kago	0	Katikiro Omuwanika	1
Theological Board	0	0	0	0	Omuwanika	3
Board of Missions	Sekibobo	0	0	2	Sekibobo Mukwenda	1
Estates Board	Sekibobo	2	0	2	Mugema	1
Finance Board	Sekibobo	2	0	3	Mugema	2
Marriage Board	not yet in existence		Katikiro Kago	0	Katikiro Omuwanika Mukwenda	0

Note: For the period 1909–12 information has been gathered from the minutes of the Synods in 1909, 1910 and 1912. For 1917 and 1919 the *Diocesan Gazette* has been consulted, August 1917 and November 1919. At first all matters concerning the economy of the church were handled by the Diocesan Council or the Estates Board. It was only at the Synod in 1912 that a special Finance Board was set up at the suggestion of Bishop Willis (see his 'Policy of the Uganda Mission', 1912, pp. 23 and 32). The Marriage Board appears to have been set up later than 1914, probably in connection with that year's revised Marriage Ordinance. As regards the title-holders, Apolo Kagwa was the Katikiro and Ham Mukasa the Sekibobo all through the period. The Kago, Yakobo Musajalumbwa, became Omuwanika in late 1917. Tefiro Kisosonkole and Nasanaeri Mayanja, the Mugema and Mukwenda respectively in 1919, had earlier been Board members as minor chiefs.

In accordance with the constitution, five – later six – Advisory Boards were created by the Synod, their members to be appointed by the Diocesan Council. Although their primary accountability was to the latter body, normal practice was that their reports were presented to the sessions of the Synod for approval. These Advisory Boards became quite influential, as they tended to function as select committees and as a forum for the preparation of recommendations for final approval. We should add that the members were not necessarily appointed from the Synod, but could be selected on the basis of their expertise or influence. Both these factors made the chiefs obvious candidates for membership, and we must therefore examine how far they were active in these bodies. It is more difficult in the case of the Advisory Boards than in that of the Diocesan Council to perform a comparative analysis in terms of the ratio of chiefs to European missionaries and African clergymen. The number of ex officio members changed constantly over the period under survey. Apart from some general remarks at the end of Table 15 (which covers six Advisory Boards), we will consider chiefly members only.[315]

The first significant thing to be noticed here is that chiefly representation was relatively stable over the years and did not reflect the changes that took place within the Diocesan Council from 1917 onwards. Secondly, a high proportion of the chiefs were of the highest rank: for instance, the two Protestant ministers in the Kabaka's government, the Katikiro and the Omuwanika, were both members of two committees in 1919. There was no decline in this high-level representation after 1917, as there was in the Diocesan Council. On the contrary, the 1919 membership suggests the opposite tendency.[316] Thirdly, all the leading chiefs were recruited from the Ganda political hierarchy; nor did any of the minor chiefs included in the table come from a non-Ganda area. As the Advisory Boards (with one or two exceptions) only had chiefs as lay representatives, and as most of the clerical members also came from Buganda, these committees remained a Ganda stronghold. Although this state of affairs was widely resented, as we have already seen, the resentment did not affect the composition of the Advisory Boards. This serves to underline the profound Ganda bias within the Church of Uganda. The Advisory Boards thus provided a significant platform for chiefly influence, and an opportunity for close contacts between the Church and the African political system, but mainly on Ganda terms.

The scope which the Advisory Boards provided for chiefly influence must be viewed against the background of the presence of European missionaries and African clergy. The Bishop was Chairman of all the Boards, and the Archdeacons, the CMS Secretary and a number of missionaries were all ex officio members, so that European missionaries in most cases were in the majority. The fact that missionaries were secretaries on all committees added to European dominance.[317] As far as the African clergy were concerned, the Advisory Boards could be divided into two groups. In the Theological Board, and even more so in the Board of Missions, the African clergy outnumbered the chiefs. On the other hand, there were no elected African clergymen on the Finance Board or the Marriage Board, while the chiefly members of the Board of Education clearly outnumbered the clerical ones. The case of the Estates Board was less clear-cut: each Rural Deanery elected one representative, but no clergymen were appointed in advance, only chiefs. This breakdown of the composition of the Advisory Boards indicates the areas where the chiefs were considered to be most needed, and where their position and influence could best be utilized.

The analysis of the most influential bodies within the church organization thus shows that there was a significant contingent of chiefs among their members. This was in keeping with the general importance attached to the chiefly office by the mission. In concrete terms it meant that a high degree of personal overlap was achieved between the lay leadership of the church and the decision-makers of the African polities. It should however be added that the overlap was not so extensive that the same person could simultaneously hold the offices of chief and clergyman. In this respect the separation of offices required at the turn of the century remained in force and was not relaxed.[318] On the other hand, the mission attached great political value to the overlap between the church and the African polities in presenting its demands to the colonial government,[319] and its reliance on the chiefs' dual role was indicated when it was confidently stated that '. . . it is well to bear in mind that in Uganda the legislative power is in *Christian* hands'.[320] One example of how this personal overlap was used as an effective political instrument was in the Marriage Board. It appears to have been no accident that this Board was set up in 1913–14 and that it included among its members the two Protestant ministers in the Kabaka's government. It should be recalled that the church was anxious in the latter part of the 1910s to have legislation passed which placed the authority of the state squarely behind Christian, monogamous marriage, and more or less outlawed polygamy (Chapter 16). The setting up of the Marriage Board, with its ministerial membership, is best seen as a further attempt to achieve this aim.

Practical use was made of the chiefly linkages in both the economic and the political spheres. It has been demonstrated that the chiefs were the economic backbone of the work of the church from the 1890s onwards, and that they were essential for the realization of self-support. There was some doubt after the turn of the century of the chiefs' continued usefulness in view of the changes which had taken place in society (p. 84), which, it was assumed, would hasten the decline of the feudal system in Buganda.[321] But reality proved these doubts unfounded, and the economic role of the chiefs continued to be crucial, especially in view of the church's need for funds to pay its growing number of African workers. The African clergy demanded more pay in 1906, and the request was directed to the chiefs at one of the first Synodal meetings.[322] At the Synod in 1909, the chiefs were again appealed to, and it was admitted that the church was to a great extent dependent on 'the generosity of individual chiefs'. People, rather than contributing themselves, looked to their local chiefs 'to make good every deficit'.[323] The Bishop too looked to the leading chiefs when he suggested in 1912 the establishment of a Clergy and Teacher's Augmentation Fund.[324] The pattern was repeated at the Synod of 1919, when the initiative was taken to set up a Church Reserve Fund, where the chiefs would deduct the necessary money from their land incomes.[325]

This dependence on the chiefs, financially and otherwise, was even more marked when it came to the realization of new initiatives within the church. In connection with the scheme for starting plantations on church land, the Baganda chiefs were asked in 1912–13 to put up 100 acres as security for an investment loan.[326] The chiefs' contribution was even more important in the case of the building of the new Cathedral. The Kabaka, the Katikiro and many leading chiefs in Buganda promised to contribute 40 per cent of the rents they received from tenants on their estates,[327] and when expenses exceeded expectations the chiefs at all levels were again the natural group to engage in the work of raising funds.[328] They continued to act as fund-raisers even after the inauguration of the Cathedral building in 1919.

The strategy of making the chiefs the ultimate fundament of the church was looked upon with some uneasiness and even deprecated on some occasions by the mission and the chiefs themselves. At the Synod in 1907, one of the Regents, Zakariya Kisingiri, remarked that the Bakopi were too willing to leave all the responsibility for church work to the chiefs; and the Sekibobo, Ham Mukasa, added that 'the people too much regard the Church as that of the chiefs only and the common people do not help'.[329] But the trend continued, and the building of the Cathedral confirmed once again the church's dependence on the chiefs. The Bishop even had to issue a statement to the effect that 'the Cathedral is not for the chiefs only but for all Christians'. The chiefs could afford to be generous because they were rich, he added, referring to Mark XII: 44, but contributions from the poorer people were much needed and deserved even more praise.[330] Yet things did not change. Only the following year it became necessary again to deprecate 'the custom of dependence as in the early days on the chiefs'.[331]

The prospects of reversing this trend seemed even poorer in the period immediately after the First World War. The financial difficulties of the CMS meant that the Uganda mission could not do much to reduce the church's dependence on the chiefs. On the contrary, the evidence suggests that in all districts the direct relationship between the chiefs' generosity and the extent of church work done remained as marked as ever. From Toro it was reported that the Omukama, the Katikiro and a couple of leading chiefs provided a third of the total contributions. At the same time, it was claimed that progress in education was largely hindered by the lack of engagement on the part of the majority of the chiefs.[332] In Ankole, the fact that fund-raising would be difficult was foreseen, as many Hima chiefs had lost their cattle in an epidemic: 'and it had been the chiefs who had for long supported the Church by their generous offers'.[333] When church workers in Bunyoro found themselves in financial difficulties because of their low wages, the Church Council immediately turned to the chiefs.[334] Bishop Willis used the same method in Buganda when he wanted to improve the clergy's inadequate salaries. He even took the extraordinary step of calling a joint conference of the leading chiefs and the Diocesan Council.[335] This not only indicated the church's continued reliance on the Ganda secular leaders, but also showed the incapacity of the Diocesan Council, as then composed, to deal with such matters. The bringing together of the chiefs and the Council was an attempt to make up for the loss which the church organization had suffered when the leading chiefs had been edged out of the Council. The change had reduced contact with the secular leaders, and communications now had to be improved again.

The chiefs' economic importance for the church thus remained unchanged over the period under survey. Neither party was happy with this situation, and some dissatisfaction was expressed, but without any visible results. In the wider perspective we may suggest that the church's links with, and dependence on, the chiefs reflected the developing stratification of society at large. This made it more of a battleground for mounting tensions than otherwise might have been the case. Two points are of particular relevance here. In the first place, when the Synod issued its Encyclical Letter in 1921, it was considered necessary to allude to the wide class differences in the country, and to the disregard in which the Bakopi were held. It was stated that such differences, which accorded ill with the message of the Gospel, should not exist within the church. In practice Bakopi participated in church meetings on an equal footing with the chiefs, and their children went to the same schools.[336] There must have been good reasons for the inclusion of such a statement in the Encyclical Letter, and it may have reflected the increasing criticism of the chiefly landed aristocracy coming from the Bataka Movement and others.[337]

While these social differences became important at a later period, it is possible to detect, even at this stage, a related social polarity within the church between the clergy and the wealthier class of chiefs. As early as the Synods in 1906, 1907 and 1909 it was pointed out that the clergy were very badly paid compared with the chiefs, and it was claimed that the chiefs did too little to give the clergy a status in the church as prestigious as their own in society.[338] This conception of the chiefs as a class which failed to fulfil its natural obligations must have grown up over the years against the background of the clergy's underprivileged position. The suggestion that there were tensions between these two groups receives some support when we consider the fierce controversy in 1919–21 about the removal of a cross placed on the altar in the new Cathedral. The presence of the cross had originally been seen as too reminiscent of Catholic practice. But the evidence suggests that the strong opposition of most of the African clergy to the presence of the cross was because, for reasons too complex to go into here, it came to stand as a symbol of chiefly dominance. The controversy about the cross may thus be taken as a manifestation of the existing tensions between the two groups.[339]

Another related source of tension which existed in the country as a whole and which was strongly manifested within the church was the conflict of interests between Buganda and the rest of the country. One reason why this is relevant in connection with the issue of the chiefs' financial importance is that their influence was to a great extent dependent on their possession of land. This put the Baganda in a privileged position, as they were the only group to have benefited from the land settlement which had granted chiefs private as well as official mailos. The composition of the Finance Board and the Estates Board clearly reflected this state of affairs, and Ganda ascendancy was further reinforced every time the Bishop called for special contributions from the Buganda landed aristocracy. The building of the Cathedral in particular showed how the tension could manifest itself within the church. The special pledge of the Ganda leaders to give 40 per cent of their rents and their leading role in the whole project meant that it was seen by many as a purely Buganda enterprise for which the rest of the Diocese had very little responsibility. At the Synod in 1917 the Bishop even had to make an explicit statement to the effect that the Cathedral was 'not for one tribe only', but for the whole Diocese. While he was grateful for the large Ganda contribution, he also appealed to other areas to support the project.[340] The Katikiro of Bunyoro, supported by representatives from Toro and Ankole, blamed the Baganda for having monopolized the building of the Cathedral from the beginning. Considerable efforts at persuasion, a public apology from the Ganda delegates and the promise of a proper inscription on the foundation stone were necessary before the non-Ganda representatives consented to engaging themselves in the project.[341]

The controversy over the building of the Cathedral was paralleled by the request for a reduction of Ganda influence in the Diocesan Council and by demands for financial independence instead of allocations channelled through the Ganda-dominated Central Fund.[342] A climate of confrontation was thus arising between Ganda and non-Ganda, and the church was placed in a serious dilemma. On the one hand the church's finances and organization appeared to be – and in fact to a great extent were – under Ganda control; but at the same time the church had to try to dispel this impression in order to preserve unity within its ranks. The dilemma remained unsolved, reflecting a major split in the country as a whole. The church was particularly susceptible to outbreaks of tension along these lines. It could easily come to function as an outlet for tensions which belonged properly in the political field, as the political field was under stricter control and was also more diversified (see below, Chapter 22).

The distance between awareness of the chiefs' financial importance for the church and the utilization of their political position was not a great one. One area where the chiefs' political power was used was that of education. The Synod discussed in 1907 how to deal with lapsed teachers who no longer performed their duties but still continued to live on the church shambas. The most favoured solution was that the chiefs should evict these teachers, if only for the sake of the ordinary people.[343] Thus the official responsibility of the chiefs for good order was invoked to solve an issue which can only be seen as an internal church one. In other words, the work of the church in the educational sphere was considered of such public importance that the chiefs' assistance could legitimately be called upon. The same premise lay behind the idea that it was the chiefs' responsibility to keep the church buildings and teachers' houses in good repair. The following account of Bishop Tucker's statement sums up his attitude to the chiefs' obligations to the church.

The Bishop thought the Chief should do a great deal towards helping in this work because he is not a chief for his own pleasure, or that he may put money into his own pocket, but that if he is a Christian man he ought to consider the good the Church is doing and help it all he can.[344]

Various claims of this kind were made over the following years. One persistent assertion was that it was part of the local government's duty to construct and keep in good repair the roads leading to the bigger churches and the main centres of Christian activity. Inevitably this led to the claim that luwalo labour, which was available to the chiefs for local, official purposes, should be employed for the benefit of the church. Although the government refused to acknowledge the church's right to luwalo, the church's close connection with the chiefs meant that the customary tribute was in fact employed for some limited purposes, such as roadmaking and the building of local schools. Concrete evidence of this is scanty, but the suggestion receives indirect support from later events, when the commutation option was introduced. Soon after the possibility of commuting the luwalo obligation into cash was allowed, an official request was filed with the government asking it to allow local administrations to use luwalo funds for the erection of schools. It was made clear that this was a legalization of what had hitherto been an informal practice.[345] Further confirmation of the use of luwalo for these purposes was provided when the Buganda Lukiko undertook in 1924 the upkeep of roads leading to important church centres, thus taking over a task for which luwalo labour could no longer be used.[346]

Although it is difficult to establish the exact details of what happened, the personal bonds with the African political systems thus seem to have been applied to gain various benefits. Two other areas where chiefly influence was important were the land grants to the church from chiefs in their official capacity and the mission's and the chiefs' joint efforts to have the chiefs' right of disposal over land recognized (see in part Chapter 10). Secondly, there was the church's drive to have special Christian legislation passed on marriage and morality in order to set

Uganda on the road towards Christian nationhood (Chapter 16). This in particular showed how personal bonds between the church and the African political systems worked to influence political processes, but it also illustrated the limitations inherent in concentrating on such linkages. One significant feature which emerged from the analysis of the drive for Christian legislation was that personal overlapping provided an easy and regular means of communication between the mission and the African leaders. The whole apparatus of Synod, Diocesan Council and various sub-committees allowed for the briefing of the political leaders, and provided a channel through which the wishes and current needs of the church could be communicated. It provided a platform for the exchange of information and for preparatory discussions before decisions were made in the political arena.

This pattern of organized contacts between the leaders of the church and the African political systems and its obvious political potential was precisely observed and described by a contemporary, if hardly impartial, outsider, the influential Catholic Omulamuzi, Stanislaus Mugwanya. Commenting on the inferior position of his party in the Buganda political structure, he gave the following account of the linkages between the Protestant church and the Protestant political leadership:

a thing the Government knows not, is the fact that some members of the Lukiko fulfil two different offices in the same time, one of State, and one of Religion, such as Yakobo when still Kago, and others, but chiefly A. Katikiro [Sir Apolo Kagwa] who is at the head of both Lukikos, that of State and that of Church, the latter having meetings at every moment. This man has indeed for a long time done good work for the Government. Well now whenever he informs the Government of what was passed at the Lukiko, the Government takes it for the good pleasure of the Lukiko, whereas often times it is not the case. Many designs he gets from the Protestant Lukiko and brings to the State Lukiko to obtain what the former is looking for. Moreover he intimidates the members of the Lukiko to prevent them from putting forth their own opinions, and even the Kabaka himself is not clear of him. If he (Kabaka) endeavours to follow right justice, as he was taught by the Government as being the lot of the Royal Power, he (Katikiro) breathes into his mind another principle, viz. to be good Kabaka he must stand by the Protestant side and in particular follow the opinion of the Katikiro alone.

This state of things enables the Church Lukiko to have its views brought forth to the State Lukiko and agreed too, as the rule of the latter is that measures are carried by the majority of votes. Now the Protestants are by far the most numerous in the Lukiko . . .[347]

Mugwanya here bears witness to the importance of the dual role of the leading Protestant chiefs, especially the Katikiro, and shows how these linkages were used politically. His own bias may have made him exaggerate, as our earlier analysis of the church's influence on moral legislation suggested (Chapter 16). Still, his claims raise the question of the government's attitude. How much scope was it willing to allow to these linkages, and did it feel the need to exercise control at any stage? These questions have been touched upon earlier but will be reintroduced here for a full discussion.

The first point to stress is that there was a marked change in the government's attitude after the First World War. Before then it was well known to the colonial administration that there were frequent and close contacts between the mission, the church and the African political leaders, especially the Baganda chiefs. As long as this remained at a reasonable level and did not involve direct interference the government was prepared to consider these contacts and personal bonds relatively harmless and to tolerate their existence.[348] In the post-war period, colonial officials became more sensitive to these linkages and their political significance as described by Stanislaus Mugwanya, although his letter does not seem to have exerted any direct influence on the course of events. One indication of the government's growing concern is the following remark made by a colonial official when the Synod sent a number of resolutions to the Lukikos in various districts.

This communication might be treated with the contempt it deserves, were it not for the fact that these Synods represent the views of the Protestant members of the Lukikos, and that they at times hold a conclave as a Synod or local Church Council before they enter the Lukiko to discuss public business.[349]

There were two reasons for the alarm among government officials. First, policy was being formulated in various church bodies by Protestant leaders. These institutions thus came to function to a certain extent as rivals of the officially recognized Lukikos. Secondly, the personal overlap between church and state opened up a channel for mission and church influence in the political arena which the government found undesirable. The government therefore decided to take action. To block the personal links between the mission and the African leaders was naturally beyond the power of the government, but it was possible to exercise greater control over the lines of communication. An opportunity of doing so came in connection with the Synod's practice of sending resolutions to the African political institutions. After the introduction of the Buganda Lukiko system to neighbouring areas, the Synod began sending resolutions to the various Lukikos. In 1921 Synod resolutions were sent to Buganda, Busoga, Ankole and Toro, asking the Lukikos to deal with certain matters concerning labour conditions, education and marriage. This led to a strong protest from the District Commissioner of Ankole, who complained that such resolutions should not be sent directly to public bodies which were under the guidance and control of District Officers.[350] The immediate issue at stake was, then, that the church was bypassing the central administration and acting as an official body with direct access to African political institutions.[351] Behind this complaint over procedural matters lay the fear that the church was exercising undue influence on the process of legislation and on the African administration in general. This was considered especially unfortunate as resolutions from the Synod were naturally taken to represent the opinions of the leading Protestant chiefs who were members of it.

The 1921 case led to a change in procedure: the government ruled that the Synod's correspondence with public bodies was to be mediated through Provincial or District Commissioners. Bishop Willis acquiesced in this demand in general, but reserved the right to communicate directly in cases where officials refused to forward communications.[352] This reservation was apparently meant as an accusation of censorship, and was therefore strongly contested by various officials.[353] It is however significant that when the next Synod in 1924 passed resolutions on education, drinking and witchcraft, with the object of obtaining legislative action, and wanted to send the resolutions to the Lukikos, the church applied for permission beforehand and duly received it.[354] This new procedural rule was not solely prompted by the government's concern over the political potential of the close personal contacts between the Protestant church and the majorities in the various Lukikos. The government's growing awareness of its own prerogatives was also due to the elaboration of the Protectorate administration, with its centralization and built-in tendency towards uniformity, supervision and control. This in itself left less room for free play between the two sub-systems and made access to political institutions less direct. But it should be emphasized that the channels of direct communication and influence along personal lines were not blocked. The range of this kind of activity and its political potential were simply reduced because of changes in the government's attitude and overall developments within the colonial system.

We may also briefly touch upon some other factors which tended to reduce the political significance of personal linkages with the African political systems. Three factors, all mentioned earlier, were important. First, the development of the administrative system was followed by a tightening-up of control. There was thus less scope for the chiefs to take initiatives and implement decisions on their own within the African political system. So they became less valuable politically to the church, as the land issue demonstrated. Secondly, the chiefly institution itself was undergoing changes. This was observed at a very early stage by leading figures both within the African polities and the colonial administration. When the Kabaka of Buganda accused the government of eroding his status he made special mention of its interference in the appointment of chiefs, adding: 'A worse consequence resulting from this practice is that individual Chiefs are now beginning to flout the authority of the Native Government and to consider themselves more as British Government Officials rather than as my native Chiefs.'[355] The Kabaka was here virtually characterizing the chiefs as 'civil servant chiefs', who no longer primarily derived their legitimacy from traditional sources. A similar change, related in more general terms to the advance of colonial civilization, was noted by the Provincial Commissioner of the Northern Province, who spoke of the gradual abolition of the feudal system in Bunyoro and the chiefs' loss of authority over their people.[356]

This leads us to a third point: the attitude of the people. It has earlier been noticed (Chapter 15) that the young, educated generation, in the first instance in Buganda, constituted an element of opposition to the chiefly oligarchy in the Lukikos. Signs of change existed, and the emergence of the new pattern was noticed by contemporary observers.[357] Probably even more important was the loosening of the bonds between ordinary people and chiefs which was evident at about the same time. The Provincial Commissioner quoted above spoke of the peasantry's growing independence of the chiefs. It should be remembered that the Encyclical Letter of 1921 referred to wide class differences in Buganda. The developing pattern of agricultural production contributed to a gradual breaking-down of the traditional system of clientship between people and chiefs.[358] It was even indicated by one of the leading missionaries that the saza chiefs no longer carried much influence with the villagers in religious matters.[359]

These various factors could have two consequences for the value of the personal linkages between the church and the African polities. First of all, the chiefs' changing status within their own system could mean that they were less able to fulfil the material expectations of the church. Their traditional standing in society, which was held to justify their dominant position in the organization of the church, was dwindling, and with it their value in terms of their official capacity. A second, even more negative, consequence was that, even though the chiefs continued to play a leading role in the church, there was a gradual shift in emphasis from their official capacity to their private one, which was more and more defined by their economic potential as landholders or salaried bureaucrats. In other words the chiefly group came to function more and more in terms of *class*, as an upper echelon in society, and less in terms of its traditional political role.[360]

The situation which faced the mission in the post-war period was part of the same pattern of events which determined the African reaction within the field of education against the smoothly-working alliance of mission and chiefs (Chapter 15). Although developments were necessarily very gradual and therefore difficult to pin down in an analysis, there were, as noted above, warning signals interpretable in the contemporary setting. The mission did not heed these warnings, and the basic principles of its policy remained unchanged, as can be seen from its various statements and actions and not least from the composition of the various Church Boards. Although the modest role of the Bakopi was regretted now and then, there was no real doubt of the validity of the basic trends in the prevailing policy. The Christianization/Protestantization of the political offices and the corresponding links between the African political systems and the church were regarded as being so valuable, and had hitherto proved so profitable, that firm commitment to this policy was never called into question, and no other approach was seriously considered. The economic straits of the mission in the post-war period also contributed to the inertia in its pattern of work.

In any final characterization of the relations with the African political system it should be emphasized that the pursuit of the policy outlined above meant that the Protestant mission and church became closely tied to a political ideology and a political structure which was increasingly criticized and opposed as time went on. As a consequence of its identification with a particular political system, the church inadvertently became involved in the political and social tensions that existed in society. It was criticized for its alignment with the hereditary chiefly class and for contributing to its dominating position. This criticism was a sign of the growing social confrontation between the landed aristocracy and the Bakopi. Related to this was a second, just as significant ethnic confrontation. As the chiefly class was virtually identical with the Ganda aristocracy the church became trapped in the general confrontation between Buganda and the rest of the country. Both these kinds of tension have been noticed earlier in this survey. Given the church's linkages with the surrounding society, increasing tension along either social or ethnic lines in society at large were bound to spill over into the church. In the end, the ecclesiastical arena could even serve as an outlet for social and ethnic forces in cases where their expression was restricted in the political arena.

Identification with the African political system in the initial phase of the colonial period was clearly seen by the mission as a means of achieving its goal of a self-supporting church and of creating a Christian nation and a quasi-Christian state. The unintended result was that the church became tied to a political and social order whose value was declining or at least changing fast. The beginning of this process has already been noticed, although the real acceleration came in the following period.

Conclusions on the issue of a Christian state

We must first recall that the concept of a Christian state was not taken to imply that the mission's goal was an officially declared Christian state with an established church. The missionaries had from the outset a less ambitious, but also less well-defined goal in mind, which was to be achieved by the use of specific approaches to the state. In order to systematize these various approaches a distinction has been made between the colonial state and the African polities. Furthermore, the concept of the Christian state has been defined as comprising the Christianization of institutions within the state, and the establishment of institutionalized linkages between church and state. In evaluating the results of this analysis the first important observation is that a number of differences have emerged in connection with the mission's approach to the two political structures. In order to interpret and compare these results the boundary concept will be employed, with special emphasis on boundary maintenance between systems.[361]

The mission gained very little ground as regards the explicit Christianization of institutions within the colonial state or the establishment of official linkages between church and state. Thus the boundary between the two sub-systems was of very limited permeability at the official level, and the government showed itself by its actions to be fully conscious of the necessity for clear boundary maintenance. This does not mean that it felt no need to cooperate with the Protestant mission and church. In view of religious factionalism and denominational rivalry, however, this cooperation could only take place in so far as it did not infringe strict boundary maintenance. This explains the importance attached to the consultative status of the mission in the foregoing analysis. A consultative status presupposed an identifiable boundary between the two systems, and specific rules to guide the exchanges between them. We have noted that consultative status was granted in practice to the Protestant mission and that this allowed it to carry out functions beyond the capacity of an ordinary interest group. This in turn contributed to the impression that the mission and church enjoyed a special relationship with the colonial state which could be of considerable propaganda value.

So far we have applied the concepts of boundary and boundary maintenance at the institutional level, that of the church–state problem. Given the government's handling of the appointment of chiefs, it is evident that the institutional level of analysis is not sufficient for the investigation of all relations. The appointments issue constitutes a separate level of inquiry, requiring emphasis on societal factors, in the sense that religious affiliation provided the basis for political identity and political groupings. In this respect the colonial administration, in spite of all its public utterances and all its efforts, failed to neutralize the religious factor. During the period under survey the political significance of religion as the main structuring principle in society remained virtually unchallenged. Denominational rivalry in particular placed such constraints on the government that religious affiliation became the major determinant in its appointments policy.

It is important to distinguish between these two levels of inquiry in order to make it clear that the appointment of chiefs on religious grounds was not due to their position within the church system. The distinction between these two levels as regards the interaction between religion and politics is parallel to the separation of the institutional and societal levels in our earlier discussion of religious liberty

(Chapter 7). It thus appears to be of general analytical value to distinguish between these two levels when inquiring into the relationship between religion and politics.[362]

Turning to the African political system, a quite different pattern emerges. It has been established that the ideal of a Christian state came close to realization, judged on the basis of the two elements included in our definition: the Christianization/Protestantization of the important political institutions; and the establishment of institutionalized linkages between church and state. These interconnections quite clearly suggest poor boundary maintenance between the two systems. Personal overlap in particular was obviously responsible for much flow of influence in both directions between the two systems. The church had a means of influencing political processes and benefited at the same time in various ways from having people of political importance in its own bodies. In evaluating the tangible results of this boundary permeability we may suggest that, although it certainly produced a number of valuable results, they were generally of more limited and short-term value, possibly apart from their propaganda effect, than might have been expected, given the amount of effort invested in them. In addition there were various negative effects on the standing of the church in society at large. In the first instance, the African political system was subject to the supervision of the colonial government. Even in Buganda, colonial officials could interfere in the decision-making process, and their final approval was necessary before any measures of importance could be implemented. A second reason follows from the above. The prohibitive powers of the government were most likely to be activated in a situation where officials became aware of the political significance of poor boundary maintenance between the two systems. This was what happened from the mid-1910s onwards, when a number of measures were taken with the aim of strengthening the boundary: the refusal to allow prayers at the Lukiko meetings; the scaling-down of the church's identification with the Kabakaship; and, most importantly, the blocking of direct access to political institutions like the Lukikos. Although these moves may have served to make the boundary less permeable they did not result in the establishment of a boundary like the one that existed between the mission and the colonial state. The poor boundary maintenance in this area remained a significant feature during the following period. But indirectly the importance of this relationship was reduced by a third, almost accidental factor. The development of the colonial system and the corresponding changes in the status and function of the African political institutions tended to reduce the political value of the boundary's permeability.

One additional aspect of the relationship between the church and the African political system is underlined by analysing it in terms of boundary maintenance. The permeability of the boundary helps to explain why the two systems were linked so closely together that tensions and confrontations within one arena were reflected in the other. Examples of this causal relationship have been given above. The types of linkage between the two systems also justifies the use later in our analysis, of that component of systems theory which deals with indirect or tacit inputs from one system to another.

PART V

Indirect inputs: parallelism and reciprocity in the relationship between church and state

12 Masters and their Ganda assistants at Mengo High School, *c.* 1905–10

13 Ganda leaders, missionaries and colonial officials at the opening of Mengo High School, January 1905. Sitting from left to right: the Kabaka Daudi Chwa, Mrs George Wilson, the Deputy Commissioner George Wilson, Bishop A. R. Tucker, the Katikiro Sir Apolo Kagwa and the leader of the Ganda Muslims, Prince Mbogo

14 Boys of the Mengo High School with Namirembe Cathedral in the background, *c.* 1905–10

18

Parallelism and coordination in the administrative pattern

The examination of direct inputs has stressed the causal dimension in the relationship between church and state by measuring the extent of the mission's and the church's influence on the political system. There is, however, another dimension in the relationship between church and state, which, in the terms used by Ali Mazrui, primarily concerns 'a relationship of parallel roles rather than functional sequence'. A wide range of cases falls within this category, which is characterized by 'coincidence of interests' and some degree of adaptation and reciprocity.[1] Only a few of these, selected on the basis of their wider political implications and their bearing on the church–state relationship, can be dealt with here.

One obvious area where we are likely to find parallelism and mutual adaptation in the relationship between church and state is in their administrative patterns, one aspect of which has been touched upon in connection with missionary expansion (Chapter 6). The outcome of the conflicts of the 1890s was that the mission finally accepted the prerogative of the state in determining the timing of missionary moves into new districts. Missionary freedom was respected, but official permission was required, and this caused delays and meant that a certain parallelism prevailed between the expansion of the colonial state and that of the missionary work. A case in point occurred when the CMS asked, and duly received, permission to work in Acholi in 1903. As the area was not yet under 'effective occupation', it was stressed that they went at their own risk. Despite this qualification, the government characteristically welcomed the missionary initiative, hoping that missionary presence in Acholi would help to make conditions more settled there.[2] This willingness to let the mission do the pioneering work was spelt out more clearly some years later, when the Governor of the neighbouring British East Africa directly encouraged the mission to start work among the Nandi, whose territory came under the Uganda Diocese at the time.[3] A number of British expeditions had been sent against the Nandi over the years, and after their final defeat the mission was clearly considered to be a useful instrument for helping to create more settled conditions.[4] The mission responded positively to this opportunity for coordinated effort, although there was considerable doubt as to the feasibility of the whole enterprise. The fact that the government had such a positive attitude was what finally swung the balance in favour of sending missionaries to the Nandi.[5] That the missionary expedition had been undertaken primarily in order to accommodate the government was a strong argument for some missionaries against withdrawal from Nandi territories when the work there turned out to be fruitless after two years.[6]

The mission's coordination of its own expansion with the government's effective occupation of the Protectorate was thus a significant and deliberate element in its strategy in the pioneering phase.[7] The mission's susceptibility to indirect influence from the political system became even more marked when both sides began to elaborate their organizational structures. Two related topics will be examined here: the geographical importance of the politico-administrative centres; and the parallelism between the administrative divisions used by the mission and the government.

At an early stage the mission was faced with the problem of whether to situate mission stations and church centres close to the administrative centres. In the case of Busoga it decided to await the government's selection of a site for its headquarters,[8] and when the main government station in Bunyoro was moved, the mission followed.[9] The erection of new buildings which these moves necessitated was very expensive for the mission, and on one occasion at least it protested over a proposed government move.[10] The main reason for the mission's desire to stay close to administrative centres was the need to maintain contact with the major chiefs, who spent a large part of the year at government centres in the various districts.[11] The close geographical placing of mission and government centres was thus a basic missionary principle over the years; and as the religious work became more settled, with large church buildings, and well-developed boarding schools, the mission became highly dependent on the permanence of the administrative structure. When the government headquarters in Bunyoro were moved from Hoima to Masindi in 1911 the vehement protests of the local missionary indicated how serious a matter this was for the mission.[12] But as far as the location of centres was concerned, the government called the tune and was clearly the stronger part in the relationship.[13]

As for the problem of administrative structure, we have seen that one guiding principle in the church constitution was to adhere to the administrative divisions established by the colonial administration. The existence of local Church Councils in Toro, Bunyoro and Busoga were thus officially recognized at the Synod in 1910.[14] In the case of the two former districts it should be added that this organizational pattern was due less to the government than to the two areas' own national feelings; for they insisted on the greatest possible control of their own affairs, and the full independence of Buganda. Here it is hardly possible to isolate the one factor from the other: both mission and government bowed, as we shall see, to the strength of the traditional and ethnic boundaries. One case which should be mentioned is that of 'the lost counties' – that part of Bunyoro which was incorporated into Buganda after the war in the late 1890s. The loss of this territory had been a sore point for Bunyoro ever since, and was one of the reasons for the outbreak of antagonism against Ganda agents in 1907.[15] In this situation the mission came down on the side of the government in its efforts to uphold the boundary once it had been delineated.

The controversy over the lost counties was related to the major question of which principles should guide the fixing of organizational boundaries, where there was a conflict between administrative expediency and traditional political, linguistic and ethnic divisions. This dilemma was not felt acutely in the Kingdoms, with their centralized political structures; but it was unavoidable in the segmentary areas in the eastern and northern part of the Protectorate.[16] The mission took the easiest course out of this dilemma by absolving itself of any responsibility. In 1914 the principle of following the boundaries demarcated by the government was laid down.[17] This decision endorsed an organizational parallelism between church and state, and constituted an admission of dependence on government criteria for fixing boundaries.

It would take us too far to go into the vast and complex problem of the criteria applied by the government in the demarcation of administrative boundaries. This question has been discussed in some detail in a different work,[18] and will only be mentioned here in so far as it helps us to establish the importance the colonial administration attached to the missionary contribution. We may consider the case of the district of Lango. When the Protectorate government began in 1909 to extend its authority to the northern areas, it planned at first to follow natural, geographical boundaries; but it was soon discovered that such a demarcation would have the unfortunate effect of dividing the Langi.[19] So the main criterion used was the tribal unit, vaguely defined in terms of the use of a common language, and the existence of common cultural and political traits. In the case of Lango this was supported by considerations of area and population. The government felt it to be rather unfortunate when the CMS mission had to divide the district into two parts because of the lack of missionary personnel. The eastern part was under the influence and guidance of Baganda teachers from Bukedi, while the western one was linked to the work in Acholi and was staffed by Banyoro evangelists.[20] The Lango district was being pulled in two opposite directions by the mission's administrative division and by the two different methods of work employed. In this respect the government felt that it was being let down by the mission, which was normally its ally. Accordingly, government officials expressed the hope that the boundaries of the district and those of the missionary unit could be made coterminous.[21] This in fact happened ten tears later, but the government reaction at the time indicates the political importance it attached to the parallelism between administrative and ecclesiastical divisions. In such cases the government appreciated the mission's supportive function, and underlined their common interests.

Elsewhere the mission complied fully with the government's administrative demarcations. The policy was officially stated in 1913, and it was emphasized on several other occasions that the framework of the civil administration was used as the basic guiding principle for the organization of the church.[22] This parallelism manifested itself at three different levels. At the highest level, the mission respected the boundary of the Protectorate as a whole. One argument in support of withdrawal from the Nandi area was the inconvenience of working in a different political unit. A similar problem arose in Mboga, which was situated in an area which was ceded to the Belgian Congo in 1911,[23] but which remained the responsibility of the Church of Uganda. On the other hand, Kavirondo, which had been part of the British East Africa Protectorate since 1902, was placed in 1919 under the Anglican Diocese of Mombasa, because the lack of congruence between political and ecclesiastical boundaries was felt to be highly inconvenient.[24]

The second level was constituted when a new ecclesiastical unit, the Rural Deanery, was created in 1915. The distribution of the Deaneries was made to follow closely the administrative demarcations; and except in Buganda they corresponded with already existing districts.[25] This continued to be the practice whenever new Deaneries were created in former missionary areas.[26] In Buganda the system was somewhat different, as the Deaneries mainly corresponded to the original pattern of missionary expansion, that is, to the territories of the major chiefs. Thus the saza became the basic unit, and the six (later seven) Deaneries in Buganda were identical with sazas – or in most cases groups of sazas – whereas the civil administration divided Buganda into four districts. This organizational pattern explains why the Ganda Protestants did not have a Church Council for Buganda as such. On the other hand, the division into six or seven Deaneries, half of the total number, meant that Buganda was ensured a dominant position in the Diocesan Council. This accentuated the difference between Buganda and the rest of the country within the church organization.

At the lowest level of the church organization, i.e. within each saza, the ecclesiastical division into pastorates and parishes (earlier called districts and sub-districts) corresponded with the secular division into gombololas and miruka (singular: muluka), both systems following the divisions within the chiefly hierarchy.[27] Because of the church's shortage of manpower, a pastorate would in many cases comprise more than one gombolola, but adherence to the civil unit was still the ideal.[28] Even in its administration of church land the mission stuck firmly to the civil pattern and appointed a katikiro for each saza and an assistant in each gombolola.[29]

The mission, then, consciously followed the lead of the government in adapting its administrative units to those of the state. In doing so it was faced with no real conflict between the colonial demarcations and the traditional boundaries from before the colonial expansion. This relatively harmonious process was facilitated first by the centralized political structures of the Bantu areas, and secondly, in the northern and eastern areas, by the government's employment of broad cultural criteria. For its part, the government was aware of the political effect of the missionary presence, but with one temporary exception it found no reason to criticize the mission or even ask for its active cooperation. From the purely organizational point of view, the mission thus helped to strengthen the government's administrative boundaries. It now remains to be seen whether the mission by its work helped to shape a popular consciousness of these boundaries which made the areas thus demarcated better able to function as effective political units.[30]

19

Centralization versus decentralization in church and state

It follows from the analysis of the mission's organizational pattern that there were both centralizing and decentralizing tendencies at work. The mission could either pursue a policy of integration by emphasizing the former tendency, or it could allow each administrative unit to follow its own course in accordance with its traditions. This would tend to reduce the church to the status of a mere coordinating agency. Whatever line was taken, it would have consequences beyond the confines of the church, and would consequently be of relevance for the state.

The CMS mission was fully aware of the linkages between the ecclesiastical and political fields when it came to the question of integration, and acknowledged at an early stage the importance of harmonizing mission and government policy. When missionary work really got under way in the Kingdom of Toro the problem unavoidably arose of defining Toro's relationship to Buganda. Some missionaries wanted to separate the two; others wanted to keep Toro under the direction of the Mengo Church Council.[1] In these discussions, which took place around the turn of the century, Archdeacon Walker, the Secretary of the CMS mission, linked the ecclesiastical issue with developments in the political field. He connected the efforts to establish a separate Toro mission with the Omukama Kasagama's wish for more independence from Buganda. Efforts to promote the cause of Toro included claims for the recognition of the Lutoro language at the expense of Luganda.[2] Walker himself was against independence in both fields and called for the extension of the Buganda hegemony. Bishop Tucker, on the other hand, was much more aware of the problems inherent in the whole situation, and envisaged Toro and the surrounding areas as a separate diocese in the distant future. But he accepted that the issue was not crucial at the time, and drew attention to the importance of the links between the political and the ecclesiastical fields: 'the policy of the Government at the present time is undoubtedly to bring together the smaller nationalities and weld them into one'. It therefore made no sense, he thought, to contest this policy.[3]

The need to harmonize mission and government policy on the integration of the various parts of the Protectorate was underlined in 1901. Once again the language issue arose, as the missionaries in Toro and Bunyoro strongly supported the use of Lunyoro as the primary language.[4] The political overtones of this issue were clearly acknowledged within the mission. Bishop Tucker stated that there was considerable national feeling in Toro, nourished by some of the missionaries, directed against dependence on Buganda and the extension of its influence. Although Tucker supported the primacy of Luganda and believed in its integrative capacity, he preferred in this case to leave more than one option open.[5] The influential Secretary, Archdeacon Walker strongly emphasized the political consequences of the language issue for both church and state. For the sake of the unity and strength of the future church and missionaries, he claimed, ought to give the connection with Buganda as much support as possible, rather than foster antagonistic feelings against the Baganda. Language differences would almost certainly divide the church in Toro and Bunyoro from that in Buganda.[6] Walker further called attention to the necessity of following the policy adopted by the government, saying that it would be a mistake to solve the language problem by encouraging disintegrative tendencies, which would work against the policy of making one country of Bunyoro, Toro and Buganda.[7] Walker went so far as to suggest that the principle of parallelism between mission and government policy ought to carry considerable weight in formulating the mission's policy.

The English Government is doing all it can to draw all the surrounding countries more and more under the influence of Uganda [Buganda] . . . In every way the Government officials are doing all they can to make the country one whole with Uganda proper as the head . . . If we adopt a different policy I am sure we are making a mistake.[8]

Walker's wish to gear mission policy to that of the government was fully appreciated when the Acting Commissioner responded to his rather unusual request for an official opinion on the language issue. F. J. Jackson expressed a strong preference for the use of an official language in the Protectorate, and if English was out of the question, Luganda was the only alternative. 'I not only think that Luganda should be the standard language, but the Buganda methods of administration though by no means perfect should be the standard.'[9] The benefit of parallelism and coordination was thus fully acknowledged by both parties, and in Walker's, and to some extent Tucker's eyes, this was a fact which ought to carry weight in framing mission policy. That this line carried the day and became practical policy up until about 1907–8 can be substantiated by two observations. In the first place, both agencies practised a policy of integration and worked for the unity of the Protectorate. The Acting Commissioner in 1906 confirmed their common interests: 'It has long been my endeavour to promote a "Federal" feeling throughout these countries, a desire which has always had the warm support of men experienced in local affairs, particularly of Bishop Tucker of Uganda.'[10] In the second place, both agencies employed the same basic principle in pursuing the 'federal policy', which meant the extension of Ganda influence. The resultant parallelism between mission and state was evident at at least three levels. First, both agencies in principle gave the primacy to Luganda as the lingua franca, and considered the language to be the most effective tool in the integrative process, despite the fact that there was some opposition to Luganda within the mission, and that the government, as will appear below, postponed its own implementation of the pro-Luganda language policy. A precise expression of this whole attitude may be found in the following statement from one of the missionaries: 'The true imperial idea is that of unity, both in the Church and in Civil life, and the more that is promoted by a common language the stronger will both the Church and the country become.'[11]

Secondly, both agencies used Ganda personnel. The government appointed Ganda agents as chiefs in those areas which it brought under its administration; and the mission sent Ganda evangelists or teachers, sometimes to be followed by Ganda clergymen, to newly opened districts.[12] Thirdly, both based their administrative systems on the Ganda model, primarily by creating Lukikos within each unit. The church in fact went a step further than the state in using the Ganda formula. Before the introduction of the church constitution the Mengo Church Council was considered superior to the other Church Councils, and functioned in the same way as the later Diocesan Council.[13]

Generally, the mission pursued the Ganda-based 'federal policy' more actively than the government did, especially as regards language. Consequently, the mission suffered a greater setback when this policy became untenable. While the government mainly experienced opposition in connection with its employment of Ganda agents, as in Bunyoro in 1907, the mission's use of the Ganda formula was completely undermined at about the same time, when it had to give up its hopes of making Luganda the sole official language, thereby losing its key instrument in pursuing the federal policy. The strength of the opposition to the federal policy, and the necessity for a new integrative formula, became evident a little later within the church organization. It has already been shown how the various ecclesiastical districts in the Bantu area achieved independent status, and how they aimed at a position of more equality with Buganda within the church.[14] Although the Ganda bias remained during the rest of the period under survey, as we have seen in the church organization, and as we shall see again in the longer-term language policy, it had nevertheless become necessary to redefine the policy of integration. The mission had to act determinedly, if centralization was to be achieved.

The mission was thus faced with the challenge of creating some kind of unity amidst widespread diversity.[15] The 'national consciousness' in the non-Ganda districts, and the granting of independence to these districts within the church organization, represented a decentralizing tendency; and this reflected the realities of the political field. In its search for a unifying force to stem the centrifugal trend the mission acknowledged that no help was to be had from the political arena. Instead, the mission considered the means which it had at its own disposal. Christianity was in itself a unifying force, and its organizational expression, the church, could by its very structure promote integration. The mission's educational work, especially with the sons of chiefs, provided one way of drawing the peoples of the Protectorate together. The establishment of an official language, which could only be Luganda, was also considered to be a viable possibility. Most important of all, the church had one institution which placed it far ahead of the colonial administration as far as national unity was concerned. The Synod brought representatives together from all parts of the Protectorate, and thereby accomplished something which the government had never even attempted.[16] It was a forum in which Christians met on equal footing, irrespective of their local origin, and made decisions which were binding for the whole Protectorate.[17] A similar integrating tendency was evident in the composition of the Diocesan Council, and this was on later occasions hailed by the missionaries as a significant contribution to the unification of the whole country in the face of the widespread decentralizing tendencies. The Synod and the Episcopacy were presented by the missionaries as a national body which gave the people themselves a dominant voice in the administration of the church.[18] Bishop Willis laid stress on the unifying capacity of the Synodal organization.[19] He explicitly compared the ecclesiastical organization with the civil administration, and drew a parallel with the early history of England by saying that it had been left to the church to unite the various parts of the country.[20]

The claim that the church was ahead of the civil administration, and performed a political function from which the government benefited, raises the question of how far the government sought integration, based on equality between the various districts, and whether it acknowledged the contribution of the church in this respect. Two issues arose at an early stage which indicated at least some awareness of the problem. In the first place, it was suggested that leaders from the three Kingdoms of Bunyoro, Toro and Ankole should meet regularly in order to break out of their isolation, and to further progress in their respective regions by mutually beneficial exchanges of information.[21] But nothing came of this suggestion. In the second place, the government expressed concern in 1910 about the impact of newspapers: the press could help in the process of integration, but was equally capable of stirring up separatist feelings. Until now, the former had been the case, as the two existing papers were in the hands of the CMS mission. The missionaries' restraining influence was even thought to be the reason why 'an independent native newspaper had not yet appeared . . . The missionaries would probably view with disfavour the appearance of an influence in the country which might be beyond their control, and which might possibly be detrimental to their work in the future.'[22] Still, the Governor expressed some doubt, in view of the spread of education, as to the mission's continued capacity to stem separatist feelings. Such feelings could undermine the unity of the Protectorate. So, as a precautionary measure, a press law (the Newspaper Surety Ordinance) was introduced, which gave the government the right to censor the press.[23]

Apart from these two early cases, little was heard over the following years of the government's concern for, or the missionaries' contribution to, the process of integration. It was not until 1921 that the problem of integration was properly discussed, and, significantly enough, it was the same two topics which again figured on the agenda: the establishment of an assembly for the African leaders, a Central Lukiko; and the starting of a newspaper. The Acting Governor suggested that a Central Lukiko should be established, composed of all the Katikiros and one or two selected chiefs from each province. Such an institution would provide a forum for communication between the colonial administration and the African authorities, and would be especially useful in explaining government policy. More importantly, it would bring the various tribes into closer contact with one another and help to unify and consolidate the Protectorate.[24]

The proposal was sent out for comment from the Provincial Commissioners and other leading officials. One group gave its full support, but another was critical. Their arguments will be dealt with in turn. One Provincial Commissioner, P. W. Cooper, was very enthusiastic in his support; he found that the Protectorate had now progressed so far that it was essential to bring all its elements closer together, but he emphasized the importance of government guidance in the selection of members and the conduct of the assembly. As for the assembly's composition, he suggested that it should include one representative from each district, and considered that the Kitikiro of Buganda, Sir Apolo Kagwa, was the obvious candidate for the chairmanship. A leading Muganda should be Secretary and Luganda the working language.[25] As a supplement to the establishment of a Central Lukiko, Cooper further recommended that the government should start a 'Native Newspaper' in order to pursue a more active information policy. This too could help to make the Africans feel that the Protectorate was an integral unit within the empire. He also emphasized that this would in no way encroach on the work of the missions, who had so far been responsible for newspapers and magazines. It would be a government newspaper, and outside their sphere; there was a need for something that could influence and unify all parts of the African community independently of the religious parties.[26] Cooper was here referring to one limitation on the Christian institutions' ability to integrate the Protectorate: they were partisan, and therefore subject to the influence of denominational rivalry.

Cooper's support for a Central Lukiko was endorsed by two other officials,[27] who predicted that, first of all, Ganda dominance would only be a risk in the initial phase. When all the other ethnic groups met the Baganda on equal terms in the new assembly, there would be no danger of this.[28] Secondly, it was wrong to fancy that the Central Lukiko would provide a forum for 'disloyal elements'. It would provide an opportunity to voice local grievances. This would be a good thing, and disruptive tendencies would be balanced by the strongly felt need for coordination between the various provinces in a period when ever greater numbers of Africans were becoming educated or detribalized.[29]

These optimistic arguments were contested by the other group of officials.[30] In the first place they pragmatically drew attention to the differences in the degree of progress which existed in the various parts of the Protectorate. This meant that some areas were unsuitable for membership of a Central Lukiko. There were grave inequalities between the Bantu and the Nilotic peoples in the north, and to bring them together in the same forum could easily give the latter exaggerated ideas of their own status.[31] The same officials also saw unfortunate consequences stemming from Buganda's influence. Apart from the risk of Ganda dominance in a Central Lukiko,[32] the catalytic effect of contact between Buganda and other regions was of special concern, as it would most likely result in the other areas adopting Ganda ideas and their chiefs requesting the same status and privileges as were granted to Ganda chiefs by the Uganda Agreement. With this would follow the same political and social evils as could now be found in Buganda. Under the system of hereditary chiefs the peasants were worse off in Buganda than in other districts.[33] From the administrative point of view, there were already enough difficulties under the terms of the Agreement. Buganda was like 'an unruly ship' which could only be handled with the greatest care, and should definitely not serve as a model for other areas.[34]

In a final argument against the Central Lukiko proposal the whole underlying idea of centralization was attacked. It was asked whether coordination and harmonization of this kind in the fields of law and custom were either possible or desirable.[35] It was considered unwise to introduce means 'whereby the possibilities of too close a combination of all tribes in the Protectorate might in the future create a united aggressive attitude with either latent or explosive results to Local Government policies'.[36] These officials added the more pragmatic point of view that the best safeguard against the creation of such a platform was the present system, with the Lukikos in every province competing with one another and thus providing the necessary stimulus for progress[37] – a roundabout way of expressing the divide-and-rule principle.

Having considered the arguments, the Governor tended to agree with the opponents of the Central Lukiko.[38] At their 1922 conference the Provincial Commissioners stated that the time was not yet ripe for a Protectorate-wide institution,[39] and the proposal then seems to have been shelved for good. On the other hand, the related plan for a government newspaper was warmly supported, not for the sake of promoting integration, but 'for the education of native public opinion and for the direction of that opinion into healthy channels'.[40] In the eyes of the government an official organ was obviously needed in view of the existence of the independent mission-controlled newspapers, and the prospects of several African newspapers starting up.[41] The proposed government paper even featured in the draft financial estimates for 1923,[42] but the plan eventually came to nothing, mainly because of lack of money and manpower.[43]

The discussion of these two proposals illustrates the government's attitude in two areas: that of the relationship to the African political sub-systems, which will be touched upon separately below; and that of the unification of the Protectorate. The government was clearly not interested in following in the footsteps of the mission by replacing the earlier 'federal policy' with a new policy of integration. On the contrary, the administration became increasingly sceptical of the value of such a policy, and rejected any steps such as the establishment of a Central Lukiko. One major factor behind its attitude was the fear of Ganda dominance and the catalytic effect of Buganda's special position. There was also growing dissatisfaction with the way things worked within Buganda itself after special rights had been conceded by the Uganda Agreement. The government settled for a policy of decentralization which would confine African administrative activity within the boundaries of each district. In this way, its own administrative system would provide the only Protectorate-wide structure. It thus combined a divide-and-rule policy with a foreign and strictly controlled superstructure of integration.[44]

In this respect the mission was right in claiming that the church was the only agency in the Protectorate which promoted unification and integration at the African level. At this point the similarity between government and mission policy broke down, in spite of the organizational parallelism that otherwise existed. Accordingly the government could not view the mission's policy of integration with much sympathy. But we must then ask why the government neither commented on nor criticized this part of the mission's policy. Although it is not possible to arrive at any definitive answer, certain observations may go some way towards an explanation. First, the government did not attach any major political importance to the Synod as a forum for representatives from all parts of the Protectorate. Secondly, it had little confidence in the mission's and the church's integrative capacity as such (illustrated by its doubts about mission-run newspapers). From the government's point of view the two churches corresponded with two politico-religious parties, each of them representing only one section of the community. Furthermore the government knew that the mission was neglecting the most powerful means of integration, a unitary language. It had given concessions to a number of local languages, thereby undermining its own plans for greater integration.

Was the government right in ascribing so little value to the influence of the Synod for the unification of the Protectorate? Or did the Synod and the church organization in general succeed in performing an integrative function in spite of the differences between church and government policy? The results obtained from the examination of the church organization and the composition of its Boards suggest that they did not succeed in this respect. On a number of occasions the meetings of the delegates from the various Deaneries were marked by opposition to Ganda dominance and demands for organizational and financial independence and equal status with Buganda (for a detailed account, see below, Chapters 20–2). The proceedings of the Synod thus appeared to confirm the pessimistic expectations of government officials about a Central Lukiko. We may say that the centrifugal forces within the political arena pulled against the centripetal aims within the ecclesiastical one. This assessment should not, however, be understood as a complete devaluation of the existence and function-ing of the Synod. As a similar institution was absent within the colonial system, the Synod easily came to be a platform for the voicing of grievances which could not be expressed in the political field. In this respect the ecclesiastical field appeared to be ahead of the political one (cf. below, p. 382 for a fuller assessment of the importance of the synodal organization within the church).

Any final judgement on the Synod's integrative capacity would have to be based on an analysis covering a longer period. But the present evidence allows us to arrive at two interrelated conclusions: one of a specific nature, the other of a more general character. First, two conflicting aims have been seen at work within the church: on the one hand the ideal of performing an integrative function, on the other the desire for regional independence and a decentralized church structure. So far the latter tendency had been by far the strongest one: the centrifugal forces had prevailed within the church. The organization of the church had helped to strengthen the politico-administrative boundaries set by the government. The integrative function which the mission had intended the Synod to perform may have gone against the government's wishes in theory, but in reality the decentralizing tendency was the predominant feature. The mainte-nance of the existing boundaries thus became the major effect of the church structure (see below, Chapter 23).

This leads to the more general point. The close links with the political environment made it impossible for the church to decide on its own which of the two tendencies should prevail. The 1910s provide a clear example of how the church had to bow to decentralizing forces in society. The church seemed bound to live with a dichotomy inherent in the nature of the surrounding society, and it could therefore not be expected to play a major role in weakening local boundaries once they had been established, or to take the lead in the process of integration. This latter point must be kept in mind, as later literature has often stressed the role of the church in neutralizing ethnic boundaries.[45]

The examination of the parallelism between church and state as regards centralization/decentralization requires an analysis of three more areas essential to the investigation of tacit or indirect inputs. Evidence from these areas may further substantiate results already obtained. First we must consider the pattern of relationships existing on the one hand between the colonial state and its African sub-system, and on the other between the mission and the African church. Secondly, the use of a common language was suggested as an essential step in furthering the policy of integration, and this whole issue deserves closer examination. Finally, we have already noted the catalytic effect of Buganda, and we must investigate the extent to which this issue linked government and mission together.

20

Parallelism and diversity in the mission's and the government's relationships with their African sub-systems

It has emerged from the examination of the centralization/decentralization issue that the government preferred African political and administrative activity to be confined to the district level. No horizontally based nationwide institutions were established and no forum was created where colonial officials and African leaders could meet formally on a Protectorate-wide basis. The only politico-administrative structure was the colonial one, which covered the whole of Uganda and was run entirely by European officials. Strict boundary maintenance was preserved by both institutions and personnel.

The ecclesiastical system presented quite a different picture. The Church Constitution of 1909 shows that a number of bodies existed in which European missionaries and African lay leaders and clergy were supposed to meet on equal footing, so that no clear distinction existed between the European agency and the African church.[1] It was also the overall aim that the missionary agency should in the not too distant future become superfluous and withdraw, leaving a sufficiently well-established church in African hands.

It follows that the pattern of relations which developed between the mission and the church was very different from the one that existed between their counterparts in the political field. This leads to the question of whether the apparent lack of parallelism in the actual pattern of work and in longer-term policy had any political significance. There is all the more reason to pose this question, as the desirability of a joint approach was discussed at an early stage by representatives from both sides. The Commissioner hinted at this prospect in an interview in 1904: 'I may say that for the present and for some time to come it will be found as necessary to maintain English supremacy in Church organization as it is found to be in administration of the country.'[2] Even earlier, some of the missionaries, discussing the proposal for a church constitution, drew a parallel with the political system and recommended that the same principles be employed in defining the relationship between a European agency and an African sub-system.[3] But in spite of these early suggestions the mission deviated substantially from the government guidelines when it integrated its personnel into the church from 1909 onwards. Remarkably enough this new departure and the resultant lack of parallelism brought no direct comment or criticism from government circles. One reason may be that the government did not fully grasp the implications of the integration of mission and church, as these only became evident at a later stage. Another explanation could be that, in spite of all constitutional niceties, the mission remained for all practical purposes the basic agency with which the government communicated and made arrangements; and the church was more or less bypassed. This suggests that the lack of parallelism in the mission's and the government's relations with their African sub-systems had little or no political effect, just as in the case of the policy of integration (cf. Chapter 19); but this suggestion must be further substantiated.

It is essential to emphasize from the outset that the colonial administration did not even contemplate following in the footsteps of the mission. If anything, it deliberately stuck to its previous policy when the issue of the proposed Central Lukiko came up for discussion. The same line prevailed when, at about the same time, a Legislative Council was established consisting of members of the colonial administration and three non-government representatives appointed by the Governor.[4] The unofficial members (two Europeans and one Indian) represented the immigrant communities, and it was not even discussed whether Africans should be members. Their interests were assumed to be represented by the government majority in the Legislative Council.[5] The same kind of thinking lay behind the establishment of another addition to the colonial machinery, the Executive Council, which was composed of the four official members of the Legislative Council, with the Governor as chairman.[6] The Provincial Commissioners strongly recommended that one member should be specifically appointed to the Executive Council to represent African interests; but they meant a Provincial Commissioner, not an African.[7] Africans were confined to the so-called 'native administration' within the existing administrative boundaries.

While the colonial administration was thus underlining the distinction between itself and the African administrative structure, and consciously clarifying and defining the role of the latter, certain developments occurred within the ecclesiastical field which necessitated some form of government response. This gives us an opportunity of examining whether and to what extent the different nature of the relationship between the mission and the church was of any concern to the government. The fact that the mission had followed its policy for a decade might be expected to have had some cumulative effect.

The controversy within the church about the placing of a cross on the altar in the new Cathedral first arose in 1919 in connection with the consecration of the new building, when a large section of the African clergy objected to its presence.[8] The controversy flared up again at the 1921 Synod and ended in a defeat for

Bishop Willis, who had to remove the cross under protest.[9] One internal observer took a very serious view of the whole incident, and feared a schism in the Anglican Church. If that happened, the opponents of the cross could easily turn anti-European, as strong feelings were involved.[10] The whole controversy came to the notice of the colonial administration, and was looked upon with some alarm. The government was first and foremost concerned with the wider political consequences of a possible split in the church;[11] but the treatment to which the Bishop had been subjected was also noticed with astonishment, and it dawned on the government that the reaction might be a negative effect of the system of government within the church. Consequently, the government began to regard the Synod with some suspicion, as it seemed to provide a platform for the expression of feelings which were difficult to control.[12]

The importance attached to the risk of a schism in the church was due to the fact that it was seen against the background of two other contemporary phenomena. One was the so-called Malaki sect, which had been started some ten years earlier by people who had broken away from the Anglican church. The Malaki church had attracted some 91,000 followers in Buganda alone, and although it had caused some trouble by its hostility to modern medicine, the government had tolerated it and had not taken its anti-European undertones too seriously.[13] Another phenomenon was an oppositional tendency among the younger generation against the chiefly hierarchy. This included demands, such as those expressed by the Young Baganda Association, for better educational facilities. Taken singly, these three highly different movements were considered relatively harmless, although a close watch was kept on them. However, if the two former movements or possibly all three combined forces, there would be every reason for alarm, as anti-European feeling would most likely be their rallying-point. Missionaries pointed out this possibility,[14] and government officials expressed considerable concern at the prospect.[15]

The government therefore kept the internal situation in the church under close surveillance in view of its possible political implications. It doubted the mission's ability, given the organizational system of the church, to control the forces that existed within its ranks. The mission was also increasingly forced to acknowledge its common interests with the government and the need for alertness and stricter control. This corresponded to the trend observed earlier towards cooperation in education.[16] We may cite two examples of this overall tendency. When the Ganda newspaper *Munyonyozi*, sponsored by the Bataka Association, vehemently attacked the Katikiro, Sir Apolo Kagwa, for his way of running official functions, the matter came to the notice of the Governor, who asked the Bishop whether he thought it expedient to impose a three months' ban on the paper. The Bishop fully supported this idea; the move could have a salutary effect by stemming 'the growing spirit of impatience at tribal authority among the young Baganda'.[17] The Governor and the Bishop thus agreed in their analysis of the situation and on the measures to be taken. A second example of the mission's awareness of the necessity for joint action and cooperation was a statement by Bishop Willis: 'Our great object is to train the Native Church, as the Government is training the Native Chiefs, to undertake responsibility.'[18]

Apart from confirming the parallelism between the two European agencies' principal goals, this statement touches indirectly on the question of the range of African responsibility and the speed of the process of Africanization. Within these fields the mission had followed different principles from those of the government, and had placed more responsibility in African hands. It will be appropriate to examine how the government responded to this difference of approach and to find out whether it tried to exert any influence on appointments within the church in view of the increased awareness of common interests which was evident from the beginning of the 1920s onwards.

In 1922 two African clergymen were nominated as trustees for the Native Anglican Church. Hitherto all land granted for church work had been invested in three European trustees – the Bishop, the Archdeacon of Buganda and the Secretary of the CMS mission. In accordance with the law these three were recognized as a corporate body by the Governor.[19] As the ecclesiastical authorities laid great weight on the fact that the land belonged to the African church rather than the mission, the Diocesan Council wanted two Africans added to the number of trustees. The Bishop duly approached the government for its approval of this change,[20] and went out of his way to emphasize that the obligations connected with church land would be fulfilled, as the majority of trustees would still be Europeans, and the Bishop would have the right to veto all recommendations.[21] The question was considered by the newly established Executive Council, which found it inadvisable to appoint Africans as trustees. The main reason given was 'their present state of development'.[22] The proposal was thus rejected, and not even a modified version with only one African co-trustee was approved.[23] When it came to the central issue of responsibility for and control of land, the colonial government thus exercised its power to prevent even a very limited extension of African influence. This indicates that it wanted to deal with Europeans only, and had no interest in the issue of the mission's integration into the church; an attitude in full harmony with that on the issue of church versus mission ownership of land granted for Christian purposes.

A further case revealed the same trend in government thinking. The CMS mission applied for permission to employ a coloured West Indian doctor, highly qualified for the job.[24] The government turned down the request, and admitted that it did so for political reasons. Employing the doctor would stimulate the aspirations of the young Baganda and increase their dissatisfaction with the present lack of educational opportunities, particularly the rather basic course for medical students at Makerere.[25] Such a violation of existing racial boundaries between mission and church would, the government claimed, have grave political consequences for the rest of society. The government was evidently concerned about how far integration between the mission and the church could progress, and was willing to interfere to limit it if it thought that it might have serious effects.

A third, more indirect case supplements this assessment of the government's attitude. The practice of paying teaching missionaries out of the government grant caused, as we have seen, a change in the decision-making processes within the church and subsequently had an adverse effect on the relationship between the mission and the church, measured against the principles laid down in the constitution. The government directly influenced this process by explicitly stating that it gave the grant solely to the CMS, not to the NAC, and that the relations between these two bodies were none of its concern. This caused some disagreement in missionary circles, and the issue was discussed once again at the Synod in 1924. A resolution was passed, calling upon the government to make the educational grant payable to the church instead of to the mission;[26] the government was unwilling to do so.[27] Even Bishop Willis' compromise formula (that the educational grant should be made to 'the Registered Trustees of the NAC') was rejected.[28] As in the case of church land, the government would not recognize any legal rights as being invested solely in the church. The relationship between the mission and the church was irrelevant, as it was a purely internal matter.[29]

Taken together, these three cases show that the government saw the ecclesiastical system in terms of its own organization. It dealt with the mission as a counterpart related to its African sub-system as the government was to the African political system, although it was fully aware of the mission's different objectives and its attempts to integrate mission and church. Sometimes the differences in policy had unwelcome consequences. In these cases the government used its powers of intervention to block proposed measures, or pointed out the mission's own interest in limiting and controlling African activities. This approach, backed by the economic strength of the government, proved most effective. In so far as the government succeeded in neutralizing the political effects of the difference between the church system and its own, it was justified in acting on the basis of an assumed parallelism. The situation was summed up in the following statement, which mentions another factor which helps to complete the picture. 'There is a strong native representation on the Council and on all sub-committees, but the Bishop and his European staff fill the post of President and other offices by the Constitution of the Church.'[30] In other words, in spite of all the missionary talk of integration and a special constitution, Europeans held all the leading posts and thus retained firm control of the church. The process of Africanization had not gone so far as to give Africans control of the leadership. The background for this state of affairs has been discussed in detail elsewhere,[31] and only two essential factors will be repeated here. First, there was a built-in inequality between missionaries and Africans in the integration process; the missionaries had a special status, as they belonged to both the mission and the church at the same time. Secondly, the missionary attitude to Africans left little scope for African advancement. Both these factors should be kept in mind as we examine some of the steps which were taken by the mission to increase African influence. We should then be able to explain why developments in the church were such that the government could still consider the mission's relationship with the church as a parallel to its own relationship with the African political systems.

As we discuss the issue of Africanization within the church, we should bear in mind the composition of its various committees. Three groups were identifiable at most organizational levels: the European missionaries, the African clergy and the lay representatives (mostly chiefs). However, most of the influential posts (Chairmen, Secretaries of Committees, and the executive offices such as Bishop, Archdeacon and Rural Dean) were held by missionaries. The process of Africanization would have meant the replacement of missionaries by African clergymen. The Anglican Church of Uganda was essentially a clergy-led institution, and an early ruling stipulated that secular leaders like chiefs could not be ecclesiastical leaders at the same time.

If Africanization of the leadership was to prevail, the Africans themselves, and especially the chiefs, must work for it. While there was some discontent among the African clergy, the chiefs were not active in this respect. It may be that the lower status of the African clergy and the perpetual problem of the clergy's low educational standard gave the chiefs less inclination to exert any pressure.[32] Also, the alliance between the chiefs and the missionaries worked so well inside as well as outside the framework of the church that it was considered inadvisable to bring in a third group which might have had diverging interests from the others.[33] Another precondition for Africanization was a positive attitude from the missionaries. When the mission might have been expected, in accordance with the spirit of the constitution, to hand over influence and responsibility to the Africans, Bishop Willis and other missionaries were hinting at the African clergy's lack of education and experience, and justifying the European presence in the church by reference to the need for someone who could take initiatives and show powers of leadership.[34] One indication of the mission's reluctance to give more responsibility to the African clergy came in 1913, when anxiety was expressed over the fact that five African priests were put in sole charge of their pastorates as against two in 1912. Even at this relatively low level, this development was seen as premature. The change was due to a shortage of missionaries rather than deliberate policy.[35]

It was typical of the situation in Uganda that it was the home authorities who noticed the lack of congruence between the ideals laid down in the constitution and their very slow implementation. A retired missionary spoke of the risk that European dominance would cripple the African pastorate,[36] and the CMS in London called for a speeding-up of the transfer of the work to African hands.[37] A member of the CMS Committee was asked to assess the situation during a visit to Uganda, and he said in his report that more could be done to phase out European control.[38] Nothing concrete seems to have materialized from these efforts. Soon afterwards, as an experiment, one of the missionaries let three African clergymen run the work in his district with no more than nominal European supervision. But others found this premature,[39] and this was typical of the missionary stand over the rest of the period. The transfer of authority, they felt, must be very gradual,[40] and for the moment the African clergy were unable to assume more responsibility than they already had.[41] The argument was that the educational standard of the prospective leaders was still too low.[42] This attitude was maintained in the face of mounting African pressure,[43] and in defiance of a new request from the home authorities to speed up the process of Africanization.[44] Dependence 'intellectually, financially, spiritually' on European help was felt to be so great that if Europeans withdrew there was a real danger of 'an Ethiopian movement on a large scale' – the formation of an independent church which would become increasingly anti-European and anti-government.[45]

During the period under discussion the only opportunities for African advancement were due to the shortage of missionaries and the need to concentrate those who were available on supervision and training – the so-called 'withdrawal upwards'.[46] It was decided, not without some misgivings, to replace the European Rural Deans in Buganda with African clergymen,[47] and in 1922 the first four African Rural Deans were appointed.[48] But it was emphasized that they were subject to the supervision of the Archdeacon and that the remaining eight Deaneries were still under the direct control of Europeans.[49]

The four Ganda Rural Deans were the only officials who realized the mission's goal of handing as much responsibility as possible over to the Africans; such a small step was hardly likely to be noticed by the government at all. The missionaries had very little confidence in the Africans' capabilities, and constantly referred to their insufficient educational standards. Since the education and training of African clergy was part of the policy of self-support, the only possible conclusion is the paradoxical one that strict adherence to one principle hindered the realization of another, that of creating a self-governing church. There was thus very little reason for the government to be concerned over the possible political effects of the difference between the ecclesiastical system and its own.

At a more subtle level another blocking mechanism was inherent in the relationship between the mission and the church. When rules were laid down in 1917 for European Anglican congregations and chaplaincies, the possibility was mentioned that at some future date Rural Deans and Archdeacons might be Africans. In that case they were not to have visitorial powers in any English church; a senior English clergyman must be appointed for this purpose.[50] The African clergy's authority was thus circumscribed from the outset, as an office-holding African could never have any supervisory powers over Europeans. That this principle could hinder the rise of an African leadership became evident a few years later. When the decision was made to pay some of the teaching missionaries out of the government grant the Uganda mission pointed out that if these payments were approved by the Diocesan Council, where Africans were in the majority, the result would be 'Native control of White men'. This possibility had been firmly rejected in 1909, and the establishment of the Missionary Committee to handle all matters concerning Europeans provided a safeguard in that respect. The solution to the problem of the educational grant and its wider consequences has already been discussed. It is, however, clear that the 1909 settlement, which granted the missionaries a dual position by allowing them to belong to both the mission and the church and providing them with guarantees against coming under African control, had the effect of preventing Africans from taking over the leadership. As long as the missionaries held the key posts in the church, there could be no real integration of mission and church. In other words, in spite of all the mission's denials, there was in practice a dual system within the church which corresponded with the distinction between mission and church and underlined the inequality between African and European workers.[51] In spite of different frameworks, the parallelism between the political and the ecclesiastical fields was clear. The distinction between the European and African areas of authority was upheld in both cases.

The government was probably unaware of these hindrances to African advancement and leadership. What mattered most to them was, as appeared from the quotation above (p. 379), the fact that government officials never had to deal with Africans in leading positions rather than missionaries. Their contacts in most cases were with the Bishop or the Secretary of the CMS Uganda mission. It was impossible to decide in any given case whether the missionary representative was acting on behalf of the mission or the church. Sometimes the same person held two official posts, and it was difficult for outsiders to know which role he was playing.[52] In the most influential bodies within the church organization, the Synod and the Diocesan Council, it is significant that all through the period missionaries were appointed Secretaries with African clergymen as Co-Secretaries.[53] In all the Advisory Boards the Bishop was the ex officio Chairman, and only missionaries functioned as Secretaries.[54] It was considered exceptional when an African was elected at the Synod in 1921 as Assistant Financial Secretary.[55] But when the missionary who held the post of Treasurer later went on leave, and the Assistant Financial Secretary might in the normal course of events have been expected to take over his post, another European (who also happened to be the Secretary of the mission) was asked to fill the vacancy. This appointment was decided by the mission without any reference to the church authorities.[56] At the next Synod in 1924 the control of finances remained in European hands.[57]

The fact that European missionaries held all the offices with which the colonial administration came into contact was almost ironically confirmed in 1925, when the mission made renewed efforts to get the government to understand the essential difference between the mission and the church.[58]

A list was made of the departments into which the work of the church was divided, and of the proper persons to whom correspondence should be addressed; in all cases the leaders of departments were European missionaries.[59] Even at the local level the local missionary was the key person irrespective of his status in the church. The government was left with a rather confusing impression: 'All such correspondence should be sent through the Senior Missionary of the District, either (if the matter concerns the C.M.S) in his capacity as Senior Missionary or (if it concerns the work of the N.A.C) as the cleryman in ecclesiastical charge of the district.'[60]

The fact that the mission failed to pursue its policy of Africanization and kept the leading offices in the hands of the missionaries gave the government the impression that the mission provided the main decision-making structure within the ecclesiastical field. Despite the different constitutional system and the mission's declared goal of making the church independent of missionary control, there was in practice a parallel between the colonial government's and the mission's relationships with their respective African sub-systems. It was thus with full justification that the government attached little political importance to the different organization of the church. This attitude was encouraged by the diffidence of the mission on the subject of its own longer-term aims. It failed to challenge the government, as it saw its own interests better served by not diverging too much from the government line. The various movements among the Africans around 1920 also made the mission acutely aware of the interests which it had in common with the government and reinforced certain tendencies which already existed within the mission. All this resulted in a parallelism between the two agencies in their relationships with their respective African sub-systems.

Hence, seen from the point of view of the colonial state, the Synod and its various committees could not be of much relevance. Judging from organizational criteria, we have claimed that the missionary structure was superior to the synodal system when it came to influence and decision-making. The composition of the various bodies within the church has also shown that the missionaries and the chiefs dominated at the expense of the African clergy. This again meant that the Synod to a great extent reflected tensions in society, not least the split between Buganda and the rest of the country, which counteracted its integrative potential (Chapter 19). This rather pessimistic assessment of the Synod needs, however, to be balanced by the introduction of three wider criteria which have not figured prominently in the present survey. First, at the concrete level the Synod served as a forum for solving grievances and raising opposition in matters internal to the church, and also in relation to conflicts which reflected tensions in society at large (see in particular Chapter 22). Secondly, in the eyes of the African population the church at least provided, unlike the colonial system, some opportunity for expressing legitimate African concerns. Thirdly, seen from the outside, not least from the neighbouring East Africa Protectorate (Kenya), the synodal system based on democratic principles was considered to be a Ugandan privilege which was not attainable for other African Christians in the near future.[61]

21

The language problem in the Protectorate

We have seen that the CMS mission considered the employment of a single language to be the best method of unifying the church and integrating the various parts of the Protectorate. The language issue linked the church with the political arena in two respects. In the first place, it was used at an early stage by African leaders, for example the Omukama and the chiefs in Toro, as a means of obtaining certain political objectives. In the second place, the mission considered that it was necessary for it to coordinate its own policy with that of the government, or even to try to influence the government in order to achieve the common goal of a unified Protectorate. During the initial years of the century both trends exerted some influence on the mission's language policy, although the two were not always complementary. As regards the first kind of linkage, we have seen how African pressure for the recognition of Lutoro/Lunyoro within the church was supported by some of the missionaries and constituted an element of opposition to the Luganda monopoly. Another group within the mission, led by Archdeacon Walker, favoured Luganda for the sake of unity within both the church and state.[1] Bishop Tucker took up the position between these two: while he was willing to grant concessions to the vernaculars in deference to the strength of national feeling in the two Western Kingdoms, he upheld the primacy of Luganda at higher levels.[2] One result of this acknowledgement of Lutoro/Lunyoro was that the missionaries were no longer obliged to pass language examinations in Luganda, nor were they required to learn another language if they had chosen to learn Lunyoro at first instead of Luganda.[3]

That some recognition was given to vernaculars other than Luganda did not mean that the mission vacillated in its longer-term aim of promoting Luganda as the primary language of the Protectorate. But it did indicate a split within the mission as regards the speed and thoroughness with which this longer-term policy should be carried out. In this situation the government's language policy became of crucial importance, as it might give some support to either of the two diverging opinions within the mission. Archdeacon Walker was fully aware of the import-ance of the government's policy, and requested at an early stage the government's support for the Luganda alternative. He was given at least verbal assurances and a declaration of intent by the Acting Commissioner, but when it came to giving practical support the government took a more passive line, deciding to await the results of the mission's efforts to promote Luganda. In the meantime, Swahili proved in practice to be an easier language than Luganda, and of more general application, and accordingly more immediately suitable for colonial officials. Swahili was therefore made obligatory, while Luganda and some other Bantu and Nilotic languages were made 'bonus languages', and special benefits were conferred for the passing of an examination in them.[4] Commenting on the upgrading of Swahili, the Commissioner said that the fact that Luganda was now a 'bonus language' helped to promote its use, and said that government policy was geared in the longer term to that of the mission. If the mission succeeded in making Luganda the most useful language, steps would be taken to reintroduce it as the obligatory language.[5]

When the Commissioner explained this wait-and-see policy to the mission and asked for its comments,[6] Bishop Tucker admitted the strength of the practical reasons for making Swahili obligatory, and expressed his appreciation of the encouragement given to the study of Luganda; but his real attitude was revealed by his shrewdly worded refusal to teach Swahili in the schools, which stated that he much preferred English to Swahili as the lingua franca.[7] Internally, he gave as his real reason the fact that 'Swahili like Arabic means Mahomedanism and all its evil influence'.[8] Faced with the Swahili threat, Tucker was obviously capitalizing on the government's natural preference for English; accordingly the mission's preference for Luganda was temporarily played down in dealings with the colonial administration. The change in government policy thus had some impact on short-term missionary policy.

A different influence which also had the result of reducing the prospects for Luganda was brought to bear a little later, when the pressure of national feeling in Toro and Bunyoro became too strong for the mission to maintain its previous policy of restricting translations into Lunyoro in order to facilitate the spread of Luganda. As early as 1905 the Omukama and chiefs of Toro demanded the whole Bible, including the Old Testament, in a Lunyoro version. This would give Lunyoro primacy in the areas in which it was spoken and a status that was equal to that of Luganda.[9] Their demand was supported by the Toro-based missionaries, and they tried to get the Bunyoro leaders to join forces with them.[10] There was some support in Bunyoro for the translation, but by far the most characteristic feature in Bunyoro was that the issue had a strong catalytic effect and sparked off strong anti-Buganda feeling which resulted in revolt against the Baganda chiefs in 1907 (see below, p. 398).[11]

The wider implications of the Lunyoro Bible translation issue were thus apparent at an early stage; a positive decision would be a turning-point for mission policy in more than one respect. It is then hardly surprising that the issue split the mission in two. The absolute majority, including most of the senior missionaries, and in particular Archdeacon Walker, held one opinion; while another group – mainly the Toro missionaries, strongly supported by Bishop Tucker – held the opposite view; and in the end the latter view was victorious.[12] The former faction raised three objections to the translation of the whole Bible into Lunyoro. First, it would mean the virtual abandonment of the previous policy of making Luganda the primary language in the Protectorate. This was to be regretted for a number of reasons: Luganda was by far the most highly-developed language of all; it was spoken by the leading and most progressive part of the population and at the centre of administration; finally, to work with more than one language in the church beyond a certain level involved severe practical difficulties as regards the printing of books.[13] The second argument was that giving up Luganda as the primary language would mean that the major instrument in binding together the various parts of the Protectorate into a more united whole was lost. The loss of one common language would help to 'keep alive all tribal differences and separations . . .'[14] In a wider sense, such a change in language policy in reality implied the complete abandonment of the 'federal policy' pursued on Ganda terms and under Buganda hegemony.[15] Thirdly, the concessions to the demands for a Lunyoro Bible translation were of a political character: the problem had become purely political, and had nothing to do with a sincere desire for an Old Testament translation; it had more to do with anti-Buganda feeling and opposition to any Ganda influence.[16] It would be a severe setback to the whole Christian effort to give any concessions to these national feelings in the Western Kingdoms.

Bishop Tucker knew all these arguments and was fully aware of the wider implications of the language issue. He conceded that by granting permission to translate the whole Bible into Lunyoro he was reversing the previous policy of making Luganda the primary language.[17] He conceded too that this reversal did nothing to further the unity and integration of the church and the Protectorate; but he could not disregard the strong feelings against Buganda dominance, and admitted that a policy of integration based on Ganda hegemony was no longer tenable.[18] In both these respects he acknowledged the need for a new policy. But the main reason for Tucker's radical change was his positive attitude to the national movements in the Western Kingdoms. He was convinced of the sincerity of the desire for a Lunyoro Bible translation, and he could not accept that the demand was solely due to political motives. It would be an outrage to disregard a genuine wish by saying: 'You shall *not* have the Word of God in your own tongue.'[19] He admitted that the demand for such a translation also sprang from national feelings; but such feelings should not be neglected, and the mission was fully justified in adopting an accommodating attitude to this kind of political movement. Tucker even went so far as to sympathize with the opposition to the tendency towards Ganda dominance inherent in the government's administrative policy. Accordingly he could not rebuke those Toro missionaries who were being accused by their colleagues of having actively supported the national movement.[20] Tucker said outright that to reject the demand for a Lunyoro Bible would in the eyes of many Batoro and Banyoro be 'to side with those who are resisting their just national aspirations . . .'[21]

Accordingly Bishop Tucker pressed the issue through the Missionary Committee in the face of strong opposition, and won his case only by using his position and authority.[22] Both opponents and supporters recognized that this move heralded a fundamental change in mission policy in the two related areas of language and federal policy. It is quite remarkable that the change came as a positive response to the national aspirations of the Western Kingdoms, with their explicit anti-Buganda bias. It now remains to examine the language policy the mission pursued from then on, and we must ask whether the government took any notice of the mission's deference to the national movement.

For the time being the mission shelved its direct, active attempts to make Luganda the primary language within the church. But it continued to give Luganda priority as the working language at the Diocesan level. It was written into the constitution of 1909 that all business at the Synod was to be transacted in Luganda.[23] The same rule was later extended to cover the proceedings of the Diocesan Council, and it was here added that the minutes should be kept in both Luganda and English.[24] Luganda was also made obligatory in the various Advisory Boards.[25] This may have been due to practical considerations, but it is worth emphasizing that the practice was likely to leave the church open to the suspicion that it nourished a Ganda bias or was even Ganda-dominated. In spite of the reversal of policy in 1907, language remained an important issue over the years and contributed to the church's problems as regards the rift between Buganda and the rest of the country (see below, Chapter 22).

African political pressure influenced the mission's policy. But we must also ask how much influence a second political factor, the wish for coordination with the government, had on the substantial changes in 1907. The available source material suggests that the government took remarkably little interest in the language controversy and the anti-Buganda feeling that lay behind it. During the Bunyoro agitation against Ganda agents the government noted that pupils in schools refused to be taught in Luganda or by Ganda teachers.[26] This was taken to indicate that the mission suffered just as much from the upheavals in Bunyoro as the colonial administration did. In other words, government officials did not see the language issue as one of the factors that sparked off the anti-Buganda rebellion, but rather as symptomatic of the same anti-Buganda feeling. As the CMS mission itself remained loyal to the government while the latter was quelling the upheavals in Bunyoro,[27] the government had no cause for alarm over the mission's handling of the demand for a Lunyoro Bible or its general language policy. The neutral official attitude to the language issue even in the face of strong national feeling was, however, in keeping with two features of government policy mentioned earlier. First of all, the government did not pursue the federal policy with the same vigour as the mission up to 1907–8, nor did it see Luganda as a major instrument in furthering the policy. Secondly, the obligatory language for officials was still Swahili, which meant that the government was unaffected by the mission's revision of its policy on the primacy of Luganda. The only linkage with the mission's language policy was the earlier promise that if Luganda gained sufficient ground in practice the government would be willing to adapt its own regulations to practical circumstances.

It was thus the concrete outcome of the mission's language policy which counted with the government, not the politically-inspired concessions sparked off by national aspirations. Within the Public Works Department it soon became evident that Luganda was a much more useful language than Swahili in most parts of the Protectorate. Consequently a request was submitted asking that Luganda be made the official language in the Department.[28] When this was granted, a similar request came from the Marine Department.[29] A process had begun which could eliminate Swahili as the obligatory language. When F. J. Jackson returned as Governor in 1911, he recognized that this process had gone so far that a change was now necessary. Swahili had not taken root in the Protectorate, and was clearly losing ground; Luganda was now a much more widely known language.[30] It should here be recalled that Jackson had at a very early stage spoken in favour of the mission's giving priority to Luganda. His decision when he returned was probably not unconnected with the now registrable effects of the mission's policy, especially the fact that the mission had firmly refused to teach Swahili in the schools. In recommending Luganda as the new obligatory language, Jackson's major argument was the status of the Baganda in the Protectorate, not only numerically, but also qualitatively. 'They are a progressive race and their language and influence are extending rapidly.'[31] Accordingly Luganda was made the obligatory language for all officials from 1912 onwards. Swahili and a number of other local languages continued to be bonus languages.[32]

There was no direct reference to the mission, but the new language policy can best be seen as a fulfilment of the old promise to gear government policy to the results of the mission's language policy. It is therefore interesting to observe that the government's move had a reciprocal effect on the mission. It was hailed as a great step forward that Luganda had at last replaced Swahili as the official language.[33] It was further added that such a lingua franca was badly needed, primarily for its unifying effect, and that Luganda was the only possibility.[34] Extra emphasis was now placed on the teaching of Luganda in elementary schools in the non-Luganda-speaking areas, while the local vernaculars were used as the medium of instruction. English was only taught in the higher-grade schools.[35] The Synod decided in 1913 that in the missionary areas, that is, in the Eastern and Northern Provinces, which were non-Bantu areas, the teaching of Luganda was begin in all schools.[36] The change in government policy in 1912 thus served as an impetus for the mission to strengthen the position of Luganda and to propagate its use as the most appropriate lingua franca in the Protectorate.

The 1913 measures in many ways represented a return to the period before the reversal of policy in 1907, and it is not surprising that the old repercussions once again came to the fore. The government had difficulties with the implementation of the new policy, and in 1914 officers serving in the Northern Province were excepted from the obligatory use of Luganda.[37] The mission for its part experienced a revival of national consciousness in the non-Ganda areas, and had to contend with widespread suspicion that the extended use of Luganda was synonymous with the increase of Buganda's influence. A request for a translation of the new policy, and in 1914 officers serving in the Northern Province were exempted from the obligatory use of Luganda.[37] The mission for its part experi- despite the fact that there were twice as many of them as there were Banyoro, they did not yet have a Christian literature in their mother tongue. Some money was allocated for the purpose, and the Omugabe continued to express interest on later occasions.[38] Later it was reaffirmed that Ankole was an independent kingdom with a language of its own.[39]

Two opposite tendencies were thus at work within the church. On the one hand, there was a drive to make Luganda the lingua franca of the Protectorate, on the other concessions to national movements allowing them to preserve their vernaculars. The inevitable result could only be that the process of making Luganda the national language was severely hampered,[40] and this in turn meant that the government had to question the advisability of linking its own language policy with that of the mission. It was on this basis that various officials argued when there was a new round of discussions of Luganda's status in 1918–19. It was claimed that the missionaries stationed in Bantu areas outside Buganda were making no real effort to introduce Luganda, but were helping to perpetuate the local Bantu languages through translations.[41] Besides this reference to the mission's language policy, two additional points were made against the suitability of Luganda as a lingua franca. First, it was a difficult language to learn, and unlikely to be taken up by non-Bantu peoples. Secondly, non-Baganda, especially those in the neighbouring Kingdoms and Busoga, were strongly prejudiced against Luganda for political reasons; the Baganda were not loved by their neighbours.[42] It was strongly recommended that Swahili should be re-established as a permanent official language, especially since it could facilitate communications with the East African Protectorate and German East Africa.[43]

Other officials claimed that the positive effects of the use of Luganda were just beginning to appear, and that it would be a step backwards to revert to Swahili. Swahili was an imported language and had much less affinity with the other Ugandan Bantu languages than Luganda. Swahili would tend to undermine the customs of the country, and to introduce it by force, as had been done in German East Africa, would inevitably create problems for the administration.[44] Jackson's reasons for making Luganda the official language were still considered valid, in particular his view of the Baganda's inherent qualities. They were not only 'the principal and most progressive tribe of this Protectorate',[45] but probably 'the most progressive race in Africa'.[46] This Ganda-biased position won the day in the first round of the language discussions. The Governor kept Luganda as the official language, except in the Northern Province, where Gang (Acholi) was recognized. He dismissed as invalid the argument that Swahili was the official language in other parts of East Africa. The Germans only encouraged it 'to facilitate exploitation for their own interests, and not those of the native inhabitants'.[47]

But the Swahili/Luganda debate did not end here. Another group, the European planters, announced its interest in the subject and argued in favour of Swahili for commercial reasons, as it facilitated communication with the rest of East Africa. At the same time they recommended that the opinion of the missions should be disregarded, as they had failed badly in their stated aims by allowing literature to be printed in so many vernaculars. It was suggested that the issue should be discussed again by officials from the district administration, the missions and the settler community.[48] This intervention sparked off a new round of talks in 1919–20. The arguments still centred on the familiar themes. How much importance was to be attached to the missions? What was the connection between Luganda and the Buganda influence? And how much emphasis should be put on ties to the rest of East Africa?

Within the colonial administration there were still two schools of thought. The first one had as its starting point the dwindling importance of Luganda, and had four main arguments.

(1) Buganda's influence had been substantially curtailed on a Protectorate-wide level. In particular the number of Ganda agents had been drastically reduced in the preceding ten years.

(2) The Baganda were unpopular among other groups because of the methods they used when they acted as agents.

(3) The missions had in fact not made extensive use of Luganda, but had instead made enormous efforts to translate the Bible into the many vernaculars. This disqualified Luganda as the universal language in the Protectorate.

(4) The Northern and Eastern Provinces had made very great progress compared with the rest of the Protectorate in the preceding eight years. In

these two provinces Swahili had gained much ground at the expense of Luganda. This disproved the accepted doctrine that there was a close correlation between the spread of Luganda and the progress of the Protectorate.[49]

The counter-arguments in favour of Swahili were as follows.

(1) In view of the growing feelings of 'national or tribal pride' it was unwise to adopt the language of any particular nation or tribe as the official language. This could provoke hostility from the others. The neutral Swahili was preferable.[50]

(2) Swahili was absolutely essential for communication with the adjacent East African territories, 'as the ultimate object of European control in East Africa is surely to weld the territory into one whole'.[51]

(3) The argument which the mission had used against Swahili since the days of Bishop Tucker, that Swahili was the language of Islam, was no longer tenable. Besides, this did not justify the choice of Luganda.[52]

(4) The outgoing Baganda agents had in the Eastern Province in particular been clerks of the courts and had kept the books in Luganda. But their young replacements from the local area were trained in the vernaculars. To secure uniformity and enable Swahili-speaking officials to inspect the books, Swahili was absolutely preferable.[53]

A second group of officials questioned both these groups of arguments and spoke in favour of Luganda as follows.

(1) In view of the number of languages in the Protectorate it would at all events be necessary to impose one language. Swahili was not the mother tongue in any part of the Protectorate, so the most sensible thing would be to select the language spoken by the greatest number of people.

(2) It was undeniable that the Baganda were unpopular, but not to the extent that other Bantu peoples would prefer Swahili to Luganda.

(3) Even though Lunyoro was spoken by more people than Luganda it was a crucial factor that 'the push and progressiveness of the Muganda is markedly greater than that of the Munyoro'.

(4) If the non-Bantu peoples of the north were to learn a Bantu language anyway, it might just as well be Luganda.[54]

So far the discussions remained inconclusive. The characteristic pattern was that officials working outside Buganda tended to support Swahili, while those connected with Buganda were in favour of Luganda. The missions do not seem to have been consulted, but the work of the Uganda Development Commission during the latter months of 1919 (see Chapter 15) provided them with a platform from which to present their views, as it did for the planters and the business community. It was in fact the first opportunity since the days of Bishop Tucker when the CMS could publicly state its views on the language issue. But internal differences prevented the mission on this occasion from presenting a united front. The Archdeacon, speaking for the Bishop, who was away at the time, made a strong plea for the use of Luganda as the official language, and argued against Swahili. He foresaw, however, that English would one day supplant Luganda.[55] Another missionary who gave evidence for the Commission was less negative towards Swahili, but he preferred Luganda.[56] Only one gave his full support to Luganda alone,[57] while another was in favour of English.[58]

Probably in order to counteract the image of vagueness which these internal differences presented, the mission took the opportunity of restating its language policy in its own magazine. At the same time it reminded the Uganda Development Commission that there was not a single missionary among its members, and that it was therefore unqualified to decide on language matters.[59] The article was strongly in favour of Luganda, first of all because it was already widely spoken and understood in all parts of the Protectorate, secondly because of the inherent qualities of the Baganda. They 'are the most intelligent people in the Protectorate and the most valuable native servants of Church, State and Commerce'.[60] The mission's admiration of and bias towards the Baganda were thus made perfectly clear. This line of argument could only serve to fuel the widespread suspicion that the spread of Luganda was inseparable from the extension of Ganda influence.

The European settler and business community continued to favour Swahili.[61] But the mission did gain some support from E. L. Scott, who by virtue of his office was considered to be well informed on so-called 'native affairs'.[62] He summarized the arguments in favour of Luganda, but at the same time pointed out the necessity for cooperation between the missions and the government. Luganda had almost become the lingua franca as the Baganda had exerted the greatest civilizing influence in the Protectorate. They had been used both by the government and the mission in all parts of the Protectorate. The missions' main mistake had been that it had committed the various local languages to writing and had used them as the medium of instruction in their schools.[63] He also emphasized Luganda's association with Christianity. Swahili was a carrier of Islam, with its dangerous political consequences, and every step should be taken to check the rising tide of 'Mohammedanism'. As for Luganda it 'was created as a written language by the Christian Missions, and has been the language through which Christian doctines have been first interpreted among the bulk of the tribes of the Protectorate . . . '[64] Scott thus implied that the government had to take religious considerations into account when adopting a language policy, and accordingly urged that the government pursue an active policy with the aim of establishing Luganda as the common language, in cooperation with the missionary societies. In other words, the missionaries were indispensable for the implementation of any language policy, especially as the schools were entirely in their hands.[65] The connection between the missionaries and the implementation of any official language policy was here recognized and formulated more precisely than ever before. There was one attempt to act upon this premise at the time, when the issue of the language of the courts in the Eastern Province came up. As the Ganda clerks had to leave in accordance with the new government policy, but the court records were still kept in Luganda, both missions were asked to teach young locals Luganda in their schools so that they could take over the posts.[66]

Faced with these conflicting views, the Uganda Development Commission came to no final conclusion.[67] The two schools of thought within the colonial administration represented by officials outside Buganda and those at government headquarters continued their discussion along the same lines as before. The Provincial Commissioners' Conference in November 1920 supported Swahili as the official language and recommended that the missions be asked to teach it in their schools.[68] The necessity of including the missions was thus acknowledged; but the suggestion was rejected, and again the missionary factor played an important role. The long-term aim was to make English the language of the country, as the CMS mission had already suggested; in the meantime Luganda was to remain the official language.[69] This policy was upheld over the next few years,[70] and in 1922 the Provincial Commissioners gave up trying to make Swahili the official language.[71] Luganda remained the obligatory language for government officers with certain exceptions (Gang in the north, Lunyoro in Bunyoro and Toro, and Swahili in Kigezi).[72]

But the problem did not end here. While Luganda held its ground against Swahili, both the government and the missions prevented a complete breakthrough for Luganda by envisaging a time when English would be the official language. The most concrete outcome of the protracted discussion of the language issue had so far been that the government had understood that its language policy had to be linked to that of the mission, especially as the missionaries ran the schools.[73]

The educational sector therefore naturally became the next area where the language issue was discussed. In connection with the increased government engagement in education in the Protectorate, E. R. J. Hussey, who later became Director of Education, said in a 1924 report that Luganda was the main medium of instruction in the schools in accordance with the government's policy of making it the official language. He suggested that it should continue to be used at the primary level (in the Elementary Vernacular Schools) all over the Protectorate, whereas English should take over at the higher levels.[74] The Provincial Commissioners also acknowledged the importance of the educational sector, and after consultation with the Director of Education they finally came out in support of using Luganda all over the Protectorate in elementary education. Their recommendation was hailed as the end of the Swahili/Luganda controversy, and it was assumed that Luganda was now becoming so widespread that its final victory could only be delayed, not stopped by government intervention.[75] The forecast, however, proved somewhat optimistic. In practice Luganda did not have the full support of the mission or the government. Both agencies differentiated between the various parts of the Protectorate, both for practical reasons, and out of respect for the use of the mother tongue in elementary education. The latter principle was especially impressed on agencies in Uganda by the Colonial Office's Advisory Committee on Native Education in Tropical Africa, although there was some disagreement as to whether the aim should be to concentrate on a few of the local languages or preserve the many.[76] In Uganda the issue came up for discussion in the newly established Advisory Council on Native Education, where both mission and government officials were members.[77] Towards the end of 1925 it was unanimously approved that instruction in elementary schools was to be given according to the three main language groups. Luganda was to be the language of the Bantu areas, Acholi (Gang) in parts of the Northern and Eastern Provinces, and Iteso in parts of the Eastern Province.[78]

The long drawn-out discussion of the single-language issue in Uganda thus seemed to have come to an end with the reorganization of the educational system. No language was given official status, and the project for linguistic unity in the Protectorate seemed to have been shelved. The principles of differentiation which had been employed in mission and government circles for the previous two decades thus proved to be the key to a settlement. The result, and the significance of the long and difficult controversy, may best be assessed by discussing the political connotations of the language issue, and the longer-term prospects for the language policy adopted in the mid-1920s.

The CMS mission had succeeded over the years, with the help of the other missions, in combating the forces within the colonial administration who favoured Swahili. But it did not succeed in making Luganda the universal language of the Protectorate. This was first and foremost due to the strength of the national movements, which made language a key issue in their campaigns, which in turn caused disunity within the mission. While the mission was thus torn between Luganda and the various vernaculars, but largely united in its opposition to Swahili, the colonial government experienced a split within its own ranks between Swahili and Luganda supporters. Both agencies were thus weakened in their capacity to pursue a uniform language policy. This helps to explain why the issue was such a protracted one. Even more significantly, internal differences within each agency opened up the possibility of informal alliances across the usually stable boundary between the government and the mission.

In the latter respect, the language issue illustrates one particular aspect of the pattern of relations between the mission and the government which is worth pursuing further, as it shows a characteristic kind of linkage between the two fields. At first the Luganda faction within the mission angled for the government's direct support, but this resulted only in a passive relationship, in the sense that the government upheld the primacy of Swahili for its officers but expressed willingness to adapt its own language policy to the palpable results of the mission's campaign for the spread of Luganda. These results were not forthcoming because of the various concessions granted to national movements in the form of Bible translations into local vernaculars. When there seemed to be no solution in sight to the Swahili/Luganda dilemma, Governor Jackson almost overnight changed the government's role to an active one by making Luganda the official language. This certainly gave a boost to the mission's efforts to promote Luganda, but the widespread preference for individual vernaculars, combined with opposition to the spread of Ganda influence through Luganda, constantly hampered missionary endeavours to promote Luganda as a lingua franca.

A decisive new phase began around 1920 with the forming of a more active alliance between the leadership of the mission and the Luganda faction within the colonial administration. The common ground for this cooperation was a high regard for the Baganda, and a positive assessment of Buganda's leading role in the Protectorate. Some officials even thought that they had so many interests in common with the mission's leadership that they were willing to take religious considerations into account in rejecting Swahili and advocating Luganda as the carrier of Christian values. This informal alliance exerted considerable influence on policy-making in favour of Luganda and worked to the detriment of support for Swahili. Missionary influence in support of Luganda came to a peak when the school system was recognized as a key instrument for pursuing any language policy, and when the government acknowledged the necessity for close cooperation between itself and the missions in questions of language. By 1924 it was no longer considered possible to halt the spread of Luganda and the mission could, after all its setbacks, see victory ahead.

But the expected victory did not materialize. Anti-Luganda factors were still at work, and both the mission and the government had to settle soon afterwards for a pluralistic solution which effectively ruled out the prospect of Luganda ever becoming the official language of the whole Protectorate. But not even this solution, which after all kept Luganda as the lingua franca in the Bantu areas, and granted Swahili no recognition, proved to be the final one. To explain the failure of the mission's language policy and to assess the extent of the mission's influence in general, we must mention the next phase of the language controversy, although it falls outside the actual period under investigation.

In the Bantu areas national feeling was still strong and found expression in an anti-Buganda attitude which militated against the extended use of Luganda. Even in the areas neighbouring Buganda, Luganda could hardly be regarded as a lingua franca. In addition, the Northern and Eastern Provinces were mixed linguistic areas where neither Acholi nor Iteso could be used as common languages.[79] This made an adjustment of the 1925 settlement necessary, and support for Swahili was renewed among colonial officials.[80] The Governor in particular was a keen protagonist of Swahili, and considered Governor Jackson's reversal of policy in 1912 to have been a mistake.[81] He suggested various steps which could be taken to promote Swahili as the primary language, for instance that it should be made the medium of instruction in the elementary schools in the north. But he was at the same time fully aware that cooperation from the people who ran the schools was indispensable.[82] When the issue was discussed in the Advisory Council on Native Education, the CMS mission was taken by surprise by the reappearance of the Swahili problem.[83] They managed to block the endorsement of Swahili as a future official language, but they had to give their reluctant approval to certain adjustments in the previous policy which allowed for Swahili in the curriculum. In the mixed language areas (the Northern and Eastern Provinces), Swahili was to be taught in the Elementary Vernacular Schools, but the vernaculars were to remain the medium of instruction. The status quo would be maintained in the Bantu areas, but Swahili would be made an optional subject in the non-Ganda districts. As for Buganda, it was underlined that the medium of instruction there would always be Luganda. Swahili was also to be taught in the Teacher Training Colleges.[84]

This 1927 compromise solution was open to different interpretations. The mission naturally considered that the status now accorded Swahili was the maximum one acceptable, and during the following years they took care that no further concessions were granted to it. Their control of most of the educational system, especially at the elementary level, allowed them to use delaying tactics, and the government actually accused them of doing so.[85] The mission interpreted the government's move as a revival of the earlier Luganda/Swahili controversy, and deplored this, as English had been agreed upon as the official language of the future. For the time being, they claimed that all arguments were in favour of retaining and extending the use of Luganda rather than Swahili.[86]

On the government's side, the settlement of late 1927 was seen as a first step towards making Swahili the official language.[87] Various measures were taken to speed up this process, by, for instance, making Swahili not only a subject but also the medium of instruction in the last three years of the elementary course in the mixed language areas.[88] The government also saw the struggle as one between Swahili and Luganda, and the suggestion was even made that the mission could be defeated if the government exploited its dependence on the educational grants-in-aid.[89] In the end, as no viable solution appeared, the 1927 compromise was reaffirmed by the government in 1932.[90] Neither side could win its case under the prevailing circumstances; in the longer term, however, English was available as a possible way out of the stalemate.[91]

One reason for the reintroduction of Swahili as a possibility was the drive for East African unity in the later 1920s.[92] But the decisive factor in shaping both agencies' attitudes during the renewed Swahili/Luganda controversy was their different assessments of Buganda's role in the Protectorate. The government's opposition to Luganda was clearly connected with Buganda's falling stock with colonial officials. Apart from the fact that Luganda had not proved itself to have lingua-franca qualities, the government found it inadvisable to make Luganda the official language in view of Buganda's dwindling importance. At the same time the government attributed the mission's strong pro-Luganda stand largely to its continued affection for the Baganda in view of Buganda's early contribution to the spread of the Gospel and its continued importance within the church.[93]

As for the mission, the Buganda factor certainly exerted a great deal of influence on its pro-Luganda language policy. The mission had great affection for the Baganda and a positive assessment of Buganda's leading role in the Protectorate; and the same was the case during the later phase of the language controversy.[94] It is further significant that, every time the mission was close to victory with its pro-Luganda policy, its success was due to a positive attitude to the Baganda on the part of the leading nucleus within the colonial administration. When Buganda's stock began to fall, the mission was unable to pursue the Luganda policy with any great success, in spite of the fact that its efforts were supported by active cooperation from the Ganda leaders in church and state. Still, even under the difficult circumstances of the later 1920s, their joint efforts proved strong enough to combat the Swahili threat. The reappearance of Swahili as an alternative thus served to strengthen bonds between the mission and Buganda, and may have prevented the mission from following the government in a critical reappraisal of its dependence on Buganda. This assessment of the situation gains support from the Ganda response. From the point of view of the Ganda leaders, it was not just the Swahili issue which confirmed the political value of their alliance with the mission.[95] The campaign for the introduction for Swahili was recognized as part of the larger issue of the unification of East Africa.[96] Under these circumstances it was to the advantage of both parties to join forces, and the alliance could only strengthen the impression that the mission identified itself closely with the interests of Buganda.[97]

Two aspects of this situation were significant. First, the mission's affection for the Buganda did not decline, as the government's did. The mission thus continued to see the language issue largely through Baganda eyes. It was still convinced that Buganda was the key to the progress of the whole Protectorate, as the Baganda were the most advanced and progressive people in the area.[98] Secondly, the mission's pro-Ganda outlook not only influenced its own policy; it affected the mission's approach to the government, and, as things turned out, weakened its influence with it. All in all, judging from the language issue, a 'Buganda syndrome' seems to have characterized the mission's policy and influenced the government's response to it. As we have met the same factor before in other contexts, a later chapter will examine the wider implications of this syndrome.

The later phase of the language issue brought some changes in the pattern of relations between mission and government. At first the mission took the lead, and the government was willing to adapt its own policy to the mission's results. When these were not forthcoming, officials attempted to disregard the mission and pursue their own policy. This led to a phase where the need for active cooperation between the two agencies was emphasized, especially in the educational sector. When the policy of cooperation in the promotion of Luganda proved unrealistic, the government's influence increased and a situation resulted where the state held the initiative and the mission had to conduct a defensive rear-guard action in the Swahili/Luganda controversy.

The mission's loss of the initiative cannot be explained solely by the weaknesses inherent in its Luganda policy, although these were in evidence all through the period. The educational sector was more important as the key to a successful language policy. The schools replaced translation work as the major method of promoting a particular language. This must be linked with the government's increased engagement in education, which began in the early 1920s (Chapter 15). The decline of missionary influence was due, first, to the government's increased involvement in education, in the form of larger grants-in-aid, accompanied by demands for increased control over standards in schools. As language learning was an important element in any syllabus, an avenue had been opened up for the government to influence the overall language policy much more decisively. Secondly, the reorganization of the educational system had as one of its consequences the establishment of an apparatus of educational administration which allowed the government to exercise influence and control. The establishment of the post of Director of Education and the Advisory Council on Native Education were examples of such institutional innovations. We have seen how influential these bodies became in policy-making, and how the implementation of language policy was no longer the sole responsibility of the missions. Thirdly, and probably most importantly, by substantially increasing grants-in-aid to the mission schools, the government demonstrated its economic power and superiority. The mission may not have been fully aware of this, or of the implications for its own language policy; but the government was certainly conscious of the pressures it could bring to bear. Not only did this awareness allow the Governor to dismiss the mission's threat of non-cooperation;[99] it was also claimed that financial support carried with it the obligation to implement the government's language policy,[100] and it was even suggested that adherence to the policy might be made an outright condition of the receipt of grants-in-aid.[101]

This confirms a suggestion made during the analysis of educational policy (Chapter 15). The language issue alone is not enough to demonstrate the effects of the mission's increased economic dependence on the government. But it accords well with the pattern we have seen in other connections. Over the years the missionaries' scope for independent action was curtailed, and they increasingly came to depend on government decisions without being able to influence them.

22

The 'Buganda syndrome' in mission and government policy

Qualitative assessments of the Baganda and the differences between Buganda and other units in the Protectorate played an important role in deciding whether to give support to Luganda as an official language in both missionary and government circles. The choice between Swahili and Luganda was to a great extent determined by conceptions of Buganda's past, present and future contribution to the progress of the Protectorate. The common problem of adopting a suitable attitude to the Buganda factor linked the political and ecclesiastical arenas, but the identification of both with Buganda sometimes incurred the displeasure of other groups in the Protectorate: both were perceived as nourishing a Ganda bias, and anti-Buganda feeling found an outlet within both fields. This raises the question of the extent to which the policy of the one agency influenced the other, and whether there was a high degree of parallelism between them.

Anti-Ganda feeling was strong within the church around the turn of the century, especially in the two Western Kingdoms of Toro and Bunyoro (pp. 367, 384). National feeling found expression in the demand for recognition of the local languages, Lutoro and Lunyoro (as opposed to Luganda); and the demand for organizational independence. Faced with these demands the mission was placed in a serious dilemma. Should it carry on using the Buganda formula, and work for unity and integration on Ganda terms, or should it attempt to accommodate the new national consciousness with its anti-Buganda overtones? There were arguments for each course within the mission, but Bishop Tucker came down on the side of linguistic devolution and organizational independence, thereby recognizing the strength of opposition to Ganda dominance.[1]

Two features stand out from these early expressions of anti-Buganda feeling, and from the mission's response to them. Antagonism against Buganda was first expressed within the ecclesiastical field, and the demands mentioned above represented the first wave of these feelings. Secondly, the issue was dealt with by the mission alone, and the government showed little or no interest. The spillover effect into the political arena was considered negligible, and the government saw no need for concerted action. It failed to see the political implications of developments within the church.

These expressions of anti-Ganda feeling within the church were paralleled by agitation outside the church against the most directly felt manifestation of Ganda ascendancy, the presence of Ganda personnel outside their own areas. When this opposition gained momentum, and specific demands were made for their withdrawal, the separation of church and state was no longer tenable, for in the eyes of the people concerned, they were closely linked together, as they pursued the same policy of 'Gandaization'. The employment of Ganda agents in the colonial administrative system, and their appointments to chiefly posts within the existing political structures in the non-Ganda areas, now remodelled along Ganda lines,[2] nourished fears that the Baganda had come 'to eat the country'.[3] As the same practice of employing Ganda personnel was widely used within the church,[4] although for quite different ends, it was inevitable that the church would also suffer from the effects of anti-Ganda agitation. That the identification of the church with the government's pro-Ganda policy was justified may be seen from the fact that certain members of the mission gave their wholehearted support to the government's policy of bringing in Baganda as chiefs, the idea being that the Baganda could teach other peoples how to administer their countries. The spread of Ganda-type administration thus came to coincide with that of Christian influence. A case in point occurred in Bunyoro, where the local leaders complained to Bishop Tucker that the missionaries were encouraging the use of Ganda personnel in various positions.[5]

It was only natural, in view of the pattern of missionary and colonial expansion, that the first reactions against the Baganda presence in both church and state appeared in the Western Province. The Ganda clergy and teachers stationed there were painfully aware of the fact that their countrymen were not loved by the local people.[6] In Bunyoro in 1905 the Church Council members demanded full control of their own catechists and of their payment, at the same time making it obvious that they thought the time had come for the Ganda teachers to return to their own country; enough local candidates were now coming forward to cover local needs.[7] As might be expected, Bishop Tucker was sympathetic towards both demands. The Church Councils in Toro and Bunyoro were given sufficient freedom of action to employ their own teachers on local terms.[8] It may be taken as a sign of his awareness of the need to 'nationalize' the clergy that Tucker had already taken the initiative to have local people trained. As early as 1907 the first two Batoro were ordained Deacons.[9]

The government responded positively to some extent to the opposition to the presence of Ganda agents. For example, there were no Ganda saza chiefs or sub-chiefs in Toro by 1907; in Ankole a couple of saza chiefs and some 20 sub-chiefs were retained for the sake of administrative efficiency despite local dissatisfaction.[10] In the latter respect Bishop Tucker clearly linked the political and ecclesiastical fields, and was in fact instrumental in pursuing a common policy. He pointed out how leaders in Toro and Ankole had resented the government's policy of placing Ganda chiefs over them, but 'by patience and due representation at the proper quarters, *largely through myself* – these chiefs have gradually been withdrawn'.[11] It was unfortunate, in Tucker's opinion, that the Banyoro had chosen a different course of action and started a near-rebellion by simply driving out the Ganda chiefs.

The situation in Bunyoro provides the best opportunity of examining how antagonism against Ganda personnel necessarily involved both church and state and forced them to clarify their positions.[12] Events in Bunyoro were clearly part of the general outburst of anti-Ganda feeling in the three Western Kingdoms (and possibly Busoga) during 1906, sparked off in particular by the language issue and the Bible translations.[13] There were even reports of attempts at coordinated action between these areas to oust the Ganda agents.[14] That the situation in Bunyoro became so serious was due to two main factors. First, during the British campaign against the Omukama Kabarega in the late 1890s, Buganda helped the government and was awarded a large part of Eastern Bunyoro, which became known as 'the lost counties'. This annexation was a sore point with the Banyoro, and one aim of the anti-Ganda action was to regain the lost counties.[15] Secondly, Bunyoro was treated as a conquered country after the war. In order to re-establish the administration, Ganda agents were introduced in large numbers from 1901 onwards, and in 1907 one saza chief and 20 sub-chiefs were Baganda.[16] This system was considered to work well. Any progress in Bunyoro was largely ascribed by colonial officials to the presence of the Baganda. Bunyoro was one of the places where the system of using Ganda agents was employed most thoroughly, and was considered to be a model state by the official who introduced the system, Deputy Commissioner George Wilson.[17]

Agitation against the Ganda chiefs peaked in May 1907, when a number of Banyoro chiefs took matters into their own hands, and either forcibly ejected the Ganda chiefs or forced the government to withdraw them temporarily. The government demanded their immediate reinstatement and sent an expeditionary force under George Wilson. As a result, 52 Banyoro chiefs were deported.[18] The Anglican church was involved in these upheavals in two main ways. In the first place, there was also opposition to the presence of Ganda teachers, and the Protestant work was almost brought to a complete standstill.[19] Secondly, the church became politically involved; at first the leaders of the anti-Ganda campaign sought the support of the resident CMS missionary, A. B. Fisher, and asked him to identify himself with the Nyoro cause. That he firmly refused to do so made him seem pro-Ganda,[20] and this probably explains the strong reaction against the Anglicans.[21] The Catholic mission managed to steer a more neutral course, which for some observers bordered on an alliance with the Banyoro.[22] The mission played an active political role by winning over the Omukama, who at one stage vacillated in his attitude. In the end, following Fisher's advice, he came down firmly on the side of the government.[23] Thirdly, the mission responded to an appeal for help from the colonial government. Fisher had no doubt that it was his duty to offer his good offices to help to restore conditions to normal, and this meant the reinstatement of the Ganda chiefs.[24] Thus the CMS mission in Bunyoro officially identified itself both with the cause of the Baganda and the practice of employing Ganda personnel, in view of the good work they had done. Fisher was acting in full accordance with his stand on the language issue, and his firm support for the government placed the church in a position where its policy was in conflict with the national aspirations of most Banyoro, and seemed to support Ganda hegemony.

Bishop Tucker's support for the Bible translation into Lunyoro may have served to counterbalance the impression of a one-sided pro-Ganda attitude. But it was difficult for him to go a step further and state publicly that he had great sympathy with the Banyoro and their dissatisfaction with the presence of Ganda chiefs. He deplored the fact that the Banyoro had taken the matter into their own hands, and he acknowledged that the government had to reinstate the Ganda chiefs in order to affirm its authority.[25] But he considered this a temporary solution, and foresaw that the government would soon be obliged to withdraw them by 'a gradual process of elimination'. Tucker understood the reasons for the national movement, and knew that the government too had to respond positively and eventually change its administrative practice of employing Ganda agents. He therefore supported the idea of 'de-Gandaization' of both church and state.[26]

There were thus two opposing views within the mission on the issue of the Ganda agents, just as there were in the controversy over the Lunyoro Bible translation. In the latter case Tucker succeeded in steering the church away from its pro-Ganda image. But the Bunyoro controversy, at least among the Banyoro, strengthened the impression that the church still nourished a strong pro-Ganda bias. Whether one or the other line prevailed in the end would depend on a number of decisions, for example on the status of Luganda and the degree of autonomy which would be allowed to the church in Bunyoro. But, as the issue of the Ganda agents showed, the church's range of action was to a great extent conditioned by the government's policy on Ganda influence in the other parts of the Protectorate. In Bunyoro the church and the government were equally the targets of anti-Ganda antagonism. The government's use of Ganda personnel drew attention to the same practice within the church, and exposed it to more criticism than would otherwise have been the case. It was therefore important for the future of the mission and the church that there existed great scepticism among government officials as to the soundness of the continued use of Ganda personnel.[27] One result of this was a promise made to the Banyoro that the Ganda agents would be withdrawn in due time.[28] But at present the continued use of Ganda agents by the state drew undue attention to the church's similar practice and gave the impression that its work revolved around Buganda. In this respect the two fields were clearly interdependent, and the church was just as liable as the state to become the butt of anti-Ganda feeling. In order to improve this situation it was necessary for the line taken by Bishop Tucker to be implemented as practical policy, so that the Ganda factor would be neutralized within the church.

A very similar pattern of events occurred in the Eastern Province. As there was harassment of Baganda there at the same time as anti-Ganda feeling was growing in the Western Province, there may have been some contact between the two areas.[29] On the other hand, the local situation in itself contained enough elements to explain this harassment. Bukedi and other parts of the Eastern Province, and Lango in the Northern Province, had for years been subject to Ganda influence and Ganda immigration. This was mostly the work of one outstanding Ganda chief, Semei Kakungulu. After a period of rivalry with the Katikiro, Apolo Kagwa, he moved to Bukedi and, with the support of the government, established what was almost an empire, based on the Buganda model and using Baganda as chiefs. Although he came into conflict with the government at one stage, he still succeeded in extending his influence over a large area and provided a channel for Ganda expansion. He laid the foundation of the system approved in 1904 of using Ganda agents. When the CMS mission moved in, the Ganda presence provided a network for Christian expansion, so in the beginning Christian activities revolved around the Baganda and there was an extensive use of Ganda evangelists.[30]

Tension was thus bound to arise between the local people and the immigrant Baganda, and the first serious episode affected both church and state. In June 1905 two Ganda evangelists and a Ganda tax collector were killed.[31] The resident missionary, J. B. Purvis, said that the real reason for the incident was a strong distaste for the Baganda among the local people, and he was critical of the use of Ganda agents.[32] He was supported by some officials who were particularly unhappy about Kakungulu's position, but other officials, especially the Sub-Commissioner, George Wilson, defended the practice of employing Ganda agents.[33] Only a year later a new controversy flared up over the Ganda presence in connection with a new killing, the one which sparked off the Purvis affair referred to above (p. 309). During the inquiry the government's use of Ganda agents was again defended, on the grounds that no other administrative system was possible at present. It was also argued that the mission also used Baganda in their work.[34] In spite of this parallelism the government was sensitive to any criticism from the mission of the Ganda agent system. As more agents were murdered during 1907, the main protagonist of the system, George Wilson, expressed the fear that he would be forced to a premature withdrawal of the agents, and that this could have serious repercussions in the Western Province so soon after the Bunyoro revolt. Among the system's critics Wilson listed not only people within the administration but also Bishop Tucker, of whose earlier criticism of the continued employment of Ganda agents he was apparently aware.[35]

Summarizing the events in Bukedi in 1905–7, we can see the same factors at work as in Bunyoro. State and church alike were the targets of anti-Baganda agitation, and in this situation the attitude of the mission counted as an important political factor for the government. Scepticism towards, and even outright rejection of, the process of 'Gandaization' came from some missionaries, headed by Bishop Tucker; and the colonial officials were also divided among themselves. Nevertheless, in the end the case for the Ganda agents was the strongest one. They were considered indispensable, and continued to be used after a minor reorganization. Most officials thought anyway that the peoples of the Eastern Provinces were a heterogeneous group with virtually no organization of their own.[36] Clashes between the Ganda agents and the local people continued to occur over the following years,[37] but in spite of this the system was used again when Lango, in the Northern Province, was brought under colonial control. The results there were no different from anywhere else.[38]

A fundamental change in government policy only came when George Wilson left and F. J. Jackson returned as Governor in 1911. He denounced the use of Ganda agents, as it was based on the premise, which had never been proved, that the people in the Eastern and Northern Provinces were savage and difficult to control. He therefore demanded the withdrawal of the agents, and recommended that people should in future be ruled through their own chiefs, who were fully capable of taking over responsibility.[39] The withdrawal started immediately; within the first year eighteen agents had left. Jackson then back-tracked a little and introduced a more gradual process, but the aim remained unchanged. He still considered that the agent system was wrong and that it made the Baganda unpopular. For the sake of good administration some Ganda agents should stay on; but their numbers should constantly be reduced, and they should be kept under much closer control than before.[40]

The colonial officials were still divided on the issue of Ganda agents. Some of them, especially those from the Northern Province, fully supported Jackson, not least because of the agents' deplorable behaviour towards the local people;[41] others protested, saying that the agents would remain indispensable for years to come. Most significantly, the opponents also had support from within the mission from Archdeacon Buckley, who was against any sudden withdrawal of the agents.[42] The end result was that the need for a gradual withdrawal was emphasized even more.[43] When Jackson suggested a change of policy, he was faced like his predecessor with two opposing factions within the administration. The CMS mission was in the same dilemma, and this was considered to be of political importance, and was exploited by the parties involved. In spite of all opposition, Jackson carried on with the policy of gradual withdrawal, following principles suggested by Bishop Tucker six years before,[44] and taking some practical steps to facilitate the implementation of the new policy.[45] It remained the official one over the following years, and was reaffirmed during the controversy over Swahili and Luganda.[46] Although this policy suffered setbacks, it produced some notable results.[47] A survey in 1919 showed that Ganda influence was on the wane in almost all districts of the Protectorate. This was due both to the progress made by the respective people themselves 'in civilisation and in the management of their own affairs', and to the Baganda's continued unpopularity.[48] While Bukedi and Teso had been run entirely by Ganda agents in 1910, only five were now left in each area, and the same tendency was evident in other districts.[49] A somewhat paradoxical proof that the new policy was in fact being implemented may be taken from Toro. Toro was considered to be lagging behind its neighbours because of inefficiency and maladministration; so Governor Jackson quite explicitly appointed a Muganda to a vacant saza chieftainship as a punitive measure and to set an example for the Omukama and his chiefs.[50] We have already discussed how unpopular his appointment was in Toro, and how strenuously the Omukama worked to be rid of the Ganda chief (p. 329). When it considered that it had made its point, the government itself recommended his withdrawal.[51] This type of measure could, however, hardly fail to provide an impetus to the already existing anti-Ganda feelings.

In conclusion, the state adopted a policy which Bishop Tucker had recommended as early as 1907; the process of withdrawing the Ganda agents may have been slow, and may have worked differently in the various parts of the Protectorate, but the tendency in government policy was clearly in favour of those forces which were working against Ganda dominance. One predictable effect of this was that some of the steam was taken out of the agitation against Ganda agents. As this issue had provoked the strongest reaction and had been the rallying point for much of the anti-Ganda agitation we might expect some of the pressure to be taken off the government. There was certainly an increasing awareness among government officials of the political implications of the Ganda factor; for a number of officials the existing prejudice against Buganda and their desire not to provoke these feelings further were given as main reasons for their opposition to the use of Luganda as a lingua franca. This was especially so during the discussions in 1919. The government did very little to pursue a policy of integration. At the African level there was rather a policy of decentralization, while the colonial administration itself was the sole unifying structure at the higher level (see p. 372). There was thus no horizontal structure within the state which could serve as a nationwide outlet for anti-Ganda feeling. When overall policy on integration was eventually discussed in connection with a proposal for a Central Lukiko, the Ganda factor was the main stumbling-block. The project could not be realized because of the government's fear of Ganda dominance and the catalytic effect on other groups of contact with the Baganda. Indeed, government officials became increasingly critical of the whole Buganda system. They were dissatisfied both with the way the system worked on the basis of the Uganda Agreement, and with the behaviour of the Ganda leaders. Thus the positive assessment of Ganda qualities which had been the underlying premise for the use of the Buganda model and Ganda agents, and which had been used as an argument for making Luganda the official language, was no longer valid.

It is clear from this that the Ganda bias in government policy became less and less marked in the period from the 1910s to the mid-1920s. But anti-Ganda feeling did not decrease correspondingly. Buganda's declining stock with government officials did nothing to neutralize the Baganda's privileged position within the Protectorate, which had been laid down in the Uganda Agreement in 1900, and which was epitomized by the special Ganda system of private landholding. In one sense the Baganda continued to serve as a reference group for other parts of the Protectorate. Their enjoyment of certain benefits tended to set goals and provide grounds of comparison for the other groups. Conversely, Ganda superiority placed the other groups on the defensive, so that they were hypersensitive to any attempt to promote the spread of Ganda ascendancy. In both cases a profound imbalance was ingrained in the whole colonial fabric. Irrespective of officials' increasing discomfort with the situation, the imbalance caused by Buganda's special position remained a permanent feature for years to come.[52] Accordingly, anti-Ganda feeling stayed alive, as its roots remained untouched. Government policy was only capable of reducing the possibilities of confrontation in its own field. The change of policy as regards Ganda agents was so intended, and other more general measures were taken later.

It seems natural to pose the question of whether religious leaders were as aware of the Ganda factor as the government, and whether they did anything to reduce anti-Buganda feeling. In addition we should ask whether the policy of the state had any spillover effect on the church, in view of the links that existed between church and state as regards the Buganda problem. The church's employment of Ganda personnel is a relevant issue in this respect. The government progress in taking the pressure off helped to improve conditions for the same practice within the church. The use of Ganda teachers became much less of a target for opposition. Also, to return to a subject touched upon earlier, Bishop Tucker had already, for reasons different from those of the state, laid down the policy of employing local people in each district. This was an obvious procedure for establishing ground-level contacts in the early phase of the introduction of Christianity. Measures were taken to recruit catechists locally, and to prepare candidates for ordination. There was thus already a clear trend within the church, although Ganda personnel were still employed.[53] But there was no longer an all-out reliance on Baganda church workers, so there was less likelihood of controversy arising.

However, in the post-Tucker period the mission did not follow the Bishop's line of 'de-Gandaization'. Three other interrelated features of missionary policy intervened and helped to nourish suspicions of continued strong Ganda bias within the church.

(1) Although the mission was divided internally on language policy, it revived

its efforts to make Luganda the lingua franca from 1912 onwards, concurrently with the government's shift from Swahili to Luganda. The pro-Luganda policy was based on the mission's great affection for the Baganda and their assumed importance for the spread of the Gospel.[54] This was the mission policy for the rest of the period, and the more the government tried to promote Swahili, the more determinedly the mission pursued its pro-Luganda policy. Developments in the late 1920s showed that the church suffered more from the Buganda syndrome when it was fighting against the introduction of Swahili, as it was forced to identify itself still more closely with the Baganda. Not only did the Swahili issue force the mission to reaffirm its positive assessment of Buganda's leading role in the Protectorate; it also helped to cement the alliance between the mission and Buganda in practical political matters. Thus the church became even more identified in the eyes of the people with the cause of Luganda and the supposed extension of Ganda influence than the government. The church therefore had to bear the brunt of anti-Ganda feeling, as far as the language issue was concerned.

(2) As regards the organization of the church itself, we have discussed the details of how the church was constantly haunted throughout the 1910s by the problem of Buganda's relationship to the rest of the country. There were accusations of Ganda dominance in the Diocesan Council and the various Advisory Boards, and although some measures were taken to alleviate the conditions which caused these accusations, Ganda dominance remained a fact of life. The church still relied heavily on the chiefly class economically, and its political alliance with it inevitably meant that the chiefs played a leading role in the church too.[55] Thus the church fell victim to the ethnic tensions in Uganda society and became much more sensitive to them than the government was.

(3) The mission's vulnerability was increased by the fact that it, unlike the government, proclaimed and pursued a policy of integration, and the most important expressions of this policy were the Synod and other Diocesan institutions. Through its own organization the church sought to promote unity and equality in all Uganda. But the means actually applied gave the non-Ganda Christians the impression that unity was mainly to be achieved on Ganda terms. The disparity between ends and means left the church wide open to expressions of anti-Ganda feeling, and its very organization provided an obvious platform for such expressions. Paradoxically, the mission's policy of integration and unity thus had the effect of activating partisan feeling and exposed the church more than ever to accusations of Ganda bias (see Chapter 19).

We may draw two conclusions on the linkage between church and state on the basis of this issue. First, the church was more likely than the government to become a target for anti-Ganda feeling, and it was by virtue of its structure more likely to function as a platform for its expression. This conclusion is fully confirmed by the events at the Synod in 1917. Anti-Ganda feeling had been mounting steadily in the years leading up to the Synod,[56] and there was a serious outbreak during this session.[57] The problem was the central theme in the Bishop's Episcopal Charge,[58] and it appears from the agenda that the whole register of explosive issues was touched upon during the discussions: the economic independence of the districts; hostility towards contributing to the church in Buganda and having the money allocated by Ganda-dominated organs; organizational independence and the rejection of any kind of Ganda dominance; the controversy over the symbol of Ganda hegemony, the new Cathedral building.[59] A compromise was reached with various concessions to the outlying districts, but the Synod of 1917 was long remembered as the one where the tendencies towards separatism and insularity were strongest.[60] In spite of the 1917 compromise, anti-Buganda feeling continued to manifest itself within the church both locally and at the Synods.[61] The campaign against the cross in the Cathedral in 1919 and 1921 was an expression of the gulf between Buganda and the rest of the country, although it also grew out of social tensions between the chiefs and the clergy.

The second conclusion is more tentative, and is based on the linkage between church and state in the face of anti-Buganda agitation. It was not only because of its own apparent policy of 'Gandaization' that the church came to serve as a major outlet for anti-Ganda feeling. The government's different policy and different organization directed these feelings away from the state and put extra pressure on the church. Thus the church was directly, if unintentionally, affected by the government's policy, and found itself in a much more exposed position than would otherwise have been the case. The close causal relationship between these factors was not recognized by the participants, and it is of course difficult to substantiate the suggestion on the basis of empirical evidence. But we have earlier observed how sensitive the church was to tensions in society at large. When these tensions could find no outlet in the political field, it was natural for the church to be used instead.

This kind of interdependence between church and state gave the relationship a character of its own. By existing and functioning in the same society, both church and government were likely to become victims of the same tensions, and both had to respond in one way or another. What the Buganda issue illustrates is that the one agency was affected by the response of the other. Under certain circumstances the links between the two could become so close that changes in government policy would inevitably have certain effects on the church. No neutral zone with an absorbing capacity could exist between the two when they were faced with tensions such as those due to the gulf between Buganda and the rest of the country.

This brings us back to what was initially termed 'the Buganda syndrome', which we have met at three different levels. First, Buganda was an important determinant in the policy-making process. Secondly, identification with Buganda accounted in various contexts for the government's attitude and its response to the mission's suggestions and actions. Thirdly, the Buganda factor influenced the attitude to the mission and the church of other parts of the community. Put in stronger terms, it was instrumental in squeezing mission and church between Buganda and the rest of the country.[62]

23

Conclusions on parallelism and reciprocity in the church–state relationship

By using the concept of indirect or tacit input as an analytical category, it has been possible to examine a number of issues which showed the two agencies acting in parallel roles, and revealed various processes of exchange and mutual influence. Some special features of the relationship between church and state have thereby emerged, and a more far-reaching effect of missionary activity has become apparent within the field of ethnicity.

The nature of the church–state relationship

In dealing with a relationship of parallel roles and adaptation and less with the causal aspects of the situation, the topics which have been examined may seem to have little coherence and little representative value, but they nevertheless represent areas where there was a coincidence of interests between the two institutions.[1] The parallels in policy and practice between church and state could be explained more simply by the fact that the two agencies functioned in the same society and were both trying to accomplish tasks that might differ in degree, but not in kind. They were faced to a great extent with the same problems, and were, independently of one another, responding to them in the same way. Thus the factors which produced parallelism were external to both agencies, and originated in the African surroundings and the colonial situation. Cases in point have been the two agencies' parallel ways of drawing their administrative boundaries and the centralization/decentralization issue, where both sides failed to implement a policy of integration. Some aspects of the language issue and the agitation against Buganda's influence likewise illustrated the importance of external factors.

Yet this does not suffice to explain the dynamic nature of the church–state relationship, which we have seen in action on several occasions. Some of the cases examined clearly demonstrated a flow of influence in both directions.[2] The government could not regard the mission and church as neutral, as their presence and activities clearly had a political dimension. A clear example of this was the government's anxiety over anti-European feeling stemming from the church's internal problems. Furthermore, on some occasions, as for example in the case of early developments in the language issue, the government was willing to gear its own policy to that of the mission, or at least to take the mission's views into account when deciding policy. This was the case with the efforts to start newspapers. Conversely the mission/church could not act independently of the government, but acknowledged its impact on its own sphere of activity and showed readiness to take the government's attitude into account, as with the Nandi case (p. 364). In some instances the government's attitude could carry so much weight that the mission accepted restraints on its own freedom of action, as with the appointment of African trustees and the educational grants to Africans (pp. 378–9). In these cases the mission's ties to the state affected the extent to which it could attain its own goals.[3]

These mutual attempts at adaptation and coordination explain a number of cases where parallelism was a significant feature of the policy and practice of both agencies. The early attempt to pursue a 'federal policy' was one clear case (Chapter 19). In addition, some degree of active coordination and even positive cooperation was achieved in connection with the Buganda agents. Active cooperation was sometimes facilitated by correspondence between attitudes on both sides, and there were even informal alliances between sections from each side, for example during the agitation against the Ganda agents and during the language controversy.

A more negative way of measuring the concern for parallelism is to look for cases where it was absent. One example was the centralization/decentralization issue, where the mission differed significantly from the government in its approach to the problem of integration. Although the government deliberately pursued a decentralization policy from the 1910s onwards, no attempt was made to coordinate it with the mission's integrative policy, which was not considered to be making headway or having any effect within the administrative arena. An even more remarkable lack of parallelism appeared in connection with the integration of the European mission and the African church, and the promotion of Africans. Within these fields the mission's policy differed greatly from that of the state. If the government failed to react to this obvious lack of parallelism, it was simply because the mission pursued its Africanization policy halfheartedly and with little efficiency. As far as the government was concerned, the difference in policy was of no real consequence, and it could take a detached view of the theoretical policy differences between itself and the mission. But whenever the Africanization policy seemed about to bear fruit, as with the appointment of a West Indian doctor and of Africans as trustees, or the receipt of educational grants by Africans, the government felt obliged to warn the mission against too much deviation from the government line – and the mission complied. But the opposite happened in the later stages of the language controversy. The lack of parallelism between government and mission policy became so obvious that it brought the two parties into conflict. When this happened, neither could pursue its own policies with any chance of success. In negative terms, their interdependence proved so close that it exerted a blocking power on both sides, so that a situation of interlocking balance and control arose.

While we have in some instances seen a pattern of balance and mutual control, most of the cases examined give the impression that the advantage was on the side of the government. The mission/church accommodated itself to government policy and allowed the government to take the lead more frequently than vice versa. The fixing of administrative boundaries and the overall church organization illustrated this. In other words, the mission conceded that the government was the stronger partner by making efforts not to deviate too much from government policy. In general the church's range of action and ability to implement its goals were more affected by the various linkages to the political arena than vice versa. Viewing the course of events from the chronological perspective, we may suggest that the tendency for the state to be the stronger partner gained momentum as conditions became more settled and spheres of activity were defined more precisely. On the basis of the present evidence, however, we cannot go as far as to conclude that the government's concern for parallelism and coordination with the mission/church in areas of mutual interest declined correspondingly.

One effect of these developments which has already been mentioned in other contexts (p. 257) was that the mission assumed a supportive function in relation to the state. We have even seen that the government sometimes saw the mission's function as a directly auxiliary one, as was the case when new areas were opened up, and at some points during the language controversy. It should however be added that the mission's supportive or auxiliary function need not be taken as an indication of submissiveness. The pattern of parallelism cannot be explained simplistically by saying that the mission and church followed submissively in the footsteps of the state. The language issue in particular militates against such an interpretation.

Missionary activity and ethnic consciousness

In spite of the wide range of interaction between church and state, and in spite of the apparent lack of cohesiveness between the cases examined, there is one theme which runs through all the issues so far discussed under the heading of indirect inputs, the complex problem of ethnicity (seen at that time in terms of 'national feeling') and, more specifically, the emergence of ethnic groups. It is therefore relevant to raise the question of how far the activities of the mission and the church and their pattern of work contributed to the formation of the ethnic groups which have been such a significant feature in Uganda politics in the colonial period as well as in the period of independence. I have discussed the political role of ethnicity at length in an earlier work, and will here employ some of the analytical categories developed there.[4] In order to clarify the role of the mission and church within the field of ethnicity we may then concentrate the discussion on two key elements: the establishment and maintenance of boundaries between ethnic groups, and the politicization of the ethnic groups.

With regard to the establishment and maintenance of boundaries between the ethnic groups, we have seen that the mission implicitly accepted the Protectorate boundaries fixed by the colonial authority. Apart from one case (Mboga in the Belgian Congo) they actually found it inconvenient to depart from the political demarcation lines. Furthermore, the organizational structure of the mission and church contributed significantly to the structuring of the whole region, and thereby to the founding of a wider society which had not existed before. Within the arena thus constituted two types of process were at work in the establishment and maintenance of boundaries. First, there was the actual introduction of administrative divisions, in which respect the mission worked in close coordination with the government. By having a parallel pattern of organizational structure, the mission clearly helped to strengthen the new boundaries. Later, by developing its organization with due respect for the new boundaries, the mission assisted considerably in binding the new units together. These units formed the basis for a number of activities. Especially in societies with a high degree of centralization the mission fulfilled an integrating function by identifying the work closely with the institutions of kingship and chieftainship.

Secondly, and undoubtedly more significantly, the mission contributed to an awakening of ethnic consciousness, defined as a process by which a community comes to see itself as distinct from others, with a group identity and common interests. We are thus concerned, not just with the group's inward-looking awareness of its common cultural tradition, but with its outward-looking perception of its boundaries with other groups, and with the interaction between the groups thus established.[5] Original cultural elements like language and existing political structures did of course play a substantial role in the shaping of an ethnic identity, and in establishing boundaries *vis-à-vis* outsiders; but they did not constitute an end in themselves, nor did they represent a static commitment to traditional patterns of culture. The point was that the common consciousness should be capable of reaching out to the administrative boundaries without cutting too much across them, especially in situations of confrontation with similar units within the wider arena.

The mission and church contributed in various ways to the acceleration of this whole process, and even to the confrontation of the various units with each other. The previous examination of parallel roles showed how contact and confrontation with Buganda, whether in the organizational sense or within the field of language, had a clear catalytic effect. On the one hand, it put people on the defensive against any kind of Ganda dominance; on the other, the Baganda came to serve as a reference group possessing desirable goods and institutions, and served as a spur to other groups. The mission's pro-Ganda orientation helped to provoke both kinds of reactions, and thus to increase people's awareness of the boundaries existing between the Baganda and the other inhabitants of the country.

More specifically, the language issue served as a central ingredient in the emergence of ethnic consciousness. The political use of the vernaculars was by no means an invention of the mission. It came in response to already-existing pressures; but the mission's 'going vernacular' helped to stimulate local 'national feelings' so that it unavoidably became part of the awakening of ethnic consciousness. Bible translations into the vernaculars were not only a means of spreading the Gospel; they were among the earliest formulated demands from ethnic groups. This dual function of the use of local languages, the instrumental and the consciousness-raising, later became important in the elementary schools, with the significant addition that the mission, faced with the government's campaign for Swahili as the universal language, emphasized even more the use of the vernaculars as mediums of instruction. In connection with the spread of literacy the mission contributed substantially to the development of norms for the vernacular languages by printing tracts and books in these languages. This in itself became an important factor in the rise of national feelings. Generally speaking, there is hardly any field other than that of language which provides more insight into the process of boundary-fixing and the corresponding rise of ethnic consciousness. Language was simultaneously an instrument in, and a manifestation of, the process. It helped to create a common identity as a basis from which to interact with other groups.

Yet, however crucial, the language factor cannot be taken in isolation. We have met cases where a local language was spread over larger units than those defined by administrative boundaries. One example was the introduction of Lunyoro as the joint language of Bunyoro, Toro and Ankole. The local languages from these areas were considered to be so close to one another that one of them would suffice as the working language. The fact that there was a united front against Luganda also helped participants to arrive at a solution which cut across organizational divisions. Yet it was characteristic that each area demanded its own church council with the highest possible degree of autonomy in its own affairs. There was an early example of this in Bunyoro, and it was later emphasized in Ankole that the local ruridecanal council was to have the proper title 'the National Church Council of Ankole'. Each area wanted its own platform from which to express its own particular interests as against those of other groups. In spite of the fact that linguistic and political boundaries were not coterminous, the outward expression of a common identity thus followed the administrative boundaries. This is further confirmed by the fact that the Ankole Church Council, despite the existence of the Lunyoro Bible translation, a little later demanded a Bible translation into Lunyankore, on the grounds that Ankole was an independent kingdom with a language of its own, an effect of the spread of literacy and the appearance of books in the vernacular. In the end, there was thus still a tendency for linguistic and organizational demarcations to correspond with one another. This in turn had the reciprocal effect that personnel, whether for the church or the schools, were recruited on a local basis.

A number of factors operating within the ecclesiastical field thus worked together both to raise ethnic consciousness and to confine it within the administrative boundaries.[6] The contribution of the mission and church to the resultant 'sense of ethnic loyalty and identification' was both direct, first and foremost through the extensive use of the local languages; and indirect, through the creation of a framework for interaction between the various units. Coming into contact with one another, and especially with Buganda, the groups became conscious of their different interests, and of the value of formulating demands on a communal, local basis, through the ethnically constituted institutions.

This brings us to the politicization of the groups. The question at issue here is how the groups came to function as political units, that is, how demands were essentially presented to the political system through the ethnic groups, and how the ethnic mechanisms provided a basis for the allocation of goods. An analysis of the ecclesiastical field alone cannot do justice to this kind of question, which belongs properly to the wider political arena. What is relevant in this connection is to ask whether conditions in the church were conducive to the expression of interests and the channelling of demands through the ethnic structure and thus set precedents for a pattern of political activity which was later to be employed, when the time was ripe, by the state.

An examination of indirect inputs showed us three areas where the ethnic groups were in the centre of activity, or where the church structure facilitated such a pattern of activity. First, as regards the allocation of funds within the church, each of the various districts wanted to retain its own authority rather than relinquish its allocative powers to a central institution. Money collected was claimed for the districts, and should not go through a central fund; this demand was to a great extent met. Local authority was thus enhanced at the expense of the power of the centre. Secondly, it is characteristic that the distribution of seats in the most important assembly, the Diocesan Council, was ethnically determined, and that there were conscious attempts to achieve a better balance in the representation of the various districts. Thirdly, because of the two foregoing factors, and given the significant lay element in the church organization, the leaders in the various districts acquired the habit of articulating their specific demands, and taking care of the interests of their groups *vis-à-vis* the other actors within the ecclesiastical arena. Some experience was thus gained of operating the ethnic apparatus. All in all, the church's extensive activity along ethnic lines blazed the trail for the politicization of the ethnic groups.

It is, however, natural at this stage to raise the question of whether there were opposite tendencies within the church, or even deliberate attempts to neutralize some of the effects of the ethnic factor, and thus within the wider arena to reduce the importance of the ethnic framework. More specifically, it may be asked whether Christianity as such and the church as its organizational expression tended towards integration rather than differentiation. This topic has been discussed in earlier connections, and need only be summarized here.[7]

In the first instance, we may look at Christianity's unifying capacity in an ideological context, a feature that was occasionally emphasized by the mission. It could be argued that Christianity, conceived of as an ideology, might tend to supplant ethnic consciousness and generate a stronger vertical line of division to replace the horizontal division along ethnic lines. One mobilizing factor in that respect would be the constant polarization between the two Christian denominations. The present analysis provides us with little evidence either to support or invalidate such a suggestion; but the indications we have suggest that Christianity was not capable of neutralizing ethnic consciousness. In particular the discussion of the language issue showed how important it was felt to be that Chrisitianity was mediated first in the mother tongue. This meant that the Gospel after all appeared in a local guise, and became identified with expressions of the local value system. Christianity did not, as we have noticed in connection with the institutions of kingship and chieftainship, undermine the tribal political institutions.[8] Hence, the specific form of Christianity practised in each area was not likely to lead to any community of interest beyond the boundaries of the local cultural unit. It is worth recalling in this connection what Bishop Tucker pointed out at an early stage: that the demands for Bible translations into the vernaculars could not be regarded reductively as purely political manifestations, as they were expressions of a sincere desire to have the Gospel in the most readily accessible form.

Turning to the organizational expression of Christianity, the church, we are on more secure ground in passing judgement on its capacity to weaken the ethnic lines of division. It has been shown earlier how the church was torn between the two opposing tendencies of integration and decentralization (Chapter 19). It was observed that, because of its organizational structure, the church did not have the capacity to halt the latter force or further the former. By virtue of its ethnically determined allocation of offices in central bodies, the church was itself so much an integral component in the prevailing ethnic configuration that it lacked the power to break it down. It was also noticed that the church became a platform for the expressions of ethnic tensions in society at large, especially those between Buganda and the rest of the Protectorate. Two more specific organizational traits demonstrated the church's powerlessness in the face of the ethnic factor. First, there remained an ethnic asymmetry within the church, not least as a result of the mission's continued orientation towards Buganda, as manifested by its preference for Luganda and the Ganda dominance in bodies like the Diocesan Council and the various Advisory Boards. This lack of balance could only serve to keep ethnic factionalism very much alive. Secondly, and perhaps more subtly, we may suggest that the mission remained for all practical purposes, and in spite of all constitutional niceties, the real ecclesiastical superstructure, with the missionaries in leading positions *qua* missionaries, and not in their capacity as members of the church. Not even the Bishop, despite his office and his special position in the church, managed to avoid giving the image of belonging primarily to a European agency. Parallel with the colonial administrative structure the missionary organization provided the main unifying element within the ecclesiastical field, and this naturally had a dual effect. In the first place, it weakened the church's potential to perform an integrative function. Secondly, it supported the tendency to confine the handling of as many church matters as possible to the local level, thus emphasizing the local focus at the expense of the centre.

PART VI

An outline of the church–state relationship in a colonial setting: summary, conclusions and evaluation

15 Kabaka Daudi Chwa at Namirembe Cathedral on the day of King Edward VII's Coronation, 1902, accompanied by two missionaries, a colonial official, a leading Ganda chief and the senior African clergyman, Rev. Henry Wright Duta Kitakule.

"It will be a unique opportunity for those who govern and those who are governed to meet together as members of the Christian Church professing a Common Creed"

24
The capacity of the church

A number of case studies have been examined within each of the three main categories of interaction outlined in the Introduction. The focus of the investigation has been the mission's and the church's wants and explicit demands, as presented to the political structures, the mechanisms used to present these demands, and the resultant responses. The central topic of investigation has been the interactions between the political structure and its environment with 'arrows of causation' pointing in both directions. The aim is now to measure the impact of the church institution and thus to characterize the relationship between church and state in the special colonial setting. This includes both an assessment of the capacity of the church in its dealings with the state and a discussion of the resultant responses of the state, which may be termed the government's religious policy.

A recurrent theme has been the capacity of the church institution to define its wants and present its demands to the state, and in this respect the church has been acting in a political role. We must now systematize some of the factors which influenced its ability to perform that role. Some of the forces at work were clearly internal, especially those stemming from organizational features; but it is also important to investigate the external perspective by asking whether and to what extent the act of presenting demands to the state, that is, political participation, created a dependence on the political structure which could affect the autonomy of the church institution through time and impose limitations on its capacity. In other words, the potential of the church institution was rooted in its internal structure, but could also be affected by external forces.[1]

From this latter perspective some of the factors earlier shown to have influenced the capacity of the church will be discussed once more in order to arrive at some basic conclusions. As we do so, it should be remembered that we cannot define the capacity of the church without reference to the principal goals which it had set out to achieve. Hence, its capacity is defined both by its basic objectives in the political sphere, and by its power to achieve them.[2]

Structural aspects: the importance of the distinction between mission and church

During this survey the ecclesiastical arena has been presented in a somewhat undifferentiated way: the terms 'mission' and 'church' have been used almost interchangeably, but with the mission as the predominant actor. But in order to assess the capacity of the church institution it is essential to unravel this two-skeined structure. The events of the 1890s showed the inevitability of this type of structure in a missionary situation, and we must point out how it affected the capability of the church to act *vis-à-vis* the state. The principal aim of the whole missionary enterprise was to establish an independent church and thereby make the mission redundant. This again meant that a great deal of the mission's resources were directed towards the task of placing the African church on a solid economic footing, of seeking certain rights and privileges from the political authorities, and in general of securing for the church a status and position within the fabric of society. A number of demands were thus directed towards the state in order to realize the primary goal, and this accounts for the fact that the African church was from the outset placed in a special situation of interaction with its social and political surroundings.

It will be appropriate to begin with an analysis of the African church. Internally, the boundary between mission and church must be defined in order to clarify their separate functions. It is here taken for granted that the potential of a church organization is rooted in its internal structure. Externally, the capacity of the African church was greatly influenced by the nature and extent of its linkages with the political system, in this case primarily the African system. It is thus assumed that the realization of potential was affected by external forces. It follows that in both respects the organizational distinctiveness and autonomy of the church functioned as a major variable.[3]

The internal structure: the African church *vis-à-vis* the mission

As regards the internal dimension, we have seen that the boundary between mission and church in the formative period was maintained with no provision for permeability in either direction. Apart from the Bishop, the boundary ran along racial lines, with Europeans on one side and Africans on the other. At the same time the mission made no headway in gaining official recognition for the African church. The major new departure in the period under survey came in 1908–9 with the passing of a church constitution. This topic has been dealt with in a separate work,[4] and has been touched upon briefly in the present survey (Chapter 20). It will be sufficient here to emphasize two features. From the structural point of view, the boundary between the two bodies had become blurred. While the missionaries on the one hand had become full members of the church on equal footing with the Africans, they had nevertheless preserved their own missionary organization to deal with matters which only affected Europeans. They thus had two sources of authority and two types of status, and it became difficult to tell in which capacity they acted on various occasions. Turning to the permeability of the boundary, we may say that, although the boundary had not been removed, it had become semi-permeable. The flow of influence was running from the European mission to the African church, but not in the opposite direction. The mission remained a closed system to Africans. This could only have the effect of placing Europeans and Africans on an unequal footing and limiting the prospects for African advancement; such a situation was bound to cast doubt upon the autonomy of the church.

The decision-making machinery within the church did nothing to improve this situation. It has earlier been shown how influential the missionaries were within various parts of the church organization, and how they occupied all the posts of major importance for decision-making. Moreover, the executive functions, where interaction was necessary with the political authorities, were largely in the hands of the missionaries. In such cases it was difficult for outsiders to see whether they were acting in their capacity as missionaries or as officeholders in the church.[5]

To these organizational features should be added some significant trends within the church which helped to prevent African advancement. The chapter on relations with African sub-systems (Chapter 20) revealed a number of blocking mechanisms of a structural and attitudinal nature which worked against African leadership and thus deprived the church of genuine independence by concentrating focus on the mission. All this leads to the conclusion that the potential of the newly constituted church to play a political role was limited, mainly because its organizational distinctiveness and autonomy were badly developed, given its poor boundary maintenance with the mission. The position may best be summarized by borrowing an illustration from another context: although some amount of responsibility had been transferred to the church following the passing of the constitution, 'this reallocation of duties had not been accompanied by corresponding amounts of decision-making power'.[6]

External relations: the African church *vis-à-vis* the state

The potential of the church in relation to the African system has been discussed at some length in the chapter on attempts to achieve a Christian state (Chapter 17). It will be important in the present context to recall two aspects of that discussion. In the first place, there was the question of the position and status of the African church in relation to the African political system. This was mainly assessed by looking at the degree of Christianization of essential political institutions like the Kingship and the chieftainships, and the Lukikos, so that in the period under survey the politically centralized societies were the predominant ones, seen from the perspective of the ecclesiastical arena. We found a high degree of Christianization with a significant Protestant dominance, even to the extent that a Protestant establishment could be seen at work on some occasions. But it is just as important to emphasize that this Protestant hegemony was based on unwritten rules of custom and practice, and did not provide the church with any constitutional or established position. Its position could rather be characterized as semi-established. An image of establishment was projected, rather than an officially recognized status.

There were two obvious circumscribing factors which restrained any such ambitions. First, the aim of the principal actors, the missionary leaders, was not to have a real state church. This was at one stage even rejected explicitly as unrealistic. Nor did they seek an established church in the Anglican sense.

Furthermore, they did not seek a direct political role for the church by promoting its officeholders as official representatives to political institutions. What they worked for was the more limited goal of a 'most-favoured' position with the African political system. All this helped to enhance the status of the church in society and to preserve and extend its material basis. They succeeded to a great extent in this more limited aim, as the boundary between the two systems was characterized by a high degree of permeability.

It is in this latter respect that the second circumscribing factor comes in. The colonial government sought by various means to have the boundary maintained more strictly. While not entirely successful in its efforts to encourage more distance in the relationship between the Anglican church and the African political system, the government was able, by using its controlling and supervisory powers, to reduce the effects of the special relationship, especially as the colonial system became more established over the years (see Chapter 17). One indication of the government's attitude to the church emerged from the ongoing discussions of alienation in connection with land and labour services (Chapter 11). The church was not recognized as an African institution to the extent that customary privileges and legal rights could be invested in it.

The second criterion for establishing the capacity of the church, the extent of the institutionalized linkages between it and the African political system, has mainly been discussed in terms of personal overlap, and has been seen as an effect of the Christianization/Protestantization of the African political institutions. The most obvious manifestation of this was the presence of a substantial number of political officeholders on boards, committees and councils, and their participation in the policy- and decision-making processes. These connections secured substantial material resources by linking the church with the most privileged stratum in society. Secondly, they afforded direct access to African officeholders and the chance to influence the selection of issues to be put on the agenda as well as overall policy and decisions. It is, however, important to emphasize that these linkages were not utilized to give the church a direct political role or the clergy outright political influence. They were geared more generally to the needs of the church in fulfilling its tasks. It was assumed that the chiefs as Christians and Protestants had an obligation to help in this respect.

Thus, although the linkages with the African political system constituted a great potential for the church, the alliance with the chiefs, as the most important linkage, involved some built-in restraints on the realization of the potential. First, the value of these linkages was largely dependent on the chiefs' financial and political position. If this changed, the capacity of the church was bound to be affected. It has been pointed out in various connections how a process of erosion affected the chiefs' capacity and range of action. The colonial system's more established position, the process of bureaucratization and the government's tightening of control were all factors to be reckoned with. In addition the government became increasingly aware of the significance of this channel for church influence and intervened accordingly to limit its scope. In the wider perspective, the capacity of the church was dependent on a political and social order whose durability was somewhat questionable. As a general conclusion, we may then suggest that the realization of the church's potential was to a great extent influenced by that of the African political system.[7]

There was a second limitation involved in the relationship with the African political system. Basically, it was the church which was the dependent partner.

The political officeholders, as lay representatives, constituted an influential element within the church organization, while there was no such linkage in the opposite direction. African clergymen were not allowed, both for practical reasons and as a matter of principle, to hold political office. In more concrete terms, the chiefs were instrumental for the church, not vice versa. It is important to remember that the newly constituted church did not provide the basis for the Protestant chiefs' holding of office, nor was it involved in the Christianization/ Protestantization of the majority of the political offices. This whole process predated the church and, as we saw in part II, was rooted in the fact that the existence of the two Christian denominations constituted the most important stratifying principle in society. In other words, these Protestant officeholders were in power prior to and independently of the church institution, and they did not have their power base in the church. Conversely, the church had the function of signifying and confirming the Protestant hegemony and providing it with a certain outward legitimacy. The church helped to cement the existing state of affairs, but did not provide the foundation under it. This dependent position was bound to affect the church's influence with the political system, and it underlines the fact that the church was still at an early stage in its development. Its function was more an auxiliary than an instrumental one.

The nature of the linkages with the African political system thus limited the capacity of the church, but the chiefly presence within the church organization also had another aspect which did little to improve the situation. While the African clergy were designated as the coming leaders of the independent church, they were generally of a different, usually lower, status than the chiefs, measured by the value system prevailing in the surrounding society. This gap was later increased by differences in educational standards. As they also stood in the shadow of the missionaries, they were prevented from exercising much leadership. The natural leaders of the African church were caught in a no-man's-land between the two other groups. Conversely, the other two groups worked together within the framework of the church and took joint action in approaching the political authorities – the protests against the land policy in 1914 were a case in point. But this was not always done in the name of the church, and when the Anglican establishment took action, it was not necessarily identical with the church institution. Nor did the reduction of the number of chiefs on church boards necessarily indicate any change in the internal power structure, or a weakening of the alliance between the mission and the chiefly hierarchy. All in all, the church did not emerge as an institution with real African leadership, and in some cases it served merely as a forum for contacts and exchanges between missionaries and chiefs, both of whom had their own means of access to the political system.

The interaction with the African political system as such had its own impact on the capacity of the church. The nature of the linkages between the two systems tended to reduce the capacity of the church *vis-à-vis* the state. The special position of the African political system also became an important variable as, increasingly in its dealings with the church, it came under the guidance and control of the colonial government. Secondly, this external effect was reinforced by certain features of the internal structure connected with the church's relationship with the mission. It emerges clearly that, within the ecclesiastical field itself, it was the mission which took the lead and made the vital decisions in dealing with the state.

Both trends worked together to reduce the organizational and functional autonomy of the church. It is at the same time striking how much they bear witness to the continued validity of the quadrangle established in connection with the events of the 1890s, characterizing the patterns of relations between church and state in a colonial setting (see p. 105). It has further been reaffirmed that the mission must remain the primary factor in any analysis of the capacity of the ecclesiastical field in its dealings with the state.

The capacity of the mission

In establishing the capacity of the mission in its dealings with the state one primary criterion must be the degree of goal implementation it achieved: to what extent did the mission during the period under survey succeed in realizing its principal objective of founding an independent church with a recognized position within the state and society? With this as a point of departure we will be able to identify the major factors which influenced the mission's stand *vis-à-vis* the state, whether internal to the missionary organization or external. The pattern of analysis will thus be similar to the one used in connection with the African church.

An assessment of the mission's goal implementation: the drive for official recognition

It has frequently been underlined that the primary goal to which a considerable portion of the mission's activity was geared was a recognized and legally valid status for the church as distinct from the mission within the colonial system. The government was asked to grant the church enough legitimacy to establish a binding relationship. This meant an official and recognized position *vis-à-vis* the colonial state which would enable the church to ask for and receive endowments and other types of support and privileges. Furthermore, the church was to be accepted as an institution within African society, entitled to status, rights and privileges originating from that context. According to this approach to the political system, constitutional, legal and economic factors were thus inseparable. This should be borne in mind when the means employed to achieve these goals are discussed.

Two areas in particular were important for the realization of the principal goal, and results achieved in these areas are indicative of more general success. A major part of the survey has been devoted to the issue of church land (see Part III), because land ownership was acknowledged from an early stage to be necessary for the establishment of the church and its functioning on an independent economic basis. Land ownership was at the same time the best way of integrating the church firmly into society and the state. After the allotment of a number of square miles under the Uganda Agreement of 1900, the mission constantly and energetically worked to increase the amount of land available for church work, and to improve the conditions on which the land was held, especially as regards the people living on the land, in order to increase its value as a source of revenue. In both respects it was seen as crucial that land granted for Christian purposes was invested in the church, not in the mission. This presupposed that the church was recognized as a legitimate holder of such land. The first aim of the mission was thus to have the church recognized as an African institution, in order to avoid the restrictions placed on land owned by non-Africans. The crucial argument was that church land was not alienated from the African system; on the contrary it carried with it all the rights and privileges originating in the African tradition.

The theme of non-alienation was developed further when the mission claimed certain of the chiefly rights connected with the ownership of land: first, that church land should be subject to a special system of authority, distinct from and in some respects independent of the administrative system of the chiefs, with church katikiros holding office; secondly, that tenants on church land should be exempted from certain obligations, and be able to fulfil others by working for the church. The church as such, the mission claimed, should be recognized as an institution with a certain autonomy within the African system.

The demand for recognition went further, in that it was also directed towards the colonial system. It was requested that the land grant should be considered as an endowment, usable for whatever purpose was most profitable, whether for sub-letting or plantation agriculture. Furthermore, the concept of ownership should not be limited to the intrinsic value of the land, but should be widened to comprise rights over people living on church property. This meant that the church would be entitled to labour services otherwise due to the government over and above the rents from the tenants. This latter type of recognition obviously implied that the church was to be accepted as an institution of national importance qualifying for state support. The mission thus sought recognition for the church at three different levels, all closely related and overlapping in some respects. By using this comprehensive argumentation, the mission clearly ran the risk of weakening its own chances of success, as its objectives thus became less clear-cut and more difficult to comprehend in detail. This implication of the mission's strategy will be considered further below.

The government conceived of the whole alienation issue differently from the mission. Its major concern was the preservation of chiefly authority as the linch-pin of the administrative system in the Protectorate. However the chiefs' authority was defined, there could be no question of allowing church katikiros to represent an alternative system of authority, nor of transferring tributes to the church. In principle, there could be no exemptions from obligations to either of the two political systems. Working for the church was *not* equivalent to fulfilling obligations towards the nation. When land and labour concessions were given in spite of this, they were in each case granted for a well-defined purpose, not related to the church as such, and a maximum limit was fixed to their extent. Secondly, the government adhered firmly to the 'mission formula' as it had been laid down as early as 1900. It dealt with the mission: how the mission organized things itself was an internal matter. Consequently, land granted for Christian purposes was the legal responsibility of the mission, even if it was said to be held in trust for the Native Anglican church. Therefore, the land was necessarily classified as privately-owned or non-African-owned, and any entitlement to rights and obligations was determined by this legal framework.

The church was thus not granted any legitimacy as regards landholdings. The result was equally negative when the mission attempted to use the educational sector in the battle for recognition. As we have noted on several occasions, the educational work was related to the land issue. The mission relied on a secular argument by claiming that the heavy drain on its resources which its educational activities represented justified an increased land grant on more profitable and liberal terms. This argument did not work with the government, which took a comprehensive view of the missionary enterprise, and could not see the general educational work as belonging to a separate category undertaken by the church. The land allotment was considered to be a block grant covering all aspects of missionary work, and was not earmarked for educational activities in particular. Consequently, these activities did not justify additional grants of land and labour.

When the government eventually undertook some degree of responsibility for educational work, its support was given directly to identifiable and accountable aspects such as the poll-tax reimbursement in the case of teachers. As the government's engagement in education increased substantially in the post-war period, the growing grants-in-aid were given directly to the mission as the agency in charge of education, and were even earmarked for specific purposes. Inevitably, this greater government involvement had among its repercussions an increased separation of the evangelizing and the educational work, and the latter came to be seen as a specialized missionary activity distinct from the church's work. The drifting apart of these two sectors was underlined in 1922–3 when those missionaries who were solely engaged in educational work began to be paid out of the government grant. On this occasion it was made absolutely clear by the colonial government that the educational grant was given to the CMS mission and not to the church (Chapter 15).

Alarmed by the wide-ranging consequences of this development, the Synod made an attempt to have the educational work recognized as the responsibility of the church. If the church was acknowledged as the receiver of grants-in-aid, it would imply some degree of official recognition from the government and an endorsement of the distinction between mission and church. As no result was forthcoming, the mission pursued the matter energetically on its own by setting up a special sub-committee; it was considered to be crucially important that the church be recognized at last[8] – 'their failure to do so is a constant hindrance in all sorts of ways'.[9] To ease the way for the government – although this may have caused some confusion – the Bishop suggested that the educational grant should be paid to the Registered Trustees of the Native Anglican Church, the idea being that this would secure European control over the money for a long time to come, but in the name of the church.[10] It was also suggested that the NAC should appoint representatives through the Diocesan Council to the newly established educational boards.[11] The educational sector was here being used as a device to obtain from the government 'the recognition of the Native Anglican Church as a self-governing body with responsible officers, quite distinct from the Mission'.[12] The mission thus reiterated its familiar arguments, but on this occasion also went a significant step further: 'We suggest that the time may now have come for the drafting of an ordinance defining the position of the Native Anglican Church in Uganda, its powers over its own members, and its relations to Government.'[13] This rather surprising demand represented the culmination of all the mission's efforts to have the church officially recognized, and indicated that the mission considered it necessary after all to establish constitutional linkages between church and state, and to obtain a formalized position for the church within the state along English lines. The government was asked to endorse the church constitution legally, which also involved pledging the church to adhere to Anglican doctrines and to follow certain ecclesiastical rules and regulations. This in fact amounted to asking that the state pass legislation for the church and undertake responsibility for its doctrines. In this way the church would be recognized as a corporate body within the state.

This interpretation of the mission's request is borne out by the government's response. It was specifically stated that any kind of legislation for the church was out of the question. Irrespective of the labels 'mission' or 'church', both bodies were non-corporate associations, and as long as they followed the laws of the Protectorate there was no reason for government intervention. As regards establishment, the Church of England model could not be extended to Uganda, despite the fact that the mission and the church were in ecclesiastical communion with the Church of England: these links did not place the church in a position different from that of any other religious body.[14] The government, faced with this bold – and rather unexpected – initiative from the mission, thus took this opportunity to clarify its own position, now that the issue of establishment had for once come right to the surface. But its response was in full accordance with its attitude on previous occasions, when there had been more indirect demands for institutionalized linkages between church and state. Minimal religious engagement was the ideal of the colonial state (see Chapter 17).

Apart from the legislatory aspects, the mission did not with this latest gambit succeed in conveying to the government the gist of its argument, the distinction between the mission and the church. The whole issue was considered by government officials to be very complicated, 'almost metaphysically so'. Because the land issue was involved, the mission's distinction was seen as a device to obtain more acreage – 'sighting shots at the land-target'.[15] This last incident justifies more than anything else the conclusion that the mission achieved a very low degree of goal implementation in the period in question.[16] This lack of success indicates at the same time the limits within which the substance of the relationship between the mission and the colonial state must be established. Before moving on to this issue, however, we must examine some of the factors which proved decisive for the mission's capacity in its engagements with the state.

Factors influencing the capacity of the mission

The mission's strategy in approaching the government

In its attempts to achieve its major goal the mission harped constantly on the theme of the distinction between the mission and the church, claiming that the church was an African, non-alienated institution. But we also saw how the mission failed to convey the gist of its argument to the government.[17] The strategy employed did not have the desired effect on the government, which did not understand the issue at stake or its implications. It tended to interpret the mission's arguments as a pretext for obtaining objectives incompatible with its own, or even as expressions of pure self-interest.

We may first assess the way the message was communicated to the government. The mission sought, as we have just seen, recognition of church land as such, and of the accompanying rights simultaneously at three different levels. This comprehensive approach weakened the impact of its arguments on the government by making its stand less clear and more liable to misunderstanding. Secondly, frequent references were made to the educational work and its increasing drain on resources, on the assumption that a secular argument of this type would work better with the government. But this concentration on the educational argument tended to blind the missionaries themselves to the real reasons for the government's support of their work (see in particular p. 256). It also made it difficult for the mission to convince the government later that education was integrated with the rest of the Christian work, or that it was a church-sponsored activity. This would have meant that educational grants would be given to, and administered by, the church. But the government considered education to belong in the European sphere of work, and held the mission to be the sole educational agency to which support could be granted. A lack of cohesion in the mission's presentation of its position is further put into perspective when we consider also the extent to which the mission in fact qualified its own arguments. Although the church was presented as an African institution and a self-governing body with its own constitutional apparatus, when it came to the question of state support it was pointed out that the disposal of resources was to remain under European control for a long time to come. References were made to the Bishop's veto rights on legislation and expenses. The NAC trustees, too, were Europeans, and a majority of them would still be Europeans in the foreseeable future. Thus the mission tended to qualify the value of its own arguments.

The discrepancy between the mission's official policy and its actual practice in its everyday work made the mission's position less convincing. First, it has been pointed out how the mission pursued its ideals only halfheartedly and with great diffidence. Africans were seldom placed in positions of leadership, and if they were, it was out of necessity (see Chapter 20, where the parallelism between church and state was the most significant factor). Secondly, as a consequence of this the government dealt only with missionaries, who held all the executive posts. This again cast doubt upon the claim that the church was an independent institution. Thirdly, despite all claims to the contrary, the mission accepted its role as an educational agency and sole receiver of government grants, and some missionaries consequently had to be paid out of public funds. This was equivalent to allowing the evangelizing and educational aspects of the work to be placed in different categories. The mission and the church thus tended to drift away from each other, and this could only devalue the role of the church.

Perhaps underlying all the other weaknesses in the missionary strategy was their peculiar internal organization, with its semi-permeable boundary between mission and church. The mission admitted that it was difficult to explain this structure to the government, and that any attempt to do so was likely to create confusion.[18]

All in all, the mission's strategy did not facilitate its goal implementation or help to present its real objectives properly. It rather provided the government with the opportunity to dismiss its arguments as either incomprehensible or incompatible with government policy. It was then easy for the government to continue with the 'mission formula' and to refrain from taking much notice of the newly constituted church.

Links with the colonial state and channels of influence

It follows from our examination of the concept of a Christian state that the mission was not able to act from a position of establishment. Nor was it possible to any noteworthy extent to find any institutionalized linkages between the mission and the colonial state. In that respect the government practised a restrictive policy with much concern for proper boundary maintenance; but this did not prevent the mission from nurturing the image of a special relationship with the government, for instance by exploiting the presence of the Governor on selected occasions. In view of the government's restrained attitude and its concern for neutrality in its relations with the two denominations, the mission had little opportunity to play what has earlier been called its third political role, based upon its common nationality and creed with the government. Towards the end of the period it was even made quite clear that the mission's relationship with the Church of England did not make its position any different from that of any other religious body.[19]

It is therefore necessary to look for other channels of influence than these in order to establish the capacity of the mission. On the basis of the two political roles frequently ascribed to the mission, its advisory function with African leaders and its function as intermediary to the colonial administration, we have suggested that the mission had assumed a consultative status within the colonial system. This accords well with the mission's own perception of its role *vis-à-vis* the colonial state, as it saw itself as an intermediary between those who governed and those who were governed (p. 308). Our examination of this consultative status proved the best way of describing the channels of missionary influence, and establishing the extent of that influence. We saw how the capacity of the mission was dependent on both internal and external factors. Internally, the mission consciously geared itself to playing its two roles by instituting organizational, procedural and personal measures. At the same time it was fully aware of the limitations under which it had to act. The external forces obviously had a constraining effect on the mission's ability to act. This was the case when the government accused the mission of interference, and deliberately tried to limit its consultative role. What should be suggested here is that the mission, judged on the basis of its consultative status, in spite of all the constraining factors, retained a considerable capacity to act *vis-à-vis* the government. In other words, it had sufficient organizational autonomy to represent a challenge to the state.

The mission's capacity was related to the kind of issues it chose to raise with the government. Whether the government considered the issues to be within the mission's legitimate sphere of interest was particularly important. This complex interrelationship has in various parts of the analysis been used as a variable in measuring the mission's success with the government, and the arguments will not be repeated here. However, one overall structural factor helps to explain the variety of subjects raised and the variations in the strength the mission could muster. Together with the other missionary societies, the CMS mission had a monopoly-like position in the colonial state, because the missions were the only institutions besides the government with an organizational structure that covered the whole Protectorate. This brought the CMS mission to a certain extent into competition with the political sphere, particularly as it had its own newspapers and educational system. It was thus within its power to ensure loyalty towards the political system, a factor which the leadership could not overlook.

Two areas in particular illustrated this source of power, and also its fragility. First, much of the activity the mission directed towards the colonial government was connected with its special position in relation to African society and its ability to act as its advocate. This was noted especially in connection with the mission's alliance with the leading chiefs (p. 315 ff.). Changes in the outer system meant that this role became less important. Consequently, the mission's position as the only alternative to the colonial system was weakened. The second area was that of education. As the only educational system available, the mission obtained an educational monopoly which put it in a strong position because of education's socializing effect and its potential for providing trained manpower. But this position was somewhat eroded when the government began to take an active interest in the educational enterprise. The mission's role changed to that of an educational agency, in which capacity it no longer held the initiative. In both cases the state expanded its range of activity and correspondingly devalued the mission's position as the only alternative structure, although it by no means deprived it of all influence and power. The educational work in particular continued to provide a platform for political influence, as we saw from the later phases of the language issue.

Apart from these overall structural considerations, which helped to define the mission's position and capacity within the colonial system, two further channels of influence should be considered. In both cases we are concerned with the actual means of establishing contacts. The normal procedure was the exchange of official letters and memoranda, sometimes supplemented by *ad hoc* meetings. Great care was taken to observe the proper procedures. But an additional formal channel of contact appeared in the late 1910s, when an Advisory Board was set up on education including representatives of all three missions and government officials. This measure was clearly indicative of the government's stronger involvement, and of the need for closer cooperation between all the agencies involved. In one sense this brought the mission closer to the centre of power and it thus had better opportunities to exert its influence before decisions were made – one example was the issue of language policy in elementary schools. On the other hand, the government's intention with this measure must have been to impose some restraints on the mission. With it came closer control, so that education was no longer an independent area of activity for the mission. The channel of influence thus had a dual nature.

The second avenue of influence was personal, informal contacts. In an analysis based on the kind of material we have used, this type of contact is unlikely to be brought to light to any great extent. There are, however, in the missionary material, and especially in private letters, references to the close personal relations and frequent informal contacts between officials of the two agencies at both district and headquarters levels. Most significantly, there were the relations between the Governor and the Bishop. A number of factors must certainly have facilitated such contacts, in particular their common cultural and educational background, and their common creed. In assessing the importance of this possible channel of influence and interest articulation, two aspects should be distinguished. In the first place, there was the image-creating effect, in the sense that the apparent special relationship between the colonial administration and the CMS could have wider ramifications, especially as regards the Catholic mission's attitude (see in particular the conclusions, p. 343f). Secondly, the actual scope for influence via these informal channels must be considered in order to assess the value of personal contacts. As pointed out earlier, there was in government circles awareness of the risk of preferential treatment in view of the CMS's contacts with the Anglo-African establishment. This prompted the government to attempt to neutralize the effects of these links by assuming a position of neutrality, which reduced the benefits to be obtained from personal contacts (see Chapter 25). Again, not only the government, but also the mission, laid great stress on adherence to the existing procedural rules. This inevitably left less room for informal exchanges. This was reinforced by the mission's internal hierarchical structure. Authority emanated from the top (from the Bishop and/or Headquarters), and each missionary was obliged to obey his superiors and to find his own place on the hierarchical ladder. This structure functioned smoothly with few exceptions – one exception occurred in connection with the revision of the Marriage Ordinance, and the outcome confirmed the strength of the established order more than it suggested that any benefits were to be obtained by deviating from it (see the case of W. E. Owen, p. 274). Another example was the informal alliances between various sections within both mission and administration on the question of an official language (p. 392). These internal divisions cannot, however, be ascribed primarily to personal contacts. They were due rather to each group's separate registration of such differences of opinions as were voiced publicly. It is also noticeable that all the missionaries later fell into line behind the official missionary language policy. As the colonial administration was based upon a similar hierarchical order, the two agencies reinforced each other in this respect. In general, a hierarchical pattern of authority, backed as it was by an ecclesiastical tradition typified by the status of the Bishop, certainly strengthened the mission in its dealings with the government, as the officeholders' power, primacy and right to rule were not disputed internally. On the other hand, the scope for political influence via personal contacts was limited. Finally, looking at actual results within fields of importance for the mission, one is led to the negative conclusion that personal relations and informal exchanges cannot have been of much significance. In key areas like land, labour services and education the mission suffered several setbacks. As regards the distinction between the mission and the church, the Bishop does not appear to have used the personal approach to help the mission to explain this complicated matter; when informal lines of contact appear to have been activated, on the issue of chaplains (p. 307), the matter was decided by general guidelines laid down in London, and the personal contacts proved of little value.

On the basis of these examples it may be concluded that although personal, informal contact cannot be ruled out as part of the relationship between mission and the colonial government, we are not justified in ascribing much explanatory value to it. The mission's capacity and its impact on the government can be sufficiently explained by reference to other factors.

Links with the European arena

During the first part of the analysis, which covered developments before 1900, a double line of connection was described, running from the African to the European arena. The same two lines, running from the mission and government respectively, continued to operate during the first quarter of the twentieth century, and we must now evaluate the extent to which these linkages influenced the capacity of the mission. One necessary first step is to assess the independence of the local CMS mission as part of a larger missionary organization centred in London. The CMS headquarters had two instruments of control in its hands: it provided finances and manpower. Furthermore, both money and men had to be deployed in accordance with the key principle of self-support and the other principles upon which the whole CMS activity was based. In spite of these guidelines our survey has shown that the Uganda mission had ample room for independent action. The two instruments of control were naturally decisive for the extent and quality of the work, as we have seen in connection with the transfer of the payment of educational missionaries to government grants, and the possibility of the agricultural development of church land; but both the actual pattern of the everyday work and policy aimed at the founding of the future independent church were in general left to the local leaders' discretion. This wide range of independent action can be illustrated by the devolution of authority and the corresponding acceleration of the Africanization process, when headquarters brought pressure to bear on the local representatives, indicating that the time for such measures seemed overdue. Despite this, the Bishop and the Missionary Committee argued against any such moves for the time being, and wanted instead to deploy more missionaries (Chapter 20). Another illustration is the resistance to the home authorities when they warned against too much engagement in educational work, especially in the high schools, as this could put serious hindrances in the way of the church's future self-government and self-support. The mission in Uganda was bent on continuing and even expanding its educational work, and chose to disregard the warnings from home.

It is difficult to describe accurately the degree of the mission's independence of the home authorities; but it is obvious that the CMS mission in Uganda had greater scope for independence in policy- and decision-making than the government did. In the case of the government, the question was not simply one of budgetary control. Policy on central issues like land was laid down in London, to an extent that sometimes surprised or dismayed local officials, and its implementation was closely guided and controlled by the Colonial Office. The mission, on the other hand, had ample scope to pursue its own line within the African arena, to take its own initiatives and to respond to government actions relatively independently of the home board. In other words, the missionary system was more decentralized than the government one, so the European-based authorities assumed a more instrumental value, in the sense that they provided access to the European arena and its potentialities.

Pursuing the latter point, we may say that the Uganda mission's main targets within the European arena were the Colonial Office and the Colonial Secretary, who was approached either through the CMS headquarters or directly by the Bishop, who thus bypassed the local authorities. Depending on the nature and gravity of the subject, the next step on the path of recourse was the parliamentary system itself, either the House of Commons, to which access could be obtained through the CMS establishment, or the House of Lords, which could be reached via the established position of the Church of England as personified by the Archbishop of Canterbury, who could also be deployed in his capacity as guardian of Christian moral principles.

It was only a small step further to activate another element in British public life which might exert influence on the parliamentary system and on public opinion: lobbying or pressure groups. Examples of this were the Anti-Slavery and Aborigines' Protection Society and later the Conference of British Missionary Societies under the leadership of J. H. Oldham. Finally there was more direct access to public opinion through newspapers (in particular *The Times*) and, for some selected issues, through the CMS' wide organizational structure and many publications.[20]

The extent to which the potential of the European arena enhanced the mission's capacity in its dealings with the colonial government can best be established if we look at the results of their use of this mode of action. The issues which were taken to the European arena may broadly be divided into two categories: those concerned with concessions and the conditions of missionary work; and those connected with the safeguarding and defending of African rights. As regards the former, the issues of land and labour concessions and of education were occasionally raised in London. This was no more than logical as long as their overall policy was laid down in London by the Colonial Office. In spite of both Bishops' energetic efforts over the years to increase landholdings and to acquire the land on better terms, the mission had very little success in this. The most likely explanation is that the mission here came up against two barriers: first, there was the overall colonial policy on land, with its strict limits on state support to missionary work; secondly, government concessions to missionary work were in general a sensitive issue in Parliament and were likely to provoke outspoken opposition. As regards increased educational support, the results were just as meagre at first, the major difficulty being that the mission's demands came into conflict with the goal of making the Protectorate self-supporting. It was only in the post-war period that substantial educational support began to be granted. More significantly, it was only then that the principle of cooperation between mission and government was endorsed, thanks to lobbying from the CMS headquarters and pressure from Oldham (p. 246 ff.).

Turning to the question of the safeguarding of African interests, we have seen how Bishop Tucker in particular made use of the whole range of possibilities in the European arena in connection with the labour issue (Chapter 12 on kasanvu and Chapter 13 on forced labour) and with the upholding of the chiefs' rights (Chapter 14 on excess land). Tucker certainly succeeded in stirring up opinion and making an impact which caused certain policy changes. At the same time both issues also illustrate the limitations inherent in invoking the European arena. Tucker himself was fully aware that this means of recourse should be employed with great care. Certain issues could lead to accusations of undue interference, and in such cases the involvement of the European arena could backfire. Nevertheless, in view of its potentialities, it is significant that under Tucker's successor reference to the London office was made more sparingly to defend African interests. A different, less positive perception of African interests, and a more positive attitude to the colonial government, led to the falling-off of interest in the European arena as a political factor.

In view of the few registrable results and the untapped possibilities it is somewhat difficult to arrive at a final assessment of the value of the European arena for the mission. One additional aspect has, however, to be mentioned. Even if Tucker did not produce all that many results, and even if his successor did not follow the same line, the 'demonstration effect' was not lost on the government. It was clearly aware of the latent importance of the European arena, and this may have had a deterrent effect on some of the colonial government's decisions.[21]

Yet, although an appeal to London could work both ways, it is conceivable that it increased the mission's capacity *vis-à-vis* the state in some ways, as it directly or indirectly imposed some constraints on the local government. Probably the most significant feature of this whole relationship is that it provided access, however little it was used, to a parliamentary system and to public opinion. These essential ingredients for the functioning of a political system were virtually absent in the colonial setting. What characterized the African arena more than anything else during the period under survey was the fact that the two European agencies were to a great extent uninhibited by the controlling and restraining forces normally attributed to parliamentary processes and the pressure of public opinion.

Economic resources

The Uganda mission was dependent for its resources, mainly funds and manpower, on the London headquarters. Frequent appeals for more men indicated that the support granted was not adequate to keep up with expanding missionary activity. The mission was faced with this situation even in the pre-war period, and this meant that when founding the church it was more dependent than it had expected on the politico-economic developments in African society. The situation was aggravated by a rigoristic adherence to the principle of self-support in church work. Secondly, as regards its most state-related activity, teaching, the mission had difficulty in coping with the needs which its self-assumed educational monopoly imposed. This weakness did not go unnoticed by the colonial government, as the educational argument was constantly used to try to obtain increased public support.

At first a precarious balance was preserved, in spite of everything, between the means at hand, the standard of the work and the potential expansion. In the post-war period two developments contributed jointly to the destruction of this balance. First, the demands of the educational sector increased substantially with the government's active involvement. Secondly, the CMS' financial crisis and corresponding austerity measures made the local mission less capable of meeting the educational demand. The result was that a severe discrepancy arose between goals and ambitions on the one hand and the actual resources at hand on the other. As education was by then the most state-related of the mission's activities, its weakened position could not remain unnoticed by the government, and the capacity of the mission vis-à-vis the state was reduced. This became evident when the mission had to accept the transition from an educational monopoly to an educational agency, with its overtones of tighter state control. And it had to accept certain intra-organizational consequences of its changed position and consequent setbacks for its overall goal implementation. Hence, it may be concluded that, as far as economic resources were concerned, the capacity of the mission to act independently of the state was reduced, both from an objective point of view and in the eyes of the government.

External factors affecting the mission's capacity

The mission's capacity to engage with the state was related to the interplay between internal factors and external forces, and consequently could not remain constant. One illustrative example has just been mentioned: the mission's diminishing economic resources, combined with changes in the government's education policy. As in the case of the African church, the potentialities were rooted in the internal structure; but their actualization was influenced by socio-political structures in society, and related to the policies of the government and the orientation of colonial officials.[22]

One clear case of interdependence of the latter kind was connected with the mission's objective of establishing an independent church in the African setting. This aim more than any other exposed the mission to the influence of external factors, and the same was true to a lesser degree of a state-related activity like education. In general, the bonds established with the state made the mission susceptible to changes originating in the political sphere. While the implications of this for the mission's freedom of action and the qualitative aspects of its engagement will be discussed later, it will be appropriate here to identify the variables we have met which actually constituted these external forces.

The most comprehensive factor influencing the mission's capacity to act in a political role was the colonial state's development towards a more established and well-defined status. One particular aspect of this was the process of bureaucratization. First, the chiefs became more and more part of the colonial administrative hierarchy, so that their source of authority was increasingly the colonial system rather than the African tradition. This was marked, for instance, by the Native Authority Ordinance of 1919. The chiefs came under ever greater state control, while the colonial officials at the same time took pains to secure their authority against any rival systems of authority, not least in the ecclesiastical field. All this meant that the mission's lines of connection with the African political system were weakened and became less profitable. Secondly, as regards the general process of formalization, we have noticed the transition from custom to law (Chapter 11) leading to less scope for informal action and *ad hoc* decisions. Matters had to be dealt with in accordance with the established code, and more emphasis was put on procedural rules in relations with the mission.

With the process of bureaucratization came a change in the colonial officials' attitude to the mission, as we saw in connection with the various aspects of the drive for a Christian nation (Chapter 16). A certain scepticism developed towards the mission's activities and demands, and the result was closer scrutiny and control. All in all, these various changes meant that there was less room for the mission to play a political role; the whole scope of missionary influence was reduced. Issues became more complicated for various reasons, and more technical expertise was needed for the formulation of demands (Chapter 14). The areas of interaction and the means of contact became more formalized and codified as time went on.

Some of the factors discussed above have been seen as reinforcing the mission's capacity, while others clearly had a constraining effect. No single factor can be taken as a decisive one, given the prevailing pattern of interplay between internal potentialities and external forces, and the significant changes over time. To characterize this process further, we may on the one hand say that a number of interreacting factors tended to produce an erosion effect resulting in a gradual decline of the mission's capacity to act *vis-à-vis* the state. On the other hand, in spite of this process of reduction, the mission still preserved so much autonomy that, in Milton Yinger's words, it had 'the independent power to challenge the state'.[23] All through the period the CMS mission, together with the other missions, provided the only alternative organizational structure in society beside the colonial state. The CMS mission distanced itself enough from the government to be able to challenge it, and it never lost this perception of its own role.[24] In spite of the erosion effect stemming from the various forces enumerated above, its power was neither neutralized nor annihilated; it changed in degree, but not in kind.

25

The colonial government's religious policy

W e will now examine the church–state problem from the government's own perspective: how did it conceive of the mission and church within the colonial setting, and what position was it prepared to grant the mission under these special circumstances? Thus, our focus will be on the processes within the political system and the results on the output side, that is, the religious policy of the colonial state.

For a full assessment of the government's point of view it is, however, essential to widen our perspective by including comparative aspects of the issue. In order to assess the position of the Anglican church properly and to establish whether its activities and results can be explained in terms of a Christian bias on the part of the colonial government, it is necessary to take the government's attitude towards the traditional African religion and Islam into account. It is one of the shortcomings of the analytical schema employed in the present survey that it has focused on inputs from the Christian, mainly Protestant institutions, but paid little attention to the other religions which existed in the colonial state. To fill out this gap and arrive at a balanced picture of the government's policy towards the Anglican church, it will be appropriate once more to introduce some of the issues raised in the earliest part of the survey when we employed religious liberty as the analytical concept. This will also involve some discussion of the denominational factor, in view of the cleavage between the Catholic and Protestant missions.

The significance of non-Christian factors

The African traditional religion

Earlier, when we reviewed the government's religious policy on the basis of developments in the 1890s, our conclusion was that, apart from guaranteeing minimum rights to the large section of the population labelled variously 'Traditionalists' or 'pagans', the government took no active interest in their position within the state (Chapter 7). The African traditional religion had no influence on the shaping of government policy, and its lack of leaders and spokesmen did nothing to help it in this respect. The natural leaders who could have defended and championed the interests of this group had converted to Christianity. It is typical that, when this section of the community was mentioned at all, it was by colonial officials who pointed out the risk of forgetting non-Christians in connection with the expansion of the mission's educational activities. While the Muslims were in the forefront when it came to government initiatives, the people 'without any religion' were also alluded to. In the longer term the reference seems to have been an isolated one, and of a cosmetic nature; it was more due to scepticism towards the mission's educational monopoly than any real regard for African traditions and rights (see the interpretation of the Acting Governor's dispatch in 1905, p. 226). Consequently, this group was not taken into account when the educational policy was worked out. The low esteem in which the traditional religion was held was underlined when this issue was discussed at the Colonial Office. It featured as a poor third when the religions were arranged on a hierarchical ladder, with Christianity at the top and Islam in the middle. Islam was considered to be far ahead of 'paganism' and preferable as a transitional stage.[1]

The next example of the policy on traditional religion came in connection with the complex of marriage laws. Priority was here clearly given to the Christian marriage institution, while the question of the status and validity of customary marriage was left in abeyance. When the issue of the recognition of these marriages was eventually raised it was only because of the need for clarification in cases of transition from marriage under customary to marriage under statutory law. Although some concern was expressed with regard to the proper functioning of African institutions, the government yielded to missionary opinion and appeared to favour monogamous Christian marriage, whereas customary marriage received no legal status, but was left to function as before outside government jurisdiction. When the two types of marriage were after all given equal legal status it was more due to the need to formalize actual existing practice than to any real recognition of African customs. Although this change was accompanied by colonial officials' expressions of concern at the disruption of African institutions by the mission's over-zealous approach, their major worry seems to have been that their administrative task might be made more difficult by the mission's activities.

This administrative self-interest in the approach to African institutions was paralleled by the government's efforts to uphold the chiefs' authority. If non-Christians were found on the lists of chiefs, it was not due to any attempt to strike a balance between the various religions. This group of mainly lower-level chiefs played no real role in the distribution of chieftainships. As their number decreased over the years, their function might justifiably be described as that of a stopgap, until people with sufficient education, that is, Christians, could take over. All in all, the traditionalists were not conceived of as representatives of the traditional religion. Their main qualification was that they were carriers of a traditional authority which was in great demand within the administrative ranks (see Tables 6–11).

This interpretation of the official attitude to African traditional religion is confirmed when we consider the revision of the educational policy in the post-war period. The fact that government officials reintroduced the issue of non-sectarian schools was due to their dissatisfaction with the missionary educational work and a desire for closer government involvement in the educational sector. The non-Christians as such were hardly mentioned. When the actual pattern of cooperation between mission and government was later hammered out, the Director of Education cited the existence of the Muslims as a major reason for starting government elementary schools. Although the Traditionalists were mentioned, their plight was not in itself considered sufficient grounds for action. In any case, the government settled once again for a denominationally based educational system.

Although evidence is scanty on the status of the African traditonal religion we are justified in concluding that the large section of the population who retained their original religion did not constitute an important element in the government's religious policy. The traditional religion was not considered worthy of protection or as a force to be cooperated with. While individuals were defended against oppression and protected from having to perform religious obligations against their will, as will be seen below, the fate of their religion itself was of no interest to the government, as long as its decline did not result in any administrative inconvenience. The traditional religion was a factor of virtually no significance in the overall religious policy; it did not even have any restraining influence on the pro-Christian policy and cooperation with the missions.

Islam

Islam was often mentioned together with the African traditional religion, but with quite different connotations. It has already been noted that Sir Harry Johnston regarded the spread of Islam with some alarm. Hence, although the Muslims were covered by the principle of religious liberty at the individual level, and in addition were guaranteed a few offices, they were not given equal status with the Christians, and were kept under careful observation by the government. It is therefore noteworthy that the Muslims were singled out in 1905 as a group for whom the government ought to take special educational responsibility, as they had been left behind educationally by the Christians, who had the missionaries to teach them. It was proposed that the government should start a couple of non-sectarian schools to cater for them, and the proposal was duly approved by the Colonial Office. In order to evaluate this initiative in the proper perspective two points should be made. First, the plan for two government schools came to nothing. It was quietly shelved for many years, and was never at any point pursued with enough vigour to overcome missionary opposition and the general shortage of funds. Secondly, other motives were certainly involved. The Muslim community was 'notoriously non-progressive' when left to its own devices. The improving effect of secular education was considered necessary if Muslims were to serve any useful purpose within society.[2] In other words, the move to start non-sectarian schools was not simply meant to secure equal status for the Muslims, but was to serve as a preventive measure in the interests of the government.

Another, similarly double-edged, attitude was evident at about the same time in connection with the marriage laws. While Muslim marriage was legally recognized on equal footing with Christian monogamous marriage, it was all the same placed in a disadvantageous position because of the marriage fees and various procedural rules. The colonial government left no doubt that it gave priority to the Christian marriage institution, and ascribed greater prestige to it than to others. The same was true of the allotment of land to the Muslim community in 1913–14. Arguments based on administrative convenience carried much weight whereas the question of equality counted for little. Another testing-ground was the appointment of chiefs, where the government had on one occasion even been presented with direct demands from the Muslim leaders for more equality. At first the government made an attempt in 1913 to redress the Muslim community's numerically unbalanced position by appointing a Muslim to a vacant saza chieftainship (p. 327). There is no doubt that this move sprang from a genuine desire to secure a higher degree of religious tolerance, but there was also some desire to penalize the Protestant and Catholic parties in Buganda because of their constant rivalry. As things turned out, the first idealistic motive was soon forgotten, while the more pragmatic attitude prevailed, in the sense that the status quo policy continued, with its inherent Christian ascendancy. This was underlined in 1923, when the government was faced with a direct demand from the Muslim leaders for the same rights as the Christians to the religious monopoly of gombolola chiefs within their allocated saza. The request was rejected, and the status quo reaffirmed. The government more or less washed its hands of the whole affair and refused to readjust any imbalance.

In order to explain this ambivalence towards the Muslims, it is necessary to look more closely at the government's basic perception of Islam's position within the colonial framework. What was implicit in Johnston's attitude in 1900 was spelt out explicitly and publicly by his successor in 1904 when he made it clear that 'paganism' was bound to yield to either Christianity or Islam, in which case the former was preferable: 'To those who fear the possibility of a Mahomedan revival, the importance of Uganda as a strong bulwark in equatorial Africa, gradually spreading Christianity to its surroundings, must be at once apparent.'[3]

In this case, as on later occasions, the presence of the Muslims and Islam's prospects of advancement were carefully watched.[4] Islam was considered a negative, even dangerous, factor, which made it an important influence on policy-making. The government saw clearly the instrumental value of Christianity in this respect, and the work of the missions thus had a special dimension in the government's eyes as a means of containing Islam.[5] Both the concern for the political implications of Islam and the mission's instrumental value came to the forefront in 1917. In that year there was a lengthy discussion between the missions and the government about financial and moral support for the educational work, which resulted in the first educational conference ever held. In a circular it was stated that equal tolerance should be extended to every form of religious belief (see below), and Islam was singled out:

With reference to Mahomedanism it is to be borne in mind that the Moslem faith, although entitled in itself to the same tolerance as other religions, is peculiarly liable to fanatic development and as such must be judiciously watched by those who are responsible for the preservation of law and order.[6]

Three not fully compatible trends stand out as possible determinants of government policy: adherence to religious tolerance, a leaning towards Christianity and its missions, and anxiety over the spread of Islam. Actual policy towards Islam depended on which of these determinants was given priority. At first there was an emphasis on the last trend in view of the events of the war. The Colonial Office, alarmed by the growth of Muslim fanaticism and revivalism during the war in Tanganyika, inquired if there was a similar risk in Uganda, not least in view of possible link-ups with outbreaks of Ethiopianism.[7] The Acting Governor took a relaxed view, and saw no risk in Uganda. Provided the Muslims were reasonably handled they represented 'a mildly elevating moral force'. Although he did not believe in the theory of Uganda 'as a kind of buffer Christian state', he was adamantly against the Colonial Office's proposal to establish secular schools in order to combat Islam, as they would almost certainly become hotbeds of Muslim propaganda, and then there would be real reason for anxiety. In addition, they would be regarded by the people as Muslim schools opposed to the Christian ones, and the establishment of government schools would be seen by the missions as direct government support for Islam.[8]

It appears from this that, while the third consideration in government policy, the political implications of Islam, was of less importance in Uganda than elsewhere, it was none the less an active factor, in the sense that the government was not prepared to take any measures which might further the cause of Islam and redress existing inequities. One deterrent factor was clearly the risk of a collision with the missions. Furthermore, the pattern of interrelationships between the three strands in government policy changed in the immediate post-war period, when the 'perils of Islam' once again came to the forefront and constituted an important element in policy-making. When the so-called Allah Water cult gained ground in the West Nile District, and a number of people had to be deported, one major concern was whether there was any connection between this movement and 'Mohammedan propaganda', but the theory was duly repudiated.[9] Again, when the government nurtured the idea of starting a newspaper in Luganda, one of its objectives was to combat the spread of Islam.[10] Finally, at about the same time, the District Commissioners in the Northern Province called for equal concessions for ministers of all religions and the abolition of special privileges for European missionaries. They also recommended the separation of religious and secular education, with the government undertaking the latter. This resolution was condemned by headquarters as undue and untimely interference, as it showed 'an anti-Mission feeling which is unfortunate in an area where Mohammedan influence is already so strong'.[11] Soon afterwards it was recommended that the officers in the Northern Province should take the Muslim presence and the risk of fanaticism into account, and respond positively when the missions asked for land to start schools. Christian doctrines and ideals were seen as the best way of combating Muslim influence.[12] Thus, the greater the anxiety over the political implications of Islam, the more the instrumental value of the missions was emphasized, and the ideas of tolerance and equality were put aside. Earlier we have seen exactly the same attitude in connection with the language issue.

The above-mentioned recommendation from the District Commissioners in the Northern Province indicates, however, the different attitude which seems to have gained ground among officials during the first half of the 1920s. Officials serving in the Northern and Eastern Provinces in particular dismissed as invalid the usual arguments about the political risks inherent in Islam, and some of them spoke up in favour of a policy of greater equality, especially in the field of education, which from now on provided the most important platform for the various groups who were in favour of a more balanced religious policy. As early as 1919 the Uganda Development Commission recommended that the government should make provisions for the elementary education of Muslims,[13] and this recommendation was later repeated by the Young Baganda Association, who at the same time pointed out that the government ought not to wait for an initiative from leaders of the Muslim community, who did not realize the value of education.[14]

The sense of an obligation towards the Muslim community gained momentum when Governor Archer took over in 1922–3. For him it was sufficient reason for a government initiative that no one until then had catered for the educational needs of the Muslim population.[15] This opinion was later clearly reflected in reports from the educational advisor to the Uganda government, E. R. J. Hussey, who, with the Muslim community in mind, suggested a separate system of non-sectarian state schools. But the issue was mixed up with the overall issue of future educational policy – whether the government would start its own educational system or continue its close cooperation with the missions by using them as government-supported educational agencies. While this matter of principle was solved independently of the Muslim issue, it was considered to be a minimum requirement that the government provided educational facilities for the Muslim community along the lines suggested by Hussey.[16] This decision was upheld, in spite of fierce opposition from the CMS mission, which accused the government of breaching the accepted principle of religious neutrality, in that it was giving the Muslim community preferential treatment by granting it more privileges than the Christians.[17] The latter criticism shows where the real problem lay. First of all, the government's range of action was curtailed by its cooperation with the missions. This gave education in Uganda a Christian stamp at the expense of the non-Christians, in particular the Muslims. The only way out of this situation was to practise some form of positive discrimination and thereby to secure 'a road to social advancement' for a minority group whose interests no one else protected. The mission was partially right in accusing the government of lack of neutrality, but it failed to see that the mischief was rooted in the overall policy of cooperation with Christian agencies, and that this preferential treatment was an attempt to make some small amends for the unfortunate effects of the long-term policy.

This development in the government's educational policy illustrates the three trends in the religious policy mentioned above. It is quite clear that the assumed political implications of Islam were substantially played down, and this had two effects. First, the instrumental role of the Christian missions in making Uganda a bulwark against Islam's progress was correspondingly reduced in the eyes of officials. Secondly, the sense of obligation towards the Muslim community had a positive effect on the importance of the Islamic factor in government policy-making. Still, in spite of the readjustment in priorities between the three trends in government policy, commitment to the Muslim cause and to neutrality in general was not strong enough to override the continued close educational cooperation with the missions and bring about the introduction of an entirely secular system of education. The government's commitment went no further than a desire to even out inequalities to a limited extent within the already existing framework. The actual results of the policy of making provisions for the Muslims – or the non-Christian community – prove this. The number of government elementary schools was reduced from the proposed six to one, and the ones started both at this level and at the secondary level were short-lived.[18] When they were closed down the few Muslim students were often transferred to mission schools.[19] One obvious explanation of this reduced programme was lack of funds. Resources were tied down elsewhere, especially in the support of mission-run institutions, and the education of Muslims was not given enough priority to change that.[20] In addition, there were still a number of leading officials who were opposed to any form of Muslim progress because of the political risks. These spoke in favour of encouraging people to embrace Christianity instead of Islam.[21] It may further be taken as indicative of the very limited scale of the secular educational system that the mission seems to have acquiesced in the new policy.[22]

Probably the most decisive factor of all was the very poor response from the Muslim community itself. This may partly be ascribed to its own leaders' failure to appreciate general education beyond what was supplied by the Koran schools, as the Young Baganda Association had suggested a few years earlier. But there were also some traits inherent in government policy which may have had a constraining effect on the Muslim response. First of all, by not introducing an entirely secular system of education, and by leaving the bulk of the work to be run on Christian principles by the missions with state support, the government could not avoid giving the impression that education was a Christian activity. This inevitably served to nourish Muslim suspicion.[23] Secondly, while the Christians had denominational schools, the Muslims were offered a secular system. Although this was done deliberately to attract the Muslims, it was nevertheless only a gesture towards providing equal facilities, and may in fact indicate failure to understand the ingrained Muslim antagonism to Western education. A more direct approach would have been to support a Muslim missionary society. But this possibility was firmly rejected when the opportunity actually presented itself in 1925 in the shape of a missionary movement from India. It was envisaged that the presence of such an agency would almost certainly mean political trouble, and the government would not support it officially by granting it exemptions from poll tax, a privilege the Christian missionaries enjoyed.[24] Instead, the principle of equality was upheld to some extent by cancelling the concessions to the Christian missionaries and by reference to the planned secular schools.[25]

A process of change occurred throughout the years under survey. The Muslim factor played an increasingly positive role in shaping policy, as opposed to its negative one in the first part of the period. After 1920 in particular the government became more concerned with the situation of the Muslim community and took active measures to ameliorate it. Still, the last case mentioned has shown that constraining factors were at work. In the first place, although now less significant, the old fear of the political repercussions of the Muslim factor lived on, and limited the extent to which the government would pursue a policy of positive discrimination. Again, the ascendancy of Christianity was still strong, and this in itself tended to limit the government's range of action towards the Muslims. The measures taken to secure more equality of opportunity for the Muslims were meant to relieve their inferior status, and represented no substantial changes in the government's overall religious policy.

Tolerance and neutrality in government policy

This analysis of the government's attitude towards the African traditional religion and Islam has made it clear that there existed in government policy an inherent Christian bias, in the sense that Christianity enjoyed a position of privilege over the other religions, and special concessions were granted to their missionary work. On the other hand, there were also in government policy both a balancing tendency towards religious tolerance and concern for the rights of non-Christians. Hence, there was an element of paradox in the situation, and we must ask how far the two trends were compatible. The question may be framed differently in terms of the concept of religious liberty. How important was religious liberty for government policy? During the formative period (the 1890s) the government made efforts to safeguard religious liberty at the individual level, but beyond that there was a tendency to apply the concept only within the Christian denominational framework. Thus, while it safeguarded people's rights to worship as they wished and extended tolerance to all religions, the government was not strictly neutral in its policy towards each religion. We must therefore ask whether the government widened its concept of religious liberty in the first quarter of the twentieth century.

The issue of religious liberty arose only occasionally in this period. The evictions from land on religious grounds, which had earlier been so controversial, were now almost a thing of the past.[26] The next step was to protect people from having to contribute to religious work against their will. This issue is inextricably bound up with the conflict between individual rights as represented by the concept of religious liberty and communal obligations firmly rooted in the African tradition. The government took the side of individual rights and approved a law passed by the Buganda Lukiko which stipulated that no one could be forced to work on a mosque or a church if he did not wish to do so on religious grounds.[27] This law was later extended to other parts of the Protectorate.[28] It did not, of course, apply in the case of paid work, where individuals could decide for themselves; but it was a different matter when people were expected to do this type of work as part of their tribute to their chief. Then it became crucial to decide whether communal obligations took priority over individual rights. The government opted for individual rights in one specific case, when it ruled that a chief could not use his tenants' one month's busulu labour to erect a church; the Bakopi were not to be forced to do work on religious buildings.[29] Although it protected individual rights, this ruling did not solve the wider problem of how far the chiefs were to be allowed to use their feudal authority to support the religious work, if this was defined as being for the benefit of society at large. The issue arose sporadically over the next few years.

As for reliance on the chiefs' prestige and influence in society, the Anglican church was naturally in the forefront as it had the leading Ganda chiefs in its fold. We have already seen how this relationship worked in connection with the rebuilding of the Cathedral in 1910–19, when the Ganda leaders committed themselves substantially to its funding (see p. 351). It is significant that this caused some alarm within the European arena. It was asked in Parliament whether the chiefs forced their subordinates to contribute money, causing them to believe mistakenly that the government had introduced a new tax. The matter was investigated, and the allegation was disproved, but the fact that the issue had arisen made the government aware of the wider attention which the protection of individuals attracted.[30] The potential element of indirect coercion by secular leaders was brought into focus a few years later, when a leading Protestant chief equated obedience to God with obedience to the Kabaka. Of the newly founded Malakite sect (see below) he stated: 'I think that his [Malaki's] teaching is a rebellion but not a religion. Because the religion orders to obey the Kabaka and the rulers, but that [sic] who does not obey them resists God.'[31] This was close to advocating a state church model, and the ideal came close to realization at the end of the period. A gombolola court sentenced a man who had refused to organize a collection for the Protestant King's College, Budo. The legal basis for its decision was a letter from the Kabaka in which he recommended that chiefs should use their influence for such purposes. When the matter was investigated, it appeared that the Kabaka's letter could easily assume the character of law, which meant that the collection was no longer a voluntary one. That some pressure was in fact involved was later confirmed by the Katikiro, Sir Apolo Kagwa. If someone refused to pay, he was called to the gombolola chief, who explained to him the benefit of King's College. If he remained adamant, he could be sent to the Katikiro, but most people paid when the situation was explained to them. The Governor objected strongly to this, and characterized it as an abuse of the chiefs' influence, no matter how laudable the ends were. The government suspected that the CMS mission was behind the whole affair.[32]

For the mission it was only natural to make use of the chiefs' influence because of their leading role within the church, their prestige in society and their economic potential. But in practice it was difficult to tell whether they were acting in their private or their official capacity. The issue became more sensitive for the government when the chiefs became civil servants rather than traditional officeholders. In view of the linkages between the Anglican church and the Protestant majority in the Lukiko, the chiefs' engagement in fund-raising gave the impression that the machinery of the state was being activated for religious purposes. This was an example of the poor boundary maintenance between the church and the African political system which the government deplored. The government stepped in in the case in question because the use of the African leaders' position and authority represented an encroachment on individual liberty in religious matters. Reference to the common good was not enough to justify this encroachment.

It was more difficult to harmonize these two principles in the case of the Bakopi's obligations towards the chiefs. The first opportunity to clarify the issue came when the Malakite movement was flourishing in the Eastern Province under the guidance of the veteran Ganda leader, Semei Kakungulu (see pp. 399).[33] Besides asking for freedom of movement for his teachers, he also requested the district administration via the chiefs to order his Malakite followers to build houses.[34] The colonial administration now took the opportunity to clarify its policy. Freedom of movement was granted to teachers of religion in all administered areas, but it was specifically stated that 'the chiefs had no power either to order or compel their people to erect Churches or Schools or to work for religious propaganda'.[35] Instead, voluntary or paid labour must be used. As an explanation of this ruling, and in order to clarify the principles underlying the government's policy on religion and educational initiatives, the following statement was prefaced to the ruling:

The Government will do all possible to promote religion and education among the native inhabitants of the Protectorate, but does not concern itself with the religious beliefs or teachings of the people, in other words complete 'religious toleration' is to prevail.[36]

Attempts to implement this policy in the Eastern and Northern Provinces, especially in the Lango District, however, put it to a test which it could not pass. When a zealous District Commissioner pursued the policy to the letter, it became evident that on this basis cooperation with the missions on Christian education was logically ruled out. As the government would not start an educational system of its own, or give direct support to the missions, the only alternative was to use the authority and labour services of the chiefs. The mission saw this as fully justifiable, as educational initiatives were for the general welfare of the people and in the government's own interests.[37] But the District Commissioner disagreed: such an approach would involve forced labour, and would thus violate the rights of individuals, and would be inconsistent with the neutrality of the administration.[38] The reason for this strong stand on neutrality and the ban on the chiefs' involvement was almost certainly the fact that the government was faced with two versions of Christianity, missionary and Malakite.[39] But the whole government attitude was contrary to familiar practice in the Bantu areas, not least in Buganda, and the CMS mission quickly pointed out that the line pursued in the Eastern and Northern Provinces represented a significant new departure in government policy.[40] Criticizing this new departure, they then further pointed out that it hindered the educational work and could be interpreted as deliberate opposition to the mission's aims. A distinction ought to be drawn between encouraging education and putting pressure on individuals. While the latter was naturally precluded, the former was certainly permissible, as it was for the general welfare of the people. Consequently, the chiefs ought to be allowed to use their authority and a reasonable amount of their labour tribute for educational purposes. This would be for the benefit of the people and could not be regarded as coercion for religious purposes.[41]

The missionary argument was based on two crucial principles. First of all, it involved a distinction between tolerance and neutrality. While the mission fully acknowledged the value of tolerance, the state's neutrality bordered on passivity or outright indifference. This argument anticipated by a year the joint call from all three missions mentioned above, when they urged the government to work for a Christian nation. The rejection of the state's version of neutrality and the call for the chiefs' active involvement implied that priority and official acknowledgement should be granted to Christian education. The second crucial point raised by the CMS mission confirms this interpretation. Bishop Willis specified explicitly the options facing the government: either it must settle for a truly secular system of education, with a sharp distinction between secular and religious teaching, or it must endorse the coexistence of secular and religious, i.e. Christian education. These two crucial points defined the dilemma with which the government was confronted in its attempts to pursue a policy of religious tolerance and neutrality, as manifested by its ban on the use of chiefly labour tributes for religious purposes.

First, the government reaffirmed the principles laid down when the issue first arose with Kakungulu's request for chiefly services.[42] Bishop Willis could, however, threaten to stop educational work in the Eastern and Northern Provinces. At that juncture he could be confident that the government, because of general inertia, the pattern established elsewhere in the Protectorate, and financial limitations, was bound to modify its policy.[43] His confidence was justified. The controversy caused the government to call the first ever educational conference with representatives from both the three missions and the government.[44] A number of practical issues requiring cooperation between the missions and the government – such as the establishment of sites for churches and schools – were settled, and the government backed down somewhat, if only tacitly, on the question of the chiefs' involvement.[45] The most important decision on religious policy was that 'The Government of the Uganda Protectorate, while desirous of encouraging the spread of Christian principles by all legitimate means, extends an equal toleration to every form of religious belief.'[46]

First of all, this statement of policy should be compared with the equivalent statement from the foregoing year (p. 441). While it still professed religious toleration, the government was now clearly committing itself to Christian principles and legitimizing their extension. Secondly, the distinction between tolerance and neutrality was now tacitly recognized. Thirdly, the statement gave priority to an educational system based on Christian principles. Fourthly, it implicitly legitimized the use of the chiefs' authority and tributes for Christian purposes, provided that such use did not violate the principle of tolerance.

All in all, the decision meant a religious policy on Christian foundations or with a Christian bias. This was not a new policy, but because of the events in the north and the east it was spelt out in more definite terms than before. Over the next decade it remained the most authoritative expression of the government's religious policy, and officials had occasion to cite it from time to time.[47] Yet its content was somewhat paradoxical. The policy was based on an inherent dichotomy between two principles: toleration and neutrality. Consequently, the government was constantly faced with the problem of striking a balance between these two principles. In other words, it had to decide to what extent the religious neutrality of the state could be dispensed with without violating the principle of tolerance. How the problem was solved in practice can be illustrated by five different cases.

(1) As stated above, the Malakite movement constituted one of the determinants in policy-formation, and this movement gave rise to one of the first occasions where the Circular of 1917 was invoked. The principle of tolerance was extended to the Malakites as far as freedom of teaching and the movement of teachers were concerned; and even when the CMS mission tried to induce the government to impose restrictions on the new sect, the government stood by the principle of tolerance.[48] It made efforts to ensure that the Protestant hegemony within the Buganda political system could not be used to limit religious freedom for the Malakites.[49] When the mission made an attempt to politicize the issue by pointing out the risk of anti-government and anti-European feelings, the government saw no immediate danger and confined itself to keeping the movement under observation. It would only take action if the anti-medical element in Malakite teaching gained ground and presented a danger to public health.[50] So far the government's record with regard to tolerance had been impeccable, although its motives had been partly pragmatic.

A new phase began when the Malakites in Ankole asked for Temporary Occupation Licence plots of the type held by the missions. Dealing with this request, officials referred to two clauses in the Circular of 1917. In the first place, the provision about 'encouraging Christian principles' was considered invalid, as it was questionable whether the Malakites represented genuine Christian principles. Secondly, the sect had not attempted to found any educational establishments, and consequently was not covered by the Circular. As a general criterion for handling such issues, a distinction was drawn between 'opposing and encouraging an institution'. While the movement should not be opposed, as it had the right to exist, encouragement was quite a different thing. Both the final decision and the underlying arguments were upheld by the central authorities, and no sites were granted.[51] The same thing happened a couple of years later when the Malakites asked for exemptions from kasanvu. Although persecution should be avoided the religion was not to be encouraged in any way, as its doctrine was not 'to the best interests of the country'.[52] The government would only intervene if it found the sect's opposition to medical treatment to be a danger to public health.[53]

The Malakite movement did not present much of a problem for the government as far as the last issue was concerned. The right to profess the new creed was clearly guaranteed in spite of the mission's efforts to have it circumscribed. On the other hand, the government was not over-concerned with the question of neutrality. Qualitatively assessed, the Malakite creed was not considered to be in accordance with Christian principles, and therefore qualified for no special support or encouragement. Hence, there was for the government no conflict between the principles of tolerance and neutrality in its handling of the Malakite movement; on the contrary, a reasonable tolerance was considered to have prevailed, and the government stood firm against any attempts to encroach on this principle.

(2) In the second case, the government was requested to abandon the principle of neutrality altogether. As mentioned in Chapter 16 on the Christian nation, the three bishops' letter of 1918 claimed that the government's strict neutrality amounted to religious indifference in the eyes of the people, which was incompatible with its position as a Christian government in a Christian nation. It was requested that the government abandon the principle of neutrality and actively support and encourage the Christian cause. This was to be done by supporting Christian education, ensuring that the chiefs' moral standards were satisfactory, and in general by encouraging Christian morality, first and foremost through the marriage laws. In short, the bishops asked the government to follow more strictly its own ruling in the Circular of 1917, implying that the principles of tolerance and neutrality were not necessarily interdependent.

The education issue will be tackled separately below, but the government's response on the marriage issue was that it would not allow itself to be forced to play a more active role as a Christian government. It stood by its preference for Christian, civilizing principles, but it was not prepared to move any further from its position of neutrality by supporting Christianity more actively. Having examined this request for more explicit support of the Christian cause (which was not presented in denominational terms), we may suggest that there was a limit to the extent to which the government was willing to reduce the amount of neutrality in its policy by identifying itself with Christian principles. Adherence to the principle of tolerance combined with pragmatic factors in policy-making helped to fix this limit.

(3) While there was an upper limit for the government's active support of Christian principles, it was still doubtful how the government proposed to fulfil its pledge to further the Christian cause. The CMS mission's request in 1922 for luwalo resources to erect school buildings takes us one step towards answering

this question. As already pointed out (p. 197), it was requested that the government, after the abolition of kasanvu, should provide the necessary school buildings and allocate luwalo labour for the purpose. The underlying line of reasoning was that these buildings were for the benefit of all, not just a limited section of the community, and further that they were important for the development of the whole country.[54] What this amounted to was a claim that educational work at ground level was beyond religious categories, and that the government could therefore dispense with restrictions based on concepts like tolerance and neutrality. However sympathetic it was to the Christian cause, the government could not accept such a suggestion. The schools were clearly denominational, and had an evangelizing function. It was even questioned whether they were of any real educational value.[55] To use compulsory unpaid labour (luwalo) for such a purpose would mean forcing people to work for a religion different from their own, and this was an infringement of the right to religious liberty granted in earlier laws. Had education been state-run and open to all, the employment of luwalo labour would have posed no problem.[56]

While it thus defined the educational work primarily in religious terms and recognized the principle of religious liberty as a limitation on its range of action, the government was now faced with the problem of whether it was reasonable for the state to find an alternative way of supporting the mission's work, in view of the fact that it was Christian evangelizing activity, however much it also benefited the community at large. Two considerations helped to secure a positive response. In the first place, the mission's educational work was considered after all to have national and societal dimensions over and above the evangelizing aspect.[57] Secondly, it was reaffirmed that a decisive factor in policy-formation was 'the sympathy of the government with the work of the Missions', whether the usefulness of the missions to the government was defined positively in terms of their civilizing function, or negatively, as a means of combating Islam.[58] The government was thus prepared to act on the principles laid down in the Circular of 1917, and the only problem was to find a formula for doing so without violating the rights of individuals in matters of religion. It was left to provincial officers to find solutions at the local level, but one recommendation was that money collected from the commutation of luwalo could be used to help the missions to build schools.[59] It was even added in the government's Circular that in 'primitive districts' with little luwalo labour and no commutation, luwalo labour could occasionally be used to build schools 'if and when this can be done without offending the religious susceptibilities of the natives'.[60] The government had certainly moved beyond its statement of policy in 1917, which had been prompted by the situation in the north. The emphasis on religious liberty had been moderated, while the commitment to encouraging Christian principles was now stressed.

(4) Yet the educational sector, by combining religious and secular teaching, still constituted a sore point for the government. This can be illustrated by looking more specifically at the field of education, where attempts were made to broaden the concept of neutrality and increase its importance in policy-formation. We have seen on more than one occasion that education was considered to be important for the general welfare and morality of the country. Christian principles in general could also contribute to the public good, and the government's support for Christian education was therefore not considered to be in breach of the principle of neutrality. However, the increased government engagement in the educational sector raised doubts about the combination of Christian and

secular training, especially from the qualitative point of view. One disadvantage was the admitted lack of equality and the failure to provide people with equal opportunities. The issue of the Muslim community more than any other raised the question of whether insufficient neutrality in government policy meant unfair treatment of people. It was increasingly being urged that religious and secular education should be separated and that the government should run its own system. Still, financial considerations, the fear of the political implications of Islam, and appreciation of Christian values in education won the day. It was decided that it was compatible with the principle of neutrality to run the educational system on Christian lines. The guidelines laid down in the Circular of 1917 were thus upheld, and educational cooperation with the missions was continued.

Developments in the educational sector, not least the discussion of the Muslim issue, revealed the inherent tension between the principle of tolerance and the narrow definition of the concept of neutrality. At the beginning of the 1920s the government was faced with a difficult question: should it accept the consequences of its own religious policy by favouring the Christians and thus creating unequal conditions and opportunities in society? Although a few attempts were made to rectify the situation, the government chose to tie its policy to Christian principles, although it was fully aware of the policy's negative effects.

(5) An area where the government was prepared to accept the consequences of its policy all through the period was the appointment of chiefs. Within this area the question may be posed whether the government accepted the possibility that its religious policy inevitably tied the right to office to Christianity. In Buganda, after the events of the 1890s and the conclusion of the Uganda Agreement, the government inherited a situation where the chiefly offices were tied to religious affiliation; the chieftainship had virtually become a Christian institution with a built-in Protestant dominance. There was no improvement in this situation in the following period. Apart from a short interval when an attempt was made to neutralize the religious factor, the main aim of government policy was to preserve the status quo. At one stage it was even admitted that the religious criterion meant that the best candidate for the chieftainship would not always be chosen. It was therefore difficult for the government to defend this criterion publicly; but it could always fall back on the explanation that changes in the system would have disturbing effects on the peaceful functioning of the country. The religious factor itself was played down, and it was maintained that factionalism now represented party feeling rather than religious differences. Still, the government was uneasy about the whole situation. It knew that its status quo policy was inconsistent with the principles of religious tolerance and neutrality.

It is therefore striking that the same pattern was found in the non-Ganda areas, where no Agreement existed to hinder the government in pursuing its own aims. The same politicization of the religious factions occurred, with slight differences in the individual districts, so that religious allegiance became the major criterion in appointments and the chiefly institution became predominantly Christian with a tendency towards a Protestant monopoly of power. In spite of all its claims to the contrary, the government was unable to prevent a Buganda-like situation arising in other parts of the country. One important factor for which the government was fully responsible was that the Buganda administrative model was exported to other districts. As the Ganda agents were the instruments of this system, it is not surprising that it had both advantages and disadvantages. Another factor was missionary expansion. Competition between the two denominations constituted the major structuring principle in society, and the resultant differences were increased by their different methods of work, particularly as regards the question of whether education should concentrate on the future ruling class. Thirdly, and as a consequence of the two foregoing factors, Protestant hegemony became ingrained in the local political systems, especially in the Lukikos, so that a strong element of inertia was at work in the political systems.

It would have required considerable determination and authority to stem these forces, and the government displayed neither. Instead it tried to play down the importance of the religious factor by emphasizing the primacy of either educational criteria or traditional qualifications. But this was overlooking the fact that these factors reinforced rather than weakened the religious basis for appointments. Appointments were at any rate interpreted in essentially denominational terms by the people involved.

The situation both in Buganda and the non-Ganda areas shows that one factor was at work which helped to distract the government's and others' attention from the tying of office to religious adherence. The whole debate was conducted within a narrow denominational framework, and only the two Christian communities had spokesmen to protect their interests. Accordingly, the government's main concern became the Protestant–Catholic ratio, rather than the pursuit of equality on an overall basis. The inequities stemming from the Christian bias in the government's religious policy could easily be ignored as long as the government was faced with vociferous demands from both Christian parties. By dealing with these more obvious demands, the government gave the impression of promoting equality. The overall principle in religious policy were thus implemented within a narrow denominational framework with an implicit Christian bias, and the government's attitude almost amounted to support for the institutionalization of the Christian chieftaincy. We will later ask whether the government practised sufficient neutrality within the denominational framework, but in this context it should be emphasized that the government, although it did so with some hesitation, allowed its policy, with its inherent Christian bias, to have the effect that the absolute majority of chiefly offices were tied to Christianity. Very little had changed since the 1890s. The explanation may simply be that priorities in religious policy were quite clear. The encouragement of Christian principles was clearly favoured, and this left the government in a situation where it could do little to prevent the Christianization of offices.

How did the government manage to pursue the policy of tying civic rights to Christianity without meeting strong opposition from guardians of the ideal of religious liberty? These, faced with the effects of government policy, would have been justified in asking for a higher degree of tolerance and neutrality. First, as we have shown, the denominational factor helped the government, as it diverted attention from other issues and allowed the government to make visible efforts to preserve neutrality and ameliorate the Catholics' minority position. Secondly, as we saw with the Malakite and luwalo issues, the ideal of tolerance and the principle of neutrality were applied at two different levels. When the government guaranteed the religious freedom of individuals and actively sought to protect their rights, it gained some room for manoeuvre as regards the granting of special concessions to the Christians. In short, the government had an alibi for neglecting its neutrality as far as non-Christians were concerned as long as it carefully guarded their rights as individuals. It should be added that the distinction between these two levels in government policy corresponds in many ways with the one established during the analysis of the events in the 1890s between the individual and societal levels.

The five cases just examined have helped to show how the government implemented a religious policy with an inherent Christian bias and a dichotomy between tolerance and neutrality. We have answered the questions: how far could the government dispense with its neutrality, and how could it achieve an appropriate balance between tolerance and neutrality in practical policy? Religious policy can hardly be described in terms of a single formula, in view of the results achieved so far. But it is helpful to see the various phases in terms of a continuum running between two extremes. At one end we have absolute religious liberty, manifested by tolerance and neutrality. At the other we find religious (Christian) monopolism.[61] The government never placed itself at either extreme; neither principle had exclusivity or primacy, but both simultaneously exerted influence on policy and decisions. Where the government placed itself on the continuum, or for that matter where individual officers placed themselves, was decided both by normative and pragmatic criteria, and by political considerations directed towards the maintenance of order and security.[62] Exemplifying the use of the continuum analogy, we may say that the government in its Circular of 1917 made a formal move in the direction of Christian monopolism, but did not go all the way, given its rejection of the three bishops' demands that it should abandon its neutrality. There was a movement in the opposite direction in 1919 when the District Commissioners in the Northern Province recommended equal concessions for all ministers of religion, whether they were Muslim walimu, Malaki priests or African Traditionalists. At the same time they called upon the government to separate religious and secular education by taking over the whole educational system.[63] This tendency was later reinforced in connection with a proposed revision of the educational policy, when it was suggested that a government-run system would create more equality of opportunity. The decision to continue with the combination of religious and secular education demonstrates the inertia that overwhelmed any movement along the continuum. The movements (changes within government policy) took place within a narrow range. The government's policy was remarkably stable over the whole period, with close adherence to the guidelines laid down during the 1890s. It may even be suggested that the two extremes of the continuum were rooted in the contradictory principles found in the Berlin Treaty of 1885 (Chapter 3). As a final assessment of government religious policy it may be said that by accepting the inequality of opportunity which existed, and tying civic rights to Christianity, the government was closer to Christian monopolism than to the other extreme, given its ability to operate at two different levels as regards religious liberty.

We may finally ask what type of state was emerging as a result of this religious policy. Ali Mazrui has suggested three categories which are useful in this context: the secular state, the state with an established church, and the ecumenical state.[64] The first two types may safely be dismissed in this context. There was no established church, and the state did not recognize itself as a Christian state. It could not be seen either as a secular one. Its appreciation of Christian values, its preference for and support of Christian principles and its cooperation with and utilization of the Christian missions, especially in the field of education, indicated an active engagement in religious affairs which was inconsistent with a secular state, in the normal sense of the term. Turning to Mazrui's ecumenical category, two criteria are relevant. First, such a government is not monopolistic, favouring one belief against others, but it is bent on upholding religious pluralism. This distinguishes such a state from one with an established church. Secondly, in an ecumenical, as opposed to a secular state, the government maintains a role in religious affairs, frequently serving as an arbitrator among the various religions for the sake of overall harmony. Both these criteria were fulfilled in colonial Uganda, and some, if not all, of the government's policies were carried out in accordance with them. This classification is unable to deal, however, with the fact that essential parts of government policy, as for example the arbitration function, were conducted within a narrow Christian denominational framework. We thus have to expand the definition to include the fact that the state had a clear Christian bias, and gave some support to the emergence of a Christian nation, but not to the exclusion of other religions and not to the extent of having a Christian state with an established church. Hence, the colonial state must be placed somewhere between the ecumenical state and the state with an established church. On the basis of the present evidence it is difficult to say whether this categorization is valid for colonial situations other than the one in Uganda, but it would be worthwhile to pursue this line of analysis elsewhere.

The Christian factor in government policy

So far we have pointed out the Christian bias in the government's religious policy, in particular its commitment to encouraging the spread of Christian principles, even at the expense of its neutrality. We must now examine how the government demonstrated this commitment, and in particular how it defined its relationship with the executive wing of Christianity in Uganda, the missions. On the pattern of the analysis of the formative period (Part II), these issues may be dealt with under the headings: general policy towards the Christian missions; neutrality and equality within the context of Christian pluralism; and government support for missionary work.

General policy towards the Christian missions

The conclusion of the analysis of the formative period was that the supremacy of the secular authority was generally accepted as regards missionary movements to new areas, as was its power to determine the status of the missions within the colonial state. These limitations were not considered to constitute an encroachment on the principle of missionary freedom. The events of the following period would show whether this commitment to missionary freedom was strong enough to absorb any unfortunate effects of missionary activity. We have seen that the official attitude to the Muslims was influenced by assumptions that Islam constituted a political risk. We must therefore establish whether similar political risks arising from the dual missionary presence coloured the government's attitude to missionary freedom.

The question became acute in 1905–6, when an Austro-Hungarian Catholic missionary society asked for permission to operate in northern Uganda in the region bordering on the Sudan, where the CMS had already started work.[65] There was a risk that denominational rivalry and corresponding political confrontations familiar from other parts of the Protectorate would be extended to this new area. The government seriously considered denying the Catholics access, but such a step was ruled out as incompatible with the provisions of the Berlin Act, which guaranteed freedom of missionary enterprise. The stipulations of the Act were taken so seriously that they were considered to prohibit the official allotment of spheres of action to the respective missions. This was the practice in the Sudan, which lay beyond the zone covered by the international treaty.[66] Although the risk of political repercussions could not be ruled out entirely, the government felt that it would be going beyond its jurisdiction to be party to any comity agreement between the missions.

A few years later 'an unseemly scramble for adherents' in Bukedi prompted the administration once more to discuss the possibility of allocating spheres to each mission.[67] The Governor himself, after a tour to the Eastern Province, deplored in strong terms the religious rivalry he found there, as it clearly caused feuds and dissension.[68] However, although he could criticize and appeal to the missions, he could not commit the government to any action.[69] When the Governor-General of the Sudan later appealed for the allocation of spheres of activity in the border area, it was reaffirmed that there were no official missionary spheres in Uganda, and that there were no restrictions on the movements of missions, nor could any such step be contemplated.[70] There was an opportunity to make this policy public soon afterwards. After the controversy over the chiefs' involvement in the building of schools in the north, the risk of missionary rivalry was used as a justification for strict control of the missionary enterprise.[71] But this policy was discontinued when the government's religious policy was formulated in the Circular of 1917. Two principles were stated: first, the demarcation of spheres of missionary influence was to be left to the societies concerned; secondly, officials were to refrain from intervening except when the maintenance of public order was at stake.[72] This policy was upheld by the Uganda administration, even when the Colonial Office suggested that only one denomination should be allowed to work in each ethnographic area. Any such step would be opposed by the mission, and it would be a step backwards, as it was contrary to a well-established practice which had worked well for many years in Uganda.[73]

It is beyond all doubt that the government adhered strictly to the principle of missionary freedom and allowed freedom of enterprise within the Christian framework. The government abjured any restrictive supervision which might undermine the principle of missionary freedom. In pursuing this policy the government was guided both by the provisions of the Berlin Act and pragmatic considerations, although it was fully aware that the policy meant the export of politico-religious factionalism to all parts of the Protectorate.

Neutrality and equality in the context of Christian pluralism

It was one thing to remain passive and allow almost unrestricted scope to the two denominations in spite of possible political repercussions. But it was another matter when it came to active encouragement of the missionary enterprise by way of granting concessions and direct support. The question arose of whether the government could maintain a neutral stand in the face of denominational pluralism and practise a policy of equality.

Land was from the outset the most important element in direct support. When Sir Harry Johnston settled the issue of missionary land with the 1900 Agreement he did so impartially by granting each of the three missions a number of square miles in accordance with the range of their activities. This was one possible formula, but the result was that overall Catholic landholdings were more extensive than Protestant ones. Bishop Tucker later deplored this and demanded denominational equality. The government granted his request, and gave him some extra square miles, enough to even out the difference between the Protestant and Catholic holdings.

Only a decade later the government was faced with exactly the same problem again in connection with educational grants. Over the years a somewhat lenient practice had developed which gave the CMS mission more than twice as much money as the two Catholic missions combined. When a further increase was requested the government suggested that a policy of equality was desirable, as all the missions did work of equal value.[74] But in more detailed proposals the principle of equality was extended only to the CMS and the White Fathers. The Mill Hill Mission had its own grant, determined by the extent of its work.[75] It was immediately pointed out from London that this constituted denominational inequality,[76] whereupon the local administration went back to giving equal grants to both denominations.[77] Thereafter the government remained neutral and pursued a policy of equality in the two important fields of land concessions (Chapter 10 on the new land policy of 1914) and educational grants (Chapter 15 on the new educational policy in the 1920s). How deeply rooted the principle was in government policy was symbolically confirmed in 1919. It was suggested that all three missions should be presented with a 'brass eagle lectern' in appreciation of their wartime assistance. At the same time it was underlined that all three societies must be treated alike.[78] This illustrates the precautionary element in the policy of denominational equality.

So far we have analysed the government's policy at a level where its concessions were easily measurable, and where it was accountable to public opinion. At another level, preferential treatment was less obvious, and the commitment to denominational equality and equal treatment was put to a subtler test. This was the issue of the Christianization of offices within the African political system, where there was a substantial Protestant dominance, and where the two missions clearly had competing vested interests. First of all, the CMS mission had monopolized the kingships, and thereby the centres of power, in the various polities. This was clearly done at the expense of the Catholics, and the government occasionally tried to intervene to reduce the scale of the Protestant ascendancy. Yet on the two occasions when strong Catholic opposition was expressed, in connection with the Kabaka's visit to Britain and his investiture, the government failed to tackle the problem. The Protestant hegemony remained unchallenged, and the Catholics were secured minority rights rather than equality. The government was not prepared to act more vigorously in spite of its frequently expressed annoyance with the Protestant exploitation of the centres of power.

The Catholic mission also urged the government to improve Catholic representation in chieftainships, and the government made some attempts to give the Catholics a fairer share, but at the same time gave up the idea of neutralizing the denominational factor in appointments. But the government was not determined enough or powerful enough to neutralize the Protestant hegemony. Its efforts hardly went beyond the 'demonstration point', hence, as far as appointments and offices were concerned, the Catholics were left in an inferior position. They were granted only minority rights, and the government showed little determination to work for real equality.

Finally, we may analyse the government's approach to the two denominations from a third point of view. We have already asked whether personal relations between the CMS mission and members of the colonial administration could account for the government's acceptance of denominational imbalance, but it transpired that it was unnecessary to resort to this explanation. This of course did not rule out the possibility that outsiders had the impression that there was a special relationship between the CMS mission and the government. We may then conclude that the government maintained a position of neutrality in areas where it had to respond publicly to direct demands from the missions, and had to account for its policy and actions in a wider context. In areas where it was less accountable its commitment to a policy of equality seems to have been less strong, and it accepted and maintained an inherited situation of denominational inequality. As far as its referee role was concerned, it played it as neutrally as possible in areas where it was accountable. Otherwise, there was a tendency to accept the advantages given to the Protestant side.

Government support for missionary work

It has been a recurring theme throughout the whole survey that the government became actively engaged in the furtherance of Christianity by supporting the missions. The support mainly took the form of land grants and labour service concessions. The government also provided grants for education and allowed a number of other concessions and privileges. The bias towards Christianity thus found concrete expression. We must now discuss the extent to which the government actively engaged itself in the missions' work, and its motives and aims.

Most of these questions were raised earlier in connection with developments in the 1890s. It will be useful to recall the factors from that period which prompted the government to respond positively and establish material links with the missionary work by providing various kinds of support. One major concern was to get away from all forms of indirect support such as exemptions. Instead, direct and identifiable concessions were granted, so that there could be upper limits for the extent of support, and clearly defined objectives. As for the government's reasons for supporting the Christian work, the presence of the missionaries was seen as a natural element in the colonial setting, and the government therefore felt itself to be under an obligation to provide adequate conditions for their work. This meant that the government supported missionary work in general, with its mixed activities, without singling out specific activities like education as qualifying the missions for support. This principle has been termed 'the mission formula', and it was not prompted by purely utilitarian considerations. By acting on the assumption that utilitarian arguments would produce better results with the government, the CMS mission made a strategic mistake, and failed to understand the government's position.

The extent to which these themes remained the basic ones over the following years indicates the great consistency in government policy towards the Christian missions. The government could not include an annual grant for missionary work in its budget, for this would have been tantamount to saying that the promotion of Christianity was a state activity. But the state did acknowledge an obligation to create reasonable conditions for the missions by relieving them of some of their burdens. Support and concessions took the form of a block land grant accompanied by rights to labour tributes, so that conditions for people living inside and outside church land were almost the same. The survey has shown how indispensable a source of income this land grant was for the mission's realization of its major goal, the establishment of an independent church. Two indications of its crucial importance were the fact that the mission constantly asked for more land on better terms, and the fact that the mission was so sensitive to changes in the conditions on which the land was held.

Obviously this type of support, which placed the missionary work firmly within the fabric of society and tied it to general socio-economic developments, was somewhat difficult to quantify. As we saw in connection with the land issue there was a major trend in government policy towards defining the proper limits on concessions granted to comply with the obligation to secure reasonable conditions for missionary work. First the government wanted to establish a ceiling for the actual acreage to be put at the disposal of the missions, and did so with its land policy of 1914. Combined with this was the need for limitations on labour services and indirect forms of support such as exemptions. The overall aim was clearly to stop the escalation of government support. Secondly, it was important to define whether the land was granted as revenue-producing endowment which could be used for plantations, the growing of cash crops and subletting; or simply as a provision for purposes narrowly defined as religious, such as securing housing and food for religious workers. The government settled for the last option, and this led to conflict with the mission, whose interpretation of the concept of landholding was different. The government could not accept the mission as a major economic factor in society, either as a great landowner or as a pioneer of agricultural development.

This leads us to the third criterion: the limitation of concessions was partly a precautionary measure, as the government had to defend its own interests and preserve its position of supremacy. The right to landholders' tributes and privileges could give the mission a special status in society which might have wider repercussions. The government was on its guard against the mission's constituting a 'government within the government' when special rights to labour services on church land were requested. One specific aspect of the problem was the issue of alienation. As defined by the government this meant that the mission, as a landholder, enjoyed chiefly rights to traditional tributes, thus depriving the chiefs of some of their power and authority. All through the period, a basic theme in government thinking was that no concessions should be granted which could cause this kind of alienation or tend to diminish the chiefs' position. In short, while certain privileges and concessions were granted, there was always the proviso that the mission should not achieve a status which enabled it to compete with state institutions.

By applying these three criteria the government managed to fix an upper limit to the extent of its support for the missions, although this was an ongoing process because of the unspecified nature of the block grant of land and labour. One further point is that arguments in favour of an upper limit for the government's concessions to the mission have so far been derived from the local setting, although the details of the land policy of 1914 were worked out in London. The question of support and land grants must, however, be discussed within the context of overall colonial policy and support for missionary work. It has earlier been hinted that the British government was averse to granting direct financial support, even for chaplains, who were working for the benefit of the colonial officials themselves (p. 307). In 1907, for example, the local administration recommended that a site of two acres should be provided for the building of a new church near government headquarters, together with a grant of £500. The site was granted, but the money grant was refused by the Colonial Office.[79] A grant from public funds was thus considered to be in a quite different category from land grants. This distinction and the underlying policy were upheld over the following years, and no government money was provided directly for religious purposes.[80] In fact, the principle behind this policy was explicitly formulated in 1924 as being 'the gradual withdrawal of state aid for purely religious purposes in the Colonies'. This was a response to 'Parliamentary pressure against the endowment of a particular form of Christianity'.[81] On a later occasion the Colonial Office went to great lengths to emphasize that the Uganda government's grant of £50 to the Muslim Khadi, to cover his expenses on a pilgrimage to Mecca, was for the purely secular purpose of further training.[82]

When we thus consider the influence of the European arena, two aspects of government policy emerge. First, the granting of land and labour services was considered less of a commitment to the missionary cause, and less of an official confirmation of a close alliance with Christianity, than the granting of money from public funds. The state could therefore with little hesitation endorse the system of missionary landholding developed during the 1890s and confirmed by Sir Harry Johnston in 1900. The British government could even be instrumental in framing a new policy in 1914 which, with minor adjustments, upheld the mission's land rights. Secondly, by making land available instead of public funds, the government was only using the surplus gained from the establishment of the colonial state. Land was in abundance from the government's point of view, and it was easy to give the missions a small share as a one-off block grant, provided that doing so did not erode the traditional system of authority or have negative budgetary consequences because of exemptions. This type of support was less demanding for both sides, as it did not figure in the annual budget, and no annual account was necessary.

It was the government's intention in providing this type of support on these terms to ease the mission's working conditions and to promote the cause of Christianity and the advancement of Christian civilization, as opposed to, say, an Islamic culture. The expected result was progress in the country. It was at this juncture that the mission misinterpreted the government's motives. Behind the government's benevolence it saw more utilitarian motives, which it assumed would favour the mission's secular activities. The mission failed to understand that the state's general conception of Christianity's civilizing influence was rooted in the idea of the responsibility of a European colonial power as expressed in the Berlin Act. The mission therefore referred frequently to the educational work's drain on its resources, arguing that education was the mission's major contribution to the general progress of the country, and qualified it for more land on better terms. But from the government's point of view the educational enterprise was not, and could not be, related to the land grant, which was given for much more general purposes.

When grants-in-aid were provided for the mission's educational work, they could be taken from public funds because they were ear-marked for an easily identifiable activity which happened to be run by the mission. In principle the money was only granted for this secular purpose, not for religious activities, although the distinction was difficult to maintain in practice. Still, no principle was violated as long as the assistance was on a small scale and amounted to no more than a tax rebate for a specified number of teachers. This situation only changed after the First World War, when the government took a more active interest in education and was constantly faced with the mission's demands for increased support. Then the mixture of educational and evangelizing work became a problem, as the government could easily be seen as financing missionary propaganda, which would violate a fundamental long-standing principle.[83] In this situation the first, and most logical course for the government would have been to secularize education and start its own non-sectarian system, an option which was favoured by some officials and later by the prospective Director of Education. But the inertia of two decades, financial problems, and the mission's lobbying activity in Britain made this course of action unrealistic. The second option was to continue cooperation with the missions by using them as education-al agencies, at the same time making sure that education and evangelizing activities were separated in principle. This could be achieved by stipulating certain qualitative requirements. The latter option was chosen, and the govern-ment managed to separate the mission's two activities to some extent by making sure that the money was primarily spent on education rather than evangelizing (Chapter 15). In spite of increased scrutiny the government was only partially successful in this separation, mainly because of two counterproductive factors inherent in its policy. First, the mere acceptance of an educational system run on a denominational basis worked against the government's own stated intentions, and meant that public funds were inevitably used for narrow religious purposes, if only indirectly. Secondly, the implicit premise for employing the missions as educational agencies was still the state commitment to the idea that Christian principles were most beneficial to the development of African society.

In spite of this it is essential when we discuss the government support for, and concessions to, the missions to maintain the distinction between support in land and labour for general missionary activity, and grants for a more specialized, mainly secular, undertaking. Only the former illustrates the positive and active relationships between the state and the missions; the latter belongs in a different category, as the mission was here undertaking a more technical activity for which it happened to be qualified. Hence, the distinction between the two kinds of support reflects two distinct types of relationship between the state and the mission. The difference lay in the extent to which the state publicly and officially committed itself to the furtherance of Christianity. This commitment was clear when land and labour were granted, but was played down when support was granted from public funds, as such support was given for an ostensibly secular activity. Yet, as we have already indicated, even the mode of granting the former allowed the government to keep a low profile as regards support for the Christian missions. It was helped in this respect by the Christian pluralistic situation and denominational rivalry. The government's handling of this situation gave an impression of neutrality which counterbalanced the Christian bias that otherwise characterized its policy.

Conclusions on the Christian factor in government policy

Having examined three aspects of the relations between government and mission, we may now venture some conclusions on the significance of the Christian factor in the government's religious policy and assess how it defined its relationships with the missions.

One first point to be emphasized is that this relationship had to be established within a Christian, pluralistic framework, and this engendered some ambivalence in the government's approach. On the one hand, its policy was based upon the ideal of neutrality in the pluralistic situation. It tried to achieve a higher degree of equality by distributing land and other concessions fairly. On the other hand, permissiveness towards continued Protestant dominance prevailed in day-to-day policy, so that the imbalance between the two denominations was maintained. These two conflicting trends characterized government policy over the years, and a number of factors helped the government to gloss over the inconsistencies.

The investigation of state support for missionary activity and of reasons for such support has helped us to clarify the role that the government assigned to Christianity and the Christian institutions within the colonial state. If we follow the categories suggested by Ali Mazrui (p. 447) we may say that while the government did not acknowledge the African church, it clearly favoured the spread of Christian principles in society, a process in which the missions were seen as instrumental. The government was concerned with the encouragement of Christian principles, not with Christianity's institutional aspects. It follows that the government did not envisage a Christian state. Instead it preferred the gradual development of a Christian nation, based not on narrowly defined Christian moral norms, but on the more broadly defined and less demanding Christian principles which had been filtered through European civilization. The gradual nature of the process was emphasized. The government was opposed to any abrupt changes or reforms initiated and guided from above, with the mission as agent and the government as sponsor. This could easily cause disruption and make administration difficult.

Hence, the government's focus was directed mainly towards the mission to which it ascribed an instrumental and auxiliary function. We may further clarify the government's conception of the mission's role by introducing a terminology used earlier (p. 78). One trend in government policy was to dissociate itself from the mission's more ambitious goals, such as the recognition of Christian institutions, whether mission or church, or the promotion of strictly Christian norms. On the other hand, it was committed to the furtherance of Christianity's civilizing value for society, and thereby to cooperation with the mission, although not as much as the mission expected. It was this policy of cooperation which was officially endorsed by the Circular of 1917, the most important statement on religious policy during the period. In this latter respect the government followed the guidelines of the Berlin Act, which provided the bias towards Christianity with some legal foundation.

It was important for the government to combine 'institutional separation' with 'functional interaction' between church and state.[84] Basically, the colonial state and the mission had many shared interests, and from the state's point of view the mission had an auxiliary and instrumental function. This provides us with an overall framework within which to investigate the anatomy of the relationship between mission and state.

26

The nature of the relationship between mission, church and state

In order to view our results in a wider perspective and to add to the comparative value of this study, an attempt will be made to present and interpret the results in terms of concepts and categories generally used in analyses of the church–state problem.

The dynamics of the church–state relationship: the question of secularization

One recurrent feature of the relationship between church and state has been the interplay between factors internal to the mission and church, and external forces activated by the attitude and policy of the state. The relationship was dynamic rather than static, and was subject to changes over the years. In order to examine this dynamic aspect further, we will follow analytical concepts suggested by S. N. Eisenstadt in his examination of the relationship between religious and political systems in centralized, bureaucratic empires, as there are clear similarities between colonial Uganda and the kind of empire he studied.[1]

According to Eisenstadt the first and basic question which must be asked in analysing such a relationship is whether a religious system contributes to the continued existence of the political system. In the Uganda situation this can only be answered in the affirmative: it was explicitly acknowledged by the mission and taken for granted by the colonial government. Even in its criticism the mission did not question the justification of the colonial state, and in general it recognized the colonial framework as the basis for its activities. In this respect the mission clearly performed a state-affirming function. There were basic points of contact and a clear foundation for a positive relationship between the mission and the colonial state, based upon a wider range of common interests and mutual dependence.

Within this overall framework there appears, still according to Eisenstadt, a striking parallel between the positions of the two sides. There are within each system a positive and negative element which decide the nature of the relationship and account for its dynamics. In Uganda the two opposing tendencies in the colonial state can be described as, on the one hand, the need for the mission's supportive and legitimizing function, and for cooperation in concrete cases. On the other hand, it was necessary for the colonial state to confine the mission's activities to certain areas, and to exercise a controlling function, in short, to keep the mission at a distance and to arrive at an ever more accurate definition of its activities within the state. The mission accepted its legitimizing function, and was fully aware of the advantages of a strong state, and of establishing cooperation with it; while at the same time it clearly had a critical role to play, as the protagonist of the state's African subjects. The latter role required a more distanced, autonomous relationship with the state.

As long as the two opposing tendencies within each system balance each other out there will be a state of equilibrium and mutual accommodation between the religious and political institutions. This situation may be said to have arisen in Uganda after the conclusion of the Uganda Agreement in 1900, and to have extended through the period of Bishop Tucker, although even then there was a somewhat precarious balance. Later shifts in the balance meant changes in the relationship between the mission and state. The state became less dependent on cooperation with the mission, and had less use for its supportive, legitimizing function. The dichotomy between the two tendencies was not completely neutralized, and the pendulum swung in favour of the state's independence of the mission. Cooperation would now be much more on the state's terms. The issue of education and the language problem illustrate these changes in the balance between the positive and negative elements. The situation was the reverse for the mission. Mainly for economic reasons, its dependence on the state increased, and this affected its ability to perform its critical role. For more technical reasons its capacity to perform an advisory and intermediary function was reduced (p. 315 ff). In general the mission's scope for independent action *vis-à-vis* the state was curtailed, as the two opposing tendencies no longer balanced each other out.

It follows that the nature of the relationship between mission and state had to be redefined; the state had taken the lead and the mission was on the defensive. The state had extended its area of control, although the ties binding the two systems together had not been broken. The basic orientation of the mission towards the colonial state had not changed, but it was now more dependent and had lost some of its political potential and bargaining power. All in all, the mission had more to gain from the relationship than the state.

Such an analytical approach puts the dynamic aspect of the relationship between mission and state into perspective. Developments favoured the state, while the mission was subjected to a process of erosion, as we have seen before in connection with its dwindling capacity (Chapter 24). But it is important to emphasize that this process was not allowed to go too far, given the joint interests and mutual dependence still existing. The mission's position within the state was not completely undermined. The changes amounted to a reduction in the scale and range of its activities, but did not constitute a completely new basis for the relationship.

The concept of secularization is frequently employed when the changing relationship between church and state is analysed, and it may prove useful to view the changes in Uganda from that point of view. It should, however, be made clear from the outset that the term will be used here on the basis of a somewhat narrow definition. Normally, when it is employed in African studies – and for that matter in the study of developing countries in general – the focus is on the secularization of traditonally-rooted values and traditional politico-religious systems, and involves a process of modernization and a radical alteration of 'the traditional relationship between society, polity and religion'.[2] The emphasis is thus on traditionalism versus modernization, and the process of secularization involves the progressive exclusion of religion from almost every form of social life and from political processes. In the present context the concept will be employed only in connection with the colonial polity on the one hand and Christianity, represented by the CMS mission, on the other. Within this framework, a distinction may be drawn between the valuational aspect, that is, the change in the value system accompanying dissociation from religious values, and the institutional aspect, the relational changes between religious and secular institutions.[3] Most attention will be given to the latter dimension: but the former one cannot be excluded, of course, from an overall analysis of the relationship between church and state.

It will also be useful, following Donald E. Smith, to speak of a multi-faceted process of secularization, and to distinguish between four types.[4] In view of the foregoing outline of church–state relations we may safely exclude the most wide-ranging and radical model of secularization, polity-dominance secularization, which recognizes no areas of religious autonomy, and which involves a drastic change in the value system accompanied by efforts to eliminate the influence of religion from society. No attempts of this kind were made in colonial Uganda. Hence, we may confine ourselves to Smith's three remaining types of secularization: (1) polity–separation secularization; (2) polity–expansion secularization; and (3) polity–transvaluation secularization.

(1) Polity–separation secularization 'involves the severance of connections, or the decision not to create the connections in the first place, between religion and the polity'.[5] Here, besides an active aspect, a passive, preventive element is present in the relationship between church and state. As we saw in Chapter 17, the passive, preventive element characterized the colonial state's approach to the mission. The government's first concern was the maintenance of the existing boundary between itself and the mission, and it was on the alert for any attempt to create an established or semi-established position for the mission or church within the colonial political system. The important objective was to establish the mission's legitimate sphere of interest and to define its proper role within the colonial state. As regards the active aspects of polity-separation secularization, there was no question of severing connections between the colonial polity and the mission, as there were no constitutionally formalized linkages between the two, and no direct financial support was granted to the Christian work as such. On the other hand the few, mainly ceremonial, bonds were left untouched, and indirect support was given in the form of land and labour.

The situation was somewhat different in the relations between the church and the African political system. Here the Christianization/Protestantization of offices was remarkably high, and the linkages between the Protestant church and the

African polities were correspondingly numerous. Hence, the colonial government took active measures to achieve a higher degree of separation, both for its own sake and in order to create equality between the two Christian denominations. One means at its disposal was a more centralized system of administration with stricter control of the African polities. But the government's success in reducing the political potential of the linkages between the church and the African political system was limited. One major reason for this was that it did not attack the root of the matter by secularizing the underlying political processes.[6] At this level, which goes beyond the institutional dimension, political processes remained rooted in the religious structure. Religious differences constituted the major structural principle in society, and religion provided the basis for political identity and political groupings. These factors dictated government policy to the extent that a number of offices were tied to certain religions, so that a Protestant ascendancy arose within the African political system. However uncomfortable the government felt, and however many efforts it made to neutralize the religious factor, it did not succeed in dissociating political processes from their religious foundation.

We may then conclude that the degree of polity–separation secularization was rather low. Even when the government pursued an active line with the African polities it may have increased the extent of its control, but it could not sever the existing connections between Christianity and the African political system.

(2) Polity–expansion secularization may accompany the separation process. Here 'the polity expands its functions at the expense of religion', that is, the political system extends into areas of life formerly regulated by religion, but now considered as rightly belonging under the authority of the state.[7] It is also relevant here to consider the negative, preventive aspects of state policy, in the sense that the state can make efforts to prevent the intrusion of religious institutions into areas of life which are of special interest to the polity, in order to anticipate the necessity of state expansion. Smith mentions four major areas where the expansionist process may frequently be observed. These four areas correspond accurately with issues discussed in the present survey, and each will be taken in turn.

(a) The secularization of the economy was in Uganda virtually confined to the preventive measures mentioned above, and was mainly directed towards land-holdings. In the first place it was important for the government to limit the mission's accumulation of wealth in the form of land by stipulating a maximum acreage. Secondly, church land was conceived of as a means of providing minimum facilities for the mission's work and relieving it of some of its expenses, not as a revenue-producing endowment involving chiefly rights over those living on the land and subletting rights. Thirdly, the church was not to assume the role of a leading agency in economic development. Consequently, the government was opposed to any large-scale mission engagement in agricultural development. All in all, the state tried to prevent the mission and church from becoming an economic force in society by virtue of their landholdings.

(b) The secularization of the social structure may be surveyed first in terms of the position of the chiefs. With the growth of the colonial bureaucracy and the bureaucratization of the chiefs their authority was no longer solely rooted in traditional structures and values. First, the chiefs could no longer be monopolized by the missionaries, as the colonial administration took a greater interest in them and exercised stricter control; the state now moved into an area where missionaries, as confidants of the chiefs, had earlier had a free hand. Secondly, the chiefs' right to dispose of land was severely curtailed by the state, which meant that the mission and church could no longer freely receive gifts of land. Only the initial phases of this change in the chiefs' position were apparent in the period examined in this survey, but even here the state's tighter grip on the chiefly institution had registrable effects. We may observe a similar tendency if we examine the preventive aspect of the actions of the state. The government saw itself as the regulator of society, and would not allow any church-related group to achieve a special status and constitute an alternative centre of power. Therefore, no exemptions were to be granted to church workers, and katikiros on church land were to have no special rights which would make them equivalent to secular officeholders such as chiefs. In general, people on church land were to have no special status which could sequester them from the power of the secular authorities. All these issues can be subsumed under the wider category of alienation which, according to the government, was incompatible with its role as regulator of the functions of society. The state was clearly motivated by the desire to maintain full internal supremacy and control.

(c) This principle was put even more crucially to the test when it came to the secularization of law.[8] Vital areas of life, in particular those involving the family, are often based on and regulated by religious principles. The question arises of whether the state should uphold this religious foundation, and whether it should allow religious institutions to administrate, or even pass, laws touching on these areas. In the Uganda situation attention has been drawn to the marriage laws in particular. Just after the turn of the century, the state attempted somewhat haphazardly to pass a Marriage Ordinance which made monogamous marriage a civil institution under the jurisdiction of the state, thus excluding the church. A remarkably strong missionary campaign blocked this expansionist attempt, and the final result was that ordinances were passed allowing marriages according to the laws of each religious community present in the Protectorate (Christian, Muslim and later Hindu). Thus two concessions were granted to the mission: first, a marriage law was passed based upon Christian principles, and monogamous marriage was not considered to be an exclusively civil institution. Secondly, the church was given the right to perform legal marriages. Thus the state granted the church a legitimate role, and even gave it moral support by showing a preference for monogamous, Christian marriage. On the other hand, Christianity achieved no monopoly, as the state respected the principle of religious pluralism. In particular the state reserved a role for itself by legalizing civil, monogamous mariage without any Christian ceremony, and later by introducing and exclusively administering a divorce ordinance (Chapter 16).

While the state thus allowed the extension of Christianity and the influence of the church into the area of marriage law, and even to some extent committed itself to the further extension of Christian principles, the vast field of customary marriage was still left outside official jurisdiction. Two interrelated problems became crucial here: first, should customary marriage be considered equal to religious marriage and receive full recognition by the state, or should the state also actively support the extension of Christian values in this field? Secondly, how far should the state, in cases of conversion to Christianity and transition to Christian, monogamous marriage, support such conversions by legislation?

Attempts to solve the first problem ended in a stalemate, as customary marriage occasioned intense controversy between mission and state. The realities of life forced the missionaries to recognize the validity of customary marriage, but they did so only on the condition that no more than one wife was involved. In other words, recognition involved the utterly foreign concept of a customary, monogamous marriage, and the state was asked to support this step towards monogamy by introducing a system of registration. The state wished to retain customary marriage in its original form without restrictions, but the mission prevented a special ordinance from being issued placing customary marriages on an equal footing with Christian ones – which would have amounted to an official recognition of polygamy. The customary marriage institution was not incorporated into the statute book, but was left to be guided solely by customary law. This inconclusive state of affairs left the way open for attempts from both parties to swing the pendulum to one side or the other. The state tried to preserve the traditional marriage institution, with its polygamy option, and came close to recognizing it officially when it stated that Christians had the right to marry in the traditional way, and that they were under no obligation to marry under the Christian Ordinance. This amounted virtually to granting not only equal legality but also equal prestige to the two types of marriage, and would have meant the extension of secular principles into the field of family law. It was naturally vehemently contested by the mission, and the government retreated somewhat. Conversely, the mission made an attempt to combat polygamy by having the Christian mongamous ideal endorsed by legislation. In order to erode the dominance of customary marriage, the mission recommended that legal protection should be denied people who had contracted polygamous marriages, and that Christians should be obliged to marry in church. The government found both recommendations unacceptable, and was unwilling to pass legislation which Christianized the marriage institution to such an extent at the expense of the customary system.

Hence, each of the two parties was able to prevent the other from arriving at an exclusive solution to the problem of customary marriage. The church did not gain exclusive control of marriage, while the state's opposition to the extension of Christian norms did not lead to the introduction of exclusively secular legislation. This is in accordance with the conclusion that the state did in fact favour monogamous Christian marriage, in the sense that its legislation allowed for a gradual development in that direction. The process was thus the opposite of polity–expansion secularization. The state was not opposed to the extension of Christian principles into a social institution like marriage, provided that it was a gradual process, and provided that the legislative and judicial authority remained the state's prerogative and was not left to ecclesiastical courts. Hence, within the field of marriage the polity did not expand at the expense of Christianity and its institutions, although it did try to control the Christian expansion.

This leads to the second question posed above. To what extent was the state to support the spread of Christian values, for instance in cases of conversion to Christianity? As regards the marriage laws, part of the answer has already been given: the state rejected the mission's proposal that Christians should be compelled to marry under the Christian Ordinance. The state would go no further than to provide in the law for the conversion of a customary marriage to a Christian one in order to meet the church's conditions for baptism. All this remained optional, and the government refused to attach legal consequences to conversion to Christianity. Secular law and Christian doctrine were not made to correspond to the extent that baptismal requirements were endorsed by legislation (p. 295 f.).

This qualification of the state's active role in furthering Christian monogamy is further put into perspective when two later developments are taken into account. In the first place, doubts increased among government officials as to the expedience of a sudden transition to monogamy. This could have disruptive effects on African society which would be unfortunate from an administrative point of view. Secondly, it was increasingly doubted whether legislation was the proper way to further the monogamous ideal. This was demonstrated by the government's unwillingness to prosecute in accordance with the law (see p. 277). The state's active role in furthering Christian principles in society was thus reduced.

It will be easier to discuss the problem if we broaden our perspective to include the general legislative process and the corresponding administrative measures. The state was on several occasions faced with demands from the mission and the Synod for support in introducing Christian norms into African society. The African leaders in particular had a tendency to call upon the civil authority to pursue this course of action. It is characteristic of the government's response that it was rather hesitant to commit itself with administrative measures beyond the moral level (as in the case of Sunday labour). As far as the appointment of chiefs was concerned it refused more or less directly to apply strict Christian norms, regarding administrative expedience as more important than the chiefs' role as moral mentors for the people. When Christian principles were involved in laws and regulations, the main element in the government's response was the distinction between the optional and the compulsory (see p. 301). While the mission, and in particular the Synod, advocated compulsory measures, the government insisted on optional ones. The government, while professing commitment to Christian principles, confined itself to moral support in furthering them by providing options and facilitating the transition to Christianity; but it was not willing to engage itself beyond that level. This caused all three missions to accuse the government of hiding its lukewarmness and religious indifference behind a cloak of neutrality. They claimed that it was not acting as a Christian government in a Christian nation.

Having examined the field of law in terms of polity-expansion secularization, we may conclude that there was no expansionist drive at the expense of the Christian institutions. On the contrary the state accepted that certain vital areas of social life fell within the legitimate sphere of the church, allowed for Christian values in its laws and administrative measures, and allowed the church some degree of influence and control within this sphere. The scope of Christian influence was, however, restricted by two factors. First, the state doubted the value of the legislative method and settled for an optional approach rather than a compulsory one. Secondly, the state retained control of the Christianization of the legislation and the way in which the laws were implemented. The blocking of the direct lines of contact between the church and the Buganda Lukiko was one example of the state's concern for full control of the legislative process (p. 356). The state was thus in an ambivalent position, as it was committed on the one hand to the furtherance of Christian principles in vital areas of social life, while on the other it went to great lengths to control all aspects of the process. Before arriving at any final conclusions, however, we must discuss the last and most crucial form of secularization.

(d) The secularization of education is a field where the expansionist mood of any government is easily assessable.[9] In the Uganda context it was even more so in view of the fact that we began at a point where the missions held an educational monopoly. The erosion of that monopoly can best be seen as part of a process of secularization, and we must then assess how far the process actually went. The government's move into the educational sector may be seen in terms of three different patterns of secularization.

The first pattern runs along horizontal lines: the state undertook responsibility for technical training and higher education. From the point of view of the state it was here that the need for well trained manpower with special skills was felt most acutely. From the point of view of the mission this specialized education required a large-scale investment of resources and manpower which was not possible in the post-war period. The resultant division of work is put into perspective when we recall that the mission was adamant in keeping more general secondary education under its full control, but beyond this level a non-sectarian educational system was started and operated by the state.

At the same time the influence of the state also expanded along vertical lines. The same problems existed at other levels of the educational system, especially in the high schools from which the future African leaders and business class were supposed to emerge. But the missionary system was biased in favour of non-manual skills. Its training of manpower was not considered professional enough, which meant that the missionary schools were not functioning well as a source of recruitment for government institutions. In this respect the state expected from any educational system that it should accommodate itself to plans for the general development of society and the prevailing pattern of production (in this case agriculture); and that the interests of the state should be taken into consideration. Education should have a socializing effect by fostering loyalty towards the state and neutralizing tendencies towards unrest and discontent.

In both cases stricter state supervision was essential. The first, most radical solution would be to nationalize the educational sector, or at least to start a parallel, and thoroughly secular, educational system. The second, more moderate, solution would be to settle for cooperation between church and state with built-in controlling mechanisms. The colonial state chose the last option in the middle of the 1920s, but it had in fact begun to implement it much earlier. This solution meant that the Christian, and in practice denominational, basis of the educational system was upheld. Although the government provided a substantial part of the funding, it continued to rely on missionary manpower. The state and the mission exerted influence together and neither of them gained a monopoly. This in itself constituted a significant change, by which, first, the state exercised considerable influence on standards, the curriculum and organizational features through the conditions attached to its grants-in-aid. Secondly, administrative reforms such as the establishment of a government department headed by a Director of Education and Advisory Committees at the central as well as the local level increased the state's formal influence on the mission's educational work.

The state's moves to exercise greater influence and control met with willingness on the part of the mission to comply with its demands, a willingness that was prompted to a great extent by severe financial difficulties. Nevertheless, the engagement of the state in educational work was clearly part of a process of polity–expansion secularization, and was accompanied by relational changes between mission and state. The balance shifted in favour of the state as the final authority in the field of education within the given framework of cooperation,[10] and the mission was assigned the role of an educational agency undertaking a function that was primarily the responsibility of the state. In order to evaluate properly the degree of secularization that had thus taken place it will be useful to discuss the rejected, more radical model, and the reasons for its rejection.

The more radical model would have meant the establishment of secular government schools and the removal of responsibility for education from the missions. The teaching of religious knowledge would be dealt with separately. Two solutions were discussed.[11] The more moderate of these involved making the existing institutions interdenominational, in order to reduce the waste of money and energy caused by duplication and introduce more flexibility into the whole educational sector. While this proposal was aimed at reducing the direct missionary influence on educational institutions, it did so mainly at the organizational level, as the schools would still be run on a Christian basis and under the supervision of the missions. The missions flatly refused even to consider this solution, but some government officials were sympathetic to the idea. In the end the proposal was considered unworkable. It would have meant excluding the missions altogether, as it was impossible for them to separate the two aspects of their work.

The second solution, the establishment of proper government schools, was therefore the most logical and consistent one. The first and most far-reaching option open to the state was either to nationalize the existing schools and to run them along non-sectarian lines, or to start a government system from scratch, leaving the missionary schools as a privately run, unsubsidized system. The second option was to introduce a dual system which, with government support, catered for Christians as well as non-Christians. This would help to reduce denominational rivalry and it was implicitly assumed that a state secular system would prove superior in the long run to the mission one. In both cases a considerable state expansion into the educational field at the expense of the Christians would be necessary.

Both options were seriously considered, and found some support among government officials. In the end the radical solution was ruled out, and the state settled for continued cooperation with the missions, with the reservation that the Muslim community must be catered for. Thus the state in fact refrained from taking any real steps towards expansionist secularizaton, due to lack of finance, the inertia of the previous two decades, and the inability to counterbalance the pro-missionary pressure groups in Europe. However, one positive element of great importance in the policy-making process must also be included. Certain forces were at work which brought the state closer to a Christian educational system than to a purely secular one. First, the government acknowledged and appreciated the effect of Christian teaching on people's morality and discipline. Secondly, as long as the mission ran the educational sector, it promoted a value system which the colonial state largely shared, and which helped to promote loyalty and acceptance of the government's legitimacy. Thirdly, a mission-run educational system was in full harmony with the Christian bias in the state's religious policy and with a firmly rooted trend in its general policy. Thus, one necessary condition for a real policy of secularization, the displacement of the prevalent commitment to Christian values by a purely secular ideology, was lacking. This takes us from the institutional level to the valuational dimension covered by Smith's third type of secularization.

(3) Polity–transvaluation secularization is a far more complex matter, and can in the present context only be touched on rather sketchily.[12] The colonial state never faltered in its overall commitment to the furtherance of Christian values.

On the contrary, the policy statement of 1917 (p. 442) reaffirmed its acceptance of Christianity as the most appropriate guiding principle for the future African society. Within the political arena this manifested itself in two ways. First, the government tolerated Christianity all through the period as the cohesive principle of group identity, and the resultant groupings were accepted as the basis for political action. In the second place, the government's goals were inspired, and to some extent determined, by Christianity, as we have seen in connection with the legislation issue. The furtherance of Christian values was seen as a source of legitimacy for the colonial government. All in all, the colonial state was closer to the Christian ideology than to any secular one such as, for example, nationalism.[13]

It is one thing to adhere to Christian principles rather than secular ones. But, as the whole complex problem of the Christian nation has shown (Chapter 16), it is quite a different matter to clarify one's commitment to Christian values when they are transformed into practical policy. Contemporary missionary opinion, as expressed in the three bishops' letter in 1918 (pp. 288–9), was certainly not appreciative of the state's record in that respect. The bishops deplored its open failure to support the Christian cause and its hiding behind a cloak of neutrality, and they accused the government of religious indifference, implying that its aims were really purely secular. Part of this difference of opinion can be seen as a disagreement on ends: the mission employed a narrow definition of the Christian nation which emphasized Christian morality as the principal criterion. The government had a wider concept, not specifically geared towards the Christian way of life, but rather towards civilizing society along broad Christian lines, as in Europe. Consequently, the state would not grant demands of a specifically Christian nature. Secondly there was disagreement on the means by which a Christian nation should be promoted and on the pace of the process. While the mission advocated an active lead from the state by way of legislation and administrative measures, the government favoured a gradual process where its responsibility was to provide options, not to force developments in a strictly Christian direction. The government obviously envisaged a Christian nation, but in the longer term and on a different scale from the mission (p. 303 f).

At this point the position of the colonial state may be more easily interpreted in terms of 'civil religion', developed in the Tocquevillean tradition by Robert N. Bellah, with special reference to the American situation.[14] He defines civil religion in terms of two criteria which correspond remarkably well with the way the colonial government in Uganda defined its commitment to Christian principles. In the first place, civil religion is not associated with any church institution, but is operative over and above any links that exist between church and state. Civil religion is an expression of the state's religious interest in the sense that it is an important part of the value core which constitutes the cohesive principle in society. We have already seen how a similar distinction between Christianity and its organized expression could be applied to the colonial government's relationship with the African church (p. 455). In the second place, a distinction must be made between civil religion and Christianity. Although the former comprises elements selectively derived from the latter, it is not in any specific sense Christian – Bellah even goes so far as to speak of 'an utter incompatibility between civil religion and Christianity'. The same distinction existed in Uganda and reflected the different conceptions of a Christian nation mentioned above. While the mission adopted a strictly qualitative approach and emphasized Christian morality and the Christian way of life as the essential and indispensable expressions of Christian belief, the government conceived of Christianity in more utilitarian and functional terms, expecting religion to produce good citizens and to provide the state with legitimacy. A significant expression of this attitude was the following statement from one of the colonial officers:

What is required out here is practical religion such as is preached by some of the finest men in the Church of England which teaches a man to work not only for his own good but for the good of his country . . . If all missionaries would instil this into their people and loyally support the Government in their measures to create it, both the country would advance and the moral tone of its people would be improved.[15]

The utilitarian approach certainly determined which elements the government selected from Christianity, and the role it assigned to the Christian religion within the colonial state. Thus we may claim that, just as there exists an elaborate civil religion based on Christian elements in the American political realm, there existed within the colonial state a similar Christian dimension in the sense that 'Christianity furnishes many of the "first premises" ' on which the colonial government based its value decisions.[16] The colonial state even went so far as to sanction the development of Uganda towards a Christian nation 'in the broad sense that Christian principles underlie its laws and values'.[17] To that extent Christianity functioned as a civil religion according to Bellah's definition. A Christian dimension of this kind was fully compatible with the pluralistic Christian presence in Uganda, but was far from meeting the Christian leaders' qualitative demands for the state's Christian engagement. At the same time Christianity's status as a civil religion was decisive for the role the state could play in supporting and encouraging Christian values in society. This meant that it could provide moral support for the promotion of some Christian values, which would later be reflected in laws and administrative measures. But the state could not take the lead by passing compulsory legislation in generating and upholding a carefully defined Christian morality and a specifically Christian way of life. Any closer links between church and state were ruled out as the furtherance of Christian norms was not identical with the furtherance of any church institution.

It is indicative of the attitude of the colonial state to Christianity that an analytical concept developed in the American setting can be usefully employed to assess the situation in Uganda, where the key issues, as in America, were neither the problem of establishment or disestablishment, nor the separation of church and state, but the degree of the state's commitment to Christian values, and the means of putting this commitment into practice. The central issue was how far the colonial state should support the Christian missionary activity. We may conclude that the colonial state hardly went beyond the level of civil religion in its commitment to the furtherance of Christian principles. On the other hand, this confirms that the belief system guiding the government's policy was rooted in Christian rather than in secular values.[18]

A first conclusion is that the strengthened position of the state at the expense of the mission and the church, which we saw was the most significant trend in their changing relationship, can only with certain qualifications be called a process of secularization. Commitment to Christian values, even if it is reduced to the level of civil religion, is bound to slow down the secularization process. Two factors in particular were important in the policy of the state. First, certain areas properly belonged in its domain, to the exclusion of the Christian institutions. Education was the most clear-cut example, but even there the state's expansion was limited and it deliberately refrained from taking the most decisive step towards secularization. Furthermore, its limited expansion here was outweighed by Christian intrusion into certain areas of legislation. The second and most important factor was the negative, preventive element in the state's actions. Its major concern was to maintain the status quo by preventing escalation in one or the other direction, and most importantly by preserving the political sector's position of control and supremacy. No bipolar balance of power was allowed to emerge. This is the most significant result of the analysis of secularization. The controlling function of the government was strengthened at the expense of the mission mainly because of changes in the mission's capacity. But the process of secularization did not go much beyond that point. Although its range of action was narrowed, Christianity's legitimate function within the colonial state was not undermined. The state expected certain benefits to accrue from the mission's presence and even relied on it in some respects.

The mission's role and function within the colonial state

The mission's functions within the colonial state may be divided into three categories. The first one has to do with the legitimacy of the colonial state and its institutions. The mission did not at any time question the existence or justification of the colonial state, but accepted it as a given framework for its enterprise. It availed itself of colonial institutions and identified with them on official occasions, thus exhibiting a state-affirming attitude in spite of occasional tensions and conflicts over particular issues. In general the mission supported government policy, even the less agreeable parts of it, as we saw in connection with the forced-labour issue. This positive attitude counted for much, as it came from the only non-governmental organizational structure existing in the country. The legitimizing effect was further reinforced by the fact that the state and the mission largely shared the same value system. In spite of differences in definition and scale Christianity was a privileged religion from which ultimate norms and values were taken. Hence Christianity and the mission provided a source of legitimacy for the colonial state.

Moving on to its more active role, the mission also performed a supportive function. As we saw in our analysis of indirect inputs, the pattern of parallelism and coordination implicitly had a supportive effect for the colonial state (Chapter 23). This function was more obvious in the field of education than elsewhere. The government was aware of the educational sector's socializing potential, and the mission responded positively to its expectations by adopting as one of its principal goals the fostering of loyalty to 'the parental rule of the British Government'.[19] Such considerations were also extended to other areas and were generally applied when certain kinds of activity were evaluated.[20] Later the mission became even more conscious of its supportive function, when African initiatives and reactions raised doubts about the younger generation's attitude to the 'parental' colonial system (p. 234 ff). Again the common value system was as apparent as the mission had joint interests with the state as far as their supposed civilizing function was concerned. This was evident in the discussion of the issue of the Christian nation.

It is worth adding that the subject of support is an element in Easton's scheme of analysis which has not figured prominently in the present survey. In discussing inputs we have mainly concentrated on the demands presented by the mission, but the supportive dimension was clearly present and helps to explain the state's basically positive attitude and response.[21]

This brings us to the mission's directly instrumental function. The basis for undertaking such a role was, first, that the ecclesiastical system constituted the only administrative organization existing in the Protectorate apart from the state; secondly, that the nature of the church's work gave it well-developed channels of communication. The educational sector served naturally as the major instrument for this kind of activity, but other aspects of the missionary work also contributed (Chapter 23). In various ways the mission helped to create future leaders and furnished the state with trained personnel. In general it helped to develop a stratum in society which could form the backbone of future socio-economic progress. At another level, Christian activity promoted discipline and morality, a factor not to be disregarded by the state, and helped to control the emergence of critical independent opinion, not least through the medium of the church magazines and other publications. The government was also appreciative of the mission's instrumental value in other ways. For example, it helped to stem the Muslim tide. These joint interests and a common value system brought mission and state close together.

Combining the effects of these three overlapping roles, we may conclude that the mission performed a useful and even indispensable function within the colonial state. Accordingly, the government provided some of the means of fulfilling this function. But we must not forget the second trend in government policy. As we saw in connection with secularization, the government's main concern was to maintain a controlling authority, and to limit the independence of the mission in order to minimize its chances of becoming an independent centre of power. So far the state had managed to strike a balance between these two somewhat contradictory tendencies in its policy towards the mission, and had even, as suggested above, been able to turn the tide in its own favour. The mission was recognized as a fully legitimate actor on the colonial stage, but it was the state which increasingly set the scene and assigned the mission its role.

Using the present mode of analysis we can do no more than assess the mission's instrumental function in relation to the colonial state. Recently, however, alternative analytical approaches have been suggested which interpret the role of the mission and Christianity in qualitative terms and within an evaluational framework. Stimulated by recent theories of colonialism and imperialism, some works on colonial Uganda now tend to place the mission among those forces which paved the way for the special type of state formation represented by the colonial state. These works stress the dual role of the mission as an element intermediate between the metropole and the colony, and as a force within the colony itself.[22] Within such an evaluational framework Ronald Robinson has suggested that a central mechanism in the functioning of imperialism and the European management of the non-European world was the system of collaboration, in the sense that there emerged among the indigenous ruling élite a group of collaborators. Their status and authority were rooted in local institutions, and the policy of collaboration was due to an awareness on both sides of mutual interests and interdependence. This two-way process means that the term is not used in a pejorative sense. It indicates rather the pragmatic response of ruling groups to a new and difficult situation.[23] Terence Ranger has argued in particular that it is necessary in the African context to consider collaboration and resistance as related aspects of a complex situation, and that it is difficult to decide whether a specific society should be described as 'resistant' or 'collaborative' in analysing the various responses to colonial intrusion.[24] This is borne out by events in Uganda. The situation in Bunyoro after the Kanyangire episode in 1907 (p. 398) has been characterized as 'enforced collaboration' underneath which resistance continued.[25] In general the theme of collaboration has naturally been used to explain developments in centralized societies like the interlacustrine kingdoms,[26] especially Buganda.[27] Within this area Christianity and the Christian missions have been included as variables. Michael Twaddle has argued that Christianity 'facilitated political collaboration' between British officials and the Ganda chiefs, as it provided the framework for close personal contacts and gave the chiefs an ideology which was also shared by the colonial rulers.[28] Semakula Kiwanuka takes the argument a step further when he says that, compared to the Catholics, the Protestant establishment was so closely associated with colonialism that its position was one of servile collaboration. This reflected the closeness of the links between the CMS mission and British colonialism. Thus Kiwanuka holds the CMS largely responsible for the presence of the Protestant collaborators among the ruling Ganda élite.[29]

The theme of collaboration has not been pursued in the present survey, but a number of the results produced so far support such an evaluative theory. While the presence of the mission was neither a sufficient nor a necessary condition for the emergence of a group of collaborators, it was certainly instrumental in sustaining the collaborative apparatus and making the policy of collaboration work. The mission deliberately took upon itself a mediating role which was initially accepted by both parties. It concentrated on the traditional hierarchies and power structures, and African ruling groups used Christianity and the good offices of the mission to obtain their share of the available benefits. Consequently the mission acted as a spokesman for the interests of the chiefs, for instance in connection with one pillar of their power, their right to dispose of land. Through the educational system the mission also contributed to the continuation of collaboration into the next generation by concentrating on the sons of the chiefs and meeting the needs of the colonial state for trained manpower. Thus the mission's work also had a socializing effect: it predisposed the élite to an acceptance of alien suzerainty and colonial ideology. But it should be added that two trends during the period under survey necessitate a reappraisal of the mission's role. As the chiefs became more and more integrated into the colonial bureaucracy, and as the mission moved closer in many ways to the colonial government (to the extent that they could be seen as constituting a moral community) less scope was left for the mission, through no fault of its own, to take part in the politics of collaboration. Still, for most of the period under survey we may accept the theory of collaboration and ascribe this wider function to the mission within the colonial system.

Other writers, such as E. A. Brett (1973), Tarsis B. Kabwegyere (1974 and 1976) and Mahmoud Mamdani (1975 and 1976) have emphasized specific features of the colonial state and focused on its linkages with the metropole. A colonial state like Uganda was run by a foreign ruling class which monopolized authority, and which incorporated the colonial dependency into the world capitalist economy. Local production was restructured to meet metropolitan demands, and this led to an underdeveloped economy. Internally, this kind of exploitation had an impact on indigenous social structures and initiated a process of class formation which again facilitated imperial control. The mission is counted more or less explicitly among those organizations that sustained the colonial state.[30]

The method of analysis used in this survey hardly allows us to see the missionary work in these terms or to make it the subject of such a qualitative evaluation. In particular too little attention has been paid to economic development and the modes of production to enable us to either refute or confirm such a judgement. We may, however, venture the suggestion that Bishop Tucker in some of his interventions with the government and in his interpretation of government policy came close to modern theories of colonialism. In his campaign against forced labour, forced cotton cultivation and a settler economy, he showed awareness of the oppression and exploitation which could accompany any link with the metropolitan economy, and which could result in a form of satellite position with dependence and subordination in the economic field. This was not in accordance with the priority which ought to be given to African interests. Instead the society's economy should be geared to its own needs and put on a basis which would eventually make it independent of the metropolitan economy. On the other hand, in the post-Tucker period there was a significant absence of missionary comment on the long drawn-out discussion of the future system of landownership and the resulting pattern of production – whether it should be a plantation system under European settlers or African peasant production. Even more significant was the change in the attitude to forced labour from the Tucker to the Willis epoch. In accordance with modern theories of colonialism this can be seen as a reflection of the overall process which perpetuated African underdevelopment, and in which the mission was a partner.

As regards the process of social stratification, we have discussed the mission's connection with two differentiating factors, landholding and education. A distinction was created between landowners and the Bakopi, and a group of tenants emerged who paid tribute to land- and officeholders in the form of poll tax, or busulu (labour).[31] The educational system helped to create a gap between the élite and the masses, although not to the extent that we are justified in speaking of real class differences in the Marxist sense.[32] One could with as much justification mention the mission's awareness of the process of social stratification and even its concern about the creation of what it called 'class differences'. Furthermore, the mission itself suffered from these forces. It failed to interest the newly educated generation in offices within the church. It was blinkered by its belief in its own diffusionist theory that a Christian chieftaincy and a new Christian middle class would act as the leavening in creating a Christian society. The effect of this theory was that the mission identified its own interests with those of the chiefs, even to the extent that 'the Church's fortune rested with a limited section of society and one which, in terms of rapidly growing social trends, was on the decline'.[33]

These various interpretations of the effects of missionary activity must remain speculative in the present context; but they serve to underline the fact that the same course of events can produce widely differing interpretations according to the theoretical framework applied. We have in the present work focused on political processes and specific forces at work within the colonial system rather than on the wider consequences of missionary enterprise or of colonialism as such. The type of evaluative, even critical, approach to missionary and colonial enterprise suggested by the authors mentioned above is difficult to apply in the present context as a number of necessary components have not figured in the survey.

The mission's approach to the colonial state: the special nature of their relationship

So far we have mainly analysed the changing relationship between the mission and the state from the viewpoint of the colonial state. It is equally important, if we are to establish the special nature of the interrelationship, to consider the mission's own attitude. How did it perceive its role within the colonial state, and how far were its expectations met by the actual response of the state? In other words, how far did the mission's assumed and assigned roles correspond to one another?

To answer these questions we must first look at the factors which determined the mission's basic attitude to the colonial state and then identify its basic political objectives in relation to the state. First, mission and state shared a common value system, although they defined it differently, and had different attitudes to its actual impact on policy and decisions. Still, as we saw when we discussed the concept of civil religion, Christianity was an important source of the colonial state's belief system.[34] Secondly, the African context itself presented them with similar problems, and they often arrived at the same solutions. This made parallelism and coordination a significant feature of their relationship. Out of this grew the third factor, the utilitarian aspect in the mission's perception of its relationship with the state. At the more abstract level, cooperation with the colonial government had a legitimizing effect on the missionary work. Again, as noted on various occasions, exchanges with the government had an image- and prestige-creating effect, which gave the Protestant work a special standing in society. At a more concrete level, the mission enjoyed the benefits of the *Pax Britannica* – peaceful conditions and improvements in the infrastructure and communication. Finally, the mission benefited directly from the colonial presence in that it received various kinds of support which enabled it to carry on its work on a larger scale and in more sectors than otherwise would have been the case.[35] These three factors inclined the mission to a positive orientation towards the colonial state, and paved the way for a cooperative approach. This becomes even more evident when we summarize the mission's main political objectives, which can conveniently be systematized in five categories.[36]

(1) The first objective was the recognition and protection of the state. Judged on the basis of the position of Christianity as such, the mission was quite successful. Christianity, though not the established religion, was granted a protected and privileged position compared to other religions, so we are concerned with something more than an ecumenical state. It is another matter when we consider the institutional expressions of Christianity. Denominational pluralism precluded any established status, and the mission, in spite of great efforts, failed to obtain any official recognition of the future independent church. The church was not considered a legal body, entitled for example to own land, and the

government refused to be drawn into legislation in the ecclesiastical field. The mission, rather than the church, was recognized as the main religious unit in the colonial state, and a special relationship was established with it.

(2) Closely related to the first objective was the preservation and expansion of the material base of the Christian bodies and the consequent enhancement of their position and capacity. We have seen that it was a recurrent theme in the mission's approach to the government that it asked for more land on better terms, with particular emphasis on tenant labour rights, and in general for more concessions and direct support for parts of the work, with reference to its national importance. We have also seen that the government responded sparingly to these demands, as it clearly did not want extensive material links to exist between church and state. As regards the land, its major concern was to limit acreage and to impose restrictions on the use made of the land. Direct state support for mission work was ruled out. Only clearly identifiable and primarily secular activities like education could be granted support. Material linkages between the two spheres must not become so close that the general missionary work could in any sense be considered a state activity or the direct responsibility of the state.

(3) At another level the mission sought to extend Christian principles in society by Christianizing the fundamental premises of the polity and by pursuing policies based on Christian values. This objective has been dealt with in a special chapter, and, as we have just seen, the process leading to the emergence of a Christian nation began. But the mission and state did not agree on ends and means. The government kept a lower profile, interpreting its own role in terms of civil religion, while the mission stood firmly on the ground of Christian doctrine and morality.

(4) In order to increase its capacity and its chances of realizing its major goals, the mission tried to move into positions of political and administrative import-ance. This theme has been dealt with most extensively in the chapter on the Christian state. It will be recalled that there was never any question of the clergy being elevated to political offices, nor of the mission or church having an established position in relation to the state. The mission's objective was simply to institute various linkages with the African polities and the colonial state as channels for contact, information and influence. While the mission succeeded in establishing institutionalized linkages between the church and the African poli-ties, the colonial government remained wary of formalized ties between itself and the mission. Instead the mission assumed a consultative status which enabled it to exercise some influence on policy-making within certain fields of relevance for its work, and it was in this capacity that missionaries could undertake an advisory role with African leaders and function as intermediaries to the colonial govern-ment. But the consultative status was reduced in the latter part of the period. The expansion of the government's controlling function in particular, which was a key element in the secularization process, worked against the mission's position of influence.

(5) The last and most fundamental objective of the mission was to maintain enough autonomy to perform its functions. This issue has been discussed in connection with the mission's capacity to act *vis-à-vis* the state (Chapter 24). We saw there that the mission's autonomy was relative, both because it was dependent to a great extent on external forces, and because the state aimed at extending its controlling influence in various ways (cf. the secularization analysis). In this situation it became crucial to maintain sufficient power to challenge the state and

to strike a balance between the need to cooperate with it on the one hand and to remain independent on the other. The process of change over the years did not favour the mission. It had to decide how far it was able and determined to act with sufficient autonomy in view of the many constraining linkages to the state and the surrounding society.

Comparing the mission's objectives with the government's response, we can make two observations. First, there was a discrepancy between objectives and achievements, and consequently between the mission's assumed and assigned roles. Secondly, a process of change was at work which was not in the mission's favour. Hence the mission was faced with a basic dilemma. Should it give priority to cooperation with the state in spite of its failure to achieve the expected results; or should it place the major emphasis on maintaining its own autonomy and range of action? The mission's options can be seen as ranging along a continuum running between the two polar concepts of dissociation and cooperation, involving a critical, challenging role, and a supportive, legitimizing role respectively. In even stronger terms, we may speak of a conflict between a desire for independent power to challenge the state and the risk of being 'twisted to its purposes'.[37]

We have identified three types of determinants which decided the mission's position on this scale. First, there were internal factors like finances, organizational structure and other elements which determined the general capacity of the mission in its engagement with the state. Secondly, there were external forces such as the social and political structures in society and the policies and orientation of the colonial state. As a third determinant we must take into account certain more subjective factors which achieved greater importance over the years. We have seen the development of an increasingly positive and appreciative orientation towards the state and a recognition of joint interests prompted in particular by changes in African attitudes and reactions. This was accompanied by an increasing awareness of the utilitarian benefits of various kinds of support which allowed the mission to operate on a larger scale than otherwise would have been the case. All these determinants account for the mission's position on the continuum. There was never any question of moving to one or the other of the extremes. Basically, the mission settled for the cooperative approach, and this placed certain constraints on its autonomy. During the first (mainly Bishop Tucker's) part of the period, the mission managed to maintain a reasonable balance between the two poles, where it had the ability to challenge policies and have some say in political decisions. In the subsequent period, the mission moved closer to the cooperative end of the scale, which had an erosive effect on its capability to influence and challenge policy, while its supportive functions assumed greater significance.

On the basis of these mechanisms and trends in the relationship between the mission and the colonial state, we may move on to assess the mutual strength of the two parties and to offer an explanation of the special nature of their interrelationship. Four modes of explanation will be suggested and the value of each of them discussed in turn.

(1) The simplest explanation of the mission's one-way move along the continuum towards a position of less autonomy is that such a development is predetermined or inevitable. J. Milton Yinger comes close to suggesting such a solution when he discusses the separation of church and state. In his opinion separation is characterized by the church's role of 'challenging, modifying or denying the claims of politics'. This is only likely to occur where power is

diffused, in the sense that there exists some measure of economic freedom and freedom to express judgement and criticism, and where there is unrestricted public access to information. All these factors create a setting in which religious challenges to secular power structures are most likely to occur. Where these conditions are lacking, 'church and state are not likely to be effectively separate, whatever the formal institutional structures may be'.[38] Yinger is in other words stating the necessary conditions which must exist for a church to possess sufficient autonomy and power to challenge the state. In Uganda two features indicate that the basic conditions for the mission's performing of an independent political role were not met. First, the political system could be characterized as a centralized bureaucracy, with little room for alternative centres of political activity. Secondly, the state was bent on maintaining its internal supremacy and expanding its controlling function. In view of the prevalence of these two traits, virtually only one basic mode of relationship was possible in the long run, that of government over church;[39] consequently few options were open for the ecclesiastical sphere. The form which this state supremacy took might vary, but the basic nature of the relationship cannot be doubted. According to Yinger's conceptual apparatus, the colonial state's special structure and its search for internal supremacy combined with greater potential predestined the church to a position of dependence. By this interpretation there is some degree of automatism in the relationship between the ecclesiastical sphere and the colonial state, and no alternative development was possible.

(2) A second way of explaining the nature of the mission/church–state relationship is of a more comprehensive type. According to S. N. Eisenstadt, it is necessary to consider not only the state's strength and structure, but also the church's basic objectives, orientations and characteristics. While its potentialities are rooted in the ecclesiastical field, their realization is dependent on the policy of the state, which means that the focal point becomes the element of interplay between the two actors.[40] It is mainly this analytical approach which has been employed in the foregoing survey. It involves a large number of variables, and gives a very complex picture of the relationship. Even if we reduce the number of variables to two summary ones, the capacity of the church and the policies of the state, the emphasis on the interplay between internal factors and external forces precludes a single-factor explanation or a simplified characterization of the relationship. It is rather the dynamic and processual features which are most significant.

(3) The latter type of explanation maximizes the complexity of the relationship. The third method of explaining the mission's moving closer to the state narrows the focus to the special circumstances inherent in the colonial situation. As we saw in connection with the analysis of indirect inputs, these circumstances created a special kind of interdependence between mission and government. The colonial situation was significant for the high degree of parallelism which prevailed between the two European agencies: their mutual adaptation, consultation and cooperation within fields of common interest. Such a high degree of interdependence naturally had an impact on the mode of relationship between the two. We have further seen that the mission, as the only non-government organization present, undertook a wide range of mainly secular tasks either assigned by the state or pursued with a view to fulfilling the requirements of the state. This meant that the mission, in the absence of intermediary structures, faced the state directly with its centralized bureaucracy and its clear intention of controlling and supervising most activities in society. This somewhat exposed position was

further underlined by the economic ties which such state-related activities created. These special features of the colonial situation emphasized as time went on the necessity for collaboration and induced the mission to move closer to the state. The state appeared more and more as the stronger partner which dictated the terms for its relations with the mission.

(4) This explanation, based on the concept of interdependence in the colonial situation, is related to a more subjective one. It has on more than one occasion been underlined that the common value system and the basic attitudes of the missionaries and the government officers were important elements in the relationship between them. They were instrumental in making the two European agencies complementary partners with common interests. We may say that the actors involved constituted a moral community, a category of people whose guiding values were known and largely accepted by all members.[41] They were held together not only by obvious economic ties and mutual dependence, 'but also by cross-cultural links, which helped to create a climate of understanding and trust'.[42] The concept of a moral community explains the mission's basically positive attitude towards the colonial state and the state's appreciation of the missionary enterprise within the colonial system. It constituted a force that promoted acceptance of fundamental common aims and consequent collaboration. It would take very strong hindrances to annihilate this effect.[43]

These four models provide explanations of varying adequacy for the mission's move towards collaboration with the colonial state. The first three concentrate on the supremacy of the state – the fact that the state is the stronger partner in the relationship. Assessing their explanatory value in relation to one another we may say that the first one is in a category by itself. It is self-sufficient, in the sense that it can dispense with additional means of explanation, given its deterministic character. It can ignore other variables and is based first on a special conception of the colonial state and its inherent supremacy, and secondly on the overriding power of material and economic interests. Our analysis does not allow us to generalize to this extent. But this does not mean that the notion of the innate supremacy of the state and the inherent strength of economic ties are negligible factors.

The best solution is a combination of the three remaining types of explanation. The second type works with a complex set of variables in order to establish the capacity of each of the actors involved, and the resultant relationship between them. The two latter types provide necessary interpretative aids by widening the scope to include both the peculiar colonial environment and subjective, attitudinal factors. Given these three factors, we are able to analyse the relationship between the mission and the colonial state in a wider perspective and to produce a more coherent picture of their mutual strength and power.

The price of cooperation: the question of dependence

In view of the special nature of the relationship between the mission and the colonial state, it is only natural to ask what price the mission had to pay for its association. This issue has been touched upon in several connections (especially p. 249 ff). Within 'the collaborative relationship',[44] directly state-related activities, primarily education, had the most profound impact on the ecclesiastical field. This sector was given high priority, and attempts were made to preserve as much as possible of the previous monopoly. But when the mission had to meet educational demands from both the colonial state and the Africans, an increasing disparity grew up between the mission's objectives and the means available. The mission opted for continuing with its educational role, and accepted the fact that it was no longer so much participating in a joint venture as becoming an educational agency subsidized by the state and subject to certain conditions. A channel was opened up for direct government intervention and control of some aspects of the work. A similar dependence stemmed from the economic ties with the state represented by concessions in the areas of poll tax and land and labour services. As we saw in connection with the issue of forced labour, the mission's dependence on the cheap public service labour available influenced its attitude to government policy and crippled its ability to act in a political role. Hence, collaboration with the state and state-related activities forced the mission into a network of dependence in the following ways.

(1) It lost its goal achievement, as the establishment of an independent church was delayed. The lines of contact with the government constituted blocking mechanisms for the development of the church and served to emphasize the role of the mission itself, thus reinforcing the pattern of missionary dominance.

(2) Consequently relations with the state had intra-organizational repercussions in the ecclesiastical field. The growth of the state-subsidized educational sector increased the mission's influence on decisions and policy at the expense of the church and altered their relationship. The payment of teaching missionaries from the government grant was an example of this. The boundary between the two was defined more precisely and the planned integration of the two organizations became more difficult. At the same time the process of Africanization within the church was hindered by bonds between the mission and the government (see Chapter 20).

(3) These organizational changes were accompanied by structural repercussions for the pattern of the work. The transfer of teaching missionaries to the government payroll created a formal distinction between two categories of missionaries and meant that the mission had to postpone the integration of evangelizing and educational work which was otherwise a hallmark of the missionary enterprise in Uganda. The balance between religious and secular work had been skewed. The differentiation was made more explicit by placing the two kinds of work on a different footing. The secular work relied on state support, while the missionary work was still determined by the principle of self-support. The most profound effect of this differentiation was that the two sectors were aimed at different social groupings. While the educational work was directed towards society at large, and had as its goals the creation of a Christian ruling class and middle class, the evangelizing work had as its target a self-governed and self-supporting church. But the balance between serving state and church could not be maintained, and the disparity between these two aims was the most serious consequence of the mission's engagement in secular activities.

(4) The mission was thus faced with a paradox problem stemming from its ties with the surrounding society and the emerging pattern of social differentiation. In justification of their secular activities the missionaries maintained that they aimed at creating a new political and commercial élite which could serve as the backbone of a Christian society. The mission thus became the captive of its own society-

orientated efforts in two ways. In the first place, the church was unable to recruit the best-trained people to its own ranks. The gap which arose between the church personnel and the new educated wealthy élite proved almost impossible to bridge. Secondly, the Christian work became dependent on the new élite, which then became the economic backbone of the church. The church could not afford to dissociate itself from this new stratum without setting its work at risk. In short, the mission relied financially on the new status group, while it relied on quite different sources for its personnel. Furthermore the mission became identified with the colonial socio-political order, and could not extricate itself because of its economic dependence, even if it had wanted to do so.

The mission had thus to make great sacrifices for the sake of cooperation with the state. The educational engagement in particular constituted a major opening for external influence and trapped the mission in a network of dependence. In Biblical terms, one may say that the mission sold part of its soul for a mess of educational pottage. The colonial state, too, had to pay for its collaboration, although this did not lead to a similar kind of dependence, because of the state's superior strength in the interrelationship. All the same, cooperation with the Christian agencies meant that the state had to dispense with the principle of religious neutrality as this was applied strictly within the Christian domain. Even within that narrow framework the state was unable to separate religion and politics. It had to accept religious factionalism as the major structuring principle in society, so it could not pursue a policy of full equality. Acceptance of the mission's state- and society-related activities had a constraining effect on the religious policy the state was able to conduct, and it had to live with a certain discrepancy between its official principles and its practical policy.

Focusing on the concept of dependence illustrates the complexity of the mission's and the church's relationship to the colonial state and the effect of their engagement in secular, state-related activities. In sum, we may make two generalizations originally employed in another context. These sustain and elaborate the generalizations which summed up the analysis of the educational linkages between church and state (pp. 257–8).

First, the autonomy and scope of the ecclesiastical field for independent action were affected by its linkages with the colonial state. They exerted a restrictive influence in the sense that political participation was reduced in scale and to a level acceptable to the state. Developments in this direction were characterized by a certain inertia. The stronger the linkages with the state were, the less scope there was for independent action and for challenging the state. The tendency was further reinforced since the church and the state shared a common value system and the state had the advantage as regards potential and resources.[45]

Secondly, within this basic framework, state- and society-related activities placed the mission and church in a vulnerable position and made them susceptible to state influence. The more this engagement and the 'social servant function' took the church beyond its means and capacity, the more dependent it was on the state, and the more it had to yield to external influence. The resultant dependence was bound to have negative effects on internal structure and goal achievement.[46]

Special features of the colonial situation

The two generalizations on the church–state problem indicate one primary objective of the present survey: the perception of specific factors in a colonial setting within a general analytical framework, and the examination of how far methods and concepts usually employed in studies of the church–state problem may prove helpful in explaining and interpreting the colonial situation. To pursue that aim, we have employed concepts like the Christian nation and the Christian state; and as interpretative aids we have employed general concepts like secularization and civil religion. We have widened our comparative perspective further by placing the relationship between mission, church and state within the general framework of political analysis. A simplified model from systems analysis has been used to define the relative positions of the two actors and to view the activities of the mission and the church in political terms, as inputs to the political system. The present analysis has thus been raised to a certain level of generalization, and this suggests that the study of the church–state problem in a colonial setting need not fall within its own particular category or require a specific conceptual framework. Yet, beyond the comparative and generalizing framework the church–state problem in a colonial situation presents certain problems of its own. The special African background with its political systems, patterns of society, culture and religion must be taken into account, and a number of additional factors must be included in the analysis. Thus a more specific approach is necessary in order to account fully for the peculiarities of the colonial situation.

(1) One must work with parallel tripartite structures within both the ecclesiastical and political fields. In the first place, it is essential to analyse the relationships and lines of authority between all three components within each sphere – between European headquarters, the local European agency and the African institutions. In this respect things are complicated further on the church side in view of the fact that the European mission's major task was to lay the foundations of a future independent church and make itself superfluous. It thus had to be decided how much autonomy was to be allowed to the embryonic church at any given time, or, more negatively, how much supervision and control it was to be subject to. Secondly, in exchanges between the two sides there were many potential lines of contact and communication, the relative importance of which must be examined in order to assess the nature of the interrelationship.

(2) It is thus necessary to make a distinction between the European and the African arenas within each sphere. Focus will then be on the interrelationship between the two, and in particular on the importance and function of Europe in the colonial situation. Naturally, the final authority in a colonial situation will be with the metropole, and the African arena will have some form of satellite status. But we must clarify how the metropole exercised its authority, and how far it influenced policy- and decision-making. Or, from the angle of the African arena, we must ask how much autonomy the local agencies have. As regards the function of the European arena, there is also a movement in the opposite direction. An actor in Africa could activate the European arena in order to influence political processes or to use it as a court of appeal in order to have decisions reversed, or to bring about a change in the attitudes of other actors. For such purposes 'Europe' comprises several elements, such as the government apparatus, the parliamentary system, the news media, lobbying and pressure groups, and public opinion. Thus some form of democratic parliamentary influence may be brought to bear on the political and administrative processes affecting the African dependency.

(3) While these mechanisms operate within Europe, the local governing bodies within both the political and ecclesiastical fields virtually operate in a parliamen-

tary and democratic vacuum. The colonial arena is not subject to checks and restraints originating from parties or other specific groups, from the press, or from a legislature. A bureaucratic system prevails, and the interest articulation of an organization like the mission goes directly to the political system without intermediary structures. In Uganda, this direct line of access to policy-makers gave a special status to the ecclesiastical organizations, as they were almost alone in the field during the period under survey, when a kind of dual system prevailed. Only African political leaders like chiefs could exert any pressure in the initial stages, often in concert with the CMS mission; but their capacity to do so decreased as the colonial system became more established and their offices were integrated into the colonial bureaucracy. Towards the end of this period a more differentiated situation arose, and this was bound to affect the mission's monopoly-like position as regards interest articulation. On the one hand a Legislative Council and settler organizations were established. On the other, embryonic African groups began to make their voices heard, for instance by starting newspapers. But the government still maintained undisputed control and could still act almost undeterred by democratic restraints. The mission could not step in to fill this gap either, as the situation forced it to move closer to the government.

In discussing the absence of democratic means of control within the colonial arena, it is natural also to assess the importance of the democratic elements within the church's synodal constitution, where the electoral principle was practised at various levels, especially at the level of the lay members. But we have seen that, except in rare cases, there was limited scope for democratic processes of control and policy-making during the period under survey. It follows from these two lines of reasoning that it was, at least initially, the two European agencies who were the dominant actors in the African arena, and that they were to a great extent free of the constraints of parliamentary and public accountability.

(4) The organizational structure of the political and ecclesiastical fields must also be taken into account. In both cases it may be said that they were monolithic systems with a hierarchical pattern of authority. Power and authority emanated from the Governor and the Bishop respectively, and final decisions rested with them, although they occasionally had to refer to the European arena. Under such an order internal divisions are unlikely. If they occur they will be of great significance, as they may weaken the position of the agency concerned, and thus affect its ability to pursue its policy or interests. In such cases of internal disunity (for instance, within the ecclesiastical sphere, disagreements on the handling of national movements and the marriage laws, and, in the case of the colonial administration, differences over the language problem), the familiar pattern of authority prevailed, and each agency was after all able to present a unified outward front. Neither side exploited the disunity in the other's ranks; each respected the other's internal autonomy. This tells us much about the unwritten laws which guided the relationship between the two major actors in the colonial setting.

(5) We must also consider whether a colonial situation involving two European agencies tends to create something like a moral community between them, in spite of the differences between their objectives and means. The first factor in favour of such a moral community will be a situational one: they experience the same pressure from their African surroundings and are faced with the same problems. In short, the specific type of society created by the colonial situation

makes the same impact on both agencies and emphasizes their coincidence of interests. The second factor is a qualitative one. They are attracted to each other because of their common national, cultural and denominational background, and this accounts for their attachment to a common value system. These forces appear to be significant in the colonial situation, and it will be useful to consider in more detail, how strong they actually were, as they were bound to influence the pattern of interaction between European agencies.

(6) Finally, underlying all these factors, there is the general problem that in a colonial situation the church is not working in a state or a nation as these terms are normally understood in a European context. First, a superstructure is imposed by an external agency on societies and polities which have hitherto existed independently of one another. It is important to assess how far they are able to continue to function on their own terms. Correspondingly, we must ask to what extent colonial structures penetrate local societies, that is, the extent of centralization and the levels at which it works. Naturally, a Christian mission is part of, and works within, this whole framework, and it is within this context that its objectives and methods of work should be assessed. Secondly, although the society in question is held together by external forces, there is at least in the early phase no national spirit and no nation-wide movement apart from the European agencies. Nor is there any infrastructure which can exert such an influence. Accordingly, the conflict between the desire for integration on the one hand, and decentralization and respect for local feelings and characteristics on the other, provides the mission from the outset with a problematical situation to which it has to adapt. It must consider its own policies, establish its own priorities, and decide how far they should differ, if at all, from those of the state.

These six factors have been significant for the study of the colonial situation in Uganda. At the same time they typify more general factors of some relevance for an analysis of the church–state problem in other colonial situations. They emphasize once more what has emerged as a general theme of the present survey, the fact that the relationship between church and state in a colonial setting is of special complexity, and that its analysis requires a greater number of variables than the study of most other areas.

Appendix 1 The analytical approach: theoretical aims

An elementary and somewhat traditional model from systems analysis has served as the guiding and selective principle during the investigation of the lines of connection running between mission, church and state in a colonial setting. One reason for introducing such a model was that I did not consider it sufficient to select a single topic and examine it over a certain period of time. The educational sector or the land and labour issues might have constituted such topics; but each of these only touches on isolated aspects of the relationship between church and state, and neither of them can produce the more comprehensive picture we require. Nor is there any other single topic or episode which will furnish such a picture.[1] Hence, the development of this relationship must be seen as a multi-faceted process, and a substantial number of issues varying in type and significance have to be included. This has had two implications for the analytical approach. In the first place, a thematic study had to be pursued and placed within an overall framework, which provide the necessary criteria for the selection and categorization of the various themes and for establishing empirical relationships between them. In the second place, it was not possible to employ a diachronic principle; a synchronic approach was necessary. While particular issues were examined diachronically, the overall analytical framework dispensed with the chronological perspective. It was only introduced again when I systematized results and assessed the process of change affecting the relationship between church and state.

Two further features of this thematic, synchronic approach should be mentioned. First, very little research has been done on the church–state problem along these lines. No conceptual apparatus was available beforehand, and though there is a vast amount of source material, it is not organized with this type of study in mind. The solution was to conceive of the church–state problem in terms of systems analysis.[2] The colonial state, with its various structures and authorities, was defined as a political system to whose environment the ecclesiastical sphere belongs. The political dimension of ecclesiastical activity was then seen in terms of inputs to the political system. I further specified the role of the church by conceiving of it in terms of an 'interest group'. The ecclesiastical sphere constituted an institutional interest group which articulated widely varying interests to the political system. The primary focus was on the input function, answering such questions as what demands did the church address to the political system, and what were its objectives? It was also necessary to discuss the capacity of the church as an interest group to engage with the political system. The conversion of these inputs within the political system and the outputs into the environment (the response of state authorities to ecclesiastical demands) also figured in the scheme of analysis. In short, the focal point of the study was the interaction between the church as an institutional interest group and the political system.[3]

One necessary condition for the deployment of this scheme was that the two actors involved had suitably consolidated positions: each needed a proper organizational base and reasonably well-developed administrative structures in order to carry out their functions; and orderly procedures for their interrelations had to be established. While these conditions were met during most of the period under survey (the first quarter of the twentieth century), this was not the case in the formative period of the early colonial phase in the 1890s. But it has been necessary to include this early phase in order to identify the issues which divided the two actors and to describe their common interests and different objectives. This also provided us with a provisional outline of the church–state problem in the colonial setting, upon which the subsequent analysis could be based. Here a different conceptual apparatus proved necessary. In order to characterize the embryonic church–state relationship the almost classic concept of religious liberty was chosen as an analytical aid, for reasons which appear in Chapter 3, and was used to cover the special circumstances of the early colonial situation.

The analytical framework has been used to introduce three categories for the interactions between the ecclesiastical and political fields (cf. Chapter 1). While the first category, the material basis of the church–state relationship, is self-explanatory, and the direct-input category deals with the question whether and to what extent the mission and church were able to influence, challenge, modify or even hinder any given policy, the third category of indirect input goes beyond the causal dimension in the relationship between church and state (cf. Chapter 18).[4] It is based on the assumption that neither system was unaffected by the existence of the other, even if no direct demands were presented. The political system would in certain cases gear its policy to the presence and activities of the mission and church, which resulted in a certain parallelism in decisions and actions. At the same time the pattern of interdependence also meant that the church and the mission made allowances for the line followed by the state, which was expressed in a willingness to harmonize policy and activities with those of the state. It follows that the question of adaptation becomes a major issue in this part of the analysis.

Apart from being founded in general systems theory, this approach has been inspired by that field of research which deals with inter-organizational or inter-institutional relations. Following this latter tradition, one aim of the analysis has been to establish the extent to which organizations had ties with, or were otherwise affected by, other organizations in their environment, and in particular the extent to which such indirect and informal ties influenced policy- and decision-making, or accounted for restraints on behaviour. The study of such interlinkages has revealed a pattern of interdependence or a structure of inter-locking balance and control.[5]

The employment of such an analytical model imposes certain limitations on the scope of the survey. In the first place, any model presents a simplified picture of reality and cannot do full justice to all its variety and complexity.[6] In the second place, such a mode of analysis involves some element of eclecticism, as it influences the choice of cases to be examined. Only those inputs with some impact on the political system, and which elicited some response from it, are taken into account. This means that a number of factors which might be significant if another approach was employed are either left out or taken as constants, so that what emerges is to some extent an abstraction. The advantage of such an approach is, however, that it becomes possible to see much more clearly the processes and mechanisms at work in the interactions between the two systems in question. In the present case this conceptual apparatus has helped us to interpret exchanges between mission, church and state and to pose questions about the nature of their relationship.[7]

Having outlined the analytical approach, we may now summarize and explain in more general terms the theoretical aims of this survey, especially as regards theoretical propositions and generalizations. Theoretical concepts were used in four ways. First, they served functionally as selective and organizing principles in relation to the source material. They thus guided the survey and were instrumental in raising questions and formulating problems. Secondly, theoretical propositions served as interpretative aids and enabled us to move beyond the purely descriptive level. Instead of describing isolated features we were able to identify the processes and underlying forces involved and gain some understanding of the complexity of developments. A third, more general function was to demonstrate the application of a conceptual apparatus which could be of value in the study of other Afro-colonial situations, and be used in the comparison of the colonial situation with other areas as far as the church–state problem is concerned. Fourthly, an analytical rather than a narrative approach at the same time enabled us to demonstrate that it can be useful to employ concepts and theories from political science and other social sciences in the interpretation of historical source material. Ultimately, this approach allowed us to attain a higher degree of generalization than otherwise would have been the case.

As regards generalizations, I would like to make one final point about the aims of the present study. It clearly falls within the category of case studies, and in this field we may employ Arend Lijphart's classification, and distinguish between six types.[8] The present study clearly goes beyond Lijphart's first type, the atheoretical case study, which is purely descriptive and 'moves in a theoretical vacuum'. My principal aim has been to carry out an interpretative case study, where explicit use is made of established theoretical propositions in order to throw light on the subject matter. Hence its aim and value cannot be seen in terms of theory formation. It was not my intention to contribute to the formulation of general theory, nor to the improvement of existing generalizations. In this respect this survey represents neither a theory-confirming nor a theory-infirming case study. Yet we may say that the study conforms to some extent to two other types which again correspond to the analytical themes outlined in the Introduction. On the one hand the aim was to develop a conceptual apparatus and an analytical approach which are generally applicable to the study of church–state problems in a colonial setting. In this respect the present survey will involve a certain amount of theoretical generalization, and we may thus to a limited extent speak of a hypothesis-generating case study. On the other hand the study set out to ascertain how far theoretical notions and generalizations drawn from analyses of the church–state problem in traditional areas are of any value in explaining the situation in colonial Uganda. In this respect we may speak of a deviant case analysis, as the aim is both to reveal how the colonial situation deviates from generally accepted propositions, and to assess whether it contributes to the process of refining current definitions of the church–state problem. Thus, three types of case study are of some relevance in categorizing the present study. This serves to underline its multi-purpose nature as regards theoretical propositions.

Appendix 2   A survey of related works

This study has been stimulated by and is indebted to a great variety of earlier works to which reference has been made. The range of studies has become too extensive to allow more than a brief outline of the main tendencies, with the emphasis on more recent works. I shall aim at an assessment of how the present study, in view of my definition of the church–state problem, is related to and differs from other works which deal either with the wider African setting or more specifically with Uganda.

It is remarkable how early two themes, or approaches, crucial for the church–state problem in a colonial setting, were formulated. As early as 1952, the Norwegian church historian Fridtjov Birkeli drew attention in his work on politics and missionary activity in Madagascar[1] to the necessary connection between missionary work and politics, and the need to consider the political dimension in studies of missionary work, the specific features of the colonial situation, and the connections between missions and colonialism, and the need to take African political systems and local political situations into account. Given these three topics, Birkeli's main focus of study became the relations between the various missions and the colonial powers, the role of the missions in the process of colonial establishment and as intermediaries to African polities, and the assessment of the colonial powers' religious obligations, based on the concept of the Christian state. In more theoretical terms, he called for a systematic study of the organic relationship between missionary activity and colonialism. He outlined four possible solutions to the problem, using common national origins and confessional affiliations as his major determinants. He found that in many cases missionary activity and politics were not kept distinct. Missionaries and colonialists shared the same interests and worked together for the same ends on the basis of their common nationality. At the same time missionaries sometimes misused political influence, especially as regards African polities, behaviour which Birkeli explained by reference to their confessional traits. On other occasions, denominational differences proved stronger, and the missions and the colonial power were openly antagonistic to one another. Birkeli thus identified a number of variables which must be taken into account in studies of the admittedly complex relationship between mission work and colonialism. The problem was, however, usually seen from the missionary point of view.

In the same year as Birkeli's book appeared, Roland Oliver published his pioneer study, *The Missionary Factor in East Africa*. Oliver expanded the scope of the study by explicitly formulating the problem of the relationship between mission, church and state (Chapter 5). He defined the position of the European missionary as that of an intermediary between the African church and the European state (p. 246), and emphasized the need to study the relationship between the mission and the church, especially in terms of the former's engagement with the colonial state (pp. 286ff). Oliver did not focus on colonialism as such, but emphasized the institutional aspects of the colonial situation. In this respect his point of departure was primarily events taking place in the African setting, although he attached great importance to the mission's access to the European arena as a valuable precondition for its capacity to act in a political role. Within this framework the main target was to identify the most important issues which exercised the mission and the colonial power, and then to assess how far the mission influenced policy and decision-making. Hence, the major analytical aim was to measure the impact of the missionary factor on political processes in the colonial state, and in a wider sense to account for the political and social effects of the missionary presence in society.

These two themes or approaches, first outlined in 1952, have since either singly or in combination provided the point of departure and the conceptual framework for a series of studies which either present an overall outline of the main topics,[2] or deal in more detail with various parts of tropical Africa. Within the latter group the area formerly known as the Congo Independent State naturally attracted early interest. We have over the years had three historical studies along the lines suggested by Birkeli,[3] and we may also mention the contribution of a political scientist.[4] West Africa presents a more varied picture. Many accounts have appeared which touch on and expand these themes. Here we find many early African contributions which ascribe great significance to the African setting in order – in the Oliver tradition – to assess the political and social impact of the missions.[5]

In the Central African region there is again emphasis on and expansion of the Birkeli theme, probably because of the white-settler presence. As argued by Terence Ranger, 'Missionaries now operated within the total context of colonial white activity', and he asks 'how far and in what ways churchmen, whether missionaries or independent leaders, were the creators of the colonial situation'.[6] Several answers have been suggested by scholars in various disciplines, beginning with Robert I. Rotberg, and so far ending with John McCracken.[7] We may also in this context include Ian Linden and his studies from Malawi and Rwanda.[8] The Central African region provides evidence of widespread reaction against the missions and the colonial system from Africans who formed their own churches or societies.[9] Here the crucial issue was how much scope the missions and the colonial state allowed for independent African initiatives. These reactions are typical of a general African evaluation of the relationship between the missions and the colonial state, as formulated by the Kenyan nationalist leader Oginga Odinga, who had also experienced a white-settler situation: 'It dawned that administration and Church were different representations of the same White authority. The policy of the Church was ever in accord with that of the administration'.[10]

This assessment prompts us to ask whether we are justified in assuming a similar state of affairs when we turn to Uganda. There is a remarkable lack of research on developments in Uganda as far as the two major themes outlined above are concerned. We have studies on the initial and later phases of the colonial period, but the intermediate period has not really been dealt with systematically. D. A. Low has laid the foundations for all later studies with his account of the political impact on the Buganda polity of the arrival of the two missions,[11] and he has been followed by a number of other scholars who have analysed various aspects of the process of transformation which took place in Buganda society before the turn of the century.[12] Low has in his later writings touched on the church–state problem in the subsequent decades,[13] and Carl-J. Hellberg, writing of the frontier area between Uganda and Tanganyika, has made a valuable contribution to the study of the interplay between missions and colonialism, with important side-lights on Uganda.[14] But we have to move on to the decolonization phase and the transition to independence before more specific studies appear. F. B. Welbourn was the first to give a general acount of religion and politics in the crucial years 1952–63,[15] and his work has been followed by more specialized studies by a number of scholars in various disciplines: Colin Leys (1967), Akiiki B. Mujaju (1976), A. G. G. Gingyera-Pinycwa (1976), and Michael Twaddle (1978), all of whom have concentrated on the political effects of religious pluralism and more specifically on the correlation between religious allegiance and voting behaviour. The same themes have been pursued by Kathleen Lockard in her study of the post-independence period.[16]

No really comprehensive study has been made of the colonial period dealing with the two basic themes suggested above and answering the qualitative questions about the relations between the missions and the colonial state raised by Africans. This gap has provided one point of departure for the present study, and has been decisive for the demarcation of the period to be studied. There is, however, also a more methodological problem which arises from previous works on Uganda, especially the later ones. They call implicitly for more stringency in framing the problem of religion and politics and for a more precise conceptual apparatus than the two thematic studies by Birkeli and Oliver allow. This change of attitude to the analytical approach was echoed by D. A. Low in a later work, when he asked whether the time had not come, after the many studies of the so-called 'missionary factor', 'to open up some other issues in some rather different directions'.[17] Low himself suggested the inclusion of a wider societal dimension in the study of the interaction between empire and Christianity, with more emphasis on African response, and called for a qualitative assessment of the mutual benefits each of the parties gained from their association.

In this book, a deliberate attempt was made to move beyond the limitations of the purely descriptive case study and to apply a more systematic analytical approach. Secondly, it involves a higher degree of conceptual rigour than is usually seen in studies on the question of religion and politics – or Christianity and politics. Kathleen Lockard in particular has, in her study of religion and political development in Uganda, emphasized the need to distinguish between various levels of inquiry, and before that Victor C. Ferkiss outlined three aspects of religion which have political relevance: religion as institution, as idea, and as the basis of interest groups. Michael Twaddle's recent study of a confessional political party in Uganda demonstrated how different one's conclusions can be according to the political significance one ascribes to religion.[18] Thirdly, the present study confines itself to the institutional level, and focuses on the interaction between religious and political institutions within the colonial framework. In this respect we may draw a parallel to the typology of church–state relations in independent Africa which Adrian Hastings has recently suggested, where he calls for a systematic study of the issues involved and of the factors which account for the special nature of the relationship.[19] This book employs a related typology.

Appendix 3 Danish Summary

Del I: Indledning: problemformulering og metode

Afhandlingen er udformet som et 'case study', der omhandler udviklingen i Uganda fra 1890, hvor såvel det europæiske kolonisystem som den europæiske missionsvirksomhed tog sin egentlige begyndelse, frem til ca. 1925, hvor der i forholdet mellem den statslige og den kirkelige sektor var opnået en rimelig grad af afklaring og stabilitet. Afhandlingens tema er forholdet mellem kirke og stat i en kolonisituation, og den tager sit udgangspunkt i det forhold, at der ikke hidtil er foretaget nogen omfattende og systematisk behandling af denne problemstilling i en afrikansk sammenhæng. Hensigten med nærærende studium er derfor med udgangspunkt i et konkret område dels at analysere og vurdere den løsning på kirke-stat problemet, som kolonisituationen gav anledning til, dels at fremdrage de træk, som er specielle for den koloniale situation. Studiet får herved i to henseender et generaliserende og komparativt sigte. For det første fastholdes det som en grundlæggende tese, at et case study fra Uganda vil vise sig at være af generel værdi for kolonitidens Afrika som helhed, både hvad angår problemformulering, metodisk tilgang og konkret analyse af kirke-stat-forholdet. For det andet arbejdes der ud fra den antagelse, at kolonisituationen er sammenlignelig med mere traditionelle analyser af kirke-stat forholdet, og at den netop kan tjene til at udvikle kirke-stat problematikken gennem tilføjelsen af en ny og hidtil upåagtet dimension.

Kolonisituationens kirke-stat problem udmærker sig i særlig grad ved sin kompleksitet og dynamiske karakter. Der er inden for begge sfærer tale om to europæiske aktører, der optræder samtidig i Afrika. Selv om de forfølger hver sit mål, henholdsvis stat- og kirkeopbygning, kan de ikke optræde uafhængigt af hinanden, og der er derfor et stadigt behov for at udforme og definere forholdet mellem dem, ikke mindst i pionerfasen, hvor der findes meget få eller slet ingen regler for deres indbyrdes adfærd. Samtidig er såvel kolonisitaten som missionen på den ene side underordnet hjemlige myndigheder, henholdsvis regering og missionsselskab, og på den anden side må der tages hensyn til de forskellige afrikanske organer, hvad enten det er de eksisterende afrikanske politiske systemer eller den afrikanske kirke, som det er den kristne missions mål at opbygge. Man er derfor nødsaget til inden for begge sfærer at arbejde med et trestrenget, hierarkisk system af organer, hvilket i sig selv nødvendiggør, at et stort antal variable inddrages i studiet. Dette tjener også til at forklare, at afhandlingens titel er udvidet til at være: mission, kirke og stat i kolonitidens Uganda.

Det store antal variable og problemstillingens kompleksitet har nødvendiggjort dels en præcisering af det niveau, undersøgelsen foregår på, dels en afgrænsning og strukturering af analysen gennem den metodiske tilgang. Hvad det første angår, begrænser analysen sig konsekvent til det institutionelle aspekt af kirke-stat-forbindelsen og udelukker andre, lige så relevante dele af kristendommens politiske dimension. Da der ikke fra andre studier kan overtages et egnet begrebsapparat, og da samtidig materialets omfang nødvendiggør et udvælgende og organiserende princip, anskues kirke-stat problemet – efter inspiration fra især den politiske videnskab – i en systemteoretisk ramme, således som den specielt er udformet i traditionen fra David Easton. Den koloniale stat med dens forskellige strukturer og autoriteter defineres som et politisk system, til hvis omgivelser mission og kirke hører. Den kirkelige sfære kan endda opfattes som en interessegruppe, der artikulerer sine interesser og krav til det politiske system. Netop disse input bliver studiets væsentligste objekt, og de opdeles efter den Easton'ske tradition i tre kategorier, der samtidig bestemmer afhandlingens disposition: den materielle basis for kirke-stat relationerne, direkte input og indirekte input.

Det skal understreges, at der er tale om en strukturerende og problemformulerende analysemodel. Afhandlingen bevarer stadig karakteren af et historisk case study, hvor de anvendte teorier har en instrumental of interpreterende funktion. Den instrumentale funktion træder ikke mindst frem i organiseringen af det omfattende dokumentariske kildemateriale, der ligger til grund for afhandlingen, og som for størstedelens vedkommende er indsamlet i Uganda og suppleret med materiale fra England.

Del II: Den formative period, 1890–1900

Der gives en kort introduktion til scenariet i Uganda i 1890. Som det mest karakteristiske træk fremhæves eksistensen af tre religiøse partier: protestanter, katolikker og muslimer. Disse udgør det væsentligste strukturerende princip i samfundet, hvorigennem al politisk aktivitet foregår og de forskellige goder fordeles. Desuden introduceres de to europæiske aktørgrupper: dels repræsentanter for det engelske kolonisystem, dels missionærer fra det anglikanske missionsselskab Church Missionary Society (CMS). Det bemærkes, at afhandlingen kun i begrænset omfang inddrager den tilsvarende katolske mission.

Den formative periode spænder over kolonialismens første manifestationer: fra kompagnistyre via den formelle etablering af officielt kolonistyre frem til indgåelsen af Uganda Agreement i 1900, der formaliserer en konstitutionel, politisk og økonomisk ordning. Denne aftale omfatter alene kongedømmet Buganda, den største provins inden for Protektoratet, og giver det en særstilling, som er medvirkende til den efterfølgende manglende balance i Protektoratet og til udviklingen af en art Buganda-syndrom i relation til andre områder, der først senere inddrages i Protektoratet Uganda.

Det er tesen i dette afsnit, at de fleste af de problemer, som siden konstituerer forholdet mellem kirke og stat, fremstår allerede i denne periode. Med henblik på at identificere disse problemer og karakterisere udviklingen i forholdet mellem mission, kirke og stat i perioden anvendes begrebet religionsfrihed som analytisk instrument. Religionsfrihedens omfang og indhold var i sig selv en væsentlig faktor i udviklingen, ikke mindst under Frederick Lugard's virke i Uganda fra periodens begyndelse. De løsninger, der blev forsøgt, afspejler, at der gennem 1890'erne skete en stigende politisering af religion, hvilket manifesterede sig i, at kolonistyret nødtvungent måtte anerkende de tre religiøse partier (protestanter, katolikker og muslimer) som den nødvendige forudsætning for sin politik. Dette rejste straks problemet om regeringens neutralitet, ikke mindst i relation til de to kristne grupper. På dette punkt peger undersøgelsen på et protestantisk hegemoni, foranlediget af det nationale, konfessionelle og politiske fællesskab mellem koloniregering og mission. På den anden side prøver kolonistyret bevidst at begrænse missionens rettigheder, ikke mindst hvad angår statsstøtte i form af koncessioner og specielt jordtilliggender, som de lokale høvdinge stillede til rådighed for det protestantiske arbejde som gaver. Missionen måtte således anerkende den sekulære myndigheds supremat og opnåede ikke den autonome status for sig selv eller for den afrikanske kirke, som man havde arbejdet for.

Del III: Den materielle basis for kirke-stat relationerne: jord og arbejde

I årene efter 1900 stod det klart for såvel koloniregeringen som missionen, at jord var det største økonomiske aktiv i det afrikanske samfund. Derfor blev spørgsmålet om ejendomsret til jord og ikke mindst definitionen heraf det væsentligste politiske spørgsmål i årene frem til 1925 (kap. 9–12). Imidlertid blev det hurtigt klart, at jordens værdi alene fremkom gennem de mennesker, der boede på jorden, og under forudsætning af, at der med ejendomsretten fulgte rådighed over en del af deres arbejdskraft. Herved bliver det klart, at der ikke primært er tale om en europæisk defineret ejendomsret, hvor købs- og salgsværdien er afgørende, men derimod om et afrikansk ejendomsforhold, hvori mennesker og arbejdskraft indgår.

Da den engelske mission som sit primære mål arbejdede for at opbygge en selvunderholdende afrikansk kirke, blev det af afgørende betydning at sikre, at den nye kirke fik rådighed over så megen jord som muligt på de bedst mulige betingelser. Dette mål gav i årenes løb anledning til en intens statsrelateret aktivitet. Alene af den grund udgør denne del af analysen afhandlingens tyngdepunkt, men samtidig findes der her et væsentligt materiale både til at aflæse de to aktørers respektive mål og til at måle udviklingen i deres indbyrdes forhold.

I første række søgte missionen at opnå rådighed over så store landområder som muligt og allierede sig herunder med de afrikanske ledere, høvdingene, idet man forsvarede deres ret til frit at disponere over jord inden for deres jurisdiktion, herunder at give den som gave til kirken. I denne forbindelse argumenterede missionen stærkt for, at jorden alene tilhørte den afrikanske kirke, og at der derfor ikke kunne være tale om en 'fremmedgørelse' (alienation) af jorden, idet denne netop tilhørte en afrikansk institution og ikke et europæisk organ som missionen. Af samme grund krævede man også høvdingerettigheder over jorden, d.v.s. ret til at råde over arbejdskraften på traditionel vis. Missionen var dog ikke ganske konsekvent i sin argumentation, idet man også arbejdede med et europæisk ejendomsbegreb og krævede ret til at anlægge plantager og ret til videreudlejning.

Regeringen havde derimod som sit afgørende mål at begrænse kirkens rådighedsret over jord. Det manifesterede sig i en håndfast begrænsning af omfang og udnyttelse, idet man ønskede både at begrænse de økonomiske tilskud, som jordtilliggender var udtryk for, og at hindre, at kirken kunne udvikle sig til en økonomisk magtfaktor i samfundet. Samtidig var det regeringens politik ikke at give den afrikanske kirke status som en afrikansk institution. En sådan anerkendelse ville have indebåret risikoen for, at beboerne på kirkens jord faldt uden for de afrikanske høvdinges jurisdiktion, det centrale element i det koloniale, bureaukratiske system. Koloniregeringen arbejdede ikke med nogen distinktion mellem mission og kirke og fastholdt derfor, at de rettigheder, der var forbundet med rådighed over jord, svarede til dem, som andre ikke-afrikanere havde.

Missionen vandt således ikke genklang for sit synspunkt, at det samfundsrelaterede arbejde til fordel for afrikanerne, ikke mindst inden for uddannelsesområdet, begrundede tildelingen af store jordområder. Tværtimod skete der gennem de første to årtier af 2o. årh. en stramning af regeringens politik, hvilket skal ses i sammenhæng med udbygningen af det koloniale, administrative system, der levner mindre råderum såvel for de afrikanske ledere som for de kirkelige organer. Alt i alt viser denne del af undersøgelsen, at missionens og kirkens arbejdsbetingelser er stærkt afhængige af den økonomiske, sociale og politiske udvikling i det afrikanske samfund og underkastet de skiftende konjunkturer.

Del IV: Direkte input: kirkens krav til den koloniale stat

Denne del af undersøgelsen omhandler de forventninger og krav, som mission og kirke direkte rettede til det politiske system. En undersøgelse af en række af disse krav og statens reaktion herpå giver svar på spørgsmålet om den politiske rolle, kirkeinstitutionen formåede at spille, og videre i hvilken grad missionen var i stand til at influere, modificere eller direkte hindre en bestemt politik.

Tæt forbundet med spørgsmålet om rådighed over afrikansk arbejdskraft er problematikken omkring *tvangsarbejde* (kap. 13). Når folk var forpligtet til arbejdsydelser over for deres egne traditionelle ledere og siden til kolonimagten, og når arbejde kunne erstatte skattebetaling eller afgift på jord, involverede det uundgåeligt en stillingtagen til tvangsarbejde, herunder om traditionelle arbejdsydelser kan betragtes som sådan. Ved periodens begyndelse førte den daværende biskop, A. R. Tucker, en hårdnakket kampagne mod enhver form for tvangsarbejde, hvorunder han også inddrog humanitære organisationer i England. Hans indsats undermineredes i nogen grad af, at missionen samtidig ikke undså sig for at drage nytte af tvangsarbejdet. Hertil kommer, at hans efterfølger, J. J. Willis, afgørende ændrede kurs. Dels anmodede han om en udvidet kvote af tvangsarbejde, dels advarede han mod en ændring i regeringens politik, der betød en begrænsning af de arbejdsforpligtelser, som bønderne kunne pålægges. Willis lagde sig tættere op ad koloniregeringen end forgængeren, og han tillagde ikke varetagelsen af afrikanske interesser den samme prioritet. Den underliggende bevæggrund viser sig dog at være en stigende afhængighed af de ressourcer, som tvangsarbejde repræsenterer, ikke mindst på baggrund af den stadige udvidelse af arbejdet inden for uddannelsessektoren, som fandt sted i det andet tiår af århundredet.

Netop på *uddannelsesområdet* (kap. 15) kommer denne stigende afhængighed endnu tydeligere frem. Omkring århundredskiftet satte CMS i Uganda stærkt ind på at opnå et uddannelsesmæssigt monopol, således at statens indsats begrænsedes til at yde tilskud. Koloniregeringen accepterede med glæde denne ordning, der bestod frem til slutningen af 1.verdenskrig. Missionen så det som en meget væsentlig opgave at uddanne ledere til både stat og kirke, og statstilskuddene muliggjorde tillige et samlet højere aktivitetsniveau, end hvis man havde været henvist til egne midler.

Efter første verdenskrig begyndte den hidtidige monopolstilling at udhules på grund af stigende skepsis fra koloniembedsmænd, voksende tvivl om missionens kapacitet fra unge afrikanere og ikke mindst CMS' finansielle krise, der medførte nedskæringer i Uganda. Koloniadministrationen overtog selv den videregående tekniske uddannelse og begyndte at fastlægge en egentlig uddannelsespolitik. Et så radikalt skridt som at starte et sekulært skolesystem, evt. ved at nationalisere missionens skoler, veg man dog tilbage for på grund af stærk pression fra missionscirkler såvel i Uganda som i England og på grund af de store investeringer, som ville have været nødvendige. Samtidig trak ønsket om kontrol af den unge generation i retning af fortsat samarbejde med missionen på grund af dennes moralske og karakterdannende indflydelse. Resultatet blev, at der i 1924 blev indgået en ny aftale om fortsat samarbejde på uddannelsesområdet. Aftalen bar dog stærkt præg af, at missionen nu var i defensiven. Parallelt med øget statsstøtte blev regeringskontrollen langt stærkere såvel organisatorisk som hvad angår indhold og kvalitet af undervisningen.

Uddannelsessektoren, der indebærer et tæt samarbejde mellem stat og kirke og en høj grad af statsstøtte for en del af missionens arbejde, udgør et velegnet grundlag for at vurdere den virkning, som et engagement med staten kunne have på mission og kirke. For det første opstår der for mission og kirke en paradoks-situation. Det viste sig umuligt for kirken som oprindelig planlagt at rekruttere de bedst uddannede, som var produkter af missionens eget apparat. De søgte i stedet til koloniadministrationen eller den lokale afrikanske administration. Der fremkom således en uddannelsesmæssig og økonomisk kløft mellem de afrikanske ledere i stat og kirke. En væsentlig årsag hertil var den ringe betaling, som kirken kunne tilbyde på grund af princippet om selvunderhold. Konsekvensen blev en ubestemt udsættelse af afrikaniseringen af kirkens ledelse, fordi der ikke var kvalificerede folk, og dermed en udsættelse af den selvstændiggørelse af kirken, som var missionsarbejdets primære mål.

For det andet bevirker statsstøtten en manglende balance mellem de to sektorer af missionsarbejdet, idet de køres efter forskellige principper. Missionen tilpasser i nogen grad sit arbejde efter, hvor støtten kan hentes, d.v.s. inden for uddannelsessektoren, mens det pastorale arbejde fortsat er undergivet selvunderholdets princip. Da statsstøtten ligesom i spørgsmålet om jord gives til det europæiske organ, sker der en forvridning af forholdet mellem mission og kirke, hvilket også udsætter realiseringen af målsætningen om kirkens selvstændighed. Alt i alt medfører samarbejdet om skolerne en formindskelse af missionens handlefrihed og en øget afhængighed af staten, der igen åbner for en statslig indflydelse på arbejdet. Konklusionen bliver, at samtidig med at missionen økonomisk og ideologisk gennem årene rykker tættere på kolonistaten, svækkes dens position, fordi den ikke har ressourcer til at køre en sekulær aktivitet ud over pioner-stadiet.

De to andre områder, der undersøges under afsnittet direkte input, har overvejende karakter af forventninger til koloniregeringen og ønsket om at influere den langsigtede politik i en kristen og en for kirken gunstig retning. Under begrebet *en kristen nation* (kap. 16) diskuteres såvel missionens krav til koloniregeringen om at basere samfundsudviklingen på kristne værdier som statens villighed til at lade sin politik lede af kristne principper. Som grundlag for denne del af undersøgelsen benyttes lovgivningsprocessen, specielt familieområdet og herindenfor ægteskabslovgivningen. Det kan konstateres, at staten gav primat til det kristne, monogame ægteskab, administreret af kirken. Derimod blev status for og lovligheden af polygame ægteskaber, indgået efter traditionelle regler, et kontroversielt punkt. Spørgsmålet kompliceredes af, at det i praksis viste sig vanskeligt at trække grænsen mellem kristne ægteskaber og traditionelle ægteskaber, idet folk hyppigt legitimerede deres ægteskaber ud fra begge former eller jævnligt ønskede at konvertere fra det ene til det andet. Koloniadministrationen ville ikke følge kravet om at lovgive mod polygame ægteskaber, både fordi man frygtede et socialt opbrud i samfundet, og fordi man fastholdt princippet om, at lovgivningen skal følge, ikke lede udviklingen og ikke anvendes som tvangsmiddel.

Denne holdning fik i 1918 den protestantiske biskop til sammen med sine to katolske kolleger at beskylde koloniregeringen for at krybe i ly bag en velvillig neutralitet og svigte sin forpligtelse som en kristen regering i en kristen nation til at fremme en kristen moral i samfundet. Trods dette angreb fastholdt regeringen, at der er og bør være forskel på civil lov og kristen lov, og at statsapparatet ikke kan bruges til at fremme specielt kristne doktriner. Nok vedkender kolonistaten sig målsætningen om en kristen nation, men den arbejdede for det ud fra en anden definition end missionerne. Dens interesse lå i at civilisere det afrikanske samfund frem for direkte at kristianisere det.

I undersøgelsen af spørgsmålet om *en kristen stat* (kap. 17) drejer det sig ikke om, at staten gennem sin forfatning erklærer sig for kristen of anerkender en bestemt kirke som statskirke. Begrebet en kristen stat omhandler her dels spørgsmålet om kristianisering af institutioner inden for det politiske system, hvorved kristendommens og især den protestantiske kirkes specielle status kan måles, dels hvilke institutionaliserede forbindelser der eksisterede mellem staten og kirken, idet kirken herigennem kunne have en platform til at øve indflydelse på det politiske system. For at undersøge disse to aspekter af begrebet en kristen stat sondres mellem den koloniale stat og de afrikanske politiske systemer.

Hvad den første angår, realiseres ingen af de nævnte muligheder. Derimod har det vist sig frugtbart at indføre begrebet konsultativ status, der omfatter dels den direkte adgang til kolonistatens beslutningstagere med henblik på at udtale sig om aktuelle spørgsmål, dels rollen som advokat for afrikanske interesser i kraft af en formidlerstilling mellem dem, der regerer, og dem, der bliver regeret. Undersøgelsen viser, at missionen på disse punkter opnår en semi-officiel status, der rækker ud over, hvad man almindeligvis forbinder med en interessegruppe. Alligevel viser det sig vanskeligt at finde den rette balance i denne form for politisk rolle, ikke mindst når missionen går i brechen for afrikanske interesser. På den anden side optræder missionen hele tiden på det koloniale systems præmisser og sætter ikke spørgsmålstegn ved dette. Derfor er hele denne position undergivet de samme skiftende konjunkturer, som allerede er nævnt i tidligere sammenhænge, og man kan gennem årene registere en indsnævring af den konsultative aktivitet og en bevægelse fra en kritiserende til en legitimerende rolle.

I relation til de afrikanske politiske systemer er graden af kristianisering/ protestantisering helt anderledes markant. Alle fire konger i det sydlige Uganda var protestanter efter en bevidst indsats fra CMS–missionen. Ikke mindst markeredes det ved enhver given lejlighed, at Kabaka'en af Buganda var en kristen konge i et kristent land. I endnu højere grad blev høvdingeinstitutionen et næsten kristent embede. Talmateriale fra de forskellige distrikter viser klart, at langt de fleste høvdinge var kristne, og blandt disse udgjorde protestanterne den overvældende majoritet. Den protestantiske missions oprindelige satsen på de afrikanske ledere havde således båret frugt, og koloniregeringen formåede ikke at bryde den protestantiske inerti, men måtte begrænse sig til at sikre status quo i det etablerede, konfessionelle partisystem. Det betød også at regeringen måtte leve med et område, hvor den religiøse faktor gang på gang influerede politik.

Protestantiseringen af høvdingeembedet manifesterede sig tydeligt i personlige forbindelseslinier mellem de afrikanske politiske systemer og kirken og i en direkte protestantisk brug af afrikanske politiske institutioner. Det var et led i den anglikanske tradition at have læge medlemmer af kirkens styrende organer, og kirkens pyramidalske opbygning og vidtstrakte brug af komité-princippet frembød store muligheder for afrikanske politiske ledere til at spille en prominent rolle som lægmænd i kirkens styrende organer. En gennemgang af disse organers sammensætning viser et betydeligt kontingent af høvdinge, og selv kongerne er i mange tilfælde medlemmer. Der er således en betydelig personlig overlapning i lederskabet inden for kirken og de afrikanske politiske systemer, hvilket foruden klare politiske fordele, som har vist sig i jord- og lovgivningsspørgsmål, medførte en betydelig økonomisk afhængighed af høvdingene og gjorde kirken til offer for den begyndende klassedannelse i samfundet. Samtidig bidrog dette til at forstærke modsætningen mellem læg og geistlig, som allerede eksisterede på grund af den tidligere nævnte forskel i uddannelse og aflønning. Høvdingeindflydelsen medførte samtidig en Buganda-dominans inden for kirken, der herved blev genstand for det dybtliggende modsætningsforhold mellem Buganda og resten af Protektoratet. I det hele taget betød alliancen med den traditionelle ledergruppe, at såvel mission som kirke blev bundet til en politisk ideologi og en politisk struktur, som i stigende grad blev genstand for kritik og opposition.

Del V: Indirekte input: parallelisme og reciprocitet i forholdet mellem kirke og stat

Netop den just omtalte sammenhæng mellem kirken og det omgivende samfund leder frem til en særlig dimension i forholdet mellem kirke og stat, som her betegnes som indirekte eller tavse input. Herved forstås, at selv i tilfælde, hvor der ikke kan tales om direkte krav til det politiske system, er de to systemer i kolonisituationen så tæt forbundne, at det ene ikke kan være uanfægtet af det andets eksistens og handlinger, hvorfor det bliver nødvendigt med et vist mål af koordination og gensidig tilpasning. Det bliver derfor et mål for undersøgelsen at analysere karakteren af den gensidige påvirkning og fremdrage de virkninger, den måtte have på de to aktører og forholdet mellem dem. Et stort antal emneoråder falder inden for denne kategori, og fem er blevet udvalgt til nærmere undersøgelse under hensyntagen til deres vidergående politiske betydning og deres indflydelse på kirke-stat forholdet.

Med hensyn til *den administrative inddeling af Protektoratet* (kap. 18) viser der sig en høj grad af parallelitet mellem de to parter, idet der fra begge sider tages store hensyn til de oprindelige etniske opdelinger. Dette fører videre til en undersøgelse af *spørgsmålet om centralisering versus decentralisering* inden for de to områder (kap. 19). Oprindeligt førte begge en centraliseringspolitik, væsentligst gennem brug af Buganda-modellen, hvad angår sprog, lokalt ansatte og administrativ praksis. Imidlertid viste de centrifugale kræfter med udgangspunkt i de etniske grupper sig for stærke til at gennemføre en integrationspolitik med brug af Buganda-formelen. Mens koloniregeringen accepterede en decentral politik, søgte kirken gennem den organisatoriske opbygning at tilvejebringe en ny formel for en integrationspolitik med det formål at skabe en national kirke, der overvandt den etniske opdeling. Missionen fandt her, at den også udøvede en politisk virksomhed, som staten forsømte. Kirken havde dog ikke kapacitet til alene at gennemføre sin integrationspolitik, idet modsætningerne i det omgivende samfund klart slog igennem inden for kirkens egne vægge.

Dette sidste leder til en undersøgelse af den måde, hvorpå henholdsvis koloniadministrationen og missionen definerede *forholdet til deres respektive afrikanske organer*, idet der her findes en slående mangel på parallelisme (kap. 20).

Hvor koloniadministrationen udgjorde den eneste landsdækkende struktur, og de enkelte afrikanske enheder var begrænset til distriktsniveau, tilstræbtes der en integration af mission og kirke, idet målet var at gøre kirken selvstændig og missionen overflødig. Koloniregeringen så ved flere lejligheder med nogen bekymring på denne politik, ikke mindst på grund af de afrikanske avancementsmuligheder og vanskeligheden ved at kontrollere afrikanske oppositionelle kræfter. Regeringen greb endda ind for at standse en accelerering af udviklingen, men beroligede sig i øvrigt med, at effekten af missionens forskellige politik var meget begrænset. De europæiske missionærer sad stadig på alle nøgleposter, og som tidligere påpeget var der ringe mulighed for en afrikaniseringsproces. Hertil kommer, at alliancen mellem missionen og høvdingene var så velfungerende, at den kun levnede ringe plads for de afrikanske præsters overtagelse aft lederfunktionerne. I praksis var der således udmærket parallelisme mellem den politiske og kirkelige sfære.

Spørgsmålet om indførelsen af *et nationalsprog i Uganda* (kap. 21) repræsenterer derimod et område, hvor missionen havde mulighed for at føre sin politik igennem, mens regeringen forholdt sig afventende og rede til at acceptere resultatet. Missionens mål var at fremme luganda (sproget i Buganda) som enhedsprog gennem brug af det i kirke og skole. Bestræbelserne svækkedes imidlertid af, at der som resultat af lokale selvstændighedsønsker og anti-Buganda følelser måtte gives tilladelse til brug af forskellige lokalsprog inden for kirken, eksempelvis ved bibeloversættelser. Denne uklarhed i sprogpolitikken fik regeringen til at sætte spørgsmålstegn ved tilrådeligheden af at indrette sin egen politik efter missionens. I stedet var der bestræbelser for at gøre swahili til nationalsproget, hvilket missionen, stærkt støttet af Buganda, gik imod på grund af en mulig muslimsk indflydelse. Sprogpolitikken blev således fanget mellem på den ene side en anti-Buganda stemning, der gjorde det umuligt for missionen at vinde støtte for luganda, og på den anden side en anti-muslimsk stemning, der umuliggjorde fremgang for swahili. Skolernes sprogundervisning blev det område, hvor kampen især kom til udtryk, og resultatet blev nærmest uafgjort, idet de to parter blev enige om en differentieret løsning, der tillod anvendelsen af flere sprog. Udfaldet afspejler et eksempel på en blokerende balance mellem mission og koloniregering, idet ingen af dem kunne føre sin egen politik igennem, men alene blokere modpartens.

Bag luganda-swahili kontroversen lå det problem, der mere end noget andet var afgørende for udviklingen i kirke og stat: *Buganda's rolle* (kap. 22). Et 'Buganda-syndrom' karakteriserede gennem årene missionens politik, og dens pro-Buganda-holdning bevirkede, at kirken i langt højere grad end det politiske system blev valplads for de stærke anti-Buganda følelser, der herskede i den øvrige del af Protektoratet. Et særligt stridspunkt var spørgsmålet om Buganda personel, som både stat og kirke anvendte i hele Protektoratet. Mens der efterhånden blandt koloniembedsmænd bredte sig en stigende skepsis over for Buganda og dets dominerende position, spillede Buganda-faktoren stadig en afgørende rolle i kirken. Kontroversen omkring swahili cementerede båndene mellem missionen og Buganda, der yderligere forstærkedes af Ganda-ledernes økonomiske og organisatoriske position inden for kirken. Denne blev således i særlig grad offer for de etniske modsætninger i samfundet og tjente endda til at gøre situationen lettere for koloniadministrationen.

Netop sidstnævnte punkt leder frem til en sammenfattende diskussion af hovedtema'et i denne sektion, *den etniske faktors betydning* (kap. 23). Kirken bidrog selv gennem sin organisatoriske opbygning, gennem sin brug af de lokale sprog og ved inden for sine rammer at konfrontere grupperne med hinanden og specielt med Buganda til at fremme den etniske bevidstgørelse og til at give de etniske grupper en politisk funktion. Kirken blev selv en integreret del af det etnisk opdelte samfund, således at den ikke kunne bidrage til at neutralisere betydningen af den etniske faktor hverken inden for sine egne rammer eller i relation til kolonistaten.

Del VI: Opsummering og konklusioner omkring kirke-stat-forholdet i en kolonisituation

I slutningsafsnittet drøftes først den kirkelige sektors kapacitet til at handle i relation til staten (kap. 24). Med hensyn til den nyetablerede afrikanske kirke reduceres dens kapacitet af de forskelligartede bindinger til det afrikanske politiske system. På samme vis virker også den tætte relation til missionen begrænsende, og missionen fremtræder derfor som den ledende aktør i relation til kolonistaten. Den afrikanske kirkes organisatoriske og funktionelle autonomi var således begrænset af såvel interne som eksterne faktorer.

I henseende til missionen anskues dens rolle først ud fra en vurdering af, i hvor høj grad det lykkedes at realisere dens vigtigste målsætning, en anerkendt og legaliseret status for den afrikanske kirke. Især undersøgelsen af jordproblematikken og uddannelsessektoren har vist, at missionen på dette felt opnår en ringe grad af målopfyldelse. Årsagerne hertil må søges i en række faktorer, der hver for sig bidrager til at svække missionens kapacitet i dens handlen over for staten, herunder ikke mindst svigtende økonomiske ressourcer. Trods dette udgjorde missionen den eneste alternative organisation i samfundet ved siden af kolonistaten, og CMS-missionen distancerede sig tilstrækkeligt fra staten til at være i stand til at udfordre den på trods af de skiftende konjunkturer.

For at komplettere billedet er det lige så nødvendigt at gøre status for den anden hovedaktør i kirke-stat-forholdet, koloniregeringen. Dette gøres gennem en undersøgelse af dens religionspolitik (kap. 25). Bortset fra en sikring af individuelle rettigheder spillede den traditionelle afrikanske religion og islam en ringe rolle i religionspolitikken. Mod slutningen af perioden var der nogle bestræbelser for at skabe mere lighed for muslimerne, men det ændrer ikke ved det faktum, at koloniregeringen førte en klar pro-kristen politik, hvilket udmøntede sig i forskellige privilegier og koncessioner. Dette rejser spørgsmålet om neutralitet og tolerance i regeringens politik, ikke mindst i lyset af den indbyggede konflikt mellem individuelle rettigheder og traditionelle forpligtelser, som meget let opstod i forbindelse med høvdingenes ret til at disponere over deres undersåtters arbejde, som kunne skænkes til religiøse formål. Koloniregeringen måtte her erkende, at den stod for tolerance, men at den ikke kunne praktisere neutralitet, når den støttede udbredelsen af kristne, civiliserende normer i samfundet. Spørgsmålet blev i højere grad at drage grænsen for den aktive støtte for ikke helt at underminere tolerance-elementet. End ikke i spørgsmålet om embedsbesættelser praktiseredes neutralitet, idet høvdingeinstitionen i overvejende grad var forbundet med kristendommen.

Samtidig afslørede regeringens holdning til de to kristne konfessioner en anden form for ulighed. Mens man praktiserede lighed i henseende til tildeling af jord og statsstøtte til skolerne, accepteredes på andre områder et klart protestantisk hegemoni, ikke mindst i forbindelse med høvdingeinstitutionen, hvor katolik-kerne var i en klar minoritetsstilling. Imidlertid var det et gennemgående træk i kolonipolitikken, at kolonistaten ved at sikre gode arbejdsbetingelser for de kristne missioner så det som sin opgave at fremme kristendommen med dens civiliserende indflydelse og dermed gradvis bane vej for en kristen nation. Kolonistaten tolker dog mål og midler på en mindre specifik kristen måde end missionen. Nok ligger statens politik inden for en kristen dimension, men den når i sit engagement og i sin støtte til fremme af kristne normer næppe længere end til, hvad der med en amerikansk terminologi kan rummes inden for begrebet 'civil religion', som udtrykker statens positive religiøse interesse med fremhævelse af de utilitaristiske og funktionelle aspekter af religion.

Afslutningsvis (kap. 26) gives en sammenfattende karakteristik af forholdet mellem mission, kirke og stat gennem anvendelse af begreber og kategorier almindeligvis anvendt i studier af kirke-stat problematikken. Mission og kirke bidrog til det politiske systems fortsatte eksistens og havde således en statsbe-kræftende funktion. Missionen stillede ikke spørgsmål ved den koloniale stats eksistens, men accepterede det koloniale system som basis for sine aktiviteter. Når der blev fremført kritik, gik den overvejende på at hindre misbrug og sikre afrikanske interesser. Vurderes udviklingen i et tidsperspektiv, er tendensen, at staten bliver den stærkere partner, mens missionen kommer i defensiven og får vanskeligere ved at spille sin kritiske rolle. I forbindelse med dette dynamiske aspekt i forholdet mellem mission, kirke og stat indføres begrebet sekularisering, og det diskuteres, om ændringerne i forholdet kan betegnes som en sekularise-ringsproces. Det konkluderes, at der på visse områder kan tales om en sekularise-ringsproces, men at den væsentlige ændring består i en styrkelse af statens kontrollerende funktion.

Dette fører videre til en drøftelse af missionens og kirkens funktion inden for den koloniale stat. I almindelighed havde missionen en positiv holdning over for koloniregeringen og udøvede som sådan både en legitimerende og støttende funktion, ikke mindst gennem uddannelsessystemet. Dette peger igen på den instrumentale funktion, som missionen havde ved at uddanne kommende ledere, ved at fremme disciplin og moral i samfundet og ved at kontrollere fremkomsten af en mere kritisk afrikansk opinion.

Nærværende analytiske apparat tillader næppe videregående tolkninger af missionens og kirkens rolle inden for det koloniale system, men det understreges, at der ved brug af andre analysemåder, inspireret af nyere kolonialisme- og imperialismeteorier, fremkommer mere kvalitative tolkninger af specielt mis-sionens rolle. Den ses som medvirkende til opkomsten af en gruppe af kollabo-ratører og af et klasseopdelt samfund, der er afgørende forudsætninger for kolonial kontrol og udbytning. I videre forstand er missionen medansvarlig for koloni-statens fortsatte beståen og for dens satellit-position i relation til metropolens økonomi.

Hvis man imidlertid som vurderingsgrundlag vælger missionens egen selvfor-ståelse af sin rolle i kolonistaten, ser man, at den ud fra et fælles værdisystem og på grund af de goder, som kolonistaten bragte med sig, orienterede sig i retning af et samarbejde. Dog ligger der her et dilemma for missionen: skulle den give prioritet til sin autonomi og muligheden for at spille en kritisk rolle, eller skulle den i højere grad satse på sin legitimerende rolle? Af såvel interne som eksterne grunde valgte missionen samarbejdslinien, der imidlertid gennem årene skabte afhængighed of udhulede den selvstændige politske rolle, som missionen var i stand til at spille. Bag dette valg kan fremdrages nogle karakteristiske determinanter og mekanismer, som har almen gyldighed for kirke-stat problematikken.

Ved siden af en sådan generaliserende tolkning, der understreger, at kirke-stat-problemet i en kolonisituation ikke udgør en kategori for sig selv, er der grund til at fremdrage de specielle faktorer, som indgår i en kolonisituation med dens specielle afrikanske baggrund. Der må på begge sider arbejdes med en tredelt struktur, som på den ene side nødvendiggør inddragelse af de øverste organer i Europa og på den anden side tager hensyn til de specielle afrikanske strukturer og reaktioner, herunder ikke mindst at der i den afrikanske sammenhæng ikke er tale om en stat eller nation i gængs forstand. Hertil kommer, at de to europæiske organer, koloniregering og mission, optræder i et parlamentarisk vacuum, hvorved en organisation som missionen får en særlig status med direkte adgang til koloniregeringen uden om de bindinger, der findes i andre former for politisk system. Der er således i kolonisituationen en lang række særlige variable, som der i en analyse må tages hensyn til, og som tjener til at understrege, at kirke-stat problemet i en kolonisituation er særlig komplekst.

Notes

Abbreviations

Ag.	Acting
Arch.	Archives
Ch. of Ug.	Church of Uganda
CMS	Church Missionary Society
CO	Colonial Office
DC	District Commissioner
Diary I, II, III	Diaries of Lord Lugard, vols. I–III
ESA	Entebbe Secretariat Archives
FO	Foreign Office
FOCP	Foreign Office Confidential Print
IBEA Co.	Imperial British East Africa Company
LO	Land Officer
MP	Minute Paper
MUL	Makerere University Library
NAC	Native Anglican Church
PC	Provincial Commissioner
PP	Parliamentary Paper
PRO	Public Record Office, London
Rs	Rupees
SMP	Secretariat Minute Paper
TOL	Temporary Occupation Licence
WF	White Fathers

Part I   Introduction

1 General introduction

1 Archdeacon R.H. Walker to his brother, 31 July 1898, Walker Papers, CMS Arch.

2 See the three Ugandan bishops' joint letter to the Governor, 19 April 1918, and the colonial officials' comments, in SMP 5368, ESA. See also below, p.288ff.

3 See the emphasis on applicability of traditional or universal concepts in the study of religion and politics in Africa in Victor C. Ferkiss (1967), p.1 See also Richard Gray (1978), pp.90ff.

4 Re conceptual framework developed here see Talcott Parsons (1960), ch. 10.

5 On this whole conceptual framework see in particular Kathleen Lockard (1974, unpubl. thesis) and Ferkiss (1967); cf. also H.B. Hansen (1979, conference paper).

6 cf. Jarle Simensen's remarks about the tyranny of the source material; Simensen (1970), section 13.

7 M. Louise Pirouet (1978); A.D. Tom Tuma (1973, unpubl. thesis), J.M. Waliggo (1976, unpubl. thesis); cf. also comparative study by A. Hastings (1969). A number of the authors mentioned in this chapter have contributed to the useful collection, 'A Century of Christianity in Uganda, 1877–1977', edited by Tom Tuma and Phares Mutibwa, and publ. in connection with the centenary celebrations of the Church of Uganda in 1977.

8 For this point of view see J.F.A. Ajayi & E.A. Ayandele (1969), pp. 90ff. See also Gray (1968).

9 cf. Roland Oliver (1968) and Simensen (1970). For a recent comment on the controversial question of dealing with 'Whites in Africa', see Terence Ranger (1979). See also Donald Denoon & Adam Kuper (1970).

10 For a related argument see Gray (1968), T.O. Beidelman (1974), and John McCracken (1977), pp. viiff.

11 Beidelman (1974), p. 235.

12 Andrew Porter has in recent works (1976 and 1977) discussed the socio-political consequences of the evangelical tradition. In a similar way F. Birkeli (1952) had earlier explained the missionaries' differing approaches to the colonial political system by reference to their confessional traits.

13 cf. D.A. Low & R.C. Pratt (1960); and Vincent Harlow & E.M. Chilver (1965).

14 See special issue of *Journal of African History* 19, 1, 1978, on World War I and Africa, in particular the Introduction.

15 The most accessible examples can be found in the reports from two conferences on Christianity in Africa held in 1965 and 1975. See C.G. Baëta (1968) and E. Fashole-Luke, R. Gray, A. Hastings & G. Tasie (1978).

16 Fridtjov Birkeli (1952), Introduction on problems and method (English summary, pp.465ff). This book has suffered from appearing only in Norwegian.

17 D.A. Low (1957a, unpubl. thesis), later expanded in Low (1968) and Low (1971a).

18 In particular F.B. Welbourn (1965) and Kathleen Lockard (1974, unpubl. thesis). See also Appendix 2 below.

19 The employment of systems analysis has been inspired by Ole Karup Pedersen (1970), pp.22ff. In developing the analytical approach I have consulted D. Easton (1965a and b) and E. Rasmussen (1971), chs. 3 and 4. The use of the concept of capacity in developing the relationship between church and state has been stimulated by S.N. Eisenstadt (1962), cf. also L. Lundquist (1976, seminar paper).

2 The Buganda setting

1 cf. R. Oliver (1952), pp.39f.

2 On the introduction of Islam, see A. Katumba & F.B. Welbourn (1964). On the Zanzibarian penetration into the interior, see D.A. Low (1963), pp.323ff.

3 Low (1963), pp.332f.

4 Oliver (1952), pp.44f.

5 The period in the history of Buganda from the arrival of the first missionaries in 1877 until 1890 when Captain Lugard arrives is well covered in the literature. The following account has especially drawn on several works by D.A. Low, who has done the pioneer research into the history of Buganda, especially in his thesis (1957a); M. Kiwanuka (1972); J.V. Taylor (1958); C. Wrigley (1959); Å. Holmberg (1966), pp.313–97; and S.R. Karugire (1980), ch.2.

6 D.A. Low (1957b) has dealt with this problem of integration into the socio-political structure of Buganda.

7 This two-tiered structure in Buganda is described in Low (1971a), pp.14ff, pp.29f, and aptly summarized in M. Twaddle (1972), pp.57f.

8 Remarks by a Ganda chronicler quoted by Twaddle (1972), p.58.

9 The missionaries' position in Buganda in the eyes of Mwanga is described in R.H. Walker to L.G.W., 28 Febr. 1888, Walker Papers; cf. R. Ashe to CMS Committee, n.d. (must be 1887 or 1888), G/AZ 1/6, CMS Arch.

10 Walker to L.G.W., 3 June 1888, Walker Papers.

11 Gordon to Lang, 7 Nov. 1888, in Low (1971b), pp.12f; Walker to L.G.W., 8 Nov. 1888, Walker Papers.

12 The reign of Mwanga and the position of the various religions are dealt with in three articles supplementing each other excellently: M.S.M. Kiwanuka (1969), John A. Rowe (1964) and M. Twaddle (1972).

13 cf. Twaddle (1972) versus C.C. Wrigley (1959).

14 The treaty is described in the Macdonald Report (see below), copy in ESA, A1/1 (Part 3); quotation from Oliver (1952), p.143. cf. E.C. Gordon to Euan Smith, 25 Oct. 1889, copy in MSS. Brit. Emp. s.43, Rhodes House, Oxford. See also John A. Rowe (1969), p.4.

15 D.A. Low (1957a, unpubl. thesis) has a detailed account of the position of Buganda within the colonial setting and the establishment of British colonial rule from 1890 onwards. For the concept of 'informal British Empire', see R. Robinson & J. Gallagher (1965), ch.1; and R. Robinson (1972).

16 Walker to L.G.W., 20 Sept. 1889, Walker Papers.

17 Walker to L.G.W., 1 Nov. 1890, Walker Papers.

18 See Oliver (1952), p. 148; and Rowe (1969), p.7.

19 Walker to L.G.W., 1 Nov. 1890, Walker Papers. For a brief account of the Catholic position see J. Cussac (1955), pp.60f.

20 Walker to L.G.W., 5 March 1890, Walker Papers.

21 Walker, op.cit. Apolo Kagwa, Katikiro of Buganda, to Col. Euan Smith, British Consul-General, Zanzibar, 25 April 1890, in D.A. Low (1971b), pp.25f. Copy of translation in MSS. Brit. Emp. s.43, Rhodes House, Oxford.

22 Walker, op.cit. The increasing tendency to political involvement can be seen by comparing this letter with his letter to Basil, 10 Oct. 1889, Walker Papers.

23 cf. R.H. Walker's observation in a letter to Ashe, 20 March 1890, Walker Papers. Also R.H. Walker to Euan Smith, 21 Oct. 1889, copy in MSS. Brit. Emp. s.43.

24 See remarks by Bishop A.R. Tucker in his autobiography: Tucker (1908), pp.110ff. On the missionaries' general attitude see Walker to Euan Smith, 21 Oct. 1889.

25 R. Ashe to CMS Committee, n.d. (must be 1887 or 1888), G/AZ 1/6, CMS Arch. cf. Tucker, op.cit., pp.142ff. This problem has been discussed by Åke Holmberg (1966), ch. 15 and pp.350ff.

26 Walker to L.G.W., 5 March 1890, Walker Papers.

27 Apolo Kagwa in Lowe (1971b); Rowe (1969), p.30.

28 Tucker (1908), ch.10; F.D. Lugard (1893), vol. II, pp.18ff. It is interesting to notice that the term 'Ba-Ingelisa' also applied to Congolese Protestants in the former Belgian Congo; Ruth Slade (1959), p.400.

29 The basic patterns permeating Buganda society are developed by D.A. Low (1971a), pp.139ff; cf. also Low (1962), pp.9ff.

30 For a clear and short description of this politicization of religion, see Ali A. Mazrui (1975, conference paper), pp.5ff; cf. also discussion of religious parties in Karugire (1980).

31 cf. L.A. Fallers (1964), esp. ch.2.

32 This utilitarian principle in the traditional religion has been used in a political analysis of modern Ghana; cf. Maxwell Owusu (1970), esp. pp.241ff. Tom Tuma has pointed to a utilitarian trait in Busoga traditional religion; Tuma (1973, unpubl. thesis), pp.64, 125.

33 Walker to L.G.W., 5 March 1890, Walker Papers.

34 The suggestion to divide the relationship between religion and politics into three dimensions and subsequently to operate with three levels of inquiry has been made in an earlier conference paper, H.B. Hansen (1979), pp.16ff. cf. also K. Lockard (1975, unpubl. thesis), ch.1.

35 The quality of the new Christians has been taken up by J.V. Taylor (1958), ch.2 and 3; and discussed by D.A. Low (1968) and (1971a), ch. 1. A contemporary, Rev. J.J. Willis (Bishop of Uganda from 1912), who around the turn of the century worked as a pioneer missionary in Ankole, deliberately drew a distinction between conversion and what he called 'a political move', when the Omugabe (King) and his chiefs chose to adopt Protestantism. It was not meant in any derogatory sense. J.J. Willis' Journal, 9 Jan. 1901, MUL.

36 Mwanga's purge has been discussed by Rowe (1964); cf. Taylor, op. cit. The 'revivalist attitude' of the Protestant missionaries is well treated by Taylor, especially in his reference to George Pilkington. The extent to which the question of morality and a true Christian life engaged the missionaries and the newborn church can be seen from the minutes of Mengo Church Council, enclosed in Kitakule Journal, 27 July 1895 – 12 Sept. 1896. The issues on the agenda dealing with this subject are numerous. Kitakule Journal, Namirembe Arch.

37 The problem of divine kingship in relation to the Kabakaship has been discussed in H.B. Hansen (1966).

38 cf. Low (1971a).

Part II The formative period

3 *The concept of religious liberty*

1 A general discussion of recent origin can be found in L.H. Gann & P. Duignan (1969), pp.119ff; and C.P. Groves (1969), pp 462ff.

2 Åke Holmberg (1966), pp.313ff; D.A. Low (1957a, unpubl. thesis, *passim*), John S. Galbraith (1972), esp. pp.192ff.

3 Touched upon in D.A. Low (1957b) and briefly discussed in F.B. Welbourn (1965), ch.2; and Kathleen Lockard (1974, unpubl. thesis), pp.17ff.

4 I have dealt with the problem of religious liberty as a factor in development in the 1890s in Hansen (1966). In the following some of the same material will be used, but seen from a different angle. For a recent general outline with special reference to the idea of equality, see J.R. Pole (1978).

5 This is part of the broader question of universal history discussed in H.B. Hansen (1974).

6 An accurate description of what is meant by religious liberty at this level is found in the proclamation in which Queen Victoria in 1858 accepted British responsibility for rule and administration in India: 'We declare it to be Our royal will and pleasure that none be in anywise favoured, none molested or disquieted by reason of their religious faith or observance, but that all alike shall enjoy the equal and impartial protection of the law . . . And it is Our further will that, so far as may be, Our subjects, of whatever race or creed, be freely and impartially admitted to offices in Our service, the duty of which they may be qualified by their education, ability and integrity, duly to discharge.' Quoted by Stephen Neill (1964), p.323. cf. also J.F.A. Ajayi (1965), p.173.

7 The pursuit of equality constitutes the main theme in Pole (1978), from which many of the concepts used here have been taken, particularly equality of opportunity and equality of attainment or result, the latter combined with the idea of affirmative action.

8 cf. a similar use of the term 'church' by D.E. Smith (1970, p.7) in spite of the particular Christian history of the word.

9 Examples of these references to art. 6 in the Berlin Act can be found in Ruth Slade (1959), pp.143, 274; and in Marvin D. Markovitz (1973), pp.17, 35 and 65.

10 General Act of the Berlin Conference is reproduced *in extenso* in A.K. Keith (1919), app.1. Article 6 is quoted in M.D. Markowitz (1973), app.A, and in David Lagergren (1970), p.70.

11 Ruth Slade (1959), pp.75ff. The italics are mine. For a short general assessment of the Berlin Conference, see Suzanne Miers (1975), p.181, and O. Karup Pedersen (1963), pp.29ff.

12 The Act of Brussels, Article 2, is quoted in Markowitz (1973), app.A. cf. M. Searle Bates (1945), p.99, and in particular Slade (1959), pp.92ff. The Brussels Act is reproduced *in extenso* in Miers (1975) app.I. cf. also renewed controversy about Muslim missions, this time between France and Turkey: Miers, p.254.

13 P.L. McDermott (1893) has the full text of the Charter in app. III, pp.282ff. cf. John S. Galbraith (1972), ch.5, about the origin of the Charter.

14 The Agreement is reproduced in McDermott (1893), app. VIII.

15 cf. John Flint (1963).

16 The italics are mine. Sir F. de Winton's Letter of Instruction, 16 Sept. 1890, is reproduced in M. Perham (1959), vol.I p.327; henceforth quoted as Diary I, etc.

4   *The era of Company rule*

1 George S. Mackenzie, Zanzibar, to Lugard, 22 April 1890, MSS. Brit. Emp. s.40, Lugard Papers.

2 The following is not intended as a full account of Lugard's actions in Uganda, but limited to aspects related to the problem of religious liberty. For a full account see Margery Perham (1956); D.A. Low (1957a, unpubl. thesis), pp.228ff; John A. Rowe (1969); S.R. Karugire (1980). The two contemporary accounts, Lugard's own (1893) and the CMS missionary R.P. Ashe's (1894), are useful, but coloured by the authors' roles in the events in Uganda.

3 The Treaty is reproduced in Diary II, pp.42ff. On the signing and the importance of the chiefs, see entry 26 Dec. 1890.

4 This interpretation of the Treaty is different from the one given by Perham (1956, p.232). She finds that freedom of religion as such is guaranteed.

5 Numerous letters were exchanged between Lugard and the leaders of the two parties of missionaries within the first week of his arrival. Lugard tried to explain his intentions and the content of the coming treaty with Mwanga so as to enlist the cooperation of the missionaries. His statements on religious liberty are very clear, especially in Lugard to Mgr Hirth (the Catholic bishop), 20 Dec. and 22 Dec. 1890, MSS. Brit. Emp. s.42, Lugard Papers. Even Captain Macdonald in his critical report on Lugard's actions in Uganda admitted that Lugard adhered to the principle of religious liberty: The Macdonald Report, part 4, copy in ESA, A1/1.

6 Diary II, 23 Dec. 1890.

7 This can be seen from the correspondence with the missions, now in MSS. Brit. Emp. s.42, Lugard Papers; and from Lugard's diary from the first months after his arrival.

8 Minutes of some meetings of the Church Council in 1890s can be found in Minute Book of the Eastern Equatorial African Diocese, CMS Arch. For chiefs as Church Elders see G.K. Baskerville's Journal, 6 Oct. 1891; and D.A. Low (1957b), p.12.

9 Minutes in same minute book (n.8); cf. Baskerville's Journal, 6 July 1891.

10 Diary entries from last week of December, letters to missionaries (see n.7), Baskerville's Journal, 2 Jan. 1891.

11 Rowe (1969) has emphasized this point of view *passim*.

12 In Diary II, e.g. 23 Dec. 1890, 5 Jan. 1891 and 28 Febr. 1891; cf. also Low (1957a), pp.228ff.

13 Just after the event by one of the missionaries, R.P. Ashe (1894), p.160, and later by Perham (1956) and Low (1957a).

14 e.g. Walker to Mrs S., 9 March 1891; to Basil, 6 March 1891; to Salter Price, n.d. (most likely Aug. 1891), Walker Papers.

15 Walker to Salter Price, Aug. 1891, Walker Papers. Extracts of the letter were read to the secretary of the IBEA Co. in London and then sent to Lugard in Kampala, enclosed in Secretary to Lugard, 29 Jan. 1892, Lugard Papers.

16 See Lugard's Diary for the first 3 months of 1891.

17 So Ashe (1894). It is interesting that people in the IBEA Co. headquarters in London had the same impression of the Protestant reaction: Ag. Secretary to Lugard, 29 Jan. 1892, Lugard Papers.

18 Diary II, 5 March 1891, cf. 28 Febr. 1891.

19 Treaty clause 3, cf. Lugard to Mgr Hirth, 20 Dec. 1890, Lugard Papers.

20 Hirth to Lugard, 21 Dec. 1890, Lugard Papers.

21 Lugard to Hirth, 22 Dec. 1890, ibid.

22 This was first brought up in a personal conversation and repeated in Hirth to Lugard, 21 Dec. 1890. An answer is found in Lugard to Hirth, 20 and 22 Dec. 1890, ibid.

23 Mackenzie to Lugard, 10 Aug. 1891, Lugard Papers; and Mackenzie to CMS London, 10 Aug. 1891, G/Y A7/1, CMS Arch.

24 Lugard himself (1893, pp.104ff) in retrospect discussed this problem of the status of the missionary under British authority.

25 Mgr Hirth in conversation with Lugard and later in writing, Hirth to Lugard, 21 Dec. 1890, Lugard Papers.

26 The newly arrived CMS missionary, G.K. Baskerville, admits this in his Journal, 8 Jan. and 2 Febr. 1891 (copy in MUL). 'Is this country [Busoga] to be lost to protestant England! Where are the men to go in and possess the land.' On the sending of Ganda evangelists to Busoga: 'it is hard to tell how far this is prompted by a love of souls: one fears that desire for power and wish to exclude RCs prompts them a good deal'. cf. Walker to T.S., 6 March 1891; and to Basil, s.d., Walker Papers.

27 This dilemma is evident in Lugard's letters to Mgr Hirth, 20 and 22 Dec. 1890, Lugard Papers.

28 ibid.

29 Diary II, 25 Febr. 1891, and *passim*.

30 Diary II, 15 Febr. 1891; cf. Lugard (1893), p.102. Walker to L.G.W., 10 Febr. 1891; and to Basil, 19 May 1891, Walker Papers.

31 The minutes of CMS Finance Committee in the Buganda Mission bear witness to frequent reversals of decisions, esp. concerning Busoga in 1891 and 1892; minutes in Minute Book of the Eastern Equatorial African Diocese, CMS Arch. Concerning lack

of consensus among the missionaries, see Walker to Basil, 19 May 1891; and to L.G.W., 27 Dec. 1891. The weakness in leadership is expressed in Walker to Father, 31 Oct. 1891; and to L.G.W., 27 Dec. 1891. Walker has this gloomy comment: 'Now we all do exactly as we like' (31 Oct., Walker Papers).

32 In his diaries Lugard comments frequently on the missionaries' personalities and actions, e.g. Diary III, 11 Febr. 1892.

33 This policy on the part of the Company emerges from the correspondence which Rev. John Roscoe in his capacity as chairman of the CMS Finance Committee had with Lugard and his deputy, Captain Williams, in Jan. 1892; letters in Lugard Papers. cf. Lugard (1893), pp.102ff. Lugard did not have time to keep a diary in most of January 1892 and he left a lot of petty business to Williams (cf. Diary III, introduction). His policy on missionary expansion is clearly set out in Diary III, 27 April 1892. Copies of all letters between Lugard and CMS missionaries in Janaury 1892 concerning missionary extension were sent by Lugard to the IBEA Co. headquarters from where they were forwarded to the CMS, G3. A5/08, no. 340, CMS Arch.

34 Roscoe to Lugard, 21 Jan. 1892, Lugard Papers, where the rest of the correspondence between mission and Company can be found for this period. The threat to refer the matter to Parliament haunted Lugard during the following months; see Diary III, 27 April and 30 May 1892.

35 Roscoe to Lugard, 23 Jan. 1892, ibid. Lugard had noticed the apparent disagreement between the missionaries; see Diary III, 11 and 12 Febr. 1892.

36 Minutes of Finance Committee, 9 and 11 Febr. 1892.

37 Minutes of the Finance Committee, 14 June 1892; and Lugard's disapproving comments in Diary III, 15 June 1892.

38 Thus indicated by Walker in W. to Father, 29 Aug. 1891, and directly stated in W. to Father, 29 Sept. 1891: 'To write fully all that is done here is just the one check we have on men like Captain Williams.'

39 Walker to Lugard, 16 Febr. 1891, MSS. Brit. Emp. s.42, Lugard Papers; Diary II, 16 and 23 Febr. 1891.

40 Walker to Mother, 2 Dec. 1890, Walker Papers; Baskerville's Journal, 18 Febr. 1891.

41 cf. Walker to Lugard, 16 Febr. 1891.

42 Diary II, 18 Febr. 1891.

43 Lugard admitted later that it was questionable whether the Sese Islands belonged to Buganda (1893, pp. 75ff).

44 Diary II, 25 Febr. 1891.

45 Diary II, 18 Febr. 1891.

46 In Diary II, Jan.–March 1891, Lugard is constantly occupied by this issue. See also correspondence from the same period in Lugard Papers.

47 Thus Walker to Basil, 13 July 1891, Walker Papers.

48 Walker to Father, 29 Sept. 1891. cf. Baskerville's Journal, 13 and 15 July 1891.

49 Thus outlined in the Macdonald Report, par. 3 (A1/1, ESA). Captain J.R.L. Macdonald, chief engineer on Uganda railway survey, was in 1892 ordered by the British government to draw up a report on the causes of the dramatic events and the religious war in Uganda in 1892. cf. Perham (1956), pp. 325ff and ch. 19.

50 Mentioned in Walker to Lugard, 3 March 1891, Lugard Papers.

51 Diary II, 17 Febr. 1891.

52 Diary II, 18 and 25 Febr. 1891.

53 This constitutes the major theme in David Apter (1961).

54 Diary II, 3 March 1891.

55 Diary II, 5 March 1891.

56 Diary II, 6 March 1891; Walker to Lugard, 7 March 1891, MSS., Brit. Emp. s.42.

57 Diary II, 9 March 1891.

58 The Protestants' line of argument can be studied in Walker to Lugard, 7, 8 and 13 March 1891, loc. cit., and Diary II, 5 March 1891.

59 Walker to Basil, 6 March 1891, Walker Papers; and Diary II, 9 March 1891.

60 Walker to Mrs S., 9 March 1891, Walker Papers.

61 Diary II, 9 March 1891.

62 ibid. cf. Walker, op. cit., and Baskerville's Journal, 16 March 1891.

63 In his inquiry into the events in Buganda during Lugard's period of command Captain Macdonald pronounced a strong verdict on this particular arrangement. Macdonald Report, par. 5 (A1/1, ESA).

64 Mgr Hirth to Williams, 14 July 1891, in Lugard (1893), pp. 660ff.

65 Walker is alluding to this point when he states: 'The IBEA Co. seeing the strength of the RC influence weaken the Protestant party so as to make the King stronger and the country easier to rule.' Walker to Salter Price, Aug. 1891, Walker Papers; cf. also Walker's review of the events during 1891 in W. to Father, 29 Sept. 1891, Walker Papers.

66 Lugard even got the impression that Williams was biased towards the Catholics. Diary II, 15 Nov. 1891.

67 Williams' own account is expressed in Williams to Lugard, 12 Sept. 1891, in Diary II, pp. 400ff.

68 Walker to Lang, 5 Aug. 1891; and W. to Father, 29 Sept. 1891, both in Walker Papers.

69 Walker to Father, 29 Sept. 1891; Baskerville's Journal, 19 July 1891.

70 Baskerville, loc. cit.

71 Walker to Basil, 13 July 1891; and W. to Lang, 5 Aug. 1891, Walker Papers; Baskerville's Journal, 13 Aug. 1891.

72 Thus Baskerville, loc. cit.

73 Walker to Salter Price, Aug. 1891, Walker Papers.

74 One example appears in G.L. Pilkington to Williams, 28 Aug. 1891, MSS. Brit. Emp. s.42. The same position may be found in a number of Walker's letters from the same period, e.g. W. to Basil, 13 July 1891; to N.N.14 July 1891; to Lang, 5 Aug. 1891; to Father, 29 Aug. 1891. Lugard himself expressed concern because of the bad relations between Williams and the missionaries, cf. Diary II, 15 Nov. 1891, and his report from a meeting with Walker in Masaka, 19 Dec. 1891.

75 It is useful to give one example of how the communication with Europe actually worked: Walker started the process by writing a strong letter to his brother (W. to Basil, 13 July 1891, Walker Papers). The brother sent the letter to Prebendary H.E. Fox of the CMS who forwarded it to Gen. Hutchinson, a leading member of the CMS Parent Committee (Fox to Hutchinson, 22 Jan. 1892, G/Y A7/1, CMS Arch.). At the same time Walker's brother and a Uganda missionary on leave, Rev. E.C. Gordon, approached the office of the IBEA Co. and read various letters from Uganda. Headquarters then took action and sent a dispatch to Lugard (Ag. Secretary to Lugard, 29 Jan. 1892, MSS. Brit. Emp. s.45, Lugard Papers).

This chain of events also illustrates the time factor in the communication between Uganda and Europe; 5–6 months for a letter was not abnormal, and almost one year might, therefore, pass before those in Uganda could receive a response and renewed instructions.

76 Ag. Secretary to Lugard, 29 Jan. 1892 (cf. previous note).

77 Walker to Basil, 13 July 1891. In his letter to his father, 29 Sept. 1891, W. was even suggesting that steps should be taken to secure the country against misrule and 'to strengthen the hold the Protestant faith has on the land'. The CMS ought to complain to the IBEA Co. he added.

78 Baskerville's Journal, 22 July 1891.

79 The missionaries' third political role (p. 17). It is clearly expressed in Walker to Father, 29 Sept. 1891.

80 Baskerville's Journal, 13 and 15 July 1891; cf. letter by G.L. Pilkington, 11 Aug. 1891, in C.F. Harford-Battersby (1898) pp. 141ff.

81 ibid.; and Walker to Father, 29 Sept. 1891.

82 Diary II, 15 Nov. 1891.

83 Walker to Mrs S., 2 March 1892, Walker Papers.

84 Diary II, 18 Dec. 1891. cf. Baskerville's Journal, 27 and 29 Dec. 1891.

85 Diary III, 27 Jan. 1892.

86 ibid.

87 Lugard to Mwanga, 15 Jan. 1892, Lugard Papers.

88 Walker to Mrs Stanley, 8 Dec. 1891, Walker Papers.

89 A detailed account of the battle of Mengo can be found in Rowe (1969); cf. also Perham (1956), ch. 15; Åke Holmberg (1966), pp. 363ff; and Semakula Kiwanuka (1971), pp. 224ff. A Catholic account of the events appears in J. Cussac (1955), pp. 69ff.

90 Re Macdonald Report, see n. 51. Lugard himself published in 1893 *The Rise of our East African Empire* in two volumes. For two opposite evaluations of Lugard's role in Uganda see Perham (1956), and Kiwanuka (1971).

91 See substantial number of letters in MSS. Brit. Emp. s.44, Lugard Papers. See also Cussac (1955).

92 See Perham (1956), pp. 327ff.

93 Baskerville's Journal, 5 Oct. 1892.

94 Diary III, 23 March and in particular 14 April 1892. Walker was fully aware of Lugard's concern for his image, see W. to Basil, 28 March 1892; and to Mother, 6 April 1892, Walker Papers.

95 See missionaries' letters to Lugard in MSS. Brit. Emp. s.42, Lugard Papers. See also Walker's letters to his family, Febr.–March 1892, Walker Papers, and Parliamentary Paper (henceforth PP) C. 6848, pp. 30ff. cf. Holmberg (1966), pp. 366ff.

96 Perham (1956), pp. 327ff.

97 cf. John S. Galbraith (1972), pp. 212ff; and D.A. Low (1971a), pp. 55ff.

98 This campaign has been carefully analysed in Low (1971a). See also D.A. Low (unpubl. thesis, 1957a), ch.4. For economic motives in retaining Uganda see W.G. Hynes (1979).

99 An illustrative example is found in a discussion between Lugard and the CMS missionary Ashe, reported in Diary III, 20 April 1892; cf. also 12 April 1892.

100 Diary III, 1 April 1892.

101 cf. Diary III, 20 April 1892.

102 Diary III, 27. Jan., 11 Febr. 6 March and 11 April 1892.

103 cf. Diary III, 1 and 6 April 1892; see also Holmberg (1966), pp. 366ff, quoting Ashe and Bishop Tucker in support of the Protestant claim.

104 Diary III, 28 March 1892.

105 cf. Diary III, 6 March 1892. For Catholic opinion see Cussac (1955).

106 The treaty appears in Diary III, 11 May 1892; in Lugard (1893), pp.434ff; and in P.L. McDermott (1893). It is dated both 30 March and 11 April, but it was finally concluded on the latter date.

107 cf. H.W. Duta to missionary in Zanzibar, 5 April 1892, quoted by Low (1957b), p. 10. See also Baskerville's Journal, 1, 17, 25 and 30 April 1892; Diary III, 16 April 1892; Walker to Mother, 2 May 1892, Walker Papers.

108 Diary III, 6 and 7 April 1892.

109 Diary III, 20 April 1892.

110 ibid.; cf. Ashe to Lugard, 19 April 1892, Lugard Papers.

111 Diary III, 23 March 1892.

112 Diary III, 1, 7 and 25 April 1892.

113 Baskerville's Journal, 19 April 1892.

114 Diary III, 29 April and 11 May 1892.

115 Diary III, 5 April 1892; cf. also 23 May 1892.

116 Diary III, 3 Febr. 1892; cf. Walker to Basil, 8 Febr. 1892, Walker Papers. About the inclusion of the Muslims in the negotiations see in particular Diary III, entry 7 April 1892.

117 Diary III, 3 Febr. and 28 March 1892.

118 Diary III, 7 April and especially 14 April 1892. Mgr Hirth to Lugard, 23 Febr. 1892, Lugard Papers.

119 Diary III, 6 March 1892; Walker to Mother, 6 March 1892, Walker Papers; Père Achte to Lugard, 22 Febr. 1892, Lugard Papers.

120 The treaty is printed in Lugard (1893), pp.427ff.

121 cf. Diary III, 7 April and 26 May 1892; and Lugard (1893), p 425

122 Diary III, 1 April 1892. cf. Cussac (1955), pp.72ff.

123 Diary III, 7 April 1892.

124 Diary III, 3 June 1892.

125 Diary III, 20 April 1892.

126 Diary III, 14 April 1892. See map in B.W. Langlands & G. Namirembe (1967), p.8.

127 Diary III, 26 May 1892, and Lugard (1893), p.425.

128 This is made explicit in one of Lugard's reports (1893), p.427; cf. Diary III, 6 April 1892.

129 Diary III, 7 April 1892.

130 Baskerville's Journal, 23 April 1892.

131 ibid., 17 July 1892.

132 Diary III, 7 and 14 April 1892.

133 Diary III, 7 April 1892; cf. also Lugard's later account in PP C. 6848, Africa no. 2 (1893), pp.61ff.

134 cf. Lugard (1893), vol. II, pp.559ff.

135 Diary III, 7, 12 and 29 April 1892.

136 Lugard frequently uses the term *futabangi* (bhang-smokers), either for Ganda rebels

who do not belong to either Christianity or Islam, or in a wider sense for heathens in general. Both ways can be read out of Diary III, 29 April 1892. It is not possible always to decide where the term is used in one way or the other, cf. 5, 20 and 25 April 1892.

137 Diary III, 5 and 29 April 1892, 2 June 1892.

138 cf. Lugard's later explanation in PP C. 6848, p.68.

139 Diary III, 26 May and 14 June 1892.

140 Diary III, 7 April and 25 May 1892.

141 Diary III, 23, 25 and 26 May, 14 June 1892.

142 Baskerville's Journal, 31 Oct. 1892.

143 Diary III, 2 and 6 April 1892.

144 Diary III, 24 and 29 May, 1 June 1892.

145 Diary III, 3 May and 1 June 1892.

146 John A. Rowe has made the interesting observation that Lugard after the battle of Mengo replaced to a large extent the religious names of the parties with the terms 'Fransa' and 'Ingleza'. Rowe (1969), p.24.

147 Perham (1956), p.382.

148 Baskerville's Journal, 31 Oct. 1892.

149 This strategy of using the chiefs as the cornerstones has been mentioned several times. An outstanding cxample, although it is back in 1891, can be seen from the endeavour to work out a list of 37 chiefs who were willing to support an English missionary. Baskerville's Journal, 6 July and 28 Aug. 1891, Minutes of Church Council.

150 cf. Diary III, 18 April 1892.

151 PP C. 6848, Africa no. 2 (1893), pp.58ff; cf. Lugard (1893), vol. II, pp.427ff. Bishop Hirth was in doubt with regard to the content of clause two: 'Absolutely arbitrary and contrary to the Conventions of Berlin and Brussels.' Memorandum 28 Dec. 1892, in PPC. 7109, Africa no. 8 (1893), pp.20ff. See also Cussac (1955), p.73.

152 Practically every entry in the Diary from the month of April 1892 reflects the increasingly strained relations between Lugard and the CMS missionaries.

153 Diary III, 20 April 1892; Baskerville's Journal, 3 March 1892; Walker to Mother, 6 April 1892, Walker Papers.

154 Walker to Mother, 6 April 1892. An example of a less involved person, who from his own observation on the spot got the impression that the missionaries expected every backing from the Company, can be found in 'Evidence by Dr J.S. Macpherson, Med. Officer IBEA Co. Uganda Expedition, 1891–2', enclosed in Lugard to FO, March 1894, MSS. Brit. Emp. s.45, Lugard Papers.

155 Diary III, 14 April 1892.

156 ibid.; see also 15, 16 and 20 April 1892.

157 Diary III, 14 April 1892.

158 Diary III, 15 April 1892.

159 Walker to Mother, 6 April 1892, Walker Papers; Baskerville's Journal, 22 July 1892; cf. CMS missionaries' direct question to Lugard whether he is acting in the name of the Queen or in the name of the Company, Walker to Lang, 29 Sept. 1892, quoted by Holmberg (1966), p.367.

160 Diary III, Febr.–April 1892 *passim*; cf. Ashe to Lugard, 19 Febr. 1892, Lugard Papers; Walker to Basil, 28 March 1892; and to Mother, 6 April 1892, Walker Papers.

161 Diary III, 12, 14 and 18 April 1892. cf. Lugard to Sir William Mackinnon, 13 April

1892; and Ashe to Mackinnon s.d., copies forwarded by the IBEA Co. headquarters, G.A5/08, nos. 342 and 343.

162 It was first discussed in Jan. 1892 (see pp.35f) and a new round came in June when the CMS mission asked Lugard to make his own position absolutely clear: whether he issued a definite order or only gave advice. See collection of missionaries' letters in MSS. Brit. Emp. s.42, Lugard Papers; cf. also Baskerville's harsh comments in his Journal, 10 June 1892, where he refers to Gladstone's remarks in Parliament about missionary freedom.

163 Diary III, 29 and 30 April 1892. Ashe to Lugard, 30 April 1892 (Lugard Papers) contains the missionaries' answer, cf. Baskerville's Journal, 30 April 1892.

164 Diary III, 13 April 1892, cf. Baskerville's Journal, 13 April 1892; and Walker to Mother, 2 May 1892, Walker Papers.

165 Diary III, 14 and 30 April 1892; Ashe to Lugard, 30 April 1892; cf. Baskerville's Journal, 14 April 1892, Walker to Mother, 6 April and 2 May 1892, Walker Papers.

166 Diary III, 12, 29 and 30 April 1892.

167 Ashe to Lugard, 30 April 1892.

168 An important element was the clash of personalities between Lugard and R.P. Ashe, who during this period was chairman of the local Finance Committee. However, I have here concentrated on the more fundamental aspects which can be deduced from the material. That Ashe also lost the confidence of the CMS Home Board due to disagreement over his attitude towards the Company can be seen from the fact that he had to resign from the CMS; see Ashe to Africa Secretary (of the CMS), Buganda, 12 Dec. 1892, no. 60, G3. A5/09, and later correspondence in the same file.

5 The introduction of direct British rule

1 See D.A. Low (1971a), ch. 2; cf. W.G. Hynes (1979).

2 This period has been dealt with in Åke Holmberg (1966), ch. 17; D.A. Low (1957a, unpubl. thesis), ch.4; R. Oliver (1952), pp.140ff.

3 All treaties are printed in E. Hertslet (1967), vol. 1, pp.393ff.

4 Williams to Portal, 25 March 1893, A 32/1, ESA, and Portal to Williams, 2 April 1893, A 3/1, ESA; cf. Portal's own remarks in his private letter to Lord Rosebery, 22 March 1893, MS. Afr. s.109, Portal Papers, that with the exception of Bishop Tucker all the CMS missionaries were drawn from 'the lower middle classes'.

5 Portal to his wife, 4 April 1893, MS. Afr. s.113, Portal Papers, cf. Lugard, p.561.

6 cf. Portal to Lord Rosebery, 9 April 1893, MS. Afr. s.109, Portal Papers.

7 cf. Williams to Portal, 25 March 1893. Portal was not particularly consistent in his private reports and his official dispatches (cf. Holmberg (1966), pp.383ff). He refers in one of his later letters to the amicable attitude of the CMS missionaries; Portal to Sir Percy Anderson (FO), 9 April 1893, MS. Afr. s.109, Portal Papers.

8 The Portal mission is dealt with in detail in Holmberg (1966) and in Kenneth Ingham (1958), pp.51ff.

9 Captain Williams' Memorandum of 11 Jan. 1893, enclosed in Tucker to Portal, 5 April 1893, A2/1, ESA.

10 cf. Lugard, Diary III, 15 June 1892, and Macdonald to Williams, 17 Jan. 1893, A3/1, ESA.

11 The case of the two nephews is clearly set out in A.R. Tucker (1908), vol. I, pp.244ff, and will be discussed below.

12 Captain Williams, Memorandum on Catholics, dated 10 or 18 March 1893, A2/1, ESA.

13 Williams' point of view and goals are set out in the Memorandum just referred to and in that of 11 January to Bishop Tucker (see n.9). cf. Williams' review of the whole matter in a letter to Lugard, 23 Dec. 1893, MSS. Brit. Emp. s.45, Lugard Papers. Bishop Tucker's points of view can be found in Tucker to Portal, 5 April 1893, including among other papers his Memorandum of 7 January 1893 to Williams, A2/1, ESA. cf. also Williams' renewed attempt to reach a settlement in February 1893, correspondence with Protestant missionaries in A32/1, ESA and Zachariah Kisingiri (Muganda chief) to Lugard, 3 March 1893, MSS. Brit. Emp. s.43, Lugard Papers.

14 Williams' Memorandum of 10 or 18 March 1893.

15 cf. Portal to Sir Percy Anderson, 9 April 1893 (see n.7).

16 Portal to Lady Charlotte Portal, 7 April 1893, in Sir Gerald Portal (1894).

17 Portal to Earl of Rosebery, 24 May 1893, in PP C. 7303.

18 ibid., Portal to his wife, 4 April 1893 (see n.5); cf. Portal's Diary, 27 March 1893 (in Portal (1894), p.215), and Tucker (1908), vol. I, pp.265ff.

19 Tucker to Wigram (sec. CMS), 24 April 1893, no. 241, G3. A5/09. Portal's account of the meeting with the two bishops can be found in Portal to Earl of Rosebery, 8 April 1893, in PP C. 7109, Africa no. 8 (1893). Portal pays a special tribute to Tucker for his contribution in arriving at a settlement.

20 Tucker's report of the meeting differs somewhat from the one given by Portal, as pointed out by Holmberg (see Tucker to Wigram, 24 April 1893). cf. Tucker's own comment to Portal's report from the meeting in Tucker (1908), vol. I, p.266. The agreement with the bishops is enclosed in Portal to Earl of Rosebery, 8 April 1893.

21 cf. Tucker to Portal, 15 April 1893, A 2/1, ESA, asking for a change in the clause about the doubling of chieftainships.

22 Tucker to Wigram, 24 April 1893.

23 Portal's Diary, 22 April 1893, in Portal (1894), p.229.

24 The agreement is printed in PP C. 7708, p.8; cf. Tucker to Wigram, 24 April 1893. See also map in Langlands & Namirembe (1967), p.11.

25 cf. Holmberg (1966), p.385. Hirth's primary conditions are set out in 'Garanties au sujet des deux neveux catholiques de Mwanga', n.d. (presumably between 6 and 22 April 1893), A2/1, ESA; cf. Portal to Macdonald, Mumia's, 26 July 1893, A31/1, ESA.

26 The treaty of 29 May 1893 is printed in Hertslet (1967). The quotation is from clause 10 (italics mine). This clause is repeated in the final treaty by which Britain acknowledges the Buganda Protectorate.

27 Tucker to Wigram, 24 April 1893.

28 Tucker to Baylis, Mombasa, 31 Aug. 1893, no. 242, G3. A5/09.

29 e.g. Portal to his wife, 22 March 1893, MS. Afr. s.113, Portal Papers.

30 Holmberg (1966) has rightly pointed to the difference between Portal's private letters and his official dispatches, and he finds Bishop Tucker's account of the negotiations to be the most reliable (pp. 385ff).

31 Portal to Earl of Rosebery, 8 April 1893, in PP C. 7109.

32 He admits that this question was brought up in his discussion with the two bishops; Portal to Sir Percy Anderson, 9 April 1893 (see n.7).

33 Baylis (secr. CMS) to Tucker, 29 Sept. 1893, p.35, G3. A5/L 7 and various telegrams during September.

34 Tucker to Baylis, Mombasa, 27 and 29 Sept. (nos. 264 and 215); and 20 Oct. (no. 287) 1893, G3. A5/09.

35 Baylis to Roscoe and Tucker, 3 Nov. 1892, p.422, G3. A5/L6.

36 Tucker to Baylis, 18 April 1893, no. 218, G3. A5/09.

37 The first case concerns Singo, a saza in Buganda: Tucker to Baylis, 21 Febr. 1893, no. 194; cf. Tucker to Baylis, 18 April 1893, no. 218, where permission had been granted. The second area is the Kingdom of Toro where Tucker promised Capt. Williams not to send missionaries for a period of six months starting in January 1893; in return the Catholics were also excluded: Tucker to Baylis, 27 Sept. 1893, no. 264, all letters in G3. A5/09.

38 Tucker, last mentioned letter.

39 This political element in Tucker's approach can be deduced from his letters of 21 Febr. and 27 Sept. 1893.

40 The treaty of 29 May 1893 is printed in Hertslet (1967).

41 A detailed comparison of Lugard's and Portal's treaties appears in Holmberg (1966), pp.388ff.

42 In his welcoming letter to Portal, Bishop Hirth raises the question of religious liberty in strong terms by quoting from European conferences on the subject: Hirth to Portal, 24 March 1893, A2/1, ESA.

43 Tucker to Baylis, Mombasa 31 Aug. 1893, no. 242, G3. A5/09.

44 ibid.

6 Official colonial rule: the organizational phase

1 This period is especially dealt with in D.A. Low (1957a, unpubl. thesis), ch.5; Kenneth Ingham (1958), ch.2; and D.A. Low, in Harlow & Chilver (1965). cf. also A.D. Roberts (1963).

2 PP C. 7708, p.8.

3 Macdonald to Hirth, 20 July 1893, A3/1; and to Portal, 18 July 1893, A33/1; cf. Notes on Mgr Hirth's letter of 21 July 1893, A3/1, all in ESA.

4 First in connection with the independent chieftaincy Koki, south of Buganda: Colvile to Kamswaga (King of Koki), 12 Dec. 1894, A3/2, ESA. The second case concerns the southern part of Bunyoro, to which we refer below.

5 Colvile to Hirth, 28 April 1894, A3/2 ESA, in PP C. 7708, p.86.

6 Hirth to Colville, 9 and 10 Dec. 1893, A2/1, ESA; cf. H.P. Gale (1959), p.81. The whole correspondence and the resultant proclamation are printed in PP C. 7708, Africa no. 7 (1895), pp.12ff.

7 Colvile to Consul General, Zanzibar, 13 Dec. 1893, A3/1, ESA, also in Foreign Office Confidential Print (henceforth FOCP), part 37, no. 75, p. 52. The problem of evictions was in fact brought up only a couple of weeks after Portal's conclusion of the agreement with the chiefs. The Protestant Katikiro, Apolo Kagwa, reported an eviction in a Muslim-held shamba and asked for help from the colonial administration to reinstate the man. Apolo Kagwa to Berkeley, 6 May 1893, A2/1, ESA.

8 Proclamation of 11 Dec. 1893 signed by Colvile and Mwanga, and 'Draught of Policy' of 12 Dec. 1893, signed by Colvile, both in A3/1, ESA; cf. also FOCP, op.cit., and PP C. 7708. See also L.L. Kato (1971), pp.154ff.

9 The documents were forwarded via the Consul General, Zanzibar. The reply from the FO is in Earl of Kimberley to Mr Craknall, 30 April 1894, in FOCP, part 37, no. 117, p. 78; and Consul General, Zanzibar, to Colvile, 4 June 1894, A31/2, ESA. The FO reserves for itself the right to see how it works in practice before pronouncing a definite opinion. It is interesting to notice that the answer from FO does not include any reference to the policy in other parts of the empire.

10 In this interpretation I differ from Gale (1959), who talks about Colvile's removing the strongest weapon the Protestants had so far had (p.81).

11 Archdeacon Walker mentions two cases from 1896. In the first one he reports that 'the cry of religious liberty is raised' if a Protestant chief refuses to let the Catholics build a church within his area (Walker to Harriett, 25 Oct. 1896). In the second case a Catholic chief comes to the Protestant Church Council and asks for Protestant teachers to take care of the many Protestants within his area (Walker to Harriett, 25 Nov. 1896). It should be added that Walker later reports that Bishop Tucker induces Protestant chiefs to refuse Catholics to build churches on their estates, a step which Walker deplores on the ground of religious liberty (Walker to Wilfred, 31 July 1898, all letters in Walker Papers).

12 Proclamation of 11 Dec. 1893, A3/1, ESA. It is interesting that Archdeacon R.H. Walker as early as 1891 raised this question and advised the Protestant chiefs to refuse to assist in building a Catholic church: Walker to Father, 29 Sept. 1891. An example of the administration of this ruling can be found in Gale (1959), p.130.

13 Walker to Wilfred, 17 Sept. 1894 (Walker Papers) mentions that some of the Bakopi are unhappy about building Protestant churches and have declared themselves to be Catholics.

14 The close relationship between the position of the chiefs, the prevailing economic system in the country and the expansion of the mission and the church will be further developed below.

15 Colvile to Consul General, Zanzibar, 13 Dec. 1893, A3/1, ESA, in FOCP, part 37, no. 75, p.52.

16 'Draught of Policy'; see n.8.

17 Berkeley to Marquess of Salisbury, 19 Nov. 1896, in FOCP, part 48, no. 63, p. 89. A copy is in G3. A5/L 8, p.125.

18 Berkeley to Marquess of Salisbury, 14 May 1896, FOCP July–Sept. 1896, no. 86, p. 105, cf. Memorandum on Conversation with Mgr Hirth, 18 July 1893, A3/1, ESA.

19 Thus Colvile to Consul General, Zanzibar, 13 Dec. 1893.

20 cf. Macdonald's letters to Portal in June 1893, Portal Papers, and his later account of the campaign against the Muslims and the reallocation of Muslim sazas to the Christians in Macdonald (1897). See also Ingham (1958), pp.54ff, and A.T. Matson's introduction to the 1973 ed. of Macdonald (1897).

21 Macdonald kept Portal informed about the rearrangement of the Muslim sazas: correspondence in FOCP, part 36, no. 123; cf. map in B.W. Langlands & G. Namirembe (1967), p.12.

22 Memorandum of Conversation with Mgr Hirth, 12 and 18 July 1893, A3/1, ESA; Macdonald to Portal, 18 July 1893, A33/1, and 21 Oct. 1893, A32/1, ESA.

23 Berkeley to Marquess of Salisbury, 19 Nov. 1896; cf. Walker to Father, 22 Nov. 1896, Walker Papers. The FO gives its approval both to the arrangement itself and to the language used by Berkeley; FO to Berkeley, 24 Febr. 1897, in FOCP, part 48, no. 91, p.109. See also A.D. Roberts (1962) and M.S.M. Kiwanuka (1968).

24 Memorandum of Conversation with Mgr Hirth, 12 July 1893.

25 Baskerville's Journal, 15 April 1893.

26 'A R.C. chief . . . has recently become Protestant, but has voluntarily resigned his chieftainship and estates.' Macdonald to Portal, 21 Oct. 1893, A32/1, ESA. cf. for the same practice in Busoga, Baskerville's Journal, 29 April 1893.

27 Walker to Mother, 25 June 1896; cf. Walker to Mother, 10 April 1897; to Parents, 9 June 1897; and to Basil, 12 Nov. 1897, all in Walker Papers.

28 Ternan to Marquess of Salisbury, 14 Aug. 1897 (see n. 43).

29 Especially during 1896–7 this theme of social status and the many nominal Christians is much in the minds of the Anglican missionaries: cf. Walker letters dated 7 Febr., 27 March, 26 June 1896, and 9 May, 12 Nov. 1897 (Walker Papers).

30 Colvile to Consul General, Zanzibar, 12 Dec. 1893, A32/1, ESA, in PP C. 7708, p.12.

31 Colvile to Consul General, Zanzibar, 8 Dec. 1893, A32/1, ESA, in PP C. 7708; cf. Colvile (1895), pp.71–81.

32 Hirth to Colvile, 11 Dec. 1893, A2/1; Earl of Kimberley to Consul General, Zanzibar, 1 May 1893, enclosed in Hardinge to Colvile, 4 June 1894, A32/2, ESA. Colvile had suggested as a reward to Mwanga if he kept his word against his own wishes 'the Companionship of the Order of St Michael and St George', but the FO found this bestowal of a decoration unsuitable.

33 Mwanga to Colvile, 24 July 1894, A3/2, ESA.

34 Colvile to Mwanga, 25 July 1894, A3/2, ESA.

35 Report from Captain Gibb, 3 Aug. 1894, A2/2. Colvile to Consul General, Zanzibar, 19 Aug. 1894, A32/2, ESA.

36 An extensive correspondence is in A2/1, A2/2, A3/1, A3/2, A31/2, A32/1, A32/2, ESA, covering the years 1893–4. cf. Gale (1959), pp.78ff. Parts of the correspondence may also be found in PP C. 7708.

37 Colvile to Consul General, Zanzibar, 15 April 1894, in FOCP, part 37, no. 341, p.258. cf. Colvile (1895), pp.238ff.

38 The Catholics offered to baptize the child without any preconditions but in the end Mwanga wrote a letter handing over the child for 14 years 'to be taught the Protestant faith'. Walker to Wilfred, 31 July 1898, Walker Papers; E. Millar to Baylis, 12 Aug. 1896, no. 308, G3. A5/012.

39 Already in the beginning of 1894 Walker comments on Mwanga's limited power and combines it with his wish to change his religion. Walker to Basil, 3 Jan. 1894, Walker Papers.

40 Mwanga accuses the Protestant chiefs, especially the Katikiro, of squeezing him out. Walker to Basil, 16 July 1897, Walker Papers; cf. analysis of Mwanga's position under colonial rule in Semakula Kiwanuka (1971), pp.263ff.

41 Walker to Basil, 18 Nov. 1896; and to Father, 17 Dec. 1896, Walker Papers.

42 The events in 1897–9 are described in D.A. Low (1965), pp.72ff. The mixture of anti-religious and anti-European feelings is emphasized by Archdeacon Walker; Walker to Parents, 9 June 1897; cf. Walker to Parents, 4 (14) July 1897; and to Stockdale, 8 Aug. 1897. He even goes as far as to say: 'The word "European" includes all our readers and the adherents of all Missions.' Walker to Cyril, 7 Aug. 1897, all in Walker Papers. For the Catholic point of view see J. Cussac (1955).

43 Walker describes the coronation in a letter to Cyril, 15 Aug. 1897 and emphasises the importance of a Protestant household for the young Kabaka in a letter to Parents, 29 Aug. 1897; cf. Major Ternan to Marquess of Salisbury, 14 Aug. 1897, in PP C. 8718; also Walker to Baylis, 16 Aug. 1897, no. 297, G3. A5/013, CMS Arch. (the other Walker letters in Walker Papers). Sir Harry Johnston later deplored the Protestant monopoly on the infant Kabaka's upbringing; Johnston to Marquess of Landsowne, 10 July 1901, in PP Cd. 671, Africa no. 7 (1901), p.18. Also Ternan to Salisbury, 23 July 1899, FO 2/203.

44 When rebellion was still only a faint threat Walker pointed out how dependent the government was on the Christian leaders in Buganda and their attitudes: Walker to Parents, 9 June 1897 and to anon., 11 May 1897; cf. Walker to Parents, 23 Oct. 1897, Walker Papers.

45 Walker's letters in 1897 and 1898 illustrate this fact, in particular Walker to Cyril, 15 Aug. 1897; and to Parents, 23 Oct. 1897.

46 Ham Mukasa's sermon is reported in Walker to Stockdale, 8 Aug. 1897.

47 cf. Minutes of Finance Committee, 25 and 27 Jan. 1894 regarding Kavirondo; Tucker to Berkeley, 16 and 20 June 1898 re Bunyoro, A6/4 and A6/5 respectively, ESA. Ag. Commissioner Ternan to Tucker, 3 July 1899; and Tucker to Ternan 4 July 1899, A6/6 and A7/5 resp., ESA.

48 The examples are legion, e.g. Walker to Baylis, 4 Aug. 1899, no. 176, regarding Kavirondo (G3. A7/01).

49 Minutes of Finance Committee, 9 July 1894. The letter to the CMS headquarters is quoted in the minutes and is also found in G3. A5/010, no. 249. The minutes of the Finance Committee are included in Minute Book of the Eastern Equatorial Diocese, CMS Arch.

50 Minutes from the same meeting (9 July 1894) show a direct reference to the Parliamentary Paper from which Portal's interpretation can be read. At the same time Colvile granted the White Fathers permission to set up a station in Toro with the explicit argument that Toro fell within the Catholic sphere of influence in accordance with Portal's agreement with the two bishops: Gale (1959), p.118.

51 Roscoe to Baylis, 1 July and following days 1894; Walker to Baylis, 9 July 1894, no. 245, both in G3. A5/010.

52 Walker, op.cit.

53 Baylis to Walker, 19 December 1894, G3. A5/L7, p.294. The principle of self-support is constantly brought up in these years. In the Buganda context it is developed extensively in Tucker to Baylis, 8 November 1895, no. 48, G3. A5/012.

54 Walker, op.cit.; Roscoe to Baylis (see n.51).

55 Baylis to Tucker, 23 November 1894, G3. A5/L7, p.251.

56 cf. Gale (1959), pp.85ff; and Cussac (1955), pp.85ff.

57 Colvile to Earl of Kimberley, London, 4 April 1895, in FOCP, part 41 (April–June 1895); cf. Gale (1959), pp.112ff.

58 Sir Percy Anderson, FO, to CMS London, 18 April 1894, copy in G3. A5/L7, p.344.

59 This is directly indicated by Sir Percy Anderson in an interview with CMS secretary Baylis; see report of interview in Baylis to Tucker, 5 July 1895, G3. A5/L7, p.399.

60 ibid.

61 Sir Percy Anderson to CMS London, 18 July 1895, copy in G3. A5/L7, p.408.

62 Baylis, op.cit. Foreign Office to CMS, 27 June 1895, in FOCP, op.cit.

63 Tucker, who at this time was in Mombasa, was in contact with the Consul General at Zanzibar who forwarded the correspondence to the Foreign Office.

64 Tucker to Consul General, Zanzibar, Mombasa, 15 May 1895, copy in Tucker to Baylis, 17 May 1895, no. 180, G3, A5/011.

65 This is directly stated by Sir Percy Anderson, cf. n.59.

66 Berkeley to Marquess of Salisbury, 19 November 1896, in FOCP, part 48, no. 63, p.89.

67 Walker to Baylis, 1 June 1898, no. 152, G3 A7/01; Walker to Cyril, 28 July 1898, Walker Papers; cf. Walker to Ag. Commissioner Ternan, 22 September 1899, no. 242, G3. A7/01, where it is indicated that the colonial administration was interested in the extension of the Protestant work to Buddu. A general reference to the desirability of the promotion of Christianity may be found in Ternan to Marquess of Salisbury, 3 June 1899, FO 2/202.

68 Walker to Wilfred, 31 July 1898, Walker Papers. It has not been possible to trace this controversy anywhere else, e.g. in CMS Arch.

69 cf. Walker to Mother, 2 March 1895, Walker Papers.

70 cf. Walker to Ashe, 15 Nov. 1894, Walker Papers.

71 e.g. Walker to Father, 2 March 1896: the Katikiro and later Kabaka Mwanga ask for advice in connection with registration of guns. Walker to Cyril, 18 Oct. 1896: the Katikiro asks for advice with regard to a question of compensation, both letters in Walker Papers.

72 One example is connected with the issue of a Government Savings Bank: Walker to Basil, 17 Sept. 1896, Walker Papers.

73 Thus Archdeacon Walker in connection with the agreement with Koki: W. to Mother, 15 Nov. 1896; cf. W. to Mother, 19 Aug. 1895, Walker Papers.

74 Walker to Colvile, 28 Sept. 1894, A2/3, ESA; Walker to Cyril, 15 Aug. 1897, Walker Papers.

75 Walker to Mother, 2 Dec. 1895, Walker Papers.

76 The examples are legion: e.g. Tucker to Baylis, 31 Aug. 1893, no. 242, G3. A5/09, concerning a Protestant chief who is also a licensed lay evangelist. From 1894 a number of cases are found in A2/3, ESA. Re missionaries' general approach to interventions, see Walker to Mother, 29 Oct. 1894 and to Wilfred, 28 June 1896.

77 In Walker's opinion government officers ought also to attend language courses. Walker to Father, 29 Nov. 1896, Walker Papers.

78 Examples in Walker to Harriet, 12 June 1896; and to Stockdale, 28 June 1896, Walker Papers.

79 Colvile in a memorandum to the FO, dated London, 2 April 1895, FO 2/92, in FOCP, part 41, no. 3, p.2. In his memorandum Colvile refers to matters dealt with in an earlier correspondence with the CMS missionaries; the letters may now be seen in A2/3, ESA. A number of cases were brought to the attention of various people and public bodies in Europe, e.g. Aborigines' Protection Society to the Earl of Kimberley, 10 April 1895; and Colvile's blunt answer in C. to FO, 12 April 1895, FO 2/92, in PP. C. 7708, Africa no. 7 (1895), pp.142ff.

80 Behind many of these often trivial matters it is possible to see misunderstandings and clash of personalities. Dr Ansorge, who in 1894 was in charge of the fort in Kampala, was the stumbling-block in the eyes of the missionaries, while the Rev. G. Pilkington had the same role in the opinion of government officials. Colvile's explanation of controversies with the missionaries was met with approval in the FO, where it was minuted that the CMS missionaries still pursued 'the course of antagonism to the administration which they adopted in Capt. Lugard's time'. FO minute, 3 April 1895, FO 2/92.

81 Thus Macdonald's memorandum of conversation with Mgr Hirth, dat. 12 July 1897, A3/1; Colvile to Hirth, 10 June 1894, A32/2, both in ESA.

82 e.g. Macdonald to Hirth, 20 July 1893, A3/1. cf. Walker to Maud, 22 Sept. 1895, Walker Papers.

83 cf. Walker, op.cit.

84 Berkeley to Marquess of Salisbury, Lake Naivasha, 22 Jan. 1897, in FOCP, part 49, no. 47, pp.55ff.

85 Colvile to Father Superior at Villa Maria, 30 Aug. 1894, A22/2. Walker consents to this and points to the advantage which the French fathers enjoy. Walker to Colvile, 2 Nov. 1894, A2/3, both in ESA.

86 Walker mentions that the Catholic Bishop in 1896 accuses the Commissioner, as well as Lugard before him, of being led by the CMS: Walker to Father, 2 March 1896, Walker Papers.

87 Minutes of the Finance Committee, 26 March 1893 (see n.49).

88 Walker to Mother, 29 Oct. 1894; and to Father, 2 Dec. 1894, Walker Papers.

89 Walker to Colvile, 2 Nov. 1894; Walker to Baylis, 30 Dec. 1894, no. 111, G3. A5/011.

90 Walker to Father, 2 Dec. 1894; and to Wilfred, 18 Sept. 1896, Walker Papers.

91 Walker to Cyril, 16 Dec. 1896, Walker Papers.

92 Walker to Father, 9 Jan. 1896 and to Wilfred, 18 Sept. 1896, Walker Papers.

93 Walker to Mother, 10 Feb. 1897; and to Basil, 30 June 1897. At that time he had reversed his earlier detached view of the matter: cf. Walker to Father, 9 Jan. 1896; cf. also the anxiety expressed in connection with the growth of the number of Europeans present in the Protectorate: Walker to Cyril, 6 March 1898, all in Walker Papers.

94 An example may be seen in the eagerness which the missionaries exhibited with regard to the officers' participation in services; cf. Walker to Father, 27 July 1895; and to Mother, 11 April 1897, Walker Papers.

95 Walker to Basil, 1 July 1895; and to Father, 24 Nov. 1896, Walker Papers.

96 Father Streicher to Sub-Commissioner of Buganda, 3 May 1897, A4/8 ESA; and Walker to Parents, 9 June 1897, Walker Papers.

97 Walker, op.cit.

98 The Sub-Commissioner of Buganda, George Wilson, points to this cause of the unrest, especially with regard to the French fathers in Buddu. George Wilson to Lugard, 30 March 1899, MSS. Brit. Emp. s.45, Lugard Papers.

99 cf. Walker to Parents, 7 (14) July 1897, Walker Papers; Walker to Baylis, 9 July 1897, no. 268, G3. A5/013; and again 18 Dec. 1897, no. 63, G3. A7/01.

100 Walker to Parents, 6 Aug. 1895, Walker Papers. 'To eat' is a verb frequently used in Luganda to indicate that someone requires in an excessive way something at the expense of others. See also Walker to Baylis, 3 Aug. 1897, no. 296, G3. A5/013; and again 18 Dec. 1897, loc. cit.

101 Walker to Stockdale, 8 Aug. 1897, Walker Papers; cf. also Walker to Baylis, 3 Aug. 1897.

102 Walker to Baylis, 30 Aug. 1897, no. 323, G3. A5/013.

103 cf. Walker to Parents, 9 June 1897, Walker Papers.

104 cf. Walker to Stockdale, 8 Aug. 1897.

105 Walker to Parents, 28 Oct. 1897; Tucker to Rev. H.E. Fox, Mombasa, 24 Jan. 1898, no. 27, G3. A5/014.

106 Walker, op. cit. Major Macdonald to Walker, 20 Dec. 1897, A7/3, ESA (the original under no. 70, G3. A7/01). See also Commissioner to Walker, 22 March 1898, A7/4, ESA.

107 Thus Macdonald, op. cit.

108 Walker to Parents, 2 Dec. 1897, Walker Papers.

109 Walker to Parents, 9 June 1897; Walker to Baylis, 9 July 1897, no. 268, G3. A5/013.

110 cf. Walker to Wilfred, 17 Nov. 1897; to Tucker, 23 Feb. and 10 March 1898, all in Walker Papers.

111 Walker to Parents, 21 July 1897; cf. Walker to Parents, 4 (14) July 1897.

112 cf. Walker to Basil, 2 March 1898, Walker Papers. In 1899 Walker is anxious to correct some statements published by CMS missionaries implying that the government is not successful. On the contrary, there has been 'progress of civilization and Christianity'. Walker to Baylis, 31 March 1899, read after the Precis, G3. A7/P1 (the original missing); and Walker to Father, 1 April 1899 (with a copy of the letter to

Baylis included), Walker Papers. The colonial administration's dissatisfaction with the missionaries' news reports is expressed by George Wilson to Lugard, 30 March and 7 April 1899, MSS. Brit. Emp. s.45, Lugard Papers. Evidence of the improved relations may be found in Ag. Commissioner Ternan's letter to Walker at his departure from Uganda in which he expresses his appreciation of the good relations between the government and the CMS – quite the opposite was the case at Colvile's departure five years earlier: Ternan to Walker, 20 Jan. 1900, encl. in Walker to Father, 21 Jan. 1900, Walker Papers.

113 One indication is Bishop Tucker's complaint against two government officials in 1898 and 1899. Tucker to Berkeley, 24 May 1898, A6/4; and Tucker to Ternan, 24 Oct. 1899, A6/7, ESA.

114 cf. p.75 above. See also Tucker to Baylis, 17 May 1895, no. 180, G3. A5/011.

115 Tucker to Baylis, 14 Jan. 1896, no. 102, G3. A5/012.

116 Walker to Ashe, 23 Sept. 1895; cf. Walker to Basil, 29 Dec. 1895, Walker Papers.

117 Portal to Macdonald, Mumia's, 26 July 1893, A31/1, ESA.

118 Thus Walker to Stockdale, 25 March 1896, Walker Papers.

119 Tucker (see n.115); Walker to Parents, 22 Aug. 1898, Walker Papers. With regard to government officials' point of view see George Wilson to Lugard, 24 March 1899, MSS. Brit. Emp. s.45, Lugard Papers.

120 Various officials' private letters to Lugard in the latter half of the 1890s may be seen as such examples, especially the letters from the Sub-Commissioner of Buganda, George Wilson (cf. previous note). Wilson later complained that both he and Berkeley in regard to their career had suffered from 'the indiscreet paper reports' of 'some of the injudicious members' of the CMS mission. Wilson to Rev. Fisher, 8 Oct. 1901, Fisher Papers, Misc.

121 That Colvile at that time happened to be in London on leave is immaterial.

122 For a similar analysis of the relationship between the local administration and the FO see Low (1965), pp.58ff., 62ff.

123 This topic has been touched on in H.B. Hansen (1980).

124 The lack of leadership within the CMS mission has earlier been hinted at. R.H. Walker, whose letters have been used as a major source, was appointed an Archdeacon in 1893. In this capacity he functioned as secretary for the Finance Committee and acted as a substitute for the Bishop, but his authority was not clearly defined. The colonial officials hinted often at the difference in the CMS mission's approach when Bishop Tucker was present; e.g. George Wilson to Lugard, 30 March 1899, MSS. Brit. Emp. s.45, Lugard Papers.

125 Walker to Basil, 20 Sept. 1895; to Parents, 29 Aug. 1897; and to Harriett, 20 June 1898, all in Walker Papers.

126 Walker to Wilfred, 31 July 1898; cf. Walker to Parents, 29 Aug. 1897.

127 One example is the baptism of the infant King of Bunyoro, see Tucker to Baylis, 16 March 1899, no. 87, G3. A7/01.

128 Walker to Basil, 1 July 1895, Walker Papers.

129 Walker to Mother, 6 Aug. 1896, Walker Papers.

130 Walker to Parents, 29 Aug. 1897.

131 e.g. Walker to Baylis, 9 April 1896, no. 204, G3. A5/012, in which the issues concerning the number of Mwanga's wives, their right to leave and their being baptized are raised. The example reveals a clash between 'native law' and Christian principles, and it shows also that the colonial administration preferred to stand aloof on this whole issue.

132 Walker to Parents, 29 Aug. 1897, cf. above p.7.

133 Walker to Father, 27 April (11 May) 1899, Walker Papers.

134 Walker to Mother, 2 March 1895; and again in Walker to O. Sibley, 12 Febr. 1896, Walker Papers.

135 Walker to Basil, 1 July 1895, Walker Papers.

136 Walker to Cyril, 18 Oct. 1896; cf. Walker to Mother, 11 April 1897; he reports how he explained to Wilson that 'it is the Mission that had given them [chiefs] the superiority . . .' Walker Papers.

137 Thus George Wilson to Lugard, 30 March 1899 (see n.124).

138 cf. Low (1965), pp.63ff. Baskerville mentions in his Journal (12 June 1897) that George Wilson 'has started a kind of Parliament or weekly senate and the chiefs are all required to be present'. Wilson himself presents a list of administrative and judicial reforms he is working on in a letter to Lugard, 12 Sept. 1895, MSS. Brit. Emp. s.45, Lugard Papers. cf. Wilson's later account of the administrative system in the Protectorate in a lecture to the Society of Arts, in *Journal of the Society of Arts*, vol. 55, Febr. 1907 (copy under no. 44, G3. A7/05).

139 Walker to Basil, 25 March 1896 (Walker Papers), where a concrete case is reported involving the Katikiro, Apolo Kagwa.

140 Thus Walker to Mother, 6 Aug. 1896, where he mentions that he has promised in future to go first to the Kabaka before contacting the colonial officials; cf. also Walker to Cyril, 18 Oct. 1896, where he refrains from advising the Kabaka in a particular case.

141 Walker and Baskerville were initially both stationed outside the capital in response to requests from chiefs. Re economic set-up in Buganda in the 1890s, see C.C. Wrigley (1959), ch. 1; Wrigley (1964), pp.21ff; and C. Ehrlich (1965).

142 In 1891 the Church Council drew up a list of 32 major chiefs who wanted a missionary to live close to their headquarters; cf. Baskerville's Journal, 6 July and 28 Aug. 1891. Walker comments later that the number of missionaries now exceeds the chiefs' capacity: Walker to Parents, 22 Aug. 1898, Walker Papers.

143 Walker to Wilfred, 17 Sept. 1894; cf. Walker to Mother, 25 June 1896, Walker Papers. About that time Walker estimated the value of this work at about £200 a year; Walker to Baylis, 8 June 1897, no. 224, G3. A5/013.

144 An impression of the pattern of work can be gained from Baskerville's Journal, see for instance 20 March, 16 April, 6 Nov. and 7 Dec. 1894. See also Minutes of the Mengo Church Council, 27 July 1895 – 12 Sept. 1896, in Kitakule Journal, Namirembe Arch. cf. J.V. Taylor (1958) pp.68ff.

145 Walker to Mother, 2 March 1895; cf. Walker to Mother, 3 May 1896. Minutes of Mengo Church Council, 9 May 1896. Walker estimates the number at about 150 shambas; Walker to Baylis, 8 June 1897.

146 Walker to Mother, 3 May 1896; Walker to Parents, 22 Aug. 1898, Walker Papers.

147 Bishop Tucker describes in his autobiography the growth of the work and start of the church fund. Tucker (1908), pp.306ff.

148 Walker to Wilfred, 9 May 1896, Walker Papers.

149 cf. Minutes of Mengo Church Council, 30 May 1896. It was estimated that about 400 teachers were sent out in 1896, and that £300 was collected during 1895. The last figure should be compared with the pay of a teacher, about £1.5.0 a year, and that of the ten ordained clergymen, each £2.12.0 a year. Walker to Wilfred, 9 May 1896, Walker Papers; Walker to Baylis, 11 May 1896, no. 222, G3. A5/012. The Church Council in 1897 approved that teachers who were not supported by the church were free to work four months and teach eight months. Minutes from 16 Oct. 1897.

150 Walker to Mother, 2 March 1895, Walker Papers; cf. Wrigley (1964).

151 Walker's letters from 1894–7 touch frequently on the question of how to match the demands following the growth of the work, the available church funds and the adherence to the principle of self-support; cf. summary in Walker to Baylis, 8 June 1897, no. 224; and 17 June 1897, no. 223, G3. A5/013.

152 Walker to Wilfred, 9 May 1896; Walker to Baylis, 11 May 1896; cf. also Walker to Baylis, 14 Jan. 1897, no. 110, G3. A5/013. The chiefs at all levels got a share of the tax they had collected. Walker gives an outline of the chiefs' sources of income in letters to Basil and Baylis, 12 Nov. 1897, Walker Papers (the two letters are identical).

153 cf. Walker to Wilfred, 9 May 1896; and to Baylis, 11 May 1896. Late in 1897 Walker fixed the number of Europeans at about 80 and the Nubian soldiers at some 1500; Walker to Basil and Baylis, 12 Nov. 1897.

154 Walker to Baylis, 27 Jan. 1896, no. 140; and 19 Sept. 1896, no. 403, G3. A5/012; Walker to Mother, 25 June 1896, Walker Papers. cf. J.V. Taylor (1958), pp.78ff.

155 Walker to Bishop Tucker, 10 March 1898, copy in Walker Papers; Walker to Baylis, 15 March 1898, no. 112, G3. A7/01. See also Baskerville's Journal, 15 June 1898, where he ascribes the difference between two areas to the two chiefs' different attitudes and interests.

156 A number of Walker letters from 1898 dwell upon this new development: to Harriett, 2 March; to Cyril, 6 March, to Parents, 27 May and 12 Dec., all in Walker Papers. Also W. to Baylis, 21 June 1898, no. 166; and 12 Dec. 1898, no. 49, G3. A7/01.

157 Walker to Baylis, 31 March 1899, copy in Walker Papers.

158 Walker to Parents, 22 Aug. 1898, Walker Papers.

159 Walker to Baylis, 21 June 1898, no. 166, G3. A7/01; cf. Walker to Harriett, 2 March 1898; and to Father, 21 Jan. 1900, both in Walker Papers. Baskerville's Journal, 4 June 1898 and 2 Febr. 1899. A.G. Fraser comments on the low level of church workers' salaries compared to common labourers, Journals of A.G. Fraser, 11 Nov. 1901, MSS. Brit. Emp. s.283, Rhodes House.

160 Walker to Cyril, 6 March 1898; and to Father, 12 Dec. 1898. cf. Baskerville's Journal, 1 March 1898.

161 Thus Wrigley (1964), p.27.

162 Walker to Basil and Baylis, 12 Nov. 1897, Walker Papers. cf. Wrigley, op.cit. The different use of Christian names by the Protestants and the Catholics made it possible to identify people according to their creed.

163 Walker to Wilfred, 28 March 1897, Walker Papers.

164 Walker to Mother, 10 Febr. 1897, Walker Papers.

165 Walker to Father, 10 April 1897. A protest from the mission was only concerned with the date from which the new ruling should take effect; cf. Walker to Wilfred, 28 March 1897, Walker Papers; and to Baylis, 4 April 1897, no. 183, G3. A5/013. Also Walker to Ag. Commissioner Ternan, 27 March 1897, A6/3, ESA.

166 Walker to Baylis, 20 Nov. 1895, no. 52, G3. A5/012; Walker to Basil, 29 Dec. 1895, Walker Papers; cf. minutes of Finance Committee, 4 March 1895. See also Walker to Ternan, 26 Sept. 1899, FO 2/204 and A6/7, ESA.

167 See Walker to Colvile, 17 Oct. 1894, A 2/3, ESA, in which W., in accordance with an official request, makes a distinction between shambas given to teachers and to the CMS; cf. also previous note.

168 Walker to Colvile, 2 Oct. 1894, A2/3, ESA.

169 Walker to Mother, 2 March 1895, Walker Papers.

170 Walker, op.cit.

171 Walker to Mother, 3 May 1896, Walker Papers, gives an example of this rather one-sided point of view.

172 Walker to Father, 8 Nov. 1895, Walker Papers.

173 Walker to Mother, 3 May 1896; cf. minutes of Mengo Church Council, 9 May 1896, Kitakule Journal.

174 Minutes of Mengo Church Council, 9 May 1896; Walker to Mother, 3 May; and to Wilfred, 9 May 1896, Walker Papers; Walker to Baylis, 11 May 1896, no. 222, G3. A5/012.

175 Walker to Mother, 3 May 1896.

176 Minutes of Mengo Church Council, 9 May 1896.

177 Walker indicates in 1899 that nobody is allowed to take a shamba without the consent of the Katikiro: Walker to Baylis, 24 April 1899, no. 114, G3. A7/01.

178 The missionaries were not members of the Mengo Church Council, but acted as advisers and kept the minute book. cf. Walker to Baylis, 3 Aug. 1895, no. 317, G3. A5/011; Walker to Ternan, 26 Sept. 1899 (see n. 166).

179 Archdeacon Walker's wish to possess a shamba is prompted by his need of labour supply; Walker to Basil, 29 Dec. 1895, Walker Papers.

180 Walker to R.P. Ashe, 28 Sept. 1894, Walker Papers.

181 Colvile to FO, 12 April 1895, answering queries from the Aborigines' Protection Society, FO 2/92, in PP C. 7708, Africa no. 7 (1895), pp. 143ff. Colvile's accusation was clearly in reprisal for the missionaries' complaints about the colonial government's harsh treatment of Africans, cf. above. For Walker's comments, see W. to Father, 8 Nov. 1895; cf. W. to Wilfred, 19 Sept.; and to Basil, 20 Sept. 1895, all in Walker Papers.

182 This result can be read from Walker to Basil, 20 Sept. 1895; and to Father, 8 Nov. 1895.

183 'Here in Uganda all work is forced labour.' Walker to Parents, 9 June 1897, Walker Papers.

184 Walker to Basil and Baylis, 12 Nov. 1897.

185 Minutes of Finance Committee, 16 Sept. 1899.

186 Walker to Baylis, 22 Sept. 1899, no. 219, G3 A7/01. 'We find it false economy to accept forced labour.'

187 ibid. and Walker to Baylis, 11 Oct. 1899, no. 241, G3. A7/01.

188 H.W. West (1964), p. 4. Ch. 1 gives a general introduction to the traditional system of land tenure. See also H.W. West (1972) and J.A. Rowe (1964a).

189 West (1964), p. 2.

190 Walker to Ternan, 26 Sept. 1899 (see n.166).

191 Aptly summarized in Walker to Baylis, 24 April 1899, no. 114, G3. A7/01.

192 See summary in Walker to Baylis, 17 June 1897, no. 243, G3. A5/013. The distinction between mission and church constitutes a major theme in Hansen (1980).

193 cf. Walker to Baylis, 22 June 1899, no. 151, G3 A7/01.

194 Walker to Baylis, 17 June 1897; cf. minutes of the Finance Committee, 6 May 1897.

195 Walker to Baylis, 18 Dec. 1897, no. 63; and 23 Dec. 1897, no. 65, G3. A7/01.

196 The matter is aptly summarized in Walker to Parents, 20 Oct. 1898, Walker Papers; and Tucker to H.E. Fox, 7 June 1899, no. 149, G3. A7/01. cf. Hansen (1980).

197 Walker to Baylis, 20 Sept. 1898, no. 187; and 22 June 1899, no. 151, G3. A7/01.

198 Berkeley to Marquess of Salisbury, Lake Naivasha, 26 Jan. 1897, in FOCP, part 49,

no. 47, p. 55; cf. D.A. Low & R.C. Pratt (1960), p. 17. Berkeley drew a distinction between private land and public land, but he did not make himself clear as to the implications of such a distinction. Concerning Colvile's ruling see L.L. Kato (1971), pp.155ff.

199 Walker to Basil, 29 Dec. 1895, Walker Papers; Walker to Ternan 26 Sept. 1899 (see n. 166). cf. Low & Pratt, op. cit., where no distinction is made between church land and mission land.

200 See Low & Pratt, op. cit., pp.17ff.

201 For general land policy see Low & Pratt, op. cit., and Kato, op. cit.

202 Low & Pratt, op. cit.; cf. Walker to Baylis, 24 April 1899, no. 114, G3. A7/01.

203 Walker, op. cit., contains his review of the situation.

204 ibid. See also Walker to Baylis, 22 June 1899.

205 cf. Ternan to Sir Clement Hill, 27 June 1899, FO 2/202. These considerations took a concrete form in Ternan's proposal that 'in future the ownership of all land should be jointly exercised by the Government and the inhabiting tribe . . .' Land must be set aside for government purposes; no gifts were in future to be made, and all sales and leases should be under official control. Ternan to Marquess of Salisbury, 22 July 1899, FO 2/203; cf. Walker to Harriett, 23 July 1899, Walker Papers. See also Low & Pratt (1960), p. 19, and Kato (1971), p. 157.

206 Walker to Baylis, 11 Oct. 1899, no. 241, G3, A7/01.

207 Walker to Father, 22 Oct. 1899, Walker Papers.

208 Walker is close to admitting this in his letter of explanation to Ternan, 26 Sept. 1899.

209 The whole case is reported in Walker to Baylis, 11 Oct. 1899.

210 Ternan to Sub-Commissioner, Bunyoro, 19 Sept. 1899, A5/7, ESA.

211 cf. Tucker to Baylis, 22 Sept. 1899, no. 216, G3 A7/01.

212 'Memorials of Instruments Affecting Land' is printed in H.W. West (1969), pp.10ff; the seven sites are mentioned on p. 12. cf. also Walker to Father, 22 Oct. 1899, Walker Papers, and Tucker to Baylis, 2 Oct. 1899 with enclosure, no. 217, G3. A7/01.

213 Walker to Ternan, 26 Sept. 1899. The number of shambas amounts to 83, cf. Ternan to FO, 28 Sept. 1899, FO 2/204, in which Walker's letter is enclosed.

214 Ternan to Walker, 28 Sept. 1899, A7/5, ESA.

215 Ternan to Marquess of Salisbury, 28 Sept. 1899, FO 2/204, in FOCP, part 59, no. 82, p. 96.

216 Walker to Father, 22 Oct. 1899.

217 Tucker to Baylis, 2 Oct. 1899; and Tucker to H.E. Fox, 2 Oct. 1899, G/AC 4/30. The divergence between Walker and Tucker has been dealt with in detail in Hansen (1980), pp.246ff.

218 Ternan, op. cit.

219 Walker to Ternan, 26 Sept. 1899.

220 Ternan, op. cit.; and Ternan to Walker, 28 Sept. 1899.

221 The background for the appointment of Sir Harry Johnston can be found in R. Oliver (1957), ch. 10, and in Low & Pratt (1960), pp.13ff.

222 Note by Sir Harry Johnston on Ternan's dispatch, 28 Sept. 1899, FO 2/204. Johnston's note is not dated, but it is presumably written in the last part of October or the beginning of November, while he camped at Naivasha or Eldama Ravine; cf. Oliver, op.cit.

223 Johnston, op. cit., supplemented by the analysis of his first proposals in Low & Pratt (1960), pp.22ff. cf. also Oliver (1957), pp.299ff.

224 Johnston, op.cit.

225 ibid.

226 Johnston confined himself to the remark that all three missions considered the allotment of 92 sq.m 'a perfectly fair settlement of their claims'. Johnston to Marquess of Salisbury, 12 March 1900, FO 2/297. Bishop Tucker's and Archdeacon Walker's official letters to the CMS headquarters contain nothing about this issue within the actual period, nor do Walker's letters to his family. Almost as an afterthought Tucker tells about the grant of 40 sq.m as an endowment to the church. His only worry is whether in case of surplus, Johnston will reclaim any over and above the 40 sq.m, but in that case Tucker will object. Tucker to H.E. Fox, 15 Febr. 1900 (private letter), G/AC 4/30, CMS Arch. Otherwise it is remarkable that so little is said about this vital matter. For the question of church land see also Tucker (1908), vol. II, pp.268ff, and Low & Pratt (1960), pp.74ff.

227 The Uganda Agreement, which incidentally only deals with Buganda, is reproduced in Low & Pratt, op.cit., app. II (quotation from clause 15). See also J.V. Wild (1955). A few days after the conclusion of the Agreement Walker reports that the CMS holds 40 out of the 92 sq.m. Walker to Baylis, 14 May 1900, no. 88, G3. A7/02. cf. also Johnston to Tucker, 2 May 1900, copy in Bishop's Files: K–L. Land 1912–1913. Subfile: Land General.

228 Johnston to Marquess of Salisbury, 12 March 1900; Walker, op. cit.

229 Tucker's main concern was that it would be difficult and expensive for the church when the teachers had to pay the hut tax of 3 rupees annually; see below.

230 cf. Low & Pratt (1960), p. 106. Tucker reckons that the 40 sq. m, allotted to the CMS amounts to about 1,000 shambas spread over the country. This represents a higher figure than the Protestants had before; cf. Tucker to Baylis, 15 Sept. 1900, no. 172, G3. A7/02. It appears later that the 40 sq.m are supposed to meet the claims for land also in the neighbouring areas. Johnston to Tucker, 4 Oct. 1900, A23/1, ESA. See also below, ch. 10.

231 Tucker (1908), vol. II, p. 259; Baskerville's Journal, 9 May 1900; cf. Walker to Commissioner Hayes Sadler, 22 July 1902, A22/1, ESA. cf. also H.B. Thomas & A.E. Spencer (1938), pp.65ff.

232 cf. Low & Pratt (1960), p. 148.

233 Tucker to Deputy Commissioner F.J. Jackson, 10 Sept. 1900; and to Johnston, 17 Sept. 1900, both in A22/1, ESA. Archdeacon Walker had at that time been invalided home and could not report on this phase of the land question.

234 Otherwise Tucker stuck to his proposal that the missionaries should be full members of the church; cf. Hansen (1980) and above, p.97.

235 Tucker to Baylis, 15 Sept. 1900; J. Roscoe (ag. secr. for the CMS mission) to Baylis, 14 Sept. 1900, no. 180, and 23 Nov. 1900, no. 24, G3. A7/02.

236 Johnston to Tucker, 4 Oct. 1900.

237 e.g. Jackson to Rev. Millar, 8 March 1901: 'please keep the two lots apart and separate, otherwise we will get confused, I fear'. cf. Jackson to Tucker, 12 Sept. 1900, both in A 23/1, ESA. A further confusing element was that some of the missionaries possessed their own plots and wanted to have them registered as private property. See Baskerville to Cunningham (secr. to colonial administration), 9 and 31 Aug. 1900; Roscoe to Cunningham, 16 Aug. 1900, both in A22/1, ESA. cf. minutes of Finance Committee, 5 March 1900; and Tucker's and Walker's strong opposition to this practice, Tucker to Baylis, 14 March 1900, no. 83; and Walker to Baylis, 14 March 1900, no. 88, both in G3. A7/02.

238 Cunningham to K.E. Borup (CMS missionary), 10 Oct. 1900, A23/1; and Tucker to Cunningham, 17 Jan. 1901, A22/1, ESA.

239 The Deputy Commissioner, F.J. Jackson, seems at one stage to have accepted a formula which included the Mengo Church Council, but this is significantly, though tacitly, cancelled later. Jackson to Tucker, 12 Sept. 1900, A23/1, in answer to Tucker to Jackson, 10 Sept. 1900, A22/1, ESA.

7   Colonial rule established

1 I am especially indebted to D.A. Low, Part I in D.A. Low & R.C. Pratt (1960). Use has also been made of R. Oliver (1957), D.A. Low (1957a, unpubl. thesis), J.V. Wild (1955). A good summary may be found in M. Twaddle (1969): cf. also D.A. Low (1971a), pp.40ff, and S.R. Karugire (1980), pp.75ff. On the land question see J.A. Rowe (1964), H.B. Thomas & A.E. Spencer (1938), ch. 13.

2 Johnston made an attempt to solve the difficulty of mixing the names of the Protectorate and the Kingdom of Buganda by recommending that *Buganda* be reserved for the latter, while *Uganda* meant the whole Protectorate, but his proposal was only adopted in 1908. Walker to Cyril, 11 Jan. 1900, Walker Papers; Governor Hesketh Bell to Secr. of State, 10 March 1908, CO 536/18–13464, and Wild (1955), p.95.

3 See in particular Low & Pratt (1960), pp.142ff; and D. Apter (1961), pp.112ff.

4 Tucker to H.E. Fox, 15 Febr. 1900, G/AC 4/30, CMS Arch. For the wider social implications of the land settlement, see T.B. Kabwegyere (1976).

5 cf. E. Hertslet (1967), pp.397ff.

6 The Uganda Agreement is printed in Low & Pratt (1960), app. II; in Wild (1955) and in M.S.M. Kiwanuka (1971), app. C.

7 Bishop Hanlon to Johnston, 26 March 1900, quoted in D.A. Low (1957b), p.12.

8 Johnston to Hanlon, 2 April 1900, quoted in Low & Pratt (1960), p. 97. Johnston expressed himself in similar terms in Johnston to Marquess of Salisbury, 6 April 1900, FO 2/298.

9 This principle was repeated to the Protestants in a similar case in Toro; Johnston to Tucker, 19 Aug. 1900, A23/1, ESA.

10 Tucker to Johnston, 29 Nov. 1900, A22/1, ESA. The whole issue is dealt with in T. Tuma (1973, unpubl. thesis), pp.207ff.

11 Johnston to Tucker, 1 Dec. 1900, A 23/1, ESA. On another occasion Johnston expressed himself in similar terms: 'It is not in the interest of the British Government that Mohammedanism should receive any more adherents than we can help in Uganda as Muslims are proverbially difficult to manage . . . ' Quoted by K. Lockard (1974, unpubl. thesis), p. 112.

12 cf. Johnston to Marquess of Salisbury, 6 April 1900.

13 With regard to the first visit of a Catholic missionary to Ankole in late 1900, the Omugabe's and his leading chiefs' hostile reaction, and the Collector's interference to avoid a Buganda-like situation with two religious parties, see Rev. H. Clayton's Journal, 8 Jan. 1901, and Rev. J.J. Willis' Journal, 23 Dec. 1900, 9 Jan 1901, MUL. The Ankole chiefs' protests were forwarded to Bishop Streicher who took strong exception to the government's handling of the issue; Streicher to Secr. to the Administration, J. Cunningham, Villa Maria, 23 Febr. 1901, A24/1, ESA. The official ban on Catholic missionary work in Ankole was issued in Oct. 1901; see Dep. Commissioner Wilson to Streicher, 5 Oct. 1901; and lifted in March 1902; see Wilson to Streicher, 11 March 1902, both in A24/1. But Wilson had as early as August 1901 indicated that it was not possible for long to keep the Catholics out of Ankole as they had appealed home; cf. Clayton's Journal, 11 Aug. 1901. See also about this whole incident T.S.M. Williams (1965, unpubl. MA thesis), pp.163ff. For a general account of the arrival of the two missions in Ankole and the wider effects of the dual missionary

presence, see M.R. Doornbos (1978), ch. 3, esp. pp. 86ff; and M.L. Pirouet (1978), ch. 4.

14 Johnston to Marquess of Salisbury, 6 April 1900. In one respect Johnston changed Portal's arrangement: he abolished the system of two Katikiros and placed the administration of justice in the hands of the saza chiefs, thus separating the administration of justice from the religious divisions within each saza. See Tucker to H.E. Fox, 15 Febr. 1900.

15 Low (1957b), p. 12; Low & Pratt (1960), pp.95ff; cf. also Johnston, op.cit.

16 Table compiled on the basis of results produced by D.A. Low and presented in Low & Pratt, op.cit., ch. 4 and 5. For the membership of the Lukiko cf. also D.A. Low (1959), pp.64ff. On the official list the religious affiliation is marked after each name. See also list of saza chiefs indicating their religion in Johnston, op.cit., and the map drawn in B.W. Langlands & G. Namirembe (1967), p.14.

17 This line of reasoning is based on Low & Pratt, op.cit., pp.122ff.

18 The rent was in 1902 fixed to 2 Rs a year for each plot. In comparison the annual hut tax was 3 Rs. Walker to Commissioner Hayes Sadler, 22 July 1902, A22/1 ESA, gives a thorough description of the position of the minor chiefs.

19 cf. Low & Pratt, op. cit., pp.123ff. The number of allottees is increased from 1,000 specified in the Agreement to a figure of 3,900 (ibid., p.116). See also H.W. West (1964), p.11, and West (1972), pp.18ff.

20 These comparisons can be read out of the tables in Low & Pratt, op.cit., pp. 123–6.

21 This comparison between the Protestant/Catholic and the pagan elements within the sazas is based on the tables in Low & Pratt, loc. cit.

22 cf. Tucker to Baylis, 8 June 1900, no. 128; and 20 June 1900, no. 137; Roscoe to Baylis, 23 Nov. 1900, no. 24; all in G3. A7/02. See also A.R. Tucker (1908), vol. II, pp.260ff.

23 cf. Low & Pratt, op. cit., pp.108ff.

24 cf. Low (1971a), p.48.

25 cf. Twaddle (1969), p.313; and Twaddle (1974).

26 Characteristically expressed by Bishop Tucker: 'It is entirely due to the work of the Mission that these men are at all qualified to undertake the work which the Government is placing in their hands.' Tucker to H.E. Fox, 15 Febr. 1900, G/AC 4/30.

27 The outcome is summarized in Twaddle (1969), p.310.

28 cf. C.C. Wrigley (1964), p.31.

29 David Apter has discussed the relevance of applying the concept of class in describing this system of stratification, but has come to a negative conclusion in view of the great mobility that comes to prevail between the various strata. Apter (1961), pp.110ff.

30 Johnston to Marquess of Salisbury, 12 March 1900, FO 2/297. cf. Tucker's own account of relations with Johnston during the negotiations, in Tucker to Fox, 15 Febr. 1900.

31 See Low & Pratt (1960), chs. 2, 3 and 4 *passim*; cf. Johnston to Walker, 17 Febr. 1900, Walker Papers.

32 Low & Pratt, op. cit., pp.83ff; Johnston to Walker, 4 April 1900, Walker Papers.

33 One example appears in Walker to Father, 30 Jan. 1900, Walker Papers. See also Tucker to Fox, 15 Febr. 1900 and in particular 14 Jan. 1900, where the chiefs' anxiety with regard to Johnston's first proposals is reported. Extracts of the letter in FO 2/378. In the internal minutes in the FO Tucker was called 'an alarmist', and Lord Salisbury bluntly called him 'a meddlesome man – a pestilent priest'.

34 Walker to Father, 18 Febr. 1900, Walker Papers.

35 Walker to Johnston, 10 Febr. 1900, A6/8, ESA, cf. Low & Pratt (1960), p.76.

36 cf. Low & Pratt, op. cit., pp.50ff and 62.

37 'The chiefs seem fairly satisfied which is the main consideraton. How it will affect our work remains to be seen.' Bishop Tucker seems here to present the position of the CMS in the negotiations. Tucker to Baylis, 13 March 1900, no. 81, G3. A7/02.

38 H.P. Gale (1959), pp.203ff.

39 cf. Low & Pratt (1960), pp.38 and 88.

40 Thus Johnston to Tucker, 19 Aug. 1900, A23/1, regarding Toro; and Johnston to Bishop Streicher, Mumia's, 14 April 1901, A24/1, regarding two sazas in Buganda (both letters in ESA).

41 One example can be found in Johnston to Tucker, 19 Aug. 1900, where he expresses much sympathy with and preference for the work of the CMS and where he refers to his cordial relations with Tucker.

42 Sir John Kennaway to CMS secretary at headquarters, 10 July 1900; Baylis to Tucker, 27 July 1900; Tucker to Baylis, 31 Oct. 1900, no. 1, all in G3. A7/02 & L1. A reflection of this discussion appears in Walker to M.J.W., 6 Febr. 1902, Walker Papers.

43 Tucker to Baylis, 15 Febr. 1900, no. 77, G3. A7/02. Tucker brought this matter forward even before the conclusion of the Agreement.

44 Walker to Father, 18 Febr. 1900, Walker Papers. Walker figures out that the double taxation means 6 Rs, compared to the usual pay of 10 Rs from the church.

45 Low & Pratt (1960), p. 98. Tucker was beforehand very pessimistic about the outcome. Tucker, (see n.43).

46 Roscoe (Ag. Secretary) to Jackson (Dep. Commissioner), 23 Aug. 1900, A22/1, ESA.

47 Commissioner's Office to Roscoe, 30 Aug. 1900, A23/1, ESA.

48 Cunningham (secr. to the colonial administration) to Père Bresson, 10 Oct. 1900, copy in A23/1. Copies were sent to all missions, thus one in Ch. of Ug. Arch., MUL.

49 Tucker to Johnston, 29 Oct. 1900, A22/1, ESA.

50 Report by HM's Special Commissioner, encl. in Johnston to Marquess of Lansdowne, 10 July 1901, in PP C. 671, Africa no. 7 (1901), p.18.

51 Johnston, op. cit.; cf. also Preliminary Report by HM's Special Commissioner, encl. in Johnston to Marquess of Salisbury, 27 April 1900, in PP C. 256, Africa no. 6 (1900), p.12.

52 Tucker to Johnston, 17 Sept. 1900, A22/1; Johnston to Tucker, 4 Oct. 1900, A23/1, both in ESA. cf. West (1972), pp.54ff. The authorized fee for each estate was £2.

53 Hanlon to Johnston, 26 March 1900, quoted in Low (1957b), p.12; cf. also Low & Pratt (1962), p.97.

54 cf. E. Millar (Ag. Secr. CMS Uganda) to Baylis, 10 April 1901, no. 118, G3. A7/02. Millar discusses here the vacant saza chieftainship of Buyaga and the Catholic bid for it. cf. also Baskerville's Journal, 22 June 1900.

55 Thus Tucker to Baylis, 8 June 1900, no. 128; Report of Conference of Missionaries in Uganda, 6 Nov. 1901, no. 254; cf. also E.C. Gordon's letter to the conference, dat. 3 Nov. 1901, no. 255, all in G3. A7/02. See also Walker to Father, 24 Nov. 1901, Walker Papers; and Journals of A.G. Fraser 1900–1903, 6 Oct. 1901, MSS. Brit. Emp. s.283, Rhodes House.

56 Gordon, op. cit.

57 Journals of A.G. Fraser, 11 Nov. 1901.

58 Millar to Baylis, 19 June 1901, no. 165, G3. A7/02. *Mengo Notes* July 1901 (a monthly magazine issued by local CMS missionaries, later called *Uganda Notes*. Copy in MUL).

59 Millar to Baylis, 21 May 1901, no. 141, G3. A7/02. *Mengo Notes*, June 1901.

60 Millar to Baylis, 27 March 1901, no. 111, G3. A7/02. *Mengo Notes*, April 1901.

61 Baskerville's Journal, 22 June and 11 July 1900.

62 Tucker to H.E. Fox, 7 June 1899, no. 149, G3. A7/01.

63 The minutes of the Mengo Church Council from the 1890s are in two different minute books: (1) Meetings of Church Elders April 1892 – Oct. 1892, Minute Book of the Eastern Equatorial African Diocese, now in CMS Arch. (2) Minutes of the Mengo Church Council Sept. 1893 – Oct. 1899, also called Kitakule Journal (after the Rev. H.W. Duta Kitakule), Ch. of Ug. Arch., MUL. Until Oct. 1896 the minutes are in English, thereafter in Luganda. Mr D. Senono has assisted in the translation.

64 Thus J.V. Taylor (1958), pp.70ff; and D.A. Low (1965), p.115.

65 D.A. Low (1957b, pp.13ff) has made a careful analysis of the chiefs' and clergymen's background in about 1900.

66 Taylor (1958), p.68.

67 Low, op.cit.

68 Tucker to Baylis, 23 Jan. 1901, no.77, G3. A7/02.

69 When Walker in 1897 listed ten men as participants in the ordinands' class, it appears that only one had been a chief. Walker to Stockdale, 18 Aug. 1898, Walker Papers.

70 Walker to Baylis, 12 Nov. 1897, G3. A5/014. cf. also Walker's 'The Native Clergy in Uganda' dat. 3 Aug. 1900, Walker Papers.

71 This came to the surface at the first meetings of the Diocesan Synod, 1906 and 1907. Minutes of the Diocesan Synod, Ch. of Ug. Arch., MUL.

72 The contradiction in the mission's attitude is already evident by 1892 when Henry Wright Duta refuses a chieftainship, while the missionaries advise Mika Sematimba to become a chief. See Baskerville's Journal, 14 March 1892; cf. M.L. Pirouet (1978), pp.21ff. In 1897 Walker reports with satisfaction that Tomasi Semfuma will give up a chieftainship on ordination. At the same time he is faced with the Katikiro's request to have an ordained man appointed to a leading chieftainship. Walker to Wilfred, 9 May 1897; and to Parents, 9 June 1897, Walker Papers.

73 Tucker to Baylis, 16 Oct. 1899, no. 239 (read after the Precis), G3. A7/P1. Tucker mentions specifically that the Katikiro participates in the meeting of the Church Council at which the scheme for a church organization is passed. Tucker to Baylis, 15 Sept. 1900, no. 172, G3. A7/02. Quite significantly the legal document is signed both by the Katikiro and the leading clergyman, H.W. Duta.

74 Tucker to Jackson, 10 Sept. 1900, A22/1, ESA.

8 A case-study from Toro

1 The most extensive account of the start of Christian work in Toro can be found in M.L. Pirouet (1978), ch. 2; cf. also O. W. Furley (1961).

2 About Toro in general see D.A. Low (1957a, unpubl. thesis), chs. 5–7; Low (1965), pp.66ff; K. Ingham (1975), ch. 3; E.I. Steinhart (1973); Steinhart (1977), ch. 4. The basic account of Kasagama's whole reign may be found in Furley, op.cit.

3 cf. Steinhart (1973), pp.269ff. This opinion was generally held by the Catholic mission; see for instance Bishop Hirth to Colvile, 27 April 1894, in PP C. 7708, Africa no. 7 (1895), p.840.

4 cf. Pirouet (1978), pp.42ff.

5 See Ashburnham's own report in A. to Commissioner, 18 Dec. 1895, A4/3 in ESA (henceforth references to A-series all in ESA); and Archdeacon Walker's in W. to Mother, 2 Dec. 1895; to Basil, 29 Dec. 1895; to Father, 9 Jan. 1896, all in Walker Papers.

6 Ashburnham to Commissioner, 12 Nov., 11 Dec., 18 Dec. and 26 Dec. 1895; cf. also Walker Correspondence (see n.5).

7 Walker to Cyril, 3 March 1896, Walker Papers.

8 cf. Tucker to Commissioner, 27 Nov. 1895, A6/1, and Tucker to Baylis, 14 Jan. 1896, no. 102, G3. A5/012.

9 cf. Walker's account in W. to Cyril, 3 (and 6) March 1896, Walker Papers.

10 ibid. and Ashburnham to Commissioner, 18 and 26 Dec. 1895, A4/3.

11 cf. Ashburnham to Commissioner, 26 Dec. 1895. See also Steinhart (1977), p.113.

12 cf. Ashburnham to Commissioner, 11, 18 and 26 Dec. 1895.

13 These two political motives were clearly expressed in Walker to Baylis, 2 (and 7) March 1896, no.182, G3. A5/012.

14 ibid., and W. to Cyril, 3 March 1896. cf. Berkeley's own account in B. to Marquess of Salisbury, 14 March 1896, FOCP, part 45, p.225.

15 Walker to Basil, 2 (and 15) March 1896, Walker Papers. Tucker to Baylis, 19 March 1896, no. 180, G3. A5/012.

16 See Tucker's own account of the visit in T. to Mr Stock, 14 and 30 April, 9 and 12 May 1896, no. 352 & 353, G3. A5/012. cf. Ingham (1975), pp.82ff.

17 See Tucker to Mr Stock, 9 May 1896; Walker to Baylis, 16 Aug. 1897, no. 297, G3. A5/013. cf. Pirouet (1978), pp.43ff, and Steinhart (1977), *passim.*

18 About the temporary appointment see Berkeley to Marquess of Salisbury, 14 March 1896.

19 See Walker to Baylis, 9 April 1896, no. 204, G3 A5/012, and W. to Mother, 3 May 1896, Walker Papers.

20 See Tucker's account of the visit in Tucker, op. cit.; cf. also A.B. Fisher's later account in Book VI, p.21, Fisher Papers (on microfilm in MUL).

21 Guillermain to Berkeley, 12 Jan. and 28 Febr. 1896, A6/2, in FOCP, part 45, p.226.

22 Berkeley to Guillermain, 24 Jan. and 14 March 1896, A7/2, in FOCP, loc. cit.

23 Capt. Ashburnham to Commissioner, 4 May 1896, enclosing Fr Achte's complaints, dat. 30 April 1896; and Tucker's denial of the allegations, dat. 1 May 1896; all in A4/5. cf. also Kasagama's opposition towards appointing Byakweyamba's Catholic substitute to any office, reported in Sitwell to Commissioner, 1 June 1896, A4/5.

24 Sitwell to Commissioner, 30 June 1896. He reiterated later 'how one's time and patience is wasted here'; Sitwell to Commissioner, 10 Aug. 1896, both in A4/5.

25 Reported in Sitwell to Commissioner, 30 June 1896.

26 cf. Sitwell to Commissioner, 1 Aug. 1896, A4/5, and 16 Sept. 1896, A4/6.

27 Thus Bishop Streicher to Commissioner, 13 Aug. 1896, reproducing a report from Fr Achte, in A6/2. cf. also Sitwell to Commissioner, 16 Sept. 1896.

28 cf. Sitwell's allegation against Fisher in S. to Commissioner, 16 Sept. 1896. See Book VI and VII in Fisher Papers for tensions seen from the CMS point of view.

29 Sitwell, Report on Toro District 1897–1898, dat. 4 June 1898, in FOCP, part 56, p. 77; cf. also the Commissioner's plan to raise the issue of Fisher's attitude with the CMS leaders in the capital; Berkeley to Sitwell, 11 Nov. 1896, A5/2.

30 Sitwell had occasionally to admit such mistakes; see for instance S. to Commissioner, 6 Dec. 1896, A4/6. He indicated also that it was difficult to know whom to believe 'in such a collection of liars'. S. to Commissioner, 30 June 1896, A4/5.

31 See Sitwell to Commissioner, 2 June 1896, A4/5; Berkeley to Sitwell, 25 Aug. and 26 Aug. 1896, both in A5/2; Sitwell to Berkeley, 16 Sept. 1896, A4/6.

32 cf. Sitwell to Commissioner, 9 Oct. 1896, A4/6.

33 Berkeley to Sitwell, 18 May 1896, A5/2.

34 Berkeley, op.cit., cf. also Sitwell's report on his lecture to the Toro leaders in S. to Berkeley, 19 and 30 June 1896, A4/5.

35 Berkeley to Sitwell, 25 Aug. 1896, A5/2.

36 Berkeley to Sitwell, 11 Nov. 1896, A5/2; and Berkeley's general report on the Uganda Protectorate, dat. 26 Jan. 1897, in FOCP, part 49, p.55.

37 Thus Sitwell to Berkeley, 1 Aug. 1896; cf. also Sitwell to Berkeley, 30 June 1896, both in A4/5.

38 cf. Steinhart (1977), pp.116ff, where also a certain correspondence between religious and ethnic divisions has been suggested.

39 cf. Sitwell to Commissioner, 10 Aug. 1896, A4/5.

40 Reported in Sitwell to Commissioner, 1 Aug. 1896, A4/5.

41 Sitwell to Commissioner, 16 Sept. 1896, A4/6.

42 Commissioner to Sitwell, 25 Aug. and 11 Nov. 1896, A5/2.

43 Sitwell to Commissioner, 30 June 1896, A4/5; Berkeley to Sitwell, 25 Aug. 1896, A5/2; and Berkeley's report of 26 Jan. 1897 (n.36).

44 cf. Sitwell to Commissioner, late May 1896 and 30 June 1896, both in A4/5.

45 cf. Sitwell to Commissioner, 30 June 1896, A4/5.

46 Sitwell to Commissioner, 10 Aug. 1896, A4/5.

47 See Steinhart (1977), p.115. A parallel situation occurred five years later in Ankole, where the Omugabe explicitly referred to the experiences from Buganda and settled for Protestantism to the exclusion of the Catholic mission: see J.J. Willis' Journal, 9 Jan. 1901, MUL.

48 The colonial administration ascribed the improvement to the departure of Mr Fisher on leave; cf. Sitwell, Report on Toro District 1897–1898 (n.29).

49 cf. Sitwell to Ag. Commissioner, 10 Febr. and 20 Nov. 1897, A4/7 and A4/9.

50 Baskerville's Journal, 2 Oct. 1898.

51 Fr Roche to Capt. Bagge, 23 June 1899, A6/6 (Fr Roche had replaced Fr Achte, and Capt. Bagge had replaced Capt. Sitwell). About the Ganda influence see Steinhart (1977), pp.120ff. cf. also Walker to Baylis, 17 Dec. 1899, no. 27, G3. A7/02.

52 Fr Achte to Ag. Commissioner Ternan, 20 July 1899, A6/6.

53 Ternan to Fr Achte, 22 July 1899, A7/5.

54 Ternan to the French Mission, 16 Oct. 1899, A7/5; cf. Ternan to Bagge, 19 Oct. 1899, A5/8; and Bishop Streicher to Ternan, 21 Oct. 1899, A6/7.

55 See for instance Sir Harry Johnston to Tucker, Fort Portal (Toro), 19 and 21 Aug. 1900, A23/1; cf. Steinhart (1977), p.120. The collector in Toro later recommended his removal from the district, cf. Wylde to Commissioner, 27 Dec. 1901, A14, and Ingham (1975), p.108.

56 Ternan to Bagge, 8 Sept. 1899, A5/7.

57 Bagge to Ternan, 20 Aug. and 22 Sept. 1899, A4/20 and A4/21.

58 One of the CMS missionaries, Rev. H.E. Maddox, emphasized later that Bagge always ruled through the chiefs. Maddox to Ag. Commissioner George Wilson, 3 Sept. 1904, A22/1.

59 Thus expressed in Ternan to Bagge, 8 Sept. 1899; cf. also the issue of permitting the Catholics to erect a chapel within the area of a Protestant chief; Fr Roche to Bagge, 21 Aug. 1899, A6/6; Bagge to Ternan, 23 Aug. 1899, A4/20.

60 cf. Maddox's account in M. to George Wilson, 3 Sept. 1904. A copy of the Agreement

can be found in Owen Papers: Land Question in Toro, CMS Arch., acc. 83; cf. also Ingham (1975), ch. 4, and Steinhart (1977), pp.177ff.

61 Steinhart, op. cit., pp.122, 228ff.

62 In an addendum to the Agreement, see Ingham, op. cit., p.92.

63 Fr von Wees to Johnston, 10 Oct. 1900; and Johnston to Fr Bresson, 19 Oct. 1900, both in A24/1.

64 For the post-Agreement period see Furley (1961), pp.194ff; Ingham (1975), ch. 4; Steinhart (1977), pp.224ff.

65 See the list of Toro chiefs in 1906 in Steinhart, op. cit., p.236. Of the 10 county chiefs 3 were Catholics, but only one was left in 1907. See also below, ch.17.

Part III Land grants and labour services

9 *Mission and church land*

1 F.G. Bailey (1969), pp.9ff.

2 Walker to Sadler, 22 July 1902, A22/1, ESA. Sub-Commissioner Jackson had earlier reported the discontent among the minor chiefs regarding their remuneration; Jackson to Secr. of State, 25 Jan. 1902 FO 2/589.

3 Johnston to Tucker, 4 Oct. 1900, A22/1.

4 Johnston to Tucker, 13 and 18 Sept. 1901, copies with min. 108, SMP 470^I. The whole matter has been summarized in CO 536/100–30631/1920; cf. H.B. Thomas & A.E. Spencer (1938), p. 52, and H.W. West (1972), p.54.

5 Eastern Province Minute Papers, unnumbered file: Misc. Corresp. 1903, ESA; cf. also memorandum by the three Ugandan bishops to the Educational Conference, Sept. 1917, min. 29, SMP 4844.

6 e.g. Secr. of State to Governor, 30 May 1914, SMP 470^I, and CO 536/68–16978/14; cf. also CO memorandum, 10 Aug. 1915, SMP 4915, copy in CO 536/79–37090/1915.

7 See Trustees of Native Anglican Church to Land Officer, 30 March 1914, CO 536/68–16978. The enclosed CO minutes indicate that exchanges of land held in Buganda with land in other districts were a normal practice.

8 e.g. Bishop Willis to PC Eastern Province, 17 Nov. 1914, SMP 470^I. cf. also the three bishops' memorandum of Sept. 1917.

9 Memorandum on land held by the Native Anglican Church, 12 Nov. 1917, min. 108, SMP 470^I; cf. also Willis to Governor, 19 April 1918 (draft), Bishop's Files: K–L. Land 1912–13. Subfile: Land. Memoranda.

10 Minutes in CO 536/68–16978/1914.

11 cf. Willis to PC, 17 Nov. 1914.

12 Willis to Governor, 24 Nov. 1924, SMP 470^{II}. Ag. Chief Secr. to Willis, 12 Dec. 1924, with enclosure; Ag. Ass. Land Officer to Land Officer, 10 Dec. 1924, Bishop's Files: K–L. Land 1912–1913. Subfile: Land, General; cf. also West (1972), p.54.

13 For discussion see D.A. Low & R.C. Pratt (1960), ch.6.

14 West (1972), pp.34ff, 54ff, and figure 2 (p. 67). This distinction between mailo land and freehold land, the latter originally vested in the Crown and thus a Crown grant, appeared as early as 1923 in connection with the prohibition of sale of land to non-natives (minutes in SMP 9561), and was fully explained in 1929 in H.B. Thomas, Land Officer, to Chief Secr., 16 July 1929, SMP 4917.

15 cf. Buganda Land Law 1908, s.2(c), in H.W. West (1964), app. A.

16 Copy of Certificate of Claim in Bishop's Files (see n.12).

17 e.g. discussion between Archdeacon Walker and colonial officials in 1906, SMP 501/1906.

18 The CMS even took legal advice from Sir R.B. Finlay; copy of his memorandum, dat. 16 Jan. 1907, in Bishop's Files (see n.12). This should probably be seen as a response to a statement from the Crown Advocate, 19 June 1906, min. 5, SMP 501/1906.

10   Mission land demands: the government response

1 It proved to be an enormous and time consuming task to accomplish the surveying programme, and it was in fact only finalized in 1936. H.B. Thomas & A.E. Spencer (1938); and H.W. West (1972), p.35.

2 cf. D.A. Low (1965), pp.91ff.

3 West, op.cit., *passim*. See also A.B. Mukwaya (1953), ch. 2.

4 See precis of the 7 reports in SMP 2198, Notes by Perryman, 11 Jan. 1922. See also K. Ingham (1958), pp.95ff., and D.A. Low & R.C. Pratt (1960), pp.228ff.

5 For a thorough discussion of this problem see C.C. Wrigley (1959), pp.27ff. cf. Low & Pratt (1960), pp.227ff; H.F. Morris & J.S. Read (1966), pp.44ff; and G.F. Engholm (1968, unpubl. thesis), ch. 1.

6 CO minute 9 April 1915, CO 536/75–14664/1915, cf. memorandum by Mr Bottomley of the Colonial Office, 10 Aug. 1915, CO 536/79–37090/1915, also in SMP 4915.

7 For instance, Ordinance of Church of England Trustees 1908, CO 536/15–1844/07–08, and draft of Buganda Land Law 1908, CO 536/19–16358/1908.

8 e.g. exchange of letters in 1908 re Bukedi between the Collector, the Dep. Commissioner and the Governor, SMP 318/1908; cf. also Baylis to Tucker, 19 Nov. 1909, with an account of an interview with Governor Hesketh Bell, who especially complained of the rivalry when the mission opened stations in new districts: G3. A7/L2, pp.460ff.

9 When Governor Jackson in 1911 sought the approval of the CO to sell 800 acres of Crown land in Ankole to the White Fathers, officials in the CO expressed surprise that they were brought into the matter as the amount of acres was below 1,000 and therefore could be disposed of in accordance with the Crown Land Ordinance of 1903. Governor to Secr. of State, 13 Dec. 1911, CO 536/43–1288/1911–12.

10 The right procedure initiated in 1911 was clearly set out in a CO minute, 2 Oct. 1913, CO 536/61–33458/13. The CO was at that time, in contrast to the Protectorate government, rather restrictive with regard to Europeans' acquisition of freehold land; see for instance, Ag. Governor Tomkins to CO, 31 May 1910; and CO to Governor, 18 Aug. 1910, in CO 536/33–19313. See also Wrigley (1959), pp.28ff; and West (1972), pp.56f.

11 cf. Archdeacon Walker to Tomkins, 9 June 1906, SMP 501/1906; W. to Baylis, 1 Jan. 1912, no. 18, G3. A7/09.

12 This situation was summarized by the newly installed Bishop J.J. Willis in his first charge to the missionaries; Policy of the Uganda Mission, dat. July 1912, copy under no. 157, G3. A7/010 (in the following called Willis (1912)).

13 At the Synod in 1912 a Finance Board consisting of three missionaries and three Ganda chiefs was set up to consider the financial position and especially the utilization of church land. Minutes of the Synod 1912, Ch. of Ug. Arch. MUL. One missionary, A.B. Fisher, in Bunyoro, saw considerable danger if the church as such undertook the development of its estates. Fisher to Bishop, no date, but prior to the Synod in July 1910, Fisher Papers.

14 cf. Wrigley (1959); and Engholm (1968).

15 Rev. Tegart to Walker, 12 Dec. 1911, no. 19. Industrial Missions Sub-Committee to Willis, 2 April 1912, no. 78, both in G3. A7/09.

16 F. Rowling to Secr. Industrial Missions Committee, 23 Dec. 1912, no. 30, with a manuscript of Willis and Rowling encl.; Col. Kenyon (Chairman of Industrial Committee) to G.T. Manley (Baylis' successor), 9 July 1913, no. 140; cf. also Rowling's Memorandum on Uganda Church Lands Development, 18 Aug. 1913, no. 166, all in G3. A7/010. On this issue see further *Uganda Notes*, March, April and Aug. 1913; Minutes of the Board of Land to the Synod in July 1913; and Archdeacon Baskerville to Manley, 17 Oct. 1915, no. 135, G3. A7. A valuable statement of the Uganda Mission's general policy can be found in NAC Trustees to Land Officer, 30 March 1914, CO 536/68–16978.

17 See correspondence from 1913 in SMP 470[I].

18 Ag. Chief Secr. Jarvis to Secr. of State, 30 Aug. 1913, CO 536/61–33458. cf. also Governor to Secr. of State, 21 July 1911, recommending a grant to the CMS for agricultural training; CO 536/41–28663.

19 Governor to Secr. of State, 13 Dec. 1911, CO 536/43–1288/1911–12. Dep. Governor to Secr. of State, 26 March 1914, CO 536/68–14907. It is interesting to notice that the White Fathers also used the argument of becoming self-supporting by getting an income from the land; see H. Hunter to Chief Secr., 5 Jan. 1912; and Land Officer to Chief Secr., 10 Jan. 1912, SMP 2338.

20 This positive attitude was in line with the contemporary policy of encouraging European plantations; cf. John A. Rowe (1964), pp.10f; but see also the reference in n.10 with regard to divergent attitudes among colonial officials. With regard to the mission's attitude to sale of land to Europeans see below, Ch.14.

21 Ag. Chief Secr. Jarvis to Secr. of State, 30 Aug. 1913, CO 536/61–33457/1913.

22 Dep. Governor to Secre. of State, 26 March 1914, CO536/68–14907.

23 CO minute 3 Oct. 1913, CO 536/61–33458.

24 Secr. of State Harcourt to Governor, 10 Oct. 1913; cf. CO minute 6 Oct. 1913, loc. cit.

25 CO minute 30 Sept. 1913, loc. cit.

26 cf. CO minute 19 May 1914, CO 536/68–16978/14.

27 The Trustees' original letter, dat. 30 March 1914, is in CO 536/68–16978/14.

28 Ag. Chief Secr. to Secr. of State, 30 Aug. 1913, CO 536/61–33457 (in some places numbered 33407).

29 CO minute 2 Oct. 1913, loc. cit.

30 Secr. of State to Governor, 10 Oct. 1913, loc. cit. Governor Jackson to Secr. of State, 9 Jan. 1914; and Secr. of State to Governor, 13 Febr. 1914, CO 536/67–4461/14.

31 cf. CO minute 2 Oct. 1913; CO 536/61–33458/13 (written at the same date as the minute on land to the Muslims and by the same official; see n.29). cf. also Secr. of State to Governor, 2 Oct. 1914, CO 536/70–36107.

32 Summarized from CO minutes from Sept. and Oct. 1913; and Secr. of State to Governor, 10 Oct. 1913, CO 536/61–33458.

33 See extensive CO minute (by Mr Bottomley), 19 May 1914, CO 536/68–16978/1914.

34 Secr. of State to Governor, 30 May 1914, loc. cit.; further specified in Secr. of State to Governor, 2 Oct. 1914, in which answers are given to some comments from the Ag. Governor, CO 536/70–36107/1914.

35 See memorandum by Mr Bottomley of the CO, 10 Aug. 1915, CO 536/79–37090/ 1915, copy in SMP 4915.

36 cf. Secr. of State to Governor, 2 Oct. 1914, (see n.31).

37 Under the 1,000 acres' limit the Mill Hill Mission was still entitled to 591 acres. To put the two other missions on an equal footing, and enable them to receive gifts of land, they were permitted to take up an extra 591 acres in freehold. This rather illogical

ruling caused considerable confusion within the colonial administration in Uganda; cf. Ag. Governor to Secr. of State, 17 Aug. 1914, CO 536/70–36107.

38 Secr. of State to Governor, 16 April 1915, SMP 470^I; cf. CO minute 9 April 1915, CO 536/75–14664/1915; and memorandum by Mr Bottomley (n.35); cf. also Wrigley (1959), p.28, and other references in n.10.

39 K. Ingham (1959), pp.142ff; cf. also CO minute 26 Oct. 1917, which summarizes the whole matter, CO 536/86–49903/1917.

40 Wrigley, op.cit. The move was advertised as early as 1915 in Secr. of State to Governor, 16 April 1915, SMP 470^I; cf. also Henry Lambert (for the Under Secr. of State) to Land Officer Uganda, 19 Aug. 1915, SMP 4915.

41 Wrigley, op. cit., pp.31ff; Low & Pratt (1960), pp.227ff.

42 cf. Secr. of State to Governor, 16 April 1915, SMP 470^I.

43 This consequence is directly stated in Secr. of State to Governor, 22 Jan. 1917, CO 536/82–1935/1916–17.

44 Trustees of the NAC to Land Officer, 30 March 1914, CO 536/68–16978/1914.

45 This was clearly stated in Mr Bottomley's memorandum of 10 Aug. 1915.

46 The discussion continued during most of the 1910s and the beginning of the 1920s; e.g. Governor to Secr. of State, 9 Aug. 1917 with enclosures, CO 536/86–49903/1917.

47 e.g. Hesketh Bell to DC, 31 Oct. 1906 with regard to Bunyoro; and minutes by F.J. Jackson in 1911, all in SMP 1019/06.

48 The climax of this controversy seems to have been reached in 1923; cf. Governor to Secr. of State, 24 Dec. 1923, CO 536/127–4290/1923–24. With regard to Bunyoro Rev. A.B. Fisher reveals inadvertently how much excess land the mission had acquired, and how one leading motive had been 'to block the advance of the RCs'. This had even created a certain resentment with the Omukama and the chiefs who had not yet acquired any land. Fisher to Rev. Tegart, 27 Nov. 1911; Fisher to the Bishop, no date, but prior to the Synod in July 1910, both in Bunyoro Correspondence 1905–1912, Fisher papers. See also DC Bunyoro, R.D. Anderson, to Crown Advocate, 13 June 1912, SMP Conf. 32/1909. Still in 1921 the mission held much more than the authorized amount of acres; PC Northern Province to Bishop Willis, 21 June 1921, Bishop's Files: K–L. Land 1921–1933 (Bunyoro). The situation was similar in Ankole in 1923; see M.R. Doornbos (1978), p.82.

49 See notes by Rev. T.B. Fletcher, Superintendent NAC Estates, on a letter from the Land Officer, dat. 18 July 1922; and Fletcher, 'A Report upon the Present Situation re Church Lands in Busoga', April 1926, both in Bishop's Files: K–L. Busoga Land 1912–1932.

50 Willis to PC Eastern Province, F. Spire, 17 Nov. 1914, SMP 470^I.

51 In reviewing the issue of mission lands the Land Officer, H.B. Thomas (minute 6 Febr. 1926, SMP 2125), points out that the letter from Secr. of State with the new guidelines was forwarded to the CMS, 25 Nov. 1914. The date should be compared with Willis' letter to PC, 17 Nov. 1914.

52 Willis to PC, 17 Nov. 1914. In 1918 about one sq.m was added in transfer for a plot in Jinja: Governor to Secr. of State, 3 May 1918, CO 536/89–29328/1918.

53 Willis to PC, 17 Nov. 1914.

54 ibid.

55 PC Eastern Province, F. Spire, to Chief Secr., 12 Febr. 1915, SMP 470^I.

56 First Ass. Secr. to Chief Secr., 23 Febr. 1915, loc. cit.

57 Land Officer to Chief Secr., 22 Febr. 1915, loc. cit.

58 Memorandum on land held by the NAC by Archdeacon Baskerville, dat. 12 Nov. 1917, SMP 470^I.

59 Proceedings of Education Conference, 22–28 Sept. 1917, min. 29, SMP 4844.

60 Land Officer to Chief Secr., 26 Nov. 1917, SMP 470^I.

61 Ag. Chief Secr. to Governor, 12 Oct. 1917; min. by Ag. Governor, 1 Nov. 1917; Chief Secr. to the three bishops, 17 Nov. 1917, all in SMP 4844. cf. Land Officer to Chief Secr., 26 Nov. 1917.

62 cf. Governor to Secr. of State, 3 May 1918 (see n.52).

63 Ag. DC Busoga, Postlethwaite, to PC Eastern Province, 28 May 1919, Eastern Province Minute Paper 58/1913. Land: CMS Mission Estates in Busoga – re exchange of, ESA.

64 The Secr. of State had even made it clear that he was not prepared to agree to any new grants of freehold land to the missions Secr. of State to Governor, 22 Jan. 1917, CO 536/82–1935/1916–17.

65 Land Officer to Trustees of the NAC, 14 June 1919; cf. Land Officer to Bishop Willis, 9 July 1919, Bishop's Files (see n.49).

66 Willis to Land Officer, 11 July and 21 July 1919, copies in Bishop's Files loc.cit.

67 Willis referred in a different context to the difficulties of starting work in areas where the chiefs possessed no land; W. to PCs Northern and Eastern Provinces, 15 July 1916, SMP 4844.

68 Land Officer to PC Eastern Province, 9 July 1919 (see n.63).

69 Spire to Chief Secr. 15 April 1916, encl. in Ag. Governor to Secr. of State, 9 Aug. 1917, CO 536/86–49903/1917.

70 Ag. Governor, op. cit.

71 See Ag. Governor to Secr. of State, 17 Aug. 1914 with regard to a misunderstanding of this clause, CO 536/70–36107/1914. Somewhat later a disagreement occurred between the Attorney General and the Land Officer regarding the interpretation of the clause; Ag. Governor to Secr. of State, 26 Oct. 1916, CO 536/82–1935/16–17.

72 Ag. Governor to Secr. of State, 4 Oct. 1921, CO 536/114–55957/21.

73 PC Northern Province, Eden, to Chief Secr., 20 June 1917, reporting on a DCs' conference, SMP 5139.

74 The minutes in SMP 2198 contain reports from various commissions and present different features of the land policy. An extensive and useful summary may be found in 'Notes' by P.W. Perryman, dat. 11 Jan. 1922, SMP 2198. See also Wrigley (1959), pp.27ff, 42f; Thomas & Spencer (1938), ch. 12; and R.C. Pratt (1965), pp.477ff.

75 See especially their careful analysis in Annexure to the Minutes of the PCs' Conference 1922: Native Land Policy, SMP 2198.

76 This was directly stated by the Ass. Secr. for Native Affairs in his minute dat. 14 June 1922, SMP 2198.

77 Ag. Governor to Secr. of State 12 Sept. 1922, CO 536/120–52981/22, copy in SMP 2198, min. 302. Ag. Governor to Secr. of State, 7 Nov. 1922, CO 536/121–63837/1922.

78 Statement on land policy, Dec. 1923, min. 359, SMP 2198.

79 Ass. Secr. for Native Affairs to Archdeacon Kitching, CMS, 9 April 1923, min. 331, SMP 2198.

80 See minutes from PCs during the first part of 1922, SMP 7168. The Land Officer complained that this matter of unregistered plots had all too long been left in abeyance; Land Officer to Fletcher, 14 Febr. 1922, Bishop's Files (see n.49). It has earlier been described how the mission over the years had taken up much more land than authorized by the government; see n.48.

81 Circular Memorandum, 5 July 1922, copy under min. 40, SMP 7168, and in Bishop's Files (see n.49).

82 Even the Superintendent of NAC Estates found it necessary to start from scratch in making a list of unregistered plots; Fletcher to Land & Survey Office, 27 March 1922, min. 25, SMP 7168.

83 cf. PC Eastern Province to Ass. Secr. for Native Affairs, 10 Oct. 1922, min. 50, SMP 7168.

84 Chief Secr. to Willis, 20 Febr. 1924, Bishop's Files (see n.49). The same was clearly expressed in Governor to Secr. of State, 24 Dec. 1923, in which dispatch Busoga is mentioned as an extremely bad example. CO 536/127–4290/1923–24.

85 Rev. A.E. Clarke to Willis, 11 March 1925; Fletcher, 'A Report of the Present Position re Church Lands in Busoga', April 1926, both in Bishop's Files (n.49).

86 Bishop Willis, Memorandum on Native Lands in Uganda (draft), sent to Governor, n.d., but presumably middle of 1926, Bishop's Files: K–L. Land 1912–1913. Subfile: Land. Memoranda. The Busoga case was later mentioned as an example of an anti-missionary trend in the government's land policy. Willis to Under-Secr. of State, Ormsby-Gore, 29 Dec. 1926, copy in Bishop's Files: R (1). Kabaka 1926–1927.

87 Willis, Memorandum, op.cit.; cf. minute by Chief Secr., 3 Febr. 1926, SMP 8897.

88 Fletcher, op. cit.

89 e.g. Willis to Chief Secr., 1 Febr. 1926; and Chief Secr. to Willis, 2 March 1926. The Land Officer, H.B. Thomas, commented on Willis' letter: 'The Bishop appears to be launching another offensive on behalf of "unregistered plots".' SMP 2125.

90 Ag. Governor to Secr. of State, 19 Jan. 1926, CO 536/139–1815/1926 (original destroyed, read from index).

91 Willis to Mr Bottomley of the CO, 29 June 1923, CO 536/129–Mi. 35014/1923; cf. about the same issue the discussion in the Estates Board's report to the Synod, Jan. 1924 (in minutes of Synod).

92 Governor to Secr. of State, 24 Dec. 1923, CO 536/127–4290/23–24; copy sent to Bishop Willis, now in Bishop's Files (see n.49).

93 Secr. of State to Governor, 11 April 1924, CO 536/127–4290/23–24; cf. also Secr. of State to Governor, 28 Dec. 1923, CO 536/129–Mi. 35014/1923.

94 ibid., incl. the internal CO minutes.

95 This is clearly alluded to in Rev. A.E. Clarke, Ag. Rural Dean of Busoga, to Willis, 14 March 1925, Bishop's Files (see n.49).

96 Busoga Lukiko to PC Eastern Province, 12 Jan. 1926; Busoga chiefs to Governor, 8 June 1926; Busoga Lukiko to Secr. of State, 29 Dec. 1926, and again to PC, 12 Jan. 1927, all in SMP 2125. It is significant that copies of these letters were sent to CMS, now in Bishop's Files: loc. cit.

97 Thus Busoga Lukiko to Willis, 1 and 14 April 1926, 30 May and 23 June 1927, all in Bishop's Files: loc. cit. Willis then raised the issue with the Under-Secr. of State, W. to Ormsby-Gore, 29 Dec. 1926 (n.86).

98 A.E. Clarke, op. cit.

99 For example in Willis to Chief Secr., 1 Febr. 1926, SMP 2125.

100 Chief Secr. to Willis, 2 March 1926, loc. cit.

101 Willis' Memorandum of 1926 (see n. 86). In his reply, dat. 8 June 1926, the Governor revealed that Willis planned to send his memo to J.H. Oldham of the International Missionary Council in London. For the role of J.H. Oldham see R. Oliver (1952), ch. 5.

102 Memorandum by P.W. Perryman, 17 Jan. 1922, SMP 7168.

103 Minute by Ag. Ass. Chief Secr., 3 Nov. 1926, SMP 2125; cf. Rev. Fisher's support for the Omukama and chiefs in Bunyoro (n.47).

104 Minute by Governor, 30 March 1927, SMP 2125.

105 A modification of the land settlement, following the opposition from the Busoga chiefs, was first mentioned as early as 1924; Chief Secr. to Governor, 26 May 1924, SMP R18/1.

106 e.g. E.L. Scott, Ass. Secr. for Native Affairs, to Chief Secr., 2 May 1927, SMP 2125; and the final decision in Governor to Secr. of State, 20 April 1928, CO 536/149–20104/ 1928.

107 It seems that Willis at one stage admits that the church in Busoga has got more land than necessary, and he is therefore willing to accept a reduction in accordance with the new regulations. Willis to Clarke, 14 March 1925, Bishop's Files (see n.49).

108 CO minute 16 July 1923, CO 536/129–Mi. 35014/1923.

109 See Engholm (1968, unpubl. thesis), p.44; and C. Ehrlich (1965), pp.423ff.

110 *Uganda Notes*, Jan. 1920, cf. minutes of Educational Advisory Board, 14 May 1920, min. 76, SMP 4844. See also D.A. Low (1965), p.120.

111 The Educational Advisory Board was set up in Dec. 1917, SMP 5264.

112 Minutes of the Educational Committee, London, 29 Nov. 1916, no. 131, G3. A7.

113 Memorandum to Group III Committee (dealing with Africa), 9 Dec. 1913; Manley to Rowling, 15 Dec. 1913, no. 193, G3. A7/010. A similar anxiety was expressed by Fisher (see n.13).

114 Report of the Sub-Committee, 21 Oct. 1918, no. 59; Memorandum of Interview between Maj.-Gen. Kenyon, Canon Rowling and Rev. Manley, 2 Nov. 1918, no. 61, G3. A7. The arguments put forward here are in disagreement with J.V. Taylor, who explains the shelving of the agricultural scheme by referring to the possible eviction of tenants. J.V. Taylor (1958), p.157.

115 This change of policy is aptly confirmed by Archdeacon Baskerville's Memorandum to Uganda Development Commission, Dec. 1919, in which the agricultural scheme is not mentioned, but only industrial and agricultural education as the mission's contribution. Bishop's Files: K–L. Land. Subfile: Land. Memoranda. The same emphasis on the educational aspects may also be found in the report on the agricultural scheme in Bunyoro which was first suggested in 1911–12, and in fact got started with the help of money borrowed locally (the Kiryanga Estate). It proved unsuccessful and became after a few years a liability for the mission and the church, only justifiable for its educational values. Rev. F. Rowling to Manley, 29 Oct. 1917, with enclosure: Memorandum on Development of Uganda Church Lands, G/Y A7/1, CMS Arch.

116 Notes by Baskerville and Rowling, no date, but presumably June 1920, no. 133; cf. minutes of Missionary Committee, 2 June 1920, no. 140, both in G3. A7. The same connection between the church's educational contribution and the intrinsic and rental value of church land was already expressed by CMS London in 1918, Memorandum of Interview between Kenyon, Rowling and Manley (see n.114).

117 At the PCs' Conference 1919 it was asked whether the government's policy was 'for the native to develop the Country in his own interest or whether he is to be exploited in the interest of the White settler'. The governor answered that this question was not likely to come up for a long time. 'The policy of the Government is to encourage both the native and the European settler.' Minutes in SMP 3841; cf. Wrigley (1959), ch. 3.

118 See above p.139. See also various minutes and drafts from 1923 in CO 5636/129–35014/1923.

119 e.g. Land Officer to Chief Secr., 10 Aug. 1917, min. 26, SMP 4844. The LO makes it clear that 'mission purposes' cover schools as well as churches.

120 cf. Conference of the DCs in Northern Province, Masindi, Oct. 1919, SMP 5959. Ag. PC Eastern Province to Ass. Secr. for Native Affairs, 10 Oct. 1922, SMP 7168.

121 cf. Wrigley (1959), p. 28. For a general discussion of this topic see E.A. Brett (1973), pp.53ff.

122 CO minute 12 May 1914, CO 536/68–16978/1914; Governor to Secr. of State, 12 Aug. 1919, CO 536/95–54985/1919. See also CO minute from 1921 in CO 536/117– C.59722.

11   The nature of landholding

1 A general account of the whole surveying operation may be found in H.B. Thomas & A.E. Spencer (1938). A scale of survey fees was drawn up as early as 1902, Sub-Commissioner Jackson to Secr. of State, 25 Jan. 1902, FO 2/589.

2 cf. Rev. Ernest Millar to Bishop Willis, 12 Febr. 1912, Bishop's Files: K–L. Land. Subfile: Land, General. Encl. is a copy of Johnston to Tucker, 4 Oct. 1900 in which J. estimates that the survey fee will not exceed one pound a plot.

3 cf. Land Officer's record of a meeting with CMS representatives in LO to Chief Secr., 10 Febr. 1913, SMP 3065.

4 Chief Secr. to Willis, 15 Febr. 1913, Bishop's Files (see n.2).

5 Rev. F. Rowling to Chief Secr., 25 Sept. 1919, SMP 3065.

6 Ag. Governor to Secr. of State, 16 Dec. 1919, CO 536/97–5152/1919–20.

7 cf. CO minute 30 Jan. 1920 (see n.6); cf. summary of the whole issue in Ag. Governor to Secr. of State, 20 April 1920, CO 536/100–30631.

8 Ag. Chief Secr. to Governor, 10 Oct. 1919, SMP 3065.

9 cf. Ag. Chief Secr. to Governor, 29 Oct. 1919, and the Governor's comments, SMP 3065. cf. also dispatch to the CO recommending a reduction of survey fees, 16 Dec. 1919, CO 536/97–5152/1919–20.

10 The final cost of the survey of church land amounts to £1,500 for the 40 sq.m. held under the Agreement and £450 for the extra 12 sq.m. obtained later. Director of Surveys to Treasurer NAC, 7 Sept. 1921. The total of £1,950 should be compared with the original estimate of about £3,000. The limited value of the reduction was hinted at when the survey operation was extended to Bunyoro; cf. Land Officer to DC Bunyoro, 12 Dec. 1922 (copy to the secr. of the NAC Land Board). All in Bishop's Files: K–L. Land 1912–32 (Bunyoro).

11 Archdeacon Walker to Sub-Commissioner Leakey, 18 Febr. 1903, SMP 501/1906.

12 Walker to Tomkins, 18 March 1903, loc. cit.

13 Tomkins to Walker, 20 March 1903, loc. cit. Tucker said later that it might be necessary to take the issue right to the CO; Tucker to Baylis, 27 Nov. 1905, no. 258, G3. A7/04.

14 Walker to Tomkins, 9 June 1906, SMP 501/1906.

15 Minute by Crown Advocate Allison Russell, 19 June 1906, loc. cit. His opinion was clearly based upon the Certificate of Claim; see above, pp.139.

16 Commissioner Hesketh Bell to Walker, 7 July 1906, loc. cit.

17 Memorandum by Sir R.B. Finlay (former Attorney General of England), 16 Jan. 1907, Bishop's Files (see n.2), copy in SMP 6274. cf. also ch. 9, n.18.

18 Chief Secr. Jarvis to Secr. of CMS Ladbury, 14 Oct. 1918, SMP 6274. The 2,343 rupees were equivalent to £160.

19 Ladbury to Chief Secr., 25 Nov. 1918, loc. cit.

20 Attorney General to Chief Secr., 27 Nov. 1918; Governor to Chief Secr., 7 Dec. 1918, SMP 6274.

21 Letter to the three missions, 3 April 1919, in *Diocesan Gazette* 4, 6, 1919, p. 57; cf. also rejections of later applications in SMP 7639.

22 In Oct. 1919 the Governor admitted that he could not legally stop the CMS building shops for leases on a piece of land bought in 1912 with the purpose of growing food for Mukono Theological College. SMP 6274.

23 Minute by Land Officer, 15 Dec. 1922, SMP 7639. Regarding the whole issue of the use of mission land see also H.W. West (1972), pp.54ff.

24 See also D.A. Low & R.C. Pratt (1960), pp.148ff.

25 See for instance the study of Lango by John Tosh (1973) and Tosh (1978), chs. 5 and 6.

26 cf. Low & Pratt (1960), pp.176ff.

27 The term 'indirect rule' has not been applied in the present study. For a thorough discussion of this problem see Low & Pratt, op. cit., ch. 7; R.C. Pratt (1965), pp.470ff. Cf. also H.F. Morris & J.S. Read (1972), *passim*.

28 Correspondence from the first half of 1907, in SMP 175/1907 and SMP Conf. 14/1907.

29 H.B. Lewin to Ass. Collector Speke, 23 Jan. 1907, SMP 175/1907.

30 Speke to Sub-Commissioner Buganda, 4 March 1907, SMP Conf. 14/07.

31 Dep. Commissioner George Wilson to Commissioner, 1 March 1907, SMP 175/1907.

32 Sub-Commissioner Leakey to Dep. Commissioner, 14 Febr. 1907, loc cit.

33 Ass. Collector Speke, op. cit.

34 Dep. Commissioner George Wilson to Commissioner, 1 March 1907, SMP 175/1907.

35 Archdeacon Walker to Sub-Commissioner, 11 April 1907, loc. cit.

36 See the 3 Regents' letter to the 3 missionary societies, 20 May 1907, SMP 520/1907. The Regents clearly considered the mission estates to be a large reservoir of labour.

37 This case from Bunyoro is reported in Sub-Commissioner Bunyoro to Dep. Commissioner, 22 June 1908, SMP 1160/1908.

38 Chief Secr. to Crown Agent, 11 and 25 March 1909, SMP Conf. 32/1909.

39 It is noticeable that the Crown Agent does not make a distinction between obligations rooted in the African system and those introduced by the colonial system. He confines himself to considering the authority of the chief as customary in all cases.

40 The Crown Agent is here quoting clause 20 in the Uganda Order of Council.

41 Crown Agent Allison Russell to Chief Secr., 17 April 1909, min. 4, SMP Conf. 32/1909.

42 PC Buganda to Chief Secr., 15 June 1909; Chief Secr. to PC Buganda, 6 Oct. 1909, SMP Conf. 1007/1909.

43 PC Buganda to Mr Sturrock, 5 Nov. 1909, loc. cit.

44 Sturrock to PC Buganda, 7 Nov. 1909, loc. cit.

45 Chief Secr. to Governor, 10 Nov. 1909, loc. cit.

46 PC Buganda to Chief Secr., 2 Febr. 1910, SMP 279/1908.

47 PC Buganda to Chief Secr., March 1910, loc. cit.

48 They date from 1909; see D.A. Low (1965), p.95; and Tosh (1973), pp. 478ff. See also Governor to Secr. of State, 1 June 1908, where he points out that the sub-chiefs in each saza are 'a kind of native Civil Service' which is becoming more and more indispensable with regard to collection of tax. CO 536/20–24968/1908.

49 Report of Ass. DC's tour through Bugerere, 14 Febr. 1911, SMP 1759/1911.

50 Busoga Monthly Reports, Febr. 1911, SMP 169 A/1911.

51 Initially the main problem was whether the head men on church estates should act as tax collectors on church estates and get a certain percentage of the tax collected; cf. Rev. Tegart to Rev. Fisher, Masindi, 25 Oct. 1911, Fisher Papers: Bunyoro 1905–12. For the government's reaction see DC Bunyoro, R.D. Anderson, to Crown Advocate, 13 June 1912, SMP Conf. 32/1909.

52 Correspondence in SMP 4563.

53 Ag. Ass. Chief Secr. to Chief Secr., 30 Aug. 1915, and following minutes, SMP 4563.

54 e.g. Attorney General to Chief Secr., 11 Oct. 1913; and Chief Secr. to Governor, 14 Oct. 1913, SMP Conf. 32/1909.

55 This position was in fact sketched by Bishop Willis in his first outline of 'Policy of the Uganda Mission' after taking office. He warned that the mission should beware of establishing 'an *Imperium in Imperio*', for instance by securing for tenants on mission land exemptions and privileges which other tenants had not got. The charge was printed as a pamphlet: J.J. Willis, 'Policy of Uganda Mission', 1913, copy under no. 157, G3. A7/010. This line of policy was later written into the 'Laws and Regulations of the Church of Uganda', passed by the Synod, 1917. It was here stated that tenants on church estates were supposed to do necessary work for the state (par. G.48 and 50) and also to provide food for European caravans paid for at the regular rates (par. G. 49).

56 Dating from 1916; see Low (1965), p. 98.

57 Minutes of the Synod, June 1917. The 'Laws and Regulations' were printed as a booklet in 1917. Church katikiros are dealt with in section G (pp.73ff).

58 Archdeacon Baskerville to PC Buganda, 9 Oct. 1917, Provincial Commissioner Kampala no. 1380: Native Anglican Church: official recognition of Katikiros, ESA.

59 The PC circulated the request and asked for comments from the DCs in Buganda, 26 Oct. 1917, loc. cit.

60 The answer to the Archdeacon's request is contained in PC P.W. Cooper to Baskerville, 12 Dec. 1917, loc. cit.

61 Baskerville to PC, 19 Dec. 1917, loc. cit.

62 The 3 Ugandan bishops to Governor, 19 April 1918, SMP 5368. The letter was drafted by Bishop Willis; cf. draft in Bishop's Files: K–L. Land. Subfile: Memoranda. The same anxiety was expressed by the Synod of the NAC, 1919; minutes in *Uganda Notes*, Oct. 1919, p. 99.

63 PC Buganda, P.W. Cooper, to Chief Secr., 17 May 1918, SMP 5368.

64 Memorandum by J.C.R. Sturrock, n.d., loc. cit.

65 Governor Coryndon to Chief Secr., 31 May 1918, loc. cit. Coryndon took office in 1918.

66 PC Western Province, Browning, to Chief Secr., 12 Sept. 1918, loc. cit. For kasanvu and luwalo, see below, ch. 12.

67 Cooper to Chief Secr., 1 July 1918, supplementing his letter of 17 May, loc. cit.

68 Cooper to Chief Secr., 17 May 1918. Cooper mentions that he has taken a special interest in this whole issue, which again parallels his handling of the question of church katikiros in 1917. See also Cooper to DC Masaka, 6 July 1917, where his general policy of administration is outlined (in D.A. Low (1971b), pp.49ff). Mr Cooper was considered by the CMS mission to be sympathetic towards missionary work; Rowling to Manley, 2 April 1917, no. 63, G3. A7.

69 No minutes exist from the meeting, but it is mentioned in Willis to Cooper, 19 June 1918, in the file: PC Kampala (see n.58). cf. also Cooper to Chief Secr., 1 July 1918, SMP 5368.

70 cf. Lucy Mair (1934), pp.200f.

71 Cooper, 'Memorandum for guidance of the Bakatikiro of Native Anglican Church Estates', dat. 18 June 1918, SMP 5368; also in the file: PC Kampala (see n.58).

72 Willis to Cooper, 19 June 1918, SMP 5368.

73 cf. Cooper to Chief Secr., 1 July 1918, loc. cit.

74 The Native Authority Ordinance is in *Laws of the Uganda Protectorate*, 1936 edition. A copy is enclosed in Governor to Secr. of State, 17 Febr. 1919, CO 536/93–20076/1919. See also Low & Pratt (1960), pp.209ff., and Pratt (1965), pp.488ff.

75 The Governor (op. cit.) made it clear that the measure should cover the whole Protectorate, but he found it improbable that the powers provided in the Ordinance would be applied in Buganda. His successor, however, was in no doubt that 'the Native Authority Ordinance has no real application to Buganda where full control and authority over the native population is vested, under the terms of the Agreement, in the Native Government. Thus our hands are rather tied.' Governor Archer to Secr. of State, 18 July 1924, CO 536/131–34019/24.

76 cf. Low (1965), pp. 98f.

77 Minutes of the Synod, 19 Sept. 1919, par. 43, MUL.

78 Willis to Ag. Chief Secr. T.S. Thomas, 25 Sept. 1919, SMP Conf. 1007/1909.

79 Memorandum to Uganda Development Commission by Archdeacon Baskerville, Dec. 1919, p.9. Bishop's Files: K–L. Land. Sub-file: Memoranda.

80 T.S. Thomas to Willis, 6 Oct. 1919, SMP Conf. 1007/1909.

81 Thus Ag. PC Northern Province, Haddon, to Chief Secr., 25 Febr. 1920, min. 189, SMP 529¹.

82 ibid., including Chief Secr.'s answer to Haddon.

83 Low & Pratt (1960), p. 177. cf. the careful analysis of this process of change with regard to Lango in Tosh (1978), ch. 7.

84 Pratt (1965), p. 492.

12   Usufructuary rights to tenant labour

1 cf. L.A. Fallers (1964), p.68.

2 The introduction of the new poll tax is extensively reported in *Uganda Notes*, Nov. 1904, pp.169ff. See also Governor to Secr. of State, 27 April 1909, CO 536/26–20092/1909.

3 cf. Governor to Secr. of State, 16 March 1909 (telegr.), CO 536/25–9254/1909.

4 Governor to Secr. of State, 27 April 1909, loc. cit. cf. J.A. Atanda (1969), p.156.

5 Minute by Governor (in London), June 1909, CO 536/26–19220/09. See agreement on poll tax in Toro, 7 April 1910, signed by the Omukama, chiefs, government officials and missionaries; SMP Conf. 29/1910.

6 Governor to Secr. of State, 27 April 1909, (see n.2).

7 ibid. Exactly the same worry was expressed two years earlier by the Ganda leaders; see Three Regents to Ag. Sub-Commissioner, 19 April 1907, SMP 520/1907.

8 The causal relationship between poll tax and the supply of labour has been emphasized by P.G. Powesland (1957), ch. 1.

9 cf. Uganda Agreement clause 12; and Ag. Governor to Secr. of State, 7 June 1909, CO 536/26–22250/1909.

10 cf. Governor to Secr. of State, 1 June 1908, CO 536/20–24968/08.

11 ibid.; and Governor to Secr. of State, 27 April 1909, CO 536/20–24968/08.

12 CO minute 25 March 1909, CO 536/25–9254/1909; Governor to Secr. of State, 27 April 1909, loc. cit. cf. also *Uganda Notes*, Nov. 1904.

13 cf. C. Ehrlich (1965), pp.400ff.

14 cf. CO minute, 8 Sept. 1919, CO 536/94–50670/19.

15 Governor to Secr. of State, 30 June 1919, loc. cit.

16 Kabaka and his ministers to Secr. of State, 8 May 1919, loc. cit.

17 The CO officials blamed the Governor for having acted with lack of diplomacy and were at pains not to weaken his authority unnecessarily; CO minutes in loc. cit.

18 See also D.A. Low (1971b), pp.45ff.

19 Accurately expressed in the words of the Dep. Commissioner George Wilson: 'to educate the country to conduct its affairs upon the more enlightened Uganda [Buganda] system . . . ' Wilson to Secr. of State, 25 June 1907, CO 536/13–25631/07.

20 See minutes in SMP Conf. 346; cf. Ag. Chief Secr. to Governor, 22 Jan. 1918, SMP 1371. Regarding kasanvu in general see J.B. Kakwenzire (1976, unpubl, thesis), pp.3ff.

21 cf. Archdeacon Walker to Regents and Members of the Lukiko, 29 March 1909, Walker's Letterbook I (copy book), MUL.

22 Walker to PC Buganda, 28 May 1909, loc. cit.

23 PC Buganda, Knowlcs, to Secr. CMS, 29 June 1909, Special File: 1909/10. Re Compulsory Labour in Buganda, MUL.

24 cf. Powesland (1957), pp.18f; C.C. Wrigley (1959), p. 35; Ehrlich (1965), pp. 428f.

25 Tucker to Ag. Governor Boyle, 20 Dec. 1909; Tucker to DC Kampala, Haldane, 16 Febr. 1910, both in SMP Conf. 144/09. Archdeacon Walker had already touched on the same issue in his letter to PC Buganda, 28 May 1909.

26 See conflicting opinions in minutes encl. in PC Buganda to Chief Secr., 1 March 1910. Leading officials were extremely annoyed that Tucker got so many different answers from officers; see Chief Secr. to Ag. Governor, 3 March 1910, both in SMP Conf. 144/1909.

27 Haldane to Tucker, 17 Febr. 1910, encl. in PC Buganda to Chief Secr., 1 March 1910, loc. cit.

28 Tucker to Ag. Governor Boyle, 20 Dec. 1909, loc. cit.

29 ibid.; and later Tucker (in London) to R.V. Vernon of the CO, 15 Dec. 1910, CO 536/38–38735/1910, copy in SMP Conf. 144/09.

30 Tucker to Under-Secr. of State for the Colonies, Col. Seely, 3 Febr. 1911, CO 536/47–U 3722/11, copy in SMP Conf. 144/09.

31 This point of view was most clearly expressed in Tucker to Col. Seely, 3 Febr. 1911.

32 Ag. Governor Boyle to Tucker, 4 Jan. 1910, SMP Conf. 144/09; Ag. Governor Tomkins to Secr. of State, 27 March 1911, CO 536/40–13005/11.

33 Tomkins, op. cit.

34 Boyle, op. cit.; and Tomkins, op. cit.

35 CO minute 26 April 1911, CO 536/40–13005/11.

36 The CO confined itself to reproducing the Ag. Governor's dispatch in the reply to Bishop Tucker; cf. draft dated 29 April 1911 in loc. cit.

37 cf. Walker to DC Kampala, P.W. Cooper, 18 March 1912, Walker's Letterbook vol. II, MUL. About the increased demand for labour as from 1912 see Powesland (1957), pp.20f.

38 cf. *Uganda Notes*, July 1919, p. 76.

39 See minutes from 1916–17 in SMP 1371; and memorandum by PC Buganda, P.W. Cooper, dat. 28 Nov. 1917, SMP Conf. 346.

40 cf. Cooper to Chief Secr., 27 Aug. 1917, SMP 1371.

41 Minute by Cooper, Dec. 1917, SMP Conf. 346.

42 See minutes re Ankole in SMP 1371, and re Eastern Province in 1919 in SMP Conf. 393.

43 See Cooper's memorandum, 28 Nov. 1917.

44 ibid.

45 Governor to Secr. of State, 17 Febr. 1919, CO 536/93–20076, with a draft copy of the Ordinance encl.; cf. PC Eastern Province to Chief Secr., 8 April 1919; and Governor to Chief Secr., 23 April 1919, both in SMP Conf. 393.

46 First expressed by Chief Secr. to Governor, 5 Dec. 1917, SMP Conf. 346. See later A.M. Watson (posted in West Nile District) to Governor Coryndon, 4 Nov. 1918, MSS. Afr. s.633, file 4, Coryndon Papers, Rhodes House, Oxford. (I am grateful to Dr Michael Twaddle for drawing my attention to the Coryndon Papers.)

47 Memorandum by Cooper, 8 Sept. 1918, SMP Conf. 346.

48 The Omuwanika and 11 leading Ganda chiefs to PC Buganda, Cooper, 25 June 1918; Anderea L. Kimbugwe (a saza chief) to Cooper, 13 July 1918 (in the translation the year is erroneously given as 1917), Both letters were enclosed in Bishop Willis to Governor Coryndon, 15 July 1918. Willis summarized the chiefs' point of view and supported the abolition of kasanvu. All letters in Coryndon Papers. For later moves by the Ganda chiefs see Powesland (1957), pp. 27 and 32. In April 1920 the Lukiko passed a detailed set of rules with a view to improving conditions for people called up to do kasanvu and in order to clarify the exemption rules (published in *Diocesan Gazette*, Dec. 1920, pp.108ff). In 1921 the Lukiko voted in favour of abolishing kasanvu (Minutes in SMP 5116).

49 cf. Governor to Chief Secr., 10 Nov. 1921, SMP Conf. 346. See also A. Clayton & D.C. Savage (1974), ch. 4,

50 Labour Commissioner to all heads of department and PCs, 7 Dec. 1921, SMP 5116. It took effect 1 Jan. 1922 in Buganda, Bunyoro and Toro, and one year later in Busoga, Bukedi and Ankole. cf. summary in Dep. Governor, E.C. Eliot, to Secr. of State, 9 Febr. 1922, CO 536/118–14109. The process of decline and final abolition of kasanvu is described in Powesland (1957), ch. 2. cf. also Governor to Secr. of State, 30 May 1922, CO 536/119–33120/22, where it is pointed out that the increased labour supply was also an effect of the decline in economic activity caused by the fall in cotton prices.

51 cf. Ag. Commissioner George Wilson to Secr. of State, 22 June 1907, later reproduced in an answer to Parliament in connection with a question related to forced labour, CO 536/13–25629/07. For the extension to Lango in the north, see J. Tosh (1978), pp.166f.

52 This was clearly expressed in a long article on labour problems in *Uganda Notes*, July 1919, pp. 72–80, presumably written by Bishop Willis, cf. p.212.

53 ibid., p. 76.

54 CO minutes 31 May and 11 June 1919, CO 536/93–20076/19.

55 cf. Powesland (1957), pp. 28, 34.

56 PC Buganda to Chief Secr., 24 June 1919, SMP 1371; and *Uganda Notes*, (see n.52). also R.C. Pratt (1965), p. 493.

57 Thus PC Buganda to Chief Secr., 24 June 1919. About the reorganization of the

luwalo system see J.R.P. Postlethwaite (1947), pp.84f. (Postlethwaite was DC of Kampala at the time.)

58 cf. Governor to Secr. of State, 14 Oct. 1919, CO 536/96–70586/19.

59 See minutes in SMP 6111; cf. also R.C. Pratt (1965), pp.224f.

60 cf. Governor to Secr. of State, 30 May 1922, CO 536/119–33120/22.

61 These two factors were pointed out by the PC Western Province, P.W. Cooper, to Chief Secr., 7 Nov. 1921, SMP 6111. Cooper had moved from Buganda to the Western Province, but he was still concerned with the position of the chiefs, although he admitted that the feudal system 'is bound to slip away naturally'.

62 See minutes in SMP 7577; and Governor to Secr. of State, 20 May 1922, CO 536/119–33120.

63 cf. H.W. West (1972), p. 69.

64 cf. Ag. Governor to Secr. of State, 25 Sept. 1914, CO 536/70–42065/14. See also H.B. Thomas & R. Scott (1935), pp.100f.

65 Ag. Commissioner F.J. Jackson to Marquess of Lansdowne, 25 Jan. 1902, FO 2/589; cf. also D.A. Low & R.C. Pratt (1960), pp.102ff; and J.A. Atanda (1969), p. 152.

66 Compare the divergent points of view expressed by H.W. West (1964), pp.19f, and by J.A. Rowe (1964), pp.6f (esp. n. 24). The latter takes the same view as sketched above.

67 F.J. Jackson (see n.65); Archdeacon Walker to Commissioner Sadler, 22 July 1902, A22/1, ESA.

68 For this transition see D.E. Apter (1961), ch. 5, esp. p. 112.

69 cf. Tucker to Under Secr. of State for the Colonies, 3 Febr. 1911, CO 536/47–U 3722, copy in SMP Conf. 144/09 (see also above p.179).

70 This was explicitly stated by the Ag. Governor in his dispatch to the Secr. of State, 25 Sept. 1914, CO 536/70–42065/14.

71 ibid.

72 cf. PC Buganda, P.W. Cooper, to Chief Secr., 27 Aug. 1917, SMP 1371.

73 PC Eastern Province to Chief Secr., 30 March 1918, min. 77, SMP 1371. cf. L.A. Fallers (1965), pp.147ff.

74 Ag. Chief Secr. Jarvis to Land Officer, 10 April 1918, min. 78, SMP 1371.

75 See minutes from 1920 to 1925 in SMP 6025[f]. It was at one stage suggested linking busulu exclusively to the system of landholding and define it as rent for the use of land. Consequently tenants on Crown land should, just as people on privately owned estates, pay rent, but to the Crown. See notes by Governor Coryndon Sept. 1920, file 2, Coryndon Papers (see n.46); and Ag. Governor Jarvis to Secr. of State, 16 July 1921, CO 536/112–44590; and 31 Jan. 1923, SMP R 18/1. cf. attempt at clarification in a minute by Ass. Secr. for Native Affairs, dat. 7 April 1923, where it is emphasized that in Toro and Bunyoro busulu is a tribute, though often incorrectly translated as rent. SMP 2198.

76 This is most definitely expressed by the DC Bunyoro, Sandford, in 'Notes on the Obusulu Payment in Bunyoro', dat. 27 Oct. 1924, SMP 6025 C. Re introduction of busulu in the Nilotic parts of Eastern and Northern Provinces, following the establishment of colonial administration, see 'Report on Dues or Tributes', no signature, n.d., but presumably 1924, SMP 6025[I].

77 The outcome of the busulu question is aptly summarized in Chief Secr. to PC Northern Province, 3 March 1926, SMP 6025[I].

78 As the only district outside Buganda, commutation of busulu to 5 Rs in cash payment

in place of one month's labour was allowed in Bunyoro from 1913, see 'Report on Dues or Tributes', p.4.

79 See comparison between Buganda and the Eastern Province in Wrigley (1959), pp.44ff and Wrigley (1964), pp.35ff.

80 cf. Governor to Secr. of State, 14 Oct. 1919, CO 536/96–70586/19. See also Powesland (1957), pp.26f.

81 cf. 'Report on Dues or Tributes'.

82 Thomas & Scott (1935), pp.101f; cf. also H.B. Thomas & A.E. Spencer (1938), p. 59. The principle was well developed at the PCs' Conference 1922; see Annexure to the Minutes of the PCs' Conference, par. 10, SMP 2198[II]. Archdeacon W.E. Owen of Kavirondo, Kenya, formerly a Uganda missionary stationed in Toro, sparked off a heated discussion with the colonial administration about the change of busulu from rent to tribute and the accompanying land settlement policy. He called the plan to make all land in Toro Crown land confiscation of land to the Crown, as it broke all promises earlier given to the Batoro, and he considered the new tribute to be simply a taxation on all holdings of land. Owen was not backed by his Ugandan colleagues, and it will be a subject for another analysis whether he was right in his criticism. Evidence about this controversy, which started in Jan. 1923, may be found in Owen Papers: file on the land question in Toro, acc. 83, CMS Arch., and in CO 536/124–11423.

83 cf. Governor to Secr. of State, 14 Oct. 1919, when he commented on a report on the labour problems in the Eastern Province, CO 536/96–70586. See also Ag. Chief Secr. to PC Western Province, 28 Jan. 1920, SMP 6025[I].

84 It was reported that this process had been accomplished by the end of 1923; Governor to Secr. of State, 8 Dec. 1923, CO 536/127–1650/1923–4. See also precis of minutes 22–42 for the years 1924–5, and 'Report on Dues or Tributes', both in SMP 6025[I]. Re Eastern Province in particular, see SMP 6025 A. Re Toro: this whole process of transforming busulu from a rent to landholders to a tribute to the local government, and the close connection between the issue of busulu and the general land settlement have been aptly illustrated in the report 'Enquiry into the Grievances of the Mukama and People of Toro', dat. 28 July 1926, copy in Owen Papers (see n.82).

85 cf. West (1972), pp.42f.

86 Thomas & Spencer (1938), p. 69; Postlethwaite (1947), pp.99f; Wrigley (1959), p. 49. The Kabaka defended strongly the nvuju custom cf. Kabaka to Governor, 25 June 1926, copy in Bishop's Files: R (1), Kabaka 1926–7.

87 'Report on Dues or Tributes', p.6, presumably from 1924, SMP 6025[I]. West (1972), p. 70, and Low & Pratt (1960), p. 237.

88 cf. Wrigley (1959), pp. 53f.

89 cf. Low & Pratt (1960), pp. 237f.

90 Wrigley (1964), p. 42.

91 cf. M. Twaddle (1969), pp.311ff; D.A. Low (1971a), pp.144ff.

92 Based upon Bishop Tucker's list of obligations in T. to Ag. Governor Boyle, 20 Dec. 1909, suppl. with DC Kampala, Haldane, to Tucker, 17 Febr. 1910, both in SMP Conf. 144/09; cf. also Atanda (1969) about the burdens on the Bakopi in the first decade of the twentieth century.

93 Based upon a list set up by Bishop Forbes, White Fathers' Mission, in his memorandum to Uganda Development Commission, dat. 8 Dec. 1919, SMP 5860; cf. also PC Buganda, P.W. Cooper, to Chief Secr., 27 Aug. 1917, SMP 1371. Bishop Forbes lists 2 months for kasanvu, but it is rightly one month with the possibility of an extra month call-up. He mentions a few other obligations and arrives at an annual amount of labour of about 7 months.

94 cf. 'Report on Dues or Tributes' (see n. 87).

95 See in particular Thomas & Spencer (1938), pp.70ff; Twaddle (1969), pp.314f; Low (1971a), pp.144ff.

96 cf. Archdeacon Walker to Ag. Chief Secr. Tomkins, 4 March 1909, SMP 356/1909. He fixes the number of unmarried teachers at about 400. No material directly connected with the introduction of the new poll tax in 1904–5 has been found, but it is well documented in the references from 1909. The question of exemption of teachers is hinted at in *Uganda Notes*, Nov. 1904, p. 172.

97 Tucker to Ag. Governor Tomkins, 11 May 1909, SMP 356/1909, copy in CO 536/26–24876.

98 Thus Governor Hesketh Bell, when he commented on Walker's letter of 4 March 1909, SMP 356/1909.

99 Tucker to Ag. Governor Tomkins, 11 May 1909.

100 Ag. Governor Tomkins to Secr. of State, 7 June 1909, CO 536/26–22250.

101 Ag. Governor Tomkins to Secr. of State, 23 June 1909, CO 536/26–24876.

102 Governor Hesketh Bell to Secr. of State, 6 Jan. 1909, CO 536/25.

103 cf. Tucker to Ag. Commissioner George Wilson, 13 Dec. 1905, A22/1, ESA.

104 Ag. Governor to Secr. of State, 7 Dec. 1909, CO 536/28–118/1909–10.

105 Tucker to Chief Secr., 16 June 1909, SMP 356/1909.

106 The Treasury approved of £700 to all three missions in Uganda; minute in CO 536/26–24876/1910.

107 cf. Ag. Chief Secr. to Tucker, 23 Dec. 1909, in Special File 1909/10: Compulsory Labour in Buganda, Ch. of Ug. Arch., MUL.

108 Governor to Secr. of State, 27 Dec. 1911, CO 536/43–2757/1911–12. cf. also *Uganda Notes*, April 1913, where it is emphasized that £300 is returned in the form of teachers' poll tax.

109 cf. 'Report of the Sub-Committee . . . on Education in Uganda', July 1917, no. 102, G3. A7. For a more detailed account see below, ch. 15.

110 Secr. of State to Governor, 16 Febr. 1912 (draft), CO 536/43–2757/11–12. Otherwise the officials in Uganda praised the missionary management of education in the period under survey; cf. Governor Jackson to Secr. of State, 27 Dec. 1911, (see n.108). The Secr. of State saw no reason in 1918 why the government should take direct responsibility for education in view of the missions' good work; Secr. of State to Governor, 28 March 1918, min. 200, SMP 1912.

111 CO minute 16 Dec. 1912, in CO 536/53–39566.

112 Ag. Governor to Secr. of State, 18 Nov. 1912, CO 536/53–39566; cf. minutes in SMP 944/09. See also the Tax Amendment Ordinance 1913, min. 1. SMP 3288; the minutes from 1917 in SMP 3864; and *Uganda Notes*, April 1913, p. 77.

113 See suggestion in Chief Secr. Wallis to Secr. of State, 16 April 1912, and negative reaction in the CO minutes 15 and 18 May 1912, CO 536/49–14313.

114 Willis to Governor Corydon, 9 May 1919, min. 209, SMP 1912[I].

115 Ag. Secr. CMS, Boulton Ladbury, to Chief Secr., 25 June 1919, min. 213, loc. cit.

116 Governor Corydon to Secr. of State, 14 Nov. 1919, CO 536/96–73439/19. The grant then amounted to £500 (7,500 Rs) which corresponded to 1,000 teachers (7.50 Rs each in poll tax), the same number as in 1910.

117 Treasury Chambers to Under Secr. of CO, 24 Febr. 1920, CO 536/106.

118 See minutes of meeting of DCs in Northern Province, Oct. 1919, SMP 5959. The DCs

demanded that the privilege should be extended to teachers and priests of the non-Christian religion.

119 The file dealing with this issue in 1919 has not been found, but the matter is explained in Chief Secr. to Governor, n.d., but must be early October 1925. SMP Conf. 865.

120 Memorandum by Governor Gowers, 7 Oct. 1925, loc. cit. Gowers emphasized that 'to limit the tax on the ground of anyone's race or occupation seems to me open to objection'. Bishop Willis saw this annulment as indicative of an anti-missionary trend in the Governor's educational policy. Willis to Ormsby Gore of the CO, 29 Dec. 1926, copy in Bishop's Files: R (1). Kabaka 1926–1927.

121 This may be inferred from W. Holden, Secr. NAC, to Chief Secr., 8 June 1925, SMP 1912^{II}.

122 Archdeacon Walker to Regents and members of the Buganda Lukiko, 29 March 1909; W. to PC Buganda, Knowles, 28 May 1909, copies of both in Walker's Letterbook I, MUL.

123 PC Buganda to Secr. CMS, 29 June 1909, Special File 1909/10 (see n.107); and Millar to Baskerville, 5 July 1909, loc. cit.

124 Ag. PC Browning to Chief Secr., 29 July 1913, SMP 3424.

125 The three Ugandan bishops to Governor, 10 April 1918, SMP 5368.

126 PC Buganda Knowles to Secr. CMS, 29 June 1909 (see n.123).

127 Walker to DC Kampala, P.W. Cooper, 18 March 1912, copy in Walker's Letterbook II, MUL.

128 The direct answer to Walker's request has not been found, but the ruling can be deduced from W. to Paske Smith, 30 June 1912, copy in Walker's Letterbook IV, MUL. cf. also restatement of the condition in the three bishops' joint letter, 19 April 1918; and in P.W. Cooper's memorandum on Katikiros on church estates, SMP 5368.

129 See first minutes in SMP 5116; and PC Buganda, P.W. Cooper, to Chief Secr., 17 May 1918, par. 8 and 9, SMP 5368.

130 The tightening of the policy regarding kasanvu is described in the three bishops' joint letter, 19 April 1918, and commented upon in P.W. Cooper, op. cit. It is also described by the missionary in charge of church estates; see T.B. Fletcher, 'The Estates of the Native Anglican Church', *Uganda Notes*, April 1920, pp.69f.

131 The joint letter from the three bishops has been quoted earlier, and the question of people deserting the church estates has been dealt with in connection with the issue of katikiros on church land. The joint letter had been drafted by Bishop Willis; cf. draft in Bishop's Files: K–L. Land. Subfile: Memoranda. Re double duty see also T.B. Fletcher, op. cit.

132 Governor Coryndon to Chief Secr., 31 May 1918; cf. P.W. Cooper to Chief Secr., 1 July 1918, both in SMP 5368.

133 This wider aspect has already been discussed and references given, see above pp.180ff.

134 This can be detected from Bishop Biermans to Governor, 18 Dec. 1919; Ag. PC Buganda, Sturrock, to Chief Secr., 29 Dec. 1919, followed by Minute by Ag. Chief Secr. T.S. Thomas, all in SMP 1371. In a report to the Synod 1919 from Bwekula Deanery it was stated that there were 1,416 male tenants on church land (124 plots), but when teachers, katikiros, people in permanent employment, were deducted, only 650 tenants could be called up for kasanvu. Reports from Deaneries 1919, Namirembe Arch.

135 cf. T.S. Thomas, op. cit. T.B. Fletcher (see n.130) confirms that tenants on church land are under the same laws and regulations as people on private estates.

136 This was clearly pointed out by Sturrock, op. cit.

137 For instance in 1920 it was recommended that kasanvu labour amounting to 100 men per month was required for the building of Mukono Theological College; Minutes of Theological Board, 11 June 1920, in *Diocesan Gazette*, Sept. 1920, p. 78. It was later stated that tenants on church land gave the first month's kasanvu labour to the mission and the second to the government; minutes of Advisory Educational Board, 10 May 1922, min. 111, SMP 4844.

138 As late as at the 1921 Synod there was a call for a better use of kasanvu labour on church estates and a warning against misuse by the government in its call on church tenants. On the 40 sq.m of land (mainly in Buganda) there were 2,593 rent-paying tenants who would also be liable for kasanvu. Minutes of Synod 1921: report from Estates Board, Synod File, Namirembe Arch. T.B. Fletcher (see n.130) states that in one year 866 were available for kasanvu and the church called upon 687, but neither year nor district is mentioned.

139 Willis to Ag. Chief Secr. Eliot, 6 March 1922, min. 96; minutes of meeting in Advisory Educational Board, 10 May 1922, min. 111, both in SMP 4844; cf. also Ag. Chief Secr. to all PCs, 17 May 1922, SMP 7545. The suggestion to build schools with the help of luwalo labour was raised as early as August 1921; cf. 'Report of Educational Conference 1921', printed copy under no. 119, G3. A7/1921. After the abolition of kasanvu it also became difficult in the districts for the mission to recruit its own tenants. cf. Archdeacon Lloyd to DC Toro, 27 Jan. 1923. DC's Files, Fort Portal, MP 73.

140 cf. Tucker to Ag. Governor, 20 Dec. 1909, SMP Conf. 144/1909.

141 cf. PC Buganda, P.W. Cooper, to Chief Secr., 27 Aug. 1917, SMP 1371.

142 cf. PC Buganda to Chief Secr. 24 June 1919, loc. cit.

143 The three bishops' joint letter to Governor, 19 April 1918, SMP 5368.

144 ibid.

145 P.W. Cooper to Chief Secr., 17 May 1918; and Memo for guidance of Bakatikiro of NAC Estates, 18 June, SMP 1371.

146 Cooper to Chief Secr., 1 July 1918; PC Western Province to Chief Secr., 12 Sept. 1918, SMP 1371.

147 Memorandum by P.W. Cooper, 8 Sept. 1918, SMP Conf. 346.

148 cf. G.K. Baskerville, Memorandum to Uganda Development Commission, Dec. 1919, Bishop's Files: K–L. Land. Subfile: Memoranda.

149 cf. PC Western Province to Chief Secr., 24 June 1919, min. 104, SMP 1371.

150 F. Rowling, Secr. CMS Uganda, and Archdeacon Baskerville to Ag. Governor, 22 April 1920, followed by letter from the two Catholic bishops, 28 April, both in SMP 6111.

151 ibid., cf. also notes of meeting of Advisory Educational Board, 14 May 1920, SMP 4844. It is notable how similar this wording is to the report of the Uganda Development Commission from Febr. 1920. It recommends in par. 92 that 'some measure of relief from customary national work' should be granted to tenants on church land, as they were already performing work useful to the country. Copy of report in CO 536/99–17962/1920.

152 Chief Secr. to Governor, 7 June 1920; and the Governor's approval, both in SMP 6111. The decision was communicated to the missions in Ag. PC Buganda to the missionary societies, the Lukiko and DCs, 11 Oct. 1920, in *Diocesan Gazette*, Nov. 1920, p.90.

153 Bishop Willis complained that the DC of Mbarara (Ankole) had ordered clergy and catechists to do luwalo as from 1 Jan. 1923. Willis to Chief Secr., 27 Nov. 1922; and PC Western Province to Chief Secr., 8 Dec. 1922, both in SMP 7577.

154 Minute by Governor, SMP 7577.

155 Ag. Chief Secre. to PC Western Province, 20 Dec. 1922, SMP 7577. See also minutes of Missionary Committee, 4 Jan. 1923, AR N3/3, Ch. of Ug. Arch., MUL.

156 cf. Ag. Chief Secr. Sturrock to PC Northern Province, 27 Nov. 1924, SMP 6025^I.

157 Ag. Chief Secr. Scott to PC Eastern Province, 30 Dec. 1924, loc. cit.

158 Willis to Ag. Chief Secr. Jarvis, 20 Oct. 1921, encl. a resolution from the Diocesan Council, SMP 6111.

159 PC Western Province, P.W. Cooper, to Chief Secr., 7 Nov. 1921, loc. cit. (see earlier, p. 183).

160 This number is calculated on the basis of the 10,000 rupees which CMS estimated as their extra expenses in connection with a cash payment of 5 Rs in luwalo and 2.50 Rs in extra poll tax; cf. Rowling and Baskerville, 22 April 1922 (n.150).

161 Willis to Ag. Chief Secr. Eliot, 2 June 1922, SMP 7545; minute of Advisory Educational Board, 10 and 25 Oct. 1922, SMP 4844. The request for luwalo labour was later extended to include specific church purposes like the carriage of clergy loads, which the Buganda Lukiko approved of, but the Governor vetoed. See Willis to Under-Secr. of State, Ormsby-Gore, 29 Dec. 1926, Bishop's Files: R (1). Kabaka 1926–7.

162 cf. *Diocesan Gazette*, March 1916.

163 Governor Jackson to Secr. of State, 20 May 1914, CO 536/69–22508/14.

164 This was later regretfully confirmed by T.B. Fletcher, 'The Estates of the Native Anglican Church, *Uganda Notes*, April 1920, pp.69ff.

165 Secr. of State to Governor, 30 June 1914, (see n.163).

166 Ag. Governor Wallis to Secr. of State, 25 Sept. 1914, CO 536/70–42065/1914.

167 cf. Governor Jackson to Secr. of State, 29 Jan. 1915, CO 536/75–11779/1915.

168 Two minutes in CO, both dated 10 Nov. 1914, CO 536/70–42065/14.

169 The drain of revenue away from the chiefs was clearly pointed out when it was estimated that 25% of revenue from rent was absorbed in 'the mission revenue'. PC Northern Province to Bishop Willis, 21 June 1921, Bishop's Files: K–L. Land (Bunyoro) 1912–32. cf. also the warning against the transfer of busulu to the missions and the subsequent erosion of the chiefs' power, incl. in Ag. PC Northern Province, Haddon to Chief Secr., 25 Febr. 1920, SMP 529^I.

170 Circular Memorandum to PCs and DCs, 5 July 1922, SMP 7168; cf. Ag. Chief Secr. Scott's memorandum to PC Eastern Province, 17 Nov. 1924, SMP 6025^I.

171 DC Busoga, Sullivan, to PC Eastern Province, 31 Oct. 1924, loc. cit.; cf. also PC Northern Province to Willis, 21 June 1921, describing the same practice in Bunyoro (cf. n.169).

172 Ag. Chief Secr. Scott's memorandum, 17 Nov. 1924, supplemented by Ag. Chief Secr. Sturrock to PC Northern Province, 27 Nov. 1924, loc. cit.

173 DC Bunyoro, Sandford, to PC Northern Province, 9 Jan. 1925, SMP 6025^I. Even before the ruling of 1924 Sandford pointed to the abuse of busulu on the part of the CMS in his 'Notes on the Obusulu Payments in Bunyoro', dat. 27 Oct. 1924, SMP 6025C. Even 3 years earlier the colonial administration unofficially made Bishop Willis aware of the same dilemma: see PC Northern Province to Willis, 21 June 1921.

174 PC Northern Province to Chief Secr., 14 Oct. 1925, SMP 6025^I.

175 Chief Secr.'s draft answer to PC, no date, and the final answer dat. 3 March 1926, both in SMP 6025^I.

176 For Eastern Province, SMP 9313A; for Western Province, SMP 6025B, and for Northern Province, SMP 6025C.

177 For CMS reaction see especially Willis to Under-Secr. of State, Ormsby-Gore, 29 Dec. 1926, where he called the ruling on busulu a severe blow to the missionary work by the Uganda government; Bishop's Files: R (1). Kabaka 1926–1927. Also Willis to Chief Secr., 16 Febr. 1928, SMP 5368; Willis to Governor, 17 Dec. 1928, SMP R18/1.

178 Confirmed by Bishop Willis when he says that rent from tenants constitutes 'a substantial and permanent source of income to the Church'. 'Notes on Requirements and Policy of the Mission', dat. 17 Dec. 1918, no. 9, G3. A7/1919. The Rural Dean of Bunyoro, Rev. H. Bowers, pointed to the severe loss of labour and added that by losing control of busulu the church lost 'a large recruiting agency'. Bowers to Willis, 24 Oct. 1924. The revenue from busulu in Bunyoro was 8,000 shs p.a. Bowers to Willis, 5 Dec. 1924, both in Bishop's Files: K–L. Land (Bunyoro) 1912–34; cf. also Willis to Ormsby-Gore, 29 Dec. 1926.

179 This was admitted in *Diocesan Gazette*, March 1916. A great number of tenants even evaded payment, cf. secr. to the Finance Board, Rev. Rowling, 'Finance of the Uganda Church', *Uganda Notes*, Jan. 1916. In Report from Bwekula Deanery 1919, it was urged that a reform re collection of revenues from church lands was badly needed. Reports from Deaneries to the Synod 1919, Synod Files, Namirembe Arch.

180 An example is given in Report from Bwekula Deanery 1919, loc. cit.

181 These and other reasons are clearly listed in the Estates Board's report to the Synod 1924, dat. Jan. 1924, Synod Files, Namirembe Arch.

182 ibid., and T.B. Fletcher, (see n.164). Comparing figures in reports from Estates Board from 1921 and 1924, the number of rent (busulu) payers decreased, with 473 on the 40 sq.m in Buganda.

183 cf. G. Hewitt (1971), pp.431ff. See also below, ch. 15.

184 'Report of Uganda Mission 1921', *Uganda Notes*, April 1921; and Financial Report 1922, copy in SMP 7998.

185 ibid.

186 Aptly expressed by Fletcher, (see n.164).

187 Thus summarized when Bishop Willis presented grievances of Uganda Mission to CO in 1926. Willis to Under-Secr. of State, Ormsby-Gore, 29 Dec. 1926 (see n.177).

Part IV   Direct inputs: demands to the colonial state

13   The issue of forced labour

1 Files in ESA combined with CO records have provided the basic material supplemented with mission and church archives in Uganda and London.

2 A.R. Tucker (1908) vol. I, pp.261ff; cf. also Portal (1894), p.222.

3 Tucker, op. cit., vol. II, ch. 29 and pp. 99ff. cf. A. Clayton & D.C. Savage (1974), pp. 3f; also his intervention re passing of Bill for Abolition of the Legal Status of Slavery in the British East Africa Protectorate, correspondence encl. in Tucker to Baylis, 17 Sept. 1907, no.229; and 1 Oct. 1907, no. 241, G3. A7/05. He intervened also re position of concubines on Zanzibar through the Anti-Slavery and Aborigines' Protection Society; Tucker to its secr. Travers Buxton, 11 Dec. 1909, G138, in collection in Rhodes House, Oxford: MSS. Brit. Emp. s.22. See account by one of his contemporaries, F.J. Jackson (1930), pp. 337f.

4 *The Times*, 18 March 1903; cf. also 24 March 1903 with report of visit of deputation to the Foreign Secretary. See also *Uganda Notes*, Jan. 1903.

5 FO to Commissioner Sadler, 25 July 1903, FO 2/735; cf. also Clayton & Savage (1974), pp.30f.

6 Tucker to Rev. Tegart, 3 Jan. 1909 (copy), no. 220; Tucker to Baylis, 31 May 1909, no. 219, both in G3. A7/07.

7 Tucker to Secr. of Committee on Indian Immigration, 7 Sept. 1909, no. 300; Tucker to Baylis, 9 Sept. 1909, no. 299, in which he mentions that he will contact the Anti-Slavery and Aborigines' Protection Society and send a copy to the Archbishop of Canterbury (letters in G3. A7/07). Later he became even more convinced about the damaging effects of forced labour; see Tucker to Baylis, 3 Jan. 1910, G3. A7/08.

8 See, e.g., Ag. Governor Boyle to Tucker, 4 Jan. 1910, SMP Conf. 144/1909.

9 Tucker to Baylis, 31 May 1909.

10 Tucker to Baylis, 21 Dec. 1909, no. 37, G3 A7/08.

11 About migration as an effect of the increased burdens on the Bakopi, see J.A. Atanda (1969). F.J. Jackson had some years earlier noticed the same effect after the introduction of the hut tax; Jackson to Secr. of State, 25 Jan. 1902, FO 2/589.

12 Tucker to Ag. Governor Boyle, 20 Dec. 1909, SMP Conf. 144/09. It is significant that Tucker sent a copy of the letter to CMS London and asked them to inform Sir T.F. Victor Buxton, chairman of the Group III Committee (Africa); see Tucker to Baylis, 21 Dec. 1909.

13 Tucker to Boyle, 23 Dec. 1909, marked private and confidential, copy under no. 46, G3. A7/08.

14 Tucker to Baylis, 3 Jan. 1910, no.45, G3.A7/08. Sir Victor Buxton was again informed and it appears that he informed the Under-Secr. of State, Col. Seely, at an early stage about Tucker's criticism and anxiety; cf. Buxton to Seely, 3 Febr. 1910, copy under no. 91, loc. cit. It is interesting to notice that a copy of the same letter is kept among the papers of the Anti-Slavery and Aborigines' Protection Society (see n.3).

15 Ag. Governor Boyle to Tucker, 4 Jan. 1910.

16 Tucker commented on Boyle's answer in Tucker to Baylis, 14 Jan. 1910, no. 89, G3. A7/08. He made it clear that he was prepared to pursue the matter, which he did in private correspondence with Sir Victor Buxton; cf. Baylis to Tucker, 6 May 1910, Letterbrook II, p.501, G3. A7/L2. The Anti-Slavery and Aborigines' Protection Society was also informed, and Tucker asked it to get a public assurance in Parliament that no forced labour would be used on the construction of the railway in Busoga. Tucker to Travers Buxton, 3 May 1910 (see n.3).

17 Tucker hinted at this possibility while still in Uganda; see Tucker to Travers Buxton, 5 July 1910, (see n.3).

18 Minutes of interview between Under-Secr. of State, Col. Seely, and Bishop Tucker, 24 Nov. 1910, CO 536/38–36727/1910. Tucker to R.V. Vernon of the CO, 15 Dec. 1910, CO 536/38–38735.

19 cf. Clayton & Savage (1974), ch. 2.

20 Tucker to Vernon, 15 Dec. 1910; Tucker to Col. Seely, 3 Febr. 1911, CO 536/47–U 3722, copy in SMP Conf. 144/09.

21 See also comments in Annual Report for Buganda 1909–10, SMP 1138.

22 Ag. Governor Tomkins to Secr. of State, 27 March 1911, CO 536/40–13005/1911.

23 CO minute 26 April 1911, loc. cit.

24 Tucker paid a farewell visit to Uganda in April and May 1911 before the final answer from the CO had come.

25 Tomkins to Secr. of State, 27 March 1911, later repeated in CO's answer to Tucker, 29 April 1911 (see n.22).

26 Walker to Sub-Commissioner Buganda, Leakey, 14 Febr. 1907, SMP 175/1907.

27 Walker to Regents and Members of the Lukiko, 29 March 1909, copy in Walker's Letterbook I, p. 201, MUL.

28 Walker to Leakey, 20 May 1912, copy in Walker's Letterbook IV, p.11.

29 Willis to Governor Jackson, 22 July 1913, SMP 3424.

30 cf. Ag. PC Buganda, Browning, to Chief Secr., 29 July 1913, SMP 3424.

31 The Governor pointed out that all three missions had made use of kasanvu: Governor to Secr. of State, 17 Febr. 1919, CO 536/93–20076/19.

32 Busoga Planters Association to Chief Secr., 26 Nov. 1917, SMP 1371.

33 Ag. Chief Secr. Jarvis to Governor, 22 Jan. 1918, SMP 1371.

34 Ag. PC Eastern Province, Jervoise, to Chief Secr., 30 April 1919; Governor to Chief Secr., 6 May 1919, SMP Conf. 393.

35 cf. Anderea L. Kimbugwe to PC Buganda, P.W. Cooper, 13 July 1918 (incorrectly written 1917 on the translation copy), deploring this practice; and A.M. Watson, government official in West Nile, to Governor, 4 Nov. 1918, both in file 4, MSS. Afr. s.633, Coryndon Papers, Rhodes House, Oxford. See also reference in Annual Report Western Province 1917–18, SMP 3314.

36 The matter was raised by the Ag. PC Eastern Province, Jervoise, when he first took office, in a dispatch to Chief Secr., 8 April 1919, SMP Conf. 393.

37 Governor to Chief Secr., 24 April 1919, letter forwarded to Jervoise, SMP Conf. 393; cf. Governor to Secr. of State, 17 Febr. 1919, CO 536/93–20076/1919.

38 For the work of the Uganda Development Commission see C. Ehrlich (1965), pp.423ff. cf. G.F. Engholm (1968, unpubl. thesis), pp. 104ff. Re post-war labour policy, see J.B. Kakwenzire (1976, unpubl. thesis), part II.

39 Report of the Uganda Development Commission, Febr. 1920, par. 46–105, copies in SMP 5860 and CO 536/99–17963/20.

40 ibid. par. 104. Willis' memorandum was published in *Uganda Notes*, July 1919. The article is unsigned, but Archdeacon Baskerville identified Willis as the author in his memorandum to the Development Commission, Dec. 1919, Bishop's Files: K–L. Land. Subfile: Memoranda.

41 Thus Willis to Governor Coryndon, 15 July 1918, Coryndon Papers, (see n.35).

42 Willis, Memorandum 1919.

43 Baskerville's Memorandum to the Development Commission (see n.148). Notes of evidence to the Commission: 11th witness Canon G.R. Blackledge (member of Labour Conference), 55th witness Rev. T.B. Fletcher (secr. of the Estates Board), SMP 5860. Blackledge's statement was reported in *Uganda Herald*, 19 Dec. 1919.

44 CO minute, 9 Nov. 1920 in connection with Governor Coryndon's comments on Uganda Development Commission's report, CO 536/102–50506.

45 cf. R. Oliver (1952), pp.222ff; and Gavin White (1970, unpubl. thesis).

46 For Kavirondo see J.M. Lonsdale (1964, unpubl. thesis).

47 For a recent analysis of the settlers' position in the economy see E.A. Brett (1973), ch. 6; and R.M.A. van Zwanenberg (1975), *passim*.

48 The October circular is printed in N. Leys (1924), pp.295ff.

49 The labour issue in Kenya in 1919–20 is dealt with in Clayton & Savage (1974), pp.112ff, and van Zwanenberg (1975), esp. ch. 4.

50 The three missionary leaders' memorandum, soon called the Bishops' Memorandum, can most conveniently be found either in Leys (1924), p. 397, or in the CMS magazine *Church Missionary Review*, vol. 71, 1920, pp.142ff. cf. also Oliver (1952), pp.248ff.

51 See G. Bennett (1965), pp.291ff; Brett (1973), pp.188ff; Clayton & Savage (1974), pp.112ff; Oliver (1952), pp.248ff; A.J. Temu (1972), pp.122ff; and van Zwanenberg (1975), pp.126ff.

52 This is clearly expressed in Archdeacon Owen to Rev. Rowling, secr. of the Uganda mission, 20 Aug. 1920, Owen Papers, acc. 83, CMS Arch.: Papers on Forced Labour, file I.

53 cf. Secr. of State Viscount Milner's dispatch of Febr. 1920. See also Oliver (1952), p.250; and Brett (1973), p.188.

54 Quoted by Temu (1972), p. 125.

55 See J.W. Cell (1976), Introduction; cf. also D. Wylie (1977).

56 See correspondence between Norman Leys and J.H. Oldham, in 1920s, esp. Leys to Oldham, 10 June 1920; cf. also Leys to John Harris, 30 June 1923, all printed in Cell (1978). cf. also Leys' article 'Christianity and Labour Conditions in Africa' under pseudonym Fulani Bin Fulani in *International Review of Missions*, vo. 9, 1920, p. 544.

57 See in particular Oliver (1952), pp.250ff; and Cell (1978).

58 Oldham to Leys, 9 June 1920.

59 Leys to Oldham, 23 July 1920 and accompanying note. But Oldham failed, cf. Leys' article from 1920 (see n.56).

60 Oldham to Leys, 5 Oct. 1920.

61 See reference to the Bishops' Memorandum in the document 'Labour in Africa and the Principle of Trusteeship' from Dec. 1920, signed by all Protestant churches in Britain and 32 missionary societies; copy in CMS Archives Nairobi.

62 cf. Oldham to Leys, 5 Oct. 1920. More evidence re Oldham–Willis relations may appear from a closer examination of the Oldham papers.

63 Oldham was closely involved when the dispatch to Kenya was drafted, see the correspondence between Under-Secr. of State, Edward Wood, and Oldham, Aug. 1921, file 3 in Coryndon Papers (see n.35). cf. Oldham's comments in letter to Norman Leys, 5 Sept. 1921, in Cell (1978), p. 191.

64 Copy of dispatch to Ag. Governor of Kenya may be found in Coryndon Papers.

65 Secr. of State to Ag. Governor Uganda, 5 Sept. 1921, encl. dispatch to Kenya, copies in Coryndon Papers.

66 Ag. Governor Eliot to Secr. of State, 9 Febr. 1922, CO 536/118–14109/22.

67 See minute by Batterbee of the CO, dat. 1 April 1922 (see n.66). The restriction to 'exhortation' was later reiterated cf. Governor Archer to Secr. of State, 22 Febr. 1923, CO 536/124–15909.

68 Eliot, op. cit.

69 Batterbee, op. cit.

70 Governor Coryndon to Secr. of State, 30 May 1922, CO 536/119–33120/1922.

71 Under-Secr. of State, Edward Wood, to Oldham, 19 Aug. 1921, Coryndon Papers.

72 See remarks by Edward Wood after having reached agreement with Oldham re dispatch to Kenya: 'we may hope to have the Missionary Societies and their friends with us instead of against us'. Wood to Coryndon, 25 Aug. 1921 (n.71). Re revision of legislation Governor Coryndon recommended that there was no need for any change; Coryndon to Secr. of State, 30 May 1922. But the CO was not happy with compulsory labour, because it was banned in Kenya, and requested that the Native Authority Ordinance be altered; CO minute in CO 536/119–33120/22. The rules about luwalo remained unchanged, but re kasanvu it was written into the Ordinance that the sanction of the Secr. of State was necessary in each case, and public purposes were

clearly defined. See text in cap. 112, *Laws of the Uganda Protectorate*; and Governor Archer to Secr. of State, 22 Febr. 1923, CO 536/124–15909. Only a little later the Governor resorted to compulsory labour for road building in Eastern Province, and the CO reluctantly gave its permission; cf. Archer to Secr. of State, 30 July 1923, CO 536/131–34109, and his telegram, 22 July 1924, CO 536/131–34981: cf. also Kakwen-compulsory labour in the project, and the CO was very pleased with the outcome. Ag. Governor Jarvis to Secr. of State, 9 Jan. 1924, and the corresponding CO minute, CO 536/130–5998/24. Governor Archer later made the same suggestion re Buganda, but the matter failed for various reasons; cf. Archer to Secr. of State, 18 July 1924, CO 536/131–34109, and his telegram, 22 July 1924, CO 536/131–34981, cf. also Kakwen-zire (1976) pp.15ff.

73 See report of the Estates Board to the Synod in Jan. 1921, in which the major concern was the prevailing misinterpretation of the kasanvu rules, not their abolition. Synod Files, Namirembe Arch.

74 Minutes of Missionary Conference, 22 Jan. 1921, no. 33, G3.A7/21.

75 Minutes of the Synod, Jan. 1921, MUL.

76 Rev. T.B. Fletcher to Bishop Willis, 16 Febr. 1923, Bishop's Files: K–L. Land. Subfile: Memoranda. Fletcher was secr. to the Estates Board and had not earlier been opposed to coercion as such; cf. n.43.

77 cf. Oldham to Edward Wood, 15 Aug. 1921, Coryndon Papers.

78 Tucker to Baylis, 31 May 1909, no. 219, G3. A7/07.

79 Willis, 'The Policy of the Uganda Mission', July 1912, pr. as a pamphlet, 1913.

80 'A Members Report', Synod 1921, *Uganda Notes*, 1921, p. 45.

81 Archdeacon Walker made the difference between Tucker and Willis clear in his 'Report on Education Work done by NAC, April 1911–March 1912', copy in Walker's Letterbook III, p.69, MUL.

82 This judgement is fully confirmed by Willis himself. In 1923 he pointed to increased difficulties for the educational work, because the chiefs no longer were at liberty to use forced labour as earlier; work on buildings and repairs which earlier cost nothing would now have to be paid in cash. Memorandum of Bishop Willis' interview with Group Committee, 4 May 1923, no.46, G3. A7/1923. In 1926, when Willis complained of the Uganda government's anti-missionary policy and presented his mission's grievances to the CO, he was quite explicit about the difficulties in obtaining labour from tenants on church land any more as the kasanvu obligation had been abolished and luwalo labour was not allowed for church purposes. Willis to Under-Secr. of State, Ormsby-Gore, 29 Dec. 1926, draft in Bishop's Files: R (1). Kabaka 1926–1927.

14   Excess land and alienation

1 cf. H.B. Thomas & A.E. Spencer (1938), pp.42ff, p.69.

2 Some of these aspects are touched upon in Ag. Governor Tomkins to Secr. of State, 31 May 1910, CO 536/33–19313. The CO was more restrained in its attitude to the granting of freehold land to Europeans and preferred leasehold. For the issue of excess land seen in its wider context see esp. C.C. Wrigley (1959), pp.21ff (esp. p.26). cf. also C. Ehrlich (1965), p.412; and H.W. West (1972), pp.22f.

3 Ag. Governor Tomkins to Secr. of State, 13 June 1910, CO 536/34–22024/1910. The positive attitude to sale of land to European settlers represents a reversal of policy from the previous Governor, Sir Hesketh Bell, who argued that Uganda is 'a black man's country and European settlement is out of the question'. H.H.J. Bell (1946), pp. 159f. Bell, who was Governor 1905–1909, has in his autobiography reproduced parts of his diary from his time in Uganda.

4 Tucker to Ag. Governor Boyle, 23 Dec. 1909 (copy), no. 46, G3. A7/08.

5 Major W.A. Burn to Ag. Chief Secr., 10 Nov. 1910, copy in CO 536/40–13005/11. Burn's clients were the two Protestant Regents, the nine Protestant saza chiefs and one Muslim saza chief. cf. also Governor Jackson to Secr. of State, 6 July 1911, CO 536/41–25553/1911. The call on Johnston is mentioned in the accompanying CO minute.

6 Summarized in Burn, op. cit., p. 4.

7 Interview between Bishop Tucker and Under-Secr. of State, Col. Seely, 24 Nov. 1910, CO 536/38–36727/1910.

8 Thus Tucker to R.V. Vernon of the CO, 15 Dec. 1910, CO 536/38–38735/1910; Tucker to Col. Seely, 3 Febr. 1911, CO 536/47–U 3722, copy in SMP Conf. 144/09.

9 Tucker to Col. Seely, 3 Febr. 1911.

10 ibid. See also Tucker to Vernon, 15 Dec. 1910.

11 Thus expressed in CO to Tucker, 2 Dec. 1910 (draft), CO 536/38–36727/1910, and later in Ag. Governor Tomkins to Secr. of State, 27 March 1911, CO 536/40–13005/1911.

12 F.J. Jackson to Secr. of State, 6 July 1911. It appears from the accompanying CO minute that 21 sq.m had already been given to Europeans.

13 Jackson to Mr Read of the CO, 19 July 1911 (marked private letter), CO 536/41–27129. Officials in the CO were dissatisfied with the Governor's outburst, cf. their minutes.

14 cf. CO minute in CO 536/41–25553/1911.

15 The new edition appeared later in 1911; Jackson to Secr. of State, 19 Dec. 1911, CO 536/43–1366/1911–12.

16 The new rules were formalized in a supplementary agreement made in 1913, called The Buganda Agreement (Allotment and Survey), 1913. Thomas & Spencer (1938), pp. 67, 69.

17 Trustees of the NAC to Chief Secr., 5 Nov. 1920, Bishop's Files: K–L. Land. Subfile: Land, General.

18 Chief Secr. to NAC Trustees, 16 Dec. 1920, loc. cit.

15 *Education as an issue between church and state*

1 Education in general in Uganda is dealt with in: F. Carter (1967a, unpubl. thesis); O.W. Furley & T. Watson (1978); A. Wandira (1972); T. Watson (1968, unpubl. thesis).

2 Minutes of Conference of Missionaries, 28–30 June 1899, no. 99, G3. A7/01; the report, 'The Uganda Mission in 1904', *Uganda Notes*, Febr. 1905. See also Carter (1967a), pp.37ff.

3 See report by Archdeacon Walker, encl. in Commissioner Sadler to Marquess of Lansdowne, 2 July 1902, FO 2/591.

4 ibid.

5 See report by Archdeacon Walker and Superintendent K. Borup, encl. in Sadler to FO, 2 July 1902. See also Furley & Watson (1978), p. 104.

6 Commissioner Sadler to Marquess of Lansdowne, 9 Sept. 1903, FO 2/736; see also Bishop Tucker to Ag. Commissioner George Wilson, 1 Nov. 1904, A22/1, ESA. This whole issue of training sons of chiefs in relation to Busoga has been thoroughly dealt with in T. Tuma (1973, unpubl. thesis), pp.131ff.

7 Commissioner Sadler to Marquess of Lansdowne, 13 Aug. 1903, with General Report

– Uganda Protectorate for the year ending 31 March 1903, enclosed in PP Cd. 1839 – Africa no. 15 (1903). See also Commissioner Sadler to Secr. of State, 19 Aug. 1905, encl. Uganda Annual Report 1904–05, CO 536/2–34350.

8 FO minute 1902 in FO 2/591; FO minute 1903 in FO 2/736.

9 FO minute, 24 Dec. 1902, FO 2/732.

10 Commissioner Sadler to Marquess of Landsowne, 14 Nov. 1902, loc. cit. cf. Furley & Watson (1978), pp.105ff.

11 Commissioner Sadler to Secr. of State, 27 Oct. 1905, CO 536/3–42516/1905. For education for Muslims see F. Carter (1965); and A.B.K. Kasozi (1970).

12 Tucker to Ag. Commissioner George Wilson, 13 Dec. 1905, A22/1, copy in CO 536/3–5447/1905–06.

13 cf. Governor Hesketh Bell to Secr. of State, 6 Jan. 1909, CO 536/25, cf. SMP 1567/08. On an earlier occasion Tucker had even spoken of the government's discouragement and lack of support for educational work. Tucker to Sadler, 7 May 1903, A22/1.

14 Uganda Men's Conference, June 1904, no. 158, G3. A7/04.

15 Minutes of the Synod, 21–22 April 1909, MUL.

16 Minutes of the Synod, 12–16 July 1910, loc. cit.

17 Willis, 'The Policy of the Uganda Mission', 1913, p. 12.

18 Ag. Commissioner George Wilson to Secr. of State, 31 Dec. 1905, CO 536/3–5447/1905–06.

19 cf. CO minutes, 1 and 2 Dec. 1905, CO 536/3–42516/1905; and minutes by Ellis, 17 Febr. 1906; and by Read, 20 Febr. 1906, CO 536/3–5447/1905–06. The CO forgot to discuss the matter with the new Commissioner before his departure for Uganda; minute Nov. 1905, loc. cit.

20 ibid.

21 Governor Hesketh Bell to Secr. of State, 5 Jan. 1907, CO 536/12–4763/1907 (file destroyed, read from index).

22 See notes by Governor Hesketh Bell, Dec. 1908 (SMP 1576/08) with regard to technical instruction of Muslims, a field where Bishop Tucker was fully prepared to leave the full responsibility to the government.

23 See newly appointed Governor Hesketh Bell to Archdeacon Walker, 7 July 1906, SMP 691/06.

24 Bell to Secr. of State, 5 Jan. 1907; Bell to Secr. of State, 6 Jan. 1909, encl. Draft Estimates of Revenue and Expenditure 1909–10, CO 536/25.

25 cf. Carter (1967a), pp.58ff.

26 e.g. Governor Jackson to Secr. of State, 27 Dec. 1911, CO 536/43–2757/1911–12.

27 Ag. Governor Boyle to Secr. of State, 7 Dec. 1909, encl. Draft Estimates 1910–11, CO 536/28–118/09–10.

28 Chief Secr. Wallis to various heads of departments, 24 Jan. 1912, SMP 2351.

29 Secr. of State to Governor, 16 Febr. 1912, CO 536/43–2757/1911–12.

30 Thus expressed by J.J. Willis (1925), p. 10, and later repeated in Report from the Educational Conference 1915, p. 13 (copy in MUL).

31 Thus Willis, op. cit., p. 12, and esp. Minutes of the Education Committee, CMS London, 29 Nov. 1916, in which the leading educationist among the Uganda missionaries took part; no. 131, G3. A7/1916.

32 Walker to Ag. Chief Secr., 18 July 1912, min. 60, SMP 1912.

33 Bishop Willis, 'The Educational Work of the CMS in the Diocese of Uganda', encl. in

dispatch to CO, 7 Jan. 1913, CO 536/58–3900/1913. In 1917, 12 male missionaries were appointed to high schools; the cost was estimated at £2,630; see Report of Sub-Committee on Education in Uganda, 2 July 1917, no. 102, G3. A7/1917.

34 Interview between Colonial Secretary and Bishops Tucker and Willis, 13 March 1914, CO 536/73–9243/14; Report of the Educational Conference 1915 (n.30); Baskerville to Manley, 17 Oct. 1915, asking the CMS to put pressure on the government; no. 135, G3. A7/1915; interview with Rev. E. Millar, 5 April 1916, asking for the same; no.57, G3. A7/1916; Minutes of Educational Committee, 29 Nov. 1916, loc. cit.; Willis to Manley, 2 July 1917, requesting the CMS to take up the matter of government grants; no. 107, G3. A7/1917.

35 Willis to Chief Secr. Wallis, 18 July 1912, min. 51, SMP 1912, copy forwarded to Secr. of State, 1 Sept. 1912, CO 536/52–33217. The proposal was also put forward in Willis, 'Policy of the Uganda Mission', 1912, and repeated in Willis to Manley, 2 July 1917, no. 107, G3. A7/1917.

36 This understanding is apparent in Chief Secr. Wallis to Secr. of State, 16 April 1912, CO 536/49–14313/12, and repeated in the Report of the Educational Conference 1915.

37 Chief Secr. Wallis to Secr. of State, 21 Sept. 1912; and Secr. of State to Wallis, 6 Nov. 1912, CO 536/52–33217/12.

38 £1,000 was approved for 1913/14, but came to nothing. The CO agreed that the £850 was 'a mere trifle', but felt powerless *vis-à-vis* the Treasury. See esp. Minutes from interview with Tucker and Willis, 13 March 1914 (n.34).

39 See table in H.B. Thomas & R. Scott (1935), app. III. Willis dismissed the war argument as invalid; Willis to Manley, 2 July 1917.

40 Willis to Manley, 2 July 1917.

41 Chief Secr. to Governor, 13 July 1917, min. 10, SMP 4844.

42 Proceedings of the Educational Conference, 22–28 Sept. 1917, app. C, min. 29, SMP 4844.

43 ibid. app. A, introductory remarks by Chief Secr. Jarvis.

44 Dispatch to Secr. of State, 3 Nov. 1917, min. 47, cf. Chief Secr. to the three bishops, 17 Nov. 1917, min. 43, SMP 4844.

45 cf. Chief Secr. to Governor, 12 Oct. 1917, SMP 4844.

46 Ag. Governor Wallis to F.G.A. Butler, 1 Oct. 1917 (marked secret), CO 536/86–2457/1917–18. Wallis was even opposed to the establishment of secular schools as, both by Africans and the missions, it would be looked upon as government support for Islam.

47 Secr. of State to Governor, 28 March 1918, min. 200, SMP 1912.

48 Governor Coryndon (in England) to Secr. of State, 23 May 1920, CO 536/107–C. 25635/1920; cf. also Coryndon to Secr. of State, 4 Sept. 1920, SMP 4844.

49 cf. Notes of interview with Sir Robert Coryndon, 3 May 1920, no. 97, G3. A7/1920. Coryndon suggested a new letter to the CO which he himself would then comment upon. cf. his letter of regret to the CMS, 3 June 1920 when his intervention turned out to be unsuccessful (no. 113, loc. cit) We have earlier met Governor Coryndon's positive attitude towards the missions, when he, quite surprisingly, exempted the missionaries from poll tax.

50 e.g. resolutions from the Synods, Sept. 1919 and Jan. 1921, Minutes of the Synod, MUL. Archdeacon Baskerville, Memorandum to the Uganda Development Commission, Dec. 1919, Bishop's Files: K–L. Land. Subfile: Memoranda. G.T. Manley to Under-Secr. of State, 7 May 1920, expressing disappointment that the grant for 1920/1 had only been increased by £200 CO 536/106–Mi. 22941/1920. It was also at this time that the mission asked for an increase in the poll-tax rebate. A development

loan of £1 mill. was given to Uganda, and of this £10,000 was earmarked for the missions' educational work; cf. minutes in SMP 6478.

51 Thus expressed by Baskerville, op. cit.

52 Willis to Manley, 17 Dec. 1918, no. 8, G3. A7/1919.

53 This was clearly expressed by Governor Coryndon to Secr. of State, 6 Sept. 1919, min. 1, SMP 5839, and again Coryndon to Under-Secr. of State, 5 April 1920, SMP 5998. See also Carter (1967a), ch. 2; and Furley & Watson (1978), pp. 187f.

54 cf. Report of Committee appointed to consider Terms of Service of Native Civil Service, dat. 30 Dec. 1919, SMP 5998. See esp. N. Motani (1972, unpubl. thesis) and Motani (1975).

55 ibid. cf. M. Macpherson (1964).

56 See various minutes from 1920 in SMP 5839. See also Governor Coryndon to Secr. of State, 15 April 1920, SMP 5998; and interview with Coryndon at CMS headquarters, 3 May 1920, no. 97, G3. A7/1920.

57 Appointed in Nov. 1920, cf. minutes in SMP 6558.

58 Thus Ag. Governor Carter to Secr. of State, 15 Jan. 1920, CO 536/99–12187/20, copy in SMP 5998.

59 Minutes of Meeting of the Technical School Board, 3 Dec. 1920, min. 20 and following minutes, SMP 5839.

60 Scheme for Technical Education, dat. 5 Jan. 1922, by H.O. Savile, newly appointed superintendent of government education, SMP 5839.

61 See minute of Makerere College Board, 12 Dec. 1922, min. 114 and following minutes by government officials in SMP 5839. Relevant are also the reassuring remarks by the PC Buganda at the Anglican educational conference Aug. 1921; Report of Educational Conference 1921, copy under no. 117, G3. A7/1921.

62 cf. Baskerville's memorandum to Development Commission (see n.50).

63 This point of view was clearly expressed by the leading educationist within the CMS mission, Canon H.T.C. Weatherhead, in his memorandum to the Development Commission, n.d., but must be late 1919, SMP 5860.

64 ibid.; interview with Sir Robert Coryndon, 3 May 1920; Report of Education Conference 1921.

65 See minutes of Missionary Committee, 6 Oct. 1921, where the plans for mission institutions in each province are cancelled. Minute Book, MUL.

66 Thus within clerical training, cf. minutes of Technical School Board, 29 June 1921, SMP 5839.

67 cf. Report of Committee . . . on Native Civil Service (see n.54).

68 Thus expressed by Ag. Governor Carter to Secr. of State, 15 Jan. 1920, CO 536/99–12187/20. Carter was commenting on the report on a Native Civil Service.

69 cf. Ag. Governor Carter, op. cit.

70 Report . . . on Native Civil Service.

71 PC Buganda, P.W. Cooper, to Chief Secr., 24 Jan. 1919, min. 66, SMP 3597.

72 cf. Governor Coryndon to Secr. of State, 29 April 1919, CO 536/93–37282/19.

73 CO minute 13 Aug. 1919; Secr. of State to Governor, 29 Aug. 1919, loc. cit.

74 Coryndon, op. cit.

75 Northern Province: minutes of DCs' Conference, Masindi, Oct. 1919, SMP 5959.

76 This and other proposals from the conference were considered to indicate an anti-mission feeling; Chief Secr. to Governor, 24 Nov. 1919, loc. cit.

77 PC Northern Province, Haddon, to Willis, 21 June 1921, Bishop's Files: K–L. Land, Bunyoro 1921–1933.

78 Annual Report, Northern Province, 1921, SMP 2135 K; Memorandum from PC Northern Province to Chief Secr., 22 March 1922, SMP 7168.

79 Memorandum from PC Northern Province, loc. cit. Ag. PC Eastern Province to Ass. Secr. for Native Affairs, 10 Oct. 1922, min. 50 and following minutes, SMP 7168.

80 PCs' Conference, 18 July 1923, min. 25, SMP 6215.

81 Report of Uganda Development Commission, 1920, section on education, ch. 7, copies in SMP 5860 and CO 536/99–17962/20.

82 Minutes of Advisory Educational Board, 14 May 1920, min. 76, SMP 4844. It was the Board's first meeting since its start in 1917; cf. Chief Secr. to Governor, 29 April 1920, loc. cit.

83 Chief Secr.'s comments on the meeting, min. 77, loc. cit.

84 Attorney-General to Chief Secr., 28 May 1920, min. 78, loc. cit. In his comment on the report from the Development Commission Coryndon could rightly emphasize that education was of 'interest and some controversy'. Coryndon to Secr. of State, 14 Sept. 1920, CO 536/102–50506/20.

85 Kabaka and ministers to Secr. of State, 8 May 1919, encl. in Coryndon to Secr. of State, 30 June 1919, CO 536/94–50670/19.

86 Reflected in Willis to Manley, 17 Dec. 1918, no. 8, G3. A7/1919.

87 ibid.; Ag. Governor to Governor General of Sudan, 18 May 1920; Omukama of Toro to Governor, 3 June 1921; DC Kampala, Postlethwaite, to PC Buganda, 28 April 1923; PCs' Conference, 18 July 1923, all in SMP 6215.

88 Thus Governor Coryndon to Chief Secr., 2 April 1921, min. 12, SMP 6538.

89 Governor Coryndon to Secr. of State, 30 May 1922, CO 536/119–33310/22; cf. also minutes from PCs' Conference, 18 July 1923, and Postlethwaite, op. cit.

90 Postlethwaite, op. cit.

91 II.O. Savile, Superintendent Technical School Makerere, to Chief Secr., 28 Jan. 1922, SMP 6538; PCs' Conference, 18 July 1923; and Governor Coryndon to Secr. of State, 14 Aug. 1923, CO 536/126–46563/23.

92 Governor Coryndon to Secr. of State, 30 May 1922; cf. also Postlethwaite, op. cit., and PCs' Conference, 18 July 1923 (see n.87).

93 Minutes of Advisory Educational Board, 13 May 1921, SMP 6538. Memorandum by H.T.C. Weatherhead, Principal King's College, Budo, 16 May 1923, SMP 6215. See also Weatherhead's lecture to Ganda chiefs in which he warned them against sending their sons to America, reported in the magazine *Ebifa mu Buganda*, Sept. 1921.

94 Weatherhead, op. cit.; Chief Secr. Jarvis to Rev. H.M. Grace, CMS Uganda, 27 April 1923; PC Western Province, P.W. Cooper, to Ass. Secr. for Native Affairs, 23 Oct. 1923, both in SMP 6215.

95 Weatherhead, op. cit. W. had earlier suggested that in the meantime the government should equip the leading Anglican public school, King's College, Budo, to meet the needs for higher education. It should even be open to Catholic students. Memorandum from W. to PCs' Conference 1922, SMP 6538. A further proposal was for the government to take over the school, make it undenominational (with access for Muslims), and run it as supplementary to Makerere. Governor Archer to Secr. of State, 18 Aug. 1923 (secret), CO 536/126–46564/23.

96 cf. Annual Report for 1922: Buganda, SMP 1138 M. A similar suggestion had earlier been made with regard to technical education by the Bunyoro chiefs.

97 cf. Annual Report for 1918–19: Buganda, SMP 1138 J. See also Secr. Young Baganda

Association to Rev. C.F. Andrews, 22 Dec. 1919, copy in CO 536/107–7701/1920; and to Negro Farmers' Conference, Tuskegee Industrial and Normal Institution Alabama, 13 Sept. 1921, in D.A. Low (1971b), pp.53ff. See also minute by PC Buganda, J.C.R. Sturrock, encl. in Governor to Secr. of State, 30 Sept. 1921 (marked secret), CO 537/949–55782/21.

98 cf. Notes of Evidence before the Uganda Development Commission, 1919: 48th witness, J.C.R. Sturrock; and 51st witness, Prince Joseph (cousin of the Kabaka), SMP 5860. See also support for this observation in Commission's report, par. 325 (see n.81). D.A. Low (1971a), pp.89f, has commented on this development in about 1920.

99 Memorandum from Young Baganda Association to Development Commission, 18 Dec. 1919, SMP 5860.

100 Young Baganda Association to Rev. C.F. Andrews, 22 Dec. 1919 (on the occasion of his visit to Uganda), loc. cit. Andrews was a British clergyman with close associations with Mahatma Gandhi; see Low (1971b), p. 52. During a second visit to Uganda in 1921 he was called 'an Indian Christian Missionary' and a professor at an Indian university; cf. SMP Conf. 585.

101 Young Baganda Association to Chief Secr., 12 March 1921, SMP 6538. One government official, Mr Sullivan, took this letter as a token that the Baganda wanted the missionary influence to be removed from their education; Sullivan to Chief Secr., 25 April 1921, SMP 5839.

102 The Governor's immediate understanding was that the letter suggested that the government took over all schools; minute by Governor, 2 April 1921. This impression was later corrected, Young Baganda Association to Chief Secr., 10 May 1921, both in SMP 6538.

103 Minute by Governor Coryndon, 2 April 1921; and the official answer to the Young Baganda Association, 11 April 1921, loc. cit.

104 Minutes of Educational Advisory Board, 13 May 1921; cf. also Chief Secr. Jarvis to Young Baganda Association, 27 May 1921, both in SMP 6538.

105 See minutes in SMP 6812 and 7405. The appearance of indigenous newspapers is dealt with in J.F. Scotton (1973).

106 Z.K. Sentongo, Open Letter to Canon Weatherhead, dat. 8 Sept. 1921, in *Ebifa mu Buganda*, with copies to the three other vernacular newspapers. The colonial administration had the article translated into English, now in SMP 6812. *Ebifa mu Buganda* was started by CMS in 1909 and invited contributions from Africans; cf. Governor Hesketh Bell to Secr. of State, 12 April 1909, CO 536/26–16222/1909. For Sentongo, see Scotton, op. cit.

107 Sentongo, op. cit. Weatherhead answered in the same issue of *Ebifa*, but he commented only on the question of education in America.

108 For a general account of the East and Central African attitude to and criticism of the missions' educational efforts see T. Ranger (1965). The Ganda criticism started earlier than suggested by Ranger (p. 62).

109 cf. Annual Report from 1922: Buganda, SMP 1138M; cf. the contemporary observations of the DC of Kampala, J.R.P. Postlethwaite, in his autobiography; Postlethwaite (1947), pp.81f. See further H.B. Thomas & A.E. Spencer (1938), and D.A. Low & R.C. Pratt (1960), pp.234ff.

110 See especially Willis to Manley, 22 Sept. 1919, no. 122, G3. A7/1919, and Willis to Manley, 7 Febr. 1921, no. 38, G3. A7/1921. I hope to develop this long controversy within the church in a forthcoming article.

111 Directly stated by the leading educationist in the Uganda mission, H.T.C. Weatherhead, to Chief Secr., 6 July 1920, SMP Conf. 499; cf. also minute by PC Buganda,

Sturrock, 27 Sept. 1921 (see n.97). For Weatherhead see Furley & Watson (1978), p.110.

112 This problem was already touched upon in the 'Report of the Educational Conference', April 1915 (see n.30).

113 See statement from Young Baganda Association in 1922, where they make it one of their objectives to unite young people from all three religions; for the moment they think 'that each religion is a tribe'. Encl. in min. 1, SMP Conf. 625.

114 One reason why the Native Authority Ord. was introduced in 1919 was the situation of unrest in the aftermath of the war. Governor Coryndon to Secr. of State, 17 Febr. 1919, CO 536/93–20076. In connection with Rev. C.F. Andrews' visit, 1919, the government was very much on the alert for any sign of unrest. See CO minute April 1920, CO 536/107–7701/1920; cf. also minutes by Ass. Secr. for Native Affairs, E.L. Scott, 7 April 1922; by PC Buganda, Sturrock, 16 April 1922; by the Governor, 24 April 1922, all commenting upon Young Busoga Association and Eastern Baganda Association: SMP Conf. 625.

115 In 1923 the Governor consulted Bishop Willis with regard to 'the growing spirit of impatience at tribal authority among the young Baganda'. They both agreed that some kind of action was necessary. Minute by Governor Archer, 28 Nov. 1923, SMP 956.

116 The idea that schools should instil 'into the minds of the pupils a sense of loyalty to the British Crown' was clearly emphasized in the report of the Uganda Development Commission, par. 229.

117 e.g. Governor Archer to Secr. of State, 18 Aug. 1923 (marked secret), CO 536/126–46564/23. The attitude was aptly summarized in Annual Report Buganda 1926, par. 94, written by Ag. PC Delmege; SMP 1138 Q.

118 See minutes from Missionary Committee, 22 Jan. 1920, regretting shortage of staff to combat the anti-European feeling emerging in Uganda. See also Rowling to Manley, 24 Jan. 1920, no. 55, G3. A7/1920. Interesting is Report from Singo Deanery 1919 by Rev. S.R. Skeens, who states that the anti-European feeling will grow 'under the modern spread of Nationalism'. Minutes of Synod 1919, Synod File, Namirembe Arch.

119 cf. Intelligence Officer to Governor, 11 July 1922, quoting from personal letter from Rev. Grace, CMS, dat. 27 June 1922, SMP Conf. 625.

120 cf. Willis to Manley, 17 Dec. 1918 and enclosure, no. 8 and 9, G3. A7/1919. For this section see G. Hewitt (1971), pp.243ff.

121 Report of Uganda Educational Sub-Committee, 23 April 1919, no. 48, G3. A7/1919. Among the members were people very familiar with Uganda, like Sir T.F. Victor Buxton, the former Archdeacon R.H. Walker, and the former Africa secr. in CMS, Rev. F. Baylis.

122 Minutes of Missionary Committee, 11 Sept. 1919. Archdeacon Baskerville's memorandum to Uganda Development Commission, Dec. 1919 (see n. 50). Baskerville refers directly to the proposal from the CMS Headquarters.

123 e.g. Rev. F. Rowling, Secr. CMS Uganda, to Manley, 22 Dec. 1919; cf. also Baskerville, op. cit.

124 cf. Baskerville, op. cit.

125 See notes on interview with Bishop Willis, 12 Jan. 1920, no. 15, G3. A7/1920.

126 The CMS pressure on the Uganda mission is most clearly set out in Manley to Secr. CMS Uganda, Rev. Boulton Ladbury, 20 July 1922, copy under no. 94, G3. A7/1922. 8 male missionaries and 11 female missionaries gave their full time to education; cf. CMS London to Under-Secr. of State, 27 Oct. 1922, CO 536/123–Mi. 53554 (destroyed, but copy under no. 94, G3. A7/1922). See also statistics in Ladbury to

Chief Secr., 10 Aug. 1922, min. 314, SMP 1912, where the total cost of the educational missionaries is estimated to be £8,400.

127 Summarized in CMS London to Under-Secr. of State, 27 Oct. 1922; cf. also CMS London to Under-Secr. of State, 16 Oct. 1922, and Manley to Ladbury, 1 Nov. 1922 (see n.126). The problem was presented to the Ugandan government at a meeting in the beginning of August 1922; Notes from Meeting with CMS, min. 308, SMP 1912.

128 ibid.

129 Report Uganda Mission 1922, section on education, sgd. H.T.C. Weatherhead, SMP 7998.

130 CMS London to Under-Secr. of State, 27 Oct. 1922 (n.126).

131 Secr. CMS Uganda, Ladbury, to Manley, 15 Aug. 1922, no. 94, G3. A7/1922.

132 See H.B. Hansen (1980); also G. Hewitt (1971), pp.219ff.

133 Manley to Ladbury, 1 Nov. 1922, copy under no. 94, G3. A7/1922.

134 ibid.

135 The official communication from the government has not been found, but content in Ladbury to Manley, 30 Nov. 1922, no.2, G3. A7/1923.

136 Minutes of Missionary Committee, 7 Dec. 1922. Decision confirmed in Report Uganda Mission 1922 (see n.129).

137 In the first place it was characteristically the Financial Secr. of the NAC, Mr Holden (a missionary), who raised the matter, and he was later joined by four others; see minutes of Missionary Committee, 7 Dec. 1922 and 4 Jan. 1923. cf. also Ladbury to Manley, 16 Jan. 1923, no. 13, G3. A7/1923.

138 cf. Appeal for Recruits, March 1923, no. 38, G3. A7/1923. Appeal approved by the Missionary Committee, 1 March 1923.

139 Under-Secr. of State to CMS London, 15 May 1923, CO 536/129–Mi 21875.

140 Resolutions adopted by Executive Committee, 13 June 1923, no. 48, G3. A7/1923.

141 A clear reference to the importance attached to the CO's decision in Manley to Uganda Mission, 30 April 1924, Letterbook V, G3. A7/L5. It has not been possible to clarify to what extent this was a deliberate policy on the part of the CO. The relevant minutes may have been in CO 536/123–Mi 51605/22 and Mi 53554/22, but both files have been destroyed.

142 See minutes of Missionary Committee, 2 Aug. 1923.

143 ibid.; and minutes of Missionary Committee, 6 March 1924.

145 See Manley, op. cit.

146 Procedure confirmed by the Missionary Committee, 6 Nov. 1924. It may have been of some importance that Bishop Willis was absent at the meetings of 2 Aug. 1923 and 6 March 1924, when the educational missionaries were in the majority. He was present on 6 Nov. 1924 after his return from London where he had discussed the matter; cf. Manley, op. cit.

147 e.g. Manley to Willis, 1 Febr. 1922, encl. 'Certain Questions regarding the Devolution of Responsibility in the Church of Uganda' raised by the Parent Committee, copy under no. 42, G3. A7/1922. cf. also Hewitt (1971), pp.228f.

148 Ladbury to Manley, 15 Aug. 1922 (see n.131); cf. also Ladbury's preface to Report Uganda Mission 1922, dat. 25 Sept. 1923, SMP 7998; and Willis to Manley, 7 March 1922, no. 42, G3. A7/1922.

149 Hansen (1980).

150 cf. Archdeacon Baskerville, Memorandum to Uganda Development Commission, Dec. 1919 (see n.50); Notes of meeting with CMS, Aug. 1922, min. 308, SMP 1912.

The mission's withdrawal as a 'general educational institution' was mentioned on that occasion.

151 Secr. CMS London to Under-Secr. of State, 27 Oct. 1922 (n.126).

152 Expressed in Manley to Ladbury, 10 July 1922; and Ladbury's answer, 15 Aug. 1922, both under no. 94, G3. A7/1922.

153 Governor Coryndon to Secr. of State, 23 Sept. 1922, copy in SMP 1912, recommends the 25% increase. See Under-Secr. of State to Secr. CMS London, 15 May 1923, CO 536/129–Mi 21875. The figure of £4,688 should be compared with the expenses for education paid by mission and church, amounting to £16,000; cf. Kitching (Commissary to the Bishop), Ladbury (secr. Uganda Mission) and Weatherhead (secr. Board of Education) to Chief Secr., 19 July 1923, min. 238, SMP 1912.

154 Baskerville, Memorandum to Development Commission (n.50); Kitching, Ladbury and Weatherhead, op. cit. See also Under-Secr. of State to CMS London, 15 May 1923, CO 536/129–Mi 21875/23.

155 Demand explicitly made in Under-Secr. of State to CMS, 15 May 1923.

156 cf. PC Western Province, P.W. Cooper, to Missionary Committee urgently requesting European missionaries for schools in Toro and Ankole; Minutes of Missionary Committee, 6 Sept. 1923.

157 Thus expressed by the newly arrived Governor, Geoffrey Archer, to Secr. of State, 18 Aug. 1923, CO 536/126–46564/23. The same point of view was publicly voiced by the Governor in address to Legislative Council, 16 Nov. 1923, SMP 7835.

158 These options were suggested by PCs' Conference, 18 July 1923, SMP 6215, and later repeated in Governor to Secr. of State, 14 Aug. 1923, CO 536/126–46563/23; cf. also minute from 1923 by Ass. Secr. for Native Affairs, Scott, commenting on a memorandum on Native Affairs in East Africa submitted to Parliamentary Commission 1924, SMP 7725.

159 The conclusion reached on the basis of the evidence here presented runs contrary to that drawn by F. Carter, who points to the mission's strong position in relation to the government within the field of education. Carter (1967b), pp.259ff.

160 Clearly stated by Governor Coryndon to Chief Secr., 2 April 1921, SMP 6538.

161 Governor Archer to Secr. of State, 18 Aug. 1923 (n.157).

162 cf. Young Baganda Association to Chief Secr., 12 March 1921, SMP 6538. Governor Archer, op. cit.

163 cf. Governor Archer's outline of these plans, based on two reports from government's educational adviser, E.R.J. Hussey, in Archer to Secr. of State, 14 April 1924, CO 536/130–23441.

164 See esp. R. Oliver (1952), pp.263ff, and Carter (1967a, unpubl. thesis), ch. 3.

165 Governor Archer to Secr. of State, 18 Aug. 1923 (n.157).

166 ibid. For new educational departure see Carter, op. cit., pp.148ff, and Furley & Watson (1978), pp.188ff. See also Hewitt (1971), pp.243ff.

167 cf. Kitching, Ladbury and Weatherhead to Chief Secr., 19 July 1923 (see n.153) and the following minute by the Chief Secr., both in SMP 1912.

168 Governor Archer to Secr. of State, 14 April 1924; Hussey's memorandum of 18 Jan. 1924 and his interim report of 23 Febr. 1924, all in CO 536/130–23441. Most important is Hussey's final Report on Education, dat. 10 June 1924, CO 536/134–Mi 27294 (esp. p.20). The Governor made the new policy public in his address to Legislative Council, 28 May 1924, SMP 7835.

169 It was also the opinion of the CMS' educational secr., Dr Garfield Williams, after his visit to Uganda; see Oliver (1952), p. 267.

170 Governor Archer, 'A Considered Reply . . . to Bishop Willis' Criticisms of the Proposed Government Educational Policy', dat. 14 April 1924, CO 536/130–23442.

171 Governor Coryndon to Young Baganda Association, 11 April 1924, SMP 6538.

172 Governor to Secr. of State, 22 Sept. 1922, draft in SMP 1912.

173 Governor Archer to Secr. of State, 18 Aug. 1923 (n.157); cf. public statement in address to Legislative Council, 16 Nov. 1923, SMP 7835.

174 Thus indicated by Governor Archer to Secr. of State, 14 April 1924, CO 536/130– 23441; and Archer, 'A Considered Reply', p.3 (see n.170). See also Hussey's final report, pp.21ff (see n.168).

175 ibid. This point of view was later emphasized by Advisory Committee on Native Education in Tropical Africa, dat. Oct. 1924, CO 536/134–Mi 38673.

176 In commenting upon Hussey's scheme of 1924 Bishop Willis pointed out how dependent the government was on the educational work of the missions. J.J. Willis and H.T.C. Weatherhead, Memorandum on Native Education in Uganda, 14 April 1924, CO 536/130–23442.

177 See notes of meeting with CMS, Aug. 1922, min. 308, SMP 1912; Secr. CMS London to Under-Secr. of State, 27 Oct. 1922, copy under no. 94, G3. A7/1922. The value of this argument in discussions with government representatives is borne out by J.H. Oldham's use of it in his attempt to influence colonial educational policy; see Oliver (1952), p. 268.

178 cf. Ladbury, secr. Uganda mission, to Manley, 18 March 1924, no. 35, G3. A7/1924. The mission also felt the time of change when it was asked to submit a memorandum on the present status of CMS education to be used in a review of future government policy; minutes of Missionary Committee, 4 Oct. 1923, Minute Book, MUL.

179 Apparent in the report from the first Phelps–Stokes Commission and later emphasized by J.H. Oldham in his memorandum on future educational policy, May 1923; cf. Oliver (1952), pp.264ff. The same point of view appeared later in a report on education in Uganda from the newly established Advisory Committee on Native Education in Tropical Africa; cf. draft letter to Secr. of State, Sept. 1924 and final edition of report, dat. Oct. 1924, in CO 536/134–Mi 38673.

180 See Hussey's memorandum of 18 Jan. 1924 and his final report of 10 June 1924 (cf. n. 168). The importance of this aspect was later testified by the Governor in his address to the Educational Advisory Board, n.d., but presumably late 1925, SMP 7835. This whole issue was summarized by Bishop Willis in his memorandum on Educational Policy in Uganda, from the middle of 1925, no.93, G3. A7/1925.

181 Governor Archer to Secr. of State, 18 Aug. 1923, CO 536/126–46564/23.

182 cf. Willis and Weatherhead, Memorandum on Native Education in Uganda, 14 April 1924 (see n.176).

183 Wandira (1972), p. 270.

184 cf. Oliver (1952), pp.266ff; Carter (1967a), pp.114ff.

185 Clearly expressed by Willis in his Educational Policy in Uganda, 1925 (n. 180).

186 The second Phelps–Stokes Commission visited Uganda in March 1924; cf. Ladbury to Manley, 18 March 1924, no. 35, G3. A7/1924, and reference to visit in Governor's address to Legislative Council, 28 May 1924, SMP 7835. During the visit Governor Archer received some interim notes from the chairman, Dr Jesse Jones, about suggestions to be made in the final report. These notes emphasized the need of cooperation between mission and government: cf. Archer, 'A Considered Reply' from April 1924 (see n.170).

187 Re implementation of policy of cooperation, see, e.g. Willis' memorandum on Educational Policy in Uganda, 1925 (n.180).

188 Pointed out with regret by J.H. Oldham to Major Hans Vischer of the CO, 30 Sept. 1924, with enclosure, and is reflected in Advisory Committee's memorandum on education in Uganda (n. 179), all in CO 536/134–Mi 38673/24.

189 cf. Bishop Willis, Memorandum on Position of NAC Schools, dat. 20 Oct. 1925, no. 131, G3. A7/1925.

190 See report by Dr Garfield Williams on Education in Uganda, first draft, Dec. 1924, pp. 9f, where Hussey's plans are interpreted in this way. cf. also Carter (1967a), pp.161ff. In his final report from June 1924 Hussey left himself open to suspicion when he wrote that he was convinced that undenominational schools eventually would swamp the others (p. 25).

191 This rather unpleasant perspective for the Uganda mission was outlined by the CMS educational secr., Dr Garfield Williams, who visited Uganda with Phelps–Stokes Commission in March 1924. See Special Meeting of Africa Committee, 4 and 19 Febr. 1925, reports in the Precis, G3. A7/P3. The Uganda mission soon started to act on the recommendation; see Report of Sub-Committee, 13 March 1925, no. 27, G3. A7/1925.

192 See observation in Annual Report Buganda 1924, where the jealousy directed towards the government's intrusion into the educational sector is mentioned, and where 'a lurking dread of secularism in education' is noticed. SMP 1138 P.

193 The Makerere problem was discussed by the Advisory Committee on Native Education in Tropical Africa, Minutes 30 July 1924; Oldham advocated the Uganda mission's point of view; CO 536/134–Mi 54620/1924. See summary in Report of Sub-Committee, 13 March 1925 (n.191); and Willis' memorandum on Educational Policy in Uganda, July 1925 (n.180).

194 Hussey emphasized in particular the need to start undenominational schools at a meeting of Advisory Committee on Native Education in Tropical Africa, 30 July 1924.

195 Re Hussey's intentions and plans see Carter (1967a), pp.155ff, and SMP 7914.

196 Willis and Weatherhead, Memorandum on Native Education in Uganda, April 1924 (see n. 176); and Willis to J.H. Oldham, 21 April 1924: 'that to establish schools for the Muslim community was to practice a form of religious discrimination in favour of the least progressive element in the population'. Quoted by Carter, op. cit. pp.161ff.

197 Evidence in SMP 7914, especially minutes from educational conferences in Jan. and Febr. 1924. cf. also summary of mission's position in Report of Sub-Committee, 13 March 1925.

198 ibid.; and Carter (1967b), p. 262.

199 Carter, op. cit. p. 263.

200 See motion proposed by the Kabaka and seconded by the Katikiro at the Synod 1924, which impressed on the government the need to expand education via the existing schools. Minutes of Synod, Jan. 1924, MUL. It was later admitted that the missionary leaders had a difficult time 'in endeavouring to get the policy of full cooperation with the Government accepted by the Baganda, and they have been to some extent supported in their attitude by members of the mission'. Ag. secr. Uganda mission, Kitching, to Manley, 8 Sept. 1925, no.114, G3. A7/1925.

201 Willis and Weatherhead, Memorandum on Native Education (see n.176), called attention to the chiefs' protests. Oldham attached great importance to this reaction and put it on the agenda for Advisory Committee on Native Education in Tropical Africa; see Oldham to Major Hans Vischer of the CO, 30 Sept. 1924, with enclosure, CO 536/134–MI 38673/1924. The Governor dismissed African opinion as the voice of a minority in his comments on Willis' memorandum; see Archer, 'A Considered Reply' (n. 170).

202 Witness his participation in meeting of Advisory Committee on Native Education in Tropical Africa, 30 July 1924 (n.194).

203 Testified in Oldham to Vischer, 30 Sept. 1924 (see n.201).

204 Re Catholic approach to education see J.M. Waliggo (1976, unpubl. thesis). pp. 241ff, 334; cf. also Bishop Willis, Memorandum on the Position of NAC Schools, 20 Oct. 1925, no. 131, G3. A7/1925.

205 Thus expressed in Report of Educational Conference, April 1915, copy in MUL. Later repeated by Bishop Willis in the CMS periodical *Church Missionary Review*, Dec. 1915, p. 721.

206 cf. H.T.C. Weatherhead, 'Principles of Education in Uganda', Nov. 1908, no. 154, G3. A7/07.

207 Educational Scheme for Uganda, June 1909, no. 280; and Bishop Tucker's letter of explanation, 18 June 1909, no. 279, G3. A7/07. In a review of CMS educational work Bishop Willis quoted at length from the June 1909 scheme; letter encl. in Governor to Secr. of State, 7 Jan. 1913, CO 536/58–3900/1913.

208 Expressed by Mr Ecob during session on education at Uganda Men's Conference, June 1904, report under no. 158, G3. A7/04.

209 Point of view stated in connection with start of King's College, Budo; discussion summarized in King's School Budo: Annual Report 1908, dat. 31 Dec. 1908, sgd. H.W. Weatherhead and H.T.C. Weatherhead, SMP 2157/08. cf. T.B. Fletcher to Baylis, 6 April 1907, no. 118, G3. A7/05. Weatherhead commented on the problem and referred to insufficient pay of clergy and teachers; W. to Baylis, 1 April 1909, no. 153, G3. A7/07.

210 For the early Catholic approach to education see Waliggo (1976), pp. 187f, 240ff; and Furley & Watson (1978), pp.112f.

211 For missionary aims in education see Wandira (1972), pp.247ff; and Carter (1967a), *passim.*

212 Willis, Policy of the Uganda Mission, 1912, pp.10ff.

213 Willis to Manley, 2 July 1917, no. 107/1917; and Willis to Manley, 17 Dec. 1918, no. 8/1919, answering the accusation that educational work is not proper work for missionaries. Later repeated in Ladbury to CMS, London 25 April 1922, no. 53/1922, all in G3. A7 for the respective years.

214 Notes on Requirements and Policy of the Mission, Dec. 1918, no. 9, G3. A7/1919.

215 Report of Sub-Committee on Education in Uganda, appointed by Missionary Committee, 2 July 1917, no. 102, G3. A7/1917.

216 It should be remembered that it was an old trend in CMS policy to concentrate on the sons of chiefs. For the implementation of this policy in Busoga, see Tom Tuma (1976), p. 289.

217 Archdeacon Walker to Chief Secr., 16 Jan. 1912, SMP 1912.

218 This goal was already formulated in 1904 by Rev. H.W. Weatherhead at the Uganda Men's Conference (see n. 208).

219 Argument put forward by Walker, op. cit. It also appears frequently in CMS correspondence on industrial training.

220 Thus expressed by F. Rowling, secr. CMS Uganda, to Manley, 22 Dec. 1919, no. 25, G3. A7/1920.

221 Term explicitly used in H.T.C. Weatherhead to Chief Secr., 6 July 1920: 'I think education is bound to form a new middle class in the country.' SMP Conf. 499/1920.

222 See minutes in SMP 768/1908, esp. Governor Hesketh Bell to Chief Secr., 5 Dec. 1908. A few years later it was explicitly stated that most office interpreters and native

clerks were drawn from King's College, Budo. Annual Report Buganda 1910–1911, SMP 1138 A.

223 Re Bunyoro, see Annual Report Northern Province 1911–1912, by the PC, Guy Eden.

224 In Annual Report Northern Province 1915–1916 it is pointed out that all candidates from Bunyoro High School have entered King's College, Budo, incl. two future saza chiefs; also the White Fathers are doing a good job, 'especially among the peasants, most of the Chiefs following the Protestant religion'. SMP 2135.

225 Report of Sub-Committee of Uganda Standing Committee (Missionary Committee) on Dr Garfield Williams' Report on education in Uganda, n.d., but presumably June 1925, no. 59, G3. A7/1925.

226 Report of Educational Conference April 1915, p. 13, copy in MUL. Later printed in Bishop Willis' name in *Church Missionary Review*, Nov. 1915, pp.654ff.

227 ibid., p. 18.

228 Report of Educational Conference, Aug. 1921, p.9, copy under no. 119, G3. A7/1921. It should be added that a characteristic feature of the conference was that the question of 'the training of a Native Ministry' was dealt with by the Europeans only (p.1).

229 See Waliggo (1976), p.187, with regard to Catholic practice initiated by Bishop Henri Streicher (Bishop of Central and Western Uganda 1897–1933). His predecessor, Mgr Hirth, who in 1894 had moved to the German area, held the same view; cf. Ian Linden (1977), p. 76; and Furley & Watson (1978), pp.112f.

230 Repeated in Report for the Diocesan Council 1921–23, presented to the Synod 1924, Minute Book in MUL.

231 Touched upon by Bishop Willis in his charge to the Synod 1917, MUL. cf. also Archdeacon Baskerville and Dr A.R. Cook, Review of the Year 1916, pp.13f, no.54, G3. A7/1917. A general reference should be made to L.A. Fallers (1964), ch. 4.

232 Educational Conference 1915, report, pp.17f, makes this point clear. The same is clearly stated by the Uganda missionary, J. Britton, in his article 'Elementary Education in Uganda', *Church Missionary Review*, April 1917, p.186. cf. also Minutes of CMS Education Committee, 29 Nov. 1916, no. 131, G3. A7/1916.

233 Baskerville and Cook, op. cit., p. 14.

234 Thus formulated by Educational Conference 1921, report, p.8. But the problem was pointed out as early as 1904; cf. Uganda Men's Conference, June 1904 (n.208).

235 Educational Conference 1915; Baskerville and Cook, op. cit., pp.13f.

236 Willis to Manley, 7 March 1922, no. 42, G3. A7/1922. cf. also Willis, 'On Education in Uganda', *Church Missionary Review*, Dec. 1915, p.721.

237 e.g. Meeting of CMS Education Committee, 29 Nov. 1916; and Willis to Manley, 7 March 1922. cf. also educational conferences, 1915 and 1921.

238 Uganda Men's Conference, June 1904 (n.208).

239 Britton, op. cit (n.232).

240 Educational Conference 1921, pp.8f.

241 ibid., p.9

242 Willis to Manley, 7 March 1922 (n.236).

243 cf. Report of Educational Conference 1921, p.10.

244 The causal relationship between the clergy's low educational standard and the prospects for the Africanization of church leadership was suggested as early as 1901, when introduction of a church constitution was debated: see Rev. E.C. Gordon to Conference of Missionaries, 6 Nov. 1901, no. 255, G3. A7/02. Same opinion held 20

years later by Archdeacon Kitching in 'The Present Situation in Uganda', *Church Missionary Review*, 1921, p. 303; and touched upon in Manley to Willis, 1 Febr. 1922, which encloses 'Certain Questions regarding the Devolution of Responsibility in the Church of Uganda', no. 42, G3. A7/1922.

245 Minute by Chief Secr. Jarvis, July 1921, SMP 6876.

246 See, e.g., Educational Scheme for Uganda, June 1909 (n. 207); CMS Educational Code for 1910, SMP 1890/09; Willis to Governor Coryndon, 9 May 1919, min. 209, SMP 1912.

247 As early as 1907 Weatherhead pointed out how King's School, Budo not only fostered 'one common loyalty' among boys from various districts of the Protectorate, but the loyalty was also directed towards 'the parental rule of the British Government': H.W. Weatherhead, 'Education in Central Africa', *Church Missionary Review*, June 1907, pp.337ff. In 1921 the Missionary Committee recommended that the Boy Scout Movement should be started, so as to strengthen loyalty towards the state. The government was against it, as it feared that boy scouts would ally with the Young Baganda Association 'and be a possible danger in case of a native rising'. Minutes of Missionary Committee, 20 Jan. 1921; Rowling to Manley, 24 Jan. 1921, no. 27 and 28, G3. A7/1921.

248 This generalization and the whole discussion of dependence owe much to Ivan Vallier (1970).

249 ibid., and Emanuel de Kadt (1971), p.38.

16   The Christianization of law and administration

1 Later confirmed in Annual Report 1904–1905, encl. in Commissioner Sadler to Secr. of State, 19 Aug. 1905, CO 536/2–34350.

2 In a concrete case from Toro, Tucker deliberately emphasized that the church could only exercise spiritual power with regard to 'offences against morality'. Tucker to Sadler, 4 Sept. 1903, A 22/1, ESA. The main interest was to have all marriages registered and to ensure that both partners were baptized. Minutes of Mengo Church Council, 25 Sept. 1897, in *Kitakule Journal*, MUL.

3 Archdeacon Walker to Father, 28 Febr. 1900, Walker Papers. He refers to the law of 26 June 1893, mentioned in a memorandum drawn up by the 3 Ganda Regents, 'Our Old Customs and New', dat. 18 March 1903, SMP 991/1909; also in A 24. Sub-Commissioner George Wilson refers to this law; Wilson to Sadler, 6 Jan. 1903, A 24, ESA.

4 Official Gazette of the East Africa and Uganda Protectorates, 15 Nov. 1902. J.V. Taylor cannot be correct in suggesting that Bishop Tucker was largely responsible for the terms of the Ordinance; Taylor (1958), p.180.

5 FO to Commissioner Sadler, 17 Sept. 1902, A 24; Special File: Marriage Ord., Correspondence 1902–1904. The course of events was later clearly summarized by Lord Percy of the FO in a memorandum dat. 26 Dec. 1903, FO 2/906. See in general H.F. Morris & J.R. Read (1972), pp.216ff; and H.F. Morris (1979), pp.44ff.

6 See note by Judge Ennis on letter from FO, loc. cit. A discussion of the Marriage Ord. of 1902 can be found in H.F. Morris & J.S. Read (1966), ch. 16 and pp.395ff, and in H.F. Morris (1968).

7 Tucker to Sadler, 24 Dec. 1902, A 24.

8 Tucker to Baylis, 27 Dec. 1902, no. 43, G3. A7/03, encl. copies of all letters to the Commissioner.

9 cf. Tucker to Baylis, 13 Jan. 1903, no. 43, loc. cit.

10 Tucker to Secr. of Marriage Law Defence Union, 3 June 1903, copy encl. in Secr. to

Archbishop of Canterbury, 27 July 1903, Davidson's Correspondence: 1903, U 1: Uganda, Lambeth Palace Arch.

11 Tucker to Archbishop of Canterbury, 3 Sept. 1903, loc. cit.

12 Tucker to Sadler, 18 Dec. 1902 (telegr.); Tucker to Sadler, 19 Dec. 1902, both in A 24.

13 ibid.

14 Tucker to Sadler, 22 Dec. 1902, loc. cit.

15 Ag. Sub-Commissioner, Tomkins, to Sadler, 3 June 1903, A 27, Item 10, with a report of a meeting with the chiefs and the Buganda Lukiko.

16 cf. Sadler to FO, 11 June 1903, FO 2/906.

17 cf. *The Times*, 18 March 1903; Archbishop of Canterbury to Tucker, 16 Oct. 1903, Lambeth Palace Arch., (see n.10).

18 Baylis to Tucker, 7 March 1903, G3. A7/L1.

19 Tucker to Sadler, 22 Dec. 1902, A24.

20 ibid.

21 Tucker to Sadler, 24 Dec. 1902, A24.

22 Tucker to Sadler, 22 Dec. 1902. cf. above, ch.7.

23 Tomkins to Sadler, 3 June 1903 (n.15).

24 Tucker to Sadler, 22 Dec. 1902; Tucker to Baylis, 27 Dec. 1902, no. 43, G3. A7/03.

25 cf. Tucker to Sadler, 19 Dec. 1902, A 24.

26 Indirectly admitted by Commissioner Sadler when he indicated that after the Ord. had come into operation Christian marriages not celebrated in accordance with the Ord. would be illegal. Sadler to Secr. of State, 19 Dec. 1902 (telegr.), A 24.

27 Tucker to Sadler, 18 Dec. 1902 (telgr.), A 24; Tucker to Baylis, 27 Dec. 1902 (n.8).

28 Tucker to Baylis, 27 Dec. 1902.

29 George Wilson to Sadler, 6 Jan. 1903, A 24.

30 Sadler to FO, 19 Dec. 1902 (telegr.).

31 cf. Sadler's internal note, dat. 7 Jan. 1903, A24; and Sadler to FO, 11 June 1903, FO 2/906, copy in A 27, Item 10, ESA, later pr. in FOCP.

32 cf. Tucker to Baylis, 13 Jan. 1903, no. 45, G3. A7/03, reporting from an interview with Sadler. The Commissioner also went out of his way to explain why objections were raised in Uganda and not in other Protectorates like the East Africa Protectorate. He ascribed this solely to the strong missionary presence and the unparalleled zeal with which the Baganda had taken to Christianity. Sadler to FO, 11 June 1903.

33 cf. Tucker to Baylis, 4 May 1903, no. 93, G3. A7/03; and Sadler to FO, 11 June 1906.

34 The 3 Regents' note on 'Our Old Customs and New' (see n.3). Sadler did not agree with Tucker on the interpretation of the Uganda Agreement, but clearly refrained from a collision course. See Sadler to FO, 11 June 1903 (n.31). For wider aspects of this issue see D.A. Low & R.C. Pratt (1960), pp.150ff.

35 Tucker to Sadler, 22 April 1903, A 24.

36 cf. Judge Ennis to Sadler, 1 May 1903, with the draft Ordinance encl., A 24.

37 cf. Tucker to Sadler, 22 April 1903; and Sadler to FO, 11 June 1903, with a copy of the new draft Ordinance encl.

38 Sadler to FO, 11 June 1903 (see n.31).

39 Tucker to Archbishop of Canterbury, 4 Dec. 1903, Lambeth Palace Arch., (see n.10). cf. also Tucker's public comments on the new Marriage Ordinance in *Uganda Notes*, Jan. 1904.

40 Archbishop to Tucker, 16 Oct. 1903 (see n.10).

41 See memorandum by Lord Percy, dat. 26 Dec. 1903, FO 2/906.

42 Tucker to Secr. of Marriage Law Defence Union, 3 June 1903; Tucker to Archbishop of Canterbury, 3 Sept. 1903, both in Lambeth Palace Arch. (see n.10).

43 cf. FO minute, 6 Aug. 1903, FO 2/906.

44 See report in *The Times*, 1 Aug. 1903. See also Archbishop of Canterbury to Prebendary Fox of the CMS, 29 July 1903, Lambeth Palace Arch., and notes on interview between Archbishop and Fox, 31 July 1903, no. 145, G3. A7/03.

45 Material on Parliamentary debates in FO 2/906.

46 FO minutes of 25 July and 6 Aug. 1903, FO 2/906. The course of events may also be detected from Lord Lansdowne to Sir C. Eliot (Commissioner East Africa Protectorate), 15 Aug. 1903, draft in loc. cit., copy in A 27 Item 10, ESA.

47 The Prime Minister's memorandum is dated 1 Jan. 1904, FO 2/906.

48 See minute by Lord Percy, 5 Jan. 1904; Lord Lansdowne to Sadler, 12 and 29 Jan. 1904 (telegrams), all in FO 2/906. Before the final outcome Sadler suggested that the clause legalizing marriage with a deceased wife's sister should only be repealed as far as the native Christians were concerned. Sadler to FO, 3 Febr. 1904 (telegr.), loc. cit. FO refused to allow any distinction in the law between Europeans and Africans; FO to Sadler, 6 Febr. 1904, loc. cit. Finally Sadler forwarded Uganda Marriage (Repeal) Ord. of 1904, Sadler to FO, 22 Febr. 1904, A 27/Item 10, ESA.

49 All the time Tucker was confident of the final outcome; cf. T. to Baylis, 26 Nov. 1903, no. 227, G3. A7/03; and T. to Archbishop of Canterbury, 4 Dec. 1903, Lambeth Palace Arch. (see n.10).

50 FO to Sadler, 21 Sept. 1903, A 27, Item 10. cf. also FO minutes, 25 July and 6 Aug. 1903, FO 2/906.

51 Tucker to Sadler, 25 Nov. 1903, A 27, Item 10; *Uganda Notes*, Jan. 1904.

52 Judge Ennis to Sadler, 1 May 1903, A 24.

53 Sadler to FO, 11 June 1903, A 27, Item 10.

54 Thus Archdeacon Walker to Father, 21 Nov. 1903, Walker Papers.

55 The racial distinction inherent in the existence of two separate ordinances does not seem to have been noticed at the time. It was later vehemently denounced by the churches in Uganda; cf. Report of Commission on Marriage, Divorce and Status of Women, 1965, Government Printer, Entebbe, 1965, pars. 85 and 88.

56 cf. FO to Sadler, 17 Sept. 1902, A 24; and Sadler to FO, 6 Nov. 1902, A 22, Item 11. See also Morris & Read (1972), pp.241ff.

57 March 1903, copy in loc. cit.

58 Judge Ennis, Comments on draft Divorce Ordinance, dat. 22 May 1903; Sadler to FO, 9 Sept. 1903, FO 2/906.

59 ibid.

60 ibid.

61 Sadler to Tucker, 4 Sept. 1903.

62 At exactly the same time there was a controversy between Tucker and Sadler regarding the power of government officials to grant a divorce to Christians married in church. Tucker to Sadler, 31 Aug. 1903, A22/1; Sadler to Tucker, 3 Sept. 1903, A23/1, both in ESA.

63 Tucker to Sadler, 7 Sept. 1903, A22, Item 11. cf. also Morris (1968), p.37; and Morris & Read (1966), pp.362f.

64 cf. Sadler to FO, 9 Sept. 1903.

65 Re Divorce Ordinance, See H.F. Morris (1960), pp.198f.

66 This was apparent only half a year after the enactment of the Ordinance; cf. Sadler to FO, 31 Aug. 1904, FO 2/906.

67 Sadler pointed to 'the easy mode of life' which Islam permitted. Interview with CMS Committee in *Church Missionary Intelligencer*, Dec. 1904, pp. 914ff.

68 Ag. Commissioner George Wilson to Tucker, 26 Febr. 1906; and Wilson to Secr. of State, 21 April 1906, both in CO 536/6–21728.

69 Wilson to Secr. of State, 21 April 1906.

70 Tucker to Wilson, 1 March 1906, A22/1, copy in CO, loc. cit.

71 Wilson to Secr. of State, 21 April 1906. cf. also Morris & Read (1966), p.363. A Christian who turned Muslim in 1913 was convicted of bigamy and sentenced to five months' imprisonment by the District Magistrate's Court in Toro (see below, n.114).

72 cf. Wilson to Secr. of State, 21 April 1906, on Native Marriage Fees, CO 536/6–21727/06.

73 See Report of the Commission on Marriage, Divorce . . . , chs. II and III (n.55).

74 Tucker to Wilson, 1 March 1906 (n.70).

75 Report on Uganda Mahomedan Marriage and Divorce Ordinance, dat. 14 March 1906, encl. in Wilson to Secr. of State, 21 April 1906 (n.68); cf. Sadler to FO, 31 Aug. 1904, FO 2/906.

76 ibid., and CO minute, 30 June 1906, CO 536/6–21728.

77 cf. Tucker to Sadler, 22 April 1903; and Bishop Streicher to Sadler, 17 May 1903, both in A24. Sadler to FO, 11 June 1903, A22, Item 10. It is noteworthy that such unity between the three missions could be established at this early stage. It is further significant that it was Tucker who took the lead in the intervention with the government. The intervention re marriage laws was later hailed as a major success for the mission; see report to World Missionary Conference, Edinburgh 1910, in Conference Proceedings, Vol. VII, p.77.

78 cf. Sadler's four letters to Archdeacon Walker, July 1902, Walker Papers, and the mission's message to Sadler on the occasion of his going on leave; *Uganda Notes*, Oct. 1904. Sadler's own account of his cooperation with the CMS mission is printed in *Church Missionary Intelligencer*, Dec. 1904, pp. 914ff. cf. also General Report Uganda Protectorate for the year ending 31 March 1903, in Cd 1839 – Africa no. 15 (1903).

79 The dowry practice has aptly been described in Report of the Commission on Marriage, Divorce . . . , pars. 85, 97 and ch. V (see n.55). A.W. Southall (1960) discusses the changes caused by economic development.

80 cf. Taylor (1958), pp.176f.

81 cf. Archdeacon Walker's different view of the dowry system. He admits that there are objections to it, and that it has its advantages. He is fully aware that 'it is not selling the girl, for she goes of her own free will'. He also considers it to be a stimulus to work. 'To marry a couple when the money has not been paid to the father or relations would be like elopement in England.' Walker to Cyril, 4 Dec. 1899, Walker Papers; and Walker, Annual Letter Nov. 1899 in *Church Missionary Intelligencer*, May 1900, pp.339ff.

82 Walker, op. cit. The decision of 18 Nov. 1899 is mentioned in the 3 Regents' memorandum, 'Our Old Customs and New', dated 18 March 1903, SMP 991/09. Also quoted in J.F. Cunningham (1905), pp.150ff.

83 When the memorandum just mentioned was forwarded to the Commissioner it was simply called 'the Native Marriage Law'; cf. Leakey to Sub-Commissioner Tomkins, 20 March 1903; and Tomkins to Sadler, same date, A24. Also Bishop Tucker,

Minutes of the Synod, April 1909, par. V; Cunningham (1905) adds that these measures had not received official sanction.

84 George Wilson to Sadler, 6 Jan. 1903, A24.

85 cf. Morris (1960), pp.197ff; and Morris (1968), p.37.

86 Report of Missionary Conference, June 1904, *Uganda Notes*, July 1904, p.101.

87 In 'Our Old Customs and New' it is specifically stated that the description does not represent a law; SMP 991/09. J.M. Waliggo (1976, unpubl. thesis) calls the rates of dowry a recommendation (p.286), and Cunningham (1905) reaffirms that it has not received official sanction.

88 Wilson to Tucker, 26 Febr. 1906; and Tucker to Wilson, 1 March 1906, copy of both in CO 536/6–21728.

89 Minutes of Synod, April 1909, Minute Book, MUL. In an actual case Tucker would draw the attention of the Buganda government to the matter.

90 In Annual Report Buganda 1916–1917 a law in draft concerning Native Marriage Dowry is mentioned, but in the report for 1917–1918 it is directly stated that such a law has been shelved as it was found impractical to administrate; instead the matter is left to a gradual change in public opinion. SMP 1138 G and 1138 H. As a witness before the Uganda Development Commission, Canon Blackledge pointed out that the dowry rate now stood at 25 rupees. As great sums were involved and as the practice represented a serious obstacle to legal marriages, the dowry ought to be limited. See *Uganda Herald*, 19 Dec. 1919 and SMP 5860. Sir Apolo Kagwa favoured a legal maximum dowry and was supported by Bishop Forbes of the Mill Hill Mission; SMP 5860. Nothing materialized however, and the PCs' Conference 1919 voted firmly against fixed rates except in extraordinary circumstances, SMP 3841.

91 Minutes of the Synod, 1909, loc. cit. The comment quoted was made by one of the leading Protestant saza chiefs, the Sekibobo Ham Mukasa.

92 cf. Anderea Batulabudde to Rev. W.A. Crabtree, Mbale, 2 June 1902, photocopies of Letters to Crabtree, Ch. of Ug. Arch., MUL.

93 Missionary Conference, June 1904, report in *Uganda Notes*, July 1904, p.101.

94 cf. George Wilson to Sadler, 6 Jan. 1903, A24.

95 Walker to Father, 28 Febr. 1900, Walker Papers, commenting on discussions between Sir Harry Johnston, Bishop Tucker and himself.

96 This interpretation of the outcome of the discussion of the marriage problem has been compiled from Archdeacon Walker's report of the Missionary Conference 1904, no. 158, G3. A7/04, and the report in *Uganda Notes*, June 1904, p.101.

97 cf. Morris & Read (1966), pp.395f; and Morris & Read (1972), pp.219f, 230f.

98 A change in practice appears to have prevailed. At one stage both husband and wife had to appear before the clergyman and confirm their marriage; the customary marriage was then considered binding. The only alternative would be to conceive of the customary marriage as non-existent. See secr. for marriages, CMS, to J.F. Cunningham, Registrar General, 12 Aug. 1905, in special box: Marriage Registers etc., Ch. of Ug. Arch., MUL.

99 Minutes of Diocesan Synod, June 1907, Minute Book, MUL.

100 Minutes of Synod, April 1909, par. V d, loc. cit.

101 Willis had been a missionary in the Uganda mission since 1900, posted first to Ankole and later to Kavirondo (East Africa Protectorate).

102 W.E. Owen to Willis, 3 May 1912, Bishop's Files: Mac–Mar. Marriage Questions 1912–1940. No year is given on the letter, but taking Owen's period of work in Toro and the whole context of the letter into account we may fix it to 1912. At the same time

Owen wrote an article along the same lines, 'Prosecution in Toro for Bigamy under Uganda Marriage Ordinance', *Uganda Notes*, March 1912. (I have only learned about Owen's article from contemporary references and not had access to it, as this issue of *Uganda Notes* was not available in Uganda or in London.) ·

103 Willis, 'The Policy of the Uganda Mission', delivered to Missionary Conference, July 1912, in 1913 pr. as a pamphlet (quotation, p.19).

104 ibid., p. 21.

105 ibid., p. 20.

106 Minutes of Synod, July 1912, Minute Book, MUL (the section on marriage translated from Luganda by Daudi Senono).

107 cf. Walker to Father, 28 Febr. 1900, Walker Papers; and Willis, op. cit., p. 21.

108 Willis, op. cit. pp.21f.

109 See handwritten comments by Archdeacon Baskerville and Dr A.R. Cook on a copy of Willis (1913), p. 21, now under no. 55, G3. A7/1917. See also Willis to Chief Secr. Wallis, 9 Dec. 1912, Bishop's Files (see n.102).

110 Whole issue summarized in editorial, *Uganda Notes*, March 1913.

111 Directly stated by PC Buganda to Chief Secr., 27 Nov. 1912, copy in Bishop's Files, loc. cit.

112 cf. Ag. Chief Secr. to Willis, 8 Oct. 1912, acknowledging Willis' official letter of 30 Sept. Relevant file in ESA missing, and colonial administration's minutes only seen as far as they appear in copies in mission's files.

113 Ag. Ass. Chief Secr. to Chief Secr., 3 Oct. 1912; cf. also Owen to Willis, 3 May 1912, Bishop's Files (see n.102).

114 ibid. This point of view clearly expressed by District Magistrate in a rare case where a man in 1913 was prosecuted for bigamy under Marriage Ordinance of 1902. The magistrate blamed religious teachers who indiscriminately encouraged people to enter into a lifelong contract without knowing the consequences. Criminal Case no. 35 of 1913 in District Magistrate's Court at Fort Portal, copy in Owen Papers: Miscellaneous, acc. 83, CMS Arch.

115 PC Western Province to Chief Secr., 2 Nov. 1912; PC Buganda to Chief Secr., 27 Nov. 1912, Bishop's Files, loc. cit.

116 Thus PC Buganda to Chief Secr., 27 Nov. 1912.

117 ibid.

118 Willis to Chief Secr. Wallis, 9 Dec. 1912, Bishop's Files (see n.102).

119 ibid.

120 PC Western Province to Chief Secr., 2 Nov. 1912. The Ag. Governor later endorsed this point of view and considered the mission's policy to be very drastic. In his opinion the so-called Malakites' recent secession from the Anglican Church had to a large extent been caused by investigations into people's private lives. Minute by Ag. Governor Wallis, 11 Nov. 1914, SMP 4219.

121 PC Buganda to Chief Secr., 27 Nov. 1912 Bishop's Files (see n.102).

122 Willis (n.118). Willis may also have been influenced by the teaching of the Malakites, who by reference to the Old Testament allowed polygamy. For Malakites see below, ch. 25.

123 Governor Jackson to Secr. of State, 12 April 1913, CO 536/59–15985/13 (file destroyed, seen in Register). Minutes of Missionary Committee, 1 Febr. 1913, where secr. of the mission, Rev. E. Millar, was appointed as mission representative.

124 Internal missionary correspondence re work of Committee not found. The following

is based upon discussions and quotations in correspondence from 1914 when Owen took the matter to the Parent Committee.

125 Millar to Owen, 16 June 1914, quoting Owen's letter of 18 March 1913, copy under no. 122, G3. A7/010. cf. also Owen to Manley, 29 April 1914, no. 81, G3. A7/010.

126 Owen, Statement re Registration of all Native Marriages, July 1914, Bishop's Files (see n.102).

127 Owen to Willis, Tonbridge (England), n.d., original in Bishop's Files (see n.102). Copy encl. in Owen to Manley, 30 April 1914, no. 81, G3. A7/010.

128 Quotation of Millar's answer in Owen to Manley, 4 May 1914, no. 81, loc. cit. cf. also Owen's Statement, July 1914.

129 Millar to Owen, 16 June 1914, quoting his own answer to Owen's letter of 18 March 1913, copy under no. 132, loc. cit.

130 Memorandum of interview between Owen and Manley, 22 April 1914; Owen to Manley, 28 April 1914, no. 78; cf. Owen to Manley, 4 May 1914, no. 81, all in G3. A7/010.

131 Owen's Statement, July 1914 (see n.126).

132 ibid.

133 Millar to Owen, 16 June 1914, quoting his own answer to Owen's letter of 26 Aug. 1913, copy under no. 132, G3. A7/010.

134 He sent a petition addressed to the Chief Secr. through the secr. of the CMS mission; reported in Owen to Manley, 4 May 1914. cf. also Millar to Owen, 16 June 1914.

135 Millar to Owen, 16 June 1914, quoting his own letter of 26 Aug. 1913, where Willis' position is set forward.

136 Owen himself mentions the split, but does not indicate whether others among his colleagues supported him. He confines himself to maintaining that the older missionaries, at present in power, were opposed to him. Owen to Manley, Tonbridge, 28 April 1914, no. 78, G3. A7/010.

137 The only report available from the Committee's work appears in Attorney General, Donald Kingdon's comments on the new draft ordinance, dat. 22 Oct. 1913, encl. in Jackson to Secr. of State, 28 Oct. 1913, CO 536/62–41879/13.

138 Memorandum of interview between Owen and Manley, 22 April 1914; Owen to Manley, Tonbridge, 28 April and 4 May 1914, no. 78 and 81, G3. A7/010.

139 ibid., and Owen to Willis, April 1914 (see n. 127).

140 cf. Owen to Manley, 2 Febr. 1915, no. 18, G3. A7/011; Group Committee's interview with Owen, 24 Febr. 1915, taken from Precis, G3. A7/P; Owen to Manley, 25 Febr. 1915, no. 31, G3. A7/011.

141 Owen to Willis, Tonbridge, 18 July 1914, Bishop's Files (see n.102); and Owen to Manley, 29 Dec. 1914, no. 194, G3. A7/010.

142 See minutes of Missionary Committee, 25 April 1915, when Owen under certain conditions was allowed to be editor of pamphlets dealing with polygamy. Owen's old contestant, Ernest Millar, commented that 'the Committee did not wish to discourage Mr Owen and so allowed him to do this work which he is so interested in'. Millar to Manley, 7 May 1915, no. 89, G3. A7/011.

143 Owen became well known only a few years later, as Archdeacon of Kavirondo in British East Africa, for his defence of African interests and campaign against labour recruitment practice; see esp. J.M. Lonsdale (1964, unpubl. thesis), *passim*.

144 *Uganda Official Gazette*, 30 May 1914, p. 257. cf. Millar to Owen, 16 June 1914, no. 132, G3. A7/010. Morris & Read (1966), who otherwise examine in detail the introduction of marriage laws in Uganda, do not mention the Ordinance of 1914,

though Taylor does (1958, pp.181ff). In more general terms the conversion of marriages in Uganda is touched upon in A. Phillips & H.F. Morris (1971), pp.169f.

145 Clearly the interpretation given in Laws and Regulations of the Church of Uganda 1917, C. 294–299, pp.58f.

146 Nothing is said about this in Attorney General's comments on the Ordinance (cf. n.137). He calls the changes in the law very slight, the main aim being to avoid any kind of remarriage and to recognize customary marriage as a permanently binding union.

147 A provisional draft ordinance covering all native marriages appears among the papers dealing with the marriage law 1912–1914, Bishop's Files: Mac–Mar. Marriage Questions 1912–1940.

148 Clearly borne out by Bishop Willis blocking Owen's attempt to make direct contact with the colonial administration.

149 Owen, Statement, July 1914 (see n.126).

150 Laws and Regulations of the Church of Uganda 1917, C. 298, p.59.

151 The DC, Entebbe District, mentioned specifically that during the first year only 6 people had had their marriage ratified; Annual Report Buganda 1914–1915, SMP 1138 E.

152 Baskerville, Memorandum to Uganda Development Commission, Dec. 1919, Bishop's Files: K–L. Land. Memoranda.

153 Minutes of Synod, Jan. 1921, Minute Book, MUL. It is not reported whether the motion addressed to the Governor was carried or lost.

154 Willis to Bishop of Mombasa, 1 Dec. 1931, Bishop's Files: Mac–Mar. Marriage Questions 1912–1940.

155 Horace K. Banks to Millar, Mbale, 16 Oct. 1914, Bishop's Files, loc. cit.

156 These points are stated in Banks, op. cit., which gives a leading chief as an example.

157 ibid.

158 Owen to Willis, Masaka, 16 March 1916, Bishop's Files, loc. cit.

159 ibid.; and Owen to Puisne Judge, Masaka, 10 May 1916, loc. cit. (0. dated the letter 1915; later correspondence indicates clearly 1916).

160 He indicated that he acted in an unofficial capacity in Owen to Puisne Judge, 10 May 1916.

161 This was directly stated by Archdeacon Baskerville and Dr A.R. Cook when they updated Willis, Policy of the Uganda Mission, in 1917 (see n.109). See their comments on Ordinance of 1914 and use of penal powers.

162 cf. Ag. DC Gulu to Rev. Wright, 15 Febr. 1915; and Willis to Wright, 30 March 1915. Again Wright to Willis, 18 Febr. 1917; and Willis to Wright, 28 March 1917, all in Bishop's Files (see n.154).

163 Documents from court case not seen, but the remarks by Puisne Judge quoted in Owen to Baskerville, Masaka, 10 Febr. 1920. Owen to Puisne Judge, 10 May 1916 serves as an explanation of his course of action, both in Bishop's Files (see n.154).

164 W. Maurice Carter to Owen, 26 June 1916, unofficially answering Owen's letter of 10 May 1916, Bishop's Files, loc. cit.

165 Canon Blackledge as witness before the Development Commission, SMP 5860.

166 Quotation of Ham Mukasa, loc. cit.

167 Minute by E.L. Scott, Ass. Secr. for Native Affairs, 23 April 1914, supported by PC Eastern Province, F. Spire, Eastern Province Minute Paper 10/13, 1913/14, ESA (seen by courtesy of Dr Michael Twaddle).

168 Northern Province Annual Report 1915–1916, written by Ag. PC P.W. Cooper, SMP 2135 E.

169 PC Buganda, P.W. Cooper, to Chief Secr., 17 May 1918, SMP 5368.

170 e.g. DC Toro, Sullivan, to Ass. Secr. for Native Affairs, 11 June 1923, SMP 6013.

171 Uganda Men's Conference, June 1904, report in *Uganda Notes*, July 1904.

172 Minutes of the Synod, July 1910, Minute Book, MUL.

173 cf. Baskerville's and Cook's comments on Willis, Policy of the Uganda Mission, esp. p.17 (see n.109 and n.161). See also Encyclical Letter from the Synod, Jan. 1921, Minute Book, MUL. Baskerville earlier singled out drunkenness and immorality as crucial problems within the church, and it appears that a kind of investigation into people's private lives was started in 1912, not least with regard to marriage; Baskerville to PC Buganda, Knowles, 20 Febr. 1913, SMP 3155, and minute by Ag. Governor Wallis, 11 Nov. 1914, SMP 4219.

174 Minutes of Synod, Sept. 1919, par. 39. Moral issues were frequently brought up when missionaries gave evidence before the Uganda Development Commission in 1919, cf. SMP 5860. Some of the measures recommended to combat immorality were backed by the Development Commission in its report, but in general the Commission was sceptical of the value of the legislative method. cf. Report, pars. 194–218, copy in CO 536/99–17962 (see also below, n.217).

175 See minutes of Synods, 1919 and 1910; and Tucker to Baylis, 18 July 1910, no. 213, G3. A7/08.

176 Minutes of Synod, June 1917, par. 53; minutes of Synod Jan. 1924, par. 21, MUL.

177 The report, presented to Synod in 1912 and acted upon by Synod in 1913, may be found *in extenso* with Minutes of Synod 1912. It contains valuable analysis of prevalence of old customs and Christian attitude towards them. Committee consisted of 3 Africans and a missionary as secretary.

178 Minutes of Synod, July 1913.

179 Minutes of Synod, April 1909, section V.

180 ibid., and Synod 1912.

181 Minutes of Synod, Jan. 1924, par. 4b. cf. also secrs. of Synod to Chief Secr., 5 Febr. 1924, SMP 8152.

182 Procedure described by Low & Pratt (1960), pp.241ff.

183 See above where dowry rates were discussed. It is also significant that what are called laws and said to have been passed by the Buganda Lukiko do not always appear in the official edition of 'Native Agreements and Buganda Native Laws', Vol. VI of Laws of Uganda Protectorate, 1935–36 edition. See also Waliggo (1976, unpubl. thesis), p.286, who mentions that the Sub-Commissioner called some of the laws 'obsolete' and ordered them rewritten and revised.

184 When Committee on Customary Behaviour examined succession ceremonies, final recommendation about involvement of chiefs was worked out in consultation with Sir Apolo Kagwa and had his approval beforehand; see minutes of Synod 1912. When drunkenness was discussed in 1917 the Katikiro could inform the Synod that the Lukiko had already taken steps to combat this evil; minutes of Synod 1917, par. 53. Also when recommendations from the Central Women's Conference on various moral issues were discussed in 1910 it proved valuable to have the Katikiro's comments before the final decisions were taken; cf. minutes of Synod, July 1910.

185 See remarks from editorial, *Uganda Notes*, March 1913, p.53: 'In this connection it is well to bear in mind that in Uganda [Buganda] the legislative power is in *Christian* hands.'

186 cf. Morris & Read (1966), pp.371ff.

187 The law is dated 12 Nov. 1901; SMP 991/09, Annexure.

188 Sub-Commissioner Kampala, Tomkins, to Commissioner, 18 Sept. 1903, loc. cit.

189 Commissioner to Tomkins, 18 Sept. 1903, loc. cit. cf. *Mengo Notes*, Sept. 1901, where it was stated that the CMS favoured 14, while the leading Baganda preferred a higher age. But the paper added: 'It is a question for the Country, not for the Church, to decide.' Relationship to Guardianship Law of 1904 was not made clear; cf. Morris & Read, op. cit. p.371.

190 W.E. Owen to DC Masaka, 18 April 1917; Archdeacon Baskerville to PC Buganda, Cooper, 24 April 1917, SMP 5093.

191 Cooper to Chief Secr., 24 April 1917 and subsequent minute.

192 Buganda Native Laws, p. 1481 (cf. n.183). See also Morris & Read, op. cit. p.371.

193 Law of 18 Aug. 1902, SMP 991/09.

194 cf. Waliggo (1976, unpubl. thesis), p.285.

195 Law of 20 May 1901, SMP 991/09. Waliggo, op. cit, pp.275ff has discussed at length the problem of Christianity and women in the first two decades of the twentieth century.

196 The law is dated 7 Oct. 1901, SMP 991/09.

197 Buganda Native Laws, p. 1435: The Prevention of Abortion Law, 1904.

198 The law is dated 18 March 1902, SMP 991/09. cf. Waliggo, op. cit., pp.284f.

199 Buganda Native Laws, p. 1477. cf. Morris & Read (1966), pp.290ff.

200 ibid. p. 1438.

201 Re Adultery and Fornication Law, 1917, the case is straightforward. In the Annual Report Buganda 1916–1917 it is mentioned that such a law is in draft; in the Annual Report for the following year the passing of the law is confirmed. SMP 1138G and 1138H.

202 SMP 991/09; and Waliggo, op. cit. p. 284.

203 Minutes of Synod, April 1909, par. V c, MUL.

204 Buganda Native Laws, p. 1473. The Ganda law should be seen in connection with the Liquor Ordinance, 1916, for the whole Protectorate, Laws of Uganda Protectorate, vol. II, Cap. 98.

205 No comments were made when the resolution was received by the colonial administration, and no action appears to have been taken; see minutes in SMP 8152. There is some evidence that officials considered the Anglicans' concern about alcohol to be exaggerated and biased. cf. Sturrock to PC Buganda, P.W. Cooper, 3 Dec. 1918, encl. in Cooper to Governor Corydon, 12 Dec. 1918, File 4, Coryndon Papers, MSS. Afr. s.633, Rhodes House.

206 Laws of the Uganda Protectorate, vol. I, Cap. 40. cf. Morris & Read, op. cit., p. 302.

207 See minutes in SMP 2156.

208 ibid., and Laws of Uganda Protectorate, loc. cit.

209 See minutes in SMP 2156.

210 Buganda Native Laws, p. 1470 'Other dances' meant in particular that performed at twin birth and the nightly celebration marking the end of the period of mourning; cf. PC Buganda, Knowles, to Chief Secr., 13 Dec. 1915, SMP 4648.

211 'This thing [the Tabulu Dance] spoils the loyalty of the Nation and religious precepts and civilization in such a young country as this.' Extract from Lukiko Resolution, 4 Nov. 1915, SMP 4648.

212 Buganda Native Laws, loc. cit.

213 In updating Bishop Willis, Policy of the Uganda Mission (1912), Archdeacon

Baskerville and Dr A.R. Cook remarked: 'The Mission's policy is to abstain from seeking aid from the Government, but the Native Christian leaders have a tendency to desire civil authority.' Copy under no. 55, G3. A7/1917 (cf. n.109).

214 The fact that the Adultery and Fornication Law, 1917, is mentioned in two consecutive annual reports may be taken as an indication of greater concern and greater interest for the legislative process (cf. n.201).

215 cf. Waliggo (1976, unpubl. thesis), p.286, quoting a letter from the Sub-Commissioner, 26 April 1904.

216 P.W. Cooper to Chief Secr., 17 May 1918, SMP 5368.

217 This point of view was later endorsed by the Uganda Development Commission, pars. 194–218, copy of report in CO 536/99–17962/1920.

218 Circular letter dat. 20 July 1905, copy encl. in Tucker to Commissioner Sadler, 29 Sept. 1905, A22/1, ESA.

219 Samwili Mukasa to Tucker, 28 Sept. 1905, loc. cit.

220 Tucker to Sadler, 29 Sept. 1905, loc. cit.

221 Sadler to Tucker, 1 Oct. 1915, loc. cit.

222 Minutes of Synod, June 1906, Minute Book MUL. cf. Walker to Commissioner Hesketh Bell, 26 June 1906, emphasizing the same points and asking for markets to be closed on Sundays. SMP 501/06.

223 Minutes of Synod, June 1907.

224 Reported by Tucker in Synod, April 1909, par. V e.

225 ibid.

226 Reported by Tucker in Synod, July 1910. This whole issue also mentioned in mission's report to World Missionary Conference, Edinburgh 1910: see Conference Proceedings, vol. VII, pp.75f.

227 Minutes of Synod, July 1910.

228 Minutes of Synod, June 1917, par. 51.

229 Minutes of Synod, Jan. 1921, par. 3b, and Synod's Encyclical Letter, dat. 25 Jan. 1921, both in Minute Book, MUL.

230 This suggestion was made by Sir Apolo Kagwa when he witnessed for the Uganda Development Commission 1919; cf. also statement by Canon Blackledge, both in SMP 5860.

231 Minutes of Synod, April 1909.

232 Report of Tucker's speech at Synod 1909, in Minute Book, MUL.

233 Minutes of Synod, July 1910. The quotation represents the opinion of the Sekibobo, Ham Mukasa, Rev. Owen, Rev. Weatherhead and Mr Hattersley.

234 Willis, Policy of the Uganda Mission 1912 (1913), p. 18.

235 Comments by Baskerville and Cook, when they revised Willis, op. cit, in 1917; see n.213.

236 Secrs. of Synod, Daniell and Luboyera, to Chief Secr., 5 Febr. 1924, SMP 8152; cf. minutes of Synod, Jan. 1924, par. 26e.

237 This concern was fully shared by the Catholic missions; cf. report from Catholic mission in Iganga, Busoga, where it was revealed in 1919 that out of 20 Catholic chiefs only 9 were admitted to the Sacrament. See Tom Tuma (1973, unpubl. thesis) pp. 241ff.

238 One clear indication of this attitude may be found in Sub-Commissioner to Dep. Commissioner, 4 Jan. 1908, SMP Conf. 104/1907.

239 See minutes in SMP Conf. 272^I. See also H. Boulton Ladbury, Secr. of CMS Uganda, to Manley, 7 Aug. 1922 (marked conf.), and the enclosed cutting from *East African Standard*, no. 88, G3. A7/22.

240 Thus Willis to Ag. Governor Scott, 2 Sept. 1932; and Scott to Willis, 7 Sept. 1932, Bishop's Files: Mac–Mar. Marriage Questions 1912–1940.

241 Hesketh Bell (1946), quoting his diary entry, 5 Dec. 1908 (p. 193).

242 Willis, Policy of the Uganda Mission (1913), p. 18.

243 PC Buganda, Cox, to Willis, 9 July 1932, Bishop's Files, loc. cit.

244 Joint letter by Bishops J. J. Willis, J. Biermans and John Forbes to Governor, 19 April 1918, SMP 5368. The letter was sent after a personal interview with the Governor. Draft in Bishop's Files: K–L. Land 1912–1913. Subfile: Land. Memoranda. From the whole context it is beyond doubt that the initiative to this whole enterprise was taken by Bishop Willis.

245 Almost the same analysis of the situation and the same remedies were suggested in material presented to Uganda Development Commission the following year. See esp. Archdeacon Baskerville's memorandum of Dec. 1919, copy in Bishop's Files, loc. cit.; and Bishop Forbes on Morality and Education, dat. 21 Nov. 1919, SMP 5860.

246 Bishops' joint letter (see n.244).

247 ibid.

248 P.W. Cooper to Chief Secr., 17 May 1918, SMP 5368.

249 ibid.

250 ibid.

251 Cooper, op. cit.; and even stronger J.C.R. Sturrock, Memorandum on Bishops' letter, n.d., SMP 5368.

252 Thus Sturrock, op. cit.

253 The relationship between the two legal systems has been discussed by Morris (1960); and Morris & Read (1972), ch. 7.

254 cf. Baskerville to Willis (in England), 13 Jan. 1920, Bishop's Files: Mac–Mar. Marriage Questions 1912–1940. Southall (1960) refers to the Omulamuzi's circular and maintains that it has guided the Ganda courts ever since. As will appear from the following, the material used here causes a substantial re-evaluation not only of the circular, but of the whole course of events. H.F. Morris refers briefly to the circular and tends to agree with Southall; cf. Morris & Read (1972), p. 227, n.31.

255 Whole course of events summarized by Ag. Governor, W.M. Carter, to Chief Secr. 20 Jan. 1920, SMP 6013.

256 Baskerville to Chief Secr., 13 Jan. 1920 refers to these rumours. SMP 6013.

257 Baskerville in memorandum to Uganda Development Commission Dec. 1919 (see n.245), quoted in Baskerville to Chief Secr., 13 Jan. 1920.

258 Copies of letters to the government were exchanged between the two missions. cf. Bishop Forbes to Archdeacon Baskerville, 23 Jan. 1920, Bishop's Files (see n.245).

259 Thus Baskerville to Willis (in England), 13 Jan. 1920, loc. cit.

260 Baskerville was fully convinced that the document, in spite of its unclear administrative status, represented official policy and had the government's full sanction. Baskerville to Chief Secr., 13 Jan. 1920, SMP 6013.

261 Willis (in England) to Governor Coryndon (in England), 13 March 1920, Bishop's Files, loc. cit.

262 ibid.

263 Willis to Bishop Forbes, 8 Dec. 1920, Bishop's Files, loc. cit.

264 Willis to Coryndon, 13 March 1920, copy in Bishop's Files (see n. 245).

265 Bishop Forbes to Chief Secr., 12 Jan. 1920, SMP 6013, copy in Bishop's Files, loc. cit.

266 See correspondence between Bishop Forbes and Bishop Willis, 1920. Forbes to Willis, 1 Dec., Willis to Forbes, 8 Dec., Bishop's Files, loc. cit. Willis adheres strongly to the validity of customary marriages, even when contracted by Christians, and quotes from the Laws and Regulations of the Church of Uganda, 1917.

267 The Uganda mission's reaction appears in Archdeacon Baskerville (in absence of Bishop) to Chief Secr., 13 Jan. 1920, SMP 6013; and in Willis to Coryndon (both in England), 13 March 1920, copy in Bishop's Files, loc. cit.

268 Thus claimed by Baskerville in memorandum to Uganda Development Commission, Dec. 1919 (see n.245).

269 Baskerville to Chief Secr., 13 Jan. 1920, SMP 6013.

270 ibid.

271 cf. Baskerville to Willis (in England), 13 Jan. 1920, Bishop's Files, loc. cit.

272 Baskerville to Chief Secr., 13 Jan. 1920, SMP 6013.

273 ibid.; cf. Willis to Coryndon, 13 March 1920, Bishop's Files, loc. cit.

274 Minutes of Synod, Jan 1921, section VI: Moral and Social Questions; cf. also Encyclical Letter from Synod, both in Minute Book, MUL.

275 Minutes of Synod, Jan. 1924, par. 26 (transl. by Daudi Senono).

276 Memorandum by Ag. Governor Carter, 20 Jan. 1920, reproduced in Chief Secr. to Bishop Willis and Bishop Forbes, 24 Jan. 1920, SMP 6013 and Bishop's Files, loc. cit.

277 ibid. These instructions were carefully complied with; cf. PC Buganda, Sturrock, to Chief Secr., 9 Febr. 1920, SMP 6013.

278 cf. Willis to Bishop Forbes, 8 Dec. 1920, Bishop's Files (n.245). Before then Willis had raised the issue with Governor Coryndon (both were in England), who took the matter to the CO from whence it was referred back to Uganda. cf. Coryndon to Willis, Surrey, 3 April 1920, Bishop's Files, loc. cit.

279 It was very difficult for Bishop Forbes to accept this outcome; cf. Forbes to Chief Secr., 28 Jan. 1920, SMP 6013, and see above p.293.

280 PC's statement in Lukiko, 4 Nov. 1920, with further clarification, 8 Dec. 1920, both quoted at great length in PC Buganda, Sturrock, to Chief Secr., 26 April 1922, SMP 6013. Luganda version in Bishop's Files, loc. cit.

281 Willis to Bishop Forbes, 8 Dec. 1920, Bishop's Files, loc. cit.

282 Statement in Buganda Lukiko, 8 Dec. 1920.

283 The Bishop's Charge, Minutes of Synod, Jan. 1921, Minute Book, MUL.

284 ibid., section VI: Moral and Social Questions. Resolution in Secrs. of Synod, Daniell and Luboyera, to local governments, 15 Febr. 1921, SMP 6876.

285 PC Western Province, Cooper, to Chief Secr., 4 May 1921, SMP 6876. Cooper had since 1918 moved from Buganda to the Western Province.

286 See Bishop Willis' remarks at Synod 1921, when he expressed special appreciation of Lukiko's efforts. Copy of draft law in SMP 6013.

287 The Kabaka, the Katikiro and the Omuwanika to PC Buganda, 20 May 1922, SMP 6013.

288 The Omulamuzi, Andeleya Kiwanuka, to his two ministerial colleagues, 23 May 1922, SMP 6013. Kiwanuka thus follows the line earlier taken by Bishop Forbes.

289 PC Buganda, Sturrock, to Chief Secr., 26 April 1922, quoting *in extenso* the statements in the Lukiko, 4 Nov. and 8 Dec. 1920 (see n.280), SMP 6013. It should be

recalled that Sturrock was a participant in the discussion of the three Bishops' joint letter in 1918.

290 Although no direct veto has been found the situation is later made clear by PC Buganda, Sturrock, to Ass. Attorney General, 21 Dec. 1923, SMP 6013.

291 Instructions regarding illegitimate marriages contracted by Christian men, sgd. by the Omulamuzi, 1 Sept. 1923, SMP 6013.

292 DC Mengo, A.H. Cox, to PC Buganda, 20 Dec. 1923, encl. a letter of complaint from Ezera Mukasa, SMP 6013.

293 cf. Sturrock, op. cit.

294 But it was not ruled out that Christian chiefs could discourage the hearing of such cases in local courts. Southall (1960) shows how common such a practice was.

295 Rev. A.B. Lloyd, Toro, to DC Toro, Sullivan, 11 June 1923, copy in SMP 6013.

296 Minutes of Synod, Jan. 1924, section 26, Minute Book, MUL.

297 H.F. Morris (1968, p.38) has drawn attention to Bishan Singh v. R.; and in Morris & Read (1972), pp.228ff. Morris mentions that the case has not before been reported in detail. Hence, it is still open to question what impact it really had, especially to what extent it affected the jurisdiction of the native courts and the validity of the Adultery and Fornication Law.

298 The two concepts of a Christian nation and a Christian state owe much to Professor Ali A. Mazrui. A number of his works stimulated the concept of the church–state problem suggested here. See especially Mazrui (1966–7).

299 Interestingly enough this point was made quite clear at a very early stage when the Commissioner stated that there existed complete accord between the administration and the three missions, as all had one common aim, 'the moral and material progress of the people'. Hayes Sadler, General Report for the year ending 31 March 1904, in PP Cd 2250–Africa no. 12 (1904). For the wider Anglo-Anglican background to the idea of a Christian nation, not least alliance of 'godliness and good learning', see D. Newsome (1961), esp. Introduction.

300 This discussion of government officials' attitude to African institutions is closely related to the major topic of indirect rule, not included in the present analysis. For a recent discussion see Morris & Read (1972), *passim*; and S.R. Karugire (1980), pp. 116ff.

301 It is characteristic that Sadler, op. cit., refers to the missions' 'civilizing and progressive influence' without defining their contribution in Christian terms.

17 The Christianization of political institutions

1 cf. Ali A. Mazrui (1966–67).

2 The suggestion was put forward by some of the leading clergymen. The details of the whole discussion about the status of the Anglican church are on present evidence difficult to sort out. An important issue was to what extent the Bishop was the head of the church, and his relationship with the secular head, the Kabaka. See minutes of Synod, June 1906, Minute Book, MUL.

3 ibid. The Katikiro, Apolo Kagwa, supported Walker by emphasizing the distinction between the religious and the secular authority.

4 C.W. Hattersley's account of Archdeacon Walker's speech at the ceremony in Entebbe, *Uganda Notes*, Jan. 1904, p. 2. cf. also Walker to Basil, 1 June 1902, where he attaches similar importance to the presence of government officials on official occasions in the church (Walker Papers).

5 See various notices in *Uganda Notes* over the years where special attention is paid to the Governor. Interestingly the CMS mission considered it important to pay a visit to

newly arrived Commissioner Sadler as early as the Catholic representative; see Walker to Father, 23 Febr. 1902, Walker Papers.

6 See minutes of Synods, July 1912, July 1913 and June 1915. During all three sessions F.J. Jackson was Governor. cf. also minutes from Synod, Sept. 1919. Minute Book, MUL.

7 Minutes of Synod, June 1917. This rather blunt formulation appeared in the first draft, but was later modified.

8 Archdeacon Baskerville to Mr Cox, 20 Febr. 1919, SMP 4491.

9 Note by Governor, 21 Aug. 1919, SMP 4491.

10 ibid.

11 In 1919 two government officials, the principal medical officer and the director of education, were elected to Synod as representatives for European congregations at Nakasero and Entebbe. Minutes of Synods, Sept. 1919 and Jan. 1921. When the former and the Ag. Chief Secr. were asked to join a committee of European residents with the aim of supporting the CMS during its financial crisis they found it necessary to put their participation on 'official record'. See minutes from May 1922 in SMP 7351.

12 cf. Commissioner Sadler to FO, 23 Febr. 1904; and FO's answer, 21 April 1904, FO 2/856.

13 Ag. Governor Russell to Secr. of State, 28 June 1910, CO 536/54–23535 (file destroyed, see Register). See also minutes in SMP 811.

14 See declarations by Bishop Willis, 13 Jan. 1917 and 18 March 1918, in special box with no label, Ch. of Ug. Arch., MUL. Also discussed at Missionaries' Conference in 1919; cf. Rowling to Manley, 9 Sept. 1919, no. 112, G3. A7/1919.

15 Ag. Governor Jarvis to Secr. of State, 20 Febr. 1924, CO 536/130–14020/24, cf. SMP 811.

16 CO minute 29 March 1924; and Secr. of State to Governor, 7 April 1924, loc. cit. Re long tradition behind this CO policy see E.R. Norman (1976), pp.202f.

17 Archdeacon Walker expressed this point aptly: 'Amongst a simple minded people the outward sign is of much importance.' Walker to Father, 21 Nov. 1903, Walker Papers.

18 cf. Tucker to Ag. Governor Boyle, 23 Dec. 1909, copy under no. 46, G3. A7/08.

19 *Church Missionary Review*, Aug. 1914, p.489.

20 e.g. Walker to Sub-Commissioner Leakey, 11 April 1907, SMP 175/1907. In general, quest for consultative status and the various tasks connected with it within the colonial state were clearly outlined in report which the Uganda Mission submitted to the first World Missionary Conference in Edinburgh in 1910. Report presumably written by either Bishop Tucker or Archdeacon Walker. See World Missionary Conference: Report of Commission VII. Missions and Governments, pp.73ff.

21 The argument was used in connection with the first Marriage Ordinance of 1902; see Tucker to Baylis, 15 Aug. 1904, G3. A7/04. cf. H.B. Hansen (1980), pp.244f.

22 Thus Walker to Baylis, 6 June 1907, no. 164; cf. also Millar to Baylis, 7 May 1907, no. 143, both in G3. A7/05. This rule was reaffirmed in the mission's Executive Committee 7–8 Sept. 1908, no. 243, G3. A7/06. The problem came up as early as 1902 in connection with Rev. Fisher in Toro; cf. Commissioner Sadler to Walker, 23 June 1902, and Walker to Sadler same date, A23/1 and A22/1, ESA.

23 Minutes of Executive Committee 7–8 Sept. 1908 (n.22). cf. also Baylis to Tucker, 4 July 1907, Letterbook II, p.273, G3. A7/L2. The controversy between the Secr. of the Missionary Committee and Rev. Owen about the marriage law in 1913 touches on the same problem.

24 Walker, op. cit.

25 Tucker to Baylis, 13 Jan. 1908, no. 57, G3. A7/06. Another reason was the growth of the work.

26 Walker, op. cit.

27 Tucker apologized immediately when one of the missionaries, after accidentally killing a woman, reported the case to the head of the mission station and not to the Collector of the district. Commissioner Sadler to Tucker, 5 May 1905, A23/1; Tucker to Sadler, 7 May 1905, A22/1, both in ESA. Elsewhere Tucker bears witness to the importance which Sadler attached to 'strict official procedure'; Tucker to Baylis, 30 Dec. 1904, no. 19, G3. A7/04.

28 The incident has been thoroughly dealt with by M. Twaddle (1967, unpubl. thesis), pp.235ff.

29 See correspondence between Purvis, Walker and Collector Ormsby in 1906, now in Special File: Purvis – re Punitive Expeditions in Busoga and Bugishu, 1906, Ch. of Ug. Arch., MUL. See also Walker to Baylis, 6 June 1907, no. 164, G3. A7/05. See also Purvis' own brief account (1909, ch. 17).

30 Tucker to Baylis, 9 Aug. 1907, no. 213, G3. A7/05.

31 ibid. cf. also Twaddle, op. cit. p. 237, where the quotation of the Commissioner fully confirms Tucker's suspicion.

32 cf. Baylis to Tucker, 4 July 1907, Letterbook II, p. 273, G3. A7/L2.

33 Also recognized within government circles; cf. statement by Sub-Commissioner George Wilson, 20 Oct. 1907: 'Bishop Tucker is all that moderation and consideration should require in this matter, but he reasonably hints that his hands will be forced if this sort of thing goes on.' Quotation in Twaddle, op. cit. p. 245.

34 A large dossier on this rather trivial case may be found in A27–Item 7–1902–05: Special File. Allegations by Mr Lloyd against Nile Officers, ESA.

35 Tucker to Baylis, 30 Dec. 1904, no. 19, G3. A7/04.

36 Tucker to Baylis, 13 Jan. 1908 (see n.25).

37 The Collector Mbarara, Edward Treffry, to Commissioner Hesketh Bell, 14 May 1908, SMP Conf. 61/1908. The latest accounts of the incident in Ankole in 1905 can be found in E.I. Steinhart (1977); and M.L. Pirouet (1978), pp.132f.

38 Hesketh Bell to Ag. Secr. CMS mission, John Roscoe, 20 May 1908, loc. cit.

39 cf. Roscoe to Bell, 4 June 1908, loc. cit. The Executive Committee of the mission had to reverse an earlier decision, and it was decided to explain to Bell how Clayton's involvement in the murder case and its aftermath had been misunderstood. Minutes of EC, 6 July 1908, no. 202, G3. A7/06.

40 Walker to Bell, 7 April 1909; and Bell to Walker, 8 April 1909, loc. cit.

41 The internal correspondence from 1912 concerning A.B. Fisher is in SMP Conf. 109/1912.

42 Tucker to Baylis, 8 June 1909, no. 226, G3. A7/07; cf. Ag. Governor Tomkins to Secr. of State, 7 June 1909, CO 536/26–22250.

43 Tomkins to Secr. of State, 29 May 1909 (telegr.); and CO minute 31 May 1909, CO 536/26–18227/1909.

44 One example was in Toro in 1910, where the Governor expressed his appreciation of the cooperation with the mission; SMP Conf. 29/1910.

45 See report from Bunyoro in Rev. Tegart to Fisher, Masindi, 25 Oct. 1911, Fisher Papers: Bunyoro 1905–1912, in CMS Arch.

46 Tucker to Commissioner Sadler, 30 July 1904, forwarding a letter from missionary in charge of Toro, Rev. H.E. Maddox, dat. 5 July 1904. This initiative started a long

correspondence, as Sadler wanted more detailed information from the mission. All letters in A22/1 and A23/1, ESA. Copies enclosed in Ag. Commissioner Wilson to Secr. of State, 21 April 1906, CO 536/6–19337.

47 cf. Tucker to Wilson, 16 Sept. 1904, loc. cit.

48 cf. Maddox to Wilson, 3 Sept. 1904, loc. cit.

49 Maddox to Sadler, 5 July 1904, loc. cit.

50 cf. Tucker to Wilson, 6 Oct. 1904; and 12 Febr. 1906, A22/1. See also Wilson to Secr. of State, 21 April 1906 (cf. n.46).

51 Ag. Sub-Commissioner F.A. Knowles to Wilson, 19 April 1906; and Wilson, op. cit., both in CO 536/6–19337. The content of the 1906 Agreement and the whole process leading to its conclusion have been described by O.W. Furley (1961), pp.195ff. cf. also K. Ingham (1975), pp.103f.

52 Clearly acknowledged by the CO; see Minute in CO 536/6–19337.

53 cf. Sadler to Tucker, 5 June 1904, A23/1.

54 Tucker to Governor, n.d., but in view of the content presumably 19 Dec. 1907, SMP 1367/1907, min. 21 and following minutes.

55 Rev. A.B. Lloyd to Chief Secr., n.d.; and Ass. Secr. to Chief Secr., 16 April 1914, SMP Conf. 186/1914.

56 Two examples may be taken from M. Twaddle (1967, unpubl. thesis), pp.196ff, 209ff, the latter describing the formal alliance between the Ganda chief Kakungulu and the CMS in the Eastern Province.

57 Another example: in Bunyoro Rev. A.B. Fisher intervened and acted as spokesman for the chiefs in order to secure for them the land promised by the government in freehold. Fisher to Archdeacon Walker, 25 Aug. 1911, Fisher Papers: Bunyoro 1902–1912.

58 e.g. joint platform with the chiefs in the Busoga land controversy meant that the colonial administration later was inclined to interpret other moves by the mission as 'sighting shots at the land-target'. Minute by Attorney General, dat. 16 Nov. 1925, SMP. 8897, cf. below pp.422ff.

59 Thus defined by Archdeacon Walker in letter to Sub-Commissioner Buganda, Leakey, 11 April 1907, SMP 175/1907.

60 Minutes in SMP Conf. 44/1907.

61 Question raised by Archdeacon Walker during the Purvis controversy. cf. references in Special File: Purvis – re Punitive Expeditions (n.29).

62 For example, Fisher in Toro forced a chief by threats to pay back the fine which he, with the approval of the colonial resident, had imposed on a man after a court case. Fisher was convinced that the man was innocent, but his intervention dismayed the colonial officials. Minutes from 1910 in SMP Conf. 102/1910. The same role later precisely defined 'as mediator or advocate in obtaining redress or relief, where the Laws of the Government are unjust, or appear so, or are ignorantly applied'. Report from Singo Deanery 1919 to Synod 1919, written by Rev. S.R. Skeens, Synod Files, Namirembe Arch.

63 Dep. Commissioner George Wilson to Commissioner, Nimule, 16 June 1904; and Hoima, 12 Aug. 1904, A27–Item 7–1902–05, ESA.

64 Tucker to Ag. Collector Wyndham, Wadelai, 2 April 1904, loc. cit.

65 Ag. Commissioner George Wilson thanked the Bishop and commented carefully on his letter (Tucker's letter is missing); Wilson to Tucker, 14 June 1907, SMP 710/1907.

66 Dep. Commissioner George Wilson to Commissioner, 16 June 1904 (cf. n.63).

67 ibid.

68 Indicated by Wilson, op. cit., who quoted some of his colleagues. See also Ag.

Collector Wyndham to Tucker, Wadelai, 31 March 1904, A27–Item 7–1902–05.

69 Tucker to Sadler, 5 Oct. 1903, re Toro, A22/1.

70 Tucker to Wyndham, 2 April 1904 (cf. n.64). See tribute which F.J. Jackson, Dep. Commissioner around 1900 and later Governor of Uganda, paid in his autobiography to Bishop Tucker's and the CMS Mission's policy of non-interference. F. Jackson (1930), ch.23.

71 George Wilson, op. cit.

72 Ag. PC Western Province, Anderson, to Chief Secr., 20 Aug. 1912, SMP Conf. 109/1912. The missionary was Rev. A.B. Fisher, earlier singled out as a thorn in the flesh of the colonial administration.

73 Ag. Commissioner George Wilson to Secr. of State, 31 Dec. 1905, CO 536/3–5447/ 1905–06. On that ground Wilson even supported a secular system of education run by the government.

74 It is significant that Bishop Willis considered it necessary to make a distinction between intervention and interference, when he explained the mission's defence of Africans' interests. Willis (1913), Policy of the Uganda Mission, 1912, p. 28.

75 The Ag. Commissioner George Wilson thus paid tribute to assistance rendered by Mr Lloyd in administrative work in Acholi; Wilson to Commissioner, Nimule, 16 June 1904 (see n.63). See also Archdeacon Walker's remarks about relationship between Bishop Tucker and colonial government in obituary in *Church Missionary Review*, Aug. 1914, p. 489.

76 e.g. Fisher's assistance during the Bunyoro chiefs' rebellion against Ganda agents in 1907 (see below, ch. 22). Minutes in SMP 710/07 and corresponding letters in Fisher Papers: Book XVIII.

77 George Wilson to Secr. of State, 31 Dec. 1905 (see n.73).

78 As a further example, after the First World War the colonial government wanted to present a brass eagle lectern to all three missions in appreciation of their assistance during the war, with the additional argument that it was essential to maintain good relations with them. Governor Coryndon to Secr. of State, 10 April 1919, CO 536/93–28729/1919.

79 One example may be found in Twaddle (1967), p.246. In the wake of the Purvis controversy the need for an exhaustive report was emphasized as the whole incident surely would be subject to missionary inquiries.

80 It is interesting to notice that some of the same points have been made with regard to independent Africa. This serves to generalize the church–state problem in an African setting. See Adrian Hastings (1973, unpubl. paper), pp.16ff.

81 Most of the constraining factors may be seen in action in 1923 when Archdeacon W.E. Owen of Kavirondo raised the issue of making all land in Toro Crown land, which in his opinion meant a new tax on people and a breach of promises earlier given to the Toro chiefs on the allocation of private estates. The CMS Uganda mission and the colonial authorities deplored in particular Owen's violation of all procedural rules. Correspondence in CO 536/124–11428/1923, and in Owen Papers, acc. 83, CMS Arch. (cf. also n.82, ch.12).

82 Assessment based upon Bishop Willis' first charge as a bishop in 1912; Willis (1913), Policy of the Uganda Mission, p. 27. Later Willis reaffirms his positive view of the contribute, so that people considered it a new tax levied by the government. The Ag. Governor answered that there was no ground for the allegation. Secr. of State to Governor, 3 May 1912; and Ag. Governor to Secr. of State, 24 June 1912, SMP 1142, cf. CO 536/50–23591/12.

83 Assessment based upon Bishop Willis' first charge as a bishop in 1912; Willis (1913), Policy of the Uganda Mission, p. 27. Later Willis reaffirms his positive view of the

colonial government and praises in general the happy cooperation between mission and government: 'The Reflections of Bishop J.J. Willis of Uganda', pp.20–30, copy of manuscript, written 1950–4, in Royal Commonwealth Society's Library, London.

84 See report from Singo Deanery 1919, quoted above (n.62).

85 Memorandum on Education of His Highness, Daudi, King of Buganda, dat. July 1901, G/Y A7/1, CMS Arch. No signature, but writer presumably Preb. H.E. Fox, Bishop Tucker's confidant within CMS Headquarters. Tucker was on leave in England at the time.

86 ibid.

87 About the same time Sir Harry Johnston recommended as a tutor a person who was independent of any of the missionary societies and appointed directly by the British government. Johnston to Marquess of Lansdowne, 10 July 1901, in PP C. 671 (Africa no. 7), 1901.

88 See approval from Crown Agents, mid-1905, CO Register, CO 682/1.

89 *Mengo Notes*, Sept. 1900.

90 *Uganda Notes*, Sept. 1905. cf also Sept. issue of *Uganda Notes* during the following years.

91 Ag. Governor Boyle to Secr. of State, 31 Dec. 1909, CO 536/28–3038/1909–10. See also A.R. Tucker, Postscript, in second edition of his autobiography (1911), pp.347ff.

92 Boyle, op. cit.

93 A report by J.C.R. Sturrock, the Kabaka's tutor, is enclosed in Ag. Governor Tomkins to Secr. of State, 12 Aug. 1910, CO 536/34–28001/1910. See also Rev. E. Millar to Baylis, 12 Aug. 1910, no. 230, G3. A7/08; and *Uganda Notes*, Sept. 1910.

94 *Uganda Notes*, Sept. and Oct. 1910; Tucker, op. cit.

95 ibid., and Millar, op. cit.

96 Minutes starting in July 1910 in SMP Conf. 77/1910.

97 PC Buganda to Chief Secr., 24 Jan. 1911, loc. cit.

98 Chief Secr. to Governor, 25 Jan. 1911, loc. cit.

99 Secr. of State to Governor, 17 March 1911 (telegr.), loc. cit.

100 Minutes from 1911 to 1913 in SMP Conf. 77/1910, especially Regents to PC Buganda, 3 March 1913.

101 See minute by J.C.R. Sturrock, June 1911, loc. cit.

102 Minute by Ag. PC Buganda, March 1913; and PC Buganda, Browning, to Chief Secr., 8 April 1913, loc. cit.

103 cf. Chief Secr. to Governor, 4 April 1913, loc. cit. Bishop Willis' letter is not included in the file, probably because it was a private letter to the Governor.

104 Bishop Biermans to PC Buganda, 8 April 1913, loc. cit.

105 PC Buganda, Browning, to Chief Secr., 8 April, 1913, loc. cit.

106 PC Buganda to Chief Secr., 16 April 1913, loc. cit. cf. *Uganda Notes*, April 1913. Accordingly the Synod of the NAC could in July 1913 congratulate theKabaka upon his safe arrival in England; Minute Book, MUL.

107 Minute by Governor F.J. Jackson, 9 April 1913, SMP Conf. 77/1910.

108 Apolo Kagwa and Zakariya Kizito Kisingiri to Governor, 21 April 1913, loc. cit.

109 Interview between Secr. of State, Harcourt, and Tucker and Willis, 11 March 1914, CO 536/73–9243/1914.

110 See Baskerville to CMS London, 14 April 1914, under no. 95, G3. A7/010. See also J.H. Cook (see n.111). The separation in time between the two ceremonies caused

some confusion in the CO. When report of official ceremony was received it was asked whether any religious ceremony had taken place, such as Tucker and Willis had requested. cf. Ag. Governor Wallis to Secr. of State, 13 Aug. 1914; and CO minute 22 Sept. 1914, CO 536/70–36106/1914.

111 cf. J.H. Cook, 'Investiture of the Kabaka of Buganda', *Church Missionary Review*, 1915, pp.115ff.

112 It should be added that between the accession ceremony and the coronation ceremony the Kabaka married a daughter of one of the senior Anglican clergymen, Rev. Yonasazi Kaiza. See report in *Uganda Herald*, 29 Sept. 1914.

113 cf. Britton, Ag. Secr. Diocesan Council, to Manley, 14 April 1914, no. 95; and Millar, Secr. Uganda Mission, to Manley, 7 May 1914, no. 102, both in G3. A7/010. See also R.A. Snoxall (1937), who gives a contemporary Ganda account of the Coronation.

114 cf. J.H. Cook, op. cit.

115 See draft copy of plan for the Coronation ceremony in Bishop's Files: R (1), and account of the event in Snoxall, op. cit.

116 As early as 1912 a committee was set up to examine the implications of the old beliefs and rites; Minutes of Synod July 1912, Minute Book, MUL (cf. above p.280). See also interpretation of the event by D. Apter (1961), pp.139ff; and F. Welbourn (1961), p. 218 n.23. John Roscoe has given a full account of the customary Coronation ceremonies; Roscoe (1965), pp.190ff.

117 cf. J.H. Cook, op cit. The interpretation suggested here represents a variation on the one given by David Apter. He makes a distinction between a European and a customary ceremony, but it seems more correct to talk about an official ceremony and a Christian/traditional one.

118 See Millar (n.113). No internal Minutes by colonial officials have been seen which deal with this aspect. It must have been a last minute decision as the Governor's name appears on the draft copy of the programme (see n.115).

119 Even the *Uganda Herald* commented on the absence of officials: issue 13 Nov. 1914.

120 Minutes of the Synod, June 1915, loc. cit.

121 It is interesting that the Commissioner as early as 1904 regarded Buganda as 'a Christian kingdom, because its native rule is formulated on practically Christian principles, and its King, Regents, and most of its chiefs and leading persons are Christians by profession'. Hayes Sadler, General Report on the Uganda Protectorate for the year ending 31 March 1904, PP C. 2250 (Africa no. 12), 1904.

122 cf. Apter, op. cit. pp.141ff; and M. Twaddle (1969), p. 315.

123 See Rev. G. Blackledge, 'The King of Toro's Baptismal Anniversary', *Uganda Notes*, May 1908, p. 71.

124 ibid. For a thorough description of the Coronation ceremony and its wider impact see Pirouet (1966); and Pirouet (1978), pp.68ff.

125 Note that Toro High School was opened in 1913 on the Omukama's accession day with great festivities; see *Uganda Notes*, June 1913. For a general evaluation of the importance of the Omukama for the cause of the church in Toro, see *Uganda Notes*, July 1913.

126 Pirouet (1978), p. 82.

127 cf. Rev. A.B. Fisher, Bunyoro Notes, entry April 1900, Book XIV, Fisher Papers.

128 Pirouet (1978), p.89; Steinhart (1977), pp.169f; cf. also A.R. Dunbar (1965), p. 108; J. Beattie (1971), p.79; and G.N. Uzoigwe (1972), pp. 185f.

129 cf. Fisher to Baylis, Hoima, 19 Febr. 1905, no. 90, G3. A7/04. See also A.B. Lloyd (1906), pp.50f.

130 ibid. cf. also importance attached to the Omukama in Fisher to H.E. Fox, 30 Nov. 1905, Book XVI, Fisher Papers.

131 cf. Pirouet, op. cit., pp.105f; and Uzoigwe, op. cit., p. 199. See also below, ch. 22.

132 See Fisher's account, 'Celebrations at Hoima', encl. in Fisher to Baylis, 21 Nov. 1908, no. 251, G3. A7/06. See also A.B. Lloyd's remarks regarding opportunities for mutual help; Lloyd, op. cit., p. 38.

133 Report on the event in SMP 7098.

134 This can be deduced from Ag. PC Weatherhead to Chief Secr., 11 Aug. 1924, loc. cit.

135 ibid.

136 ibid.

137 Copy in SMP 7098.

138 Ass. Chief Secr. to Chief Secr., 20 Aug. 1924, loc. cit.

139 For a full account of Ankole see Pirouet (1978), ch. 4. On the kingship see M.R. Doornbos (1978), pp.96ff. cf. also T.S.M. Williams (1966), and the Clayton and Willis Papers, MUL.

140 Minutes of Ankole Church Council, 26 May 1916, Minute Book, Bishop's Office, Mbarara (transl. from Luganda by D. Senono).

141 At the Synod in 1912; see Fisher to Secr. of Synod, Daniell, Hoima, 22 May 1912, Bunyoro Correspondence 1905–1912, Fisher Papers.

142 The course of events is given in Willis to Ag. PC Buganda, P.W. Cooper, 3 Jan. 1917, Bishop's Files: Ab–Ar. Archbishop of Canterbury, Correspondence 1913–1938.

143 cf. Archbishop of Canterbury to Willis, 5 Oct. 1916, loc. cit.

144 Cooper to Willis, 2 Jan. 1917, loc. cit.

145 See summary by J.A. Rowe (1970), p. 43.

146 cf. Streicher to Dep. Commissioner, George Wilson, Villa Maria, 5 Dec. 1907, SMP Conf. 104/1907; see account of Bishop Streicher's work in Uganda by J. Cussac (1955).

147 Mentioned in George Wilson to Governor, 8 Jan. 1908, SMP Conf. 104/1907.

148 Sub-Commissioner Tomkins to George Wilson, 4 Jan. 1908, loc. cit.

149 Tomkins to Wilson, 1 May 1908, loc. cit.

150 Tomkins to Wilson, 13 June 1908, SMP Conf. 16/1909.

151 George Wilson to Governor, 18 June 1908, loc. cit.

152 Governor Hesketh Bell to Wilson, 19 June 1908, loc. cit.

153 Hesketh Bell to George Wilson, 8 July 1908, loc. cit.

154 Wilson to Governor, 18 June 1908, loc. cit.

155 Andereya Bagenda to Ag. Chief Secr., 19 July 1910, SMP 898.

156 Mugwanya to PC Buganda, 1 Aug. 1910, loc. cit. With regard to M's central role in the Catholic church see Cussac, op. cit. p.156f.

157 PC Buganda to Chief Secr., 16 Aug. 1910, loc. cit.

158 See memorandum by Crown Advocate, 26 Aug. 1910, loc. cit.

159 Governor to Chief Secr., 9 Sept. 1910, loc. cit.

160 PC Buganda to Chief Secr., 20 Dec. 1910, loc. cit.

161 Apolo Kagwa and Zakariya Kizito Kisingiri to PC Buganda, 11 Sept. 1913; and Mugwanya to PC, 11 Sept. 1913, both in SMP Conf. 156/1913.

162 Mugwanya, op. cit.

163 See Ag. PC Browning to Chief Secr., 15 Sept. 1913, loc. cit.

164 This aspect was the subject of the three Catholic saza chiefs' complaint to the colonial administration re Apolo Kagwa's treatment of Mugwanya in the case of the Kabula saza. Cyprien M. Luwekula, Nyasi Lule Kyambalange and Aleni Kiimba to PC Buganda, 31 Oct. 1913, SMP Conf. 160 A. For reaction of colonial administration see Ag. PC Browning to Chief Secr., 3 Nov. 1913, loc. cit., and minute by Governor Jackson, 4 Nov. 1913, SMP Conf. 156/1913.

165 Ag. PC Browning to Chief Secr., 15 Sept. 1913 loc. cit.

166 Minute by Governor Jackson, 4 Nov. 1913, with reference to art. 11 in Uganda Agreement. cf. also PC Buganda, Knowles, to Chief Secr., 15 Dec. 1913, SMP Conf. 156/1913.

167 D.C. Baines to PC Buganda, 28 Nov. 1913, loc. cit.

168 Thus PC Buganda to Chief Secr., 6 Dec. 1913, loc. cit.

169 PC Buganda, Knowles, to Chief Secr., 14 Nov. 1913, SMP Conf. 160 A; cf. also Knowles to Chief Secr., 6 Dec. 1913, SMP Conf. 156/1913.

170 Thus stated by PC Buganda, Knowles, to Chief Secr., 15 Dec. 1913, SMP Conf. 156/1913.

171 F.J. Jackson had been Dep. Commissioner to Sir Harry Johnston at the time of the conclusion of the Agreement, 1900. He took office as Governor in 1911.

172 Secr. of State's notes from the interview, dat. 11 March 1914, in CO 536/73–9243/ 1914.

173 cf. CO minute in loc. cit.

174 See PC Buganda, P.W. Cooper, to Chief Secr., 16 Nov. 1916, min. 318, SMP 1483. The question of the Ganda agent was first raised by DC Toro to PC Western Province, 23 Sept. 1915, SMP 330. Re his appointment in 1913 as a punitive measure against Kasagama, see minutes in SMP 3385 (and below, ch.22).

175 Annual Report Buganda 1916–1917, SMP 1138G.

176 Omukama's letter is encl. in Cooper (see n.174).

177 The post fell vacant when the previous holder, Yacobo Musajalumbwa, was appointed Omuwanika (Minister of Finance) instead of Zakariya Kizito Kisingiri who had died. It was even discussed within the colonial administration which candidate would act most independently of religious bias. PC Buganda, P.W. Cooper, much preferred Ham Mukasa, but was overruled by Ag. Governor. Minutes in SMP Conf. 343.

178 cf. Kabaka to PC Buganda, 3 Dec. 1917, min. 352, SMP 1483.

179 Mugwanya's position was made clear in PC Buganda, Cooper, to Chief Secr., 5 Dec. 1917, min. 353, loc. cit.

180 Cooper, op. cit.

181 Mugwanya et al. to Governor, 30 Jan. 1918, SMP 5310 (the letter is six pages long). Parts of this letter are quoted below p.355.

182 Chief Secr. to Governor, 6 Febr. 1918, loc. cit.

183 PC Buganda, Cooper, to Chief Secr., 31 Jan. 1918.

184 Chief Secr. to Governor, 6 Febr. 1918.

185 Minute by Ag. Governor H.R. Wallis, dat. 8 Febr. 1918, loc. cit. F.J. Jackson had left Uganda for good before the vacancy in Kyadondo came up.

186 Ag. Chief Secr. Jarvis to Mugwanya, 9 Febr. 1918, loc. cit.

187 PC Buganda to Chief Secr., 23 Febr. 1918, min. 378, SMP 1483.

188 Ass. Chief Secr. to PC Buganda, 1 March 1918, loc. cit.

189 Mugwanya to Kabaka, 11 June 1919, encl. in PC Buganda, Sturrock, to Chief Secr., 18 July 1919, min. 427, loc. cit.

190 Kabaka to Mugwanya, 16 June 1919, loc. cit. Sturrock commented that the Kabaka on this occasion apparently repeated certain generalizations from his tutor's (Sturrock's) lectures: cf. Sturrock to Chief Secr., 8 Aug. 1919, SMP 5310.

191 Memorandum by Deputy to Governor, Sir W. Morris Carter, dat. 26 July 1919, SMP 5310.

192 Ag. PC Buganda, Sturrock, to Chief Secr., 8 Aug. 1919, loc. cit.

193 Mugwanya to Governor Coryndon, 4 Sept. 1919, loc. cit.

194 It is characteristic that Ag. Governor Wallis in his statement of policy in 1918 recommended open discussion and explanation instead of correspondence which committed the government much more (see n.185).

195 Ag. Chief Secr. T.S. Thomas to Mugwanya, 13 Oct. 1919, loc. cit. See also Thomas to PC Buganda, 18 Oct. 1919, enclosing a copy of Sir Harry Johnston's letter to FO, 6 April 1900.

196 cf. Ag. PC Buganda, Sturrock, to Chief Secr., 1 March 1920, min. 444, SMP 1483.

197 cf. Sturrock to Chief Secr., 22 March 1920, with enclosures, min. 448, loc. cit.

198 Chief Secr. Jarvis to Sturrock, 1 April 1920, min. 449, loc. cit.

199 The Governor instructed that the religion of candidates should not appear on nomination lists from the Lukiko, but only in the PC's covering letter, cf. min. 451, loc. cit.

200 Established by examining relevant minutes in SMP 1483.

201 Ten Muslim leaders to Governor, 8 June 1923, SMP 5310 (official translation). Among the signatories were Prince Badru Kakungulu and the two Muslim saza chiefs.

202 ibid.

203 Letter 30 July, loc. cit.

204 The Lumama of Kabula to Governor, 1 Jan. 1924.

205 Minute in loc. cit., written while on tour in the Masaka District.

206 See census list from 1921, encl. in Ag. Chief Secr. to Governor, 19 July 1927, SMP 5310.

207 See above, p.132. The colonial administration was fully aware of the political significance of the religious distribution of offices. When one of the leading chiefs in 1904 changed from Protestantism to Islam the Dep. Commissioner immediately inquired if he should attach any political consequences to this change. cf. Ag. Sub-Commissioner, Western Province, to Commissioner, 16 Febr. 1904, A14, ESA. See also Steinhart (1977), pp.184f.

208 Hesketh Bell to Dep. Commissioner George Wilson, 13 Febr. 1908, SMP Conf. 46/1908.

209 Collector Haldane to George Wilson, 8 April 1908, loc. cit.

210 Dep. Commissioner George Wilson to Governor, 24 April 1908, loc. cit.

211 Note by George Wilson, 3 June 1908, loc. cit.

212 Hesketh Bell to George Wilson, 26 April 1908, loc. cit. Bell, on the basis of his autobiography which includes passages from his diary, appears to have had closer relations with the Catholic missionaries than with the CMS missionaries. See Bell (1946), esp. ch. 26. Cf. also Cussac (1955), pp.210ff.

213 The rule dat. 8 April 1910 may be found in SMP 541.

214 Re CMS activities in Toro see report by Rev. A.B. Fisher to Commissioner Sadler, 28 May 1902, A22/1, ESA.

215 cf. Chief Secr. to DC Toro, 5 Aug. 1911, SMP 330.

216 Bishop Coadjutor John Forbes to Governor, 24 Oct. 1919, loc. cit.

217 See comments by Pirouet (1978), pp.67f.

218 For some recent accounts see Dunbar (1965); G.N. Uzoigwe (1970); Steinhart (1977), ch. 3; Pirouet (1978), ch.3.

219 cf. Pirouet, op. cit. pp.88ff; Steinhart, op. cit., pp.67–77.

220 Fisher to H.E. Fox, Hoima, 30 Nov. 1905, Book XVI; later repeated in Fisher's Annual Letter to CMS, dat. 30 Nov. 1910, Book XVIII, both in Fisher Papers. cf. also government's appreciation of these trends in the mission's work in Annual Report Northern Province 1910–11 and 1911–12, SMP 2135.

221 George Wilson touched upon the administrative measures introduced in 1905 in his dispatch to Secr. of State, 25 June 1907, CO 536/13–25631/1907.

222 Fisher to Tucker, Hoima, 20 Nov. 1905; and Fisher to Tucker, n.d., but must be from late Nov. 1905, Book XVI. cf. also George Wilson to Fisher, 24 Nov. 1905 (copied); and Wilson to Fisher, Entebbe, 18 March 1906 (original), Correspondence Bunyoro 1905–12, all in Fisher Papers.

223 Fisher to Tucker, Hoima, 4 Dec. 1905, Book XVI, Fisher Papers.

224 ibid.

225 See below, ch. 22. cf. also Pirouet (1978), pp.103ff.

226 cf. Fisher to Baylis, 12 July 1907, no. 190, G3. A7/05. Fisher emphasizes that the new chiefs were much more favourable to the Protestant work, and that several of their best teachers were among the newly appointed, whereas the Catholics only got a few minor appointments.

227 Dep. Commissioner George Wilson to the Collector, Hoima, 14 Jan. 1908, SMP Conf. 7/1908.

228 ibid.

229 Annual Report Northern Province, 1915–1916, SMP 2135 E.

230 Bishop Coadjutor John Forbes to Chief Secr. Jarvis, 20 March 1919, min. 259, SMP 1251.

231 PC Northern Province, Watson, to Chief Secr., 31 May 1919, min. 261; and note by Chief Secr., 14 June 1919, both in SMP 1251.

232 Ag. Chief Secr. T.S. Thomas to Forbes, 25 June 1919, min. 262, loc. cit.

233 Thus Ag. PC Northern Province, Haddon, to Chief Secr., 21 June 1920, min. 273, loc. cit.

234 ibid., and Haddon to Chief Secr., 6 Jan. 1921, loc. cit.

235 See excerpt from Governor's speech to Bunyoro Rukurato, March 1923, SMP 7835; and report in *Uganda Herald*, 30 March 1923.

236 cf. Governor's lack of understanding of the Catholic position in his minute, 7 June 1923, SMP 7835.

237 The colonial administration had reluctantly to admit this when in 1927–8 at the recommendation of the Omukama it approved a Buganda-type solution and allocated one saza to the Catholics. See Omukama and Katikiro of Bunyoro to DC Bunyoro, 30 Aug. 1927; PC Northern Province to Chief Secr., 3 Sept. 1927; and Ag. Chief Secr. to PC, 25 Sept. 1928. The government reserved for itself the option 'at any time if it thinks fit [to] appoint a Protestant chief to Buruli [the saza in question]'. SMP 5310. See also J.R.P. Postlethwaite (1947), pp.114f.

238 See table in Richards (1960), p.124. cf. also Beattie (1971), pp.211f.

239 For one of the latest accounts of Ankole, see Pirouet (1978), ch.4. See also Williams (1966). Primary sources for the start of Protestant work in Ankole are entries 1900–1902 in Journals of Rev. H. Clayton and Rev. J.J. Willis, MUL.

240 See Bishop Streicher to Mr Cunningham, Villa Maria, 23 Febr. 1901; Cunningham to Johnston, 7 March 1901, both in A24/1, ESA; J.J. Willis' Journal, 9 Jan. 1901, MUL. See also Pirouet, op. cit., p.125; and Williams (1965, unpubl. thesis), pp.153f.

241 See S. Karugire (1970), and the thorough discussion of the structure of Ankole society in Doornbos (1978), chs. 2 and 3. See also Steinhart (1977), pp.191ff, 211ff.

242 Doornbos (1978), pp.21f; and Doornbos (1970), p.1111.

243 Doornbos (1978), pp.93ff.

244 For extent of Bahima preponderance in 1907 and also large contingent of non-Banyankore officeholders, see Doornbos (1978), pp.74ff.

245 Bishop Forbes to Governor Coryndon, 18 Sept. 1920, SMP 2071.

246 PC Western Province, P.W. Cooper, to Chief Secr., 30 Sept. 1920, loc. cit.

247 cf. Cooper, op. cit.; and the list of appointments made in Sept. 1920, SMP 2071. Re appointment of a Muslim as saza chief of Bukanga see minutes starting June 1921. The whole issue was mixed up with foreign, especially Ganda, influence in Ankole.

248 See Cooper, op. cit., and Chief Secr. to Bishop Forbes, 8 Oct. 1920, loc. cit.

249 Ankole chiefs to PC Western Province, Cooper, 31 Aug. 1921; and Cooper's answer 29 Sept. 1921, loc. cit.

250 cf. Richards (1960), p.171.

251 Doornbos (1978), pp.86–96, esp. pp.93f; see also pp.75f which gives the ethnic composition of chiefs in 1942 and indicates the Bairu's rather modest progress.

252 See map 2. The administrative division mentioned here appears at least from 1911, cf. minutes in SMP 2070. See also H.B. Thomas & R. Scott (1935), pp.434ff (dealing with Eastern Province). Bukedi district was divided into three districts in 1923. M.L. Pirouet (1978) takes Bukedi to include Teso and Lango following missionary practice prior to 1914 (pp.172, 225, n.14). See also F.G. Burke (1964), p.204. No group of people called themselves Bakedi; it was a nickname adopted by the Baganda; cf. Report of Archdeaconry of Busoga, Sept. 1919, Bishop's Files: Synods.

253 See analysis in J. Tosh (1973, 1978) presenting a case study from Lango. Re terminology see Elizabeth Colson (1969).

254 See L.A. Fallers (1965), *passim.*

255 Section on Busoga is mainly based upon Tom Tuma (1973, unpubl. thesis), and Tuma (1976). See also D. Mudoola (1978).

256 Archdeacon Walker to Commissioner Sadler, 15 March 1904, explaining the project and asking for support to build a house for the six chiefs. See also Tucker to Sadler, 13 June 1904, thanking for a grant of £60, both in A22/1, ESA.

257 See table V: principal chiefs in Busoga 1907, in Tuma (1973).

258 Note the very different impressions which the Basoga had of the two missions; Tuma, op. cit., pp.132ff; see also Bishop Biermans to Chief Secr., 29 Jan. 1913, SMP 3091. The conviction that if a man became a Catholic he could not obtain a chieftainship was widely held even in the middle of the 1920s; cf. Bishop Campling to Chief Secr. Jarvis, 5 May 1926, SMP 5310.

259 See memorandum by Governor Jackson, 30 July 1913, where he added that this was the only right left to the Busoga 'Kabakalets', SMP 1760/08.

260 Bishop Biermans to Chief Secr., 29 Jan. 1913; Fr Matthews to Chief Secr., 26 Febr.

1913, both in SMP 3091. The incident is reported by Tuma (1973), pp.228ff.

261 PC Eastern Province, F. Spire, to Chief Secr., 2 May 1913, SMP 1561/08.

262 See Ag. Chief Secr., T.S. Thomas, to PC Eastern Province, Guy Eden, 27 Febr. 1920, min. 307, SMP 2070.

263 Besides the list produced by Mudoola (1978), see Tuma (1973), p. 256 for 1940, and Richards (1960), p.95 for 1960.

264 When the Catholic Bishop Campling in 1926 again voiced Catholic grievances and pointed to the very small number of Catholic (even minor) chiefs, the colonial administration restated its policy of selecting the best man and did not take any further action. Campling to Chief Secr. Jarvis, 5 May 1926; Jarvis to Campling, 5 June 1926, both in SMP 5310. cf. Mudoola, op. cit., pp.27f.

265 Clearly experienced by the colonial administration re the establishment of native courts; cf. memorandum by P.W. Perryman, Native Courts in Bukedi, dat. 21 Dec. 1921, min. 181, SMP 907/08. For Lango see J. Tosh (1973) and (1978).

266 For this point and for the whole section on Bukedi I am indebted to Dr Michael Twaddle (1967, unpubl. thesis, *passim*); see also Twaddle (1969a), pp.194ff. Re other districts see Pirouet (1978), ch. 6 (esp. p. 182) on Teso; and John Tosh, op. cit. on Lango.

267 See esp. Pirouet, op. cit. pp.183f, 186 on Teso; Tosh (1978), pp.192ff on Lango.

268 See esp. Twaddle (1967), ch. 10.

269 It was advertised that from the middle of 1920 the withdrawal of Buganda agents from Teso would start, but the number of Protestant chiefs was the same in 1920 and in 1925. cf. PC Eastern Province, Guy Eden, to Chief Secr., n.d., but from position in file must be July 1920, min. 326, SMP 2070.

270 See figures in Eden to Chief Secr., 2 May 1921, min. 343 (Bukedi), 4 May 1923 (Bukedi), 6 June 1925, min. 453 (Teso), all SMP 2070. See also optimistic forecast in Report of Archdeaconry of Busoga, Sept. 1919, Bishop's Files: Synods.

271 In 1926 it was pointed out that there was not a single Catholic saza chief in the whole of the Eastern and Northern Provinces; cf. Fr Kiggen, Ngora, to DC Soroti, 14 April 1926, min. 20, SMP 5310; cf. also Campling (see n.264).

272 See also more recent figures in A.I. Richards (1960), p.275 (the Gisu); and F.G. Burke (1964), p.153 (Teso).

273 This point has recently been strongly emphasized by Pirouet (1978), pp.181ff. See also Burke, p.154; and Tosh (1973), p.483.

274 Re Teso see Joan Vincent (1977), p.153.

275 Policy aptly outlined by Bishop Willis in 1925; see Willis (1925), pp. 64–8. cf. also Willis' 'Charge to the Missionaries 1917', *Uganda Notes*, Oct. 1917; and his contemporary account of pioneer work in Ankole, Willis' Journal, 9 Jan. 1901.

276 Chief Secr. Weatherhead to Bishop Willis, 8 Sept. 1932, in file called Uganda Diocese. Deaneries B. 9. Bwekula 1932–35, Namirembe Arch.

277 The difference between 'the balance of power policy' in Buganda and 'the selection of the best man policy' in other areas was clearly outlined when in 1927 a plan was mooted to divide Bunyoro into religious spheres of interest; cf. Chief Secr. to Governor, 20 Oct. 1927, SMP 5310 (see above, n.237).

278 The difficulty in coming to grips with the religious factor is revealed in various statements connected with appointments of chiefs; cf., for instance, PC Western Province, P.W. Cooper's outline of policy to the PCs' conference 1923, dat. 26 June 1923, SMP 3841C. See discussion of the perpetual Catholic inferiority by S.R. Karugire (1980), pp.134ff.

279 This qualitative approach has been hinted at by Pirouet (1978), pp.67f (Toro), p.186 (Teso). See also Tuma (1973, unpubl. thesis), *passim*.

280 Tucker to Baylis, 16 Oct. 1899 (original missing, see Precis, G3. A7/P1). See also Hansen (1980), pp.244f.

281 Tucker to Baylis, 29 May 1909, no. 211, G3. A7/07.

282 cf. Laws and Regulations of the Church of Uganda, 1917.

283 See minutes of Synods, Jan. 1921 and Jan. 1924, Minute Book, MUL.

284 Minutes of Synod, Sept. 1919, MUL. cf. report in *Uganda Herald*, 26 Sept. 1919, and in *Uganda Notes*, Oct. 1919. Re office as President of Busoga Lukiko see minutes in SMP 7318.

285 Synod Agenda 1924, encl. in Minute Book, MUL.

286 See minutes from 27 June 1903, Toro Church Council Minute Book, in local church arch., Kabarole, Toro. See also Steinhart (1977), p.121, and Pirouet (1978), pp.57f.

287 See statement from 1907 by Rev. G.R. Blackledge, quoted in A. Wandira (1972), p.74; and Report of Toro Deanery 1919, submitted to Synod 1919, in Bishop's Files: Synods.

288 Rev. A.B. Fisher to Bishop Tucker, 20 Nov. 1905, Book XVI, Fisher Papers.

289 Meeting 20 Jan. 1905; the Omukama agreed to write to the chiefs asking them to support the building of a new church in Hoima. Meeting 6 Dec. 1916: the Omukama's support was called upon re building of churches and schools; cf. also meeting 1 June 1920. Meeting 2 July 1919: the Omukama was informed that there was no money to pay church workers. Minute Book of Bunyoro Church Council in Church Office, Hoima.

290 Report from Bunyoro Deanery 1919, written by Rural Dean, Rev. Bowers (cf. n.287).

291 Minute Book of the National Church Council of Ankole, minutes from April 1914 onwards, Bishop's Office, Mbarara.

292 Report from Ankole Deanery, written by Rural Dean, Rev. Lewin (cf. n.287).

293 Fisher to Tucker, 20 Nov. 1905.

294 The Minute Book which I have seen ends in Dec. 1904 (see n.286). cf. Steinhart, op. cit., p.121; and Pirouet, op. cit., pp.57f.

295 cf. Minute Book (n.291).

296 cf. Bishop Tucker's suggestion at Synod meeting, June 1907, which was really a meeting only of missionaries and Ganda representatives; it was approved to replace the words 'Mengo Church Council' with 'Synod' in the provisional constitution. See Minute Book of Diocesan Synod, MUL. See also Tucker to Baylis, 29 June 1907, no. 181, G3. A7/05; and E. Millar to Baylis, 1 Oct. 1908, no. 229, G3. A7/06. At the meeting in 1909 Tucker made it clear that the Mengo Church Council could no longer legislate for the whole church.

297 Laws and Regulations of the Church of Uganda, 1917, p. 103.

298 Commenting on the participation in the constituting Synod in 1909, Bishop Tucker emphasized in particular that Bunyoro, Toro, Ankole and Busoga, which in earlier days had been hostile towards Buganda, had sent both clergy and laymen to the meeting. Tucker to Baylis, 24 April 1909, no. 173, G3. A7/07.

299 See minutes from Synod meetings 1909–23.

300 e.g. report of Synod, June 1917, in *Uganda Notes*, July 1917, listing Katikiros of Buganda and Bunyoro as participants. See also *Uganda Notes*, April 1921, with report of 1921 Synod.

301 See report in *Uganda Herald*, 26 Sept. 1919, where the presence of four Kabakas and four Katikiros is especially mentioned.

302 Minutes in SMP 4124. e.g. Secr. of Synod, Rev. Daniell, and Secr. CMS Mission, Rev. Rowling, to Chief Secr., 31 Dec. 1920; and Chief Secr. to Secr. CMS, 6 Jan. 1921.

303 Synod Agenda 1924, encl. in minutes of Synod 1924, MUL.

304 Quotation from account of 1909 Synod, *Uganda Notes*, June 1909.

305 Minutes of Synod, April 1909, MUL. cf. also *Uganda Notes*, June 1909.

306 Members of the mission were clearly aware of the lack of equal representation in the central body; see editorial, *Uganda Notes*, May 1913, p. 110; see also minutes of Synod, July 1912, par. 28.

307 Resolutions passed by Synod, July 1913, copy under no. 146, G3. A7/010. cf. Laws and Regulations, pars. 41, 42.

308 This was admitted in the report of the 1917 Synod, *Uganda Notes*, July 1917. In his Charge to the Missionaries, 1917, Willis admitted that there was not a single representative from Bunyoro, neither layman nor clergy: *Uganda Notes*, Oct. 1917.

309 In its report from the 1917 Synod *Uganda Notes* (July 1917) hinted at 'certain difficult racial differences that had threatened the unity of the Church in Uganda'. In his charge to the Synod Bishop Willis admitted openly that Bunyoro and Toro did not approve of the Diocesan Council being composed entirely of Europeans and Baganda. Minutes of Synod, June 1917.

310 See minutes from 1917 Synod.

311 cf. Bishop's opening speech to Synod. In his manuscript, encl. in the Minute Book, he expressed himself in even stronger terms.

312 Minutes of Synod, June 1917; cf. also *Uganda Notes*, July 1917.

313 The list of Diocesan Council members after the Synod 1924 is less complete than the previous ones. It is only possible to identify two minor chiefs and no saza chief, which emphasizes the trend registered from 1917. Minutes of Synod, Jan. 1924.

314 See report of Synod 1917, *Uganda Notes*, July 1917. When *Uganda Notes* (July 1919, p.63) commented on the change it was even implied that the influence of the Diocesan Council had declined.

315 Re advisory boards and their special functions, see Laws and Regulations of the Church of Uganda, 1917.

316 Lists of members from the following years would have been useful to sustain this suggestion, but they have not been found.

317 Re Board of Education see Wandira (1972), pp.240ff. Concerning the Board of Missions it was requested at the Synod in 1913 that more non-Europeans should be nominated as most members were Europeans. cf. report from the Board of Missions, encl. in minutes of Synod 1913.

318 When the Bunyoro Church Council in 1916 asked whether clergy and catechists could hold chieftainships, the Diocesan Council answered that only honorary chieftainships were permitted, but nobody was allowed to receive payment in both capacities: *Diocesan Gazette*, May 1916. In 1921 it was discussed whether a clergyman rightly could hold the position of chief. In the actual case a chief who had been an ordained deacon for 20 years now wanted to function as a priest along with his chiefly duties 'and thus become the leader of his people both spiritually and civilly'. The Diocesan Council rejected by a great majority the suggestion that anybody could hold two offices which were really incompatible; it was necessary to make a choice between the two. Report in *Uganda Notes*, Jan. 1921, p. 4.

319 cf. Bishop Tucker to Governor Hesketh Bell, 3 Dec. 1907, copy in CO 536/26–24876; Archdeacon Baskerville, Memorandum to Uganda Development Commission, Dec. 1919, Bishop's Files: K–L. Land. Memoranda. In both cases the members of the

Board of Education were listed in order to emphasize the church's capacity and its close links with African society.

320 Editorial, *Uganda Notes*, March 1913.

321 *Uganda Notes*, July 1904, with report from Missionaries' Conference.

322 Minutes of Diocesan Synod, 5 June 1906.

323 See resolutions from Synod 1909, no. 223, G3. A7/05; and report of the proceedings, *Uganda Notes*, June 1909.

324 Willis (1913), pp.24f.

325 Minutes of Synod, Sept. 1919.

326 Minutes of Finance Board, 7 Jan. 1913, presented to Synod July 1913, Minute Book, MUL.

327 *Uganda Notes*, April 1913 and Dec. 1913.

328 See Katikiro Apolo Kagwa's circular, dat. 8 Jan. 1914, encl. in Millar to Manley, 30 Jan. 1914, no. 38, G3. A7/010.

329 Minutes of Synod, June 1907.

330 The Bishop's Charge to the Synod, June 1917.

331 Editorial, *Uganda Notes*, July 1918.

332 Report of Toro Deanery to Synod 1919, Bishop's Files: Synods.

333 Minutes of National Church Council of Ankole, 31 July 1919, Minute Book, Bishop's Office, Mbarara.

334 Minutes of Bunyoro Church Council, 28 Dec. 1922, Church Office, Hoima.

335 The plan is mentioned in Willis to Manley, 7 March 1922, no. 42, G3. A7/1922; and its first phase is recorded in report of Diocesan Council for 1921–23, presented to Synod, Jan. 1924, encl. in Minute Book, MUL.

336 Encyclical Letter from Synod dat. 25 Jan. 1921 and enclosed in minutes of Synod 1921.

337 cf. Twaddle (1969); D.A. Low (1971a), pp.144ff.

338 See minutes dealing with financial matters from Synods 1906, 1907 and 1909. cf. also Hansen (1980). Tom Tuma (1973, unpubl. thesis) has touched on the strained relations between chiefs and church workers in Busoga (pp.244f).

339 This controversy is still in need of a scholarly investigation. Besides material in the CMS Arch. the course of events appears from the Minutes of Synods 1919 and 1921. Other elements are the tension between Buganda and the rest of the Protectorate and the clergy's dissatisfaction with missionary leadership, not least the Bishop himself.

340 From Bishop's Charge to the Synod, June 1917.

341 Minutes of Synod, June 1917, pars. 21–2.

342 ibid.

343 Minutes of Synod, June 1907.

344 Minutes of Synod, April 1909.

345 Willis to Ag. Chief Secr. Eliot, 2 June 1922, SMP 7545.

346 Report to Synod 1924 from Estates Board, in Synod's Minute Book, MUL.

347 The Omulamuzu, Stanislaus Mugwanya, and other leading Catholic chiefs to Governor, 30 Jan. 1918, SMP 5310. The context of the letter was given earlier (pp.329f). The Kago mentioned is Yakobo Musajalumbwa, recently appointed Omuwanika. When he speaks about the Church Lukiko he must have the Diocesan Council in mind, of which Apolo Kagwa was a member until 1917.

348 e.g. PC Buganda, when he comments on the Kabaka's complaint that the Katikiro, Sir Apolo Kagwa, takes all matters to the missionaries before they have been discussed in the Lukiko. Kabaka Daudi Chwa to Protectorate Government, April 1915, and subsequent minutes, SMP Conf. 255/1915.

349 Minute to Chief Secr., 11 May 1921, in which a letter of complaint from the PC Western Province, P.W. Cooper, 4 May 1921, is commented upon. SMP 6876.

350 Cooper (n.349) forwards the DC's criticism. A little later Cooper again expressed uneasiness when Diocesan Council passed a resolution dealing with commutation of luwalo and wanted it forwarded to Buganda Lukiko. Bishop Willis to Ag. Chief Secr. Jarvis, 20 Oct. 1921; and Cooper to Jarvis, 7 Nov. 1921, both in SMP 6111.

351 Minute to Chief Secr., 11 May 1921 SMP 6876.

352 See Bishop Willis' instructions about new procedure in Willis to the Secr. of Synod, Rev. E.S. Daniell, 15 July 1921, SMP 6876.

353 See various officials' comments on Willis' letter of instruction, in SMP 6876. It was on that occasion that the Chief Secr. pointed out that in case of friction the government had the possibility of blocking the grant-in-aid to the mission's educational work.

354 Secrs. of Synod, Daniell and Luboyera, to Chief Secr., 5 Febr. 1924, and the following minutes, in SMP 8152. Even as early as 1921 Willis acted in accordance with the new procedure, when he first forwarded resolution from Diocesan Council regarding commutation of luwalo to the Chief Secr. Willis to Chief Secr., 20 Oct. 1921, SMP 6111.

355 Kabaka Daudi Chwa to Governor Coryndon, 12 March 1918, SMP Conf. 363/1918.

356 Annual Report Northern Province 1913–1914, by PC, Guy Eden, SMP 2135 C. Tosh (1978), ch. 7, has in relation to Lango given a detailed analysis of the shift of emphasis in the chiefs' dual source of legitimacy.

357 See, e.g., the following witnesses, who gave evidence before the Uganda Development Commission in 1919: 48th witness J.C.R. Sturrock, and 51st witness Prince Joseph (cousin of the Kabaka), in SMP 5860.

358 In the case of Buganda this development has in particular been emphasized by Low (1971a), pp.144ff.

359 Reported by P.W. Cooper, PC Buganda, in letter to Chief Secr., 31 Jan. 1918, SMP 5310.

360 Tuma (1973, unpubl. thesis) touched upon some of the same factors and speaks of a process of disengagement on the part of Christian chiefs (pp.244ff).

361 The employment of the boundary concept has been stimulated by readings in political science and social anthropology, especially D. Easton (1965a and b), and F. Barth (1969). I have in earlier works discussed its employment in more detail; Hansen (1977, 1980).

362 In making the distinction between the institutional and societal levels of analysis I have been stimulated by K. Lockard (1975, unpubl. thesis), esp. introductory chapter. cf. also distinction between the two topics church–state and religion–politics in A. Mazrui (1966–7).

Part V   Indirect inputs: parallelism and reciprocity

18 *Parallelism and coordination in administration*

1 See Ali A. Mazrui (1973) and Susan Eckstein (1977).

2 Bishop Tucker to Commissioner Sadler, 9 Dec. 1903, A22/1, and Sadler to Tucker, 5

March 1904, A23/1, both in ESA. See also Tucker to Baylis, 30 Dec. 1904, no. 19, G3. A7/04. For general account of start of work in Acholi see M.L. Pirouet (1978), ch. 5.

3 For the Nandi and their conflicts with the advancing colonial system see A.T. Matson (1972); cf. also D.A. Low (1963), pp.26ff.

4 cf. Governor of British East Africa to Tucker, 7 Febr. 1908, extract under no. 128; and Tucker to Baylis, 7 April 1908, no. 123, both in G3. A7/06.

5 See minutes of Executive Committee of Uganda Mission, 9 March 1908 and 1 Febr. 1909 for a positive response; Minute Book, MUL. For a more critical attitude see Walker to Baylis, 16 Febr. 1909, no. 111, G3. A7/07; and minutes of Executive Committee, 5 July 1909.

6 Minutes of Missionary Committee, 1 May 1911, no. 102; and Memorandum on the Nandi Mission by C.W. Hattersley, dat. 16 Aug. 1911, no. 134, both in G3. A7/09. Reference to the failure in Ag. PC Nyanza Province to Chief Secr., 7 Nov. 1913, PC/NZA 1/66/1, Kenya National Archives, Nairobi.

7 cf. also reopening of work in Acholi in 1913 and the selection of Gulu as headquarters parallel with the government; Pirouet, op. cit., pp.162f.

8 Minutes of Executive Committee, 1 Oct. 1900 (Minute Book, p.254).

9 Ag. Secr. of Uganda Mission, Rev. J. Roscoe, to Baylis, 8 Nov. 1900, no. 4, G3. A7/02.

10 See reference to an incident in Toro in 1901 in Dep. Commissioner George Wilson to Commissioner, Hoima, 17 Oct. 1905, CO 536/6–19337/1906.

11 This point was emphasized by E. Millar, Ag. Secr. of Uganda Mission, to Baylis, 14 Febr. 1901, no. 89, G3. A7/02. See also, re situation in Acholi, Kitching to Baylis, 2 June 1904, no. 154, G3. A7/04.

12 Rev. A.B. Fisher's protest was even recorded in the Annual Report Northern Province 1912–1913, SMP 2135B.

13 When the colonial administration gave up the station at Patiko, the CMS mission found it necessary to move its own headquarters in the Nile Province, and select a new site near the government station at Nimule. Minutes of Executive Committee, 8 April 1907, no. 124; and Walker to Baylis, 13 April 1907, no. 125, both in G3. A7/05.

14 Minutes of the Synod, July 1910, Minute Book, MUL.

15 See also A.D. Roberts (1962); and M.S.M. Kiwanuka (1974).

16 See Joan Vincent (1977) for an illustrative case study of location of boundaries in Teso District; cf. also J.R. Postlethwaite (1947), p.44.

17 Minutes of Board of Missions 1912–1913, encl. in Minutes of Synod, July 1913, and as such endorsed by the Synod.

18 H.B. Hansen (1977), ch.5.

19 See Ag. Governor Tomkins to Secr. of State, 26 May 1909, CO 536/26–22204/1909. For Lango in general see esp. D.A. Low (1965), pp. 104ff; and J. Tosh (1978), one of the latest accounts. See also H.B. Thomas & R. Scott (1935), pp.466ff. For establishment of colonial administration see K. Ingham (1955) and J. Tosh (1973).

20 cf. Pirouet (1978), p.165; and Tosh (1978), pp.192f.

21 Memorandum by E.L. Scott, dat. 23 April 1914, Eastern Province Minute Paper 10/13, ESA. I am grateful to Dr Michael Twaddle, who has kindly given me access to his personal notes from this file.

22 e.g. Report of Educational Conference 1915, pp. 3f, copy in MUL; and under no. 122, G3 A7/1915; J.J. Willis (1925), pp.29f.

23 One difficulty was landholdings under the different colonial systems; see correspond-

ence in SMP 1899. cf. also discussion of whole issue in Board of Missions, minutes enclosed in minutes of Synod July 1913.

24 Minutes of Synod, Sept. 1919.

25 The system is described in Willis to Manley, 8 Oct. 1917, no. 140, G3. A7/1917.

26 In the report from the Diocesan Council for the years 1921–3 it was stated that Bukedi and Teso had become full deaneries; report enclosed in minutes of Synod, Jan. 1924.

27 Report of Educational Conference 1915 (see n.21). See also Tom Tuma (1973, unpubl. thesis), pp.185f.

28 Thus Willis, op. cit. See also J.V. Taylor (1958), pp.77f.

29 Laws and Regulations of the Church of Uganda, 1917, pp.74f. See also Archdeacon Baskerville to PC Buganda, 9 Oct. 1917, Office of the PC Kampala, no. 1318, ESA.

30 The distinction between the organizational definition of boundaries and the consciousness of a boundary has been developed in my earlier work; Hansen (1977).

19 Centralization versus decentralization

1 The divergencies within the mission are clearly spelled out in Walker to Baylis, 26 Aug. 1899, no. 196, G3. A7/01; cf. also M.L. Pirouet (1978), pp.56ff.

2 ibid.

3 Tucker to Baylis, 23 March 1899, no. 101, G3 A7/01.

4 A.B. Lloyd to Baylis, Bunyoro, 2 Sept. 1901, no. 219; and H.E. Maddox to Baylis, Toro, 29 Sept. 1901, no. 225. See also ms. by Dr A.R. Cook from the same period under no. 211 (later pr. in *Church Missionary Intelligencer*, Feb. 1902), all in G3. A7/02. Lutoro and Lunyoro were considered to be very close to each other and the term Lunyoro was then preferred because the language was spoken by most people: see Tucker to Baylis, 10 Aug. 1900, no. 170, G3. A7/02.

5 Tucker, op. cit., enclosing a memorandum on the language in Toro, dat. Febr. 1900. Tucker allowed two missionaries to pass their language examination in Lunyoro instead of Luganda; see Walker to Baylis, 9 Sept. 1901, no. 204, G3. A7/02.

6 Thus Walker to Baylis, 19 Aug. 1901, no. 199; 24 Aug. 1901, no. 200; and 26 Sept 1901, no. 218, all in G3. A7/02.

7 Walker to Baylis, 24 Aug. 1901.

8 Walker to Baylis, 19 Aug. 1901.

9 F.J. Jackson to Walker, 6 Nov. 1901, copy under no. 257, G3. A7/02; cf. reference to Walker's letter in Jackson to Secr. of State, 25 Jan. 1902, FO 2/589.

10 Dep. Commissioner George Wilson to Secr. of State, 21 April 1906, copy in CO 536/6–19340. This represented an old trend in government policy, as a scheme for a Central Council was discussed as early as 1899; see Wilson to Berkeley, Kampala, 8 Febr. 1899; Berkeley to Ag. Commissioner Ternan, 12 April 1899; and Ternan to Wilson, 4 May 1899, all in Buganda Residency Arch., ESA.

11 Article on language issue by Rev. F. Rowling in *Uganda Notes*, Aug. 1907; cf. Governor Jackson to Secr. of State, 4 July 1912, min. 16, SMP 134.

12 This aspect of mission policy constitutes the main theme in Pirouet (1978). With regard to government policy see A.D. Roberts (1962).

13 For the Toro situation, esp. the question of language, see Tucker to Baylis, 10 Aug. 1900, no. 170; and memorandum of interview between Tucker and Baylis, 8 Nov. 1901, no. 216, both in G3. A7/02. Another feature is that the Parent Committee questioned the suitability of the Mengo Church Council to perform such an overall function; see Baylis to Walker, 18 Nov. 1901, Letterbook I, p. 270, G3. A7/L 1.

14 Besides the recognition of local Church Councils in Bunyoro, Toro and Ankole, at the Synod 1910 the three areas also got permission to have their own church funds; cf. Tucker to Baylis, 24 April 1909, no. 173, G3. A7/07. The principle that each district should raise and administer its own funds was reaffirmed at the Synod 1913, cf. *Uganda Notes*, Dec. 1913.

15 The dilemma was described with remarkable clarity and frankness in an unsigned article in *Uganda Notes*, May 1913; cf. also Willis (1913), 'Policy of the Uganda Mission, 1912', p.9. In Review of the Year 1916 the same theme was touched upon under the heading 'Relation to daughter Churches', p. 9 (under no. 54, G3. A7/1917). Willis returned to it in his 'Charge to the Missionaries 1917', *Uganda Notes*, Oct. 1917.

16 The integrating capacity of Christianity and the church was discussed in *Uganda Notes*, July 1917, p. 94, in connection with a report from the recent Synod.

17 ibid.

18 See Bishop Willis, 'A United Church in Uganda', *The East and West*, vol. 12, 1914, pp.199–208.

19 At the Synod in 1919, and hailed as a remarkable event, four Kabakas and four Katikiros from various parts of the Protectorate were brought together: *Uganda Herald*, 26 Sept. 1919.

20 J.J. Willis (1925), pp.30f.

21 Ag. Commissioner George Wilson to Secr. of State, 21 April 1906, CO 536/6–19340/1906.

22 Governor Hesketh Bell to Secr. of State, 12 April 1909, CO 536/26–16222/1909.

23 ibid.; and Ag. Governor to Secr. of State, 27 May 1910, CO 536/33–19361/1910.

24 Ag. Chief Secr. Eliot to PCs, 20 July 1921, SMP 6956.

25 PC Western Province, P.W. Cooper, to Chief Secr., 16 Aug. 1921, loc. cit.

26 ibid.

27 PC Eastern Province to Chief Secr., 1 Sept. 1921; and P.W. Perryman, 20 Sept. 1921, both in SMP 6956.

28 Perryman, op. cit.

29 ibid.

30 PC Eastern Province, Guy Eden, to Chief Secr., 29 July 1921; Labour Commissioner E.L. Scott to Chief Secr., 16 Aug. 1921; PC Buganda, Sturrock, to Chief Secr., 23 Sept. 1921, all in SMP 6956.

31 Eden, op. cit., and Scott, op. cit.

32 Eden, op. cit.

33 Scott, op. cit.

34 Sturrock, op. cit.

35 ibid.

36 Eden, op. cit.

37 ibid., and Sturrock, op. cit.

38 See memorandum by Governor Coryndon, 7 April 1922, SMP 6956.

39 Minutes in SMP 3841B.

40 ibid.

41 See minute by Ass. Secr. for Native Affairs, E.L. Scott, 11 Aug. 1922, SMP 7405.

42 See dispatch to CO, 22 Sept. 1922; cf. also the so-called 'Editorial' from Jan. 1923 inviting subscriptions; both in SMP 7405.

43 cf. PCs' Conference 1924, SMP 3841; Ag. Chief Secr. Perryman to Chief Secr., 7 March 1924, SMP 7405.

44 For a similar characteristic see R.C. Pratt (1965), pp.505f.

45 The dichotomy within the church between a centralizing and a decentralizing tendency and subsequently its limited capacity to neutralize ethnic boundaries has been discussed in H.B. Hansen (1977), pp.40, 57, and ch.11.

20 Relationships with the African sub-systems

1 The defining of the boundary between the mission and the church has been the subject of H.B. Hansen (1980).

2 Memorandum on interview between CMS Parent Committee and Col. Hayes Sadler, *Church Missionary Intelligencer*, Dec. 1904, p.914.

3 cf. J.B. Purvis to Baylis, 18 Oct. 1898; and Archdeacon Walker to Baylis, 22 June 1899, no. 151, both in G3. A7/01.

4 See G.F. Engholm (1968, unpubl. thesis), pp.50ff; and R.C. Pratt (1965), pp.527ff. cf. also D. Apter (1961), pp.161ff.

5 Engholm, op. cit. The Ganda leaders expressed strong opposition to the establishment of the Legislative Council as they feared that it would violate the Uganda Agreement. See Apter, op. cit., pp.165f.

6 ibid.

7 PCs' Conference 1922 and 1923. No action was taken; cf. Chief Secr. to PCs, 4 March 1924, all in SMP 3841 B and C.

8 See in particular Willis to Manley, 22 Sept. 1919, no. 122, G3. A7/1919.

9 cf. *Uganda Notes*, April 1921, reporting on the 1921 Synod.

10 Rev. J. Roscoe to Ass. Chief Secr. T.S. Thomas, 20 Nov. 1919, SMP Conf. 462. Willis admitted that the strife had brought the church closer to a split than ever before; Willis to Manley, 22 Sept. 1919 (n.8).

11 T.S. Thomas to Roscoe, 1 Dec. 1919, SMP Conf. 462.

12 Minute to Chief Secr., 11 May 1921, SMP 6876.

13 A number of files in ESA dealing with the Malaki church from 1914 onwards have been consulted. See also F.B. Welbourn (1961), ch. 3 (for the figures, p. 43); and below, pp.440ff.

14 Roscoe, op. cit.; extracts of letter from Rev. Grace, 5 July 1922, encl. in Intelligence Officer RCS to Governor, 11 July 1922, SMP Conf. 462.

15 See in particular PC Buganda, J.C.R. Sturrock, to Chief Secr., 27 Sept. 1921, copy encl. in Ag. Governor to Secr. of State, 30 Sept. 1921 (marked secret), CO 537/949. The same point is made by J.H. Driberg in his otherwise grossly exaggerating memorandum on the Young Baganda Association, 23 April 1920 (secret), CO 537/947–57581.

16 Roscoe, op. cit; Grace, op. cit. The latter stated bluntly: 'I feel that after education, a well informed Intelligence Dept. is one of the most effective forces in the growth and government of a country. Nothing fills a native with more confidence or healthy fear than to know that you know all about him . . . '

17 Minute by Governor, 28 Nov. 1923, SMP 956; cf. minutes from same year in SMP 6812.

18 Willis to Ag. Chief Secr., 25 Oct. 1922, SMP 9555.

19 Land (Perpetual Succession) Ordinance of 1909, Laws of Uganda Protectorate,

p.1147. The three European Trustees were appointed in 1913; see Willis' memorandum on relations between mission, church and government, dat. 2 Nov. 1925, SMP 8897.

20 Willis to Ag. Chief Secr. Eliot, 10 Oct. 1922, SMP 9555. It seems that Willis here made a mistake by referring to the Church of England Trustees Ordinance of 1908, which only covered churches for Europeans and specifically stated that trustees should be Europeans; the mistake did not influence the final outcome.

21 Willis to Eliot, 25 Oct. 1922, loc. cit.

22 Excerpts from meeting of Executive Council, 20 Oct. 1922 and 17 Nov. 1922, loc. cit.; cf. also Eliot to Willis, 18 Nov. 1922, Bishop's Files: K–L. Land 1912–1913.

23 Included in Willis' memorandum on relations between mission, church and government (see n.19).

24 Dr A.R. Cook to Principal Medical Officer, 13 May 1923, SMP 4689.

25 Ass. Secr. for Native Affairs, E.L. Scott, to Chief Secr., 29 May 1923, loc. cit.

26 Minutes of Synod, Jan. 1924; Secrs. of Synod, E.S. Daniell and F. Luboyera, to Chief Secr., 5 Febr. 1924, SMP 8152.

27 Ag. Chief Secr. to Secr. CMS, Boulton Ladbury, 4 July 1924; and Ladbury to Chief Secr., 20 Aug. 1924.

28 Willis, Memorandum . . . (see n.19) and the officials' comments, in SMP 8897. It is remarkable that Willis admitted that 'a mixed body like the Board of Education, in which the native members largely preponderate, should not be trusted with the increasingly large sums of money given in the form of educational grants'. Willis, Memorandum on Position of NAC Schools, dat. 20 Oct. 1925, no. 131, G3. A7/1925.

29 Directly stated by Attorney General in minute to Chief Secr., 16 Nov. 1925, loc. cit.

30 E.L. Scott to Chief Secr., 20 Dec. 1925, SMP 8961.

31 Hansen (1980).

32 Both points are explicitly singled out in J. Britton, 'Elementary Education in Uganda', *Church Missionary Review*, April 1917, pp.186ff.

33 The apparent absence of African pressure, which to a large extent may be ascribed to the chiefs' dominant position in the church, has been discussed in Hansen, op. cit., pp.268ff.

34 Willis (1913), 'Policy of the Uganda Mission, 1912', pp.1, 5. cf. Willis, 'Need of Reinforcements', *Church Missionary Review*, Febr. 1913, p. 88. See also Willis to Manley, 17 Dec. 1918, no. 8, G3. A7/1919.

35 Review of 1912, *Uganda Notes*, 1913, pp.10f.

36 Rev. J. Roscoe to Manley, Norfolk 19 Sept. 1912 (marked private and confidential), no. 154, G3. A7/09.

37 Recommendations of Sub-Committee on Lines of Future Action, 18 April 1913, no. 93, G3. A7/010.

38 Memorandum by Col. Kenyon, Aug. 1913, no. 159, G3. A7/010 (precis).

39 Rev. Blackledge to Manley, 1 April 1915, no. 70, G3. A7/1915, commenting on Archdeacon Baskerville's experiment in Kyagwe.

40 The CMS Africa Secr. quoted Bishop Willis as holding such an opinion in Manley to Willis, 17 July 1917, Letterbook III, p. 404, G3. A7/L3.

41 Rev. Rowling to Manley, 9 Sept. 1919, no. 112, G3. A7/1919, reporting from the Missionaries' Conference.

42 A.L. Kitching, 'The Present Situation in Uganda', *Church Missionary Review*, 1921, p. 303. See also Willis to Manley, 7 March 1922, no. 42; and minutes of Missionary Committee, 3 Aug. 1922, no. 86, both in G3. A7/1922.

43 ibid.

44 Manley to Willis, 1 Febr. 1922, with memorandum from CMS Committee enclosed: Certain Questions regarding the Devolution of Responsibility in the Church of Uganda (copy in Willis to Manley, 7 March 1922, no. 42, G3. A7/1922). See also Ladbury to Manley, 15 Aug. 1922, no. 94.

45 Willis, Kitching and Boulton Ladbury to Manley, 10 Jan. 1922, no. 19, loc. cit.

46 Minutes of Missionary Committee, 8 Dec. 1921, no. 5, loc. cit.; and J.V. Taylor (1958), p. 89.

47 Willis, Kitching and Ladbury to Manley, 10 Jan. 1922. The issue was discussed and approved by the Rural Deans' Conference in 1921, see report in *Uganda Notes*, April 1921.

48 Report Uganda Mission 1922, copy sent to government, now in SMP 7998.

49 Willis *et al.* to Manley, 10 Jan. 1922; Willis to Manley 1922 (ns. 44, 45).

50 The rules concerning English congregations were later printed in *The Diocesan Gazette*, May 1919.

51 Willis protested strongly against any attempt to introduce a system of dual government, but he had to admit that for the time being some kind of dual control existed in view of the function of the Missionary Committee; Willis to Baylis, 4 April 1917, no. 78, G3. A7/1917.

52 In 'Review of 1912', *Uganda Notes*, Jan. 1913, it was pointed out that Archdeacon Walker until his departure in 1912 had held the posts as Secr. of the mission and as Secr. for the ecclesiastical work, the latter in his capacity as Archdeacon. Later Rev. Rowling complained that it was too much for one person to perform both CMS duties and NAC duties. Rowling to Manley, 6 Febr. 1917, no. 42, G3. A7/1917; and 7 July 1919, no. 90, G3. A7/1919.

53 See report from Diocesan Council in *The Diocesan Gazette*, Oct. 1919. We have earlier seen that the Synod's correspondence with the government was signed by both a European and an African secretary.

54 e.g. list of advisory boards in *The Diocesan Gazette*, Nov. 1919.

55 Minutes of Synod Jan. 1921, par. 11. cf. Bishop Willis' report, *Uganda Notes*, April 1921, p. 48.

56 See minutes of Missionary Committee, 8 Nov. 1923, Minute Book p. 287, MUL.

57 Minutes of Synod, Jan. 1924. See also Ladbury to CMS London, 3 Aug. 1922, no. 86, G3. A7/1922, bluntly stating: 'Result of leaving accounts in hands of natives has been chaos.'

58 Willis to Chief Secr. Jarvis, 2 Nov. 1925, encl. memorandum: Government, Mission and Church, SMP 8897.

59 cf. Jarvis, Notes on interview with Bishop Willis, 3 Febr. 1926, and Ag. Secr. CMS Uganda, Kitching, to Jarvis, 8 Febr. 1926, loc. cit.

60 Willis, Memorandum (see n.58). When it was listed with which church department a government department was supposed to correspond a colonial official added in handwriting: 'the Advocatus Diaboli with the Attorney General', SMP 8897.

61 cf. J.M. Lonsdale (1964, unpubl. thesis), pp. 226ff, and F.B. Welbourn & B.A. Ogot (1966), ch. 4.

21 The language problem

1 cf. Walker to Father, 22 Oct. 1899, Walker Papers. A very strong pro-Luganda attitude was expressed in Rev. C.H.T. Ecob to C.W. Hattersley, 14 Aug. 1901, no.

201, G3. A7/02. For a general, short account of the historical background to the language problem in Uganda see P. Ladefoged, R. Glick & C. Criper (1972), pp. 22f, 88f.

2 cf. Memorandum of interview between Tucker and Baylis, 8 Nov. 1901, no. 216, G3. A7/02.

3 ibid.; Walker to Baylis, 9 Sept. 1901, no. 204, G3. A7/02; Baylis to Walker, 10 Jan. 1902, with the Parent Committee's Minute on language of 4 Jan. 1902 encl., Letterbook I, pp.280ff, G3. A7/L 1. cf. later discussion regarding Rev. Purvis *et al.* not being obliged to pass an examination in Luganda or Lunyoro, as they were posted to the Eastern Province. Purvis to Baylis, 19 June 1906, encl. in Millar to Baylis, 25 June 1906, no. 158, G3. A7/05; and resolution of Committee of Correspondence, 2 Oct. 1906, Letterbook II, G3. A7/L2.

4 Commissioner Sadler to FO, 4 Febr. 1903, FO 2/732. See also Sadler to FO, 18 April 1903 (telegr. in Register); and 14 May 1903, FO 2/753, copy in FO 2/792. The Treasury approved of this new arrangement.

5 Sadler to FO, 1 Dec. 1903, FO 2/792.

6 Sadler to the three missions in Uganda, 7 Oct. 1903, A23/1, ESA.

7 Tucker to Sadler, 30 Nov. 1903, A22/1, ESA, copy in FO 2/792.

8 Tucker to Baylis, 30 Dec. 1904, no. 19, G3. A7/04. Tucker's attitude to Islam has been touched upon by J.D. Holway (1972), pp. 204f.

9 cf. Rev. A.B. Fisher to Rev. H.E. Maddox (in Toro), Hoima, Christmas 1905 (reproduced in M.L. Pirouet (1978), p. 104); Fisher to Tucker, 27 July 1906; and to Archdeacon Walker, 8 March 1907, all in Fisher Papers: Bunyoro Correspondence 1905–12; cf. also A.R. Tucker (1911), pp.331f.

10 cf. Fisher to Walker, 8 March 1907; and to Tucker, 25 May 1907, Fisher Papers.

11 The link between the language issue and anti-Buganda feeling was clearly observed by Tucker in his letter to Baylis, 9 Aug. 1907, no. 213, G3. A7/05. See also Fisher to Walker, 23 July 1906 and 8 March 1907; and to Tucker, 25 May 1907, all in Fisher Papers (n.9). A general reference should be made to Pirouet (1978), pp.101ff.

12 Clearly revealed in Rev. E. Millar, Ag. Secr. of Uganda mission, to Baylis, 5 Aug. 1907, no. 204, G3. A7/05. It is remarkable that the Bunyoro missionaries, as opposed to the Toro missionaries, were against the Lunyoro Old Testament.

13 See especially the strongly worded article by Rev. F. Rowling in *Uganda Notes*, Aug. 1907.

14 ibid.

15 Almost directly stated by Rowling, op. cit. See also Fisher to Tucker, 25 May 1907.

16 This political interpretation of the issue was strongly voiced by the former Toro missionary, Rev. A.B. Fisher, now in Bunyoro. See Fisher to Tucker, 27 July 1906; to Walker, 8 March 1907; and to Tucker, 25 May 1907, all in Fisher Papers (see n.9), cf. also Fisher to Baylis, 11 May 1907, no. 149, G3. A7/05.

17 Specifically raised by the CMS Home Committee; see Baylis to Secr. of Uganda Mission, 4 July 1907 (copy to Tucker), Letterbook II, p. 275, G3. A7/L2. Tucker's answer is in his letter to Baylis, 9 Aug. 1907, no. 213, G3. A7/05.

18 Tucker to Baylis, 9 Aug. 1907.

19 Tucker to Fisher, 30 May 1907, Fisher Papers: Bunyoro Correspondence 1905–12; cf. also Tucker to Baylis, 9 Aug. 1907; and Millar to Baylis, 5 Aug. 1907 (n.12).

20 When Fisher expressed strong criticism of the Toro missionaries' involvement Tucker did not answer that part of the letter. Fisher to Tucker, 25 May 1907 and 28 May 1907; Tucker to Fisher, 30 May 1907, all in Fisher Papers, loc. cit.

21 Tucker to Baylis, 9 Aug. 1907.

22 This is clearly reflected in Millar (see n.12); cf. also Fisher to Tucker, 25 May 1907. Rowling, op. cit., expressed even in public strong criticism of the Bishop's concession to a minority of the missionaries. For the actual decision see minutes of Executive Committee (Missionary Committee), 6 May 1907, no. 146, G3. A7/05. Tucker's own account of the change of language policy appeared in the second edition of his autobiography; Tucker (1911), pp.331f.

23 See clause 11 in Constitution of the Church of Uganda, adopted by Synods 1907 and 1909. The actual text of the clause uses the phrase 'in the Vernacular', but the whole context as well as the Luganda version of the Constitution confirms that Luganda is the sole language to be used (copies in possession of the author). See also 1917 edition of Laws and Regulations of the Church of Uganda, clauses 30 and 36.

24 Laws and Regulations, clauses 49 and 51.

25 ibid., clauses 71–3.

26 Collector L.H. Cubitt to Dep. Commissioner, Hoima, 21 Febr. 1907; Collector Eden to Dep. Commissioner, 11 May 1907; Dep. Commissioner George Wilson to Secr. of State, 25 June 1907 (p. 11), all in SMP 710/1907 (original dispatch in CO 536/13–25631).

27 Clearly stated in Wilson, op. cit. See also Fisher to Wilson, 20 April 1907, Book XVIII, Fisher Papers. Re Bishop Tucker's support of the government's handling of the situation and his view of the longer-term policy of using Ganda agents see below, p.399.

28 Ag. Governor Boyle to Secr. of State, 15 Dec. 1909, CO 536/28–1729/1909–10.

29 cf. Dispatch, 6 Febr. 1911, CO 536/40–7154/1911.

30 Jackson to Secr. of State, 4 July 1912, copy in SMP 134.

31 ibid.

32 Secr. of State to Jackson, 10 Aug. 1912, loc. cit.

33 *Uganda Notes*, April and May 1913.

34 ibid.

35 *Uganda Notes*, Febr. and May 1913.

36 Minutes of Synod, July 1913, under report from Board of Missions. It appears that the Board of Missions first placed the vernacular and Luganda on an equal footing, but this decision was revised by the Synod; cf. report from Board of Missions, *Uganda Notes*, May 1913. In the 1917 edition of Laws and Regulations it was written into the section on education that Luganda should be taught in all the high schools; see section B, clause 121.

37 Minute of July 1914 in SMP 134. Bunyoro, which at that time belonged to the Northern Province, was not included in the exception.

38 Minutes of National Church Council of Ankole, 22 July 1915 and 26 May 1916. At the same time Ankole protested against official documents being written in Luganda; reported in Ag. PC Northern Province, Watson, to Chief Secr., 14 Febr. 1919, SMP 134; Watson recalls an experience from 1915.

39 Minute of National Church Council of Ankole, 30 May 1917.

40 Acknowledged within the mission's own circles, where doubt was expressed as to Luganda ever becoming the official language in Uganda like Swahili in the East Africa Protectorate; cf. Rev. Blackledge to Manley, Worthing, 10 May 1916, no. 68, G3, A7/1916.

41 Ass. Chief Secr. Sullivan to Chief Secr., 21 Nov. 1918, SMP 134. Sullivan had earlier been stationed in Ankole.

42 DC Gulu, McDougall, to PC Northern Province, 11 Febr. 1919; Ag. PC Northern Province, Watson, to Chief Secr., 14 Febr. 1919, both in SMP 134.

43 Sullivan (n.41), McDougall and Watson (n.42) were all in favour of Swahili. Blackledge, (see n.40), has earlier registered that many government officers strongly wanted Swahili. The three officers all had relations with the Northern Province.

44 PC Buganda, P.W. Cooper, to Chief Secr., 21 Febr. 1919, SMP 134. Cooper emphasized that his experiences were drawn from all provinces and not just Buganda; cf. also Chief Secr. Jarvis to Governor, 2 March 1919, loc. cit.

45 Cooper, op. cit.

46 Jarvis, op. cit.

47 Governor Coryndon to Chief Secr., 12 March 1919, SMP 134.

48 Mengo Planters represented by C.W. Hattersley to Governor, 12 March 1919, min. 106, SMP 134. To assess Hattersley's denunciation of the missions in the right perspective it should be added that until 1911 he was a CMS missionary working with education. In that year he resigned to take up employment with a business firm in Uganda. cf. G. Hewitt (1971), pp.222ff.

49 These points were aptly presented by the Ag. PC Eastern Province, Jervoise, to Chief Secr., 26 May 1919, SMP 134, after consultation with the DCs.

50 cf. DC Lyall to Chief Secr., 30 May 1919, SMP 134.

51 ibid.

52 ibid., supported by PC Western Province, Browning, in a following Minute and by the Ag. DC Gulu, 1 July 1919, both in SMP 134.

53 Jervoise, op. cit.

54 These arguments were put forward by Ag. PC Buganda, Sturrock, to Chief Secr., 1 July 1919, SMP 134.

55 Archdeacon Baskerville, Memorandum to Uganda Development Commission, Dec. 1919, Bishop's Files: K–L. Land. Memoranda.

56 12th witness, Dr A.R. Cook, SMP 5860.

57 5th witness, Dr E. Cook, loc. cit.

58 11th witness, Rev. Blackledge, loc. cit. Canon H.T.C. Weatherhead, Secr. of the Board of Education under the Synod, in his memorandum to the Commission recommended that the teaching of English should start in the village school; Memorandum no.23, loc. cit.

59 Editorial, *Uganda Notes*, Jan. 1920.

60 ibid.

61 See various statements to Development Commission, reported in the *Uganda Herald*, 19 Dec. 1919. E.L. Scott commented that European opinion was mainly in favour of Swahili (see next note).

62 E.L. Scott had been in the Protectorate for 11 years and had for most of the time been Ass. Secr. for Native Affairs; see *Uganda Herald*, 19 Dec. 1919.

63 Scott pointed out that in the Eastern Province a good chance was lost by not continuing systematically the use of Luganda after Kakungulu's departure from the area. See M. Twaddle (1967, unpubl. thesis) re Kakungulu.

64 E.L. Scott, Statement to Uganda Development Commission, dat. 10 Dec. 1919, SMP 134 (transferred from SMP 5860); cf. also report in *Uganda Herald*, 19 Dec. 1919.

65 ibid.

66 Ag. Chief Secr. to PC Eastern Province, 18 Dec. 1919, in answer to the PC's letter of 26

May 1919 (see n.49). On the same day letters were written both to the CMS mission and the Mill Hill Mission to ask for their cooperation, but they were not sent as they had to await a decision on the issue of Luganda versus Swahili. Material dealing with this aspect of the language problem is in a special envelope encl. in SMP 134[II], which contains correspondence for and against preservation of Luganda as the official language.

67 The only reference to language appears in the section on education, where a certain caution with regard to English is recommended; par. 230. Copy of report in CO 536/99–17962/20; cf. subsequent discussion between Bishop John Forbes and Chief Secr. Jarvis about the teaching of English. It was here emphasized that only a few selected boys should be trained in English to fill government jobs. Forbes to Jarvis; and Jarvis to Forbes, 5 May 1920, SMP 6538.

68 Report under min. 136, SMP 134.

69 Chief Secr. to Governor, 21 Dec. 1920, min. 137, loc. cit., subsequently confirmed by Governor.

70 cf. Chief Secr. to PC Western Province, 7 Febr. 1922, min. 147, loc. cit., responding to a demand from the DCs' conference that the question of introducing Swahili should be reopened.

71 Swahili was turned down at the PCs' conference by a vote of 3 to 1; E.L. Scott to Chief Secr., 22 June 1922, min. 153, loc. cit.

72 ibid.

73 It is interesting that without any explanation an excerpt of Bishop Tucker's autobiography from 1908 appears in SMP 134. Tucker deals here with the danger which Swahili constitutes for Christianity, and underlines the importance of Luganda for the progress of the Church of Uganda, although he foresees a time when it will be supplanted by English.

74 E.R.J. Hussey, Report on Education in Uganda, dat. 10 June 1924, CO 536/134–Mi 27294/1924, pp.12, 22, 27f.

75 PCs' Conference 1925; and the Chief Secr.'s comments, SMP 8655.

76 Memorandum no. 3: The Place of the Vernacular in Native Education, July 1925, copy in SMP 8139; cf. accompanying minutes with reports of the Committee's discussions. The representative for the Conference of British Missionary Societies, J.H. Oldham, emphasized strongly the practical aspects and advised that it was necessary to concentrate on a couple of languages.

77 The Advisory Council was established during the first months of 1925; see minutes in SMP 8601 and min. 20 in SMP 8139.

78 Minutes of the third meeting, 30 Nov. 1925, and the following meeting, SMP 8636; cf. also Director of Education, E.R.J. Hussey, to Chief Secr., 8 Dec. 1925, SMP 8139.

79 cf. Director of Education, Hussey, to Chief Secr., 31 Dec. 1927, SMP 8636.

80 Memorandum from PC and DCs in Eastern Province, 26 Oct. 1927, recommending that Swahili be the official language in the Eastern Province: SMP 49[I].

81 Memoranda by Governor Gowers, 10 June 1927, SMP 134; and 25 Nov. 1927, SMP S. 49[I]. cf. also Gowers to Secr. of State, 26 Sept. 1927, CO 536/147–14340/1927. For new phase of language controversy in 1927 see K. Ingham (1958), pp.163ff.

82 Memorandum, 25 Nov. 1927.

83 Minutes of 7th meeting of Advisory Council on Native Education 28 Nov. 1927, SMP 8636. The meeting was adjourned for one month, and when it was reassumed the two Protestant bishops had drawn up a memorandum on the issue.

84 ibid. While Bishop Willis voted for the final resolution, the four other Protestant members were against.

85 Thus Director of Education to Chief Secr., 2 Jan. 1932, SMP S. 49.

86 cf. Minutes of 4th meeting of Advisory Committee on Education (a NAC Committee), 5 Nov. 1931, Ch. of Ug. Arch., MUL. See also Memorandum on the Teaching of Swahili in Elementary Schools in the Protectorate of Uganda, dat. Nov. 1931 and signed by the two Anglican and the two Catholic bishops, SMP S. 49.

87 Thus Governor Gowers to Secr. of State, 10 Dec. 1927, CO 536/148–20003/1928; and Gowers to Secr. of State, 19 Nov. 1928, SMP 134. This policy was endorsed by the CO, cf. Secr. of State to Governor, 29 Sept. 1928, SMP S. 49.

88 Memorandum by Director of Education, 27 Aug. 1928, SMP 134; cf. also question put forward in the Legislative Council, 27 Nov. 1930, extract in min. 52, SMP S. 49, and answer by Mr Amery to a question in Parliament, reported in dispatch of 12 July 1928, SMP 1845. The colonial administration later denied that the policy had been to introduce Swahili as the medium of instruction, but in view of the evidence this matter is in need of further investigation. See minutes in CO 536/170–22023/1932.

89 Thus Director of Education to Chief Secr., 2 Jan. 1932, SMP S. 49. cf. also memorandum by Ag. Dep. Chief Secr., E.L. Scott, dat. 7 April 1927, min. 196, SMP 134.

90 Ag. Chief Secr. E.L. Scott to the four bishops, 30 Jan. 1932; Director of Education to all members of Advisory Council on Native Education, 7 Nov. 1932, SMP S. 49. For preceding controversy between missions and government, see minutes in CO 536/170–22023/1932.

91 See comments to this whole development in Tarsis B. Kabwegyere (1974), pp.216ff.

92 See R.C. Pratt (1965), p. 525; cf. also D.A. Low & R.C. Pratt (1960), pp.254ff, and D.E. Apter (1961), ch. 8.

93 The Buganda factor was clearly hinted at in Director of Education to Chief Secr., 2 Jan. 1932; and Governor to Secr. of State, 13 Febr. 1932, both commenting on the Bishops' Memorandum (n.86); minutes in CO 536/170–22023/32.

94 cf. Bishops' Memorandum of Nov. 1931.

95 See, for instance, Ganda newspaper *Ddobozi lya Buganda*, 4 July 1928, extract in SMP S. 49, min. 35; cf. also Governor to Secr. of State, 12 June 1929, where he comments on and reprimands the Kabaka's pamphlet against the use of Swahili, which appeared earlier in the year and was quoted *in extenso* in the vernacular press; min. 46, SMP S.49.

96 cf. Kabaka's pamphlet, and statement by Serwano Kulubya, Omuwanika of Buganda, to Joint Committee on Closer Union in 1931, in D.A. Low (1971b), pp.87ff. The Bishops' Memorandum (n.86) refers to both these expressions of Ganda opinion.

97 The Kabaka seems to have put matters straight when he frankly stated 'that ever since the Governor [Gowers] came to this Country, he has openly shown himself to be "anti-Missionary" and consequently "anti-native", as is amply instanced by his ideas on the question of Native Education'. The Kabaka further listed a number of grievances which he asked Willis to pursue with the authorities while in London, which he duly did. Kabaka to Willis, 27 Sept. 1926 (strictly confidential); and Willis to Ormsby-Gore of the CO, 29 Dec. 1926. The Kabaka appealed even more to the mission's and Buganda's joint interests against the Governor and his administration in a letter, 7 Sept. 1926, cf. Willis' positive answer, 1 Nov. 1927. Letters in Bishop's Files: R (1). Kabaka 1926–1927.

   Buganda is treated as an entity in the present analysis, and no account is taken of internal divisions or the mission's handling of, e.g., the resignation of the Katikiro, Sir Apolo Kagwa, in 1926.

98 cf. Bishops' Memorandum of Nov. 1931 (n.86).

99 Governor Gowers to Secr. of State, 13 Febr. 1932 (n.93).

100 Director of Education to Chief Secr., 2 Jan. 1932, SMP S. 49.

101 Memorandum by Ag. Dep. Chief Secr., E.L. Scott, 7 April 1927, min. 186, SMP 134.

22   The 'Buganda syndrome'

1 One early example has been met re recognition of autonomy of Bunyoro Church Council in 1906; see the rather detailed Rules for the Bunyoro Church Council, dat. 30 June 1906 and drawn up during a visit of Archdeacon Walker. Copy in Fisher Papers, Bunyoro Correspondence 1905–12.

2 The extended use of Ganda agents has been thoroughly dealt with by A.D. Roberts (1962). See also S.R. Karugire (1980), ch. 4. cf. remark by F.J. Jackson quoted above, p.368.

3 A common expression in the Protectorate directed against the colonial power as well as the Baganda. It was for instance used by Archdeacon Walker when he described the Batoro's fear of Ganda 'designs on their country'. Walker to Baylis, 26 Sept. 1901, no. 218, G3. A7/02.

4 For mixture of spiritual and political motives behind Baganda's desire to extend Christianity to neighbouring areas, see M.L. Pirouet (1978), pp.36f. An account of use of Ganda evangelists in early years may also be found in Pirouet, op. cit., under sections dealing with individual areas. For a case study from Ankole see T.S.M. Williams (1966).

5 See Rev. C.T. Ecob to C.W. Hattersley, 14 Aug. 1901, no. 201, G3. A7/02; and Pirouet, op. cit., p. 92. An Ankole missionary gave the following account of how the system worked: 'Our collector, Mr Racy, seems anxious to help us as much as he can. He has just imported 3 keen Christian men from Buganda and has given them chieftainships in different parts of the country, that they may have a good educational influence on the people. They will of course build Churches at once at their places and will probably act as teachers without pay, so I hope they will be of great use.' Rev. H. Clayton's Journal, entry Mbarara, 2 June 1901, MUL.

6 e.g. Letter from Rev. Nuwa Nakiwafu, April 1902, *Church Missionary Intelligencer*, Oct. 1902, p.775; cf. also Nakiwafu to Jemusi Kago, Hoima, 6 Febr. 1907, transl. copy in SMP 267/1907.

7 Fisher to Tucker, 12 June 1905, Book XV; and Fisher to Tucker, 8 June 1905, Book XVI; cf. also strong demand for financial independence reported in Fisher to Tucker, 20 Nov. 1905, Book XVI, all in Fisher Papers.

8 cf. Rules for Bunyoro Church Council, dat. 30 June 1906 (cf. n.1).

9 A.R. Tucker (1908), vol. II, p. 354; cf. also Tucker to Baylis, 9 Aug. 1907, no. 213, G3. A7/05.

10 Information given by Sub-Commissioner Knowles, Western Province, to Dep. Commissioner Wilson, 25 June 1907, as part of the inquiries made after the Bunyoro disturbance, SMP 710/1907, part II; cf. also Ag. Collector Mbarara, A.H. Watson, to Dep. Commissioner, 18 June 1907, SMP 267/1907. Re Ankole see also M.R. Doornbos (1978), p. 74; and T.S.M. Williams (1966), who emphasizes the early parallelism between the political and ecclesiastical fields.

11 Tucker to Baylis, 9 Aug. 1907, no. 213 (italics mine). Tucker's decisive involvement has not been confirmed by other sources, but is in full harmony with his general attitude towards the national aspirations in the non-Ganda areas; cf. re Toro, Fisher to Baylis, Hoima, 11 May 1907, no. 149, both in G3. A7/05.

12 The best account of the so-called Nyangire revolt in 1907 is in G.N. Uzoigwe (1972).

He emphasizes that the Bunyoro reaction was not solely a revolt against Ganda chiefs, but must be seen in the wider context of opposition against British overrule; cf. also E.I. Steinhart (1977), pp.239ff.

13 See Fisher to Archdeacon Walker, 23 July 1906 and 8 March 1907; Fisher to Tucker, 27 July 1906, all in Fisher Papers, Bunyoro Correspondence 1905–12. Also Fisher to Tucker, 20 May 1907, copy under no. 155, G3. A7/05.

14 Dep. Commissioner George Wilson's report on disturbance in Bunyoro, encl. in Wilson to Secr. of State, 25 June 1907, CO 536/13–25631 (copy in SMP 710/1907). See also Ass. Collector Bunyoro, Haddon, to Collector Bunyoro, 19 May 1907, encl. in Wilson, op. cit.; Ag. Collector Mbarara, A.H. Watson, to Dep. Commissioner, 18 June 1907, SMP 267/1907. See also Pirouet (1978), p.139; and Uzoigwe, op. cit., pp.194ff.

15 This factor was stressed by both government and mission. cf. Petero Nsuhya, Kadoma of Kakonda, to Apolo Kagwa, 26 April 1907, SMP 267/1907; Wilson, op. cit.; Ag. Sub-Commissioner F.H. Leakey to Wilson, 25 May 1907, encl. in Wilson, op. cit.

16 Wilson's own account of his introduction of Ganda chiefs into Bunyoro may be found in Wilson, op. cit. W. estimated that there were in all 140 sub-chiefs in Bunyoro. cf. Uzoigwe, op. cit., pp.188, 197.

17 Clearly expressed by Wilson himself in his report on the Bunyoro disturbance (see n.14).

18 cf. Wilson's 1907 report, with enclosures.

19 Collector Bunyoro, Eden, to Ag. Dep. Commissioner, 11 May 1907, SMP 710/1907; Wilson, op. cit.; Fisher to Wilson, 20 April 1907, Book XVIII, Fisher Papers, cf. also Pirouet, op. cit., pp.104f.

20 Noticed by Wilson, op. cit., and confirmed by Fisher to Tucker, 20 May 1907 (n.13).

21 See also Tucker's observations during his visit shortly after; Tucker (1908), vol. II, p.354.

22 Fisher to Tucker, 20 May 1907; Fisher to Baylis, 12 July 1907, no. 190, G3. A7/02; Collector Bunyoro, Eden, to Dep. Commissioner, 11 May 1907, SMP 710/1907; Wilson, op. cit. See also Pirouet, op. cit., p. 106.

23 Fisher to Tucker, 20 May 1907. cf. also Collector L.H. Cubitt to Dep. Commissioner, 21 Febr. 1907, encl. in Wilson, op. cit.; Eden, op. cit.; Wilson, op. cit. See also Uzoigwe, op. cit., pp.198f.

24 See Fisher to Wilson, 20 April 1907; Fisher to Baylis, 11 May 1907, no. 149; Fisher to Tucker, 20 May 1907, copy under no. 155, both in G3. A7/05. This impression is fully confirmed by Wilson in his 1907 report. cf. also Uzoigwe, op. cit., p.203.

25 This explains how Tucker could express sympathy with the way George Wilson handled the matter; see above, p.313.

26 cf. Tucker to Fisher, 30 May 1907, Fisher Papers, Bunyoro Correspondence 1905–12; Tucker to Baylis, 9 Aug. 1907, no. 213, G3. A7/05.

27 Wilson's (n.14) 1907 report, indirectly accused some of the officials of being in sympathy with Banyoro's demand for a withdrawal of Ganda agents. This impression was confirmed by Cubitt, op. cit., and Tomkins to Dep. Commissioner, 15 April 1907 (encl. in Wilson's 1907 report). Fisher criticized some of the officials for their lukewarm attitude to the Ganda agents; Fisher to Wilson, 20 April 1907, Book XVIII, Fisher Papers; Fisher to Tucker, 20 May 1907, no. 155, G3. A7/05.

28 Wilson, op. cit.; and reintroduced by Ag. PC Northern Province, Guy Eden, to Chief Secr., 9 Aug. 1911, SMP 2083. cf. Uzoigwe, op. cit., p. 206.

29 The evidence is scanty, but Wilson hinted in his 1907 report at Banyoro connections with Busoga and Northern Uganda; cf. Steinhart (1977), p. 251.

30 This brief account of Ganda penetration of Bukedi has been extracted from M. Twaddle (1967, unpubl. thesis), *passim*; cf. also statement by one of the officials involved, J.R.P. Postlethwaite, in his autobiography (1947), pp.31ff, and by one of the missionaries, A.L. Kitching, 'The Teso Country', *Church Missionary Review*, March 1909, p. 160. See also G. Emwamu (1967) and J. Vincent (1977) on Teso, and J. Tosh (1973 and 1978) on Lango.

31 Twaddle, op. cit., pp.211ff. cf. also Roscoe to Baylis, 11 July 1905, no. 163, G3. A7/04.

32 ibid. Purvis later repeated his point of view in P. to Baylis, 19 June 1906, no. 159, G3. A7/05.

33 Twaddle, op. cit., pp.217ff, 228f.

34 ibid., pp.240f.

35 Wilson's report of 20 Oct. 1907 is summed up in Twaddle, op. cit., pp.245f.

36 Twaddle, op. cit., pp.247ff.

37 Minutes from 1909–1911 in SMP 2020.

38 Minutes in SMP 519/09 under heading: Buganda Agents in Lango District.

39 Jackson to Chief Secr., 26 June 1911, SMP 519/09; Jackson to Secr. of State, 14 July 1911, CO 536/41–26752. General reference should be made to Twaddle, op. cit., ch. 10; and to J. Tosh (1978), pp.142ff.

40 Memorandum by Jackson, 9 Dec. 1911, SMP 519/09, and Jackson to Secr. of State, 18 June 1912, CO 536/50–22189; cf. also T.B. Kabwegyere (1972), pp.309f.

41 DC, J.O. Haldane: Report from Lango District, dat. 12 June 1911; PC Northern Province, Guy Eden: Annual Report 1910–1911, both in SMP 2135. cf. also Tosh, op. cit., pp.142f. For an example of implementation of policy in Teso see J.C.D. Lawrance (1955), pp.35f.

42 cf. Twaddle, op. cit., pp.267ff.

43 Ag. Governor Wallis to Secr. of State, 28 Oct. 1912, CO 536/52–37001, where a clear scepticism is expressed against Jackson's plans for withdrawal of Ganda agents.

44 Jackson to Secr. of State, 11 April 1913, CO 536/59–15984.

45 Jackson to Secr. of State, 11 April 1913, CO 536/59–15983.

46 Chief Secr. to PC Eastern Province, 18 Dec. 1919, in envelope in SMP 134[II]. It follows that when J.R.P. Postlethwaite in 1918 took over as DC of Busoga he could with the PC's approval start to remove all Ganda agents, which gave an immense impetus to the progress of the district. See Postlethwaite (1947), p.74

47 Roberts (1962) and Twaddle, op. cit. have both emphasized the slow process of withdrawal. cf. also Tosh, op. cit., pp.146ff.

48 One expression of this antagonism occurred in 1914 when a Mill Hill mission house was burned because of the presence of a Ganda teacher; see Ag. Governor Jarvis to Secr. of State, 3 Febr. 1914, CO 536/67–8194/1914.

49 Ag. PC Eastern Province, Jervoise, to Chief Secr., 26 May 1919, SMP 134. For Teso see Emwamu (1967), pp.176ff and Vincent (1977), p.153. Roberts, op. cit., pp.445f, states that in Ankole the number of Ganda chiefs remained high for a long time. None the less, the trend to reduce Ganda influence prevailed also in Ankole. While, as Roberts states, 3 out of 12 saza chiefs in 1913 were Baganda, in 1922 there was only one, whose appointment was due to a special and customary concession to the Muslim, mainly Ganda, community in Ankole. cf. Ankole chiefs to PC Western Province, P.W. Cooper, 31 Aug. 1921; and Cooper to Ankole chiefs, 29 Sept. 1921, SMP 2071. See also M.R. Doornbos (1978), pp.74ff.

50 PC Western Province to Chief Secr., 23 June 1913; Memorandum by Governor Jackson, dat. 31 July 1913, both in SMP 3385.

51 DC Toro to PC Western Province, 22 Sept. 1915, SMP 330.

52 This aspect has been discussed in more detail in H.B. Hansen (1977), *passim*.

53 The practice of mixing local and Ganda workers is clearly set out in H.G. Dillistone, CMS missionary in Teso, to CMS Headquarters, Ngora, Febr. 1914, extracted for the Committee of Correspondence, G/Y A7/1. CMS Arch.

54 This attitude was clearly reaffirmed in a series of review articles on the situation of the Native Anglican Church, *Uganda Notes*, Febr. and March 1913.

55 Bishop Willis himself pointed to the danger of close alliance with the chiefs. See Willis, 'Charge to the Missionaries, 1917', *Uganda Notes*, Oct. 1917.

56 e.g. Minutes of National Church Council of Ankole, 26 May 1916 and 30 May 1917; Archdeacon Baskerville and Dr A.R. Cook, Review of 1916, p. 12, referring especially to Toro and Bunyoro, copy under no. 54, G3. A7/1917.

57 It was later admitted that the most outstanding feature of the Synod was the 'racial differences' that emerged. Report in *Uganda Notes*, July 1917.

58 Minutes of the Synod, June 1917. cf. also Willis' 'Charge to the Missionaries, 1917', where he singled out Bunyoro as the most clear-cut example.

59 Minutes of Synod, June 1917, supplemented by report in *Uganda Notes*, July 1917. See also Bishop Willis' reference to this session in his 'personal notes', 'The Reflections of Bishop J.J. Willis of Uganda, 1872–1954', written 1950–4, copy in Royal Commonwealth Society's Library, London.

60 Report to Synod 1919 from Toro Deanery, Bishop's Files: Synods.

61 ibid.

62 The conclusions presented here are somewhat provisional and solely related to the relationship between church and state and the accompanying political implications of Buganda's special role. To assess all aspects of the relationship between mission, church and Buganda a different approach is necessary.

23   Conclusions on parallelism and reciprocity

1 For the terminology employed here see Susan Eckstein (1977), p.464.

2 For this way of framing the problem see K. Lockard (1974, unpubl. thesis), pp. 461f.

3 For a general discussion of the relationship between *inter*-institutional ties and *intra*-organizational relations see Eckstein, op. cit.; and L. Lundquist (1976, seminar paper).

4 H.B. Hansen (1977), esp. chs. 4 and 5 where a tripartite scheme of analysis for describing the origins of ethnic groups was developed, largely inspired by the Norwegian social anthropologist F. Barth.

5 ibid., pp.33ff, 45ff.

6 ibid., pp.50f, where the relation between these two criteria has been discussed in more detail; cf. also M.R. Doornbos (1978), p.95.

7 For a more theoretical discussion based on the development in the 1960s, see Lockard, op. cit. pp.429ff; and Doornbos, op. cit., ch. 5.

8 cf. R.C. Pratt (1965), p. 519.

Part VI   The church–state relationship in a colonial setting

24   The capacity of the church

1 This way of framing the problem has been influenced by S.N. Eisenstadt (1962), p.

292. I have been inspired by various works on interest groups, for instance G.A. Almond & J.S. Coleman (1960); D. Easton (1965a and b); G.A. Almond & G.B. Powell (1966); E. Rasmussen (1971).

2 cf. Eisenstadt, op. cit., p.281.

3 For this dual approach see Eisenstadt, op. cit., p. 291; and D. E. Smith (1970), pp.14ff.

4 H. B. Hansen (1980).

5 In certain situations the Missionary Committee on its own made decisions which rightly were the responsibility of the church, for instance in connection with the transfer of educational missionaries to be paid out of government grants (p.240f).

6 I. Vallier (1970), pp. 33f.

7 Eisenstadt, op. cit., p. 292; cf. Smith, op. cit., pp. 14ff.

8 See Ag. Secr. Uganda Mission, Kitching, to Manley, 6 Oct. 1925, with enclosures, nos. 120, 121 and 123, G3. A7/1925.

9 Kitching to Manley, 8 Dec. 1925, no. 4, G3. A7/1926.

10 Bishop Willis to Manley (CMS Africa Secr.), 20 Oct. 1925, with a long memorandum, The Position of NAC Schools, encl., nos. 381, 130 and 131, G3 A7/1925. cf. above p. 381.

11 Willis, op. cit.

12 Kitching to Manley, 2 Febr. 1926, no. 23, G3. A7/1926.

13 Willis, Memorandum on Government, Mission and Church, dat. 2 Nov. 1925, SMP 8897.

14 See in particular minute by Attorney General, dat. 16 Nov. 1925, loc. cit.

15 ibid. See also minutes by Land Officer, 9 Nov. 1925; and by Chief Secr., Jarvis, 3 Febr. 1926, after a meeting with Bishop Willis, all in SMP 8897.

16 As mentioned earlier (pp.381f,) the only result of this last initiative was a new procedure of communication between mission and government.

17 Not even a centrally placed official like the Land Officer understood fully the distinction between mission and church and its implications for landholdings. See Land Officer, E. Richardson, to Rev. Daniell, 14 Nov. 1921, and to NAC Trustees 22 Sept. 1922, Bishop's Files: K–L. Land 1912–1913. Subfile: Land at Mukono. cf. also Land Officer to Ass. Secr. for Native Affairs, 18 June 1923, SMP 9561, and minute by Land Officer, 9 Nov. 1925, SMP 8897. H.B. Thomas, who served in the Land and Surveys Department from 1911 to 1942, in the latter years as Land Officer and Director of Surveys, has confirmed that it was only towards the end of his period in Uganda that the colonial administration began to understand that the church and the CMS were two different things. Interview with H.B. Thomas, OBE, in his home in Sussex, 13 July 1968.

18 cf. Willis, Memorandum on Government, Mission and Church, Nov. 1925, SMP 8897; and Willis, Memorandum on the Position of NAC Schools, dat. Oct. 1925, no. 131, G3. A7/1925.

19 See minute by Attorney General, 16 Nov. 1925, SMP 8897.

20 Bishop Tucker's campaign against the first Marriage Ordinance in 1902–3 represents a most illustrative example of all the means available; ch. 16 above.

21 For example, when Bishop Willis in 1917 strongly disputed the conditions laid down by the government for missionary work in Lango, he added that if these matters were not adjusted the only alternative was to withdraw the teachers, 'pending reference to the home authorities'. But he sincerely hoped that matters could be settled in Uganda. The Ag. Governor, H.R. Wallis, remarked in the margin, 'The usual threat.' But soon after the first educational conference was held: Willis to Chief Secr. Jarvis, 9 July 1917,

min. 9; and following minutes in SMP 4844. The whole issue of links with the European arena in the 1920s has been discussed by E.A. Brett (1973), pp.53ff.

22 cf. Eisenstadt (1962), p. 292. See also Vallier (1970), p. 15.

23 J.M. Yinger (1970), p. 434.

24 The Secr. of Uganda Mission, H. Boulton Ladbury, at the end of our period of survey clearly outlined such an independent role for the CMS mission in particular. Amidst doubts from the CMS headquarters, Ladbury maintained his 'very great faith in the influence of the CMS with the British Government'. Ladbury to Hooper (Africa Secr.), 20 July 1926, no. 72, G3. A7/1926.

25 The colonial government's religious policy

1 cf. CO minutes, Febr. 1906, CO 536/3–5447/1905–06.

2 Ag. Commissioner George Wilson to Secr. of State, 31 Dec. 1905, loc. cit. The mission on several occasions took strong exception to those officials who nurtured such feelings towards the Muslims and appeared to favour them by employing them in the district administration. cf. report of Uganda Mission to World Missionary Conference in Edinburgh 1910, in Conference Proceedings, vol. VII, pp. 76f.

3 General Report on Uganda Protectorate for year ending 31 March 1904, in Cd 2250 – Africa no. 12 (1904). It is noteworthy that parts of the report, including the above quotation, were reproduced in the CMS magazine *Church Missionary Intelligencer*, Dec. 1904, pp.914ff. cf. survey of Uganda mission's attitude to Islam in the same period by J.D. Holway (1972), pp.203f.

4 See for instance Annual Report Buganda 1913–1914, section on Masaka District, SMP 1138D. See also Report on Archdeaconry of Busoga, Sept. 1919, where the DC is quoted as saying 'that he felt uneasy at the rapid spread of Islam among the Bagesu'. Reports of Deaneries to Synod 1919, Namirembe Arch.

5 The PC Northern Province, Guy Eden, called in 1911–12 for more Christian schools to cater for government employees and members of the army. In view of Islam's advancement over the latter years, 'I am of opinion that this matter should have earnest consideration.' Annual Report for Northern Province 1911–12, SMP 2135.

6 Circular no. 16 of 1917, dat. 1 Nov. 1917, min. 34, SMP 4844.

7 cf. Minutes in CO 536/86–2457/1917–18.

8 Memorandum on the Subject of Mohammedanism and Ethiopianism in Relation to Future Administration in East Central Africa, encl. in Ag. Governor Wallis to Secr. of State, 30 Oct. 1917 (marked secret); and Wallis to F.G.A. Butler (in the CO), 1 Oct. 1917 (marked secret), all in loc. cit.

9 See Ag. Governor Carter to Secr. of State, 21 Febr. 1920, CO 536/99–16053/1920. The same theme figured in reports from West Nile District; see Memorandum by Ag. DC, A.C. Weatherhead, 3 Febr. 1919; and Weatherhead, 5 Aug. 1919, both in SMP 5592.

10 Governor Coryndon to Sir Horace Byatt (administrator of Tanganyika), 17 Jan. 1919, SMP Conf. 397.

11 DCs' Conference, Masindi, Oct. 1919; Chief Secr. to Governor, 24 Nov. 1919, SMP 5959.

12 Ag. Chief Secr., T. S. Thomas, to PC Northern Province, 4 Febr. 1920, min. 187, SMP 529.

13 Report of Ugunda Development Commission, par. 228, p. 35, copy in CO 536/99–17962/1920.

14 Young Baganda Association to Chief Secr., 12 March 1921 and 10 May 1921, SMP 6538.

15 Archer to Secr. of State, 18 Aug. 1923, CO 536/126–46564. cf. Archer to Chief Secr., 30 Aug. 1923, quoted by F. Carter (1965), p. 196; and Archer, 'A Considered Reply by the Governor to Bishop Willis' Criticisms of the Proposed Government Educational Policy in Uganda', dat. 14 April 1924, CO 536/130–23442.

16 cf. Archer to Secr. of State, 14 April 1924; and Archer, 'A Considered Reply', both in loc. cit.

17 Bishop Willis and Canon Weatherhead, memorandum on Native Education in Uganda, April 1924, CO 536/126–46564; and Governor Archer's reply (see previous note). The NAC Board of Education had earlier spoken against special schools for Muslims. Minutes of Board of Education, 9 Febr. 1924, MUL.

18 cf. Carter, op. cit.

19 See e.g. Deputy Governor, E.L. Scott, to Secr. of State, 24 Dec. 1931, SMP S. 63.

20 ibid.

21 The Ass. Secr. for Native Affairs, E.L. Scott, repeated in 1922 his earlier opinion: 'I am very much in favour of the spread of Christianity in Central Africa as I believe this to be the only means of combating Mohammedanism, which I consider to be politically a dangerous form of religion.' Scott to Chief Secr., 8 Nov. 1922, SMP 7545. A similar opinion can be found in Ass. Chief Secr. to Dep. Chief Secr. Perryman, 14 Sept. 1925, SMP Conf. 685. Chief Secr. Jarvis held the same opinion; Carter, op. cit., p. 196.

22 cf. Bishop Willis' summary of the new educational policy in Educational Policy in Uganda, July 1925, no. 93, G3. A7/1925.

23 This background for the Muslim attitude has been emphasized by Ali A. Mazrui (1968).

24 The issue of a Muslim missionary agency is dealt with in SMP Conf. 865, in particular in a memorandum by Director of Education, dat. 10 Sept. 1925; and in Ass. Chief Secr. to Dep. Chief Secr. Perryman, 14 Sept. 1925.

25 Memorandum by Governor, 7 Oct. 1925, loc. cit.

26 Emphasized by Dep. Commissioner George Wilson to Secr. of State, 6 Febr. 1906, CO 536/5–7458.

27 Law passed by Lukiko, 25 Nov. 1901, SMP 991/09.

28 For instance by Ankole Lukiko; see Ag. Collector, Watson, to Dep. Commissioner, Mbarara, 20 Jan. 1908, SMP 131/08.

29 The issue was raised by the Catholic Father Laane in a letter to the Commissioner, 10 July 1907. The answer referred to the law of 1901 and to a memorandum sent to the Buganda Regents, 20 Oct. 1905, in which they were requested to stop chiefs forcing Bakopi to erect churches. See Sub-Commissioner Leakey to Dep. Commissioner, 29 July 1907, SMP 894/1907.

30 Secr. of State to Governor, 3 May 1912, referring to a question in Parliament, 30 April: Ag. Governor Wallis to Secr. of State, 26 June 1912, SMP 1142; CO 536/50–23591 (destroyed, summary in Index).

31 The Sekibobo, Ham Mukasa, to E.N. Nanfumbani (a sub-chief), 8 Jan. 1915, encl. in PC Buganda, Knowles, to Chief Secr., 27 Jan. 1915, min. 26, SMP 4219 (seen in official translation).

32 The Governor's memorandum of 24 Oct. 1925 and the rest of the material are under min. 276, SMP 1912[II].

33 For Malakite movement see F.B. Welbourn (1961), pp. 44ff. M. Twaddle (1967, unpubl. thesis) has dealt extensively with Kakungulu's activities in the Eastern Province.

34 Kakungulu to DC Soroti, Adams, 11 Aug. 1915, encl. in PC Eastern Province, F. Spire, to Chief Secr., 19 Aug. 1915, min. 45, SMP 4219.

35 First stated when Adams forwarded Kakungulu's letter; Adams to PC Eastern Province, loc. cit. The original document outlining the policy on religion has not been found, but it seems to have been included in letters from the Chief Secr., 12 Jan. 1916 and 31 May 1916; see DC Lango, Driberg, to PC Northern Province, 12 June 1917, min. 6, SMP 4844. The general principles of the policy on religion, which Governor Jackson approved, were repeated in Chief Secr. Jarvis to Bishop Willis, 29 June 1917, min. 8, SMP 4844.

36 See Jarvis to Willis, 29 June 1917.

37 Bishop Willis had earlier made this position absolutely clear in a letter to the PCs Eastern and Northern Provinces, 15 July 1916, encl. in Willis to Governor Jackson, 18 July 1917, SMP 4844 (min. 1).

38 Exchange of letters between Driberg and Kitching: Kitching to Driberg, 14 March 1917; Driberg to Kitching, same date; Kitching to Driberg, 3 April 1917; copies forwarded in Kitching to Willis, 26 April 1917, who again sent the correspondence to Chief Secr. Jarvis, 21 May 1917, min. 3, SMP 4844. cf. also Rev. Wright, Gulu, to Willis, 28 Febr. 1917, Bishop's Files: Mac–Mar. Marriage Questions. J. Tosh (1978), pp.194f, has given a brief account of Driberg's administrative practice in Lango.

39 This was indirectly admitted by Ag. Governor H.R. Wallis, 14 July 1917, min. 11, SMP 4844.

40 Kitching to Willis, 26 April 1917; and Willis to Jarvis, 21 May 1917 and 9 July 1917, all in SMP 4844.

41 See Kitching to Driberg, 3 April 1917, and Willis (see n.38).

42 Jarvis to Willis, 29 June 1917, min. 8, SMP 4844.

43 Willis, op. cit.

44 First suggested in Jarvis to Governor, 13 July 1917, and endorsed by Ag. Governor Wallis, minute 14 July 1917, SMP 4844. (cf. ch. 24, n. 21.)

45 Clause 6 in the rules reads: 'The Government is desirous of extending every reasonable encouragement to genuine Insitutions of an educational character.' Circular no. 16, dat. 7 Nov. 1917, SMP 4844.

46 Clause 1, loc. cit.

47 Thus in connection with the question of Islam in the north. Ag. Chief Secr. T.S. Thomas to PC Northern Province, A.H. Watson, 4 Febr. 1920; and Watson to Chief Secr., 2 March 1920, both in SMP 529. Chief Secr. Jarvis quoted clause 1 of the Circular of 1917, when the government before the 1926 conference of the East African Governors should clarify its policy towards religious societies. Jarvis to Governor, 23 Dec. 1925, SMP 8961.

48 cf. Minutes from 1914–15 in SMP 4219.

49 DC Kampala, J.C.R. Sturrock, to the Sekibobo, Ham Mukasa, 29 Jan. 1915; Kabaka to all saza chiefs, 8 Febr. 1915; Kabaka to Bishop Willis, 1 April 1915, all in Bishop's Files: Ab–Ar. File: Abamalaki or KOAB.

50 cf. DC Kampala to PC Buganda, Sturrock, 23 June 1915, SMP 4219.

51 Ag. DC Mbarara to PC Western Province, 29 Oct. 1918; PC Browning to Chief Secr., 6 Nov. 1918; Chief Secr. to Browning, 13 Nov. 1918. Correspondence in SMP 4219, and Western Province MP 277 in Provincial Archives, Fort Portal, Toro.

52 PC Buganda to Chief Secr. Jarvis, 25 Jan. 1921; and Governor Coryndon to Chief Secr., 3 Febr. 1921, SMP 4219.

53 See minutes from 1921 in SMP 4219, and Welbourn (1961), pp.42f.

54 Bishop Willis to Ag. Chief Secr. Eliot, 2 June 1922; Archdeacon Lloyd, Toro, to PC Western Province, Cooper, 5 Sept. 1922, SMP 7545. Even a colonial official had the

previous year made the same suggestion to Bishop Willis; PC Northern Province to Willis, 21 June 1921, Bishop's Files: K–L. Land. Bunyoro 1912–1932. He too considered the educational work to be of 'national importance'.

55 Ass. Secr. for Native Affairs, E.L. Scott, to Chief Secr., 8 Nov. 1922, SMP 7545.

56 Cooper to Lloyd, 12 Sept. 1922, loc. cit.

57 Cooper, op. cit. cf. also Chief Secr.'s comments in Willis to Eliot, 6 March 1922, min. 96, SMP 4844.

58 Scott, op. cit.

59 cf. Scott to Chief Secr., 12 Oct. and 8 Nov. 1922, SMP 7545.

60 The final decision appears in Chief Secr.'s circular to all PCs, 11 Nov. 1922, loc. cit. The practice was later confirmed in Chief Secr. to PC Eastern Province, copy in Western Province MP 319, Fort Portal. cf. also application to use luwalo labour for upkeep of schools in Ankole; DC Ankole to PC Western Province, 6 March 1926, loc. cit. MP 387.

61 The employment of this category has been inspired by Ali A. Mazrui (1974), and Mazrui (1975), p. 1.

62 The expression 'normative and pragmatic criteria' has been adapted from F.G. Bailey (1969), pp.14, 189.

63 Minutes in SMP 5959.

64 Mazrui (1974), *passim*; see also Mazrui (1975).

65 Baron Mensdorff to FO, 4 Dec. 1905; correspondence between FO and CO; and CO's dispatch to Uganda, 14 Dec. 1905, CO 536/4–43485/1905 and SMP 529 (min. 5).

66 Ag. Commissioner George Wilson to Secr. of State, 22 Jan. 1906, encl. a copy of Governor General Sudan, Reginald Wingate, to Wilson, 30 Nov. 1905. See also CO minute 17 Febr. 1906, all in CO 536/5–5450/1906 and SMP 529. In 1910 reference was made to the Berlin Act in connection with developments in the Eastern Province: Eastern Province MP 65/1912 (seen by courtesy of Dr M. Twaddle).

67 cf. Collector Ormsby to Dep. Commissioner, 24 Febr. 1908 and subsequent correspondence in SMP 318/1908.

68 Governor Hesketh Bell to Secr. of State, 11 Sept. 1908: Report on tour to Eastern Province. The report was later printed in PP Cd 4524, 1909, with exception of par. 35 on missionary rivalry; cf. minute by H.J. Read of the CO, 25 Febr. 1909: 'in the context it is an onslaught on the CMS and the Mill Hill Fathers'. CO 536/21–37925.

69 Hesketh Bell drew special attention to the state of affairs in an interview at the CMS Headquarters; cf. Baylis to Tucker, 19 Nov. 1909, Letterbook II, p. 460, G3. A7/L2. Tucker called the Governor 'strangely ignorant of the facts'; Tucker to Baylis, 14 Dec. 1909, no. 30, G3. A7/08.

70 See minutes 80, 81 and 93 in SMP 529; and Ag. Governor Jarvis to Governor General, Sudan, 5 Febr. 1914, copy encl. in Jarvis to Secr. of State, 20 Oct. 1916, CO 536/82–57749.

71 Ag. DC Lango, Driberg, to PC Eastern Province, 12 June 1917, SMP 4844.

72 Circular no. 16 of 1917, dat. 7 Nov. 1917, min. 33, loc. cit.

73 Ag. Governor Wallis to Secr. of State, 30 Oct. 1917: Memorandum on the Subject of Mohammedanism and Ethiopianism in Relation to Future Administration in East Central Africa, p. 7. CO 536/86–2457/1917–18.

74 Governor Jackson to Secr. of State, 27 Dec. 1911; and discussion within the CO, CO 536/43–2757/1911–12.

75 Ag. Governor Wallis to Secr. of State, 16 April 1912, CO 536/49–14313.

76 cf. Treasury Chambers to Under-Secr. of State, CO, 5 June 1912, copy under min. 47, SMP 1912; and CO to Governor, 11 June 1912, loc. cit.

77 Ag. Governor Wallis to Secr. of State, 21 Sept. 1912, and CO's approval 6 Nov. 1912, CO 536/52–33217.

78 Governor Coryndon to Secr. of State, 10 April 1919, and CO minute 26 May 1919, CO 536/93–28729.

79 Ag. Commissioner George Wilson to Secr. of State, 20 July 1907; Commissioner Hesketh Bell, 24 Aug. 1907; and the subsequent CO minutes, CO 536/14–29327.

80 Ag. Governor Russell to Secr. of State, 28 June 1910, CO 536/34–23535.

81 Dep. Governor Jarvis to Secr. of State, 20 Febr. 1924, CO minute 29 March 1924; and dispatch to Governor, 7 April 1924, CO 536/130–14020/1924; cf. above p.307.

82 Governor Archer to Secr. of State, 7 Nov. 1924 and subsequent CO minutes, CO 536/133–57026/1924.

83 cf. Governor Archer, 'A Considered Reply' (see n.15).

84 For these expressions see F.H. Littell (1967), p.34.

26 *The nature of the relationship between mission, church and state*

1 S.N. Eisenstadt (1962).

2 D.E. Smith (1970), ch. 1; and Smith (1974), part 1. See also G.A. Almond & J.S. Coleman (1960), pp. 284ff, 536ff; G.A. Almond & G.B. Powell (1966), *passim*; K. Lockard (1974, unpubl. thesis), pp. 440ff.

3 cf. Almond & Coleman, op. cit.; and Smith, op. cit.

4 Smith (1970), pp.10ff; and ch. 4.

5 ibid. p. 91.

6 In a later revision of his typology D.E. Smith singled out political–process seculariza- tion as a special category, defining it as the decline in political saliency of religious groups, parties and leaders and in general the weakening of religious identity among actors (Smith (1974), p. 8). In the present context, where the emphasis is on what the state tried to implement, this process is included under the separational aspect and under polity–transvaluation secularization.

7 cf. Smith (1970), p. 97; and Smith (1974), p. 8.

8 Smith (1970), p. 97.

9 ibid., p.104.

10 ibid., pp.108f.

11 The same distinction has (re 1960s) been suggested by Lockard (1974), p. 351.

12 cf. the more elaborate use of the concept in Smith (1970), pp. 113ff.

13 See Smith, op. cit., pp.117f, re distinction between religion and nationalism.

14 R.N. Bellah (1967); and Bellah (1978). cf. also J.M. Yinger (1970), pp.436ff.

15 Annual Report Buganda 1909–1910, by DC Kampala, P.W. Cooper, SMP 1138. This attitude resembles the so-called 'public school ethos' and the call for an alliance of 'godliness and good learning': cf. D. Newsome (1961).

16 Phrase borrowed from Yinger, op. cit., p. 436.

17 Yinger, op. cit., p. 436, quoting a declaration by the US Supreme Court in 1892.

18 A parallel may be drawn to the ideal within nineteenth-century Anglicanism that it is 'the function of the State to enable and to encourage its members to aspire to the highest standards of Christian living', Newsome, op. cit., p.2. The use of the term 'belief system' has been inspired by G. Sjöblom (1980), but a corresponding analytical

approach has not been the intention in the present work.

19 Thus expressed by Rev. H.W. Weatherhead in 'Education in Central Africa', *Church Missionary Review*, June 1907, pp.337ff.

20 For instance, start of the Boy Scout Movement: cf. minutes of Missionary Committee and Ladies Committee, 20 Jan. 1921; and Rev. Rowling to CMS Headquarters, 24 Jan. 1921, no. 27, G3. A7/1921.

21 D. Easton (1965b), part 3.

22 For this approach see J. Lonsdale & B. Berman (1979), p. 490, in an article which deals with Kenya.

23 R. Robinson (1972). He singles out Buganda as a very appropriate example (p. 121).

24 T.O. Ranger (1969).

25 G.N. Uzoigwe (1972).

26 The theory of collaboration constitutes the analytical framework for the recent work on Toro by E.I. Steinhart (1977).

27 See, first, M. Twaddle (1969). cf. also D.A. Low (1971a), pp. 232f; and S.R. Karugire (1980), p. 62.

28 Twaddle, op. cit., p. 312.

29 M.S.M. Kiwanuka (1971), ch. 10, in particular pp. 246f, 259ff.

30 See, for instance, M. Mamdani (1975), p. 28.

31 See in particular Kabwegyere (1976). See also M.R. Doornbos (1978), pp.84f; and Karugire, op. cit.

32 The gap between élite and masses is not necessarily identical with a class difference; see P.C. Lloyd (1966), Introduction.

33 I. Vallier (1967), p. 195.

34 This point of view was aptly expressed by a Uganda missionary in 1903: 'A Christian Government and a Christian mission shall work hand in hand and they always will exactly in proportion as each is true to its position and profession.' *Uganda Notes*, Dec. 1903, p. 65; cf. parallel opinion held by the government, *Uganda Notes*, Jan. 1904, p. 2.

35 Most of the elements inherent in the utilitarian aspect have been aptly summarized in an article from 1904 by J.J. Willis, who in 1912 became Bishop of Uganda, 'Administration and Mission: A Mutual Debt', *Uganda Notes*, April 1904. Willis touched later on the same theme in his first charge to the missionaries, 'Policy of the Uganda Mission, 1912' (1913).

36 Typology suggested by Eisenstadt (1962), p. 281; cf. also Eisenstadt (1963), p. 185.

37 cf. Yinger (1970), p. 447.

38 ibid., pp. 433f. A. Hastings (1973), p. 12, introduces the distinction between democratic and non-democratic countries and relates the independent voice of the church to the former.

39 For this expression see D.E. Smith (1970), pp.68ff.

40 Eisenstadt (1962), p. 281 and Conclusion.

41 For this terminology see J.S. La Fontaine (1969), p. 187.

42 A.G. Hopkins (1973), p. 109.

43 The concept of moral community and its explanatory value corresponds with David Easton's 'belief in a common interest'. Easton (1965b), ch. 20.

44 Vallier (1967), p. 466.

45 See Eisenstadt (1962), esp. p. 292.

46 cf. I. Vallier (1970); and E. de Kadt (1971), pp.37f.

Appendix 1

1. On the single issue approach as opposed to the thematic approach see J.H. Whyte (1971), pp.22ff.

2 The employment of systems analysis in this survey has been inspired by Ole Karup Pedersen (1970), pp.22ff. For terminology, see Erik Rasmussen (1971), section 2.4.6. and ch. 3.

3 In developing this analytical approach I have consulted D. Easton (1965a and 1965b); Rasmussen, op. cit.; G.A. Almond & J.S. Coleman (1960), pp.26ff; and G.A. Almond & G.B. Powell (1966), pp. 74ff.

4 The employment of indirect or tacit input has been inspired by Easton, op. cit., and F.G. Bailey (1969). R. Hodder-Williams (1978) has used the same concept, though with a different definition, in a study of the political links between the settlers and the central government in Rhodesia. See also Ali A. Mazrui (1973).

5 See Susan Eckstein (1977) for a thorough discussion of the theory of inter-organizational relations with special reference to the church–state problem. cf. also L. Lundquist (1976, seminar paper).

6 cf. Easton (1965b), p. 23; and Rasmussen (1971), p. 254.

7 Some of the phrases used here have been taken from Easton (1965a), p. 34.

8 Arend Lijphart (1971). cf. discussion of the use of case studies within history and political science in Hans Mouritzen (1979).

Appendix 2

1 Fridtjov Birkeli (1952), Introduction on problem and method (English summary, pp. 465ff). This book has suffered from appearing only in Norwegian.

2 See, for instance, H.W. Gensichen (1962), Stephen Neill (1966), C.P. Groves (1969). Within the Scandinavian setting we have Bengt Sundkler (1963) and Torben Christensen (1976), pp.700ff. Also stimulating for the present study has been Max Warren (1966), who specifically raised the question whether 'the Church of England as by law established was fit for export' to the colonies. See also Max Warren (1965), esp. ch. 3.

3 Ruth M. Slade (1959), David Lagergren (1970), and Marvin D. Markowitz (1973); cf. summary by Ruth Slade Reardon (1968).

4 Crawford Young (1965), esp. pp. 12ff, and pp. 148ff.

5 See in particular J.F. A. Ajayi (1965), E.A. Ayandele (1966), F.K. Elkechi (1971), G.O.M. Tasie (1978).

6 Terence Ranger in T.O. Ranger & John Weller (1975), pp.85f.

7 Robert I. Rotberg (1965) and John McCracken (1977), which has a useful bibliography covering the Central African region.

8 Ian Linden (1974, 1977).

9 See George Shepperson & Thomas Price (1958), later to be followed by many others; cf. classification in Bengt Sundkler's pioneer work (1961).

10 Oginga Odinga (1967), p. 75; cf. D.A. Low (1973), p. 140.

11 D.A. Low (1957a, unpubl. thesis), later expanded in Low (1968) and Low (1971a).

12 Thus C.C. Wrigley (1959); David Apter (1961), ch. 3; Michael Twaddle (1972); and S.R. Karugie (1980), ch. 2. See also ch. 2 above.

13 See in particular Low (1971a); cf. also Apter, op.cit., ch. 5.

14 C.J. Hellberg (1965).

15 F.B. Welbourn (1965).

16 Kathleen Lockard (1974, unpubl. thesis).
17 D.A. Low (1974), p. 120.
18 Michael Twaddle (1978).
19 Adrian Hastings (1973, seminar paper).

Bibliography

Primary sources

The survey is based primarily on unpublished documents dating from the first quarter of the twentieth century; little oral evidence has been collected from that period. As far as the later period is concerned, a number of interviews have been conducted, in particular with Africans, whose experiences have greatly stimulated the present inquiry. The unpublished documents are contemporary with the events concerned and comprise several types: official correspondence between various institutions, official dispatches, committee minutes, the internal minutes of various organizations and administrative bodies, informal notes, private letters and diaries.

Colonial administration: Uganda

In Entebbe

The bulk of the governmental material was preserved in the former Secretariat of the Chief Secretary in Entebbe, now known as the Uganda National Archives. Apart from the colonial government's records, the collection also includes some material from the provincial and district administration which was later transferred to Headquarters. This material also includes a number of commission reports which were printed locally. A vast number of files has been examined in this well-organized archive. As the archives were consulted in the 1960s the previous name and the old system of classification have been retained in the present study, and are designated ESA in the notes. The records consulted may be divided into five categories:

i. Until 1906 the A-series, mainly organized according to the location of the correspondent: FO in London, districts in the Protectorate, missions, etc. There are in each case files for inward and outward correspondence.

ii. From 1906 records are arranged in Secretariat Minute Papers (SMP) according to the nature of the topic and in most cases covering a considerable number of years. No proper cataloguing system existed at the time of inspection. These files constitute the most important material as regards exchanges between the colonial government and the Anglican mission and church.

iii. Some of the records by Protectorate officials were classified as 'Confidential files' (SMP Conf.). In the mid-1960s I consulted a number of these in cooperation with Dr Michael Twaddle. However, it was not possible to obtain access to all confidential files relevant to the subject.

iv. Some records from the Provincial Administration were transferred to ESA towards the end of the colonial period. Two of these collections have been consulted: Buganda Residency Archives, also cited as the Provincial Commissioner's Office, Kampala, and Eastern Province Minute Papers (in collaboration with Dr Michael Twaddle). Only a limited number of records remains in these two collections.

v. Annual, quarterly and monthly reports from Provinces and Districts can mainly be found in special SMP files, but they have in some cases been catalogued separately. Annual reports from the Protectorate as a whole were printed in Britain (see below). As many ESA files as possible concerning contacts between mission, church and government have been examined. It amounts to more than 500 files, but because of the cataloguing system it is impossible to be sure that all records relevant to the topic have been consulted. The files are not listed here, but a reference has in each case been made in the notes; for the more voluminous files, the minute number for the particular item is quoted.

Provincial and District archives

The archives are located in the former Provincial and District headquarters. Those consulted contain only a few records for the period before 1920–5, and they vary in value according to treatment by departing colonial officials in 1962. The following archives have been consulted:

i. Ankole District, DC's Office, Mbarara: a substantial collection of records, mainly for the period after 1925.

ii. Toro District, DC's Office, Fort Portal: a large and disorganized collection, mainly dating from 1920 onwards. It is mixed up with records from the Provincial Headquarters, Western Province.

iii. Bunyoro District, DC's Office, Hoima: only a very limited collection is left.

iv. Western Province Archives: a large collection from the 1920s onwards is in the DC's Office, Fort Portal (the former PC's Headquarters), mixed up with the Toro Archives. Copies of some records from the Northern Province Headquarters, Masindi, may also be found here.

Mission and church records: Uganda

The ecclesiastical sphere presents a less clear-cut picture, as the organizational system here was more elaborate. I employ material related to the Church Missionary Society's Uganda mission and to the emerging church organization, which was first given a constitution in 1909. No sharp distinction was made between the two organizations at the time, because of the overlap of persons between them, and the same confusion characterizes the documentary material preserved. Central to the mission was the Missionary Committee, whose minutes and subsequent correspondence provide useful sources. On the church side we have the synodal constitution with its elaborate system of councils and boards, which have allowed me to conduct the analysis at both the central and the local levels. Still, it is often difficult to establish from which of the two organizations, mission or church, the executive power to deal with the state originated. It was thus necessary to examine a substantial amount of material in order to assess the position of the church *vis-à-vis* the state. The task was not made easier by the division of the church collection of documents in the early 1960s without any clear criteria. Some files and Minute Books were deposited in Makerere University Library, while most of the official and internal correspondence, called Bishop's Files, was kept at the Headquarters of the Church of Uganda on Namirembe Hill. While the former material has been used by other scholars, the latter collection was not subjected to any substantial examination before I had the opportunity in the mid-1960s.

These two collections of unpublished documents have been particularly valuable. The extent of the church archives and the standard of record-keeping are in no small amount due to the scheme for the preservation of historical records which the Department of Religious Studies at Makerere University initiated in the 1960s. I took part in this scheme during my research work and benefited substantially from its results. This work also involved the preservation of locally-produced mission and church magazines, notably *Uganda Notes*.

The Bishop's Files in the Namirembe Archives
The Bishop's Files are organized according to the nature of the topic and arranged alphabetically in accordance with the first letter of the title, e.g. under K–L: Land, and under Mac–Mar: Makerere College and Marriage Questions. Each file may be divided into sub-files. Almost all the Bishop's Files have been examined, with due respect for the rules of access.

Apart from the Bishop's Files there are in Namirembe Archives a few packets and boxes dealing with the various Deaneries, the Synod (to be supplemented with records in MUL), the Diocesan Council and other Boards, and with topics such as education.

Church of Uganda Archives, Makerere University Library
This collection contains various records relating to the work and personnel of the Church

of Uganda and the CMS Uganda mission. The records originate mainly from three sources: the main part of the collection was transferred from Namirembe Archives; records from Deaneries and local Church Councils deposited in MUL; letters, journals, diaries and other personal papers written by missionaries, African clergymen and laymen. The records consulted include the following:

i. Minutes of the Missionary Committee: the minutes covering the period 1891–1934 are organized in the following way:

1891–1901: Finance Committee, Minute Book of the Eastern Equatorial African Diocese, CMS Arch., London.

1902–9: Executive Committee, Minute Books in MUL, AR N3/3.

1909–24: Missionary Committee, Minute Books in MUL.

1924–34: Standing Committee, Minute Books in MUL.

Minutes from each meeting were regularly forwarded to the CMS headquarters and may be found in the CMS Arch. in the series G3. A5 (until 1898) and G3. A7.

Supplementary material: Ladies' Missionary Committee, 1910–24; CMS Missionary Conference 1927:

ii. Minutes of Mengo Church Council: minutes for the period 1892–9 are found in: Meeting of Church Elders April–Oct. 1892, Minute Book of the Eastern Equatorial African Diocese, pp.350ff, CMS Arch., London.

Sept. 1893–Oct. 1899: minutes in *Kitakule Journal*. From Oct. 1896 kept in Luganda. Translated by Daudi Senono Lubowa.

iii. Records of the Diocesan Synod 1905–28: the material consists of Minute Books, reports from boards and committees under the Synod, the Bishop's charges, resolutions etc. Most of these valuable records are in MUL, but a few files are still kept in Namirembe Arch. The minutes were kept in Luganda from 1912 and have been translated by Daudi Senono Lubowa.

iv. Minute books of boards, councils and committees:

a. Diocesan level:

Theological Board 1919–25; Board of Education 1923–36 (in English and Luganda); Diocesan Church Building Committee 1919–29 (in English and Luganda).

b. Local level:

Women's Ruridecanal Conference, Namirembe, 1919–39 (in Luganda); Women's Parochial Council, Namirembe, 1912–26 (in Luganda); Ngogwe Saza Council (Olukiko lwe Saza) 1912–26 (a district church council, minutes in Luganda); Ngogwe Church Council 1905–18 (a ruridecanal council, minutes in Luganda).

The last two Minute Books may have been returned to Ngogwe Church Office. The Minute Books in Luganda have been translated by Daudi Senono Lubowa.

v. Misc. Mission and church correspondence from the 1890s onwards, in two special boxes:

a.   27 files. Of special relevance are no. 11: Purvis – re Punitive Expeditions in Busoga; no. 13: 1909/10, re Compulsory Labour in Uganda.

b.   Marriage registers, Luganda examinations and 14 files enclosing some correspondence with the colonial government.

Documents written in African languages

The working language within the church was Luganda, the language of the largest single Ugandan group, the Baganda, and many Minute Books were kept in Luganda. Furthermore, many of the local church councils kept their records in the local vernaculars – first and foremost, for the purposes of this survey, Lutoro, Lunyoro and Lunyankore – as the districts where these were spoken established their own Church Councils during the period concerned. This type of material, supplemented by official and private letters, has been used as much as possible, as it gives the best reflection of the attitudes and reactions of the Africans. During this part of the research work I was greatly assisted by students from Makerere University, who provided me with the necessary translations.

The following items have been examined:

i. Minute Book of Toro Church Council 1898–1904, kept in the Church Office, Kabarole, Fort Portal. The minutes from the last year in Lutoro have been translated by Moses Nyakazingo. Two Minute Books in Lutoro for the period 1911–29 have not been consulted.

ii. Minute Book of Bunyoro Church Council 1905–40, kept in the Church Office, Hoima. Parts of the Minute Book have been translated by Keren K. Kabadaki. Minute Book of the District Council of Masindi 1909–16, kept in the same place, has been consulted briefly.

iii. Minute Book of the National Church Council of Ankole 1914–22, kept in the Church Office, Mbarara. Translated from Luganda by Daudi Senono Lubowa.

iv. Minute Book of the Gulu Church Council 1918–25, now deposited in MUL. Translated by J. Ocaya.

Government and church administration: Kenya

CMS Regional Office, Nairobi
A number of files has been examined mainly relating to the Kikuyu Controversy, 1914–18, the issue of forced labour around 1920 and the question of closer union in East Africa in the late 1920s. Some files have since been transferred to the Kenya National Archives.

Kenya National Archives, Nairobi
A few files have been examined covering areas of common interest to the two Protectorates: missionary work among the Nandi and in the Nyanza Province, education and closer union.

Government records: England

It was in the nature of the colonial and missionary situation that political and ecclesiastical agencies in Uganda were under the direction of their respective metropolitan authorities and had to keep them reasonably well informed. Hence there was a flow of dispatches and letters between Uganda and Britain.

As regards the colonial government, extensive use has been made of Foreign Office and Colonial Office material in the Public Record Office in London (PRO). Until 1905 when the Uganda Protectorate was transferred from the Foreign Office to the Colonial Office, the files dealing with mission and church matters in Uganda are mainly found in the FO 2 series. For the period after 1905 files in the CO 536 series have been examined systematically in order to identify the issues at stake between mission and government in Uganda and to establish the role of the European arena. A few files from other series have also been consulted, notably CO 537. In some cases, when files have been destroyed, the Registers of Correspondence, CO 682, have proved useful. Records are quoted by series/box no. – file no./year, e.g. CO 536/3–5447/1905–6. In some cases duplicates may be found in ESA.

In addition the following printed documents have been consulted:

i. Foreign Office Confidential Prints: a printed selection of FO correspondence, useful for the study of developments in Uganda in the 1890s. These are in the PRO series FO 403. They are also available at the Institute of Commonwealth Studies, University of London, and in ESA.

ii. Colonial Office Confidential Prints: in PRO series CO 879 from 1905ff. They have not been extensively used as the original material is readily available in ESA and PRO.

iii. Parliamentary Papers: a selection of dispatches on special topics printed for the use of Parliament. A number of Parliamentary Papers (PP) for the period 1890–1910 has been studied. They were published in the Command Series (Cd) and are available e.g. in Senate House Library, University of London.

iv. Annual Reports for the Uganda Protectorate: besides appearing in Parliamentary Papers up to 1918–19 they were also published after 1904 in the series Colonial Reports – Annual, available in Senate House Library.

Mission records: England

As regards the Uganda mission, a huge and meticulously organized collection of Uganda correspondence was kept in the Church Missionary Society's Archives in London, and has lately been transferred to Birmingham, notably the series G3. A5 and G3. A7. A few of the missionaries' letters, together with their shorter notes and articles, were occasionally printed in CMS magazines, particularly in the *Church Missionary Intelligencer* (up to 1906) and the *Church Missionary Record* (from 1907 onwards).

In accordance with the 50-year rule, correspondence between the Uganda Mission and the CMS Headquarters has been examined from the establishment of the mission in 1877 until the late 1920s. Series G3. A5 covers correspondence until 1897; in this period Uganda was part of the Eastern Equatorial Africa Mission. Series G3. A7 covers correspondence after 1898, when a Ugandan Diocese was established. There are three types of records in these series:

i. Incoming letters: reference is made to the number of the letter and the packet, after 1915 the year (e.g. G3. A7/1920).

ii. Outgoing letters: copied in Letterbooks (L).

iii. The Precis (P): a register of correspondence with extensive summaries of each letter.

Apart from the main series the following records have been examined:

G/AC 4: Misc. correspondence concerning the campaign for the retention of Uganda in the early 1890s. Letters about missionary work in Uganda.

G/Y A7/1: Minute Book of the Eastern Equatorial African Diocese. Records of the campaign for the retention of Uganda 1891–2, and later misc. correspondence concerning Uganda.

G/AZ 1/6: Circulars and other Papers, 1886–91.

G/AZ 1/7: Circulars and other Papers, 1902–4.

G/AZ 1/8: Circulars and Printed Papers, 1908–13.

G/CS 2–4: Minutes of Sub-Committees (incl. Special Sub-Committee on the Constitution of the Church of Uganda).

Baylis Papers: Sub-Committee on Native Church Organization, 1889–1901; Sub-Committee for Mission Administration in the Field, 1908–9.

Minute Book, Group III Committee (Africa), 1904–17.

Semi-official letters, private letters, journals and diaries

In the first place, there are private and semi-official letters from the Uganda mission to various institutions or associations in Britain. One means of recourse for the missionaries was to write to the Archbishop of Canterbury, and as a consequence the Lambeth Palace Archive has been consulted. Another means of exerting influence on political processes in Britain was via pressure groups like the Anti-Slavery and Aborigines' Protection Society, whose papers are now deposited in the Rhodes House Library, Oxford. The collection of papers left by Sir Robert Coryndon (Governor of Uganda 1918–22) is also to be found there.

Secondly, we have the private letters written by both missionaries and colonial officials. A number of collections have been consulted, first and foremost Archdeacon R.H. Walker's numerous and valuable letters to his family and friends over the years from 1887 to 1906. Among the papers of government officials, we may also mention the letters of R.W. Moffat, Medical Officer until 1906.

Thirdly, there are the diaries kept by people who were involved in various capacities with events in Uganda. F.D. Lugard's diaries, easily accessible in Marjorie Perham's printed edition, have proved an invaluable source for the tumultuous 1890s. Sir Gerald Portal's and Rev. A.G. Fraser's journals, both in Rhodes House Library, and Rev. A.B. Fisher's papers, deposited in the CMS Archives, have also proved useful. To the same category belong the journals of Rev. G.K. Baskerville from the 1890s, copies of which are in both Makerere University Library and the CMS Archives, and the papers of J.J. Willis (first missionary and from 1912 onwards Bishop of Uganda), which are available in xerox copies in Makerere University Library.

Some of the leading actors in Uganda later wrote their autobiographies. Notable within the ecclesiastical sphere were the first two Anglican Bishops of Uganda, A.R. Tucker (*Eighteen Years in Uganda and East Africa*, 1908), and J.J. Willis ('The Reflections of Bishop J.J. Willis', MS. written between 1950 and 1954 and now deposited in the Royal Commonwealth Society's Library). A number of government officials also wrote auto-biographies, notably one of the early governors, Sir Hesketh Bell (1946), and one of the provincial commissioners, J.R.P. Postlethwaite (1947). But it should be emphasized that these autobiographies have been used only to a limited extent, and with some caution, and only as a supplement to primary documentary evidence, as, with the exception of Bishop Tucker's, they post-date the actual events considerably.

In Makerere University Library, Uganda

i. Journals of the Rev. G.K. Baskerville, 1890–1901; G.K. Baskerville: 'The History of the Uganda Mission of the CMS from 1876 to 1927', typed manuscript, 265 pp.

ii. Extracts from letters of Rev. H. Clayton, 1897–1904.

iii. Various letters to Rev. W.A. Crabtree, 1895–1909 (xerox copies in MUL).

iv. Letterbooks and journals of Rev. H. Boulton Ladbury, 1903–50.

v. Letters of Dr R.U. Moffat, 1891–1906. Moffat was a Medical Officer in Uganda, 1893–1906.

vi. Archdeacon R.H. Walker's Letterbooks I–IV, 1909–12.

vii. Dr C.A. Wiggins' reminiscences, written about 1960. Wiggins had been a Medical Officer and later the Principal Medical Officer in Uganda, 1906–23.

viii. Collection of Bishop J.J. Willis' papers: letters, journals, articles, cuttings from the Kikuyu controversy, 1914–17, etc. (xerox copies in MUL).

In CMS Archives, London

i. Rev. A.B. Fisher papers: a collection of notebooks, letters etc. from Fisher's period as a missionary in Uganda, 1892–1914. Most of the notebooks are not original, but written up during the 1950s. Parts of the original correspondence are preserved, notably Bunyoro Correspondence, 1905–12. (The Fisher Papers are also available on microfilm in MUL.)

ii. The papers of Archdeacon W.E. Owen: a large collection (in 6 boxes) of documents from Owen's period as a missionary in Uganda from 1904 to 1918 and later in Kenya as Archdeacon of Kavirondo. Selected files on matters relating to Uganda have been examined. Dr C.G. Richards kindly granted me access to these.

iii. Archdeacon R.H. Walker's papers: a collection of more than 500 letters from Archdeacon Walker to his family and friends in Britain over the years 1887–1906. As secretary of the Uganda Mission and as the first Archdeacon of Uganda, Walker played a key role in the missionary work and his letters are extremely important sources for the period.

In Lambeth Palace Library, London

The archive contains the correspondence between the mission and church in Uganda and the Archbishop of Canterbury. Of special interest is the correspondence with Bishop A.R. Tucker in the Letters of Archbishop Benson (1883–96) and in Randall Davidson's Correspondence, series U 1: Uganda, and T 10. I am grateful for the assistance of the Librarian of the Lambeth Palace Library.

In Royal Commonwealth Society Library, London

'The Reflections of Bishop J.J. Willis of Uganda, 1872–1954', ms., 200 pp., written between 1950 and 1954.

In Rhodes House Library, Oxford

i. Anti-Slavery and Aborigines' Protection Society: G 138: 1910: Uganda Forced Labour.

ii. Papers of Sir Robert Coryndon, Governor of Uganda, 1918–22: box 1 holds material related to Uganda. (Seen by kind permission of Mr Peter Coryndon. I am grateful to Dr Michael Twaddle for calling my attention to the Coryndon papers.)

iii. A.G. Fraser's papers: Fraser was missionary in Uganda 1900–3, later known as Fraser of Trinity and Achimota: box 1: Journals 1901–3.

iv. Papers of Ernst Gedge, employed by the IBEA Co, and from 1893 correspondent for *The Times*: correspondence with Uganda missionaries in the early 1890s.

v. Lord Lugard's papers: material and correspondence relating to Uganda in the 1890s.

vi. Sir Gerald Portal's papers: letterbooks, diaries and correspondence relating to Uganda, 1892–3.

Periodical publications

Mengo Notes, 1900–2, followed by *Uganda Notes* 1902–21: a local missionary magazine started by the CMS Uganda Mission, for most of the period appearing monthly. The publication represents a valuable source on many aspects of development in Uganda. The only complete series known is held by MUL. Incomplete series are found in Royal Commonwealth Society Library and in CMS Library and Archives (G3. A7 series).

The Diocesan Gazette: first published together with *Uganda Notes*, 1913–15; from 1916 separate monthly issues.

Uganda Protectorate Gazette: published fortnightly from 1908. Only consulted on particular points, e.g. the Marriage Ordinance 1914. Available in PRO and in Royal Commonwealth Society Library.

Uganda Herald: a daily newspaper in English, started 1912.

Church Missionary Intelligencer: a missionary magazine, published by the CMS, London, 1849–1906.

Church Missionary Record: succeeded the previous magazine and was published 1907–26. Both magazines frequently carried letters or articles by Uganda missionaries.

Oral information

Interviews have been conducted with African clergy (ordained in the 1920s) and laymen and with a few colonial officials, notably H.B. Thomas, who served in the Land and Surveys Department, 1911–41, in his last period as Land Officer. While this kind of information has been stimulating for the whole inquiry, little direct use has been made of it in the present context as it has a more direct bearing on events after 1925.

Secondary sources and references

The list of references contains only books and articles quoted in the notes; it does not pretend to be a complete bibliography covering all aspects of the church–state problem in Uganda during the period.

Published material

Almond, Gabriel A. & J.S. Coleman (eds.) (1960): *The Politics of the Developing Areas*. Princeton University Press, NJ.

Almond, Gabriel A. & G. Bingham Powell (1966): *Comparative Politics: a development approach*. Little, Brown, Boston.

Ajayi, J.F.A. (1965): *Christian Missions in Nigeria 1841–1891. The making of a new elite.* Longman, London.

Ajayi, J.F.A. & E.A. Ayandele (1969): 'Writing African Church History', in Beyerhaus, Peter & C.F. Hallencreutz (eds.): *The Church Crossing Frontiers. Essays on the nature of missions. In honour of Bengt Sundkler*, pp. 90–108. Studia Missionalia Upsaliensia XI. Gleerup, Uppsala.

Apter, David (1961): *The Political Kingdom in Uganda.* Princeton University Press, NJ.

Ashe, R.P. (1894): *Chronicles of Uganda.* Hodder & Stoughton, London.

Atanda, J.A. (1969): 'The Bakopi in the Kingdom of Buganda 1900–1912', *Uganda Journal* 33(2), pp. 151–62.

Ayandele, E.A. (1966): *The Missionary Impact on Modern Nigeria 1842–1914. A political and social analysis.* Longman, London.

Baëta, C.G. (ed.) (1968): *Christianity in Tropical Africa.* Oxford University Press.

Bailey, F.G. (1969): *Stratagems and Spoils: a social anthropology of politics.* Oxford University Press.

Barth, F. (ed.) (1969): *Ethnic Groups and Boundaries.* Little, Brown, Boston.

Bates, M. Searle (1945): *Religious Liberty: an inquiry.* Harper, London.

Beattie, John (1971): *The Nyoro State. A study of social and political change.* Oxford University Press.

Beidelman, T.O. (1974): 'Social Theory and the Study of Christian Missions in Africa', *Africa* 44, pp. 235–49.

Bell, Sir Hesketh H.J. (1946): *Glimpses of a Governor's Life.* Low, Marston, London.

Bellah, R.N. (1967): 'Civil Religion in America', *Daedalus* 96(1), pp. 1–21.

(1978): 'Religion and Legitimation in the American Republic', *Society* 15(4), pp. 16–23.

Bennett, G. (1965): 'Settlers and Politics in Kenya, up to 1945', in Harlow & Chilver (1965), pp. 265–332.

Birkeli, Fridtjov (1952): *Politikk og misjon. De politiske og interkonfesjoneele forhold på Madagaskar og deres betydning for den norske misjons grunnlegging 1861–1875.* Egede Instituttet, Oslo.

Brett, E.A. (1973): *Colonialism and Underdevelopment in East Africa. The politics of economic change 1919–39.* Heinemann, London.

Burke, Fred G. (1964): *Local Government and Politics in Uganda.* Syracuse University Press.

Carter, Fay (1965); 'The Education of African Muslims', *Uganda Journal*, 29, pp. 193–8.

(1967b): 'Cooperation in Education in Uganda: mission and Government relations in the inter-war period', *Bulletin of the Society for African Church History* 2(3), pp. 259–75.

Cell, J.W. (ed.) (1976): *By Kenya Possessed. The correspondence of Norman Leys and J.H. Oldham 1918–1926.* University of Chicago Press.

Christensen, Torben & Sven Göransson (1976): *Kyrkohistoria 3.* Scandinavian University Books, Lund.

Clayton, A. & D.C. Savage (1974): *Government and Labour in Kenya 1895–1963.* Cass, London.

Churchill, Winston S. (1908): *My African Journey.* Hodder & Stoughton, London.

Colson, Elizabeth (1969): 'African Society at the Time of the Scramble' in Gann & Duignan (1969), pp. 27–65.

Colvile, Henry (1895): *Land of the Nile Springs.* Edward Arnold, London.

Cunningham, J.F. (1905): *Uganda and its Peoples.* Reprinted Cass, London, 1969.

Cussac, J. (1955): *Évêque et Pionnier Monseigneur Streicher.* Éditions de la Savane, Paris.

Denoon, Donald & Adam Kuper (1970): 'Nationalist Historians in Search of a Nation', *African Affairs* 69, pp. 329–49.

Doornbos, Martin R. (1970): 'Kumanyana and Rwenzururu: two responses to ethnic inequality', in Rotberg, R.I. & A.A. Mazrui: *Protest and Power in Black Africa.* Oxford University Press, New York, pp. 1088–136.

(1978): *Not All the King's Men. Inequality as a political instrument in Ankole, Uganda.* Mouton, The Hague.

Dunbar, A.R. (1965): *A History of Bunyoro Kitara.* Oxford University Press, Nairobi.

Easton, David (1965a): *A Framework for Political Analysis.* Prentice-Hall, NJ.

(1965b): *A Systems Analysis of Political Life.* John Wiley, New York.

Eckstein, Susan (1977): 'Politics and Priests. The 'iron law' of oligarchy and interorganizational relations,' *Comparative Politics* 9(4), pp. 463–81.

Ehrlich, C. (1965): 'The Uganda Economy, 1903–1945', in Harlow & Chilver (1965), pp. 395–475.

Eisenstadt, S.N. (1962): 'Religious Organizations and Political Process in Centralized Empires', *Journal of Asian Studies* 21, pp. 271–94.

(1963): *The Political Systems of Empires.* Free Press of Glencoe, London.

Ekechi, F.K. (1971): *Missionary Enterprise and Rivalry in Igboland 1857–1914.* Cass, London.

Emwanu, G. (1967): 'The Reception of Alien Rule in Teso, 1896–1927', *Uganda Journal* 31(2), pp. 171–82.

Fallers, L.A. (ed.) (1964): *The King's Men.* Oxford University Press.

(1965): *Bantu Bureaucracy. A century of political evolution among the Basoga of Uganda.* University of Chicago Press.

Fashole-Luke, E., Gray, R., Hastings, A. & G. Tasie (eds.) (1978): *Christianity in Independent Africa.* Rex Collings, London.

Ferkiss, Victor C. (1967): 'Religion and Politics in Independent African States: a prolegomenon', in Butler, J. & A.A. Castagno: *Boston University Papers on Africa. Transition in African politics.* Praeger, New York, pp. 1–38.

Flint, John (1963): 'The Wider Background to Partition and Colonial Occupation', in Oliver & Mathew (1963), pp. 352–90,

Furley, O.W. (1961): 'Kasagama of Toro', *Uganda Journal* 25(2), pp. 184–98.

Furley, O.W. & Tom Watson (1978): *A History of Education in East Africa.* NOK Publishers, London.

Galbraith, John S. (1972): *McKinnon and East Africa 1878–1895.* Cambridge University Press.

Gale, H.P. (1959); *Uganda and the Mill Hill Fathers.* Macmillan, London.

Gann, L.H. & P. Duignan (eds.) (1969): *Colonialism in Africa 1870–1960*, vol. I, Cambridge University Press.

Gensichen, H.W. (1962): 'Die Deutsche Mission und der Kolonialismus', *Kerygma und Dogma* 8, pp. 136–249.

Gingyera-Pinycwa, A.G. (1976): *Issues in Pre-Independence Politics in Uganda. A case-study on the contribution of religion to political debate in Uganda in the decade 1952–62.* East African Literature Bureau, Kampala.

Goldthorpe, J.E. & F.B. Wilson (1960): *Tribal Maps of East Africa and Zanzibar.* East African Studies no. 13. East African Institute of Social Research, Kampala.

Gray, Richard (1968): 'Problem of Historical Perspective: the planting of Christianity in Africa in the nineteenth and twentieth centuries', in Baëta (1968), pp. 18–33,

(1978): 'Christianity and Religious Change in Africa', *African Affairs* 77, pp. 89–100.

Groves, C.P. (1969): 'Missionary and Humanitarian Aspects of Imperialism from 1870 to 1914', in Gann & Duignan (1969), pp. 462–96.

Gulliver, P.H. (ed.) (1969): *Tradition and Transition in East Africa.* Routledge & Kegan Paul, London.

Hansen, Holger Bernt (1974): 'Fra Missionhistorie til Universal Kirkehistorie', *Dansk Teologisk Tidsskrift* 37, pp. 280–307.

(1975): 'Forholdet mellem mission–kirke–stat' (Mission–Church–State: Early tensions in Uganda). *Svensk Missionstidskrift* 63(4), pp. 252–66.

(1977): 'Ethnicity and Military Rule in Uganda, a study of ethnicity as a political factor in Uganda, based on a discussion of political anthropology and the application of its results'. Scandinavian Institute of African Studies Research Report no. 43, Uppsala.

    (1980): 'European Ideas, Colonial Attitudes and African Realities: the introduction of a Church constitution in Uganda 1898–1908', *The International Journal of African Historical Studies* 13(2), pp. 240–80.

Harford–Battersby, C.F. (1898): *Pilkington of Uganda*. Marshall, London.

Harlow, Vincent & E.M. Chilver (eds.) (1965): *History of East Africa*, vol. II, Clarendon Press, Oxford.

Hastings, Adrian (1969): 'From Mission to Church in Buganda', *Zeitschrift für Missionswissenschaft und Religionswissenschaft* 53, pp. 206–28.

    (1979): *A History of African Christianity 1950–1975*. Cambridge University Press.

Hellberg, Carl. J. (1965): *Missions on a Colonial Frontier West of Lake Victoria*. Studia Missionalia Upsaliensa VI. Gleerups, Lund.

Hertslet, Sir E. (1967): *The Map of Africa by Treaty*. Reprint of 3rd ed. Cass, London.

Hewitt, Gordon (1971): *The Problems of Success. A history of the Church Missionary Society 1910–1942*, vol. I: *In Tropical Africa, the Middle East, at Home*. SCM Press, London.

Holmberg, Åke (1966): *African Tribes and European Agencies: colonialism and humanitarianism in British South and East Africa 1870–1895*. Studia Historica Gothoburgensia VI. Akademiförlaget, Göteborg.

Holway, James D. (1972): 'CMS Contact with Islam in East Africa before 1914', *Journal of Religion in Africa* 4 (3), pp. 200–12.

Hopkins, A.G. (1973): *An Economic History of West Africa*. Longman, London.

Hunter, L.S. (ed.) (1966): *The English Church: A new look*. Penguin, Harmondsworth.

Hynes, W.G. (1979): *The Economics of Empire. Britain, Africa and the new Imperialism 1870—1895*. Longman, London.

Ingham, Kenneth (1955): 'British Administration in Lango District, 1907–1935', *Uganda Journal* 19(12), pp. 156–68.

    (1958): *The Making of Modern Uganda*. Allen & Unwin, London.

    (1975): *The Kingdom of Toro in Uganda*. Methuen, London.

Jackson, Frederick (1930): *Early Days in East Africa*. Edward Arnold, London.

Journal of African History (1978): 19(1). Special issue: Whites in Africa.

Kabwegyere, Tarsis B. (1972): 'The Dynamics of Colonial Violence: the inductive system in Uganda', *Journal of Peace Research* 9(4), pp. 303–14.

    (1974): *The Politics of State Formation. The nature and effects of colonialism in Uganda*. East African Literature Bureau, Nairobi.

    (1976): 'Land and the Growth of Social Stratification', in *History and Social Change in East Africa. Proceedings of the 1974 Conference of the Historical Association of Kenya* (ed. B.A. Ogot), pp. 111–33.

Kadt, Emanuel de (1971): 'Church, Society and Development in Latin America', *Journal of Development Studies* 8(1), pp. 23–43.

Karugire, S.R. (1970): 'Relations between the Bairu and Bahima in Nineteenth-Century Nkore', *Tarikh* 3(2), pp. 22–33.

    (1980): *A Political History of Uganda*. Heinemann Educational Books, Nairobi.

Kasozi, A.B.K. (1970): 'Impact of Koran Schools on the Education of African Muslims in Uganda 1900–1968', *Dini na Mila* 4(2), pp. 1–21.

Kasozi, A.B.K., Noel King & Ayre Oded (1973): *Islam and the Confluence of Religions in Uganda 1840–1966*. Studies in Religion Series. American Academy of Religion, Florida.

Kato, L.L. (1971): 'Government Land Policy in Uganda 1889–1900', *Uganda Journal* 35(2), pp. 153–60.

Katumba, A. & F.B. Welbourn (1964): 'Muslim Martyrs of Buganda', *Uganda Journal* 28(2), pp. 151–64.

Keith, A.K. (1919): *The Belgian Congo and the Berlin Act*. Oxford University Press.

King, Noel (1971): *Christian and Muslim in Africa*. Harper & Row, New York.

Kiwanuka, M.S.M. (1968): 'Bunyoro and the British: a reappraisal of the causes for the decline and fall of an African Kingdom', *Journal of African History* 9(4), pp. 603–19.

(1969): 'Kabaka Mwanga and his Political Parties', *Uganda Journal* 33(1), pp. 1–17.

(1971): *A History of Buganda from the Foundation of the Kingdom to 1900*. Longman, London.

(1974) 'The Diplomacy of the Lost Counties Question: its impact on the foreign relations of the Kingdoms of Buganda, Bunyoro and the rest of Uganda, 1900–1964', *Mawazo* 4(7).

Ladefoged, P., R. Click & C. Criper (1972): *Language in Uganda*. Oxford University Press.

La Fontaine, J.S. (1969): 'Tribalism among the Gisu', in Gulliver (1969), pp. 177–93.

Lagergren, David (1970): *Mission and State in the Congo. A study of the relations between Protestant missions and the Congo Independent State authorities with special reference to the Equator District, 1885–1903*. Almqvist & Wiksell, Uppsala.

Langlands, B.W. & G. Namirembe (1967): *Studies on the Geography of Religion*. Occasional Paper no. 4, Dept. of Geography, Makerere University, Kampala.

Lawrance, J.C.D. (1955): 'A History of Teso to 1937', *Uganda Journal* 19(1), pp. 7–40, *Laws and Regulations of the Church of Uganda* (1917). Namirembe, Kampala.

Leys, Colin (1967): *Politicans and Policies. An essay on politics in Acholi, Uganda 1962–65*. East African Publishing House, Nairobi.

Leys, N. (1924): *Kenya*. Hogarth Press, London.

Lijphart, Arend (1971): 'Comparative Politics and the Comparative Method', *American Political Science Review* 65, pp. 682–93.

Linden, Ian (1974): *Catholics, Peasants and Chewa Resistance in Nyasaland 1889–1939*. University of California Press.

(1977): *Church and Revolution in Rwanda*. Manchester University Press.

Littell, Franklin H. (1967): 'The Churches and the Body Politic', *Daedalus* 96, pp. 22–42.

Lloyd, A.B. (1906): *Uganda to Khartoum. Life and adventure on the Upper Nile*. Collins, London.

Lloyd, P.C. (ed.) (1966): *The New Elites of Tropical Africa*. Oxford University Press.

Lonsdale, J. & B. Berman (1979): 'Coping with the Contradictions: the development of the colonial state in Kenya, 1895–1914', *Journal of African History* 20, pp. 487–505.

Low, D.A. (1957b): *Religion and Society in Buganda 1875–1900*. East African Studies no. 8. East African Institute of Social Research, Kampala.

(1959): 'The Composition of the Buganda Lukiko in 1902', *Uganda Journal* 23(1), pp. 64–8.

(1962): *Political Parties in Uganda 1949–1962*. Athlone Press, London.

(1963): 'The Northern Interior 1840–1900', in Oliver & Mathew (1963), pp. 297–351.

(1965): 'Uganda: the establishment of the Protectorate, 1894–1919', in Harlow & Chilver (1965), pp. 57–122.

(1968): 'Converts and Martyrs in Buganda', in Baëta (1968), pp. 150–64.

(1971a): *Buganda in Modern History*. Weidenfeld & Nicolson, London.

(1971b): *The Mind of Buganda. Documents of the modern history of an African Kingdom*. Heinemann, London.

(1973): *Lion Rampant. Essays in the study of British imperialism*. Cass, London.

Low, D.A. & R.C. Pratt (1960): *Buganda and British Overrule*. Oxford University Press.

Luckham, A.R. (1971): 'A Comparative Typology of Civil–Military Relations', *Government and Opposition* 6(1), pp. 5–35.

Lugard, Frederick D. (1893): *The Rise of Our East African Empire*, vols. I–II. Blackwood, Edinburgh.

McCracken, John (1977): *Politics and Christianity in Malawi 1875–1940. The impact of the Livingstonia Mission in the Northern Province*. Cambridge University Press.

McDermott, P.L. (1893): *British East Africa or IBEA*. Chapman & Hall, London.

Macdonald, J.R.L. (1897): *Soldiering and Surveying in British East Africa 1891–1894*. Reprinted Dawson, Folkestone & London, 1973.

Macpherson, Margaret (1964): *They Built for the Future*. Cambridge University Press.

Mair, Lucy (1934): *An African People in the Twentieth Century*. Routledge, London.

Mamdani, Mahmood (1975): 'Class Struggles in Uganda', *Review of African Political Economy* 4, pp. 26–61.

(1976): *Politics and Class Formation in Uganda*. Heinemann, London.

Markowitz, Marvin D. (1973): *Cross and Sword. The political role of Christian missions in the Belgian Congo 1908–1960*. Hoover Institution Press, Stanford University, Cal.

Matson, A.T. (1972): *Nandi Resistance to British Rule, 1890–1906*. E.A. Publishing House, Nairobi.

Mazrui, Ali A. (1966–67): 'Islam, Political Leadership and Economic Radicalism in Africa', *Comparative Studies in Society and History* 9, pp. 274–91.

(1973): 'The Lumpen Proletariat and the Lumpen Militariat: African soldiers as a new political class', *Political Studies* 21(1), pp. 1–12.

(1974): 'Piety and Puritanism under a Military Theocracy: Uganda soldiers as Apostolic successors', in *Political-Military Systems.Comparative Perspectives* (ed. Catherine McArdle Kelleher), Sage Publications, Beverly Hills, pp. 105–24.

(1977): 'Religious Strangers in Uganda: from Emin Pasha to Amin Dada', *African Affairs* 76 (302), pp. 21–38.

Miers, Suzanne (1975): *Britain and the Ending of the Slave Trading*. Africana, New York.

Morris, H.F. (1960): 'Marriage and Divorce in Uganda', *Uganda Journal* 24(2), pp. 197–206.

(1968): 'Marriage Law in Uganda: 60 years of attempted reform', in Anderson, J.N.D. (ed.): *Family Law in Asia and Africa*. Praeger, New York, pp. 34–48.

(1979): 'The Development of Statutory Marriage Law in Twentieth-Century British Colonial Africa', *Journal of African Law* 23(1), pp. 37–64.

Morris, H.F. & J.S. Read (1966): *Uganda. The development of its laws and constitution*. Stevens, London.

(1972): *Indirect Rule and the Search for Justice: essays in East African legal history*. Clarendon Press, Oxford.

Motani, Nizar (1975): 'The Ugandan Civil Service and the Asian Problem 1894–1972', in Twaddle, M. (ed.): *Expulsion of a Minority: essays on Ugandan Asians*. Athlone Press, London.

Mouritzen, Hans (1979). 'Politologisk egenart – også i case-studier?', *Statsvetenskaplig Tidskrift* 61(3), pp. 179–90.

Mudoola, D. (1978): 'Religion and Politics in Uganda', *African Affairs* 77(306), pp. 22–35.

Mujaju, Akiiki, B. (1976): 'The Political Crisis of Church Institutions in Uganda', *African Affairs* 75(298), pp. 67–85.

Mukwaya, A.B. (1953): *Land Tenure in Buganda. Present-day tendencies*. East African Studies, no. 1. Eagle Press, Kampala.

Mulira, E.M.K. (1950): *Troubled Uganda*. Fabian Colonial Bureau, London.

Neill, Stephen (1964): *A History of Christian Missions*. Penguin, London.

(1966): *Colonialism and Christian Missions*. Lutterworth, London.

Newsome, David (1961): *Godliness and Good Learning. Four studies of a Victorian ideal*. Murray, London.

Norman, E.R. (1976): *Church and Society in England 1770–1970. A historical study*. Oxford University Press.

Odinga, Oginga (1967): *Not Yet Uhuru: an autobiography*. Heinemann, London.

Ogot, B.A. (1963): 'British Administration in the Central Nyanza District of Kenya', *Journal of African History* 4 (2), pp. 249–74.

Oliver, Roland (1952): *The Missionary Factor in East Africa*. Longman, London.

(1957): *Sir Harry Johnston and the Scramble for Africa*. Chatto & Windus, London.

(1968): 'Western Historiography and its Relevance to Africa', in Ranger, T.O. (ed.): *Emerging Themes of African History*. Proceedings of the International Congress of African Historians, Dar es Salaam, Oct. 1965. E. A. Publishing House, Nairobi, pp. 53–60.

Oliver, Roland & G. Mathew (eds.) (1963): *History of East Africa*, vol. I. Clarendon Press, Oxford.

Owusu, Maxwell (1970): *Uses and Abuses of Political Power: a case study of continuity and change in the politics of Ghana*. University of Chicago Press.

Parsons, Talcott (1960): *Structure and Process in Modern Societies*. Free Press of Glencoe, Illinois.

Pedersen, Ole Karup (1963): *Afrikansk Nationalisme*. Internationale Studier IV. Selskabet for Historie og Samfundsøkonomi. Copenhagen.

    (1970): *Udenrigsminister P. Munchs opfattelse af Danmarks stilling i international politik*. Gads forlag, Copenhagen.

Perham, Margery (1956): *Lugard: the years of adventure*. Collins, London.

Perham, Margery and M. Bull (eds.) (1959); *The Diaries of Lord Lugard*, vols. I–IV. Faber, London.

Phillips, Arthur & H.F. Morris (1971): *Marriage Laws in Africa*. Oxford University Press.

Pirouet, M.L. (1966): 'The Coronation of the Omukama of Toro', *Makerere Journal* 12, pp. 16–24.

    (1978): *Black Evangelists. The spread of Christianity in Uganda 1891–1914*. Rex Collings, London.

Pole, J.R. (1978): *The Pursuit of Equality in American History*. University of California Press.

Portal, Sir Gerald (1894): *The British Mission to Uganda in 1893*. Edward Arnold, London.

Porter, Andrew (1976): 'Cambridge, Keswick and late Nineteenth-Century Attitudes to Africa', *The Journal of Imperial and Commonwealth History* 5(1), pp. 5–34,

    (1977): 'Evangelical Enthusiasm, Missionary Motivation and West Africa in the Late Nineteenth Century: the career of G.W. Brooke', *The Journal of Imperial and Commonwealth History* 6(1), pp. 23–46.

Postlethwaite, J.R.P. (1947): *I Look Back*. Boardman, London.

Powesland, P.G. (1957): *Economic Policy and Labour*. East African Studies, no. 10. East African Institute of Social Research, Kampala.

Pratt, R.C. (1965): 'Administration and Politics in Uganda 1919–1945', in Harlow & Chilver (1965).

Purvis, J.B. (1909): *Through Uganda to Mount Elgon*, T. Fisher Unwin, London.

Ranger, Terence O. (1965): 'African Attempts to Control Education in East and Central Africa, 1900–1939', *Past and Present* 32, pp. 57–85.

    (1969): 'African Reactions to the Imposition of Colonial Rule in East and Central Africa', in Gann & Duignan (1969), pp. 293–324.

    (1979): 'White Presence and Power in Africa', *Journal of African History* 20, pp. 463–69.

Ranger, T.O. & John Weller (eds.) (1975): *Themes in the Christian History of Central Africa*. Heinemann, London.

Rasmussen, Erik (1971): *Komparativ Politik*, vol. I. Gyldendal, Copenhagen.

Reardon, Ruth Slade (1968): 'Catholics and Protestants in the Congo', in Baëta (1968), pp. 83–100.

Report of the Commission on Marriage, Divorce and the Status of Women (1965). Uganda Government, Entebbe.

Richards, A.I. (ed.) (1960): *East African Chiefs*. Faber, London.

Roberts, A.D. (1962): 'The "Lost Counties" of Bunyoro', *Uganda Journal* 26(2), pp. 194–99.

    (1962a): 'The Sub-Imperialism of the Baganda', *Journal of African History* 3(3), pp. 435–50.

    (1963): 'The Evolution of the Uganda Protectorate', *Uganda Journal* 27(1), pp. 95–106.

Robinson, Ronald (1972): 'Non-European Foundations of European Imperialism: sketch for a theory of collaboration', in Owen, R. & B. Sutcliffe (eds.): *Studies in the Theory of Imperialism*. Longman, London, 1972, pp. 117–42.

Robinson, Ronald & John Gallagher (1965): *Africa and the Victorians. The official mind of imperialism*, 3rd ed. Macmillan, London.

Roscoe, John (1965): *The Baganda. An account of their native customs and beliefs*, 2nd ed. Cass, London.

Rotberg, Robert I. (1965): *Christian Missionaries and the Creation of Northern Rhodesia 1880–1924*. Princeton University Press, NJ.

Rowe, John A. (1964): 'The Purge of Christians at Mwanga's Court', *Journal of African History* 5(1), pp. 55–72.

 (1964a): 'Land and Politics in Buganda, 1875–1955', *Makerere Journal* 10, pp. 1–13.

 (1969): *Lugard at Kampala*. Makerere History Papers. Longman, Kampala.

 (1970): 'The Baganda Revolutionaries', *Tarikh* 3(2), pp. 34–46.

Sanderson, Lilian Pasmore & Neville Sanderson (1981): *Education, Religion and Politics in Southern Sudan 1899–1964*. Ithaca Press, London.

Scotton, J.F. (1973): 'The First African Press in East Africa – protest and nationalism in Uganda in the 1920s'. *International Journal of African History* 6(2), pp. 211–28.

Sekamwa, J.C. & S.M.E. Lugumba (1973): *Educational Development and Administration in Uganda 1900–1970. Selected topics*. Longman, Kampala.

Shepperson, George & Thomas Price (1958): *Independent African. John Chilembwe and the origins, setting and significance of the Nyasaland native rising of 1915*. Edinburgh University Press.

Simensen, Jarle (1970): 'Fra Utforskningen av Afrikas Historie', *Historisk Tidsskrift* 3, pp.311–56.

Slade, Ruth M. (1959): *English-Speaking Missions in the Congo Independent State (1878–1908)*. Academie Royale des Sciences Coloniale, Brussels.

Smith, Donald Eugene (1970): *Religion and Political Development. An analytic study*. Little, Brown, Boston.

 (ed.) (1974): *Religion and Political Modernization*. Yale University Press.

Smith, Elwin A. (1972): *Religious Liberty in the United States. The development of church–state thought since the revolutionary era*. Fortress Press, Philadelphia.

Snoxall, R.A. (1937): 'The Coronation Ritual and Customs of Buganda', *Uganda Journal* 4(4), pp. 277–88.

Southall, A.W. (1960): 'On Chastity in Africa', *Uganda Journal* 24(2), pp. 207–16.

Steinhart, E.I. (1973): 'Royal Clientage and the Beginnings of Colonial Modernization in Toro', *International Journal of African Historical Studies* 6, pp. 265–85.

 (1977): *Conflict and Collaboration. The Kingdoms of Western Uganda, 1890–1907*. Princeton University Press, NJ.

Stock, Eugene (1916): *The History of the Church Missionary Society*, vol. IV. CMS, London.

Sundkler, Bengt (1961): *Bantu Prophets in South Africa*, 2nd ed. Oxford University Press.

 (1963): *Missionens Värld. Missionskunskap och Missionshistoria*. Diakonistyrelsens Bokförlag, Stockholm.

Tasie, G.O.M. (1978): *Christian Missionary Enterprise in the Niger Delta 1864–1918*. Brill, Leiden.

Taylor, John V. (1958): *The Growth of the Church in Buganda*. SCM Press, London.

Temu, A.J. (1972): *British Protestant Missions*. Longman, London.

Thomas, H.B. & R. Scott (1935): *Uganda*. Oxford University Press.

Thomas, H.B. & A.E. Spencer (1938): *A History of Uganda Land and Surveys and of the Uganda Land and Survey Department*. Government Press, Entebbe.

Tosh, John (1973): 'Colonial Chiefs in a Stateless Society: a case-study from northern Uganda', *Journal of African History* 14(3), pp. 472–90.

 (1978): *Clan Leaders and Colonial Chiefs in Lango. The political history of an East African stateless society c. 1800–1939*. Clarendon Press, Oxford.

Tucker, A.R. (1908): *Eighteen Years in Uganda and East Africa*, vols. I–II. Edward Arnold, London.

 (1911): *Eighteen Years in Uganda and East Africa* (new ed.). Edward Arnold, London.

Tuma, Tom (1976): 'African Chiefs and Church Work in Busoga Province of Uganda, 1900–1940 – part I', *Kenya Historical Review* 4(2), pp. 283–95.

    (1977): 'African Chiefs and Church Work in Busoga Province of Uganda, 1900–1940 – part II', *Kenya Historical Review* 5(1), pp. 93–106.

Tuma, Tom & Phares Mutibwa (eds.) (1978): *A Century of Christianity in Uganda 1877–1977*. Uzima Press, Nairobi.

Twaddle, Michael (1969): 'The Bakungu Chiefs of Buganda under British Colonial Rule, 1900–1930', *Journal of African History* 10(2), pp. 309–22.

    (1969a): 'Tribalism in Eastern Uganda', in Gulliver (1969), pp. 193–208.

    (1972): 'The Muslim Revolution in Buganda', *African Affairs* 71, pp. 54–72.

    (1974): 'Ganda Receptivity to Change', *Journal of African History* 15(2), pp. 303–15.

    (1978): 'Was the Democratic Party of Uganda a purely Confessional Party?' in Fashole-Luke *et al.* (1978), pp. 255–66.

Uzoigwe, G.N. (1970): 'Kabalega and the Making of a New Kitara', *Tarikh* 3(2), pp. 5–21.

    (1972): 'The Kyanyangire, 1907: passive revolt against British overrule', in Ogot, B.A. (ed.): *War and Society in Africa – 10 studies*. Cass, London, pp. 179–214.

Vallier, Ivan (1967): 'Religious Elites: differentiations and development in Roman Catholicism', in Lipset, S.M. & Aldo Solari: *Elites in Latin America*. Oxford University Press, pp. 190–232.

    (1967a): 'Church Development in Latin America: a five-country comparison', *Journal of Developing Areas* 1, pp. 461–76.

    (1970): 'Extraction, Insulation and Re-entry: toward a theory of religious change', in Landsberger, H.A. (ed.): *The Church and Social Change in Latin America*. University of Notre Dame Press, pp. 9–35.

    (1970a): *Catholicism, Social Control and Modernization in Latin America*. Prentice-Hall, Englewood Cliffs, NJ.

Vincent, Joan (1974): 'Visibility and Vulnerability: the politics of pacemakers', *Africa* 44(3), pp. 222–34.

    (1977): 'Colonial Chiefs and the Making of Class: a case-study from Teso, Eastern Uganda', *Africa* 47(2), pp. 140–59.

Wandira, A. (1972): 'Early Missionary Education in Uganda; a study of purpose in missionary education'. Dept. of Education, Makerere University, Kampala.

Warren, Max (1965): *The Missionary Movement from Britain in Modern History*. SCM Press, London.

    (1966): 'The Church of England as by Law Established – Unfit for Export?' in Hunter (1966), pp. 129–43.

Welbourn, F.B. (1961): *East African Rebels. A study of some independent churches*. SCM Press, London.

    (1965): *Religion and Politics in Uganda 1952–62*. E.A. Publishing House, Nairobi.

Welbourn, F.B. & B.A. Ogot (1966): *A Place to Feel at Home. A study of two independent churches in Western Kenya*. Oxford University Press.

West, H.W. (1964): *The Mailo System in Buganda. A preliminary case study in African land tenure*. Government Printer, Entebbe.

    (1969): *The Transformation of Land Tenure in Buganda since 1896*. African Social Research Documents, vol. II, African Studies Centre, University of Cambridge.

    (1972): *Land Policy in Buganda*. African Studies Series 3, Cambridge University Press.

Whyte, J.H. (1971): *Church and State in Modern Ireland, 1923–1970*. Macmillan, Dublin.

Wild, J.V. (1955): *The Story of the Uganda Agreement 1952–1962*. Macmillan, London.

Williams, T.S.M. (1966): 'The Coming of Christianity to Ankole', *Bulletin of the Society for African Church History* 2(2), pp. 155–73.

Willis, J.J. (1925): *An African Church in Building*. CMS, London.

Wilson, George (1907): 'Lecture to the Society of Arts', *Journal of the Society of Arts*, 55, pp.281–302.

World Missionary Conference (1910). *Report of Commission VII. Missions and Governments*. Oliphant, Anderson & Ferrier, Edinburgh.

Wrigley, C.C. (1959): 'The Christian Revolution in Buganda', *Comparative Studies in Society and History*, 2, pp. 33–48.

(1964): 'The Changing Economic Structure of Buganda', in Fallers (1964), pp. 16–63.

Wylie, D. (1977): 'Confrontation over Kenya: the Colonial Office and its critics 1918–1940', *Journal of African History* 18(3), pp. 427–47.

Yinger, J.M. (1970): *The Scientific Study of Religion*. Macmillan, New York.

Young, Crawford (1965): *Politics in the Congo. Decolonization and independence*. Princeton University Press, NJ.

Zwanenberg, R.M.A. van (1975): *Colonial Capitalism and Labour in Kenya 1919–1939*. E.A. Literature Bureau, Nairobi.

Unpublished theses, conference papers, etc

Carter, Fay (1967a): 'Education in Uganda, 1894–1945'. PhD thesis, University of London.

Engholm, G.F. (1968): 'Immigrant Influences upon the Development of Policy in the Protectorate of Uganda 1900–1952, with particular reference to the role of the Legislative Council'. PhD thesis, University of London.

Hansen, Holger Bernt (1966): 'British Administration and Religious Liberty in Uganda 1890–1900'. Conference Paper no. 373, East African Institute of Social Research, January 1966.

(1979): 'Religion and Politics in Independent Uganda: the role of the religious factor in Ugandan politics and a discussion of the conceptual framework'. Conference Paper: Workshop on Religion and Politics, European Consortium of Political Research Joint Session, Brussels, April 1979.

Hastings, Adrian (1973): 'A Typology of Church–State Relations'. Discussion Paper on 'Christianity in Post-Colonial Africa'. School of Oriental and African Studies, London, 25 Oct. 1973 (later publ. in the author's *The Faces of God*, Chapman, 1975).

Hodder-Williams, Richard (1978): 'Politics from the Marandellas Grass-Roots'. Annual Conference, African Studies Association of the United Kingdom, 21 Sept. 1978.

Kakwenzire, Joan B. (1976): 'Colonial Labour Policy in the Uganda Protectorate, 1919–1939'. MA thesis, University of London.

Lockard, Kathleen (1974): 'Religion and Political Development in Uganda 1962–1972'. PhD thesis, University of Wisconsin.

Lonsdale, J.M. (1964): 'A Political History of Nyanza, 1883–1945'. D. Phil. thesis, University of Cambridge.

Low, D.A. (1957a): 'The British and Uganda, 1862–1900'. D. Phil. thesis, University of Oxford.

Lundquist, Lennart (1976): 'Organisationskapabiliteter och Omgivningsrestriktioner'. Arbejdspapir, Institut for Samfundsfag, University of Copenhagen.

Mazrui, Ali A. (1968): 'Islam and the English Language in East and West Africa'. 9th International African Seminar of the International African Institute, University College, Dar es Salaam, Dec. 1968.

(1975): 'Religious Strangers in Uganda. From Emin Pasha to Amin Dada'. Conference paper on 'Christianity in Independent Africa', Jos, Nigeria, 1975.

Motani, Nizar (1972): 'The Growth of an African Civil Service in Uganda, 1912–1940'. PhD Thesis, University of London.

Pirouet, M.L. (ed.) (1969): 'A Dictionary of Christianity in Uganda'. Dept. of Religious Studies, Makerere University, Kampala.

Sjöblom, Gunnar (1980): 'Some Problems of the Operational Code Approach'. Conference Paper on 'Perception and Misperception in International Politics', European

Consortium of Political Research Workshop, Florence, Italy, 22–30 March 1980.

Tuma, A.D. Tom (1973): 'The Introduction and Growth of Christianity in Busoga 1890–1940; with particular reference to the roles of the Basoga clergy, catechists and chiefs'. PhD thesis, University of London (a revised version publ. 1980: *Building a Ugandan Church. African participation in Church growth and expansion in Busoga 1891–1940*. Kenya Literature Bureau, Nairobi).

Twaddle, Michael (1967): 'Politics in Bukedi, 1900–1939'. PhD thesis, University of London.

     (1968/9): 'The Religion of Malaki Revisited'. Social Sciences Council Conference 1968/9, History Papers, Makerere Institute of Social Research.

Waliggo, J.M. (1976): 'The Catholic Church in the Buddu Province of Buganda'. D. Phil. thesis, University of Cambridge.

Watson, Tom (1968): 'A History of Church Missionary Society High Schools in Uganda, 1900–24'. PhD thesis, University of East Africa.

White, Gavin (1970): 'Kikuyu 1913: an ecumenical controversy'. PhD thesis, University of London.

Williams, T.S.M. (1965): 'The Protestant Church in Nkonde – The establishment of the Protestant church in an Ankole village and its social relevance today', MA thesis, Makerere University College, University of East Africa.

Willis, J.J. (1913): 'Policy of the Uganda Mission, 1912'. Pamphlet, Kampala.

INDEX

The index includes personal names, places and subjects appearing in the text. Authors are indexed only if they are mentioned in the text.